BRITISH WRITERS

BRITISH WRITERS

Edited under the auspices of the British Council

IAN SCOTT-KILVERT

General Editor

VOLUME VI

THOMAS HARDY

TO

WILFRED OWEN

CHARLES SCRIBNER'S SONS / NEW YORK

Library of Congress Cataloging in Publication Data (Revised)

Main entry under title:

British writers.

Includes bibliographies and index.
CONTENTS: v. 1. William Langland to the English
Bible—v. 2. Thomas Middleton to George Farquhar—
[etc.]—v. 6. Thomas Hardy to Wilfred Owen.
1. English literature—History and criticism.
2. English literature—Bio-bibliography.   3. Authors,
English—Biography.   I. Scott-Kilvert, Ian.
II. Great Britain.   British Council.
PR85.B688   820'.9   78-23483
ISBN 0-684-15798-5 (v. 1)   ISBN 0-684-16635-6 (v. 4)
ISBN 0-684-16407-8 (v. 2)   ISBN 0-684-16636-4 (v. 5)
ISBN 0-684-16408-6 (v. 3)   ISBN 0-684-16637-2 (v. 6)

1 3 5 7 9 11 13 15 17 19   V/C   20 18 16 14 12 10 8 6 4 2
PRINTED IN THE UNITED STATES OF AMERICA

Excerpts from poems copyright 1915 by Rudyard Kipling, copyright 1919 by Rudyard
Kipling, copyright 1926 by Rudyard Kipling from *Rudyard Kipling's Verse: Definitive
Edition*. Reprinted by permission of the National Trust and Doubleday **and Company,**
Inc. Permission also granted by Macmillan and Company, London Ltd.

Thanks are due to the Estate of W. Somerset Maugham and to Messrs. William Heinemann Ltd. for permission to quote from *Ten Novels and Their Authors*, *Home and
Beauty*, *The Casuarina Tree*, *Tellers of Tales*, and *The Moon and Sixpence*.

Editorial Staff

List of Subjects in Volume VI

Introduction

British Writers is designed as a work of reference to complement *American Writers,* the eight-volume set of literary biographies of authors past and present, which was first published in 1974. In the same way as its American counterpart, which first appeared in the form of individual pamphlets published by the University of Minnesota Press, the British collection originates from a series of separate articles entitled *Writers and Their Work.* This series was initiated by the British Council in 1950 as a part of its worldwide program to support the teaching of English language and literature, an activity carried on both in the English-speaking world and in many countries in which English is not the mother tongue.

The articles are intended to appeal to a wide readership, including students in secondary and advanced education, teachers, librarians, scholars, editors, and critics, as well as the general public. Their purpose is to provide an introduction to the work of writers who have made a significant contribution to English literature, to stimulate the reader's enjoyment of the text, and to give students the means to pursue the subject further. The series begins in the fourteenth century and extends to the present day, and is printed in chronological order according to the date of the subject's birth. The articles are far from conforming to a fixed pattern, but speaking generally each begins with a short biographical section, the main body of the text being devoted to a survey of the subject's principal writings and an assessment of the work as a whole. Each article is equipped with a selected bibliography that records the subject's writings in chronological order, in the form both of collected editions and of separate works, including modern and paperback editions. The bibliography concludes with a list of biographical and critical publications, including both books and articles, to guide the reader who is interested in further research. In the case of authors such as Chaucer or Shakespeare, whose writings have in-spired extensive criticism and commentary, the critical section is further subdivided and provides a useful record of the new fields of research that have developed over the past hundred years.

British Writers is not conceived as an encyclopedia of literature, nor is it a series of articles planned so comprehensively as to include every writer of historical importance. Its character is rather that of a critical anthology possessing both the virtues and the limitations of such a grouping. It offers neither the schematized form of the encyclopedia nor the completeness of design of the literary history. On the other hand it is limited neither by the impersonality of the one nor the uniformity of the other. Since each contributor speaks with only one voice out of many, he is principally concerned with explaining his subject as fully as possible rather than with establishing an order of merit or making "placing" comparisons (since each contributor might well "place" differently). The prime task is one of presentation and exposition rather than of assigning critical praise or censure. The contributors to the first volume consist of distinguished literary scholars and critics—later volumes include contributions by poets, novelists, historians, and biographers. Each writes as an enthusiast for his subject, and each sets out to explain what are the qualities that make an author worth reading.

The fourth volume of *British Writers* deals in the main with the romantic poets and critics and with the fiction and other prose of the Regency period. But because of the chronological dovetailing of the romantic era and its successor, the same volume also includes authors such as Tennyson, the Brownings, Disraeli, Carlyle, and Macaulay, who, although sufficiently close to the romantics to have felt their influence strongly, are generally regarded as characteristically Victorian.

The fifth volume consists of essays on "Victorian literature" in the sense that scarcely any of the writers discussed had begun to publish before the beginning of Queen Victoria's reign, and almost all of them had ceased to do so by the time of her death. Volumes V and VI likewise overlap, but for the opposite reason to the one mentioned above. This is that while a number of major authors, notably Hardy, James, Shaw, Kipling, and Conrad, had already established a reputation before the end of the nineteenth century, their literary achievements may be regarded as extending to a significant degree into the twentieth.

Queen Victoria's reign was the longest of any English monarch, and by the 1870's many of the features that had originally characterized the so-called Victorian era had changed or passed away, in particular the confident belief in a future of uninterrupted material progress. This had been widely shared by the generation of Thomas Babington Macaulay and was founded on the fact that the "Hungry Forties" had been followed by two decades of continuous expansion in industry and trade. Government had encouraged the creation of wealth with the minimum of interference from the state, and the creed of the entrepreneur was reinforced by the conviction that society was best served by competition, and also by the comforting biological doctrine of the survival of the fittest. Social reform was limited to the extension of education and to measures inspired by the Victorian dedication to charity, philanthropy, and self-help.

But by the mid-1870's it had become clear that higher production no longer sustained prosperity, as the British industrial revolution encountered competition from Europe and America. In the countryside the depression was even more severe, as the common land of villages was enclosed and many village crafts and ancillary occupations were swept away. Country life in Britain had always been hard and never idyllic, but it had possessed a genuinely communal quality to which Thomas Hardy's early novels bear witness. This fabric was not only weakened by the drift of agricultural laborers to the cities, but torn apart by the ethic of competition, which was quite alien to the mutually supportive quality of village life.

As unemployment rose and poverty spread, the socialist movement, of which little had been heard since the demise of Chartism, began to attract increasing support. One of the most influential books of the period was the American Henry George's *Progress and Poverty*; the lecture that he delivered in London in 1882 converted the young Bernard Shaw to socialism. Victorian writers of conscience, such as Elizabeth Gaskell and Charles Dickens, could attack the abuses of their day without questioning the principles on which society was established: their successors now felt obliged to challenge its very foundations. The question that had so urgently engaged the mind of Thomas Carlyle in the second quarter of the century—"The Condition of England"—reappeared to confront his grandchildren. It provided the title of C. F. Masterman's famous book in 1909, which discusses the subject on the political and economic plane. But it also provided a central theme for the fiction and drama of the post-Victorian era: Rudyard Kipling's *Puck of Pook's Hill*, E. M. Forster's *Howards End*, Shaw's *Heartbreak House* all explore the subject in imaginative terms.

In the literary and artistic fields, the period is dominated by the two movements known as naturalism and symbolism. Britain, traditionally insular in her culture, became increasingly susceptible to continental influences. Naturalism may be seen as the logical outcome of developments in the material world, of man's advances in science, biology, industry, and communications. The term is used not only with reference to the accurate rendering of physical detail, but in its full philosophical sense—the post-Christian acceptance of scientific laws as the sole governors of all forms of life, and a view of heredity and environment as exerting an overpowering influence on the individual. The leading apostles of this doctrine were Henrik Ibsen and Émile Zola, and in some respects Hardy: the writer locates his characters in a minutely specified setting and records their behavior.

Symbolism may be seen as a logical sequel to the romantic movement. Just as William Blake and his successors sought to break down the scientist's duality of body and spirit and to transfer the writer's vision from the universe, conceived as a machine, to the soul of the individual, so the symbolists sought not to specify or catalog, but to evoke or suggest images. Since the poet's sensibility is prized as a unique vision of experience, he must devise a special language to express it, a language depending on symbols or images placed in association as much as on words. The result was to create a deliberately somewhat blurred vision of what was described; the purpose was to mingle the imaginary with the real and also to blend the perceptions of the five senses. Some of the composers of the period, notably Richard

Wagner, aimed at a parallel effect. In Ibsen's plays both naturalism and symbolism can be seen at work. The so-called problem plays of his middle period, such as *An Enemy of the People* and *A Doll's House,* are classic examples of dramatic naturalism; the later pieces, beginning with *The Wild Duck,* are increasingly shaped by the symbolist approach. As it happened, it was the former category that first gained acceptance in England, so that when a serious drama appeared in the work of Shaw, John Galsworthy, and Granville Barker, it was irrevocably cast in the problem-play mold.

The symbolist approach was strengthened by a widespread belief that in the light of scientific discoveries, certainty on ethical, intellectual, and aesthetic questions was becoming unattainable and, hence, judgments must be relative. Walter Pater, the English critic who was most sympathetic to symbolism at this time, in fact invoked scientific support for his position. "The philosophical conception of the relative," he wrote, "has been developed in modern times through the sciences of observation. . . . The faculty for truth is recognized as a power of distinguishing and fixing delicate and fugitive details."

Symbolism flourished most actively in France, and was not at this stage, as will be seen, absorbed into the mainstream of English poetry: it influenced only a few writers living in London in the 1890's— Oscar Wilde, William Butler Yeats, the coterie known as the Rhymers' Club, and the critic Arthur Symons, author of *The Symbolist Movement in Literature.* These writers created a life style and a personal mythology of extreme sophistication, artificiality, and weary self-consciousness, but the period was, on any showing, a decade of remarkable and diverse literary vitality. The most popular poet was undoubtedly Kipling, a writer at the opposite pole to the Rhymers. His imperial and patriotic muse brought back into use, as William Wordsworth had claimed to do, a simple and colloquial diction—"the language really used by men"—and made verse a living influence among a huge middle-class readership. The same period also produced A. E. Housman's *A Shropshire Lad,* George Moore's naturalistic classic *Esther Waters,* and Shaw's *Plays Pleasant and Unpleasant.* Nevertheless the fin-de-siècle spirit, a mood of ennui and exhaustion, was pervasive and touched the work of writers who had no connection with symbolism, for example Hardy's novel *Jude the Obscure,* with its tragic character Old Father

Time—the child totally unequipped for the world into which he is born—or Wells's *The Time Machine,* with its prophetic vision of the Eloi, a parasitic upper class of "flower people." The death of Oscar Wilde at the turn of the century did indeed mark a turning point. As Yeats described it: "Then in 1900 everybody got down off his stilts; henceforth nobody drank absinthe with his black coffee; nobody went mad; nobody committed suicide; nobody joined the Catholic church; or if they did, I have forgotten."

The final phase, from 1900 to 1914, was nominally a period of world peace and tranquillity, but in fact, especially in Britain, these were years of breathless change and innovation in intellectual matters and of vigorous controversy and reform in politics. Internationally the country passed through a time of notable unpopularity, partly due to the Boer War, partly due to envy of the heyday of her power; and these developments caused some writers to withdraw into isolationism or Little-England chauvinism. The other great powers likewise found themselves threatened by the aspirations of national minorities, industrial unrest, international terrorism, and the clash of rival imperialist ambitions.

The death of Queen Victoria and of so many eminent Victorians signaled an inevitable break with the past and a challenge to custom and authority. In particular, the posthumous publication in 1903 of Samuel Butler's *The Way of All Flesh* had the effect of a time bomb in demolishing many long-accepted assumptions concerning family life and parental infallibility. In broader terms Butler had noted the power of "that mysterious drive towards greater power over our circumstances" which Shaw was already interpreting as the Life Force. In short, the atmosphere of the new age was to accept it as new, to question the existing moral and social order at every turn, and to attempt to reshape it by deliberate effort.

In 1906 a Liberal Government won a large majority and, in the years that followed, carried through a program of radical measures that embraced the powers of the House of Lords, the rights of trade unions, taxation, and social insurance. Two of the most controversial issues of the day for which solutions were not found were women's suffrage and Irish Home Rule. Nevertheless the climate of these years was set for reform.

In literature and the arts the changes in taste and technique, especially in poetry, were gradually transformed into the energies that created the modern movement and extended well into the years between the two world wars. These are therefore reviewed in Volume VII. The lifetime of Yeats is spread over both periods, and indeed by 1914 he had barely reached the midpoint of his long career. Still there are good reasons for surveying his work in the present volume.

One function that especially distinguishes the writers of the first years of the century—not least Yeats himself—was that of public controversy. The spirit of dissent and challenge, so strongly in evidence on all sides, was made all the more articulate by the revolution in education, the huge increase in readership, and the appearance of mass newspapers and new periodicals. Editors, leader-writers, and journalists became persons of consequence; politicians possessed of literary gifts, such as Winston Churchill, became aware that they might make and record history simultaneously. Writers were tempted to see themselves as molders of opinion, and so they sharpened their powers of communication. Some authors, for instance G. K. Chesterton and Hilaire Belloc, flourished on debate; even those who were far more highly endowed with original creative gifts, such as Yeats and Shaw, spent much of their time and energy on public platforms or conducting campaigns in prefaces, essays, and articles. These years have aptly been dubbed the most talkative epoch of English literature.

Hardy and Henry James are the two literary giants whose careers span the Victorian and Edwardian eras. Hardy, who grew up in a conservative rural society, seems in some respects to belong to an earlier generation. James, settling in London as a young man and making the acquaintance of the great figures of the day, immediately finds an observer's role on the Victorian literary scene, of which his *Partial Portraits* is a brilliant record. Yet it would be difficult to find two more dissimilar contemporaries; and neither held a high opinion of the other's work. Hardy remarked of James that he was occupied with subjects one could be interested in only when there was nothing better to think of; James regarded Hardy as a writer of inescapably minor stature because of his provincial culture, and referred to him patronizingly as "the good little Thomas Hardy."

R. A. Scott-James's essay presents Hardy the novelist in terms on which his reputation can securely rest: first, as the chronicler and painter of the countryside, "Hardy's Wessex," which endures in the imagination more vividly than any other region described by an English writer; and second, as the creator, in both the tragic and comic dimensions, of country men and women whose destinies form an integral part of the Wessex tapestry and whose speech and vitality can bear comparison with the creations of Shakespeare. As a poet Hardy is a remarkably isolated figure. He published his first volume when he was nearly sixty years old and continued to write verse prolifically for the rest of his life. He was largely self-taught, and his diction and technique are simple and archaic to the point of crudity, yet they possess great strength of expression. The majority of his poems are personal in inspiration—love-lyrics, evocations of distant memories, meditations on old age, short stories in verse. Cecil Day Lewis, the former poet laureate, praises Hardy's verse above all for its integrity and clear vision, its refusal to overstate an emotion or falsify a situation.

Hardy as both novelist and poet was a deeply conservative writer. James, though consciously indebted to various European masters, remains one of the great innovators of his age, who radically altered the conception of what the novel could be and do. Tony Tanner's essay surveys the full range of James's immensely varied oeuvre. He draws attention to the analytical subtlety that distinguished James's writing from the outset and the critical opposition he encountered in winning acceptance for his concept of fiction. The discussion of the novels and stories is interwoven with a biographical sketch, which touches upon one of the central problems of James's artistic life—the choice of the most suitable base from which to work within the mainstream of the European tradition and the English language. England eventually prevailed over the alternatives of France and the United States. The biographical survey also gives an account of James's travels, the success or lack of recognition of his writings at different points in his career, and the factors that influenced his choice of subject. In estimating James's achievement Tanner does not attempt any grading of the novels, nor does he seek to place the familiar three phases of James's writing in order of merit. But the emphasis of his appreciation makes it clear that he places *The Portrait of a Lady* and *The Wings of the Dove* high among James's successes.

In a famous correspondence between James and Wells on the aims of the novelist, the latter wrote: "To you literature, like painting, is an end. To me, literature like architecture is a means, it has a use. I had rather be called a journalist than an artist, that is the end of it." The antithesis throws some light on the contrasting objectives of the two leading groups of novelists who succeeded the generation of James. The one (not necessarily disciples of the master) placed a Jamesian emphasis on the unique importance of the individual record of experience and tended to create characters who are endowed with exceptional awareness and whose feelings and speech are refined so as to yield the most delicate shades of meaning. The other group tended to regard fiction as a record of social change: hence they accumulated facts and circumstances and depicted characters in terms of their material position—in other words, as social units. Wells in his *Experiment in Autobiography* wrote of himself as "an individual becoming the conscious Common Man of his time and culture." James's reply was that it is Art that makes Life, not the other way round: after you have cataloged in the minutest detail the external qualities and situations of your characters, is that all? The materialist school commanded attention more quickly and won a wider readership because their novels responded to the energy and excitement of a period of rapid and dramatic change. The successors of James include Joseph Conrad, Ford Madox Ford, E. M. Forster, and, arguably, Kipling. The materialists include Wells, Arnold Bennett, Galsworthy, and Somerset Maugham. It is noteworthy that the writings of the first group, if far less popular before 1914, attract far more critical interest today.

Conrad is a difficult author to fit into any historical scheme. This is not so much because of his unusual career—a refugee Polish aristocrat who spent nearly twenty years in the British Merchant Service and did not begin to write until he was almost forty years old—but rather because his fiction now seems more closely related to the modern age than to the Edwardian. His sea stories introduce us to the pessimism of his outlook, when he portrays an enclosed professional world, dependent on skill, endurance, and discipline, but perpetually threatened by the uncontrollable forces of nature. But it is on his later novels that his high reputation rests, and to them he brings imaginative insights on Central Africa, international terrorism, and the clash between business enterprise and Third World revolutionary forces. In these novels he shows an extraordinary awareness of the precarious nature of modern organized society. Bertrand Russell wrote that Conrad gave the impression of one "who thought of civilised

. . . human life as a dangerous walk on a thin crust of barely cooled lava which at any moment might break." Brian Cox's essay argues that he rejected the Victorian belief that man can control matter and establish a permanent civilized order and that he created new forms in fiction to express humanity's predicament in an uncomprehensible universe.

Kipling's writing has obvious points of similarity to Conrad's. Both wrote of Europeans in the East placed in situations of command or administration and struggling against the implacable forces of nature; both approached English life to some extent as visitors, the one from Europe, the other from India. Alan Sandison observes that Kipling's literary gifts are apt to be obscured by his association with the idea of empire, and his essay stresses Kipling's highly original qualities as a prose writer. He dwells on Kipling's family connection with Burne-Jones and the Pre-Raphaelites, a connection that deeply influenced his early life. From this artistic strand in his upbringing, Kipling derived his sharp observation and his precise use of naturalistic detail. But the factor that links his work most closely to Conrad's is his attitude to nature, which he likewise sees as an alien and menacing force; and the corollary of this view, also shared with Conrad, is that the threat of chaos exists not only outside man but within him, and is kept at bay only by unremitting discipline and devotion to duty. Kipling's best writing, the author considers, is found in his short stories, and in order to analyze Kipling's qualities, the essay is focused on a representative selection of nine of his stories and on *Kim*. These include the famous "Without Benefit of Clergy" and one of the most imaginative of Kipling's tales, "The Short Ride of Morrowby Jukes," which he wrote at the age of nineteen. The essay deals only with Kipling's prose. The poetry is discussed in a chapter reprinted from the late Bonamy Dobrée's study *Kipling: Realist and Fabulist*.

Conrad and Ford Madox Ford shared with James a profound interest in the form of the novel and a reverence for the French masters. Conrad and James habitually conversed in French; Conrad and Ford hammered out a common approach to style and technique. These discussions took place when the latter was still under thirty, but did not in his case bear fruit until many years later. Kenneth Young explains how Ford began his career as a writer of historical novels. In 1908 he was made editor of the *English Review*, which published Hardy, James, Wells, Conrad, and Tolstoy; discovered, among others, Ezra Pound, Wyndham Lewis, D. H. Lawrence, and Norman Douglas; and rapidly became the most brilliant literary journal of the age. But Ford's masterpiece, the Tietjens tetralogy, was not written until the mid-1920's, by which time the author was able to arrange his experiences, both during World War I and in the years preceding it, into a panoramic design. The series is conceived on two planes, the historical and public and the personal and private, and Ford succeeded in combining the large dimensions of the nineteenth-century epic novel with the impressionistic, sharply focused type of description that he and Conrad had discussed.

The career of E. M. Forster follows in some respects the opposite pattern to that of Ford: he had written all his novels by the age of forty-five. Forster often explained that his imagination did not feel at home in post–World War I society. Philip Gardner points out that this was not the only reason why Forster published no more fiction in the second half of his life. The novel *Maurice,* which creates a full-length portrait of a homosexual relationship, and a number of short stories were posthumously issued only for the reason that Forster felt he could not publish as an avowed homosexual and would not publish under the pretense that he was not. The essay identifies three principal concerns in Forster's novels: the individual's search for self-realization, the attempt to harmonize different life styles and schemes of values, and the individual life set against something larger than itself—a country or the universe. Forster's famous appeal—"Only connect"—applies to all three: it is the epigraph to *Howards End,* which gives us Forster's fullest statement of his view of English society. It is to an important degree a "Condition of England" novel. The house, Howards End, with its ancient wych-elm, embodies for Forster both a countryside and a set of ideals that are threatened by the advance of urban, materialist, and selfish values.

George Moore occupies an intermediate position between the two groups of novelists described above, and his work shows at different times the influence of both the naturalist and the symbolist movements. His first novel to attract attention was *A Mummer's Wife,* in which he used Zola's technique of detailed observation to describe the life of an English theatrical touring company, but the book that established his reputation in the naturalist mode was *Esther Waters.* In the next decade he moved closer to the symbolist approach with *The Lake,* and

later still he developed a peculiarly limpid and flowing style for the writing of his two historical novels, *The Brook Kerith* and *Héloise and Abélard.* Autobiography was also a form of writing that came naturally to him, and the best of these chronicles, *Hail and Farewell,* is probably still the most widely read of his books. He was an active and eloquent member of the world of letters in Dublin, London, and Paris, and may well survive as a historical figure rather than as a literary one.

Writing in 1914 in "The New Novel," James described Wells and Bennett as "saturation novelists," writers who deluge their readers with external data at the expense of the inner life and truth of their creations. "Life" or "truth" are in this sense flexible terms, and James, Wells, and Bennett all held different conceptions of them. The criticism, if accurate at the time, is rather less than fair to Wells, whose writings passed through several distinct phases. It is certainly also relevant to the writings of Galsworthy and Maugham. But it is worth noting that in spite of his minute interest in the rural environment, the phrase has never been applied to Hardy.

With the passing of time, Wells has come to be regarded as an ideologist and a prophet of change as much as a literary artist. He first made his mark in the 1890's with such scientific fantasies as *The Time Machine;* here he could tap a romantic, even poetic, vein that none of the other materialist novelists possessed. His realistic fiction, written between 1900 and 1916, includes *Kipps, Tono-Bungay,* and *Mr. Polly,* the three exuberant picaresque novels on which his reputation mainly rests. Much of the raw material for these, as Kenneth Young points out, consisted of thinly disguised autobiography: two of the heroes of these books escape, as Wells did, from the drudgery of a draper's shop. Wells was an extremely keen observer, and James himself praised *Kipps* for having treated for the first time the English lower middle class "without the picturesque grotesque interference of which Dickens is so misleadingly full." Wells became immensely popular at this time because he was prominent in the revolt against Victorian mores and social conventions, and he spoke for the rising generation, especially the less privileged, who longed to free themselves from such constrictions. He was always a popularizer of ideas rather than a thinker, and in later life his interest shifted increasingly from fiction to social engineering and plans for the future of mankind. His outlook in this direction became increasingly gloomy and culminated in his autobiographical *Mind at the End of Its Tether*, the final testament of his pessimism.

His contemporary Arnold Bennett shared a similar determination "to get out of this"—to escape from the commercial drudgery of his adolescence, get on, and make money—though not the Wellsian impulse to change society. He trained himself to be a far more meticulous literary craftsman, studying such models of naturalism as Zola, Turgenev, Guy de Maupassant, and George Moore. Even Virginia Woolf, who disliked Bennett's technique, praised his books for their solidity and deftness of construction. Kenneth Young's essay stresses the importance in Bennett's oeuvre of his knowledge of provincial life, in particular of the Potteries region, where he grew up and which forms the background of his first work of distinction, *Anna of the Five Towns,* and of his major works, *The Old Wives' Tale* and the Clayhanger trilogy. "Saturation" in Bennett's case signifies his immersion in the physical presence of the world he conjures up. Kenneth Young judges *The Old Wives' Tale* to be the finest example of Bennett's art. The book gradually reveals a portrait of two sisters from their youth to old age, and its theme—the slow changes wrought by time—is perfectly adapted to the dropping of some unobtrusive fact into the narrative to clinch the message—"that is what life does." The last of his novels, *Imperial Palace,* is a tour de force that pushes his fictional method to its logical conclusion: the scene is a grand hotel, the London Savoy, a subject that commended itself to Bennett for the rich diversity of human interest that the affairs of clients and management presented.

Unlike most of the novelists and dramatists included in this volume, John Galsworthy had an inherited income and no urgent economic incentive to write. He trained himself to become a professional author, but was impelled by conscience rather than material reward. The years 1900–1914 mark the prime of his creative life (after World War I something of the ardor went out of his writing), and this, as we have seen, was a period of great intellectual ferment, when writers were intensely critical of the composition of society. Galsworthy strove to hold the balance between the struggle for change and the defense of the status quo, but certainly much of his sympathy went out to the reformers. Writing of his drama, Margery Morgan describes him as the outstanding British adherent of naturalism (in the full sense of the word as used above). Galsworthy's plays documented various burning issues of the day: *Strife*

(mass industrial action), *Justice* (the inhumanity of the criminal code), *Loyalties* (class-consciousness and anti-Semitism). Such pieces were well-constructed and successful in box-office terms, but they lack the originality of thought and the literary vitality of Shaw's problem plays, and have lost, as "committed" literature is apt to do, much of their original urgency and appeal. Galsworthy has enjoyed a revived popularity through the television adaptation of *The Forsyte Saga.* There is irony in this, since *The Man of Property,* the novel that launched the Saga in 1903, was written in strongly satirical terms, but in the later episodes, written in the 1920's, Galsworthy himself became more identified with "Forsyte values." Margery Morgan surveys the whole of Galsworthy's fiction and drama and makes a good case for renewed study of an unduly neglected author.

Somerset Maugham shared with Galsworthy the distinction of combining great success as both a novelist and a dramatist in the first quarter of the twentieth century. He could likewise be described as a critic of society, though certainly not as a crusader for social reform. He also possesses a number of qualities in common with Arnold Bennett. Both desired financial success and studied the book-buying market; both admired the French naturalist novelists and made France a second home; both were fascinated by the diversity and paradox of the human comedy, without expressing the desire to change society. Anthony Curtis notes that Maugham began his career as a dandy and an aesthete and draws two conclusions from this. The first is that Maugham remained highly conscious throughout his life of the sacrifices that art demands of the artist, and made this theme prominent in his work, notably in *Of Human Bondage* and *The Moon and Sixpence.* The second is that Maugham discovered as a young man that he was homosexual, and in order to conceal this he developed the image of the detached, sardonic raconteur and man of the world as the authorial stance that would serve him best. Elsewhere Curtis develops the view that Maugham, like Maupassant, was a born short-story writer who also wrote some excellent novels. He sums up with the judgment that Maugham was a literary conservative who believed in the power of linear narrative and descriptive realism, at a time when greater writers were breaking with this tradition, and who succeeded in demonstrating what was worth preserving in it.

W. B. Yeats is the only great poet discussed in the

present volume, and his greatness was slow to reveal itself. He early developed a style that seemed at first to label him—as an erotic poet in the Pre-Raphaelite tradition, with special interests in Irish mythology and the literature and ritual of the occult. Yet, seen in perspective, his whole life was devoted to creating a succession of styles that could match the gradual enlargement and deepening of his vision. His participation in the Irish literary renaissance did much to mature his writing. Yet he repeatedly baffled critics by the apparent limitation of his intellectual range and by his indifference to so many of the scientific, political, and religious issues that his contemporaries regarded as supremely important. How could a writer who took trances and magic, ghosts and fairies seriously have anything of great consequence to say to the modern mind?

George Fraser deals with this central question by considering Yeats's self-education and the construction of his personal mythology. He discusses *A Vision*, Yeats's formulation of the cyclical movement of religions and civilizations, and how this system of thought gave him access to the worlds of ancient Greece, Byzantium, and the Quattrocento, which play so important a part in his later poetry. In the end, so far from being out of touch with his century, poems such as "The Second Coming," or the two songs from his play *Resurrection*, prove that Yeats possessed a clearer, more prophetic view of the crisis of modern civilization than any of his contemporaries, and could express this insight in lyrics of genius. In discussing the construction and style of the poems, Fraser concludes that Yeats made himself master of a diction that was at once aristocratic and colloquial; such obscurity as the poems present is an obscurity of allusion, not of language.

Fraser's essay is devoted in the main to Yeats's lyrical poetry and nondramatic prose. In discussing his contribution to the theater, he points out that throughout his life Yeats remained the visionary of the Irish dramatic movement, working toward a marriage of poetry and drama that was different in kind from that of his collaborators—more lyrical in diction, more stylized and ceremonious in movement and staging. J. M. Synge and Lady Gregory by contrast aimed at a regional naturalism, which culminates in the plays of Sean O'Casey.

In her study of Synge, Elizabeth Coxhead explains how the energies of the nationalists, frustrated by the fall of their leader, Charles Stewart Parnell, found an outlet in the 1890's in the Irish literary renaissance.

Starting from the desire to free the creative powers of their compatriots from the alien English culture, the pioneers turned to Irish mythology and epic. They discovered that many among the peasantry, whose first language was Irish Gaelic, still spoke a musical and vivid English based on mental translation from the Gaelic. At this date nothing resembling an Irish theater existed. Dublin was dominated by English plays and English actors, and so a twofold creative feat was required. A repertory of Irish plays had to be written and an Irish company trained to perform them. Many hands contributed to the task, but Lady Gregory, Yeats, and Synge were the prime architects. The fact that these two aims were achieved in the few years of Synge's lifetime, with the slenderest resources and in the teeth of violent opposition, is little short of a miracle.

Synge was the only great poetic dramatist of the movement. He believed that the speech of city-dwellers had become "pallid and joyless," and hence that the modern drama, for all its intellectual penetration, had failed. By drawing upon the imagination and vocabulary of the peasantry, he succeeded in creating dramatic speech of immense vitality. Nominally, his plays are written in prose, but in both the tragedy *Riders to The Sea* and the comedy *The Playboy of the Western World*, his language achieves an imaginative strength and tension that are the property of poetry. The solution was of course a partial one: it could not have served an English dramatist of the same period, but in Ireland it was what the historical context demanded.

Bernard Shaw's plays have never ceased to succeed in the theater or to attract generations of distinguished directors and performers, and they continue to be adapted as popular films and musicals. Yet since his death, Shaw, in England at least, has received surprisingly little attention from the critics. Besides surveying Shaw's dramatic achievement, Margery Morgan presents his career as a connected whole, tracing the links between his early resolve to train himself as a public speaker, his novels, his years as a critic of music, art, and drama, his championing of such controversial contemporaries as Ibsen and Wagner, and his political writings. Shaw's command of the arts of controversy and his tendency to disparage the profession of playwright have sometimes encouraged the view that his plays are little more than dramatized debates. Margery Morgan examines Shaw's dramatic technique and the many varieties of play or dramatic effect he

INTRODUCTION

devised for the exposition of different ideas. *The Doctor's Dilemma* and *Pygmalion* are classic examples of the problem play. *Major Barbara* combines drawing-room comedy with Dickensian melodrama. *Misalliance* demonstrates Shaw's gift for fantasy and burlesque, forms of writing that were related to the futurist and other movements of the time. *St. Joan* blends the modes of chronicle play and courtroom drama. *Heartbreak House* approaches a symbolist dramatic technique, replacing logical plotting with a patterning of the principal themes. In his late plays farflung and exotic milieux replace the English domestic scene, and it is the planet as a whole that becomes the setting for his plots. But to the end of his career, Shaw continued to create scenes and characters that could stretch the virtuosity of his performers.

Both the historians included in this volume are admired for their powers of expression as well as for the mastery of their material. G. M. Trevelyan, son of Sir George Otto Trevelyan and great-nephew of Lord Macaulay, belonged to a dynasty of historians. As to why he chose to apply his literary gifts to history rather than to any other form of writing, Sir John Plumb finds the answer in Trevelyan's passionate interest in Time. Trevelyan defined it himself when he wrote of the historian's "ardour to know what really happened in that land of mystery which we call the past." The essay points out that the appearance of the book that established Trevelyan's reputation, *Garibaldi's Defence of the Roman Republic*, coincided with the electoral triumph of the British Liberal party. The Garibaldian epic was felt to symbolize the victory of liberal humanism and was thus completely in harmony with the spirit of those years. Apart from Trevelyan's other achievements in historical scholarship, the essay pays tribute to two works that have become popular classics for the layman, *The History of England* and *English Social History*.

John Connell's essay on Winston Churchill notes the paradox that, while from the beginning of his career Churchill earned his living as a journalist, biographer, and historian, it is impossible to consider Churchill the writer and Churchill the statesman in separate compartments. No other historian has been called upon to lead his nation at a moment of world crisis: no other national leader has had recourse to his literary powers to confront such a crisis as Churchill did through his oratory in 1940. His histories of both the First and the Second World

Wars are of course vulnerable on many counts, since they are also political documents that blend the functions of historian and advocate. But they are also unique as the simultaneous creation of the artist and the participant. Churchill, as the author sums up, was a man of words and deeds: the word did not fail to inform, mold, and fortify the deed.

Between the passing of the last of the Victorian poets—Tennyson, Browning, Morris, and Swinburne—and 1914, English poetry was in a phase of near stagnation. The springs of the romantic tradition were all but exhausted, and no strong fresh current was discernible. The most vigorous voice was that of Kipling, but he was addressing a different audience. With the solitary exception of Yeats, the poets of this period were followers rather than innovators, setting themselves limited tasks in which craftsmanship played an important part. In describing the work of Robert Bridges, John Sparrow remarks that he is the author of the largest body of entirely beautiful poetry in the language. He is referring to Bridges's conviction that art is the creation of beauty, that beauty can be explained only as a form of goodness; these beliefs were the creative purpose to which Bridges dedicated his career. This devotion, he points out, is a rare phenomenon among English writers and cuts off the poet from a wide range of human experience. Bridges's career was singleminded and biographically uneventful. He was a classical scholar, a lover of music, a fine linguist, and was highly sensitive to the subtleties of prosody and meter. He devoted himself to his art with ascetic fervor, to the extent that his undoubted lyrical delicacy at times takes on a mannered air, as if constrained by his austere and disciplined temperament.

Some of these generalizations could also be applied to the career of A. E. Housman. But Housman was a great classical scholar whose academic work absorbed a high proportion of his time and energy. His muse was a rare visitant and he certainly did not regard poetry as his vocation. The composition of *A Shropshire Lad* was, he admitted, a painful process: this must surely be self-evident from the contents. Many of Bridges's poems are serene expressions of his poetic creed. Many of Housman's poems are cast in dramatic or narrative form, lyrics of outcry against a tragic order of things. Housman's original inspiration sprang from the emotions of youth, the period when untried ideals and untutored desires, at their strongest, first encounter a hostile or indifferent world. At his best he voices these passions with an extraordinary force in which feeling, language, and meter are completely fused. But at this stage of emotional development he stops short, so that the verses he wrote at sixty and later display almost exactly the same qualities, wonderfully unimpaired yet also undeveloped, as those he was writing as a young man.

The poetry inspired by World War I might appear to belong to an easily defined category, but this is not the case. John Press's careful classification of his material plays an important part in his critical judgment. As many of the combatants have testified, fighting was an experience that cut them off from civilians and from their own past and future. Some of the survivors succeeded in blocking off the memory from their later lives, others did not: some died too early in the conflict to experience its full horror, others could not transmute their experiences into poetry until years later. It is especially noticeable that the prewar poetic trends—imagism, Georgianism, the early budding of the modern movement—had a negligible influence upon war poetry, while the latter scarcely affected the modern movement when it flowered in the 1920's.

The essay draws a broad dividing line between those who died in the first two years of the war—the "morning heroes," for whom some illusions concerning the chivalry of the struggle were still possible— and those who encountered the mass slaughter of the Somme and the nightmare of the trenches. The best known in the first category were Rupert Brooke, Julian Grenfell, and Charles Sorley, whose war poems have their roots in a peacetime conception of fighting. The foremost names in the latter group, whose poetry sprang directly from the ordeal of trench warfare, gas, and mud, were Siegfried Sassoon, Robert Graves, Isaac Rosenberg, Wilfred Owen, and David Jones. Although Sassoon survived the war by nearly half a century, his fame as a war poet rests very largely on the powerful, often satirical lyrics that he wrote between 1916 and 1918. Robert Graves, now almost the sole survivor of his generation, composed little war poetry, but wrote the most vivid memoir in English of active service, *Goodbye to All That*; his subsequent distinguished literary career is the subject of a separate essay in Volume VII.

To read any of these writers is to marvel that poetry could be composed at all under such condi-

tions. But the work of Isaac Rosenberg and David Jones must remind us that the difficulties were even greater for private soldiers than for officers. "Nobody but a private in the army knows what it is to be a slave," Rosenberg wrote, with justification; but posterity at least has recognized his true stature. David Jones, like Rosenberg a painter, poet, and private soldier, did not publish his *In Parenthesis* until 1937. This epic, part prose, part verse, which describes the march of his battalion to the Somme and the annihilation of his platoon in the battle, is the most difficult poem to come out of World War I, but it has stood the test of time.

Wilfred Owen has long been considered the outstanding British poet of the war. One of his most striking innovations was the use of pararhyme and assonance. He was already experimenting with these in 1913 and the application of them to war poetry was a discovery of genius, the unfulfilled rhymes echoing the unfulfilled lives and aspirations of the combatants. Dominic Hibberd considers that Owen's major contribution to the poetry of war is to be found not in his sonnets or satirical poems but in his elegies, and he notes that his finest poems are laments for the dead rather than exposures of the horrors of war. The dating of Owen's poems is a difficult task, and since the order given in earlier editions is largely arbitrary, the probable order of composition is set out here. Hibberd concludes that Owen's poetry at its best belongs to English literature, and not just to a historical event.

The series was founded by Laurence Brander, then director of publications, at the British Council. The first editor was T. O. Beachcroft, himself a distinguished writer of short stories. His successors were the late Bonamy Dobrée, formerly Professor of English Literature at the University of Leeds; Geoffrey Bullough, Professor Emeritus of English Literature, King's College, London, and author of *The Narrative and Dramatic Sources of Shakespeare*; and since 1970 the present writer. To these founders and predecessors *British Writers* is deeply indebted for the design of the series, the planning of its scope, and the distinction of their editorship, and I personally for many years of friendship and advice, and invaluable experience generously shared.

—Ian Scott-Kilvert

Chronological Table

CHRONOLOGICAL TABLE

John Ruskin's *Modern Painters* (1843–1860)

Wagner's *The Flying Dutchman* performed in Dresden

Death of Robert Southey

Edvard Grieg born

Henry James born

1844 Rochdale Society of Equitable Pioneers, one of the first consumers' cooperatives, founded by twenty-eight Lancashire weavers

James K. Polk elected president

Elizabeth Barrett Browning's *Poems*, including "The Cry of the Children"

Dickens' *Martin Chuzzlewit*

Disraeli's *Coningsby*

Dumas's *The Three Musketeers*

Turner's *Rain, Steam and Speed*

Gerard Manley Hopkins born

Robert Bridges born

Friedrich Wilhelm Nietzsche born

Henri (Le Douanier) Rousseau born

Paul Verlaine born

1845 The great potato famine in Ireland begins (1845–1849)

Disraeli's *Sybil*

Dumas's *The Count of Monte Cristo*

Poe's *The Raven and Other Poems*

Wagner's *Tannhäuser* performed in Dresden

Death of Thomas Hood

1846 Repeal of the Corn Laws

Mexican War (1846–1848)

The *Daily News* founded (edited by Dickens the first three weeks)

Elias Howe's sewing machine patented

Standard-gauge railway introduced in Britain

Balzac's *La Cousine Bette*

The Brontës' pseudonymous *Poems by Currer, Ellis and Acton Bell*

Lear's *Book of Nonsense*

Melville's *Typee*

1847 The California gold rush begins

The Mormons, led by Brigham Young, found Salt Lake City

The Ten Hours Factory Act

James Simpson uses chloroform as an anesthetic

Anne Brontë's *Agnes Grey*

Charlotte Brontë's *Jane Eyre*

Emily Brontë's *Wuthering Heights*

Emerson's *Poems*

Tennyson's *The Princess*

Balzac's *Le Cousin Pons*

1848 The year of revolutions in France, Germany, Italy, Hungary, Poland

Marx and Engels issue *The Communist Manifesto*

The Chartist Petition

The Pre-Raphaelite Brotherhood founded

Zachary Taylor elected president

Anne Brontë's *The Tenant of Wildfell Hall*

Dickens' *Dombey and Son*

Dumas's *La Dame aux camélias*

Elizabeth Gaskell's *Mary Barton*

Macaulay's *History of England* (1848–1861)

Mill's *Principles of Political Economy*

Thackeray's *Vanity Fair*

Death of Emily Brontë

Paul Gauguin born

1849 Bedford College for women founded

Arnold's *The Strayed Reveller*

Charlotte Brontë's *Shirley*

Ruskin's *The Seven Lamps of Architecture*

Death of Anne Brontë

Death of Frédéric Chopin

Death of Edgar Allan Poe

August Strindberg born

1850 The Public Libraries Act

First submarine telegraph cable laid between Dover and Calais

Millard Fillmore succeeds to the presidency after the death of Taylor

Elizabeth Barrett Browning's *Sonnets from the Portuguese*

Carlyle's *Latter-Day Pamphlets*

Dickens' *Household Words* (1850–1859) and *David Copperfield*

Nathaniel Hawthorne's *The Scarlet Letter*

Charles Kingsley's *Alton Locke*

The Pre-Raphaelites publish the *Germ*

Tennyson's *In Memoriam*

Thackeray's *The History of Pendennis*

Wordsworth's *The Prelude*

Death of Honoré de Balzac

Death of William Wordsworth

CHRONOLOGICAL TABLE

Guy de Maupassant born
Robert Louis Stevenson born
1851 The Great Exhibition opens at the Crystal Palace in Hyde Park
Louis Napoleon seizes power in France
Elizabeth Gaskell's *Cranford* (1851–1853)
Melville's *Moby Dick*
Hawthorne's *The House of the Seven Gables*
Meredith's *Poems*
Ruskin's *The Stones of Venice* (1851–1853)
Verdi's *Rigoletto* produced in Venice
1852 The Second Empire proclaimed, with Napoleon III as emperor
David Livingstone begins to explore the Zambezi (1852–1856)
Franklin Pierce elected president
Arnold's *Empedocles on Etna*
Harriet Beecher Stowe's *Uncle Tom's Cabin*
Thackeray's *The History of Henry Esmond, Esq.*
George Moore born
Augusta (Persse) Gregory born
1853 Crimean War (1853–1856)
Arnold's *Poems*, including "The Scholar Gypsy" and "Sohrab and Rustum"
Charlotte Brontë's *Villette*
Elizabeth Gaskell's *Ruth*
Hawthorne's *Tanglewood Tales for Girls and Boys*
Verdi's *Il Trovatore* and *La Traviata*
Vincent Van Gogh born
1854 Frederick Denison Maurice's Working Men's College founded in London with more than 130 pupils
Battle of Balaklava
Dickens' *Hard Times*
Theodor Mommsen's *History of Rome* (1854–1856)
Tennyson's "The Charge of the Light Brigade"
Thoreau's *Walden*
Florence Nightingale in the Crimea (1854–1856)
Arthur Rimbaud born
Oscar Wilde born
1855 Robert Browning's *Men and Women*
Elizabeth Gaskell's *North and South*

Tennyson's *Maud*
Thackeray's *The Newcomes*
Trollope's *The Warden*
Whitman's *Leaves of Grass*
Death of Charlotte Brontë
1856 Henry Bessemer's steel process invented
James Buchanan elected president
Flaubert's *Madame Bovary* (new edition in book form, 1857)
Death of Robert Schumann
Sigmund Freud born
George Bernard Shaw born
1857 The Indian Mutiny begins; crushed in 1858
The *Atlantic Monthly* founded
Dred Scott decision, involving legal status of slaves
Baudelaire's *Les Fleurs du mal*
Charlotte Brontë's *The Professor*
Elizabeth Barrett Browning's *Aurora Leigh*
Dickens' *Little Dorritt*
Elizabeth Gaskell's *The Life of Charlotte Brontë*
Thomas Hughes's *Tom Brown's School Days*
Trollope's *Barchester Towers*
Joseph Conrad (Józef Korzeniowski) born
Edward Elgar born
George Gissing born
1858 Carlyle's *History of Frederick the Great* (1858–1865)
Arthur Hugh Clough's *Amours de voyage* first published
George Eliot's *Scenes of Clerical Life*
Morris' *The Defence of Guinevere*
Trollope's *Dr. Thorne*
Giacomo Puccini born
1859 John Brown raids Harper's Ferry and is executed
Edwin Drake drills the first oil well, in Pennsylvania
Charles Darwin's *The Origin of Species*
Dickens' *A Tale of Two Cities*
George Eliot's *Adam Bede*
FitzGerald's *The Rubaiyat of Omar Khayyam*
Meredith's *The Ordeal of Richard Feverel*
Mill's *On Liberty*

xix

Tennyson's *Idylls of the King*
Death of Thomas De Quincey
Death of Thomas Babington Macaulay
A. E. Housman born
Francis Thompson born

1860 Giuseppe Garibaldi's "Thousand" liberate Sicily and Naples
Abraham Lincoln elected president
The *Cornhill* magazine founded with Thackeray as editor
Wilkie Collins' *The Woman in White*
George Eliot's *The Mill on the Floss*
James Matthew (J. M.) Barrie born
Anton Chekhov born
Gustave Mahler born

1861 American Civil War (1861–1865)
Victor Emmanuel II of Sardinia proclaimed king of Italy
Louis Pasteur presents the germ theory of disease
Arnold's *Lectures on Translating Homer*
Dickens' *Great Expectations*
George Eliot's *Silas Marner*
Meredith's *Evan Harrington*
Francis Turner Palgrave's *The Golden Treasury*
Trollope's *Framley Parsonage*
Peacock's *Gryll Grange*
Death of Prince Albert
Death of Elizabeth Barrett Browning
Death of Arthur Hugh Clough

1862 George Eliot's *Romola*
Victor Hugo's *Les Misérables*
Meredith's *Modern Love*
Christina Rossetti's *Goblin Market*
Ruskin's *Unto This Last*
Trollope's *Orley Farm*
Turgenev's *Fathers and Sons*
Death of Henry David Thoreau
Claude Debussy born

1863 Thomas Huxley's *Man's Place in Nature*
Lincoln's Gettysburg Address
Emancipation Proclamation
Ernest Renan's *La Vie de Jésus*
Berlioz's *Les Troyens* produced in Paris
Manet's *Le Déjeuner sur l'herbe*
Tolstoy's *War and Peace* (1863–1869)
Death of William Makepeace Thackeray

1864 The Geneva Red Cross Convention signed by twelve nations

Robert Browning's *Dramatis Personae*
John Henry Newman's *Apologia pro vita sua*
Tennyson's *Enoch Arden*
Trollope's *The Small House at Allington*
Death of Nathaniel Hawthorne
Death of Walter Savage Landor
Richard Strauss born
Henri de Toulouse-Lautrec born

1865 Assassination of Lincoln; Andrew Johnson succeeds to the presidency
13th Amendment abolishes slavery in the United States
Massachusetts Institute of Technology opened
Arnold's *Essays in Criticism* (1st series)
Carroll's *Alice's Adventures in Wonderland*
Dickens' *Our Mutual Friend*
Meredith's *Rhoda Fleming*
A. C. Swinburne's *Atalanta in Calydon*
Wagner's *Tristan und Isolde* produced in Munich
Death of Elizabeth Gaskell
Rudyard Kipling born
Jean Sibelius born
William Butler Yeats born

1866 Alfred Nobel invents dynamite
Austria at war with Prussia
First successful transatlantic telegraph cable laid
Dostoyevsky's *Crime and Punishment*
George Eliot's *Felix Holt, the Radical*
Elizabeth Gaskell's *Wives and Daughters*
Ibsen's *Brand*
Swinburne's *Poems and Ballads*
Death of Thomas Love Peacock
Herbert George (H. G.) Wells born

1867 The second Reform Bill
Arnold's *New Poems*
Bagehot's *The English Constitution*
Carlyle's *Shooting Niagara*
Marx's *Das Kapital* (vol. I)
Ibsen's *Peer Gynt*
Trollope's *The Last Chronicle of Barset*
Verdi's *Don Carlos* produced in Paris
Death of Charles Baudelaire
Arnold Bennett born
John Galsworthy born

CHRONOLOGICAL TABLE

Luigi Pirandello born

1868 Gladstone becomes prime minister (1868–1874)

Johnson impeached by House of Representatives; acquitted by Senate

Ulysses S. Grant elected president

Robert Browning's *The Ring and the Book* (1868–1869)

Collins' *The Moonstone*

Dostoyevsky's *The Idiot*

Wagner's *Die Meistersinger* produced in Munich

Norman Douglas born

1869 The Suez Canal opened

Girton College, Cambridge, founded for women students

Arnold's *Culture and Anarchy*

Flaubert's *L'Education sentimentale* (dated 1870)

Mill's *The Subjection of Women*

Trollope's *Phineas Finn*

Wagner's *Das Rheingold* produced in Munich

Death of Hector Berlioz

André Gide born

Henri Matisse born

1870 Franco-Prussian War (1870–1871)

Elementary Education Act establishes schools under the aegis of local boards

Heinrich Schliemann begins to excavate Troy

Dickens' *Edwin Drood*

Disraeli's *Lothair*

Morris' *The Earthly Paradise*

Dante Gabriel Rossetti's *Poems*

Death of Charles Dickens

Death of Alexandre Dumas (père)

Vladimir Ilyich Lenin born

1871 The Paris Commune

Trade unions legalized

Newnham College, Cambridge, founded for women students

Carroll's *Through the Looking Glass*

Darwin's *The Descent of Man*

Meredith's *The Adventures of Harry Richmond*

Swinburne's *Songs Before Sunrise*

Verdi's *Aida* produced in Cairo

Theodore Dreiser born

Marcel Proust born

John Millington Synge born

Paul Valéry born

1872 Samuel Butler's *Erewhon*

George Eliot's *Middlemarch*

Grant reelected

Hardy's *Under the Greenwood Tree*

Turgenev's *A Month in the Country* first performed

1873 E. Remington and Sons begins manufacturing typewriters

Arnold's *Literature and Dogma*

Mill's *Autobiography*

Pater's *Studies in the History of the Renaissance*

Tolstoy's *Anna Karenina* (1873–1877)

Trollope's *The Eustace Diamonds*

Death of John Stuart Mill

Ford Madox Hueffer (Ford) born

1874 Disraeli becomes prime minister

Hardy's *Far from the Madding Crowd*

James Thomson's *The City of Dreadful Night*

Gilbert Keith (G. K.) Chesterton born

Winston Churchill born

William Somerset Maugham born

Gertrude Stein born

1875 Britain buys Suez Canal shares

Trollope's *The Way We Live Now*

Bizet's *Carmen* produced in Paris

Death of Hans Christian Andersen

Death of Georges Bizet

Carl Jung born

Thomas Mann born

Maurice Ravel born

Rainer Maria Rilke born

1876 Bell transmits first message on the telephone

F. H. Bradley's *Ethical Studies*

George Eliot's *Daniel Deronda*

Henry James's *Roderick Hudson*

Meredith's *Beauchamp's Career*

Morris' *Sigurd the Volsung*

Trollope's *The Prime Minister*

Mark Twain's *The Adventures of Tom Sawyer*

Brahms's *First Symphony*

Wagner's *Götterdämmerung* and *Siegfried* produced in Bayreuth

George Macaulay (G. M.) Trevelyan born

1877 Russia and Turkey at war

Edison invents the phonograph record
Rutherford B. Hayes elected president after Electoral Commission awards him disputed votes
Ibsen's *Pillars of Society*
Henry James's *The American*
Zola's *L'Assommoir*
Cézanne shows sixteen pictures at the third impressionist exhibition

1878 The Congress of Berlin ends the Russo-Turkish War
Electric street lighting introduced in London
Hardy's *The Return of the Native*
James's *The Europeans*
Swinburne's *Poems and Ballads, Second Series*
Edward Thomas born

1879 Somerville College and Lady Margaret Hall opened at Oxford for women
The London telephone exchange built
Gladstone's Midlothian campaign (1879–1880)
Browning's *Dramatic Idyls*
Ibsen's *A Doll's House*
Henry James's *Daisy Miller*
Meredith's *The Egoist*
Albert Einstein born
Edward Morgan (E. M.) Forster born
Paul Klee born
Josef Stalin born
Leon Trotsky born

1880 Gladstone's second term as prime minister (1880–1885)
James A. Garfield elected president
Louis Pasteur discovers streptococcus
Browning's *Dramatic Idyls, Second Series*
Disraeli's *Endymion*
Dostoyevsky's *The Brothers Karamazov*
Hardy's *The Trumpet-Major*
James Thomson's *The City of Dreadful Night*
Zola's *Nana*
Death of George Eliot
Death of Gustave Flaubert
Jacob Epstein born
Lytton Strachey born

1881 Garfield assassinated; Chester A. Arthur succeeds to the presidency
Ibsen's *Ghosts*

Henry James's *The Portrait of a Lady* and *Washington Square*
D. G. Rossetti's *Ballads and Sonnets*
Death of Thomas Carlyle
Death of Benjamin Disraeli
Béla Bartók born
Pablo Picasso born

1882 Triple Alliance formed between German empire, Austrian empire, and Italy
Married Women's Property Act passed in Britain
Britain occupies Egypt and the Sudan
Ibsen's *An Enemy of the People*
Wagner's *Parsifal*
Deaths of Charles Darwin, Ralph Waldo Emerson, Dante Gabriel Rossetti, Anthony Trollope
James Joyce born
Franklin Delano Roosevelt born
Igor Stravinsky born
Virginia (Stephen) Woolf born

1883 Uprising of the Mahdi: Britain evacuates the Sudan
Metropolitan Opera opens
Royal College of Music opens
T. H. Green's *Ethics*
Nietzsche's *Thus Spake Zarathustra* (1883–1891)
Stevenson's *Treasure Island*
Deaths of Edward Fitzgerald, Karl Marx, Ivan Turgenev, Richard Wagner
Franz Kafka born
John Maynard Keynes born

1884 The *Oxford English Dictionary* begins publishing
The Fabian Society founded
Hiram Maxim's recoil-operated machine gun invented
Ibsen's *The Wild Duck*
Mark Twain's *Adventures of Huckleberry Finn*
Ivy Compton-Burnett born
Percy Wyndham Lewis born
Sean O'Casey (John Casey) born

1885 The Mahdi captures Khartoum: General Gordon killed
Gottlieb Daimler invents an internal combusion engine
Pasteur perfects vaccine for rabies
Marx's *Das Kapital* (vol. II)

Meredith's *Diana of the Crossways*
Maupassant's *Bel-Ami*
Pater's *Marius the Epicurean*
Tolstoy's *The Power of Darkness*
Zola's *Germinal*
Death of Victor Hugo
David Herbert (D. H.) Lawrence born
Ezra Pound born
Sinclair Lewis born

1886 The Canadian Pacific Railway completed
Gold discovered in the Transvaal
The Statue of Liberty dedicated
Linotype first used in the New York *Herald Tribune*
Hardy's *The Mayor of Casterbridge*
Ibsen's *Rosmersholm*
Henry James's *The Bostonians* and *The Princess Casamassima*
Kipling's *Departmental Ditties*
Nietzsche's *Beyond Good and Evil*
Rimbaud's *Les Illuminations*
Stevenson's *The Strange Case of Dr. Jekyll and Mr. Hyde*
Siegfried Sassoon born
Death of Franz Liszt

1887 Hardy's *The Woodlanders*
Verdi's *Otello*
Zola's *La Terre*
Rupert Brooke born
Edith Sitwell born

1888 Henry James's *The Aspern Papers*
Kipling's *Plain Tales from the Hills*
Rimsky-Korsakov's *Scheherazade*
Strindberg's *Miss Julie*
Death of Matthew Arnold
Death of Edward Lear
Thomas Stearns (T. S.) Eliot born
Thomas Edward (T. E.) Lawrence born
Kathleen Beauchamp (Katherine Mansfield) born
Julien Grenfell born
Eugene O'Neill born

1889 George Eastman produces a celluloid roll film
Henri Bergson's *Time* and *Freewill*
Yeats's *The Wanderings of Oisin*
Death of Robert Browning
Death of Gerard Manley Hopkins
Marc Chagall born
Charles Chaplin born
Adolf Hitler born

1890 Morris founds the Kelmscott Press
Robert Bridges's *Shorter Poems*
Ibsen's *Hedda Gabler*
William James's *The Principles of Psychology*
Henry James's *The Tragic Muse*
Morris' *News From Nowhere*
Tolstoy's *The Kreutzer Sonata*
Ivor Gurney born
Isaac Rosenberg born
Death of John Henry Newman
Death of Vincent Van Gogh
Charles De Gaulle born

1891 Debussy's *L'Après-midi d'un faune*
Gissing's *New Grub Street*
Hardy's *Tess of the d'Urbervilles*
Wilde's *The Picture of Dorian Gray*
Death of Herman Melville
Death of Arthur Rimbaud

1892 Conan Doyle's *The Adventures of Sherlock Holmes*
Kipling's *Barrack-Room Ballads*
Shaw's *Widowers' Houses*
Toulouse-Lautrec's *At the Moulin de la Galette*
Zola's *La Débâcle*
Wilde's *Lady Windermere's Fan*
Death of Alfred, Lord Tennyson
Death of Walt Whitman

1893 The World's Columbian Exposition opens in Chicago
Munch's *The Scream*
Tchaikovsky's Pathetic Symphony
Verdi's *Falstaff*
Wilde's *A Woman of No Importance* and *Salomé*
Death of Guy de Maupassant
Death of Peter Ilyich Tchaikovsky
Wilfred Owen born

1894 Trial and conviction of Alfred Dreyfus
Kipling's *The Jungle Book*
Moore's *Esther Waters*
Marx's *Das Kapital* (vol. III)
Aubrey Beardsley's *The Yellow Book* begins to appear quarterly (1894–1897)
Shaw's *Arms and the Man*
Deaths of Walter Pater, Robert Louis Stevenson, Christina Rossetti
Aldous Huxley born
John Boynton (J. B.) Priestley born

CHRONOLOGICAL TABLE

1895   Trial and imprisonment of Oscar Wilde
Roentgen discovers X rays
Marconi sends first wireless telegraph signals
The National Trust founded
Conrad's *Almayer's Folly*
Hardy's *Jude the Obscure*
Wells's *The Time Machine*
Wilde's *The Importance of Being Earnest*
Yeats's *Poems*
Deaths of Friedrich Engels, Louis Pasteur, and Arthur Rimbaud
Robert Graves born
Frank Raymond (F. R.) Leavis born
Charles Sorley born

1896   The Nobel Prizes established
First modern Olympic Games held in Athens
Chekhov's *The Seagull*
Housman's *A Shropshire Lad*
Ibsen's *John Gabriel Borkman*
Puccini's *La Bohème*
Wells's *The Island of Dr. Moreau*
Death of William Morris
Death of Alfred Nobel
Death of Paul Verlaine
Edmund Blunden born
John Dos Passos born
F. Scott Fitzgerald born

1897   The Klondike Gold Rush begins
Conrad's *The Nigger of the Narcissus*
Havelock Ellis' *Studies in the Psychology of Sex* begins publication (1897–1936)
Henry James's *The Spoils of Poynton* and *What Maisie Knew*
Kipling's *Captains Courageous*
Rostand's *Cyrano de Bergerac*
Shaw's *Candida* and *The Devil's Disciple*
Wells's *The Invisible Man*
Death of Johannes Brahms
William Faulkner born

1898   Pierre and Marie Curie discover radium
Count von Zeppelin builds an airship
Chekhov's *Uncle Vanya*
Hardy's *Wessex Poems*
Henry James's *The Turn of the Screw*
Moore's *Evelyn Innes*

Shaw's *Caesar and Cleopatra* and *You Never Can Tell*
Wells's *The War of the Worlds*
Wilde's *The Ballad of Reading Gaol*
Death of Lewis Carroll
Death of William Ewart Gladstone
Bertolt Brecht born
René Magritte born

1899   Boer War (1899–1902)
Conrad's *Heart of Darkness* first published (in book form, 1902)
Elgar's *Enigma Variations*
Ernst Haeckel's *The Riddle of the Universe*
Kipling's *Stalky and Co.*
Tolstoy's *Resurrection*
Noel Coward born
Ernest Hemingway born

1900   British Labour party founded.
Boxer Rebellion in China
Reginald A. Fessenden transmits speech by wireless
First Zeppelin trial flight
Max Planck presents his first paper on the quantum theory
Joseph Conrad's *Lord Jim*
Edward Elgar's *The Dream of Gerontius*
Sigmund Freud's *The Interpretation of Dreams*
William Butler Yeats's *The Shadowy Waters*
Deaths of Friedrich Nietzsche, John Ruskin, and Oscar Wilde

1901–1910   **Reign of King Edward VII**
1901   Marconi transmits messages by wireless telegraph from Cornwall to Newfoundland
Chekhov's *Three Sisters*
Freud's *Psychopathology of Everyday Life*
Rudyard Kipling's *Kim*
Thomas Mann's *Buddenbrooks*
George Bernard Shaw's *Captain Brassbound's Conversion*
August Strindberg's *The Dance of Death*
Death of Giuseppe Verdi
Death of Henri de Toulouse-Lautrec
André Malraux born

xxiv

1902 J. M. Barrie's *The Admirable Crichton*
Arnold Bennett's *Anna of the Five Towns*
Cézanne's *Le Lac D'Annecy*
Conrad's *Heart of Darkness*
Henry James's *The Wings of the Dove*
William James's *The Varieties of Religious Experience*
Kipling's *Just So Stories*
Maugham's *Mrs. Craddock*
Times Literary Supplement begins publishing
Deaths of Samuel Butler, Cecil Rhodes, and Émile Zola

1903 At its London congress the Russian Social Democratic Party divides into Mensheviks, led by Plekhanov, and Bolsheviks, led by Lenin
The treaty of Panama places the Canal Zone in U.S. hands for a nominal rent
Motor cars regulated in Britain to a 20-mile-per-hour limit
The Wright brothers make a successful flight in the U.S.
Burlington magazine founded
Samuel Butler's *The Way of All Flesh*
George Gissing's *The Private Papers of Henry Ryecroft*
Hardy's *The Dynasts*
Henry James's *The Ambassadors*
Shaw's *Man and Superman*
Synge's *Riders to the Sea* produced in Dublin
Yeats's *In the Seven Woods* and *On Baile's Strand*
Death of James McNeill Whistler
George Orwell (Eric Blair) born

1904 Russo-Japanese war (1904–1905)
Construction of the Panama Canal begins
The ultraviolet lamp invented
The engineering firm of Rolls Royce founded
Chekhov's *The Cherry Orchard*
Conrad's *Nostromo*
Henry James's *The Golden Bowl*
Kipling's *Traffics and Discoveries*
Georges Rouault's *Head of a Tragic Clown*

G. M. Trevelyan's *England Under the Stuarts*
Puccini's *Madame Butterfly*
First Shaw–Granville Barker season at the Royal Court Theatre
The Abbey Theatre founded in Dublin
Deaths of Anton Chekhov, Leslie Stephen, and Antonín Dvořák
Salvador Dali, Graham Greene, Christopher Isherwood born

1905 Russian sailors on the battleship *Potemkin* mutiny
After riots and a general strike the czar concedes demands by the Duma for legislative powers, a wider franchise, and civil liberties
Albert Einstein publishes his first theory of relativity
The Austin Motor Company founded
Bennett's *Tales of the Five Towns*
Claude Debussy's *La Mer*
Forster's *Where Angels Fear to Tread*
Strauss's *Salome*
Wells's *Kipps*
Wilde's *De Profundis*
Arthur Koestler, Anthony Powell, and Charles Percy (C. P.) Snow born

1906 Liberals win a landslide victory in the British general election
The Trades Disputes Act legitimizes peaceful picketing in Britain
Captain Dreyfus rehabilitated in France
J. J. Thomson begins research on gamma rays
The U.S. Pure Food and Drug Act passed
Churchill's *Lord Randolph Churchill*
Galsworthy's *The Man of Property*
Kipling's *Puck of Pook's Hill*
Shaw's *The Doctor's Dilemma*
Yeats's *Poems 1899–1905*
Deaths of Pierre Curie, Paul Cézanne, Henrik Ibsen
Samuel Beckett born
John Betjeman born

1907 Exhibition of cubist paintings in Paris
Henry Adams's *The Education of Henry Adams*
Bergson's *Creative Evolution*

Conrad's *The Secret Agent*
Forster's *The Longest Journey*
André Gide's *La Porte étroite*
Shaw's *John Bull's Other Island* and *Major Barbara*
Synge's *The Playboy of the Western World*
Trevelyan's *Garibaldi's Defence of the Roman Republic*
Death of Edvard Grieg
Death of Francis Thompson
Wystan Hugh (W. H.) Auden born
Louis MacNeice born

1908 Herbert Asquith becomes prime minister
David Lloyd George becomes chancellor of the exchequer
The Young Turks seize power in Istanbul
William Howard Taft defeats William Jennings Bryan and is elected president
Henry Ford's Model T car produced
Bennett's *The Old Wives' Tale*
Pierre Bonnard's *Nude Against the Light*
Georges Braque's *House at L'Estaque*
Chesterton's *The Man Who Was Thursday*
Jacob Epstein's *Figures* erected in London
Forster's *A Room with a View*
Anatole France's *L'Ile des Pingouins*
Henri Matisse's *Bonheur de vivre*
Edward Elgar's *First Symphony*
Ford Madox Ford founds the *English Review*

1909 The Young Turks depose Sultan Abdul Hamid
The Anglo-Persian Oil Company formed
Louis Bleriot crosses the English Channel from France by monoplane
Admiral Robert Peary reaches the North Pole
Freud lectures at Clark University (Worcester, Mass.) on psychoanalysis
Serge Diaghilev's Ballets Russes opens in Paris
Galsworthy's *Strife*
Hardy's *Time's Laughingstocks*

Claude Monet's *Water Lilies*
Trevelyan's *Garibaldi and the Thousand*
Wells's *Tono-Bungay* first published (book form, 1909)
Deaths of George Meredith, John Millington Synge, and Algernon Charles Swinburne

1910–1936 **Reign of King George V**
1910 The Liberals win the British general election
Marie Curie's *Treatise on Radiography*
Arthur Evans excavates Cnossus
Edouard Manet and the first post-impressionist exhibition in London
Filippo Marinetti publishes "Manifesto of the Futurist Painters"
Norman Angell's *The Great Illusion*
Bennett's *Clayhanger*
Forster's *Howards End*
Galsworthy's *Justice* and *The Silver Box*
Kipling's *Rewards and Fairies*
Rimsky-Korsakov's *Le Coq d'or*
Stravinsky's *The Fire-Bird*
Vaughan Williams' *A Sea Symphony*
Wells's *The History of Mr. Polly*
Wells's *The New Machiavelli* first published (book form, 1911)
Deaths of William James, Leo Tolstoy, Henri (Le Douanier) Rousseau, and Mark Twain

1911 Lloyd George introduces National Health Insurance Bill
Suffragette riots in Whitehall
Roald Amundsen reaches the South Pole
Bennett's *The Card*
Chagall's *Self Portrait with Seven Fingers*
Conrad's *Under Western Eyes*
D. H. Lawrence's *The White Peacock*
Katherine Mansfield's *In a German Pension*
Edward Marsh edits *Georgian Poetry*
Moore's *Hail and Farewell* (1911–1914)
Strauss's *Der Rosenkavalier*
Stravinsky's *Petrouchka*
Trevelyan's *Garibaldi and the Making of Italy*
Wells's *The New Machiavelli*
Mahler's *Das Lied van der Erde*

CHRONOLOGICAL TABLE

William Golding born
1912 Woodrow Wilson elected president
SS *Titanic* sinks on its maiden voyage
Five million Americans go to the movies daily; London has 400 movie theaters
Second post-impressionist exhibition in London
Bennett and Edward Knoblock's *Milestones*
Constantin Brancusi's *Maiastra*
Vasili Kandinski's *Black Lines*
D. H. Lawrence's *The Trespasser*
Lawrence Durrell born
Patrick White born
1913 Second Balkan War begins
Henry Ford pioneers factory assembly technique through conveyor belts
Epstein's *Tomb of Oscar Wilde*
New York Armory Show introduces modern art to the world
Alain-Fournier's *Le Grand Meaulnes*
Freud's *Totem and Taboo*
Lawrence's *Sons and Lovers*
Mann's *Death in Venice*
Proust's *Du Côté de Chez Swann* (first volume of *À la recherche du temps perdu*, 1913–1922)
Ravel's *Daphnis and Chloe*
Angus Wilson born
1914 The Panama Canal opens (formal dedication on 12 July 1920)
Irish Home Rule Bill passed in the House of Commons
Archduke Franz Ferdinand assassinated at Sarajevo
World War I begins
Battles of the Marne, Masurian Lakes, and Falkland Islands
Joyce's *Dubliners*
Shaw's *Pygmalion* and *Androcles and the Lion*
Yeats's *Responsibilities*
Wyndham Lewis publishes *Blast* magazine and *The Vorticist Manifesto*
Dylan Thomas born
1915 The Dardanelles campaign begins
Britain and Germany begin naval and submarine blockades
The *Lusitania* is sunk
Hugo Junkers manufactures the first fighter aircraft
Poison gas used for the first time

First Zeppelin raid in London
Rupert Brooke's *1914: Five Sonnets*
Norman Douglas' *Old Calabria*
D. W. Griffith's *The Birth of a Nation*
Gustave Holst's *The Planets*
Lawrence's *The Rainbow*
Wyndham Lewis's *The Crowd*
Maugham's *Of Human Bondage*
Pablo Picasso's *Harlequin*
Sibelius' *Fifth Symphony*
Deaths of Rupert Brooke, Julian Grenfell, and Charles Sorley
1916 Evacuation of Gallipoli and the Dardanelles
Battles of the Somme, Jutland, and Verdun
Britain introduces conscription
The Easter Rebellion in Dublin
Asquith resigns and David Lloyd George becomes prime minister
The Sykes-Picot agreement on the partition of Turkey
First military tanks used
Woodrow Wilson reelected president
Henri Barbusse's *Le Feu*
Griffith's *Intolerance*
Joyce's *Portrait of the Artist as a Young Man*
Jung's *Psychology of the Unconscious*
Moore's *The Brook Kerith*
Wells's *Mr. Britling Sees It Through*
Death of Henry James
Death of Lord Kitchener
1917 U.S. enters World War I
Czar Nicholas II abdicates
The Balfour Declaration on a Jewish national home in Palestine
The Bolshevik Revolution
Georges Clemenceau elected prime minster of France
Lenin appointed chief commissar; Trotsky appointed minister of foreign affairs
Conrad's *The Shadow-Line*
Douglas' *South Wind*
Eliot's *Prufrock*
Modigliani's *Nude with Necklace*
Sassoon's *The Old Huntsman*
Prokofiev's *Classical Symphony*
Yeats's *The Wild Swans at Coole*
Death of Edward Thomas
Death of Edgar Degas

Anthony Burgess born

John Fitzgerald Kennedy born

1918 Wilson puts forward Fourteen Points for World Peace

Central Powers and Russia sign the Treaty of Brest-Litovsk

Execution of Czar Nicholas II and his family

Kaiser William II abdicates

The Armistice signed

Women granted the vote at age thirty in Britain

Rupert Brooke's *Collected Poems*

Gerard Manley Hopkins' *Poems*

Joyce's *Exiles*

Wyndham Lewis's *Tarr*

Sassoon's *Counter-Attack*

Oswald Spengler's *The Decline of the West*

Lytton Strachey's *Eminent Victorians*

Béla Bartók's *Bluebeard's Castle*

Elgar's *Cello Concerto*

Charlie Chaplin's *Shoulder Arms*

Deaths of Claude Debussy, Wilfred Owen, and Isaac Rosenberg

Muriel Spark born

1919 Versailles Peace Treaty signed

J. W. Alcock and A. W. Brown make first transatlantic flight

Ross Smith flies from London to Australia

National Socialist party founded in Germany

Benito Mussolini founds the Fascist party in Italy

Sinn Fein Congress adopts declaration of independence in Dublin

Eamon De Valera elected president of Sinn Fein party

Communist Third International founded

Lady Astor elected first woman Member of Parliament

Prohibition in the U.S.

John Maynard Keynes's *The Economic Consequences of the Peace*

Somerset Maugham's *The Moon and Sixpence*

Shaw's *Heartbreak House*

The Bauhaus school of design, building, and crafts founded by Walter Gropius

Amedeo Modigliani's *Self-Portrait*

Death of Theodore Roosevelt

Death of Pierre Renoir

Margot Fonteyn, Edmund Hillary, Doris Lessing, and Iris Murdoch born

1920 The League of Nations established

Senate votes against joining the League and rejects the Treaty of Versailles

The Nineteenth Amendment gives women the right to vote

Warren G. Harding elected president

White Russian forces of Denikin and Kolchak defeated by the Bolsheviks

Karel Čapek's *R.U.R.*

Galsworthy's *In Chancery* and *The Skin Game*

Sinclair Lewis's *Main Street*

Katherine Mansfield's *Bliss*

Matisse's *Odalisques* (1920–1925)

Ezra Pound's *Hugh Selwyn Mauberly*

Paul Valéry's *Le Cimetière marin*

Yeats's *Michael Robartes and the Dancer*

Paul Scott born

1921 Britain signs peace with Ireland

First medium-wave radio broadcast in U.S.

The British Broadcasting Corporation founded

Braque's *Still Life with Guitar*

Chaplin's *The Kid*

Aldous Huxley's *Chrome Yellow*

Paul Klee's *The Fish*

Lawrence's *Women in Love*

John McTaggart's *The Nature of Existence*, vol. I (vol. II, 1927)

Moore's *Héloïse and Abélard*

Eugene O'Neill's *The Emperor Jones*

Luigi Pirandello's *Six Characters in Search of an Author*

Shaw's *Back to Methuselah*

Strachey's *Queen Victoria*

1922 Lloyd George's Coalition government succeeded by Bonar Law's Conservative government

Benito Mussolini marches on Rome and forms a government

William Cosgrave elected president of the Irish Free State

The BBC begins broadcasting in London

Lord Carnarvon and Howard Carter discover Tutankhamen's tomb

The PEN club founded in London

The *Criterion* founded with T. S. Eliot as editor

Eliot's *The Waste Land*

A. E. Housman's *Last Poems*

Joyce's *Ulysses*

Lawrence's *Aaron's Rod*

Sinclair Lewis's *Babbitt*

O'Neill's *Anna Christie*

Pirandello's *Henry IV*

Virginia Woolf's *Jacob's Room*

Yeats's *The Trembling of the Veil*

Death of Marcel Proust

Kingsley Amis born

Philip Larkin born

1923　The Union of Soviet Socialist Republics established

French and Belgian troops occupy the Ruhr in consequence of Germany's failure to pay reparations

Mustafa Kemal (Atatürk) proclaims Turkey a republic and is elected president

Warren Harding dies; Calvin Coolidge becomes president

Stanley Baldwin succeeds Bonar Law as prime minister

Adolf Hitler's attempted coup in Munich fails

Time magazine begins publishing

E. N. da C. Andrade's *The Structure of the Atom*

Bennett's *Riceyman Steps*

Churchill's *The World Crisis* (1923–1927)

J. E. Flecker's *Hassan* produced

Paul Klee's *Magic Theatre*

Lawrence's *Kangaroo*

Rainer Maria Rilke's *Duino Elegies* and *Sonnets to Orpheus*

Sibelius' *Sixth Symphony*

Picasso's *Seated Woman*

William Walton's *Facade*

Death of Katherine Mansfield

1924　Ramsay MacDonald forms first Labour government, loses general election and is succeeded by Stanley Baldwin

Calvin Coolidge elected president

Noel Coward's *The Vortex*

Forster's *A Passage to India*

Mann's *The Magic Mountain*

Shaw's *St. Joan*

Sibelius' *Seventh Symphony*

Deaths of Joseph Conrad, Anatole France, Franz Kafka, Giacomo Puccini, Woodrow Wilson, and Lenin

1925　Reza Khan becomes shah of Iran

First surrealist exhibition held in Paris

Alban Berg's *Wozzeck*

Chaplin's *The Gold Rush*

John Dos Passos' *Manhattan Transfer*

Theodore Dreiser's *An American Tragedy*

Eisenstein's *Battleship Potemkin*

F. Scott Fitzgerald's *The Great Gatsby*

André Gide's *Les Faux Monnayeurs*

Hardy's *Human Shows and Far Phantasies*

Huxley's *Those Barren Leaves*

Kafka's *The Trial*

Sean O'Casey's *Juno and the Paycock*

Virginia Woolf's *Mrs. Dalloway*

Brancusi's *Bird in Space*

Shostakovich's *First Symphony*

Sibelius' *Tapiola*

1926　Ford's *A Man Could Stand Up*

Gide's *Si le grain ne meurt*

Kafka's *The Castle*

D. H. Lawrence's *The Plumed Serpent*

T. E. Lawrence's *Seven Pillars of Wisdom* privately circulated

Maugham's *The Casuarina Tree*

O'Casey's *The Plough and the Stars*

Puccini's *Turandot*

Death of Claude Monet

Death of Rainer Maria Rilke

John Fowles born

1927　General Chiang Kai-Shek becomes prime minister in China

Trotsky expelled by the Communist party as a deviationist; Stalin becomes leader of the party and dictator of the USSR

Charles Lindberg flies from New York to Paris

J. W. Dunne's *An Experiment with Time*

Freud's *Autobiography* translated into English

Albert Giacometti's *Observing Head*

Ernest Hemingway's *Men Without Women*

Fritz Lang's *Metropolis*

F. W. Murnau's *Sunrise*

Proust's *Le Temps retrouvé* posthumously published

Stravinsky's *Oedipus Rex*

Virginia Woolf's *To the Lighthouse*

1928 The Kellogg-Briand Pact, outlawing war and providing for peaceful settlement of disputes, signed in Paris by sixty-two nations, including the USSR

Woman suffrage granted at age twenty-one in Britain

Alexander Fleming discovers penicillin

Bertolt Brecht and Kurt Weill's *The Threepenny Opera*

Eisenstein's *October*

Huxley's *Point Counter Point*

Christopher Isherwood's *All the Conspirators*

D. H. Lawrence's *Lady Chatterley's Lover*

Wyndham Lewis's *The Childermass*

Matisse's *Seated Odalisque*

Munch's *Girl on a Sofa*

Shaw's *Intelligent Woman's Guide to Socialism*

Virginia Woolf's *Orlando*

Yeats's *The Tower*

Death of Thomas Hardy

1929 The Labour party wins British general election

Trotsky expelled from USSR

Museum of Modern Art opens in New York

Collapse of U.S. stock exchange begins world economic crisis

Robert Bridges's *The Testament of Beauty*

William Faulkner's *The Sound and the Fury*

Graves's *Goodbye to All That*

Hemingway's *A Farewell to Arms*

Ernst Jünger's *The Storm of Steel*

Hugo von Hoffmansthal's *Poems*

Henry Moore's *Reclining Figure*

Priestley's *The Good Companions*

Erich Maria Remarque's *All Quiet on the Western Front*

Shaw's *The Applecart*

R. C. Sheriff's *Journey's End*

Thomas Wolfe's *Look Homeward, Angel*

Virginia Woolf's *A Room of One's Own*

Yeats's *The Winding Stair*

Second surrealist manifesto; Salvador Dali joins the surrealists

Epstein's *Night and Day*

Mondrian's *Composition with Yellow and Blue*

Walton's *Viola Concerto*

John Osborne born

1930 Allied occupation of the Rhineland ends

Mohandas Gandhi opens civil disobedience campaign in India

The *Daily Worker*, journal of the British Communist party, begins publishing

J. W. Reppe makes artificial fabrics from an acetylene base

W. H. Auden's *Poems*

Coward's *Private Lives*

Wyndham Lewis's *The Apes of God*

Maugham's *Cakes and Ale*

Ezra Pound's *XXX Cantos*

Evelyn Waugh's *Vile Bodies*

The Blue Angel and *All Quiet on the Western Front*

Deaths of Robert Bridges, Arthur Conan Doyle, and D. H. Lawrence

Ted Hughes born

Harold Pinter born

1931 The failure of the Credit Anstalt in Austria starts a financial collapse in Central Europe

Britain abandons the gold standard; the pound falls by twenty-five percent

Mutiny in the Royal Navy at Invergordon over pay cuts

Ramsay MacDonald resigns, splits the Cabinet, and is expelled by the Labour party; in the general election the National Government wins by a majority of 500 seats

The statute of Westminster defines dominion status

Ninette de Valois founds the Vic-Wells Ballet (eventually the Royal Ballet)

Chaplin's *City Lights*, René Clair's *Le Million*, and Leontine Sagan's *Mädchen in Uniform*

CHRONOLOGICAL TABLE

Coward's *Cavalcade*
Dali's *The Persistence of Memory*
O'Neill's *Mourning Becomes Electra*
Antoine de Saint Exupéry's *Vol de nuit*
Walton's *Belshazzar's Feast*
Death of Arnold Bennett

1932 Franklin D. Roosevelt elected president
Paul von Hindenburg elected president of Germany; Franz von Papen elected chancellor
Sir Oswald Mosley founds British Union of Fascists
The BBC takes over development of television from J. L. Baird's company
Basic English of 850 words designed as a prospective international language
The Folger Library opens in Washington, D.C.
The Shakespeare Memorial Theatre opens in Stratford upon Avon
Faulkner's *Light in August*
Huxley's *Brave New World*
F. R. Leavis' *New Bearings in English Poetry*
Boris Pasternak's *Second Birth*
Ravel's *Concerto for Left Hand*
Rouault's *Christ Mocked by Soldiers*
Yeats's *Words for Music Perhaps*
Death of Lady Augusta Gregory
Death of Lytton Strachey
V. S. Naipaul born

1933 Roosevelt inaugurates the New Deal
Hitler becomes chancellor of Germany
The Reichstag set on fire
Hitler suspends civil liberties and freedom of the press; German trade unions suppressed
George Balanchine and Lincoln Kirstein found the School of American Ballet
André Malraux's *La Condition humaine*
Orwell's *Down and Out in Paris and London*
Gertrude Stein's *Autobiography of Alice B. Toklas*
Death of John Galsworthy
Death of George Moore

1934 The League Disarmament Conference ends in failure
USSR admitted to the League

Hitler becomes Führer
Civil war in Austria; Engelbert Dollfuss assassinated in attempted Nazi coup
Frédéric Joliot and Irene Joliot-Curie discover artificial (induced) radioactivity
Einstein's *My Philosophy*
Fitzgerald's *Tender Is the Night*
Graves's *I, Claudius*
Toynbee's *A Study of History* begins publication (1934–1954)
Deaths of Marie Curie, Frederick Delius, Edward Elgar, and Gustav Holst

1935 Grigori Zinoviev and other Soviet leaders convicted of treason
Stanley Baldwin becomes prime minister in National government; National government wins general election in Britain
Italy invades Abyssinia
Germany repudiates disarmament clauses of Treaty of Versailles
Germany reintroduces compulsory military service and outlaws the Jews
Robert Watson-Watt builds first practical radar equipment
Karl Jaspers's *Suffering and Existence*
Ivy Compton-Burnett's *A House and Its Head*
Eliot's *Murder in the Cathedral*
Barbara Hepworth's *Three Forms*
George Gershwin's *Porgy and Bess*
Isherwood's *Mr. Norris Changes Trains*
Malraux's *Le Temps du mépris*
Yeats's *Dramatis Personae*
Klee's *Child Consecrated to Suffering*
Benedict Nicholson's *White Relief*
Death of T. E. Lawrence

1936 **Edward VIII accedes to the throne in January; abdicates in December**

1936–1952 **Reign of George VI**
German troops occupy the Rhineland
Ninety-nine percent of German electorate vote for Nazi candidates
The Popular Front wins general election in France; Léon Blum becomes prime minister
The Popular Front wins general election in Spain
Spanish Civil War begins

Italian troops occupy Addis Ababa; Abyssinia annexed by Italy

BBC begins television service from Alexandra Palace

Auden's *Look, Stranger!*

Auden and Isherwood's *The Ascent of F-6*

A. J. Ayer's *Language, Truth and Logic*

Chaplin's *Modern Times*

Huxley's *Eyeless in Gaza*

Keynes's *General Theory of Employment*

F. R. Leavis' *Revaluation*

Mondrian's *Composition in Red and Blue*

Dylan Thomas' *Twenty-five Poems*

Wells's *The Shape of Things to Come* filmed

Deaths of A. E. Housman, Rudyard Kipling, G. K. Chesterton, Maxim Gorky, and Luigi Pirandello

1937 Trial of Karl Radek and other Soviet leaders

Neville Chamberlain succeeds Stanley Baldwin as prime minister

China and Japan at war

Frank Whittle designs jet engine

Picasso's mural *Guernica*

Shostakovich's *Fifth Symphony*

Magritte's *La Reproduction interdite*

Hemingway's *To Have and Have Not*

Malraux's *L'Espoir*

Orwell's *The Road to Wigan Pier*

Priestley's *Time and the Conways*

Deaths of J. M. Barrie, Ivor Gurney, Ramsay Macdonald, Ernest Rutherford, and Maurice Ravel

Tom Stoppard born

1938 Trial of Nikolai Bukharin and other Soviet political leaders

Austria occupied by German troops and declared part of the Reich

Hitler states his determination to annex Sudetenland from Czechoslovakia

Britain, France, Germany, and Italy sign the Munich agreement

German troops occupy Sudetenland

Edward Hulton founds *Picture Post*

Cyril Connolly's *Enemies of Promise*

Faulkner's *The Unvanquished*

Graham Greene's *Brighton Rock*

Hindemith's *Mathis der Maler*

Jean Renoir's *Le Grande Illusion*

Jean-Paul Sartre's *La Nausée*

Yeats's *New Poems*

Anthony Asquith's *Pygmalion* and Walt Disney's *Snow White*

Death of Karel Čapek

Death of Mustafa Kemal (Atatürk)

1939 German troops occupy Bohemia and Moravia; Czechoslovakia incorporated into Third Reich

Madrid surrenders to General Franco; the Spanish Civil War ends

Italy invades Albania

Spain joins Germany, Italy, and Japan in anti-Comintern Pact

Britain and France pledge support to Poland, Romania, and Greece

USSR proposes defensive alliance with Britain; British military mission visits Moscow

USSR and Germany sign nonaggression treaty, secretly providing for partition of Poland between them

Germany invades Poland; Britain, France, and Germany at war

USSR invades Finland

New York World's Fair opens

Eliot's *The Family Reunion*

Isherwood's *Good-bye to Berlin*

Joyce's *Finnegan's Wake* (1922–1939)

Deaths of Ford Madox Ford, Sigmund Freud, and William Butler Yeats

1946 Death of H. G. Wells

1950 Death of George Bernard Shaw

1952– **Reign of Elizabeth II**

1952 Death of Norman Douglas

1962 Death of G. M. Trevelyan

1965 Death of Winston Churchill

Death of Somerset Maugham

1970 Death of E. M. Forster

List of Contributors

JOHN CONNELL. Journalist and biographer. Leader writer, *Evening News*, London (1945–1959). Publications include *Winston Churchill the Writer; Auchinleck; Wavell, Scholar and Soldier*. **Winston Churchill.**

CHARLES BRIAN COX. John Edward Taylor Professor of English Literature, University of Manchester (1976–   ). Publications include *The Free Spirit: A Study of the Novel; Joseph Conrad, The Modern Imagination;* and *Every Common Sight* (poems). Editor of *Critical Quarterly* and The Black Papers on Education. **Joseph Conrad.**

ELIZABETH COXHEAD. Novelist, biographer, and critic. Publications include *Lady Gregory, A Literary Portrait; Daughters of Erin* (biography); and *One Green Bottle* (novel). **J. M. Synge and Lady Gregory.**

ANTHONY CURTIS. Journalist and critic. Literary editor, *Financial Times*, London. Publications include *The Pattern of Maugham* and *Somerset Maugham*. **W. Somerset Maugham.**

CECIL DAY LEWIS, CBE, FRSL. Poet Laureate (1968–1972). Clark Lecturer, Trinity College, University of Cambridge (1946); Professor of Poetry, University of Oxford (1951–1956); Vice President, Royal Society of Literature (1958–1972); C. E. Norton Professor of Poetry, Harvard University (1964–1965). Publications include *A Hope for Poetry; Collected Poems, 1954; The Poetic Image; The Gate and Other Poems; The Room and Other Poems; The Whispering Roots; The Eclogues, The Georgics,* and *The Aeneid of Virgil* (translations). **Thomas Hardy: The Lyrical Poetry.**

GEORGE SUTHERLAND FRASER. Reader in Poetry, University of Leicester (1958–1980). Publications include *The Modern Writer and His World; Vision and Rhetoric; Metre, Rhyme and Free Verse; Essays on Twentieth Century Poets; A Short History of English Poetry; Home-Town Elegy; The Traveller Has Regrets; Conditions* (poems); and *Poems of G. S. Fraser, 1981*. **William Butler Yeats.**

PHILIP GARDNER. Professor of English, Memorial University of Newfoundland, Canada. Publications include *Norman Nicholson* (criticism); *The Deserted Village; A View of the Island* (poems); (with Averil Gardner) *The God Approached: A Commentary on the Poems of William Empson*. Editor of *E. M. Forster: The Critical Heritage*. **E. M. Forster.**

IAN GORDON GREENLEES, OBE. Reader in English, University of Rome (1934–1936); Director, The British Institute, Rome; Deputy Representative, The British Council, Italy (1948–1954); Director, The British Institute, Florence (1958–1981). Commendatore dell'Ordine del Merito della Republica Italiana. **Norman Douglas.**

DOMINIC HIBBERD. Lecturer in English, University of Keele (1973–   ). Editor of *Wilfred Owen: War Poems and Others; Poetry of the First World War: A Casebook*. Articles on Owen and Siegfried Sassoon in academic journals. **Wilfred Owen.**

MAURICE CHRISTOPHER HOLLIS. Member of Parliament for Devizes (1945–1955). Publications include *A Study of George Orwell; The Papacy: A History of the Jesuits; The Mind of Chesterton; The Seven Ages* (autobiography). **G. K. Chesterton.**

ALEXANDER NORMAN JEFFARES, FRSL, FAHA. Professor of English Language and Literature, University of Adelaide (1951–1956); Professor of English Literature, University of Leeds (1957–1974); Professor of English Literature, University of Stirling (1974–   ). Editor of *A Review of English Literature* (1960–1967) and *A Review of International*

Literature (1970–1972); Vice Chairman, Scottish Arts Council; Life President, International Association for the Study of Anglo-Irish Literature. Publications include *W. B. Yeats, Man and Poet; A New Commentary on the Collected Poems of W. B. Yeats;* (with A. S. Knowland) *A Commentary on the Collected Plays of W. B. Yeats;* and editions of *Fair Liberty Was All His Cry,* a tercentenary tribute to Jonathan Swift; *Jonathan Swift,* Modern Judgments series; *In Excited Reverie,* a centenary tribute to W. B. Yeats; *W. B. Yeats: The Critical Heritage; A Goldsmith Selection: She Stoops to Conquer;* and *Restoration Drama* (4 vols.). **George Moore.**

MARGERY M. MORGAN. Reader in English, University of Lancaster. Publications include *A Drama of Political Man: A Study in the Plays of Harley Granville Barker; The Shavian Playground: An Exploration of the Art of G. B. Shaw; York Notes on Shaw's "Pygmalion" and "Major Barbara."* **George Bernard Shaw; John Galsworthy.**

JOHN HAROLD PLUMB, FBA. Master of Christ's College, University of Cambridge (1978–1982); Lecturer in History, University of Cambridge (1946–1962); Reader in Modern English History (1962–1965); Professor of Modern English History (1966–1974); Chairman, Faculty of History (1966–1968); Visiting Professor, Columbia University (1960); Distinguished Visiting Professor, City University of New York (1971–1972, 1976); Historical Adviser, Penguin Books (1960–   ). Publications include *Chatham; Sir Robert Walpole; The First Four Georges; The Growth of Political Stability in England, 1625–1725; New Light on the Tyrant George III.* **G. M. Trevelyan.**

JOHN PRESS, FRSL. Formerly Literature Adviser, The British Council; Visiting Professor, University of Paris (1981–1982): Publications include *The Fire and the Fountain; The Chequer'd Shade; Rule and Energy; A Map of Modern English Verse;* and *The Lengthening Shadows.* **Poets of World War I.**

ALAN G. SANDISON. Professor of English Literature, University of Strathclyde, Glasgow (1974–1982). **Rudyard Kipling.**

ROLFE ARNOLD SCOTT-JAMES, OBE, MC. Literary Editor, *Daily News,* London (1906–1912). Leader writer, *Daily Chronicle* (1919–1930); Editor, *London Mercury* (1934–1939); Editor, *Britain Today* (1940–1954). Publications include *Modernism and Romance; The Making of Literature; The Day Before Yesterday; Fifty Years of English Literature.* **Thomas Hardy: The Novels, The Dynasts.**

IAN STANLEY SCOTT-KILVERT, OBE. Director of Publications, Recorded Sound, and Literature Department, The British Council (1962–1977). Publications include *John Webster;* and translations of *The Rise and Fall of Athens, Makers of Rome, The Age of Alexander* (Plutarch's *Lives*), and *The Rise of the Roman Empire* (Polybius' *Histories*). **A. E. Housman.**

JOHN SPARROW. Warden, All Souls' College, University of Oxford (1952–1977). Publications include *Sense and Poetry; Independent Essays; Controversial Essays; Mark Pattison and the Idea of a University; Visible Words.* Co-editor (with A. Perosa) of *Renaissance Latin Verse: An Anthology.* **Robert Bridges.**

ANTHONY TANNER. Fellow of King's College, University of Cambridge; University Lecturer in English, King's College. Publications include *Conrad's Lord Jim; The Reign of Wonder; Saul Bellow; City of Words; Adultery and the Novel: Contract and Transgression.* **Henry James.**

KENNETH YOUNG, FRSL. Former Editor, *Yorkshire Post;* Political Adviser, Beaverbrook Newspapers. Publications include *Dryden* (criticism); *Balfour; Baldwin* (biography); *The Greek Passion; Chapel* (history). Editor of *The Journals and Letters of Sir Robert Bruce Lockhart.* **Arnold Bennett; Ford Madox Ford; H. G. Wells.**

BRITISH WRITERS

THOMAS HARDY
(1840-1928)

R. A. Scott-James and C. Day Lewis

THE NOVELS

Suddenly an unexpected series of sounds began to be heard in this place up against the sky. They had a clearness which was to be found nowhere in the wind, and a sequence which was to be found nowhere in nature. They were the notes of Farmer Oak's flute.

SUCH were the notes that set the key in chapter 2 of *Far from the Madding Crowd* (1874). They are the same notes that were heard as distinctly in *Under the Greenwood Tree* (1872), the first of Thomas Hardy's novels to win the attention of a large public, though the second in order of appearance. That book introduces us to a place, a scene, set in a region the particularities of which were to be gradually unfolded in a series of novels, a region to become familiar in the mind's eye as the "Wessex of Thomas Hardy," centered in the hamlets, villages, towns, woods, meadows, and heathland of Dorset, and overflowing into the adjoining counties. It is a countryside inhabited by country people living, for the most part, under the conditions that prevailed when Hardy was a boy. The character of the region and still more the habits of the people have suffered many changes since then; and these outer and inner changes, already perceptibly beginning a hundred years ago, are again and again linked with the tragedies of his heroes and heroines. But the memory of the Wessex described by Hardy is fixed for posterity as long as English fiction continues to be read. It lives in the imagination more distinctly than any other region described by an English writer, perhaps any writer. Not thus do we know even the Scottish country described by Walter Scott. The Lake country associated with William Wordsworth is to Hardy's Wessex as a poetic symbol is to a human reality—a reality charged with all that is intimate and poignant in human experience. Not only have we been made to see the wild expanse of Egdon Heath, the rich meadowland of Talbothays, where Tess milked her cows and Angel Clare made love to her, the fir plantations and orchards of the Hintocks among which moved Giles Winterbourne and Marty South, the houses and streets and cornmarket of Casterbridge, frequented by all the farmers of the neighborhood; but also we have become aware of these places as influences subtly entering into the lives of the men and women born and bred there, who inherit memories, habits, and instincts handed on through the centuries. Those born in the Hintocks, with

an almost exhaustive biographical or historical acquaintance with every object, animate and inanimate, within the observer's horizon . . . know all about those invisible ones of the days gone by, whose feet have traversed the fields which look so grey from the window; recall whose creaking plough has turned those sods from time to time; whose hands planted the trees that form a crest to the opposite hill; whose horses and hounds have torn through that underwood; what birds affect that particular brake; what bygone domestic dramas of love, jealousy, revenge, or disappointment have been enacted in the cottages, the mansions, the street or on the green.

(*The Woodlanders*, ch. 17)

This Wessex country, inhabited by simple people and the ghosts of their ancestors, and no less by animals, trees, and grasses,[1] is the background never wholly absent in Hardy's work, fiction or poetry.

What he says of Clym Yeobright, walking on Egdon Heath in *The Return of the Native* (1878), might have been said of himself:

If anyone knew the heath well, it was Clym. He was permeated with its scenes, with its substance, with its odours. He might be said to be its product. His eyes had first opened thereon; with its appearance all the first images

*In this essay R. A. Scott-James wrote the sections The Novels and *The Dynasts* ; C. Day Lewis wrote The Lyrical Poetry.

[1]It is curious that songbirds occur rarely in the novels.

of his memory were mingled; his estimate of life had been coloured by it; his toys had been the flint knives and arrowheads which he found there, wondering why stones should "grow" to such odd shapes; his flowers, the purple bells and yellow gorse; his animal kingdom, the snakes and croppers; his society, its human haunters.

(bk. III, ch. 2)

Hardy was born in 1840 in Higher Bockhampton, in the parish of Stinsford. His father was a stonemason and builder who inherited from the grandfather a love of instrumental music and the care of the church choir; carol singing at Christmas, as described in *Under the Greenwood Tree*, and festive occasions celebrated with jigs, hornpipes, reels, and other country dances, lived in the memory of the novelist; again and again in his novels his style acquires a wonderful liveliness where he tells the story of a dance. As a small child, Florence Hardy says, he was "of ecstatic temperament, extraordinarily sensitive to music"; he was so moved by some of the tunes that he had to dance on to conceal his weeping. In his childhood his life was never far from that of the folk; he lived continuously in Dorset until he was twenty-two, attending first the village school, then schools at Dorchester. At the age of sixteen he began to study architecture under an architect much of whose work was concerned with church restoration. He read books omnivorously, studied Latin and French, and later, with the help of a friend, Greek; and he wrote poetry. It was in Dorchester that he came to know William Barnes, who as pedagogue gave him advice on grammar, and as poet stimulated his poetic interest in Dorset.

In literature, poetry was Hardy's first love, as it was his last. When he went to London at the age of twenty-two to pursue his profession of architecture, he worked conscientiously at it but continued to write poetry, though he had no success in getting it published. He was by no means unpractical. His supreme interest, he felt, lay in the composition of poetry, and throughout his earlier and middle creative period he constantly wrote verse to please himself; but he did not turn his back on the necessity of earning a living. He continued his regular work as an architect until he had made sure he could succeed in literature. In the field of literature, since the editors and publishers did not want his poems but did, in time, come to demand his novels, he gave his energies to fiction and found there his means of self-expression. He was to prove that a poet could write

fiction in prose and would do it the better for being a poet. But often the task was irksome. Many of his novels had to be written on schedules to suit the journals in which they were published serially. When he was at the height of his powers (by the age of forty-six), he complained that his novel writing was "mere journeywork," and in later years he was impatient with those who did not think his verse superior to his fiction. But one need not overstress this self-criticism. Earlier, he was dissatisfied with cramping conditions; later, enjoying freedom, he remembered years when he had written under duress. Again and again he spoke seriously enough of his art, meaning the art of fiction, as when he wrote on 3 January 1886: "My art is to intensify the expression of things, as is done by Crivelli, Bellini, etc., so that the heart and inner meaning is made vividly visible."

Nonetheless, one must remember that for more than twenty years, during most of his novel-writing period, Hardy was, in a certain sense, writing for a living; that is to say, he was not in a position to rest on his oars and stop writing. This means that though we shall see him developing his essential powers and writing from inner necessity, we shall also find him producing work in which he is below himself, in books parts at least of which are irrelevant to his genius. His first venture in fiction, "The Poor Man and the Lady" (1867–1868), was never published, though a much shortened version of it was printed later in a magazine. It was read and criticized by two publishers' readers, none other than John Morley and George Meredith, the latter advising him, probably rightly, against publication, but less rightly telling him how to set about the writing of a novel. Hardy took the advice and exaggerated it in the thrills and surprising episodes that he heaped one on another in *Desperate Remedies* (1871)—a clever experiment in fiction, but not what we have come to think of as characteristic of Hardy.

Yet in the very next book, *Under the Greenwood Tree*, the real Hardy is present unmistakably. Already we strike the authentic note. No one could have done this book but Hardy, and, for what it is, it could scarcely have been done better. Here we have not yet reached the philosophy of Hardy; there is no sense of overwhelming destiny, no note of tragedy, no deep hint of the tears of things. It is not one of his greater books, yet I should profoundly regret it if he had not written it. It is a picture, an idyll, of Dorset country life as the author remembered it from his boyhood and before reflection had tinged it with bitterness. Here is Wessex—the Dorset country and people, the fir trees sobbing in the breeze, the ash hissing, the beeches rustling, the procession of villagers proceeding in the dark to the tranter's cottage, the rustic choir singing under Fancy Day's window, the dancing, the lovemaking that goes awry and ends gaily—all of this, the lovely raw material of rustic life as it might have been if no Spirit Sinister had left its mark, no "viewless, voiceless Turner of the Wheel" had been discerned working havoc. It is the Garden of Eden before Adam fell; and if Fancy Day had ever so little of Eve's naughtiness, it was not more than enough to make her human. The scenes are real, the characters true to life; yet the book is not so much a novel as an idyll of English country life, a pastoral poem in prose.

The next book was to be a more ambitious essay in fiction, but far less satisfying. *A Pair of Blue Eyes* (1873) has received from many critics higher praise than I am able to give it. The total impression that this book leaves does not carry for me the unmistakable, unforgettable note of the essential Hardy. Several critics have divided Hardy's novels into three or four classes, and Hardy himself distinguished between kind and kind. Thus, Lionel Johnson, the earliest important critic of the novels, arranged them into three groups: the tragic; the idyllic; and the comic, ironic, satiric, romantic, extravagant. This division is well enough, but takes no account of a distinction that in my opinion is more important—a distinction of quality between the books that spring from Hardy's essential genius and those that do not. The former come from the inner core of his creative imagination; the latter are fabricated. In the first he is possessed by his subject; in the second he is using his inventive talent to carry him as best it can through an ingenious story.

From first to last, Hardy—observant, percipient, sensitive, and thoughtful as he was—was a person of great simplicity. There was something of the peasant in him that sophistication did not wholly eliminate. He grew up to know, as only an observant, percipient, and sensitive person could have known, a world of a certain kind, filled with a certain life, human and natural—to know it in all its beauty, its contrariness, and its perplexing painfulness. That life, as he had known it from his childhood, he absorbed imaginatively, and it became the raw material of his art. He would never be at his best except when near to the life that he had thus absorbed, though he was to transcend it and put it into a vaster context. Even as a

boy and young man he was being modified by his reading of English literature, the classics, and history, by his careful study of architecture, by his interest in pictures and in acting, by his disturbing contacts with Charles Darwin, Herbert Spencer, and Arthur Schopenhauer, and by his puzzled study of the Oxford Movement theologians and their opponents. As a man he became more and more uneasy with innovations that were displacing rustic customs and with social ideas at variance with the older codes of life. He found evils aggravated by the intolerant judgment of society, as if there were not enough that are beyond human control and inherent in human life. Percipient, meditative, contemplative, he remained simple, a peasant burdened with knowledge that magnified the problems, heightened the significance of the emotions, and enlarged the objects of perception until they seemed to be coexistent with all the world and the infinite. The problems that were thus revealed were to become insoluble and almost unbearable, and the more so as men and women—the raw material of life, continuing their plodding existence with primitive passions and developing consciousness—were converted into tragicomic realities of the imagination. "The business of the poet and novelist," he wrote on 19 April 1885, two days after he had written the last page of *The Mayor of Casterbridge* (1886), "is to show the sorriness underlying the grandest things, and the grandeur underlying the sorriest things."

The people and the countryside of what he called Wessex, seen through the prism of a romantic imagination, provided for Hardy the archetypal forms of human existence. During the whole of his novel-writing period, the life of this kind that he portrayed became, when he was at his best, like the notes and chords in an orchestral composition moving from theme to theme as the motive dictated. He might be clumsy in individual passages, the plot might creak under the excessive use of coincidence, but the essence of the movement is there, the sureness of the motive unerring. Hardy is possessed by his subject. His assimilating and constructive imagination is engaged. And this is just as true in the case of a slight masterpiece, such as *Under the Greenwood Tree*, as in the grand tragedy of *The Return of the Native*, or *Tess of the d'Urbervilles* (1891), or *The Mayor of Casterbridge*. But it was not always thus. At one moment, as we have seen, Hardy was diverted from his inclination by advice offered by the great Meredith. At another time, as Mrs. Hardy says, when "he was committed by circumstances to novel-writing as a regular trade," he felt constrained to look about for material in social and fashionable life; his "gloomy misgivings" on this score were confirmed in a talk with Anne Isabella Thackeray, who told him that "a novelist must necessarily like society." Moreover, the "journeywork" of writing thrust upon him commitments to editors of magazines demanding that he write another book before his creative imagination was ready for the task. Under these circumstances it is easy to understand that he should have written a number of books that, though they would have been creditable to a lesser novelist, lack the mark of the real Hardy. The sum total of his work would not be much impoverished if we removed altogether *A Pair of Blue Eyes*, *The Hand of Ethelberta* (1876), *A Laodicean* (1881), and *Two on a Tower* (1882)— books that were interspersed among the finest of his novels.

This is not to say that there are not many excellencies in these books, and passages in which the writer reveals his distinctive power. *A Pair of Blue Eyes* commands the reader's interest from beginning to end. The theme is that of a woman's inconstancy, one not likely to be dully treated by Hardy, who idealized the opposite quality, that of long-suffering constancy in love, in Tess, Giles Winterbourne, Marty South, Gabriel Oak, the Trumpet-Major. Hardy found the making of much tragedy in the possession or lack of that virtue. In *Jude the Obscure* (1895), passion for Sue began with "the love of being loved"; for Elfride in *A Pair of Blue Eyes*, it began in "the love of admiration." In retrospect there is the memory of a first entanglement, the young man whom she had kissed at the tomb; he had died. In the early part of this book she becomes secretly engaged to the young architect, for he is of humble origin; she runs away to be married, but does not marry. In the next phase she succumbs to the superior qualities of her lover's rather priggish friend. By a series of accidents the third lover discovers all that has happened, suspects more, and leaves her. Lovers number two and three travel together to Elfride's village on a train, and find that it carries a hearse and her body. She had married a fourth lover and then died. Thus baldly outlined, the story sounds melodramatic and absurd, and in fact it is not without these defects. Yet Elfride is done well enough to gain our sympathy, and Knight to earn our dislike. The narrative is alive and often exciting, as in the episode on The Cliff without a Name; and though the scene is in

Cornwall, and not in Hardy's more intimately known Dorset, there are passages of description that show he had already intuitively discovered a way of conveying through the medium of words what a painter conveys in a picture, but by devices appropriate to the art of letters. Hardy knows that by writing you cannot "paint" a scene; to attempt to do by successive words what a painter does by coexistent images in a picture is merely to bewilder the reader, as by a catalog; he prefers to describe through action, to show things moving, breathing, appearing; to give us as much that can be *heard* as *seen*; to record the effect left on the mind of a spectator. Though we can find much finer passages in Hardy's other books, this power of literary description is exhibited many times in *A Pair of Blue Eyes*, as thus in chapter 24, when Stephen stands at the door of the church porch looking for Elfride:

> The faint sounds heard only accentuated the silence. The rising and falling of the sea, far away along the coast, was the most important. A minor sound was the scurr of a distant night-hawk. Among the minutest where all were minute were the light settlement of gossamer fragments floating in the air, a toad humbly labouring along through the grass near the entrance, the crackle of a dead leaf which a worm was endeavouring to pull into the earth, a waft of air, getting nearer and nearer, and expiring at his feet under the burden of a winged insect.

In such passages as that we have the authentic note that is Hardy's.

The Hand of Ethelberta is one of those books that I have spoken of as being "fabricated." When he wrote it, Hardy was taking Miss Thackeray's advice— he was entering society, describing a life that he could report but not build up through his own vision. It is incidentally interesting as affording an example of Hardy's consciousness of class distinction, discernible in greater or lesser degree in most of his novels.

A Laodicean is generally, and rightly, spoken of as the worst of his novels. Much of it was written when he was ill but under contract to provide chapters month by month for an editor. Hardy had doubtless intended to write a book illustrating the contrast between the ancient and the modern, the inherited and the acquired, the dignity of the old order and the indignity of modern progress. He produced in fact a crudely thrilling melodrama in which villainy, blackmail, eavesdropping, and violence produce a succession of reversals of fortune ending happily in marriage. Hardy sufficiently described the book himself in the preface to the 1896 edition: "*A Laodicean* may perhaps help to while away an idle afternoon of the comfortable ones whose lines have fallen to them in pleasant places; above all, of that large and happy section of the reading public which has not yet reached ripeness of years."

Two on a Tower is not very much better than *A Laodicean*, though a series of coincidences that thwart hero and heroine is less absurd. It concerns a love affair between a young man of peasant birth who is becoming a brilliant astronomer, and a lady of aristocratic family who has been deserted by her husband; and the love scenes take place on a lonely tower where the young man introduces Lady Constantine to the fixed stars. "This slightly-built romance," wrote Hardy thirteen years later, "was the outcome of a wish to set the emotional history of two infinitesimal lives against the stupendous background of the stellar universe."

The books of which I have just been speaking may be considered minor episodes in Hardy's work. Like his other and greater books they are love stories depending for their development on the external incidents of plot. Hardy firmly believed that a novel should tell a story, and with him the story always turned upon actual events in the lives of his personages. He spoke slightingly about Henry James's preoccupation with "the minutiae of manners": "James's subjects are those one could be interested in at moments when there is nothing larger to think of." What Hardy sought was an action exhibiting the simple, elemental emotions, such as had been chosen by the Greek tragedians and Shakespeare. In the lesser books, where his imagination was not fully engaged, the story is just a story, ingeniously contrived, whose incidents afford occasions for exhibiting individual characters; but the characters do not stand in symbolic relationship to a pattern of life. The poet in him asserted itself from time to time, but did not control the situation. He told his story with a sort of ingenuous fidelity to his task, and that was all. But when the grand moment came, Hardy the poet-novelist took charge. The dividing line between his greater work and his lesser is absolute. To the former belong unmistakably *Under the Greenwood Tree*, *Far from the Madding Crowd*, *The Return of the Native*, *The Trumpet-Major* (1880), *The Mayor of Casterbridge*, *The Woodlanders* (1887), *Tess of the d'Urbervilles*, and *Jude the Obscure*.

Hardy had the mind of a poet. He was reading and writing poetry through all the years of his novel writing, and he turned finally to poetry when he had said his say in the appropriate form of fiction and came to the grand summing-up. He had the imagination of Samuel Taylor Coleridge's creative poet who seeks to externalize all the world that he is aware of in terms of his understanding of it. That being so, his art was from its nature progressive, revealing the successive stages of his discovery of life. No author's work reveals a clearer pattern, moving on stage by stage in the elucidation of life, not by argument or teaching, but by exhibiting life itself, human beings in action, driven by forces they do not understand. It begins with the simpler material of human life, men and women shown under stress of emotion, generally in a rustic setting. It ends with all history in time, all the universe in space, and the Kosmos, which includes all space and time and the possible beyond. His real creative work shows a steady progression from perception of an individual to perception of the Universal. In the latter case it is *perception*, not *conception*, for even the Universal is individualized and perceived through the eye of the artist.

Each of Hardy's finer novels may be taken as a projection of his state of awareness at a certain stage of his development; its material is the world that he felt to be real. The content of that world, when he wrote *Under the Greenwood Tree*, was that Wessex life of which I have spoken and all the memories of youth it included. It was still such that it could be presented idyllically, with the rhythmic pattern of a pastoral poem. If the course of true love is not quite smooth, it is only so little troubled as to make the smoothing pleasant. The village, which is the scene of action, stands for all the English villages where life is cast in the traditional mold. But Hardy has moved on when he comes two years later to *Far from the Madding Crowd*. The country life is in essentials the same, though we see it on a larger scale. It is more consciously conceived as something that does not change, remaining "ancient" when so much else is becoming "modern."

In Weatherbury three or four score years were included in the mere present, and nothing less than a century set a mark on its face or tone. Five decades hardly modified the cut of a gaiter, the embroidering of a smock-frock, by the breadth of a hair. Ten generations failed to alter the turn of a single phrase.

(ch. 22)

The more important persons, with one exception, might have behaved as they do here a century or two ago. The exception is Bathsheba herself, the first example that Hardy gives us of a partly emancipated woman, who farms her own farm and demands equal status with the men when she goes to Casterbridge market. The story, as in most of Hardy's novels, is essentially a love story. It touches a deeper note that has the quality of tragedy, but the disturbance arises not, as we are to feel later, from any cruelty in the nature of things, but from the conflict between the characters and their responses to impulse or to those accidents that play too frequent a part in all Hardy's plots. For Hardy, love is always treated as the major passion in life, and constancy in love is shown as the major virtue, accompanied by other excellencies that it implies. Gabriel Oak stands side by side with John Loveday, Giles Winterbourne, Marty South, and the Reddleman among the heroes and heroines whose love is proof against all shocks.

Farmer Oak is slow, deliberate, moving with quiet energy, though if occasion demanded he could "do or think a thing with as mercurial a dash as can the man of towns . . . his special power, morally, physically, and mentally, was static, owing little or nothing to momentum. . . ." When he looked at the sky he drew practical conclusions about the time and the weather, but "being a man not without a frequent consciousness that there was some charm in this life he led, he stood still after looking at the sky as a useful instrument, and regarded it in an appreciative spirit, as a work of art supremely beautiful" (chapter 2). He does not hesitate to criticize Bathsheba when she has offended his sense of right, and can help her as none other can in moments of crisis, yet he has not that sort of masterfulness that would compel her to love him. He will not, like Farmer Boldwood, press his claims because she has flirted with him. He is not the man to plead where he is not wanted. Bathsheba, for all her strength and good sense, proves to be at the mercy of her own impetuosity where the heart is involved, and falls all too easy a prey to the handsome, adventurous seducer, Troy. Once again, however, it is an accident that plays its part in leading her to marry him. The story pursues its way rhythmically through incidents that stir the emotions of three men and a girl amid the rustic events of sheepshearing, stacking, marketing, in calm and in storm, to a running commentary of gossip from the chorus of workers. The ending is a compromise between that of tragedy and comedy. Gabriel marries Bathsheba, but not until his rivals have been tragically removed.

Far from the Madding Crowd established Hardy's reputation, but it was to be followed disappointingly by *The Hand of Ethelberta* and then by a masterpiece, *The Return of the Native*. But first, a word about *The Trumpet-Major*, a novel that might well have come before rather than just after *The Return of the Native* in Hardy's natural development. We know from his memoranda that in 1875, five years before *The Trumpet-Major* was published and three years before *The Return of the Native*, Hardy's mind was moving toward the theme that was to become that of *The Dynasts* (1903–1904; 1906; 1908). "Mem:" he wrote at that time, "a Ballad of the Hundred Days. Then another of Moscow. Others of earlier campaigns—forming altogether an Iliad of Europe from 1789 to 1815." And two years later he wrote, "Consider a grand drama, based on the wars with Napoleon, or some one campaign (but not as Shakespeare's historical dramas). It might be called 'Napoleon' or 'Josephine,' or by some other person's name." But long before then Hardy had been deeply interested in the recollections of old persons whom he had known in childhood, who had been eyewitnesses of the events that occurred in Dorset when the invasion of England by Napoleon was daily expected. As a boy he had studied the "casual relics" of the preparations for defense—"a heap of bricks and clods on a beacon-hill," "worm-eaten shafts and iron heads of pikes," "ridges on the down thrown up during the encampment, fragments of volunteer uniform, and other such lingering remains." These discoveries profoundly affected the imagination of the young Hardy, and gave him an insight into the condition of England at the time of the Battle of Trafalgar (1805). This early knowledge was to be extended later by close study of the history of the period. Already, before he wrote *The Trumpet-Major*, Hardy was imaginatively seeing the history of his native district in the larger perspective of England and Napoleon's Europe, just as so often in his stories of individuals living in a Wessex homestead we find the pressure of a wider humanity surging round and beyond. "A certain provincialism of feeling is invaluable," he wrote in the very year of *The Trumpet-Major*. "It is the essence of individuality, and is largely made up of that crude enthusiasm without which no great thoughts are thought, no great deeds done."

And so it is with *The Trumpet-Major*. Though in a certain sense it is the story of love affairs written in the spirit of light comedy, its lightness is that of the provincial scenes in *The Dynasts*—it is the relief to a vaster background of historic events; it is the village commentary on life the day before the battle. The slight love story will stand on its own merits, but it becomes something more when it is an interlude in a world conflict. Not that Hardy presses upon us these sterner reflections. In this historical novel we are much nearer to *Under the Greenwood Tree* than to *Jude*. There is enough to entertain us in the succession of lively pictures that Hardy draws—the cavalry soldiers on their bulky gray chargers, ascending the down and preparing the camp, while the romantic Anne looks on from the miller's cottage; the excitement in the village; the party at the miller's; the behavior of the solid John Loveday, the soldier, and his lively, mercurial brother, Bob; the King's visit to Budmouth; the false alarm when the beacon is lit; and the ups and downs of Bob's affections. There are touches of melodrama, such as when the bully Festus has too many opportunities for playing the villain or when Matilda exceeds herself as the scarlet woman. But it is all part of the play—vigorous, zestful— whose romance takes a deeper note when it describes the simple fidelity of John to his unattainable beloved and his unstable brother. Though not a major novel, this has its place in the sequence of Hardy's works in which he is genuinely possessed by his subject.

The five greater novels, which it remains to consider, are all tragedy—tragedy on the grand scale. They are all of them love stories, as before, but the men and women who suffer this passion in its extremity, individual as they are, become also representatives of the human race. We are to see them through Hardy's eyes, as Aeschylus saw Prometheus chained to a rock, against a vast background of nature, the victim of "the President of the Immortals." His magnificent beginning of *The Return of the Native*, showing in the description of Egdon Heath what sort of place it is in which the persons are to suffer, creates an impression of nature more somber than we have had before, indeed a nature that appears to share the suffering of men. "Fair prospects wed happily with fair times; but alas, if times be not fair. . . . Haggard Egdon appealed to a subtler and scarcer instinct, to a more recently learnt emotion . . . wearing a sombreness distasteful to our race when it was young." "The storm was its lover, and the wind its friend." It could become "the home of strange phantoms." "Like man, slighted and enduring," it was "colossal and mysterious in its swarthy monotony." In *The Woodlanders*, too, though there are some gentler pictures, "the bleared

white visage of a sunless winter day emerged like a dead-born child," and in the wood we observe "the Unfulfilled Intention, which makes life what it is," working havoc underground—"the leaf was deformed, the curve was crippled, the taper was interrupted; the lichen ate the vigour of the stalk and the ivy slowly strangled to death the promising sapling." Though nature assumes a far sweeter aspect at Talbothays during those months when Tess and Clare are working among the cows and the meadows, the sweetness of it becomes a foil to the horrors that are to follow.

Hardy peoples this alternately lovely and sinister world with men and women, the more ordinary of whom play the chorus. The exceptional ones, some capable of intense emotion, others, in a worse plight, equally emotional but also acutely conscious and self-conscious, sense in themselves what Tess "was expressing in her own native phrases—assisted a little by her Sixth Standard training—feelings which might almost have been called those of the age—the ache of modernism." In *The Return of the Native* Clym Yeobright's face reflects "the view of life as a thing to be put up with, replacing that zest for existence which was so intense in early civilizations." Henchard in *The Mayor of Casterbridge* perceives more simply but passionately. The shape of his ideas in time of affliction was simply "a moody 'I am to suffer, I perceive'"; his superstitious nature led to the grim conclusion that his misfortunes were due to "some sinister intelligence bent on punishing him." In *Jude the Obscure* the perception of the new type of human being reaches an extremity where it is unbearable. Even as a boy Jude showed that he was "the sort of man who was born to ache"; he was at moments "seized with a sort of shuddering." As a man he is a victim of "the modern vice of unrest." Sue—the ethereal, the fine-nerved, the idealist—has the same sensitiveness and becomes almost masochistic in her love of suffering. Hardy pursues the theme to a point where it becomes almost horrible in reproducing the affliction of the parents in their children. "I ought not to be born, ought I?" says Little Father Time, working himself up to the mood that ends in his hanging himself and his baby brother and sister. "The doctor," it is reported, "says there are such boys springing up amongst us—boys of a sort unknown in the last generation. . . . It is the beginning of the coming universal wish not to live."

These five books are not to be taken as a statement of Hardy's philosophy. But in giving body to human life, as this meditative man finds it, a pattern appears, a pattern in accordance with which human nature manifests itself; the pattern yields a philosophy, imposed on Hardy by his intuitive reading of experience. There emerges a sort of theory of society into which the facts, as he sees them, fit; it widens into nothing less than a view of the universe. Already in *The Return of the Native* we are faced with the problem of a young man of bucolic origin moving too quickly to intellectual and sophisticated aims, reaching a condition of unbalance between the two elements in himself. In *The Mayor of Casterbridge* we have in Lucetta the half-emancipated woman—"I'll love whom I choose." The old superstition still strong in her, however, she shrinks and withers to her death before the terrors of the skimmington-ride. In *The Woodlanders* we are introduced to the deficiencies of the divorce laws; in *Tess* to the cruelty of public opinion toward those who have offended against its decrees; and in *Jude* Sue Bridehead, so clear-sighted in vision, though so unreasonable in action, makes her explicit protest against "the social moulds civilization fits us into," and asks whether a marriage ceremony is a religious thing or "only a sordid contract, based on material convenience in householding, rating, and taxing, and the inheritance of land and money by children." "When people of a later age look back upon the barbarous customs and superstition of the times that we have the unhappiness to live in, what *will* they say?" she exclaims. And before then even Jude, with his more conventional views, finding his life ruined by marriage with the coarse, dissolute Arabella, had reflected on the fundamental error of "having based a permanent contract on a temporary feeling."

In these, Hardy's subtlest and most tragic books, we have a searching criticism of modern life and finally of all life. We have still the chorus of ordinary men and women, with rustic minds not yet unhinged, accepting life and judging it, gaily or sadly, in accordance with the older standards. But in the forefront we have others, born in the same milieu, who have come to put everything to the question; who have acquired the self-consciousness that is the distinctive characteristic of modern man; who question the fundamentals of the society we live in, the rightness of social conventions, the sanctity of the marriage contract, the goodness of a progress and a civilization that bring so much misery to man, and finally, the benevolence or the omnipotence of the power that rules the universe. Clym Yeobright saw "the whole creation groaning and travailing in pain." Henchard feared "some sinister intelligence." Tess

supposed that we live on a star that is "a blighted one"; she questioned the "use of learning," though she added, "I shouldn't mind learning why—why the sun do shine on the just and the unjust alike. . . . But that's what books will not tell me." Sue Bridehead had once imagined that "the world resembled a stanza or melody composed in a dream," but her fully awakened intelligence concluded that "the First Cause worked automatically like a somnambulist, and not reflectively like a sage." "All the ancient wrath of the Power above us has been vented upon us, His poor creatures, and we must submit." Sue comes near to expressing the developed cosmology of *The Dynasts*. The characters, more sinned against than sinning, are those of human beings set in a framework of universal destiny.

Hardy did not set out to give us a pessimistic philosophy. He did set out to show how certain persons, selected because they were interesting and had certain characters, would behave under certain circumstances, arbitrarily conceived, but not impossible. In bringing them to disaster he is prone to weight the chances against their prosperity by too many coincidences. His frequent use of the unlucky accident is a blemish in nearly all of his plots—the accident that Giles Winterbourne should fail to notice the writing that Grace chalked on his wall, or that grim mishap in *The Return of the Native* that prevents the opening of the door when Clym's mother had made her dreary journey over the heath to be reconciled with her son and his wife: "'Tis too much, Clym. How can he bear to do it? He is at home; and yet he lets her shut the door against me!" Hope turns to gloom and disaster.

It has been claimed, and I think rightly, that Hardy has elevated the function of the novel, and succeeded in placing it among the greatest of the literary art forms. He has told in each case a tale, and in that respect it stands on the merits proper to a tale. Each also contains characters who are faithfully and subtly exhibited. But that is not all. The action is significant. It moves according to a pattern that is part of the pattern of all life, and so yields an account of the world and the universe we live in. This visible tract of life unfolded before our eyes springs from Hardy's vision of life as a whole; it is nothing less than his conception of the universe expressing itself at given moments of time and in a given place, and the time and even the place itself participate in his cosmic conceptions. Just as Shakespeare calls upon the whole of his imagination when he makes a Macbeth or a Lear, and Milton in his quite different way when he presents the Archangels at War, so does Hardy when he shows Mrs. Yeobright striving to overcome her prejudices, or Michael Henchard proceeding headlong to a doom brought down on him by his own arrogance and obstinacy, or poor Tess harassed and killed by the avenging Furies of conventional opinion.

The tragedy, however, does not always follow the Aristotelian rules. A good plot (in spite of the coincidences); characters, serious and deserving of our attention; action, calling forth pity and fear; all of these are present. But Hardy sometimes violates the rule that forbids the shocking spectacle of a virtuous person brought through no fault of his or her own from prosperity to adversity. In *Jude the Obscure*, Hardy goes to extremes in showing men and women pursued relentlessly by a cruel "Universe" through no fault of their own. This novel, I think, immense as it is in dissecting the problems of Jude and Sue and in describing their relationship, does leave a sense of horror at the end that is incompatible with the highest art, but in this case alone. In *The Return of the Native* the two characters who matter are Clym and his mother, Mrs. Yeobright. The tragedy is brought about by the error of Clym, who misconceives his mission in life, and above all by Mrs. Yeobright, whose prejudice and obstinacy are not atoned for by her gestures of forgiveness. In *The Mayor of Casterbridge* it is the recklessness, the pride, the unforgiving obstinacy of Henchard's nature that cause his downfall. His tragedy, like Lear's, is the tragedy of his own soul.

There is no comparable fault or error in the protagonists of *The Woodlanders* or *Tess*; yet we are not disgusted, unless it be by the violence with which Tess's life is ended. If in these cases we are not shocked, but on the contrary are profoundly moved by the behavior of the persons and the sublimity of the scene, I think we shall discover that that is because the disaster is not complete. Destiny may seem pitiless and cruel, but the nobility of the characters facing it with courage and sympathy toward one another evokes a compensating admiration. In *The Woodlanders* the devotion of Giles to Grace is unfailing, and at the end the tragedy of his death is softened by the triumph of his self-sacrifice for her sake, and beautified by the unfailing and apparently unrewarded love of Marty South. Marty's patient love, serenely in the background throughout the story, breathed only to the young larches, is immortalized in the book's silences and in the lyrical whispered cry with which it ends.

Even in *Tess*, when "'Justice' was done, and the President of the Immortals, in Aeschylean phrase, had ended his sport with Tess," and had shown the last of her so grimly on the gallows, the penultimate scene had its compensation. It brought happiness—Tess called it happiness—in the final reunion and understanding between herself and Clare. When the pursuers at last find them at Stonehenge, "'It is as it should be,' she murmured. 'Angel, I am almost glad—yes, glad! This happiness could not have lasted. It was too much.'" She faces the end with her habitual courage. "'I am ready,' she said quietly."

Hardy is pessimistic about the governance of the universe, but not about human beings. In his lesser books there are villains playing their melodramatic parts, but in his greater novels there are no villains. There are weak, and volatile, and selfish people like Wildeve or Fitzpiers; but they are not simply scoundrels. There can be a coarse, unscrupulous creature like Arabella, but even she is not wholly bad. The chorus of ordinary men and women is full of good humor and the milk of human kindness. The heroes and heroines have noble and lovable qualities; they stand in sublime contrast to the supreme powers. Giles Winterbourne, "born and bred among the orchards," who "looked and smelt like Autumn's very brother," is endowed with the qualities that Christians have allotted to the saints. And with what wonderful words does Mrs. Cuxsom reveal both herself and the dead woman of whom she speaks.

"And she was as white as marble-stone. And likewise such a thoughtful woman, too—ah, poor soul—that a' minded every little thing that wanted tending. 'Yes,' says she, 'when I'm gone, and my last breath's blowed, look in the top drawer o' the chest in the back room by the window, and you'll find all my coffin clothes; a piece of flannel—that's to put under me, and the little piece is to put under my head; and my new stockings for my feet—they are folded alongside, and all my other things. And there's four ounce pennies, the heaviest I could find, a-tied up in bits of linen, for weights—two for my right eye and two for my left,' she said. 'And when you've used 'em, and my eyes don't open no more, bury the pennies, good souls, and don't ye go spending 'em, for I shouldn't like it. And open the windows as soon as I am carried out, and make it as cheerful as you can for Elizabeth-Jane.'"

(*The Mayor of Casterbridge*, ch. 18)

The grimly comic is not lacking when she tells how Christopher Coney dug up and spent the pennies. The passage ends with one of those lyrical sayings that abound in the prose of this poet:

"Well poor soul, she's helpless to hinder that or anything else now," answered Mother Cuxsom. "And all her shining keys will be took from her, and her cupboards opened; and little things a' didn't wish seen, anybody will see; and her wishes and ways will all be as nothing."

Hardy, a meditative poet, gave to the novel a sublimity which in his own country it had not attained before. His procedure is architectural. Out of all the elements in life that he knows, he builds up, through a series of novels, a whole that embraces the kind of men and women he has observed, the beautiful English country they have lived in, the memory of the past that has haunted them, and the whole panorama of life and earth filled with love and jealousy, ambition, fear, and unfulfilled ideals. His style moves for the most part slowly and cumbrously, sometimes awkwardly, like Gabriel Oak's walk. He has no scholarly fastidiousness of language; yet in moments of excitement or tension or deep emotion it breaks through its impediments, becoming now vivacious, now brilliant, now lovely in its still depths. But for the most part the effects are cumulative; he assembles piece by piece the elements that go to the making of a vast panorama.

THE DYNASTS

I have said that Hardy's art was progressive, revealing the successive stages in his discovery of life. When he had written *Jude*, he probably felt that he had said all that he had to say in novel form. The torrent of invective that the book drew down upon him from the critics was an experience that, he said seventeen years later, completely cured him of further interest in novel writing. But the invective can scarcely be the whole or even the main reason for his abandoning prose fiction. He had always known himself to be a poet, and he was a poet whether he wrote in prose or verse; and he was now free to follow his bent. But there were overwhelming reasons, inherent in his own development, why he should turn from novels to the epic drama of *The Dynasts*. He had spent twenty-five years in the effort to state life in terms of life; the novels were an objective expression of the raw material of experience; his gradual discovery of what life consists of led to those novels; experience, intuition, meditation gave birth to those tracts of human experience there exposed;

and already, before he had done with them, they were revealing themselves in a wider context: the history of the human race and its place in the universe. It remained for him to state his conclusions—not philosophically, for his mind worked imaginatively, but in a poem. *The Dynasts* is the summing-up of all that he had done before.

"Ay; begin small, and so lead up to the greater. It is a sound dramatic principle." Thus the Spirit Sinister in *The Dynasts* replies to the Spirit of the Years, who had called the attention of the assembled Spirits to some human beings traveling in a stage-coach over a ridge in Wessex in March 1805. Hardy's own literary work had proceeded in this way, beginning small with light poems and *Under the Greenwood Tree*, gaining volume and depth as the novels progressed, and culminating in his great epic drama. He had for many years been preparing himself for the subject he treats here, "the Great Historical Calamity, or Clash of Peoples" in the Napoleonic wars, for the use of verse as a literary medium, and for a cosmological survey of the human race. I have already alluded to his studies of the Napoleonic wars, which he used in the small beginnings of *The Trumpet-Major*, and of his growing interest in the scheme of an epic of Napoleon. It was natural that he should link this up with his studies of individual human beings whom he had observed tragically out of harmony with the "social moulds" of modern life and as the victims of a fate that appeared to dog them senselessly and pitilessly.

In form *The Dynasts* is both epic and drama. It uses both narrative and dialogue, mainly in verse, but partly in prose. Its subject in the narrower sense is that of the Napoleonic wars from 1805 to 1815 (followed in strict accord with historic evidence), with special reference to the part played by England in the European conflict. There are many scores of persons, conspicuous among them Napoleon, William Pitt (the Younger), Horatio Nelson, George III, Pierre Villeneuve, the emperors Francis and Alexander, the empress Josephine, Lady Hester Stanhope, and many admirals, marshals, politicians, priests, court ladies, and humble sailors, soldiers, burgesses, beacon-watchers, and rustics seen and heard on the continent of Europe, in England, or at sea. Regarded as historic epic the work presents a colossal, and I believe accurate, historic pageant of the leaders and common people of Europe in the greatest human conflict prior to the two world wars. But it is much more than that; it follows the classic examples of Homer's *Iliad* and Milton's *Paradise Lost* in introducing extraterrestrial powers, and allotting to them an integral part in the action. But there are significant differences, corresponding to the differences in thought, which put a gulf between Hardy and the poets of less skeptical ages. The gods in Homer are like men and intervene in their affairs; the Archangels of Milton are also anthropomorphically conceived and intervene benevolently or malignly in the affairs of men. The Immanent Will of *The Dynasts,* however, from the nature of its being cannot appear at all as a person or a speaker. As for the Spirits—the Ancient Spirit and Chorus of the Years, the Spirit and Chorus of the Pities, the Shade of the Earth, the Spirits Sinister and Ironic with their Choruses, and the Rumours, Spirit-Messengers, and Recording Angels—they do not, with two or three exceptions, interfere at all in the human sphere; they are observers, recorders, commentators. We are to discover that it is not we human beings who are primarily the audience, the spectators, of the drama. The play is played to the Spirits; it is they who watch it, they who judge it and express their sympathy or indifference. The vast panoramic struggle is thrown as it were on a terrific screen that embraces the whole of Europe and seen through the eyes of nonhuman Intelligence. Behind all is the Immanent Will and its designs:

> It works unconsciously, as heretofore,
> Eternal artistries in Circumstance,
> Whose patterns, wrought by rapt aesthetic rote,
> Seen in themselves Its single listless aim,
> And not their consequence.
>
> (Fore Scene)

"In the Foretime," adds the Spirit of the Years,

> Nothing appears of shape to indicate
> That cognizance has marshalled things terrene,
> Or will (such is my thinking) in my span.
> Rather they show that, like a knitter drowsed,
> Whose fingers ply in skilled unmindfulness,
> The Will has woven with an absent heed
> Since life first was; and ever will so weave.
>
> (Fore Scene)

The Spirit of the Years, aloof and passionless, presides among the Spirits as the play goes on before them; the Pities, as Hardy pointed out, approximate what August von Schlegel called "the Universe Sympathy of human nature—the Spectator idealized" of

the Greek chorus. The speeches of the Spirits constitute a sublime play beyond the play; they are in strong, rhythmic, sonorous verse appropriate to their dignity, the vocabulary strangely compounded of long Latin words and terse, pithy Anglo-Saxon words such as

> You'll mark the twitchings of this Bonaparte
> As he with other figures foots his reel,
> Until he twitch him into his lonely grave.
>
> (Fore Scene)

The stage descriptions embrace all Europe and the scene gives us people in millions. "The nether sky opens, and Europe is disclosed as a prone and emaciated figure, the Alps shaping like a backbone, and the branching mountain-chains like ribs, the peninsula plateau of Spain forming a head. . . ." "The peoples, distressed by events which they did not cause, are seen writhing, crawling, heaving, and vibrating in their various cities and nationalities." What a foreglimpse, in 1903, of the world wars to follow, as seen from the onlookers' stall.

The human play is methodically pursued, with varying power. Some of the "small" things are among the best, where Hardy, in appropriate prose, writes of his Wessex folk, talking with their native humor in the vernacular; or Wessex soldiers, fighting in Spain, recalling their old loves at home; or French soldiers, in their distracted retreat from Moscow. His love of the gruesome comes out in the *Mad Soldier's Song* (sung in the retreat):

> What can we wish for more?
> Thanks to the frost and flood
> We are grinning crones—thin bags of bones
> Who once were flesh and blood.
> So foolish life adieu
> And ingrate leader too.
> —Ah, but we loved you true!
> Yet—he-he-he! and ho-ho-ho!—
> We'll never return to you.
>
> (pt. III, I.xi)[2]

To meet the ends of an action that covers so wide a field, in so many representative scenes, the language varies in power and dignity. The verse is always vigorous, but not always at a high level of poetry. But who before has attempted in verse the task of reporting a parliamentary debate? Even so, Pitt in

[2]References are to part, act, and scene.

one of his speeches talks in successful verse almost as Winston Churchill talked in prose.

> The strange fatality that haunts the times
> Wherein our lot is cast, has no example.
> Times are they fraught with peril, trouble, gloom;
> We have to mark their lourings, and to face them.
>
> (pt. I, I.iii)

The speeches of Napoleon are usually rhetorical, but there are vivacity and force in the rhetoric. The strategists, statesmen, and courtiers all talk in character. The action proceeds from scene to scene with swiftness and unfailing energy, and we can read on as we would read a story, eager to follow the thrilling narrative, and stirred by the dark adventures and bold exhibitions of character. Sometimes—even on the battlefield of Waterloo—we are gripped by the poetic sense of the continuing life of the earth, the earth that Hardy knows in Wessex, but here grimly threatened by the human conflict:

> Yea, the coneys are scared by the thud of hoofs,
> And their white scuts flash at their vanishing heels,
> And swallows abandon the hamlet-roofs.
>
> (pt. III, VI.vii)

It is a singular fact that in this drama of a European war Hardy should so write that we can never forget that Wessex coast and the people who live in the Wessex villages. Though Hardy is a good world citizen, and once said that the sentiment of "foreignness" should "attach only to other planets and their inhabitants, if any," we feel nonetheless that he is stirred by English patriotism, that he admires the patriotic sentiments that Pitt expresses, and loves the innate and ineradicable patriotism—provincialism, if you like—of the English countryman. Though he is completely objective in his treatment of friends and enemies of the English and rejects nationalism in his sympathy and in his pity for human beings, nonetheless the pulse of the poet seems to beat a little faster when he exhibits the reflections of a Pitt, the emotions of a Nelson, or the sentiment and humor of the English rustic. He has not set himself to praise England as Vergil in the *Aeneid* sang the praises of Rome; nonetheless there emerges in the course of the epic a sort of personality, which is that of the English people, with qualities very dear to the poet, compounded of good and bad, serious and comic, but, in the sum, both noble and lovable. But these qualities are also those of the human race. Much of the tragic

irony lies in this contrast between the essential goodness and kindliness of human beings and the blank indifference, the unkindness, of the irresistible universe. The Spirit of the Pities recalls the words of Sophocles, who

> . . . dubbed the Will "the gods." Truly said he,
> "Such gross injustice to their own creation
> Burdens the time with mournfulness for us,
> And for themselves with shame."
>
> (pt. I, V.iv)

The Dynasts is a large-scale action, planned to project the situation of the whole human race, which consists of individuals possessing a sense of justice and noble aspirations, frustrated, as it seems to them, by an irresistible and indifferent destiny. The whole is an imaginative picture, not a set of dogmas; but it yields the conclusion that arises irresistibly from those samples of life Hardy has given in the novels.

The novels are as full of poetry as is this epic. The epic itself contains many prose passages, and some of the speeches written in verse would have been equally, sometimes more, satisfactory in prose. Hardy traverses the low ground of less distinguished speech and high ground where his verse becomes equal to the strain and exhibits extreme vigor and sometimes a rare and forceful imagery that touches the higher peaks of poetry. He is not a fastidious writer with a sure touch in the use of words, and yet in a few passages the words could not be bettered—that occurs when he is fully possessed by the emotional content of his theme, and the words seem to pour from him irresistibly in their own right.

The Dynasts is the indispensable culmination of his work. It is as necessary as *War and Peace* is to Leo Tolstoy, combining, as that book does, the individual and the universal. The private tragedies, which in Tolstoy were interwoven with the world catastrophe, are more subtly treated by the Russian and more poignant. Tolstoy's individuals are more individual, more alive. But all this, the human side of life, had already been presented by Hardy in his novels with less aloofness but with consummate power. *The Dynasts* has an advantage over *War and Peace* in its unity and orchestration. It is the finale of the great body of work that had begun in his youth, matured in his middle age, and concluded itself here. He had surpassed any other English novelist in using the novel as an artistic vehicle for projecting life in its totality realistically, emotionally, meditatively; in doing with it what hitherto only poetry had done; and in fitting it into a structure sublimely conceived and capable of summary in a final work that, in form as well as substance, is poetic.

THE LYRICAL POETRY

It is related of Thomas Hardy's infancy that, one hot afternoon, his mother returned to the cottage at Higher Bockhampton to find the baby asleep in his cradle, with "a large snake curled up upon his breast, comfortably asleep like himself." It had come in, no doubt, from the wild country nearby, which he would immortalize one day as Egdon Heath. To strangle snakes in his cradle is a very proper symbol for the future hero of action. For one destined to be a hero of another kind—a contemplative who saw less good than evil in the human condition, but, by taking that evil to heart, by accepting it into his poetry, disarmed or purified it a little; a man of great compassion, a man who preserved through journey-work, fame, obloquy, and disillusionment a singular innocence—for such a hero the image of the sleeping snake on the infant's breast is strangely fitting.

Personalities, as a rule, should be kept out of the criticism of poetry. But it is extraordinarily difficult, and possibly undesirable, to dissociate Hardy's poetry from his character. Those who knew him best have all borne witness to his patience and modesty, his tenderness, and the magnanimity that gave grandeur to a somber cast of mind. We know about the moral courage without which a mind so sensitive as his might well have closed up against experience in despair and the integrity that insisted that what seemed true of life, however terrible, should not be excluded from art. We have human witnesses to these qualities; but we do not need them, for they are manifest in the poems themselves. But in other respects we may misinterpret or undervalue the poems unless we realize the complicated nature, so oddly compounded of naiveté and erudition, ardor and melancholy, that produced them. For example, if we ignore the inherited peasant streak in Hardy, we shall fail to catch the countryman's raw humor and his love of a story for its own sake.

There is another reason why personality must enter any discussion of Hardy's verse. Almost all his finest poems are deeply, nakedly personal: the love poems of 1912–1913, for example, or the meditations in old age—"Surview," "Afterwards," "An Ancient to Ancients." It is the tone of such poems that, perhaps more than any other facet of his genius, awakes in the reader a feeling of affectionate veneration for the man who wrote them. Hardy put everything he felt, everything he noticed, everything he was into his poetry. As a result he wrote many indifferent poems; but because what he gave so unreservedly were the impressions of a magnanimous heart—the thoughts of a mind closely engaged in the problems of its own time and possessed of a strong historical sense, the experience of a man thoroughly versed in human suffering—his poetry has that breadth of matter and manner that only a major poet can compass.

We must not, however, be led by the importance of the personal in Hardy's verse to judge him as a sort of well-meaning, ham-handed titan who somehow blundered into poetry now and then by sheer force of personality. This is a superficial judgment, albeit a common one still. Though I sympathize with F. R. Leavis' feelings of dismay at Hardy's "gaucherie, compounded of the literary, the colloquial, the baldly prosaic, the conventionally poetical, the pedantic and the rustic," I believe that, in common with other critics who do not write verse, he has failed to notice the great technical skill that Hardy commanded and the amount of experiment in versification that he undertook. Often, it is true, Hardy seems to lose all touch with his medium, and will dress up his subjects in the shoddiest, hand-me-down verse. But it is of the utmost significance that whenever he comes to write of something near to his heart, of personal experience, he finds his touch again, and his technique becomes masterly. Consider this enchanting picture of his childhood home:

> Here is the ancient floor,
> Footworn and hollowed and thin,
> Here was the former door
> Where the dead feet walked in.
>
> She sat here in her chair,
> Smiling into the fire;
> He who played stood there,
> Bowing it higher and higher.
>
> Childlike, I danced in a dream;
> Blessings emblazoned that day;
> Everything glowed with a gleam;
> Yet we were looking away!
> ("The Self-Unseeing")

This lilting, serious, elegant poem illustrates several of the salient qualities in Hardy's lyrical poetry. We see here, for example, what has been justly termed his "natural piety"—the "he" and the "she" are his father and mother. We notice how the subject of beloved things in retrospect calls out here, as it seldom failed to do, the poet's lyrical tenderness. The poem illustrates, too, that love of music and the dance that affected Hardy from an early age and clearly influenced his style. It shows his delicate skill in suffusing pathos with gaiety, his sense of the transient haunting all scenes of present happiness. Although it is not strongly marked by his well-known idiosyncrasies of manner, it could not be mistaken for any other poet's writing—"Blessings emblazoned that day;/Everything glowed with a gleam" has the authentic Hardy ring.

The first thing we notice about Hardy's manner is that he seems to have been born with it. It can be detected in his earliest surviving poem, "Domicilium." Hardy wrote a fair number of poems during his young manhood, very few in his middle novel-writing period, and returned happily to verse—the medium he had always preferred—after the publication of *Jude the Obscure* and *The Well-Beloved* (1897). It was during the last thirty years of his life that the bulk of his verse, including *The Dynasts*, was written. His first volume of verse, *Wessex Poems*, was not published until 1898. Here, as in each subsequent volume, he included a number of earlier poems with poems composed at more recent dates. The former he sometimes, but not always, dated. His development would therefore have to be traced by internal evidence for the most part: luckily for the critic, there was no development in the sense of a change from one style to another or from one field of subject matter to another. Throughout, he was chiefly concerned with love, transience, death, and what the newspapers would call "human-interest stories." If we compare the poems dated between 1865 and 1875 with those poems of a later date, we find little alteration in manner: what we do notice is that most of the earlier ones are in the iambic ten-syllable meter, and many of them sonnets. It seems that Hardy did not experiment widely in the complex stanza forms and flexible rhythms that represent his greatest technical achievement until he returned to poetry in his late fifties.

Not only in idiosyncrasy but in more general aspects of style Hardy's poetry shows little alteration through the years. We know he read Vergil when young, admired Crabbe, Shelley, Keats, Scott, and, of his contemporaries, Barnes, Swinburne, Meredith, and Browning. But it is extremely difficult to detect any stylistic influence that these writers had upon him other than his use of certain of Barnes's stanza forms and his affinity with Browning. Browning is the only poet whose idiom is strongly echoed from Hardy's own verse. For example, these famous lines ironically sum up Hardy's attitude to life:

> Let him in whose ears the low-voiced Best is killed by
>   the clash of the First,
> Who holds that if way to the Better there be, it exacts
>   a full look at the Worst,
> Who feels that delight is a delicate growth cramped
>   by crookedness, custom, and fear,
> Get him up and be gone as one shaped awry; he
>   disturbs the order here.
>
> ("In Tenebris II," st. 4)

The shyness that prevented Hardy from meeting Browning and other contemporaries during his young days in London may well have contributed to the persistence of his own early idiom; certainly, had he met them, he might have become a more self-critical poet. But he gained more than he lost by not being thrown, so young and immature as he was then, into the deep end of literary society. For Hardy's is a classic example, if ever there was one, of the self-made manner: not just a manner made largely out of his self, and in that sense full of character, full of flavor; but also as it were a self-taught manner with the roughness, the naiveté, the vigor, the uncertainty of taste that we might infer from the term "self-made." He was not, however, altogether uncritical about his own work: for instance, when his first wife died, he wrote a considerable number of poems about their past: of these he selected twenty-one to appear in *Satires of Circumstance* (1914) as "Poems of 1912–13"; the remainder we find scattered about in later publications. If we compare these with the original twenty-one, we find that the latter are noticeably superior: his first choice was, in fact, a sound one; and to have chosen so well from a body of poems so intimately personal as these surely argues a genuine critical detachment.

We learn something about his attitude to poetry from Hardy's own *Life of Thomas Hardy*. He approved Leslie Stephen's judgment that "the ultimate aim of the poet should be to touch our hearts by showing his own; and not to exhibit his learning, or his fine taste, or his skill in mimicking the notes of his predecessors." Elsewhere he says, "To find beauty in ugliness is the province of the poet." He made "quantities of notes on rhyme and metre: with outlines and experiments in innumerable original measures," his tendency being always against too regular a beat. Again, writing of his prose method, he says:

The whole secret of a living style and the difference between it and a dead style, lies in not having too much style—being, in fact, a little careless, or rather seeming to be, here and there. . . . It is, of course, simply a carrying into prose the knowledge I have acquired in poetry—that inexact rhymes and rhythms now and then are far more pleasing than correct ones.

Hardy's poems are less rich than his novels in fresh, attentive description of natural objects; nor, except in *The Dynasts*, do we often find the panoramic views that form the great poetic images of his novels. In another respect, however, the novelist and the poet were one. Nothing was too small to escape Hardy's notice, or too great to daunt his powers, whether it was a hedgehog crossing a lawn at night or Europe's armies on the march. In his poetry no less than in his novels, he shows a genius for focusing together the great and the small, for feeling and revealing "infinite passion, and the pain/Of finite hearts that yearn," through some little glimpse or brief episode that, prosaic or trivial on the surface, he transmutes into a moment of vision.

Much has been written about Hardy's philosophy. He himself was at pains, though he spoke of the poet's task as "the application of ideas to life," to contradict those who found a philosophy of life in his work. What critics called his philosophical tenets were, he said, only "impressions" or rationalizations of moods. He vigorously disclaimed the title of pessimist, preferring to be thought of as a meliorist, and showing in his idea of an emergent consciousness in the universe a certain affinity with the doctrine of Emergent Evolution. It is, indeed, not difficult to sympathize with critics who found the deepest-dyed pessimism in his work. But we must not coagulate a poet's moods into a philosophical system, anymore than we must demand consistency from his ideas. Nor should we disregard the more positive and brighter aspect of Hardy's beliefs. He himself gave us the ideal groundwork of his art when he said that human nature is "neither ghastly, hateful, nor ugly; neither commonplace, unmeaning, nor tame, but . . . slighted and enduring; and withal singularly colossal

and mysterious"; or when he jotted down in his diary of August 1882: "An ample theme: the intense interests, passions, and strategy that throb through the commonest lives." We may disagree with this generous humanism of his, but if we disregard it, we shall lose much of the value of his poetry. For it is part of the pattern as he saw it, about which he said in a note for *The Dynasts*: "The human race to be shown as one great network or tissue which quivers in every part when one point is shaken, like a spider's web if touched."

In the compass of this essay, I shall confine my remarks to the shorter poems. They are the ones that put the greatest strain upon our allegiance to Hardy: often trivial, grotesque, or merely quaint in subject, these potted melodramas are all the more difficult to take because they tend to be written in a sort of album verse that ranges between the inept and the perfunctory. Moreover, they are apt to get laughs in the wrong places:

> "Then, where dwells the Canon's kinswoman,
>   My friend of aforetime?"
> I asked, to disguise my heart-heavings
>   And new ecstasy.

or

> We late-lamented, resting here,
>   Are mixed to human jam. . . .

There is a certain monotony of theme in these poems, and we feel that the poet is all the time shepherding his characters remorselessly toward the tomb. Once or twice, as in "The Trampwoman's Tragedy," Hardy deepens the implications of an episode and tautens the verse form, so that we get powerful poetry. But too often he found a story so absorbing as gossip that he could not or would not see any necessity for heightening it poetically. To a friend who remonstrated with him about one such poem, Hardy replied, "Oh, but it was a true story." Again and again this interest in gossip lures Hardy on to blithely tackling the most intractable subjects. Such narratives—and there are dozens of them—are not the products merely of idle curiosity about folktales and provincial contretemps: they show us how Hardy was touched by the little accidents that change human lives; and therefore, though they are often laughable, the laughter they provoke in us is affectionate.

Sympathy like this is the seed of poetic imagination. We get the full harvest in the vast imaginative vistas of *The Dynasts*, but one of the shorter poems offers us in miniature the same grandeur: "The Convergence of the Twain," subtitled "Lines on the Loss of the *Titanic*." It describes how the Immanent Will shapes an iceberg, "a sinister mate" for the great liner, and designs them to be "twin halves of one august event."

> In a solitude of the sea
> Deep from human vanity,
> And the Pride of Life that planned her, stilly couches she.
>
> Steel chambers, late the pyres
> Of her salamandrine fires,
> Cold currents thrid, and turn to rhythmic tidal lyres.
>
> Over the mirrors meant
> To glass the opulent
> The sea-worm crawls—grotesque, slimed, dumb, indifferent.
>
> Jewels in joy designed
> To ravish the sensuous mind
> Lie lightless, all their sparkles bleared and black and blind.
>
> Dim moon-eyed fishes near
> Gaze at the gilded gear
> And query: "What does this vaingloriousness down here?"...
>
> Well: while was fashioning
> This creature of cleaving wing
> The Immanent Will that stirs and urges everything
>
> Prepared a sinister mate
> For her—so gaily great—
> A Shape of Ice, for the time far and dissociate.
>
> And as the smart ship grew
> In stature, grace and hue,
> In shadowy silent distance grew the Iceberg too.
>
> Alien they seemed to be:
> No mortal eye could see
> The intimate welding of their later history,
>
> Or sign that they were bent
> By paths coincident
> On being anon twin halves of one august event,
>
> Till the Spinner of the Years
> Said "Now!" And each one hears
> And consummation comes, and jars two hemispheres.

Theme, language, and rhythm are perfectly congruous here; the weird submarine imagery of the opening stanzas deepens the imaginative reach of the subject. It is one of those poems, like Tennyson's "The Kraken" or Browning's "Childe Roland to the Dark Tower Came," that, although they are recognizably in the poet's idiom, seem to lie outside his canon and compel us to speculate how different that canon might be had the poet explored this particular vein more persistently.

But Hardy, in his shorter poems, evoked his genius most successfully through the personal and the lyrical. His lyrics are seldom pure; they are nearly always clouded by personal experience, and, even when the poem seems to be a pure distillation, it almost certainly had its sources in some real incident or flesh-and-blood person. The exquisite poem "To Lizbie Browne," for instance, is not addressed to any ideal or composite rustic charmer: Lizbie Browne was a gamekeeper's daughter with whom Hardy fell in love as a boy.

In his old age Hardy said that "his only ambition, as far as he could remember, was to have some poem or poems in a good anthology like the Golden Treasury." The model he had set before himself was "Drink to Me Only," by Ben Jonson. We remember that Hardy from childhood was devoted to music, could tune a fiddle at the age of six, and learned to refine in his verse rhythms the lilting, pausing, lolloping measures he had first loved in country dance tunes. So it is not after all very surprising if he took the Ben Jonson poem as his model. What is remarkable is that he should have written so many of his most beautiful lyrics in old age. If Hardy's mind was born old, his heart remained young:

> But Time, to make me grieve,
> Part steals, lets part abide,
> And shakes this fragile frame at eve
> With throbbings of noontide.
> ("I Look into My Glass")

The idealisms of his youth were never quite extinguished. They can be heard in the wistful last stanzas of "The Oxen" and "The Darkling Thrush," both of which are strainings after "some blessed Hope" in a bleak world. The passion that moves behind his love poems is the passion of young manhood seen through a golden haze of retrospect. We must allow that this backward-looking stance is vulnerable to criticism. Nostalgia, we are told, is an enervating emotion, likely to corrupt a poet's work. I can readily believe it; indeed any emotion is dangerous to a poem: there is only one thing more dangerous—the lack of it. The poet has somehow to distance himself from his emotions and the objects that gave rise to them without losing touch with them altogether. Hardy distanced himself by the simple device of writing most of his poetry in old age: he kept in touch because—again I can think of no more scientific phrase for it—his heart remained young; also, he evidently had what we might call a good sensuous memory. He was a nostalgic, both in the strict sense of one who feels homesickness—this is part of the emotional tone of his natural piety toward his parents, friends, and places of his youth—and in the looser sense of brooding constantly over the past. But the verse in which he embodies such brooding seldom shows the tenuousness or oversweetness that are signs of a morbid nostalgia. It is saved from them partly by deliberate roughness of technique and his habit of weaving homely images and colloquial phrases into the poetical texture, partly by sheer force of sincerity.

There are times, indeed, when we feel that the sense of the transience of things has become a monomania with Hardy; but at least his variations on this theme are extremely diverse, ranging from some of the best of the intimate poems to such unusual lyrics as "The Five Students" or "During Wind and Rain." Both of these offer us a subtle use of refrain, a technical device that Hardy employed in a masterly way to underline the pathos and inevitability of things passing. In both, the romantic and plangent refrain lines are balanced by the hard, factual, forthright imagery of the lines that precede them.

Another technical skill can be seen in Hardy's blending of the gay and the humorous with the poignant, an extremely difficult thing to do without breaking up the legato of the poem or ruining its texture. A good example of this is "He Revisits His First School":

> I should not have shown in the flesh,
> I ought to have gone as a ghost;
> It was awkward, unseemly almost,
> Standing solidly there as when fresh,
> > Pink, tiny, crisp-curled,
> > My pinions yet furled
> From the winds of the world.
>
> After waiting so many a year
> To wait longer, and go as a sprite
> From the tomb at the mid of some night

> Was the right, radiant way to appear;
> > Not as one wanzing[3] weak
> > From life's roar and reek,
> > His rest still to seek:
>
> Yea, beglimpsed through the quaint quarried glass
> Of green moonlight, by me greener made,
> When they'd cry, perhaps, "There sits his shade
> In his olden haunt—just as he was
> > When in Walkingame he
> > Conned the grand Rule-of-Three
> > With the bent of a bee."
>
> But to show in the afternoon sun,
> With an aspect of hollow-eyed care,
> When none wished to see me come there,
> Was a garish thing, better undone.
> > Yes; wrong was the way;
> > But yet, let me say,
> > I may right it—some day.

That charming poem, with so much of his personality in it, brings us to the most personal of all his poems—and the best. A little must be said about the human situation behind them. Hardy's first marriage went wrong. There were faults, very possibly, on his side that made him a difficult man to live with. When the glamour of their Cornish courtship faded, his wife was seen to be snobbish, small-minded, and incapable of living gracefully in the shadow of Hardy's genius. But a greater shadow fell upon her and darkened their relationship. Some mental derangement of hers has been hinted at, and veiled references may be found in a number of the poems: for instance, "Near Lanivet," "The Blow," "The Interloper," "The Man with a Past," or here, in "The Division":

> > But that thwart thing betwixt us twain,
> > > Which nothing cleaves or clears,
> > Is more than distance, Dear, or rain,
> > > And longer than the years!

Whatever "that thwart thing" may have been, his wife's death when the poet was seventy-two[4] swept away the long estrangement there had been between them, releasing a gush of reminiscence and poetry. I believe the best of these 1912–1913 poems to be some of the finest love poetry in our language: indeed, one

---

[3]Wanzing: wasting, diminishing.

[4]Two years later Hardy married his second wife, Florence Emily Dugdale, who was also a writer.

may wonder if there is in any language a parallel to this winter flowering of a poetry or sentiment that had lain dormant in the poet's heart throughout the summer of his age. The emotional range of the poems is remarkable, from the agony of bereavement and remorse in "The Going" to the almost ecstatic acceptance of "After a Journey"; from the delicate pathos of "The Haunter," in which the dead wife is speaking, to the no less delicate melancholy, strengthened by sinewy phrasing and a few clear-cut images, that makes "At Castle Boterel" so haunting a farewell to love. The variety of emotion is equaled by that of stanza form: it is as though the diverse molds had been preparing through a lifetime, and now those scenes from the past ran freely into them, each recognizing its own. Tricks of technique, which had at times been wasted on inferior material or had called too much attention to themselves, now came into their own—such as the triplet rhyming of "The Voice":

> Woman much missed, how you call to me, call to me,
> Saying that now you are not as you were
> When you had changed from the one who was all to me,
> But as at first, when our day was fair.
>
> Can it be you that I hear? Let me view you, then,
> Standing as when I drew near to the town
> Where you would wait for me: yea, as I knew you then,
> Even to the original air-blue gown!

Beneath their grace and appealing diversity, the 1912–1913 poems have good bone, formed by the sincerity, the refusal to overstate an emotion or falsify a situation, that we have noticed before. There might so forgivably have been flecks of self-pity, or sentimentality, even, in the best of these poems. That there are none is due not to the carefulness of a poet who has feared to give too much of himself away lest it muddy the stream of his verse but to the unselfconscious recklessness with which Hardy did give himself. The moral quality of that self may be gauged, I believe, by the poetic quality of what was thus created:

> Hereto I come to view a voiceless ghost;
>   Whither, O whither will its whim now draw me?
> Up the cliff, down, till I'm lonely, lost,
>   And the unseen waters' ejaculations awe me.
> Where will you next be there's no knowing,
>   Facing round about me everywhere,
>   With your nut-coloured hair,
> And grey eyes, and rose-flush coming and going.

> Yes: I have re-entered your olden haunts at last;
>   Through the years, through the dead scenes I have tracked you;
> What have you now found to say of our past—
>   Scanned across the dark space wherein I have lacked you?
> Summer gave us sweets, but autumn wrought division?
>   Things were not lastly as firstly well
>   With us twain, you tell?
> But all's closed now, despite Time's derision.
>
> I see what you are doing: you are leading me on
>   To the spots we knew when we haunted here together,
> The waterfall, above which the mist-bow shone
>   At the then fair hour in the then fair weather,
> And the cave just under, with a voice still so hollow
>   That it seems to call out to me from forty years ago,
>   When you were all aglow,
> And not the thin ghost that I now frailly follow!
>
> Ignorant of what there is flitting here to see,
>   The waked birds preen and the seals flop lazily;
> Soon you will have, Dear, to vanish from me,
>   For the stars close their shutters and the dawn whitens hazily.
> Trust me, I mind not, though Life lours,
>   The bringing me here; nay, bring me here again!
>   I am just the same as when
> Our days were a joy, and our paths through flowers.
>   ("After a Journey")

Such, then, is the tenderness of Thomas Hardy. I do not know any other English poet who strikes that note of tenderness so firmly and so resonantly. With Hardy at his best, it is the poem—the whole poem, not any high spots in it—that makes the impression. We shall be offended by his frequent use of archaic, uncouth, or stock-poetic words if we detach them from their contexts—words such as "domicile," "denizenship," "subtrude," "thuswise," "hodiernal," "fulgid," "lippings," "unbe." But if we allow the momentum of the poem to carry us over them, as often it can, they will seem very small obstacles; and without them his poetry would lose something of its characteristic flavor. It cannot, of course, be denied that the massive deployment of a simple idea, though apt enough for a work on the scale of *The Dynasts*, becomes in a short poem grandiose and cumbrous: circumlocution is a serious danger to Hardy's lyrics. Yet he often, by a secret formula in which craft and innocence are somehow combined, manages to absorb his circumlocutions in the body of the poem. One can think of few less promising lines to start a poem—or more ponderous ways of saying "When I am dead"—than "When the Present has latched its postern behind my tremulous stay": yet the poem it begins is one of Hardy's finest. The language of poetry is, after all, an artificial language, whether the poet uses a poetic diction throughout a poem or whether he varies it with colloquial phrases. The only question is, has he achieved balance and congruence; and the final test of this is whether the poem survives as a whole or in fragments.

I believe that where personal poetry is concerned the wholeness of a poem must depend not only upon technical skill, not even upon technical skill backed by imaginative power, but also—and perhaps most—on a certain wholeness in the poet himself. Great poems have been written by immature, flawed, or unbalanced men; but not, I suggest, great personal poetry; for this, ripeness, breadth of mind, charity, honesty are required: that is why great personal poetry is so rare. It is an exacting medium: false humility, egotism, or emotional insincerity cannot be hidden in such poetry; they disintegrate the poem. Thomas Hardy's best poems do seem to me to offer us images of virtue; not because he moralizes, but because they breathe out the truth and goodness that were in him, inclining our own hearts toward what is lovable in humanity:

When the Present has latched its postern behind my
    tremulous stay,
    And the May month flaps its glad green leaves like
        wings,
Delicate-filmed as new-spun silk, will the neighbours
    say,
    "He was a man who used to notice such things"?

If it be in the dusk when, like an eyelid's soundless
    blink,
    The dewfall-hawk comes crossing the shades to
        alight
Upon the wind-warped upland thorn, a gazer may
    think,
    "To him this must have been a familiar sight."

If I pass during some nocturnal blackness, mothy and
    warm,
    When the hedgehog travels furtively over the lawn,
One may say, "He strove that such innocent creatures
    should come to no harm,
    But he could do little for them, and now he is
        gone."

If, when hearing that I have been stilled at last, they
    stand at the door,

Watching the full-starred heavens that winter sees,
Will this thought rise on those who will meet my face
    no more,
    "He was one who had an eye for such mysteries"?

And will any say when my bell of quittance is heard
    in the gloom,
    And a crossing breeze cuts a pause in its
        outrollings,
Till they rise again, as they were a new bell's boom,
    "He hears it not now, but used to notice such
        things"?

                      ("Afterwards")

SELECTED BIBLIOGRAPHY

I. BIBLIOGRAPHY. C. Wilson, ed., *A Descriptive Catalogue of the Grolier Club Centenary Exhibition* (Waterville, Me., 1940); C. J. Weber, *The First Hundred Years of Thomas Hardy, 1840–1940* (Waterville, Me., 1942), a centenary bibliography of Hardiana; R. L. Purdy, *Thomas Hardy: A Bibliographical Study* (London, 1954); K. Carter, comp., *Thomas Hardy Catalogue* (Dorchester, 1968), a list of the books by and about Hardy in the Dorset County Library.

II. COLLECTED WORKS. *Works in Prose and Verse*, 20 vols. (London, 1895–1913); *The Writings of Thomas Hardy in Prose and Verse*, 21 vols. (New York–London, 1895–1903), the Anniversary ed.; *Works in Prose and Verse*, 25 vols. (London, 1906–1919), the Pocket ed.; *Works in Prose and Verse*, 23 vols. (London, 1912–1913), the Wessex ed.; *Works in Prose and Verse*, 37 vols. (London, 1919–1920), the Mellstock ed.; *Poetical Works*, 2 vols. (London, 1919–1921), vol. I: *Poems*, vol. II: *The Dynasts*; the 2nd and subsequent eds., each in one vol., do not include *The Dynasts*; the first one-vol. ed. of *The Dynasts* was published in 1910, and there is a deluxe ed. in three vols. (1927); *Short Stories* (London, 1928); *The Novels* (London, 1949–1952); J. Gibson, ed., *Complete Poems* (London, 1974), the New Wessex ed.

III. SELECTED WORKS. G. M. Young, ed., *Selected Poems* (London, 1940); W. E. Williams, ed., *Selected Poems* (London, 1960); J. C. Ransom, ed., *Selected Poems* (New York, 1961); C. J. Weber, ed., *Love Poems* (London, 1963); P. N. Furbank, ed., *Selected Poems* (London, 1964); J. Wain, ed., *Selected Shorter Poems* (London, 1966); J. Wain, ed., *Selected Stories* (London, 1966); G. Grigson, ed., *Choice of Poems* (London, 1969); T. R. M. Creighton, ed., *A New Selection* (London, 1974); J. Gibson, ed., *Chosen Short Stories* (London, 1976); J. Moynahan, ed., *The Portable Thomas Hardy* (London, 1979); D. Wright, ed., *Selected Poems* (London, 1979).

IV. SEPARATE WORKS. *Desperate Remedies*, 3 vols. (London, 1871), novel, first published anonymously; *Under the Greenwood Tree: A Rural Painting of the Dutch School,* 2 vols. (London, 1872), novel, first published anonymously; "A New Edition with a Portrait of the Author and Fifteen Illustrations" [by Thomas Hardy] was published in 1891; *A Pair of Blue Eyes: A Novel,* 3 vols. (London, 1873); *Far from the Madding Crowd,* 2 vols. (London, 1874), novel; *The Hand of Ethelberta: A Comedy in Chapters,* 2 vols. (London, 1876), novel; *The Return of the Native,* 3 vols. (London, 1878), novel; *The Trumpet-Major: A Tale,* 3 vols. (London, 1880), novel; *A Laodicean, or, The Castle of the De Stancys: A Story of To-day,* 3 vols. (London, 1881), novel; *Two on a Tower: A Romance,* 3 vols. (London, 1882), novel; *The Dorset Farm Labourer Past and Present* (Dorchester, 1884), essay; *The Romantic Adventures of a Milkmaid* (New York, 1884), short story; *The Mayor of Casterbridge: The Life and Death of a Man of Character,* 2 vols. (London, 1886), novel; *The Woodlanders,* 3 vols. (London, 1887), novel; *Wessex Tales: Strange, Lively and Commonplace,* 2 vols. (London, 1888), short stories.

Tess of the d'Urbervilles: A Pure Woman Faithfully Presented, 3 vols. (London, 1891), novel; *A Group of Noble Dames* (London, 1891), short stories; *The Three Wayfarers: A Pastoral Play in One Act* (London, 1893), a dramatization of the short story "The Three Strangers"; *Life's Little Ironies. A Set of Tales with Some Colloquial Sketches Entitled "A Few Crusted Characters"* (London, 1894), includes "The Melancholy Hussar," first printed in *Three Notable Stories* (London, 1890), and "To Please His Wife," first printed in *Stories from "Black and White"* (London, 1893); *Jude the Obscure* (London, 1895), novel; "The Spectre of the Real," short story written in collaboration with F. Henniker, printed in *In Scarlet and Grey* by F. Henniker (London, 1896); *The Well-Beloved: A Sketch of a Temperament* (London, 1897), novel; *Wessex Poems and Other Verses* (London, 1898), with thirty illustrations by Hardy.

Poems of the Past and Present (London, 1901); *The Dynasts: A Drama of the Napoleonic Wars,* 3 parts (London, 1903–1904, 1906, 1908), J. Wain, ed. (paperback) (London–New York, 1965), verse drama; *Time's Laughingstocks and Other Verses* (London, 1909), verse; *A Changed Man, The Waiting Supper, and Other Tales* (London, 1913), short stories; *Satires of Circumstance: Lyrics and Reveries* (London, 1914), verse; *Moments of Vision, and Miscellaneous Verses* (London, 1917), verse.

Late Lyrics and Earlier. With Many Other Verses (London, 1922), verse; *The Famous Tragedy of the Queen of Cornwall at Tintagel in Lyonness* (London, 1923), verse drama; *Compassion: An Ode* (London, 1924), verse; *Human Shows, Far Phantasies, Songs and Trifles* (London, 1925), verse; *Life and Art* (New York, 1925), essays and letters, not previously printed in book form, ed. with intro. by E. Brennecke; *Winter Words, in Various Moods and Metres* (London, 1928), verse; *Old Mrs. Chundle* (New York, 1929), short story not in the collected short stories; *An Indiscretion in the Life of an Heiress* (London, 1934), short novel, adapted by the author from his first novel, "The Poor Man and the Lady," it was privately printed in a limited edition for Mrs. Hardy (London, 1934), first published separately (Baltimore, 1935) with an intro. by C. J. Weber; *The Intruder* (Fairfield, Me., 1938), short story not in the collected short stories.

Revenge Is Sweet: Two Short Stories (Waterville, Me., 1940), this limited edition contains "Destiny and a Blue Cloak" and "The Doctor's Legend," previously unpublished in book form; *Maumbury Ring* (Waterville, Me., 1942), essay, limited edition, not published elsewhere; *Our Exploits at West Poley* (London, 1952), story; E. Hardy, ed., *Notebooks, and Some Letters from Julia Augusta Martin* (London, 1955); C. J. Weber, ed., *Dearest Emmie* (London, 1963), letters from Hardy to his first wife; *The Architectural Notebook* (Dorchester, 1966), with intro. by C. J. P. Beatty; H. Orel, ed., *Thomas Hardy's Personal Writings* (Lawrence, Kans., 1967).

V. LETTERS. R. L. Purdy and M. Millgate, eds., *Collected Letters,* vol. I: *1840–1892* (London, 1978), vol. II: *1893–1901* (London, 1980).

VI. BIOGRAPHICAL AND CRITICAL STUDIES. L. P. Johnson, *The Art of Thomas Hardy* (London, 1894; rev. ed., 1923), the latter adds new material, also contains a bibliography by J. Lane of 1st eds. to 1922 and an added ch. on the poetry by J. E. Barton; C. G. Harper, *The Hardy Country: Literary Landmarks of the Wessex Novels* (London, 1904); F. O. Saxelby, *A Thomas Hardy Dictionary* (London, 1911); L. Abercrombie, *Thomas Hardy: A Critical Study* (London, 1912); D. H. Lawrence, "Study of Thomas Hardy," in *Phoenix* (London, 1914); H. Child, *Thomas Hardy* (London, 1916); H. D. Duffin, *Thomas Hardy: A Study of the Wessex Novels* (Manchester, 1916).

J. M. Murry, *Aspects of Literature* (London, 1920); J. W. Beach, *The Technique of Thomas Hardy* (London, 1922); E. Brennecke, *Thomas Hardy's Universe: A Study of a Poet's Mind* (London, 1924); R. Williams, *The Wessex Novels* (London, 1924); E. Brennecke, *Life of Thomas Hardy* (London, 1925); H. B. Brimsditch, *Character and Environment in the Novels of Thomas Hardy* (London, 1925); M. Chase, *Thomas Hardy, from Serial to Novel* (Minneapolis, 1927; repr., New York, 1962); A. Symons, *A Study of Thomas Hardy* (London, 1927); P. Braybrooke, *Thomas Hardy and His Philosophy* (London, 1928); V. H. G. Collins, *Talks with Thomas Hardy at Max Gate 1920–1922* (London, 1928); P. d'Exideuil, *Le Couple humain dans l'oeuvre de Thomas Hardy* (Paris, 1928), English translation from rev. text by F. W. Crosse, with an intro by H. Ellis (London, 1930), the French ed. contains a list of French translations of Hardy's works; F. E. Hardy, *The Early Life of Thomas Hardy, 1840–1891* (London, 1928); H. M. Tomlinson, *Thomas Hardy* (New York, 1929).

F. E. Hardy, *The Later Years of Thomas Hardy, 1892–*

1928 (London, 1930), this work and the previous one of 1928, which purport to be by Hardy's widow, were actually written by Hardy himself, a fact that he went to some lengths to conceal; the two books were repr. in one vol. entitled *The Life of Thomas Hardy, 1940-1928* (London, 1962); F. L. Lucas, *Eight Victorian Poets* (London, 1930); A. S. MacDowall, *Thomas Hardy: A Critical Study* (London, 1931); F. R. Leavis, *New Bearings in English Poetry* (London, 1932); A. C. Chakravarty, *The Dynasts and the Post-War Age in Poetry* (London, 1938); W. R. Rutland, *Thomas Hardy* (Oxford, 1938).

C. J. Weber, *Hardy of Wessex: His Life and Literary Career* (New York, 1940; rev. and exp., 1965); E. Blunden, *Thomas Hardy* (London, 1941); D. Cecil, *Hardy the Novelist: An Essay in Criticism* (London, 1943), the Clark Lectures, 1942; C. Clemens, *My Chat with Thomas Hardy* (Webster Groves, Mo., 1944), with an intro. by C. J. Weber; C. M. Bowra, *The Lyrical Poetry of Thomas Hardy* (Nottingham, 1946), the Byron Lecture, 1946; J. G. Southworth, *The Poetry of Thomas Hardy* (New York, 1947); H. C. Webster, *On a Darkling Plain: The Art and Thought of Thomas Hardy* (Chicago, 1947); A. J. Guerard, *Thomas Hardy: The Novels and Stories* (London, 1949).

D. Hawkins, *Thomas Hardy* (London, 1950), although the ed. bears this date, publication was in the following year; R. A. Scott-James, *Fifty Years of English Literature, 1900-1950* (London, 1951), contains an assessment of Hardy as a lyric poet; see also Scott-James's *Modernism and Romance* (London, 1908); C. Day Lewis, *The Poetry of Thomas Hardy* (London, 1951), a lecture delivered before the British Academy, June 1951, and published in the *Proceedings*; J. Holloway, *The Victorian Sage* (London, 1953); W. Allen, *The English Novel* (London, 1954); M. D. Brown, *Thomas Hardy* (London, 1954; 2d ed., rev., 1961); E. Hardy, *Thomas Hardy: A Critical Biography* (London, 1954); C. M. Bowra, *Inspiration and Poetry* (London, 1955); J. O. Bailey, *Thomas Hardy and the Cosmic Mind: A New Reading of The Dynasts* (Chapel Hill, N. C., 1956); G. Ford, ed., *The Pelican Guide to English Literature*, vol. VI: *Dickens to Hardy* (London, 1958).

J. Paterson, *The Making of "The Return of the Native"* (Berkeley-London, 1960); Emma Hardy, *Some Recollections*, Evelyn Hardy and R. Gittings, eds. (London, 1961), recollections of Hardy's first wife, together with fourteen of Hardy's poems that inspired them; S. Hynes, *The Pattern of Hardy's Poetry* (London, 1961); M. D. Brown, *Hardy: The Mayor of Casterbridge* (London, 1962), a close critical analysis of the novel; J. S. Cox, *Monographs on the Life, Times and Works of Thomas Hardy* (St. Peter Port, Guernsey, 1962-), a large collection of memorabilia by various authors; A. J. Guerard, *Hardy: A Collection of Critical Essays* (Englewood Cliffs, N. J., 1963); H. Orel, *Thomas Hardy's Epic Drama: A Study of "The Dynasts"* (Lawrence, Kans., 1963); J. I. M. Stewart, *Eight Modern Writers, Oxford History of English Literature*, vol. XII

(Oxford, 1963); G. Wing, *Hardy* (London, 1963); R. C. Carpenter, *Thomas Hardy* (New York, 1964); L. Dacon, *Hardy's Sweetest Image: Thomas Hardy's Poetry for His Lost Love, Tryphena* (Chagford, 1964); R. Morell, *Thomas Hardy: The Will and the Way* (Kuala Lumpur, 1965); D. Lodge, *Language of Fiction* (London, 1966); A. Kettle, *Hardy the Novelist: A Reconsideration* (Swansea, 1967); H. Orel, ed., *Thomas Hardy: Personal Writings* (London, 1967); E. Gosse, *Thomas Hardy, O.M.*, R. Knight, ed. and annot. (Bulpham, 1968); I. Howe, *Thomas Hardy* (London, 1968); T. Johnson, *Thomas Hardy* (London, 1968); L. Lerner and J. Holmstrom, eds., *Thomas Hardy and His Readers: A Selection of Contemporary Reviews* (London, 1968), with commentary; F. B. Pinion, *A Hardy Companion: A Guide to the Works of Thomas Hardy and Their Background* (London, 1968); D. Daiches, *Some Late Victorian Attitudes* (London, 1969); K. Marsden, *The Poems of Thomas Hardy* (London, 1969).

J. O. Bailey, *The Poetry of Thomas Hardy* (Chapel Hill, N. C., 1970); R. G. Cox, ed., *Hardy: The Critical Heritage* (London, 1970); J. H. Miller, *Thomas Hardy: Distance and Desire* (Cambridge, Mass., 1970); M. Millgate, *Thomas Hardy, His Career as a Novelist* (London, 1971); F. R. Southerington, *Hardy's Vision of Man* (London, 1971); J. I. M. Stewart, *Thomas Hardy: A Critical Biography* (London, 1971); F. E. Halliday, *Thomas Hardy: His Life and Work* (Bath, 1972); E. Hardy and F. B. Pinion, *One Rare Fair Woman* (London-Coral Gables, Fla., 1972); P. Meisel, *Thomas Hardy: The Return of the Repressed* (New Haven, Conn.-London, 1972); M. Williams, *Thomas Hardy and Rural England* (London-New York, 1972); D. Davis, *Thomas Hardy and British Poetry* (London, 1973); F. B. Pinion, ed., *Thomas Hardy and the Modern World* (London, 1974); P. Vigar, *The Novels of Thomas Hardy: Illusion and Reality* (London, 1974); M. Drabble, ed., *The Genius of Thomas Hardy* (London, 1975); R. P. Draper, ed., *Hardy: The Tragic Novels. A Casebook* (London, 1975); R. Gittings, *The Young Thomas Hardy* (London, 1975); D. Kramer, *Thomas Hardy: The Forms of Tragedy* (London, 1975); G. Thurley, *The Psychology of Hardy's Novels: The Nervous and the Statuesque* (St. Lucia, Queensland, 1975); D. Hawkins, *Thomas Hardy: Novelist and Poet* (Newton Abbot-New York-Vancouver, 1976); H. Orel, *The Final Years of Thomas Hardy* (London, 1976); T. O'Sullivan, *Thomas Hardy: An Illustrated Biography* (London, 1976); F. B. Pinion, *A Commentary on the Poems of Thomas Hardy* (London, 1976); L. St. J. Butler, *Thomas Hardy After Fifty Years* (London, 1977); F. B. Pinion, *Thomas Hardy: Art and Thought* (London, 1977); J. Bayley, *Essay on Hardy* (Cambridge, 1978); R. Gittings, *The Older Hardy* (London, 1978); A. Enstice, *Thomas Hardy: Landscapes of the Mind* (London-New York, 1979); R. Gittings, *The Second Mrs. Hardy* (London, 1979); J. Grundy, *Hardy and the Sister Arts* (London, 1979); D. Kramer, *A Critical Approach to the Fiction of Thomas Hardy* (London, 1979); D. K. Robinson, *The First*

Mrs. Thomas Hardy (London, 1979); A. Smith, ed., *The Novels of Thomas Hardy* (London, 1979); P. Boumelha, *Thomas Hardy and Women: Sexual Ideology and Narrative Form* (Sussex, 1982).

LIST OF SHORT STORIES

(The title in italics refers to the volume in which the story appears.)

"Absent-Mindedness in a Parish Choir," *Life's Little Ironies;* "Alicia's Diary," *A Changed Man;* "Andrey Satchel and the Parson and Clerk," *Life's Little Ironies;* "Anna, Lady Braxby," *A Group of Noble Dames;* "Barbara of the House of Grebe," *A Group of Noble Dames;* "A Changed Man," *A Changed Man;* "A Committee-Man of 'The Terror,'" *A Changed Man;* "The Distracted Preacher," *Wessex Tales;* "The Duchess of Hamptonshire," *A Group of Noble Dames;* "The Duke's Reappearance," *A Changed Man;* "Enter a Dragoon," *A Changed Man.*

"Fellow-Townsmen," *Wessex Tales;* "A Few Crusted Characters," *Life's Little Ironies;* "The Fiddler of the Reels," *Life's Little Ironies;* "The First Countess of Wessex," *A Group of Noble Dames;* "For Conscience' Sake," *Life's Little Ironies;* "The Grave by the Handpost," *A Changed Man;* "The History of the Hardcomes," *Life's Little Ironies;*

"The Honourable Laura," *A Group of Noble Dames;* "An Imaginative Woman," *Life's Little Ironies* (first published in *Wessex Tales*); "Incident in the Life of Mr. George Crookhill," *Life's Little Ironies;* "Interlopers at the Knapp," *Wessex Tales;* "The Lady Icenway," *A Group of Noble Dames;* "Lady Mottisfont," *A Group of Noble Dames;* "The Lady Penelope," *A Group of Noble Dames.*

"The Marchioness of Stonehenge," *A Group of Noble Dames;* "Master John Horseleigh, Knight," *A Changed Man;* "The Melancholy Hussar of the German Legion," *Wessex Tales* (first published in *Life's Little Ironies*); "A Mere Interlude," *A Changed Man;* "Netty Sargent's Copyhold," *Life's Little Ironies;* "Old Andrey's Experience as a Musician," *Life's Little Ironies;* "On the Western Circuit," *Life's Little Ironies;* "The Romantic Adventures of a Milkmaid," *A Changed Man;* "The Son's Veto," *Life's Little Ironies;* "Squire Petrick's Lady," *A Group of Noble Dames;* "The Superstitious Man's Story," *Life's Little Ironies.*

"The Three Strangers," *Wessex Tales;* "Tony Kytes, the Arch-Deceiver," *Life's Little Ironies;* "To Please His Wife," *Life's Little Ironies;* "A Tradition of Eighteen Hundred and Four," *Wessex Tales* (first published in *Life's Little Ironies*); "A Tragedy of Two Ambitions," *Life's Little Ironies;* "A Tryst at an Ancient Earthwork," *A Changed Man;* "The Waiting Supper," *A Changed Man;* "What the Shepherd Saw," *A Changed Man;* "The Winters and the Palmleys," *Life's Little Ironies;* "The Withered Arm," *Wessex Tales.*

HENRY JAMES
(1843-1916)

Tony Tanner

I

In November 1882, the authoritative and esteemed American critic William Dean Howells published an article on Henry James, Jr., in the *Century* magazine that helped to precipitate, or rather exacerbate, a controversy, not only about the respective virtues of English and American writing, but about the very nature and future of fiction itself. He praised Henry James in the following terms:

His race is Irish on his father's side and Scotch on his mother's, to which mingled strains the generalizer may attribute, if he likes, that union of vivid expression and dispassionate analysis which has characterized his work from the first. . . . We must agree, then, to take what seems a fragment instead of a whole, and to find, when we can, a name for this new kind of fiction. Evidently it is the character, not the fate, of his people which occupies him; when he has fully developed their character, he leaves them to what destiny the reader pleases.

The analytic tendency seems to have increased with him as his work has gone on. . . . No other novelist, except George Eliot, has dealt so largely in analysis of motive, has so fully explained and commented upon the springs of action in the persons of the drama, both before and after the facts. These novelists are more alike than any others in their processes, but with George Eliot an ethical purpose is dominant, and with Mr. James an artistic purpose. . . . The art of fiction has, in fact, become a finer art in our day than it was with Dickens and Thackeray. We could not suffer the confidential attitude of the latter now, nor the mannerism of the former. . . . The new school derives from Hawthorne and George Eliot rather than any others; but it studies human nature much more in its wonted aspects, and finds its ethical and dramatic examples in the operation of lighter but not really less vital motives. The moving accident is certainly not its trade; and it prefers to avoid all manner of dire catastrophes. It is largely influenced by French fiction in form. . . . This school, which is so largely of the future as well as the present, finds its chief exemplar in Mr. James; it is he who is shaping and directing American fiction, at least. . . . Will the reader be content to accept a novel which is an analytic study rather than a story, which is apt to leave him arbiter of the destiny of the author's creations?

Something of the background to these remarks—which caused much offense, anger, and attempted rebuttal—should be sketched in, if we are to understand and appreciate in what ways Henry James was the "chief exemplar" of a new school of fiction, the future of which (not only in America) he was to be so instrumental in "shaping and directing." To quote a friend of Howells', George Pelles, writing in 1888, "For a long time a wordy war has raged in the magazines and the newspapers between so-called realists and romanticists. . . . The ground is strewn with dead and dying reputations." It is this "war" we should say a word about, to comprehend something of what Henry James was trying to do in and with the novel that seemed so new—and at times incomprehensible—at the time.

The terms of the controversy were crude, and a word like *realism* now begs more questions for us than it answers. But the opposition seemed clear enough at the time. The great majority of readers wanted novels that, to put it tersely, were either sentimental or sensational. The popular novels were "dramatic" and "romantic"; they concentrated on externalities of action and deployed stereotypical characters and emotions. In a debased use of the term, these novels were thought to be "idealistic," inasmuch as they showed ideal characters experiencing ideal emotions. Anything written under the name of "realism" was thought to be a threat to this "idealism." What this popular novel distinctly avoided was "psychological" analysis—that was "scientific," anti-idealistic, heartless. In the majority of contemporary reviews, the very word *analysis* was invariably used in a pejorative sense. So James's novels would be castigated for offering "what may be stigmatized as super-subtle analyses, ultra-refined phrases, fine-spun nothings" (Annie R. M. Logan).

We may note the tacit but prevailing assumption that "story" and "analysis" were antipathetic, if not mutually exclusive phenomena, the latter working to the detriment of the former.

I have stressed this early resistance to James's work because we have come to think of him mainly as "the Master," admired and deeply respected by a whole range of major twentieth-century writers. It is important to realize what he had to struggle *against* as he gradually developed a new kind of fiction that played a major part in what Henry Nash Smith calls "the liquidation of nineteenth-century culture," and served to effect radical changes in the conception of what a novel could be and do.

II

HENRY JAMES was born in New York City in 1843, an urban beginning that from the start left him relatively untouched by the dominant American influences of the Transcendentalist writers of New England (best represented by Ralph Waldo Emerson and Henry David Thoreau). His whole education and upbringing were calculated to give him a multiple and international perspective on various cultures, and to ensure that he would not, or could not, be contained within the orthodoxies of any one school of thought or theory of fiction, American, English, or European. His father, himself a remarkable and independent figure, had rejected the Calvinism of his father (an Irish immigrant), and was influenced mainly by the philosophy of Emanuel Swedenborg, traces of whose thought have been detected in his son's work. Henry James, Sr., gave his children an unusually free rein during their childhood, which doubtless contributed to the notable "freedom" of their thought. (Henry's brother, William, was to become a major American philosopher and psychologist whose ideas about the "stream of consciousness" can be related to the fictional practice of his brother.) Henry was taken abroad when he was six months old, and his earliest impressions and memories were of Europe (one of his first memories was of the Napoleonic column in the Place Vendôme). He returned to Albany and New York when he was nearly three and spent his boyhood in a number of private schools in New York; by the age of twelve he was well steeped in the atmosphere of Manhattan. Then, in 1855, his father took the family abroad, and for three years the children had a number of tutors and governesses in Geneva, London, and Paris. What kind of formal education Henry absorbed during these years would be hard to estimate; he not only became an avid reader of the fiction of France and England, as well as of America, but was acquiring a sense of the value of individual freedom and a habit of detachment from any kind of group commitment. He lived among, and off, literature, museums, galleries, and the variegated impressions of the changing cultural scenes through which he passed.

In 1858 the family returned to America; then, a year later, Henry went to Geneva. He returned, and the family settled in Newport, Rhode Island. During this period he sustained a strange back injury (while helping to put out a fire) about which there has been much speculation, since, among other things, it prevented him from taking any active part in the Civil War. In 1862 he entered Harvard Law School but soon withdrew: he had already started writing articles and short stories, and he realized that he was not cut out for any of the orthodox professions. He was to stay in America until 1870, when he made his first adult journey to England (where he met Dante Gabriel Rossetti, William Morris, and John Ruskin), France, and Italy, and it was in that year in Boston that he wrote his first novel, *Watch and Ward*, which was serialized the next year. Between 1872 and 1874 he was again in Europe, particularly Rome, and it was there he began *Roderick Hudson*. Again he returned to America, where he attempted to make a living from literary journalism in New York. *Roderick Hudson* was published in 1875, as were a number of important short stories and a book of travel sketches. From 1875 to 1876 he was back in Paris (where he met such eminent writers as Ivan Turgenev, Gustave Flaubert, Émile Zola, Edmond de Goncourt, Alphonse Daudet, and Guy de Maupassant). It was there he wrote *The American*, published in 1877.

This year seems to have been decisive, for in December 1876 he decided to settle in London, which was to remain his base, if not his home, for the rest of his life. During these years, James had learned a great deal about the "art of fiction" from English and European writers—one might single out Honoré de Balzac, Turgenev, and George Eliot—but it is worth remembering that he was still an American, albeit a very unusual and unanchored one, with a unique multinational tone. A passage from a letter to Thomas Sergeant Perry is worth keeping in mind:

We are Americans born—*il faut en prendre son parti*. I look upon it as a great blessing; and I think that to be an American is an excellent preparation for culture. We have exquisite qualities as a race, and it seems to me that we are ahead of the European races in the fact that more than either of them we can deal freely with forms of civilization not our own, can pick and choose and assimilate and in short (aesthetically etc.) claim our property where we find it. To have no national stamp has hitherto been a regret and a drawback, but I think it not unlikely that American writers may yet indicate that a vast intellectual fusion and synthesis of the various National tendencies of the world is the condition of more important achievements than any we have seen. We must of course have something of our own —something distinctive and homogeneous—and I take it that we shall find it in our moral consciousness, our unprecedented spiritual lightness and vigour.

(20 September 1867)

These are sentiments that would be echoed by subsequent American expatriate writers, such as Ezra Pound and T. S. Eliot, who were to be instrumental in shaping a new kind of modern poetry. They are not the words of an "outsider," as we have come to understand that word, but rather of a supranationalist, a would-be synthesist of the best achievements of various cultural forms, a citizen primarily of literature itself, his real domain the endless empire of the word.

Given his upbringing, and the multiple cultural perspectives it afforded him, it is hardly surprising that Henry James should have developed what came to be known as the "international theme," often introducing the fine "moral consciousness" of the American into the rich cultural atmosphere of Europe, thus dramatizing the confrontation of different schemes of values, showing the "provincialism" of the American groping his way through the European social landscape, dense with moral ambiguities, saturated in history, and dominated by old precedents, manners, and sophistications. But we would be making a mistake to see his work as simply contrasting American "innocence" with European "experience." As he said of himself, it was a "complex fate" to be an American living in Europe, and his sense of that complexity carried over into his fiction, so there is never (or seldom) any melodramatic sense of American goodness succumbing to European intrigue, deviousness, and evil. Indeed, some of his morally culpable and evil intriguers are expatriate Americans, as we can see in *The Portrait of a Lady* (1881), a novel rightly reckoned, in my opinion, to

mark his greatest achievement during what might be termed the first phase of his fictional writing, while he was still to some extent trying to "synthesize" all he had learned from the existing fiction of three cultures, as well as developing the style that was becoming distinctively his own.

III

It is worth taking note of a few of James's very early short stories before moving on to a consideration of the novels. From the start, love appears as potentially lethal—as in his very first, rather crude story ("A Tragedy of Error"), in which a woman plans to murder her lame and unloved husband (James would scarcely be so crude again—the plottings and "killings" become much more subtle and devious). Other stories are mainly pegs on which to hang his accumulated clusters of impressions of Europe, gathered and hoarded by his "sympathetic retina" and habit of "trembling observation" (though one, "Travelling Companions," with its Venetian scenes, its young American heroine with "the divine gift of feeling," and her rich, affectionate father, carries tiny adumbrations of his last major novels).

But perhaps most interesting are the stories that concern themselves with the terrible silent rapacity of civilized people, the concealed jostlings for emotional power that take place with furtive intensity just below the social surface (see, for example, "A Light Man," in which the ruthless competitive egoism of two different men—both trying to ingratiate themselves with a foolish, rich old man in order to become his heir—masquerades, on the one hand, as exquisite, entertaining social manners, and, on the other, as a pious pseudoreligious dedication: in the event, both of them lose). In "De Grey: A Romance," James uses a Hawthornesque family curse for its psychological possibilities, touching on an idea which, later, he would explore more deeply: that in any relationship one partner battens onto, and drains, the life energy of the other. Thus, all the women ever loved by a man of the De Grey family have died young: the heroine, in love with the young De Grey, rejects the curse and goes ahead with her love affair—and this time, the man withers: "As she bloomed and prospered, he drooped and languished. While she was living for him, he was dying for her." What is here streaked with gothic melodrama is later to become a subtler and arguably more frightening aspect of James's vision of human relationships. For we perhaps too often forget—charmed by his civilized tone—that for James there were beauty *and* terror in "conditions so highly organised," that is, in civilized society. "Our imagination is always too timid," says one of his wiser characters. We prefer not to envisage the possibility of hidden atrocity under the smooth social surface, but for James it was a perpetual possibility—one that he developed his art in order to explore more fully.

IV

Watch and Ward was Henry James's first novel, written in 1870 and serialized in the following year in the *Atlantic Monthly* (it did not appear in book form until 1878, by which time it had been heavily revised). It is often ignored, as James himself disregarded it when he came to assemble a collected edition of his work; yet he had high hopes for it when he wrote it (it was to be that elusive entity "The Great American Novel"), and it is worth glancing briefly at the theme and arrangement of the novel, as it contains, albeit embryonically, seeds of some of his future work. A young-to-middle-aged man, Roger Lawrence, who is not notably active, attractive, or passionate, and who has failed in his one attempt at a love affair, "adopts" a young girl, Nora Lambert, who is orphaned (in a rather melodramatic way—her father shoots himself in the hotel at which Lawrence is staying; one of the few actual pistol shots in James's fiction). His motives for this kindly act of adoption are complex, overdetermined, as we say after Freud. There is pity and there is generosity (though James was well aware of the concealed predatory nature of much of what passes for generosity); on the other hand, Lawrence is consciously conducting an experiment, determined to bring Nora up as a perfect wife who will feel so indebted to him that she will choose to marry him—thus his act of kindness is not disinterested, as it is also a form of investment on which he expects to collect a return. Such treatment of another person, as part of an experiment or as a form of investment, is always highly ambiguous in James. Lawrence has a "strenuous desire to fathom the depths of matrimony. He had dreamed of this gentle bondage as other men dream of the free unhoused condition of celibacy," so he chooses to "use" the in-

itially rather plain and not very bright Nora to satisfy this dream. He sees himself as "a protector, a father, a brother," and he aspires to allow Nora all the freedom she needs to develop in her own way. As he "cunningly devised her happiness" he feels that "his small stale merits became fragrant with the virtue of unselfish use." At times, he thinks of Nora "as a kind of superior doll, a thing wound up with a key" (and there is much play with the idea of keys in the book, not only keys that unlock the heart, but also unconscious sexual ones, as in one famous scene in which Nora tries to find a key the right size to wind up her watch).

As is often the plight of the young girl seeking to be "free" in the world at large, Nora finds herself at the mercy of plausible but exploitative egoists who have no real concern for her as a unique and precious "other," but simply seek to use her for their own ends (this is to be one of the main themes of *A Portrait of a Lady*). Paradoxically, all of Roger's "planning" and "scheming" for her are mainly to allow her to be free to be herself and develop her own potential to the utmost—though, to be sure, the plan includes a hope that in that freedom she will choose Roger as her husband. As she finally does. After her defection, he is ravaged by illness and prepares himself to accept a life of renunciation (another key theme in James), but Nora, after her experience of other men and the harsh heartlessness of the world at large, feels that she has come to perceive a secret truth: "Yes, she was in the secret of the universe, and the secret of the universe was that Roger was the only man in it who had a heart." For this to happen, Roger has to cease to regard himself as her guardian, which imposes on her "the terrible burden of gratitude," and she has to forget her wardship and the sense that she is acting as his "debtor," and choose him freely, as she finally does. This largely forgotten first novel in fact contains in embryo many of the themes and some of the methods—the half-revealing, half-concealing conversation; the detailed summary of shifting states of consciousness and interior ratiocination—that, in more complex forms, will be encountered in James's subsequent work.

V

Roderick Hudson was started in Europe in 1874 and was to be the first of many works in which James explored the problems of what it was to be an artist in his own time, problems of material and audience: *what* was he producing, exactly, and *for whom* was he producing it? What was the morality of the artist, and what was his relation to the artistic wealth of the past? Where Nathaniel Hawthorne was visibly nervous about introducing his American artists into a Europe in which it was difficult to tell the richness from the rottenness (see *The Marble Faun*), Henry James found in the situation the perfect theme for his first exploration of the problems of the American artist. The novel traces the short career of an American sculptor who opens himself up fully, indeed greedily, to European experience, with fatal results. It was F. Scott Fitzgerald who said that the lives of American writers contained no second acts. The remark hardly applies to James, but there is something almost prophetic in his picture of an American artist moving at such a pace that he will have no energy left after the crowded first act of his artistic life.

From the beginning, when he is seen as a discontented student of law in a provincial American town, Hudson is seen as doing "everything too fast," and he characterizes himself as being driven by a "demon of unrest." Upon seeing one of his statues, Rowland Mallett, a rich friend who appreciates art but cannot produce any himself, offers to take Hudson to Europe and become his patron. Mallett is one of James's observers, and it is worth noting that James made, thus early, a clear distinction between the artist and the observer. In the preface to the novel written for the twenty-six volume New York edition of his works James says,

My subject, all blissfully, in face of difficulties, had defined itself . . . as not directly, in the least, my young sculptor's adventure. This it had been but indirectly, being all the while in essence and in final effect another man's, his friend's and patron's, view and experience of him. . . . The centre of interest throughout "Roderick" is in Rowland Mallett's consciousness, and the drama is the very drama of that consciousness.

Thus James defines, retrospectively, what was to become a crucial subject for him—the drama of consciousness of the observer.

To illuminate some aspects of Roderick's doomed career it is helpful to notice the changing subjects of his sculpture. His first piece seen by Rowland is of a youth standing naked, drinking deeply from a gourd, and it is called "Thirst." Rowland asks whether the drinker represents an "idea" or is a "pointed symbol," and Hudson agrees that his work represents innocence, youth, curiosity, drinking deeply of knowledge, pleasure, and experience. The one thing that Roderick does not mention as being represented by his symbolic work is any actual drink, such as wine. Yet when he gets to Europe he soon discovers the pleasures of real champagne as well as the inspiration of high ideals. In these early days his talk is always about ideas or ideal forms, including a prospective "magnificent image of my native land." It is at this time that Rowland first sees that problematical lady Christina Light, who is for him "a glimpse of ideal beauty." If such beauty is wrong, he says, then he is happy to see her as the "incarnation of evil." Christina, although nominally American, has been brought up in Europe and is a deeply disturbing, ambiguous female (James was to employ her again, in *The Princess Casamassima*). She is a mixture of passions, while presenting a totally indifferent face to the world. She may be the epitome of corruption, as she herself says, or the finest bloom of a fusion of cultures; she is capable of unpredictable metamorphoses.

In his feeling of adoration for Christina, Roderick goes beyond socially recognized good and evil. When she withdraws from him, he cannot return to a form of life governed by those categories; he can only collapse into apathy and die. One general point made about Roderick summarizes something important about the American artist. As Rowland sees Roderick: "the great and characteristic point with him was the perfect separateness of his sensibility. He never saw himself as part of a whole; only as the clear-cut, sharp-edged, isolated individual, rejoicing or raging, as the case might be, but needing in each case to affirm himself." A perfectly separate sensibility is one that cannot truly be socialized: the affirmation of the artist is inseparable from his isolation, perhaps finally from his destruction—these are two propositions that James's novel may fairly be said to bear out. The difficulty for the artist to see himself as "part of a whole" is not restricted to Americans, but it seems to have remained for American artists a more constant problem. It is relevant to note that a perfect separate self is unlikely to be in harmony with the democratic mass. And, in its way, this was to remain a problem for James himself.

One more quotation from the later preface should be added here, since it was to be a problem for James from the start, and often a source of criticism of his work:

Where, for the complete expression of one's subject, does a particular relation stop—giving way to some other not concerned in that expression? Really, universally, relations stop nowhere, and the exquisite problem of the artist is eternally but to draw, by a geometry of his own, the circle within which they shall happily *appear* to do so. He is in the perpetual predicament that the continuity of things is the whole matter, for him, of comedy and tragedy; that this continuity is ever, but the space of an instant or an inch, broken, and that, to do anything at all, he has at once intensely to consult and intensely to ignore it.

It was this awareness that gained for James the reputation of offering inconclusive conclusions, open-ended and indeterminate terminations, and a sense that while certain incidents or relations achieve their natural end or foreclosure, life is meanwhile streaming on, generating ever-new complexities. In this he was avoiding the endings of the popular novel, in which the author felt he had the right, or obligation, to tie up all the loose ends and offer a conclusion in which everything was neatly concluded. Here again we can see James rebelling against the well-made, popular novel in which the conventions of the form effectively concealed or dismissed the actual complexities of life.

VI

The American (1877) is in many ways one of James's simpler works, since it is based on an almost schematic opposition between the American innocent—Christopher Newman could hardly be more obviously named—and some genuinely evil Europeans, the Bellegardes, who ruthlessly plot to prevent him from marrying their daughter, Claire de Cintré. The story is a mixture of melodrama and romance, a combination James was certainly to use quite often, but perhaps never so blatantly or obviously. However, Newman is not simply an innocent: "It was our friend's eye that chiefly told his story; an eye in which innocence and experience were singularly blended." If he is amusingly inaccessible to the artistic heritage of Europe, he still has his own kind of knowledge, confidence, and even nobility. He was not contented by what America had to offer—"I seemed to feel a new man inside my old skin, and I longed for a new world." Though, as one character says of him, he is "the great Western Barbarian, stepping forth in his innocence and might, gazing a while

at this poor effete Old World, and then swooping down on it." "Swooping" is not exactly what he does, but he has come on a determined search for a perfect wife—"My wife must be a magnificent woman."

What annoys the Bellegardes about Newman is that he has no sense of social hierarchy:

his sense of human equality was not an aggressive taste or an aesthetic theory, but something as natural and organic as a physical appetite which had never been put on a scanty allowance and consequently was innocent of ungraceful eagerness. His tranquil unsuspectingness of the relativity of his own place in the social scale was probably irritating to M. de Bellegarde.

(ch. 13)

When, later, Newman enters the room of Madame de Cintré, who has been more than half won over to him, "he felt, as soon as he entered the room, that he was in the presence of something evil." She has in fact succumbed to the ruthless pressure and "authority" of her parents and agreed to renounce Newman. The Bellegardes cannot accept a "commercial person." Newman feels "sick, and suddenly helpless . . . to lose her by the interference and the dictation of others, by an impudent old woman and a pretentious fop stepping in with their 'authority'! It was too preposterous, it was too pitiful." But the power of the house is too strong for Madame de Cintré, and she cannot break away: she has accepted the idea of becoming a nun (always a kind of living death in James). "The idea struck Newman as too dark and horrible for belief, and made him feel as he would have done if she had told him that she was going to mutilate her beautiful face, or drink some potion that would make her mad."

A kind of nausea sets in—"What a horrible rubbish heap of iniquity to tumble in!" Soon after—and here the plot becomes somewhat Gothic—Valentin de Bellegarde puts him in possession of an old secret that would effectively discredit, if not socially destroy, the Bellegardes. Newman is given a letter that incriminates the Bellegardes in murder. At first determined to have his revenge, Newman finally decides to let the whole matter go. The pages of the novel in which James describes him coming to his decision are curiously moving and quite transcend the gothic mode. After going to look at the convent/prison of the Carmelites in which Madame de Cintré is immured, he turns away, sad but relieved. "He turned away with a heavy heart, but with a heart lighter than the one he had brought. Everything was over, and he at last could rest."

Newman's last thought was that of course he would let the Bellegardes go. If he had spoken it aloud he would have said that he didn't want to hurt them. He was ashamed of having wanted to hurt them. They had hurt him, but such things were really not his game.

(ch. 26)

He burns the damning letter, and his friend Mrs. Tristram comments with reference to the Belle-gardes: "Their confidence, after counsel taken of each other, was not in their innocence, nor in their talent for bluffing things off; it was in your remarkable good nature! You see they were right."

The antiromantic conclusion of this novel disappointed many readers, including Howells. It seemed to violate the premises on which the narrative was set up, though we can see now that it was part of James's "realism" not to capitulate to the expected norms of the genre. In his later preface James made a very important distinction that is relevant for all his work and worth quoting in full:

The real represents to my perception the things we cannot possibly *not* know, sooner or later, in one way or another; it being but one of the accidents of our hampered state, and one of the incidents of their quantity and number, that particular instances have not yet come our way. The romantic stands, on the other hand, for the things that, with all the facilities in the world, all the wealth and all the courage and all the wit and all the adventure, we never *can* directly know; the things that can reach us only through the beautiful circuit and subterfuge of our thought and desire.

And he goes on:

The only *general* attribute of projected romance that I can see, the only one that fits all its cases, is the fact of the kind of experience with which it deals—experience liberated, so to speak; experience disengaged, disembroiled, disencumbered, exempt from the conditions that we usually know to attach to it and, if we wish so to put the matter, draw upon it, and operating in a medium which relieves it, in a particular interest, of the inconvenience of a *related*, a measurable state, a state subject to all our vulgar communities. . . . The balloon of experience is in fact of course tied to the earth, and under that necessity we swing, thanks to a rope of remarkable length, in the more or less commodious car of the imagination; but it is by the rope we know where we are, and from the moment the cable is cut

we are at large and unrelated: we only swing from the globe—though remaining as exhilarated, naturally, as we like, especially when all goes well. The art of the romancer is "for the fun of it," insidiously to cut the cable, to cut it without our detecting him. What I have recognized then in "The American," much to my surprise and after long years, is that the experience here represented is the disconnected and uncontrolled experience—uncontrolled by our general sense of "the way things happen"—which romance alone more or less successfully palms off on us.

As to what extent James's novels move toward pure romance as he describes it (cutting the cable "for the fun of it"), that is something we have to decide individually, but we can readily see that much of his work operates from a tension between the "real," as here described, and the "romantic"; between the "earth" of unavoidably knowable reality and the "balloon" of romance and "disconnected and uncontrolled experience." Perhaps no other writer derived so much so subtly from operating between the earth of reality and the balloon of romance.

VII

AFTER the comparative disappointment of *The American,* James promised the *Atlantic Monthly* a novel that would better please its readers. This novel was *The Europeans* (1878), which varied James's basic narrative situation of bringing an American to Europe by bringing foreign characters to America. It concludes with no less than three happy marriages, though even so it failed to please his fellow countrymen, who found it weak or false in its local realism, while William James found it "insignificant." Yet it is without doubt a minor masterpiece in its own way and deserves considered attention. We might say that in *The Europeans* there is a crucial question of "dress," or the status of all cultivated appearance, that involves the problem of how the individual is to bear himself or herself in society. In a letter to Howells, James outlined the idea for the novel:

I shall probably develop an idea that I have, about a genial, charming youth of a Bohemianish pattern, who comes back from foreign parts into the midst of a mouldering and ascetic old Puritan family of his kindred . . . and by his gayety and sweet audacity smooths out their rugosities, heals their dyspepsia and dissipates their troubles. . . . It would be meant, roughly speaking, as the picture of the

conversion of a dusky dreary domestic circle to epicure-
anism.

(30 March 1877)

So much, roughly speaking, is in the book, though
the conversion is by no means complete. James had
already explored the bewilderments and difficulties
of the American trying to make his way through
European territories saturated with culture and
tradition, and he clearly found it comparably stimulating to imagine the progress of two quintessential
Europeans through the comparatively blank spaces
of America of the 1840's, and to depict not only their
own intermittent bafflement and uncertainty, but
also their impact on local Puritanism. It is worth
noting that the main European of the book, Eugenia
(well born), is not mentioned in James's outline.
Without her, the ensuing confrontation of Puritan
and European might well have been a little obvious.
In adding her, James added immeasurably to the
novel's depth and complexity; it now becomes a
searching engagement of different values—values of
costume and conduct—as well as a provocative encounter between different visions of life—life seen as
discipline or opportunity.

From the start the Europeans are connected with
art and artifice. In the opening scene Felix is drawing
one of those effortless sketches that testify to his
ability to extract pictorial values from the New
World simply by accepting it with an uncritical
serenity. Eugenia, characteristically restless because
of a personal energy that as yet cannot find any expressive form, is looking in the mirror, checking her
dress and the set of her hair. Through the window
the visible landscape is unmitigatedly grim. It is in
this bleak, negative landscape that she is to try to
find a place, a home. Perhaps the main question of
the book is: Can that colorless, styleless landscape
find room for her? She is from the beginning depicted
as the careful mistress of her own person. She has
many dresses and earrings, which she wears "in alternation," and she is referred to as dark, foreign, exotic,
with an oriental aspect. These two, Felix and Eugenia, are almost generic foreigners, now homeless
and seeking to find a life and make their fortunes in
the capaciousness of the New World. If this makes
them seem like adventurers (as it does to most
critics), it should also be noted how much they can
contribute in the way of culture, costume, brilliant
conversation, and an unfailing wit that testifies to
an exhilarating play of mind.

The virtues of their American relatives, the Wentworths, are sufficiently intimated by their dwelling.
This overlit, underfurnished house is the very image
of that pale, blank New England of the 1840's that
James elsewhere describes as being composed of
"high vertical moral light, the brightness of a society
at once very simple and very responsible." The
house is also, as so often in James, indicative of the
mind inhabiting it. When Eugenia asks to be admitted to Mr. Wentworth's house, she is also asking to
be admitted into the American consciousness of the
time. But her advent is felt as a threat: "The sudden
irruption into the well-ordered consciousness of the
Wentworths of an element not allowed for in its
scheme of usual obligations required a readjustment
of that sense of responsibility which constituted its
principal furniture." Mr. Wentworth cannot quite
see Eugenia as part of his house; nor, indeed, can
Eugenia herself. The decision to lodge her in a
separate house "over the way" represents a compromise—hospitality without assimilation. It also
keeps the threat of foreignness somewhat at bay. The
young daughter, Gertrude, welcomes the idea: "It
will be a foreign house." To which Mr. Wentworth
replies: "Are we very sure that we need a foreign
house?" Inevitably, to him, as to others, Eugenia and
Felix seem like a species of actors, mountebanks,
who derive an immoderate pleasure from indulging
in an irresponsible free play of the self made possible
through words—and clothes, costumes, gestures. "I
shall keep them in the other house," resolves Mr.
Wentworth firmly. This, in effect, is the Puritan rejection of the expressive delights of style in favor of a
few rigidly simple concepts of obligation and responsibility. When Felix asks Mr. Wentworth for the
hand of Gertrude, he says that she needs a place in
the world "that would bring her out." "A place to do
her duty," counters Mr. Wentworth, thus implicitly
revealing the opposition between self-exfoliation
and self-contraction that lies at the heart of the book.

But America in this book is not simply the house of
innocent, dutiful purity, any more than Eugenia—
for all her confessed "fibs," schemes, and simula-
tions—is an incarnation of Old World duplicity and
immorality. Mr. Wentworth's daughter, Gertrude,
is as restless as Eugenia, and she too bridles at the
church spires that menacingly confront her. Like
Eugenia, she has an instinct for colorful clothes and
the more exotic, oriental side of life (she takes down
the *Arabian Nights* while the others attend church).
And it is Gertrude who brings out into the open one
of the book's crucial issues when she cries out to the

importunate clergyman Mr. Brand, concerning her relationship with Felix: "I am trying for once to be natural! . . . I have been pretending, all my life; I have been dishonest, it is you that have made me so!" The Puritans' self-conceit was that their way of life represented something nakedly simple and natural, whereas the amoral Europeans were given over to concealment and pretense. But here is a spirited child revealing that it is those honest, simple Puritans who have imposed a life of concealment and pretense on her, while it is with the adorned and eloquent Europeans that she feels most "natural." The paradox is a deep one: perhaps it is precisely with the aid of art that we may most readily discover, and be, our natural selves; while the attempt to deny and expunge art in the interests of purity and radical integrity may involve a falsification of the self far more destructive than the artifice in the flexible performance of the Baroness, for instance. She is indeed effectively expelled, while the book dissolves in marriages; but this rejection reflects more damagingly on the limitations of the American consciousness, which refuses to assimilate her and the civilizing influence she incorporates.

In fact Eugenia is almost too serious, too complex for the book. With her, as with none of the others, the possibilities of real suffering are envisaged. Eugenia begins to feel a "sense of the enlargement of opportunity" in the wild American spaces; but then she learns that "the social soil on this big, vague continent was somehow not adapted for growing those plants she especially liked to inhale." Coming to America like a wearied swimmer, she finds instead "a smooth, straight wall of rock." Certainly she has come to serve herself, perhaps save herself. But she does bring with her the "seedlings" of civilization to which the American soil proves innutritive; and the wall of rock that should have been a hospitable beach indicates as much a loss for America as it does a rebuff to Eugenia. Indeed, the implied comment on the Wentworths' America is curiously severe. Since Gertrude leaves in the name of "naturalness" and Eugenia is effectively excluded from it because of her "arts," it becomes something of a problem to define exactly what does manage to flourish on that inhospitable soil. Certainly James seems here to suggest that art is indispensable for the liberation and expression of nature; and, himself a supreme stylist, he can only deplore, in his humorous, balanced way, the failure of this America gladly to accept and "take in" the natural stylishness of "the Europeans."

VIII

IN the summer of 1878, while *The Europeans* was not amusing the readers of the *Atlantic Monthly*, *Daisy Miller* most distinctly was pleasing the readers of the English *Cornhill*. It came to be described as "an outrage on American girlhood" and enjoyed a success—or perhaps *succès de scandale*—that in retrospect seems somewhat disproportionate; but whatever else, it showed that James had hit upon a subject that fascinated his readers and that he would make his own—nothing less than "the American girl," endlessly simple, endlessly complex; who could say which? This is part of the charm, enduring resonance, and still-alive ambiguity of this deceptively simple tale. First of all, it is narrated by an American who is rather "stiff" (he doesn't dance), rather too proper, too influenced by snobbish old ladies in his estimate of "the done thing," somewhat too effete in his rather shallow European veneer: he carries the appropriately chilly name of Winterbourne. When he meets Daisy, walking at large in their hotel in Vevey (Switzerland), he is immediately attracted, as, it seems, is she. (We can never be sure with Daisy—we can only trust her, which Winterbourne ultimately, and perhaps fatally, fails to do.) His descriptions of Daisy are a continuous oscillation, testifying to the fact that he cannot "read" this new kind of figure.

F. W. Dupee makes the important point that Daisy is not a product of Boston or old New York, two different types of heroine who also play their part in James's work, but whose own kind of aristocratic breeding is more assured. Daisy is a daughter of the provincial plutocracy—Schenectady in the process of taking over New York City; she is the American girl of the future. Thus at first Winterbourne has no doubts as he looks at her face: "this glance was perfectly direct and unshrinking. It was not, however, what would have been called an immodest glance, for the young girl's eyes were constantly moving," just as she is restless and likes a bit of a "fuss"—probably amounting to little more than a boat ride or a promenade with a suitable gentleman friend. But that constant facial movement puts her beyond any stable interpretation, and can worry Winterbourne as much as it can enchant him—more, perhaps. Winterbourne himself has become "dishabituated to the American tone"—another of those American expatriates who lose one set of cultural instincts without really gaining another. So he cannot work out whether Daisy is simply a pretty, social girl: "or was she also a designing, an audacious, an unscrupulous young person? Winterbourne had lost his instinct in this matter." Indeed he has, and his direct appreciations start to turn into insidious suspicions. She is pronounced common by the self-appointed censors (Americans) of this provincial European society, but "it was a wonder to Winterbourne that, with her commonness, she had a singularly delicate grace." At times she seems to him "an extraordinary mixture of innocence and crudity." What she does reveal, in her own quiet way and only when cornered, as it were, by overbearing negative advice, is a real spirit of independence: "I have never allowed a gentleman to dictate to me, or to interfere with anything I do."

This is the tone of the new American girl of the future. Winterbourne, used to traditional "nice girls," finds her "an inscrutable combination of audacity and innocence." Winterbourne is not so inclined to damn her as are the gossiping, cruel, older Americans, who pride themselves on knowing what is delicate and indelicate, and try to hurt Daisy by cutting her in the crudest way. But when she is seen walking out alone with the gallant Italian Giovanelli, Winterbourne's faith in her begins to wane, though not without sympathy: "He was very sorry for her . . . because it was painful to hear so much that was pretty and undefended and natural assigned to a vulgar place among the categories of disorder." But she needs his faith more than pity. He continues to find her ambiguous: "He asked himself whether Daisy's defiance came from the consciousness of innocence, or from her being, essentially, a young person of the reckless class." The conclusion comes when Daisy insists on visiting the Colosseum by night, a place generally considered to be a miasmic spot where it was very easy to catch malaria (perhaps through some confusion with the miasma of history that had taken place there). She is with Giovanelli, and Winterbourne, out walking, sees them together. From that point on he thinks "the riddle had become easy to read. She was a young lady whom a gentleman need no longer be at pains to respect." Effectively he drops her, and there is a hint that, in response, she simply abandons herself to the Roman fever she contracts after her evening stroll through the polluted space of the old center of European civilization, and quickly dies. It is Giovanelli who speaks the most eloquent elegy—simple and doubt-free: "She was the most beautiful young lady I ever saw,

and the most amiable . . . and she was the most innocent." He has a trust and directness of insight that Winterbourne has lost. Daisy Miller, as a figure, has become part of the folklore of America, a figure, or a reference point, often cited in isolation from the fiction in which she appears. But we should note that the story is as much about Winterbourne and his indeterminate ambivalences as it is about her disturbingly attractive mixture of innocence, apparent recklessness, and innocent but strong spirit of independence.

Mention should be made here of Henry James's beloved young cousin Minny Temple, who died while he was abroad in 1869–1870. She was as brilliant and changeable and independent as Daisy Miller, and in effect James was to re-create her character in his fiction as the young American girl of the future. Many of his heroines, right up to Milly Theale, in *The Wings of the Dove*, may be related to his memories of the figure of Minny Temple. It has often been remarked that James seemed congenitally more sympathetic to the world and minds of women than of men, and, despite his starting with Christopher Newman and Roderick Hudson, it remains true that he found more in the emerging female sensibility to engage his interest. In many ways, the world of men—particularly as equated with the world of business—was simply closed to him.

IX

PUBLISHED two years later, *Washington Square* (1881 [1880]) is a rather different kind of novel, with a very different kind of "heroine." It is James's only novel named simply and directly after a place, and this gives us an opening clue. Catherine Sloper is the daughter of Dr. Sloper, and they reside in Washington Square. As the book develops the question is: Will she ever be able to escape "Washington Square" and all that it stands for in the way of coercive, restrictive paternal authority; and despite one joyless trip in Europe—mainly forced on her to teach her a lesson—the answer is that she does not. The story also revolves around money, and how it can pervert the possibilities of human relationships. Dr. Sloper thinks his daughter is dull, plain, stupid, and thus at the mercy of any fortune hunter (she has a fortune from her mother and will inherit one from him). When the plausible, good-looking, but essentially shallow and venal Morris Townsend enters her life, her father is quite determined to stop the match. If he is a clever, correct, and even just man, he is also a sadistic and ruthlessly cold one, bringing the abstract notions of geometry to bear on the delicacies and suffering of human sensibility. He causes his daughter a great deal of pain—and he doesn't mind, as long as he keeps her from Morris Townsend. Meanwhile, Catherine's life is not being made any easier by the foolish meddlings of Dr. Sloper's sister, Mrs. Penniman, whose mind is soaked in romantic stereotypes and who attempts, as it were, to help the relationship of Catherine and Morris Townsend along the road of her fantasy: she had "a taste for light literature, and a certain foolish indirectness and obliquity of character. She was romantic; she was sentimental; she had a passion for little secrets and mysteries—a very innocent passion, for her secrets had hitherto been as unpractical as addled eggs." Catherine can see through her, and Morris finds her a bore when he discovers she cannot really help him in his plan; but her slightly wild romantic fantasying is to be put along with, or opposite, her brother's cold, calculating practicality, if we are to comprehend the kind of "frame" within which Catherine has to operate.

Catherine, for all her apparent dullness, plainness, shrinking modesty, and fear of her father, is the most interesting and—it is part of James's genius that he can make us feel it—the most human and moving figure in the book. In her quiet way, she does indeed fall in love with Morris, who in his predictable way—the doctor is always right—takes himself off when he learns that her father will not leave Catherine his fortune if she marries him. She alone is the true lover, who gives up everything for Morris and is willing to defy her father on his behalf. When they return from Europe—part of the father's plan to induce forgetfulness and fear through separation and solitude—we read: "Catherine had brought home a present to every one—to every one save Morris, to whom she had brought simply her undiverted heart." That is arguably the greatest gift that one human being can give to another, but no one, and certainly not Morris, can appreciate its worth amid the perverted money values and authority/fantasy patterns that dominate the world of "Washington Square." Catherine abandons the idea of marriage and takes refuge in silence and stoical self-retraction. But though she becomes somewhat old-fashioned,

she is firm (she has her own kind of "unaggressive obstinacy"), and when Morris comes back she is not so easily to be picked up for her residual financial value: he is calmly and quietly, but quite definitively, sent packing. And the book ends with one of James's most perfectly modulated ironies: "Catherine, meanwhile, in the parlor, picking up her morsel of fancy-work, had seated herself with it again—for life, as it were." Just so; we have seen how this apparently unattractive yet curiously moving girl has been sentenced to "Washington Square"—for life, as it were.

X

ALSO published at this time was James's most important work of literary criticism, his book on Hawthorne (1879). One of his intentions in this work was to show off his own Englishness and "Europeanness"—with comparisons to Balzac and Thackeray—by stressing, and overstressing, the provinciality of America and Hawthorne (and most other American writers mentioned in the book—Emerson, Thoreau, Edgar Allan Poe). In a famous review of the book, Howells made some fair objections in his usual temperate way:

If it is not provincial for an Englishman to be English, or a Frenchman French, then it is not for an American to be American; and if Hawthorne was "exquisitely provincial," one had better take one's chance of universality with him than with almost any Londoner or Parisian of the time.

(Atlantic Monthly, February 1880)

James had adopted an opposite point of view at the very outset of his book by affirming that "the moral is that the flower of art blooms only where the soil is deep, that it takes a great deal of history to produce a little literature, that it needs a complex machinery to set a writer in motion." He did not believe that "human life" was some abstract essence that could be seen and grasped in separation from the diverse forms through and among which it manifested itself. And these forms were, simply, society. "We know a man imperfectly until we know his society," he said in a later essay on Emerson (1887). The richer and denser the society, the greater the number of potential sources of knowledge. James's case against America was not based on any notion that it was somehow intellectually backward or morally inferior to Europe (rather the contrary); it was that, as a novelist, he found it comparatively empty. In that same essay James spoke of the curious fate of "the primitive New England character" and "its queer search for something to expend itself upon." If you consider that character and the thin society in which it had its being, James went on, you get "the impression of a conscience gasping in the void, panting for sensations, with something of the movement of a landed fish." Where America was a void, Europe was a plenitude, or, to follow his own imagery, it was an ocean in which the gasping American conscience could at least find an element to swim in. That a person, particularly an American, might well drown in those deep and dangerous waters was a part of James's sense of the complexity of the American fate. But as a novelist he clearly felt that there was more to be learned from a swimming fish than from a landed one.

To establish this image of a genius starved of adequate material to work on, James quotes passages in which Hawthorne depicts his plight in just this way. Thus:

"No author, without a trial, can conceive of the difficulty of writing a romance about a country where there is no shadow, no antiquity, no mystery, no picturesque and gloomy wrong, nor anything but a commonplace prosperity, in broad and simple daylight, as is happily the case in my dear native land."

(ch. 2)

And again: "'I have another great difficulty in the lack of materials; for I have seen so little of the world that I have nothing but thin air to concoct my stories of.'" And having established the picture of a genius starved in America, James goes on to imply that when Hawthorne did get to Europe, he was too old to take advantage of what it offered. Thus, commenting on Hawthorne's book on England (*Our Old Home*), James says:

It is the work of an outsider, of a stranger, of a man who remains to the end a mere spectator (something less even than an observer), and always lacks the final initiation into the manners and nature of a people of whom it may be said . . . that to know them is to make discoveries.

The implication is clear: James himself had come to an early realization of the paucity of material in America and had removed himself to Europe at the right age to partake of what he later called "the banquet of initiation." In such ways do we see James quietly justifying and defining his own position while sympathetically outlining the difficulties Hawthorne faced as an artist in America. There are many contradictions in the book, as James oscillates between his desire to put a distance between himself and Hawthorne, and his realization that, as a writer, he was much closer to Hawthorne than he had allowed. For instance, on the one hand, James effectively deprecates Hawthorne's work by continually attaching to it such epithets as "charming," "exquisite," "soft," "simple," "pure," "natural," "spontaneous," "childlike," and so on—as though to emphasize that Hawthorne's work was as innocent and simple as the land it emerged from (the epithets seem very incongruous and inapposite to us now). On the other hand, many of his most brilliant comments reveal that he was far from unaware of the troubling depths in Hawthorne's work, as when he says of Hawthorne's imagination that it was "always engaged in a game of hide-and-seek in the region in which it seemed to him that the game could best be played—among the shadows and substructions, the dark based pillars and supports of our moral nature." He credits Hawthorne, rightly, with "a haunting care for moral problems" and sums up by saying, "Man's conscience was his theme."

Such penetrating insights as these reveal that James was at least half-aware of those elements that were carried over into his own work; for most of the above remarks (after the patronizing words about "soft" and "childlike") would perfectly fit James's own fiction. Similarly, he speaks disparagingly of Hawthorne's use of symbols and allegory, for this was the period when James was still trying to emulate the great European realists. Yet he admitted that Hawthorne's allegories offered "glimpses of a great field, of the whole deep mystery of man's soul and conscience. . . . The fine thing in Hawthorne is that he cared for the deeper psychology." Nothing about "childlike" spontaneity here—this is the great American writer whose symbolic and allegorical power, and care for "the deeper psychology," would increasingly reappear in the work of James. And sometimes, indeed, the deeply understanding sympathy reveals itself in memorable words, as when he compares Hawthorne to Emerson: "Emerson, as a sort of spiritual sun-worshipper, could have attached but a moderate value to Hawthorne's cat-like faculty of seeing in the dark." It was just such a faculty, rather than any British or European mastery of the concretions of society, that would make James what he was to become—an unmistakably great, and an unmistakably American, novelist—a novelist who, as this little book beautifully if unconsciously reveals, owed his greatest debt not to Balzac but to Hawthorne.

XI

JAMES could now finally set to work on *The Portrait of a Lady*, which was intended as a culmination of his work to date; we can see quite clearly now that it is one of his most notable masterpieces, and one of the really major works of the nineteenth century. Once more James sends an "innocent" young American girl to Europe—the starting point, he says, was "the conception of a certain young woman affronting her destiny" (notice "affront," not "confront"—there is a certain haughty insolence in Isabel Archer as she *overconfidently*—we see how important the word is in James—takes on her destiny, with a fine disregard for the problematics of such an undertaking). Once in Europe, she is variously proposed to, planned around, plotted against: she is made rich by a bequest, and this simply adds to the dangerous illusion of a high-sailing freedom.

In the event she makes a disastrous marriage to a perverted aesthete, a "Europeanized" American named Osmond (the name having a dead, skeletal ring—the bone/the world), acting in collaboration with his ex-lover, Madame Merle, another highly elegant, deeply treacherous Europeanized American (the dangers in this book, and deepest immoralities, do not come from Europeans—James is far beyond the unsubtle polarity of American innocence ensnared by European immorality and guile: the perverted American is the real danger). Much of the book traces out the slow process by which Isabel comes to realize how she has simply been used in a scheme by the two Americans, a realization that culminates in one of the great passages in James as she sits by the fire late into the night, going over what has happened to her and just where she really is. As James says of the passage in his preface to the novel:

She sits up, by her dying fire, far into the night, under the spell of recognitions on which she finds the last sharpness suddenly wait [recognitions that she finds accompanied by

the ultimate pain]. It is a representation simply of her motionlessly *seeing,* and an attempt withal to make the mere still lucidity of her act as interesting as the surprise of a caravan or the identification of a pirate.

As any reader will agree, it is much more interesting than any number of caravans and pirates and is one of the high points to which psychological fiction reached. Isabel finally makes an effective breach with her husband by going to see her dying cousin, Ralph, who has always loved her in his own disabled, fraternal way. But, despite the urgings of her strong American suitor, Caspar Goodwood, at the end of the book she seems to be returning to her sterile marriage in Rome. The ambiguous ending has somewhat vexed some readers, but it is appropriate for the haughty girl who affronted her fate and was herself affronted by it.

It is a magnificent book—James had never yet written so majestically or with so much easy confidence. Nor had he ever been so fully in control of his material. The novel defies summary, but certain points about its themes can be mentioned. From Isabel's point of view the book is about the dream of pure space, and the subsequent experience of contaminated limitations. She speaks the language of theoretical freedom, but experiences the actuality of malign intentions. She holds on to her idea of acting in pure freedom for as long as possible, a sort of deluded existentialist who believes in absolutely unconditioned free choice. But in fact she is constantly tampered with. She insists on choice—"I wish to choose my fate"—whereas it will be mostly chosen for her by the disregarded (by Isabel) intentionality of other people. Her "love of liberty," says James, "was as yet almost exclusively theoretical"—she is not versed in the praxis of the world. Osmond deceives her by pretending to share her own attitude to her position, saying, "You can do exactly what you choose; you can roam through space."

This is an abiding American dream; but all the time she is moving into a prison composed of other people's plots. Miltonic echoes are brought in: "The world lay before her—she could do whatever she chose." But she enters what the Countess Gemini calls "a steel trap" under the illusion that she is extending her freedom. She is of course *too* theoretical, and thus unprepared for the facticity of the world. She has her system: but everybody else has his own system, and wary as she is of getting involved in anybody else's system—an abiding American dread

—she in fact involves herself in the most constricting, life-denying system of all.

James is very clear about how he saw Isabel Archer, as we can see from his introduction. "I had my vivid individual," he says, "vivid, so strangely, in spite of being still at large, not confined by conditions, not engaged in the tangle to which we look for much of the impress that constitutes an identity." Without that "impress," from which Isabel feels so privilegedly free, there can be no identity—one of the things that Isabel acquires from her great mistake is indeed an identity. To provide that tangle James said he found it came to "organising an ado about Isabel Archer." So around her "perfect isolation," and penetrating it, James duly establishes a highly complex "ado" of many variants. The uncommitted self has to commit itself in the interest of acquiring an identity. With notable exceptions, to remain in pure potential is to be nothing actual.

So Isabel has to choose. But why does she seem to make such a disastrously wrong choice? We are told of her early education, reading German transcendental philosophy, which is perhaps not the best preparation for assessing, and living in, the imperfect actual world. She is also an "egoist"; she has theories about her own nature, which she compares to a garden: she likes to wander around in her "remarkable soul" gathering roses. This suggests a dangerous, self-worshiping solipsism, so self-absorbed as to ignore the reciprocities of life. She has intimations that "there were other gardens in the world . . . a great many places that were not gardens at all—only dusky pestiferous tracts, planted thickly with ugliness and misery." And, indeed, her rose-filled garden is surrendered to, and mastered by, the sterile wasteland of Osmond's inner life. She chooses his "system" of life, having rejected other, more humane ones.

It may be that part of Osmond's secret attraction for Isabel (nobody else is remotely taken in by his posing) is that she senses that he promises a passionless life; that in his talk of "making life a work of art" she realizes that she can become part of his collection, a sort of escape from the mire and fury of human life by an act of self-reification. The lady would, as it were, rather be a portrait—and that is what she seems to become as she helps to keep up the masquerade of the "magnificent form"—as Osmond thinks of it—of their marriage. We should note that in the everyday world her most common emotion is fear. She is frightened of Caspar's sexual drive, or assertive virility; she is frightened of Warburton's social system; she is frightened of her money; and she is frightened of herself.

Madame Merle—the blackbird—is Osmond's partner in plotting, and she has acquired such an apparently civilized veneer that Isabel is still American enough to feel that she is "not natural." Yet in many ways she wishes to emulate Madame Merle's total self-control and cool detachment (Madame Merle's most chilling remark is "I don't pretend to know what people are for. . . . I only know what I can do with them"). These two ladies have one exchange that is crucial to the book. It starts when Isabel says that she does not care what kind of house Caspar Goodwood has. Madame Merle's answer is central:

"That's very crude of you. When you've lived as long as I have you'll see that every human being has his shell and that you must take the shell into account. By the shell I mean the whole envelope of circumstances. There's no such thing as an isolated man or woman; we're each of us made up of some cluster of appurtenances. What shall we call our 'self'? Where does it begin? Where does it end? It overflows into everything that belongs to us—and then it flows back again. I know a large part of myself is the clothes I choose to wear. I've a great respect for *things*! One's self—for other people—is one's expression of one's self; and one's house, one's furniture, one's garments, the books one reads, the company one keeps—these things are all expressive."

(ch. 19)

Now, there is a great deal in this that is true, but Isabel immediately disagrees:

"I think just the other way. I don't know whether I succeed in expressing myself, but I know that nothing can express me; everything's on the contrary a limit, a barrier, and a perfectly arbitary one. Certainly the clothes which, as you say, I choose to wear, don't express me; and heaven forbid they should. . . . My clothes may express the dressmaker, but they don't express me. To begin with it's not my own choice that I wear them; they're imposed upon me by society."

"Should you prefer to go without them?" Madame Merle enquired in a tone which virtually terminated the discussion.

Isabel is very American in her suspicion of "things" as "limits" and in her idea of a pure self existing apart from all materiality. But without limits you cannot have identity. And while the self is not *identical* with things, Madame Merle is right to the extent that the self must enter into commerce with things (houses, clothes, other people, etc.) to establish itself as a self and experience itself as a self. There is no self in a void. The danger, of course, is when things absorb the self, and the self abandons itself to thinghood. Isabel is dangerously one-sided—and vulnerable—in what she thinks of as her contempt for the encircling things that make up her world as much as they do anybody else's.

It is partly this error that brings her into Osmond's "prison" while she thought she had been discovering her liberty. As she says to herself in the great night meditation:

She had taken the first steps in the purest confidence, and then she had suddenly found the infinite vista of a multiplied life to be a dark, narrow alley with a dead wall at the end . . . he had led her into the mansion of his own habitation, then, *then* she had seen where she really was. . . . Between those four walls she had lived ever since; they were to surround her for the rest of her life. It was the house of darkness, the house of dumbness, the house of suffocation.

(ch. 42)

It is part of the characteristic atmosphere of the book that, while Isabel develops in her own way and sight deepens into insight, there is a growing feeling of free, spontaneous life giving way to, or turning into, mechanistic automata, art objects, instruments, masks, theatrical performances, shells containing no life. People become dry and empty, touched or blighted with that desiccation which for Shakespeare was a mark of evil or dead life—as when Madame Merle complains to Osmond, "You've dried up my soul." Even Isabel, near the end, goes into something like a catatonic state, devoid of "purpose [and] intention," envying statues and objects their insentient immobility, longing, even, for death.

The final exchange is with Caspar. Isabel is sitting on an old bench in the garden, which will become the bench of meditation and the bench of desolation in James's later work. She feels "a singular absence of purpose. . . . There was nothing to recall her to the house." By this time the garden/house contrast has taken on many ambiguous connotations: among other things, the garden is the garden of interiority, the withdrawn consciousness, while the house is, in its various forms, the house of life and active participation in the social game. Caspar speaks to Isabel in a language she would once have agreed with:

"It's too late to play a part; didn't you leave all that behind you in Rome? . . . Why should you go back?—why should you go through that ghastly form. . . . We can do absolutely as we please; to whom under the sun do we owe anything? . . . The world's all before us—and the world's very big."

(ch. 55)

Almost all are things that she has said in her past: he is the spokesman of new beginnings, of the world as possibility, of the casting off of dead forms (he sees that what Osmond insists is a "magnificent form" is in fact a "ghastly form"). The appeal is very strong, and for once, the virginal Isabel Archer succumbs to a kiss—the only one, at least, that we are told of. And at this moment the world around her seems "to take the form of a mighty sea, where she floated in fathomless waters." She feels herself drawn to the idea of sinking in his arms, in pure passion: but she also feels herself threatened by this liquidity. It is not the way for her, and the kiss seems to "free her from this pull."

She never looked about her; she only darted from the spot. There were lights in the windows of the house; they shone far across the lawn. In an extraordinarily short time . . . she had moved through the darkness (for she saw nothing) and reached the door. Here only she paused. She looked all about her. She had not known where to turn; but she knew now. There was a very straight path.

(ch. 55)

This has been taken as a form of spiritual suicide, of perverse and masochistic renunciation of a genuine chance for a new start—for where does that "very straight path" lead to? James, teasingly—maddeningly to some—does not say. But there is a realism in this last gesture of that strange and fearful girl, Isabel Archer. She has no belief in a recoverable freedom, a freedom that was initially purely theoretical. We are what we have done, and what has been done to us. Isabel, who has always been frightened of passion and the oceanic tug of released feelings, returns to the form, the play. For another character, that doorway might lead to adultery, or it might lead to the life of the artist—as James's door had led him to. And both topics occur quite frequently in his later work. Isabel goes back, so we feel, to Rome and the ruins of her life: but she has acquired a new consciousness of the whole situation, a new awareness of the world. She has had to face the fact that she has been used as a thing—"a woman who has been made use of"—finally see "the dry staring fact that she had been an applied handled hung-up tool, as senseless and convenient as mere shaped wood and iron." And she must live with that knowledge—though such knowledge brings with it a larger knowledge of life itself. She will no longer be a victim of Osmond's rigid system, nor indeed of anyone else's. At last, we feel, she will be her own woman, appreciating the part and place she must take in the world.

XII

In November 1881 Henry James was sitting in a Boston hotel. He had returned to America, while the serialization of *The Portrait of a Lady* was nearing its conclusion, out of a sudden desire to renew direct contact with his family: "I needed to see again *les miens*, to revive my relations with them, and my sense of the consequences that these relations entail." As it turned out, he had only returned to see them die, and America itself seemed barren, alien, and innutrient. While he was sitting in that Boston hotel—it was still prior to the deaths of his parents—he embarked on an extraordinary summing-up of his life so far, which he committed to his notebook. It is a mixture of retrospective definition and prospective intention, and flows on for pages as Henry James not only takes stock of his position, but clarifies to himself what it was to be Henry James at that moment. (Incidentally, and perhaps oddly, he got his own age wrong—he was thirty-eight.)

I am 37 years old, I have made my choice, and God knows that I have now no time to waste. My choice is the old world—my choice, my need, my life. . . . My work lies there—and with this vast new world, *je n'ai que faire*. One can't do both—one must choose. No European writer is called upon to assume that terrible burden, and it seems hard that I should be. The burden is necessarily greater for an American—for he *must* deal, more or less, even if only by implication, with Europe; whereas no European is obliged to deal in the least with America. . . . The painter of manners who neglects America is not thereby incomplete as yet; but a hundred years hence—fifty years hence perhaps—he will doubtless be accounted so.
(25 November 1881)

James goes on to recall his many European experiences, and then comes to the moment he decided to move to London. It was in many ways the most important decision of his life:

I don't remember what suddenly brought me to the point of saying—"Go to; I will try London." I think a letter from William had a good deal to do with it, in which he said, "Why don't you?—That must be the place." . . . I *did* try it, and it has succeeded beyond my most ardent hopes. . . . I came to London as a complete stranger, and today I know much too many people. *J'y suis absolument comme chez moi.* Such an experience is an education—it fortifies the character and embellishes the mind. It is difficult to speak adequately or justly of London. It is not a pleasant place; it is not agreeable, or cheerful, or easy, or exempt from reproach. It is only magnificent. . . . You may call it dreary, heavy, stupid, dull, inhuman, vulgar at heart and tiresome in form. I have felt these things at times so strongly that I have said—"Ah London, you too then are impossible?" But these are occasional moods; and for one who takes it as I take it, London is on the whole the most possible form of life. I take it as an artist and as a bachelor; as one who has the passion of observation and whose business is the study of human life. It is the biggest aggregation of human life—the most complete compendium of the world. The human race is better represented there than anywhere else, and if you learn to know your London you learn a great many things.

So London it was to be—for the next sixteen years, with few interruptions (a visit to Paris in 1884, where he met and talked to Zola, Daudet, Goncourt; a long stay in Italy in 1886–1887, which generated a number of his greatest stories, including *The Aspern Papers*). He was to meet most of the well-known writers of the time—Alfred Tennyson, Robert Browning, George Eliot—and many social celebrities, including the statesman Herbert Gladstone. Indeed in one winter he dined out 107 times. He was certainly getting to know his compendium! In the end he was to withdraw—retreat, perhaps—from it, exhausted and disappointed. But that is a later story. In 1882 James's visit to America was darkened by the death of his mother in January of that year. He returned to London but was almost immediately recalled by the news that his father was dying.

After the loss of his parents—*les miens* were no more—Henry James settled in London (first near Piccadilly, then in Kensington) and, immensely productive, entered into a new phase of his writing career. Indeed James's sojourn in London was to take him through three distinct phases. Having, as he thought, somewhat exhausted the "international theme," he turned away from his Daisy Millers and Isabel Archers and embarked on what were intended to be serious social novels in what was then thought of as the "naturalist" mode. The three major ones were *The Bostonians* and *The Princess Casamassima* (both published in 1886), and *The Tragic Muse* (1890). They were all pretty much failures with the public and James felt he had to try something else. He turned to writing drama for some five years (1890-1895). Here he failed even more seriously. A dramatization of *The American* had some little success, but on the first night of *Guy Domville* James came out to take a bow after the play was over, only to be booed and jeered by an angry audience.

Much has been made of this incident, and given James's sensibility there is no doubt that it was in certain ways traumatic. After this disaster he returned to fiction, but the fiction takes a new turn. It is constantly experimental, not only drawing on what he had learned from writing for the theater, but also exploiting in new ways such strange genres as the ghost story ("The Turn of the Screw" is perhaps the most famous). He also wrote a number of tales about unsuccessful writers and artists, and stories of spoiled childhoods, contaminated innocence, blighted adolescence. He was undoubtedly going through some sort of crisis in his career, and it is reflected in a number of strange devious works, full of moral dubieties and unusual, even perverse, psychological processes and behaviors, taking place in a social atmosphere that is darkening—at times toxic, mephitic. James's attitude to London had grown more somber—by which we are also saying that his attitude to life had as well; since what, for James, was life, if it was not London? Feeling estranged from his adopted city and unappreciated and unwanted by his audience, James left London and finally purchased an old house with a walled garden in Rye, Sussex. This was Lamb House, where he went in 1898, and where he was to write his final masterpieces.

XIII

I wished to write a very *American* tale, a tale very characteristic of our social conditions, and I asked myself what was the most salient and peculiar point in our social life. The answer was: the situation of women, the decline of the sentiment of sex, the agitation on their behalf.

THUS James formulated in an entry in his personal notebook the generative idea of his novel *The Bostonians*. He set about depicting a group of Bostonian women concerned, in different ways and to different degrees, with the cause of feminism—or redressing the wrongs done to women by men over the centuries. The central member of this group is Olive Chancellor, who is hysterically bigoted in her commitment to "the cause" and obsessively, pathologically unremitting in her total aggression toward men. She takes up a young girl, adopting her—indeed, effectively "buying" her from her venal, fraudulent parents (the father a charlatan faith healer, the mother a vapid, foolish, would-be social climber). The girl, Verena Tarrant, is another of those slightly magical "innocent" young girls who appear throughout James's fiction—vulnerable and yet firm; malleable and yet essentially themselves; timid and yet daring; at times loving and yet somehow unreachable; capable of deep silences and long looks and unexpected declarations; innocent and yet with some nameless knowledge all their own. Sometimes almost blanks, such figures are nevertheless often the magnetic center of the works in which they appear. And so it is with Verena Tarrant. She has some sort of a gift for apparently impromptu "inspired" public utterance—long, persuasive speeches about the sufferings and rights of women. And yet the words do not seem to come from her—she is a passive vehicle for a discourse not her own. As we say now, she does not really speak on such occasions—she is spoken.

Olive Chancellor appropriates Verena Tarrant, partly to develop her gift to further the feminist cause, and partly because—while she hardly recognizes it—she is intensely, deviantly, and perversely in love with her. James noted that his book "should be a study of one of those friendships between women which are so common in New England." It is irrelevant and limiting to consider it as a study of lesbianism. James is considering a much larger matter—the perversion (it is a common word in the book) of sexuality and emotionality, the confusion and debasement of relationships, the aberrant and extreme ideologues of "the masculine" and "the feminine," "the decline of the sentiment of sex," as James ambiguously puts it—which all pervade the book and which are signs, simply, of a society gone wrong. The drama of the book is precipitated by the arrival in Boston of a distant cousin of Olive Chancellor's—a man named Basil Ransom who is something of a refugee from the ravaged post–Civil War South. He is almost as extreme in his ideas about the respective roles and places of men and women as Olive is in her hysterical denunciations of his sex. He falls in love with Verena, and from then on it is war, almost to the death, between him and Olive as to which of them should "possess" her. In giving up, temporarily, the "international theme," James had not given up the organization of his work around complex oppositions. Instead of America and Europe, we now have the differences between the North and the South in America, and, even more importantly, an exploration of the most crucial and ambiguous (not to say controversial) difference of all—between male and female.

The note of deviancy and perversion is pervasive and touches nearly all the characters in different ways: it is as though no one is sure what constitutes his identity, what is his place in society, what exactly is his "sexuality" and what it entails. They are displaced, unplaced—products and victims and symptoms of the confused society—or nonsociety—of post–Civil War America. Olive Chancellor is the most extreme case. Although "cultured" and with a sense of her place in an elitist social coterie—one could hardly call it "society" since no one seems quite to know where that elusive entity is to be located—she is in a state of serious psychological disarray. She is morbid, nervous, fixated on her belief in "the great male conspiracy," and paranoid in her sense that there is always some base masculine "plot" being aimed at her (a paranoia triggered by her anxiety that some man will entice Verena Tarrant away). In every way she attempts to negate her own, and indeed all female, sexuality: "There are women who are unmarried by accident, and others who are unmarried by option; but Olive Chancellor was unmarried by every implication of her being"; and "she had absolutely no figure, and presented a certain appearance of feeling cold."

In no other of his novels does James pay more attention to the physical appearance of his characters. For a writer who is supposed to shy away from the body, he shows himself to be amazingly acute when it comes to registering the sheer corporeal presence of his characters and what their bodies reveal about their relations to their own sexuality. Olive speaks out of "outraged theory" and is "hungry for revenge." "She considered men in general as so much in the debt of the opposite sex that any individual woman had an unlimited credit with them; she could not possibly overdraw the general feminine account"—an attitude not uncommon in some feminist groups today. Among other things, this great novel has unexpected contemporary relevance. Ransom is right in his reply to Verena's claim that what Olive wants is "equal rights": "Oh, I thought what she wanted was simply a different inequality—simply to turn out the men altogether."

Basil Ransom is the opposition—in every way: southern male, avowedly and ruthlessly reactionary. Some people have taken him to be the approved figure in the book—the firm, sensible, old-fashioned male rescuing Verena from a bunch of demented spinsters. This is to misread the book in a serious way. Basil Ransom is "very provincial"; he operates from "narrow notions": his hero is Thomas Carlyle, preferably in his ranting, denunciatory mode. He regards women as "essentially inferior to men, and infinitely tiresome when they declined to accept the lot which men had made for them." If Olive shows the bad effects of a Puritan culture, Basil has "the unregenerate imagination of the children of the cotton states." In other words, he grew up in a society based on slavery, and while he rejects the actual use of slaves, he carries over the notion of master/slave relationship into his attitude to women. He is not only a cynic, he is "aggressive and unmerciful," as Verena perceives. He may regard himself as the one sane man among a group of aberrant women, but he is himself—as Verena sees—"perverse." He does have a strong sexual appeal, one to which Verena finally succumbs. But this is not a story of true love emerging at last. When he realizes that Verena is in love with him, under his "spell," he is quite merciless.

One particular bit of male cruelty on the part of Basil should be noted. The finale of the book is set in the Music Hall, where Verena is to give what is planned as a major speech. Her voice, we should note, is said to be particularly lovely. But Basil's thoughts run this way: "if he should become her husband he should know a way to strike her dumb." Olive is not wrong in saying to Verena that "it was because he knew that her voice had magic in it, and from the moment he caught its first note he had determined to destroy it. It was not tenderness that moved him—it was devilish malignity." Devilish or not, it is a purely repressive act, a crude assertion of power. He wants to privatize Verena, allow her no "public life." The only "platform" she will have will be the "dining-table." In a small way it is an act of pure sexual totalitarianism. James knew very well what he was doing—he always did—when he placed one of the first meetings between Basil and Verena in the Memorial Hall of Harvard, in which there is a chamber consecrated to those who died in the Civil

War. That particular war is over, but the unending war between the sexes is entering a new phase. Slavery may have been abolished, but in this confused society slavery in various forms can be endlessly reinstituted. Basil Ransom of course has his attractive qualities, and the power of his deep appeal to Verena is made quite plausible. But as Verena goes away with—is pulled away by—him, she is in tears: "It is to be feared that with the union, so far from brilliant, into which she was about to enter, these were not the last she was destined to shed." So James concludes the book, offering us the hint, as Irving Howe once put it, that "Ransom and Verena, married at last, would live unhappily ever after."

The book, on the whole, is written in a spirit of incisive satiric humor—among other things, it is simply one of James's funniest books. But the humor bites, and the issues revealed are deeply serious ones. And the fate that gathers round Verena finally gives the book a somber tone. I have not the space to indicate the skill with which James depicts a very large range of characters, nor the way in which he deploys descriptions of city settings and landscapes—but in both ways he achieves that "density of specification" he thought a social novel should have. However we wish to define the social novel, on these grounds— conveying a sense of the moral and physical condition, or malaise, of a society in a distinct historical setting—*The Bostonians* is the finest one James ever wrote.

XIV

WHEN James turned to his second attempt at a major social, "naturalist," novel he shifted his attention from a reform movement to a revolutionary one, from the feminists of Boston to a somewhat vague socialist-anarchist-revolutionary group in London. The year the book was written and published, 1886, saw the Trafalgar Square riots in London and the Haymarket killings in Chicago—revolution, in an unorganized, uncoordinated, but threatening sense, was distinctly in the air, and it was an astute choice on James's part to attempt a major novel dealing with this menacing feeling of a threat to society coming from the lower classes. James was not a very precise sociologist any more than he was a particularly factually well-informed historian—he worked through a sense of the past, his genius for registering the total

atmosphere of a place and all that was latent or impregnated in it. Thus in *The Princess Casamassima* the politics of the revolutionary group are various, inconsistent, and vague. This was not only a shrewd choice on James's part—by inclination he was not especially knowledgeable about revolutionary politics or cells, conspiracies, underground groups, and the like—but also a deliberate tactic. The vagueness of the politics was reflected in the vagueness of the threat, and it is just this sense of some possible imminent, but as yet indefinable, social upheaval that James manages to convey.

Temperamentally, as I have said, James was hardly in much sympathy with this part of his subject. Not that he had any illusions about the injustices and degradations of the English class system. At this time he wrote of the English upper class:

The condition of that body seems to me in many ways to be the same rotten and collapsible one as that of the French aristocracy before the revolution—minus cleverness and conversation; or perhaps it is more like the heavy, congested and depraved Roman world upon which the barbarians came down. In England the Huns and Vandals will have to come up—from the black depths of the (in the people) enormous misery.

(letter to Charles Eliot Norton, 6 December 1886)

Among the many things that James was inhaling in his beloved London was the vast amount of human suffering it contained. There are many passages in the novel referring to it—for example: "the season was terribly hard; and as in that lower world one walked with one's ear nearer the ground the deep perpetual groan of London misery seemed to swell and swell and form the whole undertone of life." And he undoubtedly did feel that "the people was only a sleeping lion, already breathing shorter and beginning to stretch its limbs and stiffen its claws." But, for all that, James the artist could not really get inside a political movement, nor really explore in Zolaesque detail the actual conditions of urban squalor and misery. So, while the book pays nominal respect to the revolutionaries and their cause, its real sympathies go in the opposite direction—as a brief look at the main characters and the plot will indicate.

As his hero, or central figure, James chose not a robust child of the working people, but an anomaly. Hyacinth Robinson (one can hardly imagine someone called "Hyacinth" working passionately alongside a Lenin) is the illegitimate son of a decadent English lord who was murdered by a working-class French prostitute. Thus, perhaps rather too obviously, there is a clear genetic reason for the duality in his nature: from the mother, a sense of resentment at the exploitative decadence of the upper classes; from the father, an innate tendency toward gentility and an inassuagable appetite for the elegancies of high society and aesthetic satisfactions of great art. A visit to his dying mother in prison sows in the boy's mind "the seeds of shame and rancour"; it makes him "conscious of his stigma, of his exquisite vulnerability." Both as a product and as a person he really fits in nowhere, nor does he—can he—know who or what he really is. In his person he is small, not strong, but obviously a "gentleman," very delicate, and with "something jaunty and romantic, almost theatrical, in his whole little person." "His own character? He was to cover that up as carefully as possible; he was to go through life in a mask, in a borrowed mantle; he was to be every day and every hour an actor."

James was to take up the problematical relation between acting and life in his next novel, but here we can notice one important result of Hyacinth's doubt about his own self. Given his social—not to say ontological—insecurity, he is easily influenced, led in different directions, seduced into a particular group or by a stronger person, like the revolutionary Paul Muniment. In this he resembles Verena Tarrant, who was also a lonely anomaly in her own society, easily taken over and influenced by other people. And just as Verena never really takes to the cause of feminist reform with the ardent convictions and obsessions of Olive and the others, neither does Hyacinth really take to the revolutionary cause with the passion of a genuine radical. He gives his word—which is to have important repercussions—but not his heart. They are two of James's typical characters—Hyacinth is "one of the disinherited, one of the expropriated, one of the exceptionally interesting," and so in her different way is Verena. These and many other comparable figures are near to James's heart: he himself was displaced from America to Europe, and in a subtler sense from life to art.

Hyacinth's tantalizing and disturbing contacts with the fine amenities of upper-class life come about through the mysterious woman after whom the book is named. Christina Light was the enigmatic and destructive woman in *Roderick Hudson*, and she reappears in this book, married to but separated from Prince Casamassima, to be as fatal a torment to Hyacinth as she was to Roderick. Her reappearance stretches plausibility a little, but her behavior does not. She is the rich, bored woman who has had everything and all the lovers she wants, and is always on the lookout for some new excitement and distraction. In her ennui she has turned to flirting with revolutionaries, as if they could give her a taste of the "real life" that her jaded senses no longer find in other society. Today we would call her attitude radical chic. Her companion, Madame Grandoni, calls her a *capricciosa* and warns Hyacinth not to give himself up to her. Paul Muniment calls her a "monster" but seems to be taking up with her after she drops Hyacinth, as she does near the end of the book. She first takes up Hyacinth in a theater—always a significant venue in James—and it is she who gives him a glimpse of the graces and seductions and finesses of upper-class social life, particularly at her country house, Medley. Hyacinth's visit there is a vision of earthly delights, an intoxication from which he scarcely recovers. That he is capable of being devoted to the princess is clear. That for her he is just the satisfaction of another whim is also clear: "Why shouldn't I have my bookbinder after all? In attendance, you know—it would be awfully *chic*. We might have immense fun."

Artists, bookbinders, Italian princes, revolutionaries . . . all immense fun—for a time. Hyacinth succumbs to the atmosphere around her, but he also succumbs to his experience of the world. And she can see the pathos in his position: "to be constituted as you're constituted, to be conscious of the capacity you must feel, and yet to look at the good things of life only through the glass of the pastry-cook's window!" But while it is inconceivable that he should sustain a relationship with that daughter of London, Millicent, it is also only too evident that the princess will play with him and then drop him. And while he can never be at home in his own class, he can never hope to gain lasting access to one above him. He has no one. He has nowhere to go—indeed, nowhere to *be*. It is a fitting end to the novel that he should be found dead, having used the gun given to him to kill the duke to commit suicide. This sad conclusion dramatizes a problem that becomes prominent in James's work. A person may achieve a certain refinement and subtlety of sensibility that will simply make it impossible for him to operate in any of the given social—or nonsocial—spaces of the world. There are extreme solutions: the bullet in the head, the retreat into art; both, in very different ways, involve some kind of loss of participation in life, though, to be sure, writing is more creative than suicide. But James was to go on wondering whether there were any other solutions besides the bullet and the pen.

XV

BOTH *The Bostonians* and *The Princess Casamassima* were failures with the public. To Howells, James wrote in 1888, "I have entered upon evil days, I am still staggering a good deal under the mysterious and (to me) inexplicable damage wrought—apparently—upon my situation by my last novels." So he decided to abandon the types of large public themes he had been attempting, one reason being, as he said, his "sense of knowing terribly little about the kind of life I have attempted to describe" (true of *The Princess Casamassima*, not true of *The Bostonians*). But it could also be that he had not only exhausted the themes of the naturalist social novel, he had also exhausted its form. He was to concentrate more and more on the small group, the individual, and embark on new fictional modes, but not before completing one more novel that ranges widely enough to be characterized as one of his social novels of this period. This was *The Tragic Muse*, in which he brought together the worlds—and claims—of politics, art, and theater in a rather unusual way. "*The Tragic Muse* is to be my last long novel," he wrote to his brother; so it is not surprising that he should have taken as his theme the whole problem of the relation of the artist to society and focused on the theater, the arena he intended to enter to repair his fortunes. James saw his theme as

> some dramatic picture of the "artist-life" and of the difficult terms on which it is at the best secured and enjoyed, the general question of its having to be not altogether paid for. To "do something about art"—*art, that is, as a human complication and a social stumbling block*—must have been for me early a good deal of a nursed intention, the conflict between art and "the world" striking me thus betimes as one of the half-dozen great primary motives.
>
> (*The Tragic Muse*, pp. v–vi, italics added)

The words in italics do indeed sum up a theme that generated a large number of stories and novellas by James and, in this case, a whole novel. Put at its simplest, the problem was the relationship between the artist and marriage or sexuality (the "human complication"), and between the artist and society (art as "a social stumbling block")—the problem in each case being whether to renounce or participate. James himself renounced marriage and, apart from the very late flowering of a tolerably well-controlled homoeroticism, sex; he participated in society but was mentally—artistically—detached from it. All his libidinal energy seems to have gone into the eye and the pen. But note that even James—so supremely urbane—sees a *conflict* between art and society. Not that he was thinking of art as being deliberately subversive as, say, Jean Paul Sartre might. But simply, to the extent that one was an artist, one was so much less a social being, even a citizen, even, at times, a human being. And yet, for James, art was the supreme value in life: indeed in the final analysis it gave value to life. It is hardly surprising that the conflict between art and the world struck him as "one of the half-dozen great primary motives." In his own case it was *the* primary one.

The novel is long and at times complicated, yet the organizing structure is almost diagrammatically clear. Nick Dormer (son of a great politician) is effectively offered a safe seat in the House of Commons, plus a high social position, if he marries the eminently political-social lady Julia Dallow. But, under the influence of a rather curious spokesman for art, Gabriel Nash, he turns down that life and takes up painting. At the end he has painted Julia Dallow's portrait, and it is an open question whether they will not, after all, finally marry, and—who knows—the not notably successful painter Nick Dormer might once again turn to politics. The other relationship, running concurrently with Nick's fluctuations between Julia/politics and painting, is between Peter Sherringham and Miriam Rooth. He is a successful diplomat, and she is a young actress who rapidly achieves fame. Peter is in love with her and offers to marry her if she will give up the stage (shades of Basil Ransom). In his attempt to persuade her he says: "The stage is great, no doubt, but the world is greater. It's a bigger theater than any of those places in the Strand. We'll go in for realities instead of fables, and you'll do them far better than you do the fables." She is not persuaded, but we may note that the problem of just what is "reality" and what is "fable," and how one can with any confidence draw the line between them, is very much a part of this book. Peter, somewhat perversely, asks Miriam if she would let him sacrifice his work and career and prospects to join her in the world of the theater and "simply become your appendage?" But Miriam is a quicker and more powerful girl than Verena Tarrant, and she unanswerably replies: "My dear fellow, you invite me with the best conscience in the world to become yours." Eventually Miriam marries one of her theatrical assistants, Basil Dashwood, and Peter marries the socially correct Biddy Dormer. They are true to their respective worlds.

Such is the story, and one can readily see how these relationships allow for long debates about politics and painting, social office and theater, public service and private dedications. These debates really constitute the interest of the book, because in a crucial way the book is let down by its two main men. Nick Dormer is first singled out by "the wandering blankness that sat at moments in his eyes, as if he had no attention at all," and James must have named him deliberately with the French word for "sleep" (*dormir*) in mind, for a very sleepy individual he is, marked more by vacancies than saliences as he drifts somewhat somnambulistically through the novel. He is not convincing as a politician, a painter, or a lover—not, that is, as a man. Peter is a public-service type, all right, but his sudden wild passion for Miriam—while we know that, of course, that sort of thing can happen to anyone—is somewhat implausible. He is not much less sleepy than Nick, despite all his avowed ambition. They both seem somehow to live life with their hands in their pockets—more given to a kind of elegant indolence than intensities of infatuation. No, the saving interest of the book is the girl, the actress, the Tragic Muse, Miriam Rooth, because in his study of her James managed to say a number of things about the problems of what exactly constitutes a self, a character, a subject, an identity, that were a good deal ahead of his time, though now well recognized. But if they are so recognized, it is because of the kind of pioneering psychological work that writers like James did toward the end of the last century.

Miriam is half-Jewish, a wanderer over continents, a "vagabond." She is by nature displaced in, and from, society, just as Julia Dallow incorporates the very ideal of social place and mastered hierarchy. The problem for Peter, for James, for us, is: What is *in* her? What, who, is she, really? Her face at times seems a "persistent vacancy," and she herself is thoroughly "plastic." "Miriam was a beautiful, actual, fictive, impossible young woman, of a past age and undiscoverable country." But still, what is she? Here is a key passage summarizing Peter's thoughts:

It came over him suddenly that so far from there being any question of her having the histrionic nature, she simply had it in such perfection that she was always acting; that her existence was a series of parts assumed for the moment, each changed for the next, before the perpetual mirror of some curiosity or admiration or wonder—some spectatorship that she perceived or imagined in the people about her. . . . [She was a woman] whose identity resided in the continuity of her personations, so that she had no moral privacy, as he phrased it to himself, but lived in a high wind of exhibition, of figuration—such a woman was a kind of monster, in whom of necessity there would be nothing to like, because there would be nothing to take hold of.

(ch. 10)

He tells her that she has "no nature of your own," that "your only feeling is a feigned one," that she has no character—or a hundred. "She delighted in novels, poems, perversions, misrepresentations and evasions, and had a capacity for smooth, superfluous falsification which made Sherringham think her sometimes an amusing and sometimes a tedious inventor." But she is more than that. She is a great actress with the endless recession of irresolvable ambiguities that that implies, and the unanswerable questions it raises. Because where does acting stop? Not at the door of the theater. What about the House of Commons? What about the great formal social occasions Julia Dallow loves to organize and promote? Miriam is said to be a "mountebank" (a common word in the book) associated with "mountebanks and mimes," but who exactly is, and is not, a mountebank? Are there none in politics, in high society?

This is not mere playing with paradox. James is probing very deeply into our too unexamined assumptions about the priorities of "reality," which puts our relational life above our representational life. An ontological shift of some considerable importance is going on here. And if the Miriam Rooth offstage is a mercurial, unreliable, perhaps even promiscuous person, the truth of her own statement remains: "One may live in paint and tinsel, but one isn't absolutely without a soul." As much of a soul as a politician or a society hostess—perhaps more. For they are often deceived, self-mystified, by the paint and tinsel *they* live in, live *on*—Miriam is not. She has fewer deceptions about herself than anyone in the book. She may like "superfluous falsifications," yet in the deepest sense she doesn't lie. She is, in truth, a remarkable figure of worryingly ambiguous truth and certainly the most "awake" character in the

44

book. The Tragic Muse herself remains most "real" in all her mastery of corporeal falsifications and representations. James chose his title well. (Note that the titles of all three of these "social" novels refer to women—never to men. James knew what he knew best.)

XVI

THE novel was not a great failure, but James had decided that he had to try something else. To his brother he wrote, "I know what I shall do and it won't be bad." As F. W. Dupee once remarked, it was a curious thing to say. Because what James was about to do was to attempt, exactly, to make his fortune in the theater. And what he did there was "pretty bad." I propose to say nothing about the plays, not because they are so irremediably bad, but because they are not, somehow, of the essence of James. He was trying to falsify his art to make money, and while there is nothing immoral in that, the result in James's case was a series of productions of art somehow not quite his own. Clearly he learned a lot from these years of theatrical writing. He was always brilliant at dialogue, but after writing for the theater—in which, apart from scenery and bodily gesture, everything must be revealed in speech—he became an absolute master, and indeed later wrote one of his most brilliant novels (*The Awkward Age*) almost entirely in dialogue. But he learned another lesson. One of the great powers of his art was the originality of his metaphors, often developed at great length, usually to depict elusive or crucial inner dramas or thought processes. It is just those metaphors and those accounts of inner movements that cannot be translated onto the stage. When James returned to novel writing he knew more about his own essential powers, so that his last novels are as rich in metaphor as they are in dialogue. But while avoiding the plays, I want to mention two other aspects of James's work. First of all, he was a superb travel writer. He could register the sense of a place incomparably, working not through information but through impressions, at times seemingly as able to communicate with—listen to—buildings and scenes as with people, at times more able. I will give three examples, drawn from his three main travel works (a fourth, *The American Scene*, will be discussed later), temporarily abandoning chronol-

ogy. First this, from *Italian Hours* (1909), concerning Venice, for James the most magical of cities:

It is a city in which, I suspect, there is very little strenuous thinking, and yet it is a city in which there must be almost as much happiness as misery. . . . The Venetian people have little to call their own—little more than the bare privilege of leading their lives in the most beautiful of towns. Their habitations are decayed; their taxes heavy; their pockets light; their opportunities few. One receives an impression, however, that life presents itself to them with attractions not accounted for in this meagre train of advantages, and that they are on better terms with it than many people who have made a better bargain. They lie in the sunshine; they dabble in the sea; they wear bright rags; they fall into attitudes and harmonies; they assist at an eternal *conversazione*. It is not easy to say that one would have them other than they are, and it certainly would make an immense difference should they be better fed. The number of persons in Venice who evidently never have enough to eat is painfully large; but it would be more painful if we did not equally perceive that the rich Venetian temperament may bloom upon a dog's allowance. Nature has been kind to it, and sunshine and leisure and conversation and beautiful views form the greater part of its sustenance. It takes a great deal to make a successful American, but to make a happy Venetian it takes only a handful of quick sensibility. . . . Not their misery, doubtless, but the way they elude their misery, is what pleases the sentimental tourist who is gratified by the sight of a beautiful race that lives by the aid of its imagination.

("Venice," sec. 1)

And then this, the concluding paragraph of *A Little Tour in France* (1885), since it catches James in such a characteristic posture and mood:

I think the thing that pleased me best at Dijon was the little old Parc, a charming public garden, about a mile from the town, to which I walked by a long, straight autumnal avenue. It is a *jardin français* of the last century—a dear old place, with little blue-green perspectives and alleys and *rondpoints*, in which everything balances. I went there late in the afternoon, without meeting a creature, though I had hopes I should meet the Président de Brosses. At the end of it was a little river that looked like a canal, and on the further bank was an old-fashioned villa, close to the water, with a little French garden of its own. On the hither side was a bench, on which I seated myself, lingering a good while; for this was just the sort of place I like. It was the furthermost point of my little tour. I thought that over, as I sat there, on the eve of taking the express to Paris; and as the light faded in the Parc the vision of some of the things I had seen became more distinct.

And finally, from *English Hours* (1905), part of his evocation of Rye, the place that he was to choose as his home for his final years:

I seem to myself to have lain on the grass somewhere, as a boy, poring over an English novel of the period, presumably quite bad—for they were pretty bad then too—and losing myself in the idea of just such another scene as this. But even could I rediscover the novel I wouldn't go back to it. It couldn't have been as good as this; for this—all concrete and doomed and minimised as it is—is the real thing. The other little gardens, other little odds and ends of crooked brown wall and supported terrace and glazed winter sun-trap, lean over the cliff that still, after centuries, keeps its rude drop; they have beneath them the river, a tide that comes and goes, and the mile or more of grudging desert level, beyond it, which now throws the sea to the near horizon, where, on summer days, with a depth of blue and a scattered gleam of sail, it looks forgiving and resigned. The little old shipyards at the base of the rock are for the most part quite empty, with only vague piles of brown timber and the deposit of generations of chips; yet a fishing boat or two are still on the stocks—an "output" of three or four a year!—and the ring of the hammer on the wood, a sound, in such places, rare to the contemporary ear, comes up, through the sunny stillness, to your meditative perch.
("Winchelsea, Rye, and Denis Duval," sec. 2)

The other genre in which James also excelled was the field of criticism and critical theory. He wrote many important articles on contemporary writers, such as George Eliot, Ralph Waldo Emerson, Ivan Turgenev, Gustave Flaubert, Anthony Trollope, and others (see, for example, *Partial Portraits*, 1888). He also wrote theater criticism and art criticism (as in, for example, *Picture and Text*, 1893). But most importantly, he raised the thinking about the art of fiction to a new level of self-consciousness and sophistication. His essay *The Art of Fiction*, published in 1884, is not only a crucial statement by James about his own art, as he saw it; it marks a turning point in the history of the theory of the novel. I shall run together some of the key statements from this extremely important document.

It goes without saying that you will not write a good novel unless you possess the sense of reality; but it will be difficult to give you a recipe for calling that sense into being. Humanity is immense, and reality has a myriad forms; the most one can affirm is that some of the flowers of fiction have the odor of it, and others have not. . . . Experience is never limited, and it is never complete; it is an immense sensibility, a kind of huge spider-web of the finest silken threads suspended in the chamber of consciousness, and catching every air-borne particle in its tissue. It is the very atmosphere of the mind; and when the mind is imaginative—much more when it happens to be that of a man of genius—it takes to itself the faintest hints of life, it converts the very pulses of the air into revelations. . . . The power to guess the unseen from the seen, to trace the implication of things, to judge the whole piece by the pattern, the condition of feeling life in general so completely that you are well on your way to knowing any particular corner of it—this cluster of gifts may almost be said to constitute experience. . . . If experience consists of impressions, it may be said that impressions *are* experience, just as (have we not seen it?) they are the very air we breathe. . . . A novel is a living thing, all one and continuous, like any other organism, and in proportion as it lives will it be found, I think, that in each of the parts there is something of each of the other parts. . . . What is character but the determination of incident? What is incident but the illustration of character? What is either a picture or a novel that is *not* of character? . . . A psychological reason is, to my imagination, an object adorably pictorial; to catch the tint of its complexion—I feel as if that idea might inspire one to Titianesque efforts. There are few things more exciting to me, in short, than a psychological reason, and yet, I protest, the novel seems to me the most magnificent form of art. . . . The deepest quality of a work of art will always be the quality of the mind of the producer. In proportion as that intelligence is fine will the novel, the picture, the statue partake of the substance of beauty and truth. To be constituted of such elements is, to my vision, to have purpose enough. No good novel will ever proceed from a superficial mind; that seems to me an axiom which, for the artist in fiction, will cover all needful moral ground. . . . Remember that your first duty is to be as complete as possible—to make as perfect a work. Be generous and delicate and pursue the prize.

With James, English writing about the theory of the novel comes of age.

XVII

MANY of James's more remarkable works of fiction during this period (1882–1898) emerged as short stories or novellas—indeed, we will have only one other clearly major novel to refer to. *The Aspern Papers* (1888) has come to be recognized as one of James's most remarkable pieces of work. It is a substantial novella, recounted by an unnamed narrator, and it is quite extraordinarily rich and subtle, with a stringent mixture of high comedy and telling pathos. The narrator is a critic and editor, and he is convinced that some precious papers of his adored poet, Jeffrey Aspern (Byron was probably in mind), are in the possession of Aspern's mistress, who, incredibly enough, is still alive in Venice. So to Venice he goes, prepared to stop at virtually nothing to gain possession of the putative papers. What he does stop at is the distinctly moving climax of the story. As the story is narrated in the first person, we have to work out how to take the narrator, what to make of him, morally speaking, how to assess his own rationalizations, justifications, self-exonerations (a device perfected by Browning in his monologues, which James certainly knew well)—so the story offers a particular exercise in the problematics of reading. The narrator seems honest enough about his lack of scruple: "Hypocrisy, duplicity are my only chance." He knows the old lady, Juliana Bordereau, hates any kind of inquiry or publicity, so he has to find a way to insinuate himself into her house. He does this oddly—and comically—by presenting himself at the old palazzo and begging to rent rooms there because it has a garden, and he simply must have a garden. This garden, incidentally, with all its iconographic associations, adds significantly to the incredibly rich and suggestive atmosphere of the story. It is a "garden in the middle of the sea," with the crumbling, evocative architecture of the old palazzo, of old Venice, all around it. What takes place in this setting of meeting and mingling elements is a drama concerning how the present—in one way—seeks to appropriate the past. Precious things—great loves, great buildings, great poets, great papers—are always vanishing: there is a great deal here of "the poetry of the thing outlived and lost and gone." The narrator as critic justifies his salvage operation, as in this exchange with Juliana:

"Do you think it's right to rake up the past?"
"I don't know that I know what you mean by raking it up; but how can we get at it unless we dig a little? The present has such a rough way of treading it down."

(ch. 7)

In some ways, then, the editor-critic is, if not our representative, at least our agent, as he develops his plan of campaign to penetrate the old house, bypass or buy off the old lady, and rescue the hidden, buried poetry and introduce it into the present, adding it to our culture, our heritage. But he is also a "publishing scoundrel," as Juliana remarks on one memorable occasion when she finds him actually meditating whether to force open a desk that he senses might contain the papers. And there is a central moral

problem. The narrator is positively comical as he tries to seduce the old lady and her demure niece, Tita, with endless flowers that he forces the garden to yield (he actually dislikes gardening); and when it comes to purchasing the papers indirectly—that too is fair enough. Juliana for him represents "esoteric knowledge" (it is an important part of her mystification that she wears a green eyeshade, so that—except for one terrible accusing glare when she catches him at the desk—he never "sees" her properly), and that excites his "editorial heart." In just such ways the past is ever seducing the present. And if our editor feels that "my eccentric private errand became a part of the general romance and the general glory," we may mark a note of megalomania but pass it as understandable all the same. Flowers are harmless. Money is different—that is the source of bargains, and there is a great deal of bargaining in the book. Indeed, old Juliana proves to be a ruthless bargainer, whether over the rent or over a small oval portrait of Aspern that she agrees to sell. Indeed, her avidity is her most distinctive characteristic, though the narrator admits that he was possibly responsible for having "lit the unholy flame" of her "coarse cupidity." He is himself, after all, a lesson in avidity when it comes to the Aspern papers. So bargains are fought over and more or less struck. Flowers. Money. But people.

The story changes in tone when the unworldly, helpless, friendless niece, Tita, begins to get involved. In a way—we have to decide how calculatingly, how coolly, how cruelly—the narrator does "make love" to Tita, to gain her help in getting access to the papers. He says little enough beyond certain gallantries, but then he is dealing with a lady who has no experience of the world and must be exceptionally impressionable and needy: "From the moment you were kind to her she depended on you absolutely." He is, for mixed motives, "kind"—she duly becomes absolutely "dependent." When Juliana finally dies there is an excruciatingly awkward moment when Tita intimates that her aunt had indicated that Tita could give the narrator the papers if he married her—in effect, she offers her hand to him with the promise of the papers in exchange. It is the last of many hard bargains, and this time it is a perversion, a degradation. The narrator recoils in barely concealed horror and takes himself off. He now regards Tita as a "piece of middle-aged female helplessness" that he would certainly not encumber himself with. He even loses temper with the confounded Aspern papers, those "crumpled scraps." Then he returns to visit Tita. She is oddly, momentarily "beautified," "angelic," and seems to have acquired a "force of soul," so much so that the narrator thinks to himself, "Why not, after all—why not?" Then Tita reveals that she has burned all the papers, and the "transfiguration" is over: "she had changed back to a plain, dingy, elderly person." The narrator is left with the oval portrait and his "chagrin at the loss of the letters." How much do we discern him as a scoundrel, how much do we see him as a person in whom values have become so perverted that the papers determine his assessment of another person's worth, or beauty, or simple humanity? How much do we see the "force of soul" in Tita's act of obliterating an inheritance that, as it were, threatened to be more important than her own identity? What do we make of the editor's "eccentric private errand"? These and many other matters James leaves up to the reader—and each reading of this remarkable tale brings out different nuances, different distributions of sympathy. One thing, however, we do recognize, as the narrator himself has to recognize: "I had unwittingly, but none the less deplorably, trifled."

XVIII

MUCH as he admired London and England, James could see that in many ways expressive forms had rigidified into repressive formalities; that it was a society which in its pathological devotion to external proprieties moved inexorably toward the suffocation of personal spontaneity. In such a world conscience could be at a premium, and in many of the stories of this period James shows just how hard it was to maintain a true conscience in contemporary society.

One aspect of the Victorian age is that it seemed to enforce an unusually wide gap between the passion cherished in private and the gestures demanded in public (hence so many references to the "buried life" in much poetry and fiction of the time). Concerning this phenomenon James gave a defining parable in his wonderfully deft "The Private Life" (1893). Ostensibly a mystery story—why is a certain great writer (based on Browning) so banal in public; why does a certain famous public figure (based on Lord Leighton) actually seem to vanish when left without an audience?—it has a ghostly resolution that pin-

points the latent schizophrenia of the age. The writer is in fact two people, one a genius who stays in his room and writes in the dark, the other a bourgeois who is his sufficient deputy for dining and gossiping in the "vulgar and stupid" common world. The public figure is indeed so utterly devoted to public appearance ("he had a costume for every function and a moral for every costume") that he has no private life to fall back on. The disguises have absorbed the man. In such an age how should the artist proceed, indeed survive? James returns often to the theme of necessary renunciation. It is the rather ambiguously given lesson in "The Lesson of the Master" (1892); it is in "Collaboration" (1892) and a number of other stories—a renunciation not only of public rewards but of domestic consolations. Clearly James's sense of the possibly enfeebling effects of involvement with women was not diminishing with the years, but his aesthetic is obviously earnestly conceived. Art must "affirm an indispensable truth," and the artist must, like the two collaborators in "Collaboration," sacrifice to make that affirmation. Such art "makes for civilization," ultimately "works for human happiness." James was too aware of so much around him that did not. In fact, the actual, visible reality of the age could be insufficient to stimulate true art, as is amusingly brought out in "The Real Thing" (1893), which is something of an ontological joke but with serious resonances. A typical genteel couple in need of money seek work from a book illustrator as models. But they are "all convention and patent-leather." The real thing is the dead thing: it offers no suggestion to the imagination, no scope for "the alchemy of art." The truly real is not so easily located and has to be approached by subtler means. The artist cannot confront or, indeed, embrace, his age so directly.

If the Jamesian artist can or must renounce, many of his characters can only succumb. There is little murder in James (though one, in the strange *The Other House*, 1896), but there is a surprising amount of death. In "Brooksmith" (1892), the butler (for whom the story is titled) develops an artistic imagination that he cannot employ after his sympathetic master dies, and he simply withers away. Agatha Grice, torn apart by the forces exerted on her by her English husband and her American brother, commits suicide in "The Modern Warning" (1888). Grace Mavis, the poor American girl who is trifled with and gossiped about on the ship that is taking her to an arranged and unsought-for marriage, jumps overboard in "The Patagonia" (1888). Louisa Chantry, overwhelmed by the shame of revealing a hidden passion, dies almost immediately in "The Visits" (1892). And in one of James's finest stories, "The Pupil" (1891), young Morgan Moreen's heart gives out from an accumulated burden of shame and the sudden, shattering impact of a prospective release from his wretched family. Thus society takes its victims. It is worth recalling that two of the titles of collections of stories James published during this period are *Terminations* (1895) and *Embarrassments* (1896).

XIX

In the summer of 1896 James was in a rented cottage in Rye finishing one work and beginning another. The first was to be called *The Other House* (it had an odd history, having started as a play-scenario under the title "The Promise," then being turned into a novella, and ten years later converted back again into a play). It is an unusual and powerful work in the James canon, for he presents us with an almost unmitigatedly evil female figure, the "bad heroine" Rose Armiger, who goes far beyond the other women whose complex motivations result in destruction (Christina Light, Madame Merle, Kate Croy in *The Wings of the Dove*). She not only plots and cheats and lies and deceives, she murders a child and then tries to fix the blame on the "good heroine." The action is precipitated by a vow given by a man, Tony Bream, to his wife on her deathbed—namely, that he will not marry again while their child is still alive. Rose Armiger and the "good" Jean Martle are both in love with him, so Rose decides, since she is willing to do anything to gain possession of Tony, that the only way is to kill the child and make it seem that Jean is responsible. It is not melodrama; the passions are vibrant and intense. In giving his account of what happened, Tony looks "as if he were retracing the saddest story on earth" (I wonder if Ford Madox Ford had the phrase in mind for his memorable opening sentence of *The Good Soldier*). This short and neglected novel has real power. It is worth remembering that James was ending a period in which he had immersed himself in the theater. In particular, he was at the time under the influence of Henrik Ibsen (his friend Elizabeth Robins had played Hedda Gabler in 1891), and James's comments on Hedda are, as Leon Edel noted, perfectly applicable to Rose Armiger. James wrote of Hedda:

> Her motives are just her passions. . . . She is infinitely perverse . . . one isn't so sure that she is wicked, and by no means sure that she is disagreeable. She is various and sinuous . . . complicated and natural; she suffers, she struggles, she is human, and by that fact exposed to a dozen interpretations.
>
> ("Henrik Ibsen," in *Essays in London and Elsewhere*)

The Other House is James's most Ibsen-like novel and one of the most positive yields of his period as a dramatist.

The other work James started that summer and published in 1897 was *The Spoils of Poynton.* Where the former work concentrates on the struggle for possession of a man, this one was to focus on the extraordinary human emotions that can be roused by the struggle for the possession of property, valuables, things—"spoils." James's novel—first entitled "House Beautiful," then "The Old Things"—certainly addresses itself to what he called "that most modern of our current passions, the fierce appetite for the upholsterer's and joiner's and brazier's work, the chairs and tables, the cabinets and presses, the material odds and ends, of the more labouring ages." The abiding paradox—the value of beautiful things, the enormities perpetuated on their behalf—is at the very center of this remarkable novel. As James wrote in his later preface: "The real centre, as I say, the citadel of interest, with the fight waged round it, would have been the felt beauty and value of the prize of the battle, the Things, always the splendid Things." But rather than describe the things directly, he concentrates, wisely, on the passions they arouse. "Yes, it is a story of cabinets and chairs and tables; they formed the bone of contention, but what would merely 'become' of them, magnificently passive, seemed to represent a comparatively vulgar issue." To the victor the spoils, as we say: but in this battle there are no winners in any traditional sense. Whether any other kind of victory can be secured amid "the ugliness of the whole close conflict" is a question explored by the novel.

The situation that generates the struggle is as follows: Mrs. Gereth is a widow, and it was she who built up the magnificent Jacobean house Poynton into a veritable museum of art treasures and fine things. Her husband having died, the house is now in the possession of her son, Owen. He is a powerful but philistine man who doesn't care about "the damned things" (his room, full of rifles, whips, tobacco pots—a different kind of collection—is the one "monstrosity" of Poynton). Thus his mother, who cares passionately about the things, is very concerned that he should marry the right kind of girl, one who would, as it were, maintain the spirit and tradition of Poynton. To this end, she tries to force a young girl, Fleda Vetch, to—in effect—seduce Owen into marriage by giving herself to him. Fleda is too scrupulous, but the crude, sensuous, rapacious Mona Brigstock is not, and she gets Owen and Poynton. This is too much for Mrs. Gereth, who tries various ways of keeping possession of the things, even virtually stealing them at one point. The passions of the three women effectively precipitate the action; they move the unmoving objects, human and material. In terms of a morality play, Mona Brigstock influences Owen through sexual means; Mrs. Gereth uses her worldly cleverness to plot against him; while Fleda Vetch voices the claims of spirituality. He himself, a "natural" man, seems sufficiently amenable to being Mona's romping partner, Mrs. Gereth's dutiful son, and Fleda's obedient saint. Like the cherished objects that are legally his, he tends to stay where he is put, and go where he is pushed. The owner, Owen, is variously owned. Products of nature and products of art, here in the form of Owen and Poynton, are in themselves neutral and mindless; everything depends on the resolute temperaments that seek to appropriate them (as Mona does), direct them (as Mrs. Gereth does), or influence them (which is Fleda's "heroic" ambition). In an extreme form we might say that we see physical, mental, and spiritual force variously seeking to influence the inert products of nature and art. The final result is thus of some metaphysical, as well as social, moment.

Mrs. Gereth genuinely appreciates the beauty of the things. But, as it transpires, she is another of those Jamesian collectors whose humanity has diminished in the dedicated pursuit of things. When she realizes that she has irrevocably lost her things through the marriage of Owen and Mona, she becomes "a dead gray mask," exhausted, "with empty hands in her lap." If things are "the sum of the world," then to lose them is to lose all reason to exist. Mrs. Gereth has been the guardian of her spoils for so long that, as Fleda perceives, it has "despoiled her of her humanity." Fleda disappoints Mrs. Gereth because she will not use her sexuality to catch Owen. For Fleda, things, no matter how beautiful, are not the sum of the world.

This is clearly shown when she joins Mrs. Gereth at the lowly house Ricks after their "defeat." Mrs. Gereth finds the place detestable, but when Fleda comes into the despised cottage she responds to something not on the inventory of the furniture that Mrs. Gereth draws up. Fleda tries to define it: "It's a kind of fourth dimension. It's a presence, a perfume, a touch. It's a soul, a story, a life." Fleda is aware of a dimension beyond the purely material.

James was not religious in any orthodox way, and he certainly cherished the beauties of the physical and artistic world, just as he disliked rigid asceticism; but he could see that those who lived exclusively for material ends courted a death of the heart and soul that might go far toward invalidating the beauty of the things they possessed. At the end of the book, when Fleda finds the house and all the things devoured by a fire, she says to the stationmaster, "Poynton's *gone*?" To which he makes the considerate and suggestive reply: "What can you call it, Miss, if it ain't really saved?" James leaves his hints as hints, but we are left with the feeling that pure things, unpermeated by spirit, are indeed unredeemed and unredeemable, and that world without soul will not be saved. If the conflagration at Poynton metaphorically looks back to the sacking of Troy, it also carries an anticipatory hint of the Day of Judgment.

XX

PROBLEMS of possession and conscience are dominant in James's next novel, *What Maisie Knew* (1897), his last major work of this period. The situation simply concerns a little girl, Maisie, whose parents, the Faranges, are divorced. They have their various affairs but—not an uncommon phenomenon—they exploit Maisie, either for their own ends or to anger or irritate each other. The person kindest to Maisie is Sir Claude, one of Mrs. Farange's lovers, but he is entirely feeble and spineless—no possible kind of father substitute. The other person who claims to care for her is the stern little Mrs. Wix, a type of governess figure who seeks to gain possession of her and, in the end, succeeds. What James centers on is not just the pathos of the exploited little girl, a helpless victim of the sexual games that older people play. There is something much more positive to Maisie as she tries to comprehend the world she has to move in. Her most precious attribute—it is a key one in James's work—is her capacity for wonder; as he wrote in the preface:

the active, contributive, close-circling wonder . . . in which the child's identity is guarded and preserved, and which makes her case remarkable exactly by the weight of the tax on it, provides distinction for her, provides vitality and variety, through the operation of the tax—which would have done comparatively little for us hadn't it been monstrous.

The monstrous tax on her wonder is imposed by the selfish, ambiguous, deceptive, exploitative emotions that swirl around her. Her instincts are precisely not selfish. She has "an instinct for keeping the peace," and to this end often practices "the pacific art of stupidity," cultivating a tactful "blankness" in the interests of general harmony and self-preservation. And there is a pathos in her innocence, which, because of her situation, is "an innocence so saturated with knowledge and so directed to diplomacy." Yet she is unspoiled by this knowledge: none of the surrounding dirt rubs off on her. Like Fleda Vetch (yet with none of her hysteria), like Verena Tarrant, perhaps even like Daisy Miller, she effectively represents "the only decency" in the world of the book.

But the book is about Maisie's knowledge as well—what she sees and what she makes of what she sees. As a child abandoned by her real parents and exploited by her adulterous stepparents, Maisie has more incentive and more need to use her eyes than any other Jamesian character. They are, as it were, all she has got. While Maisie would know a great deal if she were an adult, if we remember her limited outlook, her stature, her somewhat vague, indiscriminate attention, then we realize how hard it would be for her to read the signs correctly, if at all. As with what she sees, so with what she hears. Out of the confused social murmur sudden phrases detach themselves and come to her ears with a clarity as baffling as the previous inaudibility for want of a context: "she found in her mind a collection of images and echoes to which meanings were attachable—images and echoes kept for her in the childish dusk, the dim closet, the high drawers, like games she wasn't big enough to play." Precisely: she lacks the terms, the concepts, the rules of the game, a knowledge of the stakes. She is the recipient of innumerable impressions, but she lacks any coordinating key.

The novel implies that her mental grasp of the world is constantly growing stronger—"the little

girl's interpretations thickened." At the start of chapter 12 we read: "It may indeed be said that these days brought on a high quickening of Maisie's direct perceptions, of her sense of freedom to make out things for herself." Yet too often enlightenment leads to more enigma. If at one stage she is claiming insouciantly, bravely, "Oh yes, I know everything!" one of her last pathetic cries is: "I don't know—I don't know." She develops a sense rather than a sureness "of the relations of things," and it is her "reflexions" that "thicken" rather than her knowledge of verifiable facts. For James, this could be a very valuable mode of knowledge, an infinitely rich mode of cognition.

But there is one thing that determines Maisie's groping ignorance, one missing clue without which the whole tangled web of adult involvements will remain forever incomprehensible—sex. She has picked up all the terms but does not understand the matching substance (this, of course, generates a lot of the genuine comedy of the book). There is "impropriety"; people can be "compromised"; some people are called "bad." These things she knows, but it is a purely verbal knowledge; for Maisie such words remain almost nonreferential. And as long as the ramifications of sexual appetite are still a mystery to her, her world will remain phantasmagoric, full of sudden events and activities, precipitating motives, and mixed consequences that she will never fathom. In a sense the book hinges on what Maisie does *not* know.

Mrs. Wix is the embodiment par excellence of the "conscious conscience," and I think we may infer that Maisie's character might indeed "suffer much" by close association with it, by enforced subjugation to it. Mrs. Wix is constantly upbraiding Maisie for having no "moral sense." But she has something more valuable, that sense of wonder. When she visits Boulogne her first emotion is "the great ecstasy of a larger impression of life." There is no timidity or fearful holding back: this is the world, this is her world. "She recognised, she understood, she adored and took possession; feeling herself attuned to everything and laying her hand, right and left, on what had been simply waiting for her." The descriptions of the scenes as they appear to Maisie's rapt eye evoke the sensuous delight of the work of the French Impressionists. It is a world that, to Maisie's eye, "prances" with sheer joy of being.

In this novel James is not just saying something about the plight and epistemological problems of an abandoned child; he is also demonstrating what, to him, was the most valuable way of responding to experience—with generous, unselfish wonder:

the case being with Maisie to the end that she treats her friends to the rich little spectacle of objects embalmed in her wonder. She wonders, in other words, to the death—the death of her childhood, properly speaking; after which (with the inevitable shift, sooner or later, of her point of view) her situation will change and become another affair, subject to other measurements and with a new centre altogether.

(preface)

XXI

IN September 1897 James signed a twenty-one-year lease on Lamb House, in Rye. The decision to move from London and to take on, for the first time, a house—an old house—of his own obviously disturbed James as well as excited him. Certainly, in the following four months (September to December 1897) he wrote one of his strangest, most perplexing, haunting stories, "The Turn of the Screw." With a story called "Covering End"—a story version of a play he had written for Ellen Terry—James published the pair in a book with the suggestive title *The Two Magics* 1898).

Both stories center on old houses, both concern themselves with struggles of possession and dispossession, and in each one a different "magic" is operative. Covering End is a magnificent old English country house whose legal owner, Clement Yule, has had to mortgage it, so that it is completely in the possession of the unscrupulous Mr. Prodmore. Yule meanwhile has taken up radical politics and shown no interest in Covering End—indeed has never seen it prior to the action (one day) of the story. Briefly, Prodmore wants Yule to give up his radical politics, stand as a Conservative in a safe seat, and marry his daughter, Cora; in return he will cancel all the debts on Covering End and restore the house to Yule. On the day of the story he has come to close the deal, and Yule is coming to see him at Covering End. But the action is complicated, as far as Prodmore is concerned, by the unanticipated and uninvited presence of a remarkable American woman, Mrs. Gracedew. She, it turns out, is an absolute Anglophile who has made a study of old English country houses and knows more about Covering End than the owner,

the old servant, and indeed anybody actually connected with the place. She wins the struggle for possession of the house and, in the event, also wins Yule. Her name sufficiently indicates the kind of "magic" James associates with her—she is a force for regeneration and renewal, effectively reanimating both the house and its owner, bringing new life—and salvation and "grace"—to both. James was to revert to this theme in *The Golden Bowl* (1904), though in an infinitely more ambiguous manner. One statement of Yule's concerning Covering End will lead us into the companion tale. As he walks around the old house of his ancestors for the first time, he says: "I don't know what's the matter—but there *is* more here than meets the eye. . . . I miss the old presences. I feel the old absences. I hear the old voices. I see the old ghosts. "The Turn of the Screw" hinges precisely on someone who, in another ancient house, sees the old ghosts.

Briefly, the story is as follows. A young governess, as her first job, is taken on by a handsome man in Harley Street who wants her to go down to his country house, Bly, and look after his nephew and niece, the only condition being that she must never trouble him about them. She goes to Bly and finds the children, Miles and Flora, enchantingly beautiful, angelic, adorable. One odd note is struck when she learns that Miles has been expelled from his school with no reason given. But to her eyes he is all "love," and the pair of them are figures of absolute innocence. Then the governess sees ghosts, first a man and then a woman. She describes these apparitions to Mrs. Grose, the old housekeeper who has been there for years, and Mrs. Grose immediately recognizes them as being the figures of Quint—one of the master's ex-servants—and Miss Jessel—the former governess. Both of these characters are by this time dead. It transpires that Quint and Miss Jessel indulged in a very dissolute life together, and it is quite possible that they corrupted the children, since they had complete control over them. In any case, the governess is convinced that, as evil spirits, they are coming back to take "possession" of the children, to infect them and draw them into damnation. So she sees her struggle as an attempt to "fence about and absolutely save" the children. To this end she is not only possessive and protective; she tries in different ways, all indirect, to bring the children to the point of confession concerning their contact and dark collusion with Quint and Miss Jessel.

This is where the trouble starts, because it becomes a possibility that the governess—who admits to her "infernal imagination," her "obsession," her susceptibility to impressions, her capacity to be "easily carried away"—is imposing some kind of perverse sexual fantasy on the children. Certainly Flora rebels against her on a crucial occasion when the governess "sees" Miss Jessel, and the child turns accusingly on the governess: "I don't know what you mean. I see nobody. I see nothing. I never *have*. I think you're cruel. I don't like you." Shortly after this, Flora becomes dangerously ill with fever, and Mrs. Grose takes her away to London. Alone with Miles, the governess now struggles to save *his* soul, trying to get him to confess to what he had done at school, what really is going on under his innocent appearance. In the climactic final scene, Quint appears at the window and the governess clutches Miles, trying to prevent him from looking in that direction. He is aware of some kind of fearful presence, and there follows an entirely ambiguous exchange. He asks, "It's *he*?" She quickly asks, "Whom do you mean by 'he'?" Miles replies, "Peter Quint—you devil!" The problem here is: To whom is that "you devil" addressed—Quint, or the governess? The governess feels triumphant and says: "What does he matter now, my own? . . . *I* have you, but he has lost you forever!" But even as she holds him he is dying, and so to the final, memorable sentence: "We were alone with the quiet day, and his little heart, dispossessed, had stopped." Was he saved or suffocated, finally succumbing to a powerful evil force reaching from beyond the grave, or unable to withstand the tyrannical power of the relentless insinuations of the obsessed governess? Has she been guilty, in her own words, of "the obtrusion of the idea of grossness and guilt on a small helpless creature"? And, as she realizes, "If *he* were innocent, what then on earth was *I*?" Who "possesses" Miles at the end? Quint? The governess? We cannot say. All that is sure is that the little boy's heart is itself "dispossessed," and the ambiguities and ironies that emanate from that perfectly placed word preclude any possible single, definitive reading of this tale and the final struggle.

Critics have been quick to pounce on the governess, noting that she has obviously fallen in love with the Harley Street uncle and dreams of doing something "heroic" to please him; that she is self-confessedly anxious, excessively imaginative, and obsessive; and that she is both sexually repressed and overly possessive when it comes to the children (near

the end Miles asks her, very gently, to "let me alone"). If the children are not "angels," they are "fiends" (she was brought up in a vicarage, and so all is dramatized into salvation and damnation). Such a figure, the argument goes, would be very liable to hysterical hallucinations, and in fact it is she who effectively "haunts" the children, even to death.

There is much in the story to sustain this reading, but it leaves problems. The governess does describe Quint and Miss Jessel without ever having met them. Miles *was* expelled for something at least fairly serious (in an English public school it could easily, of course, have been for homosexuality). And when Flora is in her fever of hatred concerning the governess, Mrs. Grose admits that her language is "really shocking," so she has picked up a foul vocabulary somewhere.

We must add to this considerations of the form of the story. It is narrated by a friend of the first narrator, and this obviously honorable man has only good things to say about the governess, whom he knew in later life when she was accounted a respected and cherished governess. What he then offers is a manuscript of her own account of what happened, and in that account she speaks of "the duty of resistance to extravagant fancies." So there is much support for her honesty and reliability. But of course the question cannot and need not be settled. The whole atmosphere of the house, brilliantly evoked in all its varying moods, does somehow contain a sense of evil, of a bad past, of unsavory secrets; so perhaps the governess can fairly say, with Clement Yule: "I feel the old absences. I hear the old voices. I see the old ghosts." And somehow, through various agents perhaps, a bad magic is at work, has been at work.

Whether the governess saves the children, as Mrs. Gracedew saves Covering End, is debatable, even dubious; though whether she is responsible for in some way corrupting them with her sick imagination is also debatable and, I would say, dubious. What is certain is that, at the end, Flora is very sick and Miles is dead. This struggle for the possession of human souls has ended only in a fatal "dispossession." And so the story will continue to haunt its readers endlessly—while who knows what personal ghosts James may have been exorcising when he wrote it?

In June 1898 Henry James moved into Lamb House, in Rye. It was there that he was to remain for the rest of his life, apart from some travel, and it was there that he continued his explorations into the problematical depths and intermixings of those "two magics"—the benevolent power of regeneration, the malignant power of destruction—that so wonderfully, so worryingly, make up so much human motivation. The third magic is the art with which he conducted those explorations as he moved into his final phase.

XXII

"I've been in London for 3 weeks—came back here on the 20th; and feel the old reviving ache of desire to get back to work. Yes, I yearn for that—the divine unrest again touches me." Thus James in his notebook on January 22, 1899. "Here" was of course Lamb House, and there, for the next fifteen years or so, the "divine unrest" resulted in some of his greatest works. Not that he stayed uninterruptedly down at Rye. Although he took an active interest in local matters and involved himself a good deal in the provincial life there, he found that he experienced a new kind of loneliness and sense of deprivation; in a word, he missed London, particularly in the winter. So he moved between Rye and London (where he had a series of rooms or apartments) for a decade, finding the former place ideal for work and the latter, as always, indispensable for stimulation, distraction, and "impressions." It was, it seems, a satisfactory arrangement, and between 1902 and 1904 he produced his last three masterpieces—an extraordinary burst of creative energy. His one major interruption to that life was a visit he made to America in 1904, after an interval of some twenty years. It was, this time, a visit related not to family obligations but rather to "the idea of *seeing* American life again and tasting the American air." To his friend Howells he wrote, "I feel my going not only as a lively desire but as a supreme necessity." He was there for ten months, not only revisiting familiar places but venturing into the South and out as far as California. In many ways it was a triumphant return, but much of America he found to be, like Washington, "a spacious vacancy," and he later recorded his negative feelings and apprehensions about the present and future of his native country in perhaps his most remarkable travel book, *The American Scene* (1907). He was to spend one more year in America after the death of his brother, William, in 1910, and then he was back to Lamb House, with the attendant

fears of the sense of "immobilisation, incarceration" that he intermittently felt there. But there was still London: "Dear old London and its ways and works, its walks and conversations, define themselves as a Prodigious Cure," he wrote.

But the final years were painful. "The evening of life is difficult," he wrote and although at times he could turn, in imagination, back to "the warm and coloured past and away from the big black avenue that gapes in front of us," his life during this period is a series of steps down that black avenue in the protracted and inexorably deepening twilight of his declining years. Of course, on one level the period of 1900 to 1916 is the time of his triumph, with recognition coming, if not in the form of palpable royalties (the minute returns on his collected New York edition made him ill), then of the respect in which he came to be held by many of the most important writers of the time, the deference accorded him by a whole range of the most intelligent men and women of his day, and national honors. During this period he met, with varying degrees of pleasure, such writers as Joseph Conrad, H. G. Wells, Ford Madox Hueffer (later Ford), Stephen Crane, and Edith Wharton (with whom he had one of his most interesting friendships). Socially his contacts ranged from Prime Minister Asquith to Winston Churchill and Virginia Woolf. Among American writers he encountered figures as apparently distant in time as Mark Twain and Ezra Pound. When we remember that in his youth James knew Emerson and Flaubert, we realize what an amazing period of literary richness and innovation he lived through and contributed to.

But, of course, it is also the period of sickness and, finally, death. One by one, and with increasing rapidity, the lights were going out in the room "of the dusky p.m. of our common existence." James's own health began to let him down—gout, shingles, bad teeth, what was obviously a nervous breakdown (he insisted it was a stomach condition), and a period of intense depression ("I have really been down into hell"). He had one stroke and then another (on this occasion claiming to have heard a voice exclaim, "So here it is at last, the distinguished thing!"), and then there followed a long period preceding his death when his richly furnished imagination and memory cut adrift and he no longer knew where he was, or, indeed, who he was. At times, Napoleonic fantasies swarmed upon him, and he even signed dictated letters with the name of that emperor who had for so long occupied a unique place in his mind. James had staked out his empire in words, vast continents of them, over which he reigned as absolute master. No one knows how many compensations go into the thrust that makes an artist create ("the rarest works pop out of the dusk of the inscrutable, the untracked," he himself noted); but James's deathbed hallucinatory fusing of his own identity with that of Napoleon suggests the existence of a profound "imperial" urge in him that enabled him to go on writing, in absolute solitude, for so long and with such authority. He died on February 28, 1916.

This period of the deaths of relatives and friends culminated in World War I—"a nightmare from which there is no waking save by sleep." He felt himself to be living under "the funeral spell of our murdered civilization." (It was the war that made him apply for British citizenship, which he acquired on July 28, 1915.) And what he saw as dying was not only all the young men and the social structures of European civilization; language itself, as he understood it, would possibly never recover. It is worth quoting from a remarkable article published in the *Times* (London) on 21 March 1915 and unearthed by Leon Edel. James wrote:

The war has used up words; they have weakened, they have deteriorated like motor car tires; they have like millions of other things, been more overstrained and knocked about and voided of the happy semblance during the last six months than in all the long ages before, and we are now confronted with a depreciation of all our terms, or, otherwise speaking, with a loss of expression through increase of limpness, that may well make us wonder what ghosts will be left to walk.

However one reacts to this dire diagnosis, James was right in one thing: after World War I, literature, perhaps language, could never be the same again.

During the war James often visited the wounded in hospitals, talking to the men much as Walt Whitman had done during the Civil War. James himself made the comparison and it was in his late years that he came to love Whitman's work, which, as a youth, he had priggishly dismissed. This change is probably symptomatic of an important feature of the aging James, his avowed homoeroticism (which is not to say that, as far as is known, he was ever a practicing homosexual). Evidence has emerged in recent years of James's intense and manifestly physical (if not actively sexual) feelings for a Norwegian

sculptor, Hendrik Andersen. This relationship faded as James realized the limitations of Andersen's talent, and he warned Andersen explicitly that he was showing signs of megalomania. However, two other relationships seem to have allowed him to express those feelings that at last, and perhaps only in the comparative safety of old age, he allowed to surface. These were with Jocelyn Persse and Hugh Walpole. Passion of a kind he now certainly did feel, and Leon Edel is perhaps correct in suggesting that in allowing himself to love and tell his love, James came to reassess the supreme value he ascribed to the act of renunciation in much of his previous work. So, in the three major fictions of this period—written, amazingly, in about four years—there is a detectable sense of regret at the life not fully lived (in *The Ambassadors*), a feeling that life without love is no life at all (in *The Wings of the Dove*), and finally a recognition that, despite the many flaws and duplicities in human relationships, marriage can work and produce children who actually stay alive (in *The Golden Bowl*). There is, of course, more to these novels than this, but love and renunciation certainly come under intense scrutiny—and, arguably, revaluation—during this period. Perhaps even more remarkable is the ruthless analysis of the destructive potentialities of egoism and the terrible death-in-life that can result from the refusal of passional participation in life. This can be found in many of the novels and stories; for example, in "The Beast in the Jungle," in which a Jamesian figure has to confront "the sounded void of his life." If, as seems likely, this story was in part an act of self-examination, then it is a very remarkable and courageous one.

But a central paradox in James's life—a desire to have experience without involvement—remains to the end. Curiosity is curbed by reticence; decorum is punctured by inquisitiveness. He hated "indelicacy" above all things, but could be sedulous in his attempt to discover details about this or that scandal. As the testimony of more than one friend reveals, he yearned to know the full horrors of life but could scarcely bear to hear them named. In a letter referring to a visit to the house where George Sand had lived with her lovers, James refers to it as the place "where they pigged so thrillingly together." The uniquely Jamesian collocation of words is of course extremely amusing; at the same time it is characteristic in the absolute duality of response that it reveals. A part of James obviously experienced nausea and dread at the idea of people "honeying and making love/over the nasty sty," in the words of Yeats. Another part of him found the whole mystery surrounding the most intimate of human contacts "thrilling." In another man, the results could have been merely an unhealthy prurience. And perhaps James did suffer from an insufficiency of physical experience. (R. D. Laing's comment that "the unembodied self engages in nothing directly . . . the unembodied self becomes hyper-conscious" might be relevant here.) But there is no legislating for art, no prescribing for the artist, and James's curious combination of empathy and detachment enabled him to achieve miracles of insight into the nuanced and elusive procedures of consciousness as it attempts to cope with the mystifications and conflicts inherent in civilized living.

XXIII

THE first novel that James wrote after his move to Rye was *The Awkward Age* (1899), and interestingly—though not perhaps surprisingly—it stresses the perverse, corrupting atmosphere of London society and the blessings of a rural retreat. It is a book that hinges on two kinds of innocence—that irresistible, ambiguous state in James—as represented by two different young girls who are, precisely, at "the awkward age"—no longer children, not yet women (the state of sexual limbo is clearly intended). Nanda is like a somewhat older Maisie, though the "oppressive" social fogs, the adult "malaria" in which she lives and through which she moves is a more suffocating and sordid medium than Maisie's world. She is a girl who has been too carelessly "initiated," who "knows everything" (that ironic recurring phrase in James), and yet whose "precious freshness of feeling" seems uncorrupted by the squalid ethos to which her eyes are so candidly, so clearly, open. Yet she is rejected by the fashionable world in the character of Vanderbank (whom she loves). He feels that she has been too long steeped in a poisonous atmosphere to which, it must be stressed, he has largely contributed. The other girl, Aggie, is brought up in a state of total ignorance. She "isn't exposed to anything"; she has been kept from coming "downstairs" by her socially scrupulous mother, the duchess. Her eyes are blinkered and averted from any telltale evidence of the adult world. She reads history "that leaves the horrors out"; she is sedulously preserved from all possibly polluting contacts.

She is brought up in a garden of innocence, apart from the contaminated society in which she is subsequently to live; whereas from the start Nanda (who *has* come "downstairs"—i.e., into adult society) recognizes that "we're in society, aren't we, and that's our horizon," and she faces the fact by not feigning a sly ignorance but accepting things as they are for what they are. Hence her "crude young clearness," a clearness that is not "muddied" by what it sees and learns.

When Aggie does finally come downstairs and out into society, it is "with a bound—into the arena." Even before her honeymoon is over, she is engaging in adulterous sexual games of tooth and claw with a predatory vigor and immorality that justify James's strong animal imagery. So much for the traditional innocent. Nanda moves in the opposite direction: the more she sees and knows, the more society conspires to exclude and abandon her. There is a real pathos in the manner in which her fate starts to take on a definite shape toward the end of the book, until she finally returns "upstairs": her "punishment" for having "unlearned surprise" and for not practicing a false ingenuousness. However, she is not left to suffocate upstairs. When Vanderbank finally abandons her, Mr. Longdon comes to her rescue and invites her to come away with him to his rural paradise, though he imposes one rather stern condition: "You understand clearly, I take it, that this time it's never again to leave me—or to *be* left."

He is indeed offering a retreat: a total retreat from social life, from its battles and nightmares, but also from its possible richness and fulfillments. Nanda, however, is well schooled in renunciation. Early in the book she seems lucidly aware of her doom, and she says of marriage: "I shall be one of the people who don't. I shall be at the end . . . one of those who haven't." Henry James, in the form of Mr. Longdon, enters his own novel to rescue Nanda, as though, recognizing the value of her attitude toward life and the pathos of her predicament, he could not bear to see her so foolishly undervalued and so callously marooned. But he was to think again about renunciation and retreats.

His next novel was to be the most enigmatic he ever wrote. Indeed Edmund Wilson suggested that if we could really understand *The Sacred Fount* (1901), we would have gotten to the heart of Henry James's secret—if indeed one wants to think of a great artist having a secret rather than being aware of endless ambiguities. The novel centers on a weekend social gathering at a house in the country, Newmarch; and the first-person narrator is a solitary figure who is in some ways an outsider in the house, and who ends by fleeing from it, as if from society itself. This figure is unnamed, undescribed, more of a consciousness than a participant. What we make of this book depends on how we regard the activity of this consciousness while it is in the house, endlessly trying to work out the real relationships between the various visitors (again the problem is quite obviously, if implicitly, the matter of sexual and passional relationships). He has been variously regarded as an intolerable busybody, a sterile figure of chilling prurience, a victim of insane delusions and vanities, a veritable death's head in the house of life. On the other hand, he has also been taken to embody the whole artistic instinct, and his activities have been seen as a parable of the way the artist elicits aesthetic order out of human chaos. He has been seen as both the curse and conscience of society, and perhaps no one of these readings need necessarily exclude all the others.

James may well have been peering and probing into what his activity really was as an observer/writer. The theory that the narrator tries to apply to the tangled and concealed relationships at Newmarch is one to which James, to some extent, also subscribed. It is based on the idea of one person nourishing himself on another's life energy (a kind of vampirism), so that what one gains in vitality another may be losing. (This secret replenishing source is the "sacred fount" of the title, which also alludes to the sacred springs of the Italian goddess Egeria, who nourished King Numa; he is mentioned in the book.) The narrator notes that one lady, Grace Brissenden, seems to have grown suddenly much younger, while her husband seems to be unrecognizably old and tired; noticing also that a usually stupid man named Gilbert Long seems to be manifesting unusual wit and flair, he begins to look for some depleted victim who must be "paying" for this improvement. His speculations and searchings are sometimes dismissed as being unhealthy and intrusive, sometimes challenged and denied. Having decided that the fourth member of the algebraic pattern is one Mrs. Server, he builds his whole "palace of thought" around this surmise. In this at least he is obsessive, monomaniacal; it is clearly suggested that other pairings, groupings, relations are possible.

Quite early in the book the narrator willingly concedes:

These things—the way other people could feel about each other, the power not one's self, in the given instance, that made for passion—were of course at best the mystery of mysteries; still, there were cases in which fancy, sounding the depths or the shallows, could at least drop the lead.

(ch. 2)

Comic, pathetic, deranged, pathological, sympathetic—however the characters, or we, choose to regard the narrator, we should recognize that whether he is right or wrong (he could, after all, be correct), his attempt to find patterns in the shifting relationships around him, his efforts to sound the depths of that "power not one's self . . . that made for passion," are only another version of what James, like most great novelists, was doing himself. If this is madness, then it is, in James's own phrase, "the madness of art."

XXIV

"FRANKLY, quite the best, 'all round,' of my productions" was James's own assessment of *The Ambassadors*, written in about ten months in 1900. It centers on a man, very much of James's age and disposition, who is sent to Europe to retrieve a young man, Chad, from what his excessively moralistic mother, Mrs. Newsome, regards as inevitable corruption in Europe. But the man, Lambert Strether, has an epiphany, or a "crisis" of vision, in Paris and breaks out to another young man with these central words:

"Live all you can; it's a mistake not to. It doesn't so much matter what you do in particular so long as you have your life. If you haven't had that, what *have* you had? I'm too old—too old at any rate for what I see. What one loses one loses; make no mistake about that. . . . I'm a case of reaction against the mistake. Do what you like so long as you don't make it. For it *was* a mistake. Live, Live!"

Mistake is a key recurring word, and the question of the nature of Strether's mistake, and whether he can yet make any reparation, constitutes the central interest, and drama, of the novel. A crucial problem, or endless ambiguity, is of course: What exactly *is* it to live? So that you *have* your life? On such central questions the book, through Strether, ponders with extraordinary subtlety and delicacy. It is in *The Ambassadors* that James, for the first time, makes the consciousness of the onlooker figure the central focus of a major novel. Discussing his initial conception of Strether, James wrote: "He would have issued, our rueful worthy, from the very heart of New England," and "he had come to Paris in some state of mind which was literally undergoing, as a result of new and unexpected assaults and infusions, a change from hour to hour." It is a central Jamesian theme: a person confronting new facts with an old vision, or set of values, or system of belief, and experiencing a convulsion of values because the old vision will not adequately account for the newly perceived facts.

The book, then, is to be about an approved moral scheme challenged by confusing vivid facts, and the consequent attempt to find a new, adequate, scheme, a more inclusive vision that can contain the new range of facts even if it loses its old approval. The drama is to be "the drama of discrimination." How excessively narrow and life-denying is the New England conscience? What is fine and what is fraudulent in the rich aggregation of life's possibilities that Paris represents? The book is, as James says, about a revolution of consciousness in Strether, a revolution that has nothing to do with any carnal temptations offered by Paris, but rather its power to stimulate the sensative and appreciative imagination, to feed the senses with rich and novel impressions.

There are a number of American "ambassadors" (note the plural title), and for the most part they refuse Europe, judging and condemning, never trying to appreciate. And yet they are also enthusiastic purchasers and collectors (in its way a power gesture—reducing Europe to a shop and treating it like a contemptuous patron). Strether is a notable nonpurchaser. Behind the ambassadors is Mrs. Newsome, who is also the employer of Strether. She is—the image is used—a moral "iceberg." From her, through other characters, emanates a steady, cold force of disapproval and self-righteous negation. She gets all her money from a vulgar business that, it is implied, won its power through corrupt means. The combination of unscrupulous commercial exploitation and moral self-congratulation is clearly established. Over against her is the ultimately pathetic figure of Madame de Vionnet, who incorporates the distilled essence of an old European civilization. She is Chad's mistress. Mrs. Newsome and all the other ambassadors try—they threaten financial punishment as well as moral disapproval—to force Strether to return to America. In not returning when they

return, Strether is refusing their attitude to life. He stands firm, stands by Madame de Vionnet, stands by the perceptible, as opposed to the purchasable, values of Europe.

The worst ambassador will turn out to be Chad. He is completely egotistical: as he claims, he has always had his own way. He is a "taker" supreme, for he takes and keeps and uses all the love and care Madame de Vionnet lavishes on him, with no true reciprocation. Because Chad has acquired a European veneer and to some extent been civilized by Madame de Vionnet, Strether is initially taken in by his improved appearance. But by the end he can perceive that Chad is really just another one of those Americans who have come to Europe to exploit its valuable things before returning to America and the profits of big business. Chad's intention to return to America is not announced but clearly inferred. By the end Strether is trying to work on Chad to keep him in Europe (a major ironic reversal, since earlier Chad has had to work on Strether to gain his permission to stay longer in Europe), and he feels it necessary to utter a strong prospective indictment: "You'll be a brute, you know—you'll be guilty of the last infamy—if you ever forsake her." Chad glibly says that he will never tire of her, but "he spoke of being 'tired' of her almost as he might have spoken of being tired of roast mutton for dinner." A rank selfishness of mere appetite is hinted at here. And even while Strether is showing him how vile it would be to abandon Madame de Vionnet, Chad suddenly switches the conversation to advertising. "It really does the thing, you know"—the "thing" being to make money. He is still oblivious to intrinsic values. What is for Madame de Vionnet a real and lasting love is for him a passing amusement to be indulged in before going into business.

But she has a sort of wisdom that the egotistical American ambassadors could never attain, as when she says:

"What I hate is myself—when I think that one has to take so much to be happy, out of the lives of others, and that one isn't happy even then. . . . The wretched self is always there, always making one somehow a fresh anxiety. What it comes to is that it's not, that it's never, any happiness at all, to *take*. The only safe thing is to give."

(ch. 33)

She has given, and, we feel, she alone of the characters will achieve the dignity and stature of real suffering. But only Strether can truly appreciate her for what she is. And he too attempts to transcend "the wretched self" by a refusal to take anything that the world seems to offer, including two possible and very secure and comfortable marriages. For in the Jamesian world, those who consult and pander to the self are capable of cruel obliquities of vision and a ruthless insensitivity of conduct. Really living is a subtler affair than that. Strether *does* "have his life," in the form of accumulated treasures of consciousness and capacious generosities of vision. With his acquired subtlety of vision and refined ethical sense Strether by the end approaches very close to the Jamesian view of the world. This leaves one interesting question: Why does Strether, at the end, go back to America?

Madame de Vionnet's question is very relevant here. She asks him: "Where *is* your home moreover now—what has become of it?" The "unhoming" of Strether is important. It is not to be simply a matter of changing sides; it is getting beyond sides altogether, and the geographical equivalent of this is his refusal to seek around for a comfortable corner for himself in Europe. To show that Strether's vision has passed beyond all the demands of "the wretched self," it is important that he must not get any material loot or swag for himself (as, for instance, even his friend Maria Gostrey has her little museum of sharp acquisitions). He must be above all collecting, all purchasing, all possessing. His gain must be all of the imagination, even if there does seem to be something excessively ascetic in this attitude; what he *has* acquired are gems of appreciation, understanding, and a range of sympathy that transcends any fixed moral schemes. Thus we have our last glimpse of Strether looking, perhaps, not unlike James himself, alone, "unhomed" in a profound sense, somehow out of life, but full of a priceless vision.

XXV

JAMES had a young cousin, Minny Temple, a brilliant, life-hungry girl who died tragically young, as mentioned earlier. She became the very image of a generous but doomed consciousness, which James was to explore and dramatize in different ways. He wrote of her in his *Notes of a Son and Brother* (1914):

She was absolutely afraid of nothing she might come to by living with enough sincerity and enough wonder. . . . Life claimed her and used and beset her—made her range in her groping, her naturally immature and unlighted way from end to end of the scale. . . . None the less she did in fact cling to consciousness; death, at the last, was dreadful to her; she would have given anything to live—and the image of this, which was long to remain with me, appeared so of the essence of tragedy that I was in the far-off aftertime to seek to lay the ghost by wrapping it . . . in the beauty and dignity of art.

(ch. 13)

This he most beautifully did in *The Wings of the Dove*, which he wrote immediately after *The Ambassadors* (though it was published one year before that novel, in 1902).

Minny Temple is transformed into Milly Theale (note the identity of initials), who is a young American princess, "an angel with a thumping bank account," indeed—"a dove." But she is mortally ill when she comes over to Europe, though she is desperately eager to "live." She enters the novel only with book III, and thereafter she hardly acts but is rather acted upon. The novel in fact starts with another lady, the English girl Kate Croy, who indeed initiates much of the action—and she is one of the very great studies of a woman in English fiction. The first sentence unostentatiously points to some of the key aspects of the novel. "She waited, Kate Croy, for her father to come in, but he kept her unconscionably. . . ." "Waiting" is one of the problems of the book. Kate, for instance, is secretly engaged to a penniless journalist, Merton Densher, but as she herself has no money, they cannot get married. And they have no place to go. So they must "wait." The other problem is: Exactly what is "conscionable" or "unconscionable"? Milly has "boundless freedom" and is indeed first seen high in the Alps, climbing a path that "led somewhere, yet apparently quite into space"—she can indeed spread her wings and fly where she will. She is associated with large rooms, ample houses, and a superb elevated Italian palazzo in Venice, where she eventually dies.

Kate, however, seems condemned to cramped and mean settings: her father's squalid rooms in Chirk Street, her sister's no less squalid house—in neither of which is she wanted. She is accepted at the massively splendid house Lancaster Gate, home of Aunt Maud. But—and here is Kate's problem—Aunt Maud is a veritable "lioness," an "eagle" with predatory talons all exposed. She is "a complex and subtle Britannia," sitting imperiously among her ostentatiously material possessions: "she *was* London, *was* life—the roar of the siege and the thick of the fray." And she is determined that Kate marry not the impoverished Densher but the rich Lord Mark. Kate is a complex girl in an impossible position. She recognizes that "material things spoke to her" and is not out of this world, as the more ethereal Milly is. At the same time she is loyal to Densher and *does* commit herself to him. "I engage myself to you forever," she announces. But they are without a place. They meet in art galleries, in parks, even on the underground railway, public places of passage hardly constituted to offer lovers privacy. So Kate plots, in the subtlest way. She becomes a friend of Milly's—a "sincere" friend—and realizes that she is going to die. She also realizes that Milly, who has never really been properly loved or known love, is falling in love with Merton Densher. So she subtly suggests to Densher that they continue to conceal their engagement and that he marry Milly and thus soon inherit her fortune. "Since she's to die, I'm to marry her?" he asks. "To marry her," Kate replies. "So that when her death has taken place I shall in the natural course have money?" "You'll in the natural course have money," Kate concludes. "We shall in the natural course be free." The plot is not so purely Machiavellian as it may sound. Kate "sincerely" wants Milly to be happy for the short time she has left, but things go wrong when Lord Mark, in a spirit of revenge (he has been rejected by Milly), reveals to her the secret engagement of Kate and Densher. It is then we gather, in a famous statement, that "She [Milly] has turned her face to the wall." She does in fact leave her money to Densher, but something has happened to him; he now cannot touch it and will marry Kate only on that condition.

"I'll marry you, mind you, in an hour."
"As we were?"
"As we were."
But she turned to the door, and her headshake was now the end. "We shall never be again as we were!"

(ch. 38)

So the novel famously concludes. They have lost their love and their future. Milly has escaped into the great space of death. They are left alone, back "in the same box. Their box, their great common anxiety, what was it, in this grim breathing-space, but the practical question of life?" It might be stressed that the problems of place and space, direction and "position," "journey" and "flight," "abyss" and "laby-rinth" and "maze" are prominent throughout. The various rooms and houses and galleries through which Milly and the others pass do add up both to a kind of social atlas and a whole social, psychological, and moral geography, until the late great scene in the stormy Venice of winter—"It was a Venice all of evil that had broken out for them alike"—when Densher is turned away from Milly's palazzo and realizes that his "lie" and deception have been exposed. The final sense of desolation and loss is intense.

The problem of the lie is central to the book. No one knew better than James that society is maintained and structured on varying degrees of fiction, fabrication, suppression, misrepresentation—a whole scale of collusion and duplicity. Yet, particularly in connection with human relationships, the lie can be ruinous. The notion of lying (and "playing the game" of society) is there from the start when Kate meets her father, a man with some disgrace in his past, and realizes "there was no truth in him." In Venice, Densher, increasingly frustrated that he is having to enact Kate's plot while she still won't go to bed with him, says: "I'll tell any lie you want . . . if you'll only come to me." And go she does. But there comes a point when he can tell no more lies nor deny his love for Kate. Kate sees it differently. Milly, she says, "never wanted the truth. . . . She wanted *you*. . . . You might have lied to her from pity." It is plausible but specious. Densher has realized that there comes a point when the lying has to stop, recognizing, like various other characters in fiction (Mark Twain's Huck Finn, Joseph Conrad's Razumov) that, finally, you can't live a lie. As he says to Kate after Milly's death, "we've played our dreadful game, and we've lost." He leaves the letter announcing Milly's bequest to him unopened, signifying a renunciation of the money. Kate *has* her sincerities and her truths; she *has* been faithful to her love for Densher. But she cannot escape the "box"—of materiality and, perhaps unavoidably, of mendacity—in which she has to live. Milly, freed from the start from all material worries and restrictions, has to die. Densher is left with, perhaps, a new conscience, a memory, and the prospect of an endless solitude.

XXVI

In his last great novel, *The Golden Bowl* (1904), James concentrates on two married couples almost to the exclusion of anyone else (there are very few, and minor, other characters). The book starts with two licit relationships; these shift into illicit or unnatural relationships; then there is a "rearrangement" and a return to two legitimate relationships—though, of course, by the end the characters have all changed and are in very different situations of knowledge and power. They can never be again as they were. But—and here we do have something new in James—the two marriages *have* survived, as indeed has the one child produced by the unions. James was originally going to call the novel "The Marriages," and it is a key word, and indeed key relationship, in the book ("I want to *be* married. It's—well, it's the condition," says one of the ladies prior to actually entering that state). On what terms and in what state the marriages survive is very much a matter for debate, and indeed there has been the widest possible disagreement about this since the novel appeared. Either the characters are preserved—some say redeemed—by the maintaining of the forms, or, it has been argued, the forms are maintained at the expense of the characters.

Put very simply, the story concerns a rich American girl, Maggie Verver (some have seen a regenerative hint in the "Ver"—Latin for "spring," with more than a hint of English "verve" or "vigor"), who is married to an Italian prince, Amerigo. A former friend (lover?) of the Prince, Charlotte Stant, turns up, initially to buy them a wedding present. The Prince and Charlotte, it need hardly be said, are poor, so even if they had wanted to get married in the past it was financially out of the question—not a new situation in James. Maggie's father, Adam, joins them and—really for the sake of symmetry, or, as he thinks, for the sake of his daughter's marriage—he marries Charlotte (he is, incidentally, revealed to be sexually impotent: they can have no child). But it doesn't work out quite as it should. Maggie and Adam become closer and closer, a slightly unnatural father-daughter intimacy that is only intensified when Maggie has a child (he is a "link between a mamma and a grandpapa," but not between a wife and her husband). The Prince and Charlotte are left to themselves, indeed rather thrust at each other, and eventually they become lovers. In a way they set up a new kind of contract, since the actual marriages seem to have gone off in somewhat perverse, or at least unfulfilling, directions. "We must act in concert, Heaven knows . . . *they* do!" says Charlotte, and their passion, as demonstrated in their kiss, seems to give the "contract" a kind of validity.

"Their lips sought their lips, their pressure their response and their response their pressure; with a violence that had sighed itself to the longest and deepest of stillnesses they passionately sealed their pledge." Maggie and Adam are said, indeed, to have "imposed . . . *their* forms" on Charlotte and the Prince, so no one person can be said to be guilty of a breach of the forms. "Forms" is another key and shifting word in the book: people can "cheat each other with forms." Maggie thinks of "the funny form of our life," as well she might, and there are dangerous moments of loss of "confidence" in forms. In fact, the new illicit symmetry is arrived at by a kind of group collusion and complicity.

But it doesn't end there. Maggie, who for the first part of the story seems all innocence and passive ignorance—not to say regressive childlikeness—becomes aware of the situation and begins to take action—quiet, quiet action—to bring about the restoration of the legitimate symmetries. Quiet, apart from the breaking of the bowl, about which a word. The "golden bowl" is the wedding present Charlotte buys for the Prince and Maggie. From the start, when they are buying it in the shop, there is much question as to whether it has a crack or a flaw or a split in it, concealed by the golden veneer. There is even a question as to whether it is real crystal or glass, and the further consideration that if you cannot see the crack, does it matter? ("But if it's something you can't find out, isn't it as good as if it were nothing?") And does real crystal split?

> "On lines and by laws of its own."
> "You mean if there's a weak place?"
> (ch. 6)

In all this talk there is, of course, a clear double entendre; all that is said about the bowl is indirectly a questioning about marriage, or the two marriages in question, with their golden surfaces and concealed flaws and cracks and lines of potential breakage. It is not a symbol for us; it is one for the characters, who use it as a way of talking about what would otherwise be unmentionable. When Maggie deliberately smashes the bowl, shattering it on the floor, it is clearly a way of saying that she now knows exactly what the relationship between Charlotte and the Prince is, and that their marriages are all wrong and need to be reconstituted. She immediately starts to pick up the fragments (significantly, she can pick up only two at a time, adumbrating the final separation of the—effectively—*ménage à quatre* into proper couples). She announces her aspiration quite clearly: she wants "the golden bowl—as it *was* to have been. . . . The bowl with all happiness in it. The bowl without the crack." Her state of knowledge and power enables her to manipulate the Prince and Charlotte, who increasingly do not know what Maggie knows and therefore are increasingly her potential victims (and her father's). At the end, Maggie and the Prince are back together again, while Adam is taking Charlotte back to America (always a less than desirable fate in James's fiction). Maggie maintains that she can bear anything and do anything "for love"; on one memorable occasion she repeats the phrase three times. And perhaps she does inaugurate a needed "new system," as she intends. The marriages hold. But questions remain.

We are reminded at the start of the "machinery" and the "power"—"the power of the rich peoples" —and Adam Verver for one (who is the source of the money, and thus the power and the machinery) is a very ambiguous figure. Adam is, of course, a favorite American name to suggest innocence, but James may well be offering a telling reappraisal of that oft-celebrated American innocence. Adam may be very ignorant or he may be very knowing. He is inscrutable (based, of course, on the American robber barons), and he has all the power. His plan to build what he calls "American City" back in America and fill it with all the precious objects he has acquired in Europe may have benevolent intentions, but it reveals a more dubious aspect of his collecting instinct, namely, "his application of the same measure of value to such different pieces of property as old Persian carpets, say, and new human acquisitions."

Maggie is even more ambiguous. She can be described, metaphorically, variously as a doll, a slaughtered innocent, a resourceful settler, a divine savior. There is, as it were, an excess of metaphor around her, putting her and her actions beyond any certain judgment. But one thing is clear; however passive she may be at the start, at the end she controls the action and realizes that the others are at her mercy: "There was no limit to her conceived design of not letting them escape." There is a note of something like glee in her realization that "they're paralysed, they're paralysed." "I make them do what I like," she all but boasts to Mrs. Assingham, and it is this inquiring onlooker who decides that "it will be Maggie herself who will mete out" all the punishments. By the end she sees the Prince as being in

"prison" and "caged," and once again it is with a thrill that she notes how he is "straitened and tied" by her superior manipulation of the situation. Maggie visits and comforts him in prison—the image is sustained—but then we have learned that her "revenge" is to be a subtle thing: it will consist of "compassionate patronage." Admittedly, all this is done "for love," the motives and operations of which are fathomless enough. And there are those—many— who see Adam and Maggie as almost allegorical saviors and restorers of the crumbling relics and structures of European civilization. But that, to me, is too happy and facile a reading. There is too much awareness of the ambiguity of those forms that may be as "ghastly" as they are "necessary" (not to say "funny"), too much awareness that the new "rearrangement" rests on a felicitous "deceit" and a potentially ruthless power. This is not to say that James totally despaired of social structure and the maintaining form of marriage, nor of love, for there *is* love as well as passion (and revenge) in the book. He simply knew what they could cost to be maintained, just as he knew what the Prince tells Maggie almost at the end of the book: "Everything's terrible, *cara*— in the heart of man."

XXVII

JAMES finally published his reactions to America, after his return visit of 1904, in *The American Scene* in 1907. It is an altogether remarkable book, and it remains, as Edmund Wilson said, "one of the best books about modern America." It is interesting to note James's procedure in writing the book. Although he visited many friends and attended social functions, he cuts out almost entirely all reference to any dialogue with companions. This way he appears in the book as a "lone visionary," sending out his "lasso of observation," standing on the "verandahs of contemplation," a solitary "restless analyst" such as might have appeared in his own novels. His intercourse is with streets, buildings, vistas, and landscapes, all of which seem to address him with their murmured apologies, their aggressive boasts, or their pathetic pleas, which he in turn answers. The most important dialogue is between Henry James and the American scene. One of the things that strike him time and again is the seeming emptiness of America, an America visibly and audibly more crowded and busily pursuing "pecuniary gain" more avidly than ever before. "Void" and "vacancy" are perhaps the most frequent words in the book.

Before one judges this as a brand of patrician snobbery, it is instructive to try to discern the grounds for James's reaction to this new America of "florid creations waiting, a little bewilderingly, for their justification, waiting . . . for identity itself to come to them." He found a growing antipathy to recognizable distinctions and was struck by the strange homogenization of the emerging population—the way, for instance, an immigrant would lose the distinguishing qualities of his native identity without acquiring any new coloration from his new neighbors: "we surely fail to observe that the property washed out of the new subject begins to tint with its pink or azure his fellow-soakers in the terrible tank." This "terrible tank" is of course James's rephrasing of Walt Whitman's more optimistic image of America as a great "melting pot," and whether James is in Washington society or the New York Jewish ghetto he is everywhere struck by the power of the "terrible tank" to dissolve distinctions, producing mass without meaning. The fluid emptiness that James recoiled from was at bottom a lack of forms communicating any sense of values, any deeply felt meaning: "it is as if the syllables were too numerous to make a legible word." For James, the skyscraper (and New York City struck him as like a "broken haircomb turned up") was the negation of significant form: "*They*, ranged in this terrible recent erection, were going to bring in money." This, for James, was the featureless architecture of greed.

But as well as what Americans were putting up, it was what they were tearing down that distressed him: "What was taking place was a perpetual repudiation of the past." Seeking out the sites and buildings of his childhood, he found them all changed or obliterated. James's shock is not simply a conservative's preference for the old familiar forms. What worried him was that the new America did not seem to care enough for any of its new structures to wish to preserve them: "the very sign of its energy is that it doesn't believe in itself"—a profound observation. It was America's "inability to convince . . . that she is serious about any form whatever, or about anything but that perpetual passionate pecuniary purpose which plays with all forms, which derides and devours them" that depressed James. The basic reasons he gives for the ugliness of the new America were "the so complete abolition of *forms*" and the

production of new forms that were so "plastic," so "perpetually provisional."

Of course, there are many fond evocations in the book, and one can sense James's underlying love for the country. But where he detected ominous signs he recorded them. His observation, for instance, of "the way in which sane Society and pestilent City, in the United States, successfully cohabit" is followed by a "sense of a society dancing, all consciously, on the thin crust of a volcano"—a cluster of insights that have only gained in relevance. Or again, confronted by some young American girls on a train, and the "innocently immodest ventilation of their puerile privacies," James has occasion to reconsider the position of the "innocent" American girl who had figured so richly in his fiction. He now imagines her making a silent plea to his "inward ear": "Haven't I, however, as it is, been too abandoned and too *much* betrayed? Isn't it too late, and am I not, don't you think, practically lost?" Or again, the "haunting consciousness" of the Negro, which "is the prison of the Southern spirit," is elicited with extraordinary sensitivity.

If the scattered American syllables couldn't quite make up a word to say to James, James could listen and then try to formulate the appropriate speech. In his presence the American scene thus became, paradoxically, articulate in a unique way. And at the end James permits himself some very direct speaking to his compatriots:

> You touch the great lonely land . . . only to plant upon it some ugliness about which, never dreaming of the grace of apology or contrition, you then proceed to brag with a cynicism all your own. . . . Is the germ of anything finely human, of anything agreeably or successfully social, supposedly planted in conditions of such endless stretching and such boundless spreading as shall appear finally to minister but to the triumph of the superficial and the apotheosis of the raw.
>
> (ch. 14)

James speaks here with the license of an outraged or saddened close relation, but the deep relevance of his dialogue with the American scene is still as urgent as ever.

James's shorter fictions of this period pale somewhat beside his great novels, but they reveal, even crudely, just how bleak his late fictional world could be. Society is often less a matter for humor or idealization and more a jungle of "greedy wants, timid ideas and fishy passions" (as he wrote in *The*

Ivory Tower). "Art is our flounderings shown," says one of his characters; although the late short stories deal in the main with "small, smothered intensely private things," they often throw a thin, clear beam on human confusion and wounding.

Many late Jamesian protagonists opt for renunciation because the cruel stridency and harsh, untempered friction of modern life are simply too much for them; or, more subtly, it is intimated that their renunciation may be traced to a dangerous, solipsistic overestimation of the self. So it is in the great story "The Beast in the Jungle," mentioned above, in which James explored to the full the subtle horror that could lie in this commitment to a life of renunciation. John Marcher, convinced that a special destiny awaits him, is too aridly self-enwrapped to recognize the chance for a full human relationship that May Bartram presents to him. She loves him. He loves himself too much to perceive the fact, or indeed even to see "the other" at all. She dies, and he feels no special grief. Then he sees someone in the graveyard, someone genuinely grief-stricken. The terrible truth starts to dawn: "no passion had ever touched him, for this was what passion meant; he had survived and maundered and pined, but where had been *his* deep ravage?" The moment of truth—it is the leap of the beast—is blindingly simple and terrible: "he had been the man of his time, *the* man, to whom nothing on earth was to have happened." This story, above all, is the one to remember when reading the great novels of this period.

James left two unfinished novels at his death. *The Ivory Tower* was started in 1913 but abandoned when the advent of war made it seem impossible to continue. Nevertheless, there is enough of it to allow us to see its continuity with the previous novels. Again it concerns passions and possessions, exploitations and renunciations, and, above all, money. The book opens with scenes concerning two dying millionaires. One, rather obviously named Betterman, is lingering on to see a distant relative, a young American innocent (Graham Fielder) who has been brought up in Europe and is returning to see him. It is made clear that Betterman, having satisfied himself that Fielder is absolutely untainted by the business world, having had no contact with the "awful game of grab" that seems to dominate American society, will leave him all his money. It is made equally clear that Fielder will find a way of relinquishing that money to a mercenary and predatory "friend." Dominant is a sense of an America obsessed with the "money-passion," the spirit of "ferocious acquisition." Society is "all senseless sound and expensive futility." It is at once still "innocent" and "unspeakably corrupt"; it is, in the words of James's notes, "the dreadful American money-world." Graham Fielder is to gain a vivid impression of "so many of the black and merciless things that are behind the great possessions." And since he is, rather like Strether, by nature "an out and out non-producer" and "non-accumulator," he will find a way of dissociating himself from his inheritance—getting out of the game (the symbol of the ivory tower is used in this context). He will be another Jamesian observer-appreciator. "He really enjoys getting so detached from it as to be able to have it before him for observation and wonder as he does." Among other things, the novel would have been a quite savage indictment of an America in which James felt a man of his kind of consciousness and sensibility could no longer live, a rejection of his own American "heritage."

The Sense of the Past seems to have been started in 1900 and taken up again briefly in 1906, and it was the novel James was working on when he died. In an odd way it projects a latent horror of the European past, as *The Ivory Tower* reveals a very manifest horror of the American present. The novel has a perfect and familiar subject for James. It concerns yet another of his "passionate pilgrims" for whom Europe is an experience, ambivalent to the point of annihilation. Ralph Pendrel is a young American who has never visited Europe but has somehow developed a highly refined and appreciative "sense of the past." He inherits a Georgian house from a remote relative in England and goes over to take possession. So animated are his susceptibilities and expectations that when he finally does enter the house he "disappears into the Past." He walks into a family situation of 1820 in which he is the expected American relation. At first the adventure is exhilarating. He finds he can successfully play and "improvise" the role expected of him, and he enjoys this seemingly actual immersion in a past he had hitherto only dreamed of. But the adventure starts to turn dark: moments of rapture give place to sudden chills and fears as he realizes that his 1820 relatives are beginning to find him somehow strange. As he wrote in his notes for the novel, James intended to stress

the slow growth on the part of the others of their fear of Ralph, even in the midst of their making much of him, as abnormal, as uncanny, as not *like* those they know of their own kind etc., etc.; and his fear just *of* theirs, with his double consciousness, alas, his being *almost* as right as possible for the "period," and yet so intimately and secretly wrong.

Through maneuvers of plot it was intended that he should finally be saved: "saved from all the horror of the growing fear of *not* being saved, of being lost, of being *in* in the past to stay, heart-breakingly to stay and never know his own original precious Present again." His dread—James intended to emphasize it—was of his being "never saved, never rescued, never restored again, by the termination of his adventure and his experience, to his native temporal conditions, which he yearns for with an unutterable yearning. He has come to have his actual ones, the benighted, the dreadful ones, in horror." However James would have resolved the novel, we can note a deep ambivalence that is perhaps symptomatic of his whole work (and life?). Ralph longs for the past, but when it threatens to imprison him, he yearns for "his own original precious Present," "his native temporal conditions." And yet what the present, what those conditions were like, James had portrayed in *The Ivory Tower.* Truly, where, actually and imaginatively, was one to live? And where, anymore, for someone like James, could there be a "home"? Clearly, one answer could only be—in writing.

James's other major work during his last period was what we have come to call "The Autobiographies," which consists of *A Small Boy and Others* (1913), *Notes of a Son and Brother* (1914), and *The Middle Years*, left uncompleted at his death. Although initially intended to be an account of his family, in particular of his brother, William, James confines himself almost entirely to the history and development of his own consciousness—its confusions and gratitudes, its bewilderments and wonders, its experience of the strangeness of life, and its intimations of the grace of art. Here, in quotations from various chapters in *A Small Boy and Others*, are some of the ways in which he refers to his relationship to the past.

Remembrance steals on me. . . . I woo it all back. . . . I turn round again to where I left myself gasping. . . . Let me hurry, however, to catch again that thread. . . . I scarce know why, nor do I much, I confess, distinguish occasions —but I see what I see. . . . I lose myself under the whole pressure of the spring of memory. . . . I meet another acute unguarded reminiscence.

James apologizes for leaving "the straighter line of my narrative." He "gleans" memories from things, "not minding that later dates are involved." He is totally indifferent to external chronology, the unilinear history of physical events. He has a rarely subtle sense of the mysterious commerce between present consciousness and those past states of consciousness preserved in the intermittent brilliances of memory. He uses words like "surrendering" and "succumbing" to the past; thus "I live back of a sudden—for I insist on just yielding to it." It is rather as if James's mind was wandering through the museum of his own memory, responding to sudden gleams and forgotten echoes, alternatively wooing and yielding to the still-vibrant impressions stored in the recesses of his consciousness. The human consciousness, as long as it is still conscious, performs a great act of salvage and rescue simply by remembering, recalling the stored-up images. The human consciousness saves what life merely wastes.

James loves to evoke what he calls the "tiny particles of history." That is why he will spend pages recapturing a room, someone's clothes, a facial appearance, a sudden tremor of delight or fear; as he beautifully puts it, "the passion, that may reside in a single pulse of time." But his subject was centrally himself. So, in his "Autobiographies," James is turning his consciousness inside out, trying to recapture what went into it to turn it into the consciousness of a novelist, an artist. He writes in a twilight mood, but far from despair, a mood in which meditation, comprehension, and compassion are at one:

The beauty of the main truth as to any remembered matter looked at in due detachment, or in other words through the haze of time, is that comprehension has then become one with criticism, compassion, as it may really be called, one with musing vision, and the whole company of the anciently restless, with their elations and mistakes, their sincerities and fallacies and vanities and triumphs, embalmed for us in the mild essence of their collective submission to fate.

(*A Small Boy and Others*, ch. 9)

The past was imponderable dust, and the present (World War I) was dark indeed; and James does not at all slight or mitigate the darkness, death, and ruin in life. But over against it he continues to hold up "the wonder of 'consciousness.'" It is, in the deepest sense, an "act of life."

James sent a copy of *Notes of a Son and Brother* to his friend Henry Adams, whose response seems to have been one of extreme pessimism and melancholy. We do not have his letter to James, but we have James's marvelous reply, which includes these words, incomparably poised in their tone:

I have your melancholy outpouring of the 7th, and I know not how better to acknowledge it than by the full recognition of its unmitigated blackness. *Of course* we are lone survivors, of course the past that was our lives is at the bottom of the abyss—if the abyss *has* any bottom; of course, too, there's no use talking unless one particularly *wants* to. But the purpose, almost, of my printed divagations was to show that one *can,* strange to say, still want to—or at least can behave as if one did. Behold me therefore so behaving—and apparently capable of continuing to do so. I still find my consciousness interesting—under *cultivation* of the interest. . . . *Why* mine yields an interest I don't know that I can tell you, but I don't challenge or quarrel with it—I encourage it with a ghastly grin. You see I still, in the presence of life (or of what you deny to be such,) have reactions—as many as possible—and the book I sent you is a proof of them. It's, I suppose, because I am that queer monster, the artist, an obstinate finality, an inexhaustible sensibility. Hence the reactions—appearances, memories, many things, go on playing upon it with consequences that I note and "enjoy" (grim word!) noting. It all takes doing—and I *do.* I believe I shall do yet again—it is still an act of life.

(21 March 1914)

It would be hard to find a more eloquent justification or apologia for that queer monster, that obstinate finality—the artist.

XXVIII

In conclusion here are two quotations that speak for themselves, for James, for the whole mystery and indispensability of James's unique kind of attitude and art. The first is from a letter to Grace Norton, that most difficult kind of letter to write, one of consolation to someone recently bereaved. James speaks of the "gift of life" to one mourning in the shadow of death:

Life is the most valuable thing we know anything about and it is therefore presumptively a great mistake to surrender it while there is any yet left in the cup. In other words consciousness is an illimitable power, and though at times it may seem to be all consciousness of misery, yet in the way it propagates itself from wave to wave, so that we never cease to feel, and though at moments we appear to,

try to, pray to, there is something that holds one in one's place, makes it a standpoint in the universe which it is probably good not to forsake.

(28 July 1883)

And the other quotation is from his notebooks of 1905, after he has visited the family cemetery:

Everything was there, everything *came;* the recognition, stillness, the strangeness, the pity and the sanctity and the terror, the breath-catching passion, and the divine relief of tears. William's inspired transcript, on the exquisite little Florentine urn of Alice's ashes, William's divine gift to us, and to *her,* of the Dantean lines—

Dopo lungo exilio e martirio
Viene a questa pace—

took me so at the throat by its penetrating *rightness,* that it was as if one sank down on one's knees in a kind of anguish of gratitude before something for which one had waited with a long, deep *ache.* But why do I write of the all unutterable and the all abysmal? Why does my pen not drop from my hand on approaching the infinite pity and tragedy of all the past? It does, poor helpless pen, with what it meets of the ineffable, what it meets of the cold Medusa-face of life, of all the life *lived,* on every side. *Basta, basta!*

(29 March 1905)

SELECTED BIBLIOGRAPHY

I. BIBLIOGRAPHY. L. Phillips, *A Bibliography of the Writings of Henry James* (Boston, 1906; new ed., New York, 1930); L. Edel and D. H. Laurence, *A Bibliography of Henry James* (London, 1957; rev. ed., 1961), a masterly work; S. Kappeler, *Reading and Writing in Henry James* (London, 1980).

II. COLLECTED WORKS. *Collected Novels and Tales,* 14 vols. (London, 1883); *The Novels and Tales,* 26 vols. (New York, 1907–1909), with special prefaces and textual revisions for vols. 1–24; *Uniform Edition of the Tales,* 14 vols. (London, 1915–1919); P. Lubbock, ed., *Novels and Stories,* 35 vols. (London, 1921–1923); *The American Novels and Stories* (New York, 1947); A. Wade, ed., *The Scenic Art* (New Brunswick, N. J., 1948), collected papers on the theater; L. Edel, ed., *The Complete Plays* (London, 1949); *The Ghostly Tales* (New Brunswick, N. J., 1949); L. Edel, ed., *The American Essays* (New York, 1956); A. Mordell, ed., *Literary Reviews and Essays* (New York, 1957); L. Edel, ed., *The Complete Tales,* 12 vols. (London, 1962–1964); *The Novels* (London, 1967–   ), with intro. by L. Edel.

III. SELECTED WORKS. *Fourteen Stories* (London, 1947); M. Swan, ed., *Ten Short Stories* (London, 1948); A.

Hopkins, ed., *Selected Stories* (London, 1957), the World's Classics ed.; M. Shapira, ed., *Selected Literary Criticism* (London, 1963).

IV. SEPARATE WORKS. *A Passionate Pilgrim and Other Tales* (Boston, 1875), stories; *Transatlantic Sketches* (Boston, 1875), travel; *Roderick Hudson* (Boston, 1876 [1875]), novel; *The American* (Boston, 1877), novel; *French Poets and Novelists* (London, 1878), criticism; *Watch and Ward* (Boston, 1878), novel; *The Europeans*, 2 vols. (London, 1878), novel; *Daisy Miller*, 2 vols. (New York–London, 1879 [1878]), stories; *The Madonna of the Future and Other Tales*, 2 vols. (London, 1879), stories; *Confidence*, 2 vols. (London, 1879), novel; *Hawthorne* (London, 1879), criticism; *The Diary of a Man of Fifty and A Bundle of Letters* (New York, 1880), stories; *Washington Square*, 2 vols. (New York–London, 1881 [1880]), novel; *The Portrait of a Lady*, 3 vols. (London, 1881), novel; *The Siege of London* (Boston, 1883), stories; *Portraits of Places* (London, 1883), travel; *The Art of Fiction* (London, 1884), criticism, repr. in M. Roberts, ed., *The Art of Fiction and Other Essays* (New York, 1948); *Tales of Three Cities* (Boston–London, 1884), stories; *A Little Tour in France* (Boston, 1885 [1884]), travel; *Stories Revived*, 3 vols. (London, 1885), stories; *The Bostonians*, 3 vols. (London, 1886), novel; *The Princess Casamassima*, 3 vols. (London, 1886), novel; *Partial Portraits* (London, 1888), criticism; *The Reverberator*, 2 vols. (London, 1888), novel; *The Aspern Papers*, 2 vols. (London, 1888), stories; *A London Life*, 2 vols. (London, 1889), stories; *The Tragic Muse*, 2 vols. (London, 1890), novel; *The Lesson of the Master* (New York–London, 1892), stories; *The Real Thing and Other Tales* (New York–London, 1893), stories; *Picture and Text* (New York, 1893), criticism; *The Private Life* (London, 1893), stories; *Essays in London and Elsewhere* (London, 1893), criticism; *Theatricals* (London, 1894), plays; *Theatricals; Second Series* (London, 1895), plays; *Terminations* (London, 1895), stories; *Embarrassments* (London, 1896), stories; *The Other House*, 2 vols. (London, 1896), novel; *The Spoils of Poynton* (London, 1897), novel; *What Maisie Knew* (London, 1897), novel; *In the Cage* (London, 1898), stories; *The Two Magics* (London, 1898); *The Awkward Age* (London, 1899), novel.

The Soft Side (London, 1900), stories; *The Sacred Fount* (New York–London, 1901), novel; *The Wings of the Dove*, 2 vols. (New York–London, 1902), novel; *The Better Sort* (London, 1903), stories; *The Ambassadors* (London, 1903), novel; *William Wetmore Story and His Friends*, 2 vols. (Edinburgh, 1903), biography; *The Golden Bowl*, 2 vols. (New York–London, 1904), novel; *The Question of Our Speech and The Lesson of Balzac* (Boston, 1905), criticism, two lectures; *English Hours* (London, 1905), travel; *The American Scene* (London, 1907), travel; *Views and Reviews* (Boston, 1908), criticism; "Julia Bride" (New York, 1909), story; *Italian Hours* (London, 1909), travel; *The Finer Grain* (New York–London, 1910), stories; *The Outcry* (London, 1911), novel; *A Small Boy and Others* (New York–London, 1913), autobiography; *Notes of a Son and Brother* (New York–London, 1914), autobiography; *Notes on Novelists* (London, 1914), criticism; *The Ivory Tower* (London, 1917), unfinished novel; *The Sense of the Past* (London, 1917), unfinished novel; *The Middle Years* (London, 1917), unfinished autobiography; "Gabrielle de Bergerac" (New York, 1918), story; *Within the Rim and Other Essays* (London, 1919), essays; *Travelling Companions* (New York, 1919), stories; *Notes and Reviews* (Cambridge, Mass., 1921), criticism; R. P. Blackmur, ed., *The Art of the Novel: Critical Prefaces* (New York–London, 1934); F. O. Matthiessen and K. B. Murdock, eds., *The Notebooks of Henry James* (New York, 1947); *Eight Uncollected Tales* (New Brunswick, N. J., 1950), stories; J. L. Sweeney, ed., *The Painter's Eye* (London, 1956), essays; L. Edel and I. D. Lind, eds., *Parisian Sketches, 1875–76* (New York, 1957).

V. LETTERS. P. Lubbock, ed. and comp., *The Letters of Henry James*, 2 vols. (London, 1920); *Letters of Henry James to Walter Berry* (Paris, 1928); E. Robins, ed., *Theatre and Friendship: Some Henry James Letters* (London, 1932); L. Edel, ed., *Selected Letters* (London, 1956); L. Edel and G. N. Ray, eds., *Henry James and H. G. Wells: A Record of Their Friendship, Their Debate on the Art of Fiction, and Their Quarrel* (London, 1958), with intro. by eds.; *Switzerland in the Life and Work of Henry James* (Berne, 1966), includes hitherto unpublished letters of James to Mrs. Clara Benedict.

VI. BIOGRAPHICAL AND CRITICAL STUDIES. E. L. Cary, *The Novels of Henry James* (New York, 1905), the first critical book on James's work; F. M. Hueffer, *Henry James: A Critical Study* (London, 1913), interesting, hagiographical, and not always reliable; R. West, *Henry James* (London, 1916), a short, sharp, brilliant study; J. W. Beach, *The Method of Henry James* (New Haven, 1918), an excellent study of technique.

E. Pound, *Instigations* (New York, 1920), contains an essay on James; P. Lubbock, *The Craft of Fiction* (London, 1921), contains constant references to James; J. Conrad, *Notes on Life and Letters* (London, 1921), contains an appreciation of James; A. R. Ordage, *Readers and Writers* (London, 1922), contains an essay on James; T. Bosanquet, *Henry James at Work* (London, 1924), a portrait by James's secretary; Van Wyck Brooks, *The Pilgrimage of Henry James* (New York, 1925), a study of James as an expatriate novelist; H. L. Hughes, *Theory and Practice in Henry James* (Ann Arbor, Mich., 1925); P. Edgar, *Henry James: Man and Author* (London, 1927), a careful intro. to James's work; H. Read, *The Sense of Glory* (London, 1929), contains an essay on James.

C. P. Kelley, *Early Developments of Henry James* (Urbana, Ill., 1930); L. Edel, *Les Années dramatiques* (Paris, 1931), the only full account of James as a playwright; L. Edel, *The Prefaces of Henry James* (Paris, 1931); F. M. Ford, *Return to Yesterday* (London, 1931), the ch. "Rye Road" is about James; D. MacCarthy, *Portraits* (London,

1931), contains a portrait of James; C. H. Grattan, *The Three Jameses: A Family of Minds* (New York, 1932); E. Wharton, *A Backward Glance* (New York, 1934), Wharton's autobiography, contains many references to James; F. A. Swinnerton, *The Georgian Literary Scene* (London, 1935), contains an essay on James; R. B. Perry, *The Thought and Character of Henry James*, 2 vols. (Boston, 1935); E. M. Snell, *The Modern Fables of Henry James* (Cambridge, Mass., 1935); S. Spender, *The Destructive Element* (London, 1935), contains essays on James; E. Wilson, *The Triple Thinkers* (London, 1938), contains an essay on "The Ambiguity of Henry James."

F. O. Matthiessen, *Henry James: The Major Phase* (London, 1944), studies the symbolism of the later novels; S. N. Smith, *The Legend of the Master* (London, 1947), an anthology of reminiscences of James; F. W. Dupee, ed., *The Question of Henry James* (London, 1947), a very useful selection of essays by various hands; F. O. Matthiessen, *The James Family: A Group Biography* (London, 1948), a long book containing much new material; O. Andreas, *Henry James and the Expanding Horizon* (London, 1948); F. R. Leavis, *The Great Tradition* (London, 1949), contains an important study of James; E. Stevenson, *The Crooked Corridor: A Story of Henry James* (London, 1949).

C. Arnavon, *Les Lettres américaines devant la critique Française* (Paris, 1952); F. R. Leavis, *The Common Pursuit* (London, 1952), the first vol. of a 5-vol. definitive biography (see *The Conquest of London, The Middle Years, The Treacherous Years, The Master,* below); R. C. LeClair, *Young Henry James: 1843-1870* (New York, 1955); E. T. Bowden, *The Themes of Henry James* (London, 1956); Q. Anderson, *The American Henry James* (London, 1958); R. Chase, *The American Novel and Its Tradition* (London, 1958).

D. W. Jefferson, *Henry James* (London, 1960), Writers and Critics series; R. Marks, *James's Later Novels* (New York, 1960); W. R. Poirier, *The Comic Sense of Henry James: A Study of the Early Novels* (London, 1960); G. Willen, ed., *A Casebook of Henry James's "Turn of the Screw"* (New York, 1960); R. W. Stallman, *The House That Henry James Built* (London, 1961); O. Cargill, *The Novels of Henry James* (New York, 1962); D. Krook, *The Ordeal of Consciousness in Henry James* (Cambridge, 1962); L. Edel, *Henry James: The Conquest of London, 1870-83* (London, 1962), vol. II of the biography; L. Edel, *Henry James: The Middle Years, 1884-94* (London, 1963), vol. III of the biography; M. Geismar, *Henry James and His Cult* (London, 1964); L. Holland, *The Expense of Vision: Essays on the Craft of Henry James* (Princeton, N.J., 1964); D. W. Jefferson, *Henry James and the Modern Reader* (London, 1964); E. Stone, *The Battle and the Books: Some Aspects of Henry James* (Athens, Ohio, 1964); R. L. Gale, *Plots and Characters in the Novels of Henry James* (Hamden, Conn., 1965); N. Lebowitz, *The Imagination of Loving* (Detroit, 1965); M. Bell, ed., *Edith*

Wharton and Henry James: The Story of a Friendship (New York-London, 1965); S. G. Putt, *Henry James: A Reader's Guide* (Ithaca, N. Y.-London, 1966), repr. in paperback as *The Fiction of Henry James*; W. T. Stafford, *Perspectives on James's "The Portrait of a Lady"* (New York, 1967); J. A. Ward, *The Search for Form: Studies in the Structure of James's Fiction* (Chapel Hill, N. C., 1967); R. Gard, ed., *Henry James* (London, 1968), Critical Heritage series; T. Tanner, ed., *Henry James* (London, 1968), Modern Judgments series, an important selection of essays; E. D. Leyburn, *Strange Alloy: The Relation of Comedy and Tragedy* (Chapel Hill, N. C., 1968); H. Montgomery Hyde, *Henry James at Home* (London, 1969); L. Edel, *Henry James: The Treacherous Years* (London, 1969), vol. IV of the biography; J. Kraft, *The Early Tales of Henry James* (Carbondale, Ill., 1969).

P. Buitenhuis, *The Grasping Imagination: The American Writings of Henry James* (Toronto, 1970); C. T. Samuels, *The Ambiguity of Henry James* (Urbana, Ill., 1971) J. Goode, ed., *"Air of Reality": New Essays on Henry James* (London, 1972); P. M. Weinstein, *Henry James and the Requirements of the Imagination* (Cambridge, Mass., 1972); C. Maves, *Sensuous Pessimism: Italy in the Work of Henry James* (Bloomington, Ind., 1973); L. Edel, *Henry James: The Master, 1901-1916* (London, 1972), vol. V of the biography; H. T. Moore, *Henry James and His World* (New York-London, 1974), a pictorial biography; K. Graham, *Henry James—The Drama of Fulfilment: An Approach to the Novels* (London, 1975); H. T. McCarthy, *Henry James: The Creative Process* (London, 1975); W. Veeder, *Henry James—The Lessons of the Master: Popular Fiction and Personal Style in the Nineteenth Century* (Chicago, 1975); G. Leeming, ed., *Who's Who in Henry James* (London, 1976); M. Mackenzie, *Communities of Honour and Love in Henry James* (Cambridge, Mass., 1976); J. C. Rowe, *Henry James and Henry Adams: The Emergence of a Modern Consciousness* (Ithaca, N.Y., 1976); R. B. Yeazell, *Language and Knowledge in the Late Novels of Henry James* (Chicago, 1976); P. Brooks, *The Melodramatic Imagination: Balzac, Henry James, Melodrama and the Mode of Excess* (New Haven, Conn., 1976); R. L. Gale, ed., *The Fiction of Henry James: Plots and Characters* (London, 1977); S. Rimmon, *The Concept of Ambiguity: The Example of Henry James* (Chicago, 1977); E. A. Hovenec, *Henry James and Germany* (London, 1979); M. Bradbury, *The Later Novels of Henry James* (London, 1979); S. Donadio, *Henry James, Nietzsche and the Artistic Will* (New York, 1979); D. Gervais, *Henry James and Flaubert: A Study in Contrasts* (London, 1979); K. P. McColgan, *Henry James: A Reference Guide, 1917-1959* (London, 1979); D. Scura, ed., *Henry James: A Reference Guide, 1960-1974* (London, 1979); M. D. Springer, *The Rhetoric of Literary Character: Some Women of Henry James* (Chicago, 1979); Jean Strouse, *Alice James. A Biography* (Boston, 1980).

LIST OF SHORT STORIES AND NOVELLAS

(The title in italics refers to the volume in which the story appears. The title of the story used for original publication in a periodical is given first. If it was changed for publication in book form, the new title is given in parentheses.)

"The Abasement of the Northmores," *The Soft Side;* "Adina," *The Travelling Companions;* "The Altar of the Dead," *Terminations;* "The Aspern Papers," *The Aspern Papers;* "At Isella," *Travelling Companions;* "The Author of 'Beltraffio,'" *Stories Revived;* "The Beast in the Jungle," *The Better Sort;* "The Beldonald Holbein," *The Better Sort;* "The Bench of Desolation," *The Finer Grain;* "Benvolio," *The Madonna of the Future and Other Tales;* "The Birthplace," *The Better Sort;* "The Broken Wings," *The Better Sort;* "Brooksmith," *The Lesson of the Master;* "A Bundle of Letters," *The Diary of a Man of Fifty and A Bundle of Letters.*

"The Chaperon," *The Real Thing and Other Tales;* "Collaboration," *The Private Life;* "Cousin Maria" ("Mrs. Temperly" in *A London Life*); "Covering End," *The Two Magics;* "The Coxon Fund," *Terminations;* "Crapy Cornelia," *The Finer Grain;* "Crawford's Consistency," *Eight Uncollected Tales;* "Daisy Miller," *Daisy Miller;* "A Day of Days," *Stories Revived;* "The Death of the Lion," *Terminations;* "De Grey: A Romance," *Travelling Companions;* "The Diary of a Man of Fifty," *The Diary of a Man of Fifty and A Bundle of Letters;* "Eugene Pickering," *A Passionate Pilgrim;* "Europe," *The Soft Side.*

"The Faces" ("The Two Faces" in *The Better Sort*); "The Figure in the Carpet," *Embarrassments;* "Flickerbridge," *The Better Sort;* "Fordham Castle," *Novels and Tales* (New York ed., vol. 16); "Four Meetings," *Daisy Miller;* "The Friends of the Friends" ("The Way It Came" in *Embarrassments*); "Gabrielle de Bergerac," *Gabrielle de Bergerac;* "Georgina's Reasons," *Stories Revived;* "The Ghostly Rental," *Ghostly Tales;* "The Given Case," *The Soft Side;* "Glasses," *Embarrassments;* "The Great Condition," *The Soft Side;* "The Great Good Place," *The Soft Side;* "Greville Fane," *The Real Thing and Other Tales.*

"The Impressions of a Cousin," *The Tales of Three Cities;* "In the Cage," *In the Cage;* "An International Episode," *Daisy Miller;* "Jersey Villas" ("Sir Dominick Ferrand" in *The Real Thing and Other Tales*); "The Jolly Corner," *Novels and Tales* (New York ed., vol. 17); "John Delavoy," *The Soft Side;* "Julia Bride," *Julia Bride;* "Lady Barbarina," *Tales of Three Cities;* "A Landscape Painter," *Stories Revived;* "The Last of the Valerii," *A Passionate Pilgrim and Other Tales;* "The Lesson of the Master," *The Lesson of the Master;* "The Liar," *A London Life;* "A Light Man," *Stories Revived;* "A London Life," *A London Life;* "Longstaff's Marriage," *The Madonna of the Future and Other Tales;* "Lord Beaupre," *The Private Life;* "Louisa Pallant," *The Aspern Papers.*

"Madame de Mauves," *A Passionate Pilgrim and Other Tales;* "The Madonna of the Future," *The Madonna of the Future and Other Tales;* "The Marriages," *The Lesson of the Master;* "Master Eustace," *Stories Revived;* "Maud-Evelyn," *The Soft Side;* "The Middle Years," *Terminations;* "Miss Gunton of Poughkeepsie," *The Soft Side;* "The Modern Warning," *The Aspern Papers;* "Mora Montravers," *The Finer Grain;* "A Most Extraordinary Case," *Stories Revived;* "Mrs. Medwin," *The Better Sort;* "Mrs. Temperley," *A London Life;* "My Friend Bingham," *Eight Uncollected Tales;* "A New England Winter," *Tales of Three Cities;* "The Next Time," *Embarrassments;* "Nona Vincent," *The Real Thing and Other Tales.*

"Osborne's Revenge," *Eight Uncollected Tales;* "Owen Wingrave," *The Private Life;* "Pandora," *Stories Revived;* "The Papers," *The Better Sort;* "A Passionate Pilgrim," *A Passionate Pilgrim and Other Tales;* "Paste," *The Soft Side;* "The Patagonia," *A London Life;* "The Path of Duty," *Stories Revived;* "The Pension Beaurepas," *Washington Square;* "The Point of View," *The Siege of London;* "Poor Richard," *Stories Revived;* "The Private Life," *The Private Life;* "A Problem," *Eight Uncollected Tales;* "Professor Fargo," *Travelling Companions;* "The Pupil," *The Lesson of the Master;* "The Real Right Thing," *The Soft Side;* "The Romance of Certain Old Clothes," *A Passionate Pilgrim and Other Tales.*

"Sir Dominick Ferrand," *The Real Thing and Other Tales;* "Sir Edmund Orme," *The Lesson of the Master;* "The Solution," *The Lesson of the Master;* "The Special Type," *The Better Sort;* "The Story of a Masterpiece," *Eight Uncollected Tales;* "The Story in It," *The Better Sort;* "The Story of a Year," *American Novels and Stories;* "The Sweetheart of M. Brisieux," *The Travelling Companions;* "Theodolinde," *Stories Revived;* "The Third Person," *The Soft Side;* "The Tone of Time," *The Better Sort;* "Travelling Companions," *Travelling Companions;* "The Tree of Knowledge," *The Soft Side;* "The Turn of the Screw," *The Two Magics;* "Two Countries" ("The Modern Warning" in *The Aspern Papers*); "The Two Faces," *The Better Sort;* "The Two Magics," *The Two Magics;* "The Velvet Glove," *The Finer Grain;* "The Visits," *The Private Life;* "The Way It Came," *Embarrassments;* "The Wheel of Time," *The Private Life.*

ROBERT BRIDGES
(1844-1930)

John Sparrow

I

ROBERT BRIDGES can claim one title to preeminence among English poets: he is surely the author of the largest body of entirely beautiful poetry in the language.

What do we mean when we call a poem beautiful? First, and most obviously, we may have in mind its formal beauty; we may mean that its sounds and rhythms, its audible colors and patterns, satisfy our ear and that its language and diction give us pleasure by the way in which they express and enforce its meaning. Or we may have in mind the theme and substance of the poem, and mean that we find beauty in the images and ideas that compose it and the thoughts and feelings that it expresses and evokes—leaving unanswered, at least for the moment, the question what is meant by the "beauty" of a thought, an emotion, or an image.

Whatever the sense or faculty to which the beauty of a poem makes its appeal, if it is to be entirely beautiful there must be nothing in it—no cacophony, no harshness or infelicity of expression, no disharmony in the theme or imagery or in the tone and spirit of the composition—that mars the complex total effect.

To produce a work that is entirely beautiful is far from being the highest aim of the creative writer, but it is one that is rarely achieved. The novelist, the epic poet, the tragedian work on too large a scale, and to their kinds of work the concept really has no application; a sonnet by Shakespeare may be entirely beautiful, but it makes no sense to apply the phrase to *Hamlet*. Entire beauty can hardly be achieved by a writer whose aim is to convey or reproduce the effect of an extended segment of human experience, actual or imagined; for an entirely beautiful poem we turn rather to the lyrical writer, and to such short pieces as we find in the Greek Anthology or the Elizabethan song books—and even in those collections the entirely beautiful poem is rare enough. It is a still rarer thing for a writer (though less so for a painter or a composer of music) to be so enamored of beauty and so desirous of creating it that it pervades and characterizes the whole body of his work. Prose writers, after all, have many other things to do; even among poets there are few of whom it can be said that their work is consistently beautiful. Pindar, perhaps, was such a poet, and so were Spenser and Keats, and it was to "Intellectual Beauty" that Shelley "dedicated" his powers; the list is not a long one, but in it Bridges undoubtedly has a place.

Bridges believed quite simply that the poet's task was to create beauty in the medium of words. "The Artist," he said, in a broadcast address on poetry, "and the Poet as such, is the man who is possessed by the idea of Beauty." It was his belief that the beauty of poetry (as of all art) lies primarily in the theme, the thing expressed, and only secondarily in the expression; and that beauty of theme is ultimately and essentially ethical, and it is to our moral sense that it appeals. Art is "non-moral," he declared,

only in so far as we take Morals to mean the conventional code of conduct recognised by the society to which we happen to belong. Art, it is true, has very little to do with that. But pure Ethics is man's moral beauty and can no more be dissociated from Art than any other kind of beauty, and, being man's highest beauty, it has the very first claim to recognition.[1]

---

[1]"It must be admitted," he says, a little further on, "that no strict line of distinction [between the ugly and the beautiful] can be drawn, and that the average man's conception of beauty is absurdly limited and conventional; also that as much admirable skill may be used in the expression of crime as of virtue and so on; the portrait of a man suffering from confluent small-pox might thus be a masterpiece." But to those who argue from this that all these things are equally beautiful, or can be made so by competent expression, his scornful answer was: "We live in a free country where everyone may think and say what he pleases."

It was to this doctrine—that art is the creation of beauty and that beauty can be explained only as a form of goodness—that Bridges dedicated his career as a creative artist, and the last and most self-revealing of his poems, *The Testament of Beauty* (1929), was devoted to the exposition of it. "Beauty," he said in one of his sonnets, is "the best of all we know," and to Christopher Marlowe's question, "What is Beauty then?" he answered, in his "loose Alexandrines,"

> Beauty is the highest of all those occult influences
> the quality of appearance that thru' the sense
> wakeneth spiritual emotion in the mind of man.

Nothing could well be further from the aims of most English poets than the creation of beauty in this sense; no room here for Donne the sensualist or Pope the satirist, for a man of the world like Byron or a scavenger like Swift. Poets for whom poetry is primarily a deliverance of self, or whose aim is to reproduce some aspect of the world around them, will outlaw nothing that comes within the range of their experience. "Beauty" is not a criterion that they apply, consciously or unconsciously, in editing their raw material; it is epiphenomenal—something that may come into being if they hit their mark. But a devotion to beauty in Bridges's sense cuts the poet off from an immense range of human experience; and this was a sacrifice that Bridges was very ready to make in the interests of his art.

Bridges differs from most poets of today also in his attitude toward his calling. For him, poetry was essentially an affair of making rather than expressing, an art rather than an outlet. The craft of writing was an exacting one, demanding a concentrated discipline, and he gave so much time and thought to questions of technique that superficial and unsympathetic readers are inclined to think of him as a mere craftsman—nothing more than a poetical Fabergé, intent on manufacturing, for the delight of his customers, well-cut or well-set jewels and toys of ingenious design. And indeed some of his poetical exercises may invite, though they do not justify, this opinion.

Bridges himself described, both in prose and in verse, his attitude toward the art of poetry. In his memoir of his schoolfellow Digby Mackworth Dolben, after telling of the "equal enthusiasm" for poetry that the two friends shared at Eton, and of the "mutual divergence" of their tastes, he continued:

Our instinctive attitudes towards poetry were very dissimilar, he regarded it from the emotional, I from the artistic side; and he was thus of a much intenser poetic temperament than I, for when he began to write poetry he would never have written on any subject that did not deeply move him, nor would he attend to poetry unless it expressed his own emotion; and I should say that he liked poetry on account of the power it had of exciting his valued emotions, and he may perhaps have recognised it as the language of faith. What had led me to poetry was the inexhaustible satisfaction of form, the magic of speech, lying as it seemed to me in the masterly control of the material; it was an art which I hoped to learn. An instinctive rightness was essential, but, given that, I did not suppose that the poet's emotions were in any way better than mine, nor mine than another's. . . . There is a point in art where these two ways merge and unite, but in apprenticehood they are opposite approaches.

(*Three Friends*, 1932)

The ways do meet, and much of Bridges's best poetry, as we shall see, is born of their union. His intense desire to achieve "a masterly control of the material" was not due only to his sense of "the fascination of what's difficult" in the art of expression, to his love of words for their own sake; it sprang also from his hieratic, almost sacramental, view of the function of poetry, his feeling that the vehicle of spiritual beauty must be worthy of its content. Both aspects of his creed are revealed in one of his best-known lyrics:

> I love all beauteous things,
>   I seek and adore them;
> God hath no better praise,
> And man in his hasty days
>   Is honoured for them.
>
> I too will something make
>   And joy in the making:
> Altho' to-morrow it seem
> Like the empty words of a dream
>   Remembered on waking.
>   (*SP*, IV. 1)[2]

Here the second stanza testifies to Bridges's "joy in the making"; the first reveals what I have called his hieratic view of the poet's function.

There is another characteristic that distinguishes

[2]*SP* stands for "Shorter Poems," *NP* for "New Poems," *LP* for "Later Poems," and *NV* for "New Verse." The references are to, and the texts are taken from, *Poetical Works* (London, 1953), the Oxford Standard Authors.

Bridges's verse from most modern poetry and may make it more difficult for present-day readers to appreciate—his free use of poetic diction, of archaic and "literary" forms and words. *Ye* and *thee; singest; looketh; bedight; beauteous; bower; wanhope; jocund; stell'd; orb'd in the eterne*—such words crop up on every page, and he regularly employs what he himself calls "properties": he is lavish, for instance, of personifications and invocations of "the Muse." This was not due to unthinking acceptance of an inherited poetic jargon; his use of archaic forms, for instance, had a strictly practical purpose: "The author would explain," he says in a note to *The Testament of Beauty*, "that the use of *eth* for the 3rd per. sing. of verbs is not an archaic fancy, but a practical advantage indispensable to him, not only for its syllabic lightness, but because by distinguishing verbs from the identical substantives, it sharpens the rhetoric and liberates the syntax."

Those who contend that poetry should always and only make use of the forms and vocabulary of common contemporary speech, and eschew "poetic" images and properties, have to reckon with the practice of Shakespeare and Shelley just as much as with that of Bridges; indeed there is hardly a serious poet in English who does not invite their attack. Bridges himself met this line of criticism in a paper on "Poetic Diction in English." He admitted that "the revolt against the old diction is a reaction which in its general attitude is rational" and in line with the reaction of the Lake Poets. He answered it by contrasting Milton's *Lycidas* and Shelley's *Adonais*, in which the poetic convention is seen at its most extreme, with Matthew Arnold's *Thyrsis*, in which the diction is Wordsworthian in its plainness and the poetic convention ("Alas for Corydon!" and so on) merely ornamental and not organic: of the three elegies, he says, it is *Thyrsis*, with its rational attitude and simple diction, "that lacks in passion, as if it were a handling of emotions rather than the compelling utterance of them"; in it "the sorrow and the friendship seem least profound," and "though it is agreeable reading, it leaves one cold at the end." How far this is actually due (as he suggests) to the rational, prosaic treatment and how far to other factors ("its fanciful argument and the poet's mentality") cannot, he admits, be demonstrated, and his answer to the rationalists in the matter of diction rests ultimately upon his assertion that "Since poetic language is essentially a rarity of expression of one sort or another it is unreasonable to forbid apt and desirable grammati-

cal forms"—and he might have included words and images—"merely because they are not read in the newspapers or heard at the dinner-table." The premise that "poetic language is essentially a rarity of expression" begs the question; the truth is, as he says later in his paper, that diction cannot be considered apart from what he calls "keeping," that is, "the harmonizing of the artistic medium," so that diction, image, and theme all assist each other. Any diction is good that is effective in the given case.

There are moments in Bridges when his poetic diction rings hollow:

> The making mind, that must untimely perish
> Amidst its work which time may not destroy,
> The beauteous forms which man shall love to cherish,
> The glorious songs that combat earth's annoy. . . .
> <div align="right">(<i>SP</i>, III. 13)</div>

There is no need to point out the faults in those four lines: "poetic" words have been called in to clothe banality of thought, and swollen phrases to sustain a halting meter.

Bridges is not often guilty of such lapses: where they occur, the diction is not itself at fault; its incongruity is the symptom of a deeper trouble, revealing the momentary lack of poetic inspiration, a failure of the power to fuse feeling and image in speech. For contrast, take another stanza:

> I will not let thee go.
> I hold thee by too many bands:
>   Thou sayest farewell, and lo!
>   I have thee by the hands,
> And will not let thee go.
> <div align="right">(<i>SP</i>, I. 7)</div>

Here, the archaic and "poetic" diction is the natural and genuine language of passion, and no unprejudiced critic would complain of it.

It is not only his meticulous craftsmanship and his conscious use of poetic diction that have led critics to overlook, or to underestimate, the emotional element in Bridges's work; their mistake is due also to something in the nature of the emotion itself, something that for want of a better word one may call its impersonality. Strictly, "impersonal emotion" is a meaningless pair of words, and the phrase might be taken to suggest an absence of real feeling; but that is not what I mean. Many of Bridges's poems express passionate love or joy or delight in the world around him; one cannot doubt that they were *felt*. But, reading them, while one is made aware of the emotion experienced, one is somehow unaware of the person who is experiencing it—which is very far from being the case when one reads Hopkins, or Yeats, or Donne, or almost any poet who has left a large body of passionate work. This impersonality in Bridges's work is not due to a deliberate abnegation of self or a conscious generalizing of emotion (if, indeed, those phrases have any real meaning); nor is it that his care for his craft has stifled or frozen the feeling that made him write. His most passionate poems —"Awake, my heart, to be loved," "I will not let thee go," "Since thou, O fondest and truest," for example—for all the art that went to the shaping of them, impress one as absolutely spontaneous. His "impersonality" is no more than the normality, the simplicity, the sanity of his nature. Though he has an easily recognizable style, and the whole body of his work carries the impress of a strong personality, his emotions are devoid of idiosyncrasy, even of individuality; in his love poems, though he is speaking for himself, he speaks also for every lover; his utterance has the transparency and, in a good sense, the tastelessness of pure water. *Fieri non potest ut idem sentiant* (as Hopkins more than once reminded his friend) *qui aquam et qui vinum bibunt,*[3] and one may well ask, at times, for a more strongly flavored or a more intoxicating draft—in the words of Edward Dowden, "some dominant note, some fine extravagance, even some splendid sins." But Bridges would not have been true to his poetic creed or to his own nature had he attempted to give us that.

II

BRIDGES was born on 23 October 1844 at Walmer, in Kent. His father's family were "substantial Kentish yeomen," and his mother was the daughter of a baronet in holy orders. In two long elegies—"Recollections of Solitude" and "The Summerhouse on the Mound"—the poet himself described the beauties of the home of his childhood, with its garden looking out upon the Channel; and he recalled in prose the tradition of a family "that seemed to the younger generation to have been unusually supplied with a dignified and long lived aristocracy of generals, baronets and divines, whose features were familiar

to me among the many miniatures, silhouettes and other little portraits, mementos of personal affection, that hung in my mother's rooms, and in their eighteenth century fashions, kindled our imaginations of a strange and remote world." His father died when he was barely ten years old, leaving his future well provided for. At Eton, where he was sent before his tenth birthday, he was happy and successful, making many friends and becoming captain of his house; at Oxford he rowed for his college, Corpus Christi, and took Honours in the Schools. Leaving the university, he spent two years (1867–1869) in foreign travel and, returning home, made his plans for life.

His was an unusual ambition: he wished to be a poet. More unusual still, he intended first to embark upon an active profession in order to equip himself for fulfilling his ultimate purpose: he resolved to practice medicine until he was forty and then to retire and devote himself to the writing of poetry. So, in 1869, Bridges entered himself at St. Bartholomew's, where he worked for five years (with intervals of foreign travel) as a medical student. After taking his M.B. in 1874 he held a series of appointments as a physician at several London hospitals, until in 1881 a serious illness forced him to abandon medical practice and, after a short spell abroad, he retired with his mother (now widowed a second time) to live in the country at the Manor House at Yattendon, in Berkshire.[4] Two years later, in 1884, he married Mary Monica, daughter of Alfred Waterhouse, R.A., a successful architect, and with her he shared a happy married life—he was fortunate also in his children—until the end of his days.

In 1907 Bridges moved to Chilswell, a house he had built for himself on Boar's Hill, near Oxford, and there he passed the remainder of a life that was devoid of outward incident. He was made poet laureate in 1913, and he received the Order of Merit on the publication of *The Testament of Beauty* in 1929, a few months before his death on 23 April 1930.

From this short sketch it will be seen that Bridges was able for nearly half a century to devote himself to practicing the art of poetry, while he lived the life of a cultured country gentleman, in a comfortable and happy home set in the pastoral landscape that he

---

[3]It cannot be that water-drinkers and wine-drinkers have the same sensations.

[4]She had married, as her second husband, the Reverend J. E. N. Molesworth, Vicar of Rochdale, in Lancashire, which thus became the poet's second home—a striking contrast, one may suppose, to his Kentish birthplace.

loved, and within easy reach of his Oxford friends. He was speaking for himself when he said:

> And country life I praise
> And lead, because I find
> The philosophic mind
> Can take no middle ways;
> She will not leave her love
> To mix with men, her art
> Is all to strive above
> The crowd, or stand apart.
> (*SP*, II. 8. 49–56)

Bridges never wavered from his choice to stand apart from the crowd and not to "strive above" it.

Nonetheless, his earlier life had not been entirely sheltered: he had traveled; his home had been for a time in the industrial north; he had worked for ten years in busy London hospitals. And his sensitive and emotional nature had had its share of grief; the death of his younger brother, Edward, in 1866, plunged him, he said in after years, "into deep sorrow at the time, and considerably altered the prospects of [his] life," and little more than a year later his cousin and school friend Digby Dolben was accidentally drowned when almost on the point of joining Bridges at the university. How deeply Bridges was shaken by this loss can be gathered from the sketch of Dolben's life that he wrote nearly half a century later. Plainly, his friendships in youth and early manhood were deeply tinged with emotion, and the happiness they brought him was not unalloyed. His dearest friend at Oxford was Gerard Manley Hopkins, and though the difference in their outlooks upon life did not lessen their mutual affection, it precluded perfect sympathy and necessitated a parting of their ways; Hopkins' allegiance to the Jesuit discipline prevented them from meeting except on rare occasions during the twenty years that preceded his early death in 1889. Nonetheless, the two friends kept up, with few breaks, a correspondence (of which Hopkins' side alone survives) that shows how devoted each was to the other and how deeply each was interested in and admired the other's poetry.

There are in Bridges's poems echoes of these personal sorrows, and they reveal here and there a vein of unsuspected melancholy. But that vein, if deep, was a thin one; his temperament was sanguine, circumstances allowed him a happy life, and—in his own words—"the best of his art" was "gay."

If he was favored by circumstances, he was also richly endowed by nature. Lovers of beauty—one thinks of Pater, of Socrates, of Matthew Arnold—have not always been beautiful themselves; but Bridges, in youth and in age, was, in the words of W. B. Yeats, "an image of mental and physical perfection."

"In presence," said his friend Henry Newbolt,

Bridges was one of the most remarkable figures of his time; there is no company in which he would not have been distinguished. He had great stature and fine proportions, a leonine head, deep eyes, expressive lips, and a full-toned voice, made more effective by a slight occasional hesitation in his speech. His extraordinary personal charm was, however, due to something deeper than these; it lay in the transparent sincerity with which every word and motion expressed the whole of his character, its greatness and its scarcely less memorable littlenesses . . . none would have wished these away; they were not the flaws but the "grotesque" ornaments of his character. Behind him there was always visible the strength of a towering and many sided nature, at once aristocratic and unconventional, virile and affectionate, fearlessly inquiring and profoundly religious.

(*My World as in My Time*, 1932)

The fineness of his instincts, it may be added, showed itself in the "properties" of his life, in the beauty of his handwriting, for instance, and the careless elegance of his dress.

Bridges was a natural aristocrat not only in physique; he was aloof and independent in his attitude of mind, an eclectic in philosophy, in religion, and in literature. *The Testament of Beauty*, with its swarm of illustrations drawn from art and archaeology, from the historians and the philosophers, reveals both the range and the independence of his questing intellect; he drew upon Plato and Aristotle indifferently, and if the poem is suffused with Christian feeling it is also, as he once said in conversation, "all against the clergy." Religious by temperament, he had been led at school, together with his friends Dolben and V. S. S. Coles, far along the High Anglican paths of the Oxford movement. He had even intended, it is said, when he came up to Oxford, to take holy orders. But a natural paganism soon asserted itself, and orthodoxy was not the leading characteristic of one who could write:

The Christian churches will not leave the old ruts. The Pope still hankers after temporal power, and to get it would crown Tiglath-Pileser in St. Peter's while our Protestant church still begins its morning devotions by singing of

"God swearing in his wrath that his people should not enter into his rest."

(*The Necessity of Poetry*, 1918)

In literature too Bridges was immune from the impact of authority: by date a Victorian, he was unmoved by the "movements" and uninfluenced by the "influences" of that age; echoes of his distaste for its leading poets—Tennyson, Browning, Matthew Arnold—make themselves heard in his correspondence with Gerard Manley Hopkins, and among his contemporaries the poets who most influenced him were two isolated figures—Hopkins himself and Canon Dixon. If one asks what earlier writers he looked upon as masters, the index to *The Spirit of Man* (1916), his wartime anthology, gives the key: the authors he draws upon far more freely than any others are Shakespeare, Milton, Shelley, and Keats.[5]

Bridges was not interested in "literature" or literary history; gossip about dead men of letters and scholarly studies of second-rate performers bored him, and he would not waste his time on what he found uncongenial. But he was passionately devoted (the cliché expresses a literal truth) to the art of poetry and intensely concerned about the secret springs of the delight it gave him. The problems that intrigued him were philosophical and technical: What is it in the work that appeals to our sense of beauty, and what is it in us that responds to the appeal?

The circumstances of his life at Yattendon and Chilswell enabled him to spend years in pondering these questions and pursuing the answers to them down to the remotest detail—the setting of words to music; the parts played by accent, by quantity, by rhythm in metrical composition; the proper pronunciation of English, and the best way of expressing that pronunciation and safeguarding it from corruption by phonetic spellings and specially devised alphabets. The work that he did in these fields does not lend itself to summary treatment or to quotation; some indication of his activities will be gathered from the bibliography at the end of this piece, but special mention must be made of his connection with the Society for Pure English. The society was formed by Bridges, together with his friends Henry Bradley,

Sir Walter Raleigh, and Logan Pearsall Smith, in 1913; but owing to the intervention of World War I it did not get going until six years later. Its objects were, in the words of Pearsall Smith, its first secretary, "to safeguard our inherited form of speech from the dangers threatening it under modern conditions, to help defend its integrity and beauty, and make it, perhaps, into an even more adequate means of expression for modern ideas." So far as the aim of the society was to influence the public at large, it was, in the words of Raleigh, "rather like proposing that everyone shall dress well and move gracefully"; but its publications provided an excellent vehicle for Bridges and fellow enthusiasts (including H. W. Fowler, the author of *Modern English Usage*) to expound and urge their views on linguistic topics of general interest. Between 1919 and 1931 there appeared a stream of S.P.E. pamphlets, under Bridges's editorship, of several of which he was himself the author, on linguistic usage, idiom, vocabulary, pronunciation, spelling, handwriting, and kindred topics. In all these matters, his general attitude was (in the words of his daughter, who inherited her father's poetic gift)

at once conservative and democratic, aesthetic and rational. Besides fighting to preserve the traditional and characteristic beauties of our language from the dangers of slovenly and meaningless degradation, and from all confusion and ugliness, whether of thought or sound, he was at the same time a keen experimenter, and no one was more ready to appreciate and encourage all natural and healthy developments of the national genius.[6]

Bridges once told Pearsall Smith that his poetical inspiration came to him at intervals:

there would be periods, sometimes long periods, in which he felt no impulse to create; he could, indeed, write verses if he wished in these periods, but such verses he said would have no poetic value. Then, one auspicious morning the world would take on a new appearance; everything would be full of poetic interest, and the sight of a tree, a picture on the wall of his bedroom, would suggest subjects in such abundance that he was almost embarrassed by them. Then, after a few weeks or months or even longer periods, he would find that the capricious Muses had taken their departure.[7]

[5]Wordsworth, Blake, and Amiel (and also Dixon, in regard to whom he was no doubt influenced by personal predilection) come next, and in their cases the choice is accounted for by the avowed purpose of the anthology, which was to illustrate the belief that "spirituality is the basis and foundation of human life."

[6]E. Daryush, "His Work on the English Language," in *Robert Bridges*, Society for Pure English tract no. 35 (London, 1931).
[7]L. P. Smith, "Recollections," in *Robert Bridges*, Society for Pure English tract no. 35 (London, 1931).

The study of the technical problems that fascinated him served to occupy these periods of vacancy; but the business of his life was poetry.

III

It is difficult to praise, to criticize, even to describe except in the most general terms work so impersonal, so uniform, so lacking, as it were, in incident as are the lyrics of Bridges; there are no obscurities to explain, few allusions to identify, no "developments" to trace; the only way to convey their quality is to quote. But the attempt to detach a stanza from almost any of his poems reveals how closely woven is its texture, and if one quotes, one must, to do him justice, quote in full.

Bridges's lyrical and shorter poems are not, in fact, as uniform in kind as they might at first sight seem to be: they fall into several categories. The poems that one naturally thinks of first, and thinks of as being most characteristic, are those pure lyrics in which he expresses strong and spontaneous feeling—almost all of them poems of happy, even triumphantly happy, love:

> My delight and thy delight
> Walking, like two angels white,
> In the gardens of the night:
>
> My desire and thy desire
> Twining to a tongue of fire,
> Leaping live, and laughing higher;
> Thro' the everlasting strife
> In the mystery of life.
>
> Love, from whom the world begun,
> Hath the secret of the sun.
>
> Love can tell, and love alone,
> Whence the million stars were strewn,
> Why each atom knows its own,
> How, in spite of woe and death,
> Gay is life, and sweet is breath:
>
> This he taught us, this we knew,
> Happy in his science true,
> Hand in hand as we stood
> Neath the shadows of the wood,
> Heart to heart as we lay
> In the dawning of the day.
>
> (NP, IX)

That is not absolutely without blemish: the seventh and eighth lines, though high-sounding, are empty, and "in his science true" adds nothing to its content beyond a touch of incongruity. But surely the whole lyric conveys, with Blake-like simplicity and exaltation, the ecstasy that inspired it. By its side one may set a dozen others, for instance, "I will not let thee go" (SP, I.7); "Awake, my heart, to be loved" (SP, III.15); "Since thou, O fondest and truest" (SP, III.17); "My spirit kisseth thine" (SP, IV.28); and "So sweet love seemed that April morn":

> So sweet love seemed that April morn,
> When first we kissed beside the thorn,
> So strangely sweet, it was not strange
> We thought that love could never change.
>
> But I can tell—let truth be told—
> That love will change in growing old;
> Though day by day is nought to see,
> So delicate his motions be.
>
> And in the end 'twill come to pass
> Quite to forget what once he was,
> Nor even in fancy to recall
> The pleasure that was all in all.
>
> His little spring, that sweet we found,
> So deep in summer floods is drowned,
> I wonder, bathed in joy complete,
> How love so young could be so sweet.
>
> (SP, V.5)

Two of Bridges's best-known and most moving poems were inspired not by the passion of love but by the thought of another's death—the simple lines "I never shall love the snow again" (SP, V.2), commemorating his wife's brother, Maurice Waterhouse, and the reflective stanzas "On a Dead Child" (SP, III.4), evidently the fruit of experience at St. Bartholomew's. The last two stanzas from the latter poem may be quoted to show the mastery with which Bridges manipulates a difficult meter and the depth of feeling with which he conveys "the last curiosity":

> So quiet! doth the change content thee?—Death,
>   whither hath he taken thee?
>   To a world, do I think, that rights the disaster of this?
>   The vision of which I miss,
> Who weep for the body, and wish but to warm thee
>   and awaken thee?

Ah! little at best can all our hopes avail us
  To lift this sorrow, or cheer us, when in the dark,
    Unwilling, alone we embark,
  And the things we have seen and have known and
      have heard of, fail us.

Another poem that expresses feeling arising from a human relationship is the little-known "The Portrait of a Grandfather":

With mild eyes agaze, and lips ready to speak,
Whereon the yearning of love, the warning of wisdom
    plays,
One portrait ever charms me and teaches me when I
    seek:
  It is of him whom I, remembering my young days,
Imagine fathering my father; when he, in sonship
    afore,
Liv'd honouring and obeying the eyes now pictur'd
    agaze,
  The lips ready to speak, that promise but speak no
    more.

O high parental claim, that were not but for the
    knowing,
O fateful bond of duty, O more than body that bore,
  The smile that guides me to right, the gaze that
    follows my going,
How had I stray'd without thee! and yet how few will
    seek
The spirit-hands, that heaven, in tender-free
    bestowing,
  Holds to her children, to guide the wandering and
    aid the weak.

And Thee! ah what of thee, thou lover of men? if
    truly
A painter had stell'd thee there, with thy lips ready
    to speak,
  In all-fathering passion to souls enchanted newly,
—Tenderer call than of sire to son, or of lover to
    maiden,—
Ever ready to speak to us, if we will hearken duly,
  "Come, O come unto me, ye weary and heavy-
    laden!"

                                  (LP, XIII)

This is a poem about the filial relationship, manifested in three generations, the theme being translated from the human plane to the divine, and there too repeated, for the Son is thought of as fathering his human children. It is also about two pictures—an actual picture in the first stanza and an imagined picture in the third. The whole poem turns, as on a pivot, upon the midline of the second stanza—"How had I strayed without thee! and yet how few will

seek . . . ," and the second portrait is suggested by the opening words of stanza 3—"And Thee! ah what of thee, thou lover of men?"—and completed by the familiar quotation in the last line, a subtle touch that sets vividly before our eyes the image of the Man of Sorrows.[8]

Bridges's best-known poems are those in which he describes the visible world—the beauties of flower and field, of sky and sea; the best example of such sheerly descriptive writing is the miraculous "London Snow":

When men were all asleep the snow came flying,
In large white flakes falling on the city brown,
Stealthily and perpetually settling and loosely lying,
  Hushing the latest traffic of the drowsy town;
Deadening, muffling, stifling its murmurs failing;
Lazily and incessantly floating down and down:
  Silently sifting and veiling road, roof and railing;
Hiding difference, making unevenness even,
Into angles and crevices softly drifting and sailing.
  All night it fell, and when full inches seven
It lay in the depth of its uncompacted lightness,
The clouds blew off from a high and frosty heaven;
  And all woke earlier for the unaccustomed brightness
Of the winter dawning, the strange unheavenly glare:
The eye marvelled—marvelled at the dazzling whiteness;
  The ear hearkened to the stillness of the solemn air. . . .
                              (SP, III.2)

The anthologists have made the poem so familiar that there is no need to quote further. They have done as much for another remarkable word picture, "A Passer-by" (SP, II.2); and to the same class of pictorial writing belong a whole gallery of landscape poems, for instance: "There is a hill beside the silver Thames" (SP, II.5); "The Downs" (SP, II.7); "The Winnowers" (SP, V.1), and "The Garden in September" (SP, V.4). The following shows the poet's minute and sympathetic observation:

A poppy grows upon the shore,
Bursts her twin cup in summer late:
Her leaves are glaucous-green and hoar,
Her petals yellow, delicate.

Oft to her cousins turns her thought,
In wonder if they care that she
Is fed with spray for dew, and caught
By every gale that sweeps the sea.

---

[8]The only blemish in this strange and moving poem is the obscurity of "that were not but for the knowing" in line 8 and of the word "fateful" in the next line.

She has no lovers like the red,
That dances with the noble corn:
Her blossoms on the waves are shed,
Where she stands shivering and forlorn.

(SP, I.9)

"Her pétals yéllow, délicate": "no lóvers like the réd/That dánces with the nóble córn"—the accented syllables, both by their sound and by what they signify, enforce the contrast between the frail lemon-colored flower and its proud crimson cousin.

Not all Bridges's descriptive poems, however, consist only of description; sometimes the scene portrayed evokes or recalls a personal emotion, and the picture is charged with human feeling. Sometimes, as in "The Voice of Nature" (SP, III.3), he draws an explicit lesson from what he sees; and sometimes the natural scene prompts a comparison with the human condition or with human art:

The sea keeps not the Sabbath day,
His waves come rolling evermore;
His noisy toil grindeth the shore,
And all the cliff is drencht with spray.

Here as we sit, my love and I,
Under the pine upon the hill,
The sadness of the clouded sky,
The bitter wind, the gloomy roar,
The seamew's melancholy cry
With loving fancy suit but ill.

We talk of moons and cooling suns,
Of geologic time and tide,
The eternal sluggards that abide,
While our fair love so swiftly runs,

Of nature that doth half consent
That men should guess her dreary scheme
Lest he should live too well content
In his fair house of mirth and dream:

Whose labour irks his ageing heart,
His heart that wearies of desire,
Being so fugitive a part
Of what so slowly must expire.

She in her agelong toil and care
Persistent, wearies not nor stays,
Mocking alike hope and despair.

—Ah, but she too can mock our praise,
Enchanted on her brighter days,

Days, that the thought of grief refuse,
Days that are one with human art,
Worthy of the Virgilian muse,
Fit for the gaiety of Mozart.

(NP, II)

Bridges possesses the gift of persuading us of the truth of the pathetic fallacy: he can make us feel, simply by describing a natural scene, that nature is an organism with emotions of its own. Take, for instance, the closing lines of "The storm is over, the land hushes to rest":

The day is done: the tired land looks for night:
She prays to the night to keep
In peace her nerves of delight:
While silver mist upstealeth silently,
And the broad cloud-driving moon in the clear sky
Lifts o'er the firs her shining shield,
And in her tranquil light
Sleep falls on forest and field.
Sée! sléep hath fallen: the trees are asleep:
The night is come. The land is wrapt in sleep.

(SP, IV.23)

The personification here is not simply "poetic," a literary device; it expresses quite naturally the completeness with which the poet enters into and identifies himself with what he sees.

These lines are taken from one of several pieces in which Bridges eschews the stanza and lets the matter dictate the form, so that the meter follows, with the exactness of a draftsman's pencil, the lineaments of the thing described. "November" is another such poem, and here too, in its last lines, he makes us feel with him that nature is a sentient organism:

And now, if the night shall be cold, across the sky
Linnets and twites, in small flocks helter-skelter,
All the afternoon to the gardens fly,
From thistle-pastures hurrying to gain the shelter,
Of American rhododendron or cherry-laurel:
And here and there, near chilly setting of sun,
In an isolated tree a congregation
Of starlings chatter and chide,
Thickset as summer leaves, in garrulous quarrel:
Suddenly they hush as one,—
The tree top springs,—
And off, with a whirr of wings,
They fly by the score
To the holly-thicket, and there with myriads more
Dispute for the roosts; and from the unseen nation
A babel of tongues, like running water unceasing,
Makes live the wood, the flocking cries increasing,
Wrangling discordantly, incessantly,
While falls the night on them self-occupied;
The long dark night, that lengthens slow,
Deepening with Winter to starve grass and tree,
And soon to bury in snow
The Earth, that, sleeping 'neath her frozen stole,

Shall dream a dream crept from the sunless pole
Of how her end shall be.

(NP, XIV)

For virtuosity, the opening passage matches "London Snow": every line, almost every phrase, brings vividly before the eye and ear the object or sound that it describes:

> In an isolated tree a congregation
> Of starlings chatter and chide,
> Thickset as summer leaves, in garrulous quarrel. . . .

One *sees* the "isolated tree," the long vowels and the final monosyllable making an island of the phrase itself; one *hears* the chatter of the birds; one *feels* the thickset clustering of the leaves to which their "congregation" is compared. These effects are achieved by manipulating sounds; of course they are not due to sound alone, and a listener who knew no English would get no inkling of what was being described; but once the meaning has given the key, one appreciates the miraculous appropriateness of sound to subject. There is a touch of deeper magic in the last six lines.

> The long dark night, that lengthens slow,

changes at once the pace and the tone of the poem, and we pass from the visible and audible world to a realm of pure imagination.

The vision in "November" is apocalyptic and frightening; such glimpses—"Dim indications of the power/That doometh man to woe"—are rare in Bridges's work; they seem to come to him against his will and are perhaps a part of his experience not fully represented in his poetry. "Ah, many have my visions been," he says in "The North Wind":

> And some I know full well:
> I would that all that I have seen
> Were fit for speech to tell.

(SP, V. 15)

That poem is too long to quote in full and impossible to convey by extracts. Another midnight vision is described in "Melancholy," a poem of World War I:

> 'Twas mid of the moon but the night was dark with rain,
> Drops lashed the pane, the wind howl'd under the door;
> For me, my heart heard nought but the cannon-roar
> On fields of war, where Hell was raging amain:

My heart was sore for the slain:—
As when on an Autumn plain the storm lays low the wheat,
So fell the flower of England, her golden grain,
Her harvesting hope trodden under the feet
Of Moloch, Woden and Thor,
And the lovingkindness of Christ held in disdain.
   My heart gave way to the strain, renouncing more &
      more;
Its bloodstream fainted down to the slothful weary beat
Of the age-long moment, that swelleth where ages meet,
Marking time 'twixt dark Hereafter and Long-before;
Which greet awhile and awhile, again to retreat;
The Never-the-same repeating again and again,
Completing itself in monotony incomplete,
A wash of beauty and horror in shadows that fleet,
Always the Never-the-same still to repeat,
The devouring glide of a dream that keepeth no store.
  Meseem'd I stood on the flats of a waveless shore,
Where MELANCHOLY unrobed of her earthly weeds,
Haunteth in naked beauty without stain;
In reconcilement of Death, and Vanity of all needs;
A melting of life in oblivion of all deeds;
No other beauty nor passion nor love nor lore;
No other goddess abideth for man to adore;
All things remaining nowhere with nought to remain;
The consummation of thought in nought to attain.
  I had come myself to that ultimate Ocean-shore,
Like Labourer Love when his life-day is o'er,
Who home returning fatigued is fain to regain
The house where he was unconsciously born of yore;
Stumbling on the threshold he sinketh down on the floor;
Half-hearteth a prayer as he lieth, and nothing heeds,
If only he sleep and sleep and have rest for evermore.

(NV, IX)

It is difficult to know which to praise most in this wonderful poem, the imaginative power that communicates feeling through vision, or the art that intensifies the emotion by means of word pattern—a heavily recurring accent and changes rung through the whole length of the piece on three main vowel sounds, used both as final and as internal rhymes.

I have quoted these powerful, grim, and visionary poems partly for their quality and partly because this somber element in Bridges's work—other examples are "Low Barometer" (*NV*, 16) and "Melancholia" (*LP*, 7)—has been lost sight of in the dazzling sunlight of so much happy, extroverted verse.

Having praised the high level of his performance, it is right that I should mention his failures. In his longer formal poems, his masques and odes and dramas, the characters do not come to life, the situations lack dramatic effect, and inspiration—except in interspersed lyrics and occasional passages of descriptive beauty—is sadly deficient: we feel that we are reading a poetical exercise. In his lyrics there are two veins that he explored on occasion with unfortunate effect: the humorous and the patriotic. He rightly excluded from his own final selection, *Shorter Poems* (published by his widow in 1931), a handful of facetious and colloquial verses that had appeared in earlier collections; though his gay and mordant humor appeared to good effect in his prose criticism, he could not, evidently, marry it to verse; and he was right also in excluding such poems as "Regina Cara," a celebration of the Diamond Jubilee, "Matres Dolorosae," an elegy on the conclusion of the South African War, and "Britannia Victrix," published on the occasion of the Armistice in 1918, and several other poems of World War I included in *October* (1920). These suggest too much the patriotic cartoons of Bernard Partridge, and they prove how wise he was—in spite of popular complaints that he was not doing his duty by the office—to restrict his utterances as poet laureate.

If in his odes for music Bridges is inclined to indulge in too grandiose an organ-swell of poetic diction, they contain nonetheless some beautiful lyrical passages, for he can pull out the *vox caelestis* with an effect sometimes reminiscent of Blake:

> Open for me the gates of delight,
> The gates of the garden of man's desire;
> Where spirits touched by heavenly fire
> Have planted the trees of life—[9]

and sometimes he produces a music that is entirely his own:

> Sweet compassionate tears
> Have dimm'd my earthly sight,
> Tears of love, the showers wherewith
> The eternal morn is bright:
> Dews of the heav'nly spheres.
> With tears my eyes are wet,
> Tears not of vain regret,
> Tears of no lost delight,
> Dews of the heav'nly spheres
> Have dimm'd my earthly sight,
> Sweet compassionate tears.[10]

I must touch on one other verse form, the sonnet, before turning to the last development of Bridges's

technique. Bridges published something like a hundred sonnets; by 1890 he had swollen the series in *The Growth of Love* (1876) to three times its original size by the addition of more than fifty pieces. After that, he practically abandoned the sonnet, being increasingly preoccupied with experiments in quantitative, accentual, and syllabic unrhymed meters. But in that form he had achieved some of the most striking of his effects. Take, for instance, the sestet of the sonnet "I care not if I live":

> I have no care for what was most my care,
> But all around me see fresh beauty born,
> And common sights grown lovelier than they were:
> I dream of love, and in the light of morn
> Tremble, beholding all things very fair
> And strong with strength that puts my strength to scorn.
>   (sonnet 33)

Or take the opening of the sonnet, praised especially by Hopkins, on a portrait of his mother:

> Tears of love, tears of joy and tears of care,
> Comforting tears that fell uncomforted,
> Tears o'er the new-born, tears beside the dead,
> Tears of hope, pride and pity, trust and prayer,
> Tears of contrition; all tears whatso'er
> Of tenderness or kindness had she shed
> Who here is pictured, ere upon her head
> The fine gold might be turn'd to silver there.
>   (sonnet 40)

It is not easy to explain why these lines are so very moving. Their peculiar effectiveness is due, it seems, not only to the ideas themselves, but to their successive presentation—itself somehow suggestive of a shower of tears—and to the falling rhythm, beside which the cadence of "Drop, drop, slow tears" sounds almost crude.

In the following poem, which also won praise from Hopkins, Bridges again bends the sonnet form to unexpected uses:

> I would be a bird, and straight on wings I arise,
> And carry purpose up to the ends of the air:
> In calm and storm my sails I feather, and where
> By freezing cliffs the unransom'd wreckage lies:
> Or, strutting on hot meridian banks, surprise
> The silence: over plains in the moonlight bare
> I chase my shadow, and perch where no bird dare
> In treetops torn by fiercest winds of the skies.

[9]From the *Purcell Commemoration Ode* (London, 1895).
[10]From *A Hymn of Nature* (London, 1898).

Poor simple birds, foolish birds! then I cry,
Ye pretty pictures of delight, unstir'd
By the only joy of knowing that ye fly;
Ye are nót what ye are, but rather, sum'd in a word,
The alphabet of a god's idea, and I
Who master it, I am the only bird.

(sonnet 22)

Who, in the year 1876, except perhaps Hopkins himself, had written a sonnet even remotely resembling that?

IV

DURING the quarter of a century when he lived at Yattendon, Bridges composed a number of poetical exercises, including eight verse dramas, a masque, and several formal odes for music; but his most memorable work—apart from *The Testament of Beauty*—is to be found among his sonnets and shorter lyrical pieces.

Bridges also published criticism, which was collected after his death in ten small volumes containing thirty essays, reviews, and lectures; their subjects range from Bunyan to Kipling, and they include a famous paper, "The Necessity of Poetry," in which he stated his faith as a creative artist. In 1893 he published a study expounding his own original theories about the prosody of Milton's later works, and (two years later) a critical essay on Keats. His views are always his own, uninfluenced by the reputation of the author he is discussing or by the authority of previous critics, and they are set forth in a language that conveys the spoken word.

These critical essays, and his growing celebrity as a poet, explain why he was pressed to stand for the professorship of poetry at Oxford in 1895. He refused to allow his name to go forward, for he was not in any sense an academic, and he never had the slightest desire to become a public figure; and it was with reluctance probably, and certainly without eagerness, that he accepted the laureateship in 1913.

His critical studies influenced his own poetry; they persuaded him to experiment with verses in classical prosody and they opened his eyes to the existence of the "neo-Miltonic syllabics" in which much of his later work was composed. "Anyone may see," he wrote in 1912, "that serious rhyme is now exhausted in English verse"; and he developed, in accordance with the principles he detected in Milton, an unrhymed Alexandrine, to be measured by numbering not accents but syllables. Here is a specimen, the last lines of "The College Garden," written in 1917:

Thus hour draggeth on hour, and I feel every thrill
of time's eternal stream that passeth over me
the dream-stream of God's Will that made things as they be
and me as I am, as unreluctant in the stream
I lie, like one who hath wander'd all his summer morn
among the heathery hills and hath come down at noon
in a breathless valley upon a mountain-brook
and for animal recreation of hot fatigue
hath stripp'd his body naked to lie down and taste
the play of the cool water on all his limbs and flesh
and lying in a pebbly shallow beneath the sky
supine and motionless feeleth each ripple pass
until his thought is merged in the flow of the stream
as it cometh upon him and lappeth him there
stark as a white corpse that stranded upon the stones
blocketh and for a moment delayeth the current
ere it can pass to pay its thin tribute of salt
into the choking storage of the quenchless sea.

(NV, V)

It was in this meter that his last poem, *The Testament of Beauty*, was composed. Through four long books Bridges sustains a philosophical argument designed to show

how the mind of man from inconscient existence
cometh thru' the animal by growth of reasoning
towards spiritual conscience—

and to make plain the relation of beauty to reason:

by Beauty (he says) it is that we come at Wisdom,
but not by Reason at Beauty.

Like all philosophical poems, *The Testament of Beauty* will be read for its poetry, not for its philosophy; it is full of memorable passages, reflective, descriptive, illustrative; they grow naturally out of their context, but lose little by being detached from it; and it is these passages, and their reflection of the many-sided mind and the noble nature of the poet, that will keep the poem alive.

SELECTED BIBLIOGRAPHY

Bridges lived long and published much; many of his works first appeared in privately printed and severely limited editions and were reprinted in collections the texts of which were repeatedly revised. Some of these, not listed here separately, are included in *Poetical Works* (1898–1905), below.

I. BIBLIOGRAPHY. G. L. Mackay, *A Bibliography of Robert Bridges* (New York, 1933).

II. COLLECTED WORKS. *Poetical Works*, 6 vols. (London, 1898–1905), vol. I (1898): *Prometheus the Firegiver* (first published 1883), *Eros and Psyche* (1885), *The Growth of Love*; vol. II (1899): *Shorter Poems*, with additional section of "New Poems"; vols. III–IV (1900–1905), verse dramas: *Nero Part I* (1885), *Achilles in Scyros* (1890), *Palicio* (1890), *The Return of Ulysses* (1890), *The Christian Captives* (1890), *Humours of the Court* (1893), *The Feast of Bacchus* (1889), *Nero Part II* (1894); *Poetical Works* (Oxford, 1912) excludes the eight verse dramas but includes new poems published 1900–1912, reiss. with poems from *October, New Verse*, and *The Testament of Beauty* in Oxford Standard Authors (London, 1953); *Collected Essays, Papers, etc.*, 10 vols. (Oxford, 1927–1937), contains thirty essays, lectures, etc., ed. by Bridges's widow, special letters cut for text showing with increasing thoroughness as the series proceeds Bridges's suggested improvements in the alphabet and in phonetic spelling.

III. SELECTED WORKS. J. Sparrow, ed., *Poetry and Prose* (Oxford, 1955), in Clarendon English series, contains selections from Bridges's poetry and prose and from critical estimates of his work.

IV. SEPARATE WORKS IN VERSE. *Poems* (London, 1873), Bridges is said to have suppressed unsold copies and discouraged repr. of poems not included in subsequent eds.; *The Growth of Love* (London, 1876), anonymous, twenty-four sonnets, enl. to seventy-nine and published under same title by "C. H. O. Daniel" (Oxford, 1889); *Poems by the Author of the Growth of Love* (London, 1879), anonymous; *Poems by the Author of the Growth of Love*, 3rd ser. (London, 1890), anonymous; *Poems* (Oxford, 1884), selections from 1873, 1879, and 1880 collections with additions; *Shorter Poems*, books I–IV (London, 1890), book V (London, 1893), books I–III include poems Bridges wished to preserve from 1873, 1879, 1880, and 1884 eds., new poems in books IV and V; R. Bridges, ed., *The Spirit of Man* (London, 1916), anthology; *October and Other Poems* (London, 1920); *New Verse* (Oxford, 1925), contains first experiments in "neo-Miltonic syllabics"; *The Testament of Beauty* (Oxford, 1929, repr. 1961).

V. SEPARATE WORKS IN PROSE. "Milton's Blank Verse in *Paradise Lost*," in H. C. Beeching's ed. of book I of *Paradise Lost* (Oxford, 1887); *The Prosody of "Paradise Lost" and "Samson Agonistes"* (Oxford, 1889), rev. and repr. as *Milton's Prosody* (London, 1893), final rev. ed. (Oxford, 1966); *John Keats: A Critical Essay* (London, 1895), privately printed, published as intro. to Muses' Library ed. of Keats (London, 1896), repr. in *Collected Essays*; "On the Influence of the Audience," preface to vol. X of Shakespeare Head ed. of Shakespeare's *Works* (London, 1907), repr. in *Collected Essays*; *Society for Pure English Tracts* (London, 1921–1929), original prospectus, largely Bridges's work, appeared in 1931, many contributions on pronunciation and philological questions to subsequent series; *Address to the Swindon Branch of the Workers' Educational Association* (Oxford, 1916), on the improvement of popular education, repr. in *Collected Essays*; *The Necessity of Poetry: An Address to the Tredegar and District Co-operative Society* (Oxford, 1918), repr. in *Collected Essays*; "Poetry," broadcast delivered 28 February 1929, printed in the *Listener* (March 1929), repr. in *Collected Essays*; *Three Friends* (Oxford, 1932), repr. of memoirs of Digby Mackworth Dolben, originally prefixed to Bridges's ed. of Dolben's *Poems* (Oxford, 1911), of Richard Watson Dixon, originally prefixed to Bridges's ed. of *Poems by the Late Rev. Dr. Richard Watson Dixon: A Selection with Portrait and Memoir* (London, 1909), and of Henry Bradley, privately printed (London, 1926) and prefixed to Bradley's *Collected Papers* (Oxford, 1928).

VI. LETTERS. *The Correspondence of Bridges and Bradley, 1900–1923* (Oxford, 1940); Bridges destroyed his letters to Gerard Manley Hopkins, whose *Poems* (Oxford, 1918) he edited; Hopkins' side of the correspondence is in C. C. Abbott, ed., *Letters of G. M. Hopkins to Robert Bridges* (Oxford, 1935).

VII. BIOGRAPHICAL AND CRITICAL STUDIES. R. Brett Young, *Robert Bridges* (London, 1914); E. Thompson, *Robert Bridges 1844–1930* (Oxford, 1931), includes some personal reminiscences; N. C. Smith, *Notes on "The Testament of Beauty"* (Oxford, 1931), an excellent guide to understanding and appreciating the poem; J.-G. Ritz, *Robert Bridges and Gerard Manley Hopkins, 1863–1889: A Literary Friendship* (Oxford, 1960), a full and sympathetic account.

GEORGE MOORE

(1852-1933)

A. Norman Jeffares

LIFE

GEORGE AUGUSTUS MOORE was born on 24 February 1852 at Moore Hall, a Georgian house overlooking Lough Carra, in County Mayo in the west of Ireland. Another George Moore, his great-grandfather, had built the house out of the large fortune with which he had returned to Ireland from Alicante, after a successful period as a merchant in Spain. While there he had drawn up a pedigree that traced the family back to Sir Thomas More; the document was certainly accurate as far back as the author's own great-grandfather, Captain George Moore, the vice admiral of Connaught, and the connection with Sir Thomas More may well have been genuine. The family was originally Protestant; the first marriage into a Catholic family occurred early in the eighteenth century when John Moore of Ashbrook married Jane Lynch Athy of Renville. George Moore (1729–1799) the merchant was a son of this marriage and was accepted as a Catholic in Spain. His son John was elected president of the Republic of Connaught in the 1798 insurrection; he was captured but died before his trial began. His third son, George, was an author, who wrote a Whiggish *History of the British Revolution* and a liberal and rational treatise attacking Kant. This George's son, George Henry, returned from Cambridge and subsequent travels in the East to occupy himself with racing and hunting. But at the time of the Irish famine of 1846 he sold his stable and turned to politics, heading the poll as an Independent in 1847, a seat he retained for ten years. In 1859, however, he returned to racing and won large sums of money, some of which he spent on his sons' education, sending them to Oscott, the Catholic college where he had himself been educated in England.

His eldest son, George, went to Oscott in the winter of 1861. An attack of bronchitis in 1863 gave him a happy spell at home, fishing on the lake with his brother Maurice, shooting, and joining in the life of his father's racing stables. Both he and Maurice, who joined him at Oscott in 1865, did badly at the school, and the headmaster wrote many letters to their father about George's lack of progress. Eventually he left the school, where a younger brother, Augustus, joined Maurice; he spent a year at home and then moved to London when his father abandoned racing for a second time and was reelected to the House of Commons in 1868.

In London George Moore was influenced by the artist Jim Browne and began to attempt to paint; he was, however, sent by his father to work with a crammer who prepared pupils for entry into the army. When his father died he inherited an income of three to four thousand pounds a year from the property in Ireland, but only an income of about five hundred pounds of this was left after the payment of mortgages. He still wanted to become a painter and study in Paris, but since he was not of age and his guardians disagreed with his plans, he had to spend three years in London. He had financial scrapes, he lived a gay life, he made friends, but as soon as he was twenty-one he went to Paris.

In Paris he tried at first to obtain private tuition, but eventually became a pupil in Jullian's Academy. Lewis Weldon Hawkins—the Lewis Ponsonby Marshall of *Confessions of a Young Man* and *Hail and Farewell*—became his friend. There was a brief return to London, where he painted and lived beyond his income, but, back in Paris in 1875, he made the difficult decision to give up painting. He thought of marrying for money, also of becoming a writer; and he collaborated with Bernard Lopez on *Martin Luther,* a verse drama he had printed in 1879, a year after his poems, *Flowers of Passion,* had been printed, reviewed savagely, and later withdrawn. His friendship with Lewis diminished and Hawkins left the luxurious rooms in the rue de la Tour des Dames, so richly described in the *Confessions:*

. . . our salon was a pretty resort—English cretonne of a very happy design—vine leaves, dark green and golden, broken up by many fluttering jays. The walls were stretched with this colourful cloth, and the arm-chairs and the couches were to match. The drawing-room was in cardinal red, hung from the middle of the ceiling and looped up to give the appearance of a tent; a faun, in terra-cotta, laughed in the red gloom, and there were Turkish couches and lamps. In another room you faced an altar, a Buddhist temple, a statue of Apollo, and a bust of Shelley. The bedrooms were made unconventional with cushioned seats and rich canopies; and in picturesque corners there were censers, great church candlesticks, and palms; then think of the smell of burning wax and you will have imagined the sentiment of our apartment in Rue de la Tour des Dames. I bought a Persian cat, and a python that made a monthly meal off guinea-pigs; Marshall, who did not care for pets, filled his room with flowers—he used to sleep beneath a tree of gardenias in full bloom.

(p. 47)[1]

Moore was moving in French society now, and the period from 1877 to 1880 was also the time of his "café education," when he got to know Manet and Degas and their circle of friends, whom he met frequently in the Nouvelles Athènes in Montmartre. Yeats described him as "sitting among art students, young writers about to become famous, in some café; a man carved out of a turnip, looking out of astonished eyes." His appearance was indeed unusual. He had a receding chin, a long neck, a full if straggling moustache, and sloping shoulders; his hair was pale yellow, his prominent eyes a pale gray-green, his complexion delicately pink; in Yeats's phrase again, his body was "insinuating, upflowing, circulative, curvicular, pop-eyed."

In 1880 Moore had to face the effects of the land war in Ireland. His tenants refused to pay their rents, agricultural prices were down, and his uncle, Joe Blake, honest but chaotic, handed over the agency and was replaced by Tom Ruttledge, young, untried, but efficient. After a winter in Ireland, Moore settled down in London to write, living a very frugal and thrifty life and undertaking journalism—he wrote on the naturalistic novel, striving to bring Émile Zola's work before British readers.

Moore's first novel, *A Modern Lover*, was published in 1883, to reappear in rewritten form as *Lewis Seymour and Some Women* in 1917. This is a study of an artist who is helped throughout his life by women. Shaw remembered Moore at this time as

always telling stories about himself and women. In every story there was a room full of mirrors and chandeliers and the story usually ended with some woman throwing a lamp at George and driving him out of the house. Everybody used to laugh at George and no one believed him, but he had an imperturbable good humour and if you said: "But, George, don't talk such nonsense, you are making it all up," he was not in the least put out or angry but just said: "Don't interrupt me," and went on as before.

(Conversation cited by Charles Morgan, *Epitaph on George Moore*, pp. 15–16)

Moore realized later that his ability to write prose was questionable (as much so as were his earlier attempts to paint and to become a poet), but the story, he said, enthralled him. His novel received favorable notice, but the circulating libraries thought it unsuitable for their readers, so his next venture was a one-volume novel published cheaply by Vizetelly. This was *A Mummer's Wife*, a study of a touring company, which he began in Ireland in the winter of 1883–1884, first at Moore Hall and later in Dublin, where he went to observe and take part in the season at the viceregal court, the levee, the state ball, and other social events, thus laying the foundations of *A Drama in Muslin*.

He moved to chambers in London and there completed *A Mummer's Wife*, his active answer to the sentimental school, a novel in which he deepened his portrayal of character and successfully applied the method of the French naturalistic writers to English life. The winter of 1884–1885 he spent in Ireland, where he finished *A Drama in Muslin*. He launched an attack on the viceregal court in nationalist newspapers, as he had not been invited, despite his requests, to a state dinner party. He read Pater with great delight, then transferred himself to London and made a telling attack on the circulating libraries. He made friends with the English artists Walter Sickert and P. Wilson Steer; a neighboring landlord from Galway, Edward Martyn, recently down from Oxford, became another close friend. Martyn was portrayed in *A Mere Accident* (1887), a novel written in and about Sussex, which marks the end of Zola's influence on Moore. (This reached its zenith in *Parnell and His Island*, but its waning is perhaps best captured in his 1894 account of a visit to Médan in 1888.) The effect of J. K. Huysmans and Gustave Flaubert on his writings now became apparent.

Moore had come to Sussex as the guest of old friends, the Bridgers, and in 1887 he joined with Collyer Bridger in a rabbit-farming venture there. He en-

---

[1]Quotations from the *Confessions* are from Moore's own annotated edition (London, 1904; 1917).

joyed what he called the "Protestantism of Sussex," and *Spring Days* records this liking, captured in a Balzacian way. Edouard Dujardin's writings had a noticeable effect upon Moore, as is shown by his *Confessions of a Young Man* (1888); this rich and full account of Moore's life in Paris led to his alienation from Degas and Zola. Though his next novel, *Mike Fletcher*, proved a failure, he was already engaged upon *Esther Waters* in 1890; he laid it aside, however, to write *Impressions and Opinions*, a successful collection of essays. *Vain Fortune* was a serial for the *Lady's Pictorial*, but did not do well. The winter of 1891–1892 he spent writing *Esther Waters*.

Moore's criticism flourished, and his articles for the *Speaker* were collected in *Modern Painting* (1893). He had extended his friendships among the artists, and now knew William Rothenstein, Henry Tonks, and D. S. MacColl, who was the art critic of the *Spectator* and an equally enthusiastic supporter of the French Impressionists.

During the nineties Moore enjoyed a wider social life in London and even joined Boodles, the exclusive Tory club. Though he talked much about his love affairs, sentimental or promiscuous, and though he had set his mind against marriage, he seems to have fallen deeply in love with Mrs. Craigie, an American heiress who wrote novels under the pseudonym John Oliver Hobbes. He collaborated with her on several plays. But she dismissed him savagely, probably because she had hopes of marrying Lord Curzon.

Esther Waters (1894) proved a popular success, and Moore followed it with the volume of short stories *Celibates* (1895), in which Mrs. Craigie appears as Mildred Lawson—she is also depicted in "Lui et Elles" in *Memoirs of My Dead Life* (1921 edition), and in "Henrietta Marr" in *In Single Strictness* (1922). Joseph Hone relates in his biography the story of the third quarrel with Mrs. Craigie, which took place in 1904 after Moore and she had agreed to collaborate again in writing a play. Moore told his friend Dujardin what had happened:

"I was walking in the Green Park," he said, "and I saw her in front of me. I was blind with rage and I ran up behind her and kicked her." At first he related this story with some embarrassment, but when he grew accustomed to his invention, with relish. The scene in the Green Park was afterwards used in the sketch "Lui et Elles" . . . where a heartless woman on whose face he detected a mocking smile receives the assault "nearly in the centre of the backside, a little to the right," and seems highly gratified to find that she has aroused such a display of feeling. "It was inevitable, I said,

part of the world's history, and I lost sight of all things but the track of my boot on the black crêpe de Chine."
(*The Life of George Moore*, p. 254)

Mildred Lawson is incapable of love, her sensibility warped by her revulsion from sexuality; she turns to religion, but this is as unsatisfactory as the independent life she had sought earlier in her pursuit of art. *Evelyn Innes* (1898) also owes something to Mrs. Craigie's life, though Moore had to learn a lot about music and convents to write it, a thing he did with "pure joy." The novel seemed at the time to be very successful indeed, but its sequel, *Sister Teresa* (1901), was less so. Yeats remarked that Moore was jealous of his own creation; Sir Owen Asher, a man-about-town and materialist, added that Moore was all self and yet had so little self that he would destroy his reputation, or that of some friend, to make his audience believe that the story running in his head at the moment had happened, and only just happened. He was indeed a master of indiscretion.

By the time *Sister Teresa* was published, Moore had left London for Dublin. He was deeply disturbed by the Boer War, by Kiplingesque imperialism, and found life in England distasteful. But there were also positive reasons for his move. The formation of the Gaelic League in 1893 had stirred his imagination. As a child he had grown up in a Gaelic-speaking area. He admired Yeats; Edward Martyn was his friend; and so he sympathized with their plans for an Irish literary theater. He loathed the conventional English theater; he despised the state of English dramatic criticism; he disliked the power of the great actors and actor-managers; and, as the third director of the Irish Literary Theatre, he joined eagerly in the early work of getting Martyn's *Heather Field* and Yeats's *The Countess Cathleen* on the stage in Dublin in 1899. Indeed Yeats wrote that the Irish theater could not have been founded without Moore's help and his knowledge of the stage. Moore felt that great art could coincide with national revival, and he brought to Dublin his own cosmopolitan concept of art, literature, and music.

He hurled himself into the movement to create a culture for Ireland. He spoke at meetings; he wrote art criticism; he wrote *The Bending of the Bough*, a patriotic play begun by Martyn that he took over, and this was produced in Dublin in February 1900. With Yeats he collaborated in the writing of *Diarmuid and Grania*; it was performed in Dublin in 1901. He developed a strong if short-lived enthusiasm for Gaelic. He settled in a house in Ely Place and, though he lived a laborious life, became part of the Dublin scene. He did not lack company, for a woman friend of his, the Stella of *Hail and Farewell,* came to live in Rathfarnham, near Dublin, and he formed a friendship with AE (George Russell) and with John Eglinton (W. K. Magee), a librarian in the National Library.

The Irish Literary Theatre was replaced by the Irish National Dramatic Company in 1902; this year marked Moore's quarrel with Yeats over further collaboration and, in Yeats's phrase, he "dropped out of the movement." Then he wrote *The Untilled Field* (1903), a collection of stories that developed an earlier anticlericalism and that are also brilliant Turgenev-like pieces of observation. He demonstrated his anti-Catholicism in a letter to the *Irish Times,* declaring his conversion to the Church of Ireland, an action that led ultimately to his estrangement from his brother Maurice, whom he had invited with his family to live in Moore Hall from 1905 onward. But though he became disillusioned with Irish life, with what he saw there as an eternal conflict between literature and dogma, his return to the Irish scene gave him fresh material. *The Lake* (1905) seemed to him a triumph over the difficulty of preserving unity of scene. It also represented a new phase in his art, a continuous weaving of memories, of highly imaginative reverie, which reached its peak in the mischievous, malicious, and yet deeply appreciative vignettes of his friends and acquaintances in the trilogy *Hail and Farewell* (1911, 1912, 1914), for which *Memoirs of My Dead Life* (1906) with its memories of various love affairs had been a lively rehearsal. Joseph Hone, his biographer, remarked that in later life, Moore, when mentioning an episode with a woman, would usually say that he was now going home "to write an account of it for his new book." His brother Maurice said his adventures were "half imagination, half reality."

With the first volume of *Hail and Farewell* about to be published, it was time to leave Dublin for London. Moore sold his estate to the Land Commission, and, after repaying mortgages, received between £25,000 and £30,000; he retained Moore Hall and about 500 acres around it. He had in the 1890's shared the original settlement of the property with his brother Maurice, the second son, as they were then on good terms. But their estrangement increased steadily until, in 1911, Colonel Maurice Moore and his family left Moore Hall. (The house was never again occupied. It was burned down in the troubles in 1923, and Moore eventually received £7,000 in compensation.) A house in Belgravia, 121 Ebury Street, seemed suitable, and Moore lived there from 1911 until his death in 1933. He made a few trips to Ireland, and a visit to France was virtually an annual event, with Dujardin often acting as his host. He also visited the Holy Land in 1913. Having written *The Apostle* (1911), a melodramatic play about St. Paul's finding Jesus still alive, he wanted to deal again with the biblical past and to get the background right. He spent fourteen months writing *The Brook Kerith. A Syrian Story* (1916), concentrating now on the character of Jesus rather than that of Paul, keeping the stream of his ideas and narrative flowing continuously and melodiously.

This style of his animates *A Story-Teller's Holiday* (1918), but in these somewhat contrived tales Moore had to rely upon James Stephens' help with the dialogue. This was the first of his works to be issued in the limited and expensive editions in which the rest of his writings would be first published before going into cheaper editions. By this means of publication he generally earned at least two thousand pounds on each book.

In 1918 he began to think up *Héloïse and Abélard* (1921), spending three years on it, traveling in France to absorb atmosphere, consulting many friends on points of detail, and developing for the first time his method of dictating about 1,500 or 2,000 words a day, then later revising the whole book. This was a laborious method of writing that, as a letter to a friend put it, made his life pass "in loneliness and composition." He saw his friends by appointment only, but he enjoyed regular meetings at Tonks's house and at Sir Edmund Gosse's. Nancy Cunard, Charles Morgan, David Garnett, Mrs. Belloc Lowndes were added to his friends; there were his older friends, John Eglinton, Richard Best, Oliver Gogarty, Mr. and Mrs. St. John Hutchinson, whom he saw from time to time. There were houses he visited; he had many correspondents; the routine of his own house was watched over by his housekeeper, Clara Warville. It was an agreeable life, darkened only by kidney and prostate troubles from 1927 onward. He was not strong enough for a major operation, and his friends often found him difficult. Sir John Thomson-Walker, the surgeon who helped him a great deal, became a close friend, and Moore's last completed book, *Aphrodite in Aulis* (1930), was dedicated to him.

The last years of Moore's life were filled with work. He revised his writings constantly, always polishing, removing obstacles and obscurities that might hinder the progress of the tale. He told Geraint Goodwin that if he had a tombstone he would like this written on it: "Here lies George Moore, who looked upon corrections as the one morality." He followed *Héloïse and Abélard* with *Ulick and Soracha* (1926), a story of thirteenth-century Ireland. He made a delightful translation of *Daphnis and Chloë* (1924), which gave scope to his skill in storytelling; he wrote more essays, the *Conversations in Ebury Street* (1924) and *A Communication to My Friends* (1933), as well as plays and short stories. At eighty he was an impressive figure in the world of letters. Though he himself sometimes thought his merits had been overlooked by the world of letters, scholarship, and politics, he was praised generously in a message in the *Times* (London), signed by many distinguished writers, which recognized his single-mindedness, his toiling in the perfection of his craft, his effect upon the users of the language, and his revival of the art of narrative.

He died regretting the fact that he seemed unable to accomplish *A Communication to My Friends*, "telling the story of how writing was forced upon me and the persecution I have undergone for forty years and which is just ended, leaving me a wreck." He was fundamentally a serious artist, a conscious writer, who through his fifty years of work managed to create his own style and to make it the flexible expression of his own personality. He wrote in his *Confessions* that he came into the world

apparently with a nature like a smooth sheet of wax, bearing no impress, but capable of receiving any; of being moulded into all shapes. Nor am I exaggerating when I say I think that I might equally have been a Pharaoh, an ostler, a pimp, an archbishop, and that in the fulfilment of the duties of each a certain measure of success would have been mine.

(p. 1)

The result of his experience of life was to make him a mixture of naiveté and shrewdness, of mischievousness and an acute awareness of his own limitations. He became a personality filled with apprehensions of beauty and ecstasy, as well as of the absurd, a writer always sharply and persistently aware of the mystery and terrifying speed and shortness of human life.

THE NOVELS AND STORIES

MOORE has a secure place in the history of the English novel. Most readers, for instance, will have read or know of *Esther Waters*, with the new dimension of naturalism it brought into English writing; they will also know how he developed after 1903 a new kind of prose, a blend of the written and spoken word peculiarly his own achievement. But how many realize how much more there is to Moore the novelist than the achievement of his best-known novel or to Moore the raconteur than the apparently artless gossip of *Hail and Farewell*? Of the early works, for example, there is the unusual felicity of *A Drama in Muslin*, foreshadowing the limpidity and brilliance of *The Lake*. The maturity of *The Brooke Kerith* and the virtuosity of *Héloïse and Abélard* round off a quintet of novels extremely varied in subject matter, imaginatively rich and supremely readable. These are his outstanding novels: but there is much to be enjoyed in the others, and this survey will mention them briefly while concentrating on Moore's major work.

When Moore looked back at his first novel, *A Modern Lover*, in 1917, he thought it the book of a young man who "in a moment of inspiration, hit upon an excellent anecdote, and being without literary skill to unfold it, devised an uncouth text out of his memories of Balzac, Zola and Goncourt." He summarized the book neatly:

Three women undertake to work for a young man's welfare: a workgirl, a rich woman, and a lady of high degree. All contribute something, and the young man is put on a high pedestal. One worshipper retains her faith, one loses hers partially, and one altogether.

(*Lewis Seymour and Some Women*, p. viii)

Filled with revulsion as he reread the book, he finally decided that a new book could be molded around it, and the preface to the new version, *Lewis Seymour and Some Women*, tells us engagingly how joyously he dictated and completed the work in three months.

His early desire was to observe and record accurately: the wish to tell a story was, perhaps, a later rationalization. This novel broke new ground in its first version and allowed Moore to portray his knowledge of art and a somewhat flashy view of fashionable life. He was writing an often clumsy English, not to be compared with that of the later version, which has some urbane satire on the relations of the sexes and is more efficiently told as a story: neither version, however, is fully satisfactory.

A Mummer's Wife (1885) was begun with the hope of being, as he wrote to the French novelist, "Zola's ricochet in England." He was applying the French naturalistic method to English material, to the lives of actors in a provincial setting: he spent several weeks with a touring company, and he listened to many stories of the lives of actors and actresses. Out of this came a much more lively interplay of characters than he had achieved in his first novel. Kate Ede, who is seduced by Dick Lennox, is drawn with great sensitivity as well as realism, for Moore had developed and deepened his understanding of personality, of the effect of one sex upon the other, of the human heart; and the treatment of the scenery and the action, despite the mediocre, plain prose style, was sharper than before, more effective and indeed much more frank than anything Moore's contemporaries dared give the public. His desire to escape the bondage of the libraries (evinced in *Literature at Nurse, or Circulating Morals*, 1885) had no doubt sharpened his powers of shocking their particular audience. The realism of the early part of the book gives credence to the developing hysteria and violence of the heroine, who is always measured against the stolid matter-of-factness of Dick Lennox.

With *A Drama in Muslin* (1886), however, Moore developed a much more complex theme and treatment of it, and this novel is still most rewarding to read. In it he describes the two Irelands, of gentry and peasantry, during the tensions of the period of the Land League, which was set up in 1879. The peasants, exasperated by evictions and bad agricultural seasons, were using weapons of boycott, and their no-rent campaign was very effective. There were shootings of landlords and their agents until the 1881 Land Act at last gave the tenants a right to the land without destroying the right of the landlord; it also reduced rents by twenty percent. Further Land Acts of 1887, 1891, and 1903 were to make Ireland a country of peasant proprietors, and Moore had read the writing on the wall. He was a humane man who, though he liked the social standing of being a landlord, realized instinctively that the era of ascendancy was virtually over. The novel, therefore, draws a contrast between the social glitter and tinsel of the viceregal court in Dublin and the uneasiness, even boredom, of life in the big houses and lesser Georgian mansions, whose occupants were perpetually conscious of "the disturbed state of the country." Chapter 13, for instance, is one of the scenes, dissimilar yet interdependent, that are still technically interesting; it is a piece of montage that gives an alternating account of the arguments taking place in front of the house between peasants and their landlord and his agent and of those occurring inside the house between the landlord's wife and an army captain, an unsuccessful suitor for her daughter. The human relationship of the girl and her lover is affected by the general situation:

From the drawing-room window Mrs. Barton watched the conflict, her little selfish soul racked with individual doubt. On one side she saw her daughter's beautiful white face becoming the prize of a penniless officer; on the other she saw the pretty furniture, the luxurious idleness, the very silk dress on her back being torn from them, and distributed among a crowd of Irish-speaking, pig-keeping peasants.

(p. 127)[2]

The girl, Olive Barton, is one of several well-born (and some not quite so well-born) girls who have grown up together in Galway, and who are presented during the Dublin season. Moore hated this marriage market: he was, like Ibsen, convinced that woman was more than a domestic animal. He had read *A Doll's House* when halfway through his own story, but remarked, in the preface to the 1915 edition of *A Drama in Muslin*, that he was himself writing of a puritan heroine, "but not a sexless puritan, and if women cannot win their freedom without leaving their sex behind they had better remain slaves, for a slave with his sex is better than a free eunuch." He thought that Olive's sister, Alice Barton, was a more objective portrayal than Ibsen's Nora. Alice is drawn with dignity. She thinks for herself; she begins to write professionally because she does not regard the capture of a husband as the prime aim of her life. She is no prig, however, and supports the harum-scarum May, who has an illegitimate child; eventually she marries a dispensary doctor. To realize herself she has to resist the activities of her mother, who is drawn ruthlessly in all her vulgarity and energy.

The novel has some unevenness in style. It matches the richness, the bustle and crowding, the hectic excitements and the ensuing enervations of its social

[2]Quotations from *A Drama in Muslin* are from the most recent edition (Gerrards Cross, 1981).

scenes with a voluptuous prose. Here is a portion of the famous description of the dressmaker's shop:

Lengths of white silk clear as the notes of violins playing in a minor key; white poplin falling into folds statuesque as the bass of a fugue by Bach; yards of ruby velvet, rich as an air from Verdi played on the piano; tender green velvet, pastoral as hautboys heard beneath trees in a fair Arcadian vale; blue turquoise faille française fanciful as the twinkling of a guitar twanged by a Watteau shepherd; gold brocade, sumptuous as organ tones swelling through the jewelled twilight of a nave; scarves and trains of midnight blue profound as the harmonic snoring of a bassoon.

(p. 162)

The Misses Robinson, whom he used to visit, read him out a passage that they had added in the margin of their copy: "Everything was represented there, from the light clarinette of the embroidered lace handkerchief to the profound trombone of the red flannel pantaloons." How could he write such a thing, they asked; and he fell into their trap and defended the phrase he had never used. He later saw himself like "a hound yelping at every trace of scent" in this book. He records the serious conversations and the gossip with skill; he catches the crippled Cecilia's religious attacks on sensuous life in suitably matching tortuous prose. He contrasts the life of wretched cabin and glittering salon effectively; he describes the scenery with economical sensitivity; he analyzes the situation of women. And the story holds us with its mixture of satire, objectivity, and insight. It is an unreasonably neglected novel, and it is also a piece of highly significant social history.

When did the author of *A Drama in Muslin* change, Moore asked himself in 1915, and answered himself with 1888, the year of the *Confessions* and *Spring Days*. He wrote four novels that he did not include in his collected works. In *A Mere Accident* (1887) he attempts to capture both the monastic spirit and its opposite, the "sleepy smug-material" of Sussex. The model for the hero of the novel was Edward Martyn, and Moore drew in him a somewhat paradoxical aesthetic ascetic who runs his estates efficiently, collects Monets and Renoirs, reads medieval Latin authors as well as Pater and Schopenhauer, and likes Wagner and Palestrina. His mother tries to get him to marry and eventually he falls in love with a young girl, who is, however, assaulted by a tramp and dies melodramatically after a fall from a window. The novel shows Moore's ability to make use of his friends' characters and to get his

material in order, for he drew heavily upon his friends' knowledge, in this case of medieval Latin and music. The story appears again as "John Norton" in *Celibates,* and a comparison of the two versions shows the great speed with which Moore's technique advanced.

Spring Days (1888) was intended as a prelude to a trilogy that would give a large, sweeping survey of human nature. It tells the story of three English girls in Sussex who fail to marry, but the narrative wanders a little and the hero, Frank Escott, heir to an Irish journalist, who is a second-rate cad-about-town The trilogy was to deal, first with young men in London, next with a servant's view of servants, and finally with the attitudes of old people to their children. *Mike Fletcher* (1889) mainly describes an Irish journalist, who is a second-rate cad about town and a complete failure; the other characters are Frank Escott and John Norton. The idea of a serious novel about servants occurred to him shortly after *A Drama in Muslin* was published; it promised to be more human than *Mike Fletcher*. (Mention of this novel irritated him intensely in later life, so much had he come to dislike its lack of order and development.) He told Mme. Lanza that he intended to bathe himself in "the simplest and most naive emotions, the daily bread of humanity." But before completing this story of servants he spent the winter of 1890–1891 writing *Vain Fortune* (1891) for the *Lady's Pictorial,* where it was published serially under a pseudonym and illustrated by Maurice Greiffenhagen. This novel, not as bad as has sometimes been alleged, and, as Moore wrote in a letter, not a potboiler, has a plot dealing with the frustrations of an unsuccessful author and the girl whom he disinherits. She falls in love with him and commits suicide when he marries her companion.

By 1893 he had completed *Esther Waters;* he announced his plan to Mme. Lanza in a letter:

. . . it is all about servants—servants devoured by betting. It begins in a house in the country where there are race horses. Towards the end of the book—past the middle—the servants set up a public house. They cannot get custom unless they have betting. Then come the various tragedies of the bar—the hairdresser who cuts his throat—the servant who loses thirty years' character for six shillings—the woman who pledges the plate to give her lover money to bet with. The human drama is the story of the servant girl with an illegitimate child, how she saves the child from the baby farmers, her endless temptations to get rid of it and to steal for it. She succeeds in bringing up her boy, and the last scene is when she is living with her first mistress in the old place, ruined and deserted. The race horses have ruined masters as well as the servants.

(*The Life of George Moore*, pp. 165–166)

The book was very well received; it sold well, and the circulating libraries gave way, Mudie at first, then Smith's, after an argument in which Moore proved that they had lost £1,500 by not taking *Esther Waters*. The novel was his tribute to England, "Pecksniff done seriously, and if the feat does not seem impossible, with love."

Esther Waters contains Moore's knowledge of horse racing and of betting, and their effects upon human life. There are the great kaleidoscopic scenes of Derby day, the boom of the great mob, the cockney crowd; there is Mr. Leopold in his pantry, a picture of the butler of Moore Hall; there are the scenes, too, of the lying-in hospital, and there is the baby farmer. Balzac inspired this work, and in it Moore achieves a story of commonplace heroism. He begins with the description of the receding train as it appeared to the girl of twenty; chapter 44 begins in exactly similar words, but the train is seen now by a woman of thirty-seven or thirty-eight, and we realize now with a jolt how much has happened to her in the eighteen years since she first arrived to be a kitchen maid. His picture of how Esther is deserted and how she wrestles with life to bring up her son is realistic, but it is also written with an innate if unobtrusive compassion. It is a humane book, matching its acute observation with sensitive understanding.

In *Evelyn Innes* Moore describes the battle within an opera singer's heart between her religious feelings and her delight in the pleasures of the world. She is torn between love for Sir Owen Asher (probably modeled on a mixture of Arthur Symons' intellectualism and Sir William Eden's aristocratic sophistication) and for Ulick the Celtic musician (modeled in the first edition on Yeats and, later, on AE). The novel reflects Moore's own development: he drew upon Arnold Dolmetsch for the character of Evelyn's father, the musician; he attended some of the informal concerts held in the Dolmetsches' house in Dulwich, where he set part of the novel, and he learned much from Dolmetsch and from Arthur Symons about Renaissance and baroque music. This novel is one of the first to make use of music as a background. It reflects a good deal of fashionable aestheticism, as well as Moore's own interest in Wagner. Factual information gives solidity to the story, which is also based on Moore's own progress in the fashionable world and his financial success. The furniture and the Aubusson carpet in this novel are described with the loving attention that his own similar possessions were receiving in his new flat in Victoria Street, into which he had moved from the Temple.

Evelyn Innes is one of the novels in which he was conducting his education publicly, but the sequel, *Sister Teresa*, has less of this interest, for in it Moore, possibly stimulated by Mrs. Craigie's conversion to Roman Catholicism, was writing an account of life in a convent that allowed him to explore the religious impulse more fully, but with less certainty of touch, as though he were himself affected by Evelyn's hesitation between life in the convent or outside it. Finally, however, the novel ends with her at peace, but with the reader probably sharing the view of the priest quoted by Yeats, who remarked of the novel, "everything is there of the convent, except the religious life." In this novel Moore was echoing the current interest in the opposition of art and reality, spirit and flesh; and the heroine withdraws to the convent's ritual, disappointed by her bid for individual artistic freedom.

A reversal of this progress takes place in *The Lake* (1905), the first of Moore's fully symbolist novels. Some of the hints for it exist in *A Drama in Muslin*, where the influence of Huysmans was clear. In that novel Moore had explored the complications of character and had shown signs of matching character examination with a less drab style. Now he was to explore the complexities of style also and in so doing to create his own contribution to English prose, the melodic line. The story of *The Lake* is relatively simple. A priest drives a pregnant but unmarried schoolteacher from his parish; he later corresponds with her, and falls in love with her without ever seeing her again. His desire for the world increases, his belief diminishes, until finally he leaves his clothes beside the lake and swims across it, to leave his parish and Ireland and begin another life. Father Oliver Gogarty (the name was chosen in mockery of that unpriestlike figure Oliver St. John Gogarty, who appears as Buck Mulligan in Joyce's *Ulysses*) walks by the lakeside, and the story slowly unfolds itself with a convincing, compellingly persuasive development. The technical achievement is superb; the movement from *Esther Waters* to *The Lake* is parallel to that of Joyce from *Dubliners* to *A Portrait of the Artist* (and *Hail and Farewell* captures another aspect—Moore's life in Ely Place—of that Dublin which is also so brilliantly immortalized in Joyce's Eccles Street in *Ulysses*). The change was brought about after he had completed the stories of *The Untilled Field*, in which he had examined some of the sterility and sadness he saw in Irish life, where he attributed poverty and emigration to the work of a puritanical, priestly church. These earlier stories, especially "The Wedding Gown," "The Window," and "So On He Fares," are masterly pieces of storytelling, spare, economical, but highly emotive.

The Lake opens with a passage that shows us the kind of association Moore is to evoke throughout the novel between scene and mood; he was writing about the place in which he himself grew up, and he wrote with deep feeling:

It was one of those enticing days at the beginning of May when white clouds are drawn about the earth like curtains. The lake lay like a mirror that someone had breathed upon, the brown islands showing through the mist faintly, with gray shadows falling into the water, blurred at the edges. The ducks were talking softly in the reeds, the reeds themselves were talking; and the water lapped softly about the smooth limestone shores. But there was an impulse in the gentle day, and, turning from the sandy spit, Father Oliver walked to and fro along the disused cart-track about the edge of the wood, asking himself if he were going home, knowing quite well that he could not bring himself to interview his parishioners that morning. On a sudden resolve to escape from anyone that might be seeking him, he went into the wood and lay down on the warm grass, and admired the thickly-tasselled branches of the tall larches swinging above him.

After the priest has reached his decision to leave his parish, the lake is still there, its serenity matching the excitement with which he contemplates the oneness of nature. "Every man," he says, "has a lake in his heart," and Moore carries the symbolism forward through the novel, building up his suggestions with subtlety through the apparent simplicity of the famous melodic line:

He walked along the shore feeling like an instrument that had been tuned. His perception seemed to have been indefinitely increased, and it seemed to him as if he were in communion with the stones in the earth and the clouds in heaven; it seemed to him as if the past and the future had become one.

The moment was one of extraordinary sweetness; never might such a moment happen in his life again. The earth and sky were enfolding in one tender harmony of rose and blue, the blue shading down to grey, and the lake floated amid vague shores, vaguely as a dream floats through sleep. The swallows were flying high, quivering overhead in the blue air. There was a sense of security and persuasion and loveliness in the evening.

(pp. 267–268)

The Brook Kerith (1916) is often described as a prose epic and fully deserves the name. It is constructed with skill, and its conversational style has a directness, freshness, and spontaneity that give it warmth and color. In it Moore retells the story of the New Testament with the difference that in the account that he puts in the mouth of Joseph of Arimathea, Jesus has not died on the cross but has been rescued by Joseph. He is later discovered by Paul, who seeks refuge in the community of Essenes among whom Jesus has lived as a shepherd in the wilderness for twenty years. Paul at first believes that Jesus is a madman, then fears he may return to Jerusalem to destroy his own work. But Jesus tells him that we must learn to live for ourselves and to suffer our fellows to do likewise; all learning, he says, "comes out of ourselves, and no one may communicate his thought; for his thought was given to him for himself alone." The biblical imagery and rhythms add to the epic quality of the story: it is simple and the narrative unfolds effectively, action, description, thought, and speech blending in a pattern that provides variation and tension as well as information and reflection. It is easy to read, and it reads aloud superbly; it is spacious, dignified, and captivating, an example of the supreme flexibility of the art of a great storyteller whose essential seriousness of artistic purpose is enlivened by the subtle humor and by the inconsequential trivia that give to the novel its feelings of concrete detail:

Hast slept well, Paul, and hath sleep refreshed thee and given thee strength to pursue thy journey? Paul answered that he was very weary, but however weary must struggle on to Caesarea. Thy strength will not suffer thee to get farther than Bethennabrio, and thy sandals will need mending even to reach the village. And seating himself on a smooth stone Paul watched Jesus's hand tying new thongs, wondering if the madman's mind was still set on Jerusalem and if he would go thither as soon as he (Paul) was safely out of the ways of the Jews. Each shut himself within the circle of his own mind, and the silence was not broken till Paul began to fear that Jesus was plotting against him; and to distract Jesus's mind from his plots, if he were weaving any, he began to compare the country they were passing through with Galilee, and forthright Jesus began to talk to

Paul of Peter and John and James, sons of Zebedee, mentioning their appearances, voices, manner of speech, telling of their boats, their fishing tackle, the fish-salting factory of Magdala, Dan, and Joseph his son. He spoke a winning story of the fishing life round the lake, without mention of miracles, for it was not to his purpose to convince Paul of any spiritual power he might have enjoyed, but rather of his own simple humanity. And Paul listened, still believing his guide to be a madman. If thou hadst not run away crying: He is mad! he is mad! thou wouldst have heard how my crucifixion was brought about; how my eyes opened in the tomb and—Interrupting Jesus, Paul hastened to assure him that if he cried out: He is mad! he is mad! he had spoken unwittingly, the words being put into his mouth by the sickness in which Jesus had discovered him. And the sickness, he admitted, might have been brought about by the shock of hearing thee speak of thyself as the Messiah. But, Paul, I did not speak of myself as the Messiah, but as an Essene who during some frenzied months believed himself to be the Messiah. But shepherd, Paul answered, the Messiah promised to the Jews was Jesus of Nazareth, who was raised by his Father from the dead, and thou sayest that thou art the same. If thou didst once believe thyself to be the Messiah thou hast repented thy blasphemy. In the desert these twenty years, Jesus answered. But not till now did I know my folly had borne fruit, and that Joseph knew a story had been set going; or it may be that the story was not set going till after his death. Now it seems too late to go into the field thou hast sown with tares instead of corn. To which Paul answered: It is my knowledge of thy life among rocks that prompts me to listen to thee. The field I have sown like every other field has some tares in it, but it is full of corn ripening fast which will be ready for the reaping when it shall please the Lord to descend with his own son, Jesus of Nazareth, from the skies. As soon as the words: Jesus of Nazareth, had left his lips Paul regretted them, and upon a sudden resolve not to utter another word that might offend the madman's beliefs, he began to tell that he had brought hope to the beggar, to the outcast, to the slave; though this world was but a den of misery to them, another world was coming to which they might look forward in full surety. And many, he said, that led vile lives are now God-fearing men and women who, when the daily work is done, go forth in the evening to beseech the multitude to give some time to God. In every field there are tares, but there are fewer in my field than in any other, and that I hold to be the truth; and seeing that Jesus was listening to his story he began to relate his theology, perplexing Jesus with his doctrines, but interesting him with the glad tidings that the burden of the law had been lifted from all. If he had stopped there all would have been well, so it seemed to Jesus, whose mind was not able to grasp why a miracle should be necessary to prove to men that the love of God was in the heart rather than in observances, and the miracle that Paul continued to relate with much unction seemed to him crude; yet he once believed that God was pleased to send his only begotten son to redeem the world by his death on a cross. A strange conception truly. And while he was thinking these things Paul fell to telling his dogma concerning predestination, and he was anxious that Jesus should digest his reply to Mathias, who had said that predestination conflicted with the doctrine of salvation for all. But Jesus, who was of Mathias's opinion, refrained from expressing himself definitely on the point, preferring to forget Paul, so that he might better consider if he would be able to make plain to Paul that miracles bring no real knowledge of God to man, and that our conscience is the source of our knowledge of God and that perhaps a providence flourishes beyond the world.

(ch. 41)

Héloïse and Abélard has a rich content: in this philosophical romance Moore mixes thought and tragedy, description and story. Tension begins in Canon Fulbert's house overlooking the Seine; the lovers, the canon's niece and the brilliant academic, travel through the forests to Britanny surrounded by spring sights and sounds; there is always a background unobtrusive yet atmospheric; there is both movement and contemplation:

But to reach Chécy before nightfall they would have to hasten, and the innkeeper told them that the road through the forest looped so that the village of Lorris might be taken into the circuit; but there was no need for him to follow this winding, he would find a by-path across certain low hills which he could not miss. Abélard did not feel sure that the by-path might not be missed, but to hear the road explained out again would be merely a waste of time, and so they hastened towards the forest in a sort of half-knowledge of the way, allowing the horses to trot a little, thinking that they might draw rein when they passed through the fringe of birch-trees that encircled with their pallor the great district of pines that showed in black masses over against Etampes. Now we are well within the forest, Abélard said, as much in the forest as if we were in the middle of it; and he asked Héloïse to peep over the undergrowth that lined the rutted path down which they were riding, so that she might see the pines rising up naked and bare some fifty or sixty feet, some straight, some leaning, in endless aisles. Like the spears, Héloïse said, of Crusaders going into battle; and how penetrating is the smell of the resin. But the pines were in patches only, and the forest passed quickly into rocky hillsides overgrown with oak and beech; and so faint was the path they followed that Abélard often asked Héloïse and Madelon to draw rein while he went forward in search of the path. For if we all went forward together, he said, we should not be able to go back to where the path ends: a tree is no sure landmark; one forgets which tree, and wanders in a circle.

I've got it, he cried to them, and they came forward, the forest getting lonelier as they proceeded into it.

All bird cries have ceased, and we hear only the sighing of the boughs, Héloïse said, and the smell of the forest is different from all other smells; a more mysterious smell is about, a smell of earth and moss. There is also a warm smell, said Madelon, that reminds me of our Britanny forests, the great forest about Clisson, where we shall be—Héloïse, myself and my boy—before the month's end, should we catch a fast-sailing barge from Orléans. Did he not say that a little over three leagues from Etampes we should find the by-path that would save us several leagues' journey? Abélard asked, and some hundreds of feet after he told them to rein in while he went on ahead in search of the path. Here it is, he cried, from a clearing; we have but to follow the path that leads through the hollows yonder up to the rising ground that the innkeeper spoke of. He spoke to me of oak-trees, and here they are. And they rode beneath the boughs not yet in full leaf, following the path as it wound through hollows, losing it and finding it amid rocks, pushing their way through thickets that seemed impenetrable at a distance but did not prove so hard to force through as they had appeared. There is a rutted way under the brambles, Abélard said; cattle and horses have been through here; and stooping low in their saddles, they broke through somehow, losing bits of clothing in the passage. Soon after the path led them up hills, through thorn and hazel mingled with inter-spaces, till it brought them to a heath, and Abélard said: those pines standing so solitary at the end of the lake embedded in rocks are the trees the innkeeper told me I was to look out for. We have not missed the way, he continued; look back and see the forest that we have come through. And he pointed to a dark ragged line of pines flowing down the northern sky. But is our way to the right or to the left? Madelon asked. To the left, he answered; we have to ride southward, keeping the setting sun on our right.

(ch. 16)

Abélard's arrogant ambition, Héloïse's agonized love, their joint readiness to lie in pursuance and defense of love, are part of the whole life of the book. Moore's sensualism and his occasional mischievousness underlie the simplicity of the story; his attitude is consistent. The peasant driving his cart, and Madelon, the canon's servingwoman, are two examples of an earthy contrast opposed to the intellectualism of the lovers. The romance gains in depth because the conversations and thoughts of Héloïse and Abélard are sharply focused against a very crowded background of cities and convents, of trouvères, of classical culture, even of the contentions between nominalists and realists. Moore took immense trouble to get his picture of eleventh-century life right. Its complexity is gained through digressions and repetitions in the talk and the learning; the liveliness comes from his picture of the ceaseless sifting of the human mind on earth; the resolution rests upon a human will to believe in heaven and immortal happiness.

Ulick and Soracha deals with medieval Ireland, but it lacks the sheer beauty of *Héloïse and Abélard*; and *Aphrodite in Aulis* runs the risk of appearing disjointed, for its author's habit of digression and complication is not under the fine architectonic control he had earlier displayed.

It is perhaps fitting to conclude a brief account of Moore's fiction with some comment on the five stories—"a single narrative divided into five chapters"—of *Celibate Lives* (1927), which were based on earlier work in *Celibates, A Story-Teller's Holiday,* and *In Single Strictness.* They show Moore's developed artistry in illustrating, in smooth narrative, with calm detachment, the finer points of character, indeed his never-ceasing fascination with human motive and behavior. That the stories are about women reminds us that he had remarked in the *Confessions* that he was enthralled by "the mystery of petticoats" and confessed in the *Memoirs* that his thoughts ran upon women as the legitimate object of men's thoughts. His own thoughts he translated into an objective portrayal of women's role in a society within which they were moving to greater freedom; his apparently detached portraits were drawn not only with skill but with deep sympathy.

THE PLAYS

In all, Moore wrote eleven plays, the first two of which, *Worldliness* (about 1874) and *Martin Luther* (1879), were not performed. Several managers, including John Hare and Herbert Beerbohm Tree, refused the next of his plays, *The Strike at Arlingford,* but after a few years Moore turned its five acts into three, and it was performed in February 1893. He was greatly attracted by the Ibsen-like qualities of Martyn's *The Heather Field,* and when Martyn's next play, *The Tale of a Town,* was disappointing, he took it over and it was produced, under Moore's name, as *The Bending of the Bough* (1900). He explained the situation thus, in a letter to his brother Maurice:

I am afraid Martyn suffered a good deal. He says I spoil[ed] his play but that is an illusion. I recast the play, but not enough. I should have written a new play on the subject. . . . Then Edward said he could not sign it, and he refused to let it be played anonymously, so I had to sign it.
(*The Life of George Moore*, pp. 221–222)

The play revolves around nationalist and unionist attitudes. The potential leader gives up the struggle because of his love for a girl, and his backsliding is received with philosophical serenity by the nationalist éminence grise. It is a dull play, but in the politically charged atmosphere of the Dublin of that time it was well received.

Moore's next collaboration was with Yeats, and their work on *Diarmuid and Grania* led to much disagreement between them. The play was put on in Dublin in 1901, but the critics there regarded the treatment of the heroic legend as unsatisfactory. The susceptibilities of nationalists could be easily upset. Moore wrote to his brother that "they first of all enjoyed the play, and having enjoyed it they repented in sackcloth and ashes, and I really believe that the repentance was much greater than their enjoyment of the play."

Moore's next adventure into drama was *The Apostle*, which deals with a meeting between Jesus and Paul after the crucifixion: it was hastily published, but contains his fascinating "Prefatory Letter on Reading the Bible for the First Time." In 1906 Moore had begun work on a dramatic version of *Esther Waters*, and Lennox Robinson was called in to help with the dialogue—Moore's old weakness—in the second act. The play was performed twice, but unsuccessfully, at the Apollo Theatre. Moore, however, was not put off by its reception and resumed work on *Elizabeth Cooper* (1913), which was produced by the Stage Society in 1913. Moore had enlisted the aid of Mrs. Craigie on this play in 1904, and five years later was helped by Dujardin (who produced the French version, *Clara Florise*, at the Comédie Royale). Moore's correspondence with a foreign lady of title, begun some ten years earlier, formed the basis of the plot. In the play the foreign countess mistakes the young secretary of the author for his employer and, in one version, marries him. Another rewriting appeared as *The Coming of Gabrielle* (1920), which was rehearsed in 1921 but finally abandoned. It was a near-miss.

The Brook Kerith led to a second play entitled *The Apostle* (1923); this adds a scene to the novel, but is also lacking in good dialogue. Moore followed it

with *The Making of an Immortal* (1927), an amusing Shakespearean conceit with clever character sketches; this was well received after its production at the Arts Theatre in 1928.

The Passing of the Essenes (1930) is yet another handling of the theme of *The Brook Kerith*, and the relationship of Jesus and Paul. This time the reception was warm, the play's run extended, and Moore even went to see it himself. He came back as critical of actors as ever, since the

poor play did not come out as it should have come out, and what pleasure is it to me that other people liked it? I wanted to like it and I didn't. The uninspired actors were between me and it all the time.
(*The Life of George Moore*, p. 427)

Moore was his own best actor, and his best writing was self-dramatization. His weakness was inability to write good dialogue; his strength was in duologue, provided he was inventing both parts of the conversation.

AUTOBIOGRAPHIES AND ESSAYS

MOORE's *Confessions of a Young Man* (1888) was written when he was thirty-six; it describes his life in Paris and records his impressions of Manet, Degas, and Renoir, of Zola, and of Verlaine and Mallarmé. The book gives us an excellent impression of aestheticism and of Moore's youthful desire to shock and astonish people. It was certainly original, and the self-portrait is one of Moore as he seemed to Theodore Dorret, "a golden-haired fop, an aesthete before the days of Wilde . . . his manners were amusing and his French very funny." Always, Dorret remarked, he remained a gentleman and would never associate with those he thought to be below his rank as an Irish landlord. As a result Moore describes his early life with satiric detachment. *Memoirs of My Dead Life* contained more material likely to astonish, if taken seriously, rather than to shock. "The Lovers of Orelay" became famous as an account of an elderly man's adventure with a young woman in France, told with comic relish, as well as some naiveté, as in the account of the purchase of the silk nightshirt. The volume contains memoirs of Mayo, London, Paris, and Sussex (a moving account of Mrs. Bridger's death). The love stories reflect his comment that his thoughts ran on women: "On what would you have them run? On coppermines? Woman is the legitimate subject of all men's thoughts." When he wrote the *Memoirs* he was fifty-four; his energies were increasingly occupied by his writing and rewriting, and this gave him a reputation for cold detachment. It is true that he used his friends as material for his writing, but he used himself even more. During his stay in Ireland at the beginning of the century his style had developed from the flowing narrative of the stories of *The Untilled Field* into the complexities, repetitions, linkages, and cadences of *The Lake.* There he became the raconteur, there he moved from his livelier youth into a search for and a discovery of himself. The *Memoirs* show his flair for maintaining the fluidity of his tales, his mixture of speech and reflection, his blending of past and present thought.

Throughout the superb comedy of *Hail and Farewell,* which is his masterpiece, there runs the ground swell of his preoccupation with Protestantism as he imagined it, with the issues of life as he experienced them, emotionally and instinctively, often willfully and impatiently. He was not concerned with the reputation of Moore the man; he cared deeply for the reputation of Moore the writer. And so *Hail and Farewell* is a devastating work: ironic, witty, provocative, even at times profound in its accounts of the men and women he observed around him in Dublin. His brilliant evocation of Edward Martyn, his delicate appreciation of AE, his caustic commentary on Yeats contribute to our sense of human comedy.

The forthrightness of Moore's comments stemmed from his belief that once the veracity of a biographer (or autobiographer) is impugned, the book becomes discredited and its value depreciated. And so he gives us magnificent scenes—the dinner in the Shelbourne Hotel; the bicycling around Tara, New Grange, and Dowth with AE; as well as the account (which disturbed so many of his contemporaries) of the end of his affair with Stella. This is the artist at work—with the disciple he called Amico Moorini emerging at intervals to nudge his comic work into the risk of seeming farce—for flippancy and willfulness have never appealed greatly to critics, however much they were an almost inevitable minor part of such an unusual talent as Moore's, committed to both the artistic and the ruthless rendering of a situation, a nuance, an anecdote, which would convey his own attitude of curiosity, of almost innocent interest, to the reader. He re-creates yet again but with entirely new memories his days in the Temple, in Paris, in Mayo, in Sussex. With Whelan the coachman he avoids mass when staying with Edward Mar-

tyn, with whom he visits Bayreuth for a performance of *The Ring.* The flow of his mind is strong; he observes Lady Gregory and Yeats in the west of Ireland; he gives us vignettes of Dublin as he walks by the Liffey or the Dodder; he recounts conversations, and retells Dublin gossip: of how, for instance, Sir Thornley Stoker the surgeon collected his antiques:

. . . on the trail of a Sheraton sideboard and Naylor has been asked to keep it till an appendix should turn up. The Chinese Chippendale mirror over the drawing-room chimney-piece originated in an unsuccessful operation for cancer; the Aubusson carpet in the back drawing-room represents a hernia; the Renaissance bronze on the landing a set of gall-stones; the King Cloisonné a floating kidney; the Buhl cabinet his opinion on an enlarged liver; and Lady Stoker's jewels a series of small operations performed over a term of years.

(*Hail and Farewell,* vol. II: *Salve,* p. 437)

All of this is recounted with limpidity; the transitions from speech to thought, to memory, to speech again invite us to tour with him through reveries of rich reminiscence and ideas that are lively, stamped always with a zest and appreciation of living, with shrewdness and naiveté.

These qualities permeate his critical prose also. *Avowals* (1919), for instance, contains opinions on literary works "discovered" by Moore over the years. These are delivered with some panache, for, as Moore reminds us in chapter 16, his only affectation is complete naturalness; and on the subject of writing he held strong views. The English eighteenth-century novelists, Jane Austen, Walter Pater, Leo Tolstoy, and Ivan Turgenev are discussed with vigor and delight. Moore did not read a great deal, but he had listened and discussed; he had formed his opinions and he gave them a curiously personal flavor:

In the fifties, was the Word and it was with Flaubert, I said, and began to trace the origin of his reputation to a reaction against Byron, his going to Greece to die for an idea, to Chateaubriand's tomb, to pirates and brigands who had become so intolerable in literature that everybody welcomed the idea that a writer need not dine in a baronial hall among retainers, nor keep for pets pythons, eagles, wolves or jaguars, and of all it was pleasant to hear that Monsieur Flaubert spent much time at his window watching the Seine flowing by, thinking of the inevitable Word, which he never found till late in the evening. Everybody was delighted; fellow-feeling makes wondrous bedfellows, and when it became known for certain that *Madame Bovary* was written in a dressing-gown, the reaction against romanticism carried the book along with it, and if this explanation prove inacceptable, we shall have to fall back on the depressing belief, for which, indeed, much can be said, that the masterpiece is but our mood, and that as soon as the mood passes—all moods except the Bible, Shakespeare and Sterne pass—the inspired and the uninspired are like as twins.

(ch. 14)

Conversations in Ebury Street ranges widely. Balzac, George Eliot, and Thomas Hardy are discussed with zest. Then the artists Tonks, Steer, and Sickert are given life, followed by further literary comments and speculations, among them enlightened praise of Anne Brontë's work. There is not, however, so much concentration as in the essays of *Avowals*, which represent the flowering of Moore's literary views in the midsummer of his career, with *Esther Waters*, *The Lake*, *The Brook Kerith*, *Héloïse and Abélard*, and *Hail and Farewell* already achieved.

THE ACHIEVEMENT

MOORE's achievement needs reconsideration. His works have been allowed to drop out of print—one hopes only temporarily—but his merits should not be ignored. For he is a writer of great skill, a serious writer who can give much pleasure to his readers. He affected the course of English fiction and the style of English prose; he developed his own literary personality; he was a man in whom imagination and narrative skill, capacity for industrious work and artistic conscience so fused that he produced fiction and fictionalized autobiography that have the timeless quality of all great art. He carries us on when we read him, and that is perhaps the secret of the enjoyment he can give: it is the art of the storyteller he has developed, and he appeals to our common delight in and enjoyment of a story well told.

SELECTED BIBLIOGRAPHY

I. BIBLIOGRAPHY. I. A. Williams, *Bibliographies of Modern Authors: No. 3, George Moore* (London, 1921); J. Freeman, *A Portrait of George Moore in a Study of His Work* (London, 1922), includes H. Danielson, "George Moore: A Bibliography, 1878–1921"; H. E. Gerber, "George Moore: An Annotated Bibliography of Writings About Him," in *English Fiction in Transition (1880–1920)*, II, 2, pts. 1 and 2 (1959) and supplements; III, 2 (1960); IV, 2 (1961): the information (and sensible comments) are essential for any serious study of Moore's work; see also Gerber's article on George Moore in *English Literature in Transition*, II, 1 (1968), 50–54; J. C. Noël, *George Moore: l'homme et l'oeuvre* (Paris, 1966): the whole of Moore's work is described and analyzed with an accompanying account of its critical reception, including comprehensive bibliography and portraits.

II. COLLECTED WORKS. *The Works of George Moore*, 20 vols. (London, 1924–1933), the Uniform ed.; *The Works of George Moore*, 20 vols. (London, 1936–1938), the Ebury ed.

III. SEPARATE WORKS. *Worldliness. A Comedy in Three Acts* (London, ca. 1874); *Flowers of Passion* (London, 1878), verse; *Martin Luther. A Tragedy in Five Acts* (London, 1879), verse drama, in collaboration with Bernard Lopez; *Pagan Poems* (London, 1881); *A Modern Lover*, 3 vols. (London, 1883), novel, rewritten as *Lewis Seymour and Some Women* (London, 1917); *A Mummer's Wife* (London, 1885), novel, French trans. (Paris, 1888); *Literature at Nurse, or Circulating Morals* (London, 1885), polemic, pamphlet on selection of books at Mudie's Library; *A Drama in Muslin. A Realistic Novel* (London, 1886), largely rewritten as *Muslin* (London, 1915), the modern ed. is titled *A Drama in Muslin* (Gerrards Cross, 1981), with an intro. by A. N. Jeffares; *A Mere Accident* (London, 1887), novel, rewritten as "John Norton" in *Celibates* (1895); *Parnell and His Island* (London, 1887), sketches; *Confessions of a Young Man* (London, 1888), autobiography, ed. and ann. by Moore (1904; 1917; rev. ed., 1926), also in Uniform ed. (1933); *Spring Days. A Realistic Novel. A Prelude to "Don Juan"* (London, 1888), with preface (1912); *Mike Fletcher* (London, 1889), novel; *Impressions and Opinions* (London, 1891), criticism; *Vain Fortune* (London, 1891; rev. ed., 1895), novel; *Modern Painting* (London, 1893; enl. ed., 1898), criticism; *The Strike at Arlingford. A Play in Three Acts* (London, 1893); *Esther Waters* (London, 1894), novel, rev. and privately printed (1920), also in Uniform ed. (1932; 1964), dramatic version (1913); *Celibates* (London, 1895), stories, contains three tales, "Mildred Lawson," "John Norton," and "Agnes Lahens," rewritten as *Celibate Lives* (1927); *The Royal Academy, 1895* (London, 1895), criticism, New Budget Extra, no. 1; *Evelyn Innes* (London, 1898), novel.

The Bending of the Bough. A Comedy in Five Acts (London, 1900); "Literature and the Irish Language," in Lady Gregory, ed., *Ideals in Ireland* (London, 1901); *Sister Teresa* (London, 1901), novel, continuation of *Evelyn Innes*, entirely rewritten (1928); *The Untilled Field* (London, 1903), short stories, part of the book first published in Gaelic (Dublin, 1902; rev. ed., 1926), also in Uniform ed. (1932), and with a foreword by T. R. Henn (Gerrards Cross, 1976); *The Lake* (London, 1905; rev. ed., 1921), novel, also in Uniform ed. (1932), and with a foreword by R. A. Cave (Gerrards Cross, 1980); *Memoirs of My Dead Life* (London, 1906; rev. and enl., "Moore Hall" ed., 1921;

rev., Uniform ed., 1928), fictional autobiography; *Reminiscences of the Impressionistic Painters* (Dublin, 1906), memoirs; *Hail and Farewell,* 3 vols. (London, 1911–1914), autobiography, vol. I: *Ave* (1911); vol. II: *Salve* (1912); vol. III: *Vale* (1914; lim. ed. in 2 vols., 1925), also in Uniform ed., 3 vols. (1933), also in R. Cave, ed., *Hail and Farewell: Ave, Salve, Vale* (Gerrards Cross, 1976); *The Apostle. A Drama in Three Acts* (Dublin, 1911; rev. lim. ed., 1923); *Elizabeth Cooper. A Comedy in Three Acts* (Dublin, 1913); *Muslin* (London, 1915), novel, rev. of *A Drama in Muslin,* also in Uniform ed. (1932); *The Brook Kerith. A Syrian Story* (London, 1916), novella, 5th ed. rev. (1921), also rev. for Uniform ed. (1927), lim. ed. with engravings by S. Gooden (1929); *Lewis Seymour and Some Women* (London, 1917), novel, rev. of *A Modern Lover; A Story-Teller's Holiday* (lim. ed., London, 1918), short stories, rev. ed. in 2 vols., including *Ulick and Soracha,* also in Uniform ed. (1928); *Avowals* (lim. ed., London, 1919), criticism, also in Uniform ed. (1924).

The Coming of Gabrielle. A Comedy in Three Acts (lim. ed., London, 1920); *Héloïse and Abélard,* 2 vols. (lim. ed., London, 1921), historical romance, also in Uniform ed. (1925); *Fragments from Héloïse and Abélard: Additions and Corrections* (London, 1921); *In Single Strictness* (lim. ed., London, 1922) short stories, rev. as *Celibate Lives* for Uniform ed. (1927); *Conversations in Ebury Street* (lim. ed., London, 1924), criticism, rev. for Uniform ed. (1930); *The Pastoral Loves of Daphnis and Chloë. Done into English* (lim. ed., London, 1924), translation, from Longus, with *Peronnik the Fool* in Uniform ed. (1933); *Peronnik the Fool* (New York, 1924), short story (new lim. ed., New York, 1926; rev. lim. ed., Eure, 1928), with engravings by S. Gooden (London, 1933), with *The Pastoral Loves of Daphnis and Chloë* in Uniform ed. (1933); *Pure Poetry. An Anthology* (lim. ed., London, 1924), anthology; *Ulick and Soracha* (lim. ed., London, 1926), novel, rev. and included with *A Story-Teller's Holiday* in Uniform ed. (1928); *The Making of an Immortal. A Comedy in One Act* (New York, 1927); *A Flood* (New York, 1930), short story; *Aphrodite in Aulis* (lim. ed., London, 1930), novel, rev. for Uniform ed. (1931); *The Passing of the Essenes. A Drama in Three Acts* (London, 1930), lim. ed. of a further rev. of *The Apostle; A Communication to My Friends* (lim. ed., London, 1933), autobiography, with *A Mummer's Wife* in Uniform ed. (1933); "*Diarmuid and Grania. A Play in Three Acts by George Moore and W. B. Yeats,*" *Dublin,* 26 (April–June 1954), with intro. note by W. Becker.

Moore also wrote intros. to Zola's *Piping Hot!* (London, 1885) and Dostoyevsky's *Poor Folk* (London, 1894), among others.

IV. LETTERS. "John Eglinton" [William Magee], trans., *Letters from George Moore to Ed. Dujardin 1886–1922* (New York, 1929); *Letters of George Moore* (Bournemouth, 1942), with intro. by "John Eglinton," a frank and convincing picture of Moore as a man; R. Hart-Davis, ed., *George Moore's Letters to Lady Cunard* (London, 1957), a record of the great sentimental friendship of Moore's life, well edited; H. E. Gerber, ed., *George Moore in Transition. Letters to T. Fisher Unwin and Lena Milman, 1894–1910* (London, 1968), with commentary by ed.

V. BIOGRAPHICAL AND CRITICAL STUDIES. J. Freeman, *A Portrait of George Moore in a Study of His Work* (London, 1922), the first full-scale study of Moore's works; D. R. Gwynn, *Edward Martyn and the Irish Revival* (London, 1930), appraises Moore's work for the Irish literary revival; H. Wolfe, *George Moore* (London, 1931), enthusiastic but dated; C. Morgan, *Epitaph on George Moore* (London, 1935), extremely good brief interpretation of Moore as man and writer; J. Hone, *The Life of George Moore* (London, 1936), the most important book written on Moore, detached, accurate, and well written, an admirable biography; O. St. John Gogarty, *As I Was Going Down Sackville Street* (London, 1937), a picturesque view of Moore and Yeats; J. Hone, *The Moores of Moore Hall* (London, 1939), describes the life of Moore's brother, Colonel Maurice Moore, as well as that of the novelist; R. A. Gettman, "George Moore's Revisions of *The Lake, The Wild Goose,* and *Esther Waters,*" in *PMLA,* 69 (June 1944), points out that Moore's habit of revising his work was not confined to his old age.

S. Nejdefors-Frisk, *George Moore's Naturalistic Prose* (London, 1952); A. T. Schwab, "Irish Author and American Critic," in *Nineteenth Century Fiction,* 8 (March 1954), 256–277, and 9 (June 1954), 22–37; M. Browne, *George Moore: A Reconsideration* (Seattle, 1955), useful and appreciative; N. Cunard, *G.M.: Memories of George Moore* (London, 1956), personal memories and a friend's appreciation; H. Howarth, *The Irish Writers, 1880–1940* (New York, 1959), excellent and informative; G. Hough, *Edwardians and Late Victorians* (London, 1960), "George Moore and the Nineties," pp. 1–27, is a good survey, setting Moore in his period; E. Starkie, *From Gautier to Eliot* (London, 1960), a good account of French influence on Moore; W. F. Blissett, "George Moore and Literary Wagnerism," in *Comparative Literature,* 13 (Winter 1961), deals with Moore's use of Wagnerism and his originality; R. Pickvance, "A Newly Discovered Drawing by Degas of George Moore," in *Burlington* magazine (June 1963), useful on Moore's art criticism; F. S. L. Lyons, "George Moore and Edward Martyn," in *Hermathena,* 98 (Spring 1964), 9–32; J. C. Noël, *George Moore: l'homme et l'oeuvre* (Paris, 1966), see "Bibliography" above; G. Owens, ed., *George Moore's Mind and Art* (London, 1968), essays by various hands; J. E. Dunleavy, *George Moore: The Artist's Vision, the Storyteller's Art* (Lewisburg, Pa., 1973); R. A. Cave, *A Study of the Novels of George Moore* (Gerrards Cross, 1978); R. Welch, ed., *The Way Back: George Moore's "The Untilled Field" and "The Lake"* (Dublin, 1982), includes essays by D. Kiberd, R. Welch, R. A. Cave, T. ó Murchada, J. Cronin, C. Hart, M. E. Cordonnier, and J. S. O'Leary.

GEORGE BERNARD SHAW
(1856-1950)

Margery M. Morgan

LIFE

BERNARD SHAW created a new art of drama in the 1890's and remained the vigorous center of the British theater for half a century. For much of that period he was regarded throughout the world as the preeminent modern dramatist. After his death there came the usual critical reaction in England; and the eclipse of his reputation was a fortunate and healthy liberation for a new succession of playwrights (starting with John Osborne and Arnold Wesker) that emerged through the Royal Court Theatre in London, where Shaw himself had triumphed between 1904 and 1907. The new writers needed to bury Shaw to gain a hearing for themselves, as he had needed to bury Victorian idolization of Shakespeare. His plays continued to be performed as surefire entertainments for conventional middle-class audiences, a fate that would have exasperated but not surprised the author; and his successors carried on the work of social criticism and political debate to which he, in the wake of Ibsen, had reopened the English stage. Meanwhile, serious scholarly and critical study of his writings was left almost entirely to Americans, and the British have had to fight through years of neglect and ignorance to reach a new perspective on his work and a fresh judgment of its nature and value.

Born in Dublin of Protestant stock in 1856, Shaw became—with Oscar Wilde—the eldest of a galaxy of Irish writers, including William Butler Yeats, John Millington Synge, Sean O'Casey, James Joyce, and Samuel Beckett—who have contributed richly to modern English literature and drama. Political and economic stagnation, following the famines, poverty, and depopulation of mid-nineteenth-century Ireland, were forcing-house conditions for the imagination prior to the romantic revival of nationalism, but drove many of those with artistic talents to seek a more cosmopolitan and hopeful culture overseas.

In Shaw's case there were precipitating family reasons for his departure to England at the age of twenty. He was the son of a loveless marriage between an incompetent father, whose drinking habits won his wife's contempt and ostracism in a narrowly respectable society, and a snobbish, indifferent mother who found her emotional fulfillment in music, as an amateur singer of marked talent. She brought the teacher who trained her voice, and conducted the concerts and operas in which she sang, to live with the family. This man, George John Vandeleur Lee, had a high reputation as a musician in Dublin at the time. When he went to London to advance himself professionally, Mrs. Shaw followed him with her two daughters, the younger of whom died of tuberculosis at the age of twenty-one, while Lucy, the eldest child, made a career as a singer in light opera. For two years her son stayed with his father and worked as a clerk in a land agency. Then he left his job and joined his mother, who was now herself teaching music and becoming disillusioned over Lee's gradual abandonment of his high standards and remarkable principles of voice training.

No one had bothered to teach the rudiments of music to Bernard Shaw, but the home environment had nourished his love and need of it, and he taught himself to play operas on the piano, as he was to teach himself much else. From his father and uncles he had learned a vivid sense of the ridiculous and a quick-witted skepticism that flung reverence and conventional thinking to the winds. This was a survival kit for accommodating plagues and disasters great and small, which more Irishmen than Shaw have turned into a genius for comic fantasy. His formal education was scanty and unsystematic, and he arrived in London untrained for anything, provincial in manners, and very shy.

For the next ten years Shaw lived in his mother's house, surviving on her tolerance and with some initial help from Lee, who set him on the path of journalism by arranging for him to write and be paid for a series of articles on music commissioned from Lee himself by a satirical weekly review, *The Hornet.* Apart from this, Shaw in his twenties read widely, wrote occasional rather hopeless and usually unsuccessful letters of application for jobs, and piled up manuscripts of novels that publishers consistently refused. These "desperate days," as he later described them to Frank Harris, were a severe test of morale and determination, and undoubtedly led to his deliberate cultivation of the bold front, the self-advertising persona, "public Shaw," that was to become a familiar and sometimes exasperating feature of his art as well as a means of self-protection in social life.

Shaw was taken on for regular work by the Edison Telephone Company in the autumn of 1879, an experience reflected in his second novel, *The Irrational Knot.* But what saved him was the plunge he took, at about the same time, into the active life of London's then flourishing societies for philosophical discussion. James Lecky, a civil servant with a strong interest in phonetics, introduced him to the Zetetical Society, where he met his lifelong friend Sidney Webb. Then he joined the Dialectical Society, on which the Zetetical had been modeled. The membership of both was broadly humanist and progressive in opinion, like the congregation of the Ethical Church in South Place, which he sometimes attended. He joined literary societies, too (and through F. J. Furnivall of the New Shakespeare Society he was engaged to make an index and glossary of *The Works of Thomas Lodge*[1] for the scholarly Hunterian Club). Anxious to make his mark, he forced himself to speak at every meeting, as he forced himself to accept social invitations, until his gaucheness gave way to ease.

Shaw became a vegetarian in 1881 in the hope of curing his chronic migraine headaches; the vegetarianism, but not the continuing migraine, became another feature added to the public image, soon well known in London's intellectual circles. He worked at self-improvement: he had learned shorthand; he took drawing lessons (and showed no talent); he studied languages; with his friend Pakenham Beatty he took lessons in boxing at the London Athletic Club. His knowledge of pugilism formed the basis of

his third novel, *Cashel Byron's Profession,* and he continued to make play with the metaphysical value of personal fitness in attack and defense, notably in *Major Barbara* and, late in life, in *The Millionairess.*

Probably the most momentous event of these years was Shaw's conversion to socialism after hearing a lecture by the American Henry George in 1882. George's economic theory, concentrating on the possession and value of land, made immediate sense to one familiar with discussions of the Irish Land Question. Shaw went on to read other economists, but he had been writing and addressing meetings for the Social Democratic Federation for some time before he read the first volume of Marx's *Kapital* in a French translation in 1884. He had already met Marx's daughter Eleanor and her common-law husband, Edward Aveling, translator of *Das Kapital* into English, in the Browning Society, for they had literary and dramatic interests in common and were to share in amateur playreadings. Through the next twelve years, while he spoke as a "socialist agitator" once or twice every week all over London, Shaw became intimate with anarchists and socialists of every persuasion. Yet he and Sidney Webb had committed themselves to the Fabian Society, newly founded in 1884, and in which they soon became controlling voices: it was a deliberate move away from the proletarian element in the S.D.F. into an organization of middle-class intellectuals, "my own class," that shared Marx's "hatred . . . for the middle-class institutions that had starved, thwarted, misled and corrupted them spiritually from their cradles" (*Sixteen Self Sketches,* 1949).

How great a political influence the Fabians exerted and how socialist they were has been debated ever since H. G. Wells's attack from within in 1906, after which he left the society. (It is still functioning today.) They were planners, researchers, teachers, men and women of social conscience who, instead of forming a political party themselves, sought to promote their policies through whatever parliamentary party they could interest and involve, usually the Liberal Party, but also the Tories, before the Labour Party was formed. (Their claim to have promoted most of the progressive social legislation of this century and to have been the architects of the "Welfare State," established by the Labour government after World War II, at least deserves examination.) Although there was great variety of opinion among the early membership, Shaw's and Webb's view that socialism in Britain was more likely to come through

---

[1] Shaw declined acknowledgment for his work because he failed to finish it on time. It was completed by the Shakespearean scholar Thomas Tyler.

gradual reform than through revolution was generally accepted. But the form of Shaw's socialism, his belief in equality and his attitude to revolution, was not immutably fixed and free from ambiguousness. It gave him the purpose outside mere personal ambition that he needed—and he adopted as his telegraph address "Socialist, London"—but he never wrote or spoke simple propaganda from a doctrinaire political viewpoint. The groundwork of his politics, and what his writing expressed throughout his long life, was a faith in reason and humanity, motivating what was to seem an increasingly difficult struggle to turn men from cruel and genocidal courses. He involved himself in the practical work of local government as a councillor "vestryman" for the London borough of St. Pancras from 1897 to 1903.

Shaw's early life of political activity made him many friends, some of them already distinguished people. These included Annie Besant, already a celebrated public speaker for social reform, and William Morris, the great artist-craftsman-poet, who won Shaw's enduring love and admiration. J. L. Joynes and H. H. Champion, editors of the socialist paper *To-Day*, serialized his fifth novel, *An Unsocial Socialist*, in 1884, and *Cashel Byron's Profession* between 1885 and 1886. Annie Besant published *The Irrational Knot* in serial form in her paper, *Our Corner*, between 1885 and 1887, and the fourth novel, *Love Among the Artists*, in 1887 and 1888. However, it was his meeting with William Archer, a man of deep social and ethical convictions, well established as a critic and becoming known as translator and champion of Ibsen, that enabled him to win fame and earn a regular living as a journalist, and then led him on into his career as a playwright. Shaw had published the occasional essay and written some music criticism for the *Dramatic Review, Our Corner*, and the *Magazine of Music*, when in 1886 Archer passed over to him his own commission as staff writer of art criticism for a flourishing weekly review, the *World*. ("He didn't know much more about painting than I, but he thought he did," said Archer, "and that was the main point.") These articles were unsigned but continued from February 1886 to December 1889. Although Shaw was not offered a place on the political staff of the newly founded mass-circulation newspaper the *Star*, he was taken on as its music critic in 1888 and chose the pseudonym "Corno di Bassetto." Two years later he became music critic of the *World* under his own name and continued until the *Saturday Review* en-

ticed him to become its drama critic from 1895 to 1898.

As a critic of painting, Shaw wrote for the average man and woman uninitiated into the technicalities and more purely aesthetic qualities of the art, giving them grounds on which to approach and enjoy pictures with a degree of intelligent discrimination. Pictures that tell stories were still fashionable in this period, and his underlying concern is with the moral qualities implied in how the stories are told. The socialist origins of the Pre-Raphaelites, and John Ruskin's and William Morris' links with the movement, certainly had much to do with the generally favorable attention he gave to works of this native English school. The boxer's comments, in *Cashel Byron's Profession*, on the figure of St. George in Adrian Herbert's picture, pointing out that the artist understands nothing about the physical science of fighting, are typical of Shaw's own art reviews: observant, realistic, sensible, and limited. It was the kind of nonspecialist criticism that James McNeill Whistler, the impressionist painter, virtually killed off, in his notorious "Ten o'Clock" lecture of 1888, though it was Oscar Wilde, not Shaw, who was the object of Whistler's attack.

Shaw's music criticism, much more considerable in volume, also has greater intrinsic value, and most of it is as interesting and entertaining today as when he wrote it. He settled on a style as different as possible from the pontifical formality of the *Times*: it is personal, spontaneous, easy, and vivid, befitting a more democratic paper reaching out, as the *Star* did, toward a newly literate public. Shaw avoids isolating the musical experience from its particular context and may tell his readers about his journey to the concert hall, the chair he sat in, the coughs and fidgetings of the audience; he establishes an everyday frame of mind as natural and appropriate to the occasion.

Yet there is no mistaking Shaw's intense interest in the performance itself. He may be enraged, but he is never bored or indifferent. There is always some passage of quite precise and analytic comment, forthrightly and unhesitatingly expressed, that increases the general reader's confidence in his authority and arrests the attention of musicians. The impression of a considerable background of musical knowledge is secondary to his communication of a great appetite and enthusiasm for the art. He often criticizes with unsparing ridicule—especially famous performers giving less than their very best—yet he is equally ready to express delight in spite of imperfections. His dedication to the raising of standards and improvement in audience discrimination often resulted, even when he was writing for the *World*, in nagging or bullying passages, or comments such as a severe schoolmaster might write in a boy's report:

Richter has no right to stuff a programme with the most hackneyed items in his repertory in order to save the trouble of rehearsing. . . . The orchestra is by no means what it ought to be; and it has been getting worse instead of better for some years past.

There is a certain amount of deliberate clowning in this that can seem boorish in cold and now antiquated print; but usually the amusing exaggerations and farfetched yet curiously evocative comparisons take away some of the sting, as the attentions of a clever caricaturist may be appreciated as almost flattering by his victims.

George Carr Shaw, left alone in Ireland, died in 1885 at the age of seventy-one. None of the family went to the funeral, not even Lucy, who was in Dublin at the time. Her brother responded to the news of their father's death with the mixture of practicality and flippancy that was to serve him as a barrier against emotion on numerous other occasions. Falling in love with Alice Lockett in 1881, and for three years pursuing a volatile relationship and lively correspondence with her that are echoed in *An Unsocial Socialist*, was the beginning of a series of "philanders," as he liked to call them. He enjoyed the flattery of women's interest in him and the fun of flirtation, even the conflict to gain the upper hand, and he was not above playing off one woman against another and getting further pleasure from such intrigues.

If Shaw saw the spirit of farce hovering near all his love affairs, the women did not always share his view. In particular, Mrs. Jenny Patterson, a widow fifteen years his senior, to whom he lost his virginity on his twenty-ninth birthday, pursued him with a frustrated passion he found intolerable. Most of his erotic entanglements remained at the level of flirtation, and possibly the most delightful to both parties was his courtship of the actress Ellen Terry, conducted entirely by letter. He escaped from the threat of sexual capture into a happy celibate marriage with Charlotte Payne Townshend, a wealthy Irishwoman and fellow Fabian, in 1898, when both were over forty: "It ended the old gallantries . . . for both of us."

For Shaw there was to be one more notable exception to this.

Shaw had started the habit of theatergoing in Dublin. He enjoyed whatever was good of its kind: popular entertainment or Shakespearean tragedy. In 1890 he agreed to give a lecture to the Fabian Society on Henrik Ibsen, who had stirred Europe by his dramatic onslaughts on patriarchal society and its idealization of the home. The lecture was the germ of the first book in English on the Norwegian playwright, *The Quintessence of Ibsenism* (1891), and helped to build up interest in the formation of an Independent Theatre Society to present Ibsen's *Ghosts*, which had no chance of public production in England, in current conditions of theatrical censorship. The society mounted *Ghosts* in 1891, and its founder, J. T. Grein, then asked Shaw for a play. Shaw went back to an abortive attempt he had made in collaboration with William Archer and revised and completed it; and, under the title of *Widowers' Houses*, it was presented by the Independent Theatre in 1892. He went on writing plays. Except for one or two private performances by avant-garde groups and the presentation of *Arms and the Man* in 1894 in a short season privately financed by Miss Annie Horniman and starring one of his lady friends, Florence Farr, his plays seemed fated for the same neglect as his novels. Being no longer a poor boy, Shaw was able to publish them at his own expense in two collections under the single title of *Plays: Pleasant and Unpleasant* (1898). So they were read, often enjoyed, but dismissed as unsuitable for the stage. Until the century was over Shaw could retaliate only by citing the single example of Richard Mansfield's New York success in *The Devil's Disciple* (in the next collection, *Three Plays for Puritans*) in 1897.

It was through the campaign to establish a national theater, which had started in the 1860's, that Shaw found conditions for testing and proving the theatrical effectiveness of his drama. Archer, Professor Gilbert Murray, Shaw himself, and their young friend the actor Granville Barker (who in 1917 began to use the name Harley Granville Barker) were all involved in this campaign. Archer and Barker presented their case for a state-subsidized theater of excellence in *A Scheme and Estimates for a National Theatre*, and Barker followed this up by leasing the Royal Court theater in Sloane Square to demonstrate the higher quality of acting, production, and new drama that a theater freed from normal commercial pressures could offer. Charlotte and

Bernard Shaw put up the greater part of the money for this limited experiment; Barker trained and directed the actors, with Shaw coming in for the production of his own plays. By 1907, when the money ran out, the case was proved and the reputations were made.

Shaw lived until 1950 and continued writing almost to the end. Though he was out of public favor at times, on account of his known or supposed political views, his literary eminence was generally accepted, and his fame continued to grow. He had, he said, "no adventures"—except those of the mind, recorded in the continually changing character of his writing.

NOVELS, JOURNALISM, ESSAYS

BEFORE they started on their brief playwriting collaboration, Shaw remarked to Archer that he had difficulty in devising plots. His novels bear this out. They all contain lively scenes, but, with the exception of *Cashel Byron's Profession*, the shortest, they seem largely unplanned, even improvised. Writing to the publisher Swan Sonnenschein in defense of the first, *Immaturity* (not published until 1930), Shaw declared that he had thought of calling it *Quadrille*, as the interwoven narratives of four principal characters made the only artificial construction he cared to impose on the lifelike realism he sought. *Love Among the Artists* has a similar very general design, which does not rescue it from being the dullest of the books. There is a similar dispersal of interest in *The Irrational Knot*, though combined with a more conventional plot that gets somewhat out of hand. *An Unsocial Socialist* falls into two halves, with a number of the characters, including the extraordinary central figure, struggling through from the first half into the second.

Immaturity underwent two thorough revisions and emerged a more readable book than some of the later ones. ("People who read *An Unsocial Socialist* will read anything," said its author.) It contains plenty of good talk and amusing comment and a considerable range of figures, from Lady Geraldine Porter to the comic Irishman Cornelius Hamlet, whose histories and moral character are rapidly and vividly sketched; and it is united by the manner in which it is written, its air of good sense and sweet temper (not least in writing about bad-tempered people), its con-

sistent valuing of good fellowship and laughter at "romance." There is no evident theme beyond a very young man's discovery of society, though an egalitarian tendency is clear. *The Irrational Knot* improves on this by treating the theme of love and marriage through a contrast between two couples. There are signs that the second pair were meant to be figures of comedy, but the woman, Susannah, who is a burlesque actress under the name of Lalage Virtue, is eventually conducted through a rake's progress from strong-minded independence to alcoholic breakdown and death.

It may be that Shaw, having set himself to write a more grimly realistic type of novel, as he was to imitate conventional melodrama at the start of his play *The Devil's Disciple*, aped the conventionally narrow, moralistic attitude of the Victorian public. He shows unexpected disapproval of Susannah's profession and her freedom—not so remote from his own sister's. That he had imbibed some of his mother's puritanical and snobbish attitudes is certain (the Fabian "hatred . . . for the middle-class institutions that had . . . misled and corrupted them spiritually" may reflect his mother's influence), and this novel may well record a usually suppressed emotional shock that accompanied his youthful skepticism and intellectual boldness. There is a prevailing sourness of tone, not confined to the "bitter and flippant humour" of the spinsterish Elinor McQuinch; and characters are satirically exposed without the veil of liking that softens the ridicule through most of Shaw's comedy. Conolly, the engineer hero, and Marian, the lady born and bred, are presented in realistic detail and with a measure of sympathy, but they represent opposite temperaments, the one governed by reason, the other by emotion. Conolly comes close to being an idealized portrait of the wise and just man, but is saved from priggishness by the awareness the author lets his character share: that there is something monstrous, almost tragic, about such perfect consistency.

Cashel Byron's Profession is very different, written throughout with a much lighter and surer touch. As he was often to do later, Shaw started with an unpretentious, popular form: here a boy's adventure tale involving plenty of fistfighting. Improbably, he combined it with a novel of manners, coolly analytical of social morality and distinctly reminiscent of the work of Jane Austen. In all his novels, most of the characters speak with a rather formal precision, "as if all their speeches had been corrected by their governesses and schoolmasters," and it gives them a rather old-fashioned charm, set off in this book by the robuster boyishness of expression and occasional unselfconscious fluency of his hero, a type of the natural man. Only the inadequate development of the secondary plot, the germ of which was lifted directly from Jane Austen's *Emma*, mars *Cashel Byron's Profession*, and it was with good reason that Shaw later commented on his narrow escape from becoming a successful novelist at this point.

While publishers neglected their opportunity, Shaw went on to write the most wildly fantastic of these early works, keeping his hand in practice, but caring less than before to write an acceptable book. *An Unsocial Socialist* is an absurd farrago of incidents, mostly brought about by the "hero," who makes love to a bunch of young women and exercises his sway over them by lecturing them lengthily, but not tediously, on socialism. This character is a curious, comic variant on the psychological double made familiar in R. L. Stevenson's famous "shocker," *Dr. Jekyll and Mr. Hyde* (1886). Shaw's more particular inspiration for the wealthy Sidney Trefusis, who runs away from his young wife and puts on the burlesque disguise of the uncommon workman Jefferson Smilash, was undoubtedly Prince Hamlet in his "antic disposition": "The son of a millionaire, like the son of a king, is seldom free from mental disease," Trefusis explains. "I am just mad enough to be a mountebank." One early reader, at least, remarked on the originality of the book and recorded: "This is the most comical novel I have ever read."

Shaw's ability to create lively women characters, many of them strong-minded and sharp-tongued, is evident through all the novels. Indeed he seems more interested in the women than in his male characters. Other well-marked features that emerge again in his drama are: the governing concern with what is mockingly called "moral science," in *An Unsocial Socialist*; the interest in the philanderer-figure that starts with his first hero's imagining of himself as "Don Juan Lothario Smith"; and respect for the type of conscience that is directed toward mankind in general and runs counter to normal, domestic morality. In the form of the peculiar selfishness of the artist, this last concern provides the main interest of *Love Among the Artists*.

Shaw did not hide his personal tastes in his journalism. The music critic disliked Brahms and championed Wagner; Mozart was the musician he loved above all others. The theater critic reviewed every

kind of dramatic entertainment, including comic opera and pantomime, but identified himself firmly with the intellectual avant-garde that looked to Ibsen as the revolutionary dramatist who would sweep away the nineteenth century. Shaw coined the term *sardoodledom* to describe the "well-made plays" imported in great quantity from France, where they were slickly constructed to an established formula by Victorien Sardou, Eugène Scribe, Alexandre Dumas *fils*, and others. (These dramatists are best known today through the late-nineteenth-century operas *Tosca* and *La Traviata*, among others, based on their stories.) The most distinguished of the contemporary British dramatists that Shaw found himself reviewing, Arthur Wing Pinero, Henry Arthur Jones, and Oscar Wilde, also adopted the well-made play form and, like some of their French colleagues, had started to mix in a little of Ibsen's concern with the condition of society and its pressures on individuals. This gave their plots a superficial seriousness, but all were far from issuing any radical challenge, as Ibsen did, and as Shaw began to do.

The *Saturday Review* gave Shaw plenty of space for his critiques. Though he had not been appointed as an editorial writer, he exercised a license to comment on virtually any topical subject, and his remarks on the plays he had seen were frequently introduced by lengthy discussions of more general interest. This was the period when he acquired his reputation as a highly articulate clown, perhaps an indication that an overforceful presentation of his convictions made him less influential than a quieter, less brash advocacy would have done. But this is hard to determine: he was attacking strongly entrenched opposition, and it seems likely that his wit and liveliness started many of his readers asking new questions and looking more skeptically at old arguments. Certainly he won recognition as the most brilliant of journalists, and he sufficiently identified himself with this profession to continue as a member of the Institute of Journalists until his death. The prefaces he wrote to accompany his plays in their published form were further exercises in the genre in which he had made his name. He included them, at first, in order to sell the plays to a public unaccustomed to reading dramatic texts.

None of the three long essays Shaw published between 1891 and the end of the decade was criticism in the same sense as his regular reviews. *The Quintessence of Ibsenism* is a discussion of social morality that uses Ibsen's plays as its Bible; *The Sanity of Art*

(1895) was Shaw's answer to a sweeping attack on fin-de-siècle symbolism made by Max Nordau under the title *Degeneration* (1893), and presents the case for what we now call modernism; *The Perfect Wagnerite* (1898) translates the music-drama *The Ring of the Nibelungs* as a socialist allegory. The first of these essays isolates the theme of destructive idealism in play after play of Ibsen's. The acceptance of stereotypes and attachment to ideologies are included in "idealism," as this essay uses the term, and so is the idolization of self-righteousness that passes for "public opinion." Writing the preface to the third edition of *Quintessence*, after World War I, Shaw argued:

The war was a war of ideals. Liberal ideals . . . , bourgeois and proletarian, all heaped up into a gigantic pile of spiritual high explosive, and then shovelled daily into every house with the morning milk by the newspapers. . . .

Truthfulness to human nature was the test he saw Ibsen's realism applying to social institutions and conventional behavior, and when he came to introduce to the public his own first collection of plays (in the preface to volume II of *Plays: Pleasant and Unpleasant*), he defined his own attitude:

To me the tragedy and comedy of life lie in the consequences . . . of our persistent attempts to found our institutions on the ideals suggested to our imaginations by our half-satisfied passions, instead of on a genuinely scientific natural history.

Shaw's exposition of Wagner's *Ring* was more peculiar. He argued, with every justification, that Wagner did not write his music-drama merely for the sensual and emotional enjoyment of his audience. Indeed the Nazis were later to demonstrate horrifyingly that the work has a political message. Shaw did not read it their way, as he brought to it a concern for humanity, indeed for all life, nothing as restricted as nationalism or ideas of racial superiority; yet he was guilty, as they were, of imposing a narrow and doctrinaire meaning on an imaginative creation. Admittedly, he points out that no great allegory is ever mechanically consistent, but his whole manner of exposition raises doubts as to whether he understood why this is so. Curiously enough, the explanation is to be found in *The Sanity of Art*. Here he had employed Schopenhauer's notion of the Will as the great motive force in human psychology, inaccessible to reason. It was probably his familiarity with

evolutionary theory that allowed him to regard optimistically the power of feeling and conviction that sweeps aside personal, prudential considerations, and to view it as serving the ultimate interests of the species—or even, beyond the species, of life itself, whatever form it might take. The core of his argument in this essay is summed up in one of the Maxims for Revolutionists that he was to print with *Man and Superman:* "The unconscious self is the true genius."

Throughout his plays, this faith counterbalances the rational temperament that he had examined in his novels in the characters of Edward Conolly and of Lydia Carew, who marries Cashel Byron to make up for her own shortcomings. The result is a drama in which the discussion of public themes is combined with forms of intimate self-examination, and in which the irrational is expressed with comic passion —in laughter.

PLAYS: PLEASANT AND UNPLEASANT *AND* THREE PLAYS FOR PURITANS

BERNARD SHAW had tried his hand at writing dramatic pieces before *Widowers' Houses*, the first of his plays to be performed and published. He had dramatized a novel, *The Gadfly*, by Ethel Voynich, in 1875 (published in 1973); more significantly, he had attempted a *Passion Play* in verse in 1878 (published in 1971). There is no subtlety in Shaw's verse rhythms: only for burlesque purposes could he write effective verse at any period of his life. What is more interesting in *A Passion Play* is a determined attack on the supernatural elements in Christianity through a rather sourly naturalistic presentation of the Holy Family.

At this stage in his life, Shaw was still brashly positivist and antireligious in his outlook. The destructive aspect of his satiric and parodic impulses is still evident in the three plays he published under the general description "Unpleasant." *Widowers' Houses* offers a cynical view of young love readily collaborating with the greed and callousness of capitalist society. *The Philanderer* (written in 1893) turns its attention to the fashionable intellectuals of the day, just such enthusiasts for Ibsen as had supported the Independent Theatre production of Shaw's own previous play, and it moves to an equally disenchanted end in the announcement of a marriage that has no prospect of happiness for either party, but that society approves. Like *Widowers' Houses,* which exposes exploitation of the poor by the wealthy and respected (including the church) who draw rents from slum properties, *Mrs. Warren's Profession* demonstrates how responsibility for social evils extends through society, involving even those who think themselves innocent.

The third play was the most shocking in the means it used to bring home to his audience, or readers, their own guilty complicity. The manners of the day and the fact of theatrical censorship played into Shaw's hands by giving him grounds for suppressing the name of the profession Mrs. Warren had adopted (sexual prostitution) and advanced in (to the directorship of an international chain of brothels). There is evidence that many of the women and some of the men who saw the first performance of this play came away uncertain what the profession was, thus confirming Shaw's point that the unconscious hypocrisy of an innocence protected from knowledge of unpleasant facts can be a strong barrier against social change. Indeed the play was banned in England from public performance, as morally offensive, until World War I.

A purely aesthetic criticism tends to dismiss such works as propagandist, of a topical and so less enduring interest, and too utilitarian in their intention to be good art. Early critics' objections to these socialist "bluebook" plays, as they called them, have left a persisting echo ever since. Yet they have not lost their grip in the theater; indeed audiences of the 1960's and 1970's liked them better than some of Shaw's later, more extravagantly praised work. *Widowers' Houses* and *Mrs. Warren's Profession* further the belief on which he had based *Cashel Byron's Profession,* and that was to contribute to *Major Barbara* (written in 1905): that there is a unity, a self-consistency, in any social system that allows the nature of the whole to be discovered by study of any part. Ibsen may have helped him to this view; Mrs. Alving, in *Ghosts,* speaks of the fabric of received ideas on which society rests, in a homely simile, as like a piece of knitting that is soon totally unraveled if it comes undone anywhere. Shaw's reading of Marx is also reflected in this, though he never regarded Marx as the infallible pope of socialism.

The consequence of this way of seeing the human world is that conventional dichotomies—between private and public, individual and society—evaporate; and they seem to have been absent from the creative processes that brought the plays into being.

The title of *Widowers' Houses* is indicative: Sartorius is a widower whose emotional nature seeks fulfillment in the relationship with his daughter, and the unnatural intensity of his concern for her is the motive force behind his ruthless pursuit of wealth. In *Mrs. Warren's Profession,* Vivie is a young woman whose brittle independence corresponds to ignorance of her father's identity (an ignorance she has to live with, as no one else knows it either) and the fact that her mother, too, is a stranger, little more than a name to her. The psychological need for love and commitment to other individuals has as important a part in these plays as the revelation of how the economic structure of society determines compromises and betrayals, and gives a questionable ambiguousness to every social undertaking, every institution and profession: to marriage and family, to art, and even to the business of earning an honest living.

Shaw is able to make so comprehensive a statement with economy of method in these plays because they rest on a basically simple structure of ideas contained in a form he imitated from Ibsen's modification of the well-made play in *A Doll's House, Ghosts,* and *Rosmersholm,* particularly. The dramatic development involves a progress from apparently contented ignorance to an enlightenment that may have tragic implications for the individual in the short run. Crucial revelations are made about the past, usually in two stages, and these affect understanding of the present. The stages are marked by the appearance and reappearance of a relatively minor character: Lickcheese, in *Widowers' Houses,* has no exact counterpart in *Mrs. Warren's Profession,* though there are corresponding figures in later Shaw plays (for example, Burgess in *Candida,* Doolittle in *Pygmalion*). These features give a rather schematic effect to the plot: the choice of episodes to be presented is governed by the central idea; coincidences and sharply juxtaposed contrasts do little to suggest the unformulated experience of ordinary living, but much to direct and enforce a general argument.

Shaw blends in other styles. The supper episode in *Mrs. Warren's Profession* has a touch of the rambling naturalism to be found in *Immaturity.* Such characters as Cockane and Lickcheese in *Widowers' Houses,* Craven, Cuthbertson, and Paramore in *The Philanderer* are drawn with broad strokes, close to caricature, and they demonstrate themselves in all they say and do, in a frankly theatrical way. Shaw, discussing acting with William Archer, argued for objectivity as preferred by Denis Diderot in *Paradoxe sur le comédien* (written in 1773–1778) against psychological subjectivity, though he did not go to the theoretical extremes that his successor Bertolt Brecht was to put forward in reaction against the subjective approach of the great Russian director Konstantin Stanislavski. Yet it is not only in the major characters, notably Julia Craven and Vivie Warren, that Shaw suggests an individual temperament and some psychological complexity: Paramore is a mean creature of low vitality, and the Reverend Samuel Gardner is a figure of farce—treated as such by his son—whose alcoholic misery and degradation may have been modeled on George Carr Shaw's and set up an uncomfortable undertow to the laughter they provoke.

The inclusion of the son, Frank Gardner, in *Mrs. Warren's Profession* maintains the comic balance of the play, and indeed allows modern productions to play up the artificial coincidences in the plot and to burlesque passages that had a strained seriousness in 1892. Frank is a cool, mischievous observer who takes the world as his entertainment and ridicules the morality of a system he despises. What he objects to in the vicious characters is "their form . . . ever so slovenly," as he might say of horses, when placing his bets. Shaw's comic impulse is evident in each of the plays in this first group, but chiefly in *The Philanderer,* which echoes with the laughter of the central character, Charteris, the first of Shaw's satirical self-portraits to appear in his drama. Charteris belongs to the Don Juan type. The intrigues with women that complicate his life and give the play its bursts of farcical action are linked with a clear-sighted rationality, a combination that recalls Trefusis in *An Unsocial Socialist.* The play exposes more than the ambiguousness of his attitude to women: this is a character who playacts emotional responses and laughs at everything. Shaw has sketched the very type of a comic dramatist, but the character also represents an irresponsible man in private relationships, out of touch with his buried emotions and afraid of emotion in others. *The Philanderer* is not directly concerned with economics, as are the other two plays, but it offers a serious and subtle comment on another topic with political as well as social implications: the struggle of women toward independence and equality with men. Shaw was to return to this in *You Never Can Tell* (written in 1895–1896), one of his "pleasant" plays.

The new group represents his deliberate effort to write for the commercial theater, not just for avant-garde play-producing societies that could evade censorship and were not seeking simple entertainment first and foremost. Though he still failed to break through to the wider audience, the manner he deliberately assumed to this end was to stay with him, a mask becoming indistinguishable from his face: invariably sweet-tempered, however severe he sometimes pretends to be, essentially genial and optimistic. No doubt the ample experience of public success in another field and the welcome into a wide circle of interesting and distinguished friends modified Shaw's character, dispelling bitterness and establishing the positive aspects of his volatile temperament. This laid the foundations of an art that good-humoredly recognizes the humanity of knaves and fools and reserves its scorn for their crimes and stupidities, an art that has been accused of lacking a sense of evil. Certainly two qualities came into prominence now that must put criticism warily on its guard. These are blandness and childishness.

Each of the full-length *Plays: Pleasant* and two of the following *Plays for Puritans* contain at least one very youthful figure with which the childish view or approach can be associated: Raina (*Arms and the Man*)—who gets her own way by playing the spoiled child—and Cleopatra, the boy Ptolemy (*Caesar and Cleopatra*), the puppyish Eugene (*Candida*), Effie in *The Devil's Disciple,* and the twins in *You Never Can Tell.* Shaw was reverting to a technique he had used in the first piece he completed after arriving in London in 1876, the letter of advice to an imaginary five-year-old child, which was ultimately published in 1956 as *My Dear Dorothea.* This was informal moral reflection expressed in practical precepts and conceptually simple explanations. Treating the child as an intelligent and thoughtful being, though of limited and largely domestic experience, resulted in both a demonstration of proper respect for childhood and its rights, and a wise document that may be thoughtfully and profitably read by the adults for whom it was, in fact, intended. Shaw the theater critic had good reason to know that much of the popular, and least debased, theatrical entertainment of the day allowed audiences to relax in a simplified world of fantasy and to regress to an immature level of desire and belief. He had had a marked success in *Cashel Byron's Profession* by writing in a popular mode, while permeating it with his own critical judgment and thoughtfulness. Now he tried the same thing again, though his strong individuality made the difference from the commonplace type greater than he may have planned.

An astute publicist for his latest work, Shaw was always inclined to undervalue what he had written in earlier days. So he frequently dismissed earlier plays as potboilers and in private expressed his doubts about the worth of others that had taken considerable effort. When Alma Murray, who first acted Raina in *Arms and the Man*, was thinking of reviving the play in 1904, Shaw wrote: "I took to reading it the other day . . . and was startled to find what flimsy, fantastic, unsafe stuff it is." The words are recognition of the knife-edge that he sometimes walked and that productions of his plays need to walk, if the critical sense of reality is not to be lost in the entertainment. He claimed later that World War I need never have occurred if the lessons of *Arms and the Man* had been heeded; but how seriously he is concerned with the theme of war in this play may be overlooked by present-day audiences, who cannot even identify the war in Eastern Europe that occasioned it. Shaw does not start with actuality, but takes the then fashionable convention of Ruritanian romance (Ruritania being the imaginary European country in which Anthony Hope set his novel of 1894, *The Prisoner of Zenda*, the best-known example of the type) and attacks it with a farcical treatment in which the absurdities of the plot and puppetlike aspect of the characters are deliberately exaggerated.

Sergius Saranoff is the embodiment of honor, quixotic in his attachment to myths of militarism undoubtedly easier to sustain before World War I than after, though Shaw shows Sergius to be as ludicrously out-of-date as Cervantes' Don Quixote. Alongside this patriot of insane ideals is set Bluntschli, the Swiss mercenary, the man who knows himself to be only a tool, sees fighting as an evil to be avoided, but accommodates himself to the world as it is by soldiering simply for pay, his share of the spoils, for he has the soul of a shopkeeper. A technique of anticlimax is used to ridicule Sergius and more playfully to expose the false attitudes of the heroine, already bored with her own make-believe of romance; but it is the rather cynical subplot, involving the brutally calculating servants, that focuses the questionable nature of the alternative Bluntschli represents, and leaves Raina, the child whose toys these wooden (or candy) figures are, to hold the balance.

A similar demolition of accepted heroic values is attempted in *The Devil's Disciple* through the apparently more realistic and serious convention of melodrama. It was this play, produced in New York in 1897, that give Shaw his first taste of success as a playwright.

Shaw's competence in providing what an earlier public liked is just what may limit his appeal today; such is the risk of his chosen strategy. He did not expect a metropolitan audience of the last decade of the century to take readily to the straightforward, pious hero of old-fashioned melodrama, so he gave Dick Dudgeon a reputation for dissoluteness, evidently unearned; excluded him from decent society; filled him with hatred of his mother; and finished off the portrait with a jeering manner and a bitter tongue, to counterbalance his good looks. A soubrette type like Raina would be out of place in a melodrama; instead, Shaw includes a pathetic, oppressed, and abandoned bastard girl, and the projection of Dick Dudgeon as the scornful hero whose authentic morality is so much higher than that of orthodox society corresponds to Effie's idealizing view of him, taken over by Judith Anderson, the second sentimentalist, old enough to know better. But Dick is a sham diabolonian, a disguised example of true Christian virtue in the midst of corruption. The changing of coats that is crucial to the plot is also emblematic of Shaw's dramatic subterfuge: the parson's coat is fitly transferred to Dick, and the true rebel proves to be Anderson, the natural man of good sense, delivered from his Christian assumptions. Only near the end, with the introduction of General Burgoyne, the sophisticated wit, does the play establish itself as a comedy after all. The strategy has been to indulge childish tastes and lead through this to a more adult consciousness.

That Shaw's conception of wickedness is purely naturalistic can be gleaned through his characterization of Mrs. Dudgeon. She is unloving because unloved; the root of her malignancy is identical with that sacrifice of true love to profitable marriage to which Ibsen traces the bitterness and viciousness of a line of women characters culminating in Gunhild Borkman (*John Gabriel Borkman*, written in 1896). In the preface to *Plays: Pleasant*, Shaw declared his adherence to philosophic naturalism. Yet he rarely keeps to a naturalistic dramatic style. Of all his plays the nearest to consistent naturalism is *Candida*, where the style is part of the blandness it shares with the superficially very different *Captain Brassbound's*

Conversion. Naturalistic drama must seem to be free of domination by abstract ideas and to mean only what it shows. Like Ibsen before him, Shaw in *Candida* had to contrive to comment on dramatic situations and characters by covert means. The result was his most elaborately written and enigmatic play so far, despite its air of being as simple and straightforward as its heroine. Indeed he indirectly confessed as much, on publishing the text in 1898, when he substituted the descriptive subtitle "A Mystery" for the simple "Domestic Play" that classified it in his original manuscript. As Shaw, the working member of the New Shakespeare Society, would have known, contemporary scholarship was interested in the mystery plays of the medieval religious stage, and to Ellen Terry, the actress he wanted to play the role, he confided that Candida Morell was "the virgin mother and nobody else." Ironically, this recalls his early *Passion Play,* with its depiction of the virgin mother of Christian legend as a nagging wife; but Ellen Terry did not know that.

Though Shaw was to refer to the play as his version of *A Doll's House,* in which the man and not the woman was the doll (this being the usual state of affairs in English society as he saw it), and to declare that "Candida seduces Eugene just exactly as far as it is worth her while to seduce him," he encouraged actresses to take the character at her own estimation: as the Reverend James Morell's model wife and the motherly protector of the young poet, Eugene Marchbanks. If the other actors and the director follow the same line, *Candida* lulls audiences into accepting it as Shaw's celebration of the Good Woman and a work of distinctly conservative tendency; for the irony on which he now relies is almost silent, a matter of nuances calculated to make the conventional public just faintly uneasy in its accustomed beliefs. Both her Christian Socialist husband and the poet who loses his bid for her look on Candida with the eyes of worshippers. As neither Morell nor Candida herself shows any awareness that the great monologue in which she tells the truth about their marriage systematically humiliates him and justifies her, it is very likely that theater audiences may be mesmerized into acceptance of this version as Shaw's, forgetting the commonsense remark of the spinster secretary, Prossy, "She's very nice, very good-hearted: I'm very fond of her, and can appreciate her real qualities far better than any man can."

Shaw has been criticized for carelessness in giving Candida the stock comedy figure of Burgess, the wily cockney businessman, as a father. If he had been a thoroughgoing naturalist dramatist, social verisimilitude and realism would have excluded, or taken great pains to explain, the unlikely relationship. But the staginess of Burgess disturbs the bland surface to insinuate a political comment on Candida and the effect of the domestic ideal in delaying social reform. The character of Marchbanks offers a similar choice of interpretation that may lead to artistic failure, mawkish and embarrassing if entirely naturalistically played; or to ironic success, if authorial awareness and fey, almost puckish humor (a generic relation to Frank Gardner and to Philip in *You Never Can Tell*) break through the simple portrait of a shy boy, unused to society. Why unused, if he is indeed an earl's son and not a foundling from outside nature altogether?

Prossy's words, "very nice, very good-hearted," are even more applicable to Lady Cicely Wayneflete of *Captain Brassbound's Conversion* (a character Ellen Terry did eventually play). Not even subdued irony calls into question her selflessness, practical benevolence, and common sense. Yet much of the comedy of this play turns on her blatantly manipulative ways and the capitulation of the male characters to her moral and emotional blackmail. Certainly this makes no pretense of being a naturalistic play: it is essentially a fable, decked out as an adventure story in an exotic setting, with a cast of minor characters that looks and acts like the chorus of a comic opera. It can be argued that Lady Cicely is simply a female mask, a dramatic device for challenging the monstrous ideas of justice and punishment upheld in patriarchal society: Shaw regarded imprisonment, like poverty, as a crime committed by society against the individual, and considered all penal systems barbarous. Whereas Candida triggers speculation about her motives, no level of deep motivation, or unconscious self, is suggested in the drawing of Lady Cicely. Even so, an unpleasant aftertaste is left by Shaw's presentation of female power asserting "feminine" values through the reduction of society to a hospital or a nursery.

It is not that he does not recognize the possibility of a more open and straightforward kind of strength in women. He shows it in the able and independent Mrs. Clandon of *You Never Can Tell,* a character having qualities and experience corresponding to his own mother's, and showing a likeness also to Annie Besant and other "new" women of the day whom he numbered among his friends. She is humane and dignified, but the dramatist chastens her, instead of praising her, and his instrument to this end is the young man, Valentine, who plays a concealed game to net the young woman he desires. This is the most delicately balanced play in Shaw's early collections. The sadness of a human situation—the long-estranged family who meet again by chance only to discover that they are strangers; the unloved man confronting the unloving woman; the poignant contrast between untouched youth and soiled, defeated age—is contained within the gayest of formal comedies. The conflict of the sexes is enacted in the ritual of courtship, and, though troubles remain and problems are unresolved, all ends in a dance.

The whole is a daring, entirely successful blend of commedia dell'arte (the tradition of Italian comedy based on the stock characters of Harlequin and Columbine, young lovers; crabbed father Pantaloon; and the rest), a critique of contemporary manners, and a dialectical play that pits intellect against emotion, with the first of these elements serving to distance and simplify the more realistic content of the play. Valentine, the lover, dismisses with easy arrogance his beloved's education and good brain: "I've a better one myself: it's a masculine speciality." No other character in the play contradicts him, and the statement could pass for Shaw's own view— evidence from outside the play would raise doubts: he chose to make Vivie Warren a brilliant mathematician; he had tremendous respect for the specialist mind of Beatrice Webb. But Valentine's charm is shadowed by the brutal and bullying force of Bohun, "the very incarnation of intellect." It is a silent irony again that indicates the needful poise of thought and feeling.

The Devil's Disciple and the most trifling of the *Plays: Pleasant, The Man of Destiny,* seem to be historical plays and include what purport to be genuine historical figures: General Burgoyne in the one, Napoleon in the other. More ambitious than either of these is the remaining work in *Three Plays for Puritans: Caesar and Cleopatra.* An alternative grouping would place these "historical" plays alongside *Arms and the Man* and *Captain Brassbound's Conversion* as examples of drama that announces itself as make-believe by its use of theatrical costume and, perhaps, by exotic and decorative stage sets. The new prologue Shaw wrote for *Caesar and Cleopatra* in 1912 brushes aside the convention of the transparent fourth wall, dividing the actors from the audience whose presence they ignore; and the statue of the god Ra gibes straight out of "ancient Egypt" at the twentieth-century theatergoers. Although Shaw takes a different stretch of time, and thus different plot material, from Shakespeare in *Antony and Cleopatra,* he includes frequent allusions to, or reminiscences of, incidents and passages in the Shakespearean original.

Indeed, from the moment when Caesar, apostrophizing the Sphinx, is answered by the girlish voice calling "Old gentleman!" (the echo of a comic moment in Ibsen's moral fantasy of 1867, *Peer Gynt*), Shaw's play unfolds as a double structure of parody on heroic drama spattered with anachronisms, running parallel with a serious commentary on the action. He wrote the play with Forbes Robertson, "the classic actor of our day," in mind, but the date-eating Caesar is truly the chocolate-eating Bluntschli in a toga, while Britannus is the clown and Apollodorus is the harlequin from nineteenth-century pantomime; though it is equally true that Shaw has incorporated tragic themes. The way in which Shakespeare's play straddles two empires gave Shaw the lead toward further theatrical outrageousness: destroying the mold of conventional dramatic form in a deliberately straggling and halting action, and breaking out of the sober room, which is the typical set of modern naturalistic drama, into a frankly spectacular theater like grand opera gone mad and seeming at times like the circus, where characters dive or are pushed into a stage sea and the heroine is rolled around in a carpet. Besides the temple of Ra (in the 1912 version) and the Sphinx, the palace of Alexandria and its roof garden, the greatest library of the ancient world in flames, the Pharos and its lighthouse, and an ancient Egyptian steam-powered crane are borrowed from the pseudoclassical paintings of nineteenth-century Royal Academicians and brought to the stage. The energy of Shavian drama has burst its bounds and flowered into irregularity and extravagance, in the middle of which Caesar stands firm: not a heroic man-of-action, but a patient teacher.

MAN AND SUPERMAN

AFTER this, Shaw felt able to treat a drama of modern life with equal freedom, and the masterpieces *Man and Superman* (written in 1901–1902) and *John Bull's Other Island* (1904) were the result. The larger scale on which he worked in these plays probably reflected his hopes for the establishment of a national theater in which his drama would at last find its proper place. The campaigners certainly did not expect to have to wait until a second world war was over and a Labour government with a massive majority in office to see their plans adopted by the state; indeed Winston Churchill, a leading Liberal at the time, spoke with strong approval of the national theater cause in 1906. Shaw got on with the writing of *Man and Superman,* while Barker, with the *Scheme and Estimates for a National Theatre* already published over his name and William Archer's, proceeded in 1903 with a hilarious production for the Stage Society of *The Admirable Bashville,* a comic play in blank verse on material drawn from *Cashel Byron's Profession;* "Children in arms will find this play peculiarly suited to their taste and capacity" was one of the program notes supplied by the dramatist. Four months later, J. H. Leigh, lessee of the Royal Court theater, and his manager, J. E. Vedrenne, started a series of Shakespeare productions in which Barker was to take part, directing and acting in *Two Gentlemen of Verona,* on condition that he could also present six matinees of *Candida.* This led straight into the Vedrenne-Barker national theater experiment, in 1904. Barker had been involved as an understudy at the Avenue Theatre in 1894, when *Arms and the Man* had been presented in a double bill with W. B. Yeats's *Land of Heart's Desire.* The wealthy theater enthusiast Miss Annie Horniman had set up an Irish National Theatre at the Abbey Theatre, Dublin, by 1904. In this new theatrical climate Shaw had less need to compromise with what the public was used to, and could originate a new kind of play. Yet even in the Vedrenne-Barker seasons, the long dream sequence in the third act of *Man and Superman,* which turns a comedy of manners into a cosmic drama, was played separately.

As Shaw says in the dedicatory letter to the *Times* theater critic, A. B. Walkley, published with this play, he was answering a challenge to write about the legendary figure of Don Juan; and in his dream the millionaire socialist, John Tanner, is stripped of accidentals to reveal the type he belongs to. As we have seen, Tanner, his new satirized antihero, was not Shaw's first version of Don Juan. The outer acts of *Man and Superman* return to the matter of *Candida:* the convinced and eloquent socialist is caught in bondage, called marriage, by a woman who does not respect his principles and regards his zeal with indulgence rather than enthusiasm; *Man and Superman* deals with the process of capture, whereas *Candida* showed possession confirmed. Tanner is not

Don Juan the wayward lover of many women, but Don Juan brought low at last, in punishment for his rebellion against social and divine law. Among Shaw's remains is a two-page reading list of European literature on the Don. Unlike Morell, Tanner is treated as a figure of fun, Shaw's satiric strategy being to implicate the audience, through its laughter, with Ann against Jack, in the assimilation of the rebel by the forces of convention.

The main departure from the comedy of manners pattern is the startling change of scene involved by the motor tour—a form of chase—from England to Spain, which ends in capture by brigands. This plot element had been used in *Captain Brassbound's Conversion;* and the brigands—like the pirates of the earlier play—are a comic-opera chorus, except that these talk left-wing politics and thus offer a key to Shaw's satiric intention. Against this background Jack dreams that he is in hell, under his other identity of Don Juan in seventeenth-century garb, surrounded by other figures from the main play transformed, as in the stock transformation scene of pantomime, into other characters familiar from Mozart's opera *Don Giovanni.* They argue with brilliant, unflagging eloquence, in lengthy, rhetorically patterned speeches that call for virtuoso speaking as well as excellent memory on the actors' part.

The matter of their debate is philosophic, and for it Shaw plundered Schopenhauer (on the struggle of the sexes as a conflict between Intellect and Will) and the vitalist doctrine of Bergson. The manner is unmistakably operatic, the occasional burst of actual music backing up the effortlessly soaring dream-speech and the effervescence of ideas. Hell is defined within the episode as "the home of the unreal" (the setting is a void), and the scene serves a double purpose: as a mentally stimulating entertainment very loosely attached to the main play, a token of Shaw's expressed desire to turn his theater audience into a "pit of philosophers"; and as a satire on the inadequacy of talk and ideas (a more developed version of the attack on Morell in *Candida*), which fits closely into the general drama of Tanner and Ann Whitefield.

MAJOR BARBARA *AND* JOHN BULL'S OTHER ISLAND

IN identifying a particular social and psychological type with a recurrent figure of European legend, Shaw was moving on a general cultural tide that accompanied the decline of Christianity. The growing study of comparative religion and anthropology, as exemplified in James Frazer's *The Golden Bough* (1890), treated the Christian gospel story as one myth among others, and the ground was prepared for the deliberate use of mythic material as a kind of cultural shorthand in literature and art, as in psychoanalytic classification of human motives (most famously in the Oedipus complex).

Shaw went on to devise the plot of *Major Barbara* (1905) on lines that reflect several legends from within the Christian tradition: that of Barbara, the patron saint of gunners and miners, interlinked with a version of the mission, betrayal, passion, and ascension associated with Christ himself, and complicated with elements from the best known of postmedieval myths, that of Faust, who sells his soul to the Devil in exchange for some superhuman power in this world. He dedicated *Major Barbara* to his other close associate (along with Archer and Barker) in the campaign for a national theater and the Royal Court enterprise: Gilbert Murray, professor of Greek, whose translations of Euripides' plays were offered alongside Shaw's as new work appropriate to a national repertoire. It is well known that Professor Cusins in *Major Barbara*, nicknamed Euripides by his antagonist, the formidable Andrew Undershaft, was modeled on Gilbert Murray, to whom "my play stands indebted . . . in more ways than the way from Athens" (prefatory note to the screen version, published in 1945). Murray is known in another context as one of the small group of British classical scholars who gave wide currency to the theory of the ritual origins of Greek drama and were particularly influential on the modernist writers who incorporate myth in literature. The "way from Athens" is most directly seen in the allusions to Dionysus, god of irrational forces, linked with the birth of drama, made by Cusins in Shaw's text: Nietzsche's philosophic campaign against Christian ethics had made the name of Dionysus familiar to contemporaries by using it symbolically. But the reference was broader than that and included Shaw's indebtedness to the dialogues of Plato in his procedures for guiding others to the truth through informal debates lightened by humor and controlled with Socratic irony.

Technically, *Major Barbara* is the culmination and compendium of Shaw's work up to this point. Its three acts belong to different modes. The first is drawing-room comedy, dominated by a splendidly alive caricature of the grande dame, Lady Britomart, who is played off against three disguised clown-types: the solemn idiocy of her son, Stephen; the silly-ass antics of Charles Lomax; and the clever, ironic clowning of Adolphus Cusins. The second act switches to a Salvation Army shelter in a poor district of London and a Dickensian melodramatic action, accompanied by an intense ironic commentary embedded in the dialogue. Act III is a variation of the abstract debate, against a symbolic background, that Shaw had tried out in the dream episode of *Man and Superman*; but this time he has kept it as an organic part of the main action of the play. If the author has a persona in *Man and Superman* it is John Tanner/Don Juan himself, and the play—like *The Philanderer* before it—is in part a self-directed analysis. He has two personas in *Major Barbara*: Cusins, who grasps the meaning and understands the irony of what is going on, but is himself involved as an actor; and Undershaft, the tempter/devil in the guise of an immensely wealthy manufacturer of armaments, who directs the plot from within the play, remaining essentially detached and a totally ironic consciousness, ultimately unfathomable.

Undershaft is the most formidable character Shaw had yet created—intellectually formidable, despite the mildest of civilized manners; the play as a whole is the most intellectually taut and challenging he ever wrote and has continued to provoke rival interpretations, not because it is confused in thought, but because Shaw has succeeded in leaving it dialectically open. The vision of Perivale St. Andrews (heaven against the hell of *Man and Superman*) is an ambiguous one that points toward a social millennium but remains a cheating simulacrum: Barbara sees that "It only needs a cathedral to be a heavenly city instead of a hellish one." Metaphor and symbol are used throughout the play with a similar dangerous ambiguity, summed up in the paradox of Cusins' intention to "make war on war" and even more sharply illustrated in such explosive aphorisms as "The ballot paper that really governs is the paper that has a bullet wrapped up in it," which are scattered through the text and testify to the influence of William Blake's aphoristic and dialectical *Marriage of Heaven and Hell*, from which Shaw has taken the concept of Energy, here conflated with the Schopenhauerian concept of Will. In doing this he has been able to replace the bland, hypocritical, and self-deceived type of heroine by a new, actively committed, androgynous figure in whom energy is directed by a positive belief. It is the price of this soul that the Faustian bargaining of *Major Barbara* seeks to define.

At the Court Theatre in 1905 *Major Barbara* confirmed the reputation Shaw had achieved with the previous play, *John Bull's Other Island*, a more centrally satirical, less overwhelmingly ironic work. For this he had taken a more specifically political theme: the policy of England, and the Liberal party in particular, toward Ireland, which was then governed entirely from London through Dublin Castle. This topic in itself was calculated to bring into the theater the men of affairs whom the management wanted to win over to the national theater campaign. Shaw, the leading Fabian, together with the Webbs, followed up astute publicity with direct invitations. As a result, all the leading statesmen of the day, the king, and other members of the royal family came, were delighted (Edward VII broke his chair with his paroxysms of laughter), and in many instances repeated the visit several times. The play makes a very serious indictment, but does so in a freer, less structured form, more like a variety show with a large cast of character turns than Shaw had ventured on before. At every point comedy gets under the guard of prejudice and drives criticism home, while the central dramatic idea holds everything in unity. Shaw uses the romantic movement's interpretation of Mephistopheles as the alter ego of a Faust who is blind to reality, including the truth about himself. Both figures appear in modern form as business partners: the English Liberal, Broadbent, genial and foolish, who believes, like Voltaire's Pangloss in *Candide*, that "All is for the best in the best of all possible worlds"; and the embittered, ruthless, self-exiled Irishman, whose consciousness reflects the evil that the other does in the illusion of his benevolence. It is interesting to reflect that the play which established his stature gives the plainest indication that the genial comedian's mask Shaw showed to the world overlaid a different self, formed by the Irish experience of his early years.

THE DOCTOR'S DILEMMA, MISALLIANCE, PYGMALION, ANDROCLES AND THE LION

IN 1906, at the age of fifty, Bernard Shaw could look back on some fifteen years of increasing fame, success, and influence. The production of his plays at the Court Theatre since 1904 had established him as a superb entertainer for intelligent audiences seeking a commentary on modern life and public affairs. The long waiting period, his novels, his journalism, his public speaking and committee work had all been preparation for what now seemed his true métier—as a dramatist. He had written a dozen plays that already showed his virtuosity; a greater number lay ahead, including some of his best work. His ambition was now matched by a sense of his powers and of opportunity at last within his grasp. He saw the next step as official recognition in the form of a national theater, where his work would take its place alongside Shakespeare's, and he wrote *The Dark Lady of the Sonnets* in 1910 as propaganda, and to win campaign funds, for this cause. When the Court Theatre seasons were not immediately followed by a new, major development, he wrote to his ally Barker and encouraged him to accept the directorate of a theater in New York as a step toward the conquest of two nations: "Why not do four years there, and then come back and found the national theatre and opera house of this country? . . . Eventually, simultaneous operations on both sides of the Atlantic might be possible" (21 April 1907).[2]

Instead, Shaw had to endure a number of disappointments: not only did Barker's apparent chance prove illusory, but critical reception of the major new Shaw plays produced in 1908 and 1910 (*Getting Married* and *Misalliance*) was not so favorable, and the public was cool; while in 1909 he ran into trouble with the censorship over *Press Cuttings* and *The Shewing-Up of Blanco Posnet*. Audiences were once more delighted by *Fanny's First Play*, which had a long run at a tiny theater in 1911, but Shaw had already devised tactics to help his subsequent plays along with the right kind of publicity. Starting with *Pygmalion*, he arranged for each to be performed abroad, in translation, before the British premiere. (The translations were initially for the purpose of copyright.) Thus English critics could be refuted by reports of success abroad, and his reputation as an international dramatist was made without interference by grudging English verdicts. Siegfried Trebitsch turned each play into German as it was written; Shaw continued to be performed in Germany during the war, though his royalties were frozen, and he remained easily the most-performed modern

[2]In C. B. Purdom, ed., *Bernard Shaw's Letters to Granville Barker* (London, 1957), p. 83.

playwright in Germany—at least until the rise of Nazism, and again after World War II until the mid-1950's, when he was superseded by Brecht, his most direct successor in more intrinsic ways also.

After the sustained effort and concentration that had gone into *Major Barbara,* Shaw wrote a group of more modestly designed plays that show an easy, near-perfect mastery. These are *The Doctor's Dilemma* (1906), *Fanny's First Play* (1910–1911), *Pygmalion* (1912), and the play he wrote for children young and old, *Androcles and the Lion* (1912). *The Doctor's Dilemma* and *Pygmalion* are problem plays in a special sense: they are logically designed to examine abstract propositions of some social consequence, and much of the pleasure they offer lies in the wit and elegance of an almost mathematically exact demonstration. That Shaw had been schooled in the Platonic dialogues is suggested by his use of a fictional mode to lead others to an understanding of the questions he has isolated; the liveliness and variety of his characters are a constant challenge to the rational scheme, as the opposed parties in *The Doctor's Dilemma* try to bend logic to their own ends and those in *Pygmalion* threaten to kick it to bits. Both plays confront the question of the relative merits of human individuals. (In 1928, Shaw was to propose to readers of his *Intelligent Woman's Guide to Socialism and Capitalism* that they should think out for themselves the most equitable way to distribute the wealth of society. There he advocates economic equality because there can be no absolute judgment of what men are worth.)

The reported incident of a distinguished physician's asking "Is he worth it?" when required to take on an additional patient struck Shaw forcibly, and he devised a play that would reflect on the godlike power that some men may be tempted to exert over others. His satirical portrayal of the doctors who set themselves up as judges exposes the false pretensions of the medical profession at the same time as it delights us with their separate human foibles, rivalries, and eccentricities; and the general point is silently reinforced by the expansive amiability of the greatest fool, Sir Ralph Bloomfield-Bonington (known to his friends as B.B.), which makes him "a born healer." To set up an ironic conflict that would add savor to the play, Shaw drew on his knowledge of the art world and the half-defined debate of the late nineteenth century between ethics and aesthetics carried on through John Ruskin and William Morris, Leo Tolstoy, Henry James, and Oscar Wilde, Shaw's colleague on the *Saturday Review.* So the doctors are

provided with their match in Louis Dubedat, the artist who combines the talent and frail constitution of Aubrey Beardsley with the wit and audacity of Ruskin's antagonist, James McNeill Whistler, and the incorrigible moral carelessness of Edward Aveling. In labeling *The Doctor's Dilemma* a tragedy, Shaw was up to his games again: including a death scene as formal qualification for the description, only to treat that scene with comic poise, and at the same time indicating with full justification that the themes of comedy can be at least as serious as those of tragedy.

Pygmalion examines the assumptions of social superiority and inferiority that underlie the class system, and demonstrates how unconsciously regulated patterns of social behavior (etiquette, opposed to more spontaneous manners) help preserve class distinctions. There is good reason to believe that Shaw had read Thorstein Veblen's *Theory of the Leisure Class* (1899). In particular, this play is concerned with speech differences as hallmarks of class: a professor of phonetics sets up an experiment to prove that he can turn a slum girl into a lady by changing her speech habits, and the comic climax of this scheme—negative proof of the theory—is reached when the elegantly dressed Eliza, in the most ladylike of tones, uses the taboo expression "Not bloody likely!" in the drawing room. The play gains symmetry, and its argument is made more complex, through the introduction of a second scheme, whereby her father is elevated socially and transformed in character by a bequest of money. The schematic element is cut across by a conflict more genuinely desperate than in *The Doctor's Dilemma:* the struggle of the girl to liberate herself from the insensitive tyranny of the professor, who is himself determined to remain comfortably dominant. As in so many of his plays, Shaw guides the audience's response to *Pygmalion* by combining in it echoes of older legends that arouse particular, sometimes discordant, expectations and emotions. Here he links the Cinderella story—the classic of wish-fulfilling transformation from rags to riches in a conventionally hierarchical society—with variations on the Faust legend of the man who assumes forbidden superhuman powers: Frankenstein, who creates a monstrous form of life (a more sinister analogue of the classical Pygmalion, the misogynist sculptor whose statue is brought to life in answer to his prayers), or Svengali (a role played shortly before with much success by Beerbohm Tree, the first English actor to play Professor Higgins), who turns a young girl into a world-renowned singer by the art of hypnotic possession. In every production of the play, the lure of the Cinderella plot is so strong, and Shaw's increasing self-projection as Higgins becomes so enticing, that the theme of the degradation of women and wastage of life in patriarchal society is all but submerged, even though it is spelled out in the dialogue.

The ambivalence of Shaw's attitude to the prewar feminist movement is revealed in a group of plays worth considering alongside *Pygmalion. Fanny's First Play*, as it was produced at the Little Theatre in 1911, masquerades as the work of a suffragette—though the introduction and epilogue written to sustain this pretense soften any challenge with an avuncular playfulness, and divert attention to new, peripheral material through recognizable parodies of leading contemporary theater critics. Inset is a play as "pleasant" as *You Never Can Tell*, in which Shavian idiosyncrasy is subdued to produce a light comedy that could almost have been written by the popular Arthur Wing Pinero and that includes a footman, really the younger brother of a duke, who claims relationship with J. M. Barrie's Admirable Crichton and anticipates the Jeeves of P. G. Wodehouse. Feminist values are assumed in the characterization of Margaret Knox, as in many of the energetic young women, impatient of convention, in Shaw's later drama; perhaps feminism is there, too, in the unabashed merriment of "Darling Dora," euphemistically described as a *fille de joie*, who turns that phrase into an imaginative reality. The explicit interlinked themes are a plea for youth's freedom to live experimentally and a commentary on the folly of class distinctions; but it is the old woman, Mrs. Knox, who is promoted to oracular authority, toward the end of the play—a minor echo of Mrs. George, who, dignified by mayoral robes and fallen into a trance, carries *Getting Married* beyond the range of laws and statute books into more abstract pronouncements on human life.

Among the Fabians, Shaw put up some resistance to the campaign for votes for women, in fearful anticipation that most women would support the Tories. The neglected sketch *Press Cuttings* (1909) is a vivid example of how his own fear of women rendered the idea that they might be given greater power farcical to him. The nearest he comes in this piece to presenting a suffragette is in the entrance of the prime minister, Balsquith (a lampoon on Balfour and Asquith), to the War Office, disguised in women's clothing and having first chained himself to the railings outside. The device has the explosive economy of political caricature, but its commentary on the nervousness of the politicians over the feminist issue preludes the arrival of two women who are contrasted, yet are equally tyrannical and man-despising antisuffrage campaigners. Mrs. Banger fully appreciates the War Office's argument of force in the face of suffragism and concludes: "Give me a regiment of women with sabres, opposed to a regiment of men with votes." The younger Shaw's attitude to the power exerted by Candida Morell and Ann Whitefield (in *Man and Superman*) finds much broader expression at this period, and Androcles and Megaera, in his Roman fable play of 1911–1912, are the henpecked husband and domineering wife of popular mythology, the music hall, pantomime, and comic seaside postcards. In *Misalliance*, the motherly Mrs. Tarleton, who calms down the would-be-revolutionary, is counterbalanced by an improbable apotheosis of free womanhood in the figure of Lina Szczepanowska, who literally takes off into the skies at the end of the play—so remote was the ideal from what actually went on and was likely to go on in the world, to the playwright's way of thinking.

Though he might choose to write the occasional piece, like the self-proclaimed melodrama *The Shewing-Up of Blanco Posnet*, in a conventional guise, Shaw was now demonstrating his mastery of style and form in an increasing eclecticism and freedom of experimentation. The variousness of his output challenged audiences' powers of swift adjustment to the mode of each new work. In particular, his blatant disregard of conventional snobbish distinctions between classical and "low" art carried the principle of equality into a new area, as well as increasing the cultural range embodied in individual plays. He advertised *Getting Married*, on the eve of its first production in 1908, as a return to "the Greek form." What he meant by this—except that he had not divided the play into acts and scenes—was left obscure. It is safe to assume that the dramatist who had used a phrase from Homer in the original to make a curiously erudite joke in *Major Barbara* had again been conferring with the Greek scholar Gilbert Murray. It is generally easier to identify parallels with Aristophanic comedy and the New Comedy of Menander, in *Getting Married*, than with Greek tragedy or Plato. The play has, in effect, two choruses, one male, one female, into which the cast is divided; there is no story plot, as there is no central protagonist, only a situation, much argument, considerable stage movement, and a scatter of incidents that culminate in the "judgment" delivered by the divinely possessed coal merchant's wife; and symbols of fertility are prominent in the stage picture. Many of the actors appear in forms of institutional fancy dress, as Bishop, General, or Beadle, and present a wide range of attitudes to sexual love and marriage, against a semiallegorical stage set representing the great pillars and arches of a Norman undercroft. Some of the elements of this play recur in *The Apple Cart* (1929), where the affinities with types of comic opera may be more easily recognized.

Rehearsing the actress Lillah McCarthy in Murray's version of Euripides' *The Bacchae*[3] led Shaw to incorporate motifs from that play, and fragments of its tragic plot, in *Misalliance*, mixing them up with elements of the companion play, *The Madras House* (both written in 1909), which Barker was writing for inclusion in the same new repertory program to be given by an idealistic commercial manager at the Duke of York's Theatre in 1910. The principle of burlesque, one of the most flourishing genres of English theater in the eighteenth and nineteenth centuries, was always congenial to Shaw, who liked to recall that Henry Fielding had practiced it, before political censorship drove him to novel-writing instead. Shaw preferred improvising playful variations on the work of others, parodying conventional forms and caricaturing familiar public figures, to inventing stories and characters with the primary power of illusion to blot out the actual world. But *Misalliance* takes off from farce into fantasy as no previous Shaw play had done; his comic genius comes into its own in a scintillating blend of nonsense, radical social comment, and gnomic wisdom. No doubt he was anxious, as he had been much earlier with *You Never Can Tell*, to conceal the teacher beneath the mask of an entertainer in order to win a West End audience; he succeeded only in baffling them. The quality of *Misalliance* has been discovered by productions in the second half of the century; the androgynous character of Polish origin who descends in an airplane upon the greenhouse of a wealthy linen-draper's Hindhead mansion and asks for a Bible and six oranges, and the clerk who conceals himself in the portable Turkish bath standing conveniently on stage and emerges brandishing a pistol and declaiming lines of apocalyptic rhetoric, have obvious affiliations with the 1960's farces of Joe Orton, or the highly intelligent craziness of the Monty Python entertainments.

---

[3]Shaw was often involved in rehearsing actors for other productions when he was not at work on one of his own.

Shaw's practice seems less idiosyncratic if it is seen in a wider context that goes beyond drama and beyond the boundaries of Britain. By comparison, in opera, Hugo von Hofmannsthal and Richard Strauss combined classical legend with the comedy of Molière's *Le Bourgeois Gentilhomme* and a harlequinade, in *Ariadne auf Naxos* (1912). The hostile reception given to the postimpressionist exhibition brought to London by Roger Fry in 1910 is evidence of the contemporary English public's ignorance of the artistic ferment that led to the emergence of a variety of now celebrated avant-garde movements in Europe before World War I. (Shaw was well acquainted with Roger Fry and made a considerable financial contribution to the setting-up of the Omega Workshop, which employed Duncan Grant and Vanessa Bell, among other artists, including briefly but prominently Wyndham Lewis, whose vorticist group was England's equivalent of futurism and cubism.) The barbaric vigor of Sergei Diaghilev's Ballet Russe, seen in Paris in 1909, and influential on Granville-Barker's prewar productions of Shakespeare, may be reflected in the figure of Lina Szczepanowska. It is now possible to see that Shaw's rejection of the logic of a cause-and-effect plot and a coherently developed thesis in *Misalliance* was allied to the assaults on bourgeois order and rationality that the futurists had recently started and that were to be continued by the Dada group at the Café Voltaire, in Zurich, when Shaw was at work on his next play in the same mode, *Heartbreak House*. The anarchic zest that found expression in *Misalliance*, the clown aspect of his temperament, was averse to any carefully constructed "organic" unity in art, preferring the effects of spontaneity and improvisation; it is not fundamentally at odds with the humane reservations expressed in *You Never Can Tell* and, later, in *The Doctor's Dilemma* about the doctrinaire application of reason to human life, which he saw as a most insidious form of the supreme enemy, idealism.

WORLD WAR I

THE coming of war largely diverted Shaw from playwriting. He had attacked militarism as early as 1909 in *Press Cuttings*, which takes sideswipes at Lord Kitchener's army and ridicules the fetish of military discipline through the mouth of a conscripted orderly: "It's being made a bloomin sheep of." Incidentally, the sketch anticipates the bringing of the moon into the orbit of power politics; more centrally, it turns around the argument offered with diabolical persuasiveness by Undershaft in *Major Barbara*, four years earlier, and gives it to General Mitchener, reduced to the basic, appalling logic of war and persecution, which he offers as "the secret of government": "Public opinion is mind. Mind is inseparable from matter. Shoot down the matter and you kill the mind." (Curiously enough, Shaw was never in the technical sense a pacifist, but he was later to fall into disrepute as favoring fascism.) Aware of the dangers of intensifying trade rivalries and the arms buildup to which Britain as well as Germany was committed, he used the press early in 1912 and again in the spring of 1913 to advocate a four-power peace-keeping pact between Britain, France, Germany, and the United States. He joined with Sidney and Beatrice Webb and H. D. Harben in founding the weekly review the *New Statesman*; and from its first number, in May 1913, he seems to have regarded it as his personal organ for influencing government and public opinion, overriding the protests of Clifford Sharp, the actual editor, to insist on the publication of his articles unsigned, as though they were editorials.

Immediately upon the outbreak of war, Shaw settled down to write an extended statement of his views on the situation, internal and international, which eventually appeared as "Commonsense About the War," an eighty-page supplement to the *New Statesman*, on 14 November 1914. It was widely read, and much more widely condemned, its reception having been prepared by fragmentary reports in the American press and what was, in effect, an open letter to the American president, Woodrow Wilson, that Shaw had published on both sides of the Atlantic. Although he considered that Britain, having gotten herself into the war, must now complete the business successfully, he would have no part of the hysteria of blind patriotism then sweeping the country. Perhaps his Irish origins helped, as he claimed, to keep him emotionally detached. The fact that he was writing precisely as he would have done before the outbreak of war, with the same critical clarity, the same intention to outrage and provoke, the same humorous exaggeration and sometimes flippancy of style, was now quite intolerable to the great majority, who had embraced the absolute moral imperative of the conflict with Germany, now transformed in their minds into a diabolical power. He was quite widely branded a traitor, even forced to resign from the Dramatists' Club, and some who had been his friends broke with him temporarily or permanently.

By 1916, opinion was swinging around, and, privately at least, more people were prepared to agree with Shaw's views; early in 1917 he paid an official visit to the front, but it was certainly unrealistic of him to expect to be appointed by the British government as a member of the convention called to discuss the question of Home Rule for Ireland, in the aftermath of the Easter Rebellion in Dublin. A letter from Shaw defending the rebels and warning of the folly of reprisals had been published in the *Daily News*, and his help was sought and offered for the defense of Sir Roger Casement, eventually executed as a traitor for his part in seeking German aid for the Irish patriots. When the Irish Convention sat, in 1917, Shaw, anxious to be on hand in an advisory capacity, stayed in Dublin with its chairman, his friend Sir Horace Plunkett, and wrote the articles immediately collected under the title *How to Settle the Irish Question*, at the request of the *Daily Express*, generally the most antagonistic of newspapers to him and his views. In 1918 the Irish Recruiting Council asked him to write in support of its cause; though the armistice made it useless in any practical way, Shaw printed his characteristically devious arguments for Ireland's fighting alongside England in the European war in the pamphlet entitled *War Issues for Irishmen*, which he dated for historical interest 10 November 1918 but which was never issued to the public. Inevitably, he continued in his self-appointed task of political commentator and national adviser by issuing *Peace Conference Hints* (published in a limited edition in 1919) before Versailles.

Shaw's imaginative writing had been limited to short pieces during these war years. Light entertainment for troops home on leave seemed to be all that the theater wanted. Barker had temporized by taking a company to America in 1915, and the breakup of his marriage to Lillah McCarthy heralded the end of his work as a stage director and manager. This helps to explain the long delay before Shaw got down to writing the major play that he had been planning in 1913 and that did not appear in print or on the stage until after the war. For the Abbey Theatre, Dublin, which had put on *Blanco Posnet* when it was foolishly banned in England, he wrote the one-act *O'Flaherty, V.C.*, which may be classified among his antidomestic comedies—along with the 1913 farce *Great Catherine*—as it reveals that the Irishman's strongest motive for joining the British army is to get away from home and mother, though "home" certainly represents the troubled land of his birth, also; it is equally in line with the early *Arms and the Man* as one of Shaw's attacks on the idealization of war, and it was this aspect of the play that led to a threat from Dublin Castle that the theater's license would be revoked if it were produced. (In the absence of Yeats and Lady Augusta Gregory, who might have risen to the challenge, the theater gave in.) In addition, Shaw added to the farcical sketches he had written before the war *The Inca of Perusalem*, including a caricature of the kaiser, and *Augustus Does His Bit*, lampooning the stupidities of Whitehall bureaucrats, whom officers and men in the trenches were currently seeing as the enemy at their backs. He had also written a story for a Belgian charity, "The Emperor and the Little Girl," using a childlike consciousness for his critical purpose, as he had done in the early essay *My Dear Dorothea*.

Major events had occurred in Shaw's private life, such as it was, shortly before the war. His mother had died in 1913, and he had launched into an affair with Mrs. Patrick Campbell that may not have been wholly platonic and that caused his wife painful jealousy. As earlier in his life, the elation and flirtatious wrangling of being in love found ready expression both in letters to the lady and in his dramatic work: most immediately in *Pygmalion*, in which the part of Eliza was written for and played by Mrs. Campbell (a fact that raises the question of how far Shaw had fallen Pygmalion-like in love with his own creation); and later in his characterization of Hesione, in *Heartbreak House*, and in the "Interlude" of *The Apple Cart*. Possibly related to these events as much as to the general shattering of Edwardian complacency by the nightmare-come-true of the war itself, glimpses of emotional sensitivity appear: in private letters, as when he wrote to Stella Campbell and to Lady Gregory (when each had received the news of a son killed in action); in the general quality of *Heartbreak House*, and especially in Shotover's tenderness toward Ellie and, at last, toward Ariadne when she is troubled by her own unfeeling nature; there is emotion in Shotover's reflections on old age; and these signs anticipate the trial scene in *Saint Joan*, which the public was to find so moving.

HEARTBREAK HOUSE

SHAW had difficulty in getting on with the text of *Heartbreak House*, altering and rewriting more extensively than he was used to doing, perhaps partly because he was following no preconceived plan (as he later told Archibald Henderson). He was working on it through the greater part of 1916, the year before Guillaume Apollinaire coined the term *surréaliste* in his preface to *Les Mamelles de Tirésias (The Breasts of Tiresias)*. The names of some of the characters in the new play—Hector, Hesione (originally Hecuba), and Ariadne—indicate that Shaw was continuing whimsically to derive his work from Greek sources and, in particular, that it was in his mind to suggest an analogy between the fall of Troy and the last days of the British Empire. (The Gunner, in *Misalliance*, had already announced: "Rome fell. Babylon fell. Hindhead's turn will come.") When the text was published in 1919, it carried the descriptive subtitle "A Fantasia in the Russian Manner on English Themes," thus drawing attention to other elements in the design: the symbolist practice of replacing narrative and logical plotting with a patterning of themes in imitation of musical form (a fantastic and improvisatory patterning in this case); the assimilation of Shaw's view of the English leisure class to Anton Chekhov's treatment of the decaying provincial aristocracy of Russia in its country houses (at Shaw's prompting, begun in 1905, the Stage Society had presented *The Cherry Orchard* to London in 1911); and the volume of Shakespeare that Ellie Dunn is reading and that drops from her hand as she nods off, at the beginning of the play (a clue to the principal source from which the English themes are drawn). This is certainly not the end of the medley of materials that Shaw was now bringing together, ranging from an element of science fantasy (old Captain Shotover seeks a mind ray that will destroy his enemies) to Wagnerian cosmic allegory.

Whereas *Misalliance*, the closest anticipation of *Heartbreak House* in Shaw's drama, is generally explicable as a development out of native burlesque tradition in a climate of revolt against sober artistic conventions, the later play seems to draw imaginative and symbolic force from areas of the mind that are obscure to the playwright himself, perhaps half acknowledged in the nickname "the Ancient Mariner," which links Shotover with the weird romantic poetry of Coleridge. The humor—there is still plenty of it—is sometimes shadowed, suffused with dark moods, or clashing against them to grotesque effect. Capitalism is embodied and exposed in the character of Mangan; the more attractive, realistically drawn Mazzini Dunn, who accommodates himself happily to the strange house and its unpredictable inhabitants, represents the spirit of liberalism in its weakness and, ultimately, its strength. The rest of the vivid, strongly defined figures in the play seem for most of the time to be acting out their fantasy selves, larger than life, though occasionally coming down to earth with some commonplace admission. So the outer world of society, politics, and economics is interlocked, throughout, with the dreamlike quality of subjective life. Shaw later referred to *Heartbreak House* as his *Lear,* and indeed the character-constellation of Shotover-Hesione-Ariadne-Ellie is strikingly reminiscent of the old, mad king and his three daughters; but *The Tempest* is more substantially present in the dominant imagery of the ship driving on the rocks, the drunken sailors, the world-ordering sage who has dealt with occult powers and practices magic arts, yet watches tenderly over the young girl. Mangan, cast into a trance and cruelly persecuted, is part Caliban, part dwarfish Alberic mocked by the Rhine maidens and thwarted in his desire for Freya (Ellie) by the combination of Wotan and Loki in the guise of Shotover and Hector. For the tendency of the work is toward a kaleidoscopic quality. So, at the end in the theater, when stage and auditorium blaze in response to the call for more and more light, the mysterious sound in the air, ominously heard twice in Chekhov's *The Cherry Orchard,* is also the noise of raiding zeppelins overhead and a thrilling music: Beethoven is named in the dialogue, but it could as well be Wagner's *Ring of the Nibelungs,* the music of the flashing thunderstroke or the Ride of the Valkyries—until mind ray or "act of God" triggers the explosion.

The oracular Captain Shotover is often interpreted with some justice as Shaw's fantastic self-projection into *Heartbreak House.* Unless this is felt to some extent, the sharp dramatic jolt will be missed when he turns on Ellie: "What did you expect? A Savior, eh? Are you old-fashioned enough to believe in that?"

BACK TO METHUSELAH

THE idea that Shaw's later plays preach doctrinaire solutions to humanity's problems has done much to hamper Shaw criticism, especially in relation to his next and most ambitious play, *Back to Methuselah* (written in 1918–1920). This work's central point of reference is the recently ended European war, close to the characters of part II, which is set in the present;

the aftermath of the war is seen in remote but far from passionless perspective in the epilogue:

Mars blushed as he looked down on the shame of his sister planet: cruelty and hypocrisy became so hideous that the face of the earth was pitted with the graves of little children among which living skeletons crawled in search of horrible food.

Caricatures of Lloyd George and Asquith are introduced into the drawing-room comedy of part II to give topical focus to an exposition of the moral and intellectual bankruptcy of party politics. The design of the whole dramatic cycle is based on two principal conceptual models: Swift's satirical masterpiece, *Gulliver's Travels,* and the Judeo-Christian cosmic myth. The fact that the author called his work "A Metabiological Pentateuch" or, alternatively, a "Bible of Creative Evolution," suggests a more scientifically based replacement for the account of the creation and early history of mankind, which nineteenth-century Christians were having increasing difficulty believing as their Bible related it.

Shaw had earlier, in *Major Barbara,* written a play that took the forms of Christian legend and liturgy and changed their content. In *Back to Methuselah,* his admiration for the Bible as imaginative art is reflected in a new success in writing prose poems under its influence. The familiar story of Adam and Eve in the Garden of Eden and its continuation into the account of Cain and Abel after the Fall are retold in part I, "In the Beginning," with an economy unexpected in Shaw, and with a careful harnessing of the dramatic element to lyrical and reflective ends. The first scene introduces the themes to be developed throughout the play cycle, sounding them in succession, briefly defining them, repeating and linking them in a prose equivalent of sonata form; for the epilogue into which part V passes, the phantasms of Adam and Eve, Cain, and the Serpent return, only to be superseded by the further legendary figure of Lilith from rabbinical tradition, embodiment of the creative spirit outside time, who utters a final, sustained monologue that recapitulates all the themes in developed form. So the end circles back to the beginning and balances it in an aesthetically pleasing way.

Within this frame Shaw uses the notion of relative length (or expectation) of life as the fictive basis for his satirical perspectives, as Swift used relative physical size. The last three sections thus offer variant utopias, or speculative fantasies of human life at distances of 250, 1,080, and 30,000 years beyond the present. Far from showing any increase in wisdom, the government of the British Isles is headed in part III by a burlesque conflation of the Lloyd George and Asquith figures of the previous section viewed with a broader, more contemptuous mockery; technological advance is opportunity for greater silliness among the English, while the serious running of the state is carried on by a civil service of Chinese and blacks. The folly of the generation that had brought about the war persists in the deputation of short-livers that has traveled from the capital of the British Commonwealth at Baghdad to consult the oracle among the long-livers in southern Ireland, in part IV; indeed the Napoleonic figure of the Emperor of Turania appears to be a reincarnation of Cain much degenerated since part I.

In the last section, the vanities and illusions of humanity as we know it persist only in (physically mature) children under the age of five and, in cruder and more vicious form, reappear briefly in the automata made by the scientist-sculptor among them, who is destroyed by his own horrible creation. For the antitheses that he uses critically Shaw went to Plato: the long-livers of part IV are the totally rational Guardians of the *Republic,* who do not understand metaphor and regard imagination as a lying faculty; in part V, the state has withered away and the errors and excesses of self-government are committed by the Ancients only within the boundaries of the self, as part of an endless process of self-development and discovery. As the evolutionary direction is away from beauty toward truth, away from art toward contemplative thought and its more direct material transformations, the playwright's own activity is called into question; it is put into perspective by the miniature inset tragedy acted out by the automata when they have been partially transformed by the breath of life, and at which even the Ancients smile. The function of art is one of the main themes of the cycle, and Shaw is careful from part I to the epilogue to indicate that he belongs among those who "tell beautiful lies in beautiful words" and that what he is now presenting is not a prediction or blueprint for the future, but a fable.

Apart from a common tendency to raise overliteral objections to the substance of *Back to Methuselah,* for which Shaw's exposition of the theory of creative evolution in the preface is partly to blame, there has been much division of critical opinion over this play. In its general conception it is the most impressive, as well as the longest, of Shaw's dramatic achievements, yet critics have often shied away from it. Not surprisingly, the execution of the

scheme is uneven, and there are passages, especially in the lengthy duologues of Zoo and Zozim with the Elderly Gentleman, in part IV, when Shaw seems to have forgotten that he was writing for stage production and even falters in his differentiation of characters. It is difficult to be particularly enthusiastic about part III, "The Thing Happens" (corresponding to the Laputa section of *Gulliver's Travels*): the satire is little more penetrating than it is precise, the short-lived characters are two-dimensional, and the clownish comedy lacks engaging geniality; the carrying on of the narrative from part II holds the attention sufficiently to make a bridge to the more important fourth and fifth sections, where philosophic thought gains dominance over the satiric element, though never ousting it completely.

"Tragedy of an Elderly Gentleman" is, despite the length of its expositions, the most moving section of the whole, for the main character, who is, like Gulliver, driven to detest his own Yahoo nature, has genuine moral passion, and Shaw's rhetoric is at its most powerful and various in rhythm and tone in the sweep of his interrupted monologues:

My society has printed an editio princeps of the works of the father of history, Thucyderodotus Macollybuckle. Have you read his account of what was blasphemously called the Perfect City of God, and the attempt made to reproduce it in the northern part of these islands by Jonhobsnoxious, called the Leviathan? Those misguided people sacrificed the fragment of life that was granted to them to an imaginary immortality. They crucified the prophet who told them to take no thought for the morrow and that here and now was their Australia. . . . I accept my three score and ten years. If they are filled with usefulness, with justice, with mercy, with good-will; if they are the lifetime of a soul that never loses its honor and a brain that never loses its eagerness, they are enough for me, because these things are infinite and eternal. . . .

There is concentrated substance in this, not windy inflation, and the immediate detail also serves as commentary on the entire work.

Shaw's images of the remote future are derived from the classical past. "Their dress," he says of the children, "like the architecture of the theatre and the design of the altar and curved seats, resembles Grecian of the fourth century B.C., freely handled." All is contained in "a sunlit glade," and the use of music and formal dance contributes to the pastoral effect, the aesthetic charm and tranquility of this most distanced view of human nature. Shaw did not forget here that the characters were to be played by living actors, but offered them a distillation of familiar qualities to portray in the petulance of Strephon; the boring self-complacency of Pygmalion; the brash, soubrettish eagerness of the Newly Born (in whom both Savvy Barnabas of the twentieth century and Zoo return)—as in part I he offered the touchiness of Adam, the jealousy of Eve, the sly flattery and ironic consciousness of the Serpent. Even in his presentation of the Ancients, those grotesque embodiments of the philosophic mind, laughter and gravity are interwoven; and in part V, as in part IV, a virtually self-contained dramatic action counterbalances the discussion. The kinds of drama Shaw has written in the later parts of *Back to Methuselah* are rare in the theater, and their sophisticated artifice may be an acquired taste; but stage productions have reinforced their claim to a critical appraisal that acknowledges the care and skill with which they have been composed.

It seemed to Shaw, when he had finished *Back to Methuselah*, that he had probably written his last play. He was sixty-five years old, and he had given extended expression to the faith in Creative Evolution that he had derived from Samuel Butler and from Henri Bergson, and that he had come increasingly to speak of as his religion. It is worth noting that he did not call his socialism a religion. Having rejected Marxism, as he rejected the Darwinian version of the evolution of species, as too deterministic, he preferred to stress the pragmatic and provisional nature of his Fabian views and principles. (Incidentally, he associated himself with Ebenezer Howard's Fourierist scheme for changing society through the establishment of cooperative "Garden Cities," which resulted in the founding of Letchworth in the early years of the century and Welwyn between the wars, both within easy distance of the Shaws' country home at Ayot St. Lawrence.) The certainty of continual change, failure, decay, the necessity for renewed efforts and fresh visions were essential articles of the general faith in which he confronted the postwar world, the coming of the second major war, and the arrival of the nuclear age with its sharper threat of universal destruction.

SAINT JOAN—*SHAW'S BELIEFS*

SHAW's wife was largely responsible for interesting him in a further dramatic project: a play on the subject of Joan of Arc. Her legend had been revived in France during the war; and an ambitious Hollywood silent film, *Joan the Woman*, had been made in 1917 with the leading soprano of the Metropolitan Opera, Geraldine Farrar, in the lead. In 1920 Joan was canonized, an event that gave publicity to the original documents to which Shaw chose to go for his materials. There he found a heroine after his own heart: clearheaded and quick-witted, energetic and practical, with a personality that ruled out any crude element of sex appeal. What he produced was not a history, however, so much as another fable play that was to be the principal model for such Brechtian "historical" fables as *Mother Courage* (1936–1939)[4] and *Galileo* (1938–1939)—Brecht's *St. Joan of the Stockyards* (1929–1930) is more closely related to *Major Barbara*—and for Luigi Pirandello's theatrical demonstrations of the relativity of truth and illusion in *Six Characters in Search of an Author* (1921) and, more specifically, his *Henry IV* (1922).

To ensure the perspective of fable, Shaw combined a chronicle-play form with elements from the native tradition of pantomime. He started with a scene based on the same kind of folk legend as the familiar pantomimes of *Dick Whittington*, *Puss in Boots*, and *Mother Goose*: confronted by the insouciant audacity of the androgynous Principal Boy, whose garb Joan is eager to put on, Baudricourt stamps and fumes like a pantomime ogre; Joan's first triumph is marked by a suitably rustic "miracle," when the hens suddenly start laying in crazy abundance. The Dauphin is the clown of the play, though a particularly shrewd one; and the scattering of verbal anachronisms (from the allusion to "cowboys" in the first passage), and contemporary and often schoolboyish slang expressions, together with Joan's lapses into pantomime dialect (for example, "Coom, Bluebeard. . . . Where be dauphin?" or "Dressing up dont fill empty noddle"), are calculated controls on what might too easily have turned into a tragic pageant play. Shaw admits the possibility of a tragic vision of the materials he is using (the dialogue includes a reference to Joan's hubris), and the succession of scenes leading up to the trial, and into the immediate aftermath of Joan's death at the stake, establishes a gradual increase in gravity; but the epilogue—decried by a majority of contemporary critics, who wanted a more romantic work than the dramatist chose to give—breaks the illusion of a history play, by taking the historical events into a dream realm outside time, and reasserts the perspective of comedy in a culmination of all the earlier comic inciden-

---

[4]The years cited are those for the first versions of Brecht's plays.

tals. In fact, this last scene, which introduces a modern man in a top hat among the medieval characters, thus revealing them all as actors dressed up, is in part a return to nineteenth-century extravaganza convention, but changes into a new hybrid as it passes into the final, liturgical movement: a *Te Deum* that closes the saint's play, a passion play imitative of Christ's passion (as are all such plays within the Christian tradition), which is also assimilated into Shaw's total scheme.

The heroine is as ambiguous as the form of the play. As a human individual she is "quite innocent," as the Inquisitor privately recognizes; but a similar innocence is caricatured in the person of de Stogumber, the simpleton priest on the English side whose crude nationalism has all the excesses Shaw had deplored in the insensate patriotism he observed around him in the early years of the war with Germany. Joan is a contrast with the priest in that he lacks imagination, while hers is so vivid that it imposes itself upon her as supernatural revelation; but her vision still has its limitations, and her innocence is partly unreflecting ignorance of where her inspiration might ultimately lead. The subtle churchmen see further. Indeed, the tense conflicts of the play are essentially conflicts of perspective: Dunois, the Dauphin, and Warwick all have elements of foxy, Machiavellian political awareness beyond the range of Joan's consciousness; with a modern historian's understanding, Cauchon looks beyond the end of feudalism and the rise of Protestantism to the more distant effects of uncurbed individual self-assertion and nationalism—toward the twentieth century: "a world of blood, of fury, of devastation, of each man striving for his own hand: in the end a world wrecked back into barbarism." The Joan whose suggestion of a second coming appalls the other characters of the epilogue is both the champion of absolutes and herself an idealization, too dangerous a phenomenon to be trusted in any age. The voices she hears and stubbornly insists on obeying are tokens of her authenticity, but, though Shaw may have accepted that "The unconscious self is the true genius" (one of the Maxims for Revolutionists attached to *Man and Superman*), he was very far from equating irrationality with good. Joan's "innocent" arrogance is consequent on her lack of a self-critical faculty. According to the Serpent in *Back to Methuselah*, "The Voice in the garden is your own voice," though Adam's qualification of this claims attention: "It is; and it is not. It is something greater than me: I am

only a part of it." However altruistic its intent, the value of inspiration still needs to be tested critically, as the Inquisition, despite all its confusions and irrelevancies, tests Joan's.

A number of Shaw's plays have been classified as "religious," among them *Major Barbara*, *The Shewing-Up of Blanco Posnet*, *Androcles and the Lion*, *Back to Methuselah*, and *Saint Joan*; and certainly the adolescent Bernard Shaw who mocked all religion as crass superstition stayed, in later life, to discover the truth any religious belief might hold. He numbered among his later friends both the Anglican dean Inge and the Catholic abbess of Stanbrook, Dame Laurentia McLachlan, to whom he presented a copy of his prose fable *The Adventures of the Black Girl in Her Search for God* (1932), in expectation of an understanding it did not receive. Undershaft, in *Major Barbara*, names the subject of religion as "the only one that capable people really care for"; and Tarleton, in *Misalliance*, repudiates Ecclesiastes' association of age with the desire that fails: "Does it? By George! No, sir: it spiritualizes."

Yet an examination of Shaw's later writings makes it clear that he was not among the rebels from traditional belief who revert to some form of it as age draws on. Lavinia, in *Androcles* (the central part of which borrows the form of the sensational melodrama *The Sign of the Cross*, which was written and performed by the actor-manager Wilson Barrett and first published in 1896), discovers her readiness to die for something greater than herself but also realizes that no particular doctrine is great enough to merit total self-sacrifice. As the Archbishop explains away Joan's apparently supernatural powers in the formula "A miracle is an event that creates faith," so the dramatist rationalizes her voices and visions on a psychological basis as forms taken by natural forces, objectifications of her impulses and perceptions. *The Adventures of the Black Girl* is a critical examination of the gods that men have made for themselves that is as close to Voltaire in attitude as in its literary procedures; indeed allusions to Voltaire multiply in Shaw's late writings. Shaw was certainly in pursuit of a longer view than politics affords, but he never abandoned the rational understanding of philosophy for mysticism.

Shaw became a life member of the Royal Astronomical Society, and it fell to him to propose a toast to Albert Einstein at a celebratory dinner in 1931; at the age of ninety-three he applied to join the British Interplanetary Society, with Arthur C. Clarke, a well-known exponent of popular science, sponsoring him. He submitted the scientific material in the text of *In Good King Charles's Golden Days* (1938–1939) to Sir James Jeans and Sir Arthur Eddington for correction. In fact, he was as concerned as when he wrote *The Irrational Knot* that his view of the world and human life should be scientific. Most of his late plays offer a more distant and abstract view of their subjects (as anticipated by the last section of *Back to Methuselah*), as they take account of the major calamities of the twentieth century and, by the time he reached *Farfetched Fables* (1948), incorporate the atomic bomb and chemical warfare in their range of vision. Using a scale of astronomical change enables the playwright to maintain his philosophic and comedic poise, but as early as *Caesar and Cleopatra*, with its references to Pythagoras, and later, in *Saint Joan*, which identifies Pythagoras as "a sage who held that the earth is round, and that it moves round the sun," Shaw had used scientific theories as tokens of the relativity and provisional nature of any truth that the human mind could—indeed must—grasp.

Saint Joan proved to be the great popular favorite among Shaw's plays, though he himself never rated it so high. The first English production was beautifully staged, with decorative hangings and costumes by the great art nouveau designer Charles Ricketts, and the memory of it unluckily encouraged subsequent overromantic interpretations of the work that, in turn, helped trigger the reaction against Shaw's whole reputation as a dramatist. Meanwhile, in 1925, he won the Nobel Prize for Literature, the only public honor he agreed to accept—on the understanding that he be permitted to use the prize money for the making and publication of translations from Swedish literature, especially August Strindberg's plays, into English. After *Saint Joan* there was a gap of six years before he wrote another play. His major work within this period was the writing, at his sister-in-law's request, of *The Intelligent Woman's Guide to Socialism and Capitalism* (published in 1928; he later added chapters on "Sovietism" and Fascism for the Penguin edition in 1937), which shows the born teacher in Shaw to best advantage: master of an unforced simplicity of exposition and continual vivid yet careful illustration, staying within the bounds of the reader's likely experience. As he presents them, politics and economics are not specialist studies but the daily business of ordinary men and women. The manner he used in this book, as in many of the prefaces written to accompany his plays in printed form, was to make him a very effective broadcaster during the next decade and remained at his command for his last major work, *Everybody's Political What's What?*, published in 1944.

LAST PLAYS AND OTHER WRITINGS

Sir Barry Jackson, the wealthy theater enthusiast who gave to Birmingham between the wars a repertory theater of the first order and who was a direct inheritor of Barker's work, was responsible for the extension of Shaw's playwriting career through another eight full-length plays and a number of shorter pieces. It was he who had eventually produced *Back to Methuselah* and brought it to London, and his establishment of an annual Shaw Festival at Malvern gave the dramatist fresh impetus for the creation of new works. (Though he was once more assured of a stage and a company at his disposal in England, he continued to arrange premieres abroad, increasingly by the New York Theatre Guild; and *Geneva*—1936; revised sometime before 1939—was playing in Warsaw when Nazi troops entered the city.) The plays of the final phase still await adequate critical attention: as a group, they remain little known and tend to be briefly dismissed without differentiation as virtually senile relics of a failing talent. But the long practice of his craft stood Shaw in good stead, and although there are echoes of earlier work in most of these plays, there is no repetition of formulas, but continuing inventiveness and incisive criticism. The late work may not have the tight thematic complexity of *Major Barbara* or match the fresh exuberance of *Misalliance* or *Pygmalion*, but most of it compares well in quality with some of the plays Shaw wrote before 1900. Recent productions of *Too True to Be Good* (1931) and *On the Rocks* (1933) have held their audiences as surely as *The Philanderer* or *The Devil's Disciple*; and *The Simpleton of the Unexpected Isles* (1934) is not obviously inferior in interest or skill to *Captain Brassbound's Conversion*.

New concerns come into prominence in the late plays: above all, the theme of individual responsibility recurs in one after another. *The Apple Cart* (1928) and *On the Rocks* are Shaw's main indictments of the ineffectualness of parliamentary democracy. The first of these emulates Aristophanic

125

comedy and offers a loosely constructed satirical entertainment (with some meticulous patterning of detail) in which a chorus of cabinet members is a major element. By locating the action at an indefinite but not too distant future time, and giving classical names to the characters, Shaw is able to abstract the essentials of the situation he wants to examine. A tendency to such abstraction, which gives the plays the quality of philosophic fables, is another general characteristic of this last phase of his work. In *On the Rocks* he presents the cabinet room at 10 Downing Street on the stage, but his prime minister is not identifiable with any actual politician, and again the effect is to make the play tangential to the actual world and to emphasize the hypothetical nature of the plot. An ultimatum from America, threatening to annex Britain, breaks in upon the petty internal squabbling in *The Apple Cart;* the action of *On the Rocks* turns on the supposition that the prime minister, faced by the economic slump and mass unemployment of contemporary England, is converted to socialism by reading Marx and attempts to deal with his country's problems accordingly. Both plays demonstrate the power of vested interests at work within the party political system. *The Apple Cart* also specifically attacks the passivity of the trade union rank-and-file, which gives excessive power, without adequate accountability, to its leaders. The political maneuverings shown in *On the Rocks* are more intense and subtle, as well as more substantial, than the stylized, token equivalents in *The Apple Cart;* and it is in keeping that the old, disillusioned trade unionist, Hipney, should bring a deadlier irony into the play, as he offers the decade's most dangerous temptations:

. . . if Srarthur means business, then let him come out of Parliament and keep out. . . . The only man that ever had a proper understanding of Parliament was old Guy Fawkes. . . . Adult suffrage: that was what was to save us all. My God! It delivered us into the hands of our spoilers and oppressors, bound hand and foot by our own folly and ignorance . . . now I'm for any Napoleon or Mussolini or Lenin or Chavender that has the stuff in him to take both the people and the spoilers and oppressors by the scruffs of their silly necks and just sling them into the way they should go. . . . You cant frighten me with a word like dictator. Me and my like has been dictated to all our lives by swine that have nothing but a snout for money. . . .

But Chavender has liberal scruples that leave him anticipating some man of iron who will put through the measures he knows are needed: "I'm not the man for the job. . . . And I shall hate the man who will carry it through for his cruelty and the desolation he will bring on us and our like."

The common verdict that Shaw was pro-Fascist in the 1930's was certainly based on careless attention to his writings, a confusion between satirical technique and substance, perhaps compounded by knowledge of the close friendship he developed with the first woman (Conservative) member of Parliament, Lady Astor, whose home became a frequent meeting place for those who favored the policy of appeasing Hitler. In his public utterances Shaw tended to use the dictators as sticks with which to correct the errors of the British, while being little concerned and not very knowledgeable about the evils of their regimes. (He was certainly flattered by Stalin during the visit he paid to Russia, in a small party that also included Lady Astor, in 1931.) The term "extermination" figures quite prominently in his work of this decade; later, in *Farfetched Fables,* it is replaced by "liquidation." Defiantly, his preface to *On the Rocks* argued the case for political purges: he was certainly persisting in his efforts to shock the public into thinking, and his attitude cannot be properly appraised unless the preface is not only weighed against the testimony of the plays but seen in the context of his general opposition to judicial punishment, most fully stated in his preface to the volume on prisons in the Webbs' *English Prisons Under Local Government* (1922), several times separately reprinted. In the course of this radical document he declares that the idea of individual freedom "is as yet unformed":

we conceive Man as being either in authority or subject to authority. . . . The concept of the evolving free man in an evolving society . . . is still unusual, and consequently terrifying, in spite of all the individualist pamphlets of the eighteenth and nineteenth centuries.

His opinion that capital punishment is more humane than imprisonment received a good deal of publicity, and supplied the motivation for Joan of Arc's emotional choice of the stake in his dramatization of her story. The process of extermination, or "weeding the garden," gets its dramatic presentation in *The Simpleton of the Unexpected Isles:* useless people and mere talkers vanish, like Euphorion in the Faust legend, into air; for Shaw's abstract idea lacks the ferocity of Swift's "Modest Proposal" that the ills of Ireland might be cured by encouraging the natives to eat their children, though both display the satirist's necessary ability to be inhumanly rational about what may matter greatly to the man. The garden that is being weeded is an island utopia where the unit of group marriage embraces a blend of the cultures of East and West, subsequent to the death of colonialism. But as all fixed ideas and established systems threaten to tyrannize over "the evolving free man," the whole dream is judged and dismissed before the play ends.

Recognition that King Magnus, in *The Apple Cart*, is not a benign autocrat, but a representative figure of responsible individuality, might have come more easily if Barker's last play, *His Majesty* (1923–1928), on which Shaw drew heavily in his accustomed way in *The Apple Cart* and *On the Rocks*, had been more generally known. Yet Shaw often referred to John Bunyan as his favorite author, a fair enough clue to his own practice of allegory and a warning against overliteral interpretation that is most applicable to his later work. Concentration of the serious thought of *The Apple Cart* in the lengthy arias of the soloists, Magnus and Lysistrata, too sharply distinguishes them from the ridiculous chorus; *Too True to Be Good* may be finally less confusing because the improbabilities and absurdities of plot and matching, disjointed shifts from one stylized theatrical mode to another involve all the characters equally: from the Measles Microbe (the clown) in the prologue to the orating Elder in his cave; the Patient and the Burglar in their changing guises; and old Mrs. Mopply, who is brought to sanity by a blow from an umbrella. The whole of this latter play is acceptable as a wild fantasy version of Britain and the Empire midway between the wars; it is technically a development from *Heartbreak House*, offering Shaw's final version of Jack Tanner (of *Man and Superman*) in the compulsive preacher with nothing to say, on whom the curtain descends, but reserving respect for the energetic female, whose portrait is not now undercut with irony, as happened with Vivie Warren or Ann Whitefield in the earlier plays.

Substantially the same character appears as the Young Woman in *The Simpleton* and the similarly labeled female voice that drives through the comic duologue *Village Wooing* (1933). Amanda, the soubrette of *The Apple Cart*, Aloysia Brollikins, who emerges out of the Aristophanic chorus of *On the Rocks*, and Nell Gwynn, in *In Good King Charles's Golden Days*, are versions of the same type assimilated to vaudeville conventions. Opportunities for actors to give virtuoso displays of highly stylized acting technique are as readily to be found in most of the late work as at any earlier period of Shaw's career. The most considerable star role for an actress, in the last plays, is the part of Epifania in *The Millionairess* (1934), which requires emotional power, not simply controlled energy: a melancholy, operatic grandeur. Yet a general comparison of Epifania with Lulu, Frank Wedekind's personification in the Lulu plays of the life force, points up one aspect of Shaw's work that has particularly dissatisfied the later twentieth century: his failure to deal with sexuality, as distinct from the socially conventionalized forms of eroticism. The marriages to which several of the late plays lead are allegorical happy endings, in which efficiency and productive capacity are united with spiritual values or vision.

The voyages to distant parts of the world that the Shaws took between 1931 and 1934 undoubtedly suggested the exotic settings and elements of adventure among which the philosophic questions are posed in *Too True*, *The Simpleton of the Unexpected Isles*, *Buoyant Billions* (1936–1937 and 1945–1947), and the nondramatic fable of *The Adventures of the Black Girl*, which Shaw wrote in South Africa. (*Village Wooing* is evidently a product of shipboard experience.) In subtitling *The Apple Cart* and *Too True to Be Good* "extravaganzas," the dramatist was pointing to connections with nineteenth-century entertainments that relied as much on stage spectacle as on music and comedy. But the movement out of English domestic settings into desert, jungle, or oriental temple scenes is also a superficial token of how the world has become the true and relevant context of the plays. Internationalism is the theme of *Geneva*, the last of Shaw's plays to achieve a long run in the theater during his lifetime. Topicality may have been its chief attraction initially, though its caricatures of Mussolini, Franco, and Hitler are used as lay figures in a burlesque with a moral lesson to deliver that is even more urgent today. The political education of the audience has its surrogate in the stage action, which leads the averagely amiable, ignorant, and prejudiced Begonia Brown to summon the dictators before the World Court, the audience they cannot resist posturing before. In the literal sense the trial is "a farce," but Begonia's discovery of her own power and exposure of her inadequacy to use it wisely is more fundamental to Shaw's purpose. The Judge's verdict, "Man is a failure as a political animal," is promptly followed by news from the astronomical observatories that spells out a judicial sentence: "Humanity is doomed." Impatient of pessimism even now, and preferring to be a teacher rather than a prophet, Shaw defuses the threat of its terror in order to use it as a warning.

Shaw undoubtedly accepted the view of himself as the greatest playwright of his generation. He had taken upon himself, as if it were a public office, the characteristically Victorian role of keeper of the public conscience, criticizing the state from within and teaching its citizens how to govern; like Ibsen, he kept up a running quarrel with the majority. Being, in his generation, in revolt against Victorian earnestness and the hypocrisy it encouraged, he played the clown to carry out his task. Having inherited a theater that lent itself to the display and the mockery of rhetoric, he created for it a large repertoire of technically innovative, prolifically various, exuberant, and exhilarating works in which his passion for music found expression through torrents of cunningly orchestrated dialogue distributed among a great range of vivid, assertive characters whose home is truly the stage. His was a lopsided genius, certainly, with the virtues of its own defects: he translated his temperamental detachment into breadth of vision and public concern—for the community and, ultimately, for the species; his rejection of suffering released tremendous energy; and the buried stream of powerful feeling was signaled by his effervescent and even anarchic humor. If the intellectual thrust fails, his clowning alone can seem embarrassingly childish. Yet he remains one of the few writers who have had a complete and profound comic vision of the world: it might be "God's joke," he commented to Tolstoy, who did not understand; and being innocent of the worst confusions of the soul, he refused to romanticize as evil the ignorance and folly of men.

SELECTED BIBLIOGRAPHY

Many of Shaw's plays were published in German translations or in some cases in other languages before publication of the English texts. These foreign-language editions are not listed below.

I. BIBLIOGRAPHY.
Writings: G. H. Wells, "A Bibliography of the Books and Pamphlets of Bernard Shaw" (London, 1926; rev., enl. ed., 1929), pamphlet, from *The Bookman's Journal* Supplements (1928–1929); C. L. and V. M. Broad, *Dictionary to the Plays and Novels of Bernard Shaw, with Bibliography of His Works . . .* (London, 1929); S. Weintraub, "Shaw," in R. J. Finneran, ed., *Anglo-Irish Literature. A Review of Research* (New York, 1976); J. C. Amalric, *Bernard Shaw, du réformateur victorien au prophète édouardien* (Paris, 1977), 423–566; F. E. Loewenstein, *The Rehearsal Copies of Bernard Shaw's Plays* (London, 1950), of more specialist bibliographical interest; D. H. Laurence, comp., *Shaw: An Exhibit* (Austin, 1978), a catalog comp. for the Humanities Research Center of the University of Texas, contains much information.

Works About Shaw: "A Continuing Checklist of Shaviana," issued in the *Shaw Bulletin*, later the *Shaw Review*, published three times a year since 1950; E. Farley and M. Carlson, "George Bernard Shaw: A Selected Bibliography (1945–1955)," in *Modern Drama*, parts I and II (September and December 1959); L. C. Keough, "George Bernard Shaw, 1946–1955: A Bibliography," in *Bulletin of Bibliography* (September–December 1959, January–April 1960, May–August 1960); M. M. Morgan, "Shaw," in S. J. Wells, ed., *English Drama (Excluding Shakespeare)* (London, 1975), discusses a selection of publications on Shaw, see also J. C. Amalric and S. Weintraub, above.

II. COLLECTED WORKS. All of the following eds. were originally seen through the press by Shaw himself: *Collected Edition*, 30 vols. (lim. ed., London, 1930–1932), 3 more vols. added by 1937, lim. to 1,000 sets, known in the U.S. as the Ayot St. Lawrence ed.; *Standard Edition*, 37 vols. (London, 1931–1950), contains items not in the *Collected Edition*; *Complete Plays* (London, 1931; enl., 1934, 1938, 1950; reiss. 1965); *Our Theatres in the Nineties*, 3 vols. (London, 1932), weekly reviews contributed to the *Saturday Review* (5 January 1895–21 May 1898), in the *Standard Edition*; *Music in London*, 3 vols. (London, 1932), weekly articles contributed to the *World*, 28 May 1890–8 August 1894, in the *Standard Edition*; *Prefaces* (London, 1934), the updated and enl. ed. is entitled *Complete Prefaces* (London, 1938; reiss. 1965); *London Music in 1888–1889 as Heard by Corno di Bassetto* (London, 1937), articles originally contributed to the *Star*, in the *Standard Edition*; *The Penguin Edition*, 10 vols. (Harmondsworth, 1946), additional vol. (1956), current reprs. under editorial supervision of D. H. Laurence.

D. H. Laurence, ed., *The Bodley Head Bernard Shaw, Collected Plays and Their Prefaces*, 7 vols. (London, 1970–1974), containing previously unpublished texts in the last vol., also miscellaneous material by Shaw relating to each play, with history of composition, publication, and early performances, is new definitive ed.; D. H. Laurence, gen. ed., *Early Texts: Play Manuscripts in Facsimile*, 9 vols. (New York, 1981); D. H. Laurence, ed., *The Bodley Head Shaw; Complete Musical Criticism*, 3 vols. (London, 1981), definitive.

III. OTHER POSTHUMOUS COLLECTIONS. E. J. West, ed., *Shaw on Theatre* (New York, 1958); D. H. Laurence, ed., *How to Become a Musical Critic* (London, 1960), previously uncollected writings on music, 1876–1950; D. H. Laurence, ed., *Platform and Pulpit* (New York, 1961), previously uncollected lectures, speeches, debates, 1885–1946; D. H. Green and D. H. Laurence, eds., *The Matter with Ireland* (London, 1962), essays, 1886–1950; A. Tauber, ed., *George Bernard Shaw on Language* (London, 1963); W. S. Smith, ed., *The Religious Speeches of Bernard Shaw* (University Park, Pa., 1963); H. M. Geduld, ed., *Bernard Shaw: The Rationalization of Russia* (Bloomington, Ind., 1964); *Selected One-Act Plays*, 2 vols. (Harmondsworth, 1965), Penguin ed.; W. S. Smith, ed., *Shaw on Religion* (London, 1967); L. Crompton, ed., *The Road to Equality* (Boston, 1971), unpublished lectures and essays, 1884–1918; S. Weintraub, ed., *Bernard Shaw's Non-Dramatic Literary Criticism* (Lincoln, Nebr., 1972); L. J. Hubenka, ed., *Practical Politics: Twentieth-Century Views on Politics and Economics* (Lincoln, Nebr., 1976), speeches, 1905–1933; L. Crompton, ed., *The Great Composers: Reviews and Bombardments* (Berkeley, Calif., 1978); B. F. Dukore, ed., *The Collected Screenplays* (London, 1980); *Plays Extravagant* (Harmondsworth, 1981), Penguin ed.

IV. SELECTED SEPARATE WORKS. *An Unsocial Socialist,* serialized in *To-Day* (March–December 1884), first published in book form (London, 1887), new ed. with intro. by Michael Holroyd (London, 1980); *The Irrational Knot,* serialized in *Our Corner* (April 1885–February 1887); *Cashel Byron's Profession,* serialized in *To-Day* (April 1885–March 1886) (Harmondsworth, 1979), Penguin ed.; *Love Among the Artists,* serialized in *Our Corner* (November 1887–December 1888); G. B. Shaw, ed., *Fabian Essays in Socialism* (London, 1889), with two chs. by Shaw, new ed. with intro. by Asa Briggs (London, 1967); *The Quintessence of Ibsenism* (London, 1891), completed to the death of Ibsen (London, 1913), republished (New York, 1959); *Widowers' Houses* (London, 1893), no. 1 of J. T. Grein, ed., Independent Theatre Series of Plays; *The Sanity of Art,* in *Liberty* (New York, July 1895); *The Perfect Wagnerite* (London, 1898); *Plays: Pleasant and Unpleasant,* 2 vols. (London, 1898), vol. I: "Preface: Mainly About Myself," *Widowers' Houses* [rev. ed.], *The Philanderer, Mrs. Warren's Profession;* vol. II: "Preface," *Arms and the Man, Candida, The Man of Destiny, You Never Can Tell.*

The Admirable Bashville, in *Cashel Byron's Profession* (rev. ed., Chicago, 1901), later included in *Translations and Tomfooleries* (London, 1926); *Three Plays for Puritans* (London, 1901), contains "Preface," *The Devil's Disciple, Caesar and Cleopatra, Captain Brassbound's Conversion; Man and Superman: A Comedy and a Philosophy* (London, 1903); *Passion, Poison, and Petrification; or, The Fatal Gazogene,* in H. Furniss, *Christmas Annual* (London, 1905); *John Bull's Other Island and Major Barbara* (London, 1907), includes *How He Lied to Her Husband; Press Cuttings: A Topical Sketch* (London, 1909); *The Shewing-Up of Blanco Posnet: A Sermon in Crude Melodrama* (London, 1909).

The Doctor's Dilemma: A Tragedy (London, 1911); *The Doctor's Dilemma, Getting Married, and The Shewing-Up of Blanco Posnet* (London, 1911); *The Dark Lady of the Sonnets,* in the *English Review* (1911); *Overruled,* in the *English Review* (1913); *Misalliance, The Dark Lady of the Sonnets, and Fanny's First Play* (London, 1914); *Commonsense About the War,* supplement to *New Statesman* (14 November 1914); *Androcles and the Lion,* in *Everybody's* magazine (September 1914); *Pygmalion,* in *Everybody's* magazine (November 1914) and *Noah's* magazine (November and December 1914); *Androcles and the Lion, Overruled, Pygmalion* (London, 1916); *O'Flaherty V.C.,* in *Hearst's* magazine (August 1917); *How to Settle the Irish Question,* in the *Daily Express* (27–29 November 1917); *Peace Conference Hints* (London, 1919); *Heartbreak House, Great Catherine, and Playlets of the War* (New York, 1919).

Ruskin's Politics (London, 1921); *Back to Methuselah, A Metabiological Pentateuch* (London, 1921); *Imprisonment,* published as preface to S. Webb and B. Webb, *English Prisons Under Local Government* (London, 1922); *Saint Joan* (London, 1924); *Translations and Tomfooleries* (London, 1926), contains *Jitta's Atonement, The Admirable Bashville, Press Cuttings, The Glimpse of Reality, Passion, Poison, and Petrification; or, The Fatal Gazogene, The Fascinating Foundling, The Music Cure; The Intelligent Woman's Guide to Socialism and Capitalism* (London, 1928); "Socialism: Principles and Outlook," in *Encyclopaedia Britannica,* 14th ed. (London, 1929).

What I Really Wrote About the War (London, 1930); *Immaturity* (London, 1930); *The Apple Cart: A Political Extravaganza* (London, 1930); *Major Critical Essays* (London, 1930); *Doctors' Delusions, Crude Criminology, and Sham Education* (London, 1931); *Pen Portraits and Reviews* (London, 1931); *The Adventures of the Black Girl in Her Search for God* (London, 1932); *Essays in Fabian Socialism* (London, 1932); *Short Stories, Scraps, and Shavings* (London, 1932); *Too True to Be Good, Village Wooing, and On the Rocks* (London, 1934), *Too True to Be Good,* in *Plays Extravagant* (Harmondsworth, 1981), Penguin ed.; *The Simpleton of the Unexpected Isles, The Six of Calais, and The Millionairess* (London, 1936), *The Simpleton* and *The Millionairess* in *Plays Extravagant* (Harmondsworth, 1981), Penguin ed.; "William Morris as I Knew Him," in M. Morris, *William Morris, Artist, Writer, Socialist,* 2 vols. (Oxford, 1936); *Cymbeline Refinished* (lim. ed., London, 1937); *Shaw Gives Himself Away: An Autobiographical Miscellany* (lim. ed., Newtown, 1939); *Geneva* (London, 1939), illus. by Feliks Topolski, rev. and included in *Geneva, Cymbeline Refinished, In Good King Charles's Golden Days,* see below; *In Good King Charles's Golden Days: A History Lesson* (London, 1939).

Everybody's Political What's What? (London, 1944); *Geneva, Cymbeline Refinished, In Good King Charles's Golden Days* (London, 1946); *Sixteen Self Sketches* (London, 1949); *Buoyant Billions: A Comedy of No Manners in*

Prose (lim. ed., London, 1949), illustrated by Clare Winsten; *Buoyant Billions, Farfetched Fables, Shakes Versus Shav* (London, 1950); *Bernard Shaw's Rhyming Picture Guide to Ayot Saint Lawrence* (Luton, 1950); *My Dear Dorothea: A Practical System of Moral Education for Females* (London, 1956), written in 1878, illus. by Clare Winsten and with a note by Stephen Winsten; "Why She Would Not," in *London* magazine, III (August 1956); S. Weintraub, ed., *An Unfinished Novel by Bernard Shaw* (London, 1958); J. E. Pringle, ed., *A Passion Play, A Dramatic Fragment, 1878* (London, 1971), written in 1878.

V. COLLECTIONS OF LETTERS. *Letters from George Bernard Shaw to Miss Alma Murray*, privately printed (Edinburgh, 1927); C. St. John, ed., *Ellen Terry and Bernard Shaw, a Correspondence*, with a preface by Shaw (London, 1931); *More Letters from George Bernard Shaw to Miss Alma Murray*, privately printed (Edinburgh, 1932); C. Bax, ed., *Florence Farr, Bernard Shaw, W. B. Yeats: Letters* (lim. ed., New York–Dublin, 1941); A. Dent, ed., *Bernard Shaw and Mrs. Patrick Campbell: Their Correspondence* (London, 1952); E. J. West, ed., *Advice to a Young Critic: Letters to Golding Bright, 1894–1928* (New York, 1955); Letters to Dame Laurentia McLachlan, abbess of Stanbrook, in *The Nun and the Dramatist*, by a nun of Stanbrook, in *Cornhill* magazine (Summer 1956); C. B. Purdom, ed., *Bernard Shaw's Letters to Granville Barker* (London, 1957); P. Tompkins, ed., *To a Young Actress: The Letters of Bernard Shaw to Molly Tompkins, 1921–49* (London, 1960); "Beerbohm, Wilde, Shaw and the 'Good-Natured Critic,'" in *Bulletin of the New York Public Library* (New York, 1964), twelve letters to the critic Edward Rose; D. H. Laurence, ed., *Collected Letters*, vol. I: *1874–1897*; vol. II: *1898–1910* (London, 1972–   ), in progress; B. Forbes, *Dame Edith Evans: Ned's Girl* (London, 1978), includes letters to Edith Evans; M. Hyde, ed., *Bernard Shaw and Alfred Douglas: A Correspondence* (New Haven, Conn.–New York, 1982).

VI. SELECTIONS. J. Huneker, ed., *Dramatic Opinions and Essays*, 2 vols. (London, 1907), unauthorized ed. (New York, 1906); [Mrs.] C. F. Shaw, comp., *Selected Passages from the Works of Bernard Shaw* (London, 1912); W. R. Ellis, ed., *Bernard Shaw and Karl Marx: A Symposium, 1884–1889* (New York, 1930); *The Quintessence of G.B.S.* (London, 1949), with commentary by Stephen Winsten; H. G. Bowker, ed., *Shaw on Vivisection* (London, 1949); A. C. Ward, ed., *Plays and Players: Essays on the Theatre* (London, 1952); D. Russell, ed., *Selected Prose of Bernard Shaw* (London, 1952); C. E. M. Joad, ed., *Shaw and Society: An Anthology and a Symposium* (London, 1953); *Selected Plays and Other Writings* (New York, 1956), with intro. by William Irvine; J. F. Matthews, comp., *Dramatic Criticism, 1895–98* (New York, 1959); E. J. West, ed., *Shaw on Shakespeare* (New York, 1961); *G.B.S. on Music* (London, 1962), with a foreword by Alec Robertson; S. Weintraub, comp., *Shaw: An Autobiography*, vol. I: *1856–1898* (London, 1969), vol. II: *1898–1950: The*

Playwright Years (London, 1970); W. S. Smith, ed., *Bernard Shaw's Plays: Major Barbara, Heartbreak House, Saint Joan, Too True to Be Good* (New York, 1971), with backgrounds and criticism; H. G. Earnshaw, ed., *A Selection from Shaw's Prefaces* (London, 1977); L. Crompton, ed., *The Great Composers: Reviews and Bombardments* (Berkeley, Calif., 1978); S. Weintraub, ed., *The Portable Bernard Shaw* (London, 1978).

VII. ADAPTATIONS. *My Fair Lady* (New York, 1958), a musical play in two acts based on *Pygmalion* by Bernard Shaw, adap. and lyrics by Alan J. Lerner, illus. by Cecil Beaton; *Dear Liar: A Comedy of Letters* (New York, 1960), adap. by Jerome Kilty from the correspondence of Bernard Shaw and Mrs. Patrick Campbell.

VIII. CONCORDANCE. E. D. Bevan, *A Concordance to the Plays and Prefaces of Bernard Shaw*, 10 vols. (Detroit, 1971), with references to the *Standard Edition*.

IX. RECORD OF PRODUCTIONS. R. Mander and J. Mitchenson, comps., *A Theatrical Companion to Shaw* (London, 1954); R. Huggett, *The First Night of Pygmalion* (London, 1970); E. Stürzl and J. Hogg, *The Stage History of G. B. Shaw's Saint Joan* (Salzburg, 1975).

X. BIOGRAPHICAL AND CRITICAL STUDIES. (Note: The critical literature on Shaw is now so extensive that any selection inevitably has an arbitrary element.) H. L. Mencken, *Bernard Shaw: His Plays* (Boston, 1905), the first book on Shaw; J. G. Huneker, *Iconoclasts* (London, 1906); G. K. Chesterton, *G. B. Shaw* (London, 1909); H. Jackson, *Bernard Shaw* (London, 1909); D. MacCarthy, *The Court Theatre, 1904–1907: A Commentary and a Criticism* (London, 1907), reiss. with a commentary by Stanley Weintraub (Coral Gables, Fla., 1966); J. Bab, *Shaw* (Berlin, 1910; rev. ed., 1926); A. Henderson, *G. B. Shaw: His Life and Works* (London, 1911); A. Harmon, *Le Molière du XXᵉ siècle: Bernard Shaw* (Paris, 1913); G. Norwood, *Euripides and Mr. Shaw* (London, 1913); P. B. Howe, *Bernard Shaw: A Critical Survey* (London, 1915); E. R. Pease, *History of the Fabian Society* (London, 1916).

A. Henderson, *Table Talk of G.B.S.: Conversations on Things in General Between Shaw and His Biographer* (London, 1925); M. Ellehauge, *The Position of Bernard Shaw in European Drama and Philosophy* (Copenhagen, 1931); F. Harris, *Bernard Shaw: An Unauthorized Biography* (London, 1931), with a postscript by Shaw; E. G. Craig, *Ellen Terry and Her Secret Self* (London, 1931); A. Henderson, *Shaw: Playboy and Prophet* (New York, 1932); A. Maurois, *Magiciens et logiciens* (Paris, 1936); S. C. Sen Gupta, *The Art of Bernard Shaw* (London, 1936); C. Caudwell, *Studies in a Dying Culture* (London, 1938); C. M. Shaw, *Bernard's Brethren* (London, 1939).

J. Gassner, *Masters of the Drama* (New York, 1940; 3rd enl. ed., 1954); H. Pearson, *G.B.S.: A Full-Length Portrait* (London, 1942; new ed. with postscript, 1961); E. Strauss, *Bernard Shaw: Art and Socialism* (London, 1942; new ed., 1978); E. Bentley, *The Playwright as Thinker* (New York, 1946); S. Winsten, *G.B.S. 90: Aspects of Bernard Shaw's*

Life and Works (London, 1946), contributors include Gilbert Murray, John Masefield, Lord Passfield (Sidney Webb), H. G. Wells, Sir Max Beerbohm, James Bridie, Lord Dunsany, Lord Keynes (Maynard Keynes), W. R. Inge, Kenneth Barnes, Aldous Huxley, and others; E. Bentley, *A Century of Hero-Worship* (Boston, 1947); E. J. Hobsbawm, "Bernard Shaw's Socialism," in *Science and Society*, 11 (1947); E. Bentley, *Bernard Shaw* (Norfolk, Conn., 1947; reiss., 1967); F. E. Loewenstein, ed., *Bernard Shaw Through the Camera* (London, 1948); E. Wilson, *The Triple Thinkers* (London, 1948); W. Irvine, *The Universe of G.B.S.* (New York, 1949); A. Nicoll, *World Drama from Aeschylus to Anouilh* (New York, 1949); A. C. Ward, *Bernard Shaw* (London, 1950).

A. West, *G. B. Shaw: A Good Man Fallen Among Fabians* (London, 1950; new ed., 1974); I. Fiske, *Bernard Shaw's Debt to William Blake* (London, 1951), Shavian Tract no. 2, with a foreword by G.B.S.; D. MacCarthy, *Shaw's Plays in Review* (New York, 1951); B. Patch, *Thirty Years with G.B.S.* (London, 1951); G. Whitworth, *The Making of a National Theatre* (London, 1951); S. Winsten, *Salt and His Circle* (London, 1951), intro. by G. B. Shaw; L. Kronenberger, *The Thread of Laughter* (New York, 1952); A. Ussher, *Three Great Irishmen* (London, 1952); M. Beerbohm, *Around Theatres* (London, 1953); S. Holberg, *The Economic Rogue in the Plays of Bernard Shaw* (Buffalo, 1953); C. E. M. Joad, ed., *Shaw and Society: An Anthology and a Symposium* (London, 1953), contributors include Kingsley Martin, Leonard Woolf, S. K. Ratcliff, Benn W. Levy, Hugh Dalton; L. Kronenberger, ed., *George Bernard Shaw: A Critical Survey* (New York-Cleveland, 1953), includes commentaries by W. H. Auden, Jacques Barzun, Eric Bentley, Max Beerbohm, G. K. Chesterton, Thomas Mann, V. S. Pritchett, Dixon Scott, Stephen Spender, and others; A. Nethercot, *Men and Supermen: The Shavian Portrait Gallery* (London, 1954; rev. ed., 1966); St. J. Ervine, *Bernard Shaw: His Life, Work and Friends* (London, 1956); A. Henderson, *George Bernard Shaw: Man of the Century* (New York, 1956); G. Roppen, *Evolution and Poetic Belief: A Study in Some Victorian and Modern Writers* (Oslo, 1956); J. B. Kaye, *Bernard Shaw and the Nineteenth-Century Tradition* (Norman, Okla., 1958); L. Simon, *Shaw on Education* (1958); H. G. Farmer, *Bernard Shaw's Sister and Her Friends* (Leiden, 1959); A. Freemantle, *This Little Band of Prophets: The British Fabians* (London, 1959); E. N. Rao, *Shaw the Novelist* (Madras, 1959).

A. H. Nethercot, *The First Five Lives of Annie Besant* (London, 1960); J. Smith and A. Toynbee, eds., *Gilbert Murray, an Unfinished Autobiography* (London, 1960); M. Cole, *The Story of Fabian Socialism* (London, 1961); A. Chappelow, ed., *Shaw the Villager and Human Being* (London, 1961); G. W. Knight, *The Golden Labyrinth* (London, 1962); A. M. MacBriar, *Fabian Socialism and English Poetics* (Cambridge, 1962); R. Ohmann, *Shaw: The Style and the Man* (Middletown, Conn., 1962); M.

Shenfield, comp., *A Pictorial Biography of Bernard Shaw* (London, 1962); J. Dunbar, *Mrs. G.B.S.: A Biographical Portrait of Charlotte Shaw* (London, 1963); M. Meisel, *Shaw and the Nineteenth-Century Theater* (Princeton, 1963); C. B. Purdom, *A Guide to the Plays of Bernard Shaw* (London, 1963); J. I. M. Stewart, *Eight Modern Writers* (London, 1963); S. Weintraub, *Private Shaw and Public Shaw: A Dual Portrait of Lawrence of Arabia and G. B. Shaw* (London, 1963); F. P. W. McDowell, "Heaven, Hell, and Turn-of-the-Century London: Reflections upon Shaw's *Man and Superman*," in *Drama Survey*, 2 (1963); B. C. Rosset, *Shaw of Dublin: The Formative Years* (University Park, Pa., 1964); B. B. Watson, *A Shavian Guide to the Intelligent Woman* (New York-London, 1964; repr. New York, 1972); D. P. Costello, *The Serpent's Eye: Shaw and the Cinema* (Notre Dame, Ind., 1965); R. J. Kaufmann, ed., *Twentieth-Century Views of George Bernard Shaw* (Englewood Cliffs, N.J., 1965), contributors include Brecht, Ohmann, Bentley, O'Donnell, Crompton, Morgan, Fiske; J. O'Donovan, *Shaw and the Charlatan Genius: A Memoir* (London, 1965); J. P. Smith, *The Unrepentant Pilgrim: A Study of the Development of Bernard Shaw* (London, 1965); K. Muggeridge and R. Adam, *Beatrice Webb: A Life, 1858-1943* (London, 1967); H. Fromm, *Bernard Shaw and the Theater in the Nineties: A Study of Shaw's Dramatic Criticism* (Lawrence, Kans., 1967); F. P. W. McDowell, "Politics, Comedy, Character and Dialectic: The Shavian World of *John Bull's Other Island*," in *PMLA*, 82 (1967); W. S. Smith, *The London Heretics, 1870-1914* (London, 1968); M. Beerbohm, *More Theatres* (London, 1969); C. A. Carpenter, *Bernard Shaw and the Art of Destroying Ideals: The Early Plays* (Madison, Wis., 1969); L. Crompton, *Shaw the Dramatist* (Lincoln, Nebr., 1969); A. M. Gibbs, *Shaw* (Edinburgh, 1969); A. Mills, *Language and Laughter: Comic Diction in the Plays of Bernard Shaw* (Tucson, 1969); C. Wilson, *Bernard Shaw: A Reassessment* (London, 1969).

E. Bentley, "Ibsen, Shaw, Brecht: Three Stages," in A. Cheuse and R. Koffler, eds., *The Rarer Action: Essays in Honor of Francis Fergusson* (New Brunswick, N. J., 1970); M. Beerbohm, *Last Theatres* (London, 1970); R. F. Dietrich, *Portrait of the Artist as a Young Superman: A Study of Shaw's Novels* (London, 1970); W. B. Furlong, *G.B.S./G.K.C.: Shaw and Chesterton, the Metaphysical Jesters* (University Park, Pa., 1970); V. Pascal, *The Disciple and His Devil* (London, 1970); J. W. Hulse, *Revolutionists in London* (London, 1970); E. B. Adams, *Bernard Shaw and the Aesthetes* (Columbus, Ohio, 1971); B. F. Dukore, *Bernard Shaw, Director* (London, 1971); N. Rosenblood, ed., *Shaw: Seven Critical Essays* (Toronto, 1971), includes important essay by M. Meisel; S. Weintraub, *Journey to Heartbreak: The Crucible Years of Bernard Shaw* (New York, 1971); M. M. Morgan, *The Shavian Playground: An Exploration of the Art of George Bernard Shaw* (London, 1972); D. J. Leary, "Shaw's Blakean Vision: A Dialectic Approach to *Heartbreak House*," in

Modern Drama, 15 (1972); C. A. Berst, *Bernard Shaw and the Art of Drama* (Urbana, Ill., 1973); B. F. Dukore, *Bernard Shaw, Playwright* (Columbia, Mo., 1973); M. Hardwick and M. Hardwick, *The Bernard Shaw Companion* (London, 1973); P. A. Hummert, *Bernard Shaw's Marxian Romance* (Lincoln, Nebr., 1973); M. J. Valency, *The Cart and the Trumpet: The Plays of George Bernard Shaw* (London, 1973); M. Cole, *The Webbs and Their Work* (London, 1974); M. Goldstein, *The Political Stage* (London, 1974); J. L. Wisenthal, *The Marriage of Contraries: Bernard Shaw's Middle Plays* (Cambridge, Mass., 1974); D. Dervin, *Bernard Shaw: A Psychological Study* (London, 1975); A. Kennedy, *Six Dramatists in Search of a Language* (London, 1975); T. F. Evans, ed., *Shaw: The Critical Heritage* (London, 1976); R. Weintraub, ed., *Fabian Feminist: Bernard Shaw and Women* (University Park, Pa., 1976); A. Turco, Jr., *Shaw's Moral Vision* (London, 1976); R. N. Palmer, *Bernard Shaw's Historical Plays* (New York, 1976); R. P. Arnott, *Bernard Shaw and William Morris* (London, 1977); G. Berquist, *The Pen and the Sword: War and Peace in the Prose and Plays of Bernard Shaw* (Salzburg, 1977); R. F. Whitman, *Shaw and the Play of Ideas* (Ithaca, N.Y.–New York, 1977); B. Green, *Shaw's Champions: G.B.S. and Prize Fighting from Cashel Byron to Gene Tunney* (London, 1978); N. MacKenzie and J. MacKenzie, *The Fabians* (London, 1978); M. Holroyd, ed., *The Genius of Bernard Shaw* (London, 1979); C. D. Sidhu, *The Pattern of Tragicomedy in Bernard Shaw* (Delhi, 1979); M. Peters, *Shaw and the Actresses* (London, 1981).

XI. STUDIES OF INDIVIDUAL PLAYS. S. S. Stanton, ed., *A Casebook on "Candida"* (New York, 1962); G. A. Pilecki, *Shaw's "Geneva": A Critical Study of the Evolution of the Text in Relation to Shaw's Political Thought and Dramatic Practice* (The Hague, 1965); R. Zimbardo, ed., *Twentieth-Century Views of "Major Barbara"* (Englewood Cliffs, N. J., 1970).

XII. PERIODICALS. The leading periodical publication concerned with the study of Shaw began as the *Bulletin* of the Shaw Society of America (New York, 1951–1958) and has continued as the *Shaw Review* (University Park, Pennsylvania State University, 1959–   ). The British Shaw Society published the *Shaw Bulletin* (Dagenham, Essex, September 1946–September 1953) and the *Shavian* (1953–1959, 1960–1963). It was revived in 1976 as the *Shaw Newsletter*.

JOSEPH CONRAD

(1857-1924)

C. B. Cox

I

WHAT kind of man was Joseph Conrad? At times he could be warmhearted and generous; on other occasions he acted with a childlike irritability. Some people think of him as an efficient, capable seaman who achieved fame by transmuting his colorful experiences into material for his novels. Others regard him as a neurotic who suffered constant mental breakdowns. John Galsworthy summed up these conflicting views when he said he had never met a man so masculinely keen yet so femininely sensitive.

What was the source of these contradictions? The extraordinarily difficult circumstances of Conrad's childhood produced tensions that he never fully resolved to his dying day. Imaginative and oversensitive, he remained always unsure what kind of person he really was. In his fiction he explored his own confusions about the nature of his identity and tried to create an imaginative relation to his own past and to the outside world. In his life he adopted many roles, as seaman or novelist, as he searched unsuccessfully for a stable personality.

Conrad was born Józef Teodor Konrad Nałęcz Korzeniowski on 3 December 1857 near Berdichev in the Polish Ukraine, then under Russian rule. He was the only son of Apollo Nałęcz Korzeniowski and his wife, Evelina Bobrowski, both of landed family. Apollo was a patriot and poet who had translated Shakespeare and Victor Hugo. In 1861 he took part in clandestine political activity in Warsaw for the Polish National Committee and as a result was exiled with his wife and child to Vologda in Russia. On the journey Conrad, now four years old, suffered from pneumonia, a foretaste of the sufferings about to overwhelm the family. In a letter of 1862 Apollo described the appalling conditions of their exile:

The climate consists of two seasons of the year: a white winter and a green winter. The white winter lasts nine-and-a-half months and the green one two-and-a-half. We are now on the onset of the green winter: it has already been raining ceaselessly for twenty-one days and that's how it will be to the end. . . . The population is a nightmare: disease-ridden corpses.

In the summer of 1863 they were allowed to move to a milder climate in Chernigov, 125 miles northeast of Kiev, but the damage was done. Evelina was in an advanced stage of tuberculosis, and she died when Conrad was seven. Life alone with his father was extremely burdensome, particularly as Apollo became absorbed by morbid religiosity and a cult of his dead wife. Eventually they were allowed to return to Poland, but Apollo became ill and died in 1869. The young boy spent years in an atmosphere of death, and he never recovered from the psychological wounds. His novels reveal an understanding of depressive loneliness, which he may have learned as a child.

Conrad, now an orphan at the age of eleven, was looked after by his uncle Tadeusz Bobrowski, a stern, practical man who in subsequent years combined warm affection with firm opposition to Conrad's escapades. Conrad seems to have disliked the discipline of school life, and in 1872 he pressed his uncle to allow him to go to sea. His family was strongly opposed to the idea, but his pleas eventually succeeded, and in 1874 he left Cracow for Marseilles.

Conrad's decision to leave Poland and become a sailor has provoked much controversy. Some have argued that it created in him a feeling of betrayal and that he never overcame his guilt at deserting his country. According to this theory, in his heart he knew he had abandoned the cause for which both his parents sacrificed their lives. The desire for atonement and self-justification, therefore, dominated his life and influenced the important moments of crisis in the novels. In his excellent biography, *Joseph Conrad* (1960), Jocelyn Baines sees Jim's jump over the side of the *Patna* in *Lord Jim* (1900) and Razumov's betrayal of Haldin in *Under Western Eyes* (1911) as unconscious symbolic representations of Conrad's action in leaving Poland. He draws attention to Conrad's use of the word "jump" to describe his own case and how this recalls Lord Jim: "I verily believe mine was the only case of a boy of my nationality and antecedents taking a, so to speak, standing jump out of his racial surroundings and associations." Parallels can be drawn between Jim's efforts to vindicate himself after his desertion of the *Patna* and Conrad's own life. His sense of exile is recreated in "Amy Foster" (1903), a short story in which Yanky Goorall, from Austrian Poland, is treated with cruelty and incomprehension when he is shipwrecked on the Kentish coast.

Undoubtedly Conrad never felt at home in any environment, and a sense of alienation is continually expressed in his fiction. This tendency, however, cannot be explained simply by his rejection of Poland. As we have seen, his loneliness was part of a deep-rooted melancholia probably attributable to the death of his parents.

No one knows exactly all that happened after Conrad arrived in Marseilles. His own accounts are found in *The Mirror of the Sea* (1906), *A Personal Record* (1912), and the semiautobiographical novel *The Arrow of Gold* (1919). In 1875 he sailed to the West Indies as an apprentice and repeated the journey as a steward in 1876. He became a member of the bohemian set in Marseilles and according to his own account took part in gun-running for the Carlist Royalists in Spain. From Tadeusz Bobrowski's letters we learn that Conrad certainly went through a large amount of money. Unfortunately, in his autobiographical writings Conrad aimed to create a vivid impression of events rather than to report the facts accurately. Concerning one major crisis during his time in Marseilles we know that in later life he lied both to his friends and to his wife.

In February 1878, Tadeusz received an urgent telegram from France: "Conrad wounded, send money —come." He hurried to Marseilles, where he spent two weeks sorting out his nephew's affairs, particularly by paying his debts. Years later in England Conrad pretended that the scar on his left breast resulted from a duel. In *The Arrow of Gold*, M. George (Conrad's nickname in Marseilles) fights a duel with a Captain Blunt and is shot through the left side of the breast. The cause of the duel is Rita, a brilliant, cold, neurotic adventuress with whom they

are both in love. In the copy of *The Arrow of Gold* owned by Richard Curle, a young admirer, Conrad wrote that "all the personages are authentic and the facts are as stated." It was not until 1957, when a letter of Bobrowski's describing Conrad's attempted suicide was published in Poland, that the truth fully emerged. Although some hero-worshipers have disagreed, the evidence of three separate references in Bobrowski's writings is conclusive. The main letter was sent to Stephen Buszczyński, a close friend of Conrad's father. It describes how Conrad lost a large sum of money through smuggling and gambling:

Having managed his affairs so excellently he returns to Marseilles and one fine evening invites his friend the creditor [Mr. Fecht] to tea, and before his arrival attempts to take his life with a revolver. (Let this detail remain between us, as I have been telling everyone that he was wounded in a duel. From you I neither wish to nor should keep it a secret.) The bullet goes durch and durch near his heart without damaging any vital organ. Luckily, all his addresses were left on top of his things so that this worthy Mr. Fecht could instantly let me know, and even my brother, who in his turn bombarded me. Well, that is the whole story!

Was there a woman in the case? We shall probably never know. Bobrowski mentions no such person, and Conrad's amorous adventures in Marseilles probably had more existence in his imagination than in fact.

Conrad continued with his sea career. In April 1878 he joined an English steamer, the *Mavis*, and traveled via Constantinople to Lowestoft. He arrived in England, still only twenty years old, knowing no one and speaking only a few words of the language. He managed to sign on with a coaster running between Lowestoft and Newcastle and then obtained a berth as ordinary seaman on a wool clipper named the *Duke of Sutherland*, which ran between London and Sydney, Australia. For the next sixteen years he worked as a merchant seaman, passing his first mate's examination in 1884 and his master mariner's in 1886, the same year that he became a naturalized Briton. His examination successes are vividly described in *A Personal Record*; they prove that by this time he must have acquired a fair command of the English language.

Particular voyages were later used as material for the novels, but Conrad often altered facts to suit his fictional purposes. In 1881 he found a berth as second mate on the *Palestine*, a bark of 425 tons commanded by Captain Beard. After a disastrous voyage it eventually foundered while approaching Java Head. The adventure is recounted in "Youth" (1902), though Conrad glamorized some of the details. In the concluding sections he deliberately increased the drama by giving his young hero the chance to steer his little cockleshell for many days, whereas in fact the journey took only a few hours. In 1888 he obtained his first command, the *Otago,* which is the subject of *The Shadow-Line* (1917), and he added considerably to his knowledge of the Far East. During these years Conrad by no means overcame the neurotic condition that presumably caused his attempted suicide. While working as first mate on the *Highland Forest* on his way to Samarang in 1887 he sustained an injury when minor spars hit him in the back. He was forced to lay up for three months and suffered a kind of psychological breakdown characterized by a sudden collapse of will and inexplicable periods of powerlessness. Paul Langlois, who met him in Mauritius in 1888, called him a "neurasthénique" and noted a tic of the shoulder and the eyes. Conrad's inner conflicts were not resolved during his years at sea.

These tensions were exacerbated by his journey to the Congo in 1890. He was engaged by the Belgian Société Anonyme pour le Commerce du Haut-Congo to take command of one of the company's steamers. In Conrad's great novel *Heart of Darkness* (1902), the narrator is called Marlow; his visit to the company's office, his medical inspection by the doctor with the bizarre sense of humor, and many details of his journey to Matadi and beyond are taken directly from fact. For Conrad the journey was an unmitigated disaster. He was disgusted by the ill-treatment of the natives, by the vile scramble for loot. In his notebook he records a series of unsavory details—the horrid smell from a dead body lying by the trail, arguments with carriers, the lack of water, the heat, mosquitoes, the shouts and drumming, a skeleton tied to a post.

The steamer, *Florida,* which he was supposed to take over, had been badly damaged, and instead he journeyed as supernumerary on the *Roi des Belges* to Stanley Falls, picking up a dangerously ill company agent named Georges Antoine Klein. Klein, like Kurtz in *Heart of Darkness,* died on the return journey. In the manuscript of *Heart of Darkness,* Conrad starts by writing "Klein," and then changes the name to "Kurtz." At the conclusion of this trip Conrad suffered further frustrations in his hopes of obtaining a command, and he fell ill with fever and dysentery. Disgusted, he returned to England. It is difficult to assess the influence of the journey on Conrad's character, but there is no doubt that for many years afterward he was haunted by the Congo. He never forgot what he had witnessed of the horror of human corruption. His imagination remained obsessed by visions of native wildness, huge forests, and indescribable evil.

II

IN 1886 Conrad apparently wrote a story, "The Black Mate," for a competition in the magazine *Tit-Bits.* It was not accepted. In 1892, while working as first mate on the famous clipper *Torrens,* he showed the manuscript of his first novel, *Almayer's Folly* (1895), to one of the passengers. In 1894 he was unable to find another ship, and his enforced idleness gave him time to work on *Almayer's Folly,* which he later said he had started five years previously. He submitted the manuscript to the publisher Fisher Unwin, who accepted it. The reader was Edward Garnett, who gave Conrad valuable advice in subsequent years.

Almayer's Folly, which includes some pretentious overwriting, is a story of decadence and breakdown, of exhaustion and frustration. Almayer has married a Malay girl and taken charge of a river trading post, where he dreams of luxury and riches; but he is incompetent, a pathetic failure whose visions end in opium smoking and his eventual death. All his love is concentrated on his beautiful daughter, Nina, and when she elopes with the son of a rajah, Almayer's desolation is complete.

In *A Reader's Guide to Joseph Conrad* (1960), Frederick R. Karl draws attention to the similarities between the poetic language of the 1890's and Conrad's early work. In the writings of Arthur Symons and Ernest Dowson there is the same assortment of exhausted objects, "the drear oblivion of lost things." Almayer's ruined business premises, surrounded by the oppressive atmosphere of the jungle, provide Conrad with an image for his despair. In spite of the purple passages, *Almayer's Folly* is a remarkable achievement for a man writing a first novel in a foreign language.

Conrad served his apprenticeship as a writer with the French novelists of the nineteenth century, particularly Flaubert and Maupassant. The ironic detachment with which he treats Almayer recalls Flaubert's method in *Madame Bovary*; but already there are original touches that point forward to his future achievements. The jungle is described in typical Conradian manner—as omnipresent, heavy, vast—so that the characters are reduced to insignificance. Conrad is using fiction to express and come to terms with his own unsure hold on his personal identity.

The £20 paid Conrad by Fisher Unwin did not solve his financial problems for very long. He was still trying to find a job at sea and engaging in dubious business speculations. In this troubled time his compulsion to write remained unabated, and he finished *An Outcast of the Islands* by September 1895. This novel is very similar to *Almayer's Folly*, except that it is much more wordy. Once again there is a sense of debility and impotence. Willems is a study of a man who falls from power into a wasted life of treachery and self-disgust. He is seduced by Aissa, a native girl, and this "abominable desire" destroys his character. The whole movement of the novel is toward death. The forest trees tower over the characters, emphasizing their isolation and futility.

In 1896 Conrad married Jessie George, a quiet, sensible woman who over the years provided him with a stable home and two sons but could not match his intellect or advise him on his novels. The marriage meant that Conrad was even more urgently in need of money. On his honeymoon in Brittany he worked at a new novel, *The Rescuer* (later published as *The Rescue*, 1920), intended as a popular sea story, and wrote two short stories, "An Outpost of Progress" and "The Lagoon" (both 1898). *The Rescuer* gave him great difficulties and was not to be finished until twenty-three years later. On his return to London he went ahead fast with *The Nigger of the "Narcissus,"* his first major triumph. It was published in the *New Review* in 1897.

The story is based on Conrad's own journey on the *Narcissus* from Bombay to Dunkirk in 1884, though the novel is far from an exact transcript of his adventures. In contrast to the fetid atmosphere of his two previous novels, the style of *The Nigger* is more restrained and precise. There are some brilliant scenes of action at sea, particularly the storm sequences. Conrad was angry when he was described as just a narrator of adventures at sea. He insisted that his concern was to portray the crew "brought to a test of what I may venture to call the moral problem of conduct."

The crew of the *Narcissus* is faced by two tests, to survive the storm and to overcome the subversive anarchy represented by the waster, Donkin, and the sick black sailor, James Wait. In the storm, representative of Nature's insane violence in its dealings with man, the ship becomes an archetype for human society on its journey through an inexplicable universe. The crew survives by fidelity to its chosen calling and so exemplifies the corporate ideas of human solidarity that Conrad thought essential in any community. The old man, Singleton, saves the ship by his devotion to duty.

But the novel is not just a simple justification of the order and discipline of the ship. Donkin and James Wait tempt the crew in insidious ways that point forward to the complexities of Conrad's later fiction. Donkin tries to exploit the crew's grievances, but he is comparatively easy to resist. Wait is dying of tuberculosis, though he tries to pretend to himself that he is a malingerer. The crew is uncertain what to believe, easily blackmailed by his demands for sympathy. There is a sense that the order of the ship necessitates a withdrawal of human fellow-feeling and that a straightforward concept of duty can satisfy only simple, unimaginative men like Singleton. Similarly in the later "Typhoon" (1902), Captain MacWhirr represents the stolid, dutiful seaman whose sense of the fitness of things has to cope with the violence of the hurricane. In both novels there are hints that the ship's discipline may represent only a form of human illusion by which men evade the ultimate realities of an absurd universe. This is the frightening possibility that Conrad was to examine with so much honesty and subtlety in his later fiction.

In this essay I examine *Heart of Darkness* (first published 1899), *Lord Jim*, *Nostromo* (1904), *The Secret Agent* (1907), and *Under Western Eyes* separately, for these represent his major achievements.

III

In *Heart of Darkness*, Conrad explores his memories of his disastrous journey to the Congo. He is in search of self-understanding and perhaps trying to exorcise psychological conflicts by which he was still possessed. In this short novel he dramatizes his own conflicting attitudes toward passion and reason, savagery and civilization. *Heart of Darkness* is a truly great parable because these personal crises attain universal significance. The events of the story reflect ambiguities and tensions of central importance to Western culture. It is not surprising that T. S. Eliot was influenced by *Heart of Darkness* when he was writing "The Waste Land."

The narrative begins with a vivid evocation of the lower reaches of the Thames, with, to the west, the dark shadow of London. The sun is setting. On the *Nellie,* a cruising yawl, the anonymous narrator responds to the sense of history, to the "venerable stream" with all its immemorial associations: men such as Sir Francis Drake and Sir John Franklin set out from here on their great voyages of exploration, carrying a torch into strange lands unknown to civilization. In these opening paragraphs, as throughout the story, there is a subtle interplay between light and darkness. The language hints at symbolic meanings, as if the lurid glare of the red sun and the brooding gloom of London reflect the great conflicts of the centuries.

As darkness thickens, Marlow takes over the narration, recounting to his friends on the yawl his extraordinary adventures down the Congo in search of Kurtz, the great ivory collector who has become degraded by his lust for power over the natives. Conrad had first employed Marlow as his narrator in *Youth.* In *Almayer's Folly, The Outcast of the Islands,* and *The Nigger of the "Narcissus"* he tells the story in the conventional manner, as if he were the omniscient author who is in charge of the plot. For temperamental and ideological reasons this method did not satisfy him. He wanted to suggest his own uncertainties about the meaning of events, his own deep-rooted skepticism, his belief that illusion and reality are inextricably intertwined. This is achieved by making Marlow responsible for the story. This new indirect method means that we can never be sure how much Marlow understands, how far events are transmuted by being reflected through his consciousness.

In *Heart of Darkness,* Marlow tells us his adventure proved "the culminating point of my experience." He recalls that in Roman times England itself was a place of darkness, the very end of the world, where the Roman legionaries confronted the savage origins of their own being. At first it might seem that light and civilization are benevolent forces tackling an inferior, primitive state of human development. But the darkness retains its own potency; the civilized man may succumb to "the fascination of the abomination." Marlow's quest ends in a new awareness of the inadequacies of civilized society.

Like Conrad himself, Marlow travels to Brussels to sign on as skipper for the Belgian company. He dislikes the city, which he calls "a whited sepulcher." In the company office he is received by two women, one fat and the other slim, knitting black wool. They guard the entry to Africa, to darkness, and recall the Fates, spinning and breaking the thread of man's life. There are many references that compare Marlow's journey down the Congo to the classic expedition to the underworld, passing down like Vergil and Dante through the circles of Hell—the company station, the central station, and the inner station—to the final confrontation with the devil incarnate, Kurtz himself.

Such mythic journeys fascinated Conrad's imagination. He felt that at crises in their moral lives men enter an area of reality that normally they prefer to ignore. On such occasions the active life of the seaman may seem an illusion, an evasion of the truth. The Conradian hero must confront the ultimate meaninglessness of the forms and conventions of society. Exposure to this dark side of reality may drive him to suicide, like Brierly in *Lord Jim* or Decoud in *Nostromo.* It may persuade him to indulge in the orgies and killings apparently so attractive to Kurtz. Yet perhaps only by this confrontation with absolute darkness can the potential sources of energy repressed by the illusions of society be released. Conrad's response to the underworld voyage is ambivalent, a mixture of fascination and repulsion.

This double attitude is seen in the contradictory use of the word "reality." On arrival in Africa Marlow is shocked by the exploitation of the natives. He is disgusted by the squabblings and self-interest of the Europeans, the hollow men, the pilgrims, as he ironically calls them. He turns with relief to the task of repairing the battered, tinpot steamboat that is to carry him down the river in search of Kurtz. "I don't like work," he admits, but he believes that through his labors he can achieve self-discovery: "your own reality—for yourself, not for others—what no other man can ever know." This is one kind of test, one way in which a man may find an acceptable identity.

But Marlow is not completely satisfied with this work ethic. He admits that his absorption in keeping the steamboat afloat prevented him from responding fully to another kind of truth, to "the overwhelming realities of this strange world of plants, and water, and silences": "When you have to attend to things of that sort, to the mere incidents of the surface, the reality—the reality, I tell you—fades. The inner truth is hidden—luckily. But I felt it all the same." He too is tempted to go ashore for "a howl or a dance." This is a good example of Marlow's method of narration. He acts as a mirror of events, but what he reflects does not emerge as a rationally consistent view of reality. Marlow needs to tell his story because its conflicts remain unresolved, because Kurtz and the wilderness still tantalize and disturb his imagination.

The story is built around these oppositions and tensions between the values of work and the fascination of the wilderness. The natives enjoy degraded rites, and they foolishly worship Kurtz as a god; yet the cannibals are respected by Marlow for their endurance, for their loyalty: he says they are "men one could work with." The young Russian, Kurtz's disciple, dressed in patchwork clothes like a harlequin, retains an innocence lost by the hollow Europeans, yet in his naive enthusiasm for Kurtz he seems simple-minded. He is transported by Kurtz's eloquence, its breathtaking charm, yet the conclusion of Kurtz's seventeen-page report to the International Society for the Suppression of Savage Customs blows away such false rhetoric: "Exterminate all the brutes!" Kurtz's savage woman, with her animal vitality, contrasts with his European fiancée, who dedicates herself to a lie, in her Belgian home that resembles a cemetery. And finally, how are we to interpret Kurtz's last words: "The horror! The horror!" As he approaches death, wasted by excesses and fever, is he at last realizing the evil of his past ways and so proving that the attraction of the wilderness is indeed an abomination? Or is he looking at the horror of death, which will remove him from the scenes of his lusts and triumphs? Marlow returns to Brussels, the sepulchral city, broken down in physical and mental health by the heart of a conquering darkness.

Heart of Darkness has been interpreted in many different ways. Anti-imperialists draw attention to the suffering and torture of the natives in the scenes at Matadi and use the story as a tract against the colonial powers. From the Marxist point of view, Kurtz is an embodiment of all the evils created by free enterprise in a capitalist system. In contrast, some readers find in Kurtz a devil whose fascinations, like those of Milton's Satan, are difficult to resist. Followers of Jung discover in the story a night journey into the unconscious, a trafficking with the secret criminal energies that civilization represses. The journey down the Congo has been interpreted by Freudians as a voyage into the wilderness of sex; Marlow penetrates down a narrow channel to find in the darkness an orgiastic experience. Other readers stress the fascination with the primitive, typical of later artists such as Picasso or D. H. Lawrence. Kurtz is seen as a type of the modern artist, courageously rejecting the bland lies of civilization. The artist-outlaw dares to transgress the taboos of his society and so rediscovers a terrible new kind of imaginative energy. Kurtz foreshadows modern writers such as Hemingway and Mailer, who cultivate extreme experiences as a means of escape from the depressing conventions of contemporary life.

The wealth of interpretation arises from the symbolic force of *Heart of Darkness* achieved through the great imaginative resonance of Conrad's style. For example, on his journey to the Congo, Marlow, an idle passenger, is overwhelmed by a sense of unreality:

The voice of the surf heard now and then was a positive pleasure, like the speech of a brother. It was something natural, that had its reason, that had a meaning. Now and then a boat from the shore gave one a momentary contact with reality. It was paddled by black fellows. You could see from afar the white of their eyeballs glistening. They shouted, sang; their bodies streamed with perspiration; they had faces like grotesque masks—these chaps; but they had bone, muscle, a wild vitality, an intense energy of movement, that was as natural and true as the surf along their coast. They wanted no excuse for being there. They were a great comfort to look at. For a time I would feel I belonged still to a world of straightforward facts; but the feeling would not last long. Something would turn up to scare it away. Once, I remember, we came upon a man-of-war anchored off the coast. There wasn't even a shed there, and she was shelling the bush. It appears the French had one of their wars going on thereabouts. Her ensign dropped limp like a rag; the muzzles of the long six-inch guns stuck out all over the low hull; the greasy, slimy swell swung her up lazily and let her down, swaying her thin masts. In the empty immensity of earth, sky, and water, there she was, incomprehensible, firing into a continent. Pop, would go one of the six-inch guns; a small flame would dart and vanish, a little white smoke would disappear, a tiny projectile would give a feeble screech—and nothing happened. Nothing could happen. There was a touch of insanity in the proceeding, a sense of lugubrious drollery in the sight; and it was not dissipated by somebody on board assuring me earnestly there was a camp of natives—he called them enemies!—hidden out of sight somewhere.

(ch. 1)

Like so many famous passages in Conrad, this description is full of vivid, concrete details: the bodies streaming with perspiration, the ensign limp like a rag, the greasy, slimy swell of the sea. At the same time there are subtle hints concerning the central themes of the novel. The natives bring Marlow a "contact with reality"; they possess "a wild vitality . . . as natural and true as the surf," values that the novel suggests have been obliterated by European society. The French warship "firing into a continent" symbolizes the futility of civilized attempts to tame the wilderness. Such passages, while carrying the action forward with the excitement and speed necessary for an adventure story, evoke a whole range of complex feelings. The story haunts the imagination. Like Marlow, we return again and again to this Congo adventure to try to tease out its tantalizing and disturbing meanings.

IV

At first intended as a short story, *Lord Jim* expanded far beyond Conrad's original intention. The main episode is based closely on the scandal connected with the *Jeddah,* which left Singapore in 1880 with about nine hundred and fifty pilgrims bound for Jeddah, the port of Mecca. When the boilers began to give trouble, and she started to leak, the captain and officers abandoned the ship, leaving the pilgrims to their fate. The captain was picked up and taken to Aden, where he announced that the *Jeddah* had sunk. Shortly afterward, to his embarrassment, the *Jeddah* was towed in by another ship. As usual Conrad changes these details to suit his artistic purposes.

A new reader is likely to find *Lord Jim* difficult to understand. The first four chapters are narrated anonymously, and it is not until chapter five that Marlow takes over the story. Only in chapter seven do we learn the crucial fact that the pilgrim ship, which in the novel is called the *Patna,* did not sink. This method of narration, with its constant flashbacks, bewilders the reader. Conrad's aim is to analyze the complex influences, motives, emotions, and beliefs that determine Jim's character, rather than to tell a story in chronological sequence. Marlow's twisting, sinuous account is even more ambiguous than in *Heart of Darkness.* He calls on other characters, such as the oxlike French lieutenant or the mysterious Stein, for their viewpoints. Like Conrad himself, Marlow feels intimately involved with his story, for Jim's case holds significance for Marlow's own moral values and for his own concept of personal identity.

Jim faces two tests, first on the *Patna* and later when his adopted country, Patusan, is threatened by Gentleman Brown. The anonymous narrator of the first four chapters tells us that Jim is an inch, perhaps two, under six feet, just under the ideal requirement for the romantic hero. The son of a clergyman, Jim chooses a career at sea in the hope of romantic adventure. During his training two men are thrown in the water by a collision in rough weather. Jim stands irresolute, paralyzed by what seems to be fear, and moves only when it is too late. His imagination is horrified by the brutal violence of the gale. The other boys see *less* than Jim, but as a result can act decisively.

On a journey to the East, Jim is disabled by a falling spar. He is left behind in a hospital, and at first he regards the easygoing seamen of these hot climates with disdain. But soon he himself is bewitched by the eternal serenity of the East, by the temptation of infinite repose. He takes a berth as chief mate on the *Patna.*

On the bridge Jim listens to the regular beat of the propeller as if it were part of the scheme of a safe universe. The chart pegged out by four drawing pins is as level and smooth as the glimmering surface of the waters. He feels "penetrated by the great certitude of unbounded safety and peace that could be read on the silent aspect of nature like the certitude of fostering love upon the placid tenderness of a mother's face." Man seems in control of Nature. Suddenly the *Patna* hits a sunken wreck (a complete change from the story of the *Jeddah*). Immediately Jim's attitude changes. The calm sea, the sky without a cloud, appear "formidably insecure in their immobility, as if poised on the brow of yawning destruction." Jim's romantic quest for heroic adventure reaches its climax with the invasion of his life by a horror that lies behind the smoothness of appearances. It is a moment of recognition, of insight into ultimate reality.

About what happens next, the official inquiry demands facts, the kind of facts we have been given by the anonymous narrator about Jim's early upbringing. Jim, like Conrad himself, realizes that facts explain nothing. It is time for the assurance of the omniscient narrator to be superseded by Marlow's ambiguous account. The chronological sequences are broken; the reader is continually perplexed. The Victorian trust in an explicable, orderly universe is deliberately flouted; we are left without bearings as we try to understand the meaning of Jim's experience.

At first he behaves well. He goes below to examine the damaged bulkhead. A flake of rust as big as the palm of his hand falls off: "the thing stirred and jumped off like something live while I was looking at it," he tells Marlow. His imagination is terrified by pictures of the drowning pilgrims, the panic, the trampling rush, the pitiful screams, the boats swamped. Back on deck, paralyzed by fear, he stands stock still for twenty-seven minutes while the cowardly German captain and the other officers wrestle to launch a boat. A squall approaches, which apparently must finish the ship. The voices below, like messages from his unconscious self, call on Jim to jump. He seems to make no conscious decision but is strangely passive. He jumps.

At the end of the novel a retired sailor receives a packet of information about Jim. He is sure that Jim's jump from the *Patna* is to be condemned. He maintains that "we must fight in the ranks or our lives don't count." Marlow wavers but at times believes the real significance of the crime is in its being a breach of faith with the community of mankind, and from this point of view Jim is no mean traitor. The French lieutenant, who undertakes the highly dangerous task of taking charge of the stricken *Patna*, insists that we must control our natural fears through the habit and discipline of duty. When Jim tries to argue that it was difficult for him to decide what to do, that "there was not the thickness of a sheet of paper between the right and wrong of this affair," Marlow retorts: "How much more did you want?"

Jim looks like a reliable sailor, "one of us," as Marlow says. He should exemplify honesty, loyalty, and instinctive courage. His defection casts doubt on "the sovereign power enthroned in a fixed standard of conduct." On the other hand, Jim's imaginative awareness of the horrors awaiting the drowning pilgrims is the main reason for his cowardice. Is it only stupid people, like the French lieutenant, who can avoid the terrors thrown up by an imaginative response to the brutality of Nature and the inevitability of death?

Marlow's obsession with Jim reflects his desire to avoid this conclusion, to find some other explanation. He prefers the safe world of surface reality, controlled by a few fixed notions of conduct. Brierly, one of the assessors at the inquiry, has achieved great success in his career at sea. He is a confident, arrogant man. After the inquiry, he commits suicide. Apparently Jim acts as a mirror for Brierly, as he does for Marlow. They recognize in him hidden aspects of their own natures. Brierly cannot cope with this double awareness, this double range of values. When his self-conceit recognizes its hypocrisy in the reflecting mirror of Jim's cowardice, he kills himself.

Jim spends the rest of his life in self-justification. He works as a ship chandler's water clerk, but whenever rumors of his disgrace catch up with him, he moves on. Eventually Marlow and his old friend Stein arrange for him to work in Patusan, a country outside civilization, like some primitive Shangri-la. The people he meets there are like characters in a fairy tale, and some readers feel there is a falling away in Conrad's grip on the narrative. At first Jim seems to be accomplishing his wildest dreams. He defeats his enemy, Sherif Ali, and falls in love with the young and attractive Jewel. Patusan seems an enchanted paradise; but into this dream comes the desperado Gentleman Brown. Unwittingly Brown recalls to Jim his past cowardice, and his ability to act decisively is paralyzed. He allows Brown and his followers to leave the country unharmed if they promise to take no life. They break the pact, and Jim accepts responsibility to his community. He does not try to escape with Jewel, but allows himself to be killed.

Is this a noble act reversing his jump from the *Patna*? Or is his martyrdom a ridiculous gesture satisfying his romantic ideals? Readers disagree. In a great symbolic scene before Jim is sent to Patusan, Marlow and Stein discuss the case. Stein is a collector of beetles and butterflies, a man aware of both the evil and the beauty of life. He tells Marlow:

A man that is born falls into a dream like a man who falls into the sea. If he tries to climb out into the air as inexperienced people endeavour to do, he drowns—*nicht war?* . . . No! I tell you! The way is to the destructive element submit yourself, and with the exertions of your hands and feet in the water make the deep, deep sea keep you up.

(ch. 20)

Stein is saying that we must adapt ourselves to circumstances and that romantics who try to escape the destructive qualities of life will drown. But interpretation is not easy. At the end Marlow is still not sure he fully understands the enigma of Lord Jim.

V

CONRAD's early novels were based to a considerable extent on his memoirs of his own experiences at sea. But, as he tells us in his author's note to *Nostromo*, after he finished the final story of his *Typhoon* volume, it seemed somehow that there was nothing more in the world to write about. He had almost exhausted the material based on his own adventures and memories. In *Nostromo* he decided to base his story in South America, although he had visited this continent only briefly. The result is a brilliant work of creative imagination, dealing with both public issues and private questions of morality. For many readers *Nostromo* is his greatest achievement.

Conrad tells us that the first hint for *Nostromo* came to him in the shape of an anecdote about a man who stole single-handed a barge full of silver on the Tierra Firme seaboard during a revolution. Conrad first heard this story in 1875 or 1876 when he was in the Gulf of Mexico, then forgot it for over twenty years until he found the story in a shabby volume in a secondhand bookshop. It has now been established that this book was *On Many Seas: The Life and Exploits of a Yankee Sailor* (1897), by Frederick Benton Williams. Conrad filled in the background by reading books on South America, such as G. F. Masterman's *Seven Eventful Years in Paraguay* (1869) and Edward B. Eastwick's *Venezuela;* but the vivid flow of life that characterizes every page of *Nostromo* is his own creation. He finished this masterpiece in August 1904, after an almost continuous thirty-six-hour sitting.

As we have seen, *Lord Jim* presents major difficulties to the new reader. *Nostromo* is even more complex. The action moves backward and forward in time in a most disconcerting fashion. The opening chapter describes the town of Sulaco on the coast in the Republic of Costaguana and the Placid Gulf on which it is situated. We are then introduced to Captain Mitchell, superintendent of the Oceanic Navigation Company, and given some of his recollections about a riot in which Nostromo, head of the company's lightermen, saved the life of the dictator, Señor Ribiera. In the third chapter we meet the hotelkeeper, old Giorgio Viola, who has been an ardent follower of the Italian military leader Garibaldi, and hear about the history of the San Tomé silver mine, the coming of the railway to Sulaco, and the savage tortures and killings under a previous dictator, Guzman Bento. We move so quickly from one incident to the next that we cannot fit the happenings into a chronological pattern.

The circuitous narration is confusing, and even after many readings we remain uncertain about the exact sequence of events. The first part of the novel frustrates the normal objectives of the reader to an astonishing degree, not allowing him to identify himself with any one character or to locate himself firmly in time or place. There is no Marlow to provide us with one man's point of view of the whole action. We are sometimes given Captain Mitchell's reminiscences; toward the end of the novel we hear his confused account of the riot and of present-day Sulaco, which he retails to distinguished strangers. At one stage the narrative is mediated to us through a long letter that Martin Decoud writes to his sister in Europe. Most of the story, however, is told by an anonymous narrator, but often he precedes his words with "The story goes . . . ," or "It is said that. . . ." An impression is given that parts of the story come from hearsay and may not be true in every detail.

Why does Conrad adopt this impressionistic technique that causes so many difficulties for the reader? He believed that in real life our consciousness of a great event, such as the Sulaco riot, is invested with recollections of all that preceded it and of the results in later years. When we remember an important moment from the past, we first think of one or two striking facts and then gradually recall, in bits and pieces, the various preceding and ensuing events. The effect of the bewildering time scheme is to suggest such wayward movements of the memory, as it reflects on the past and gradually pieces together the whole story. The novel is built on a series of impressions, a great canvas of recollections and colorful scenes that create a vast panoramic picture of Costaguana and its people.

These shifts from one time to another are also of great importance in conveying Conrad's irony. We hear of the ceremonies at the banquet, with its high hopes for the future under the dictator Ribiera, after we have been told of his ignominious escape from Sulaco eighteen months later. When Charles Gould, the Englishman who runs the San Tomé mine, tells his wife, Emilia, that they will use the mine to build order and security, we know already about the riot. Repeatedly we are placed in this ironic position, able to judge the actions of the characters according to our knowledge of the outcome of events. This irony reflects Conrad's profound pessimism about human actions.

The elimination of any natural progression through time has the effect of implying that nothing is ever achieved. As we are hearing of Charles's success at the mine, these details are interspersed with others concerning the later disaster. History is made to seem repetitive, devoid of rational progression, without real progress toward a better form of society. At the end of the novel we hear that the attractive Antonia Avellanos and the fanatical missionary Father Corbelán are plotting to annex the rest of Costaguana for the new Occidental Republic, and we know that bloodshed and horror will return. History is proved to be cyclical, as the broken time scheme implies.

These determined historical processes are most clearly illustrated in the career of Charles Gould. His father has been ruined by the San Tomé silver mine; he determines to succeed where his father failed. His father died at the moment when Charles and Emilia were discovering their love, and so their devotion to the mine becomes, almost subconsciously for them, a way of repaying the father who didn't live to hear of their engagement. Charles believes in the philosophy of progressive capitalism. He tells Emilia that order and security will be a consequence of his devotion to the mine:

. . . I pin my faith to material interests. Only let the material interests once get a firm footing, and they are bound to impose the conditions on which alone they can continue to exist. That's how your money-making is justified here in the face of lawlessness and disorder. It is justified because the security which it demands must be shared with an oppressed people. A better justice will come afterwards.

(pt. I, ch. 6)

In the novel the failure of this ideal is almost total. Conrad detests the sentimentalizing of commercial power by a man such as the American captain of industry and finance, Holroyd, and shows how Gould ruins himself by allying himself with this fanatic. He becomes so obsessed by his ideals that he neglects his wife, completely insensitive to her misery. His work at the mine leads only to more riots and revolutions. Dr. Monygham, who suffered torture under Guzman Bento and is befriended by Emilia, sums up this central meaning of the novel: "There is no peace and no rest in the development of material interests. They have their law, and their justice. But it is founded on expediency, and is inhuman."

The novel might properly end with Mrs. Gould, alone in a garden, betrayed by her husband's obsession with the mine, stammering out as if in the grip of a merciless nightmare: "material interests." Silver becomes a major symbol in the novel. At the end the big white cloud hanging over the gulf is "shining like a mass of solid silver." Silver symbolizes the material interests that ruin the lives of all the major char-

acters, not only the Goulds but also Nostromo, the Italian adventurer, and Decoud, the intelligent skeptic who falls in love with Antonia.

Nostromo gives his name to the novel, but he is not the hero. In a letter of 1923 Conrad himself wrote: "I will take the liberty to point out that Nostromo has never been intended for the hero of the Tale of the Seaboard." Handsome, robust, courageous, Nostromo enjoys his reputation as the successful leader of the lightermen. He loves personal display, as he shows in the incident in which he cuts off his silver buttons for the pretty Morenita. Decoud, with his usual acumen, sees how "this man was made incorruptible by his enormous vanity, that finest form of egoism which can take on the aspect of every virtue."

This explains why Nostromo's character is transformed after his adventure with Decoud, when they try to save the silver from the revolutionaries. They escape in a lighter into the blackness of the Placid Gulf, and Conrad's descriptions make this a brilliant piece of symbolic writing. It is as if both Nostromo and Decoud journey into a strange world of darkness that obliterates their personalities. After the barge is sunk, Nostromo fears that he will lose his reputation with the people. His identity has been made up of conceit, vanity, public fame. If this is taken away he is nothing. When he realizes that the Europeans have used him for their own ends, his egoism is seriously deflated. His decision to steal the silver corrupts the very center of his identity, and he too is destroyed by "material interests." The personality he created was, in a sense, his ideal. When it is taken away from him, it is as if he has died.

Decoud could more appropriately be thought of as the main character in the novel. Intelligent, skeptical, he understands how men like Nostromo deceive themselves with a false idea of their own personality. He realizes that Charles Gould sentimentally idealizes his work at the mine, believing he is serving a noble cause. Such idealism seems dangerous to Decoud. On the journey through the blackness of the Placid Gulf, he begins to lose his faith that his own identity has any meaning or purpose. When he is stranded for ten days with the silver, solitude undermines his desire for life:

After three days of waiting for the sight of some human face, Decoud caught himself entertaining a doubt of his own individuality. It had merged into the world of cloud and water, of natural forces and forms of nature. In our activity alone do we find the sustaining illusion of an independent existence as against the whole scheme of things of which we form a helpless part. Decoud lost all belief in the reality of his action past and to come.

(pt. III, ch. 10)

Decoud's growing sense that all activity is an illusion ends in his suicide. As we have seen, this pessimism is reflected in the treatment of action in the whole novel, and some readers think Decoud has much in common with Conrad himself. The novel, however, includes many elements that do not support Decoud's skeptical nihilism. There are honest, faithful characters such as Don Pépé and General Barrios. There is Dr. Monygham's loyalty to Mrs. Gould. There are the integrity and compassion of Emilia herself.

The Placid Gulf acts as a rich symbol for the central themes, not only when Nostromo and Decoud escape in the barge, as we have seen, but throughout the novel. In the first chapter, the gulf is a place where action seems meaningless, where human beings journey back into an original state of chaos:

At night the body of clouds advancing higher up the sky smothers the whole quiet gulf below with an impenetrable darkness, in which the sound of the falling showers can be heard beginning and ceasing abruptly—now here, now there. Indeed, these cloudy nights are proverbial with the seamen along the whole west coast of a great continent. Sky, land, and sea disappear together out of the world when the Placido—as the saying is—goes to sleep under its black poncho. The few stars left below the seaward frown of the vault shine feebly as into the mouth of a black cavern. In its vastness your ship floats unseen under your feet, her sails flutter invisible above your head. The eye of God Himself—they add with grim profanity—could not find out what work a man's hand is doing in there; and you would be free to call the devil to your aid with impunity if even his malice were not defeated by such a blind darkness.

(pt. I, ch. 1)

The blackness is made to feel physically present; the scene also suggests that in this place the sailors lose their sense of connections, feel caught in a vastness that cares nothing for their activities. It is this experience that impels Decoud toward suicide.

At the end of the novel the gulf is "overhung by a big white cloud shining like a mass of solid silver." This image suggests how the silver ("material interests") has dominated the lives of all the characters. Conrad's narrative style brilliantly interweaves the concrete and the symbolic.

VI

The Secret Agent has been considered by many readers the most grim of Conrad's novels. The story is based on an attempt to blow up Greenwich Observatory in February 1894. The actual perpetrator, Martial Bourdin, did no damage but was himself killed by the bomb. In the novel Mr. Verloc is an indolent secret agent who consorts with a group of ineffective anarchists in London. His employer in a foreign embassy insists that Verloc organize the bomb outrage at Greenwich. To help him Verloc takes with him Stevie, half-crazed brother of his wife, and it is Stevie who is accidentally killed. Mrs. Verloc, whose affection for Stevie is fanatical and obsessive, kills her husband with a carving knife. Eventually she commits suicide by throwing herself into the sea from a channel steamer.

Conrad described the novel as an attempt to treat a melodramatic theme ironically. The action takes on the character of a parody of the conventional detective thriller. On the surface this is a story of a mysterious crime solved by the intelligent assistant commissioner, who visits Verloc's shop in a suitable disguise. But this linear development toward a solution is made to seem superficial by the existence of another kind of discovery. Verloc, his wife, and Ossipon, one of the revolutionaries, experience a moment of self-understanding that plunges them into despair. They discover the meaninglessness of their own self-created identity, and the shock drives them inevitably toward breakdown and suicide.

As a secret agent, Verloc thinks of himself as a preserver of civilized security, achieving this end by betraying the plans of the anarchists. He is really a typical domestic bourgeois with a strong distaste for work. His sense of security is shattered by the Greenwich outrage, and he feels that all his routines are under threat. His attempt to rediscover the illusion of domestic bliss ends in the blow from the carving knife.

Mrs. Verloc has married him not from love but to provide financial security for her brother. Her wifely pretenses hide a violent maternal passion for Stevie, exalted morbidly in her childhood by the oppression of their father. When she learns of Stevie's death, she feels as if her identity is being stripped from her. She appeals for help to Ossipon, but he betrays her. The novel ends with his breakdown. Confronted by the murder and her suicide he becomes incapable "of judging what could be true, possible, or even probable in this astounding universe."

In each case an illusion of security is destroyed. The personal fate of these three characters reflects Conrad's attitude toward society. All the characters, including the police, act from self-interest. The order of civilization is shown to be unreal; people are imprisoned in their own obsessions and, during the many interviews in the novel, continually misunderstand each other. In this novel Conrad comes closer to nihilism than ever before.

Two characters, Stevie and the Professor, might seem to stand apart from the ineffective, squalid London world. Stevie, the simpleton, is "delicately honest," with a passionate compassion for suffering. He occupies his spare time in drawing with a compass "circles, circles, circles; innumerable circles, concentric, eccentric, a coruscating whirl of circles that by their tangled multitude of repeated curves, uniformity of form, and confusion of intersecting lines suggested a rendering of cosmic chaos, the symbolism of a mad art attempting the inconceivable." The circles represent harmony of form, an ideal justice that Stevie would like to create in society, but the obsessed scribblings, the sense of cosmic disorder, suggest the impossibility of the task. He takes refuge in destructive acts, for only the annihilation of society can rid the world of its cruelties. The bomb plan enables him, or so he thinks, to put his ideas into practice; but the accident proves ironically the message of the whole novel, that anarchism means self-destruction.

The Professor is a single-minded fanatical anarchist. He wins his argument with Inspector Heat, whose comfortable domestic virtues are affronted by this puny, unhealthy specimen. The Professor clutches the detonator that will destroy himself and everyone near him if he is arrested; at least he dares to commit an act of self-destruction. But in the end he too proves a failure. Conrad's contempt for revolutionaries is powerfully expressed in this novel. The Professor's "idealism" is the result of personal vanity, and in his heart he fears the multitude who will never submit to his domination.

The story is told in a sardonic tone that is difficult to analyze. There is something unfocused and destructive about this irony, which shows no compassion toward the misfortunes of the characters. The narrator adopts an attitude of contempt that stems from no obvious moral stance. The liberal or the Marxist discerns in *The Secret Agent* only a self-destructive helplessness; and the Freudian or the Jungian finds no profound introspective analysis of character. Critics with these approaches tend to judge this a minor novel. Other critics believe *The Secret Agent* to be among Conrad's outstanding achievements. In his casebook on the play of the same title (1973), Ian Watt asks the crucial question: "How is it that a tale so deeply depressing on the face of it, a tale in which every possible card is stacked against human freedom and happiness, should be, for some readers at least, tonic rather than depressive in its final effect?" His answer is that Conrad negotiates the conflict between the ideal and the actual in his gloomy vision by means of comic style, and in this way the novel seems modern in the same way as works by Yeats, Eliot, Joyce: "All of them assume that it is the artist's voice alone which can impose some order on the vulgar folly of the modern world." In *The Secret Agent* there is a comic exuberance, particularly in the description of the anarchists, that belies the pessimism of the story. Watt writes that "the tension between what is seen and how it is presented betokens an admirable elasticity of spirit."

VII

CONRAD was not finally satisfied by this retreat into style. In *Under Western Eyes* and subsequent novels he returns to the problems of social relationships and how action can be made meaningful. In contrast to the ironic vision of *The Secret Agent*, he moves toward the ideas of fellowship and community expressed in later novels such as *Chance* (1913), *Victory* (1915), *The Arrow of Gold*, and *The Rover* (1923).

Under Western Eyes is supposedly narrated by an English teacher of languages who lives in Geneva. His complacency contrasts forcibly with the intense passions he describes. He begins with an account of how Razumov betrays his fellow-student Haldin. This is one of Conrad's most direct and dramatic passages of writing. The novel includes a terrible indictment of conditions in Russia, where Haldin has just assassinated a minister of state. He asks Razumov to help him escape. Razumov is a disowned bastard, a man without political or family ties. As a student he has tried to locate himself in society by the disciplines of work. Intelligent and self-aware, he has conceived for himself a linear kind of self-development, proceeding via the silver medal for the prize essay to the role of celebrated professor. He trusts institutions because they seem to him "rational and indestructible." They express a sense of order attractive to him because it opposes both the anarchy of revolutionaries and the loneliness forced on him by his family situation. He is proud of the lucidity of his mind and hopes to create his own future by the free use of his intelligence.

This rational existence is destroyed by the sudden appearance of Haldin, who represents the forces of irrationality, which so often in Conrad surge up from unexpected depths to confound the hero. Razumov tries to cope with this situation by giving Haldin up to the authorities, justifying his decision by appealing to rational political argument. He believes in the organic growth of institutions, which anarchism can only destroy, like a disease. He scrawls on a piece of paper:

> History not Theory.
> Patriotism not Internationalism.
> Evolution not Revolution.
> Direction not Destruction.
> Unity not Disruption.

From such a conservative idea of society it seems to him rational and just to betray Haldin.

Razumov soon discovers the inadequacy of his philosophy. Haldin asked for protection and help, and his simple human appeal was rejected. Razumov's decision to betray him is like the Ancient Mariner's killing of the albatross, an abandonment of the ties that bind man and nature, man and man. The claim Haldin made on him had fundamentally nothing to do with matters of politics or revolution. The betrayal is an archetypal sin, like the murder of a guest. Immediately afterward Razumov's character breaks to pieces under the burden of guilt.

Since no one knows about Razumov's treachery, the Russian authorities send him to Geneva to spy on the revolutionaries. He meets Natalia, sister of Haldin, and begins to fall in love with her. Conrad is never successful in depicting women, and Natalia is sentimentalized. But the portrayal of Razumov's conscience and his tortured feelings when meeting revolutionaries such as Peter Ivanovitch is brilliantly done. Razumov is cut off from all honest human relationships, and he cannot endure the strain. He is disgusted by his fantasy that he might marry Natalia without telling her of his guilt. He feels a desperate need to tell the truth.

In *Nostromo* and *The Secret Agent* Conrad often seems on the verge of suicidal nihilism. In *Under Western Eyes* he finds the answer to his pessimism by asserting the supreme importance of natural human relationships. After he has admitted his guilt to Natalia, Razumov walks back to his lodgings through the rain. "I am washed clean," he says. He goes to the revolutionaries to confess. In a violent scene the brutal revolutionary Nikita bursts Razumov's eardrums, and as Razumov leaves he is seriously injured when he does not hear an approaching tram. He proceeds from crime to punishment to redemption, but Conrad does not reward Razumov for his courage. He lives on in Russia, crippled, deaf, getting weaker every day, a broken man.

VIII

WHILE working on *Under Western Eyes*, Conrad completed his greatest short story, "The Secret Sharer" (1910). He draws on his memories of his first command on the *Otago*, when he, like the captain-narrator of this story, felt like a stranger on his own ship. He thus creates an image of himself in the captain, who is then confronted with a man very like himself in Leggatt, the mate of another ship, who appeals to the captain for help after killing a disobedient member of his crew in a storm. Both the captain and Leggatt in certain ways reflect Conrad's own character. Leggatt is both a real flesh-and-blood seaman as well as a kind of alter ego for the captain, and Conrad handles most delicately this double function. Many psychological interpretations have been advanced for this strange story in which the captain seems to be hiding a second self, a criminal doppelgänger. As the two mirrors, captain and criminal, confront each other, their roles resist clear definition. The captain is supposedly being initiated into maturity and responsibility, but, as always in Conrad's major works, there are unresolved tensions between the ideal of the efficient sailor and the ideal of the outsider whose sensitivity and imagination separate him from ordinary men. The brilliantly handled symbolism expresses rather than resolves the tensions in Conrad's own personality.

After his marriage in 1896, Conrad continued to suffer from bouts of nervous depression. His work was considerably influenced by his meeting in 1898 with Ford Hueffer (who later called himself Ford

Madox Ford). He rented from him Pent Farm in Kent, where they collaborated on two novels, *The Inheritors* (1901) and *Romance* (1903). Both are tedious, though *Romance* might be recommended as an adventure story in the Robert Louis Stevenson manner, suitable for children. In spite of these failures, there seems little doubt that Hueffer helped Conrad to understand the true nature of his genius and to develop his experimental techniques. Both were high-strung and temperamental, and their relationship passed through moods of gaiety and anger more suited to a love affair. A final quarrel broke off the relationship in 1909.

During the period from the writing of *The Nigger of the "Narcissus"* to *Under Western Eyes,* Conrad managed to find expression for the central conflicts in his life, but there is no doubt that his success imposed on him an almost intolerable strain. The collaboration with Hueffer appears to have helped him to maintain the creative drive of these difficult years. After he completed *Under Western Eyes* in 1910, the nervous tension laid him up for three months. The manuscript of the novel lay on a table at the foot of his bed, and in his delirium he held conversations with the characters. He even accused his doctor and his wife of trying to put him in an asylum. After he had recovered he wrote to Norman Douglas: "I feel like a man returned from hell and look upon the very world of the living with dread." In the following years Conrad seems to have achieved mental balance by repressing his oversensitive nature and by forcing his mind into safer, more normal channels of thought. His writings after 1910 became more superficial, without the tensions and ambiguities of his major work.

Chance, finished in 1912, proved a turning point in Conrad's financial affairs, for it became a best seller. Marlow returns as narrator, but he is now often prolix and boring. Flora, the heroine, is the daughter of a swindler, de Barral. After he is exposed she is treated abominably by her governess, and her resulting psychological breakdown almost ends in suicide. She is rescued by the romantic Captain Anthony. He fails to consummate their marriage because he wrongly thinks that she does not love him and only wishes to be rescued from her disastrous social situation. He learns of her true affection at the climactic moment when her father tries to poison him, and they live happily for several years before he is drowned in an accident. The novel is often tedious, but wakes up when Conrad is describing adventures at sea. As elsewhere there is something evasive and enigmatic about Conrad's attempts to deal with a sexual relationship.

Victory is similarly a mixture of success and failure. The villains, Jones, Ricardo, and Pedro, are caricatures portrayed in a Dickensian manner. Lena, the heroine, is another example of Conrad's failures with women. The story, in which the hero, Axel Heyst, runs off with Lena to his island paradise, at times seems an erotic fantasy for adolescents. The descriptions of passion are desperately overwritten. But the novel is saved by Conrad's most intelligent analysis of Heyst's world-weary skepticism.

Heyst inherits his beliefs from his father, who adopts a Schopenhauer-like philosophy of withdrawal from the folly of human passions and actions. The son decides to wander about the world as an "independent spectator." He drifts about the islands around Java and New Guinea, adopting a pose of polite, considerate withdrawal from the affairs of men, and determines to be loyal to himself rather than to the community. He betrays this ideal when calls are made on his compassion, first by the quixotic seaman Morrison and later by Lena, a damsel in distress. His habits of passivity render him incapable of coping with the ensuing difficulties, and he ends by committing suicide. In *Victory,* as in *Chance,* Conrad rejects the philosophical skepticism that he himself found so tempting, and tries to dramatize in fiction the need to escape the isolation of the self and to serve the community.

In this period of declining powers, Conrad managed to bring off one masterpiece. This is *The Shadow-Line,* written just after the outbreak of war in 1914. He had been in Poland when the war started and only just escaped internment. *The Shadow-Line* was begun on his return and completed by the end of March 1915. It is dedicated to his son Borys, who was serving at the front, and also to all the other young men who at that time had passed the shadow-line dividing youth from maturity, through the demands of duty, self-discipline, and devotion to an ideal.

The story, therefore, describes another case of moral initiation and, like "The Secret Sharer," is based on personal reminiscences of Conrad's first command. It is written with a vivid directness reminiscent of *Typhoon,* and there are none of the embarrassing sentimentalities typical of his later work. "The Secret Sharer" is a story of questioning and uncertainty about the grounds of being and action. In contrast, *The Shadow-Line* ends with the test satisfactorily completed. The captain has to contend with tropical fever in his crew and atrocious weather. He is a man of imagination, but, in contrast to Lord Jim, he overcomes his anxieties and obeys the seaman's code. He has to learn not to hope too much and not to expect too much, particularly from himself. Conrad is developing a new stoicism.

In his last years Conrad published *The Arrow of Gold, The Rescue,* and *The Rover. The Arrow of Gold,* as we have seen, recalls his early adventures in Marseilles. In *The Rescue* the scene is once again the Far East, where Tom Lingard tries to help a small party of society people stranded in a yacht off a dangerous coast. *The Rover* is a boy's adventure story set in the Mediterranean at the time of Nelson's blockade of Toulon. When he died in 1924, Conrad left unfinished a novel called *Suspense,* in which he hoped to express in fictional form his interest in Napoleon. These stories, with their simple trust in heroic action, are not without virtues, but they lack the depth of his major achievements.

IX

CONRAD's life and art testify to a continual, by and large unsuccessful, search for a stable identity in a universe whose cruelties he found beyond comprehension. Although his childhood and self-imposed exile must count as major sources of his depressions, just as important was his conscious philosophy, his personal response to what he considered the absurdity of the universe. His suicidal tendencies were nourished by a nihilism derived from his reading (particularly Schopenhauer) and from the climate of thought of the late nineteenth century. His doubts about his own identity were linked to philosophical skepticism about the nature of reality. In a famous letter of 1897 to his friend R. B. Cunninghame Graham, he compared the universe to a nightmarish knitting machine:

There is—let us say—a machine. It evolved itself (I am severely scientific) out of a chaos of scraps of iron and behold!—it knits. I am horrified at the horrible work and stand appalled. . . . It is a tragic accident—and it has happened. You can't interfere with it. The last drop of bitterness is in the suspicion that you can't even smash it. In virtue of that truth one and immortal which lurks in the force that made it spring into existence it is what it is—and it is indestructible!

It knits us in and it knits us out. It has knitted time [,] space, pain, death, corruption, despair and all the illusions—and nothing matters.

This belief that "nothing matters," that the universe is meaningless, gives Conrad's great fiction its startling modernity. J. Hillis Miller writes in *Poets of Reality* (1966): "The special place of Joseph Conrad in English literature lies in the fact that in him the nihilism covertly dominant in modern culture is brought to the surface and shown for what it is."

Like Franz Kafka, or the T. S. Eliot of "The Waste Land," Conrad experiments with new imaginative forms to express man's predicament in an incomprehensible universe. How can the artist impose shape and order on what is fundamentally shapeless and disordered? How can words define what is believed to be indefinable? In tackling this central twentieth-century problem, Conrad had special problems because English was not his native language. G. B. Shaw said that his style was too pure for English, too impossibly free of local idiosyncrasies. He was digging his language out of a foreign quarry. This made him doubtful about the mimetic function of words, and in this he is characteristically modern in outlook. Words for him have moved a few steps away from reality, and so on occasion he turns to image and symbol for a more mysterious and complex means of communication. In his great novels he refuses to commit himself to final explanations. The breakings of the time scheme, the multiple points of view, ensure that no ordered, coherent interpretation can be imposed on the novel. If we offer one conclusive interpretation for the behavior of Kurtz or Lord Jim, we do harm to the complexity and deliberate ambiguities of Conrad's fiction.

Conrad's response to the suicidal claims of moral nihilism is a stoical recognition of the precarious status of mind. He rejects the Victorian illusion that mind can understand and control matter, can create a permanent civilized order. The artist builds in language an acknowledgment of our incomprehension, a form of poised irresolution. Modern art, as Frank Kermode has written, goes out into the neutral air, remains in an area of noncommitment.

Conrad's efforts to put this new sensibility into words are not always successful. He found the full artistic expression of his innermost being an incalculable strain on his resources of nervous energy, and, as we have seen, this led to the simplifications of the later work. Yet in his major writings he offered to the twentieth century what Ian Watt has called "bifocal vision." His fiction presents a way of responding to life that accepts the validity of incompatible modes of apprehension and commits itself to meaning in an apparently meaningless universe. We must acknowledge that the earth seems of minimal importance in the scheme of the universe, and that it will eventually be destroyed. We must acknowledge that all the suffering and pain and killing that took place before man came on earth make the idea of a benevolent creator seem impossible. Yet, not forgetting this pessimistic vision, we put on our bifocals and look instead at the value of momentary sensations and at individual examples of trust and devotion. Conrad testifies to the reality of human dignity, even while admitting all those aspects of his thought that tend to nihilism. His success in maintaining this difficult stance was truly heroic.

SELECTED BIBLIOGRAPHY

I. BIBLIOGRAPHY. T. J. Wise, *A Bibliography of the Writings of Joseph Conrad, 1895–1921* (London, 1921); K. A. Lohf and P. Sheehy, *Joseph Conrad at Mid-Century: Editions and Studies, 1895–1955* (Minneapolis, 1957); T. G. Ehrsam, *A Bibliography of Joseph Conrad* (London, 1969); B. E. Teets and H. E. Gerber, *Joseph Conrad: An Annotated Bibliography of Writings About Him* (London, 1971).

II. COLLECTED WORKS. *The Works of Joseph Conrad*, 20 vols. (London, 1921–1927); *The Uniform Editions of the Works of Joseph Conrad*, 22 vols. (London–Toronto, 1923–1928), contains Conrad's prefaces and is complete except for the plays and *The Nature of a Crime* (1924); T. J. Wise, ed., *A Conrad Library* (London, 1928), a private ed. of twenty-five copies only; *The Collected Editions of the Works of Joseph Conrad*, 21 vols. (London, 1946–1955), repr. from the Uniform ed.

III. SEPARATE WORKS. *Almayer's Folly: A Story of an Eastern River* (London, 1895), novel; *An Outcast of the Islands* (London, 1896), novel; *The Nigger of the "Narcissus": A Tale of the Sea* (London, 1897), novel; *Tales of Unrest* (London, 1898), short stories, includes "Karain: A Memory," "The Idiots," "An Outpost of Progress," "The Return," "The Lagoon."

Lord Jim: A Tale (London, 1900), novel; *The Inheritors: An Extravagant Story* (London, 1901), novel, in collaboration with Ford Madox Ford; *Youth: A Narrative: and Two Other Stories* (London, 1902), includes "Youth," "Heart of Darkness," "The End of the Tether"; *Typhoon, and Other Stories* (London, 1903), includes "Typhoon," "Amy Foster," "Falk," "Tomorrow"; *Romance* (London, 1903), novel, in collaboration with Ford Madox Ford; *Nostromo: A Tale of the Seaboard* (London, 1904), novel; *The Mirror of the Sea: Memories and Impressions* (London, 1906), autobiography; *The Secret Agent: A Simple Tale* (London, 1907), novel; *A Set of Six* (London, 1908), short stories, includes "Gaspar Ruiz," "The Informer," "The Brute," "An Anarchist," "The Duel," "Il Conde."

Under Western Eyes (London, 1911), novel; *Some Reminiscences* (London, 1912), autobiography, appears in the collected editions as *A Personal Record*; *'Twixt Land and Sea: Tales* (London, 1912), short stories, includes "A Smile of Fortune," "The Secret Sharer," "Freya of the Seven Isles"; *Chance: A Tale in Two Parts* (London, 1913), novel; *Victory: An Island Tale* (London, 1915), novel; *Within the Tides: Tales* (London, 1915), short stories, includes "The Planter of Malata," "The Partner," "The Inn of the Two Witches," "Because of the Dollars"; *The Shadow-Line: A Confession* (London, 1917), novel; *The Arrow of Gold: A Story Between Two Notes* (London, 1919), novel.

The Rescue: A Romance of the Shallows (London, 1920), novel; *Notes on Life and Letters* (London, 1921), essays; *The Secret Agent: A Drama in Four Acts* (London, 1923), drama; *The Rover* (London, 1923), novel; *The Nature of a Crime* (London, 1924), fragment of a story, in collaboration with Ford Madox Ford, includes appendix "A Note on *Romance*," recalling details of their 1903 collaboration; *Laughing Anne, and One Day More* (London, 1924), one-act plays, the first from story "Because of the Dollars," the second from "Tomorrow," intro. by John Galsworthy; *Suspense: A Napoleonic Novel* (London, 1925), novel, incomplete at Conrad's death; *Tales of Hearsay* (London, 1925), short stories, includes "The Warrior's Soul," "Prince Roman," "The Tale," "The Black Mate," preface by R. B. Cunninghame Graham; *Last Essays* (London, 1926), intro. by R. Curle; *The Sisters* (lim. ed., New York, 1928), unfinished novel.

IV. LETTERS. G. Jean-Aubry, ed., *The Life and Letters of Joseph Conrad*, 2 vols. (London, 1927), a principal source for details of Conrad's life and friendships; *Joseph Conrad's Letters to His Wife* (London, 1927), preface by Jessie Conrad; E. Garnett, ed., *Letters from Conrad, 1895–1924* (London, 1928); R. Curle, ed., *Conrad to a Friend: Letters from Joseph Conrad to Richard Curle* (London, 1928), includes intro. and notes; G. Jean-Aubry, ed., *Lettres Françaises par Joseph Conrad* (Paris, 1930); J. A. Gee and P. J. Strum, eds. and trans., *Letters of Joseph Conrad to Marguerite Poradowska* (New Haven, 1940); W. Blackburn, ed., *Joseph Conrad: Letters to William Blackwood and David S. Meldrum* (Cambridge, 1959); Z. Najder, ed., *Conrad's Polish Background: Letters to and from Polish Friends* (London, 1964), trans. by H. Carroll; C. T. Watts, ed., *Joseph Conrad's Letters to R. B. Cunninghame Graham* (London, 1969).

V. BIOGRAPHICAL AND CRITICAL STUDIES. R. Curle, *Joseph Conrad: A Study* (London, 1914); H. James, *Notes on Novelists* (London, 1914), includes an appreciation of Conrad's early work; H. Walpole, *Joseph Conrad* (London, 1916); H. L. Mencken, *A Book of Prefaces* (London, 1917), includes an essay on Conrad; F. M. Ford, *Joseph Conrad: A Personal Reminiscence* (London, 1924), record of their relationship by Conrad's collaborator on two novels, *The Inheritors* and *Romance*; V. Woolf, *The Common Reader* (London, 1925), includes valedictory essay; A. Symons, *Notes on Joseph Conrad* (London, 1925), includes a few letters; R. L. Mégroz, *A Talk with Joseph Conrad* (London, 1926); Jessie Conrad, *Joseph Conrad as I Knew Him* (London, 1926), an appreciation by Conrad's wife; J. Galsworthy, *Castles in Spain* (London, 1927), includes reminiscences of Conrad by his oldest English literary friend, and "Preface to Conrad's Plays"; R. Curle, *The Last Twelve Years of Joseph Conrad* (London, 1928), second of two studies by a younger friend and critic.

G. Morf, *The Polish Heritage of Joseph Conrad* (London, 1930), psychological study; D. MacCarthy, *Portraits* (London, 1931), includes an essay on Conrad; F. M. Ford, *Return to Yesterday* (London, 1931), supplements Ford's 1924 *Personal Reminiscence*; R. L. Mégroz, *Joseph Conrad's Mind and Method* (London, 1931), valuable as intro. to Conrad, includes select bibliography, developed from *A Talk with Joseph Conrad* (above); Jessie Conrad, *Joseph Conrad and His Circle* (London, 1935); E. Crankshaw, *Joseph Conrad: Some Aspects of the Art of the Novel* (London, 1936); *Conrad's Prefaces to His Works* (London, 1937), with intro. by E. Garnett and biographical note on his father by D. Garnett, should be read with personal note by E. Garnett in *Letters from Conrad, 1895–1924*; as a reader for Fisher Unwin publishers, Garnett recommended publication of Conrad's first novel, *Almayer's Folly*; J. D. Gordan, *Joseph Conrad: The Making of a Novelist* (Cambridge, Mass., 1940); M. C. Bradbrook, *Joseph Conrad, England's Polish Genius* (London, 1941), scholarly analysis of Conrad's work; J. H. Retinger, *Conrad and His Contemporaries* (London, 1941); A. J. Hoppé, ed., *The Conrad Reader* (London, 1946), contains biographical intro. and large selection from Conrad's stories and other writings, title now changed to *The Conrad Companion* (London, 1948); M. D. Zabel, *The Portable Conrad* (New York, 1947), includes intro. and extensive selection, fully annotated; F. R. Leavis, *The Great Tradition* (London, 1948), includes valuable reappraisals of *Victory, Chance, Nostromo, The Secret Agent, Under Western Eyes, Heart of Darkness*.

O. Warner, *Joseph Conrad* (London, 1951); D. Hewitt, *Conrad: A Reassessment* (Cambridge, 1952); D. Garnett, *The Golden Echo* (London, 1953), Conrad seen through the eyes of a child; W. Allen, *Six Great Novelists* (London, 1955), Conrad is the sixth; E. H. Visiak, *The Mirror of Conrad* (London, 1955); G. Jean-Aubry, *The Sea-Dreamer: Life of Conrad* (London, 1957); T. Moser, *Joseph Conrad: Achievement and Decline* (Cambridge, Mass., 1957); A. J. Guerard, *Conrad the Novelist* (Cambridge, Mass., 1958); O. Andreas, *Joseph Conrad: A Study in Nonconformity* (London, 1959); J. Baines, *Joseph Conrad: A Critical Biography* (London, 1960); F. R. Karl, *A Reader's Guide to Joseph Conrad* (New York–London, 1960); L. Gurko, *Joseph Conrad, Giant in Exile* (London, 1962); E. K. Hay, *The Political Novels of Joseph Conrad* (London, 1963); H. S. Davies and G. Watson, eds., *The English Mind* (London, 1964), includes chapter on Conrad by I. Watt; J. Allen, *The Sea Years of Joseph Conrad* (New York, 1966); J. H. Miller, *Poets of Reality* (Cambridge, Mass.–London, 1966); N. Sherry, *Conrad's Eastern World* (Cambridge, 1966), see also Sherry's *Joseph Conrad's Fiction: Conrad's Western World* (below); E. W. Said, *Joseph Conrad and the Fiction of Autobiography* (Cambridge, Mass., 1966); B. C. Meyer, *Conrad: A Psychoanalytic Biography* (London, 1967); J. Guetti, *The Limits of Metaphor* (London, 1967); A. Fleishman, *Conrad's Politics: Community and Anarchy in the Fiction of Joseph Conrad* (London, 1968); P. Kirschner, *Conrad: The Psychologist as Artist* (London, 1968); J. I. M. Stewart, *Joseph Conrad* (London, 1968); J. A. Palmer, *Joseph Conrad's Fiction: A Study in Literary Growth* (London, 1968); L. Graver, *Conrad's Short Fiction* (London, 1969); P. K. Garrett, *Scene and Symbol from George Eliot to James Joyce* (London, 1969).

N. Sherry, *Joseph Conrad's Fiction: Conrad's Western World* (London, 1971), a companion vol. to Sherry's *Conrad's Eastern World* (above); R. Roussel, *The Metaphysics of Darkness* (London, 1971); B. Johnson, *Conrad's Models of Mind* (London, 1971); I. Watt, ed., *Conrad: "The Secret Agent." A Casebook* (London, 1973); C. B. Cox, *Joseph Conrad: The Modern Imagination* (London, 1974); D. Thornburn, *Conrad's Romanticism* (London, 1974); P. J. Glassman, *Joseph Conrad and the Literature of Personality* (London, 1976); N. Sherry, ed., *Joseph Conrad: A Commemoration* (London, 1976); H. M. Daleski, *Joseph Conrad: The Way of Dispossession* (London, 1977); J. Hawthorn, *Joseph Conrad: Language and Fictional Self-Consciousness* (London, 1979); F. R. Karl, *Joseph Conrad: The Three Lives. A Biography* (London, 1979); I. Watt, *Conrad in the Nineteenth Century* (London, 1980).

LIST OF SHORT STORIES

(The title in italics refers to the volume in which the story appears.)

"An Anarchist," *A Set of Six*; "Amy Foster," *Typhoon*; "Because of the Dollars," *Within the Tides*; "The Black Mate," *Tales of Hearsay*; "The Brute," *A Set of Six*; "The

Duel," *A Set of Six;* "The End of the Tether," *Youth;* "Falk," *Typhoon;* "Freya of the Seven Isles," *'Twixt Land and Sea.*

"Gaspar Ruiz," *A Set of Six;* "Heart of Darkness," *Youth;* "The Idiots," *Tales of Unrest;* "Il Conde," *A Set of Six;* "The Informer," *A Set of Six;* "The Inn of the Two Witches," *Within the Tides;* "Karain: A Memory," *Tales of Unrest;* "The Lagoon," *Tales of Unrest.*

"An Outpost of Progress," *Tales of Unrest;* "The Partner," *Within the Tides;* "The Planter of Malata," *Within the Tides;* "Prince Roman," *Tales of Hearsay;* "The Return," *Tales of Unrest;* "The Secret Sharer," *'Twixt Land and Sea;* "A Smile of Fortune," *'Twixt Land and Sea;* "The Tale," *Tales of Hearsay;* "Tomorrow," *Typhoon;* "Typhoon," *Typhoon;* "The Warrior's Soul," *Tales of Hearsay;* "Youth," *Youth.*

A. E. HOUSMAN

(1859-1936)

Ian Scott-Kilvert

INTRODUCTION

"CAMBRIDGE has seen many strange sights," remarked Housman when he bade farewell to University College, London, to become Kennedy Professor of Latin. "So the University which once saw Wordsworth drunk and once saw Porson sober will see a better scholar than Wordsworth, and a better poet than Porson, betwixt and between." The two names at first sight might appear only to emphasize how impassable a gulf is fixed between the achievements of poet and scholar at the level of genius. There have been, of course, other scholarly poets in English literature. Milton, Gray, Landor, Arnold, Fitz-Gerald, and Bridges were not only erudite men; their lives were molded by a certain precision of mind and detachment from worldly affairs that mark the scholar, and the character of their poetry reflects these qualities. But their learning was wide rather than deep, and their scholarship scarcely more than an adjunct to their poetic gifts.

Housman, on the other hand, aspired to the life of learning as early as a man can discover such an aptitude in himself. He is one of the very few English scholars to attain a European stature and the only one who is also a poet of consequence. If we can isolate a single element common to both fields, it is surely that Housman was a master of words of a very rare order. His scholarship is seldom concerned with general ideas or literary judgments: its special achievement is to concentrate his unrivaled knowledge of the classical tongues and his poetic sensibility upon the narrow front of textual criticism. His talk arrested the few who were privileged to hear it by the extraordinary aptness and penetration of the phrases he could command, when his interest overcame his reserve. His verse was deliberately limited to a few themes, which are among the most universal and timeworn in poetic currency; what strikes home immediately is the compelling power of the language, the quality of something inevitably and rightly said.

But Housman was also one of those who are born to mystify their fellows by their attitude to the human condition. In this sense he has been compared to Jonathan Swift and to T. E. Lawrence, as men gifted far above the common lot, who show themselves at once contemptuous of the admiration of others, eager for fame on their own terms, and strangely indifferent to the gift of life itself. Both in his scholarship and in his view of human relationships, Housman was a perfectionist, tormented by any falling short of his ideal, and it is the vehemence of this protest that distinctively tunes and tautens his poetry. In it the satirist, the man moved by horror and scorn and indignation, is constantly at the elbow of the love poet, and his suffering seems to spring not so much from any particular circumstance as from the very nature of human association. If Housman's life provokes a curiosity extending beyond his work, a curiosity that exceeds anything we want to know concerning most modern poets, it is not a matter of unearthing clues to his emotional experience. It is because his achievement, charged as it is with the sense of something missed and desired, raises questions that human nature is never tired of exploring, the question, for example, of what prevents such a man from rising to his full height, and of the use that men make of great gifts.

EARLY LIFE

ALFRED EDWARD HOUSMAN was born on 26 March 1859, the eldest of seven children, near Bromsgrove in Worcestershire, where his father practiced as an attorney. His mother's family was connected with the Drakes of Devon, and the Drakes's motto, *Aquila non capit muscas* (The eagle does not catch flies), could hardly have been better chosen to epitomize Housman's attitude to the world. Shropshire was never his home, nor did he at any period spend much time there. But the Shropshire hills had formed the western horizon of his childhood, and they imprinted themselves upon his memory as an imaginary world beyond the setting sun and the frontiers of everyday life. For the very reason that he did not know the county too intimately, it could later supply him with a rustic mythology and the music of place names, which served to evoke both memory and fantasy.

Housman was educated at Bromsgrove School and won a scholarship to St. John's College, Oxford. Here his true bent began to show itself, though at first with disastrous results. He was already devoted to exact and specialized study, and he could not bring himself to absorb the Greats curriculum,[1] with its widely spread interests.

One lecture from the celebrated Benjamin Jowett was enough to make him abandon the course in disgust at the professor's disregard for minutiae. Having obtained a first-class grade in the preliminary examination for Litterae Humaniores (Moderations), he may well have found the temptation irresistible to anticipate his degree and embark upon the work of a qualified scholar. At any rate when he sat for his finals his preparations proved quite inadequate, he could return only scrappy answers to some of the papers, and the examiners had no choice but to exclude him from an honors degree.

Housman's debacle at Oxford was a crucial episode in his career and resulted in the enforced relegation of his cherished classical studies to his spare time and an exile of eleven years before he could regain a position in academic life. It also offers some important clues to the austere personality he later developed, that of a man early disillusioned with the human lot, a controversialist who gave no quarter, a figure reserved and sardonic even to his closest friends, yet also capable of unexpected impulses of generosity and compassion.

Housman's biographer George L. Watson has argued persuasively that this academic disaster and its aftermath coincided and was linked with other critical stresses that had been developing for some time. Housman had been devoted to his mother, who had died on his twelfth birthday, and had become acutely conscious of the increasing incapacity of his father (who had failed in his chosen profession of attorney) to play his part as head of the family, and hence of

his own responsibilities as the eldest of seven children. The crisis in his personal life centered on his fellow undergraduate and lifelong friend, Moses Jackson. This was a friendship of opposites, Jackson being a strongly extravert "all-rounder," who rowed for Oxford and took a first-class degree in science; he was a frank and steadfast friend, but one incapable of sharing the kind of emotional intimacy that the poet's nature sought. The differences that separated them are aptly summed up in these posthumously published verses:

> Because I liked you better
> Than suits a man to say,
> It irked you, and I promised
> To throw the thought away.
> (More Poems, XXXI)

Whether this frustrated attachment contributed to the disastrous examination result can only be a matter for conjecture. But certainly Housman must have seen clearly the distress that his failure had brought upon his stricken family, and from this moment the desire to retrieve it became a consuming ambition.

After setting aside such money as he could spare for his family, Housman decided to leave home, take the civil service examination, and settle in London. Through the help of Jackson, with whom he now felt able to resume his friendship on a more pragmatic basis, he obtained a post in the patent office and moved into rooms he shared with Jackson and the latter's younger brother, Adalbert. The patent office was not an exacting employer, and Housman's main energies could now be devoted to his classical reading at the British Museum, where he proceeded to lay the foundations of his scholarship. Thus in the years when most men form their most lasting ties, his naturally reserved and solitary disposition was set in a still more inhibiting mold. According to his closest friends, his coldness of manner was imposed upon a nature that secretly craved affection, but the natural consequence was to secure his independence rather than his happiness.

Gradually his classical work began to bear fruit and his contributions to learned journals to attract attention. Finally the Chair of Latin at University College, London, fell vacant. Housman applied and was now able to support his candidature with seventeen testimonials from British, American, and German scholars. He did not fail to include the phrase, "In 1881 I failed to obtain Honours in the final

---

[1] The honors school of Litterae Humaniores, which involved the study of Greek and Roman literature, history, and philosophy.

School of Litterae Humaniores." Fortunately, the electors were unmoved, and in 1892 he took up the professorship he was to hold for nineteen years until his election to the Kennedy Chair of Latin at Cambridge.

CLASSICAL SCHOLARSHIP

HOUSMAN's appointment to Cambridge gave him the leisure and the higher standard of teaching that his gifts required for their full development. During these years he became recognized as the most eminent Latinist of the century and his name was ranked with Richard Porson's as the greatest of English scholars after Richard Bentley. Still, the nature of Housman's achievement is sufficiently remote from the interests of the general reader to require some explanation.

In the present age of mass education the public has come to expect that the distinguished scholar should, to some extent, act as a popularizer in his own field. He should not, it is held, address himself exclusively to his fellow experts. He should also communicate something of his enjoyment of his studies or pass judgment on them as literature, or relate them to the spirit or the preoccupations of his own times. The work of Gilbert Murray or C. M. Bowra might be taken as representative of this kind of scholarship. Housman's genius was of a different order. It belongs to the older, more austere tradition of scholarship, where it is assumed that the reader can supply his own appreciation and needs only to be furnished with the best possible text. The scholar, for his part, never ventures an aesthetic or moral judgment and limits himself strictly to the role of editor and to the perennial task of detecting and removing errors in the surviving manuscripts. Ideally, this work can absorb an almost unlimited measure of intellectual power, linguistic skill, and poetic sensibility: how far the results may justify the expense of so much talent is another question.

Housman upheld this point of view in his introductory lecture delivered to the combined faculties of University College in 1892. It is an eloquent address, warmer in sentiment, less waspish than his later prose, but its conclusions will fall strangely upon modern ears. The study of the arts and the sciences, he tells us, is often defended by unreal arguments. Science is not necessarily the most ser-

viceable kind of knowledge and its true aim is not to be judged by utilitarian standards. On the other hand, the humanities are praised for their power to transform our inner natures. But in practice only a tiny fraction of the human race can profit from them and they can do so "without that minute and accurate study of the classical tongues which affords Latin professors their only excuse for existence." The only genuine justification for any of these studies, he concludes, is that in their different ways they satisfy man's desire for knowledge, and this innate human appetite is part of man's duty to himself.

The reader is left to conclude that any department of knowledge is of equal value with any other. Housman evidently assumes that the classics will continue to be read, but he does not find it necessary to explain how a work becomes or remains a classic, or why, if a severe philological discipline is the sole raison d'être for professors, it would not be equally valuable for them to study the poetry of the Mayas or the Tibetans.

This, at any rate, was the narrow frame from which Housman's own work never departed. It is true, of course, that the textual expert is often ill-equipped for making literary judgments and, if a warning had been necessary, Housman always had before him the fearful precedent of Bentley's edition of *Paradise Lost* (1732).[2] But in fact Housman was keenly aware of the frontier between textual and appreciative criticism, and the intellectual pride that appears so consistently throughout his classical writings made him a relentless judge of his performance as a literary critic. He wrote explicitly on this point when he declined an invitation to deliver the Clark Lectures on English literature:

> I do regard myself as a connoisseur: I think I can tell good from bad in literature. But literary criticism, referring opinions to principles and setting them forth so as to command assent, is a high and rare accomplishment and quite beyond me. . . . And not only have I no talent for producing the genuine article, but no taste or inclination for producing a substitute. . . .

Since he thus disqualified himself from discussing poetry, his classical writings are of distinctly

---

[2] Bentley put forward the idea that Milton had employed both an amanuensis and an editor, who were held to be responsible for the clerical errors, alterations, and interpolations that Bentley professed to have found in the text.

specialized interest. The most important are the prefaces to his editions of Juvenal, Lucan, and Manilius, in which he sets out his editorial principles; a series of articles on the manuscripts of Propertius; and a paper given in 1921 to the Classical Association and ironically entitled "The Application of Thought to Textual Criticism." Besides these, he published well over a hundred articles in learned journals, notably on the Greek tragedians and on Propertius, Horace, Ovid, and Martial. Most of these papers consist of discussions of isolated textual problems. They are fragmentary reading in themselves, but to read even a few consecutively is a revelation of the intellectual discipline through which Housman developed his gifts. They display the immense range of his knowledge of the classical tongues and of the history of words, his vigilance in detecting corruption, his dexterity and insight in proposing remedies, and, above all, his unrivaled accuracy and patience, which can only have been acquired by a supreme effort of control over a brain so swift in reaching its conclusions.

While he was at the patent office, Housman published as much on Greek as on Latin poetry; after his appointment to University College he virtually ceased to write on Greek. His explanation was that he found he "could not attain to excellence in both" languages. This definition of excellence was all his own, for he certainly possessed more Greek than many professed Hellenists. What he demanded, as the bare essentials, was a complete mastery of grammar and of metrical and verbal usage, a comprehensive knowledge of manuscript history, and, beyond this, the capacity to absorb, year after year, a mass of minute detail bearing directly or indirectly on the chosen field. Judged by these standards, and remembering the far greater complexity of the Greek language and its literature, it becomes easier to understand his decision; and it must be remembered that for Housman's particular talents Latin poetry offered the more tempting prospects. For his choice of the authors he was to edit was influenced more by the ambition to build himself a monument in scholarship than by his personal literary taste.

Housman's approach to editorial problems is sketched in the paper on textual criticism already mentioned, probably the most brilliant outline of the subject that has yet been written in English. Textual criticism, he insists, is by no means a professional mystery, as it is sometimes represented, but a matter of reason and common sense. But he is equally emphatic that it is not an exact science, and nothing angered him more than the so-called scientific approach to manuscript problems, which attempted to solve by a system of rules difficulties that required an independent and flexible judgment:

A textual critic . . . is not at all like Newton investigating the motions of the planets: he is much more like a dog hunting for fleas. If a dog hunted for fleas on mathematical principles, basing his researches on statistics of area and population, he would never catch a flea except by accident. They require to be treated as individuals; and every problem which presents itself to the textual critic must be regarded as possibly unique.
("On the Application of Thought to Textual Criticism," *Selected Prose*, pp. 132–133)

The simile is characteristic. Housman was fond of testing academic generalizations by translating them into some homely and sensuous analogy, because, as he put it, the human senses have had a much longer history than the human intellect and are far less easy to deceive. Another target he singled out was the then fashionable dogma of the supreme authority of the oldest manuscript. According to this theory, the editor, having selected the earliest, is then bound to defend all its readings, unless they are hopelessly corrupt. Housman attacked it unmercifully, and he was among the first to understand, obvious though the truth may seem today, that such a doctrine was bound to become the standby of the laziest and least competent scholars.

When we come to his own editions, many lovers of the classics have found it inexplicable that a man who cared so passionately for poetry could choose for the main object of his life's work an author so little rewarding as Manilius. Lucan, we are told, was selected for him, while Juvenal is a poet entirely worthy of his gifts, whose influence on the tone of Housman's own poetry has perhaps never been fully appreciated. But Manilius, who composed a treatise on astronomy and astrology in the first century A.D., is an author whose poetic merit is less than second-rate and whose scientific value is almost nonexistent, who presents in fact the minimum of interest from any point of view but the professional scholar's. On the other hand, as Andrew Gow tells us, Housman saw in Manilius' text a better prospect "of approaching finality in the solution of the problems presented." He was an ambitious scholar, and it was no coincidence that he chose a poet previously edited by Julius Caesar Scaliger, whose Manilian commentary had been one of the most dazzling achievements of Renaissance scholarship, and by Bentley, the greatest of Housman's predecessors in England. From this point of view, he was taking up a challenge that could extend his powers to the full. This will not prevent many readers from regarding his choice as wayward and eccentric, especially since it involved the sacrifice of a commentary on Propertius, on whose text Housman had done much preliminary work and for whose poetry he cared far more.

Still, it would be wrong to suppose that Housman's poetic sensibility was shut out from his classical work. He possessed a talent excessively rare among scholars, an instinctive familiarity with the way in which poets handle words, and he succeeded in extending this so as to think poetically in the dead languages. In this way he was able to restore or to purify many lines of poetry and to perceive the deeper meaning of phrases obscured for centuries by the errors of scribes and scholiasts. Such a gift, controlled as Housman controlled it, is surely the quality that distinguishes the great from the merely competent textual critic and that guided Housman to many of his most brilliant emendations. Edmund Wilson has noted as a typical example a passage from Juvenal, where in place of the generally accepted reading, *Perditus ac vilis sacci mercator olentis* (The reckless merchant [on a stormy voyage] whose life is cheap [to himself], with his odorous bag of saffron), whose sense, if any, is obscure and labored, Housman by a small change suggests an immediately striking satirical image: *Perditus ac similis sacci mercator olentis* (The reckless merchant . . . turns as yellow as his odorous bag of saffron).

This power of responding to and recreating classical poetry found another outlet in his rare translations. Latin verse, which served as so admired a model to the Augustans, had seldom been translated by the romantics or by their Victorian successors; nor, with the exception of Landor, had it notably influenced their style. Housman's best translation is of the seventh ode of Horace's fourth book, in which his own idiom and diction, conspicuously Saxon though they are, seem perfectly matched to the original:

The snows are fled away, leaves on the shaws
  And grasses in the mead renew their birth,
The river to the river-bed withdraws,
  And altered is the fashion of the earth. . . .

But oh, whate'er the sky-led seasons mar,
  Moon upon moon rebuilds it with her beams:
Come *we* where Tullus and where Ancus are,
  And good Aeneas, we are dust and dreams. . . .
       (*More Poems*, V, "Diffugere Nives")

Housman has preserved the peculiarly Roman gift for expressing poetic commonplaces in monumental style, but his verses, while remarkably exact in their rendering, evoke a different kind of response, biblical in their vocabulary and romantic in the melody of their rhymed quatrains. The Latin speaks with a poignancy unusual in Horace, and Housman's language carries an emotional tension rarely achieved in Augustan translations.

Housman's eminence is inseparable from the moral passion that infused his studies. He possessed to a very high degree the scholar's willingness to sacrifice the present to the future; nothing could have proved this more forcibly than his career at Oxford. He put so much more into scholarship than is commonly understood by the term, making it an ideal that absorbed many of the loyalties and emotions that most men reserve for the world outside. "The faintest of human passions," he once wrote, "is the love of truth": for himself he could genuinely claim the contrary.

In consequence, his high ideal left little room for moderation. For several generations past, the elucidation of the classics had been treated as a subject deserving a calm, urbane, and tolerant approach. Housman did not see the matter in this light. He considered accuracy not a virtue but a duty. He regarded careless or lazy work as an insufferable affront to the dignity of learning, and he could seldom restrain his anger at what seemed to him the organized sloth and complacency of average scholarship. When an editor assigned to Propertius a metrically faulty line, he commented: "This is the mood in which Tereus ravished Philomela: concupiscence concentrated on its object and indifferent to all beside." And he kept a notebook in which shafts of this kind were stored up to be launched at the first deserving recipient. The layman coming fresh to his writings might feel that he was back in the age of pamphleteering, aptly described by Lytton Strachey, when "erudition was gigantic, controversies frenzied, careers punctuated by brutal triumphs, wild temerities and dreadful mortifications."

Housman was as certain of the importance of his work as he was of the rightness of his opinions, and he writes of the operations of scholars in the language of a historian surveying a line of princes:

[Palmer's] talent, like that of Heinsius, resided in felicity of instinct: it did not proceed, like Madvig's, from the perfection of intellectual power. Now the class which includes Heinsius includes also Gilbert Wakefield; and Palmer's rank in the class is nearer to Wakefield than to Heinsius. His inspiration was fitful, and when it failed him he lacked the mental force and rightness which should have filled its place. His was a nimble but not a steady wit: it could ill sustain the labour of severe and continuous thinking; so he habitually shunned that labour. . . . He had much natural elegance of taste, but it was often nullified by caprice and wilfulness, so that hardly Merkel himself has proposed uncouther emendations. . . .
("Palmer's 'Heroides' of Ovid," *Selected Prose*, p. 91)

Though he refrains from passing judgment on the classical poets, he likes to sit as a Rhadamanthus of the world of learning, issuing elaborately qualified verdicts upon dead or living scholars:

Say what you will, he [Jacob] has contributed to the *Astronomica* . . . a body of corrections not only considerable in number but often of the most arresting ingenuity and penetration. Yet the virtues of his work are quenched and smothered by the multitude and monstrosity of his vices. . . . Not only had Jacob no sense for grammar, no sense for coherency, no sense for sense, but being himself possessed by a passion for the clumsy and the hispid he imputed this disgusting taste to all the authors whom he edited; and Manilius, the one Latin poet who excels even Ovid in verbal point and smartness, is accordingly constrained to write the sort of poetry which might have been composed by Nebuchadnezzar when he was driven from men and did eat grass as oxen.
("Prefaces," Manilius I, *Selected Prose*, p. 33)

Housman's supremacy within the limits he set for himself is beyond dispute. The depth of his learning and his capacity to focus it upon minute details, the force of his intellect and the scrupulous honesty with which he applied it (a virtue for which the great Bentley was not conspicuous)—these qualities place him in the front rank of scholars.

Concerning the ultimate value of his approach to the classics, there is less agreement. Scholarship, after all, is not an end in itself; it presupposes an original literature worth preserving, and its tasks may vary greatly from one age to another. A scholar such as Petrarch seeks above all to make discoveries, to stimulate and to fertilize, and at such a moment in history it may be more valuable to kindle enthusiasm than to enforce accuracy. In Bentley's day, the first requirement was a sustained and methodical criticism, to set in order the immense classical inheritance brought to light by the three preceding centuries. In our own age, we are faced with an ominous breakdown in communication between the expert and the layman. The latter is apt to feel that the classics have no relevance for the contemporary world, while the former disdains to make that relevance felt. In such times it is arguable that the greatest need is for scholars to check the fragmentation of our culture, to concentrate upon interpretation and skilled translation as much as on specialized research. Yet to assert this, to speak of "what the age demands," is to speak of lesser men. One might argue that had Housman lived in an earlier century his talents would have produced a richer harvest. But it is idle to regret that a scholar of his caliber, who set himself the highest standards and satisfied them, did not develop differently. At any rate, in the preface to his last volume of Manilius, published very near the end of his life, the question is faced in as uncompromising a fashion as we might expect: "Perhaps there will be no long posterity for learning: but the reader whose good opinion I desire and have done my utmost to secure is the next Bentley or Scaliger who may chance to occupy himself with Manilius."

FAME AND HONORS

It would be misleading to leave the impression that Housman spent his life in unrelieved seclusion. His early years in London were no doubt a painful and lonely experience. But later his growing fame and the duties of academic life imposed more social demands and enriched his circle of acquaintance. At University College he showed himself a formidable debater and impromptu speaker. He wrote light verse, which includes his "Fragment of a Greek Tragedy" —a brilliant parody of the Greek tragic idiom that is unique in English—and a number of excellent nonsense rhymes. Although he was notoriously averse to small talk, he took pleasure in conversation that challenged his interests, and at Cambridge he was at his best in the intimate society of a dining club. He became a renowned connoisseur of wine and his letters speak of travels in Italy, Turkey, and France.

It was in fact the contrast between all that life appeared to offer him, including fame, security, and congenial work, and what he was prepared to make of its rewards that perplexed all who knew him. With scarcely any exceptions Housman kept his friends at arm's length, and his distrust of his fellow men's judgment was not relaxed even when they desired to honor him. "You should be welcome to praise me if you did not praise one another," he once wrote, and this was evidently the motive that inclined him to refuse the doctorates and degrees that many universities offered him. The final honor he declined was the Order of Merit, on the ground that it was not always given to those who deserved it, and in particular that it was already held by an author for whose work Housman felt an extreme distaste. In his letter to the king's secretary, Housman, after respectfully declining the proposed award, went on to quote the words of Admiral William Cornwallis on a similar occasion: "I am, unhappily, of a turn of mind that would make my receiving that honour the most unpleasant thing imaginable."

POETRY AND CRITICISM

When *A Shropshire Lad* first appeared in 1896, it had been rejected by several publishers, among them Macmillan on the advice of John Morley, and it was finally issued at the poet's own expense. At first it was slow to attract attention, but after the Boer War, and indeed for the first quarter of the present century, its reputation grew immensely. It appealed to the sophisticated no less than to a far larger public, for whom the greater part of contemporary verse was a closed book. By the time that *Last Poems* was published in 1922, Housman probably commanded, with the exception of Rudyard Kipling, a wider audience than any contemporary poet in our language. Indeed, on the strength of *A Shropshire Lad* alone, Sir Walter Alexander Raleigh had already referred to him as the greatest living English poet.

Such success did not take Housman unawares, but neither did it alter a mode of life in which his poetry remained a submerged activity. He scarcely ever published in periodicals, and he consistently refused to allow *A Shropshire Lad* to appear in anthologies. He neither wrote about the poetry of others nor expounded his own creative processes, and even in his correspondence, to judge by what his brother has published, poetry is scarcely ever seriously discussed. His one public pronouncement on these subjects, *The Name and Nature of Poetry* (1933), was delivered almost at the end of his life, and then not without severe misgiving before and self-reproach after the event.

Because of this reticence it was generally believed that he had suppressed or destroyed a large number of poems, and it is not surprising that the legend should have grown up of the great scholar sternly disciplining his lyrical gifts and rejecting all but the most perfectly finished products of his muse. In reality, it seems clear that the creative impulse visited him only at rare intervals, and now that all his verses are in print, we may be equally surprised at the inferiority of some of the poems he published and the excellence of others he held back.

During his lifetime, Housman's poetic career presented as much of an enigma as his personal history, and his own actions served to deepen the mystery. The quality of the verse that he consented to publish was unusually consistent both in its merits and its limitations, so that until his unpublished poems were issued posthumously, it was extremely difficult to trace any pattern of development in his work.

The poet himself stated that most of *A Shropshire Lad* was composed during a period "of continuous excitement in the early months of 1895," and that the whole book had been finished at full stretch over eighteen months. Recently, however, the remains of Housman's verse notebooks have been completely and minutely scrutinized by American scholars, and their findings tell a different story. According to his friend Dr. Percy Withers, Housman first set himself seriously to write poetry soon after he had settled in London, his preparation consisting less in practicing versification than in an intensive study of his chosen models, mainly the Border Ballads, the songs of Shakespeare, and the lyrics of Heinrich Heine. For four or five years progress was painfully slow, but the notebooks suggest that his inspiration had begun to move freely as far back as 1890. The first five months of 1895 thus represent the climax of his creative power during which twenty-three of the sixty-three *Shropshire Lad* lyrics were drafted or finished; 1895, in fact, was his *annus mirabilis,* for in its later months were written not only the remaining third of *A Shropshire Lad* but drafts of some half-dozen pieces which later appear in *Last Poems,* and a still larger number good enough to be preserved for the posthumous *More Poems* (1936). There followed a prolonged aftermath of six years, during which fewer and fewer new poems were begun, and after 1902 the creative flow dwindled to a trickle until, apparently under the excitement of preparing *Last Poems,* it returned briefly in 1922.

Grant Richards, Housman's publisher after 1897, quoted him as saying early in their association, "I am not a poet by trade. I am a professor of Latin." Behind this statement one may read something other than modesty—namely, a disinclination to commit himself to the spiritual and material hazards of a career dedicated to poetry. His creative period had flung him, we are told, into an intense emotional disturbance whose recurrence he dreaded, and after it he may well have felt that poetry for him must be an accomplishment, not a vocation, a gift to be used as circumstances might allow, not a continually dominating presence with power to shape his life according to the changing stresses of experience.

The chronology of his poetry, so far as it can be established, confirms the impression that his style was formed early and that his verses at sixty or later display almost exactly the same qualities, marvelously unimpaired and yet undeveloped, as those he wrote as a young man. There are differences in tone and in his attitude to his material, but it is difficult to fasten upon any single composition as a landmark in his development, particularly since a number of the poems that appeared after *A Shropshire Lad* contain revisions carried out at widely separate periods. Reading the posthumously published poems, one often comes upon identical epithets or turns of phrase echoed with equally striking effects in a different context, and in this sense his poetry resembles a single perpetual "work in progress."

At present Housman's verse is passing through a necessary critical revaluation; 1922 saw the appearance both of *Last Poems* and of *The Waste Land,* and the year might serve, crudely, to mark an end and a beginning in English poetry, with Housman's work standing on the far side of the rift in poetic idiom that the modern movement has produced. For the very reason that Housman presents none of the difficulties of later poets, his work has suffered from uncritical admiration and all too frequent imitation, and when a poetic revolution takes place, the penalty for contemporary popularity of this kind is apt to be overpaid.

Housman began to write at a time when the romantic tradition, as inherited by the major Victorian poets, had all but exhausted its resources, and he felt strongly how stale the current poetic jargon had

become in the hands of writers such as Andrew Lang and Arthur O'Shaughnessy.[3] Yet in the light of what was to come, his own approach might be called backward looking. He did not feel the need for fresh patterns of verbal association nor for changes in poetic structure: in later life he never became sympathetic to experiments in free verse nor to the abandonment of rhyme, and he regarded Bridges's praise of Hopkins' poetry, cautious though that was, as no more than a personal foible.

Today it is easier to recognize the traces in his work of the spirit of the 1890's; in particular the fastidiousness of expression—was there ever a period in which men trimmed and pared their writing so assiduously?—the choice of minor poetic forms and the note of weary disillusionment, the view of life as something to be endured:

> When shall this slough of sense be cast,
> This dust of thoughts be laid at last,
> The man of flesh and soul be slain
> And the man of bone remain?
>   ("The Immortal Part,"
>   *A Shropshire Lad,* XLIII)

And it is noticeable that the five-line rhyming stanza of "Bredon Hill" and other lyrics was a favorite meter of Ernest Dowson's.

Housman himself, however, remained severely aloof from the poetic coteries that flourished in London at this time. He was older than Lionel Johnson, Dowson, and most of the members of the Rhymers' Club, and in any case the leanings of this group toward ritualism combined with a Bohemian life on the Parisian model must have been thoroughly antipathetic to his temperament. Many years afterward, replying to an editor who sought permission to include him in an anthology of the period, Housman wrote that it would be as technically correct and as essentially inappropriate to reprint his poems in such a collection as to include Lot in a book on the cities of the plain.

Certainly what most impressed the early readers of *A Shropshire Lad* was its *unlikeness* to the prevailing idiom. Here apparently was a poet who could voice the familiar passions of humanity with a strange, death-dealing sweetness in sharp contrast to the current urban poetry of languor and exotic sensibility. The contrast is striking enough, yet the

---

[3]See *The Name and Nature of Poetry* (London, 1933), p. 23.

simplicity is deceptive. The primitive ballad meters, which Housman revived, are employed for a poetry not of action but of introspection. The diction is natural at some moments, artificial at others, a curious yet assured blend of the archaic and the colloquial. In Housman's hands these were genuine achievements, but they were also poetic ventures that none but he could execute—a mile farther, says William Butler Yeats of *A Shropshire Lad,* and all had been marsh.

In his early style there are echoes of the shorter poems of Bridges and of the martial measures of Kipling and William Ernest Henley, and an affinity, which cannot have been conscious, to the rustic lyrics of Thomas Hardy. Housman's poem "The Sage to the Young Man" is remarkably reminiscent of Bridges's "O Youth whose hope is high," but one has only to see the two side by side to feel the far stronger impact of the former. It is this power to communicate direct and personal emotion, through a language that lodges instantly in the brain, that distinguishes Housman from all the poets of this period.

The comparison with Hardy is more illuminating. Housman also, it might appear, sought his inspiration in a part of England that still pursued the traditions of country life, uncontaminated by the Industrial Revolution. Like Hardy, too, he had been led by the scientific materialism of the age to form a deeply pessimistic view of human destiny, judging it to be ruled by forces absolutely indifferent to moral values. But Housman's gift for exquisite description of nature has obscured the difference between his poetry and that of a genuinely rural writer such as Hardy or John Clare. Housman was not a countryman, nor did he enjoy talking or mingling with rustics. It is easily forgotten that he spent the years between twenty-three and fifty-two almost continuously in London, and that the scenes of *A Shropshire Lad* were the product of his inward eye as he walked on Hampstead Heath. His friends have noted that he was indifferent to country landscape, though he was peculiarly sensitive to the shape and characteristics of trees. When he writes of them in a poem such as "The orchards half the way," the force and beauty of his language serve not so much to describe as to intensify them as dramatic symbols of a particular state of emotion.

Thus, at first glance, *A Shropshire Lad* is written in the character of a country youth uprooted from his surroundings and exiled to a hostile metropolis where he clings to his memories of a simpler life. But it is soon clear that "Shropshire" is not a native heath with a solid existence such as Hardy's Wessex. It is rather a personification of the writer's memories, dreams, and affections. In order to make his emotions articulate, Housman apparently needed an imaginary setting and a central character who could at once be himself and not himself.

This need to construct a personal world of the imagination, perhaps as a defense against the overwhelming inhumanity of city life, seems to have been shared by other poets of the same period. The gaslit and theatrical Bohemia of Arthur Symons and Dowson, the engine room of Kipling, the world of childhood and the supernatural of Walter de la Mare are sufficiently diverse instances of the same process. Housman found his mythology in the local tragedies of rustic life, the ballads of the country youths whose sweethearts die young or desert them, who are hanged in Shrewsbury jail for crimes of passion, or who commit suicide or take the queen's shilling[4] to march away and fall on fields forgotten. In such episodes he could express his indignation at the injustice of human destiny, and he did so by infusing into the pastoral convention a new note of irony. Pastoral poetry traditionally makes its appeal by invoking a countryside where youth seems eternal, and the calm and simplicity of nature are praised by contrast with the feverish corruption of a great capital. Housman's Shropshire is a blighted Arcadia, in which the poet is constantly reminded of the limitations of mortality. Here the beauty of the countryside only intensifies the pain of his experience, since Nature, he feels, is utterly indifferent to the emotions she arouses in him. Love, which alone might redeem our lives, does no more than beguile us with hope; then it proves to be unrequited or is cut short by a harsh fate:

> His folly has not fellow
> Beneath the blue of day
> That gives to man or woman
> His heart and soul away.
> (XIV)

The brave and the true gain nothing from their virtue, and indeed they are best out of a world that will never reward their qualities:

---

[4]A recruit was paid the bounty of one shilling when he signed on. This practice continued until 1879.

Be still, be still, my soul; it is but for a season:
Let us endure an hour and see injustice done.

(LVIII)

Apart from this commerce with the outer world, Shropshire represents a more inward experience. The Shropshire hills, as we have seen, formed the western boundary of Housman's childhood, and the memory of them suggests to him a lost state of innocence and happiness. At its simplest, this feeling is communicated in the poems that lament his separation from the countryside:

Oh tarnish late on Wenlock Edge,
    Gold that I never see;
Lie long, high snowdrifts in the hedge
    That will not shower on me.

(XXXIX)

It is pursued less overtly in a group of poems that seem to gather up the various themes of the book and to form its keystone; Housman lights upon the exact metaphor for this state of mind when he discovers, with a sharp thrust of irony, that the very recollection of the countryside serves no longer to invigorate but only to torment:

Into my heart an air that kills
    From yon far country blows;
What are those blue remembered hills,
    What spires, what farms are those?

That is the land of lost content,
    I see it shining plain,
The happy highways where I went
    And cannot come again.

(XL)

Last Poems represents the gleanings of several harvests. Most of its poems date from the *Shropshire Lad* period and its immediate aftermath, while a few others are associated with the Edwardian decade and World War I. In 1920 Housman decided to set in order the work of twenty-five years, and the effort of revising and completing his drafts set him writing again. Some of these late lyrics—"Eight o'clock," for example—are an astonishing echo of his youthful style; others, such as "Tell me not here, it needs not saying," inspired by his declared farewell to poetry, touch a note of elegiac tenderness richer than anything he had written before. Compared to *A Shropshire Lad*, the book appears uneven in quality; it

contains some of Housman's tritest pieces, such as "Grenadier" or "Lancer," and it leaves an impression of less sustained power. Yet the style is more completely Housman's own, and the language at its best still more inevitable, so that the reader at times is scarcely conscious of description, so completely are the words identified with the mood and scene they create:

When the eye of day is shut,
    And the stars deny their beams,
And about the forest hut
    Blows the roaring wood of dreams,

From deep clay, from desert rock,
    From the sunk sands of the main,
Come not at my door to knock,
    Hearts that loved me not again.

(XXXIII)

Here also one meets for the first time several poems on astronomical subjects. Such imagery intensified Housman's sense of the power and indifference of the surrounding universe and of man's insignificance upon his turning planet. In "Revolution" the poet watches the alternations of day and night with the eye of a celestial mechanic:

See, in mid heaven the sun is mounted; hark,
    The belfries tingle to the noonday chime.
'Tis silent, and the subterranean dark
    Has crossed the nadir, and begins to climb.

(XXXVI)

Cold and disciplined, these are among the most faultless of Housman's poems, approaching unexpectedly close to the territory of wit, which he professed to abhor in poetry. There are echoes of them in a successor whose work bears other traces of Housman's influence, W. H. Auden.

Laurence Housman, as literary executor, was authorized to print all the finished poems that he considered not inferior to the average of those already published, and, thanks to his editorial tact, another seventy-two poems have been preserved. This collection defines the full range of Housman's verse and, since his earlier poems often take their effect in hit-or-miss fashion, it illustrates more clearly, by means of other similar attempts, the nature of his successes and failures. The full range, of course, is still a very narrow one. Housman is a repetitive writer and he was clearly right to publish only a selection of his poetry to avoid diluting its effect. *More Poems* and the "Additional Poems" (eighteen poems that have not been published separately but are included in his *Collected Poems*) consist of pieces that either could not be fitted into his thematic arrangement or that he felt echoed what he had already published. Yet both categories contain lyrics that can stand beside his finest work. It is difficult to understand why he could not find room for such truly classical pieces as "Crossing alone the nighted ferry" or the beautiful poem on Hero and Leander, "Tarry delight, so seldom met." Others, such as the "Easter Hymn" or his farewell to Venice, provoke regret that his themes are normally so restricted. Those poems devoted to battlefields and soldiers' graves, on the other hand, almost suggest a parody of his manner. Certainly the instinct to suppress these was sound, but it is impossible not to be struck by the unsureness with which Housman writes of this subject.

War is one of the dominant themes in his poetry, and the life of physical action clearly held a special excitement for him, no less strong because it was so remote from his own. In his early poems he takes pride in the martial virtues as a part of his rural heritage, and they are linked too with his feeling that youth is the supreme testing time of life. In *A Shropshire Lad*, written in an era of apparently endless peace and security, war is merely a heroic fantasy, a rumble that falls thrillingly upon the ears of rustic lovers but never approaches nearer than the frontiers of empire:

> On the idle hill of summer,
>   Sleepy with the flow of streams,
> Far I hear the steady drummer
>   Drumming like a noise in dreams.
>   (XXXV)

Last Poems, besides several excessively literary pieces on the same theme, contains others directly inspired by the Boer War and World War I. For these he chose a formal, epigrammatic style reminiscent of the classic military epitaphs of Simonides, though the tone is quite distinct:

> For pay and medals, name and rank,
>   Things that he has not found,
> He hove the Cross to heaven and sank
>   The pole-star underground.
>   ("Astronomy," XVII)

So Housman wrote of his younger brother killed in South Africa, and this note of irony is sounded still more decisively in the famous "Epitaph on an Army of Mercenaries":

> Their shoulders held the sky suspended;
>   They stood, and earth's foundations stay;
> What God abandoned, these defended,
>   And saved the sum of things for pay.
>   (XXXVII)

A Greek poet could use understatement in this context because it epitomized the Spartan code, which was the Hellenic military ideal, but the homage that Simonides wishes to communicate is quite unreserved. It is difficult for a modern poet to praise war so unequivocally. Hardy, in his Boer War poem "Drummer Hodge," is moved above all by the pathos of the ignorant country boy who never knew the meaning of the broad Karoo and the southern stars. Housman, not wishing to pay a conventional tribute, strengthens his effect by stressing the element for which all can agree the sacrifice was *not* made. War, or the trade of man, as he calls it, remained for him a subject that, at worst, demanded a certain decorum of treatment: it never presented itself, as it did to other poets, as a target for satire, yet his irony still preserves the edge of his poem, after more explicit denunciations have lost much of theirs.

Housman is often praised as a "classical" writer, but this verdict needs a good deal of qualification. He is a poet who borrows freely, though with distinction, and his style is more strongly influenced by the language of the Old Testament and of Shakespeare than by the Greek or Latin poets. The classical element, in fact, is more apparent in the outward form than in the spirit of his verse. His poems often suggest the effect of a vase painting, of a clear-cut design dexterously executed within narrow limits, and the strictness of his versification, his inversions of word order, and his skill in placing his isolated, significant epithets all strengthen this impression. Certainly classical history and mythology often enrich his imagery and provide a core for his poems. "The Oracles," for example, follows closely Herodotus' description of the Spartan sang-froid before Thermopylae, and its seven-foot lines echo the rough hexameters in which the Delphic Oracle uttered its prophecies. And the epigram on the Boer War,

> Here dead lie we because we did not choose
>   To live and shame the land from which we sprung.

Life, to be sure, is nothing much to lose;
But young men think it is, and we were young.
(*More Poems*, XXXVI)

has a possible ancestor in the epitaph attributed to Simonides on the Athenian dead at Chalcis:

A gift desired, for youth is sweet
And youth we gave, nor turned away,
Though sharp the tide of battle beat,
That darkened all our day.

Where Housman parts company from the classical spirit is in the emotional appeal of many of his poems. Though he rejects any belief in an afterlife, at the same time he rails against the very conditions of human existence. The classical poets, though they may warn us to count no man happy until he is dead, have nonetheless come to terms with the mortal state: suffering is not for them to be softened into a yearning for death, nor do they undervalue the gift of life itself:

The joys I have possessed, in spite of fate, are mine.
Not Heaven itself upon the past has power;
But what has been, has been, and I have had my hour.
(Dryden trans., Horace, *Odes* III. 29.8)

John Dryden's verses are an utterance of the classical spirit; in Housman, on the contrary, we find that aspiration constantly outruns fulfillment. There are exceptions, but these, significantly, are mostly found among those poems that he did not publish. His poetry in fact occupies an ambiguous position between two worlds of feeling; this lends them a special poignancy but also leaves them peculiarly exposed to the dangers of false or facile sentiment.

Housman works always to a simple and distinctly conceived idea of the form a poem should take. His verse is almost brutally explicit and quite contradicts the ideal of pure poetry that he upholds in *The Name and Nature of Poetry*, perhaps because he did not possess the gift of sustained melody. His poetry often came to him in snatches, the gaps having to be filled in by conscious effort, and to write in this way he needed a regular metrical framework. He has been censured for the monotony of his versification, and there is force in this criticism, for he lacks the metrical subtlety of Yeats or de la Mare. His meters are primitive and his pauses heavy, at times even mechanical. But they are appropriate for the particular tones that he wished to render, for most of his

lyrics are tinged with an element of the dramatic or the rhetorical. The four-line rhymed stanza, with the lines alternating between eight and six beats, is pressed so strongly into this service that it comes to represent the typical mood and cadence of a Housman poem, in which the note of challenge is sounded in the longer line and subsides in negation in the shorter:

June suns, you cannot store them
To warm the winter's cold,
The lad that hopes for heaven
Shall fill his mouth with mould.
(*More Poems*, XXII)

The characteristic effects are those of paradox, sudden poignancy, unexpected irony, and to achieve these, the ear needs to be led on by a smooth versification to the epithet or rhyme that is the point of stress. For this purpose too he employs a closely knit syntax in which nouns and verbs carry the main weight of his images:

Or beeches strip in storms for winter
And stain the wind with leaves.
(*Last Poems*, XL)

Their effect is often reinforced by alliteration, which creates a peculiar harmony and interdependence of sound and sense. He uses epithets sparingly, but when he does they are often inspired inventions: such phrases as "light-leaved spring," "felon-quarried stone," "the bluebells of the listless plain" perfectly combine a decorative with an emotional value in their context. His brother has pointed out how frequently Housman's capacity for self-criticism improved his poetry; how, for example, in the poem "Be still, my soul," the alternatives—vex, plague, tear, wrench, rend, wring, break, and pierce —were all rejected before the line took its final shape: "All thoughts to *rive* the heart are here, and all are vain."

The lecture on *The Name and Nature of Poetry* provoked, partly for fortuitous reasons, a considerable stir when it was delivered. Housman's personal distinction and the fact that this was his first and only venture into literary criticism had aroused high expectations. The poetic values that it defends, which Housman had long held, might be described as an extension of the position established by Matthew Arnold, and this part of the lecture, uttered twenty or even ten years earlier, would hardly have excited much comment. But by 1933 the shift in critical opinion, which had received such an impetus from Eliot, was already well under way, so that Housman's words were naturally interpreted as something of a counterattack in defense of the romantic conception of poetry. Looking back, however, and particularly in view of his avowed difficulty in writing the lecture, it seems unlikely that he was consciously entering upon controversy. In any case it is important to remember that this is a lecture, not a treatise, and that its virtues are those which belong to a formal public utterance of limited length. It is superbly phrased, it possesses wit, provocative emphasis, and felicity of quotation. It gives the verdict of a great classical scholar upon the English neoclassical poets, and it modifies Arnold's superficial and evasive estimate of Dryden and Alexander Pope. But it is not a fully developed critical position. Housman once more disclaims the office of critic, and what he offers, far from being a twentieth-century Poetics, is no more than a statement of what poetry meant to him.

He is more confident that he can feel poetry than that he can define it. He offers, in passing, various tentative definitions, none of which can be pressed very closely—"poetry seems to me more physical than intellectual," "meaning is of the intellect, poetry is not." But he is categorical in laying down what is *not* poetry, and here his taste excludes metaphysical poetry and the bulk of the verse produced between Milton's *Samson Agonistes* (1671) and William Wordsworth and Samuel Taylor Coleridge's *Lyrical Ballads* (1798). The most poetical of all writers for him is William Blake who, he says, gives us poetry "adulterated with so little meaning that nothing except poetic emotion is perceived and matters."

In saying this, Housman places himself with those critics who identify the poetic process with communication rather than with expression. He is also tacitly following the modern tendency to pass over architectonic qualities in poetry and to regard the lyric as somehow intrinsically more poetical than dramatic or narrative poetry. This point of view, he freely admits, is influenced by his own experience of composition. His description of how his own poetry came to be produced is the best-known part of the lecture, and his normal reticence gives what he had to say on this subject an authority all the more commanding. But it is plain that the process he describes could apply only to the composition of lyrics and not to the major literary forms, in which construction, balance, and sustained creative energy have an important part to play.

In the end, the only infallible criterion that Housman admits is the instinctive reaction that poetry produced upon his physical and nervous system. This verdict is startling, coming from a scholar whom one would suppose to be steeped in the teaching of Plato, Aristotle, and Horace on the moral basis of poetry; on the other hand, Housman had given warning that he regarded true literary criticism as the rarest of gifts, and any other kind as possessing no more authority than personal taste. It is not very profitable, in short, to analyze his lecture in detail. A poet often works by intuitions that he cannot explain any more satisfactorily than anyone else, and *The Name and Nature of Poetry* is best read as a statement not of critical doctrine but of a poet's instincts.

When a decisive change takes place in poetic taste, such as has been experienced in the last sixty years, not only a poet's virtues and vices, but even his aims and much that he has taken for granted, come to be differently regarded. Few writers of so slender an output can have satisfied so fully—for a time even molded—the poetic ideals of their generation as did Housman; in the event, he has suffered the fate of a minor poet thrust by popularity into the role of a major one, in that his verse has been acclaimed as much for its message as for its strictly poetic excellence, and its imperfections overlooked. In judging his work today, it is surely an advantage that our sensibility has turned to a different, more complex ideal of poetic art and that the shortcomings of Housman's pessimistic philosophy have become more apparent.

Housman's original inspiration sprang from the emotions of youth, the period when untried ideals and untutored desires at their strongest first encounter a hostile or indifferent world. At his best, he can voice these passions with an extraordinary force, with a sensuous yet cold fury—"fire and ice within me fight"—in which feeling, language, and meter are completely fused. But at this stage of emotional development he stops short. The rest of his experience is measured by the same standards, and indeed much of the emotion of his later poetry springs precisely from this vehement refusal to come to terms with life's demands and disillusionments. His choice is to reject the cup, to condemn the human situation proudly and without compromise. He would not have conceded, as Yeats could do:

I am content to live it all again
And yet again, if it be life to pitch
Into the frog-spawn of a blind man's ditch. . . .

These limitations in Housman's outlook and choice of material are familiar enough. There remain his superb powers of expression, the capacity to write verses of great poetry, if not to be a great poet. In his prose and verse alike, Housman is limited to the short flight and the minor form; but for the strength and purity of his expression, he can take his place in the company of the acknowledged masters of the English tongue. In an age of constant confusion and debasement of speech he has stood forth as one of the true heirs of the language, in whom its latent riches, the passionate simplicity of Anglo-Saxon, the splendor and eloquence of Latin, have once more found a voice. At his best he possesses the indefinable poetic faculty of conferring on words a new life, so that one turns eagerly to any new Housman fragment not so much for a fresh poetic experience as for some sudden felicity of language. Much was sacrificed for these ideals, but he possesses them securely; the command of words and the proud integrity with which he practiced it are his greatest gifts.

SELECTED BIBLIOGRAPHY

I. BIBLIOGRAPHY. J. Carter and J. Sparrow, *A. E. Housman: An Annotated Handlist* (London, 1952), annotations contain important biographical material.

II. COLLECTED AND SELECTED WORKS. *Collected Poems* (London, 1939), repr. in the Cape paperback series (1967); *Collected Poems* (London, 1956), in the "Penguin Poets" series; J. Carter, ed., *Selected Prose* (London, 1961), contains lectures mentioned below, several of Housman's most important papers on classical subjects, including critical prefaces to his eds. of Manilius and Juvenal, "On the Application of Thought to Textual Criticism," and selection of reviews, letters to the press, and other occasional writings; F. C. Horwood, ed., *Poetry and Prose: A Selection* (London, 1971).

III. SEPARATE WORKS. *Introductory Lecture*, University College, London (London, 1892; privately repr. 1933; repr. 1937); *A Shropshire Lad* (London, 1896), verse; *Last Poems* (London, 1922); A. Platt, *Nine Essays* (London, 1927), contains important preface by Housman; *The Name and Nature of Poetry* (London, 1933), the 1933 Leslie Stephen Lecture; *More Poems* (London, 1936); *The Confines of Criticism* (London, 1969), complete text of Housman's Cambridge Inaugural Lecture, 1911, with notes by J. Carter; J. Diggle and F. R. D. Goodyear, eds., *The Classical Papers of A. E. Housman*, 3 vols. (London, 1972).

IV. CLASSICAL TEXTS. *M. Manilii: Astronomicon*, 5 vols. (London, 1903–1930), repr. in 1 vol. (1932); *D. Ivnii Ivvenalis: Satvrae* (London, 1905; 2nd ed., corrected, 1931); *M. Annaei Lucani: Belli Civilis Libri Decem* (Oxford, 1926; 2nd ed., corrected, 1927).

V. LETTERS. T. B. Haber, ed., *Thirty Letters to Witter Bynner* (New York, 1957); H. Maas, ed., *The Letters of A. E. Housman* (London, 1971).

VI. BIOGRAPHICAL AND CRITICAL STUDIES. H. W. Garrod, *The Profession of Poetry* (London, 1929), includes lecture on Housman as poet and scholar; A. S. F. Gow, *A. E. Housman* (London, 1936), sketch with definitive handlist of Housman's contributions to classical scholarship, and other prose papers; *"The Bromsgrovian": Housman Memorial Supplement* (London, 1936), this supplement to Housman's old school magazine contains reminiscences and appreciations by his brother, his sister, and other hands, published in book form (New York, 1937); L. Housman, *A. E. H.: Some Poems, Some Letters and a Personal Memoir* (London, 1937), includes quotations from Housman's letters and notebooks and 18 additional poems never published separately but contained in *Collected Poems*; E. Wilson, *The Triple Thinkers* (London, 1938), contains essay on Housman's scholarship; R. W. Chambers, *Man's Unconquerable Mind* (London, 1939), contains sketch of Housman's career at University College, London; H. W. Garrod, "Housman: 1939," in *Essays and Studies*, XXV (London, 1939); P. Withers, *A Buried Life* (London, 1940); G. Richards, *Housman: 1897–1936* (London, 1941), biographical study by Housman's first publisher, includes appendix by G. B. Fletcher analyzing classical influences in Housman's poetry; C. Connolly, *The Condemned Playground* (London, 1945), contains article on Housman and the subsequent controversial letters in response, repr. from the *New Statesman*; T. B. Haber, *The Manuscript Poems of A. E. Housman* (London, 1955), publishes for the first time a large number of fragments and lines from Housman's MS notebooks (previously excluded from publication by Laurence Housman under the terms of his brother's will) in the Library of Congress; also discusses chronology of the poems; G. L. Watson, *A. E. Housman: A Divided Life* (London, 1957); N. Marlow, *A. E. Housman: Scholar and Poet* (London, 1958), sensitive study of biographical rather than critical interest; T. B. Haber, *A. E. Housman* (New York, 1967); C. Ricks, ed., *A. E. Housman: A Collection of Critical Essays* (London, 1969), in the Twentieth Century Views series; B. J. Leggett, *Housman's Land of Lost Content: A Critical Study of A Shropshire Lad* (Lincoln, Nebr., 1970); B. J. Leggett, *The Poetic Art of A. E. Housman* (Lincoln, Nebr., 1978); R. P. Graves, *A. E. Housman. The Scholar Poet* (London, 1979).

RUDYARD KIPLING

(1865-1936)

A. G. Sandison

The man Kipling, the myth Kipling, is over; but the stories themselves have all the time in the world.

(Randall Jarrell)

FOR decades it has been customary to preface any study of Kipling with either an apology or a highly specific justification for doing anything so displeasing to the clerisy and potentially damaging to the critic's own academic reputation. Yet since the 1960's a number of commentators have struggled to show that to confuse Kipling with the idea of empire is to create a barrier to understanding both. Moreover, time is on the side of those who fight against the confusion. As Britain's imperial heyday becomes more and more remote, Kipling begins to emerge from the imperial shadows as a writer of formidable talent.

This study, therefore, lays most of its stress on Kipling's artistic achievement. He was, quite simply, one of the greatest—some would say *the* greatest—short-story writer England has produced.

I

RUDYARD KIPLING was born on 30 December 1865 in Bombay, where his father had gone earlier that year to take up an appointment as a teacher of utilitarian technical crafts (designing and manufacturing terracotta pottery and architectural sculpture) in a recently established school of art. While he labored at these humble tasks in the exotic East, his friends and relatives were spearheading the increasingly successful arts and crafts movement in England.

John Lockwood Kipling was one of many children of a poorly paid Methodist minister. After leaving school he worked as a designer and modeler, and attended art school before becoming assistant to an architectural sculptor in London. In 1865 he married Alice Macdonald, whose father was also a Methodist minister. Hers too was a large family; the daughters were particularly celebrated for their beauty and wit and, ultimately, for their distinguished marriages: one to Edward (later Sir Edward) Burne-Jones, the Pre-Raphaelite painter; another to Edward (later Sir Edward) Poynter, in time president of the Royal Academy; and a third to Alfred Baldwin, an iron manufacturer (their son, Stanley Baldwin, was elected three times as prime minister of Great Britain).

In financial terms, Alice's marriage was not, initially at least, successful, and she herself wrote for magazines and local papers to eke out the family income. But though their position on the Anglo-Indians'[1] social scale was not high, they enjoyed the privileges and comforts that went with being members of the "imperial race." Consequently young Rudyard had not only his *ayah,* or nurse, but also his own manservant; and during the first five years of his life so much of his time was spent with them that they were the people he was most strongly inclined to identify with. Sharing their superstitions and their secrets, attending religious ceremonies and rituals of considerable diversity, he was rather more in their society than that of his parents, and he had learned to speak Hindi before he mastered English.

In 1871 the Kiplings returned briefly to England to leave their two children—Alice ("Trix") had been born in 1868—to be educated there. The practice was common, because of the exceptionally high mortality rate among young European children who remained in India and because of their need for an adequate education. (Sir Angus Wilson, in *The Strange Ride of Rudyard Kipling,* 1977, suggests that there was also a chauvinistic element in such a practice: the children were sent home to "make sure of their roots.")

[1]The term used by Kipling and his contemporaries to signify the British residing in India.

What was extraordinary, however, in such loving—and loved—parents was that they gave no warning of their intentions to the children. Compounding this error, they were easily reassured about the suitability of the selected foster parents. The result was that Rudyard and Trix found themselves inexplicably abandoned by their parents in a dreary house on the south coast of England dominated by a formidably disagreeable lady whom they were obliged to call Aunty Rosa. Whether she was quite as cruel as she is portrayed in "Baa, Baa Black Sheep" and *The Light That Failed* (1890) is not easy to establish, but the small boy was systematically bullied, beaten, and generally victimized by her for the next six years.

From being the center of attention of an entire household, idolized and pampered by servants, Kipling was at the age of six plunged into an environment that was almost the very opposite of the only one he had ever known. Though he survived mentally intact, surprisingly enough, he was far from being unscathed. In all sorts of ways his fiction is colored by the experience, and not just in the relatively superficial sense of dealing much in hallucinations, nightmares, and mental breakdowns. From this early time came, too, the misery of insomnia, with which he was plagued for the whole of his life and which came to play such an important part in his literary imagination.

There was one important source of relief and refuge from "the House of Desolation," as Kipling called Aunty Rosa's establishment. Each Christmas until he was ten, he and his sister went to stay with their Aunt Georgie and her husband, Edward Burne-Jones. These vacations represented an experience so totally at odds with life in Southsea that the Burne-Jones home—"the Grange" in Fulham—took on the character of a magical world. There they met other children, watched magic-lantern shows, played boisterous games (ably led by Burne-Jones himself), joined in the music-making, and generally took part in all the high-spirited fun that characterized the household at this time of year.

But the Grange was a great deal more than just a very good place to spend Christmas. For nearly thirty years it was to be a favorite meeting place of many of the most talented artists and writers of the time. It was at the heart of what might be described as the second wave of the Pre-Raphaelite movement and of that part of the arts and crafts movement which centered on William Morris and his associates in what

became known as "the Firm" (actually named Morris, Marshall, Faulkner, and Co., manufacturers and decorators).

Three men closely involved with this radical and innovative group were in a position to influence the young Kipling, and two of them, Burne-Jones and Cormell Price, undoubtedly did so; a third, William Morris, was influential, too, but in a less direct and personal way, even though the children had, at the Grange's Christmas festivities, made him an honorary uncle. Burne-Jones was the closest of all to Kipling. When he died in 1898 Kipling, then living in Rottingdean, wrote to a friend that his Uncle Ned had been "more to me than any other man. He changed my life by his visits down here."

Cormell Price ("Uncle Corm") was a friend of Burne-Jones and had been a painter of promise. More to the point, he was headmaster of the United Services College at Westward Ho! in Devon, which Kipling attended until he was nearly seventeen. Aware of the boy's enthusiasm for literature, Price gave him access to his own exceptionally well-stocked library and quite clearly helped to develop his literary taste.

Charles Carrington in *The Life of Rudyard Kipling* (1955) sums up the young Kipling and his world as he came to the end of his schooldays:

> He was a rebel and a progressive which is to say, in 1882 paradoxically—that he was a decadent. His friends, his teachers, were liberals, his tastes were "aesthetic," the writers he most admired were the fashionable pessimists. . . .
>
> In the holidays he vanished into a world that differed profoundly from that known to the average officer's family. . . . At the Poynters' or at the Burne-Jones's, as in his father's house, all the talk was of the fine arts and in the jargon of the studio.
>
> (p. 31)

Carrington refers there to the influence of "his father's house," and John Lockwood Kipling's role in shaping his son's taste must also be acknowledged. Throughout his life Kipling was exceptionally devoted to his parents and eagerly sought his father's help and advice when he wanted to talk over problems of composition. John Kipling is the model of the curator of the Lahore museum in *Kim* (1901), and the role is a peculiarly apt one for him to play; his granddaughter recalled that his "knowledge of every art and craft, even the most unusual, was amazing, while his skill with his hands was a joy to watch."

And he shared the artistic priorities and sympathies of his friends Price and Burne-Jones.

What then did these avant-garde artists, in whose ambience Kipling grew up, stand for? Among the more easily defined objectives of the original Pre-Raphaelite Brotherhood (which had been founded somewhat accidentally in 1848 by a group of young painters very resentful of the power and conservatism of the Royal Academy) was the necessity of turning the eyes of painters and of the public back again to nature and away from what they saw as a sterile classicism. But in "painting directly from nature" they were nonetheless to imbue their work with a strong ethical and narrative content and to choose for their themes subject matter that was explicitly moral and religious. Under the influence of the painter and poet Dante Gabriel Rossetti they were also encouraged to regard poetry, painting, and social idealism as organically linked.

Despite the introspective and mystical bent of much Pre-Raphaelite work, it was the painters' so-called realism, deriving from their close attention to minuteness and precision of detail, that attracted the most censure. Sir John Everett Millais' *Christ in the House of His Parents* was considered typical in its effrontery: "a pictorial blasphemy," the *Athenaeum* called it, from which all decent people would "recoil with horror and disgust." To the *Times* (London) it was "plainly revolting," having the temerity to associate "the Holy Family with the meanest details of a carpenter's shop, with no considerable omission of misery, of dirt, and even disease, all finished with the same loathsome minuteness." Even Charles Dickens, though he later made amends, joined in the general denunciation. Yet in many ways, as John Dixon Hunt points out in *The Pre-Raphaelite Imagination 1848–1900* (1968), painters like Millais and Holman Hunt were Victorian in their attempts, as Holman Hunt put it, to "make more tangible Jesus Christ's history and teaching." Dixon Hunt also makes the point that their exact and detailed representation of objects is less an end in itself than a suggestion of greater things.

In social subjects the Pre-Raphaelites were certainly capable of challenging accepted orthodoxies. Two of Rossetti's pictures have a prostitute as a central figure; Hunt's *The Awakened Conscience* shows the misery of a "kept woman"; and even Burne-Jones published a short story, "The Cousins," which in its depiction of squalor and misery could be taken as a forerunner of Kipling's excellent story—much ac-claimed for its originality and frankness—"The Record of Badalia Herodsfoot."

Other characteristics that the Pre-Raphaelite Brotherhood shared were an intensity of both feeling and color, a tendency to look back nostalgically to the past, and—increasingly—a rejection of the ugliness and materialism that industrial success had brought to Britain. Burne-Jones was closely associated with these last-named reactions, declaring uncompromisingly that "the more materialistic science becomes, the more angels I shall paint." When Burne-Jones first fell under John Ruskin's influence while at Oxford, he attempted to rally his friends by calling for "a Crusade and Holy War against this age." In the event, it was his friend William Morris who came nearer to carrying out this crusade, with his complete repudiation of Victorian "mechanism" and his championship of the craftsman.

It was not William Morris who originated the arts and crafts movement, though he is often credited with doing so. However, Morris, Burne-Jones, and other members of what the latter called the Birmingham Colony (Charles Faulkner, R. W. Dixon, William Fulford, and Cormell Price) enthusiastically adopted as central to their creed the principle John Ruskin had defined for the Pre-Raphaelite Brotherhood: "absolute uncompromising truth in all it does, obtained by working everything, down to the most minute detail, from nature only"; and having done so, they began to turn their attention to the applied arts.

In one sense this credo was a deliberate riposte to the aloofness and exclusiveness of the Academy, but it was also a natural development for them. In it they were once again consciously turning away from the materialism of their own age and back to the Middle Ages, when "the artists were more workmen and the workmen were more artists." When the possibility arose of forming a kind of cooperative to make the sort of well-designed household furnishings Morris and his friends had been unable to find for his newly built house, it was Rossetti who exclaimed, "Let's have a shop, like Giotto." Morris took the idea very seriously. He believed strongly in the redemptive force of art upon society: "You cannot educate, you cannot civilize men unless you give them a share in art," he had written.

So "the Firm" was launched in 1861. In addition to Marshall, an engineer introduced to the others by Ford Madox Brown, and the mathematician Charles Faulkner, the company consisted of the architect

Philip Webb, Rossetti, Burne-Jones, and Arthur Hughes. Against all expectations "the Firm" was a success, and its products can still serve to illustrate both the founders' faith in good craftsmanship—notably in the mediums of furniture and glass—and the idealism that found expression in, for example, their fabrics, stained glass, and ceramics.

Morris and his colleagues were attempting to express, according to Gillian Naylor,

the idea of the unity of the arts that had been latent in Pre-Raphaelite theory. To the "painterly" vision of the Pre-Raphaelites, however, there was added the ideal of the vernacular, as expressed by Philip Webb, who saw architecture as a "common tradition of honest building" and who had built [Morris'] Red House, with its great oak staircase, oak beams, red-tiled hall and large brick chimneypieces, as an expression of that vision.

(*The Arts and Crafts Movement,* 1971, p. 101)

For Morris these theories and objectives implied sweeping social changes. When he joined the Social Democratic Federation in 1883, he gave as his reason for doing so the need to "act for the destruction of the system which seems to me mere opposition and obstruction." The position, he felt, was inescapable for an artist like himself: "Both my historical studies and my practical conflict with the philistinism of modern society have *forced on* me the conviction that art cannot have a real life and growth under the present system of commercialism and profit-mongering."

Burne-Jones, though not particularly interested in politics, shared at least something of Morris' radicalism. The two of them, together with Cormell Price, organized the Workmen's Neutrality Demonstration in London in 1878 to oppose British plans to intervene in the Russo-Turkish war. Given the mood of the British public, their action required conviction and courage, for the government's bellicose attitude helped to focus the growing imperialist fervor in the country at large. The word "jingoism" itself came into the language as a direct result of the crisis, from a boastful patriotic song that became a favorite in the music halls: "We don't want to fight, but by jingo if we do. . . ."

Georgiana Burne-Jones was also of an independent and liberal opinion. Her house at Rottingdean came near to being sacked when, amid the general celebration on the night peace was concluded with the Boers, she hung a black banner from her windows with the words: "We have killed and also taken possession." Only the intervention of her nephew Rudyard saved the situation from getting seriously out of hand.

This then was the aesthetic and moral background within which Kipling grew up: forceful and influential in its pioneering of new ideas and the new aesthetic; forceful and influential, too, in its radicalism and idealism. The obvious question is: How could a writer, nurtured in this lively and original milieu, turn into "the laureate of Joseph Chamberlain's designs" (Chamberlain was colonial secretary) and "the banjo-band of empire"? But this begs another question: *Did* he?

It might seem that he did if we follow his biography a little further. In 1882, at the age of seventeen, Kipling returned to India to work as a journalist on the *Civil and Military Gazette* in Lahore. There he rediscovered the India he had known and loved as a child; and he wrote about it, perceptively and affectionately, in his paper—though it is worth noting that Kipling wrote (and thought) mainly of the Punjab. He also wrote about the political scene, drawing on club gossip, listening to the tales that soldiers—privates rather than officers—had to tell. With the arrival of Lord Dufferin as viceroy in 1894 he was even able to catch a glimpse of the innermost corridors of power, for the viceroy befriended the Kiplings and admitted them, in some small measure at least, to his circle.

All of this experience Kipling put to good use in his first volume of poems, *Departmental Ditties* (1886); in *Plain Tales from the Hills* (1888); and in his other Indian stories. But in 1889 he left India, returning only once, briefly in 1891, to see his parents. Though he settled first in London, he stayed there for less than three years. In 1892 he married Caroline Balestier, an American, and went to live in Vermont, where over the next four years he wrote some of his best stories. It was there that he first started to work seriously on *Kim,* but not until he had returned to England in 1896 and talked the subject over with his father at great length was he able to give it final shape. Finally, early in 1901, *Kim* was published. There are many (including the present writer) who believe that *Kim* marks the high-water mark in Kipling's creative achievement. Many excellent stories were to follow, but those written after 1901 lack the energy, the sharpness of eye and ear, the tightness of detail and shape, the sense of easy mastery of *Kim.*

In a number of respects Kipling never repudiated his late–Pre-Raphaelite boyhood; quite the contrary. William Gaunt surely gets the wrong end of the stick when he suggests rather archly that Pre-Raphaelitism had "whispered its enchantment into the ear of the Imperial Muse": "Perhaps some of those little golden fables spun by the painter influenced his 'beloved Ruddy,' turning him back from his sharply realist contemporary vision to those overlapping vistas of a past which was also the present in which paleolithic man, Roman legionaries, mediaeval burgesses still lived."

It is true that Kipling's interest in the past is deep and sustained (witness *Puck of Pook's Hill*, 1906); it also has something in common with the views of Burne-Jones, though a great deal more with those of Morris. Like the latter, Kipling had no solid faith in a God, Providence, or a future life, and, like him too, he found solace in what seemed to him the permanence of the country and the rural life that in his eyes enshrined the history of the race and guaranteed, so far as anything could, its future. In the attention he gives to the past, Kipling reflects a habit of mind characteristic not just of the Pre-Raphaelites but of the Victorians in general: J. S. Mill had concluded that it was their chief preoccupation to compare their own with former ages.

It is equally arguable that it was the Pre-Raphaelite influence that turned him toward what Gaunt calls his "sharply realist contemporary vision"—though some of it, at least, is also the product of continental influences. "The Record of Badalia Herodsfoot," with its emphasis on urban misery, prostitution, and exploitation, is in a direct line from Dickens, as Uncle Ned Burne-Jones's story "The Cousins" shows: "Those were [Badalia's] days of fatness, and they did not last long, for her husband took to himself another woman, and passed out of Badalia's life, over Badalia's senseless body; for he stifled protest with blows." This is really not profoundly different from the early part of "The Cousins" except in its ironic and paraded detachment, which has us at once on our guard against manipulation by what we instinctively recognize to be a very clever writer: a reaction no one is ever likely to have on reading "The Cousins."

Kipling's indebtedness to Pre-Raphaelite realism is more convincingly demonstrated in his precise use of detail, like that of the reins on the sleeping Rissaldar's wrist in *Kim*, the loaded tea-table in "The Wish House," or, paradoxically, his description of the machinery of the lighthouse in "The Disturber of the Traffic." Thomas Carlyle had praised the Pre-Raphaelites for "copying the thing as it is," and it is much the same for Kipling, even in the ideal world:

> . . . each for the joy of the working, and each, in his
>   separate star,
> Shall draw the Thing as he sees It for the God of
>   Things as They are.
>   ("When Earth's Last Picture Is Painted")

It is also possible to find other significant signs of indebtedness to Burne-Jones and his circle. There is, for example, the infusion of moral allegory into what is very often a highly pictorial composition (though part of that may also come from the Methodist background of which Kipling was very conscious). There is his overt concern with the art of the painter in so many of his stories, from *The Light That Failed* (1890) to the "Eye of Allah" (1926); and his taste for a brilliant use of color, at its most vivid in *Kim*.

Even more likely to be part of his inheritance is the intense care he took with his own craft, going over his stories again and again, paring out all that was not strictly essential. Like Morris, Kipling believed deeply that art should be committed, not divorced from the concerns of people as they busy themselves with what he considered their best means of salvation—the day's work. He says so explicitly in "The Children of the Zodiac" and in "'Teem.'" Like Morris and his friends, he was also deeply suspicious of the age's materialism and its contentment with "Idols of greasy altars built for the body's ease" ("The Islanders"). Unlike Morris, however, he did not oppose the new technology, though for unexpected reasons, as we shall see.

In one key area Kipling can be seen developing a central preoccupation of the Pre-Raphaelites to a point where it takes on for him a totally different moral significance, one that comes to underlie and give special character to his whole creative endeavor.

As anyone will realize who has ever had occasion to consult that remarkable barometer of the moral climate in nineteenth-century Britain, Thomas Carlyle, an essential consideration in the understanding of these eminent Victorians is their troubled relationship with nature. Pre-Raphaelitism and the arts and crafts movement both embodied the recognition that many of these gifted and creative men shared—most notably Edward Welby Pugin, Ruskin, and Morris—that modern progress, particularly of an industrial and technological kind, threatened to alienate man from nature. To Pugin and Ruskin in particular this meant alienation from God, since they were in no doubt that nature was ultimately a spiritual entity. But all of them believed that man's rightful and accessible domain was indeed in the bosom of nature: it was there, informed by the spirit of the Creator, that man found the roots of his being; and it was through art that he could be brought to realize this and effect a unification or a reunification with nature, thus staving off the recognized threat of alienation.

Kipling likewise is concerned, every step of the way, with man's relation to nature; only he finds the latter hostile to man and he accepts alienation as an inescapable fact of existence. Recognizing this, he sees that life will be one long battle to preserve moral integrity in a universe where there is no order and no refuge.

Kipling's conclusion is much the same as that of his contemporary Joseph Conrad. But Kipling derived his comprehensive symbol for the conflict from the idea of empire, an idea that for the world at large had a concrete and controversial political reality. Thus when he lauded the structure of empire, many of his readers assumed that he was enthralled with the political reality of empire and judged him accordingly. Such a fate was inevitable; to a certain degree there was poetic justice in it, for Kipling was prepared to put flesh, bone, and muscle on his symbol, but a symbol that shoots people and rules countries uninvited can no longer be seen simply as a literary device. One must look beyond literature to appreciate how far, and in whose company, he took part in the age's polemic. This we cannot do unless we also appreciate what he was rooted in.

II

OF Joseph Conrad, Bertrand Russell wrote:

He gave me the impression of a man who thought of civilised and morally tolerable human life as a dangerous walk on a thin crust of barely cooled lava which at any moment might break and let the unwary sink into the fiery depths.
(*Portraits from Memory*, 1956, p. 82)

The description, however, seems equally applicable to Kipling. At the heart of such a response there is an extreme, existential loneliness and fear as well as a deep pessimism.

The signs are there from the beginning, which in itself is remarkable in a man who by the time he was

nineteen had already written some of the stories in *Plain Tales from the Hills.*

> A stone's throw out on either hand
> From that well-ordered road we tread,
> And all the world is wild and strange.

So runs the epigraph to "In the House of Suddhoo," but this is the reality that governs nearly all Kipling's actions and reactions. The world of nature is hostile and threatening: it is exactly the world that Conrad's Marlow surveys when he looks over the anarchy of nature represented by the jungle in *Heart of Darkness* and wonders, "Could we handle that dumb thing or would it handle us?" In fact Kipling has something like a horror of what the French social and political theorist Georges Sorel, another distinguished contemporary, defined as "natural nature": "a mysterious, even malignant Fate, an arbitrary and meaningless force that constantly threatens to overwhelm the spheres conquered by human reason." The comparison with Sorel is strengthened by his solution, namely, to seek succor in "artificial nature," which was the construction imposed upon the chaos of reality by scientists and technicians in order to tame it. Interestingly, this is precisely the métier of the favored Kipling character. When his heroes are not literally engineers and technicians, which they frequently are, they are administrators taming the alien and menacing forces of what he calls in *Kim* "great, grey, formless India." A concern for artificial nature and its beneficent powers is also what attracts him to the machine, from which, in turn, we get stories like "The Ship That Found Herself" and ".007." To Kipling, as to Sorel, the machine is a major expression of man's ability to understand and control the forces of nature. "If there is something that is most specifically social in human activity," wrote Sorel, "it is the machine. It is more social than language itself."

So many of his stories allude to this threat from "natural nature" either centrally or peripherally that even a random dip into his works is going to illustrate its importance to Kipling. But one can choose here one or two stories where it is integral to the whole tale.

"The Disturber of the Traffic," first published in 1891, has as its epigraph a verse that is itself characteristic of the vision I have been discussing. The first stanza runs:

> From the wheel and the drift of Things
> Deliver us, good Lord;

And we will meet the wrath of kings,
The faggot, and the sword.

The story is of a lighthouse keeper, Dowse, who goes mad, seeing in the waters flowing beneath his tower the anarchy of the world. But the tale is, in a manner altogether characteristic of the author, enclosed in a context that greatly extends the power and significance of Dowse's disorienting experience. For the narrator, in true Kipling fashion, first creates an exalted notion of the mystery and exclusiveness of those (principally the lighthouse keepers) in the very special service of the Board of Trinity. He does so because they represent that selfless confederacy dedicated to the preservation of order and integrity the world over: an order that is seen quite clearly to be neither physical nor political but moral.

The great light by which the narrator and the keeper, Fenwick, are sitting when the story begins beams out through the obscurity of the darkness and the fog to bring order into what would otherwise be the chaos of coastal ships blundering about in the English Channel. Interestingly, the lighthouse is described as that of St. Cecilia-under-the-Cliff and the most powerful of the south coast lights. St. Cecilia is, of course, the patron saint of music, and the light, we are told, "when the sea-mist veils all," turns "a hooded head to the sea and sings a song of two words once every minute." But the sound undergoes what one might be forgiven for calling a sea-change: "From the land that song resembles the bellowing of a brazen bull; but off-shore they understand, and the steamers grunt gratefully in answer." Later a ship is described as "bleating like an indignant calf."

All the delicacy, charm, and harmony we might associate with St. Cecilia—backed by a vague picture of a lady of rare beauty and classical drapery—is rudely dispelled. In its place there is very deliberately planted an image of a world of brutes presided over and kept in order by the primitive, pagan force of a brazen bull. The world is a place of marauding animals—an image that recurs in Kipling's stories—dominated and disciplined by the still greater brute energy of a bull. But the fact that the bull is brazen—wrought by man, in other words—tells us something else. To control the disorder of "natural nature" Kipling turns to "artificial nature" and the world of the machine:

One star came out over the cliffs, the waters turned to lead-colour, and St. Cecilia's Light shot out across the sea in

eight long pencils that wheeled slowly from right to left, melted into one beam of solid light laid down directly in front of the tower, dissolved again into eight, and passed away. The light-frame of the thousand lenses circled on its rollers, and the compressed-air engine that drove it hummed like a blue-bottle under a glass. The hand of the indicator on the wall pulsed from mark to mark. Eight pulse-beats timed one half-revolution of the Light; neither more nor less.

In the chat that follows between Fenwick and the narrator—though it is pointedly strewn with technical jargon about dynamos, governors, and feed-pipes—the subject is mainly pilots and lights, both servants in the cause of order. As Fenwick tells his tales they are accompanied by "the roller-skate rattle of the revolving lens," the active instrument of order, and, symbolic of the anarchy of the natural world, "the sharp tap of reckless night-birds that flung themselves at the glasses."

The tale that is selected by the narrator to retell to us is of a keeper called—with rather too obvious an intent—Dowse, who is in charge of a light in a quarter of the globe where the currents are depicted as being among the most unruly, inexplicable, and destructive: "they chop and they change, and they banks the tides fust on one shore and then on another, till your ship's tore in two." An excellent example of Kipling's ability to conjure up a vivid, almost allegorical, tableau is the description of Dowse sitting up in his tower "for to watch the tigers come out of the forests to hunt for crabs and such like round about the lighthouse at low tide." This tension between order and anarchy is heightened when we are made aware of another presence in the vicinity of the lighthouse:

"There was another man along with Dowse in the Light, but he wasn't rightly a man. He was a Kling. No, nor yet a Kling he wasn't, but his skin was in little flakes and cracks all over, from living so much in the salt water as was his usual custom. His hands was all webby-foot, too. He was called, I remember Dowse saying now, an Orange-Lord, on account of his habits. You've heard of an Orange-Lord, sir?"

The narrator corrects him: the word is "orang-laut" and means, we are told, a sea-gypsy. This orang-laut, whose name is Challong, has a disturbing affinity with these unruly elements policed by the light:

"Dowse told me that that man, long hair and all, would go swimming up and down the straits just for something to do;

running down on one tide and back again with the other, swimming side-stroke, and the tides going tremenjus strong. Elseways he'd be skipping about the beach along with the tigers at low tide, for he was most part a beast; or he'd sit in a little boat praying to old Loby Toby of an evening when the volcano was spitting red at the south end of the strait. Dowse told me that he wasn't a companionable man, like you and me might have been to Dowse."

The splendid irony in the last sentence is typical of Kipling; for it is a datum with him that the wildness may be already in man's soul, whether he is civilized or not. Gradually the anarchy of the waters begins to affect Dowse, whose head "began to feel streaky from looking at the tide so long."

"The streaks, they would run with the tides, north and south, twice a day, accordin' to them currents, and he'd lie down on the planking—it was a screw-pile Light—with his eye to a crack and watch the water streaking through the piles just so quiet as hogwash. He said the only comfort he got was at slack water. Then the streaks in his head went round and round like a sampan in a tide-rip; but that was heaven, he said, to the other kind of streaks—the straight ones that looked like arrows on a wind-chart, but much more regular."

Driven to desperation and goaded by Challong, who "swum round and round the Light, laughin' at him and splashin' water with his webby-foot hands," Dowse decides that he must stop all ships from coming through the straits, because they churn up the water and make the streaks worse. He constructs, with Challong, a number of rafts (taking longer over the job than might have been needed "because he rejoiced in the corners, they being square, and the streaks in his head all running longways") on which he mounts lights so that they will serve as wreckbuoys. The captain of an admiralty survey ship hears of these mysterious buoys and goes to investigate.

When the captain gets Dowse to his ship (pursued by Challong, who "was swimmin' round and round the ship, sayin' 'dam' for to please the men and to be took aboard"), Dowse's madness becomes plain even to himself. Kipling has him suddenly catch sight of his reflection in the binnacle brasses, whereupon he realizes that not only is he stark naked but he has been so for weeks. As the ship bears Dowse away with it, Challong follows "a-calling 'dam-dam' all among the wake of the screw, and half-heaving himself out of water and joining his webby-foot hands

together." This image of the creature who "wasn't rightly a man" pursuing the boat, his "webby-foot hands" uplifted in supplication, vividly recalls the native woman's gesture of appeal to the departing Kurtz in Conrad's *Heart of Darkness;* and the significance of the two images is surprisingly similar. Challong may not be "rightly a man," but he is far too close to one for comfort. This creature who, dismayingly, does not merely survive but seems at home in the anarchy of the streaky currents, is *not* different in kind, and thereby reveals what a carefully constucted thing is one's sense of moral order, and how near one lives to what is perhaps the natural state of moral lawlessness. Conrad's Marlow, looking over the jungle landscape, had made a similar discovery:

The earth seemed unearthly. We are accustomed to look over the shackled form of a conquered monster, but there —there you could look at a thing monstrous and free. It was unearthly, and the men were—No, they were not inhuman. . . . That was the worst of it—this suspicion of their not being inhuman.

(Heart of Darkness, II)

"The Disturber of the Traffic" is by no means Kipling's best story: he fumbles a little at the beginning, and he does so again toward the end, when Fenwick comes back into the tale; and there are other blemishes, notably in the dialogue. All the same it is a powerful and serious story that for most of its length is extraordinarily well organized despite its density.

Kipling often flaws an outstanding piece of writing quite perversely, and this tale offers a good example. One can accept the slight lack of focus at the beginning because something significant and integral to the tale is going on. But Fenwick's coming into the scene again at the end and meeting up with the guilt-ridden Dowse at Fratton is a mistake. And it is all the more exasperating in that it is quite gratuitous, for there comes after it an excellent, even brilliant, coda, which is all that was needed:

Day had come, and the Channel needed St. Cecilia no longer. The sea-fog rolled back from the cliffs in trailed wreaths and dragged patches, as the sun rose and made the dead sea alive and splendid. The stillness of the morning held us both silent as we stepped on the balcony. A lark went up from the cliffs behind St. Cecilia, and we smelt a smell of cows in the lighthouse pastures below.

Then we were both at liberty to thank the lord for another day of clean and wholesome life.

The story shows something of Kipling's art as well as his disturbing vision of that menacing realm of "natural nature" which lies so close to the surface. It was published in 1891, when Kipling was twenty-five, and its central concern is common to many of his early tales, where the vision seems to find its metaphor with an ease and congruency that is much less obvious in his later work. (I agree with Somerset Maugham's view that by the end of the century and with the publication of *Kim,* Kipling had written his best work.) Of course one also finds the mawkish and the ephemeral in the early stories, just as one finds superbly integrated tales in, for example, *Debits and Credits* (1926).

"At the End of the Passage," first published in 1890, shows Kipling's keen visual sense and technical virtuosity in the very first paragraph:

Four men, each entitled to "life, liberty, and the pursuit of happiness," sat at a table playing whist. The thermometer marked—for them—one hundred and one degrees of heat. The room was darkened till it was only just possible to distinguish the pips of the cards and the very white faces of the players. A tattered, rotten punkah of whitewashed calico was puddling the hot air and whining dolefully at each stroke. Outside lay gloom of a November day in London. There was neither sky, sun, nor horizon,—nothing but a brown purple haze of heat. It was as though the earth were dying of apoplexy.

The men are in effect prisoners—at first, it seems, prisoners of their own sense of duty and stubborn dedication to the job in hand (and the story loses pace when Kipling allows his principals to have too much to say about their particular share of the white man's burden). But as the story unfolds it is clear that they are much more the prisoners of their own loneliness; and that does not mean simply the loneliness of the Englishman in India, nobly sacrificing himself far from his own kith and kin so that "the people" may have efficient administration, railways, irrigation systems, and the like. It means man's essential loneliness and isolation, an inescapable condition of his existence: "The players were not conscious of any special regard for each other. They squabbled whenever they met; but they ardently desired to meet, as men without water desire to drink. They were lonely folk who understood the dread meaning of loneliness."

The absurdist inclination of the tale is heightened when added to the picture of the four men seated in a hut, playing whist in the middle of an inferno with no distinguishable horizon, no heaven and no earth, is Mottram tinkling out London music-hall songs on the broken piano, in the middle of this same nothingness: "A dense dust-storm sprang up outside, and swept roaring over the house, enveloping it in the choking darkness of midnight, but Mottram continued unheeding, and the crazy tinkle reached the ears of the listeners above the flapping of the tattered ceiling cloth."

There is a strong feeling in this story that the chaos already exists within man and is held at bay only by the most stringent application of certain disciplines, such as unremitting work and devotion to duty. The apparent objectives (they are referred to as "trifles" in the epigraph) to which the men sacrifice themselves are ultimately of little intrinsic value: but, trifles though they may be, devotion to them gives structure and a sense of identity to the individual. Isolation, prolonged and tortured, is going to stretch their defenses to the very limit, and the destructive entropic principle that seems the only reality will more easily cause the breakup of that carefully constructed artifact—the self. Kipling's characters are haunted by the knowledge of this possibility, so that when he writes of the four young men understanding "the dread meaning of loneliness," the phrase must not be taken casually. In many stories, including "At the End of the Passage," this fear of the destruction of identity and sense of self is portrayed in terms of the most acute agony. Hummil, one of the men, is gripped by terror that has reached an uncontrollable pitch:

"For three weeks I've had to think and spell out every word that has come through my lips before I dared to say it. Isn't that enough to drive a man mad? I can't see things correctly now, and I've lost my sense of touch. My skin aches – my skin aches! Make me sleep. Oh Spurstow, for the love of God, make me sleep sound. It isn't enough merely to let me dream. Let me sleep!"

Just at a point in the story where we might suspect the author of being too closely identified with his character's crisis, the skill of the storyteller reasserts itself. The injection of morphia Dr. Spurstow administers to Hummil has only a limited effect. Preoccupied in dismantling Hummil's guns, Spurstow is as startled as we are by the engineer's wild cry from the doorway: "You fool!" The degree to which Hummil is beyond all self-control and possibly in the possession of something else is forced on us by the sheer drama of the moment; and it is followed by the deployment of an image that Kipling reserves for moments of ultimate anomic horror:

As a sponge rubs a slate clean, so some power unknown to Spurstow had wiped out of Hummil's face all that stamped it for the face of a man, and he stood at the doorway in the expression of his lost innocence. He had stept back into terrified childhood.

The doctor leaves, and almost immediately Hummil finds himself haunted again. The tale is well told: "When he came in to dinner he found himself sitting at the table. The vision rose and walked out hastily. Except that it cast no shadow, it was in all respects real."

Spurstow returns a week later and finds Hummil dead: "The body lay on its back, hands clinched by the side. . . . In the staring eyes was written terror beyond the expression of any pen." Again there is the suggestion of his whole being having been usurped by some "power unknown." "Cover up the face!" says Lowndes. "Is there any fear on earth that can turn a man into that likeness? It's ghastly. Oh Spurstow, cover it up!" And Spurstow replies, "No fear—on earth." What follows is generally regarded as a weakness in the story, though some allowance ought to be made for contemporary interest in such phenomena. Spurstow thinks he sees something odd in the dead man's eyes and, despite Lowndes's plea to "leave that horror alone," puts his camera to each eye and photographs it, afterward retreating into the bathroom to develop his film: "After a few minutes there was the sound of something being hammered to pieces, and he emerged, very white indeed."

The story ends with Spurstow turning in the doorway as he leaves (thus recalling the earlier unexpected appearance of Hummil in the doorway of the saddle room and consequently their shared doom) and quoting:

"There may be Heaven,—there must be Hell.
Meantime, there is our life here. We-ell?"

This concluding reference to hell raises an interesting question. The Kipling character's fear of moral disintegration quite frequently seems mixed up with a conviction that the hostile force in the universe is not simply its entropic principle but is actually, and actively, evil itself, and that evil expresses itself in man's essential being. This conviction diminishes the existentialist aspect of Kipling's

notion of self and replaces it with a double dose of original sin—perhaps in unconscious tribute to his double dose of Methodist ancestry.

"At the End of the Passage" can very easily be read in a way that locates it in limbo. The description in the opening paragraph supports the idea, and the epigraph is explicit:

The sky is lead and our faces are red,
And the gates of Hell are opened and riven,
And the winds of Hell are loosened and driven, . . .

But there are other pointers. Mottram's tinkling on the piano turns into the evening hymn:

"Sunday," said he, nodding his head.
"Go on. Don't apologise for it," said Spurstow.
Hummil laughed long and riotously: "Play it, by all means. You're full of surprises to-day. I didn't know you had such a gift of finished sarcasm."

The others object to Hummil's continued bitter disparagement ("You miss the note of gratitude"; "It ought to go to the 'Grasshopper's Polka'") and launch into a sentimental defense of the hymn as evoking "the most sacred recollections":

"Summer evenings in the country,—stained-glass window,—light going out, and you and she jamming your hands together over one hymn-book," said Mottram.
"Yes and a fat old cockchafer hitting you in the eye when you walked home. Smell of hay, and a moon as big as a bandbox sitting on the top of a haycock; bats—roses,—milk and midges," said Lowndes.
"Also mothers . . ." said Spurstow.
The darkness had fallen on the room. They could hear Hummil squirming in his chair.

That "darkness had fallen on the room" is worthy of Conrad. Hummil accentuates the gloom *and* gives it a more—and, indeed, curiously—precise spiritual location: "'Consequently,' said he testily, 'you sing it when you are seven fathom deep in Hell! It's an insult to the Deity to pretend we're anything but tortured rebels.'" That last is a surprise: in no way, metaphorical or any other, are they rebels, within the given terms of their setting; only in the context of man's rebelling against God's edict and being cast into hell because of the evil in his nature does it make sense. And though it surprises us, that is perhaps a criticism of our inattentiveness to what has gone before.

A few pages earlier, in a quite dense sentence,

Kipling has unobtrusively prepared the ground: "The piano was indeed hopelessly out of order but Mottram managed to bring the rebellious notes into a sort of agreement, and there rose from the ragged keyboard something that might once have been the ghost of a popular music-hall song."

"At the End of the Passage" is not wholly consistent in its quality, but Kipling shows that he can write with real power and possesses a somber vision that penetrates far below the imperial symbol he uses as a vehicle.

A considerable number of Kipling's stories have hell as their setting, some notably good ones, such as the much later "Uncovenanted Mercies" (1932); and there are others where it is offered as a clear analogue. In "At the End of the Passage," hell is an option and is well defined as such.

In "The Strange Ride of Morrowbie Jukes" (1888), hell is there, though less explicitly. This story again raises the specter of a realm of disorder and anarchy lying just under man's civilized feet. If it is true that the tale derives a good deal from Edgar Allan Poe, it does so via Robert Louis Stevenson, since it is for the most part written with a pace, concentration, and economy typical of the latter. But I see no real reason to assume either mentor, for, as must now be clear, the subject is one that nearly obsessed Kipling.

Jukes—yet another engineer, "with a head for plans and distances and things of that kind"—recovering from an attack of fever, sets out on a wild ride on horseback to silence the dogs that have been baying all night under a full moon. His horse "went forward like a thing possessed," far beyond the dogs, into what seems like uncharted desert, until, cresting a sharp rise, horse and rider find themselves rolling down a steep slope on the other side. Quite literally they have fallen into a pit—or perhaps the Pit. So steep and sandy are the sides that attempts to clamber up to the top fail. We are carefully told that the angle of the slope is about sixty-five degrees, and the sand wall about thirty-five feet high; for Jukes is an engineer and his world is symbolized by just such mathematical order. But the pit is not unpopulated; far from it. Hindu ritual, we are told, requires that when a corpse, on its way to cremation at the burning ghâts, revives from what proves to be not death but merely deep trance or catalepsy, it is not considered proper to return the man or woman to society. Such individuals are secretly transported to such a place as the pit." If you die at home," says Gunga Dass," and do not die when you come to the ghât to be burnt, you come here." One side of the pit opens to the river, but when Jukes seeks to find a way out of the trap in that direction he is fired on from a boat that is anchored in midstream to prevent escapes.

The people who emerge from the caves and holes in the sand wall are filthy and repellent. But what shakes Juke seriously is their reaction to him. He approaches the crowd with all the confidence of a sahib "accustomed to a certain amount of civility from my inferiors," as he unselfconsciously puts it. What actually happens is that they laugh at him; in fact rather more than that: "They cackled, yelled, whistled, and howled as I walked into their midst; some of them literally throwing themselves down on the ground in convulsions of unholy mirth." Kipling properly refrains from anything more explicit, but the reason for this laughter is as obvious to us as it clearly was to the shaken Jukes: a sahib, one of the lords of creation, has been reduced to the same level as themselves. The allusion is expanded when he engages Gunga Dass, whom by chance he had once known when the latter was in charge of a telegraph office, in conversation. Jukes still attempts to invoke the order of the world he has just left: "I turned towards the miserable figure and ordered him to show me some method of escaping from the crater."

Just how much the subject of the story is, in truth, the ever-present threat of the moral anarchy that Kipling sees as the essential character of nature is well established by the detail—some of it extremely subtle—in depicting Jukes's dependence on an ordered universe and in emphasizing its utter absence here. As Dass talks, Jukes is already roughing out in his mind a plan of escape: "He, however, divined my unspoken thought almost as soon as it was formed; and, to my intense astonishment, gave vent to a long low chuckle of derision—the laughter, be it understood, of a superior or at least of an equal." Jukes's character (and those of his kind) is well caught in the phrase "to my intense astonishment" and in the amazed repetition of "laughter." That a native should actually be laughing at him is almost literally world-shattering. (Kipling is by no means uniformly successful in separating himself from his first-person narrator, but here he does so wholly.) In Jukes's very next sentence he notes parenthetically that the word "sir" has disappeared from Dass's vocabulary in his near-contemptuous dismissal of Jukes's escape plans.

A "nameless terror" seizes Jukes, and he rushes blindly and vainly at the sand walls, finally collapsing by the well. There the complete disregard of the other prisoners is made strikingly manifest in all its humiliation: "Two or three men trod on my panting body as they drew water, but they were evidently used to this sort of thing, and had no time to waste upon me." The literal and moral degradation so graphically and yet so laconically described shows Kipling the short-story writer at his most effective. It is well supported in the deft touch that follows.

Jukes realizes he will starve unless he sinks his pride to some degree and gets Dass to help him. What this means in terms of the dangers to his own status and moral integrity is made clear in the sentence "being only a man after all, I felt hungry, and intimated as much to Gunga Dass *whom I had begun to regard as my natural protector*." Not only the phrase I have italicized, but its predecessor, "being only a man, after all," show Kipling working apparently effortlessly and impersonally, deep within the organic structure of his tale. He continues in this brilliant vein: "Following the impulse of the outer world when dealing with natives, I put my hand into my pocket and drew out four annas. The absurdity of the gift struck me at once." Jukes's accustomed universe has become the *outer* world, and its practices come to be seen as nothing less than absurd when viewed from his new perspective. What makes deftness into something very like genius, however, is what immediately follows. Gunga Dass, resident in the pit for two and a half years, virtually grabs the money.

I have already alluded to Kipling's strong visual sense. Here that sense is evident as the tattered, degraded Dass—he is as conscious of once having been a Brahmin as Jukes is of having been a sahib—long cast out from a world in which money has meaning, greedily snatches at it just the same. The futility of the damned in their hell, quarreling over money, is a vivid, powerful indictment, not just of Gunga Dass, but of man's ineradicably corrupt nature. "Gunga Dass clutched the coins and hid them at once in his ragged loin-cloth, his expression changing to something diabolical, as he looked round to assure himself that no one had observed us."

The nature of the world into which Jukes has entered—the true reality, perhaps, beneath the illusions of the world he has just left—is made still more explicit in the reflection, after he has surrendered all his money, that "one does not protest against the vagaries of a den of wild beasts; and my companions were lower than wild beasts." While he eats, his difficulty in coming to terms with his new status asserts itself again as he notes that the people around him "showed not the faintest sign of curiosity—that curiosity which is so rampant, as a rule, in an Indian village"; and he comes near to thinking—for him—the unthinkable: "I could even fancy that they despised me." His questions to Dass get unsatisfactory answers, though they are illuminating to us. When he asks how long this "terrible village" has been in existence, he is told, significantly, "from time immemorial," and concludes naively that "it was at least a century old." (The truth is that it is as old as man's sins.) Who the "they" are who order and maintain this system, Dass cannot or will not tell him. (In passing it is worth noting the appearance of the shadowy, menacing company who seem to patrol the outer marches of man's ordered universe and convey a sense of complicity with that world of anarchy and chaos which lies beyond. "They" appear in a number of Kipling stories and poems, in a role that reminds us of a more recent poet of law and order, W. H. Auden, with whom Kipling has sometimes been compared for largely the wrong reasons.)

Jukes endures considerable torture at the hands, or rather lips, of Gunga Dass, who takes a malicious pleasure, we are told, in telling him of the hopelessness of his plight and watching him wince. When Juke asks, "And how do you live from day to day?" the answer includes the sardonic observation that "this place is like your European Heaven; there is neither marrying nor giving in marriage."

The bitter and painful lessons that Jukes has to learn are vividly illustrated in a central section of the tale that seems to stand with the best of Kipling's writings in its imaginative insight, control of narrative, and literary tact (the fine balance between suggestive reticence and explicitness). Because of the ramifications of meaning that have been implicit from the start, although we see Jukes's tendency to appreciate the predicament in terms consistent with his more limited imagination, we ourselves are all the time aware of wider perspectives being offered and of pointers to larger dimensions. Though the order he sees repudiated is still that of the sahibs, Jukes's imagery increasingly equates himself with the less-than-human world:

Here was a Sahib, a representative of the dominant race, helpless as a child and completely at the mercy of his native neighbours. In a deliberate, lazy way [Dass] set himself to torture me as a schoolboy would devote a rapturous half-hour to watching the agonies of an impaled beetle, or as a ferret in a blind burrow might glue himself comfortably to the neck of a rabbit.

And he adds, speaking more truly than he knows, "if it were possible to forejudge the conversation of the Damned on the advent of a new soul in their abode, I should say they would speak as Gunga Dass did to me throughout that long afternoon." Then, in a skillful touch so characteristic of Kipling's handling of this tale, Jukes, the rather prosaic engineer of limited imagination, compares his ensuing struggle with "the inexplicable terror" to "the overpowering nausea of the Channel passage." Jukes sees clearly enough, though, to make the important concession that "my agony was of the spirit, and infinitely more terrible."

Kipling, however, juxtaposes this half-realization with the brilliantly conceived and told entrapment of the crows. Jukes's utter absorption in what is happening speaks volumes about his predicament, and for once Kipling resists an intrusion of his own voice in order not to spoil the effect of Jukes's severe, Swiftian understatement: "I was a good deal impressed by this, to me novel method of securing food, and complimented Gunga Dass on his skill." Dass's response is consequently all the more of a jolt, especially since it is modulated in the same cool language: "'It is nothing to do,' said he. 'To-morrow you must do it for me. You are stronger than I am.'"

In fact Dass pushes his demands a little too far, and Jukes reacts by telling him that "there is nothing on earth to prevent my killing you as you sit here and taking everything you've got," which brings Jukes dangerously near Dass's level in our eyes—as it is meant to do. The parenthesis, "I thought of the two invaluable crows at the time," is excellent, not just because of the rightness of the slightly pedantic "invaluable" but because the decoy crows are precisely what value has sunk to—survival on the lowest possible terms. Thus the victim of entrapment becomes the trapper and loses all moral distinctness.

Jukes himself in his supposed retrospective view of his behavior in the pit is explicit enough to confirm Kipling's careful structuring of detail and suggestion:

At the time it did not strike me as at all strange that I, a Civil Engineer, a man of thirteen years' standing in the Service, and, I trust, an average Englishman, should thus calmly threaten murder and violence against the man who had, for a consideration it is true, taken me under his wing.

This averageness is self-evident in the way Jukes can ingenuously employ that last metaphor, despite what, for the reader at least, has been an all-too-

indelible picture of the decoy crows going about their ferocious business. Jukes goes on:

I had left the world, it seemed, for centuries. I was as certain then as I am now of my own existence, that in that accursed settlement there was no law save that of the strongest; that the living dead men had thrown behind them every canon of the world which had cast them out.

The unconscious irony in "as I am now of my own existence" is another proof of the sustained level of Kipling's achievement here. Back in his world of sahibs he can now once again be certain of it, but in the pit he had seen its supports begin to crumble; and the reader, flattered by the discreet narrator into a perception more acute than the one by the pedestrian Jukes, has seen much further and has been made to recognize the fictions on which that certainty rests.

"I am not," says Jukes, "of an imaginative temperament—very few Engineers are"; and it is partly through Kipling's insistence on Jukes's limited sensibilities that he achieves some of his best effects: Jukes's plain account of the pegging out of the decoys and their appalling efficiency, for instance; or his account of the slaughter of his horse, Pornic. The killing of the sahib's horse is, of course, a gross violation of the order of things, at least as they were in the world he had come from. Dass rubs the message in: they killed the horse because it was better to eat than crow and "greatest good of greatest number is political maxim. We are now Republic, Mr. Jukes, and you are entitled to a fair share of the beast. If you like, we will pass a vote of thanks. Shall I propose?" Again our knowledge of Jukes's sensibilities as "an average Englishman" stands us in good stead. To him the death of his horse is bad enough (and his "How they had killed him I cannot guess" is far more sinisterly effective than full-blooded detail); but to be invited to eat it would be truly to signal the approaching end of the world: "Yes we were a Republic indeed! A Republic of wild beasts penned at the bottom of a pit, to eat and fight and sleep till we died." To us, with our wider sensibility heavily involved by this time, this sounds like a description of the reality of "natural nature."

Objection has on occasion been taken to the ending of the tale; but the ending seems to me quite justifiable. Abrupt it undoubtedly is, but Jukes, we know, is not one to elaborate even this incident. By ending it almost as though one has been suddenly awakened from a nightmare, Kipling sustains an option for the reader that was there from the beginning:

that all of what has transpired has been indeed a dream. Even the bland first sentence is slightly provocative, challenging our disbelief: "There is, as the conjurors say, no deception about this tale." It also leaves us slightly unsure about the reliability of the narrator. The slant of Jukes's own account makes certain that the door remains open: "In the beginning it all arose from a slight attack of fever." The sentence is quite dense in possibilities: the "in the beginning" is, in a purely narrative sense, syntactically inept or redundant. But Kipling does not make any such blunders in this story, and there is the clearest invitation to recall the opening of St. John's gospel, "In the beginning was the Word." It is typical of Kipling's at times sardonic humor to revise it to read, "In the beginning . . . [was] a slight attack of fever." Fever breeds dreams, and Jukes's feverishness is again alluded to in a sort of second opening (where we should note the date, 23 December, which means that the action takes place over Christmas Eve and Christmas Day). The association of the action of the tale with the birthday celebrations of a redeemer of sins once more offers a deeper perspective on Jukes's experience. Sahib though he is, he may still be of the damned, and in his subconscious, at least, he regards himself as such.

Jukes's "strange ride" has a proper claim to being considered among the best of Kipling's short stories: the control of the narrative's movement is unfailing; incident succeeds incident in a way admirably calculated to manipulate the intensity of the readers' reaction, and each is visualized with a clarity that imprints our eyes as surely as "the horror" recorded itself on Hummil's. So the mesmeric drama of the trapping of the crows gives way to the yet more Stevensonian discovery of the wound in the back of the corpse. At no time are we allowed to forget the moral significance of the story, however exciting the drama: indeed, the moral vision constantly interacts with the physical. There is, too, a plausibility in the behavior and expression of the characters that we readily accept just because these, too, are so organic to the tale's moral structure. When Gunga Dass admits without any remorse that he killed the first Englishman who fell into the pit, his explanation is an impressive indictment of the incorrigible vanity of man: "it is not advisable that the men who once get in here should escape. Only I, and *I* am a Brahmin."

Anyone who is tempted to think Kipling too extravagantly praised in this discussion should remember that when he wrote "The Strange Ride of Morrowbie Jukes," he was just nineteen.

All of the virtues mentioned above are present in yet another excellent early story, which again alludes to those inscrutable forces, inimical or at best indifferent to man, that seem to express the character of his universe. In this story, however, there is an ironic espousal—apparently above everything else—of all forms, conventions, and structures that help to give man's existence some semblance of order.

The story "Beyond the Pale" was first published in *Plain Tales from the Hills*, when Kipling was twenty-two. In essence it is simple enough: an Englishman, Trejago, while aimlessly wandering through the city, finds himself walking down what turns out to be something more like a cattle-pen than the urban cul-de-sac it is. Stumbling over some cattle food he hears a laugh from behind a grating. Since it was "a pretty little laugh," he goes forward and whispers a few lines from "The Love Song of Har Dyal," which are capped by the lady from behind the grating. In due course Trejago and Bisesa become lovers; but her father finds out and, in an exceptionally disagreeable fashion, puts an end to the affair.

One of the extraordinary things about the tale is its economy, an achievement that registers all the more forcefully when we begin to realize the density of meaning compressed within it.

Kipling was criticized in his own time as well as later for an apparent indifference to "good writing." Not only had he a tendency to start his sentences with a relative pronoun, but they could often be almost brutally abrupt. In fact, for all its apparent repudiation of finesse, his style is as carefully wrought in its own idiosyncratic way as was, say, Thomas Carlyle's; and so it is invariably part of the statement he is making. That statement usually starts with the opening paragraph, and "Beyond the Pale" is no exception:

> A man should, whatever happens, keep to his own caste, race, and breed. Let the White go to the White and the Black to the Black. Then, whatever trouble falls is in the ordinary course of things—neither sudden, alien, nor unexpected.

But before the liberal reader shuts the book in indignation, he should note the ironic tone, the provocative all-knowing worldliness, the airy espousal of segregation as something conducive to ease of body and peace of mind.

The second paragraph—to literary purists of the

day a structure hardly worth the title—cunningly stresses one word in particular: "This is the story of a man who wilfully stepped beyond the safe limits of decent everyday society, and paid for it heavily." It is hard to read the sentence in any way that does not oblige one to put an emphasis on "wilfully" (with a secondary stress on "safe"). But with the rather swaggering assurance of the narrator still provoking us from the first paragraph, we are a little suspicious of him and what *he* might regard as willful or safe. Quite deliberately Kipling has made his narrator antagonize us, and that antagonism is reinforced in the third, "simplifying," paragraph when he, the all-knowing, criticizes the hero of his tale for knowing too much: "He knew too much in the first instance; and he saw too much in the second. He took too deep an interest in native life; but he will never do so again." The narrator's "knowingness" is applied directly to the tale in a way that is both exasperating and tantalizing: he teases us not just with our own lack of knowledge but also with our strong desire to know. "Neither Suchet Singh nor Gaur Chand approve of their women-folk looking into the world. If Durga Charan had been of their opinion he would have been a happier man to-day, and little Bisesa would have been able to knead her own bread."

After his encounter in Amir Nath's Gully, Trejago receives an object-letter from Bisesa. The components of the object-letter—a broken glass bangle, a flower of the *dhak*, some cardamom seeds, and so on—intrigue us as much as they do Trejago; but he has the knowledge to read them and understand the message he has been sent, even though "no Englishman should be able to translate object-letters." He keeps the suggested assignation, and at the appointed hour the voice behind the grating once more takes up "The Love Song of Har Dyal." The narrator's flaunting of his knowledge is at its most offensive here: "The song is really pretty in the Vernacular. In English you miss the wail of it." So Trejago embarks on a double life. By day he attends to his office work and his social duties, but at night he seeks the hidden world behind the "dead walls" and the grating. The sense of a world beyond our knowing and beyond our finding (indicated partly by the alien vocabulary that helps to describe his journey there) is very well conveyed: the love that flowers in that bare little room is more intensified and sweetened by its being so shut away, so enclosed. And it is love, though the all-knowing narrator is again made to annoy us by referring to it

dismissively as "this folly." When news reaches Bisesa that Trejago has been paying particular attention to a lady of his own race—purely in the line of duty, we are given to understand—she flies into a temper, even threatening to kill herself "if Trejago did not at once drop the alien Memsahib who had come between them." Despite Trejago's rather patronizing attempt to explain "and to show that she did not understand these things from a Western standpoint," she insists on breaking off their acquaintanceship.

Trejago stays away for three weeks; then, thinking the rupture has lasted long enough, he returns to the Gully hoping that his rap on the grating will be answered. He is, we are told with heavy irony, "not disappointed":

> There was a young moon, and one stream of light fell down into Amir Nath's Gully, and struck the grating which was drawn away as he knocked. From the black dark Bisesa held out her arms into the moonlight. Both hands had been cut off at the wrists, and the stumps were nearly healed.

The effectiveness of Kipling's style could hardly be better illustrated, short sentences and all. Even so, the bland understatement of the last phrase is something of a tour de force. Our lack of knowledge, which the narrator earlier teased us with, is now a little less complete: at least we now know why Bisesa is unable to knead her own bread.

Trejago does not escape unscathed. "Something sharp"—the inexplicitness of the instrument of retribution is quite deliberate—is thrust at him through the window and hits him where retribution in this case ought to—in the groin. The hint is to be added to others that Trejago's love was—far more than Holden and Ameera's in "Without Benefit of Clergy"—compromised by an element of sexual adventuring. It confirms the suspicion raised by Trejago's remark that Bisesa did not understand these things "from a Western standpoint"; and it also allows Kipling one of his most laconic concluding sentences, presented in the syntactical form that so annoyed the guardians of literary propriety:

> But Trejago pays his calls regularly, and is reckoned a very decent sort of man.
> There is nothing peculiar about him, except a slight stiffness, caused by a riding-strain, in the right leg.

Of more importance, however, are these sentences, immediately preceding:

179

RUDYARD KIPLING

One special feature of the case is that he does not know where lies the front of Durga Charan's house. It may open on to a courtyard common to two or more houses, or it may lie behind any one of the gates of Jitha Megji's *bustee.* Trejago cannot tell. He cannot get Bisesa—poor little Bisesa—back again. He has lost her in the City where each man's house is as guarded and as unknowable as the grave; and the grating that opens into Amir Nath's Gully has been walled up.

The way that the word "knowledge" or one of its variants is made to echo through this very brief story is masterly. Of course it is a means of enhancing that tightness of organization on which the whole effect really depends, but it also keeps before us with no sense of contrivance the story's deeper moral implications. Trejago's knowledge crossed several borders and so encroached on the wild and the strange that lies on either side "of that well-ordered road we tread." Such an experience is morally shattering, and the anarchy that is the reality of "natural nature" cannot be warded off. In this light the equally knowing narrator is a sardonic young Mephistopheles. He *has* that knowledge, gained presumably by losing himself, as the epigraph has it, and in a worldly-wise manner he lectures those who will come after him against such folly. But he knows, too, that men will go on behaving foolishly, because they will always set love beyond safety, prompted at least partly by what Milton referred to as the twitching of an impetuous nerve. And they will consequently always risk losing themselves as Trejago does with Bisesa, "ignorant as a bird," whose "lisping attempts" to pronounce his name so amused Trejago: "The first syllable was always more than she could manage, and she made funny little gestures with her rose-leaf hands, as one throwing the name away."

It is important to stress that Kipling is *not* writing against an interracial love affair: to reduce it to the crass message that this is what happens to men of imperial blood who dabble with natives is a serious, though not uncommon, misreading. It is in fact about the anarchy and horror of nature and about the sanctity of well-established forms, conventions, and structures, since they are the only bulwark against the former. The self is a fragile, vulnerable, even illusory entity, and without observance of forms it cannot be sustained. Kipling was only taking a little further something that Carlyle, so much the mentor of his age, had written years before: "Formulas? There is no mortal extant, out of the depths of Bedlam, but lives all skinned, thatched, covered

with Formulas; and is, as it were, held in from delirium and the Inane by his Formulas."

"Beyond the Pale" rarely gets a place in a Kipling anthology despite all the virtuosity it displays, including its exceptionally adroit manipulation of ironic tone and its innovations vis-à-vis the role of the unreliable narrator, who first offends us and then, once we are hooked, convinces us that those of limited knowledge are the more fortunate.

Another story on a similar theme, "Without Benefit of Clergy," is usually included. Of all Kipling's early stories, this is probably the bleakest. When Holden's butler tries to comfort him after his double bereavement with the words "Moreover the shadows come and go, *sahib;* the shadows come and go," there is no lightening of the gloom for his master; and rightly, for no such equilibrium has been established in the tale. More accurate a summary is Holden's despairing, helpless cry as he rides away from the bungalow that had housed his wife and child and his happiness: "Oh you brute! You utter brute!" It is a cry directed at that hostile nature utterly without order or sympathy or anything that can be appealed to. In no little way it reminds us of Kurtz's last words in *Heart of Darkness,* "The horror! The horror," though its metaphysical pretensions are slighter and its human reality all the greater.

In fact the whole story is about the insignificance of man and the (at best) indifference of his universe toward him. The opening is tightly focused and profoundly personal. Two human beings are discussing in the seclusion of their home that momentous thing, a new birth: "But if it be a girl?" The conclusion, however, is utter desolation: "It shall be pulled down, and the Municipality shall make a road across, as they desire, from the burning ghaut to the city wall, so that no man may say where this house stood." The focus is now broader; man's life is symbolized by the road that leads from the city of his toil to the place where his body will be cremated.

From the start there is an overpowering sense of anxiety and of doom, and from the start the most strenuous efforts are made to seek some avenue of communication with the Powers that rule men's lives in order to propitiate them. But the anxiety is also in the cause of love and relationship, for Ameera finds it hard to accept Holden's protestations of his enduring love for her. Not only do they challenge the gods to do their worst in the "normal" way—by destroying their child—but they presume to sustain an enduring bond across two cultures. Thus, Ameera's

180

confidence that her prayers and her offerings at Sheikh Badl's shrine will ensure them a son paradoxically fills us with apprehension.

Kipling is at his best in suggesting the borderline on which the couple is living. Before Holden leaves for a fortnight's special duty elsewhere—directed there precisely at the time when his child's birth is due—he writes a telegraph message and bids his watchman to send it to him under certain circumstances. All the time he is away, Holden is in hourly dread of receiving the telegram, for it is not notice of whether the child is a boy or girl, but rather notice of his wife's death.

Ameera does not die, however, and Holden on his return finds he has a son. Crossing the threshold of Ameera's room, he steps on a dagger laid on it to avert bad luck. The dagger breaks, and Ameera takes the incident as a hopeful sign: "God is great. . . . Thou hast taken his misfortunes on thy head." Solemnly she assures Holden that their son is "of the Faith" and doubly blessed by being born on a Friday.

When Holden leaves he is stopped by the watchman, who hands him a sword and asks him to kill the two goats he had tethered—"otherwise, the child being unguarded from fate may die." Holden, who knows the necessary Mohammaden prayer for the sacrifice, recites it and kills the goats. The effect of all this ritual and propitiation is, however, to diminish the reader's confidence.

When we next meet Holden and Ameera they are taking their son outside for the first time, onto the flat roof of their house, to count the stars, says Ameera, "for that is auspicious." She observes the correct ritual for such an occasion, wearing her best jewelry and dressing in green. The presence of the caged green parrot—"a sort of guardian-spirit in most native households"—gives them the idea of calling the baby Tota, a word for parrot in Ameera's language. Their utter peace, security, and secluded happiness are described in one of Kipling's highly visualized set pieces:

The two sleek, white well-bullocks in the courtyard were steadily chewing the cud of their evening meal; old Pir Khan squatted at the head of Holden's horse, his police sabre across his knees, pulling drowsily at a big water-pipe that croaked like a bull-frog in a pond. Ameera's mother sat spinning in the lower verandah, and the wooden gate was shut and barred. The music of a marriage-procession came to the roof above the gentle hum of the city, and a string of flying-foxes crossed the face of the low moon.

Ameera breaks the silence by telling Holden that she has prayed both to the Prophet and to the Virgin Mary. "Will my prayers be heard?" she asks Holden. "How can I say? God is very good." Throughout these exchanges there runs Ameera's bitter consciousness of the two cultures, and she speaks "almost savagely" of the Englishwomen, one of whom, she fears, will supplant her. So Kipling with unwonted tenderness shows both the acute fearfulness of the two for their baby and the ever-present cultural barrier that also threatens their security despite the profundity of their love.

Ameera continues to invoke charms for Tota, and one of his first possessions is a silver belt "with a magic square." But, as we have come gradually to suspect, it is all to no avail. Sheikh Badl, the Prophet, the Virgin Mary, the guardian-spirit are all deaf, and Tota dies. He dies, we are told carefully, as the result not of some cataclysmic event but of "the seasonal autumn fever," and the ordinariness of his sickness not only increases the poignancy but also illustrates just how much this family—and mankind—are at the mercy of their pitiless environment.

Kipling writes well of Holden's pain in the aftermath of his son's death; of his inability to declare his sorrow; and of the unfeeling nature of events when he is forced to watch the children of others at the bandstand. At night he now returns to Ameera to go through again "the hell of self-questioning reproach which is reserved for those who have lost a child." But even now Ameera from time to time sees, and refers to, Holden as an alien, though only to correct herself in an excess of self-reproach. Nonetheless the fragility of their relationship, together with the baleful power of a hostile nature, is at once reasserted. Gradually they "touched happiness again, but this time with caution":

"It was because we loved Tota that he died. The jealousy of God was upon us," said Ameera. "I have hung up a large black jar before our window to turn the evil eye from us, and we must make no protestations of delight, but go softly underneath the stars, lest God find us out."

Once again there is attempted propitiation of these jealous and harsh gods, mixed with a recourse to folk magic. Now they hope that "the Powers" will hear their disclaimers of delight and joy in each other. Predictably, however, "the Powers were busy on other things." Famine is followed by pestilence, and "Nature began to audit her accounts with a red pencil":

Then came the cholera from all four quarters of the compass. It struck a pilgrim-gathering of half a million at a sacred shrine. Many died at the feet of their god; the others broke and ran over the face of the land carrying the pestilence with them. It smote a walled city and killed two hundred a day. The people crowded the trains, hanging on to the footboards and squatting on the roofs of the carriages, and the cholera followed them, for at each station they dragged out the dead and the dying. They died by the roadside, and the horses of the Englishmen shied at the corpses in the grass. The rains did not come, and the earth turned to iron lest man should escape death by hiding in her.

Death (always a preoccupation with Kipling) is almost visible in this description as it mows down all before it with irresistible violence. Once again destructive nature seems to be the only reality: pilgrimages, shrines, and all the paraphernalia of religion seem nothing more than a mockery of the devout.

The Englishmen, before entering the war against the rebellion, send their women to the relative safety of the hills. Holden, "sick with fear of losing his chiefest treasure on earth," does his best to persuade Ameera to go away too. Sadly, it is Ameera's consciousness of her "foreignness," declaring itself in her jealousy of the Englishwomen, that makes her refuse all his entreaties. They are going, therefore she will stay; her love for Holden is of a different, higher quality than the love of Englishwomen for their husbands.

There are not many happinesses so complete as those that are snatched under the shadow of the sword. They sat together and laughed, calling each other openly by every pet name that could move the wrath of the gods. The city below them was locked up in its own torments. Sulphur fires blazed in the streets; the conches in the Hindu temples screamed and bellowed, for the gods were inattentive in those days. There was a service in the great Mahomedan shrine, and the call to prayer from the minarets was almost unceasing. They heard the wailing in the houses of the dead, and once the shriek of a mother who had lost a child and was calling for its return. In the gray dawn they saw the dead borne out through the city gates, each litter with its own little knot of mourners. Wherefore they kissed each other and shivered.

The administrative machine of the raj gets rapidly into full gear to deal with the emergency: gaps are made in its ranks, too, and quickly filled. Holden is about to be drafted to fill such a gap when news reaches him that Ameera is dying. The scene in which Holden enters Ameera's room, the one where Tota had been born, is remarkably powerful and effective. It is both tense and subtly poignant:

She made no sign when Holden entered, because the human soul is a very lonely thing and, when it is getting ready to go away, hides itself in a misty borderland where the living may not follow. The black cholera does its work quietly and without explanation. Ameera was being thrust out of life as though the Angel of Death had himself put his hand upon her. The quick breathing seemed to show that she was either afraid or in pain, but neither eyes nor mouth gave any answer to Holden's kisses. There was nothing to be said or done. Holden could only wait and suffer. The first drops of the rain began to fall on the roof, and he could hear shouts of joy in the parched city.

Not for the first time in this story are we aware of what might be called, without disparagement, its operatic strength: emotion is manipulated in an almost formal way so that its modulations seem to transcend language. Words are superfluous as Holden, forgetful of himself, kisses Ameera on the lips, while the growing patter of rain on the roofs and the joyful cries of the populace herald the end of the epidemic. Even now, when Ameera manages a few last words, they betray her anxiety about her claim on Holden's love in the face of what she sees now—as she has all along—the inevitable triumph of her white rivals.

Three days later Holden receives orders to replace a dying colleague and goes to take a last look at his house, now decayed after the torrential rains:

He found that the rains had torn down the mud pillars of the gateway, and the heavy wooden gate that had guarded his life hung lazily from one hinge. There was grass three inches high in the courtyard; Pir Khan's lodge was empty, and the sodden thatch sagged between the beams. A gray squirrel was in possession of the verandah, as if the house had been untenanted for thirty years instead of three days. . . . Ameera's room and the other one where Tota had lived were heavy with mildew; and the narrow staircase leading to the roof was streaked and stained with rain-borne mud.

It is already as though neither they nor their great love had ever existed. But what also disappears with the house, with Ameera and Tota, and the fragile, beautiful bond between the three, is any faith in a God or gods; or indeed in any order in nature. Man is on his own; and Ameera's last words bear stark testimony to the discovery: "'I bear witness—I bear witness'—the lips were forming the words on his ear—'that there is no God but—thee, beloved!'"

Kipling repeats the first phrase for a reason; the repudiation is made all the more harsh and complete by commencing with the formal Moslem statement of faith but substituting, at the end, Holden for Allah. The gods have failed them, and the only salvation is devotion to each other and to the job in hand: to that work, so often just routine, which Holden is driven to immerse himself in after Tota's death and which "repaid him by filling up his mind for nine or ten hours a day."

The title, "Without Benefit of Clergy," refers, of course, to the illicit union of Holden and Ameera, though in no censorious mood. But the words have, or had, another sense, alluding to the law of "benefit of clergy," which allowed the clergy dispensation from prosecution through civil courts. Taken in this sense, it means that there is no dispensation from the common hard fate of mankind for these two lovers, be their love ever so profound, noble, and unselfish.

III

THE five stories we have discussed show first that Kipling was concerned with the world of "natural nature," and convinced that disorder and not order is the true inclination of his universe. He was as aware as Conrad that anarchy can be held at bay only by the forceful imposition of, and loyal submission to, conventions, codes, and rituals: structures, in other words, that the mind of man must devise for his own protection. Second, they show something of Kipling's characteristic abilities as a writer, and reveal him as a master of the short-story form. Third, they are interesting for their settings, as is Kim, which many would place in the first rank of all his writing. One of the five short stories is about the sea, where it serves in a Conradian way as an image of the moral anarchy of the world. The rest of the selections are set in India, and the juxtaposition highlights the fact that the vast subcontinent comes to have precisely the same symbolic function. With this in mind, I would argue strongly that India provides Kipling with his ideal metaphor: the vehicle through which he can best express his essential artistic, rather than political, vision.

The main character in his Indian stories is not the tired, tough administrator, the resourceful sub-altern, the resilient Other Ranks, or the ever-present engineer, but India itself. Indeed this has been established in four of the five stories we have considered. "At the End of the Passage" shows four men engaged in a relentless battle against their natural environment—India. With total commitment they throw themselves into the daily routine of work, striving to tame a tiny area of the vast space that continually threatens to engulf them, while preventing the surrounding anarchy from penetrating their own fragile integrity. In this story, however, as in many of the others, there is a whisper that anarchy may already be there, planted perhaps in original sin.

As the pattern is repeated, India comes increasingly to serve as an immensely powerful symbol of the "natural nature" that is so central a component in Kipling's moral and artistic vision: the exact equivalent of Russell's crust of barely cooled lava with the flames of destruction raging underneath. Vast and featureless, it is the enemy of form: "Great, grey formless India," as it is called in Kim, overwhelms and crushes, both physically and morally. One's own truths and moral definitions blur and diffuse themselves into meaninglessness, just as they did for E. M. Forster's Mrs. Moore in A Passage to India (1924). A character who appears in a number of early Kipling stories, Mrs. Mallowe, has, in fact, occasional flashes of Mrs. Moore's perception, observing very clearly the moral destructiveness of India, where, as she says in "The Education of Otis Yeere," "you can't focus anything." Because it is Kipling, and not Forster, we are inside India looking outward through our bars, rather than outside looking in with Mrs. Moore's cool clarity of mind.

Faced by a country that can destroy them, these beleaguered Anglo-Indians band together in pitiful, blind opposition, doomed to ludicrous failure, however much they speak of Smith as a Bengal man and Jones as a Punjabi. Herded together in the Club, in the Station, in Simla, they insist upon their "difference" from the rest of India; but even in the safety of their own community, they cannot escape the constant awareness of their vulnerability:

Everybody was there, and there was a general closing up of ranks and taking stock of our losses in dead or disabled that had fallen during the past year. It was a very wet night, and I remember that we sang "Auld Lang Syne" with our feet in the Polo Championship Cup, and our heads among the stars, and swore that we were all very dear friends.

(''The Mark of the Beast")

It is in the isolated outposts that India's malignant power is to be seen at its most active in its relentless war against the aliens.

> The night-light was trimmed; the shadow of the punkah wavered across the room, and the *"flick"* of the punkah-towel and the soft whine of the rope through the wall-hole followed it. Then the punkah flagged, almost ceased. The sweat poured from Spurstow's brow. Should he go out and harangue the coolie? It started forward again with a savage jerk, and a pin came out of the towels. When this was replaced, a tomtom in the coolie-lines began to beat with the steady throb of a swollen artery inside some brain-fevered skull.
>
> ("At the End of the Passage")

Bound on his wheel, the imperial servant struggles to reduce the hostile mass of India to governable terms, more often than not ending up as "one of the rank and file who are ground up in the wheels of the Administration; losing heart and soul, and mind and strength in the process."

Always the good these expatriates do is seen, by themselves at least, to be short-term: the bringing of some sort of law and order, the relief of famine, the improvement of agriculture, and so on. Surprisingly they show little inclination to speculate about theirs being an enduring contribution and none at all to preach the notion of a thousand-year Reich. In "The Education of Otis Yeere," for example, Mrs. Mallowe has no illusions: "We are only little bits of dirt on the hillsides—here one day and blown down the *khud* the next. . . . we have no cohesion." The raj may seek to impose its institutions on this body and domesticate it, but even they are not proof against India's inexorable power of assimilation. British justice itself is on occasion eroded, as we see in "Gemini," to the level of a useful new pawn in a very old game.

The Pax Britannica had already sowed the seeds of its own destruction:

> said Wali Dad . . . "Thanks to your Government, all our heads are protected, and with the educational facilities at my command"—his eyes twinkled wickedly—"I might be a distinguished member of the local administration. Perhaps, in time, I might even be a member of a Legislative Council."

In this story, "On the City Wall" (1898), even the narrator is, quite brilliantly, shown to be unwittingly taken over (and made a fool of) by India. The collision between the old order and the new is again well illustrated. Wali Dad—who had made "an unsuc-cessful attempt to enter the Roman Church and the Presbyterian fold at the same time" and been found out by the missionaries who had "called him names . . . but . . . did not understand his trouble"—presents the most complete picture of what has happened in this collision to people like him:

> "India has gossiped for centuries—always standing in the bazars until the soldiers go by. Therefore—you are here to-day instead of starving in your own country, and I am not a Muhammadan—I am a Product—a Demnition Product. That also I owe to you and yours: that I cannot make an end to my sentence without quoting from your authors."

Exhorted to take up his "place in the world," he becomes even more ironic:

> "I might wear an English coat and trouser. I might be a leading Muhammadan pleader. I might be received even at the Commissioner's tennis-parties where the English stand on one side and the natives on the other, in order to promote social intercourse throughout the Empire."

The mordant edge to his critique is worthy of Forster's Dr. Aziz and serves as a reminder of the famous bridge party in *A Passage to India.*

In this discussion of the role of India, however, one acknowledgment is missing: to the fascination that India continued to exert while crushing and annihilating its servants. Mrs. Mallowe sees clearly enough the bars of the cage: "I don't suppose a Russian convict under the knout is able to amuse the rest of his gang; and all our men-folk here are gilded convicts."

Outside Simla, more often than not, there was not even the gilding. Yet the color and seething abundance of life with which their enemy veiled its malevolence could still attract, quite apart from the fact that, so much having been absorbed by it, the colonials could no longer have an independent existence.

Kipling reflects the fascination in many places, but nowhere more so than in the brilliantly colored pictures in *Kim.*

IV

So far it has been the object of this essay to show how India served Kipling less as an imperial shibboleth than as a token of the anarchy of "natural nature," which was, for him, the ultimate reality. What is above all striking in *Kim* is that here Kipling for the first and only time succeeds in painting a picture of a moral universe that is balanced.

Kipling's best stories are very often those that draw their power from his awareness of the chaos and anarchy that underlie the apparently solid world in which his characters move. Indeed, the Indian empire, far from being treated as substantial and permanently enduring, is shown to be valued simply because it offers a very clear structure through which "natural nature" will be bitted and bridled and a sufficiency of order imposed for the individual to secure some sort of integrity for himself. The vast body and power of India come to stand for this anarchy, and the Anglo-Indian's struggle with India, in the form of its famines, plagues, climate, size, becomes a paradigm of man's constant struggle to retain his integrity and identity in a world where he has no natural (or supernatural) ally: where, to the contrary, he is constantly persecuted and threatened with physical and moral extinction.

To ward off this outcome, the Kipling hero is a dedicated activist, for only in constantly grappling with his enemy will he gain any sense of his own reality. So the Kipling protagonist, often quite literally a builder or engineer, toils wearily on, frequently dying in his tracks but at least having secured self-consciousness for himself in the moment of his activity. Action is seen as the antidote to anarchy, and the man of action as the hero on the side of order against cosmic disorder; those who adopt a passive mode of conduct are seen as fifth-columnists and saboteurs and are denounced by Kipling in vitriolic, at times hysterical, terms.

In *Kim*, however, we find none of this neurotic polarization; and the way in which the lama, who stands for a renunciation of action and the world, is balanced by Kim and Mahbub Ali, with their respective degrees of commitment to the activist ethic, is the best thing of its kind Kipling ever did. For the first time we find in his writing evidence of a generous magnanimity, which ordinarily he is much too fearful for his own soul to indulge in.

The book is framed by Kim and the lama. It opens with Kim sitting outside the Lahore Museum astride the gun Zam-Zammah, and it closes with the lama sitting like Buddha, his quest apparently concluded. This antithesis of activist and quietist principles illustrates a structural pattern in the work that is one of Kipling's principal methods for reinforcing its uni-

ty. In the same way, youth is balanced against age, secular against spiritual, individual against communal. Cross-references are continual, and taken together they give the book a firm intellectual shape and a compelling aesthetic symmetry.

The lama's search is the one that overarches the whole design: even Kim's is dwarfed by it, and rightly so, for the significance of Kim's search lies precisely in the fact that it remains firmly committed to life on earth, in sharp contrast to the lama's, which is from the start transcendental. As a result, Kipling is able to move easily between the material and spiritual dimensions and so make a serious comment about the meaning of life without seeming too didactic.

For those who adhere to the lama's form of Buddhism, suffering and misery stem from being bound in the perpetual cycle of life, death, and rebirth. Men are condemned to this cycle by their attachment to earthly desires and ambitions; were they able to break free from these fetters they would successfully interrupt the cycle of reincarnation and reach Nirvana, that blisssful union with the Great Soul which releases them from all suffering and reasserts the oneness of all created beings. It is this cycle the lama refers to when he talks about the Wheel of Life. Those who recognize their predicament and seek to extricate themselves from it by renouncing all earthly interests and following the Buddhist law are described as followers of the Way, and among these, of course, is the lama himself. His objective is the River that was released from the earth at that place where the arrow shot by Buddha landed. The symbolism is clear: the River will wash away sin and mark the final release for this faithful devotee of the Way from the torment of the Wheel.

The Wheel becomes the single most important and pervasive image in the book. In functioning as a symbol, it links everyone and everything in the endlessness of its form. And it emphasizes what the narrative tells us explicitly: that all men are ultimately the same, nursing the same hopes and ambitions and enduring the same fate. When the lama tells the English curator of the Lahore Museum the story of the arrow and the River, the curator acknowledges that "so it is written." But we are told that he replies "sadly." He knows the tale, and his sadness sums up all men's need for this River and the consciousness that it may never come within their reach.

The Wheel of Life is an abstraction, of course, but at the end of the discussion the lama departs, brushing through the turnstile. The effect of Kipling's deft juxtaposition of the abstraction with its concrete prototype (for the turnstile is basically a wheel) is to plant the symbol firmly in the world of men.

The physical world, it is thus made clear, will certainly not be lightly dismissed, for it has a robust argument of its own to put against the lama's asceticism. By linking the Wheel of Life with the turnstile, Kipling might at first seem to be endorsing the lamaistic view of human life on earth as that of an endless, miserable chain gang, groaning under its doom. But the turnstile can also click away merrily, reflecting something of the noise, bustle, and excitement of life: the same sort of bustle and vitality that we encounter among the innumerable wheels of the Grand Trunk Road. At times, indeed, the whole Indian landscape seems to be alive with the creaking sound of well wheels, cart wheels, train wheels. And all are helping man in that activity which Kim's excited and affectionate vision convinces us has great value. In fact Kim's own health is described in terms of a wheel. When he falls ill in chapter 15, he feels that his soul is "out of gear with its surroundings—a cog-wheel unconnected with any machinery." And his return to health is signified when he feels "the wheels of his being lock up anew on the world without."

On the other hand, once seen from the lama's exalted perspective, human activity is never likely to be viewed uncritically, or unthinkingly given absolute value. Also, near the end of the book Kipling focuses the antithesis between these two states or standpoints with great imaginative force, finely contrasting a transcendent and ageless spiritual reality in which all things find themselves in an ideal unity, and the restless flux of an earth-bound, wheel-bound humanity. The delicate, lemon-colored background throws the figure of Buddha into heavy relief, infusing into it a solid reality that reflects the assurance of the lama's faith: "[Kim] peered at the cross-legged figure, outlined jet-black against the lemon-coloured drift of light. So does the stone Bodhisat sit who looks down upon the patent self-registering turnstiles of the Lahore Museum" (ch. 15). So Kipling sympathetically balances a recognition of the vanity of man's earthly ambitions and activity with a sense of life's rich possibilities within its given limits—and symbolizes both with the Wheel.

Kim's nickname, "Little Friend of All the World" —perhaps it sounds less embarrassing in Urdu— clearly identifies him with the idea of human community, and his ready command of vernacular speech and proverbial wisdom, to say nothing of his intimate knowledge of native customs and even native secrets, greatly strengthens the association. Later, when he sets out on his own search along with the lama, he is more than a little inclined to forget all about it in the sheer pleasure of participating in the life going on around him. Given that Kim's physical being remains rather shadowy, the reader is oddly responsive to his sensations. As a result, the countryside and its people have vitality and clarity as well as richness of color, as if the whole world were new. Once more, through his skillful manipulation of perspective, Kipling makes us aware that if Kim is young, India is very, very old: the possessor of a vast history casts a light on man's absurd conceits, as, for example, when man sits astride the spoils of his latest, ephemeral, conquest.

Several of the elements of Kim's love for the life that surrounds him appear in an example of Kipling's excellent description:

The diamond-bright dawn woke men and crows and bullocks together. Kim sat up and yawned, shook himself, and thrilled with delight. This was seeing the world in real truth; this was life as he would have it—bustling and shouting, the buckling of belts, and beating of bullocks and creaking of wheels, lighting of fires and cooking of food, and new sights at every turn of the approving eye. The morning mist swept off in a whorl of silver, the parrots shot away to some distant river in shrieking green hosts: all the well-wheels within earshot went to work. India was awake, and Kim was in the middle of it, more awake and more excited than any one, chewing on a twig that he would presently use as a tooth-brush; for he borrowed right- and left-handedly from all the customs of the country he knew and loved.

(ch. 4)

The lama's search, as I have said, is for the mystical River that gushed out of the earth at the precise spot where the arrow shot by Buddha himself had landed. It is by no means fanciful to discern another parallel here between Kim and the lama, for wherever Kim's glance falls, a river of life springs up. Indeed it is precisely the phrase he thinks of when he first sets foot on the Grand Trunk Road: "The lama, as usual, was deep in meditation, but Kim's bright eyes were open wide. This broad, smiling river of life, he considered, was a vast improvement on the cramped and crowded Lahore streets" (ch. 4). And since what is reality for Kim is also reality for those who embrace an activist creed, it is appropriate that the old Rissaldar should take the same view of "the Great Road which is the back-bone of all Hind": "All castes and kinds of men move here. Look! Brahmins and chumars, bankers and tinkers, barbers and bunnias, pilgrims and potters—all the world going and coming. It is to me as a river from which I am withdrawn like a log after a flood" (ch. 3).

Now we have another river, which is opposed to the mystical River of the lama's search; and another wheel, opposed to the lama's Wheel. In the first of these three quotations, Kipling seems to go out of his way to mention wheels that are altogether mundane. The purpose is clear: the world where this wheel revolves is the workaday world where men live and where action seems to have an intrinsic value every bit as justifiable as renunciation.

One major symbol remains to be considered, that of the Great Game. The Great Game is the rather arch euphemism that Colonel Creighton and Mahbub Ali use to describe their work for military intelligence. In this role they are the vigilantes of empire, omnisciently aware of all that might threaten its security from either outside its borders or within them, and consequently ready to move at once to checkmate any advance by the enemies of law and order. Kim, with his knowledge of the country and its people, and his quick wits, is a natural recruit and is duly inducted into the Game, though with more ambivalence in his attitude to it than he is usually given credit for.

The significance of the Great Game goes beyond the limits of military intelligence, however, for it is an emblem of the deadly serious game that Kipling played all his life to secure a personal identity and integrity. In *Kim* as elsewhere in his writings, India is a metaphor for the artifact of the individual self; an entity that, as we have seen, is perpetually threatened and at risk. So these vigilantes who participate in the Great Game are certainly guarding the political structure of the Indian empire (in particular, the threat from Russian subversion, even invasion, was regarded as a real one), but they are also, once more, acting the roles of guardians of a moral structure.

From my own critical viewpoint, the intrusion of the Great Game nearly brings disaster with it. One recovers, of course, for all the other very good things in the novel are still there at the end; but one's confidence in the writer has been shaken and an element of suspicion and resentment at the damage done to such an imaginative, potentially triumphant work is also, alas, still there. To account for the harm done to

the book by the Great Game, it is necessary to recapitulate a little.

Kipling is enormously successful in creating a sense of unity and universality in *Kim*. Binding all together both morally and aesthetically is the lama's overarching search for unity with the Great Soul, whereby man's physical and spiritual destiny is universalized in the pervasive symbols of the Wheel and the River. But the chief source of the effect is Kipling's imaginative capacity for suffusing the narrative with a palpable warmth of sympathy and human love, whereby even a character as thinly drawn as Mahbub Ali becomes most real through his caring and affection for Kim. The warm, human sympathies are most effective in creating the sense of unity and universality when Kim observes the teeming life of India. Life does indeed seem an endless, intricately patterned tapestry.

Then we are subjected to a sudden and unpleasant shock. Up there, somewhere near the home of the Northern Folk, there is a frontier that puts a check on this developing comity of being; and from behind it comes a threat. There are barbarians prowling the outer marches of this "great and wonderful world." At once India seems to shrink within discernible perimeters. The beautiful submission to sense impressions seems suddenly less relaxed, and we wonder in a slightly depressed way whether we are being told that this variety of people, living amicably side by side, are doing so by virtue of the great Pax Britannica, which then becomes the (factitious) source of all unity. Rightly, I think, we suspend judgment, for we experience the more charitable effects of the lama's vision, which makes the idea of empire seem absurd, and those of Kim's humanity, which makes it seem vicious.

Kim's perceptions show us the unity in all this diversity, and as long as this impression stems from his own self-delight, his pleasure in his own senses and in his excited participation in a multitude of different actions, all is well. He is part of what he sees, and this life-affirming spirit in him is reflected in his surroundings. But something of this unity comes from Kim's precocious *knowingness;* and we are at once in what can be only, at best, the world of make-believe and, at worst, the world of the British empire. Either way, the unity seems suddenly much more artificial. Simultaneously we became aware of the reason for our dislike of Kim's nickname, "Little Friend of All the World," for in sentimentalizing the desired universal brotherhood, it compromises the writer's detachment; and we see behind Kim the pressure of Kipling's own needs. So we reject the narrator's attempt to impress us with his omniscience: "If there be one thing in the world that the small Hill-Rajahs deny it is just this charge; but it happens to be one thing that the bazars believe, when they discuss the mysterious slave-traffics of India" (ch. 4). A little of this elaborately casual parading of obscure knowledge goes a long way; and we get a great deal of it: "Few can translate the picture-parable [of the Wheel]; there are not twenty in all the world who can draw it surely without a copy: of those who can both draw and expound are but three" (ch. 11).

What is exposed by this "knowingness" is the strength of Kipling's personal desire to impose his *own* unity on his surroundings. Before, he had been saved by his literary tact, letting a sense of the inherent unity of things breathe through the luminous countryside that materializes under the purifying vision of the youthful Kim; now, his tact deserts him under pressure from his own paramount and neurotic need for security against the anarchy that is always about to destroy him.

In concluding this critique, it is profitable to discuss the ending of the novel. This, too, has been criticized on the ground that nothing has been "settled": Kim has not formally chosen between the lama and government service. Such an expectation is not only a misunderstanding of the nature of the book—which, no more than, say, Henry Fielding's *Tom Jones*, is the sort of book that ties knots or reaches a denouement—it also seems to me an oversight of the true significance and absolute propriety of the ending. Although Kipling may owe something to Miguel Cervantes for the concept of *Kim*, it is not of great help to think of it as picaresque. For Kim and his lama do not stumble out of one adventure into another; in fact the only major adventure in the book is an anticlimax, when, after a brief skirmish, the two intruders fade quickly from the scene and are overshadowed by the lama's flight from the deluding mountains.

What we get, in fact, is not a series of adventures so much as a series of pictures—and certainly not just pretty pictures, for all of them have a moral significance that is ultimately anchored in the creative antithesis provided by the contrasting visions of Kim and the lama.

The novel leaves us with a highly visual memory. Scene after vivid scene has arrested itself until we find ourselves in a superb kind of picture gallery, at the center of which is a magnificent portrayal of the Indian landscape. To paint it Kipling seems to have adopted the technique of J. M. W. Turner, for when we think of this landscape we think of a rich luminosity. Light pours over it: in the brilliant morning, when "all the rich Punjab [lies] out in the splendour of the keen sun"; at noon, when it streams through the shade of the mango tree "playing checkerwise" on the face of the lama; in "the smoke-scented evening, copper-dun and turquoise across the fields." Not even at night is light absent, for with great skill Kipling brings firelight and sunlight cleverly together:

It was a strange picture that Kim watched between drooped eyelids. The lama, very straight and erect, the deep folds of his yellow clothing slashed with black in the light of the *parao* fires precisely as a knotted tree-trunk is slashed with the shadow of the long sun, addressed a tinsel and lacquered *ruth* which burned like a many-coloured jewel in the same uncertain light. The patterns on the gold-worked curtains ran up and down, melting and reforming as the folds shook and quivered to the night wind; and when the talk grew more earnest the jewelled forefinger snapped out little sparks of light between the embroideries.

(ch. 4)

This usually golden light that continually suffuses the landscape has a coalescent effect, bringing all into one focus. It could be said that, in a very large view, the light arrests time, eternalizing Kim's youth and innocence, the lama's search, and the flux of human life, while vaguely suggesting that it has a benevolent source not entirely of this world.

Kipling's Indian pastoral is modified in an interesting and Victorian way, for these subsidiary pictures are remarkably similar to the narrative pictures, or even the parable pictures, favored by so many painters of the time, including Kipling's relatives. The parable picture is, indeed, something that Kipling excelled in, and its appearance in *Kim* links the book with two others in a trio that for many people constitutes his finest work: *The Jungle Books* (1894–1895) and *Just So Stories* (1902).

One of the most eloquent and resonant of all his pictorial compositions occurs near the end of *Kim* and strongly supports the case that the novel depends primarily on a pictorial narrative structure. It is the scene where Mahbub Ali and the lama sit beside the inert figure of Kim, who is sunk in something "deeper than sleep," and talk quietly about his future (or, perhaps, the Future, for the episode is imbued with a more universal signifi-cance):

The ground was good clean dust—no new herbage that, living, is halfway to death already, but the hopeful dust that holds the seed of all life. He felt it between his toes, pat-ted it with his palms, and joint by joint, sighing luxurious-ly, laid him down full length along in the shadow of the wooden-pinned cart. And Mother Earth was as faithful as the Sahiba. She breathed through him to restore the poise he had lost lying so long on a cot cut off from her good cur-rents. His head lay powerless upon her breast, and his opened hands surrendered to her strength. The many-rooted tree above him, and even the dead man-handled wood beside, knew what he sought, as he himself did not know. Hour upon hour he lay deeper than sleep.

(ch. 15)

Mahub Ali is anxious to save Kim for the world—which in his interpretation means government ser-vice; but the lama, regarding this concern as irrele-vant, confidently claims Kim for that Other World to which the lama has dedicated himself.

There they sit, like two presiding (and somewhat imperial-minded) deities, calmly prescribing for un-conscious and innocent Youth its destiny. But in this the picture parable does no more than repeat in a concentrated form the moral proposition advanced by the impressive diptych within which the book is enclosed: the picture at the beginning of an even more youthful Kim astride the gun; and the other one, at the end, of the lama seated, like Buddha, under his tree. Nor should it be otherwise, for it is wholly beyond the nature and scope of such a com-position to tell us of the degree to which Kim's own life will veer toward one or the other of these poles.

V

KIPLING had, as we now can see, certain prophylac-tics against the moral disorder that for him expressed the true character of the universe. Chief among these was the day's work, which teaches us what we really ought to thank our creator for:

Not for Prophecies or Powers, Visions, Gifts, or Graces,
But the unregardful hours that grind us in our places
With the burden on our backs, the weather in our faces.

Not for any Miracle of easy Loaves and Fishes,
But for doing, 'gainst our will, work against our wishes—
Such as finding food to fill daily-emptied dishes.

("The Supports")

Work, routine, discipline, law, these are the prin-cipal weapons to ward off anarchy. Without them there is, in Kipling's view, little that can be done to prevent the complete disintegration of that fragile artifact, the self. But Kipling goes a step further and includes art as yet another of the bulwarks, seeing it as the job of the artist both to tell the truth and to bring help and comfort to a mankind free of illu-sions.

A number of his stories deal either centrally or substantially with the nature and function of art and the role of the artist, stories such as "'Teem,'" "The Bull That Thought," "The Eye of Allah," "The Children of the Zodiac," and, of course, his only full-length novel in conventional form, *The Light That Failed*. There is no doubt that in the latter he is rebut-ting some of the charges made against his own art when his work erupted on the London literary scene. After the initial raptures over this startling new talent, when critics praised him in particular for his brilliance of color—J. M. Barrie, for example, de-scribed his prose as having the effect of a very bright lantern—and his creation of an exotic mise-en-scène for his tales, came the hostile attacks on the un-couthness, vulgarity, brutality, and lack of shading in his portrayal of character and events.

It is not fanciful to find something of Kipling in Dick Heldar in *The Light That Failed*, when in his absence the character is being admonished for ap-parently assuming that he can "storm up and down the world with a box of moist tubes and a slick brush," or when he is aggressively proclaiming that "real Art" is the ultrarealistic soldier in his own painting "His Last Shot":

I made him a flushed, dishevelled, bedevilled scallawag, with his helmet at the back of his head, and the living fear of death in his eye, and the blood oozing out of a cut over his ankle-bone. He wasn't pretty, but he was all soldier and very much man.

(ch. 4)

But this is not what the "art-appreciating" public wants. To them, says Dick with heavy irony, "it was brutal and coarse and violent,—man being naturally gentle when he's fighting for his life. They wanted something more restful, with a little more colour." So he has taken "His Last Shot" back and made a few alterations:

I put him into a lovely red coat without a speck on it. That is Art. I polished his boots,—observe the high light on the toe. That is Art. I cleaned his rifle—rifles are always clean on service,—because that is Art. I pipeclayed his helmet—pipeclay is always used on active service, and is indispensable to Art.

(ch. 4)

From this harangue it is fairly obvious what Dick's—and Kipling's—view is of the nature of art. It is emphatically realist, with much stress on detail and no nonsense about shutting one's eyes to what polite society might regard as offensive and unpleasant. Art "smells of tobacco and blood," says Maisie accusingly; and Dick, who knows "what life and death really mean," would not deny it, though he does not regard himself as limited to such themes. To prove it he embarks on a "head" to rival her "Melancolia," but, ironically again, it begins to take shape only when he finds a real-life prostitute to act as a model. (Predictably, and in the best fin-de-siècle manner, Kipling has this "real" creature of the gutter destroy what is possibly Dick's greatest work.)

The novel puts Dick's theory into practice, too, for two of the most memorable descriptions are of a brothel in Port Said and a battlefield that Dick visits again, after the action is over, where there has not been time to bury the twelve hundred dead. Dick says: "The sight of that field taught me a good deal. It looked just like a bed of horrible toadstools in all colours, and—I'd never seen men in bulk go back to their beginnings before."

Realism of this order demands close attention to detail and consequently a complete command over draftsmanship and materials: in Dick's words, "A great deal depends on being master of the bricks and mortar of the trade." At another point he says to Maisie: "You have a sense of colour, but you want form. Colour's a gift,—put it aside and think no more about it,—but form you can be drilled into." As a writer Kipling certainly endorses these views, as he does Dick's respect for inspiration: "Good work has nothing to do with—doesn't belong to—the person who does it. It's put into him or her from outside. . . . All we can do is to learn how to do our work to be master of our material. . . . Everything else comes from outside ourselves."

Kipling believed strongly in his "daemon," as he called his inspiration, also seeing it as something outside himself. This insistence on form and accurate drawing may, however, owe something to Burne-Jones, who, after the somewhat inspirational tuition of Rossetti, was instructed by G. F. Watts, who in turn put much greater emphasis on the discipline of drawing. Watts "compelled me to draw better," Burne-Jones said many years later, and made him realize, according to one critic, "a sounder basis for his art."

The emphasis on craftsmanship and technique is asserted again in "The Bull That Thought" (first published 1924) and "The Eye of Allah" (1926). The latter is one more of Kipling's reticent yet highly organized tales in which a great deal of affective life is going on just under the surface. The Abbot's love for the Lady Anne, now mortally sick; John's deep suffering following the death of his beloved mistress (his gift to the Lady Anne of what can only be his mistress's carnelian necklace is a delicate touch); the frustration and anguish of Roger of Salerno at being too old to make use of new scientific discoveries that the church will suppress if it can: all of this comes to light under the "eye of Allah"—an early microscope—as though the eye itself were revealing an intense world of deep, hidden, private feelings, schooled into concealment by the discipline that the characters, with difficulty and some reluctance, accept.

At the end, the wise and experienced Abbot deliberately smashes the protomicroscope to pieces despite the desperate appeals of Roger Bacon and Roger of Salerno. That it could have been put to the service of humanity there is no doubt; perhaps it could even have helped to heal people as ill as the Lady Anne. But the Abbot knows that the church will not at this time allow it, since the truth it advances would undermine the church's authority. Disorder and death would follow the premature advocacy of the invention: "Fated as dawn, but as the dawn, delayed/Till the just hour should strike." In the meantime the church contributes to a soul-saving serenity, as is noted by the party returning across the roofs of the building after having conducted their experiment on the stagnant puddle: "They walked quietly back along the leads, three English counties laid out in evening sunshine around them; church upon church, monastery upon monastery, cell after cell, and the bulk of a vast cathedral moored on the edge of the banked shoals of sunset."

In the tale, the artist-craftsman John of Burgos is twice made to say that his trade is the outside of things. (The first time there is a slight but significant difference: "There's less risk for the craftsman who deals with the outside of things.") Again it is clear that the sentiment allows some identification with Kipling: in it we find both a reply to those critics (like

Henry James and Francis Adams) who claimed that Kipling was unable to realize characters with convincing interior lives, and a statement of his interpretation of the role of the artist. The latter could *suggest* an interior life but should do so through a concentration on the things of the surface—a modus operandi that inevitably results in an aesthetic with the accent on the public and social dimensions of men's lives.

In "The Eye of Allah" Kipling once again refuses to exempt the artist from the fate of those he writes about or paints. He, too, is under the common doom, and his art will help to ease the pain that is not physical in its origins. When John of Burgos returns to the monastery after the death of his mistress, the Abbott, whose own mistress is dying, shows his understanding in a conversation with him. Of a "cake of dried poppy juice," he says to him: "This has power to cut off all pain from a man's body"; and when John assents, he adds: "But for pain of the soul there is, outside God's Grace, but one drug; and that is a man's craft, learning, or other helpful motion of his own mind." John knows this too and sinks himself "past all recollection" in his great work, the illumination of the Gospel according to St. Luke. And out of his knowledge of intense anguish and suffering comes his best work. When the senior copyist asks him how the great task is proceeding, John knows that he has at last got it fully realized: "'All here!' John tapped his forehead with his pencil. 'It has been only waiting these months to—ah God!—be born.'" Out of the deaths of his mistress and his newborn son comes the proof of his talent.

The story that illustrates most specifically and successfully the "applied" nature of Kipling's view of art, and its relation to human experience and suffering, is without doubt "The Children of the Zodiac" (first published 1891). It is really about death and dying, a subject that looms large with Kipling; but it is without the passion, savagery, and cynicism that the same subject attracts in other stories, such as the bleak and moving "On Greenhow Hill" (1890).

In the tale, the Children of the Zodiac learn mortality, having started with the belief that they were gods and having been treated as such by men. During the time when they persisted in seeing themselves as gods, they understood nothing of human affairs. When stories of death and dying and requests for help were brought to the Bull, he would only "lower his huge head and answer, 'What is that to me?'" Nor could the Children understand laughter,

and laughter, like love, is community. The first sign of their growing understanding appears when Leo kisses the Girl.

Through the kiss—the human kiss—they have opened the door to the human world and closed it on the supernatural. Immediately afterward the Girl claims understanding, and almost as soon we see the first intimations of mortality:

> "We have come to the end of things," said the man quietly. "This that was my wife—"
> "As I am Leo's wife," said the Girl quickly, her eyes staring.

It is the Girl, too, who understands why the old man, after complaining of having to live, tries to escape death. There is the growing realization that they are not immortal:

> "Leo we must learn more about this for their sakes."
> "For *their* sakes," said Leo very loudly.
> "Because *we* are never going to die," said the Girl and Leo together, still more loudly.

Their fears are confirmed when Leo asks Scorpio why he should trouble the children of men and receives the answer in Scorpio's question: "Are you so sure that I trouble the children of men alone?" The Bull, the Ram, and the Twins all admit their ultimate mortality and their need to keep working—though all explicitly find life like this unpleasant. Then Leo finds his own fate in the House of the Crab, though by this time he has realized his identity with the sons of men. There follows the final rejection of their status as gods and of their mythical immortality:

> Next morning they returned to their proper home and saw the flowers and the sacrifices that had been laid before their doors by the villagers of the hills. Leo stamped down the fire with his heel, and the Girl flung the flower-wreaths out of sight, shuddering as she did so.

And when the villagers visited them they found not gods but simply "a man and a woman with frightened white faces sitting hand in hand on the altarsteps."

Leo—it is impossible to dissociate Kipling from him here—finds it hard to accept the reality of death; and after an evening of pleasant, happy company, redolent of health, life, and vigor, he wakes up with the poignant realization:

"Every one of those people we met just now will die—"

"So shall we," said the Girl sleepily. "Lie down again, dear." Leo could not see that her face was wet with tears.

But Leo's fears cannot be stilled, and he goes in search of the Bull, who is so tired after his walk that (happily) all his contemplation is taken up by the beautiful straight furrows he has made that day. "'Well,' said the Bull, "what will you do? . . . You cannot pull a plough. . . . I can, and that prevents me from thinking of the Scorpion.'"

Leo, however, finds that he can sing, and though he would have liked "to lie down and brood over the words of the Crab," he is persuaded to continue singing. First he sings the song of the fearless, but soon discovers another, much more powerful, song.

This was a thing he could never have done had he not met the Crab face to face. He remembered facts concerning cultivators, and bullocks, and rice-fields that he had not particularly noticed before the interview, and he strung them all together, growing more interested as he sang, and he told the cultivator much more about himself and his work than the cultivator knew. The Bull grunted approval as he toiled down the furrows for the last time that day, and the song ended, leaving the cultivator with a very good opinion of himself in his aching bones.

So Leo becomes the Singer, the Poet, the Writer, or simply the Artist, whose job it is to secure just such an effect as the above quotation describes. Boldly he has confronted his destiny, and now, through his efforts, man will be helped toward dignity, integrity, and self-respect, as well as to the modicum of happiness that he is permitted.

It was after this that Leo made the Song of the Bull who had been a God and forgotten the fact, and he sang it in such a manner that half the young men in the world conceived that they too might be Gods without knowing it. A half of that half grew impossibly conceited, and died early. A half of the remainder strove to be Gods and failed, but the other half accomplished four times more work than they would have done under any other delusion.

It remains a delusion, but without it existence would not be possible.

And now the last vestiges of divinity have disappeared from the Children of the Zodiac. The Girl dies, and with her death Leo knows—in terms highly suggestive of the Fall—"all the sorrow that a man could know including the full knowledge of his own fall who had once been a god." But he continues to

sing the same song, teaching fortitude and denying any facile, mystic optimism. One of his listeners is struck down:

"It is well for me, Leo that you sang for forty years."

"Are you afraid?" said Leo. . . .

"I am a man, not a God," said the man. "I should have run away but for your songs. My work is done, and I die without making a great show of my fear."

"I am very well paid," said Leo to himself. "Now that I see what my songs are doing, I will sing better ones."

But the Artist in the middle of his work meets his own fate in Cancer, the Crab. And at the end it is emphasized that the Artist makes the same remark as all human beings, "Why have you come for me now?" Then he too draws himself up and, recalling the godhead he once thought he possessed, reaffirms his fearlessness. Kipling with a careful touch completes his story's development: "What is that to me?" said the Crab.

It is, then, the duty of the artist to "draw the Thing as he sees It for the God of Things as They are." Wreaths of marigolds presented to gods who are not gods will do nothing to ameliorate the lot of the children of men; but if the poet, the artist, can show them how to live with the maximum of fortitude and dignity, while doing nothing to minimize the stark certainty or finality of death, his contribution is precious. Above all he must be in the world of men—there is his "proper home."

> Go to your work and be strong, halting not in your
>   ways,
> Baulking the end half-won for an instant dole of
>   praise.
> Stand to your work and be wise—certain of sword
>   and pen,
> Who are neither children nor Gods, but men in a world
>   of men!
>
>   ("England's Answer")

Edmund Wilson's accusation that Kipling lacked faith in the artistic vocation seems to me a strange one, since Kipling's reverence for the artist's enduring contribution is proved in many places—even if the artist is a music-hall singer, as "A Recantation," dedicated to "Lyde of the Music Halls," makes clear:

> *What boots it on the Gods to call?*
> *Since, answered or unheard,*
> *We perish with the Gods and all*
> *Things made—except the Word.*

The last verse of "A Recantation" could very well serve as a coda to "The Children of the Zodiac":

> Yet they who use the Word assigned,
> To hearten and make whole,
> Not less than Gods have served mankind,
> Though vultures rend their soul.

VI

KIPLING's feeling for humanity as well as his sensitive portrayal of the Anglo-Indian stems from his recognition of the immeasurable preciousness of the individual self in "man," and of the unceasing battle with the Lords of Life to which man is ineluctably joined in defense of the self.

Such a realization, such a concern, can only stem from clear-sightedness. For Kipling, as for Conrad, there is a crisis of realization—such as Leo experiences—when man faces his destiny clearly and without illusions. But whereas Conrad projected this crisis in explicit artistic statements through characters like McWhirr and Mitchell on the one hand and Lord Jim on the other, Kipling leaves it largely unprojected. The crisis is part of his own experience, and though it obviously informs his work, it very rarely becomes the subject of it. (Perhaps what he lacks artistically is a reliable spokesman such as Conrad's Marlow, and Kipling's early development of the technical device we now know as "the unreliable narrator" is his attempt to find a remedy.) The fact that this crisis influences but is scarcely ever realized, in artistic terms, in his writing has an unfortunate effect upon his characterizations. In the presentation of an individual character, all traces are frequently concealed, with the result that the real dynamic of the character is largely denied him in the moment of his appearance; he arrives postcrisis with an upper lip so stiff as to preclude any explanation of his behavior. Consequently his inevitable courage, fortitude, and endurance have too often the dead unreality of a fait accompli. Kipling seems to shrink nervously from bringing the crisis into the public world of his characterization, but his awareness of it cannot be suppressed. Adherence to a code, insistence on work and discipline, are in the Kipling hero indications not of attitudinizing but of a deep sensitivity that has allowed him to see far into "the wheel and the drift of Things."

With his characters living on the Edge of Nothing,

Kipling's awareness of the abyss of "natural nature" is acknowledged in one way or another throughout his work. In the later as well as the earlier stories he returns to supernatural themes or to dealing with men who are in some way obsessed—men who are literally taken possession of by something larger and more powerful than themselves. Whether we take "The Lost Legion," "At the End of the Passage," "The Mark of the Beast," "In the Same Boat," or "The Woman in His Life," what is presented is self-possession versus possession—or the threat of possession—by the nonself. Nameless and shapeless, this malignant force, which derives from the moral anarchy that constantly threatens Kipling's carefully constructed identity, haunts his work in capitalized abstractions; it is a "Thing" or an "It"; it is "the Horror passing speech"; it is, very frequently, a Face that is faceless, depersonalized, dehumanized. Such, for instance, are the Faces, mildewed and half-eaten, that Miss Henschil sees in her nightmares in "In the Same Boat," or the Face in "A Matter of Fact," whose "horror . . . lay in the eyes, for those were sightless—white, in sockets as white as scraped bone, and blind," or the one we encounter in "La Nuit Blanche":

> Then a Face came, blind and weeping,
>   And It couldn't wipe Its eyes,
> And It muttered I was keeping
>   Back the moonlight from the skies; . . .

There are three non-Indian stories that invoke the supernatural in a particularly telling way, though the supernatural event is not what the story is about. In fact all three are about an excessive, even violent, sexual passion: in the case of two of them the principals could be said to be possessed by it. The stories could be prefaced by the poem "Gipsy Vans," which is attached to one of them. Two of these tales, "A Madonna of the Trenches" and "The Wish House," are among Kipling's later work; they were published within a few months of each other in 1924.

Almost from the outset, as has been shown, Kipling's writing is marked by a density of organization, a structuring of detail in which no item is superfluous, and a narrator far more active and independent than has been generally recognized. It is very far from the case, therefore, as has long been implied, that only the later work has sophistication of organization. As proof there is the third of the tales, the celebrated conundrum "Mrs. Bathurst" (published 1904), dense to the point of impenetrability. The effect of the exceptional degree of suppressed narrative in "Mrs. Bathhurst" is, for the most part, to tease us in the right way; that is, in a way that stimulates the reader by increasing the interpretative possibilities in action and event—the sort of thing contemporary novelists and dramatists do a little more crudely, by suggesting several possible endings to their novels and plays.

In "Mrs. Bathurst" Kipling's pictorial sense is active in a particularly dramatic and focal way. The key episode involves a quite literal picture, a new-fangled moving-picture, and the denouement is a picture of another kind: an exceptionally graphic representation of two people turned into charcoal by lightning: he standing up, she (if it is a she) on her knees in an apparent gesture of devotion—with no narrative explanation following. It is a tale, too, in which a recognition of the strength—sometimes the obsessive strength—of sexual desire is made not only explicit but far more convincing than in the conventional fin-de-siècle treatment of such a theme.

Teasing though the tale is, I do not think it is as much of a wild-goose chase as is the pursuit of the Boy Niven (with the besotted reader in the role of the credulous seamen). What few concrete impressions are left, *do* stay with us. They illustrate a permanent concern of the author, as the rest of our reading readily confirms: the power of an obsession to lure man away from the security and discipline of his craft or order to what is wild and strange and ultimately destructive. And the image of the two charcoal figures, lately possessed of such an energy of passion that it has burned them up, and still so full of a mystery from which they resolutely exclude us, is abidingly powerful. I have only one criticism: Pyecroft assumes that the crouching figure was a man; Pritchard that it was Mrs. Bathurst. For Hooper to keep silent is surely to cheat a little; for he was there and saw them.

In this story the inexplicable nature of the universe, unsusceptible to reason and law (that is what makes it such a hostile environment to man), is once more at the forefront of the picture. And here Vickery is representative of what happens when the world's disorder is allowed to enter his own mind: it destroys him, as we see when he is pointedly made to repudiate all the order, discipline, and law that are summed up in the regulations of the Royal Navy, which are recalled on every other page. In this as in other ways, we are forcefully reminded of Conrad's

Lord Jim. There Captain Brierly also is shaken to the roots of his moral being by what a fellow officer does; whereas Vickery's captain only puts on his court-martial face, Brierly commits suicide. Before he does so, however, he throws away his chronometer. We recall that Vickery's captain is said to have been seen looking like this only once before, when someone threw overboard the gunsights. Both instruments signify order and control.

That anarchy should, in this story, manifest itself in excessive physical passion is of the greatest interest. Elliott Gilbert is right, I think, in *The Good Kipling* (1972), when he relates this directly to Kipling's complex attitude to women:

Women as individuals may be charming and wholly innocent and yet at the same time may be acting, unconsciously, as the agents of a terrible power totally beyond their understanding or control. And though this power may originally have been generated by some overwhelming creative urge, its random, mindless application can just as easily be deadly and destructive.

(p. 102)

Kipling's mother, it is tempting to speculate, had much to answer for when she abandoned her son to Aunty Rosa, in that house of desolation at Southsea. On the other hand, if she had not done so, I doubt that we would ever have had Mowgli and his surrogate family of wolves, let alone Mrs. Bathurst.

In "A Madonna of the Trenches" the supernatural element is more explicit; but again it occurs as the product of an intense and illicit passion. That passion has a fundamentally disorienting effect on the principal observer and comes to reflect once more the moral anarchy that threatens to destroy the foundations of man's conventional universe.

As usual in Kipling, no detail of the environment or what is enacted within it is superfluous. Clem Strangwick, the central figure, is one of Kipling's many broken men who return from the war, their sanity undermined by the horror of their experiences. World War I, though all too real to Kipling (his only son was killed in it), was yet another vehicle for his vision of the world as a place of lawless anarchy where order, personal and cosmic, fights a losing battle against chaos. Randall Jarrell makes an interesting and perceptive remark in this connection. Quoting an observation of William James's—"The lunatic's visions of horror are all drawn from the material of daily fact. Our civilization is founded on the shambles, and each individual existence goes out in a lonely spasm of helpless agony. If you protest, my friend, wait till you arrive there yourself"—Jarrell then adds:

Kipling had arrived there early and returned there often. One thinks sadly of how deeply congenial to this torturing obsessive knowledge of Kipling's the first World War was: the death and anguish of Europe produced some of his best and most terrible stories. . . . The world *was* Hell and India underneath, after all; and he could say to the Victorian, Edwardian Europeans who had thought it all just part of his style: "You wouldn't believe me!"[2]

The framework of "A Madonna of the Trenches" is provided by the story's being set in a Freemason's Lodge—for Kipling, yet another model for order and discipline; and it is within this haven of structure that Strangwick has a recurrence of the breakdown he endured in the trenches. Apparently he cannot get out of his mind the frozen corpses under the duckboards in the bottom of the trenches: "I can't stand it! There's nothing on earth creaks like they do! And—and when it thaws we—we've got to slap 'em back with a spa-ade!"

Keede, the doctor who attends Strangwick now, was, as it happens, the medical officer at the front to whom Strangwick had been brought when he had his first collapse. Then as now Keede believes that Strangwick is using the horrors he had witnessed to protect himself against something still more terrifying; he himself gives a studiedly casual account of the same scene, in even more repellent detail, when he tells of how the French had faced both sides of their trenches with their own dead soldiers "to keep the mud back." Ordinary though he makes the scene sound, this degradation of the human body is an important detail in the story. Gradually we get at the truth.

Strangwick's family is a close-knit working-class group in which a network of relationships binds all together in an apparently solid and unbreakable order. (We are reminded that the Kiplings used to talk about their own unit as the Family Square.) Strangwick's unsettling discovery is that Sergeant Gadsoe, who has been from childhood his honorary uncle, and Strangwick's aunt, Bella Armine, have for many years been deeply in love. Because of the

"family square" it is impossible for them to desert their respective spouses and live together, and their only hope is that they will be together after death. Bella is, in fact, dying of cancer, and the brief note that she sends to Gadsoe, telling him of the date by which her "little trouble" will be over, conveys a suppressed, conspiratorial excitement—even jubilation. On the day she has appointed, her ghost appears before Gadsoe *and* Strangwick in the trenches. The latter is appalled, not just at her apparition, but at the behavior of the two lovers as well. Gadsoe's cry, Strangwick recognizes, is both of joy and relief, his "Thank Gawd" referring back to their conversation a few minutes earlier, when he quoted from the burial service, "If, after the manner of man, I have fought with beasts at Ephesus, what advantageth it me if the dead rise not?"

Strangwick's mind cannot cope with the double revelation that Bella's ghost brings with it. A new and unpleasant dimension has been added to his view of the world and its possibilities, hitherto closely regulated by his culture's totems and taboos. The words of the burial service—which have been assimilated into his background as a vaguely consoling piece of mumbo-jumbo that he does not properly understand (he talks about fighting with "beasts of officers")—in effect disturb his sense of being safely anchored. "You see . . . there wasn't a single gor-dam thing left abidin' for me to take hold of, here or hereafter. If the dead *do* rise—and I saw 'em—why —why *anything* can 'appen. Don't you understand?"

He has been permitted a sudden discomposing glimpse of the abyss, then. But what has caused him to see the chaos is almost as important as the view itself: he has discovered that sexual passion can exist on a scale of intensity that puts it outside nature; that is, outside the nature that is circumscribed and tamed by family squares, rituals of love and marriage, and the like, all rounded off with the intonation of a misunderstood burial service. Repeatedly his shock is registered in his reference to the strength of passion that he saw on his aunt's face: "All that time Auntie Armine stood with 'er arms out—an' a look on 'er face! *I* didn't know such things was or could be."

The experience demoralizes him completely: "I saw 'im an' 'er—she dead since mornin' time, an' he killin' 'imself before my livin' eyes so's to carry on with 'er for all Eternity—an' she 'oldin' out 'er arms for it! I want to know where I'm *at*." What crowns

[2]"On Preparing to Read Kipling," in E. L. Gilbert, ed., *Kipling and the Critics* (New York, 1965), p. 147.

everything for Clem Strangwick and brings final devastation with it is the fact that these lovers come from his own network of relationships. More than that, they are, so to speak, the elders of the tribe, who by virtue of their age are seen by him to be an organic part of the moral fabric of his community and coterminous with it. And Kipling carefully underlines their age. Early in the story Gadsoe is described as "an elderly bird who must have lied like a parrot to get out to the front at his age"; Bella's offense seems to be summed up in Strangwick's frequently repeated, "An' she nearer fifty than forty an' me own Aunt."

So completely is Clem's faith in women and in a moral order shattered that he has decided to break off his own engagement (and is threatened, ironically, with the law as a consequence). And once more, altogether inconspicuously, Kipling has provided a twist in the closing paragraphs of the story that deepens and complicates its meaning:

Let 'er sue if she likes! She don't know what reel things mean. *I* do—I've 'ad occasion to notice 'em. . . . *No,* I tell you! I'll 'ave 'em when I want 'em, an' be done with 'em; but not till I see that look on a face . . . that look . . . I'm not takin' any. The real thing's life an' death. It *begins* at death, d'ye see. *She* can't understand. . . . Oh, go on an' push off to Hell, you an' your lawyers.

The law and lawyers are not usually associated with hell in Kipling's writing; quite the contrary. The law and loyalty to it are what constitute Kipling's heaven. This can only spell complete demoralization for Strangwick. He, a weak and irresolute character from the start, is not just haunted by the intense, life-consuming passion he has witnessed; he is caught in its toils. Emphatically Clem is not of the Gipsy stock that can, through the intensity of feelings and the formidable strength of essentially lawless natures, survive in such a maelstrom. He, of the Gorgio race, could never inhabit the Romany world and is now unfitted for any other. We have this confirmed when the Brother who had introduced him to the Lodge tells Keede and the narrator at the end that the young lady Clem has rejected is in every way suitable: "an' she'd make him a good little wife, too, if I'm any judge." "That is all that's wanted," says Keede when he discovers the identity of the Brother: he is Armine, the widower husband of that "good little wife," Bella.

Kipling's conception and execution of the tale (dense though his working of it is) are quite remarkably authentic in psychological scope and subtlety. He is wholly convincing, too, in his portrayal of this literally supernatural love, not shrinking from investing it with a dark, grave-defeating lustfulness that has a suggestion of the demonic in it. For their awesomely long-nurtured love does not leave us with the impression of innocence. Gadsoe's carefully worded greeting, for example, as smooth and contained as their passion has been, is eloquent in its understatement: "Why, Bella . . . this must be only the *second* time we've been alone together in all these years" (italics added). And there is the look on Bella's face, which so upsets Clem: "Then he comes out an' says: 'Come in, my dear'; an' she stoops an' goes into the dug-out with that look on her face—that look on her face!"

"A Madonna of the Trenches"—the irony of the title once more cuts in many ways—is not wholly successful. It is too involuted, with its triple framing of the Masonic Lodge, the Front Line, and the Family; it is too wordy, and the clumsily handled dialect gets in the way. But what it lacks in structural clarity it makes up for in moral comprehension and complexity.

It would be unwise to leave this story, particularly considering what has yet to be said about "The Wish House," without making one thing clear. A lot has been made of the poem "Gipsy Vans" (which prefaces "A Madonna of the Trenches"), much of it quite properly approving, for the verse is well done. But it does *not* mean that Kipling is recommending Gipsy morality as a pattern for living and loving; for it leads to suffering and death. He is saying that in love—as he said before in "Beyond the Pale" and "Without Benefit of Clergy"—there are those who, given the strength of their nature and passion, will always embrace such a creed—and suffer and triumph accordingly.

> Unless you come of the gipsy stock
>   That steals by night and day,
> Lock your heart with a double lock
>   And throw the key away.
> Bury it under the blackest stone
>   Beneath your father's hearth,
> And keep your eyes on your lawful own
>   And your feet to the proper path.
>   *Then you can stand at your door and mock*
>   *When the gipsy-vans come through . . .*
>   *For it isn't right that the Gorgio stock*
>   *Should live as the Romany do.*

There are two other stories connected with World War I that are of outstanding merit, "Mary Postgate" and "The Gardener." There is not space to deal with them fully here, but their virtue is now well established, and they rightly find their way into many short-story anthologies. Again there is a considerable if inconspicuous stress on the sexual element.

Of the two, "Mary Postgate" seems the better one. There is an excellent consistency of tone throughout, slightly distanced from the event, as is proper, since it is filtered through the mind of a spinster in her early forties who "prided herself on a trained mind which 'did not dwell on these things'"—"these things" being the less pleasant aspects of life, of which Miss Postgate was by no means ignorant. As the story proceeds, the need for the cool, almost detached tone becomes greater, and the effect of the tone is much richer, both morally and dramatically.

Wynn Fowler, the nephew of Miss Postgate's employer, enlists; and in Kipling's skillful description of this event, war really does seem like the plague in the Indian stories:

It took the Rector's son who was going into business with his elder brother; it took the Colonel's nephew on the eve of fruit-farming in Canada; it took Mrs. Grant's son who, his mother said, was devoted to the ministry; and, very early indeed, it took Wynn Fowler, who announced on a postcard that he had joined the Flying Corps and wanted a cardigan waistcoat.

Mary Postgate silently dotes on Wynn and gladly serves as a slave to the demanding and not particularly grateful youth. The exact nature of Mary's emotional response is not easy to gauge in this reticent and colorless spinster. "What do you ever think of, Mary?" asks Miss Fowler, and when Mary deliberately avoids the bait and starts talking about Wynn's stockings, she persists—"But I mean the things that women think about." When Wynn is killed, however, Miss Fowler, watching as Mary takes his things to the incinerator, says to herself: "Mary's an old woman. I never realised it before." Near the incinerator, as she is about to sprinkle on "the sacrificial oil" and burn Wynn's belongings, Mary discovers the badly injured German airman who that afternoon had bombed the village, killing a child, almost right before her eyes. Repeatedly he pleads with her to get him a doctor, but all she will say is, "Ich haben der todt Kinder gesehn" (I have seen the dead child). She proceeds with her work;

Wynn's funeral pyre becomes the stake at which she is burning his enemies and the slaughterers of little children. With powerful Kiplingesque irony, she assures herself with complete confidence that "Wynn for no consideration on earth would have torn little Edna into those vividly-coloured strips and strings." And when the wounded German again calls for help, she replies using one of Wynn's favorite phrases, "Stop that, you bloody pagan." So he dies, and at the sound of his death-rattle Mary "closed her eyes and drank it in."

The story ends brilliantly:

Then the end came very distinctly in a lull between two rain-gusts. Mary Postgate drew her breath short between her teeth and shivered from head to foot. *"That's* all right," said she contentedly, and went up to the house, where she scandalised the whole routine by taking a luxurious hot bath before tea, and came down looking, as Miss Fowler said when she saw her lying all relaxed on the other sofa, "quite handsome!"

Frustrated motherhood is certainly there, but clearly the sensuality in the closing description implies more. Kipling's controlled prose is quite well-matched to the control shown by Miss Postgate.

"The Wish House," which with "Mrs. Bathurst" and "A Madonna of the Trenches" forms a trio of tales dealing with the supernatural and with obsessive physical infatuation, is the best of all his later stories. Its triumph is in part due to its very density; not the sort of opaque density we find in "Mrs. Bathurst," but the concentrated, highly organized detail that binds the story so tightly together that its intensity is communicated to us almost as a physical sensation.

The first paragraph, as so often in Kipling, tells us the most. There is enormous irony in this story of sexual rapacity, of obsessive and violent adultery, starting with the sentence: "The new Church Visitor had just left after a twenty minutes' call." But the first few lines of dialogue give us a clear lead as to the moral nature of the characters; and Grace Archer's powerful, forthright, and unsympathetic personality is etched with the most dexterous economy:

"Most folk got out at Bush Tye for the match there," [Mrs. Fettley] explained, "so there weren't no one for me to cushion agin, the last five mile. An' she *do* just-about bounce ye."

"You've took no hurt," said her hostess. "You don't brittle by agein', Liz."

The grimness of the reply, mediated through the description of her as "hostess," with its pointedly inappropriate invocation of middle-class, conventional tea-table chat, confirms the characterization. Exactly which side of the moral fence she inhabits is brought out in another brief but telling detail: "'What like's this new Visitor o' yours?' Mrs. Fettley inquired. . . . Mrs. Ashcroft suspended the big packing needle judicially on high, ere she stabbed home. 'Settin' aside she don't bring much news with her yet, I dunno as I've anythin' special agin her.'" The coarseness of the dialect, so well caught and held, has a moral and dramatic significance.

The context of their conversation, too, is well chosen. As the dialogue unfolds, the tale that is told is found to be one of ferocious sexual license and passion. But what is going on over tea in the cottage is not counterpointed against honest rural toil in the surrounding fields:

The tile-sided cottage trembled at the passage of two specially chartered forty-seat charabancs on their way to the Bush Tye match; a regular Saturday "shopping" 'bus, for the county's capital, fumed behind them; while, from one of the crowded inns, a fourth car backed out to join the procession, and held up the stream of through pleasure-traffic.

There is no such thing as rustic innocence here; people are given over to pleasure, of which the tale unfolding within the cottage is simply a denser concentration. It is a world debased and venal, a world of lost innocence.

Mrs. Archer's sixteen-year-old grandson, with "a maiden of the moment in attendance," enters, snatches up the basket his grandmother has been working on, and rushes out without acknowledgment. Mrs. Fettley's response borders on the prurient: "I lay *he* won't show much mercy to any he comes across, either." Speaking, we are told, "with narrowed eyes," she adds, "Now 'oo the dooce do he remind me of, all of a sudden?" Mrs. Archer ignores the question, and her reply to the first part is cool and hard: "They must look arter theirselves—same as we did." Mrs. Fettley concedes that Mrs. Archer always could, and slyly brings up the case of Polly Batten's husband, one of Mrs. Archer's earlier conquests. She does this in a way that suggests the two women are as much adversaries as friends; for the narrowed eyes warn us of her recognition, made explicit later, that Mrs. Archer's grandson bears a strong resemblance to Polly's husband: "Why, 'tis Jim Batten, and his tricks come to life again!" Mrs. Archer's reply is as self-possessed as ever; and she gives as good as she gets: "Mebbe. There's some that would ha' made it out so—bein' barren-like, themselves."

Mrs. Fettley admits, however, that, as Mrs. Archer says, she has had *her* "back-lookin's" too, and pauses as in reverie: "Mrs. Fettley stared, with jaw half-dropped. at the grocer's bright calendar on the wall. The cottage shook again to the roar of the motor-traffic, and the crowded football-ground below the garden roared almost as loudly; for the village was well set to its Saturday leisure." Then she confides her "satisfactions" to Grace Archer, principally, it seems, with a railwayman lover "over the four years 'e was workin' on the rail near us." In turn Mrs. Archer discloses some of her own secrets.

Kipling's introduction to these intimate confidences between the two ladies of such copious appetite is masterly in its ironies of tone and image: "The light and air had changed a little with the sun's descent, and the two elderly ladies closed the kitchen-door against chill. A couple of jays squealed and skirmished through the undraped apple-trees in the garden." There is nothing as genteel as the tone would suggest about the two women: their natures are much better represented in the second sentence of the quotation. Mrs. Archer recounts *her* skirmishing with her husband over their mutual infidelity, and deftly implicates Mrs. Fettley: "for *you* know, Liz, what a lover 'e was." Delicately as it is done, what is conveyed in a few words is a violence of passion bordering on the murderous: Grace Archer confronting Dolly Batten with a pitchfork; her husband being jailed for assaulting to the point of death his mistress's husband.

Mrs. Archer's last affair is the one that is of most significance here, for when Harry eventually falls seriously ill after he leaves her, she discovers a means of relieving him. She has learned, from a little girl who is devoted to her, how to take somebody else's pain upon herself. It is done by making contact with a Token—"the wraith of the dead or, worse still, of the living"—in what is called a Wish House. Grace Archer's wish is to "take everythin' bad that's in store for my man, 'Arry Mockler, for love's sake." From that time Harry's health improves, and the ulcer on Mrs. Ashcroft's leg begins. When she discovers that the method works, and continues to work when Harry is subsequently injured and made well through her sacrifice, Grace is exultant: "I've got ye now, my man. . . . You'll take your good from me 'thout knowin' it till my life's end. O God send me long to live for 'Arry's sake!" But the fierceness of her triumph shows that it is not so much love as jealous passion that possesses her; and indeed her only real fear is that Harry might find another woman. Here she pleads with Mrs. Fettley to reassure her that "the pain do count, don't you think?" and that this will be "counted agin" the possibility of Harry's falling prey to another woman.

Mrs. Archer's sacrifice is complete, for she knows that her ulcer has "turned," that is, it has become malignant and will bring about her death in the near future. And this last confidence provokes another from Mrs. Fettley, who has just asked her how long she has to live.

"Slow come, slow go. But if I don't set eyes on ye 'fore next hoppin', this'll be good-bye, Liz."
"Dunno as I'll be able to manage by then—not 'thout I have a liddle dog to lead me. For de chillern, dey won't be troubled, an'—O Gra'!—I'm blindin' up—I'm blindin' up!"
"Oh, *dat* was why you didn't more'n finger with your quilt-patches all this while! I was wonderin'. . . . But the pain *do* count, don't ye think, Liz?"

It is difficult not to feel a twinge of pity for Mrs. Fettley at her desertion by her thankless children and the onset of her blindness. We now see the significance of her staring so long at the grocer's bright calendar: she can no longer see it properly. But she has no real claims to her children's love or ours, for when it has suited her, she too has wantonly broken the rules that might have given her a place in her family's affections, putting her own sexual desire before loyalty to her home.

Toward Mrs. Archer we do not feel even an inkling of pity. She has gone after her various quarries with a predatory disregard for everything but her own self-satisfaction. Nothing deflects her iron will or softens her disposition. When the little girl offers her real affection or promises to take her headache away, Mrs. Archer misunderstands her: "I told her not to lay a finger on me, for I thought she'd want to stroke my forehead, an'—I ain't that make."

As the last quotation shows, Kipling never loses his command over detail and nuance. That such control should be sustained is, of course, absolutely imperative. It is essential that this passionate, iron-willed woman should be *dispassionate* in her own account, and it is important that we should not iden-

tify her with any of our own warmer emotions. And in moral terms the picture remains consistently and appropriately dark, as Kipling ensures with his deft manipulation of perspective. True, this utterly pagan story of a profane love begins with an innocuous reference to a Church Visitor, but it is not a simple opposition between smug orthodoxy and a healthy, rustic, "natural" order. The two ladies are not singular oddities, but are as corrupt as their environment. This is no Hardy-like vision of rustics living in some sort of life-embracing harmony with the rhythms of a sympathetic nature, and there is no way in which Grace Archer's story could be subtitled, like *Tess of the d'Urbervilles*, "The Story of a Pure Woman." Her invocation of the infernal powers of the Wish House to further her aims demonstrates the moral lawlessness of Grace and her community, and leaves us with a feeling that this lawlessness may well be, once more, the reality underlying all appearances.

VII

In an essay of this sort the problem is what to leave out. In such limited space one cannot do justice either to the full range of Kipling's talent or to the complexity of his moral vision. The present critique has to be seen, therefore, as a contribution to the many excellent studies already in existence, to be read along with them. I particularly regret having to leave out the beautifully elegiac story "They," told with such tenderness and restraint; the totally different tales of the "soldiers three," in which Kipling is so careful to show each of them, underneath their banter, possessed of an acute sensitivity and a capacity for suffering; the somber stories of mental sickness and healing that follow World War I and reveal yet again the fragility of mental and moral integrity; and, of course, *The Jungle Books*. In many ways, if one had been simply concerned to identify Kipling's themes, the latter could have been used to illustrate virtually all of them. In "Mowgli's Brothers," for example, Mowgli shows movingly both his (and the Kipling character's) need for community—and his isolation. On the other hand, "Tiger! Tiger!" provides a succinct summary of what Kipling means by the law, a concept of primary importance to him and one of his most misunderstood subjects: "Lead us again, O Akela. Lead us again, O man-cub, for we be sick of this lawlessness, and we should be the Free People once more."

Whatever the scale of one's enterprise, Kipling is never an easy author to write about; the many prejudices against him make it difficult to present a dispassionate consideration of his literary merit. As Randall Jarrell puts it in his excellent essay: "If people don't know about Kipling they can read Kipling, and then they'll know about Kipling." But the trouble for many years has been that people *have* "known about" Kipling; that is, they have a little, very shallow, knowledge, and for them it is sufficient. Kipling is an imperialist, and that ruins any decent palate.

Now that our pomp of yesterday *is* one with Nineveh and Tyre, and the dust of frontier skirmishes no longer obscures our vision, we are more able to see what his writing really amounts to. In some ways one could say we are beginning to catch up with him and are better able to appreciate the novelty and originality that G. K. Chesterton—so often a perceptive critic of his contemporaries—saw in Kipling's imaginative exploration of new technology and vernacular speech.

More comprehensively, he stands revealed to us as one of the greatest short-story writers England has ever produced. It is a form quite characteristically appropriate to all that he stood for morally and aesthetically, for above all it requires a craftsmanship and a discipline of the most rigorous sort. Somerset Maugham, who was influenced by Kipling and himself became a celebrated short-story writer, endorsed the view generously, perhaps establishing a claim of his own in the style he adopted for his tribute:

The short story is not a form of fiction in which the English have on the whole excelled. The English, as their novels show, are inclined to diffuseness. They have never been much interested in form. Succinctness goes against their grain. But the short story demands form. It demands succinctness. Diffuseness kills it. It depends on construction. It does not admit of loose ends. It must be complete in itself. All these qualities you will find in Kipling's stories when he was at his magnificent best, and this, happily for us, he was in story after story. Rudyard Kipling is the only writer of short stories our country has produced who can stand comparison with Guy de Maupassant and Chekov. He is our greatest story writer. I can't believe he will ever be equalled. I am sure he can never be excelled.

(*Choice of Kipling's Prose*, 1952, p. xxvii)

VIII

The following section is reprinted from the introduction to Bonamy Dobrée's Rudyard Kipling, Realist and Fabulist *(Oxford, 1967), by permission of Oxford University Press.*

Now a polo-pony is like a poet. If he is born with a love of the game he can be made.

("The Maltese Cat")

ONE day, when Beetle [Kipling] was browsing in the Head's library, rather idly conning through Isaac D'Israeli's *Curiosities of Literature* [1791–1834], suddenly

. . . at the foot of a left-hand page [there] leaped out on him a verse of—incommunicable splendour, opening doors into inexplicable worlds—from a song which Tom-a-Bedlams were supposed to sing. It ran:

> With a heart of furious fancies
>   Whereof I am commander,
> With a burning spear and a horse of air,
>   To a wilderness I wander.
> With a knight of ghosts and shadows
>   I summoned am to tourney,
> Ten leagues beyond the wide world's end—
>   Methinks it is no journey.

He sat mouthing and staring before him, till the prep-bell rang.

("Propagation of Knowledge")

What doors that would open to a boy—he was then about fifteen—poetically endowed! It would suggest that poetry works, not so much through reason, as through the intuitions, guiding our existence by awakening us to the basic, though in our daily commerce, unrecognized assumptions by which we live at all, and stirring unaccustomed levels of consciousness. Furious fancies, a burning spear, and a horse of air.

Born with the love of the game, Kipling was responsible for the verse which enlivened the amateur theatricals at Westward Ho!, jokes on the masters, and so on.[3] Most of his other verses are of the imitative kind to be found in *Schoolboy Verses,* which, unknown to him, his parents had printed in India

[3]*Stalky & Co.,* passim.

before he returned there, though he did write one poem, "Ave Imperatrix," thought by T. S. Eliot worthy of inclusion in his selection; and on one occasion he was paid a whole guinea for some verses, untraced, which he sent up to a paper, so that "the Study caroused on chocolate and condensed milk and pilchards and Devonshire Cream." Rhyme throughout his life was an essential part of verse, and he very rarely wrote anything without it. Having to "do" Horace at school, he rebelled against him and, pretending not to understand classical quantities, declared that "he could do better if Latin verse rhymed as decent verse should." When, as an imposition he was told to send up a translation of Ode III. ix, "he turned 'Donec gratus eram' into pure Devonshire dialect,"[4] the first example of a manner he could later use so effectively. The first two stanzas read:

> *He.*   Ez long as 'twuz me alone
>   An' there wasn't no other chaps,
>   I was praoud as a King on 'is throne—
>   Happier tu, per'aps.
>
> *She.*   Ez long as 'twuz only I
>   An' there wasn't no other she
>   Yeou cared for so much—surely
>   I was glad as glad could be.

He did, however, make a by no means despicable attempt at blank verse before his sixteenth birthday.[5]

How important verse was to Kipling for expressing the whole range of his ideas and emotions from the lightest to the most profound is evident from the extent to which it has been appropriate to quote it in the process of trying to elucidate his thought or emotion. It would seem that he turned for expression to verse as readily as to prose, the one medium being as natural to him as the other. As Eliot stressed, he did not try to write "poetry." When the thought lent itself to what we call poetry, or the emotion was deep enough, the "verse" became "poetry."

Thus whether he wrote in prose, or, to invert Dryden's phrase, "in the other harmony of verse," seems to have been with him not so much a matter of indifference as of the mood of the moment, sometimes, of course, of subject-matter. States of mind are not always susceptible of being conveyed in story

form, except too clumsily. What could be made of, say, "The Two-Sided Man"? But often, with his thirst to formulate, even project, what he had to say in different ways, he came to accompany his tales with a poem, either as preface or as conclusion, sometimes both. These to some degree elucidate the tale, or the tale explains the poem. Eliot went so far as to say that he invented a kind of dual form, story and poem making one whole, each being incomplete without the other: but this is rare. Occasionally there seems to be little connection. How, for instance, does "Akbar's Bridge" throw a light on "The Debt"? One may well feel that the former, good as it is, would be better as a prose story, perhaps after the manner of "The Amir's Homily."

At all events he labored at his verse as indefatigably as he did at his prose; the briefest study of the manuscripts will show this with their drafts, corrections, scribblings over, and rewriting. One extended example will illustrate the point, "A Song in Storm," already partly quoted. The manuscript version[6] has for first stanza:

> Be well assured that from our side
>   Good luck has taken flight—
> And nosing wind and raging tide
>   Make us their prey to-night.
> Our past so nearly, clearly won
>   Alas! is far removèd:
> Then welcome Fate's discourtesy
>   Whereby it shall be provèd
>   How in all time of our distress
>   (Whatever Fate shall do)
>   The game is more than the player of the game,
>   As Fame is more than the seeker after fame,
>   And the ship is more than the crew.

In the Definitive Edition this has become:

> Be well assured that on our side
>   The abiding oceans fight,
> Though headlong wind and heaping tide
>   Make us their sport to-night.
> By force of weather, not of war,
>   In jeopardy we steer:
> Then welcome Fate's discourtesy
>   Whereby it shall appear
>   How in all time of our distress
>   And our deliverance too,
>   The game is more than the player of the game
>   And the ship is more than the crew!

---

[4]"An English School," in *Land and Sea Tales.*
[5]Neither is included in the Definitive Edition. Printed in *Carrington,* ch. 15, p. 39.

[6]British Museum. Add. MSS 44841.

That was not merely correcting: the change of idea in the first four lines is radical. Nor did he cease revising. Just as in collecting his stories he would make alterations of the magazine versions, so he did when collecting his poems, even from one garnering to another—as has been marginally exampled earlier.

Whatever opinion may be held of him as a poet, it is agreed that he was brilliant in versification. Some of his verse admittedly is jingle, but of set purpose, and always disciplined, prosodically controlled. He could handle all sorts of meters, while his rhythms are complex, sometimes indeed subtle, as quotations already made will have illustrated. He was at home in the heroic couplet, common measure, ballad forms; the iambic or the rollicking anapaest, as well as more difficult prosodic units; the octosyllable or the sixteener; literally "free" verse, though rhymed; a variation of the terza rima, the varied seventeenth-century stanza, or something too readily regarded as Swinburnian, though dating from much earlier. If, however, he excelled in meter, forms beyond that of the stanza did not much attract him. His ballads are poor, his few sonnets, although one or two are good poems, are unimpressive as sonnets, lacking the structural movement, his one triumphant success in an exacting form being "Sestina of the Tramp Royal." His long poems tend to be too protracted, though exception must be made of the great monologues "McAndrew's Hymn" and "The 'Mary Gloster,'" to which may be added the semi-dialogue "Tomlinson."

There is little point in considering influences. After his *Schoolboy Lyrics* and *Echoes*, not collected, there is no trace of the Pre-Raphaelite note, except perhaps in "The Love Song of Har Dyal." It appeared in 1884 as part of "Beyond the Pale," and purports to be a rendering of an Indian poem, very moving in the original: "In English you miss the wail of it. It runs something like this—

> Alone upon the housetops to the North
>   I turn and watch the lightning in the sky,—
> The glamour of thy footsteps in the North,
>   *Come back to me, Beloved, or I die!*
>
> Below my feet the still bazar is laid—
>   Far, far below the weary camels lie,—
> The camels and the captives of thy raid.
>   *Come back to me, Beloved, or I die!*
>
> My father's wife is old and harsh with years,
>   And drudge of all my father's house am I.—

> My bread is sorrow and my drink is tears,
>   *Come back to me, Beloved, or I die!*
>   (*Definitive Edition* differs slightly)

That is clearly influenced by the Rossetti ear; we meet the vaguely evocative phrase, "the glamour of thy footsteps in the North," absent from Kipling's more characteristic verse.

The monologues may have been suggested by Browning, but the attack and versification are different. Only the very early "One Viceroy Resigns" (1888) is obviously after the manner of Browning. Parodies there are: the early one of Swinburne, where he puts the first chorus from *Atalanta in Calydon* to more mundane uses; and those in "A Muse Among the Motors." All that can usefully be said is that, widely read in English poetry, he used, or dropped into, whatever form of rhythm either came to him, or that he felt to be appropriate. When he smote "'is bloomin'" lyre he winked at all the Homers down the road of history.

More general considerations present themselves before embarking on any detailed study. Most readers will be aware of the crucial difficulty Eliot laid finger on when he said in the introduction to his *Selection of Kipling's Verse*:

While I speak of Kipling's work as verse and not as poetry, I am still able to speak of individual compositions as poetry, and also to maintain that there is "poetry" in the "verse."

Admittedly Kipling was a dazzlingly able versifier in the matter of rhythm and meter, as already said; but it will be claimed here that he was a poet in the full sense of the term. Notoriously, to try to define poetry is to rush in where angels fear to tread; it may, finally, depend upon what each person expects poetry to do for him. One may begin, however, by what Moneta said in John Keats's *The Fall of Hyperion*:

> The poet and the dreamer are distinct,
> Diverse, sheer opposites, antipodes.
> The one pours out a balm upon the world,
> The other vexes it.
>   (I.199–202)

Much of what Kipling wrote vexed the world, sometimes by direct attack upon its complacency, but more importantly, and more in Keats's meaning, by forcing the individual to face himself, the conditions of living, or the abyss of darkness which he sometimes feels may engulf him. But before he spoke with those ends in view, he vexed the secluded, self-conscious literary world of his time in a more superficial way, by using the colloquial idiom of the people. His sin was to act on Wordsworth's precept—which is more than Wordsworth did—of writing poetry in the language men (ordinary men) use in speaking to men; or, as Ben Jonson put it, animated by the same cyclical desire to purify the dialect of the tribe, to write poetry in words "such as men doe use." "Tommy" Kipling wrote in plain vernacular, then decried but now seen as contributing to that freedom of "poetic" diction that has been one of the feathers in the cap of present-century metrical writing. His was better than most, for, as Robert Bridges declared, "nothing in [his] diction is common or unclean." We get such pieces as "For to Admire," which opens:

> The Injian Ocean sets an' smiles
> So sof', so bright, so bloomin' blue:

verses in which there may not be much "poetry," except perhaps for the striking

> Old Aden, like a barrick-stove
> That no one's lit for years an' years. . . .

But there was certainly poetry in the later "Sestina of the Tramp Royal," as there was in "Chant-Pagan":

> Me that 'ave been what I've been—
> Me that 'ave gone where I've gone—
> Me that 'ave seen what I've seen—
>   'Ow can I ever take on
> With awful old England again,
> An' 'ouses both sides of the street,
> An' 'edges two sides of the lane,
> And the parson an' gentry between,
> An' touchin' my 'at when we meet—
>   Me that 'ave been what I've been.

"Danny Deever," which appeared first in February 1890, to be included in *Barrack-Room Ballads* later in the year, is now recognized as a poem proper, and a very powerful one.

But he "vexed" more deeply than that. As R. G. Collingwood noted, he "burst into the stuffy atmosphere of the aesthetes' china-shop not only by his diction, but by writing 'magical' poetry, poetry that is, that 'evokes and canalises the emotions that are to men as the steam in the engine of their daily work, and discharges them into the affairs of practical life.'"[7] That would, naturally, be repugnant in an "art for art's sake" period. There is a deal of this sort of work at a certain period of Kipling's career, "The Islanders" for instance, which vexed more than the aesthetes; "The Dykes," "The Truce of the Bear," and, though this gained considerable support to the tune of many thousands of pounds, "The Absent-Minded Beggar." There is not very much poetry to be found in these pieces, which were mainly the result of irritated impatience rising sometimes to indignation, for if in his case it was true that *facit indignatio versum*, the verse was hardly poetry. The political poems have plenty of "punch," as Mr. Hilton Brown remarks, but one cannot altogether agree with him that they make dull reading now, and would seem to have only an historical interest. Read in the context of their time, as one reads, say, John Dryden's *Absalom and Achitophel*, they take on life, while some, for example "The City of Brass," are startlingly prophetic of today. Yet it is where the "magical" fuses with the philosophic, as, to give an early, and possibly best-known, example, "Recessional," that our minds become receptive in the way that poetry induces.

A major difficulty in treating of Kipling's poetry is that he adventured along so many of the nine-and-sixty ways. He is as varied in the subject-matter of his verse as he is in his story-telling, as also in his manner. To try to simplify the discussion (though this is to be more than a little arbitrary) it might be suggested that in the main, apart from his "magical" verse, he wrote three kinds of poetry. The edges of such things are, however, always *confused*, Kipling sometimes *fusing* the kinds. These I would call the "lyric-romantic" or dreamer's poems; poems of thought and experience; and, to coin a word, "actuality" poems. It is not possible to separate these into periods. "Romantic" poetry Kipling wrote all through his life; the next group soon appeared and continued to the end; the outstanding "actuality" poems, though mainly related to his later development, are embryonically present at a fairly early date. It is only "magical" poetry that belongs to a period, that during which he was emotionally involved in politics, and it disappeared when he had reached the stage of acceptance.

[7] *The Principles of Art* (Oxford, 1938).

SELECTED BIBLIOGRAPHY

I. Bibliography. E. W. Martindell, *A Bibliography of the Works of Rudyard Kipling, 1881-1921* (London, 1922; rev. ed., 1923); F. V. Livingstone, *Bibliography of the Works of Rudyard Kipling* (New York, 1927), supp. (Cambridge, Mass., 1938); L. H. Chandler, comp., *A Catalogue of the Works of Rudyard Kipling* (New York, 1930), exhibited at the Grolier Club, New York, 1929; J. McG. Stewart, *Rudyard Kipling: A Bibliographical Catalogue,* A. W. Yeats, ed. (Toronto, 1959); *English Fiction in Transition,* Purdue University, vol. III, nos. 3, 4, 5 (Lafayette, Ind., 1960).

II. Collected Works. *Edition Deluxe,* 38 vols. (London, 1897-1937); *Outward Bound Edition,* 36 vols. (New York, 1897-1937); *Pocket Edition,* 29 vols. (London, 1907-1938), 32 vols. (New York, 1908-1932); *Bombay Edition,* 31 vols. (London, 1913-1938); *The Complete Works in Prose and Verse,* 35 vols. (London, 1937-1939), the Sussex ed., includes works not previously in book form; *Rudyard Kipling's Verse* (London, 1940; 1960), latest and most complete collection of inclusive eds. published since 1912.

III. Selected Works. T. S. Eliot, ed., *A Choice of Kipling's Prose* (London, 1941), with intro. by Eliot; W. S. Maugham, ed., *A Choice of Kipling's Prose* (London, 1952), with intro. by Maugham; W. G. Bebbington, ed., *A Kipling Anthology* (London, 1964); R. C. Green, ed., *Rudyard Kipling. Stories and Poems* (London, 1970), Everyman's Library; A. Rutherford, ed., *Rudyard Kipling. Short Stories* (London, 1971), Penguin ed.; C. E. Carrington, ed., *The Complete Barrack-Room Ballads* (London, 1973); J. Cochrane, ed., *Rudyard Kipling. Selected Verse* (London, 1977), Penguin ed.

IV. Separate Works. Fiction: *Departmental Ditties and Other Verses* (London, 1886); *Plain Tales from the Hills* (London, 1888), stories; *Wee Willie Winkie* (London, 1888), stories; *Barrack-room Ballads* (London, 1890, enl. ed., 1892), verse; *The Light That Failed* (New York, 1890; rev. ed., 1891), novel; *Soldiers Three* (London, 1890), stories; *Life's Handicap* (London, 1891), stories; *The Naulahka,* in collaboration with W. Balestier (London, 1892), novel; *Many Inventions* (London, 1893), stories; *The Jungle Book* (London, 1894), stories; *The Second Jungle Book* (London, 1895), stories; *The Seven Seas* (London, 1896), verse; *Captains Courageous* (Leipzig-London–New York, 1897), novel; *The Day's Work* (London, 1898), stories; *Stalky & Co.* (New York, 1899), stories.

Kim (London, 1901), novel; *Just So Stories for Little Children* (London, 1902), stories; *The Five Nations* (London, 1903), verse; *Traffics and Discoveries* (Leipzig-London–New York, 1904), stories; *Puck of Pook's Hill* (New York, 1906), stories; *Abaft the Funnel* (New York, 1909), stories; *Actions and Reactions* (London, 1909), stories; *Rewards and Fairies* (Garden City, N.Y., 1910), stories; *A Diversity of Creatures* (Garden City, N.Y., 1917), stories; *The Eyes of Asia* (Garden City, N.Y., 1918), fiction; *Twenty Poems* (London, 1918); *The Years Between* (Garden City, N.Y., 1919), verse; *Children's Stories* (New York, 1925), stories; *Debits and Credits* (Garden City, N.Y., 1926), stories; *A Tour of Inspection* (New York, 1928), story; *Thy Servant a Dog, Told by Boots, Edited by R. Kipling* (London, 1930); *Limits and Renewals* (London, 1932), stories; *The Maltese Cat* (London, 1936), story; *"'Teem'"—A Treasure Hunter* (New York, 1938), story.

Nonfiction: *Out of India* (New York, 1895), description; *A Fleet in Being* (London, 1898), history; *From Sea to Sea,* 2 vols. (New York, 1899), travel letters; *A History of England,* in collaboration with C. R. L. Fletcher (Oxford, 1911); "Indictment of the Government" (London, 1914), speech; *France at War* (London, 1915); "Kipling's Message" (London, 1918), speech; *The Art of Fiction* (London, 1926), criticism; *Souvenirs de France* (Paris, 1933), travel; *Something of Myself for My Friends, Known and Unknown* (London, 1937), memoir; M. Cohen, ed., *Rudyard Kipling to Rider Haggard* (London, 1965), letters.

V. Biographical and Critical Studies. W. M. Clemens, *A Ken of Kipling* (New York, 1899).

R. LeGallienne, *Rudyard Kipling, A Criticism* (London, 1900); G. F. Monkshood [pseud.], *Rudyard Kipling, the Man and His Work* (London, 1902); G. K. Chesterton, *Heretics* (London, 1909); C. Charles, *Rudyard Kipling, Life and Work* (London, 1911); G. A. Borgese, *Kipling e un sui critico* (Turin, 1913); H. Jackson, *The Eighteen Nineties* (London, 1913); D. Mantovani, *Il nuova apologio R. Kipling* (Turin, 1913); R. Durand, *A Handbook to the Poetry of Rudyard Kipling* (London, 1914); G. A. Borgese, *"Kim" di Kipling* (Milan, 1915); C. Falls, *Rudyard Kipling, A Critical Study* (London, 1915); A. Galletti, *Saggi i studi* (Bologna, 1915); H. Jackson, *Rudyard Kipling, A Critical Study* (London, 1915); W. M. Hart, *Kipling the Story-Writer* (Berkeley, Calif., 1918).

A. Chevrillon, *La Poésie de Rudyard Kipling* (Paris, 1920), and *Three Studies in English Literature: Kipling, Galsworthy, Shakespeare* (London, 1923); D. Braybrook, *Kipling and His Soldiers* (London, 1926); *The Kipling Journal,* quarterly publication of the Kipling Society (London, 1927—   ); L. C. Dunsterville, *Stalky's Reminiscences* (London, 1928); M. Brion, *Rudyard Kipling* (Paris, 1929); B. Dobrée, *The Lamp and the Lute* (Oxford, 1929; repr. New York, 1963); R. T. Hopkins, *Rudyard Kipling: The Story of a Genius* (London, 1930); T. G. P. Spear, *The Nabobs: A Study of the Social Life of the English in Eighteenth Century India* (London, 1932); G. C. Beresford, *Schooldays with Kipling* (London, 1936); G. F. MacMunn, *Rudyard Kipling, Craftsman* (London, 1937); L. Lemonnier, *Kipling* (Paris, 1939); A. M. Weygandt, *Kipling's Reading and Its Influence on His Poetry* (Philadelphia, 1939).

E. Shanks, *Rudyard Kipling* (London, 1940); H. E. Bates, *The Modern Short Story* (London, 1943); C. H. Brown, *Rudyard Kipling: A New Appreciation* (London, 1945); G. Orwell (pseud.), *Critical Essays* (London, 1946); J. I. M. Stewart, *Rudyard Kipling* (London, 1946); R.

Croft-Cooke, *Rudyard Kipling* (London, 1948); S. (Nobbe) Howe, *Novels of Empire* (New York, 1949); R. Church, *The Growth of the English Novel* (London, 1951); B. Dobrée, *Rudyard Kipling* (London, 1951; rev. ed., 1966); L. Trilling, *The Liberal Imagination* (London, 1951); E. Wilson, *The Wound and the Bow* (London, 1952); C. C. Carrington, *The Life of Rudyard Kipling* (Garden City, N. Y., 1955); R. A. Scott-James, *Fifty Years of English Literature* (London, 1956); F. Leaud, *La Poétique de Rudyard Kipling* (Paris, 1958); J. M. S. Tomkins, *The Art of Rudyard Kipling* (London, 1959).

R. Cook, *Rudyard Kipling and George Orwell* (London, 1961); R. L. Green, ed., *The Readers' Guide to Rudyard Kipling's Works* (Canterbury, 1961); R. H. Harbord, ed., *The Readers' Guide to Rudyard Kipling's Works*, 7 parts (London, 1961–1972); C. S. Lewis, "Kipling's World," in *They Asked for a Paper* (London, 1962); A. Sandison, *The Wheel of Empire* (London, 1962); J. I. M. Stewart, *Eight Modern Writers* (London, 1963); C. A. Bodelsen, *Aspects of Rudyard Kipling's Art* (New York, 1964); A. Rutherford, ed., *Kipling's Mind and Art* (Stanford, Calif., 1964); E. L. Gilbert, *Kipling and the Critics* (New York, 1965), includes R. Jarrell, "On Preparing to Read Kipling"; R. G. L. Green, *Kipling and the Children* (London, 1965); L. M. Cornell, *Kipling in India* (London, 1966); A. L. Rowse, *The English Spirit* (London, 1966); B. Dobrée, *Rudyard Kipling, Realist and Fatalist* (Oxford, 1967); T. R. Henn, *Kipling* (London, 1967).

R. L. Green, *Kipling. The Critical Heritage* (London, 1971); E. L. Gilbert, *The Good Kipling* (Manchester, 1972); J. Gross, ed., *Rudyard Kipling: The Man, His Work, and His World* (London, 1972); S. Islam, *Kipling's "Law": A Study of His Philosophy of Life* (London, 1975); J. K. Lyon, *Bertolt Brecht and Rudyard Kipling: A Marxist's Imperialist Mentor* (The Hague, 1975); P. Mason, *Kipling: The Glass, the Shadow, and the Fire* (London, 1975); A. Wilson, *The Strange Ride of Rudyard Kipling. His Life and Works* (London, 1977); K. Amis, *Rudyard Kipling and His World* (London, 1978); F. W. F. Smith, Lord Birkenhead, *Rudyard Kipling* (London, 1978).

LIST OF SHORT STORIES

(The title in italics refers to the volume in which the story appears.)

"The Amir's Homily," *Life's Handicap*; "The Army of a Dream," *Traffics and Discoveries*; "The Arrest of Lieutenant Golightly," *Plain Tales from the Hills*; "As Easy as A.B.C.," *A Diversity of Creatures*; "At Howli Thana," *Soldiers Three*; "At the End of the Passage," *Life's Handicap*; "At the Pit's Mouth," *Wee Willie Winkie*; "At Twenty-Two," *Soldiers Three*; "Aunt Ellen," *Limits and Renewals*.

"Baa, Baa, Black Sheep," *Wee Willie Winkie*; "A Bank Fraud," *Plain Tales from the Hills*; "Beauty Spots," *Limits and Renewals*; "Below the Mill Dam," *Traffics and Discoveries*; "Bertran and Bimi," *Life's Handicap*; "Beyond the Pale," *Plain Tales from the Hills*; "The Big Drunk Draf," *Soldiers Three*; "The Bisara of Pooree," *Plain Tales from the Hills*; "Black Jack," *Soldiers Three*; "The Bonds of Discipline," *Traffics and Discoveries*; "'Bread Upon the Waters,'" *The Day's Work*; "The Bridge-Builders," *The Day's Work*; "The Broken-Link Handicap," *Plain Tales from the Hills*; "The Bronckhorst Divorce Case," *Plain Tales from the Hills*; "Brother Square Toes," *Rewards and Fairies*; "'Brugglesmith,'" *Many Inventions*; "The Brushwood Boy," *The Day's Work*; "Bubbling Well Road," *Life's Handicap*; "The Bull That Thought," *Debits and Credits*; "By Word of Mouth," *Plain Tales from the Hills*.

"The Captive," *Traffics and Discoveries*; "A Centurion of the Thirtieth," *Puck of Pook's Hill*; "The Children of the Zodiac," *Many Inventions*; "The Church that Was in Antioch," *Limits and Renewals*; "The City of Dreadful Night," *Life's Handicap*; "Cold Iron," *Rewards and Fairies*; "The Comprehension of Private Copper," *Traffics and Discoveries*; "A Conference of the Powers," *Many Inventions*; "Consequences," *Plain Tales from the Hills*; "The Conversion of Aurelian McGoggin," *Plain Tales from the Hills*; "The Conversion of St. Wilfred," *Rewards and Fairies*; "The Courting of Dinah Shadd," *Life's Handicap*; "Cupid's Arrows," *Plain Tales from the Hills*.

"Dayspring Mishandled," *Limits and Renewals*; "The Daughter of the Regiment," *Plain Tales from the Hills*; "A Deal in Cotton," *Actions and Reactions*; "The Debt," *Limits and Renewals*; "The Devil and the Deep Sea," *The Day's Work*; "The Disturber of the Traffic," *Many Inventions*; "A Doctor of Medecine," *Rewards and Fairies*; "The Dog Hervey," *A Diversity of Creatures*; "Dray Wara Yow Dee," *Soldiers Three*; "Dream of Duncan Parreness," *Life's Handicap*; "The Drums of the Fore and Aft," *Wee Willie Winkie*; "'Dymchurch Flit,'" *Puck of Pook's Hill*; "The Edge of the Evening," *A Diversity of Creatures*; "The Education of Otis Yeere," *Wee Willie Winkie*; "The Enemies to Each Other," *Debits and Credits*; "An Error in the Fourth Dimension," *The Day's Work*; "The Eye of Allah," *Debits and Credits*.

"Fairy-kist," *Limits and Renewals*; "False Dawn," *Plain Tales from the Hills*; "Fatima," *Soldiers Three*; "The Finances of the Gods," *Life's Handicap*; "Friendly Brook," *A Diversity of Creatures*; "A Friend of the Family," *Debits and Credits*; "A Friend's Friend," *Plain Tales from the Hills*; "The Gardener," *Debits and Credits*; "The Garden of Eden," *Soldiers Three*; "Garm—A Hostage," *Plain Tales from the Hills*; "The Gate of the Hundred Sorrows," *Plain Tales from the Hills*; "Gemini," *Soldiers Three*; "Georgie Porgie," *Life's Handicap*; "A Germ-Destroyer," *Plain Tales from the Hills*; "Gloriana," *Rewards and Fairies*; "The God from the Machine," *Soldiers Three*; "An Habitation Enforced," *Actions and Reactions*; "Hal o' the Draft," *Puck of Pook's Hill*; "The Head of the District," *Life's Handicap*; "The Hill of Illusion," *Wee Willie Winkie*; "His Chance in

Life," *Plain Tales from the Hills*; "His Majesty the King," *Wee Willie Winkie*; "His Private Honour," *Many Inventions*; "His Wedded Wife," *Plain Tales from the Hills*; "The Honours of War," *A Diversity of Creatures*; "The Horse Marines," *A Diversity of Creatures*; "The House Surgeon," *Actions and Reactions*.

"The Incarnation of Krishna Mulvaney," *Life's Handicap*; "In Error," *Plain Tales from the Hills*; "In Flood Time," *Soldiers Three*; "In the House of Suddhoo," *Plain Tales from the Hills*; "'In the Interests of the Brethren,'" *Debits and Credits*; "In the Matter of a Private," *Soldiers Three*; "In the Presence," *A Diversity of Creatures*; "In the Pride of His Youth," *Many Inventions*; "In the Same Boat," *A Diversity of Creatures*; "The Janeites," *Debits and Credits*; "Jews in Shushan," *Life's Handicap*; "The Judgment of Dungara," *Soldiers Three*; "Judson and the Empire," *Many Inventions*; "Kidnapped," *Plain Tales from the Hills*; "The Knife and the Naked Chalk," *Rewards and Fairies*; "The Knights of the Joyous Venture," *Puck of Pook's Hill*.

"The Lang Men o' Larut," *Life's Handicap*; "The Limitations of Pambé Serang," *Life's Handicap*; "Lispeth," *Plain Tales from the Hills*; "Little Foxes," *Actions and Reactions*; "Little Tobrah," *Life's Handicap*; "The Lost Legion," *Many Inventions*; "'Love-o'-Women,'" *Many Inventions*; "The Madness of Private Ortheris," *Plain Tales from the Hills*; "A Madonna of the Trenches," *Debits and Credits*; "The Maltese Cat," *The Day's Work*; "The Man Who Was," *Life's Handicap*; "The Man Who Would Be King," *Wee Willie Winkie*; "The Manner of Men," *Limits and Renewals*; "The Mark of the Beast," *Life's Handicap*; "Marklake Witches," *Rewards and Fairies*; "Mary Postgate," *A Diversity of Creatures*; "A Matter of Fact," *Many Inventions*; "The Miracle of Saint Jubanus," *Limits and Renewals*; "Miss Youghal's Sais," *Plain Tales from the Hills*; "Mrs. Bathurst," *Traffics and Discoveries*; "The Mother Hive," *Actions and Reactions*; "Moti Guj—Mutineer," *Life's Handicap*; "The Mutiny of the Mavericks," *Life's Handicap*; "My Lord of the Elephant," *Many Inventions*; "My Own True Ghost Story," *Wee Willie Winkie*; "'My Son's Wife,'" *A Diversity of Creatures*; "My Sunday at Home," *The Day's Work*.

"Naboth," *Life's Handicap*; "Namgay Doola," *Life's Handicap*; "A Naval Mutiny," *Limits and Renewals*; "Old Men at Pevensey," *Puck of Pook's Hill*; "One View of the Question," *Many Inventions*; "Only a Subaltern," *Wee Willie Winkie*; "On Greenhow Hill," *Life's Handicap*; "On the City Wall," *Soldiers Three*; "On the Gate: A Tale of '16," *Debits and Credits*; "On the Great Wall," *Puck of Pook's Hill*; "On the Strength of a Likeness," *Plain Tales from the Hills*; ".007," *The Day's Work*; "The Other Man," *Plain Tales from the Hills*.

"The Phantom 'Rickshaw," *Wee Willie Winkie*; "Pig," *Plain Tales from the Hills*; "Poor Dear Mamma," *Soldiers Three*; "'A Priest in Spite of Himself,'" *Rewards and Fairies*; "Private Learoyd's Story," *Soldiers Three*; "The Prophet and the Country," *Debits and Credits*; "The Propagation of Knowledge," *Debits and Credits*; "The Puzzler," *Actions and Reactions*; "The Record of Badalia Herodsfoot," *Many Inventions*; "Regulus," *A Diversity of Creatures*; "Reingelder and the German Flag," *Life's Handicap*; "The Rescue of Pluffles," *Plain Tales from the Hills*; "The Return of Imray," *Life's Handicap*; "The Rout of the White Hussars," *Plain Tales from the Hills*; "A Sahibs' War," *Traffics and Discoveries*; "Sea Constables: A Tale of '15," *Debits and Credits*; "A Second Rate Woman," *Wee Willie Winkie*; "The Sending of Dana Da," *Soldiers Three*; "The Ship that Found Herself," *The Day's Work*; "Simple Simon," *Rewards and Fairies*; "The Solid Muldoon," *Soldiers Three*; "Steam Tactics," *Traffics and Discoveries*; "The Story of Muhammed Din," *Plain Tales from the Hills*; "The Strange Ride of Morrowbie Jukes," *Wee Willie Winkle*; "The Swelling of Jordan," *Soldiers Three*; "'Swept and Garnished,'" *Debits and Credits*.

"The Taking of Lungtungpen," *Plain Tales from the Hills*; "The Tender Achilles," *Limits and Renewals*; "The Tents of Kedar," *Soldiers Three*; "'Their Lawful Occasions,'" *Traffics and Diversions*; "'They,'" *Traffics and Diversions*; "Three and—an Extra," *Plain Tales from the Hills*; "The Three Musketeers," *Plain Tales from the Hills*; "Through the Fire," *Life's Handicap*; "Thrown Away," *Plain Tales from the Hills*; "The Tie," *Limits and Rewards*; "To Be Filed for Reference," *Plain Tales from the Hills*; "Tod's Amendment," *Plain Tales from the Hills*; "The Tomb of His Ancestors," *The Day's Work*; "The Treasure and the Law," *Puck of Pook's Hill*; "The Tree of Justice," *Rewards and Fairies*; "Uncovenanted Mercies," *Limits and Renewals*; "The United Idolators," *Debits and Credits*; "Unprofessional," *Limits and Renewals*; "The Valley of the Shadow," *Soldiers Three*; "Venus Annodomini," *Plain Tales from the Hills*; "The Village That Voted the Earth Was Flat," *A Diversity of Creatures*; "The Vortex," *A Diversity of Creatures*.

"A Walking Delegate," *The Day's Work*; "The Wandering Jew," *Life's Handicap*; "Watches of the Night," *Plain Tales from the Hills*; "A Wayside Comedy," *Wee Willie Winkie*; "Wee Willie Winkie," *Wee Willie Winkie*; "Weyland's Sword," *Puck of Pook's Hill*; "William the Conqueror," *The Day's Work*; "The Winged Hats," *Puck of Pook's Hill*; "'Wireless,'" *Traffics and Discoveries*; "The Wish House," *Debits and Credits*; "With Any Amazement," *Soldiers Three*; "With the Main Guard," *Soldiers Three*; "With the Night Mail," *Actions and Reactions*; "Without Benefit of Clergy," *Life's Handicap*; "The Woman in His Life," *Limits and Renewals*; "The World Without," *Soldiers Three*; "Wressley of the Foreign Office," *Plain Tales from the Hills*; "The Wrong Thing," *Rewards and Fairies*; "'Yoked with an Unbeliever,'" *Plain Tales from the Hills*; "Young Men at the Manor," *Puck of Pook's Hill*.

WILLIAM BUTLER YEATS

(1865-1939)

G. S. Fraser

I

FOR just over ten years before he died in a hotel in the south of France, at the beginning of 1939, William Butler Yeats had been universally recognized by his peers as the greatest poet of this century writing in the English language. The recognition dated from the publication in 1928 of his finest volume, *The Tower*. In June of 1939 he would have been seventy-four. He had been writing verses since his teens and had been a poet of some reputation since his twenties. Since the turn of the century, he would probably have been mentioned by any critic in a list of the four or five most distinguished English poets, and in any consideration of Irish poetry he would have headed the list. He had won the Nobel Prize for literature in 1923, he had done more than any other man to bring about the birth of the Irish theater, and he had sat in the senate of the Irish Free State. Yet every critic knows that these public honors are never the full measure of a poet's reputation. At regular intervals during his long life, shrewd critics had been convinced that Yeats was finished. To George Moore, in the Edwardian decade, it seemed that all Yeats's best poems had been inspired by his hopeless love for Maud Gonne; this love was never to find physical fulfillment, and Moore thought that Yeats's lyrical gift would wither, like cut flowers in a glass. To the young T. S. Eliot, in the early Georgian era, Yeats seemed not much more than an interesting survival from the 1890's. The young Ezra Pound, sending some of Yeats's poems to an American magazine, took it upon himself to polish and improve them. The young John Middleton Murry, one of the best poetry critics of his period, dismissed *The Wild Swans at Coole*, which came out in 1917, as the work of a used-up aesthete. The interesting generation of writers who came to Oxford after World War I thought little of Yeats. "Surely," wrote T. E. Lawrence to Pound, "Yeats is no good?" Robert Graves, in the *Pamphlet Against Anthologies*, which

he wrote with Laura Riding, made jovial hay of "The Lake Isle of Innisfree." Thus, though Yeats had never been neglected, the full recognition of his greatness, like its full flowering, came very tardily.

To many critics it seemed that Yeats, wonderful as his gifts were, did not live wholly in the real world. Thus I. A. Richards, in *Science and Poetry* (1925), commenting on Yeats's interest in magic, wrote:

Now he turns to a world of symbolic phantasmagoria about which he is desperately uncertain. He is uncertain because he has adopted as a technique of inspiration the use of trance, of dissociated phases of consciousness, and the revelations given in these dissociated states are unsufficiently connected with normal experience.

Quoting this comment, T. S. Eliot, in *After Strange Gods*, had even more severe things to say as late as 1934:

Mr. Yeats's "supernatural world" was the wrong supernatural world. It was not a world of spiritual significance, not a world of real Good and Evil, of holiness and sin, but a highly sophisticated lower mythology summoned, like a physician, to supply the fading pulse of poetry with some transient stimulant so that the dying patient may utter his last words.

The centrally important critical problem about Yeats becomes clear if we contrast these passages with the noble tribute that Eliot paid to Yeats on his death:

There are some poets whose poems can be considered more or less in isolation, for experience and delight. There are others whose poetry, though giving equally experience and delight, has a larger historical importance. Yeats was one of the latter. He was one of the few whose history was the history of our own time, who are part of the consciousness of our age, which cannot be understood without them.[1]

[1] See Eliot's "The Poetry of W. B. Yeats" in *Purpose*, XII (1940), reprinted in *On Poetry and Poets* (London, 1957).

How are these pertinent strictures to be reconciled with this deserved praise? In what sense was the mental history of Yeats, which from a superficial point of view was so odd and eccentric, more profoundly "the history of our own time"? Was Eliot, feeling that every truly great poet must in some sense be representative of his time, and feeling intuitively sure of Yeats's major qualities, merely making a formal claim that Yeats *must* be representative? Or can Yeats's representative quality be illustrated in detail?

Since the first edition of this essay was published, a great deal of scholarly work has been done, by critics such as Frank Kermode, on Yeats's sources in the 1890's and what might be called the English symbolist tradition, one deriving from William Blake and the Pre-Raphaelites rather than from Stéphane Mallarmé. F. A. C. Wilson has also written interestingly on Yeats's debts to neo-Platonic and oriental mystical ideas, and Giorgio Melchiori on his use of themes suggested by Renaissance painting. The tendency of all this criticism has been to stress the fact that, in an informal way, Yeats was an extremely learned man and to stress also his lifelong interest in the supernatural. His correspondence with Sturge Moore reveals him as an amateur metaphysician of considerable ingenuity and eloquence. But though the above writers have very much deepened my own understanding in detail of Yeats, I remain convinced that his greatness as a poet lies in his realism, in his humanity, in his power to use fantasy and abstruse speculation as metaphors for, or means of exploring, the human situation; it lies at the pole of what Yeats himself called "self" or "heart," at the pole of the "mire and blood" of human veins, rather than at the pole of what he called "soul," or dreams of an abstract eternity. He had enough earthy strength and sap to be able to digest into true poetry a great deal of what Lord Castlereagh called "sublime mysticism and nonsense." What the poems record is the continuous conflict between the claims of a prophetic wisdom, a sense of insulation against the terrors of history, and, on the other hand, the claims, rewards, and pains of the moment.

II

WHEN I. A. Richards, in *Science and Poetry*, suggested that a poet like Yeats, who took ghosts and fairies seriously, could hardly have anything quite centrally significant to say to the modern mind, he was making a crude but sensible point. The main debate of that mind, in England, since the 1880's, has been between an orthodox religious and an orthodox scientific attitude. Yeats was neither orthodoxly religious nor orthodoxly scientific; he had his own science, which was an occult one, and his own religion, or "sophisticated lower mythology," and in prose he sometimes reconciles them at the level of magic. In his better poetry, on the other hand, he often quietly jettisons both of them. The scientific attitude leads, in practice, to a kind of democratic humanitarianism. Yeats believed in aristocracy and, though his humane and fastidious temperament made him recoil from violence, he often allowed himself to romanticize violence when it was safely set in a mythological past. The modern Christian attitude tends to lead to a preoccupation with sin. From this, Yeats was quite free. In the last ten years of Yeats's life, these two contrasting attitudes were well represented in England by the work of W. H. Auden and Eliot. Auden, in the 1930's, was a kind of liberal semi-Marxist, profoundly but not always obviously affected by a Christian upbringing; Eliot was a Christian conservative, profoundly but not always obviously affected, particularly in his concern with social questions, by a liberal upbringing. These two poets, in fact, had much more in common with each other than either had with Yeats. Yet Auden, like Eliot, nobly saluted Yeats's passing:

> Earth, receive an honoured guest:
> William Yeats is laid to rest.
> Let the Irish vessel lie
> Emptied of its poetry. . . .
> ("In Memory of W. B. Yeats,")[2]

In saluting Yeats, neither Auden nor Eliot can have been merely saluting a great artist in verse. Given the deep seriousness of their critical attitudes, both must have found in Yeats's work a kind of wisdom, even though that expressed itself through ideas and gestures of which they disapproved. Yeats was as firmly set against Auden's attitude of the 1930's, which he symbolically described as "Moscow," as against Eliot's, which he symbolically described as "Rome." Just as he was never a political democrat, never at all sympathetic with the

> levelling, rancorous, rational sort of mind
> That never looked out of the eye of a saint
> Or out of a drunkard's eye,

[2]In *Collected Shorter Poems, 1930–1944* (London, 1950).

208

so he was very much farther, also, from any traditional Christian attitudes than many scientifically minded agnostics are. What may be called his morality was neither that of a diluted and imperfect Christianity nor that of a progressive humanitarianism. It could be better described as a morality of "style." It very much resembled (given that Yeats had a more genial and generous temperament) the morality of Nietzsche. Yeats's instinctive sympathies were with the strong and proud, not with the weak and humble; with the brilliant rather than the stupid, with the exceptional rather than the average. They were not, however, like those of Nietzsche, with the oppressor rather than the oppressed. Yet, as an Irish nationalist, Yeats identified himself with the liberal wing of the Protestant Ascendancy, with those like Jonathan Swift and Henry Grattan, "who gave though free to refuse," rather than with the masses of the Irish people. Yeats's frank admiration for such qualities as strength, beauty, recklessness, a dominating spirit, a "proper pride" set him against the obvious superficial currents of our age. If he does indeed have the central representativeness that Eliot claims for him, one reason may be that this aristocratic or "natural" morality—which is the morality of schoolboys, of film fans, of soldiers, a morality based on the instinctive admiration we feel for those who excel us—is more firmly rooted in us than we think, and that when we find it nobly expressed we instinctively respond to it. More broadly, for all our preoccupation today with "security," we still have hankerings after the heroic.

III

The case for Yeats's representativeness, however, has never been properly argued. The mere exposition of the meaning of many of Yeats's poems, as related to his personal history, to his social background, and to his philosophical opinions, is in itself such a complicated task that very little that can properly be called "criticism" of his poems—criticism in the sense of concrete evaluation, of distancing and placing—has been written. Maud Gonne and Mme. Blavatsky and the Abbey Theatre and Irish politics and the esoteric symbolism of A Vision tend to bulk so large in accounts of Yeats that they crowd out any consideration of his diction, his rhythms, his way of constructing a poem, the coherence and sensitivity of his responses. What John Wain wittily calls "the

Gypsy Petulengro approach"—the painstaking exposition, with diagrams, of what Yeats meant by gyres and cones and "phases of the moon"—becomes so absorbing in itself that mere literary criticism no doubt seems dull by comparison. This sketch is not primarily concerned with Yeats as a magician or a mystic. Margaret Rudd may be perfectly right when, in her book about Yeats, she says that he is a rather inferior mystic if we compare him with Blake. What is also true is that the Blake of the prophetic books is a rather inferior artist if we compare him with Yeats—these have to be approached, as even Yeats's book of occult philosophy, A Vision, need not be, with a primarily extraliterary interest. And Yeats's prose poem Per Amica Silentia Lunae, a preliminary account of some parts of A Vision, needs no apology; it is an accomplished, even a moving, artifact in its own right. But we should remember a wise remark by his wife, George: "Willie," she is reported to have said, "you are a great poet, but you are no saint." The great poet is our subject. He was, of course, no saint; but we may make out a case in passing that he had many of the virtues of Aristotle's "magnanimous man" or of the honnête homme of the French seventeenth century. His representativeness for our own age does, as I have suggested, largely depend on the fact that he both possessed and praised what we think of as archaic virtues. He was the last quite wholehearted spokesman of the aristocratic idea.

IV

Yeats came from the outer fringe of the Irish Protestant Ascendancy, from a rather better family than George Bernard Shaw's, and perhaps from not quite such a good family as Oscar Wilde's. He spent his childhood between London and Ireland, and though in Ireland his family counted as minor gentry, in London, insofar as London bothers about such things, they probably counted as shabby-genteel bohemians. Yeats's father, J. B. Yeats, was a talented but unsuccessful painter who wrote brilliant letters and had a genius for friendship. As a painter he was influenced by the Pre-Raphaelites, and he handed down to his son the idea of a "religion of beauty" and a romantic taste in art and literature that even in Yeats's youth was a slightly old-fashioned one. There are certain great writers of the type of Henrik Ibsen whom the young Yeats could never absorb; to the end of his days his attitude toward the French painters Edgar Degas and Claude Monet was rather like that of Sir Alfred Munnings toward Pablo Picasso.[3] J. B. Yeats was also influenced in his ideas by the agnostic rationalism of Thomas Huxley and John Tyndall, and this in turn effected a change in his art to a naturalist impressionist portraiture. Against such beliefs and aesthetic practices the young Yeats violently reacted.

As a boy, Yeats was dreamy and backward, fond of long solitary walks. To his dying day, he never learned to spell properly, and diffidence about his scholarship prevented him from going to Trinity College, Dublin. This lack of a formal education is important in Yeats's development. He read very widely but never systematically. He was bad at languages; insofar as the French symbolist movement influenced him at all, it was through translations made by his friend Arthur Symons, and when in later life he said that he had "almost forgotten his Hebrew," he meant that at one period, for some occult purpose, he had memorized a few words of that language. Even for himself, the map of what he knew and did not know can never have had very firm outlines. Like many poets, he probably learned much from conversations with others, and, indeed, all his life he subjected himself to mentors, sometimes younger men than himself, who supplied the deficiencies in his stock of philosophy, connoisseurship, stagecraft, or mystical experience: Lionel Johnson, Charles Ricketts, John Synge, Gordon Craig, T. Sturge Moore.

The young Yeats began writing verses very early. This early work shows much vividness of imagery, but it was some time before Yeats learned to write in regular stanzas or even to make all his lines scan. The first drafts of his poems, to the end, often show a surprising technical hesitancy—a trite choice of words, a flat shaping of the line; the poems were perfected by a habit, early acquired, of endlessly patient revision. The young Yeats was lucky in that his father encouraged him to go on with his poetry and even actively discouraged him from tying himself down to the drudgery of regular newspaper work. Yeats, however, soon became a fluent freelance journalist, chiefly on topics of Irish folklore. By his early twenties, he had begun to make a reputation. In London, he became one of a group of minor poets, among

them Symons, Johnson, and Ernest Dowson, whom today we tend to dismiss as "decadents."

This label has been attached to them partly because of their sense of the incurable materialism and philistinism of their own age, and of their self-created myth of themselves as doomed artists, and partly because of their almost exclusive devotion to their art. All of them—Lionel Johnson, Ernest Dowson, John Davidson, Arthur Symons, Aubrey Beardsley—had unhappy lives; most died young. A number were converts to Catholicism, and for them the possibility, ever present in their minds, of being damned gave not a relish but a momentousness to sin. Yeats's early poems are full of melancholy and falling rhythms, but have little to say about sin. The young Irishman was not haunted by the fear of damnation. He was chaste and temperate—the greatest love of his life, for Maud Gonne, was probably a chaste one, and his failure to win her did not drive him to prostitutes or to drink. In the middle 1890's he met a beautiful and talented woman, an unhappily married cousin of Lionel Johnson's, Olivia Shakespear, and for a short period they found happiness in their love affair. But before long, Maud Gonne appeared in London, asking for his help, and Olivia, sensing a divided loyalty, brought her affair with Yeats to an end. This renewed misery might well have brought him to the same end as the poets of "the tragic generation," had he not been rescued by the maternal kindness of Lady Gregory at the end of the decade. Shy and dreamy though Yeats was, he also was fundamentally a masterful man. Maud Gonne, dragging him at her heels on nationalist agitations, soon found that he was a natural orator and could easily dominate committees. His religion, far more than that of his companions, was genuinely a religion of poetry. Reacting against agnostic rationalism, he had not reacted in the direction of orthodoxy:

I was unlike others of my generation in one thing only. I am very religious, and deprived by Huxley and Tyndall of the simple-minded religion of my childhood, I had made a new religion, almost an infallible church of poetic tradition, of a fardel of stories, and of personages and of emotions, inseparable from their first expression, passed on from generation to generation by poets and painters with some help from philosophers and theologians.

(*The Trembling of the Veil,* 1926 ed., pp. 142–143)

How far, one wonders, was he right about himself? Was he really "very religious"? We wonder both about the word "fardel" with its dandified air and

---

[3]Munnings was a member of the Royal Academy and a painter of horses in the naturalist manner. He was intensely conservative and unsympathetic to the avant-garde work by Picasso.

about the word "stories," which shrugs off the question of whether the stories are true. The attitude is aesthetic rather than ethical or religious; in a sophisticated way the young Yeats is playing a child's game of Let's Pretend. There are late poems of his, such as "Among School Children," that do express an authentically religious attitude, one of mystical acceptance of a world experienced as contradictory; but the genuinely religious attitude that is often to be found in Yeats's poetry has little to do with—even tugs against—the pseudoreligious notions. It is not a playing with fantasies but a response to the whole. The very fact that the young man could so easily concoct a "new religion" for himself—out of Irish folklore and Blake and Mme. Blavatsky and anything that came handy—is evidence of a rather unreligious nature; evidence of a blithe and irresponsible temperament, that of a young man sure of his genius, and unconvicted of sin. The note of the 1890's, the genuinely religious note that is not to be found in Yeats's early poems, is that of Lionel Johnson's "The Dark Angel":

> Dark Angel, with thine aching lust!
> Of two defeats, of two despairs:
> Less dread, a change to drifting dust,
> Than thine eternity of cares.

Yeats's early religion, if it was properly a religion at all, was one without anguish or dread.

The charm of much of Yeats's early poetry is thus slightly equivocal—dreamy and melancholy, passive and self-indulgent, as indeed from this account of his poetical religion we might expect it to be. Robert Graves's attack on "The Lake Isle of Innisfree" is, in fact, an attack on a poet for not being properly awake. In the poem "A Faery Song" from Yeats's volume of 1892, *The Countess Cathleen and Various Legends and Lyrics*, a modern reader is embarrassed by the monotonous doleful music, by the yearning that seems neither to have nor to seek for an object:

> We who are old, old and gay,
> O so old!
> Thousands of years, thousands of years
> If all were told:
>
> Give to these children, new from the world,
> Silence and love;
> And the long dew-dropping hours of the night,
> And the stars above....
>
> (1–8)

Even throughout the 1890's, however, there was a constant, slow, hidden growth in another direction. In *The Wind Among the Reeds*, the volume of 1899, the diction does indeed seem on the surface as formal and faded, the cadences as mechanically "beautiful," as ever; and the symbolism also, increasingly intricate but not increasingly vivid,

> a coat
> Covered with embroideries,

hangs now like a rich, worn tapestry between the poet and the hard stone walls of the world. But the yearning had now an object, Maud Gonne. The individual words clutch more at particular objects. There is a movement toward active feeling, positive grasp:

> I became a man, a hater of the wind,
> Knowing one, out of all things, alone, that his head
> May not lie on the breast or his lips on the hair
> Of the woman that he loves, until he dies;
> Although the rushes and the fowl of the air
> Cry of his love with their pitiful cries.
> ("He Thinks of His Past Greatness When a Part of
> the Constellations of Heaven")

Yeats, at some time after 1909, changed the "dreamy Celtic" dying fall of the last two lines to an arrogant rhetorical question:

> O beast of the wilderness, bird of the air,
> Must I endure your amorous cries?

The poem had enough latent strength to stand the change.

We should look, in the early poems, for that latent strength. Their weary, withdrawn note is a kind of protective coloring that Yeats had taken from his friends of the 1890's. (He was often, throughout his life, ready to imitate admiringly his minor, but never his major, contemporaries. A natural leader, he liked to disguise himself as a follower, even of small men.) There is, of course, a paradox here. Yeats made himself a major poet, starting with the equipment and apparently the tastes of a good minor one —with a chaste but excessively "poetic" diction, with exquisite but trite cadences, with a tendency to use symbols in a way that was decorative and even fussy rather than deeply exploratory, with a narrow and rather willfully sad range of moods, always just on the verge of the literary pose or the stock response. He started, also, without much grasp of the outer world; his early poems rarely make us see anything; we can weave our own daydreams round them, which is another matter. And though he acquired unique rank among his contemporaries as a visionary poet, it is probable that the merely *visible* world left him, to the last, rather cold. Usually he evokes it for us by a kind of trick, not describing the thing but reminding us of our feelings about it:

> A sycamore and lime-tree lost in night
> Although that western cloud is luminous
> . . .
> Back turned upon the brightness of the sun
> And all the sensuality of the shade. . . .
> ("Coole Park," 3–4; 30–31)

We remember our feelings about staring toward a fading distance at sunset, about sharp contrasts in a garden of light and shade. We ourselves, most of the time, *make* Yeats's physical world for him. We believe in it, because we believe in Yeats, rather as we believe in a painted Elsinore when Hamlet is talking. We can, in fact, think perhaps most fruitfully of Yeats's poems as speeches made by him at crucial moments in a long noble drama. No poet lends himself so little to the cold-blooded examination of his poems as isolated objects; no poet gains more from being read as a whole, with a full knowledge of his life. Yeats, as he grows older, acts out, with growing assurance and spontaneity, the difficult part of himself. The acting in the end, having gone through the stages of lyrical mime and heroic and satirical tirade, becomes almost naturalistic.

V

THE Edwardian decade saw the masterful side of Yeats's nature coming to the surface. By 1908, when the first collected edition of his works came out, he had made a reputation not only as a poet and a dramatist, but as the man who had put the Abbey Theatre on its feet, who kept it going, and who had bravely defended Synge against local prejudice. Through Lady Gregory, who had become his patron, Yeats was now accepted by that "big house" society of which, in his childhood, he had only touched the fringes. He was becoming self-conscious about his ancestry. Some of the younger men in Dublin, and some older contemporaries like George Moore, thought him conceited and arrogant; but nobody any longer thought him a mere shy, ineffec-

tual dreamer. He had resigned himself to unfulfilled love and found public activity a distraction. Maud Gonne had made an unfortunate marriage, and though she was separated from her husband she had become a Roman Catholic, so there was no prospect of her divorcing her husband and marrying Yeats. He and she, in any case, were becoming estranged in a deeper sense. She felt that the Abbey Theatre had tempted Yeats away from the national cause. She would have liked cheaper seats and plays that were straight nationalistic propaganda. Maude Gonne remained the central figure in his poetry, a muse figure; but her presence in so many of his first lyrics should not deflect us from stressing that women played an important role as friends, even as muse figures: his wife, the young dancer Margaret Ruddock, Dorothy Wellesley (the duchess of Wellington), Lady Gregory, and, perhaps supremely, Olivia Shakespear. Their closeness survived the unhappiness of their affair in the 1890's and continued to the end of her life, a year before his own death; and it was to her that he wrote his warmest and most eloquent letters. She is also the subject of one of his most beautiful poems, "After Long Silence." Both Olivia and Lady Gregory are more sympathetic and more intelligent figures than Maude Gonne, and it is one of the achievements of later criticism that their roles in his life and art have emerged more clearly.

World War I, apart from the deaths of friends like Major Robert Gregory, hardly touched Yeats emotionally. But the Easter Rebellion of 1916, which took him by surprise (he was not in the confidence of any of the more extreme nationalists), made him regret his growing aloofness from the Irish cause. He remained a very moderate nationalist—he felt that England might still "keep faith"—and indeed the troubles of 1916 and after gave him a vivid sense of how violence can in a short time destroy values that it had taken the law centuries to build up:

> We had fed the heart on fantasies,
> The heart's grown brutal from the fare;
> More substance in our enmities
> Than in our love; O honey-bees
> Come build in the empty house of the stare.
> ("The Stare's Nest by My Window," st. 4)

Yet he felt himself more profoundly identified with the Irish people than he had been for many years.

Yeats's long romance with Maud Gonne had meanwhile ended in a kind of comic fantasy. Her husband, one of the rebels of 1916, had been shot.

Yeats felt he ought to ask her to marry him again but was probably relieved when she refused. At the same time, he fell in love with her beautiful adopted daughter, who, as a young girl, had been half in love with him. The adopted daughter could not make up her mind. Yeats gave her a date by which to do so, and when her final decision was against marrying him, he suddenly married another young lady, George Hyde-Lees. Not unnaturally, after such a complication of emotions, he was in a state of depression and anxiety after his marriage—even if there had not been the business of Maud Gonne and her daughter, he was a man in his fifties, weighed down by anxiety for his country and married, after an unusually chaste bachelor existence, to somebody much younger than himself. It was partly to distract him that Mrs. Yeats started the experiments in automatic writing that ultimately gave him the material for *A Vision*. In judging Yeats's occult philosophy, we should always ask ourselves how far, at a fundamental level, he himself took it seriously; and how far it was a necessary plaything for a powerful and distressed creative mind.

VI

MANY critics agree that it is on the volumes published in the last twenty years of his life, from *The Wild Swans at Coole* of 1917 to the posthumous *Last Poems and Two Plays* of 1939, that Yeats's future fame will mainly rest. The sharpening and hardening of his attitudes, the development of the tough, complex, and ironical later style can in fact be traced farther back, to the significantly named *Responsibilities* of 1914. There is even a hint of the new style in "Adam's Curse," from a volume of 1903, *In the Seven Woods*:

> I said, "It's certain there is no fine thing
> Since Adam's fall but needs much labouring.
> There have been lovers who thought love should be
> So much compounded of high courtesy
> That they would sigh and quote with learned looks
> Precedents out of beautiful old books;
> Yet now it seems an idle trade enough."

It can, however, be agreed that there is a remarkable new maturity, a new "realism," in the work of Yeats's last twenty years; and this can be traced to several sources.

Yeats was now writing as a married man, a man with a house and children of his own, more rooted in everyday life than he had previously been. He was writing also as a man who had seen the dream of his youth, Irish independence, come true; and who was becoming aware of certain ironies, for him tragic ironies, involved in its coming true. His own personal dream had been of a free Ireland that would be a kind of replica, without the tensions or troubles, without the injustice to the majority, of the Ireland of Grattan's Parliament.[4] He wanted to go back to the eighteenth century rather than on into the twentieth. He hoped that the "big houses" would survive, that the Protestant Ascendancy would still, because of their wealth, their wit, and their manners, constitute a dominant group. He thought of the local grandees patronizing poets and the peasants touching their hats. He was romantically innocent about politics. He found, of course, that what had come into existence was not a Protestant-dominated aristocratic republic but a Roman Catholic farmers' democracy; and the farmers did not want to touch their hats to anybody. Some of the "big houses" were burned in the troubles, others were deserted because they cost too much to keep up and because they, like even the nationalistic aristocracy, had outlived their social function. Yeats had hoped that Dublin, as the capital of a free Ireland, would become a great cultural center; he saw the "blind, bitter town" becoming more rather than less provincial. The Dublin city fathers gave the freedom of the city to a retired Tam-

---

[4]Until 1780, the Irish Parliament could reject or accept, but not amend, laws relating to Irish matters passed by the British Parliament. Irish patriots like Henry Flood and Henry Grattan took advantage of the American Revolutionary War (which involved war with France) to claim and secure legislative independence for the Irish Parliament. The Volunteer Movement, a kind of unofficial defense militia ostensibly raised to resist invasion, was in fact used to put moral pressure on the viceregal government. The viceroy and his staff, however, retained practical control of Irish affairs by offering honors and sinecures to the progovernment parliamentary majority. The new Parliament did not represent the Roman Catholic masses of the people, or even their wealthier elements. Thus the short period of Irish parliamentary independence—or really, of independence for the Protestant Ascendancy—ended in the bloody troubles of 1798 and a little later in the union, secured partly by lavish bribery, of the Irish with the imperial Parliament. Nevertheless, the short period of Grattan's Parliament was marked both by splendid oratory and by a gay and brilliant social life in Dublin, and was thus often remembered nostalgically in the nineteenth century by Irishmen who saw Dublin, both socially and culturally, becoming more and more of a provincial city.

many boss, a Mr. Croker, but rejected the suggestion of Oliver St. John Gogarty that they should also give it to Yeats. Sean O'Casey's tragic masterpiece, *The Plough and the Stars*, aroused as passionate an opposition from the Abbey Theatre audience as Synge's *Playboy of the Western World* had done. Yeats's growing bitterness comes out as early as *The Wild Swans at Coole* in one of his most powerfully sustained shorter poems, "The Fisherman":

> All day I'd looked in the face
> What I had hoped 'twould be
> To write for my own race
> And the reality;
> The living men that I hate,
> The dead man that I loved,
> The craven man in his seat,
> The insolent unreproved,
> And no knave brought to book
> Who has won a drunken cheer,
> The witty man and his joke
> Aimed at the commonest ear,
> The clever man who cries
> The catch-cries of the clown,
> The beating down of the wise
> And great Art beaten down.
>
> (9–24)

Yeats, in this new Ireland, was not, in spite of the prestige that the Nobel Prize brought him, a centrally representative figure. He became a senator, but found himself allied in the senate, a little unromantically, with rich bankers and brewers; a speech that he made protesting, on behalf of the religious minority, against a proposal to make divorce illegal made him unpopular. The esoteric philosophy of *A Vision* is partly to be understood, as we have suggested already, in terms of Yeats's need for distraction. We should not take that book more seriously than Yeats did. He had a long philosophical correspondence with Sturge Moore about hallucinatory cats and other visions of that sort. Are they real beings to which we have access only at privileged moments? Yeats would have liked to think so. Or are they, on the other hand, hallucinations? It is interesting that in this correspondence he never refers to either the "facts" or the "arguments" of *A Vision* as having any relevant authority. He explicitly states elsewhere that it is not very profitable to discuss the theories of *A Vision* in terms of "belief." Many of the ideas in the book, like that of eternal recurrence, are not new; they can be found in the Italian philosopher Giovan-

ni Vico, and in Nietzsche. Yeats, after he had written the first draft of *A Vision*, also found them in Oswald Spengler. Their truth or otherwise cannot be discussed here. They provided props for Yeats's attitude to life, which was becoming a kind of tragic stoicism. He saw life as tragic and felt that it could be acted out with the style of a tragedy. We can embrace our destiny joyfully: "Hamlet and Lear are gay."

It should be particularly noticed, however, that Yeats's attitude toward the supernatural was a profoundly ambiguous one. He wanted, from a world beyond ours, in contrasting moods, two apparently quite contradictory kinds of assurance: one, that we are in fact bound, as the Buddhists tell us we are, to the "great wheel of existence" and shall reappear upon this stage in various roles again and again; the other that, as the Buddhists also tell us, we can escape ultimately from the "great wheel"—not to nonbeing, a concept that never attracted Yeats, but to some kind of timeless perfection. He was not sure (as perhaps no Western man who studies Eastern thought ever is) that he really wanted to escape from the wheel. Thus, in the face of his "symbolic phantasmagoria," he retains the freedom of inconsistency. His images of a Byzantine heaven in which he would be transformed into a golden bird (the artist becoming an eternal work of art) symbolize his desire to escape from the disorder, the irony, the failure of life; but so also other symbols—as when he says he would like to live again, even in a "foul ditch," as a "blind man battering blind men"—stand for a craving for life at any level, the "lust and rage" of which he speaks in his *Last Poems*, that grew stronger in him as he grew older. Often he hated life for not being perfection. Sometimes, also, he feared perfection for not being life.

VII

YEATS'S early love poems are dreamily erotic, but those addressed to Olivia Shakespear, particularly through the use of hair imagery, possess a shadowy sexuality. Some of his later poems are so harshly sexual that they cease, in effect, to be erotic:

> From pleasure of the bed,
> Dull as a worm,
> His rod and its butting head
> Limp as a worm,

His spirit that has fled
Blind as a worm.
            ("The Chambermaid's
                Second Song")

A glandular operation that Yeats underwent in his last years no doubt accentuated this tendency, but it was already there. It is best considered, however, as part of a more general tendency in his later poems toward self-questioning, self-stripping:

These masterful images because complete
Grew in pure mind, but out of what began?
A mound of refuse or the sweepings of a street,
Old kettles, old bottles, and a broken can,
Old iron, old bones, old rags, that raving slut
Who keeps the till. Now that my ladder's gone
I must lie down where all the ladders start
In the foul rag-and-bone shop of the heart.
            ("The Circus Animals' Desertion," st. 5)

The man who wrote that stanza also wrote:

We were the last romantics—chose for theme
Traditional sanctity and loveliness. . . .
            ("Coole Park and Ballylee," st. 6)

Anybody who wants to get the full range of Yeats must be able to respond to both kinds of statement—must be able to accept the tautness of a great poet's terrible sincerity. In that stanza from "The Circus Animals' Desertion," Yeats has become aware that the symbols of his poetry have a Freudian meaning of which for most of his life he has been unconscious. But we should notice also that this stanza, which bids farewell to the symbolist method, is a triumphant example of it; for we know what the poet is saying here, but we cannot say it in our own words. A merely clinical interpretation will not work. Is, for instance, "that raving slut/Who keeps the till" the Freudian censor—is the money she will give us in return for old rubbish a release of libido? Are the "old iron, old bones, old rags" and the "mound of refuse" symbols for the Freudian anal-erotic hoarding instinct? Is the "foul rag-and-bone shop of the heart" merely the sexual imagination, with its accumulated scraps of lustful memory? Quite obviously not, and quite obviously what Yeats is saying here is something more general and profound. There is something basically blind, grasping, insensate in all of us; something that hoards rubbish, that shuts doors, that hides away from the light. We climb up, but we never wholly get away. All is still

under our feet, in the cellarage. And the "heart" is what grasps and is insensate but also what loves and suffers, and the "ladders"—the ways upward and outward to the free air and the life of the spirit—do start there. And when we have said all this, of course, the stanza still retains, as all great symbolist poetry does, its eternal residue of mysterious suggestiveness.

The bare honesty of such poems, even more than the rich, dark mysteriousness of "Byzantium" or "The Statues," may partly account for Yeats's hold on the young. In his last volume he asks himself more frankly than most poets have done whether he may not have done as much harm as good:

Did that play of mine send out
Certain men the English shot?

Yet he can still strike a last attitude:

Cast a cold eye
On life, on death.
Horseman, pass by!
            ("Under Ben
                Bulben")

He would not, like Rainer Maria Rilke (these lines were written out of irritation with Rilke), accept death as a final dark consummation. He would not accept life itself uncritically. And in the last thing he was working on, *The Death of Cuchulain*, the harlot (an eternal harlot, who has slept with "Conall, Cuchulain, Usna's boys") speaks of polarities and antinomies, of disgust and delight in physical love, of dread and delight in battle; speaks also of the Irish patriots of 1916, who were always in Yeats's heart, delighting in what they dreaded; speaks of gods and heroes whom we seem to embody, or who seem to stand behind us, in the crucial moments of our lives:

That there are still some living
That do my limbs unclothe,
But that the flesh my flesh has gripped
I both adore and loathe.
            (*Pipe and drum music*)
Are those things that men adore and loathe
Their sole reality?
What stood in the Post Office
With Pearse and Connolly?
What comes out of the mountain
When men first shed their blood?
Who thought Cuchulain till it seemed
He stood where they had stood?

VIII

YEATS felt that there was a tension between his life and his poetry. He thought sometimes of the poem as a kind of antipersonality that the poet builds up to compensate for or conceal personal weakness, of the poem as a "mask." This idea has something in common with Ezra Pound's idea of the poem as a persona. Pound is a poet who, according to one of his most appreciative but also harshest critics, Percy Wyndham Lewis, has no "personality" of his own worth speaking of; he can function only by pretending to be somebody else, a Provençal troubadour or a Chinese sage. Yeats's masks in poetry are not of this sort; even in his earliest work his own personality—or at least an important aspect of it, the "poetic" aspect—seems to me to come over. Similarly, no doubt, at meetings of the Rhymers' Club in the 1890's, Yeats, fundamentally a very shy and diffident young man, put on a suitable "literary dandy" or perhaps sometimes a "dreamy Celt" personality. As Yeats's poetry matures, one of the things that happens is not so much that it becomes more personal, less of a mask, as that he gets more of his personality into it. He gets in things like irony, humor, arrogant irascibility, the coaxing manners of the professional Irish conversationalist, which in the 1890's he would probably have considered "antipoetic"; he gets in more of the prosaic detail of life, transformed by a poetic apprehension of it.

We might compare the generalized evocation of Maud Gonne, from "Fallen Majesty" in *Responsibilities*,

> . . . A crowd
> Will gather, and not know it walks the very street
> Whereon a thing once walked that seemed a burning cloud,
> (6–8)

with the prose bareness of a line and a half from "Beautiful Lofty Things," in *Last Poems:*

> . . . Maud Gonne at Howth Station waiting a train,
> Pallas Athene in that straight back and arrogant head. . . .
> (10–11)

That line and a half evokes Maud Gonne, her setting, her bearing, her character (Pallas Athene, the goddess of wisdom, was severe and virginal). The more conventionally poetic phrase about "a burning cloud" tells us much about Yeats's feeling but does not evoke any image of a woman at all.

Often the force of the later poetry comes largely from this directness, like that of speech:

> Before a woman's portrait suddenly I stand,
> Beautiful and gentle in her Venetian way,
> I met her all but fifty years ago
> For twenty minutes in some studio.
>   . . .
> And here's John Synge himself, that rooted man,
> "Forgetting human words," a grave deep face. . . .
> ("The Municipal Gallery Revisited," st. 4 and 7)

> Does the imagination dwell the most
> Upon a woman won or woman lost?
> If on the lost, admit you turned aside
> From a great labyrinth out of pride,
> Cowardice, some silly over-subtle thought
> Or anything called conscience once;
> And that if memory recur, the sun's
> Under eclipse and the moon blotted out.
> (*The Tower*)

There is no rhetoric in these passages; only in the latter of them any figures of speech, and these so commonplace (a human relationship as a labyrinth, the sense of loss seeming to blot out the sun and moon) that they could occur unaffectedly in ordinary conversation. Common turns of speech are also sometimes exploited for irony. In *The Tower* we are told the story of Mrs. French (it is in Sir Jonah Barrington's *Memoirs* of 1833) and how a footman at dinner one day clipped off the ears of a farmer who was behaving boorishly and brought them to her in a little covered dish. It is with a delighted shock that we meet the lady again, in a summary of the characters in the poems, as

> Mrs. French,
> Gifted with so fine an ear. . . .

Critics who have discussed to the verge of tedium Yeats's more obscure occult fancies might have discussed with more advantage this strong simplicity of his later style. Behind the strength is honesty of statement. The lines quoted above,

> Does the imagination dwell the most . . .

express a complex of feelings that most of us have experienced but that few of us have the courage to put on record: a complex of feelings that might be called remorse or compunction. Yeats speaks for what he calls, in a poem addressed to Friedrich von Hügel, the "unchristened heart"; but with a dignity and passion that make it very unlikely that his words should ever cause scandal to Christians.

Yet if there were only pride and pagan courage and high art, only contempt for "this filthy modern tide," only the obstinate "lust and rage" of a "wild, wicked old man" in Yeats, should we turn to him as we do, not only for distraction, not only for stimulus, but for wisdom and consolation? We look in poetry for love. All great poets are more profoundly capable of love than common men, and they may be terrifyingly more capable of hate too. Yeats's capacity for hate distressed even close friends of his, like the duchess of Wellington. It was there to the last, as in the poem "A Bronze Head":

> Or else I thought her supernatural;
> As though a sterner eye looked through her eye
> On this foul world in its decline and fall;
> On gangling stocks grown great, great stocks run dry,
> Ancestral pearls all pitched into a sty,
> Heroic reverie mocked by clown and knave,
> And wondered what was left for massacre to save.
>
> (st. 4)

But he could hate like that *because* he could love. And the touchstones that I would choose from his poetry, to persuade an unsympathetic reader to reconsider it, all speak of love. I would choose these stanzas from "A Prayer for My Daughter":

> An intellectual hatred is the worst,
> So let her think opinions are accursed.
> Have I not seen the loveliest woman born
> Out of the mouth of Plenty's horn,
> Because of her opinionated mind
> Barter that horn and every good
> By quiet natures understood
> For an old bellows full of angry wind?
>
> Considering that, all hatred driven hence,
> The soul recovers radical innocence
> And learns that it is self-delighting,
> Self-appeasing, self-affrighting,
> And that its own sweet will is Heaven's will;
> She can, though every face should scowl
> And every windy quarter howl
> Or every bellows burst, be happy still.
>
> (st. 8–9)

I would choose a line or two from the gentle minor elegy "In Memory of Eva Gore-Booth and Con Markiewicz":

> Dear shadows, now you know it all,
> All the folly of a fight
> With a common wrong or right.
> The innocent and the beautiful
> Have no enemy but time. . . .
>
> (21–25)

I would choose the magnificent two last stanzas of "Among School Children":

> Both nuns and mothers worship images,
> But those the candles light are not as those
> That animate a mother's reveries,
> But keep a marble or a bronze repose.
> And yet they too break hearts—O Presences
> That passion, piety or affection knows,
> And that all heavenly glory symbolise—
> O self-mockery of man's enterprise;
>
> Labour is blossoming or dancing where
> The body is not bruised to pleasure soul,
> Nor beauty born out of its own despair,
> Nor blear-eyed wisdom out of midnight oil.
> O chestnut-tree, great-rooted blossomer,
> Are you the leaf, the blossom, or the bole?
> O body swayed to music, O brightening glance,
> How can we know the dancer from the dance?

And (though Yeats is not on the whole a poet of striking single lines, of lines that impress us out of their setting) I might choose a line and a half from "Nineteen Hundred and Nineteen":

> Man is in love and loves what vanishes,
> What more is there to say? . . .
>
> (st. 6)

Throughout his career, Yeats was a continuous reviser of his earlier work; and the student, when he quotes the work, needs to be careful that he is not basing his arguments on a text of 1908 or of the 1920's. This process is one of "making himself new." Essentially Yeats's poems are dramatic lyrics, and each of his volumes after *Responsibilities* (1914) consists of poems placed very carefully not in order of composition but in a cogent dramatic order, an unfolding, one poem commenting on its predecessor or its successor, amplifying or deflating. Each volume in turn leads on to its successor. So, for example, the last poem in *The Wild Swans at Coole*, "The Double Vision of Michael Robartes," with its figure of the dancer, is caught up in the little poem of the ensuing volume, *Michael Robartes and the Dancer* (1920).

I believe Yeats's poetry to be the centrally important part of his work. His work as a playwright is more difficult to assess.

IX

YEATS's approach is distinct from that of his contemporaries in the Irish dramatic revival. Theirs was to develop, first in the work of Synge and later in that of O'Casey, toward a drama of regional naturalism. Yeats on the other hand remained throughout his life the visionary of the movement, the one who aimed at a marriage of poetry and drama to be achieved by quite different methods. From the very beginning he took a vigorous and practical part in the artistic and technical development of the Irish theater, as well as in the day-to-day problems of administration, production, and experiment. He was by no means a Tennyson patronized by an Irving, but rather a combination of poet and man of the theater who created an integral dramatic form that was entirely new to his age. What distinguishes him from his dramatic contemporaries is his rejection of representation, a dramatic convention that had come to be accepted without question, because in Britain, at least, playwriting had for so long been overshadowed and dominated by the art of fiction. Yeats turned away not only from the large theater, with its sophisticated apparatus of illusion, and from the realistic conventions of performance, gesture, and details of staging and spectacle, but also from other conventions concerning dramatic composition:

One dogma of the printed criticism is that if a play does not contain definite character, its constitution is not strong enough for the stage, and that the dramatic moment is always the contest of character with character. . . . when we go back a few centuries and enter the great periods of drama, character grows less and sometimes disappears.
("The Tragic Theatre," in the
Mask [Florence], October 1910)

He sought, as he wrote elsewhere, "a deeper reality than any that can be reached by observation, for it is the reality of the imagination and comes from the withdrawal of the poet's mind into itself, not from the effort to see and record." His conception of the drama aimed at uncovering "not character, but those deeper forms of which character is merely a lineament."

Within these chosen limits, Yeats was to experiment for over thirty years to express his vision in dramatic form, first with the Irish Literary Theatre, then later with the Abbey; and his plays reveal a skill in the handling of his medium that increased slowly but unmistakably. In his early verse plays, such as *The Shadowy Waters* (1900), his aim is the realization of a vision of the transcendental. Next, in *Cathleen ni Houlihan* (1902)—the most popular of all his pieces—and *The Pot of Broth,* both written in collaboration with Lady Gregory, he begins to develop fluency in colloquial prose dialogue, coming down, as he put it, from the high window of dramatic verse. He returns to blank verse in a number of plays pitched in a more heroic key, notably *On Baile's Strand* (1903), centered on the episode of King Cuchulain's unwitting killing of his son, and *Deirdre* (1907), the tragic legend that was also dramatized by Synge. It is characteristic of Yeats's *Deirdre* that he contracts the action within a far smaller radius than that of Synge. Preparation is minimal and the attention of the audience is focused as soon as possible on the climax of love and death, the final tableau of queen, lover, and aged king, which constitutes the moment of insight of the play.

Yeats takes an even more radical step away from conventional dramaturgy in his *Four Plays for Dancers* (1921), which were shaped by the traditions of the Japanese *Noh* theater. "I wanted to create for myself an unpopular theatre," he wrote, and in these short pieces he strives to pare away still more rigorously what he regards as inessentials.

All imaginative art remains at a distance, and this distance must be firmly held against a pushing world. . . . Our unimaginative arts are content to set a piece of the world as we know it in a place by itself, to put their photographs, as it were, in a plush or plain frame, but the arts which interest me, while seeming to separate from the world and us a group of figures, images, symbols, enable us to pass for a few moments into a deep of the mind that had hitherto been too subtle for our habitation. . . .
(introduction to *Certain Noble Plays of Japan,* 1916)

The action in each of the four plays is framed by the presence throughout of masked musicians, who serve as prologue, chorus, and orchestra, and the plays mark a further stage in Yeats's perennial dramatic aim, to isolate particular moments of insight with the maximum of intensity.

The toughening and hardening of attitudes in Yeats's later years referred to in section VI of this essay—the replacing of music by fire, as B. Rajan has aptly put it—and its effect upon Yeats's poetic composition is paralleled by the continual effort to refine and purify his dramatic writing. Toward the end of his life his mastery of dramatic verse and dramatic prose became completely integrated, and his two finest pieces for the stage, albeit minor in scale, offer us an example of each: *Purgatory* (1939), a study of the imprisonment of people in themselves and in their heredity, is in verse; *The Words upon the Window Pane* (1934) is a histrionic tour de force in which the last days of Swift are described through the mouth of a spiritualistic medium in a state of trance.

X

YEATS wrote very delightful prose, and his reminiscences of the 1890's, in particular, are a primary document for a fascinating period. He was an erratic literary critic. His introduction to *The Oxford Book of Modern Verse, 1892–1935*, like his selection of poems in that book, is strikingly odd and eccentric; but it has the wit and charm of everything he wrote, and here and there, among statements that seem quite absurd, it has extremely penetrating paragraphs—particularly, perhaps, about his friend Ezra Pound, whose qualities and weaknesses no subsequent critic has estimated so justly. But it was into his poetry that he put himself most completely. The poetry, however, is better poetry because he gave himself to so many other things. His patriotism, his public spirit, his capacity for staunch friendship and passionate love all enrich it. The sense, which grew so strong in him in later life, that every victory he had worked for implied a defeat of something he perhaps cared about more, lends almost all his later work a pose of complex irony. The characteristics that some of his contemporaries disliked, such as his arrogance or "proper pride," are in his poems, too. Yet all true poets are fundamentally humble. Yeats was humble before the mystery of life. He never took either himself or his systems quite so seriously as some of his disciples have done. He was the last great poet in the English romantic tradition; and the only poet in that tradition, except Byron, with a genuine sense of humor and gift of wit. The true man, with the modesty and the generosity that underlay all his poses, comes out in the letters to Sturge Moore. Yeats writes about the Nobel Prize:

Yes, it will be a great help to me in several ways. Here especially it will help. I will find it easier to get the Government to listen to me on artistic things. I look upon it as a recognition of the Free State, and of Irish literature, and it is a very great help. People here are grateful because I have won them this recognition, and that is the distinction I want. If I thought it a tribute to my own capacity alone, I, being a very social man, would be far less pleased.

(23 November 1923)

All great poets tend to overawe us. They speak with "something above a mortal mouth." And they need their solitude to withdraw into. But it is as a lover, as a friend, and as a patriot, as "a very social man," that Yeats would like us to remember him. It is his broad and deep humanity that provides the substance of his art.

XI

THE first edition of this essay was published in 1954 and revised in Yeats's centenary year, 1965. How does Yeats's reputation now stand, and what light have scholarship and criticism thrown on his work since it was first printed? Only one critic, Professor Yvor Winters, has made a full-scale attack on Yeats's reputation (there has also been a skirmishing raid by Robert Graves). Professor Winters' case is that Yeats more or less invented his "romantic Ireland," that his philosophy is private and incoherent, that his images, however vivid, correspond to no clear structure of thought, that he overdramatizes and appeals to those in search of "easy emotions," and that he does not really write "pure poetry" in the tradition of the French symbolists. Professor Winters' attack is beautifully written and argued, but the brief answer is that he is wrong about Ireland—"Easter 1916" is one of the most "realistic" political poems in our language, and Yeats had a very thorough and complete understanding of Irish character and history—and that the rest of his attack is doctrinaire, an attack on Yeats for not being a kind of poet he did not set out to be.

Nevertheless, Professor Winters has put his finger on something, for it is a certain theatrical quality in Yeats, a certain occasional overeasy dramatization of certain stock attitudes, that has worried recent critics. Most contemporary critics would admit, for instance, that "Under Ben Bulben," however gallant as a deathbed gesture, is a little too stagy to be wholly satisfactory as a poem. In a lecture at Sligo in the 1960's, Professor Donald Davie suggested that the peak of Yeats's achievement lay in several late midperiod poems, like "A Prayer for My Daughter," which have a certain classical poise and balance that represent the survival in Yeats's milieu and temperament of Irish eighteenth-century decorum. The most interesting recent criticism, like that of T. Parkinson and J. Stallworthy, has made use of the variorum edition and the manuscript drafts to re-create for us Yeats's agonizingly slow, almost Flaubertian methods of composition. Yeats's first drafts, sometimes in prose, are always clear as outline sketches but remarkably hesitant and sometimes clumsy in rhythm and diction; the "grand style" was forged not easily or naturally, but with blood, sweat, and tears.

The labor that lay behind Yeats's style is perhaps one reason why, like another great, laborious poet, Milton, he has been a dangerous influence on subsequent poets. Direct imitation of him reads always like parody or pastiche; Irish poetry went through a dull period after his death and, in the work of Thomas Kinsella, Richard Murphy, and John Montague, has recently achieved a new liveliness largely by dint of resisting the temptation to overdramatize in a Yeatsian fasion. On the other hand, both Yeats's critical writings and his plays now seem much more important to his admirers than they did when I wrote the first version of this essay. We are perhaps moving away from an age of practical criticism to one of critical theorizing, and there are those who claim that as an aesthetic or philosophical critic Yeats is as important as T. S. Eliot is in the opposite field of direct scrutiny of texts. Yeats's plays have still, at least for Englishmen and Americans, to be practically tested on the stage; but Professor Peter Ure has made very high claims for Yeats's skill and readiness to experiment as a practicing playwright, and F. A. C. Wilson has emphasized the importance of the plays for the study of Yeats's "philosophy."

More recent criticism has also tended to suggest that while Yeats renewed his energies continuously throughout his career as poet, the commonly accepted notion that he somehow became a different, a finer, poet after 1908 has been overstressed. The earlier poems, particularly *The Wanderings of Oisin,* have attracted more admiration, and a number of the poems of the middle period appear to suffer from a certain dryness; the note is forced. *The Tower* now appears as the summit of the poet's achievement, although he continued to write master-

ly works. More attention has been directed to the prose works, and not simply as commentary on the poems. Argument continues as to the precise nature of Yeats's commitment to Irish politics, though we are perhaps less censorious about his alignment with bankers in the senate and his brief involvement with the Fascist General O'Duffy's Blueshirts in the 1930's.

It might be thought that the general currents of creative literature in the last ten years—the vogue of Brecht and Beckett in drama, for instance, and the vogue in poetry for low-toned or deliberately informal verse like that of Philip Larkin or Robert Lowell—as well as the tendency in all the arts toward a suspicion of the "high style" and toward the undermining of traditional standards of dignity and decorum, would have told against Yeats. I have heard T. R. Henn claim that modern undergraduates, democratic, humanitarian, anti-aristocratic, scientifically minded, practical, down-to-earth, peace-loving, are bound sooner or later to react violently against Yeats; but as a teacher of poetry to the young I have not yet come up against this hostility to Yeats. I think also that Henn perhaps underestimates the degree to which Yeats was himself, in some broad sense, a liberal; hating the violence and barbarism of the Irish troubles, stating in "Easter 1916" that "England may keep faith," and taking a firm stand in the Irish senate against the censorship and divorce laws. I find more sanity and realism about political and social affairs in Yeats than most critics have found; I think his reaction against images of violence more important than his dallying with them.

He was a poet who in his own way made as rich a use of "the tradition" as Pound or Eliot did in their ways; he could use both Donne and Spenser; there are elements in his poetry of broadsheet ballad style, Augustan formality, the self-exploration of the great romantics, Walter Pater's aestheticism and the world-weariness of the 1890's, French Symbolist mystification (as well as Blake's naked sense of symbolic mystery). He could think poetically in both emblems and abstractions. He incorporates the tradition in a new and personal way, as all great poets do. The antithetical movement of his mind, on the other hand, with its perpetual clashes against itself and its occasional precarious resolutions, is specifically modern. He combines in a strange way the virtues of two great, utterly opposite writers whom he admired: Landor's proud care for "perfection of the work"; Balzac's bursting unpredictableness (the *Autobiographies* are a great Balzacian novel). His whole oeuvre is a world, a world with elements in it of jumble, failure, pose, provinciality, but "changed, changed utterly" by his art, till "a terrible beauty is born."

SELECTED BIBLIOGRAPHY

Titles marked with an asterisk are those of books originally printed and published in limited editions by the Dun Emer (later the Cuala) Press, Dublin, founded by the poet's sisters. Yeats's texts were all republished in later editions and collections.

I. BIBLIOGRAPHY. W. M. Roth, *A Catalogue of English and American First Editions of W. B. Yeats* (New Haven, Conn., 1939); A. Wade, *A Bibliography of the Writing of W. B. Yeats* (London, 1951; rev. ed. with index, 1958), the definitive bibliography, incorporates valuable material contributed by P. S. O'Hegarty to the *Dublin* magazine (1939–1940) and includes full particulars of Yeats's contributions to books and periodicals, and a complete catalog of Cuala Press publications. Most of Yeats's poems were originally published in periodicals.

II. COLLECTED WORKS. *Collected Works in Verse and Prose*, 8 vols. (Stratford-on-Avon, 1908); *Plays for an Irish Theatre* (London, 1913), contains *Deirdre, The Green Helmet, On Baile's Strand, The King's Threshold, The Shadowy Waters, The Hour-Glass,* and *Cathleen ni Houlihan; Later Poems* (London, 1922), vol. I of the new *Collected Edition of the Works; Plays in Prose and Verse* (London, 1922), vol. II of the new *Collected Edition of the Works,* contains *Cathleen ni Houlihan, The Pot of Broth, The Hour-Glass, The King's Threshold, On Baile's Strand, The Shadowy Waters, The Unicorn from the Stars* (in collaboration with Lady Gregory), *The Green Helmet, The Player Queen, Notes and Music; Plays and Controversies* (London, 1923), vol. III of the new *Collected Edition of the Works,* contains "The Irish Dramatic Movement" and the following plays: *The Countess Cathleen, The Land of Heart's Desire, At the Hawk's Well, The Only Jealousy of Emer, The Dreaming of the Bones,* and *Calvary; Essays* (London, 1924), vol. IV of the new *Collected Edition of the Works; Early Poems and Stories* (London, 1925), vol. V of the new *Collected Edition of the Works; Autobiographies* (London, 1926), vol. VI of the new *Collected Edition of the Works,* contains *Reveries over Childhood and Youth* and *The Trembling of the Veil,* new ed. (1955), see below; *Poems* (London, 1927), the preface states that this ed. "contains what is, I hope, the final text of the poems of my youth."

The Collected Poems of W. B. Yeats (London, 1933; rev. and enl. ed., 1950); *The Collected Plays of W. B. Yeats* (London, 1934; 2nd ed., 1952); *Nine One Act Plays* (Lon-

don, 1937), contains *The Land of Heart's Desire, Cathleen ni Houlihan, The Hour-Glass, The Pot of Broth, On Baile's Strand, Deirdre, The Green Helmet, The Shadowy Waters, The Words upon the Window Pane; Poems,* 2 vols. (London, 1949), described as "the definitive edition" and lim. to 375 signed copies; *Autobiographies* (London, 1955), a new and enl. ed., the first of four vols. of Yeats's collected prose works, the others being *Mythologies, Essays and Introductions,* and *Explorations,* see below; P. Allt and R. K. Alspach, eds., *The Variorum Edition of the Poems* (New York, 1957); *Mythologies* (London, 1959); R. Pearce, ed., *The Senate Speeches of W. B. Yeats* (London, 1960); *Essays and Introductions* (London, 1961); *Explorations* (London, 1961); R. K. Alspach, ed., *The Variorum Edition of the Plays* (London, 1966).

III. SELECTED WORKS. A. N. Jeffares, ed., *Selected Poetry* (London, 1962); A. N. Jeffares, ed., *Selected Prose* (London, 1964); A. N. Jeffares, ed., *Selected Criticism* (London, 1964); A. N. Jeffares, ed., *Selected Plays* (London, 1964); J. P. Frayne, ed., *Uncollected Prose by W. B. Yeats: First Reviews and Articles, 1886–1896* (London, 1970); J. P. Frayne and C. Johnson, eds., *Uncollected Prose by W. B. Yeats: Reviews, Articles and Other Miscellaneous Prose, 1897–1939* (New York, 1976).

IV. LETTERS. H. Reynolds, ed., *Letters to the New Island* (Cambridge, Mass., 1934), letters; D. Wellesley, ed., *Letters on Poetry to Dorothy Wellesley* (London, 1940), K. Raine, ed., paperback ed. (London, 1964); C. Bax, ed., *Florence Farr, Bernard Shaw and Yeats: Letters* (Dublin, 1941); R. McHugh, ed., *Letters to Katherine Tynan* (Dublin, 1953); U. Bridge, ed., *Yeats and T. Sturge Moore: Their Correspondence 1901–1937;* A. Wade, ed., *Some Letters from W. B. Yeats to John O'Leary and His Sister from Originals in the Berg Collection* (New York, 1953), a lim. ed. published by the New York Public Library; A. Wade, ed., *Letters* (London, 1954), the fullest collection of Yeats's letters likely to be published, ed. with scholarly care by his bibliographer; R. McHugh, ed., *Ah, Sweet Dancer: W. B. Yeats and Margaret Ruddock. A Correspondence* (London–Basingstoke, 1970).

V. SEPARATE WORKS. American issues or eds., published more or less concurrently with the English, and successive reprs. of combinations of separate works are not as a general rule included in this section. *Mosada, a Dramatic Poem* (Dublin, 1886), first printed in *Dublin University Review* (June 1886), 100 copies of this pamphlet ed. printed; *The Wanderings of Oisin* (London, 1889), verse; *John Sherman and Dhoya* (London, 1891), stories, under the pseudonym of Ganconagh, no. 10 of the Pseudonym Library; *The Countess Cathleen and Various Legends and Lyrics* (London, 1892), verse, the verse drama *The Countess Cathleen* later rev. and published separately (1912); *The Celtic Twilight, Men and Women, Dhouls and Faeries* (London, 1893; rev. ed., 1903), verse, essays, stories; *The Land of Heart's Desire* (London, 1894), drama; *Poems* (London, 1895; rev. eds., 1899, 1901), verse; *The*

Secret Rose (London, 1897), stories; The Wind Among the Reeds (London, 1899), verse.

The Shadowy Waters (London, 1900), verse; Cathleen ni Houlihan (London, 1902), drama; Ideas of Good and Evil (London, 1903), essays; *In the Seven Woods (London, 1903), verse, includes the verse play On Baile's Strand; The Hour-Glass: A Morality (New York, 1904), drama, first published in the North American Review (September 1903), 12 offprints made for copyright purposes by Heinemann Ltd., London; The King's Threshold (New York, 1904), drama, 100 copies only, printed for private circulation, repr. in vol. V of Abbey Theatre series (Dublin, 1905); *Stories of Red Hanrahan (Dublin, 1904), stories; Poems, 1899–1905 (London, 1906); Deirdre (London, 1907), drama; *Discoveries (Dublin, 1907), essays; *The Green Helmet and Other Poems (Dublin, 1910), The Green Helmet, a "heroic farce," separately printed at the Shakespeare Head Press (London, 1911); *Synge and the Ireland of His Time (Dublin, 1911), with a note concerning a walk through Connemara with Yeats by J. B. Yeats; The Cutting of an Agate (New York, 1912; London, 1919), essays; Stories of Red Hanrahan: The Secret Rose: Rosa Alchemica (London–Stratford-on-Avon, 1913; New York, 1914), stories; *Responsibilities (Dublin, 1914; London, 1916), verse and a play; *Reveries over Childhood and Youth (Dublin, 1915; London, 1916), autobiography; *The Wild Swans at Coole (Dublin, 1917; London, 1919), verse and a play; Per Amica Silentia Lunae (London, 1918), essays; *Two Plays for Dancing (Dublin, 1919), contains The Dreaming of the Bones and The Only Jealousy of Emer.

*Michael Robartes and the Dancer (Dublin, 1920), verse; Four Plays for Dancers (London, 1921), contains At the Hawk's Well, The Only Jealousy of Emer, The Dreaming of the Bones, and Calvary; *Four Years: Reminiscences, 1887–1891 (Dublin, 1921), autobiography; *Seven Poems and a Fragment (Dublin, 1922); The Trembling of the Veil (London, 1922), autobiography, subscribers' ed. of 1,000 copies; "Speeches," in Parliamentary Debates Official Report, vols. I–X (Dublin, 1923); *The Cat and the Moon and Certain Poems (Dublin, 1924), drama and verse; A Vision (London, 1925), subscribers' ed. of 600 copies, rev. with additions (London, 1937), reiss. with corrections (London, 1962); Autobiographies (London, 1926) *Estrangement: Being Some Fifty Thoughts from a Diary Kept in the Year 1909 (Dublin, 1926), autobiography; *October Blast (Dublin, 1927), verse; The Tower (London, 1928), verse; Sophocles' "King Oedipus": A Version for the Modern Stage (London, 1928); *The Death of Synge and Other Passages from an Old Diary (Dublin, 1928), diary; *A Packet for Ezra Pound (Dublin, 1929), verse, an ed. of only 660 signed copies for sale; The Land of Heart's Desire [and] The Countess Cathleen (London, 1929), drama.

Stories of Michael Robartes and His Friends (Dublin, 1931), stories and a play, includes the play The Resurrec-

tion; *Words for Music Perhaps, and Other Poems (Dublin, 1932), incorporated in The Winding Stair and Other Poems (London, 1933); The Winding Stair and Other Poems (London, 1933), much enl. ed. of The Winding Stair (London, 1929) and incorporating the contents of Words for Music Perhaps . . . ; The Words upon the Window Pane (London, 1934), drama; Wheels and Butterflies (London, 1934), contains The Words upon the Window Pane, Fighting the Waves, The Resurrection, and The Cat and the Moon; The King of the Great Clock Tower: Commentaries and Poems (London, 1934), verse; A Full Moon in March (London, 1935), drama and verse, contains A Full Moon in March and The King of the Great Clock Tower; *Dramatis Personae (Dublin, 1935; London, 1936), autobiography; Modern Poetry (London, 1936), lecture, Broadcast National Lectures, no. 18; *Essays 1931–1936 (Dublin, 1937); The Herne's Egg (London, 1938), drama, published in America as The Herne's Egg and Other Plays (New York, 1938); *New Poems (Dublin, 1938); The Autobiography of William Butler Yeats (New York, 1938), autobiography, contains Reveries over Childhood and Youth, The Trembling of the Veil, and Dramatis Personae; *Last Poems and Two Plays (Dublin, 1939; London, 1940), contains The Death of Cuchulain and Purgatory; *On the Boiler (Dublin, 1939), essays and verse; *If I Were Four and Twenty: Swedenborg, Mediums and the Desolate Places (Dublin, 1940), essays; *Pages from a Diary Written in Nineteen Hundred and Thirty (Dublin, 1944), diary; D. R. Clark and G. Mayhew, eds., A Tower of Polished Black Stones: Early Versions of the Shadowy Waters (Dublin, 1971); W. H. O'Donnell, ed., The Speckled Bird (New York, 1976); G. M. Harper and W. K. Hood, eds., A Critical Edition of Yeats's "A Vision" (London–Basingstoke, 1978); P. Marcus, W. Gould, and M. J. Sidnell, eds., The Secret Rose: Stories by W. B. Yeats. A Variorum Edition (Ithaca, N. Y.–London, 1981).

VI. EDITED WORKS AND INTRODUCTIONS. W. B. Yeats, ed., Fairy and Folk Tales of the Irish Peasantry (London, 1888); W. Carleton, Stories from Carleton (London, 1889), intro. by Yeats; W. B. Yeats, comp., Representative Irish Names, 2 vols. (London, 1890), intro. and notes by Yeats; W. B. Yeats, ed., Irish Fairy Tales (London, 1892), intro. by Yeats; W. B. Yeats, ed., The Works of William Blake, 3 vols. (London, 1893), lim. ed. of 500 copies; W. B. Yeats, ed., The Poems of William Blake (London–New York, 1893; 1905), in Muses' Library series; A Book of Irish Verse (London, 1895; rev. ed., 1900), selected from modern writers with intro. and notes by Yeats; W. T. Horton, A Book of Images (London, 1898), intro. by Yeats; W. B. Yeats, ed., Beltaine. The Organ of the Irish Literary Theatre (Dublin, 1899–1900), 3 issues; W. B. Yeats, ed., Samhain (Dublin, 1901–1908), ed. for the Irish Literary Theatre from 1901 to 1908; Lady Gregory, ed., Cuchulain of Muirthemme (London, 1902), preface by Yeats; *L. Johnson, Twenty-one Poems (Dublin, 1904), selected by

Yeats; D. Hyde, trans., *The Love Songs of Connacht* (Dublin, 1904), preface by Yeats; Lady Gregory, ed., *Gods and Fighting Men* (London, 1904), preface by Yeats; *William Allingham, *Sixteen Poems* (Dublin, 1905), selected by Yeats; J. M. Synge, *The Well of the Saints* (London, 1905), intro. by Yeats; *Poems of Spenser* (Edinburgh, 1906), selected and with intro. by Yeats, in Golden Poets series; *J. Eglinton, *Some Essays and Passages* (Dublin, 1905), selected by Yeats; W. B. Yeats, ed., *The Arrow* (London, 1906–1907), 3 issues. *K. Tynan, *Twenty-one Poems* (Dublin, 1907), selected by Yeats; *W. B. Yeats and L. Johnson, eds., *Poetry and Ireland* (Dublin, 1908), essays; *W. B. Yeats, ed., *A Broadside* (Dublin, 1908); *J. M. Synge, *Poems and Translations* (Dublin, 1909), intro. by Yeats.

*J. M. Synge, *Deirdre of the Sorrows* (Dublin, 1910), intro. by Yeats; *Selections from the Writings of Lord Dunsany* (Dublin, 1912), intro. by Yeats; *R. Tagore, *The Post Office* (Dublin, 1914), a play with intro. by Yeats; *E. F. Fenellosa, *Certain Noble Plays of Japan* (Dublin, 1916), intro. by Yeats; R. Tagore, *Gitanjali* (London, 1919), intro. by Yeats; *The Complete Works of Oscar Wilde* (New York, 1923), vol. III intro. by Yeats; *J. B. Yeats, *Early Memories* (Dublin, 1923), preface by Yeats; *O. Gogarty, *An Offering of Swans* (Dublin, 1923), preface by Yeats; V. de Lisle Adam, *Axel*, H. P. R. Finberg, trans. (London, 1925), preface by Yeats; A. Ussher, trans., *The Midnight Court and the Adventures of a Luckless Fellow* (London, 1926), intro. by Yeats; *O. Gogarty, *Wild Apples* (Dublin, 1929), preface by Yeats; J. M. Hone, *Bishop Berkeley* (London, 1931), intro. by Yeats; Shri Purohit Swami, *An Indian Monk* (London, 1932), intro. by Yeats; Bhagwan Shri Hamsa, *The Holy Mountain*, Shri Purohit Swami, trans. (London, 1934), intro. by Yeats; D. Wellesley, *Selected Poems of Dorothy Wellesley* (London, 1936), intro. by Yeats; *The Oxford Book of Modern Verse, 1892–1935* (London, 1936), chosen and with intro. by Yeats; M. Ruddock, *The Lemon Tree* (London, 1937), intro. by Yeats; *The Ten Principal Upanishads* (London, 1937), put into English by Shri Purohit Swami and Yeats; O. Gogarty, *Others to Adorn* (London, 1938), preface by Yeats; Shri Purohit Swami, trans., *Aphorisms of Yoga* (London, 1938), with intro. by Yeats.

VII. BIOGRAPHICAL AND CRITICAL STUDIES. H. S. Krans, *William Butler Yeats and the Irish Literary Revival* (London, 1904), Contemporary Men of Letters series; F. Reid, *W. B. Yeats: A Critical Study* (London, 1915); P. Gurd, *The Early Poetry of William Butler Yeats* (Lancaster, Pa., 1916); J. M. Hone, *William Butler Yeats: The Poet in Contemporary Ireland* (London, 1916).

J. H. Pollock, *William Butler Yeats* (London, 1935); J. P. O'Donnell, *Sailing to Byzantium: A Study in the Development of the Later Style and Symbolism in the Poetry of William Butler Yeats* (Cambridge, Mass., 1939); *The Arrow*, W. B. Yeats Commemoration Number (Summer 1939); T. S. Eliot, "The Poetry of W. B. Yeats," in *Purpose, III–IV, XII* (London, 1940), the first Annual Yeats Lecture delivered in the Abbey Theatre, Dublin (30 June 1940), repr. in *On Poetry and Poets* (London, 1957).

L. S. Gwynn, ed., *Scattering Branches: Tributes to the Memory of W. B. Yeats* (Dublin, 1940); *J. Masefield, *Some Memories of W. B. Yeats* (Dublin, 1940); L. MacNeice, *The Poetry of W. B. Yeats* (London, 1941); J. M. Hone, *W. B. Yeats 1865–1939* (London, 1942; rev. ed., 1965), the standard biography; V. K. N. Menon, *The Development of William Butler Yeats* (London, 1942); P. Ure, *Towards a Mythology: Studies in the Poetry of W. B. Yeats* (Liverpool, 1946); D. A. Stauffer, *The Golden Nightingale: Essays on Some Principles of Poetry in the Lyrics of W. B. Yeats* (New York, 1949); R. Ellmann, *Yeats: The Man and the Masks* (London, 1949; paperback ed., 1961); A. N. Jeffares, *W. B. Yeats, Man and Poet* (London, 1949; rev. ed. and paperback ed., 1962).

J. Hall and M. Steinmann, eds., *The Permanence of Yeats: Selected Criticism* (New York, 1950); T. R. Henn, *The Lonely Tower: Studies in the Poetry of W. B. Yeats* (London, 1950; rev. ed., 1965); T. Parkinson, *W. B. Yeats, Self-Critic: A Study of His Early Verse* (Berkeley–Los Angeles, 1951); V. Koch, *W. B. Yeats: The Tragic Phase. A Study of the Last Poems* (London, 1951); A. Ussher, *Three Great Irishmen: Shaw, Yeats, Joyce* (London, 1952); M. E. Rudd, *Divided Image: A Study of William Blake and W. B. Yeats* (London, 1953); R. Ellmann, *The Identity of Yeats* (London, 1954; paperback ed., 1964); V. Moore, *The Unicorn: W. B. Yeats's Search for Reality* (New York, 1954); G. B. Saul, *Prolegomena to the Study of Yeats's Poems* (Philadelphia, 1957); F. Kermode, *Romantic Image* (London, 1957; paperback ed., 1961); F. A. C. Wilson, *W. B. Yeats and Tradition* (London, 1958); D. Donoghue, *The Third Voice: Modern British and American Verse Drama* (London, 1959).

Y. Winters, *The Poetry of W. B. Yeats* (Denver, Colo., 1960); G. Melchiori, *The Whole Mystery of Art: Pattern into Poetry in the Work of W. B. Yeats* (New York–London, 1960); A. C. Stock, *W. B. Yeats: His Poetry and Thought* (London, 1961; paperback ed., 1964); D. J. Gordon, *W. B. Yeats: Images of a Poet. Catalogue of the Yeats Exhibition at Whitworth Art Gallery, University of Manchester* (Manchester, 1961), with contributions from I. Fletcher, F. Kermode, and R. Skelton; D. J. Gordon, *W. B. Yeats: Images of a Poet* (Manchester, 1961); R. M. Kain, *Dublin in the Age of W. B. Yeats and James Joyce* (London, 1962); J. Stallworthy, *Between the Lines: Yeats's Poetry in the Making* (Oxford, 1963); P. Ure, *Yeats* (Edinburgh, 1963); P. Ure, *Yeats the Playwright: A Commentary on Character and Design in the Major Plays* (London, 1963), J. Unterecker, ed., *Yeats: A Collection of Critical Essays* (New York–London, 1963); H. Vendler, *Yeats's "Vision" and the Later Plays* (Cambridge, Mass.–London, 1963); S. M. Parrish, *A Concordance to the Plays* (Ithaca, N.Y.,

1963); E. Engelberg, *The Vast Design: Patterns in W. B. Yeats's Aesthetic* (Toronto, 1964); T. Parkinson, *W. B. Yeats: The Later Poetry* (Berkeley-Los Angeles, 1964); A. N. Jeffares and K. G. W. Cross, eds., *In Excited Reverie. A Centenary Tribute to William Butler Yeats, 1865-1939* (London, 1965); R. Skelton and A. Saddlerneyer, *The World of W. B. Yeats. Essays in Perspective. A Symposium and Catalogue* (London, 1965); E. Malins, ed., *The Dolmen Press Yeats Centenary Papers* (Dublin, 1965-); L. Miller, ed., *Yeats Centenary Papers* (London, 1965-); C. Bradford, *Yeats at Work* (Carbondale-Edwardsville, Ill., 1965); D. R. Clark, *Yeats and the Theatre of Desolate Anarchy* (Dublin, 1965); L. E. Nathan, *The Tragic Drama of W. B. Yeats* (London, 1965); B. Rajan, *W. B. Yeats: A Critical Introduction* (New York-London, 1965); C. Salvadori, *Yeats and Castiglione: Poet and Courtier* (Dublin, 1965); D. Donoghue and J. R. Mulryne, eds., *An Honoured Guest. New Essays on W. B. Yeats* (London, 1966); D. E. S. Maxwell and S. B. Bushrui, eds., *W. B. Yeats, 1865-1965. Centenary Essays on the Art of W. B. Yeats* (Ibadan, 1966); S. B. Bushrui, *Yeats's Verse Plays: The Revisions 1900-1910* (London, 1966); T. R. Whitaker, *Yeats's Dialogue with History: "Swan and Shadow"* (Chapel Hill, N. C., 1965); D. Hoffman, *Barbarous Knowledge: Myth in the Poetry of Yeats, Graves and Muir* (London, 1967); J. Stallworthy, ed., *Yeats's Last Poems: A Casebook* (New York-Oxford, 1968); R. Ellmann, *Eminent Domain: Yeats Among Wilde, Joyce, Pound, Eliot and Auden* (New York-London, 1967); J. Ronsley, *Yeats's Autobiography: Life as a Symbolic Pattern* (Cambridge, Mass.-London, 1968); A. N. Jeffares, *A Commentary on the Collected Poems of W. B. Yeats* (London, 1968; Stanford, 1969); R. Beum, *The Poetic Art of W. B. Yeats* (New York, 1969); A. R. Grossmann, *Poetic Knowledge in the Early Years* (Charlottesville, Va., 1969); J. Stallworthy, *Vision and Revision in Yeats's Last Poems* (London, 1969).

H. Bloom, *Yeats* (New York-London, 1970); P. L. Marcus, *Yeats and the Beginning of the Irish Renaissance* (Ithaca, N.Y.-London, 1970); J. R. Moore, *Masks of Love and Death: Yeats as Dramatist* (London, 1971); D. R. Albright, *The Myth Against Myth* (London, 1972); E. Domville, ed., *A Concordance to the Plays of W. B. Yeats* (Ithaca, N. Y., 1972); M. Brown, *The Politics of Irish Literature from Thomas Davis to W. B. Yeats* (London, 1973); G. Harper, *Yeats's Golden Dawn* (London, 1974); D. A. Harris, *Yeats: Coole Park and Ballylee* (Baltimore-London, 1974); R. Skene, *The Cuchulain Plays of W. B. Yeats* (London, 1974); P. Ure, *Yeats and Anglo-Irish Literature*, C. J. Rawson, ed. (Liverpool, 1974); G. Harper, ed., *Yeats and the Occult* (London, 1975); A. N. Jeffares and A. S. Knowland, *A Commentary on the Collected Plays of W. B. Yeats* (London, 1975); J. Johnson, *Florence Farr: Bernard Shaw's "New Woman"* (Gerrards Cross, 1975); W. M. Murphy, *Yeats's Early Poetry: The Quest for Reconciliation* (London, 1975); R. O'Driscoll and L. Reynolds, *Yeats and the Theatre* (Niagara Falls, N. Y., 1975); D. Young and C. Hulme, *Out of Ireland: A Reading of Yeats's Poetry* (London, 1975); D. Eddins, *Yeats: The Nineteenth Century Matrix* (University, Ala., 1976); J. W. Flannery, *W. B. Yeats and the Idea of a Theatre: The Early Abbey Theatre in Theory* (London, 1976); R. Taylor, *The Drama of W. B. Yeats: Irish Myth and the Japanese Nōh* (New Haven, Conn.-London, 1976); F. Tuohy, *Yeats* (London, 1976); A. N. Jeffares, *W. B. Yeats: The Critical Heritage* (London, 1977); L. Miller, *The Noble Drama of W. B. Yeats* (London, 1977); J. W. Flannery, *Yeats and Magic: The Earlier Works* (London, 1978); W. M. Murphy, *The Life of J. B. Yeats: Prodigal Father* (Ithaca, N.Y., 1978); A. Parkin, *The Dramatic Imagination of W. B. Yeats* (London, 1978); M. L. Rosenthal, *Yeats, Pound and Eliot: Sailing into the Unknown* (London, 1978); B. L. Reid, *W. B. Yeats: The Lyric of Tragedy* (London, 1978); A. Lynch, *Yeats: The Poetics of the Self* (Chicago, 1978).

M. H. Thuente, *Yeats and Irish Folklore* (Iowa City, 1980); E. Cullingford, *Yeats, Ireland and Fascism* (London, 1981); W. H. Pritchard, ed., *W. B. Yeats: A Critical Anthology* (Harmondsworth, 1982).

H. G. WELLS

(1866-1946)

Kenneth Young

INTRODUCTION

Who now reads H. G. Wells, critics sometimes inquire, expecting the answer: Very few. They are wrong. The scientific romances, so-called even though some of these fantasies dating from the 1890's have no element of even pseudoscience, attract yearly a new crop of young devotees in a period when science fiction has attained extraordinary popularity.

Less fashionable are the best of Wells's realistic novels, mostly written between 1900 and 1916; even so, examination of copies of *Kipps* (1905) or *Mr. Polly* (1910) in any public library shows that they are constantly taken out. Many are in paperback; they are stocked in half a dozen hardback series.

Undeniably, however, none of his politico-economico-sociological tracts, his utopias, his calls for world government are much read. As for his massive tomes *The Science of Life* (1929–1930) and *The Work, Wealth and Happiness of Mankind* (1931), which sold in millions, one might agree for once with the critics—who now reads them? Yet two or three generations ago, Wells was the great liberator, educator, visionary.

I do not suppose, either, that his 238,000-word *Experiment in Autobiography* (1934) is much in demand, which is a pity. Although, in the strictly autobiographical sense, it scarcely carries us beyond 1900, its first half is a revealing account of his early years, self-perceptive, brilliantly descriptive, frank "about my difficulties and blunders, about preposterous hopes and unexpected lessons, about my luck and the fun of the road." It is his life in those early years, repeatedly woven and rewoven, expanded here, muted there, which forms the substance, often little disguised, of his best novels, *Kipps, Tono-Bungay* (1909), *Mr. Polly*—and of some of his weakest. As time went on, his once acute interest in people other than himself and his power (or patience) to portray them declined sadly. He wrote far too much and too quickly for continuous excellence—no less than 114 volumes as well as endless journalism.

LIFE

Herbert George Wells was born a third son on Saturday, 21 September 1866, at 4:30 in the afternoon, in Atlas House, 47 High Street, Bromley ("a suburb of the damnedest") in north Kent, now part of Greater London. His parents, Sarah, then forty-three, whose ancestors came from Northern Ireland, and Joseph, thirty-eight, were poor shopkeepers. She had been brought up as a strict Protestant (which may account for Wells's apocalyptic turn of mind), had been a lady's maid, and to this sort of employment she returned, as housekeeper to the Fetherstonhaugh family at Up Park, Sussex, when her somewhat feckless husband, originally a gardener and later a professional club cricketer, drifted off.

Wells's mother, not ill-educated for her class and time, taught him the alphabet and brought him books from the public library. He was sent to a small village school, then to the Bromley Academy, one of those "frail vessels that often made more sound than sense," as the MacKenzies, his biographers, felicitously remark, or, as Wells put it, "a beastly little private school." Some parts of his holidays were spent at a riverside inn near Windsor kept by his mother's second cousin, where he learned to punt and row—"summer paradise," Wells called it. Around this time he read—significantly for his early fiction—Nathaniel Hawthorne's *The House of the Seven Gables*, Eugène Sue's *The Mysteries of Paris*, William Beckford's *Vathek*, Samuel Johnson's *Rasselas*, and Jonathan Swift's *Gulliver's Travels*.

At fourteen he left school and was apprenticed to a draper at Windsor, where he lived above the shop and had sixpence a week pocket money. He was soon discharged. The next few years he was tossed from pillar to post—a pupil teacher; back with his mother at Up Park, where he saw, albeit from below-stairs, the spacious life of the gentry, which he admired: "behind their screen of deer park and park wall and sheltered service, men could talk, think and write at their leisure." Briefly he was a chemist's assistant, studying dispensers' Latin: for six weeks a full-time pupil at Midhurst School in 1881. Once more he was apprenticed to a draper, at Southsea, "the most unhappy hopeless period of my life," working thirteen hours a day and despising the irksome, toilsome routines. He read "popular educators" from the YMCA library, and, like Mr. Polly, contemplated suicide.

When he was seventeen he abandoned his apprenticeship and became a pupil teacher at Midhurst. Here at last, in the evenings, he could read to his heart's content—Plato, Henry George's *Progress and Poverty* (1880), geology, physiology, chemistry, math. In 1884, when he was eighteen, he won a scholarship to the Normal School of Science in South Kensington, part of London University, with a maintenance grant of £1 a week. There he listened to lectures by the aging T. H. Huxley, heretical Grand Old Man of Science, at once optimistic about science and pessimistic about man, the Huxley who said in his Romanes lecture of 1900 that "the ethical progress of society depends not on imitating the cosmic process, still less in running away from it, but in combating it." Of him, Wells wrote that "he was the greatest man" he ever met. Huxley was a deep influence on his whole work.

Other lecturers were less inspiring, and Wells slacked, leaving the university with poor qualifications. But he joined the debating society (concluding one debate by saying that there was every reason to suppose that Mars had "living beings"), wrote sketches for his later science fiction, and fell in love with a cousin, Isabel, whom he married in 1891. He was small and thin, and his voice was reedy, but his ideas and enthusiasms and sheer fun attracted people throughout his life.

He became ill with tuberculosis. He worked for a London tutorial college, wrote two scientific textbooks, and began to contribute to the periodicals and newspapers then being produced in some profusion to attract the pence of the large public newly literate as a result of the Forster and subsequent educational reforms (1870).

Within months of his marriage that sexual voracity evident all the rest of his long life began to inflame and torment him. He left Isabel in 1894 and eloped with Amy Catherine Robbins (Jane), whom he later married and who, through all his many sexual adventures, remained his wife until her death in 1928.

He published his first fiction in book form in 1895. As was the custom then, these novels were serialized in advance in magazines. *The Time Machine* appeared in 1895, as did *The Wonderful Visit* and a short-story collection, *The Stolen Bacillus*, earning in all £792 that year. *The Time Machine* caused him to be hailed as "a man of genius," and in 1895 the *Bookman* published his portrait with a note about him.

These early fantasies appealed, as T. S. Eliot commented, to readers in both the first-class and third-class compartments of trains. Inside five years, with half a dozen other fantasy stories—including *The Invisible Man* (1897) and *The War of the Worlds* (1898)—behind him, he was building an expensive house, designed by the fashionable Charles F. A. Voysey, at Sandgate near Folkestone, Kent. He had "got on." At Sandgate he wrote: "I want to write novels and before God I *will* write novels." He did: the best of his work dates from these years.

His social life expanded enormously in the years from 1896. Among his acquaintances were the novelists George Gissing, Dorothy Richardson (with whom he had a brief affair), Arnold Bennett, John Galsworthy, Joseph Conrad, Ford Madox Ford, Henry James, Stephen Crane, Frank Swinnerton; though "you," he wrote to Bennett, "are the best friend I ever had." He knew the Fabian Socialists, G. B. Shaw, Sidney and Beatrice Webb, Graham Wallas; and that society mainly of aristocrats, dubbed "The Souls," among them Arthur Balfour, prime minister from 1902 to 1905, for whom he conceived an ambiguous admiration, picturing him under the smallest of disguises in his novel *The New Machiavelli* (1911) and again in *Men Like Gods* (1923). Wells was a member of the Co-efficients, a dining club to which, as well as the Socialist Webbs, belonged such diverse people as Richard Haldane (from 1906, Liberal war minister), the noted Tories Leo Amery and Lord Milner, and the maverick philosopher Bertrand Russell.

Wells had become a social lion. With the Fabians, however, he did not last long; he sought to dominate them and was opposed, especially by Shaw; and he left. With a young member of the Fabians he had a love affair and an illegitimate child, as he did later with Rebecca West. Yet his family life was usually happy. He had two small sons and enticed his many guests into charades, shadow plays, and war games, of which he gave an account in *Floor Games* (1911) and *Little Wars* (1913). But it was as much for himself as for his children that he indulged his delight in such imaginative play.

He began, too, the long series of books, fiction and nonfiction, setting the world to rights—*Anticipations of the Reaction of Mechanical and Scientific Progress upon Human Life and Thought* (1901), *Mankind in the Making* (1903), *A Modern Utopia* (1905), and so on for forty years. These were stimulating to his contemporaries; today they are valuable mainly to those who would understand the period.

Scandal about his love affairs came to a head with the publication of *Ann Veronica: A Modern Love Story* (1909), which had a heroine who seduced the hero and which implied that polygamy was justifiable. Wells had already in *Anticipations* condemned monogamy and *In the Days of the Comet* (1906) optimistically forecast the end of sexual jealousy—at least so far as wives were concerned. *Ann Veronica* and its author were denounced. "A community of scuffling stoats and ferrets," "literary filth," "this poisonous book," screamed the reviewers. The libraries banned it. Publishers—and he had always hopped from one to another—looked at him askance.

Restless as ever, he took a house at Great Easton, Essex, on the estate of Daisy, countess of Warwick, erstwhile mistress of Edward VII. When war came in 1914, he, unlike his Socialist acquaintances, welcomed it, especially in an article whose title became a national, self-comforting slogan, "The War That Will End War"—though he did not persist in that opinion.

Many of his fantasies contained accurate prophecies—of fighting in the air before the first aircraft was off the ground; of space exploration sixty years before men first visited the moon. The novel *In the Days of the Comet* describes among other things a situation very like that of Europe in August 1914. Perhaps most remarkable of all was that in 1914 in *The World Set Free* he prophesied a war with atomic bombs for 1958—a war between the "Free Nations" and the "Central Powers" that would end with the destruction of most cities, after which the survivors would meet in the Swiss Alps to plan a world state. Though the disintegration of the atom had long been a subject of speculation, it was not until 1934 that the Joliot-Curies produced radioactive phosphorus from aluminum. The book was more than prophetic. "Leo Szilard—one of the scientists whose work lay behind the Hiroshima bomb—said that when the idea of chain reaction first occurred to him in 1934 he was influenced by *The World Set Free* which he had read the year before." Thus wrote Wells's biographers Norman and Jean MacKenzie.

When war broke out, Wells was forty-eight, too old to fight. In *Boon* (1915), he savagely satirized, among others, the old and ill Henry James. He spent a few months in the Enemy Propaganda department run by Northcliffe under Beaverbrook as minister for information. His lasting achievement—and his last thoroughly worthwhile novel—was *Mr. Britling Sees It Through* (1916), although to the end his novels, however given over to his hobbyhorses, seldom failed to have flashes of his genuine gift of literary creativity. In *Mr. Britling* and *God the Invisible King* (1917) he had a brief flirtation with religion; both before and after he was agnostic, if not atheist.

After the war, the League of Nations, world government, and his huge historical compilations preoccupied him. By now he was an international figure, interviewing Lenin (whose ideas he propagated for a time), Maxim Gorki, and, later on, Stalin and Franklin Roosevelt. His accounts of these meetings were lapped up and grotesquely overpaid by the world press. Vanity and strain overcame him. His love affairs grew ever more diverse and less satisfying; yet as Beatrice Webb observed, "he is the same brilliant talker and pleasant companion—except that he orates more than he used to and listens less intelligently. . . . He has become a sort of 'little God' . . . he feels himself to be a chartered libertine." Rebecca West described him in 1922 as "practically off his head; enormously vain, irascible and in a fantasy world." At least Wells recognized his symptoms; and he describes his near-psychosis in *Christina Alberta's Father* (1925) and elsewhere.

When Wells learned in 1927 that his wife, Jane, was dying of cancer he wrote to her: "My dear, I love you much more than I have loved anyone else in the world." If love means anything more than sexual intercourse, it was the lie of a sentimental philanderer, even though he supported her and their two sons generously with money. He was always generous with money, giving away large sums from his earnings.

In the 1930's and early 1940's, though he continued to write voluminously, he felt a decline in his physical powers. He resented criticism that he was "a thinker who cannot think"; he resented the coolness of reviewers of his novels. His journalism was still remunerative; but "compulsive repetition revealed his mental sterility," as the MacKenzies comment.

The film of his novel *The Shape of Things to Come* (1933), produced in 1936, was a financial success and an artistic failure. "A mess of a film," Wells observed. All that is remembered of it now is the music by Sir Arthur Bliss, whom Wells himself proposed to the producers, the Korda brothers. It was, once more, prophetic, with its scenes of an air attack on London in 1940; ironically, it was, as the MacKenzies note, "one of the factors which created public support for the policy of appeasement."

The times had passed Wells by; there were newer idols—D. H. Lawrence, Virginia Woolf, Aldous Huxley, Evelyn Waugh. To the intellectuals Wells had become tedious; to those of them who were Communists, a petit-bourgeois humbug. In the aptly named *The Anatomy of Frustration* (1936) he revealed his dismay at death, mankind's "primary frustration." Sex was but a temporary alleviation. He was in some ways an early existentialist. *The Wonderful Visit* (1895) attacks the absurdities inherent in the human condition, as Bernard Bergonzi points out. Existentialist, too, was his perception, in *Babes in the Darkling Wood* (1940), that there was not one John Smith but many John Smiths within the single organism. The individual's belief that he is an independent personality is an illusion—the only reality lies in the collective existence of the species. More and more he despaired of the future of that species, writing in *The Fate of Homo Sapiens* (1939) that he had always been pessimistic but had tried "to live as though it were not so." The mood continued almost to the end of his life; *Mind at the End of Its Tether* (1945) prophesied that "the end of everything we call life is at hand and cannot be evaded." The dropping of the atom bomb in August 1945 seemed to affirm it.

When the Second World War began, Wells told Sir Ernest Barker that he had already composed his epitaph; it was: "God damn you all: I told you so." But quite another epitaph must be composed for the author of, among others, *The Time Machine, Tono-Bungay,* and *Mr. Britling Sees It Through.*

Wells, within a month of eighty, died at his London home in 1946.[1]

[1]For biographical information required in the writing of this essay, I am chiefly indebted to Wells's *Experiment in Autobiography* (London, 1934) and N. MacKenzie and J. MacKenzie's *The Time Traveller* (London, 1973).

FANTASY FICTION

WELLS began to write fantasy fiction because he wanted to make money and to "get on"; and, to use one of his favorite words, "woosh," he did. But why this particular genre? It was partly because in those final years of the nineteenth century there was an unusually large appetite among readers for the spine-chiller, the bizarre, the weird, and the apocalyptic. Even the great Henry James wrote "The Turn of the Screw" (1898) and William Morris, *News from Nowhere* (1890); others who helped satisfy the appetite were such half-forgotten storytellers as William Le Queux, M. P. Shiel, Edward Bellamy, Arthur Machen, and Algernon Blackwood.

The reasons why readers were avid for this kind of fiction at that time are exhaustively detailed by Bergonzi, but one he omits is that the public that had heard with astonishment of the invention of Edison's "talking machine," the first practical electric light bulb, Daimler's and Benz's internal combustion engined motorcars, Marconi's wireless transmissions, was ready to believe anything possible. They had been stampeded into credulity; to them, that a man could, for example, make himself invisible seemed no more nor less impossible than wireless communication.

Wells knew some of the early tales of the miraculous—they had been popular from classical times; he had read Mary Shelley's *Frankenstein* and *The Last Man,* and Edgar Allan Poe and Eugène Sue. From all these and others he garnered ideas like a magpie, as Ingwald Raknem has shown in *H. G. Wells and His Critics* (1962).

There was another reason why Wells wrote in this genre: he had an innate gift for it. In his preface to *The Country of the Blind, and Other Stories* (1911), he tells us how these stories originated:

I found that, taking almost anything as a starting point and letting my thoughts play about it, there would presently come out of the darkness, in a manner quite inexplicable, some absurd or vivid little nucleus. Little men in canoes upon sunlit oceans would come floating out of nothingness, incubating the eggs of prehistoric monsters unawares; violent conflicts would break out amidst the flower beds of suburban gardens. I would discover I was peering into remote and mysterious worlds ruled by an order, logical indeed, but other than our common sanity.

(p. iv)

This is like Samuel Taylor Coleridge dreaming "Kubla Khan"; or the scientist Friedrich Kekule waking from a nap in front of the fire with a clear picture of the solution to the problem that had so long teased him, how atoms are linked. In short, inspiration.

How different this was from the method of the writer to whom he was sometimes compared—Jules Verne—both men saw clearly. "There is no literary resemblance whatever," wrote Wells, "between the anticipatory inventions of the great Frenchman and these fantasies. He always dealt with the actual possibilities of invention and discovery." Verne agreed, saying of Wells: "His stories do not repose on very scientific bases. I make use of physics. He invents!" Nevertheless Wells was well aware of the latest thought in science. Also some of his fantasies *are* concerned with science in a broader sense; they express a deep pessimism about science's means and ends.

Wells's own conscious aim, however, was to write a mind-boggling, rattling good yarn. Even so, perhaps partly unknown to himself, these tales may be interpreted psychologically, symbolically, moralistically, even poetically: it was the great poet T. S. Eliot who observed that Wells's imagination was of a very high order and found the description of sunrise on the moon in *The First Men in the Moon* (1901) "quite unforgettable." It is doubtless the multiplicity of meanings to be found in the best of these tales that ensures their continuing readability.

Consider *The Time Machine*, the first and among the best of these fantasies. The book opens with a cozy dinner party in Richmond of men friends where, in the postprandial atmosphere when "thought runs gracefully free of the trammels of precision," the host explains, in a manner even now convincing to the nonmathematician, the principles of fourth-dimensional geometry. Amid their skepticism he shows them a machine which, he says, enables him to travel in time. And travel in time he does, forward to the year 802,701 A.D. and to a location resembling the Thames Valley.

There he finds decaying palaces and a little pixie-like people called the Eloi, living on fruit (cattle have disappeared), doing no work, somewhat epicene, easily fatigued, a sort of flower people, "beautifully futile," happy as the day is long—but at night fearful, huddling together. What they fear is the subterranean-dwelling, apelike race called the Morlocks, whom Wells describes in words that his novelist friend Gissing might almost have used for London slum dwellers—"those pale, chinless faces and great, lidless, pinkish-grey eyes." To his horror, the Time Traveller discovers that the Morlocks are still meat-eaters—human meat—emerging from deep shafts on moonless nights to seize their provender, the Eloi. Yet out of "an old habit of service" they still provide the Eloi with their garments "and maintained them in their habitual needs."

Wells himself—or the Time Traveller—points out the obvious symbolism: the workers, driven underground and become bestial, are taking their revenge on their former masters, who themselves over millennia had become degenerate, incapable of defending themselves, living only for the day and fearful of the night. Indeed he writes of the haves and the have-nots, observing that instead of the "great triumph of Humanity I had dreamed of," the "splitting of our species along lines of social stratification" had become complete and the "exchange between class and class" that had kept society on a more or less even keel had long ago ended. To this had post-Darwinian optimism about evolution come.

The novel is no mere Marxist parable in reverse. The Time Traveller *regrets* that he has no occasion to use his crowbar on the Morlocks. It cannot be justly said that this is Wells hating the class from which he sprang, though all these elements play a part. It is much more a cry of despair:

. . . how brief the dream of the human intellect had been. It had committed suicide. . . . Once, life and property must have reached almost absolute safety. The rich man had been assured of his wealth and comfort, the toiler assured of his life and work. No doubt in that perfect world there had been no unemployed problem, no social question left unsolved. . . . There is no intelligence where there is no change and no need of change.

(ch. 10)

The Time Traveller, after an exciting search in the best Rider Haggard style for his stolen machine, moves yet further into the future, where man has totally disappeared and the earth is left to huge white butterflies and malign crabs as big as tables: "Abominable desolation . . . the stony beach crawling with these foul, slow-stirring monsters, the uniform poisonous-looking green of the lichenous plants, the thin air that hurts one's lungs." And so, thirty million years on, to a great darkness, cold, snow, silence, the only moving object "a round thing, the size of a football perhaps, or, it may be, bigger, and tentacles trailed down from it; it seemed black against the weltering blood-red water, and it was hopping fitfully about."

When the Time Traveller has returned and told his

story to his skeptical friends, he vanishes again, this time for good, perhaps into the past of "the blood-drinking, hairy savages"; and the author himself comments in an epilogue that the Time Traveller "thought but cheerlessly of the Advancement of Mankind, and saw in the growing pile of civilization only a foolish heaping that must inevitably fall back upon and destroy its makers in the end. If that is so, it remains for us to live as though it were not so." This was Wells's own stoicism.

Yet, he adds, referring to the "two strange white flowers" the female Eloi, Weena, had put into the Time Traveller's pocket, "even when mind and strength had gone, gratitude and a mutual tenderness still lived on in the heart of man." Inconsequential? But much of *The Time Machine* is as inconsequential as a dream and that is in part due to hasty, awkward writing. Yet, eighty years on, it grips the reader no less than the centuries-older *Revelation* of St. John the Divine, with which in some aspects it may be compared.

The Wonderful Visit, published in the same year, 1895, is *The Time Machine* run backward, as it were, though it has no element of even pseudoscience in it. The vicar of a Sussex village, "Siddermorton," shoots down what he takes to be a giant bird but which turns out to be an angel or, in Wells's intention, the "natural man," the Great Simpleton. The novel is really an ironical study of life in the English countryside. "I tried to suggest to people the bitterness, the narrow horizon, of their ordinary lives by bringing into sharp contrast with typical characters a being who is free from ordinary human limitations." Thus we see Lady Hammerglow patronizing the angel, the squire warning him off for trespassing, the villagers militant against a stranger they cannot identify, and the village doctor interested only in the angel's "deformed" shoulder blades and proposing manipulative surgery to make him more human. Only Delia, the vicar's simple maid, loves the angel and with him she ascends to heaven. The satire—on ownership, on the ugliness of people's lives—is gentle, though there is a dark passage on the "readiness of you Human Beings to inflict pain" to which the vicar replies: "The whole living world is a battlefield. We are driven by Pain." From the point of view of Wells's literary development, the novel is a first sketch for some of the purely human characters he was to draw with much greater effect in *Kipps* and *Mr. Polly.*

The Island of Doctor Moreau (1896) is the most horrifying of Wells's fantasies and one of the best written and most tautly constructed. It marks the introduction into his fiction of the mad or immoral scientist. The doctor of the title is seeking to make animals half human by means of vivisectional surgery, the transplantation of organs and grafts; the pain involved is vividly described. He explains his methods by snatches of physiology that sound no less convincing than the Time Traveller's new geometry. Moreau has succeeded in making some of his ghastly man-animals talk and even read; but they tend to revert to the beast, so Moreau continues his quest to "burn out all the animal . . . to make a rational creature of my own."

As well as talking, the travesty men, the "Beast People," build huts for themselves and have certain fixed ideas implanted by Moreau known as the Law, which they chant as litany: "Who breaks the law goes back to the House of Pain":

> *His* is the House of Pain.
> *His* is the hand that makes.
> *His* is the hand that wounds.
> *His* is the hand that heals.
> *His* is . . . the lightning-flash. . . .
> *His* is the deep salt sea. . . .
> *His* are the stars in the sky.
> (ch. 12)

It was this litany with its blasphemous echoes, as much as the repulsive horrors, that caused many reviewers to castigate the novel: "to parody the work of the Creator of the human race and cast contempt upon the dealings of God with his creatures," wrote one critic. Wells, however, is more concerned with Huxley's point that suffering is "the badge of all the tribe of sentient things, attaining its highest level in man." Through this purgatory man must pass on his evolutionary way; nature itself is both cruel and blind, and the scientist himself is affected. In Moreau's words: "The study of Nature makes a man at last as remorseless as Nature."

Much of Moreau's work must inevitably remind present-day readers of the Nazi doctors' vile experiments, the even viler surgical alteration of personality in the Russian psychiatric wards, and perhaps of the more dubious of contemporary organ transplants.

After the exciting climax of the book when Moreau is killed, the grafts are gradually rejected, the Beast People's speech and carriage revert, they hold things more clumsily, "drinking by suction, feeding by gnawing," and, the females leading, begin to disregard decency, even attempting public outrages on the institution of monogamy. Finally, as Wells states in the introduction, when some years later H.M.S. *Scorpion* visits the island, there is nothing alive there except some "curious white moths, some hogs and rabbits and some rather peculiar rats."

But *The Island of Doctor Moreau* is not merely a savage attack on science and unethical experiments: "His curiosity, his mad aimless investigations . . . and the things were thrown out to live a year or so, to struggle, to blunder, and suffer; at last to die painfully." It is a broader attack—as in the fourth book of Jonathan Swift's *Gulliver's Travels*—on the nature of humanity itself.

While the narrator is still on the island he has observed "the Fox-Bear Woman's vulpine, shifty face, strangely human in its speculative cunning, and even imagined I had met it before in some city byway." And back in England:

I could not persuade myself that the men and women I met were not also another, still passably human, Beast People. . . . Prowling women would mew after me, furtive craving men glance jealously at me, weary pale workers go coughing by me, with tired eyes and eager paces like wounded deer dripping blood, old people, bent and dull, pass murmuring to themselves and all unheeding a ragged tail of gibing children. . . . [In] some library the intent faces over the books seemed but patient creatures waiting for prey.

(ch. 22)

In the end—somewhat contradictorily and after help from a mental specialist—the narrator finds solace in

wise books, bright windows, in this life of ours lit by the shining souls of men. . . . A sense of infinite peace and protection in the glittering hosts of heaven . . . in the vast and eternal laws of matter . . . [there] whatever is more than animal within us must find its solace and its hope.

(ch. 22)

The "shining souls" were conspicuous by their absence in the novel itself where there were only varying degrees of blackness.

Wells was extraordinarily versatile. In the same year as the black fantasy *The Island of Doctor Moreau*, he published the light, cheerful, literally meandering novel *The Wheels of Chance: A Holiday Adventure* (1896). This concerns a gauche young Cockney draper's assistant—a type we shall see

more of in Wells's fiction of the next decade—who sets out for a cycling[2] holiday in Surrey and Sussex and comes to the rescue of a maiden in distress—he who has always "regarded the feminine sex as something to bow to or smirk at from a safe distance."

That is no more than the gist of what plot there is. The charm lies elsewhere, especially in the character of the young draper himself, whose very name, Arthur Hoopdriver, in his dark moments seems to him as absurd as its owner. Still, he sets off blithely with four gold sovereigns in his pocket for ten whole days of freedom from the drudgery and servility of "step this way please" or "no trouble, madam, I assure you." And "his heart sang within him," within this small man "of a pallid complexion, hair of a kind of dirty fairness, greyish eyes and a skimpy, immature moustache under his peaked, indeterminate nose."

His gawkiness, of which he is all too conscious, shows as soon as he mounts his bicycle, for he—like his creator—was just learning to ride; and comical, embarrassing, small misadventures pursue him throughout the book. He "wabbles" (Wells's expressive word for a neophyte cyclist's erratic path) through a countryside most lovingly depicted: "grasses flowering, white campions and ragged robins . . . little cottages, and picturesque beerhouses with the vivid brewers' boards of blue and scarlet . . . a pebbly rivulet that emerged between clumps of sedge, loosestrife and forget-me-nots under an arch of trees": this was the premotor, prebungalow southern countryside that Wells loved.

In his new, brown cycling outfit Hoopdriver sometimes feels himself to be "a bloomin' Dook." He has always been addicted to daydreaming, and, the narrator observes somewhat sententiously: "Self-deception is the anaesthetic of life while God is carving out our beings." More down-to-earth, he adds: "His real life was absolutely uninteresting and if he had faced it as realistically as such people do in Mr. Gissing's novels, he would probably have come by way of drink to suicide in the course of a year." As indeed Mr. Polly and Wells himself almost did, though not via alcohol.

On his joyous "wabbling" jaunt, Hoopdriver keeps coming across two other cyclists, a young girl

[2]The bicycle, then being manufactured at prices only the poorest could not afford, gave the lower classes the freedom of travel; it also freed the middle-class young of chaperonage, for men and women set forth together. So the bicycle symbolized the "new freedom."

and a man in his thirties, who seem to be at loggerheads. In fact the man, Bechamel, is her would-be seducer, a typically mid-Victorian villain down even to the moustache he twirls—and married withal. The girl, Jessie, described variously as sixteen or seventeen, is a would-be emancipated maiden who has left home partly because she can no longer put up with her widowed stepmother, a literary lady of Surbiton, but also because, in the feminist spirit of the 1890's, "I want to lead a Free Life and Own myself . . . I want to do something in the world, something vaguely noble, self-sacrificing, and dignified"—perhaps, ironical as it may seem to journalists, become a journalist. As elsewhere in Wells, Jessie has curiously existential sensations: "I find myself in life and it terrifies me. I seem to be a little speck whirling on a wheel, suddenly caught up. 'What am I here for' I ask. . . . The wheels of the world go on turning, turning. It is horrible." (There is a curious parallel here with some remarks by Ursula in D. H. Lawrence's *The Rainbow*.)

Don Juan Hoopdriver, in tremulous adoration and presenting himself as a well-to-do colonial, snatches her from her would-be seducer with the usual absurdities that cling to his every action, and they cycle off together. Hoopdriver has a fight in a pub, which bucks him up enormously because his opponent (who has made a "remark" about the couple) runs away. Soon the two cyclists are being pursued inefficiently and yet more ridiculously by her stepmother, always on the edge of the vapors, and her small coterie of literary gentlemen, more concerned with winning her exclusive favors than with finding her errant stepdaughter.

The innocent pair of cyclists after a comic chase are eventually confronted. Hoopdriver is accused of abducting a girl under age but—here Wells derides suburban manners—above all everything must be kept quiet. If Jessie's escapade were to become known, ". . . you would be *ruined*," says her stepmother: "No one in Surbiton would ask you anywhere! . . . You would be an outcast."

"But I've done nothing wrong," said Jessie, "It's just a Convention—"

"But everyone will *think* you have."

"Am I to tell lies because other people *think*? stupids. And besides—who wants to know people like that?"

(ch. 39)

While this goes on, "Hoopdriver made a sad figure in the sunlight outside." Once more Jessie has become "an inaccessible Young Lady."

So they part. He dare not declare his love except to kiss her fingers. She will send him books; he will work. "What can a man make of himself in six years time?" she says. Naturally, as he leaves her, he puts his foot in a rabbit hole and almost falls. He knows it is over and done with: "Suppose a chap *was* to drive himself jest as hard as he could—what then?" As for books—"What's books?" And he returns to his apprentice quarters over the draper's shop, "the gate closes upon him with a slam, and he vanishes from our ken."

The Wheels of Chance is light, good-natured fun-poking at some diverse sections of English society—not excluding its hero—in the 1890's, a trial run for the greater *Kipps* and *Mr. Polly*. One criticism, and it applies to some later novels as well: the narrator is the old-style "buttonholer," permitting himself too many flourishes and a jocosity that can grate.

The next year, 1897, Wells returned to the fantastic genre with *The Invisible Man*. It is a less satisfactory story than *The Time Machine* partly because, for present-day readers, it has been overexposed in films and television serials often only crudely based on it; partly, however, because it lacks the poetry, the multiplication of meanings, of its predecessor. Though it was no less appreciated by its early readers, there is now an air of staleness about it; even the pseudoscientific explanation of how Griffin made himself invisible seems unconvincingly nebulous.

The first part is, like *The Wonderful Visit*, more a village comedy than anything else. Wells lovingly establishes his locals and acutely imitates their vernacular—so acutely that their talk may well baffle even an Englishman from another part of the country than Kent and Sussex. Outstanding among these characters is the tramp, Mr. Thomas Marvell.

To the villagers, Griffin—bandaged all over his head, wearing dark blue glasses and what turns out to be a false nose—is at the start merely a baffling curiosity who has, like the central figure of *In the Days of the Comet*, inexplicable outbursts of petulant rage. He is even rather comic; the tramp inquires whether he had been eating bread and cheese; he can see it in the invisible man's stomach because food does not become invisible until it is assimilated.

Gradually Griffin's frustrations, particularly his need for money, lead him to crime and violence, though much of the violence is part of the senseless rage that devours him. On the run, he enters the house of a Dr. Kemp, quietly working for his FRS

(Fellow of the Royal Society)—one of the several "normal" scientists Wells portrays. Griffin recognizes Kemp as having been at "University College" in his time and decides to trust him with his story. It is here that we learn of his ignominious, even ludicrous, adventures when he first became invisible in London; London's weather is hard on a nude invisible man, he cannot easily buy clothing and has to turn criminal to steal some. Snow will stick to his invisible body and give him away. But worse still, he is a disenchanted Faustus:

"I went over the heads of the things a man reckons desirable. No doubt invisibility made it possible to get them, but it made it impossible to enjoy them when they are got. Ambition—what is the good of pride of place when you cannot appear there? What is the good of the love of woman when her name must needs be Delilah? . . . I had become a wrapped-up mystery, a swathed and bandaged caricature of a man!"

(ch. 23)

He has sought a formula to reverse his invisibility at will but has not found it.

Now Kemp, archetype of the man of honor, breaks his word that he will not give him away; he betrays him in a note surreptitiously sent to the local chief constable, Colonel Adye; but this is what an honorable man would do since Griffin is a dangerous criminal. As Kemp waits in secret agitation for the police, Griffin confirms that he is a homicidal megalomaniac. An invisible man, he can "strike as I like, dodge as I like, escape as I like!" But why kill? "Because that invisible man, Kemp, must now establish a Reign of Terror. He must take a town, like your Burdock, and terrify and dominate it. He must issue his orders. . . . And all who disobey his orders he must kill and kill all who would defend them."

The police arrive. With a shout of "traitor," Griffin disrobes, so becoming invisible, and then begin a siege and a chase such as John Buchan might have written. The area is roused; and in the end the coup de grace for the invisible man comes from the village folk by means of the spade of a stalwart navvy.

Griffin is a less effective portrait of the amoral scientist than is Dr. Moreau. As a character he exists uneasily between farce and melodrama. He is never quite credible.[3] His return, when dying, to visibility

is imaginatively done. But to compare this tale, as does one critic, to the tragic farce of Christopher Marlowe's *The Jew of Malta* is an exaggeration.

There is at least one link between *The Invisible Man* and the otherwise very different *The War of the Worlds,* which appeared in the next year, 1898. In the former, Griffin terrorizes a county; in the latter, the Martians, arriving from their planet in ten cylinders at twenty-four-hour intervals, not only terrorize but devastate the whole country and particularly its heart, London.

The scientific background is plausible. That Mars was populated was then a scientific hypothesis. Astronomers supported the theory that the planet was drawing farther away from the sun and was therefore getting colder. Wells merely added the corollary that the Martians would naturally cast around for some warmer climate and turn envious eyes on Earth. Scientists also thought that Mars was an older spin-off from the sun than was Earth. It was therefore reasonable to deduce that its inhabitants were more developed, cleverer than men. So Wells's Martians are mainly brain floating in a brown liquid with nerves to a pair of protuberant eyes, an auditory organ, and sixteen long, sensitive tentacles arranged about the mouth. Instead of eating they suck fresh living blood from other creatures; thus, they need no apparatus of digestion, and so, unlike Mr. Polly, can suffer no dyspepsia.

Even "intellectual readers" and scientists, wrote Wells's friend Sir Richard Gregory, FRS, found the book "stimulating to thought" and were never repelled by any obvious disregard of scientific principle.

The Martian invaders fight ensconced in vast spiderlike engines a hundred feet high, mounted on a tripod and moving as fast as an express train. Their weapons include a poisonous black smoke with which they smother cities; their heat rays pulverize artillery and battleships. The ray, wrote a contemporary reviewer, was "a sort of searchlight which burned." Today we have something very like it in a laser beam.

Through such devices, the Martians quickly establish that reign of terror of which the invisible man only dreamed. Naturally it is the Martians who are the focal interest in the novel. Of human characterization there is little; the narrator and his brother are clever nonentities; and the vacuous curate is no more than a conventional anticlerical butt.

Humankind exists in the novel mainly as a mob, at first disbelieving, then panicked:

[3]Wells, despite revisions of this novel, twice uses "creditable" when he clearly means "credible." Bennett was constantly chiding him about such solecisms.

So you understand the roaring wave of fear that swept through the world just as Monday was dawning—the stream of flight rising swiftly to a torrent, lashing in a foaming tumult round the railway stations, banked up into a horrible struggle about the shipping in the Thames, and hurrying by every available channel northward and eastward. . . . By three, people were being trampled and crushed even in Bishopsgate Street; a couple of hundred yards or more from Liverpool Street station, revolvers were fired, people stabbed. . . . By mid-day a Martian had been seen at Barnes, and a cloud of slowly sinking black vapour drove along the Thames and across the flats of Lambeth, cutting off all escape over the bridges in its sluggish advance.

(ch. 16)

These scenes of what amounts to the breakup of metropolitan life are powerful; anyone who was in France in 1940 (or who has studied the history) will be irresistibly reminded of the panic-stricken civilians driven, as the Germans advanced, ever southward, jamming the roads—targets for low-flying aircraft.

There are obvious dangers for a novel without characters. An early reviewer, Basil Williams, in the *Athenaeum* (February 1898), commented: "Mr. Wells is content with describing the cheap emotions of a few bank clerks and newspapers, and the jostling in the road might very well do for an account of a Derby crowd going to Epsom." With regard to the novel's method, an American reviewer said: "It is an Associated Press dispatch, describing a universal nightmare." This is partly true; yet the narrative gains from the bulletinlike attention to time and the detailed topographical background. And the ultimate destruction of the Martians has a tellingly scientific ring: since on Mars they had long ago eliminated microbacteria, they were unprotected against the germs to which man had become largely immune. Their death agonies are unforgettably described—the howling sound, "a sobbing alternation of two notes 'Ulla, ulla, ulla, ulla,'" coming eerily across deserted, devastated London.

The War of the Worlds greatly impressed its first readers not merely because it coincided with speculation about Mars but because of regular scares about the invasion of England by France or Germany. Among the educated, too, an end-of-the-world mood was rife. The artilleryman in *The War of the Worlds* puts it thus: "Cities, nations, civilizations, progress—it's all over. That game's up. We're beat." And so—what? Of course, he says, we must fight the Martians. There must be underground resistance. But such resistance is not for weaklings; it is for able-bodied men and women willing to obey orders. And such resistance "makes life real again." But he goes on to say that "the useless and cumbersome and mischievous have to die. . . . It's a sort of disloyalty, after all, to live and taint the race."

The novel almost immediately demonstrates the ineffectualness of the artilleryman, whose contribution was added by Wells when it passed from serial form to hardback. Yet its authoritarian tone finds an echo in Wells's speculation, for example, in *A Modern Utopia*, that the country would be best dictatorially ruled by an elite.

By the end of the century Wells's creative energies began to flag, which is scarcely surprising after the almost frenzied productivity of the preceding four years; and he was also quite seriously ill. *When the Sleeper Wakes* (1899) lacks the inventiveness and the descriptive powers of the earlier fantasies. In short, it is dull; one cannot but agree with Wells himself, who called it "one of the most ambitious and least satisfactory" of his books.

By 1901 his health had been much improved by the bracing air of Folkestone, and he published *The First Men in the Moon*. Here in the descriptions of lunar scenery his imaginative gifts were at full blast—and remarkably prophetic, as we saw in the color television pictures sent back by American astronauts in the 1960's. There is narrative excitement, too—another race against time—yet something is lacking, possibly the multiple meanings I mentioned earlier. Wells has regaled us so fully that we resent any diminution in diet. The Selenites (the native inhabitants of the moon) themselves, subject from birth to systematic biological conditioning, have the sinister ring of the so-called social engineering of today. Wells himself thought it was "probably [his] best 'scientific romance.'" Certainly it is entertaining, but not the equal of *The Time Machine*.

There were several more fantasies to come, the last in this decade being *The War in the Air* (1908). But long before this his mind was elsewhere, in nonfictional visions of the future, such as *A Modern Utopia*, and in straight fiction.

This account of Wells's fantastic genre would not be complete without a note of the many short stories he wrote in it. Some are fanciful rather than imaginative (though "The Country of the Blind" is certainly the latter), and some are merely trivial. As in his full-length stories, he blends in some comedy (for

234

example, in "The Man Who Could Work Miracles"). "Lord of the Dynamos" is curiously Kiplingesque, and the psychological "The Door in the Wall" might have been no better written by Henry James. Many odd fancies fill the short stories: eyes that suddenly see the near-future; a man whose anatomy is reversed, his heart going over to the right, who becomes left-handed; a half-painted picture comes to life; an irregular movement of the planets causes catastrophe on earth. There are ghost stories, tales of the occult and the remote past.

What a feast, as Eliot said, for first-class and third-class railway travelers as they chose at the bookstall from the *Strand, Pearson's, Cassell's,* the *Windsor,* and many other magazines in that golden age of the short story.

REALISTIC FICTION

WHEN Wells turned to writing realistic fiction he did not lack for competitors. Many excellent novelists flourished—Thomas Hardy, James, Conrad, Rudyard Kipling, Galsworthy, Bennett, George Moore, Ford Madox Ford—though not all had yet done their best work. And the market was there. Not for almost half a century would fiction take second place to biography in readers' favors.

In one way Wells was an innovator. From *The Wheels of Chance* to *Mr. Britling Sees It Through*—indeed to the end of his life—his novels are about what happened to him personally and to people he knew. Before Wells, good novelists had taken a hint here, an observation there, a little introspection, and had invented their characters. Wells had many successors in sticking to more or less concealed autobiography, notably D. H. Lawrence and later C. P. Snow and Anthony Powell.

This style is no derogation. The house of fiction has many mansions. I shall not waste time by indicating upon what person such and such a character was based; in the biographical section above I have identified some real persons so blatantly portrayed as to have affected Wells's career. Who, in any case, now cares that the assistant usher at the Whortley Proprietary School on £40 a year in *Love and Mr. Lewisham* (1900) was Wells at Midhurst?

The novels today stand or fall on their literary merits. The present-day reader rightly asks only: Does *Mr. Lewisham* interest me? Is it a good read? I

think it is. It is a story of young love, mainly in adversity, joyful sometimes, quarrelsome sometimes, ending always in doubt; the only certainty in the mind of Lewisham, whose wife is pregnant, is: "The future is the child. . . . Career! In itself it is a career—the most important career in the world. Father! Why should I want more?"

Lewisham, however, *has* wanted more; he has had a schema of progress; he has wanted to be a successful science student at the Normal College in South Kensington. But he has been distracted, though sometimes resisting, by his amorous obsession for Ethel—walking her home, even occasional nights at plush restaurants in the glamorous London, vividly depicted, of the 1890's.

The novel also concerns, as K. B. Newell has shown, the corruption—or declension—of an honest assistant usher into a liar ("I'm not so honest now") or at any rate a compromiser, to the point where Lewisham observes that "the enormous seriousness of adolescence was coming to an end." Corruption is shown in a more sophisticated way in the character of Chaffery, more sophisticated since Chaffery is not merely an exposed cheat but a cheat who *defends* cheating and lying. Chaffery is a medium, with tambourine, little green box, odor of violets, and white "ectoplasmic" glove, and he is caught out. As it happens—largely from the plot point of view—Wells makes Chaffery Lewisham's stepfather-in-law, and they relax together over small beer and grog in the connubial home.

Chaffery maintains that

honesty is essentially an anarchistic and disintegrating force in society, that communities are held together and the progress of civilization made possible only by vigorous and sometimes even violent lying; that the Social Contract is nothing more or less than a vast conspiracy of human beings to lie to and humbug themselves and one another for the general good. Lies are the mortar that bind the savage individual man into the social masonry.

(ch. 23)

As for man, he is no more than a compound of "lust and greed tempered by fear and an irrational vanity." Characteristically, Chaffery abandons Ethel's mother (life at Clapham "has irked me for some time") and goes off "to live my own life."

The novel is an unusual mixture of love's young dream and disillusion. This, along with its depiction of an age so innocently inhibited about sexual relations, at least in the lower-middle and middle-middle classes, and its vivid awareness of London from the point of view of those classes, gives it a unique flavor.

Kipps was, said Wells himself, "the complete study of life in relation to England's social condition." It is not quite that; apart from a fleeting reference to the earl of Beauprès's irritability, neither the aristocracy nor the upper-middle classes come much into its purview. Where it is strongest and most observant is with its lower-middle class and shopkeepers, and the genteel and somewhat pretentious middle class.

But to speak thus is to make *Kipps* sound dull, and it never is. It is a riveting story of a young, ill-educated, but mainly happy young man, who, having become a draper's assistant, like Hoopdriver, is sacked for being late in the shop; discovers that he has been left a £24,000 legacy and a house by his natural father; begins to learn some of the mysterious "social niceties"; becomes engaged to a superior and somewhat domineering young lady whom he ditches when he meets his childhood sweetheart, now a servant girl, and elopes with her; and then finds out that the brother of his former fiancée to whom he has entrusted his financial affairs has speculated with his money, been ruined, and fled the country.

This, however, is not the end. Some of the money is rescued and, his social aspirations now comfortably shed, Kipps and his wife, Ann, settle down contentedly with their baby son to run a bookshop, after which Kipps has always hankered. As an extra bonus, the £2,000 he had invested in his affluent days in the plays of a raffish, unsuccessful playwright suddenly bear fruit; one of the plays becomes an overnight success, and so Kipps at the end of the novel "is almost as rich as he was in the beginning." A pleasurably happy ending! No wonder that a film of the novel, made in 1941, entranced its audiences, and that the musical comedy based on the book and called *Half a Sixpence* had a long run in England and abroad.

Academic critics have referred to *Kipps* as a comedy of pretenses, a study in vanity, an exposition of the operation of chance; critics at the time of its publication saw it as a fictional materialization of the "social impeachment" of Wells's *Mankind in the Making*, an essay on "spiritual squalor," and accused the novel of portraying "an utter imperviousness to ideas of any kind." These diverse attitudes can all be attested; it is a novel with many dimensions. But surely Wells's friend Henry James

comes, without any literary jargon, nearest to its essence in a letter:

A brilliancy of *true* truth. . . . You have for the very first time treated the English "lower middle" class etc. without the picturesque, the grotesque, the fantastic and romantic interference of which, e.g. Dickens is so misleadingly full. . . . Such extraordinary life; everyone in it, without exception, and every piece and part of it is so vivid and sharp and *raw*.

One can only point to particular excellences: Chitterlow, the playwright, for instance, who is pictured at first as a rambunctious alcoholic phony and turns out in the end to be heartwarmingly honest; Chester Coote, the snobbish artistic dilettante who takes Kipps in hand for his education in the ways of "society" and who toward the end is responsible for "murdering friendships." The hopelessness of Kipps's fellow drapery apprentices—"we're in a blessed drainpipe and we've got to crawl along it until we die"—is movingly shown; yet both Kipps and Buggins are lifted out of it. There is the Apemantus-like raillery of the sick socialist, Masterman, forecasting "the beginning of the Sickness of the World." Only one positive villain is depicted: Walsingham, who makes away with the bulk of Kipps's legacy.

How fresh, too, is the writing, at least in the first two-thirds of the novel. "Wanderings in the hedgeless reedy marsh, long excursions reaching even to Hythe, where the machine-guns of the Empire are forever whirling and tapping, and to Rye and Winchelsea perched like dream cities on their little hills."[4] Fine, too, the childhood love of Kipps for Ann; and, toward the end of the book, when Kipps's heart cries out for her, for "the lights that lurked in Ann Pornick's eyes," and when he revolts against the middle-class habit of "calling" when a printed card is left, and against such forgotten oddities as the anagram tea.[5]

The final part of the novel is less well done. This was due to the fact that Wells had planned and partly written the book seven years before (when he called it *The Wealth of Mr. Waddy*) and his viewpoint had changed; he wanted to make more of Masterman, have him indeed turn Kipps into a socialist, for by this time Wells was seeking how to use his characters

---

[4]The marsh is Romney Marsh; Hythe was until recently the main small-arms training school for the army.

[5]A tea party at which each guest wore an anagrammatized name tag and was given a card on which to solve as many names in the company as possible.

to voice his own beliefs. Most critics have noticed this; only one that I know of, K. B. Newell, has sought, by using themes as key signatures, to suggest that the novel *is* a unified whole. I do not think it is. All the same, *Kipps* comes up, fresh and sparkling, one of the three best novels that Wells wrote.

In the Days of the Comet, which came out a year after *Kipps,* has been variously regarded as the tail-end of his fantasies, a fictionalized version of some of his ideas in *A Modern Utopia,* and a satire on politicians. It is possibly trying to be all of these, which would account for its schematic incoherence and justifies Henry James's comment that he did not find it "an artistic fact, quite, as it is my habit to yearn to find suchlike."

The nub and the strength of it lies elsewhere: in the passion and violent jealousy, leading almost to murder, of the central character, Leadford, who sees his childhood sweetheart, Nettie, carried off by Verrall, a young, handsome sprig of the aristocracy. These passages, though occasionally perilously close to Victorian novelettish (remember the moustache-twirling seducer in *The Wheels of Chance*), have a sustained force that compels us to regard the book as novel rather than fantasy. Leadford is as furious, flailing a being as the invisible man or the devil incarnate of Elizabethan imaginings.

After the emanations of the comet—described with all Wells's gifts for evoking the weird—pacify the passions and stupidities of men, there is a great destruction of the sordid, inconvenient houses such as Leadford (and Wells) had been brought up in, and of unsanitary dress and ill-fitting boots. Men and women become "exalted," beautiful Arcadian figures.

What, then, of love and jealousy? At first Leadford proclaims to Nettie that he has "a new mistress . . . the coming City of the World." But after the death of his mother he needs human comfort and finds it in the arms of Anna, the girl who has looked after her. And Nettie? For her he retains a "hunger of the heart." . . . So? The four of them "from that time were very close, you understand, we were friends, helpers, personal lovers in a world of lovers." And, adds the narrator, it occurred to him that "the thoughts that stirred in my mind were sinister and base, that the queer suspicions, the coarseness and coarse jealousies of my old world were over and done with for these more finely living souls."

Small wonder that one periodical primly commented: "Socialist men's wives, we gather, are no less than their goods, to be held in common." It was not quite that. Leaving aside the autobiographical obtrusion, Wells was suggesting only that mutual sexual relations between "friends" were permissible, indeed welcome; he was not proposing a sexual free-for-all. Nevertheless, *In The Days of the Comet,* along with *A Modern Utopia,* is another Wells prophecy that has come true: not in respect of an appeasing comet but of the hippie commune.

Tono-Bungay is a jumble. Its narrator calls it "an agglomeration" and, in what is probably a reference to the methods of Wells's friends James, Ford, and Conrad, "comprehensive rather than austere . . . I must sprawl and flounder, comment and theorize." All the same, it is a jumble of genius, for, as Peter Quennell writes: "Despite his attitudes to art he had uncommon artistic aptitude; the gift of selecting and placing words; and unusual faculty of description and a fancy at once precise and sweeping."[6] Some have seen *Tono-Bungay* as Wells's greatest novel.

In form it is the autobiography of a man in the middle years called George Ponderevo who has seen life from butlers' pantries to the dinner tables of the titled and the great (as had Wells). Wells hoped that *Tono-Bungay* would be "a powerful instrument of moral suggestion." Perhaps, indeed, in its day it was. Now we read it as a remarkable picture of mid-Edwardian life. Here is Bladesover, the great country estate, serene yet already "overtaken by fatty degeneration and stupendous accidents of hypertrophy"; here meretricious gentry and nobility, "sold for riches"; there the poor, ill-educated masses, unkind to each other, wide open to exploitation.

Exploitation indeed, and big business followed by a financial crash is the main story line. Edward Ponderevo, the narrator's uncle, is a failed country chemist who sets up in London and begins to market a patent medicine he has invented. The medicine has little or no value and might even cause harm. The narrator has scruples about it, but eventually joins his uncle, even though he never quite accepts his uncle's argument—that all trade is good for the country, that it gives employment, and that for the consumers "we mint faith." The business booms, and Ponderevo becomes a very rich and powerful financier. Then comes the crash; he escapes to France and there dies.

Uncle Ponderevo is only a "character" in his country chemist days. In book III he changes into a rogue

[6]In *The Singular Preference* (London, 1952).

financier, based possibly on a contemporary fraudulent operator, Whittaker Wright. His wife, Aunt Susan, is always a character, human, kindly, a "natural." One is pleased with her and, when the crash comes, sorry for her.

There are many other strands to the novel. For instance, the narrator surprisingly invents a new naval destroyer said by him to be a symbol of "Truth." There is much about love, particularly with Beatrice, a young woman of the upper class—a figure almost in the mold of Hemingway's Brett—with whom the narrator has a passionate affair. She is a spoiled woman, "spoiled by this rich idle way of living . . . I'm a little cad—sold and done"; and, it is hinted, she is dependent on drugs. Despite the narrator's urgency, despite her physical passion for him, she will not marry him.

Change and decay are the keynotes that most critics have seen in the novel, certainly visible in the narrator's final remarks: "Light after light goes down. England and the Kingdom, Britain and the Empire, the old prides and the old devotions . . . pass, pass. . . . Crumbling and confusion, of change and seemingly aimless swelling, of a bubbling up of futile loves and sorrows." Yet something "drives" through the confusion: call it science, truth, austerity, beauty: "the heart of life. The one enduring thing."

But the *tone* of the novel supports neither the rhetorical pessimism nor the one ray of light presented by the narrator. It says something different. It bespeaks the brimming vitality of life—however, from the moralist's point of view, misdirected—in these Edwardian years. Of course they were not the golden years they have sometimes been painted, but certainly they seem from *Tono-Bungay* to have had energy and adventurousness.

The narrator says, "There's no humour in my blood," but there is plenty in the author's, and to that extent the narrator is *not* H. G. Wells. What one remembers of the novel is not despair, not the "witless waste" of men and of Earth's resources, but the excitement of the rise to fortune of Edward Ponderevo, of his "getting on," and of his decline. One remembers, too, the swirling, "irresoluble" complexity "of things and relations" conveyed. Nor can one deny Wells's prophetic gift once again: England and the empire *would* in the years to come crumble; "the old devotions" *would* pass.

What a worker he was! In the same year as *Tono-Bungay*, Wells published *Ann Veronica*, a novel much abused in its time for its "immorality," and

rather slighted by recent critics. Yet its evocation of middle-class life in a London suburb has a springlike quality even though the eponymous heroine finds that life excessively restrictive, because in the most innocent way, like the girl in *The Wheels of Chance*, she wants to be free.

Her father is the Victorian paterfamilias of legend and occasionally, doubtless, of reality. She escapes him but—how to live? Her experiences in murky London lodgings are unpleasant, and she throws herself upon the mercies of kind Mr. Ramage (a suburban neighbor), who tries to seduce her in the best Edwardian style, first in a Covent Garden box watching *Tristan and Isolde* and later in the private room of a restaurant—with an "obtrusive sofa" and a locked door. Her study of jujitsu comes to her aid.

Meanwhile she has been drawn into Fabian circles, some of whose members are cattily portrayed, and into love with her married biology instructor. She takes part in a suffragette escapade, is arrested, persuades her lover that she is ready for the taking—and is taken, to the Swiss Alps. Four years later the liaison is respectable—and Father comes to dinner.

This evokes a particular section of London life, seen largely from the point of view of a young girl seeking tentatively, fearfully, to become the "new woman," to shake off the excess of modesty that inhibited females at the time, to become, in brief, a person. And succeeding.

When *The History of Mr. Polly* came out in 1910, the American wit H. L. Mencken observed that it was not so much a history of Mr. Polly as of Mr. Polly's stomach; and this is only partly a joke. The novel begins with him, another unsuccessful small shopkeeper, sitting on a fence suffering from indigestion as a result of his wife's crude cooking and the unwise diet common in the lower classes of the time.[7] Wells's friend Ford Madox Hueffer (Ford) had noted of the villagers on Romney Marsh that "as children they were starved, as men they were to a man dyspeptic through eating the fat pork and cheese that form the chief of their diet. Thus, in old age, they are crabbed and crippled with rheumatism, they have no blood in their veins."[8]

So Mr. Polly's indigestion is no mere novelistic

---

[7] As John Burnett's *Plenty and Want: A Social History of Diet in England from 1815* (London, 1966) makes clear, the appalling adulteration of foodstuffs had by this time ceased as a result of stringent laws during the last quarter of the nineteenth century. But lower-middle-class cooking continued to be poor because of lack of skill and inadequate kitchen equipment.
[8] *The Cinque Ports* (Edinburgh, 1900).

device. It is reflected in his equally flatulent mental condition produced by the educational fodder at school, which had bored him yet left him no less voracious for reading, especially tales of high adventure and heroism, than his physical dyspepsia made him voracious for food. And he has, too, "an insatiable hunger for bright and delightful experiences, for the gracious aspects of things, for beauty."

The novel ends as it begins, with Mr. Polly's stomach: it ends with him happy and fit on "honest" roast beef and omelettes and wheaten bread, living in the open air, contentedly helping run a remote, riverside pub. (In this respect *Mr. Polly* belongs to that ever-lengthening literary tradition of "back to the simple life, wind on the heath.")

Mr. Polly, undeniably, *is* an escape story. It has a happy ending. Yet much in between is far from happy. Mr. Polly, like many of Wells's characters, drifts into becoming a draper's apprentice, drifts into marriage (backed by a small legacy), drifts into being a near-insolvent shopkeeper. At last he decides to act rather than drift: he will commit suicide. He gets his razor ready and in so doing knocks over an oil lamp that sets his shop on fire and ignites those of his neighbors. The fit of action once upon him, Mr. Polly turns into a hero and, forgetting his death wish, saves a deaf, comic old lady from an upper room. The fire scene is descriptively the high point of the novel—and a turning point, too, since it results in Mr. Polly's freedom. The shop is heavily insured. He gives his wife the bulk of the payment and tramps off into the countryside he has always loved. The narrator comments: "If the world does not please you, *you can change it*"—perhaps for the worse, perhaps for the better, "and at the worst for something more interesting." After all, Wells himself had proved it.

The bliss of being a handyman at the Potwell Inn is not at first unalloyed. The plump, comfortable landlady has a violent psychopathic nephew who appears from time to time to demand money with menaces; she pays. Mr. Polly, nervously, blunders once more into success; through his courage the villainous nephew ("Uncle Jim") is driven off, never to return.

Mr. Polly is related to Hoopdriver and Kipps and other, more minor, characters in the Wells opus; yet he is different in one interesting way: he is, like James Joyce, fascinated by mixed-up words. Kipps and Hoopdriver, of course, had their difficulties with the English language: Mr. Polly goes much further. Not being equipped by his education to assimilate words or to pronounce them properly, "he avoided every recognized phrase in the language, and mispro-

nounced everything in order that he shouldn't be suspected of ignorance but of whim"—an odd ambition. The results are sometimes amusingly surrealist, throwing out hints and half-suggestions, multi-forked: "Elegant Rhapsodooce," "Raboloose" (Rabelais); sometimes they are baffling even to the native English speaker—"skeptaceous," and "I'm going to absquatulate." No less recondite are Wells's phonetic renderings of the Kentish accent of his time: "Elfrid" for "Alfred," "Pass the mustid," "Swelpme." But it is notable that when important action is afoot, these dialogue condiments vanish.

The New Machiavelli is in part yet another revamping of early autobiographical material with long, discursive passages on politics and socialism. It is also reminiscent of *Ann Veronica,* except that we are given more of the pathos of the narrator Remington's relations with his wife, Margaret, once he has fallen in love with Isabel; and except that it is a political, not a teaching, career that Remington must renounce when he elopes with Isabel. The regrets of the two lovers over what they have done to Remington's wife are somewhat lachrymosely long drawn out; but genuine emotion is not lacking. And there are some very acute observations of such public figures as Balfour and the Webbs, concealed by little more than a change of name. This kind of ruminative novel could scarcely be written today; but its many felicities make it readable still.

Boon is a curious incident rather than a novel. It is a ragbag of pieces written over a decade by Wells and allegedly the work of "the popular novelist George Boon," who secretly craves the respect of littérateurs in addition to his achieved monetary success. *Boon,* wrote Lovat Dickson, is "the confession of faith of a tired, troubled and depressed mind, maintaining dispiritedly, against his own questioning, the certainties to which he has clung for so long"; Wells himself referred to it as the most revealing book he ever wrote. From the literary point of view what remains to interest the general reader today are the parodies, some of them bitter, of such writers as Edmund Gosse, George Moore, Hugh Walpole, Ford Madox Ford, G. B. Shaw, W. B. Yeats, and, most hurtful of all, Henry James, then ill, who died the year after *Boon* appeared.

The parodies *are* funny—as funny as the comedy in *The Wheels of Chance, Kipps,* and *Mr. Polly.* For instance, James and Moore returning from a stroll are both in full verbal spate, but neither heeds what the other says: Moore is describing in loving detail, Sterne-fashion, a little sexual adventure in the south of France; James, booming away in an endlessly qualified sentence. But Wells also sneers at James the writer, who regards "the whole seething brew of life as a vat from which you skim, with slow, dignified gestures, works of art. Works of art whose only claim is their art." And he describes James's style, not without some grain of truth, as being like "a hippopotamus trying to pick up a pea."

There is only one more Wells novel—there were many so-called novels still to come—that can be thoroughly recommended as fiction rather than an allegorical tract-for-the-times: *Mr. Britling Sees It Through*. It caught the mood of the well-to-do middle classes in the first months of the war and went into thirteen editions before Christmas of the year of publication. It also describes very closely Wells's own life at Easton Glebe: how Britling kept open house and how among his semipermanent guests were a young German tutor, Heinrich, and a young American sent to sign up Britling for an American publisher.

Heinrich is killed in the German army; Britling's eldest son is reported killed, and his grief and that of the boy's fiancée are told with every gift that Wells ever had as a novelist. Britling's son in fact returns from the war; and the last pages refer to Britling's sending Heinrich's violin to his parents. No less good and fresh are the evocations of the English countryside and its people during the war; the description of trench warfare (written before Wells went to France); Britling's eighth love affair, and his finding of God: "The master, the Captain of Mankind . . . God was beside him and within him and about him"; Britling says that he has thought too much "of what I would do by myself, I have forgotten *that which was with me*."

Mr. Britling is Wells's equivalent of Shaw's *Heartbreak House*. There is scarcely a false note; the argument about the future, of world government—England in the vanguard—fits naturally, not obtrusively; and he expresses English patriotism as few others have done, which was a considerable shock to some of his socialist friends, just as was his finding a semimystical religion, though in Wells himself this did not long persist.

This is his last true novel in the writing of which all his great gifts were fully deployed, though none of the later novels are totally lacking a touch here, a spark there, witty dialogue, sharp observation, not least in *Apropos of Dolores* (1938). The rest are largely written to a scheme—*Joan and Peter* (1918), for example, presents Wells's opinions on education.

Men Like Gods is not a return to the manner of the early fantasies; it is a picture of Wellsian utopia. It is perfectly possible to write propaganda that is also good fiction, for example, Charles Kingsley's *Alton Locke* or Mark Rutherford's *The Revolution in Tanner's Lane*. But Wells did not. André Malraux's proposition is generally valid: "It is not passion which destroys a work of art, but the desire to prove something."

WELLS AS THEORIST

WELLS was never in the philosophical sense a thinker, nor was he a discoverer. His mind, despite his scientific training, was too undisciplined. He was more a magpie-like picker-up of ideas that he absorbed, developed, popularized, and scattered to the four winds in the form of journalism, even if the journalism was often book length.

However stale and often ill-expressed some of these ideas—ideas that E. J. Mishan has dubbed those of the "Established Enlightenment"—seem to us today, they had enormous impact on readers of the time,[9] and not only in Britain. Indeed it is said that one French publishing house founded its fortunes on the sale of Wells in translation. It was, wrote George Orwell, not perhaps without irony, wonderful for a young person to read a man "who *knew* that the future was not going to be what respectable people imagined." Indeed it may be claimed that the reason Wells's nonfiction seems stale now is that the ideas expressed were simply assimilated into the modern mind, another example of the adage that nothing fails, in the long run, like success.

Nor, to his worldwide public, did it seem to matter that his ideas were often inconsistent and sometimes self-contradictory; he was for a quarter of a century or so taken seriously, from *Anticipations of the Reaction of Mechanical and Scientific Progress upon Human Life and Thought* until, approximately, *The Open Conspiracy: Blueprints for a World Revolution* in 1928.

We noted above the deep strain of pessimism in the famous fantasies of the 1890's. *Anticipations* is notably optimistic—a fact not perhaps unconnected with his financial success—and might have taken as

[9]Margaret Cole was only one of very many when she said that by reading Wells she had "tumbled straight into socialism overnight."

its text the sentence quoted above from *Mr. Polly:* "If the world does not please you, you can change it," or, as one critic interpreted it, "whatever is, is certain to give way to better." Wells went even further when in *A Modern Utopia* he asserted that "will is stronger than fact, it can mould and overcome fact." It was a short distance from "can" to "must." The world *must be* changed and with it human nature.

How, then, was the world to be changed? By a group of men and women, whom he sometimes called "samurai" (Japanese swordsmen) and sometimes the "new republicans," the "open conspirators," and even, later on, "the mind of the race," who would "take the world in hand" and create "a sane order." Plato's "guardians" were no doubt Wells's models. There is no reference to democratic election. Wells was that accursed being of present-day socialist demonology, an elitist.

The elite would ensure the proper education (not merely literacy or mathematical skills) of all; and such an educated community would establish rational relationships with others elsewhere. A world community[10] would develop, a sense of kinship among all men, and instead of pointless, wasteful wars, differences would be settled by negotiation and agreement. Racial, regional, and national frictions would disappear. Men would work happily together to bring each other a fair share of the world's abundant wealth. Utopia indeed.

The benevolent dictators, a sort of upper civil service on the lines of Auguste Comte's sociocrats, would ultimately operate through a world state and—sinister adumbration of the Russian dictatorship and Orwell's *1984*—would maintain a central index keeping track of every person in the world. The dictators would abjure alcohol, trade, the stage, and games, in short be a latter-day version of the Cromwellians. Indeed, in his novel *The Shape of Things to Come,* Wells refers to the dictatorship of the airmen as a "Puritan Tyranny," which by its "Act of Uniformity" would stamp out "every facile system of errors."

The books in which Wells propounded these basic thoughts are swarming with ideas; I can mention only a few. For example, the state must control procreation and eliminate the unfit. Sex should be "a straight and clean desire for a clean and straight fellow creature"—no more "uxorious inseparable-

ness." Wives were to have economic equality; husbands, however, were given sexual freedom so long as there was no "emotional offence to the wife . . . if she does not mind, nobody minds."

On less fundamental matters Wells did focus public attention on some real problems of the near future. He foresaw the age of motors, the congestion of cities, the need for throughways. Wells never believed, as G. K. Chesterton did, that the gasoline engine was the vilest invention; he pointed out that their grandfathers had hated railways, which were now everywhere accepted as a boon. So it should be with the motorcar.

He railed, too, against the conservatism that would not admit that the "ordinary domestic house" could be built with elevators and automatic sanitary appliances that would relieve servants of the worst part of their labors. To aid cleaning, rooms should be constructed without corners—a necessary innovation still far from general. Wells mapped out "human ecology"; only in the 1970's did a British government create a department of the environment. As Beatrice Webb wrote of *Anticipations,* he ranged "from the future direction of religious thought to the exact curve of the skirting round the wall of middle-class abodes."

Where doubtless he lost the sympathy of some of his socialist pacifist friends was in his justifiably hard lambasting of military men for failing to adopt "scientific appliances" with which to wage war. Perhaps he was reflecting the views of his acquaintance Balfour, who as prime minister (1902–1905) sacrificed his party's electoral future for the sake of updating Britain's defenses. As we noted in the biographical section, Wells supported Britain against Germany in 1914; it is interesting that, according to his son Anthony West, again in 1939 "Wells took the line that once the country was at war the citizen's job was to do what he was told to do without argument."[11] Wells, for all his internationalism, was at heart a patriot; he might have said, with that other rebel D. H. Lawrence, "I really think that the most living clue of life in us Englishmen is England."

Even so, though he sometimes wandered from the Fabian Socialist hard line, his basic ideas remained theirs. His methods of implementing those ideas were often *not* theirs. For example, he wanted people to have military training so as to enforce world

---

[10]Wells had perhaps been converted to internationalism, a comparatively new idea, by Havelock Ellis's *The Nineteenth Century: A Dialogue in Utopia* (London, 1906).

[11]See the perceptive essay in Anthony West's *Principles and Persuasions* (London, 1958).

government and to suppress what he calls in *The Open Conspiracy* "nationalist brigandage." The Fabians were cleverer than the impatient Wells. They saw that their aims could better be achieved by gradually infiltrating the media; by backstairs influence on politicians, industrialists, and students; by a quiet, evasive sapping. Wells, for instance, railed at Roman Catholics in *Crux Ansata* (1943) and elsewhere, and wanted them all removed immediately from any influential position. The Fabians simply penetrated them and their seminaries. It is interesting that on a visit to President Roosevelt in 1934 he noticed with pleasure the large number of open conspirators, that is, Fabians, surrounding the president. And this was true.[12]

As for Wells's Fabian aims, George Orwell was near the mark in writing in the 1930's: "Much of what Wells has imagined and worked for is physically there in Nazi Germany. The order, the planning, the State encouragement of science, the steel, the concrete, the aeroplanes." Orwell had correctly seen that the achievement of Wells's ideas would be far from the frivolity of "Utopiae full of nude women" and visions of "super garden cities." In essence, Wells stood close to both the Nazis and the Communists. There was the same millenarian rhetoric, contempt for the bourgeois, and a streak of destructiveness. In real life, despite his laudatory Stalin interview, Wells regarded the leaders of both dictatorships as "primitives," not men like gods.

His attitude to Marxism and Marx was changeable. In *New Worlds for Old* (1908) he pays tribute to Marx. Later on he refers to him as "a Jew who was kept by the tradesman Engels." A more reasoned critique of Marxism came in *The Open Conspiracy:* "In practice Marxism is found to work out in a ready resort to malignantly destructive activities and to be so uncreative as to be practically impotent in the face of material difficulties." Yet, curiously, he gave money to Communist causes and had many friends in the party. In 1945 he wrote to the *Daily Worker* saying that he was "an active supporter of the reconstituted Communist Party," but by then his mind was increasingly wandering—or revealing the true logic of his Fabianism.

Orwell also observed that Wells "is too sane to understand the modern world," by which he meant too rational. This was not quite true. What he had come to realize—and it made him very unhappy—

was that, discounting violent revolution and drastic brainwashing and surgery such as took place in Russia, human nature itself was the greatest stumbling block to the achievement of his objectives. As Conrad had told him long ago: "You do not take sufficient account of human imbecility which is cunning and perfidious"; and again, "You don't care for humanity but think they are to be improved; I love humanity but know they are not."

But Wells *did* know, even if he did not particularly love, humanity and its imbecility: he had shown it comprehensively in the novels of his Edwardian period. Was he to write as he saw or as he thought? Here was the crux of his painful dilemma; and it was not merely in the despairing and somewhat incoherent pamphlet *Mind at the End of Its Tether* (1945) that he despaired. As early as *The Undying Fire* (1919), while expressing his loathing of things as they were, he wrote: "I talk . . . I talk . . . and then a desolating sense of reality blows like a destroying gust through my mind, and my little lamp of hope blows out." It shows, writes Anthony West, "the pendulum of his mind swinging away from its natural despairing bent over to the side of determination to construct something better out of human opportunities and back, again and again."

Such doubts about the sacred cow of progress damned him in the eyes of all good progressives. But *Mind at the End of Its Tether* goes far beyond doubt. He has no doubt anymore: "The end of everything we call life is close at hand and cannot be evaded. A frightful queerness has come into life. . . . Something is happening so that life will never be *quite* the same again. The attempt to trace a pattern of any sort is absolutely futile."

Wells claimed with some justice in a letter in 1939 that all his books had insisted on "the insecurity of progress and the possibility of human degeneration and extinction. I think the odds are against man but it is still worth fighting against them." The trouble is that he fought under the wrong banner. His ideals were frequently undesirable and happily unattainable. The plain fact was that most Englishmen did not want to be regimented by Fabians or any other authoritarian, unelected group, however wise. They did not want dictatorship, nor central world government. Most particularly they did not want to change their character, except in the slow way that nature itself changes it. Only long after Wells's death were they to wake up to what was being put across them by Wells's disciples and successors.

[12]See Rose L. Martin's *Fabian Freeway* (Santa Monica, 1968).

Yet Wells's ideals sprang from goodwill and humanity; he had known poverty and all that went with it; he had been at the receiving end of bad education; he had seen the wastefulness of wars and the irresponsibility of financiers. He wanted to save others from such things, as he had saved himself (for neither wars nor economic collapse really touched him personally). During the Second World War Wells continued to write on the old themes. The MacKenzies sum it up neatly: "The world was in flames and H. G. was trying to beat them out with a Fabian pamphlet."

CONCLUSION

It was unfortunate for Wells's reputation as a novelist—and for the enjoyment of potential readers —that his fiction was given the cold shoulder by two such writers as D. H. Lawrence and Virginia Woolf, both fashionable with the literary intelligentsia in the 1920's. By that time what may be termed the snobbery of letters had gained a real hold. Writers not on the OK list were banished to critical darkness, however high their sales were. Indeed the higher the sales the more likely they were to be looked down on; it was notable that those on the approved list were usually poor sellers. The result was that when Virginia Woolf discovered Wells's work to be "already a little chilled" the word was quickly passed round: Wells is out.

Happily the tide has turned. Some first-class critics have spent time demonstrating Wells's many excellences. Some of the more academic critics, it is true, propound somewhat eccentric views of Wells. But many of them think him worth serious attention, and so they play a part in persuading contemporary readers that the best of Wells's fiction is still good reading. And it is.

I do not know whether he was a "great" writer because I am not sure, below the topmost level of, say, Dickens, Dostoyevsky, Flaubert, what "great" means; and in any case writers are not to be assessed in a sort of football league table. What I am sure of is that a reader who picks up *The Time Machine*, *Kipps*, *Mr. Polly*, and *Mr. Britling Sees It Through* will not put them aside until he has read to the end. Fiction is for enjoyment. Alas, halfway through his career Wells decided it was for teaching.

SELECTED BIBLIOGRAPHY

The H. G. Wells archive, comprising his private papers, correspondence, many MSS of his writings, etc., was acquired from his family by the University of Illinois in 1956. See LETTERS for correspondence with particular individuals published so far from this archive. The H. G. Wells Society, London, publishes occasional papers and a journal (no. 1, Spring 1972).

I. BIBLIOGRAPHY. F. A. Chappell, *Bibliography of the Works of H. G. Wells* (Chicago, 1924); G. H. Wells [G. West], *A Bibliography of the Works of H. G. Wells* (London, 1925), with notes and comments; G. H. Wells, *The Works of H. G. Wells, 1887–1925* (London, 1926), bibliography, dictionary, and subject index; G. A. Connes, *A Dictionary of Characters and Scenes in the Novels, Romances and Short Stories of H. G. Wells* (Dijon, 1926); K. R. Menon, *A Guide to H. G. Wells's Short Stories* (Singapore, 1957); H. G. Wells Society, *H. G. Wells: A Comprehensive Bibliography* (London, 1966).

II. COLLECTED EDITIONS. *The Works of H. G. Wells*, 28 vols. (London, 1924–1927), the Atlantic ed.; *The Works of H. G. Wells*, 24 vols. (London, 1926–1927), the Essex Thinpaper ed.; *Works*, 24 vols. (Geneva, 1968–1969).

III. SELECTED EDITIONS. *Tales of the Unexpected* (London, 1922); *Tales of Life and Adventure* (London, 1923); *Tales of Wonder* (London, 1923); *The Short Stories* (London, 1927); *A Quartette of Comedies* (London, 1928), contains *Kipps*, *The History of Mr. Polly*, *Bealby*, *Love and Mr. Lewisham*; *The Scientific Romances* (London, 1933), contains *The Time Machine*, *The Island of Doctor Moreau*, *The Invisible Man*, *The War of the Worlds*, *The First Men in the Moon*, *The Food of the Gods*, *In the Days of the Comet*, and *Men Like Gods*; *Stories of Men and Women in Love* (London, 1933), contains *Love and Mr. Lewisham*, *The Passionate Friends*, *The Wife of Sir Isaac Harman*, *The Secret Places of the Heart*; *The Wheels of Chance and The Time Machine* (London, 1935), Everyman Library ed.; *Selected Short Stories* (Harmondsworth, 1958); W. Warren Wagar, ed. and comp., *Journalism and Prophecy, 1893–1946* (Boston, 1964; London, 1965).

IV. SEPARATE WORKS. *Text-book of Biology*, 2 vols. (London, 1893); *Honours Physiography* (London, 1893), in collaboration with R. A. Gregory; *Select Conversations with an Uncle, Now Extinct, and Two Other Reminiscences* (London, 1895), sketches and stories, contains twelve conversations and the two short stories "A Misunderstood Artist" and "The Man with a Nose"; *The Time Machine: An Invention* (London, 1895), fantasy; *The Wonderful Visit* (London, 1895), fantasy; *The Stolen Bacillus, and Other Incidents* (London, 1895), short stories, contains "The Stolen Bacillus," "The Flowering of the Strange Orchid," "In the Avu Observatory," "The Triumphs of a Taxidermist," "A Deal in Ostriches," "Through a Window," "The Temptation of Harringay,"

"The Flying Man," "The Diamond Maker," "Aepyornis Island," "The Remarkable Case of Davidson's Eyes," "The Lord of the Dynamos," "The Hammerpond Park Burglary," "A Moth—Genus Novo," "The Treasure in the Forest"; *The Red Room* (Chicago, 1896), short story, only twelve copies printed; *The Wheels of Chance: A Holiday Adventure* (London, 1896), novel, first published serially in *Today* (London, 1896); *The Island of Doctor Moreau* (London, 1896), science fiction; *The Plattner Story, and Others* (London, 1897), short stories, contains "The Plattner Story," "The Argonauts of the Air," "The Story of the Late Mr. Elvesham," "In the Abyss," "The Apple," "Under the Knife," "The Sea-Raiders," "Pollock and the Porroh Man," "The Red Room," "The Cone," "The Purple Pileus," "The Jilting of Jane," "In the Modern Vein," "A Catastrophe," "The Lost Inheritance," "The Sad Story of a Dramatic Critic," "A Slip under the Microscope"; *The Invisible Man: A Grotesque Romance* (London, 1897), science fiction, first published serially in *Pearson's Weekly* (June–July 1897); *Text-Book of Zoology* (London, 1898), in collaboration with A. M. Davies, rev. by J. T. Cunningham (London, 1913); *Certain Personal Matters* (London, 1898), mainly autobiographical; *Thirty Strange Stories* (New York, 1897), contains three new stories: "The Reconciliation," "The Rajah's Treasure," and "Le Mari terrible"; *The War of the Worlds* (London, 1898), science fiction, first published serially in *Pearson's* (April–December 1897); *When the Sleeper Wakes* (London, 1899), science fiction, first published serially in the *Graphic* (1898–1899), rev. as *The Sleeper Awakes* (London, 1910); *Tales of Space and Time* (London, 1899), short stories, contains "The Crystal Egg," "The Star," "A Story of the Stone Age," "A Story of the Days to Come," "The Man Who Could Work Miracles."

Love and Mr. Lewisham (London, 1900), novel, first published serially in the *Weekly Times* (November 1899–1900); *The First Men in the Moon* (London, 1901), science fiction, first published serially in the *Strand* (December 1900–August 1901); *Anticipations of the Reaction of Mechanical and Scientific Progress upon Human Life and Thought* (London, [1901]), prognostication; *The Discovery of the Future* (London, 1902), lecture, given at the Royal Institution on 24 January 1902; *The Sea Lady: A Tissue of Moonshine* (London, 1902), first published serially in *Pearson's* (July–December 1901); *Twelve Stories and a Dream* (London, 1903), contains "Filmer," "The Magic Shop," "The Valley of Spiders," "The Truth about Pyecraft," "Mr. Skelmersdale in Fairyland," "The Story of the Inexperienced Ghost," "Jimmy Goggles the God," "The New Accelerator," "Mr. Ledbetter's Vacation," "The Stolen Body," "Mr. Brisher's Treasure," "Miss Winchelsea's Heart," "A Dream of Armageddon"; *Mankind in the Making* (London, 1903), education, first printed serially in the *Fortnightly Review* (September 1902–September 1903); *The Food of the Gods, And How It Came to Earth* (London, 1904), science fiction, first published serially in *Pearson's* (December 1903–June 1904).

A Modern Utopia (London, 1905), sociology, first published serially in the *Fortnightly Review* (October 1904–April 1905); *Kipps: The Story of a Simple Soul* (London, 1905), novel, first published serially in *Pall Mall* (1905); *In the Days of the Comet* (London, 1906), science fiction, first published in the *Daily Chronicle* (1905–1906); *Socialism and the Family* (London, 1906), political tract; *The Future in America: A Search after Realities* (London, 1906), sociology, first printed serially in *Harper's Weekly* (14 July–6 October 1906); *This Misery of Boots* (London, 1907), political tract, a Fabian Society pamphlet, repr. from the *Independent Review* (December 1905); *New Worlds for Old* (London, 1908), prognostication; *The War in the Air and Particularly How Mr. Bert Smallways Fared While It Lasted* (London, 1908), science fiction, first printed serially in *Pall Mall*; *First & Last Things: A Confession of Faith and Rule of Life* (London, 1908; rev. ed., 1917), philosophy; *Tono-Bungay* (London, 1909), novel, first published serially in the *English Review* (December 1908–March 1909); *Ann Veronica: A Modern Love Story* (London, 1909), novel.

The History of Mr. Polly (London, 1910), novel; *The Country of the Blind, and Other Stories* (London, 1911), contains five new stories: "A Vision of Judgment," "The Empire of the Ants," "The Door in the Wall," "The Country of the Blind," and "The Beautiful Suit"; *The Door in the Wall, and Other Stories* (New York, 1911), short stories, lim. ed. of 600 copies, eight stories selected from previous collections; *Floor Games* (London, 1911), juvenile; *The New Machiavelli* (London, 1911), novel, first printed serially in the *English Review* (May–October 1910); *Marriage* (London, 1912), novel; *Little Wars: A Game for Boys* (London, 1913), juvenile; *The Passionate Friends: A Novel* (1913); *The Wife of Sir Isaac Harman* (London, 1914), novel; *The World Set Free: A Story of Mankind* (London, 1914), fantasy, first published serially in the *English Review* (December 1913–May 1914); *The War That Will End War* (London, 1914), essays; *An Englishman Looks at the World* (London, 1914), contains twenty-six essays, thirteen repr. from the *Daily Mail* and already collected in two pamphlets, *The Labour Unrest* (1912) and *War and Common Sense* (1913), ten published in weeklies and monthlies, three in book form as occasional contributions.

Boon (London, 1915), sketches, contains "The Mind of the Race," "The Wild Asses of the Devil," "The Last Trump: Being a First Selection from the Literary Remains of George Boon, Prepared for Publication by Reginald Bliss" [H. G. Wells]; *The Peace of the World* (London, 1915), commentary, first published in the *English Review* (March 1915); *The Research Magnificent* (London, 1915), novel; *Bealby: A Holiday* (London, 1915), novel, first published serially in *Grand* (August 1914–March 1915); *What Is Coming? A Forecast of Things after the War* (London, 1916), commentary; *Mr. Britling Sees It Through* (London, 1916), novel, first published serially in the *Nation* (May–October 1916); *The Elements of Reconstruction* (London, 1916), commentary, series of articles repr. from the *Times* (July–August 1916); *The Soul of a Bishop: A Novel* (London, 1917), first published serially in *Collier's Weekly* (1917); *War and the Future: Italy, France, and Britain at War* (London, 1917), commentary; *God the Invisible King* (London, 1917), commentary; *In the Fourth Year: Anticipations of a World Peace* (London, 1918), commentary, eleven chs. mostly repr. from daily newspapers; *Joan and Peter: The Story of an Education* (London, 1918), novel; *The Undying Fire: A Contemporary Novel* (London, 1919), first published serially in the *International Review* (March–June 1919); *The Outline of History: Being a Plain History of Life and Mankind*, 2 vols. (1919–1920), originally iss. fortnightly, rev. ed. (1920), 5th rev. (1930), rev. and ext. by R. Postgate (1951).

Russia in the Shadows (London, 1920), politics, originally serialized in the *Sunday Express* (October–November 1920); *The Salvaging of Civilization* (London, 1921), politics; *A Short History of the World* (London, 1922), history; *The Secret Places of the Heart* (London, 1922), novel, first published serially in *Nash's* and *Pall Mall* (December 1921–July 1922); *Washington and the Hope of Peace* (London, 1922), commentary, articles written at the time of the Washington Arms Conference, first published in the *New York World* (November–December 1921); *Men Like Gods* (London, 1923), science fiction, first printed serially in the *Westminster Gazette* (December 1922–February 1923); *The Story of a Great Schoolmaster: Being a Plain Account of the Life and Ideas of Sanderson of Oundle* (London, 1924), biography; *A Year of Prophesying* (London, 1924), commentary; *The Dream* (London, 1924), novel, first published serially in *Nash's* and *Pall Mall* (October 1923–May 1924).

A Forecast of the World's Affairs (London, 1925), commentary; *Christina Alberta's Father* (London, 1925), novel; *The World of William Clissold: A Novel at a New Angle*, 3 vols. (London, 1926); *Meanwhile: The Picture of a Lady* (London, 1927), novel; *Democracy under Revision* (London, 1927), lecture given at the Sorbonne; *The Way the World Is Going: Guesses and Forecasts of the Years Ahead* (London, 1928); *Mr. Blettsworthy on Rampole Island* (London, 1928), novel; *The Book of Catherine Wells* (London, 1928), Wells's tribute to the memory of his wife; *The Open Conspiracy: Blueprints for a World Revolution* (London, 1928; rev. ed., 1930), politics; *The King Who Was a King: The Book of a Film* (London, 1929); *Imperialism and the Open Conspiracy* (London, 1929), politics; *The Adventures of Tommy* (London, 1929), juvenile; *The Treasure in the Forest* (London, 1929), novel; *The Common Sense of World Peace* (London, 1929), lecture, an address to the Reichstag; *The Science of Life: A Summary of Contemporary Knowledge about Life and Its Possibilities* (London, 1929–1930), biology, in collaboration with J. Huxley and G. P. Wells, originally iss. fortnightly.

The Autocracy of Mr. Parham (London, 1930), novel; *What Are We To Do with Our Lives?* (London, 1931), sociology, the final rev. of *The Open Conspiracy*; *The*

Work, Wealth and Happiness of Mankind, 2 vols. (New York, 1931; London, 1932; rev. ed., 1934), economics; *After Democracy: Addresses and Papers on the Present World Situation* (London, 1932), politics; *The Bulpington of Blup* (London, 1932), novel; *The Shape of Things to Come: The Ultimate Revolution* (London, 1933), prognostication; *Experiment in Autobiography: Discoveries and Conclusions of a Very Ordinary Brain—Since 1866*, 2 vols. (London, 1934; new ed., 1966).

The New America: The New World (London, 1935), travel; *The Idea of a World Encyclopaedia* (London, 1936), lecture given at the Royal Institution; *The Croquet Player: A Story* (London, 1936); *The Anatomy of Frustration: A Modern Synthesis* (London, 1936), commentary; *Star Begotten: A Biological Fantasia* (London, 1937), science fiction; *Brynhild* (London, 1937), novel; *The Camford Visitation* (London, 1937), satire; *World Brain* (London, 1938), essays and addresses; *The Brothers: A Story* (London, 1937); *Apropos of Dolores* (London, 1938), novel; *Travels of a Republican Radical in Search of Hot Water* (London, 1939), polemics; *The Holy Terror* (London, 1939), novel; *The Fate of Homo Sapiens: An Unemotional Statement of the Things That Are Happening to Him Now, and of the Immediate Possibilities Confronting Him* (London, 1939), commentary.

The Rights of Man: Or, What Are We Fighting For? (London, 1940), commentary; *All Aboard for Ararat* (London, 1940), commentary; *Babes in the Darkling Wood* (London, 1940), novel; *The Common Sense of War and Peace: World Revolution or War Unending* (London, 1940), commentary; *The New World Order: Whether It Is Attainable, How It Can Be Attained and What Sort of World a World at Peace Will Have to Be* (London, 1940), commentary; *You Can't Be Too Careful: A Sample of Life, 1901–1951* (London, 1941), story; *Guide to the New World: A Handbook to Constructive World Revolution* (London, 1941), commentary; *Science and the World-Mind* (London, 1942), science; *The Conquest of Time* (London, 1942), commentary, written to replace *First and Last Things* (London, 1908); *The Outlook for Homo Sapiens* (London, 1942), commentary, an amalgamation of *The Fate of Homo Sapiens* (London, 1939) and *The New World Order* (London, 1940); *Phoenix: A Summary of the Inescapable Conditions of World Reorganisation* (London, 1942), politics; *Crux Ansata: An Indictment of the Roman Catholic Church* (London, 1943), polemics; *'42 to '44: A Contemporary Memoir upon Human Behaviour During the Crisis of the World Revolution* (London, 1944), politics, lim. to 2,000 copies, Wells's doctoral thesis at London University, written in 1942 and entitled "A Thesis on the Quality of Illusion in the Continuity of the Individual Life in the Higher Metazoa, with Particular Reference to the Species *Homo Sapiens*," was printed as an appendix to this work; *The Happy Turning: A Dream of Life* (London, 1945), commentary; *Mind at the End of Its Tether* (London, 1945), commentary.

V. LETTERS. H. A. Jones, *My Dear Wells: A Manual for*

the *Haters of England. Being a Series of Letters upon Bolshevism, Collectivism, Internationalism, and the Distribution of Wealth Addressed to Mr. H. G. Wells* (London, 1921); L. Edel and G. N. Ray, eds., *Henry James and H. G. Wells: A Record of Their Friendship, Their Debate on the Art of Fiction, and Their Quarrel* (London, 1958); H. Wilson, ed., *Arnold Bennett and H. G. Wells: A Record of a Personal and a Literary Friendship* (London, 1960); R. A. Gettmann, *George Gissing and H. G. Wells: Their Friendship and Correspondence* (London, 1961). The three latter collections are from H. G. Wells papers at the University of Illinois, excellently edited and invaluable for students of Wells's relations with the literary world of his time.

VI. BIOGRAPHICAL AND CRITICAL STUDIES. A. H. G. Craufurd, *The Religion of H. G. Wells, and Other Essays* (London, 1909); J. D. Beresford, *H. G. Wells* (London, 1915); Van Wyck Brooks, *The World of H. G. Wells* (London, 1915).

E. Guyot, *H. G. Wells* (Paris, 1920); R. T. Hopkins, *H. G. Wells: Personality, Character, Topography* (London, 1922); S. Dark, *The Outline of H. G. Wells: The Superman in the Street* (London, 1922); I. J. C. Brown, *H. G. Wells* (London, 1923); G. A Connes, *Étude sur la pensée de Wells* (Paris, 1926), includes bibliography; F. H. Doughty, *H. G. Wells, Educationist* (London, 1926); H. Belloc, *A Companion to Mr. Wells's "Outline of History"* (London, 1926); H. Belloc, *Mr. Belloc Still Objects to Mr. Wells's "Outline of History"* (London, 1926), by the most acute critic of Wells's humanistic approach; P. Braybrooke, *Some Aspects of H. G. Wells* (London, 1928).

G. West [G. H. Wells], *H. G. Wells: A Sketch for a Portrait* (London, 1930); J. H. S. Rowland, *Talk with H. G. Wells* (London, 1944), with special reference to *Crux*

Ansata; N. C. Nicholson, *H. G. Wells* (London, 1950); V. Brome, *H. G. Wells: A Biography* (London, 1951); P. Quennell, *The Singular Preference: Portraits and Essays* (London, 1952); M. Belgion, *H. G. Wells* (London, 1953); V. Brome, *Six Studies in Quarrelling* (London, 1958), on the literary quarrels of Shaw, Wells, and others.

F. K. Chaplin, *H. G. Wells: An Outline* (London, 1960); W. W. Wagar, *H. G. Wells and the World State* (New Haven, Conn., 1961); B. Bergonzi, *The Early H. G. Wells: A Study of the Scientific Romances* (Manchester, 1961), illuminating and erudite; I. Raknem, *H. G. Wells and His Critics* (Oslo–Bergen, 1962); J. Kagarlitski, *The Life and Thought of H. G. Wells* (London, 1966), trans. from Russian by M. Budberg; R. Costa, *H. G. Wells* (New York, 1967); M. R. Hillegas, *The Future as Nightmare: H. G. Wells and the Anti-Utopians* (New York, 1967); K. B. Newell, *Structure in Four Novels by H. G. Wells* (The Hague–Paris, 1968); L. Dickson, *H. G. Wells: His Turbulent Life and Times* (New York, 1969), frank and entertaining account.

P. Parrinder, *H. G. Wells* (Edinburgh, 1970); W. Bellamy, *The Novels of Wells, Bennett and Galsworthy, 1890–1910* (London, 1971); J.-P. Vernier, *H. G. Wells et son temps* (Paris, 1971); P. Parrinder, ed., *H. G. Wells: The Critical Heritage* (London, 1972), well-chosen selection of reviews of Wells's works as they came out; A. Borrello, *H. G. Wells: Author in Agony* (Carbondale–Edwardsville, Ill., 1972); N. MacKenzie and J. MacKenzie, *The Time Traveller: The Life of H. G. Wells* (London, 1973), the essential full-scale biography; J.-P Vernier, *H. G. Wells at the Turn of the Century: From Science Fiction to Anticipation* (Dagenham, 1973), H. G. Wells Society Occasional Paper no. 1; G. N. Ray, *H. G. Wells and Rebecca West* (London, 1974).

ARNOLD BENNETT
(1867-1931)

Kenneth Young

INTRODUCTION

IT is not every writer who, forty years after his death, is quoted in a company report at an annual shareholders meeting. However, in April 1974, it was thought that the fictional meeting reported in Arnold Bennett's novel *Imperial Palace* (1930) was relevant to the situation of the London Savoy Hotel Limited, and so extracts were read to shareholders. Bennett, despite his inexplicable denials, had based his exhaustively detailed study of a hotel on his observation of the Savoy, from the laundry to the kitchens, the restaurant, the ballroom, and the private suites. He loved deluxe hotels, not least the Savoy, whose menu still faithfully offers "omelette Arnold Bennett" (main constituent: finnan haddie).

Fame, indeed! But, fifty years later, how goes his literary reputation? He wrote almost compulsively, publishing around eighty books of all kinds between the age of thirty and sixty-two when he died; he told friends in 1931 that "I love work . . . the only thing worth living for." One at least of his novels, *The Old Wives' Tale* (1908), is accepted as a modern classic, studied at schools and universities. Not far behind come the *Clayhanger* (1910) series and other fiction set in the Staffordshire of his youth, more particularly in the six (not, as he said, five) small towns where pottery and tableware had been manufactured for a century; thus the area was known as the Potteries.

If popularity is to be judged by paperback reprints, then Bennett is still popular: half a dozen of his novels and short story collections are available, as is his excellent journal (though abridged), which he kept from 1896. In recent years, some of his stories have been turned into plays, films, and television serials. His letters are published in three carefully edited volumes by the Oxford University Press. The literary columns he wrote for the London *Evening Standard* have been reprinted in a well-produced volume. Nor does biographical and critical interest in him flag. A young novelist, Margaret

Drabble, born eight years after his death, published in 1974 a personal, moving tribute to the man and his work; and one of the best biographies of any English writer is Reginald Pound's *Arnold Bennett* (1952).

Critics who do not care for his work always existed. Certainly he is highly criticizable, in the main because his output is extremely uneven and some of his themes are unworthy of his gifts; to other themes his inspiration would not soar. This, however, was not the real burden of complaint by such as Ezra Pound, Wyndham Lewis, and Lytton Strachey, who sneered rather than criticized. His success, his yachts, and his five shillings a word for articles in the press stuck in their maws; unlike some of his detractors, he was a public figure, the cartoonists' joy, the darling of fashionable society. Worse still, his writing, though often subtle, was never obscure; so the young intelligentsia despised him. He was also a thoroughly dangerous pricker of inflated reputations; his writing in A. R. Orage's influential Edwardian periodical *The New Age* tumbled idols and tore up reputations, as one of his biographers puts it. Between 1926 and 1931 in his weekly column in the London *Evening Standard*, he was in Hugh Walpole's words "the only man in my literary lifetime who could really make the fortune of a new book in a night"—or, of course, not. For a long time, critics, with the shining exception of Georges Lafourcade and Frank Swinnerton, blamed him for not being Virginia Woolf, a line she herself took in *Mr. Bennett and Mrs. Brown* (1924); or they suggested that nothing he wrote was any good after he lost touch with his roots in the Potteries. The one criticism was ludicrous, the other untrue.

He was five feet ten inches in height, rather burly, and, writes Swinnerton, "One shoulder was always held stiffly, rather above the other, and he walked slowly and very erect." He brushed his hair up into a quiff; below his moustache were rather prominent teeth. He affected startling bow ties and wore fobs on his watch chain. He had a lifelong paralyzing stammer. He was on terms of friendship with a very broad range of his literary contemporaries—Wells, Conrad, Buchan, Galsworthy, Gide, Walpole, Maugham, Aldous Huxley, Swinnerton. They liked him and he them. Wells wrote that Bennett "radiated and evoked affection to an unusual degree"; and the generally prickly Maugham went further: "It was impossible to know him without liking him." He was a kindly man, generous with pecuniary help to such younger writers as D. H. Lawrence (who in return referred to him as "a pig in clover") and T. S. Eliot when he was starting the famous *Criterion* magazine; he gave his time and advice to such as J. C. Squire, John Middleton Murry, the Sitwells, Noel Coward. He was almost everybody's literary uncle.

Yet in some ways he was a monster—the monster he looked when his face contorted into an almost animal snarl as a result of his stammer. His favorite sister, Tertia, wrote of his shattering silences, his "terrible" moods when she was afraid to go near him or even utter a sound in his presence.

LIFE

IN Bennett's life there was no high—nor even low—drama. It was a Jamesian or Trollopian life—though resembling in detail that of neither—rather than Wellsian or Dickensian. He was born at Shelton near Hanley, Staffordshire, on 27 May 1867, and came of a line of Methodists, such as those pictured in *Anna of the Five Towns* (1902) and *Clayhanger*, men and women cast in the Northern mold who, despite a concealed sentimentality, did not wear their hearts on their sleeves and kept the display of emotion for religious revivalist meetings, often very emotional indeed. His father, Enoch, had been a master potter, then a draper and pawnbroker; by dint of grueling nocturnal study after a long day's work (shops then were open at least twelve hours a day), he qualified as a solicitor at the age of thirty-four, when Arnold was nine. Arnold's mother was the daughter of a tailor in Burslem, one of the Potteries towns, though her grandfather had been a small farmer: by all accounts a pleasant, unassertive woman, dominated by her husband, to whom she bore nine children, three of them dying in infancy. The family situation, poor when Arnold, the eldest, was born, gradually improved, and they moved to better accommodation. Bennett's father was an autocrat, not to say bully, who appears in fictionalized form in his son's novels, as for instance *Clay-*

hanger. Arnold went to two local schools, one of which had as headmaster Horace Byatt, who was later H. G. Wells's headmaster at Midhurst. At Newcastle-under-Lyme grammar school, Arnold passed the Cambridge University local examination, but his father wanted him as his clerk, so he never went to the university.

When he was in his later teens he told his friend George Beardmore: "I'm going to get out of this." By "this" he meant in part the dirt and provincialism of the Potteries. Passing through them by train many years later, he wrote: "The sight of this district gave me a shudder," though in a letter as early as 23 December 1898, he noted "a very real beauty underneath the squalor and ugliness of these industrial districts." He also wanted to escape his father: "I hated the thought of my youth," he wrote, the fact being that he had never been allowed to be young. Escape, but how? One key to the door of his provincial prison was Pitman's shorthand, then rapidly being recognized as an important new office technique. In it he attained a speed of 130 words a minute. He was also writing gossipy notes for the local *Staffordshire Sentinel.* Above all he was reading—Ouida, George Moore, Zola, Balzac, Maupassant, Flaubert, Turgenev, who remained prime influences on his fiction for the rest of his days.

He obtained a shorthand clerkship with a firm of lawyers in London. Thus he escaped and was never again to live in his native county. The pay was poor, and his colleagues thought him "too temperamental" for the law, often gloomy, not easy to get on with. But he found rooms with congenial people, some of whom remained lifelong friends. He began buying and selling second-hand books, and in his landlord's house organized musical evenings. Bennett could play the piano; he could also sing (without a suggestion of a stammer). He practiced his hitherto schoolboy French. He began to meet artists, architects, musicians, and writers. One of them, G. K. Chesterton, remarked about Bennett at this time that he looked like a day-tripper from the provinces who had failed to go back.

His first piece published in London was a parody for the magazine *Tit-Bits;* his second was a short story for the prestigious magazine *The Yellow Book,* in which he appeared alongside Henry James, Sir Edmund Gosse, and A. E. Housman. Nothing could better symbolize his lifelong capacity for succeeding in literary fields poles apart. He worked on his first novel, *A Man from the North:* "the damnedest nerve-shattering experience as ever was." When it came out in 1898, it evoked a letter of praise from Conrad but the profit from it, Bennett said, "exceeded the cost of having it typewritten by the sum of one sovereign."

He obtained the assistant editorship of *Woman,* partly because his father inexplicably bought shares. It was a paper appealing to intelligent female readers; under the pseudonym "Barbara," Bennett did a weekly column of reviews, and this was how he first met H. G. Wells, with whom he was an intimate for the rest of his life. As "Marjorie" he did gossip and wrote "Answers to Correspondents." He said: "I learned a good deal about frocks, household management and especially the secret nature of women." He learned, too, the art of copyediting. Proofreading, however, was not his forte. It was he who, to the delight of Fleet Street, let through "Mr. Y., the rising young politician, made his first pubic speech. . . ."

Soon he progressed to editor of *Woman,* a role he greatly enjoyed, not least in its social aspects. It is the only parallel between his career and Oscar Wilde's. He wrote reviews for the superior journal the *Academy*—two worlds once more. And he played tennis, took up the craze of cycling, painted watercolors, and was a good draftsman. Always, wrote his friend the artist Frederick Marriott, Bennett was "to be found among the pioneers of any new movement." In due course he studied calligraphy, of which his manuscript of *The Old Wives' Tale* is at once a model and a miracle. He found joy in classical music and art galleries.

Once again in 1902 his versatility was demonstrated; he published the finely achieved *Anna of the Five Towns* as well as *The Grand Babylon Hotel,* which would now be called a comedy thriller and was probably influenced by the highly popular works of E. Phillips Oppenheim, a contemporary who, however, began writing ten years earlier than Bennett; Oppenheim, too, achieved the status symbol of owning a yacht.[1] *The Grand Babylon Hotel*—

first of a number of hotels described in Bennett's fiction—was written as a serial; so were other sadly undistinguished books during the next few years: *The Gates of Wrath* (1903), *Teresa of Watling Street* (1904), and *Hugo* (1906).

But the success of these potboilers enabled him to fulfill an ambition: to live in Paris. He took a flat there in 1903, when he was thirty-five. France, of course, was the land of the writers he most admired; Paris, too, was the city of liberation where sexual matters undiscussable in England were discussed— as he put it, *sans gêne*—even between the sexes. To Bennett and some of his contemporaries, Paris had glamour, sophistication, bohemian life; to others it was the sink of vice. Both aspects are portrayed in *The Old Wives' Tale.* Gradually he made friends in the city, not only with writers and artists but with demimondaines vaguely connected with the theater. He proposed to a young American girl and was turned down. He married a Frenchwoman, Marguerite Soulié, in 1907; she had been connected with the theater, though latterly and more successfully with a dress shop. It was in Paris that he conceived and largely wrote what is generally regarded as his masterpiece—*The Old Wives' Tale.* Of his years in Paris he wrote in his journal that he there enjoyed "about as near regular happiness as I am ever likely to get." Yet, as always, he suffered his neuralgia, his glooms, and the desolate feeling of time passing. "Today," he wrote on his birthday, 27 May 1904, "I am thirty-seven. I have lived longer than I shall live." His forecast was correct.

Bennett found no comfort or strength in the Christian religion, and indeed had no time for it. "Christian dogma sticks in my throat," he wrote in reference to Chesterton's Roman Catholicism. To Wells, in April 1905, he confided that "religion is done for—any sort of religion." However, he studied and to some degree practiced the stoicism learned from Marcus Aurelius and Epictetus; he was affected also by the theosophist Annie Besant's *Thought Power* (1901); he studied Christian Science. In later years he found solace in Eastern philosophy and in mystical passages in the New Testament, which, he wrote in his 1929 journal, are "perhaps the deepest source of private comfort."

Some of these influences were not entirely beneficial, since they buttressed an innate obsessional rigidity in his character, and that God-and-man-defying self-reliance that were the obverse of his kindliness and goodness. Epictetus and Annie Besant—strange coupling!—scarcely relaxed him.

---

[1]Born a year earlier than Bennett, Oppenheim, who also came from the Midlands, published his first novel when he was twenty-one and became highly successful before Bennett set pen to paper. His output was even faster than Bennett's—thirteen full-length books, for example, between 1894 and 1898. Oppenheim bought his first country house while Bennett was still in a Paris flat and before long had a villa on the French Riviera. Like Bennett he worked in the Ministry of Information during World War I. Like Bennett he had a taste for luxury. Unlike Bennett one of his lifelong luxuries was the seduction of women. Unlike Bennett he never wrote anything of lasting value, though he lived to be seventy-nine.

"Habit of work," he wrote in his 1908 journal, "is growing on me. I could get into the way of going to my desk as a man goes to whisky or rather to chloral." By October of that year, 1908, he had already written 375,000 words. The pen was his favorite narcotic. He began to boast: "My control over my brain steadily increases." That emotional ebb and flow, which most human beings know, was to him the enemy of concentration, and was "clumsy living." He wrote books with such titles as *The Human Machine* (1908) and *Mental Efficiency* (1912). In the latter he thus sternly harangued his mind: "You are nothing but a piece of machinery; and obey me you *shall.*"

His will, he thought, was all-powerful, but his flesh revolted. For his near-inhuman drive and determination he paid in sleeplessness, exhaustion, headaches, and depressions. One doctor friend had long ago told him, in a phrase then common if imprecise, that "You are one of the most highly-strung men I ever met." Bennett wrote in 1912 that, while his income had risen to £16,000 per annum, it had been a year of "intestinal failure and worldly success." He suffered several bouts of gastroenteritis, or possibly typhoid, long before the attack that killed him. He carried about with him a large collection of pills and nerve tonics. It should be added that he was rather greedy with food, though not with drink; the cocktail habit and "leaning up against bars" he particularly abhorred.

The years in France (1903–1911) were productive. Apart from *The Old Wives' Tale*—which received immediate critical acclaim, though it sold only slowly at first—he brought out a book of good short stories, *The Grim Smile of the Five Towns* (1907). He wrote the novel *Buried Alive* (1908), curious but excellent reading, the impressive *Clayhanger*, some of which was actually written during a stay in Brighton, and the ever-popular *The Card* (1911). He paid a highly profitable visit to the United States, returned to settle in England, bought a yacht, a car, and a country house at Thorpe-le-Soken in Essex. It is interesting that the larger part of his earnings just before the war came not from his novels but from his play *Milestones*, first produced in March 1912. Another play, *The Great Adventure*, a dramatized version of *Buried Alive*, ran to 673 performances in London alone.

He was forty-seven when the war broke out in 1914. In many influential articles he accepted the Allies' aims, as did Wells, while firmly rejecting war as an instrument of policy. He spoke out for soldiers, demanding that they and their dependents be adequately paid: "To say that patriotism should be above money is mere impudence in the mouths of the elderly rich." He toured the trenches and came under fire; he wrote patriotic and cheerful articles about the morale of those manning them. Yet his journal is strangely uncommunicative; he never made fictional use of what he saw at the front, though there are references to wartime London. What he saw, this hypersensitive man, was very far from cheerful; but the recording of the gore and disgust he left to Sassoon and Graves, Remarque and Owen. During the war, he lived regularly in his London clubs to be nearer the center of things and there saw the Zeppelin raids—one was vividly described in *The Pretty Lady* (1918). He sat on local and national committees with many persons well known in London society. It was not until May 1918 that through his friend Lord Beaverbrook—each found the other irresistible—he was given the top administrative post (unpaid) in the Ministry of Information, which Beaverbrook headed. Official records of what Bennett actually did are nonexistent, though he worked an eight-hour day, five days a week. When the war ended he rejected a proffered knighthood, though he would have appreciated some recognition (Companion of Honour or Order of Merit) as a writer; approached again later to accept a knighthood, he retorted, "Give it to Harry Lauder" (the Scottish comedian and singer); "they" did. Official honors were the subject of Bennett's successful comedy play, *The Title* (1918).

A first-rate novel, *Lord Raingo* (1926), came in part out of Bennett's experiences in the ministry, Beaverbrook providing the cabinet detail and without doubt some of the sketch of a character closely resembling Winston Churchill. Two more top-class novels came: *Riceyman Steps* (1923) and *Imperial Palace* (1930); and at least two eminently readable novels, *Lilian* (1922) and *Accident* (1929). His journalism proliferated though his new plays fell flat. He became chairman of a committee that made the Lyric Theater, Hammersmith, one of the theatrical highflyers of the interwar period. He was a director of the left-wing periodical *New Statesman*.

Bennett took no direct part in politics. He had an inbred and stereotyped distrust of Toryism, which, having been brought up a Methodist, he equated with the Church of England and did not understand. Though he had an antipathy to the Liberal leader, Lloyd George, he supported progressive causes such as that of the suffragettes. He wrote forcibly in many a novel about the suppressed lower orders. From the cushion of his own much-enjoyed luxury he confessed: "I am obsessed by the thought that all this comfort, luxury, ostentation, snobbishness and correctness, is founded on a vast injustice to the artisan class." Visualizing Midlands colliers boarding a tram, he says: "Set yourself to wonder why they don't use their brute force to wreck the tramcar. But they don't. They vote, many of them, Tory. Why?" However, unlike his friend Wells and the Fabians, he had no visions of utopias or benevolent dictatorships. Never in his plays or fiction did he, as did Galsworthy, starkly set the haves against the have-nots. Mildly, though probably accurately, he observed that "the uncompromising democratic idea" was felt only by a few thousand men and they were far removed from those they would help, though, he thought, "the abyss must narrow every year." *Clayhanger* vividly presents what Bennett saw as the suffering, and fortitude, of industrial England; and *Imperial Palace* was perhaps intended to picture the idle rich living on top of slaving human beings—though the strengths of the book lie elsewhere.

Bennett's marriage to Marguerite ended in 1921 by separation, not divorce, and his financial settlement for her was very generous—too generous in view of his future commitments and his relative decline in earnings. A year or so later he began a new and happy life with the attractive and intelligent Dorothy Cheston—an actress—by whom he had his only child, a daughter.

How then can it be said that this generous, hard-working man, upright and decent in his life, was a monster? Small matters first: he was a martyr to punctuality and martyrized those nearest and dearest to him who were unpunctual. He was neurotically obsessed by order, precision, and regularity, and was capable of going into aggressive sulks and silences if he thought the papers on his desk had been moved even by a fraction of an inch. He was extremely testy about the failings, real or imagined, of servants. His driving of himself to produce so many thousands of words a year was inhuman, yes, but not only to himself; his wife in particular suffered.

It was in his relations with his wife, Marguerite, that his monstrosity becomes plainest. From the early months of his marriage he went off by himself—he was a travel addict—or with friends, leaving her alone. He did not take her with him on his first triumphant trip to the United States, nor on most of his subsequent peregrinations. She languished at home while he was on his yacht with his friends, including females. At one time, though they were not on bad terms, they communicated by letter while living in the same house; they even had two separate flats in London. Doubtless Marguerite, a strikingly handsome and talented woman, had her faults and irritating foibles, but certainly during the early years of marriage she loved and cherished him and did her best to make him happy. Too often, however, he spurned the proffered marital bed and her company. It was not surprising that, during the war, Marguerite became interested in the young officers entertained at the Bennetts' country house, nor that she should have spent time abroad with a young Frenchman said to have been a neurasthenic war victim.

Yet Bennett was far from being uninterested in women; he was no cryptohomosexual. He was in fact constantly pondering the inner nature of women, as his journals show, and he shows great insight into their ways; witnesses abound—from Anna Tellwright, Hilda Lessways, Constance Baines, to Gracie Savott. He undoubtedly had intimate relations with women before he married, perhaps with those anonymities mentioned in his journals, Chichi, Jeanne, Cosette, May Elliott. Yet he was the antithesis of promiscuous.

The Beardmores, to whom he was related, claimed in *Arnold Bennett in Love*, published in the franker days of 1972 and using newly available material, that "He was dependent upon her [Marguerite] sexually, for constitutionally, out of inbuilt reserve, it is extremely doubtful whether he could have brought himself to undertake a chance liaison." Of course, if their words were carefully chosen, they would not preclude a less evanescent relationship. They note, too, that he was titillated by black lingerie and what he refers to as *nouveautés nocturnes* (novelties for the bedroom). The Beardmores quote from letters between husband and wife shortly before their separation: Marguerite refers to Bennett's "abnormal sexual habits," to which he ungallantly replies: "What about *your* sexual habits? You didn't learn anything from me." He may well have had sexual eccentricities, and in the novels there are hints of perversities. Most of his fiction, including *The Old Wives' Tale*, is drenched in implicit sexual atmosphere; later, in *The Pretty Lady* and *Imperial Palace*, episodes become nearly but not quite explicit.

But in any case it was not promiscuity that proved

the troublesome factor in his marriage. Bennett was simply not made for marital domesticity. His ideal way of living would perhaps have been that of G. J. Hoape—known like Bennett himself by his initials—in *The Pretty Lady*, visiting regularly the respectable courtesan, Christine; or Raingo with Delphine in *Lord Raingo*. Socializing and partygoing were one thing; having around him all the time a woman to whom he had duties and obligations was another. Whatever is the opposite of uxorious, he was. Even his latter happy years with Dorothy Cheston were punctuated by absences, not least when she, being an actress, was on tour; sometimes he grew impatient even with Dorothy, for, as his admiring biographer Margaret Drabble admits, "he was not an easy man to live with." It is an understatement.

In the 1920's Bennett was socially ever more in demand. Those with whom he dined or weekended read like a list compiled from *Debrett* and *Who's Who*. Hostesses such as Lady Colefax and Ottoline Morrell competed for him; his friendship with Beaverbrook grew closer, and with him he visited Berlin and Russia. Russia under the dictatorship of Communists, Bennett concluded, was "an autocracy —that is a tyranny—far more complete than that of the Czars." He was remarkably shrewd in a period when his friend Gide and the Webbs and many others of less integrity were so gullible.

Was Bennett a snob? No; but he was sought out by snobs. They wanted to hook him, not he them. He was famous, perhaps the most famous—certainly the most publicized—literary lion of his time. He enjoyed his fame and his fortune, perhaps even enjoyed seeing a drawing of himself on the sides of London omnibuses advertising his weekly review in the *Evening Standard*. But he made a nice response when the young novelist Louis Golding asked whether he was pleased to be recognized wherever he went. "It *is* rather wonderful," Bennett replied, "in a disgusting sort of way." To a few his flamboyant dressing seemed vulgar; even his friend Wells referred jocularly to his fobs as "Arnold's gastric jewellery." Others thought his retention of his Midlands accent a little ostentatious; and he did rather overdo his "grand hotel," deluxe train, yachting image. Fame brought no cessation of his neuralgia and headaches. He was often depressed, believing that his financial situation was not as secure as it once was. He gave up his yacht—"you can't have a baby and a yacht too," he decided. Yet he went on giving to funds for "starving geniuses," reading their works with enjoyment,

even those of James Joyce, though confessing he could make nothing of Gertrude Stein.

In what proved to be the last few years of his life, Bennett began to behave out of character, not to say eccentrically. He who could not suffer noise and slept badly took, against Dorothy's advice, a flat over Baker Street station in London. Lunching at Hugh Walpole's apartment, he was angered that there was no sweet course, so angered that he left abruptly, took a taxi to the Ritz, had his sweet, and returned to Walpole for coffee. He had, wrote Dorothy, become "adamant and brittle" with a "curious rigidity." His death may be ascribed to defiant obstinacy. One night in Paris, he, so fastidiously careful about health dangers, drank from the tap water, ignoring Dorothy's reproaches. When shortly afterward he did it again in a restaurant—despite the waiter's "ce n'est pas sage, Monsieur," the least Freudian-minded might be forgiven for murmuring "death wish." On his return to London, typhoid was diagnosed and—with Marguerite hanging about in the vestibule and straw strewn outside to deaden the traffic noise—he died on 27 March 1931.

The headlines thundered his death; the obituarists were gracious, even Virginia Woolf, who observed that his passing "leaves me sadder than I should have thought." Rebecca West summed it up: "All London will miss him, and some Londoners will miss him very bitterly. For he abounded in kindliness." Despite his forebodings he left £36,000, securities valued at £7,900, copyrights at £4,225; by 1975 standards, it was probably the equivalent of a quarter of a million pounds.

FICTION

FOR all his versatility in different genres of fiction, most of his novels and short stories bear trademarks recognizably Bennettian. There is the miser as early as *Anna of the Five Towns* and, twenty-one years later, in *Riceyman Steps*. He frequently and at his best analyzes, with curiosity rather than sympathy, the discord between the sexes, why men and women simultaneously hate and love each other. His heroines are either "comfy" like Alice Challice in *Buried Alive* or wayward like Hilda Lessways; his cocottes, of whom he presents quite a few, are on the whole "comfy." Elderly women are either defeated or slyly bossy. His young men are shy and repressed, the middle-aged cautious yet dreaming romantic dreams, and indeed acting them out. Old men are overbearing and distrustful.

His serious novels are slow-moving in action, almost static: Debussy, not Beethoven. This results from his calculated technique: the action of the novel must "spring out of the characters and the characters should spring out of the general environment." To this environment, events and plot are subordinate. Instead, in practice, Bennett concentrates on assembling details observed and chosen to create an impression of verisimilitude, the coherence of a character and background. He belongs in part to what Hardy calls the "life in a plain slice" school. Hence, for instance, his minute description of the diseases—ranging from measles and angina to double pneumonia and cancer—that are to carry off his main characters. And Hardy's criticism is valid: "A story must be worth the telling and a good deal of life is not worth any such thing." At the same time Bennett is deeply concerned with presentation, form, technique. Yet his austere realism and the slow build-up very far from preclude strange twists to stories and surprises for readers; and in his best fiction, this evokes not incredulity but the reader's assent, "Yes, that must have been exactly how it was."

These qualities are little evident in his first not very good novel, *A Man from the North*, about a young clerk from the Potteries failing to write a first novel, despairing, and choosing the quiet, safe suburban life. The hero, as Margaret Drabble points out, is an Arnold Bennett who failed; the Arnold Bennett who wrote it did not. Psychological shock there certainly is in his second novel, *Anna of the Five Towns*, where at the denouement the eponymous heroine realizes that she is in love not with the smooth, competent, kindly Mynors, but with Willie, the naive, lanky, pathetic son of a recently failed pottery maker who had committed suicide—"She had promised to marry Mynors and she married him. Nothing else was possible. . . . She had sucked in with her mother's milk the profound truth that a woman's life is always a renunciation, greater or less." She will face the future "calmly and genially," "be a good wife to the man whom, with all his excellences, she had never loved." She gives £100 to Willie to start a new life in Australia: "This vision of him was her stay." In fact the young man was never heard of by anyone again. And here is the last sentence of Bennett, student of Zola and Maupassant: "The abandoned pitshaft does not deliver up its secret. And

so—the Bank of England is the richer by a hundred pounds unclaimed, and the world the poorer by a simple and meek soul stung to revolt only in its last hour."

There is good stuff in *Anna*—which for some unknown reason Bennett did not later like; he quoted with approval or, at any rate complacency, the comment of a reviewer: "An entirely uninteresting tale about entirely uninteresting people." Even his friend Wells thought it "a photograph a little out of focus." It lacks Bennett's later skills, particularly those deployed in *Clayhanger*, which in one way reworks some of the material—sisterly love, Methodist society, revivalist meetings, paternal tyranny. Yet it is crisp and vivid; set against what was to become in Bennett the almost routine, depressing description of industrial Staffordshire, there is a charmingly evoked idyllic interlude on the Isle of Man, with its splendid "high teas" and comfortable lodgings, where for once two Methodists—Alderman and Mrs. Sutton—are shown as generous and warmhearted people.

"A mere lark," Bennett called *The Grand Babylon Hotel*, published after three weeks' evening work the same year as *Anna*. The "lark" sold 50,000 hardback copies in the author's lifetime. It is thin stuff full of incredible and complicated mysteries, escapes, romance, foreign princes, millionaire Americans. It does, however, introduce the luxury hotel theme he exploited most effectively in *Imperial Palace*. He was fascinated by deluxe hotels, great stores, and ocean liners, the people who worked in them and those who used them. Wealth was an element in their attraction for him, and in *Grand Babylon* we have a "good" character, Prince Aribert, observing "the value and the marvellous power of mere money, of the lucre philosophers pretend to despise and men sell their souls for." Bennett himself, born poor, never doubted the marvelous power of mere money. Hotels, too, evoked in Bennett admiration for the complex organization lying behind them; he organized his best novels no less scrupulously. Strangely enough it was this ill-organized, insubstantial *Grand Babylon* that really put Bennett on the map; it was his first work to be reviewed in the *Times*.

As well as writing serials for the magazines, Bennett was producing short stories collected under such titles as *Tales of the Five Towns* (1905) and *The Grim Smile of the Five Towns*. Most of the stories were not grim at all, but light, amusing, often ingenious if sometimes jocosely narrated. The latter collection contains his masterpiece in this genre, "The Death of Simon Fuge." Here the plot dwindles almost to nothing—merely visits from one house to another—and there are some close parallels, as Drabble points out, with Maupassant's "Le Rosier de Mme. Husson." Yet Bennett's story is no feeble imitation. The narrator, Loring, a porcelain expert on business from the British Museum, is visiting the Potteries for the first time. In the train from London he reads of the death of a distinguished if rather precious painter, Simon Fuge, whose origins were in the Potteries but whose reputation had been largely created in London. This reputation had been based upon his achievements, not only as a painter but as an impulsive amorist and a raconteur, and in particular upon his description of a romantic night in his youth with two beautiful sisters in a boat on a Staffordshire lake. Everything Loring sees as he descends from the train at Knype is, he thinks, "a violent negation" of Simon Fuge, that "entity of rare, fine, exotic sensibilities, that perfectly mad gourmet of sensations." What could such a creature have had to do with the dirt in the air, the brusque porter, the undersized potters, the advertisements for soap, boots, and laxatives?

Loring's host, an architect called Brindley, has heard of Fuge but expects, rightly, that few others in the Potteries have. Brindley, highly knowledgeable, a man of positive views, even eccentric, is "a very tonic dose"; his wife, capable and vivacious. Despite the mud and heavy vapor and glaring furnaces—"I do not think the Five Towns will ever be described: Dante lived too soon"—Loring finds himself among boisterously cultured people with not a pretension among them but with gusto and appetite for the new—and skill: Strauss's *Sinfonia Domestica*, then newly composed, is played from piano parts at sight. They eat with great appetite (including prawns in aspic—"it seemed strange to me to have crossed the desert of pots and cinders in order to encounter prawns in aspic": menus are often lovingly described in Bennett). Loring meets the two subjects of Fuge's romantic anecdotes—one now a barmaid, another the wife of a rich manufacturer who certainly remembers Fuge on the lake: he talked about neckties and his cold feet, and they were back home from the lake by 11:00 P.M.—so much for the all-night outing. Yet neither bathos nor the omnipresent irony are all that "Simon Fuge" offers. Here is realism, but lightly dealt with, an almost delicious confection, and what Bennett is saying with subtlety is that delight in the arts and in living exists among the "pots and cinders," may indeed exist more vigorously and without the pretentiousness of great cities such as London and Paris. He is also doubtless saying that the prophet has no honor in his own country, as was for long Bennett's own experience.

The Old Wives' Tale, unlike most of Bennett's serious fiction, has a theme, ancient, commonplace, and yet new for every human being: time, mutability, and death. It has been expressed throughout history in a variety of ways—in nostalgia for the past, in the Elizabethan horror at the fact of physical dissolution, in the yearning of Wordsworth for the permanence of mountains, and, more pertinently to *The Old Wives' Tale*, in François Villon's *Ballade du temps jadis*, that poignant lament that even the grace and beauty of women should be subject to the destruction of time. The centerpieces of the novel are two sisters whom we first meet as young girls—Constance, pretty, plump, and placid, and Sophia, darkly beautiful, ardent, and wayward. From their home over their parents' flourishing drapery shop in the square of a small Potteries town, we follow them through matrimony, disaster, death of relatives, some happiness, much compromise, to their physical decline and death. The gradual aging of the sisters steals on them and us like a thief in the night, until some external fact, unobtrusively dropped into the narrative, reveals it. The novel's incidents are remarkably varied whether in Bursley, where Constance lives out her life, or in Paris, where Sophia spends thirty years of hers; and the comparatively trivial events of Bursley (though they do include a murder) have no less impact on Constance than have the more dramatic events in the life of Sophia, abandoned in Paris by the faithless, spendthrift Gerald, whom she married after her youthful romantic fixation on him.

Though the two sisters occupy the center of the stage, this book of 200,000 words is thickly peopled with aunts, ancestors, and such apparently immortal persons as the thin, rasping chemist Critchlow, as harsh in voice as in character, lover of disaster, ruthless, a carrion crow. No less interesting is the humble draper's assistant, Samuel Povey, who becomes Constance's loyal husband and modernizes the shop. In Paris, we meet the charming French journalist, Chirac, who is kind to Sophia and then becomes so enamored of her as to appear foolish—and Sophia "could not admire weakness. He had failed in human dignity. And it seemed to her as if she had not previously been quite certain whether she could not love him, but that now she was quite certain." The beautiful Sophia never loves again after her husband leaves her.

Servants, babies, and dogs contribute to the rich variegation of the novel. In the days of which Bennett wrote, even the lower-middle classes could afford to employ what were in reality downtrodden maids-of-all-work. Maggie, big, gawky, charmless, is the most memorable. She has bossed Constance and Sophia as children; she is not badly treated, in the context of the time, but, says Bennett: "She was what was left of a woman after twenty-two years in the cave [the basement kitchen] of a philanthropic family." Suddenly this "dehumanized drudge" shows signs of "capricious individuality" and marries the drunken fish-hawker. Toward the end of the book servants are harder to get and far less servile; such is the "pretty and impudent" Maud, "her gaze cruel, radiant and conquering. . . . She knew she was torturing her old and infirm mistresses. She did not care. Her motto was: War on employers. Get all you can out of them, for they will get all they can out of you. On principle—the sole principle she possessed—she would not stay in a place more than six months."

How good too is Bennett with babies and children. Of him his friend Marriott said, "he loved little children and instantly won their affection." With humor and imagination he takes us inside the little world of Constance's baby boy rolling on a shawl on the hearthrug conducting experiments—"chiefly out of idle amusement"—with a ball, a doll, and Fan the dog:

He rolled with a fearful shock, arms and legs in air, against the mountainous flank of that mammoth Fan, and clutched at Fan's ear. The whole mass of Fan upheaved and vanished from his view, and was instantly forgotten by him. . . . Terrific operations went on over his head. Giants moved to and fro. Great vessels were carried off and great books were brought and deep voices rumbled regularly in the spaces beyond the shawl. But he remained oblivious. . . . An uncomfortable sensation in his stomach disturbed him; he tolerated it for fifty years or so, and then he gave a little cry. Life has resumed its seriousness.

Dogs have a considerable role in several of Bennett's novels, and he has a rare ability to see the world from what is credibly their point of view. Spot, the fox terrier puppy of Constance's later years, has been washed: "He was exquisitely soft to the touch and to himself he was loathsome. His eyes continually peeped forth between corners of the agitated towel, and they were full of inquietude and shame." But it is the chocolate-colored poodle, Fossette, cut in the French style, who has the chief canine role. We meet her first when Sophia has become the superefficient proprietor of the best pension in Paris, and Fossette is a master's last touch to the portrait of Sophia's new persona. To Fossette goes the honor of the final sentences in the book when both her mistress and Constance are dead. By now the poodle, too, is old and lame. While Constance's funeral is taking place she feels upset in her habits and neglected. The maid, however, puts her dinner before her in the usual soup plate. But Fossette, to show her derangement, sniffs and walks away and lies down "with a dog's sigh." Then she reconsiders: "She glanced at the soup plate, and, on the chance that it might after all contain something worth inspection, she awkwardly balanced herself on her old legs and went to it again." So the novel ends; so life goes on.

The *Tale* has its longueurs and its oddities: Why, for example, does the author suddenly become "I" once and once only (in referring to Samuel Povey)? But for all that, it is a true, created work of art. Its general movement, though varied in pace, is majestic and surefooted; book I is the opening statement with Constance and Sophia in their parents' home; book II is the story of Constance after Sophia has eloped; book III is the adventures of Sophia in France; and book IV is the reuniting of the sisters after thirty years—where the modulations are, in musical terms, resolved. In the telling of the story, everything is prepared for; what at first looks like chance is author's cunning. A sentence is apparently casually dropped in, rather as detective story writers scatter clues; but in Bennett the casual sentence heralds a move forward in the tale and thus adds verisimilitude, for the reader says to himself, "Yes, I remember that!"

See how skillfully the elephant (in book I, chapter 4) is used to activate great sections of the book. It is Wakes week (the annual holiday when the factories close) in Bursley; a circus arrives; an elephant goes mad and has to be shot. It is carried away and laid out pending disposal. There is great excitement among the town folk, who cut off tusks, feet, and bits of flesh for souvenirs. Even Mrs. Baines is consumed by curiosity and, accompanied by Constance and Samuel Povey, leaves her husband, who has lain stricken for fourteen years, to the care of Sophia, then in her academic mood, who professes a complete lack of interest in elephants, alive or dead. The husband cannot be left alone since, if he slides down in bed, he cannot right himself. Sophia, however, on her way to his bedroom, glimpses the attractive Gerald Scales entering the shop, leaves her father briefly, and, returning, finds him dead from asphyxia, in one of Bennett's hardest, casually brutal pages, "his head hanging, inverted near the floor . . . his mouth was open, and the tongue protruded between the black, swollen mucous lips; his eyes were prominent and coldly staring." Critchlow, who has regarded the helpless John Baines as "his property, his dearest toy," is called, and harshly he tells Sophia that she has killed her father. Her mother, herself smitten with guilt, sobs: "If it had been anything else but that elephant!" Sophia, afflicted by remorse, gives up her teaching with Miss Chetwynd because her late father had opposed the idea and returns to work in the shop. Thus she has more chance to meet Scales, who is a commercial traveler, and with him in due time she elopes. In Paris, 250 pages later, when Scales has abandoned her, she ponders sadly: "All this because mother and Constance wanted to see the elephant and I had to go into father's room! I should never have caught sight of him from the drawing-room window!" Nor can it be by chance that one of the few things Sophia recalls from her experiences of the siege of Paris by the Prussians is that, so great was the food shortage, the elephants from the zoo were killed and eaten.

How much of the novel's action flows from that elephant! Even Bennett's observations on the disappearance of early Victorian England are evoked by the death of John Baines, itself precipitated by curiosity about the dead elephant. There is considerable correlating of changes in the main characters with changes in the outer world, as in the play *Milestones*. For instance, Victorian parental authority is severely shaken when Sophia refuses to take the spoonful of castor oil her mother prescribes. Since Sophia was born in 1848, this puts her challenge around 1862—rather early, by some social historians' accounts, for young girls to be crossing their parents. Again, toward the end of the book, there is an attempt to federate the Five Towns; seeing this as an attack on the old municipal liberties, Constance struggles from her sickbed to vote. The effort is too much for her and causes her death. There is a parallel here with the death of her husband, Samuel. As she

fights for freedom, so he fought for justice. Back and forth he goes to the prison where his once jolly cousin, Dan the baker and "follower of Pan," is incarcerated for murdering his drunken, dirty wife—Dan, "the man who for thirty years had marshalled all his immense pride to suffer this woman, the jolly man who had laughed through thick and thin." Despite Samuel's efforts, Dan is hanged, and he himself dies of the pneumonia he has neglected in his efforts to prevent what he sees as a great wrong.

In this novel, there is neither melodrama nor sentimentality. The author is scarcely even sympathetic toward his characters, but he is deeply curious about them. He creates them by means of his psychological penetration, his inventiveness: "I never," he once wrote, "see a porter without giving him a hearth and a home and worries and a hasty breakfast." At the same time he is detached. Though he may sometimes be facetious, at least he never overwrites, so that the vivid phrases when they come have a forceful realism. The sickening description of the filthy *cabinets de toilette* in the house of the courtesans rivals Jonathan Swift's "A Beautiful Young Nymph Going to Bed." Striking, too, is Mme. Foucault, the fat and fading courtesan abandoned by her young (and she fears last) lover who falls sobbing in the tawdry room with its red-shaded lamp, "a shapeless mass of lace, frilled linen and corset. . . . Her face . . . was horrible, not a picture but a palette; or like the coloured design of a pavement artist after a heavy shower. . . . Her flesh seemed to be escaping at all ends from a corset strained to the utmost limit. And above her boots—she was still wearing dainty, high-heeled, tightly laced boots—the calves bulged suddenly out." This is the woman first seen by Sophia in all her smartness in a restaurant with an admiring male retinue; the woman who, too, has tended her in her illness; but a woman incurably light and irresponsible, thus differing from Bennett's later courtesans, who tend to have "hearts of gold."

French life, as seen by the disillusioned Sophia, is mainly distasteful, and this offended Bennett's most perceptive critic, Georges Lafourcade, himself French. To Sophia, France is a land of dirt, disorder, and dishonesty, whose people crave for sensation such as seeing a man guillotined. This sight inflames the crowd, among whom Sophia, led by her wanton husband, finds herself, and incites it to orgies both alcoholic and sexual. With what nostalgia does she see at Messrs. Cook's currency exchange "a little knot of English people, with naive, romantic and honest faces, quite different from the faces outside in the street. No corruption in those faces, but a sort of wondering and infantile sincerity, rather out of its element." How admirable now to the once rebellious Sophia appear all the rigid rules she had found so repressive! She thinks of "the honest workmanship, the permanence, the absence of pretence" of Bursley life. But once back in Bursley for good and unable to persuade her sister to quit the grime for the salubrious air of Buxton Spa, she reverses: "She pictured Paris as it would be that very morning—bright, clean, glittering; the neatness of the Rue Lord Byron, and the magnificent slanting splendour of the Champs Elysées. Paris had always seemed beautiful to her; but the life of Paris had not seemed beautiful to her. Yet now it did seem beautiful." She even recalls "a regular, placid beauty in her daily life there." This contrast is a part of Bennett's design that Lafourcade did not understand. The point is that Sophia has a considerable capacity for deceiving herself, just as she had deceived herself over the glamour of Gerald Scales; this capacity, the reader notes, she has in a greater degree than her far less experienced sister. Constance, too, has to the very end a stronger will than her sister; she will not leave her old home, and Sophia will not leave her. There in the square at Bursley they end their days.

To Sophia, Bennett gives the final enunciation of the grand theme of time, mutability, and death. She looks down at the dead and withered body of the once handsome young husband she has not seen for thirty years:

He and she had once loved and burned and quarrelled in the glittering and scornful pride of youth. But time had burned them out. "Yet a little while," she thought, "and I shall be lying on a bed like that. And what shall I have lived for? What is the meaning of it?" The riddle of life itself was killing her, and she seemed to drown in a sea of inexpressible sorrow.

Constance's judgment is simpler: "Well, that is what life is!" Some critics have disputed Constance's view. Henry James asked, "Yes, yes—but is this *all?*" And Walter Allen wrote of this novel: "It misses greatness, if one believes that there is that in man which transcends time." One might certainly make such criticisms of almost every other Bennett novel. Yet surely *The Old Wives' Tale*, though saying "Yes, this *is* all," raises the reader by means of its implacable hard look into what life has been for two women,

and by a sort of catharsis, to a final calm and lofty contemplation of the unchangeable facts of life.

I think we may allow Bennett his mild boast: "The effect as you finish the last page," he wrote in a letter, "is pretty stiff—*when you begin to think things over.*"

In the same year (1908) as *The Old Wives' Tale, Buried Alive* was published. Bennett referred to it as "high class humour." It is not particularly funny; though it contains some farcical scenes, these are not what the reader specially enjoys. The farfetched plot concerns a pathologically shy but very successful painter, Priam Farll, whom not even art dealers have seen, and who seizes the opportunity of the sudden death of his valet, Leek, to swap identities.[2] Leek is buried as Priam Farll in Westminster Abbey (Farll attends the occasion of his own burial and bursts into uncontrollable tears). Farll then meets and marries the woman, Alice Challice, whom Leek had been pursuing through a matrimonial agency. The comfy Alice, shrewd, innocent, patient, and practical, is the great creation of the book: "She was the comfortablest cushion of a creature" and, in the last sentence of the book, Priam travels to "a sweet exile with the enchantress Alice." Previously they lived happily together in a painstakingly accurately depicted Putney of the era. When Farll, driven by the urge to paint that is his raison d'être, starts painting again, Alice humors him and is triumphant at selling his pictures for £5 each to a local shop. She is duly astonished when a sleek art dealer, Mr. Oxford, having recognized the style of Leek as authentically that of Farll, offers him what to Alice are incredible prices. Then comes a court case over Farll's alleged bigamy. Alice performs coolly and devastatingly in the witness box. The case successfully over, the unlikely couple sail off together to Algiers.

Farll is one of the few really credible painters in fiction. A fool, perhaps "but never a fool on canvas. He said everything there and said it to perfection." Bennett had been friendly with real artists in their studios in Paris and was himself a moderately good watercolorist; he as well as Farll "knew—none better—that there is no satisfaction save the satisfaction of fatigue after honest endeavour." Once having accepted the improbabilities, the reader can scarcely not succumb to this unique novel.

Bennett lacked flair in entitling his novels. *Clay-*

---

[2]Bennett may have remembered that J. M. W. Turner lived for ten years under the assumed name of Booth.

hanger, for instance, is not exactly guaranteed to attract the stray reader: its sound is leaden, it breathes the atmosphere of a bog. The book itself seems bowed down beneath its 130,000 words. But the reader who ventures upon it will quickly forget the title, which is the surname of the chief character, Edwin; and, once into it, may find it all too short.

The young Edwin, shy, sensitive, and attracted by architecture and painting, is the son of Darius, another of Bennett's family tyrants. Once more, most of the action takes place in the Potteries, of which we are treated to yet another description. Darius is master of a small printing firm whose work is minutely described. His life has been hard and he insists that Edwin, at first reluctant, follow him in his business, in which Edwin later becomes genuinely interested. The young Edwin is at odds (or would be if he could conquer his weakness and indecision) with almost everyone—his sisters, the artificially emotional Auntie Hamps, himself—and everything. Through him, Bennett directs a blast at the deficiencies of the education of the day, at what he sees as the boredom and hypocrisy of Wesleyan Methodism, about which he is coldly sarcastic, and at the ugliness and provincialism of the Potteries and its class consciousness.

But then *Clayhanger* changes from being a near-sociological tract (with occasional lumps of sheer history) into a psychological novel. Sex, naturally, has been a worry to Edwin, inhibited no less by his nature than by his times and place. Sex—though in no very explicit terms since Bennett wished to sell to a wide public—is presaged in one of the most brilliant chapters Bennett wrote. Called "Free and Easy," it describes "a jollity of the Bursley Mutual Burial Club" (a sardonic touch) at the Dragon pub to which Edwin accompanies his father's giant chief compositor, Big James. Among the entertainments is Florence, the clog dancer with short red-and-black velvet skirts and "complete visibility of her rounded calves." As her finale she throws one foot as high as her head: "Edwin was staggered. The blood swept into his face, a hot tide."

Sexual relations—or relations between the sexes—are the main subject of *Clayhanger* and of its two sequels, *Hilda Lessways* (1911) and especially *These Twain* (1916). When Edwin first meets Hilda, he thinks her rather abrupt and unfeminine, though he is struck by her intelligence and strong personality and that kind of waywardness the young Sophia had. Then he falls in love with her despite (or

because of) her somewhat mysterious background, and the fact that she "had unfathomable grottoes in her soul." Unfathomable indeed! For, after exchanging love letters and tokens of affection, Edwin learns that Hilda has married another man (the how and why is explained in *Hilda Lessways*). She and her relationship with Edwin are full of swiftly changing contradictions: "From one extreme he flew to the other" in his view of her.

In the third of the trilogy, *These Twain*, Bennett shows with great skill the progression of domestic antagonism, and how each incident of estrangement is ended by a kiss. This divorce of sexual love from differences of opinion and downright quarreling baffles Edwin: "The heat of their kisses had not cooled; but to him at any rate the kisses often seemed intensely illogical . . . he had not yet begun to perceive that those kisses were the only true logic of their joint career." So sexual love smooths the way from differences to compromises; the trilogy admirably delineates the subtle interweaving not so much of love and hate as of passion and irritation.

Bennett had not studied Stendhal in vain. "Some women," says Gerald in *The Old Wives' Tale*, "only enjoy themselves when they're terrified." From masochism Bennett turns in *Clayhanger* to sadism:

As he looked at the wet eyes and shaken bosom of Hilda Cannon, he was aware of acute joy. Exquisite moment! Damn her! He could have taken her and beaten her in his sudden passion—a passion not of revenge, not of punishment! He could have made her scream with the pain that his love would inflict.

(bk. IV, ch. 5)

Such observations were uncommon in popular English fiction of that day. *Clayhanger* and its sequels are, however, just as much about a shy young man who becomes a success in business and of a woman, particularly in *Hilda Lessways*, who, like Wells's *Ann Veronica*, makes her own way in the wider world then still largely reserved for men.

Bennett had no very high opinion of *The Card*: "Stodgy, no real distinction of any sort, but well invented and done up to the knocker, technically," he wrote in his journal; yet it is today the Bennett story best known to the wider public. The novel narrates the rise of Denry Machin from rent collector in the Five Towns to fortune and high municipal honors. He is joker, opportunist, not invariably truthful (though he never tells lies "save in the greatest crises"), a buccaneer with his heart in the right place.

As Lafourcade noted, however, Denry is not naturally audacious; he is fundamentally shy. But he has an iron will that triumphs and turns him into a local legend. The narrative goes with great verve and is written with a curious double irony—two tongues in cheek. It is full of ingenious and comic invention, as in the incident when Denry's mule drawing the carriage containing the duchess of Chell refuses to move at the sight of squads of policemen drawn up to welcome their distinguished visitor. There are some amusing descriptions; for example, of the recently knighted local philanthropist: "Even before the bestowal of the knighthood his sense of humour had been deficient and immediately afterwards it had vanished entirely. Indeed, he did not miss it." Bennett creates some well-observed secondary characters, such as the clerk, Penkethman, and Denry's masterful and obstinate mother. Bennett, seeing the popularity of *The Card*, continued Denry's story in *The Regent* (1913), in which he becomes a London theatrical impresario; it lacks some of the bounce and brio of *The Card* but it is entertaining enough.

Though Bennett wrote a great deal during the 1914–1918 war, not until *The Pretty Lady* did he publish a novel of note. This was yet another departure, and it had successors in the Bennett canon. Since the novel largely concerns a French cocotte in wartime London, it was described in the press correctly as pornographic (writing about a harlot) but incorrectly as unsavory, wallowing in the slime of sensuality, decadent, and so on. This ensured excellent sales—20,000 in the first month. Bennett had always been intrigued by the intimacies of sex, as was noted above. Professional sex-providers also interested him. In his sketches in *Paris Nights* (1913) he observes that "some of the odalisques are beautiful. Fine women in the sight of heaven! They too are experts with the preoccupation of experts, they are at work and this is the battle of life. They inspire respect." This was not prurience, but rather that admiration for professionalism that he had earlier shown in describing the work of skilled printers and potters. At the same time, with his keen journalistic nose, he had sniffed out that the war, with its horrors and sudden death, had loosened restraints. As Christine, heroine of *The Pretty Lady*, says: "The war in London has led to the discovery that men have desires." Needless perhaps to say, Bennett treated the physical side of Christine's profession discreetly though with calm realism, as in the description of the five great plagues to which she and her colleagues are subject. Physical sex comes through atmospherically, not explicitly.

Bennett did not need or want as an artist the crude explicitness permitted (indeed demanded) in the 1980's; he was far from wishing to imitate the semi-mystical and essentially asexual frenzies described by his younger contemporary D. H. Lawrence. Nor was Bennett especially influenced (whatever that means) by Edmond and Jules de Goncourt's *La Fille Elisa*, Balzac's *Grandeurs et misères des courtisanes*, or Zola's *Nana*. He simply wanted to write about the gamut of relationships between men and women. In *The Pretty Lady* he writes not only about the religious cocotte Christine but also about the sexual natures of the war widow, Concepcion, and the aristocratic, sensation-seeking, neurotic Lady Queenie. Christine's life is presented as healthy, Queenie's as morbid. The hero (if such he is) of the book is one of Christine's clients, G. J. Hoape, the well-to-do, intelligent, self-possessed bachelor. Jealousy of Christine leads him to the wrong conclusion about her, as is revealed in the last few pages. The ending is a surprise, but this is no spurious denouement; the reader will admit that Bennett has more than adequately prepared it, far more adequately perhaps than he had done in the shock ending of *Anna of the Five Towns* sixteen years earlier. The war as reflected in London is a big element in *The Pretty Lady*—the drunken officer she succors, the leave train departing, the vividly pictured air raid, even the wartime committee meetings. The war is thought of by G. J. Hoape as "a vast dark moving entity." The novel does not quite cohere, yet even these loose ends convey the disjointedness of life in wartime London.

Lilian, the story of a poor but pretty young middle-class typist who runs away to the south of France with her middle-aged employer, is a sort of bridge to such later, better works as *Lord Raingo* and *Imperial Palace*. After the workaday early part, Bennett launches into the world of luxury hotels, dancing, cards, fine food, deluxe trains—the world of *Imperial Palace*. The hero, Felix, is a stage along the road from Hoape to Raingo. In a small role, there is a kindly French prostitute. In a sense the poor but well-brought-up Lilian herself has to choose, as Bennett points out, between starvation and prostitution; in becoming Felix's mistress she chooses what might be regarded as the latter. However, when she is pregnant, Felix marries her but shortly dies from pneumonia. Lilian, now a rich widow, returns to take over her husband's home from his spinster sister—and there in his bedroom that she has never seen before, she suddenly feels the damped-down emotion of her loss. She reacts in a strange, yet markedly Bennettian, way. She picks up one of her husband's neckties, "bit it passionately, voluptuously; the feel of the woven stuff thrilled her. . . . Lilian sobbed like a child." Yet Lilian is never less than "a nice girl" (she is shocked at being taken as one of "us girls" by the prostitute). Matter-of-factness, irony, even gentle cynicism—and a certain carelessness—imbue the book. I do not think Bennett was seeking to emulate the then popular problem novels and plays of which Galsworthy's are the best examples; but there *is* a problem raised in *Lilian*—how wise is it for a pretty young girl to marry a middle-aged man? He can indeed provide a happier life, exercise a more beneficial influence, if he is well disposed, than most impecunious young men of her own age—and Lilian is delighted to be seen dancing with Felix; but sooner rather than later she is likely to be a heartbroken, still youngish widow. At least she will be well off. The problem perhaps reflects Bennett's own.

Mr. Prohack, also published in 1922, is about a senior civil servant who has saved the treasury millions during the war while his own income has remained stationary. He is left a large legacy by a war profiteer; multiplies it by investment; and suffers from boredom and nervous ailments because he cannot find anything satisfying on which to spend his money. Eventually, he buys a papermaking business. The novel is about the rich and riches, and it is not very good; yet Prohack himself—kindly, humorous, epigrammatic, and resigned—is as interesting a character as any in Bennett's minor novels.

The stream of minor, sometimes trivial, novels and stories did not cease, but they were interrupted in the mid-1920's by three works of higher caliber. The first was *Riceyman Steps,* which was hailed on all sides as a major creation. Conrad remarked, "This is Bennett triumphant"; Wells, "A great book . . . as good as or better than *The Old Wives' Tale*"; and for it Bennett received the first literary prize of his career, the James Tait Black. It must, however, be said at the outset that *Riceyman Steps* is, overall, as gloomy as Strindberg and set entirely in a grimy bookseller's shop in Clerkenwell, one of the dingiest areas in London. It is a book entirely without hope; but it also lacks the perspective that in *The Old Wives' Tale,* at the end, after all the sadness, lifts the reader to a loftier plane.

Few readers can want to return, at any rate quickly, to a second reading of *Riceyman Steps;* it may be admired, it can scarcely be loved. Of a story line there is even less trace than usual in Bennett's serious novels. All that happens, George Moore said, is that "a bookseller crosses the road to get married." This is not quite fair; nevertheless the novel has, to an even greater degree than elsewhere, that motionlessness noted previously. As Lafourcade puts it, Bennett here carried his technique—of the casual mention of a fact that subsequently becomes an important clue—to extremes: "One feels that if the author were put on his mettle, he could write half a dozen chapters, perhaps half a dozen novels, merely to explain why one of his heroes blew his nose with his left hand, or had a wart over his right eye."

Earlforward, the antiquarian bookseller, looked after by a good-hearted, buxom young charwoman, Elsie, is a miser. He marries a widow, Violet, who has been left some money and who appears at least thrifty. Both subsequently die, in part at least because of Earlforward's meanness. A miser—yes, but Earlforward is a true original. He is not a Darius; nor is he a Shylock, Volpone, or Harpagon. He is a kind, patient, bland, and rather lazy man; with a little more effort he could make much more money. Moreover, he genuinely and sensually loves his Violet. Yet, as she sees it, "he was in love with her, but he was more in love with his grand passion and vice, which alone had power over him and of which he, the bland tyrant over all else, was the slave." He is a Jekyll-and-Hyde figure, a basically amiable man seized by a dreadful psychological disease, just as cancer physically seizes him in the end. Bennett rather overdoes Earlforward's actual worship of real gold: "'Nothing like it!' he said blandly, running his fingers through the sovereigns that tinkled with elfin music." This somewhat artificial, Jonsonian image, however, triggers off Violet's more subtle reactions: "She was astounded, frightened, ravished. . . . He was a superman, the most mysterious of supermen." Thinking of the magic gold she calls him importunately to bed; he obeys. There Bennett's psychological penetration is superb; but when in a further attempt to stress the nature of Earlforward's disease, he has him inquire of the man in charge of the vacuum-cleaning machines: "Do you sell the dirt? Do you get anything for it?" the effect is merely ludicrous.

Although Violet has some resemblance to Alice Challice, she is not much developed; her main function is to act as a catalyst. Nevertheless, like some other Bennett women, she is shown as loving and hating simultaneously: "She hated him; her resentment against him was very keen, and yet she wanted to fondle him, physically and spiritually." A subtler portrait is that of Elsie, the unselfish young char, a war widow of twenty-three who is both loyal and shy; yet in her hunger she can steal; though chaste, she is sensuous, and will take matters into her own hands when she thinks fit, not least when a former admirer, Joe, turns up, ill and unkempt. But Elsie is insufficient to alleviate the gloom that in the end permeates the novel and is what we remember of it.

Curiously enough, *Lord Raingo*, in which the dying of the eponymous hero is accorded some 200 pages, is not a gloomy book, and it is far fuller of incident than its predecessor. The basic story, however, is not complicated. Sam Raingo, millionaire and once an undistinguished member of Parliament, is called by the wartime prime minister and his boyhood friend, Andy Clyth, to be minister of records (a cover name for propaganda) toward the end of World War I. He accepts—so long as he is given a title and, because of his health, is not required to fight elections and cosset constituents. Part of the novel is devoted to the political maneuverings that persist in governments, however huge the front-line casualties become. The maneuverings wash around Sam himself, because he is popular and because he has renounced any salary; but he stoutly defeats them. Sam, like Andy Clyth, is a master of what Bennett calls "chicane"; a shrewd man who sees with a sure instinct the inner meaning of acts and remarks. The novel contains much not very covert biography: Clyth with his ruthless subtlety and his Celtic "poetry" is Lloyd George; his personal secretary, Rosie Packer, who "rules the Empire," is Frances Stevenson, later Countess Lloyd George. The belligerent minister of munitions, Tom Hogarth, was modeled on Winston Churchill (as the latter insouciantly recognized). Doubtless other of the novel's ministers are near-portraits of real persons; much of Bennett's information about the procedures involved in becoming a lord and about ministerial function came from his friend Lord Beaverbrook. Bennett is closer here than anywhere to the roman à clef. Raingo himself has certain of Bennett's characteristics—his passion for punctuality and his gaily colored bow ties (which are nearly Raingo's downfall); Bennett did briefly become nonministerial head of the Ministry of Information. There is, however, much in Raingo, as in G. J. Hoape and Felix, that is clearly not Bennett.

Raingo loves being a lord, loves running—and efficiently—a department, loves being recognized, not least by the press. Once more, Bennett scatters clues. In the novel's beginning is foreshadowed Raingo's end. The reader is casually warned that Raingo has a hypochondriac mania for doctors. The fact is, however, that this middle-aged, successful, comfortable man really does have a dubious heart, the result of infantile rheumatic fever. We wonder uneasily whether he is going to die; we are never quite sure that he will until he does. His prolonged illness, its phases and treatments so minutely described, need not necessarily be fatal. Incidentally, Bennett must surely have recalled this fictional deathbed when he himself lay ill for some weeks preceding his death in 1931; his death, too, was due to "a bit of carelessness" as was Raingo's; doubtless, too, he exhibited all the sick Raingo's suspiciousness.

Raingo has a wife, Adela, another original creation. She is vague, self-absorbed, upper-class ("she had race"), tepid, nonchalant—so nonchalant indeed that in moments of marital intimacy, she makes such remarks as "I wonder where I left my umbrella this afternoon." They have one son, a prisoner of war. Not surprisingly, Raingo has a mistress, Delphine, a young woman of voluptuous charms; not a courtesan but a poor, kind girl whom he rescued from poverty. But, like G. J. Hoape, he is suspicious of her; suspicion—or insight—plays a considerable part in his life. Though Delphine is always loving toward him, he thinks she is playing him false. Bennett cleverly works up the tension until at last Raingo catches sight of her with a young officer at the Savoy. She was once engaged to the young man and broke it off. By accident she meets him again when he is on leave from the western front. Naturally she is kind to him, though as her sister, Gwen, a pretty bus conductress, explains, kind "in a nice way if you knows what I mean. Oh yes, it was all *right*." Delphine, however, is tormented by doubt: he is at the front; ought she not to stick by him even though she does not care for him? On top of all that, after the death of Raingo's wife in a car accident, Raingo proposes marriage to her, and this exacerbates her mental torment. She disappears. It is the sick Raingo who spots in a small newspaper paragraph the report of a nameless girl found dead below the cliffs at Brighton; with his unerring instinct he knows it is she, and she it is. Raingo has loved Delphine; he thinks of "enchanted moments" with her; yet in his last minutes of life, "He murmured appealingly in the final confusion of his mind: 'Adela!' His jaw fell." Adela is his dead wife's name. As with the shock surprises at the end of *Anna of the Five Towns* and of *The Pretty Lady*, the reader accepts the shock, not as an O. Henry trick, but as a revelation of a psychological truth.

Raingo is immensely self-conscious, self-analytical, and no less controlled than his author; capable of malice, even of cynicism, but in nonaggressive ways; a man whose "sturdy rationalism" could admit that "Rationalism was as dogmatic as mysticism and superstition." And he is surrounded by cleverly delineated characters—Trumbull, Mrs. Blacklow (who is pregnant two years after her husband became a prisoner of war), the pompous Timmerson, and the general who seeks to intrigue against Raingo: thumbnail sketches, but vivid. Add to them the idiosyncratic physician, the subtly differentiated nurses, and Mayden, Raingo's confidant who in peacetime runs a chain of hotels, in whom perhaps we have a preliminary sketch of Evelyn Orcham, managing director of *Imperial Palace*.

The novel has flaws: Would Delphine be so tortured by the choice before her that she would commit suicide? Would there be an immediate affinity between Geoffrey Raingo, the ex-POW son of Raingo, and Gwen, sister of Delphine? Is there not too much coincidence (too much at any rate for fiction) in Geoffrey, twisted with neurosis, arriving home as his mother's funeral cortège passes by? These are small matters: Lafourcade is surely right in ranking *Lord Raingo* "immediately below the masterpieces."

Imperial Palace is the longest—243,000 words—and last of Bennett's novels, save for the unfinished *A Dream of Destiny* (1932). It is almost but not quite a "documentary," exposing to the reader in technical detail—as Bennett had done with a draper's shop and a printing works—every corner of the workings and organization of the grand hotel, as typical a creation of late-Victorian times as the luxury liner and the Pullman carriage. Before the grand hotel existed, the titled and rich stayed with a retinue of servants in hired villas or the palaces of friends; the discriminating middle class preferred "lodgings." These grand hotels were possibly temporary phenomena; today they are used mainly by rich actors and passing expense-account businessmen. They had always fascinated Bennett, who, when young, once wrote that his secret ambition had been to be the manager of a grand hotel. Today surely an inconceivable ambition for such as Bennett! Then, however, for an impecurious young man from the Potteries who did not believe in God, it was the temple of his substitute

God, luxury, to which he could aspire if only as an acolyte. Of course to write a novel about such an obsession required a rationale: he provided it. Observing that his earlier *Grand Babylon Hotel* was a mere lark, he went on (in his journal for 25 September 1929): "The big *hotel de luxe* is a very serious organization; it is in my opinion a unique subject for a serious novel; it is stuffed with human nature of extremely various kinds. The subject is characteristic of the age; it is as modern as the morning's milk; it is tremendous and worthy of tremendous handling."

Lafourcade claims that the hotel itself, redolent to Bennett of romance and beauty and superb intricate organization, is the real hero of the novel. This is not true; a novel cannot exist without human beings (Virginia Woolf's *The Waves* is scarcely a novel), and only a specialist researcher would read *Imperial Palace* to find out how the London Savoy was run in the 1920's. Though Bennett claims that the novel has "eighty-five speaking characters" (the figure has been disputed), there are really only three of great account. There is the precise, reserved, superefficient, long-widowed, and celibate Evelyn Orcham, managing director of the Imperial Palace. The second is Gracie Savott, daughter of a millionaire, a sophisticated, talented, untidy, capricious, sensation-seeking woman of the 1920's, akin to Lady Queenie and, in a different context, Hilda Lessways and to society women of the day. Gracie, for example, "adores" something because it is so awful; this "liking for ugliness," morbidity of taste, was part of the period that went in for primitive carvings and such perverseness of conduct as portrayed by Aldous Huxley and in D. H. Lawrence's *Women in Love*. Nor can Bennett forbear the social comment on Gracie: "Idle, luxurious, rich, but a masterpiece! Maintained in splendour by the highly skilled and expensive labour of others, materially useless to society, she yet justified herself by her mere appearance. And she knew it, and her conscience was clear."

Gracie determines to seduce Evelyn, mainly because she only wants somebody who seems not especially to want her. She succeeds—in one of those ghastly Parisian furnished flats *de convenance* such as Bennett had portrayed in *The Old Wives' Tale*—and once more there are hints of perversities. When the affair is ended by Gracie, Evelyn ponders:

A whip might keep her in order. . . . What I ought to do is to go back with a cane and rip everything off her, and give her a hiding until she fainted away, and then, when she came to, make her kneel down and beg my pardon for being thrashed.

(ch. 66)

The seduction scenes in Paris are demure by present-day criteria, yet in them Bennett went further than ever before—he knew precisely what the 1920's would tolerate—with talk of "sumptuous breasts," kissing "her open mouth," shameless visions in the bath, Gracie's appearances in knickers and camisole only. And the plain statement that she was not a virgin. The actual sexual encounters are, however, done by hint, not description. Nevertheless, Bennett was kicking over the traces: he even briefly introduces two lesbians fondling each other at a night club. There are other themes in the Evelyn–Gracie relationship: the struggle for mastery, the curious playing at homemaking.

The third personage of moment is Violet Powler, whom Evelyn transfers from the hotel laundry to the post of head housekeeper. She is a sensible, even prim girl who deals admirably with the staff, not least with one of the hotel managers; by contrast, with Gracie she is more than a little dull and submissive. Yet Evelyn comes to see her as "all woman . . . challenging and very feminine." They have a tiff, but this only increases her "passion for the welfare and efficiency of the Palace." She has determination (she saves the grill-room manager who absented himself for some days), and she is ladylike (Evelyn is agreeably assured by a "gentleman"), intelligent without education, energetic. So he marries her. She is in fact a superior Alice Challice of Buried Alive.

The other characters are foils either to the hotel theme or less often to the romantic theme: old Dennis Dover, the chairman of the hotel group, is sketched entertainingly enough, as are Long Sam the doorman, Immerson the publicity agent, and of course the Napoleonic millionaire, father of Grace, Sir Henry Savott, who precipitates the hotel merger that is an important part of the novel's action. With him, Evelyn has a revealing conversation about underdogs. Says Evelyn: "When I think for instance of you in your suite, or me here, and then of some of the fellows and girls down in the basements, I get a sort of notion that there must be something wrong somewhere." Here Bennett is being haunted by his various Maggies in their kitchen "caves." In the past he had seen no justification for their sordid servitude, but now Savott puts some points that

Evelyn (and Bennett) seems to accept. Savott says: "When there are no underdogs the world will have to come to an end, because there won't be anything to improve. Perfection's another name for death, isn't it?" Machinery is replacing the underdog, doing away with dirty, greasy, soul-destroying labor. True, the former bottle washers now unemployed and their families may die of starvation and will continue to do so for a generation or two. But, as Savott says in chapter 24, "there is a chance that mass production and machinery will abolish the underdog altogether. There's no other chance. So in the sacred cause of social progress I am determined to bear with fortitude the present and future misfortunes of your underdogs."

Imperial Palace, which incidentally started a fashion that continues to this day for novels set in hotels, is not a great work; it has dull passages and the hotel details may bore some readers; there are inconsistencies of style; and the narrative tails away. Yet as a whole it remains "a good read."

PLAYS

THROUGHOUT his writing life, Bennett toyed with the theater; toyed is the word, for he seldom spent more than three weeks on writing a play. He wrote twenty or so, of which four are adaptations of his novels. Unlike Henry James, however, he did have a few genuine successes; from Milestones, written in collaboration with Edward Knoblock, he made real money. All his plays, as Lafourcade acutely discerned, were by-products of his fictional writing.

What the Public Wants (1909) is a lively commentary on the sensational press, then in its early days, and on the avant-garde theater. It poses the far from new conflict between good taste and giving the public what it wants, between idealism and making money; and comes to no profound conclusion. The central figure, the millionaire newspaper proprietor Sir Charles Worgan, loses his fiancée but is far from losing the battle. The play is a comedy with just a touch of bitterness here and there, with irony and even epigrams. The newspaper office scenes and particularly Worgan's bright ideas for stimulating sales have lost none of their contemporaneity. He himself is ruthless, but not without a kindly heart; nor is he based at first hand on any newspaper mogul of the day, since Bennett at that time had never met one.

Part of the play is set in Bursley—where else?—whence the Worgan family comes. Sir Charles's brother, Francis, the wanderer who becomes a drama critic, observes of his critic colleagues: "We've almost all of us come from the provinces, and we try to forget it. . . . We don't even *read* about the provinces, except occasionally in *Bradshaw*."[3]

Milestones covers in three acts the fortunes of a family from 1860 to 1912 and is mainly about what is now called the generation gap—or, like *The Old Wives' Tale*, about growing old, and, subtly observed, the change it makes in character. When it was first performed, on 5 March 1912, it had a cast which, later at any rate, would have been regarded as glittering, including—and here too is a generation gap for the modern reader—such about-to-be celebrities as Mary Jerrold, Lionel Atwill, Owen Nares, and Gladys Cooper. The play, if somber at heart, is often flippant, witty, and amusing. Today it has that sort of period flavor—typists and ironclad ships, the vogue for Ouida and the bicycle were then innovations—that would make it a successful revival on television or the stage; and it is linked with national events of the time, a conception later used by Noel Coward in *Cavalcade*.

The third play, worth at least a reading, is *The Title*. It also is in part concerned with newspapers, and it has plenty of amusing dialogue about the young daughter of the wartime treasury director of accounts. Under the guise of writing cookery articles, she is really the trenchant antigovernment columnist Sampson Straight, who has recently attacked the system of honors.[4] Her mother is not without an epigrammatic gift: "I stand in queues for hours because my servants won't—it's the latest form of democracy." However, the play really revolves round the question of honors, doubtless put into Bennett's mind by the questionable behavior of the then prime minister, Lloyd George, though the honors scandal came later. The treasury director, Culver, has been offered a baronetcy. His view, however, is that governments offer honors to survive, to "placate certain interests, influence votes and obtain secret funds. . . . Honours are given to save the life of the Government." Of course the list must be skillfully done: "with about five or six de-cent names you can produce the illusion that after all the List is really rather good." He wants no part of it. The drama of *The Title* amounts to this: Culver's wife has wondered how anyone could accept a title. Immediately when it is offered to her husband, she changes her mind. He must accept. There follows an endearing scene of caresses, intramarital diplomatic finessing, then wifely fury, separate rooms: the wife wins—only to face the opposition of her children. Events become complex, even farcical; but at least they evoke two political bon mots. Says Mrs. Culver: "I consider all politics extremely silly. There never were any in my family, nor in your father's." Her husband says with fine cynicism: "No enlightened and patriotic person wants the Government to fall. All enlightened and patriotic persons want the Government to be afraid of falling. There you have the whole of war politics in a nutshell."

Not many critics would claim that, standing alone, Bennett's plays will get more than a few lines in theatrical history. As part of his opus they are worth note—and are never less than readable.

OTHER WRITINGS

There is a whole group of Bennett's nonfictional writings that the reader loses nothing by ignoring. Such are, for instance, *How to Live on 24 Hours a Day* (1908) and *Self and Self-Management* (1918). In them are trumpeted forth such bombast as "Big, strong vital thinking is contained in these pages—thoughts that make a man reach up to his highest self." Here Bennett speaks like a mixture of Émile Coué and Samuel Smiles, a gospeler of the self. Elsewhere in his collections of articles his novelistic insight reasserts itself: he is sensible enough on such matters as relations between men and women—*The Plain Man and His Wife* (1913) is quite excellent—though too frequently he falls into platitude. His travel sketches, such as *Paris Nights* and *Mediterranean Scenes* (1928), are bright and fresh, and such early books as *Journalism for Women* (1898) are full of genuinely practical advice; so is the didactic manual *How to Become an Author* (1903).

Some of Bennett's nonfictional by-products are too enjoyable to skip: the autobiographical *The Truth About an Author* (1903), the journals, and the letters. The first of these is highly entertaining and so down-to-earth as to have caused offense, not indeed

---

[3]*Bradshaw's Railway Almanack*, a standard railway timetable of the period.

[4]There was a scandal at that time over the practice of negotiating titles of nobility in exchange for cash given to party funds or charitable causes.

to the generality of readers, but to those critics of the day—they are still about—who sought to appear omniscient, leaning over the gold bar of heaven to address the mere mortals below. They would never have exposed themselves as did Bennett, revealing his reaction to the early spurning of his freelancing efforts: "I used to retire to my room with rejected stuff as impassive as a wounded Indian. . . . Mere vanity always did and always will prevent me from acknowledging a reverse at the moment: not until I have retrieved my position can I refer to my discomfiture." Worse was the awful truth he vouchsafed about reviewing: how neither he nor any competent reviewer needs to read a book all through to know its quality, and in any case regular reviewers are paid insufficiently to make it worthwhile. Bennett writes that he gave as much brainpower and time as an article demanded—"up to the limit of his pay in terms of hours at ten shillings apiece. But each year I raise my price per hour." Naturally, if he is writing purely for the advancement of his artistic reputation, he ignores finance and does it for "glory alone." He is just as open about his motive in writing his serial novels, some, though not all, of which are painfully third rate. He began by being determined to keep the "novel-form unsullied for the pure exercise of the artist in me." This went by the board "the instant I saw a chance of earning the money of shame." Such bravado did not please all his professional readers.

Bennett's journals, at least in early days when he had only aspiration and little idea of publication, are less bold-as-brass; he confesses to doubting whether he could write at all. He feels in 1896 his inferiority to, as it happens, J. M. Barrie, "a lack of bigness, and a presence of certain littlenesses." The journals, however, are among his very best productions; when he died they contained about one million words of which only 400,000 have been printed, partly because of possible offense, legal and otherwise, to some then still alive. A fuller version is now called for. The journals are full of his ravening curiosity about people and places; about himself and his neuralgia, migraines, and sleeplessness, his pleasure in clothes and new books; about his work as *Woman* editor; about his reading, which, ranging from Beaumont and Fletcher to Cellini and most of the nineteenth-century French novelists, was clearly wider in scope than he afterward professed; and about the inspiration and birth of his work—these sections are worthy to be compared with the notebooks of Henry James.

Literary historians will always study the journals for Bennett's impressions of Wells, Conrad, Maugham, Frank Harris, George Gissing, James, G. B. Shaw, Walpole, and for the whole ambience of the literary world of his day. Social historians will consult them for Bennett's impressions of, for example, hotels (the Strand Palace in 1909 cost 10s. 6d. a day for bed and all meals); the risqué comedienne Marie Lloyd; John Burns, the socialist; and for such unlikely remarks, when war broke out in 1914, as: "I agree that Russia is the real enemy, and not Germany." Later came references to Beaverbrook, Diana Manners (later Cooper), and all the notabilities of the postwar social whirl and political worlds. Good gossip, to put it at its lowest.

Bennett in his last five years was best known to the English world at large as a weekly contributor on literary subjects to the London *Evening Standard,* which on Thursdays, when his column appeared, actually rose in circulation. Most of these pieces were not strictly reviews of new books.[5] Years before, between 1908 and 1911, he had had a practice run for this kind of thing in A. R. Orage's *New Age;* a selection of these contributions had been collected in *Books and Persons* (1917). There, with discriminating gusto, he introduced the English public at large to Turgenev, Dostoyevsky, and Chekhov. He also delivered himself of the observation that "art is not the whole of life, and to adore musical comedy is not a crime." It was typical of his unstuffy approach; it ensured that he would be denigrated by the monomaniac littérateurs of his day.

Just as he educated the Edwardian public to appreciate previously unknown literary delights, so in his *Standard* column fifteen years later he spotted and made irresistible such unknowns as William Faulkner, Ernest Hemingway, Graham Greene, Evelyn Waugh, Henry Williamson, and Ivy Compton-Burnett. All proved worthy of the early boost Bennett gave them. He made best sellers of Lion Feuchtwanger's *Jew Süss* and Axel Munthe's *The Story of San Michele*—and some others that are properly forgotten now. He put his oar in on such matters as censorship, book prices, bookshops, and theaters. Bennett was not a profound critic nor did he pretend to be one. His snap judgments, however, were infrequently astray. He could be hard-hitting; he seldom failed to entertain, for, as he said of a reviewer,

[5]All are now available in A. Mylett, ed., *Arnold Bennett: The "Evening Standard" Years* (London, 1974).

"unless he is interesting he is a failure with his public. A reviewer must be a journalist before he is a reviewer." He was the first to make books "news." He had never been able to tolerate the professional de haut en bas of such as George Saintsbury and Churton Collins, Walter Raleigh and Ernest Dowden—though he granted that Saintsbury did occasionally "put on the semblance of a male human being as distinguished from an asexual pedagogue." He was often witty about writers (usually dead) for whom he did not care. Of the eighteenth-century novelist Samuel Richardson, he observed, "Life is far longer than it used to be, but it is still far too short for *Clarissa*"; of Charles Kingsley, "he never uses two words if eight or ten will do"; of James, "It took me years to ascertain that Henry James's work was giving me little pleasure." He abhorred what he termed "the lying that goes on about what you like and what you don't like." He was immune to professional jealousy, unprejudiced, magnanimous, kind whenever he could conscientiously be so. In word and deed he was against the peculiarly nauseating literary snobbism that had already begun to alienate the public from all but the most ephemeral fiction. But he never fell into the unctuous writing of such younger contemporaries as Robert Lynd or J. C. Squire.

If only one word had to serve to describe the best of Bennett's fiction and nonfiction it would be "honest." It would fit the man, too.

SELECTED BIBLIOGRAPHY

I. BIBLIOGRAPHY. N. Emery, *Arnold Bennett, 1867–1931* (Stoke-on-Trent, 1967); J. D. Gordon, *Arnold Bennett: The Centenary of His Birth: An Exhibition in the Berg Collection* (New York, 1968); A. Miller, *An Annotated Bibliography, 1867–1932* (New York, 1977).

II. COLLECTED EDITIONS. *The Clayhanger Family* (London, 1925), contains *Clayhanger, Hilda Lessways,* and *These Twain; The Minerva Edition,* 7 vols. (London, 1926); *The Arnold Bennett Omnibus Book* (London, 1931), contains *Riceyman Steps, Elsie and the Child, Lord Raingo,* and *Accident; The Penguin Arnold Bennett* (1954–   ); A. Mylett, ed., *Arnold Bennett: The "Evening Standard" Years: Books and Persons 1926–1931* (London, 1974).

III. SEPARATE WORKS. *A Man from the North* (London, 1898), novel; *Journalism for Women: A Practical Guide* (London, 1898), essay.

Polite Farces for the Drawing-Room (London, 1900), plays, contains *The Stepmother, A Good Woman, A Question of Sex; Fame and Fiction: An Enquiry into Certain Popularities* (London, 1901), criticism; *The Grand Babylon Hotel* (London, 1902), novel, published in U.S. as *T. Racksole and Daughter; Anna of the Five Towns* (London, 1902), novel; *The Gates of Wrath* (London, 1903), novel; *The Truth About an Author* (London, 1903), autobiography; *How to Become an Author: A Practical Guide* (London, 1903); *Leonora* (London, 1903), novel; *A Great Man: A Frolic* (London, 1904), novel; *Teresa of Watling Street* (London, 1904), novel.

Tales of the Five Towns (London, 1905), short stories, contains "His Worship the Goosedriver," "The Elixir of Youth," "Mary with the High Hand," "The Dog," "A Feud," "Phantom," "Tiddy-fol-lol," "The Idiot," "The Hungarian Rhapsody," "The Sisters Quita," "Nocturne at the Majestic," "Clarice of the Autumn Concerts," "A Letter Home"; *The Loot of Cities: Being the Adventures of a Millionaire in Search of Joy* (London, 1905), short stories; *Sacred and Profane Love* (London, 1905), novel, published in U.S. as *The Book of Carlotta,* dramatized version (London, 1919); *Hugo* (London, 1906), novel; *Whom God Hath Joined* (London, 1906), novel; *The Sinews of War: A Romance of London and the Sea* (London, 1906), novel, in collaboration with Eden Phillpotts, published in U.S. as *Doubloons; The Ghost* (London, 1907), novel; *The Reasonable Life: Being Hints for Men and Women* (London, 1907), rev. and repr. as *Mental Efficiency* (1912); *The Grim Smile of the Five Towns* (London, 1907), short stories, contains "The Lion's Share," "Baby's Bath," "The Silent Brothers," "The Nineteenth Hat," "Vera's First Christmas Adventure," "The Murder of the Mandarin," "Vera's Second Christmas Adventure," "The Burglary," "News of the Engagement," "Beginning the New Year," "From One Generation to Another," "The Death of Simon Fuge," "In a New Bottle"; *The City of Pleasure* (London, 1907), novel; *The Statue* (London, 1908), novel, in collaboration with Eden Phillpotts; *How to Live on 24 Hours a Day* (London, 1908); *Buried Alive* (London, 1908), novel, dramatized as *The Great Adventure* (London, 1912); *The Old Wives' Tale* (London, 1908), novel; *The Human Machine* (London, 1908); *Cupid and Commonsense* (London, 1909), play, dramatization of *Anna of the Five Towns; What the Public Wants* (London, 1909), play; *Literary Taste: How to Form It. With Instructions for Collecting a Complete Library of English Literature* (London, 1909); *The Glimpse: An Adventure of the Soul* (London, 1909), novel.

Helen with the High Hand: An Idyllic Diversion (London, 1910), novel, dramatized by R. Pryce (London, 1912); *Clayhanger* (London, 1910), novel; *The Card: A Story of Adventure in the Five Towns* (London, 1911), novel, published in U.S. as *Denry the Audacious; Hilda Lessways* (London, 1911), novel; *The Honeymoon* (London, 1910), play; *The Feast of St Friend* (London, 1911), published in U.S. as *Friendship and Happiness; The Matador of the Five*

Towns, and Other Stories (London, 1912), contains "The Matador of the Five Towns," "Mimi," "The Supreme Illusion," "The Letter and the Lie," "The Glimpse," "Jock-at-a-Venture," "The Heroism of Thomas Chadwick," "Under the Clock," "Three Episodes in the Life of Mr Cowlishaw, Dentist," "Catching the Train," "The Widow of the Balcony," "The Cat and Cupid," "The Fortune-Teller," "The Long-Lost Uncle," "The Tight Hand," "Why the Clock Stopped," "Hot Potatoes," "Half-a-Sovereign," "The Blue Suit," "The Tiger and the Baby," "The Revolver," "An Unfair Advantage"; *Milestones* (London, 1912), play, in collaboration with Edward Knoblock; *Those United States* (London, 1912), commentary, published in U.S. as *Your United States; The Regent: A Five Towns Story of Adventure in London* (London, 1913), novel, published in U.S. as *The Old Adam; The Plain Man and His Wife* (London, 1913), published in U.S. as *Married Life; Paris Nights and Other Impressions of Places and People* (London, 1913), essays, contains "Paris Nights" (1910), "Life in London" (1911), "Italy" (1910), "The Riviera" (1907), "Fontainebleau" (1904–1909), "Switzerland" (1909–1911), "England Again" (1907), "The Midlands" (1910–1911), "The British Home" (1908), "Streets, Roads and Trains" (1907–1909), illus. by E. A. Rickards; *The Price of Love* (London, 1914), novel; *The Author's Craft* (London, 1914), criticism; *Liberty: A Statement of the British Case* (London, 1914), essay; *From the Log of the Velsa* (New York, 1914), contains "Holland," "The Baltic," "Copenhagen," "On the French and Flemish Coasts," "East Anglian Estuaries," English ed. (1920), frontispiece by Bennett, illus. by E. A. Rickards.

Over There: War Scenes on the Western Front (London, 1915); *These Twain* (London, 1916), novel; *The Lion's Share* (London, 1916), novel; *Books and Persons: Being Comments on a Past Epoch, 1908–11* (London, 1917), essays; *The Pretty Lady* (London, 1918), novel; *The Title* (London, 1918), play; *Self and Self-Management: Essays about Existing* (London, 1918); *The Roll-Call* (London, 1918), novel; *Judith* (London, 1919), play.

Our Women: Chapters on the Sex-Discord (London, 1920), essay; *Things That Have Interested Me* (London, 1921), essays, distinct from those listed below in Letters and Journals, followed by a second and third series in 1923 and 1926; *Mr. Prohack* (London, 1922), novel, dramatized in collaboration with Edward Knoblock (London, 1927); *Body and Soul* (London, 1922), play; *The Love Match* (London, 1922), play; *Lilian* (London, 1922), novel; *How to Make the Best of Life* (London, 1923), essay; *Don Juan de Marana* (London, 1923), play; *Riceyman Steps* (London, 1923), novel; *London Life* (London, 1924), play, in collaboration with Edward Knoblock; *The Bright Island* (London, 1924), play; *Elsie and the Child* (London, 1924), short stories, contains "Elsie and the Child," "During Dinner," "The Paper Cap," "The Box-Office Girl," "Mr Jack Hollins Against Fate," "Nine o'Clock Tomorrow," "The Yacht," "Outside and Inside," "Last Love," "The

Mysterious Destruction of Mr Ipple," "The Perfect Creature," "The Fish," "The Limits of Dominion."

Lord Raingo (London, 1926), novel; *The Woman Who Stole Everything, and Other Stories* (London, 1927), contains "The Woman Who Stole Everything," "A Place in Venice," "The Toreador," "Middle-Aged," "The Umbrella," "House to Let," "Claribel," "Time to Think," "One of Their Quarrels," "What I Have Said I Have Said," "Death, Fire, and Life," "The Epidemic," "A Very Romantic Affair"; *The Strange Vanguard* (London, 1928), novel; *Mediterranean Scenes: Rome, Greece, Constantinople* (London, 1928), lim. ed. of 1,000, with illus.; *The Savour of Life: Essay in Gusto* (London, 1928), essays; *Accident* (London, 1929), novel; *Piccadilly: Story of the Film* (London, 1929); *The Religious Interregnum* (London, 1929), essay.

Imperial Palace (London, 1930), novel; *The Night Visitor, and Other Stories* (London, 1931), contains "The Night Visitor," "The Cornet-Player," "Murder!," "The Hat," "Under the Hammer," "The Wind," "Honour," "The First Night," "The Seven Policemen," "Myrtle at 6 A.M.," "Strange Affair at an Hotel," "The Second Night," "The Understudy," "The Peacock," "Dream," "Baccarat," "The Mouse and the Cat"; *Venus Rising from the Sea* (London, 1931), short story; *A Dream of Destiny: An Unfinished Novel, and Venus Rising from the Sea* (London, 1932), novel and short story; "The Snake Charmer," in *Eight One-Act Plays* (London, 1933); "Flora," in *Five Three-Act Plays* (London, 1933).

IV. LETTERS AND JOURNALS. *Things That Interested Me: Being Leaves From a Journal Kept by Arnold Bennett* (London, 1906), followed by two further series in 1907 and 1908 called *Things Which Have Interested Me*, all privately printed; *Journal, 1929* (London, 1930); N. Flower, ed., *The Journals of Arnold Bennett, 1896–1931*, 3 vols. (London, 1932–1933); *Arnold Bennett's Letters to His Nephew* [Richard Bennett] (London, 1935); *Arnold Bennett: A Portrait Done at Home. Together with 170 Letters from A. B. to D. C. B.* [Dorothy M. C. Bennett] (London, 1935); F. Swinnerton, ed., *The Journals of Arnold Bennett* (London, 1954; new ed., 1971), the latter includes vol. VI of journal, recently discovered, and Florentine journal; H. Wilson, ed., *Arnold Bennett and H. G. Wells: A Record of a Personal and Literary Friendship* (London, 1960), letters between the two, 1897–1930; L. F. Brugmans, ed., *Correspondance André Gide–Arnold Bennett: Vingt ans d'amitié littéraire, 1911–1931* (Geneva, 1964); J. Hepburn, ed., *Letters of Arnold Bennett*, 3 vols. (London, 1966–1970); *Florentine Journal, 1st April–25th May 1910* (London, 1967), illustrated by Bennett.

V. BIOGRAPHICAL AND CRITICAL STUDIES. F. J. Harvey Darton, *Arnold Bennett* (London, 1915; new ed. 1924); G. West [G. H. Wells], *The Problem of Arnold Bennett* (London, 1923); L. G. Johnson, *Arnold Bennett of the Five Towns* (London, 1924); Virginia Woolf, *Mr Bennett and Mrs Brown* (London, 1924), anti-Bennett study; M. Bennett, *Arnold Bennett* (London, 1925), by his wife; W. L. Cross, *Four Contemporary Novelists* (New York, 1930), study of Conrad, Bennett, Galsworthy, and Wells; M. Bennett, *My Arnold Bennett* (London, 1931), not always factually accurate; P. Smith, *"A. B.": A Minor Marginal Note* (London, 1933); R. Jaeschke, *Arnold Bennett und Frankreich* (Breslau, 1934); D. C. Bennett, *Arnold Bennett: A Portrait Done at Home* (London, 1935), by Dorothy Cheston; E. Drabert, *Frauengestalten in Arnold Bennetts Romanen* (Bonn, 1936); J. B. Simons, *Arnold Bennett and His Novels: A Critical Study* (Oxford, 1936); E. Massoulard, *Die romantischen Elemente in Arnold Bennett* (Bonn, 1938); G. Lafourcade, *Arnold Bennett* (London, 1939), still the most acute analysis of Bennett's writings; M. Locherbie-Goff, *La Jeunesse d'Arnold Bennett, 1867–1904* (Avesnes-sur-Helpe, 1939); W. Allen, *Arnold Bennett* (London, 1948).

F. Swinnerton, *Arnold Bennett* (London, 1950), sympathetic study; R. Pound, *Arnold Bennett* (London, 1952), the best biography, less satisfactory on the works; V. Sanna, *Arnold Bennett e i romanzi delle Cinque Città* (Florence, 1953); J. W. Hall, *Arnold Bennett: Primitivism and Taste* (Seattle, 1959); J. G. Hepburn, *The Art of Arnold Bennett* (Bloomington, Ind., 1963); D. Barker, *Writer by Trade: A View of Arnold Bennett* (London, 1966); O. H. Davis, *The Master: A Study of Arnold Bennett* (London, 1966); E. J. D. Warrillow, *Arnold Bennett and Stoke-on-Trent* (Hanley, Stoke-on-Trent, 1966); *Arnold Bennett Centenary, 1867–1967* (Hanley, Stoke-on-Trent, 1967), illustrated brochure; L. Tillier, *Arnold Bennett et ses romans réalistes* (Paris, 1967); S. Hynes, ed., *The Author's Craft and Other Critical Writings of Arnold Bennett* (Lincoln, Neb., 1968); L. Tillier, *Studies in the Sources of Arnold Bennett's Novels* (Paris, 1969), revealing, scholarly study; W. F. Wright, *Arnold Bennett, Romantic Realist* (Lincoln, Neb., 1971); G. Beardmore and J. Beardmore, eds. and trans., *Arnold Bennett in Love: Arnold Bennett and His Wife Marguerite Soulié: A Correspondence* (London, 1972); M. Drabble, *Arnold Bennett: A Biography* (London, 1974), enthusiastic, well-informed appreciation; F. Swinnerton, *Arnold Bennett: A Last Word* (London, 1978); J. Hepburn, ed., *Arnold Bennett: The Critical Heritage* (London, 1981).

JOHN GALSWORTHY

(1867-1933)

Margery M. Morgan

I

JOHN GALSWORTHY is commonly, and rightfully, regarded as one of the most English of writers, both on account of his descent from southern English yeoman stock, without any known racial admixture of Scottish, Welsh, or Irish blood, and—more importantly—because his focus as a writer was on English society and culture, its manners, morals, prejudices, and institutions, in some historical depth. In his best-known work, *The Forsyte Saga* (1906),[1] he set out to delineate a section of the upper middle class that he saw as culturally dominant at the end of the nineteenth century. The Forsytes, as he called them, played a crucial part in capitalism—as investors, shareholders, company directors, speculators in various forms of property: real estate, objets d'art (though collecting was a sophistication beyond the simpler Forsytes), even the lives of human beings over whom they had power. He shows the group as including the solicitors who tied up the property deals and drew up the wills, the barristers, the magistrates, and other functionaries of law who guarded and guaranteed Forsyte power, wealth, and status. No true and complete Forsyte is ever creative or productive; parasitism is the norm against which Galsworthy sets a few hybrids, half-traitors to their kind, perhaps outcasts, too. In studying Forsyte values, which he represented as permeating the culture they presided over, he was especially concerned with the place of art as commodity or dilettantism, a form of weakness in the stock, and with the opposition between the true Forsyte and the creative artist. He used the irritatingly vague and

general term "Beauty" for an element in life with which both Forsytes and artists are confronted, and he created its embodiment in the character of a woman to whom he gave the Greek name Irene ("peace," or the name of the goddess of peace), quite an unusual name at the turn of the century, though Henrik Ibsen had bestowed it on the strange, white-robed heroine of his last play, *When We Dead Awaken* (William Archer's English translation, published in 1900): Irene, who had been the model for an artist and returned as from the dead, after many years, to avenge her exploitation—or bring life at last to the soul of her exploiter.

At the time when Galsworthy began to write, Ibsen's name was generally associated in England with radical attacks on the most respected social institutions and on the hypocrisy that supported them. Galsworthy was rightly to stress how unlike his work was to that of Ibsen or George Bernard Shaw, with whom he was, as a playwright, often carelessly grouped; and he denied the influence of either upon him. Even the liking he had for single-word titles (such as *Joy, Strife, Justice, Windows*) points to a native tradition of drama established in the mid-nineteenth century by T. W. Robertson (1829–1871), with such plays as *Society, Caste, School*, that Galsworthy was continuing: drama that employed a slightly stagy realism, in contrast to the melodrama then popular, in order to scrutinize critically aspects of contemporary society. (The young people in *The Eldest Son* are rehearsing *Caste*.) Refinements and updatings of the style of Robertson and Arthur Wing Pinero gradually attracted the label "naturalistic," in what is still the predominant English usage of the word, not implying the philosophical basis of European naturalism: the post-Christian acceptance of scientific laws as sole governors of all forms of life, including the human, and a view of heredity and environment (including the social forces of history and tradition persisting in institutions and prejudices) as

---

[1] This essay treats the works of Galsworthy in chronological order of composition. In some cases publication or production of works occurred many years after their completion. For these works the text provides the dates of composition and the bibliography lists the years of publication. The dates of publication are cited for all other works discussed in the text.

exerting overwhelming pressure on individuals. Galsworthy, in fact, was the outstanding British adherent of naturalism, in both senses, working in the dramatic genre. (George Moore was primarily a novelist who made a minor excursion into drama.) He stated his faith in the preface to the Manaton edition of his plays: "I do not know if it is a discovery of mine that society stands to the modern individual as the gods and other elemental forces stood to the individual Greek." The words are surprising because the thought is such a commonplace of European naturalism, informing the social tragedies of Ibsen and August Strindberg, familiar in Émile Zola, and surely known to Galsworthy from the novels of Thomas Hardy, if not from the writings of Moore. This suggests that he absorbed the idea through impressions of a general tendency in the intellectual life and literature of his time rather than from acute, analytical reading of any particular author or work.

The particulars of his own experience certainly fed his imaginative work more than did any study of earlier authors. It is most unlikely that interest in literature would have led to his becoming a writer. It took more personal influences to bring that about; and a knowledge of the key circumstances and events of his life can lead to astonishment at how close he sometimes kept to actual situations and incidents. There is an element of devotion in the fictional re-creating of his recent forebears and their way of life. Through the strength of his feeling for his father, the model for old Jolyon Forsyte, the balance between affection and satire shifted, as he went on with the writing of the Forsyte chronicles, until nostalgia seems to be the most potent force at work. His experience as a young man, in love with the woman who ultimately became his wife and finding himself a social outsider, was of such evident value to his career as a writer that it gives rise to twin dangers: of supposing that, where the work most resembles the life, it can be used straightforwardly as biographical evidence; and of underestimating the differences of treatment and significance he introduced into his variations on the same source material.

II

JOHN GALSWORTHY was born on 14 August 1867, at Kingston in Surrey, and lived in that part of the country, in a succession of mansions built for his father, until his undergraduate days. A preparatory school at Bournemouth and then Harrow took him away during the terms. When he went up to New College, Oxford, his family moved to London (as though to the proper arena for adult life). Neither at school nor at the university did he give any indication of the kind of career he would follow, and follow with considerable success, in later life. He read law at Oxford with no particular interest or enthusiasm, but he never practiced. The training was certainly not wasted, but the uses he would ultimately make of it were unforeseen.

As a schoolboy, he was a sound athlete and sportsman. The impression he gave as an undergraduate was of considerable youthful self-conceit: too well dressed; wearing a monocle; mixing in a select, like-minded, and unselfcritical set; free-spending; and noted mainly for his knowledge of horse racing. The story "The Buckles of Superior Dosset," included in the collection *On Forsyte 'Change* (1930), clearly draws on memories of the life he had led as an undergraduate and extends more gentle irony than condemnation toward his younger self. He obviously enjoyed his privilege, and nothing moved his thoughts toward the serious purpose of making a living; his elders had done that for him, and he accepted his complete dependence upon his father as too natural to be questioned or to chafe him in any way. When his father arranged for him to travel, in suitable company, to North America, the South Seas, and Russia on business pretexts, he went happily and without demur, as if he were doing the Grand Tour of an earlier day. So he collected exotic material for his first volume of stories. A legendary chance meeting of Galsworthy and Joseph Conrad aboard the S.S. *Torrens*, on the return from the Pacific to South Africa, would have had little significance if they had not continued to develop the acquaintance through later years; for initially they did not know each other as even potential writers.

Galsworthy now had his own apartment in London, which he shared with a friend from Oxford days. This man, George Harris, later testified to his companion's ostentatious disdain for his own political interests. Though never politically astute or with the born politician's enjoyment of the game, it was a different Galsworthy who traced the parliamentary career of Michael Mont in *A Modern Comedy* (1929), a different Galsworthy who shared his wife's excitement over the election of 1905, which produced a crucial Liberal landslide.

Perhaps the chief factor in bringing about the change was the habit he developed of wandering through the London slums (he had been sent there to collect rents for his father)—much as did the fictional Dorian Gray, in search of sexual and other experiences, or, as the modern feminist writer Nell Dunn (author of *Poor Cow, Talking to Women, Steaming,* and more), who is also from a moneyed and privileged background, has described herself as doing, with the excited sense that among the poor is the richness of life. Galsworthy started to think with a truly Victorian earnestness about the misery and sharp social contrasts he saw around him, and he went on thinking with deep moral and practical concern about these matters to the end of his life.

It is as though he woke up. He might have done so sooner, if it had not been for the prevailing convention of conducting the education of boys separately from their sisters. For John Galsworthy's sisters, especially the elder, Lilian, were remarkable people. He could hardly have portrayed the Forsytes as perceptively as he did without those years of his own unconsciousness; but there may have been more to his acknowledged models—to the class the Forsytes represent—than he was entirely successful in capturing, something that produced Lilian and Mabel Galsworthy. The unexpected qualities were latent in John until his mid-twenties. Surprise has sometimes been expressed that a man of his class should have become a famous novelist, dramatist, and minor poet. There is more cause for wonder that it was not Lilian or Mabel but their philistine brother who developed in this way.

Part of the explanation is implied in Lilian's response to reading the manuscript of *The Man of Property* (1905): her effort to dissuade her brother from publishing a book that revealed secrets and expressed a coldly detached view of their father, the family circle, and their way of life; however free-ranging her intellect, she was still a loving and dutiful daughter in the accepted mold. John's reply claimed that she could not understand the kind of integrity and dedication that make the creative writer's loyalty to his work the highest morality he recognizes:

... artistically we are not the same in our cravings. ... I feel more like a sort of chemist, more cold, more dissective, always riding a philosophical idea. ... I can't bear the idea of the beautiful character. ... There are things I like, there are things I love in people, but if I start out to treat them be sure I shall do more than justice to their darker side. This is my genre.

(R. H. Mottram, *John Galsworthy*, p. 181)

The vitality of both sisters emerges vividly from all accounts of them, as it never does from the published portraits of their brother: enthusiasm, decisiveness, and overflowing interest in the world about them and—in the case of Lilian, at least—the world of the mind. She had a speculative intellect that fed on German philosophy, and she was fearless of being thought a bluestocking. Her marriage to a German painter with small command of English, who was at first admitted to the household almost as a servant (commissioned to paint her father), was typically unconventional. How intriguing the views of a foreigner and an artist were to John shows in many of his novels and plays—most notably in *The Island Pharisees* (1904) and *The Pigeon* (1912)—where he puts to good use the challenging effect that the introduction of such a figure into a self-complacent, unselfquestioning middle-class group can have.

The big development in his own life that came when the early travels were over fits conventionally enough into the picture of the idle London bachelor, if we think of it in terms of a liaison with a married woman. But the quality of the relationship had at least as much in common with John Stuart Mill's passionately high-minded association with Mrs. Harriet Taylor as with the fictional George Pendyce's attachment to Helen Bellew, in *The Country House* (1907). In her own way, the married woman, Ada, his cousin's wife, was as remarkable as John's sisters, who were her friends from the first and kept the secret of the liaison with generous sympathy. John and Ada were always reticent about the causes of the latter's unhappiness in her marriage to Arthur Galsworthy. The explanation young Jolyon Forsyte eventually writes to Jon concerning Irene's experience may reflect part of the truth at least: that she, like so many Victorian girls, had been unprepared emotionally for the physical realities of sex. Whether or not Arthur Galsworthy was in fact crudely of his time in his sexual approaches to his wife, the damage was not mended, and she continued to suffer from having to share the bed of an unwelcome partner. But her instincts, her sensuality, were not dead, and she was something of a romantic. So the way out of the trap was to fall in love with the personable young man so ready to fall in love with her.

271

One of the unexpected elements in Galsworthy's work is its freedom from the kind of puritanism about sex that afflicted greater and lesser writers of the turn of the century, even if it showed only in their nervousness over possible public reaction. Helen Bellew, in *The Country House*, is an instance of the strong, level-headed, sexually free woman, untroubled by guilt or fears of retribution, whom he presents with considerable respect. Though this is not the kind of woman character most commonly associated with his fiction, the type recurs in the striking study of Leila, in *Saint's Progress* (1919), grasping at life and the last of youth, as the shadows of middle age gather threateningly about her (a character who greatly impressed the aged Thomas Hardy). To be able to write like that Galsworthy had first to live his way through the miasma of Victorian fear of woman's sexuality.

When they began their love affair, neither he nor Ada could have had any idea of how long it would continue, illicit and clandestine, perhaps self-perpetuating largely because of those very conditions. Not until Galsworthy senior died ten years later, at the end of 1894, was it arranged for Ada's husband to divorce her so that the lovers could marry, as they did without a day's delay when the decree was made absolute.

As long as she lived, Ada guided and influenced Galsworthy's biographers, putting certain facts in their way, not stressing others. More recently, it has been realized that there was something unconventional about her origins. When one reads the last chapters of *The Forsyte Saga*, with an awareness of the tragic machinery the author is employing and noting the recurrence of the word "nemesis" in these pages (the manuscript records it as a previous choice of title for the book, now known as *To Let*), it is hard to stifle speculation on whether he was at all preoccupied, as he wrote, with the fact that his beloved wife's second name was Nemesis. She was an adopted child, adopted by a fashionable Norwich physician, Dr. Emmanuel Cooper, and the second name is just such as might be given to an illegitimate child in the world of Hardy's novels.

John was twenty-eight and Ada over thirty when their love affair began. Although they avoided the public scandal of divorce proceedings (which Galsworthy was to take as his ostensible subject in *Over the River*, 1933, his last novel), it is hard to believe that in the years before they married they never encountered anyone who knew them on the holidays they regularly took together in England and Europe; or that Ada's visits to the successive studio apartments John (like George Pendyce in *The Country House*) took in London went unremarked. Lilian and Mabel, his sisters and her friends, were in on the secret, and there was certainly some talk: John was cut by acquaintances in his club, though he did not feel it necessary to resign until Ada's divorce proceedings were about to start and he was taking her abroad to await the issue. His protectiveness toward both Ada and his aged father may have contributed equally to the long clandestinity: any moderately sensitive persons of their time would have shrunk from exposure in the courts and press; if Galsworthy senior had known of the affair, he might well have insisted that it should be stopped, and his son's dilemma would have been cruel, financially dependent as he was on his father and with a deep emotional attachment to him. Young John was not bred to poverty and the necessity of making his way. He did buckle down to literature, but the material rewards were slow in coming. Meanwhile, his temperament was such that he would surely have tried to give up Ada rather than see her risk hardship. So they waited until she was over forty, and the wait largely determined the form of their subsequent marriage: childless, with frequent, restless moves from place to place, the dogs who shared their lives being of obvious importance to their happiness. As time passed, John markedly took on the role of paterfamilias to a more extended family, including Lilian, whose husband, Georg Sauter, was interned during the war, and then her son, Rudolf, and his wife, with whom they shared a home, chosen and bought by Galsworthy during the last years of his life.

At the time of his marriage to Ada, John was already the author of *The Man of Property*. Though he had started to write before they became lovers—some of his first work was certainly written under the influence of Conrad's Malay stories, as well as, more generally, of Rudyard Kipling—the fact that he stuck to his apprenticeship with such determination and learned so much in the next few years testifies to the general change in his outlook. He himself attributed his becoming an author to Ada. It is worth noting that he was an undercover writer at first, as well as a secret lover: the four books he published between 1897 and 1901 were issued under the pseudonym John Sinjohn. Though St. John (pronounced "Sinjohn") was the name of a college friend, the budding author had in fact started on a habit of using disguised forms of his own name, particularly its first and last letters, at first suggesting John, son of

John (as he was), later including old and young Jolyon; Jon; and the feminine Jocelyn, making that the title of his second book, with its variant Joy becoming the title of his second play. Galsworthy is not famed for his sense of humor, but it existed and was surely at work when for once he bestowed the simple name John on a character, that character being a dog. Not until he had completed a book that he could be proud of, *The Island Pharisees*, did he expose his family name to literary critics and the reading public.

Ada, who became the typist for all his manuscripts, took a deep and often critically acute interest in everything he wrote; but he soon found a stricter mentor in Edward Garnett, the famous publisher's reader who saw his task as that of nurse and academic tutor to literary genius. Garnett schooled him virtually sentence by sentence through the sequence of novels that began with *The Island Pharisees* and continued through *The Patrician* (1910), turning him into a meticulous craftsman and complete professional. He had met Garnett through Conrad.

Their associating with Conrad and Garnett opened a new society to the Galsworthys in which they were fully accepted: the literary establishment, which gave them status and recognition in an alternative aristocracy of culture and intellect. (They also had access to the circle of young musicians and artists that Mabel Galsworthy, now Mrs. Reynolds and a model for June Forsyte, gathered around herself in Holland Park.) The mutual consultation and communication in which members of the group engaged certainly relieved the isolation of a writer's life. Even the moving between London and the country, from houses to hotels, and away on holidays abroad (continuing the pattern of his and Ada's earlier years together), must have diminished any sense that authorship involved a shutting of the door against busy living. Through a suggestion of Garnett's, a new involvement with the theater began in 1906 that was to bring him a second, distinct reputation, and from start to finish he visited the theaters and took a hand in the direction wherever his plays were professionally performed.

Galsworthy had been a fairly inconspicuous member of the Oxford University Dramatic Society as a student and had begun a play, "The Civilised," concerning James Forsyte, his son, and his son's wife (whose names, George and Helen, were to be used in *The Country House*, while their situation became central to *The Man of Property*), but he abandoned it in 1901. When he wrote *The Silver Box* (1910), a

London theatrical management whose artistic director was Harley Granville Barker was actually looking for this kind of work. It was the spearhead of a revived campaign for a national theater. Based at the Court Theatre in Sloane Square, with the best-trained acting company in Britain at that time, it was concerned to discover new playwrights and dedicated to the service of the dramatist's idea. Intellectuals, lovers of the arts, and men of affairs were regularly to be found together in the audiences, sometimes joined by members of the royal family. The central figures involved with it artistically, including Shaw and the Greek scholar, playwright, and internationalist Gilbert Murray, were themselves in some measure politically committed. Indeed, one current gibe was that this was a branch of the Fabian Society, undertaking to permeate opinion from Sloane Square.

Galsworthy was never a Fabian socialist, but made common cause with the Fabians in the attempt to change public consciousness and bring about political action on social issues. In 1907 he was a leader of the campaign against theatrical censorship, working together with Murray, J. M. Barrie, Granville Barker, and other prominent allies, and he brought out a pamphlet on the subject as part of the agitation for parliamentary action. This experience of combining with other literary men to form a political pressure group was preparation for the work he was to do from 1921 until his death in 1933 as first president of the international P.E.N. Club.

Even before World War I, his chief concern was the humanitarian wish to eradicate the worst callousness, cruelty, and oppression from society. The impulse that drove him had found earlier expression in the great tradition of nineteenth-century liberal reform and also in the strain of Toryism derived from Benjamin Disraeli's view of an England ruinously divided into the two nations of rich and poor. It found contemporary articulation in C. F. G. Masterman's book *The Condition of England* (1909). Galsworthy now wrote a series of plays that with single-minded clarity made a more direct assault on the inequalities of the class system and the oppression of the vulnerable by the powerful, moneyed, and privileged than either Shaw or Granville Barker managed to do in their more complex work. At the same time, he quixotically engaged in a number of single-handed investigations and agitations.

The most celebrated of his efforts was in the cause of prison reform; the performance of his play *Justice* (1910) was the culmination of a program of approuching prison governors, patiently interviewing many prisoners, writing letters to the press, and privately and publicly approaching members of Parliament and the home secretary, Winston Churchill. The latter seems to have made up his mind to introduce a bill for a change in the law governing solitary confinement before *Justice* opened, but was able, in presenting that bill to Parliament, to cite the public clamor the play had aroused. "It is a fine thing to have achieved," wrote Gilbert Murray to his friend, "a really great thing. . . . How much greater it is to have saved a lot of men and women from two months of solitary confinement than to have sent any number of over-fed audiences into raptures."

Galsworthy, who had spoken and published in support of women's suffrage, was—naturally—concerned with reform of the divorce laws, as well as with conditions and pay in the sweatshop industries and with slum clearance; perhaps most startling, he agitated for international agreement to ban the use of airplanes in war. Much of his later campaigning was on behalf of abused animals—horses, ponies used in mines, birds, performing animals, animals confined in zoos and vivisected in laboratories; and he set himself to visit slaughterhouses and compile reports as he had earlier made his prison survey. The nice balance of scruples in this man appears endearingly comic in his practice of sending his spaniel to a shooting party in Scotland each September, so that the dog might continue to enjoy a sport instinctive to him, but which his master had given up on principle, excellent shot though he was.

Through Galsworthy's interest in the theater and the love of opera he shared with Ada, they both came to know Margaret Morris, the young exponent of "Greek" dancing who in 1910 designed and choreographed a production of Gluck's *Orpheus* at the Savoy Theatre. It was arranged that she and a group of children trained by her should dance in Galsworthy's *The Little Dream* (1911) at the Gaiety Theatre, Manchester. Following that, she was cast in the straight acting role of Mrs. Megan in his new play, *The Pigeon*. Both John and Ada had interested themselves in the establishment of the Margaret Morris School of Dance; and, when the young woman fell in love with John and he with her, the three of them were prepared to consider a triangular arrangement. Ada wrote to Margaret: "You must not be unhappy, but very happy—first love at your age—can there be anything more holy! And you must not think of me—I am content." However, the strain was too great. Ada was, in fact, deeply disturbed. John could see no sign of her distress passing and brought his nascent relationship with Margaret to an end. What had happened bore a curious resemblance to events in the novel *Fraternity*, which Galsworthy had written in 1909. It was also to give him the material for the final episode in his three-part love story *The Dark Flower* (1913), where the second episode is yet another fictional variation on the story of Ada and his love for her.

The works from his pen accumulated: novels, plays, short stories, essays, pamphlets, and miscellaneous writings, all collected and published. In addition there were volumes of poems of an entirely premodernist kind, simply and straightforwardly written, using traditional, rather rigid syntax and standard meters, often rather awkwardly handled. The inclination to link up stories and sometimes plays by using the same characters in different works, thus suggesting a consistent and continuous fictional world, became evident quite early when James Forsyte, subordinate to the main character in the story "The Salvation of Swithin Forsyte" (1901), moved to greater prominence in the unfinished play "The Civilised," before the introduction of the whole Forsyte family in *The Man of Property*. Again the questioning French outsider Ferrand (based on an actual acquaintance) was introduced in *The Island Pharisees* and turned up again in the play *The Pigeon*.

The war, with the additional bitterness caused by his brother-in-law's incarceration, which all his efforts and all the influence he tried to bring to bear could not end, was not more traumatic for him than for most others. He was able to give considerable sums of money to good causes, and he and Ada spent three months, from late November 1916 to early March 1917, working voluntarily in a privately run hospital in France (he worked as a masseur and she took charge of the linen); and then he was furious at being called up for medical examination on his fiftieth birthday, in 1917.

After the war the creative energy was gone, and he went back to an old idea, settling down to a routine of writing book after book on the Forsytes and their friends and connections by marriage: With *In Chancery* (1920) and *To Let* (1921), and the story "Indian Summer of a Forsyte," he completed the group he titled *The Forsyte Saga*; he carried the family, especially Soames and his daughter, Fleur, on into more recent times in *The White Monkey* (1924),

The Silver Spoon (1926), and *Swan Song* (1928), comprising *A Modern Comedy*; after that, he branched off to follow the fortunes of members of Fleur's more aristocratic connections by marriage in the final trilogy, *End of the Chapter* (1933), consisting of *Maid in Waiting* (1931), *Flowering Wilderness* (1932), and *Over the River* (1933). In 1930 he had published an assortment of tales filling in gaps in the family history, calling the volume *On Forsyte 'Change* (with reference to Timothy's house as the meeting place for gathering and passing on personal news and gossip). Even so, works remain outside that extend the world further: Nicholas Treffry, later established as old Jolyon's friend, was featured as early as John Sinjohn's *Villa Rubein* (1900); another of the same generation, Sylvanus Heythorp, emerges in the story "A Stoic" (1918) and returns in the late play *Old English* (1924); young Jolyon had appeared in the first version of *The Country House* (then called "Danae"). The nature of the world Galsworthy created was not so much Balzacian as reminiscent of Anthony Trollope.

Galsworthy continued to write plays regularly, experimenting with structures but generally keeping to a naturalistic style. Some of the plays of the second half of his career won him success in the commercial West End theater, under the management of Leon M. Lion. In particular, these were *The Skin Game* (1920), *Loyalties* (1927), and *Escape* (1926). In addition to the Order of Merit, Galsworthy was honored with the Nobel Prize for Literature shortly before his death in 1933.

III

AT the end of *To Let*, the last short novel in *The Forsyte Saga*, the elderly Soames Forsyte finds himself in the picture gallery where the watercolors of his cousin Jolyon, recently dead, are on exhibition. He reflects: "There was certainly a body of work! And now that the fellow was dead it did not seem so trivial. The drawings were pleasing enough, with quite a sense of atmosphere, and something individual in the brushwork. . . ." It is characteristic of Galsworthy to insert an occasional passage of half-humorous self-reflection into his fiction, thinning the illusion a little for the alert reader. In this instance, the comment modestly sums up his own achievement in literature; younger writers, eager to

sweep aside his work to make room for a very different kind of art, would not be so kind.

Virginia Woolf's vigorous rejection of England's realistic novelists in the cause of modernism, in *Mr. Bennett and Mrs. Brown*, published in 1924, is established in literary history as a great step forward; while the evidence of some influence from Galsworthy operating on her own work in *Mrs. Dalloway* (1925) and *To the Lighthouse* (1927), at least, is overlooked. What has come to pass as a result is a great split in the older novelist's reputation: his popularity as a social chronicler—and a source of scripts for a superior brand of soap opera—has advanced rather than declined from the days when his investiture with the rarely given Order of Merit marked him out as the head of his profession in the public eye; meanwhile he has disappeared from view as a subject of discriminating criticism more completely than any of his major contemporaries, including Arnold Bennett himself, the chief literary arbiter of his time.

The offense that D. H. Lawrence's essay in 1928 on Galsworthy gave to the latter's admirers can be measured by the absence of any mention of it by R. H. Mottram in his monograph on Galsworthy (who was Mottram's friend and literary patron). Yet there is no better starting point than Lawrence's critique for a reexamination of his subject. His attitude is not at all close to Virginia Woolf's: his essay is not a demolition job, but a perceptive and deeply probing discussion. Lawrence acknowledges *The Man of Property* as a masterpiece: "The greatness of the book rests in its new and sincere and amazingly profound satire . . . done with really consummate skill and sincere creative passion, something quite new." And, on the basis of a rereading of most of Galsworthy's fiction, he is warm in praise of the other early novels, where "it looked as if Mr. G. might break through the blind end of the highway with the dynamite of satire." He accepts that what he hates in the books may be what the author's quiet exposure has led him to hate: "It looks as if Mr. Galsworthy set out to make that very point." In making the reservation within his comment on *To Let*—"It is one great fake. Not necessarily of Mr. Galsworthy. The characters fake their own emotions"—Lawrence is clearly aware of what Galsworthy himself called his "negative method" and the responsibility it lays on the reader to look carefully and thoughtfully at what is shown. Instead of deploring the other's pessimism, as many contemporaries did, Lawrence points to his "utter failure to see what you were when you weren't a Forsyte," his profound involvement in the very society that is the object of his radical attack. Lawrence brings his own diagnosis of the malaise of modern civilization to his reading of Galsworthy. Here he sees "the collapse from the psychology of the free human individual into the psychology of the social being." He explains: "When the human being becomes too much divided between his subjective and objective consciousness, at last something splits in him and he becomes a social being." This division, which finds expression through an unusual linking of objective and subjective methods, is illustrated in much of Galsworthy's writing. In this respect Lawrence's own double novel of the generations, *The Rainbow* (1915) and *Women in Love* (1920), fulfills the role of the other party in a general cultural dialogue with *The Forsyte Saga*.

The myth of the lost golden age, imaged in the lushness of long-cultivated rural England, informs the work of both writers. It is the receding world in *The Rainbow*. In Galsworthy's short story "The Apple Tree" (published in *Five Tales*, 1918), it is explicitly associated with the pagan world of Greek pastoral—the hero is reading Gilbert Murray's version of *Hippolytus*. Implicitly it suggests the Garden of Eden, but it is firmly identified with the youthful dream of free and spontaneous sexuality. This tale is complex in its hints that civilized, sophisticated man has betrayed nature, indeed has no option but to betray it, as the young student has in one way or another to betray the country girl who personifies the rural tradition. It may be pertinent that "The Civilised" was the title of the play Galsworthy was writing in 1901.

Stockbrokers' Surrey turns briefly into a similar idyllic scene when Irene meets her lover at Robin Hill in *The Man of Property*: "the copse where the Spring was running riot with the scent of sap and bursting buds, the song of birds innumerable, a carpet of bluebells and sweet growing things, and the sun caught like gold in the tops of the trees." Robin Hill is also the setting of the dream come true at last of old Jolyon Forsyte: the return of the emotions of youth, a freshening of the heart in old age. Such is the theme of "Indian Summer of a Forsyte" (the story counterbalancing "The Apple Tree" in *Five Tales*), which became Galsworthy's bridge from *The Man of Property* into the Forsyte chronicles that took over so much of his later career as a novelist. The figure of Irene who comes back into this story is only partly a

human character, the beautiful woman who can stir the old man's senses; even more, she is a projection of his love of the natural world he is about to leave, the love of life itself, which it is his salvation to have found after the years devoted to property.

IV

From the Four Winds (1897), the first of the books Galsworthy published under the pseudonym John Sinjohn, is a collection of stories sufficiently miscellaneous to indicate that the author was uncertain what direction to take. No dominant personal manner emerges. The variety of subjects testifies to a considerable range of reading as well, perhaps, as an abundance of ideas. Many of the tales are conventionally strange, with elements of horror and violence and experiences close to the supernatural. Although some of the plots hardly escape the preposterous, there are signs in the shaping of most of the stories that this beginner is not altogether naive technically. He frequently employs a narrator and centers his stories as carefully as he establishes the point of view. Virtually all offer some moral perception. The exotic stories, set in Malaya, Africa, and other distant parts, belong to a genre that Galsworthy's travels obviously encouraged him to try, but that he was to leave behind almost immediately. (A late exception is the play *The Forest*, written in 1922, set in the City of London and the Congo and loosely derivative from Conrad's *Heart of Darkness*, 1902.)

Other stories distinctly anticipate the author's later career, none more plainly than "According to His Lights," concerned with a "member of the leisured class" just released from Rochester Prison and soon spying his Uncle Stephen ahead of him:

The close, humping set of the shoulders, the head set stiffly forward, the walk of a man who goes straight to his object, and that object money . . . stopping every now and then before a picture or a china shop; "Four miles a day, and seventy," thought Eugene disgustedly, "he'll live to be a hundred."

A Forsyte patriarch seems to be emerging out of a Dickensian world. Furthermore, the Galsworthy cast of thought is evident in the narrator's reflection on Eugene's crime: "I myself could never see that the offence was more than a chance effect of circumstances upon a formed character. It seemed to me futile to punish a chance effect, seeing that it was the formed character you wanted to get at."

His next book, *Jocelyn* (1898), dedicated to Joseph Conrad, is a love story, the first extended treatment of a situation resembling his own and Ada's, though this is a variation involving two women and one man (the pattern that would emerge again in *Fraternity*, 1909). Irma and Giles are caught in an unsatisfactory marriage: "The friction between their two natures was endless and incurable." Giles and Jocelyn fall in love with each other. Irma's suicide eventually frees them to marry, but also loads them with a burden of guilt. John Sinjohn contemplates a fully tragic close to the story but turns aside to affirm the positive resolution and vitality of the lovers, who seize their happiness and put remorse aside.

Galsworthy thought well enough of *Villa Rubein*, which followed, to rewrite it and republish it later under his own name (1909). It is a more ambitious novel than *Jocelyn* in its plot, the range of characters, and its generally wider intellectual horizons. The European setting is not very convincingly established, and the attempt to make characters charming that results in making them irritating or silly is a fault that recurs in later works, for instance the play *Joy* (written and produced in 1907; published in 1910). The contrast of attitude between the artist hero and the English businessman is another theme that the mature author returned to. The considerable advance found in the story "The Salvation of Swithin Forsyte," the high point of the last John Sinjohn book (*A Man of Devon*, 1901), lies in the piquancy of treating a deathbed reverie as high comedy, setting the romantic encounter that is the core of the story within the consciousness of a satirically drawn character. Old Swithin amuses us to the last, both as a querulous elder and in his younger character as the nineteenth-century Englishman abroad.

What makes *The Island Pharisees* Galsworthy's first considerable novel is the firmness and strong sense of direction with which he presents the coming to birth of a moral conscience and the artistic tact that keeps the writing poised on a borderline between subjective and objective presentation. The novelist is very close to his hero or, more precisely, the central consciousness of the book, Shelton, who seems to be the conventional young man just at the point of maturity and firmly set within conventional upper-middle-class society—until a chance meeting with a down-at-heels Frenchman on a train. The emotional stirrings of being in love with an entirely appropriate young woman are brought up sharply against the requirement of a marriage contract, and the questioning process begins. Galsworthy adapts the convention of the "open road" type of novel, narrating the hero's wanderings on foot through England, especially the English countryside, to survey English life and cultural values. He denies himself the license to comment on the scenes presented from a viewpoint superior to Shelton's, with a broader, more informed, and more strongly defined vision. At the same time, he refrains from direct and coherent presentation of Shelton's critical views: the young man has not reached the point of having anything more definite than uncomfortable feelings. The portrait of Shelton that Galsworthy offers reveals a typical pose, head bent, eyes averted, expressive of embarrassment, doubt, and uncertainty, not least the uncertainty of his own opinions and unformulated judgments. Eventually Shelton extricates himself from his engagement, though he has not lost the yearnings that drew him into it. He is still scarcely a potential rebel, though he has slowly realized, while still hardly able to credit, the gulf between his private world of values and the social world he lives in. This consciousness separates him from the rest; to go into the marriage now, with a girl who is entirely innocent of any doubts about her place in the social scheme, would be a cynical accommodation and the smothering of his newborn, responsible selfhood. In this context, alienation is health.

In the first manuscript version, later rewritten, Galsworthy's title for this book was "The Pagan." More emphatically than the Kipling-derived title he ultimately chose, it indicates his focus on English society's official identification of itself with Christian beliefs. A similar focus was in his mind as he proceeded to compose *The Man of Property*, which he had thought of calling *The Forsyte Saga* (the title kept in the American edition), and he consulted Garnett on the advisability of giving the book a subtitle: "some such addition as this:

National Ethics I
or Christian Ethics I
or Tales of a Christian People I

in other words, to foreshadow a series upon that central idea." Fortunately, he was persuaded against such ponderousness; but a survey of the novels he wrote over the next dozen years, outside the scheme of Forsyte chronicles, reveals the persistence of some such continuity of idea.

The Man of Property, dissecting a wealthy and powerful section of urban society outside the ranks of the aristocracy, was followed by *The Country House*, a study of the well-to-do landowning squire-archy, its place in the rural community, and its obsession with inheritance. This book is deliberately and appropriately written in the tradition established by Henry Fielding. In tone and structure the whole work is a comedy, often close to pastiche—of William Makepeace Thackeray and, perhaps, Trollope, as well as of the eighteenth-century novel—particularly in the treatment of Horace Pendyce, the squire himself, and his ally, the Reverend Hussell Barter. Pendyce's dog, the spaniel John, as important as the human denizens of the Hall, is developed as a character in his own right, one whose attitudes and reactions contribute vitally to an understanding of the mode of life and the principles of his master and the rural community centered on him. It is not so much that the dog is anthropomorphized as that the reader is persuaded to see Pendyce and his cronies as quite closely related to their dogs, horses, and farm stock. It is in this relationship that they are most readily acceptable. The story line is provided by the son and heir, George Pendyce, his gambling debts, his horse racing, and his passion for a married woman who tires of him before he does of her.

Horace Pendyce's wife, Margery, is one of the most attractive characters Galsworthy ever created. She is more of a lady than Virginia Woolf's Mrs. Ramsay (in *To the Lighthouse*), but otherwise fully comparable with her as a realization of the wifely and motherly ideal in a human being; and, as with Mrs. Dalloway, the young woman whose hopes of love were not fulfilled in her marriage is alive and sometimes visible within the older self. Edward Garnett liked *The Country House* better than *The Man of Property* because its characters were more affectionately regarded by the author. Neither he nor Lawrence (who found Mrs. Pendyce "lovable" at first) observed the stylization of the book as a particular kind of comedy that needs a character such as Margery Pendyce to preside over it. The problems are resolved, and all turns out right in the end. It is essential to Mrs. Pendyce's character that she should act to save her son from the consequences of his folly and to save son and father from the consequences of

the latter's obstinate pride. She even leaves her husband so as to regain her independence of action. The irony in the fact that the situation virtually works itself out without her efforts is part of the general comic spirit: in a place called Worsted Skeynes, troubles pass like a bad dream, the unwise are chastened, and, after the thunderstorm, a new-washed England is hardly distinguishable from an earthly paradise:

> Every green thing glittered . . . Mrs. Pendyce's shoes were soon wet through.
> "How happy I am!" she thought—"how glad and happy I am!"
> And the feeling, which was not as definite as this, possessed her to the exclusion of all other feelings in the rain-soaked fields.
> The cloud that had hung over Worsted Skeynes so long had spent itself and gone. Every sound seemed to be music, every moving thing danced. . . . It was a home-field she was in now, and right before her lay the country house. Long and low and white it stood in the glamorous evening haze . . . and behind it, to the left, broad, square and grey among its elms, the village church. Around, above, beyond, was peace—the sleepy, misty peace of the English afternoon.

Continuing with the visual method, Galsworthy then safeguards the idyllic effect by highlighting its artifice with a detail that has the oddity and stiffness often found in peasant art:

> . . . she saw the Squire and Mr. Barter. They were standing together looking at a tree and—symbol of a subservient under-world—the spaniel John was seated on his tail, and he, too, was looking at the tree. The faces . . . were turned up at the same angle, and different as those faces and figures were in their eternal rivalry of type, a sort of essential likeness struck her with a feeling of surprise.
>
> (III. 9)

This is a book that uses literary conventions to comment on life, rather than to pass off an illusion of life as the thing itself.

In very different vein, Galsworthy went on to deal with class inequalities in *Fraternity*, before turning his attention to the governing class in *The Patrician*, which again looks at inheritance and again tells the story of a secret love affair involving a woman who has been unhappily married. Political ambition and public commitment triumph over the private attachment in this version of the author's own story. At the time Galsworthy called it the last of his "social studies" in novel form. Yet two subsequent books, *The Freelands* (1915), finished with difficulty after the outbreak of war in order to earn money for war relief, and *Saint's Progress*, written in 1917, are evidence that his mind was still playing over the social panorama: in *The Freelands* he lines up representatives of different professions to confront Christian morality as it affects a farm laborer for whom they feel in some degree responsible; in *Saint's Progress* he approaches institutional Christianity and Christian idealism more directly.

The most powerful of this group of novels is *Fraternity*. E. M. Forster's classic study of Edwardian England in the novel *Howards End* (1910) limits its range carefully to the confines of the middle class with the famous comment on the very poor that "They are unthinkable . . . only to be approached by the statistician or the poet." Galsworthy's book is bolder in challenging the strange invisibility of the "submerged tenth," the desperately poor, to whom the respectable clerks represented by Forster's Leonard Bast would seem comfortable and secure. As Forster was to do after him, Galsworthy examined the adequacy of the response that liberal humanitarianism makes to the underprivileged. The Dallisons are highly civilized, enlightened, and well intentioned, but the effect of their half-hearted attempt to interfere helpfully in the lives of their "shadows," their poor counterparts, is ultimately appalling and throws into relief the fragility of their own entente and the desperation concealed within it. The book anticipated Virginia Woolf's *Mrs. Dalloway* in its counterpoint of lives.

The Dallison family has its own prophet and visionary in its oldest member, Mr. Stone, a retired professor, now at work on his great *Book of Universal Brotherhood*. He is the voice of humanitarian tradition, and his eccentricity is the tormented sanity of one who knows the right way for society, how things ought to be, and—equally clearly—how impossible it is for human nature in its present state to take this way. Mr. Stone can survive only by projecting himself mentally into an infinitely remote future and writing and speaking of the early twentieth century as a Neanderthal condition. Living in the same house, and ironically contrasted with him, is his son-in-law, Hilary Dallison, an author of a different sort, "with that bone-deep decency, that dislike of violence, nowhere so prevalent as in the upper classes of a country whose settled institutions are as old as its roads, or the walls that insulate its

parks." He is utterly self-ironical, "so that to think a definite thought, or do a definite deed, was obviously becoming difficult to him." As for Hilary's practice of his profession, Galsworthy surely had his own in mind:

He earned an income by it, but he was not dependent on that income. As poet, critic, writer of essays, he had made himself a certain name—not a great name, but enough to swear by. Whether his fastidiousness could have stood the conditions of literary existence without private means was now and then debated by his friends; it could probably have done so better than was supposed, for he sometimes startled those who set him down as a dilettante by a horny way of retiring into his shell for the finish of a piece of work.

(*Fraternity*, ch. 3)

Hilary's wife is a painter, tightly controlling great depths of bitterness. In calling her Bianca, which suggests a "white" or unconsummated union, and presenting their marriage at the start of the book as a polite and "desiccated" arrangement, Galsworthy implies what a present-day author would more overtly state to be Hilary's sexual impotence. He does remark on Bianca's decisive rejection of any future possibility of a sexual relation between them, and describes a revealing scene in which Hilary, terrified, chill, and rigid, also rejects the "little model" (her surname, Barton, slipped into the early pages, is easily forgotten, as for most of the book she is nameless), whose grateful response to his kindness is to offer him love. This scene impressed and troubled Conrad, who assumed that Galsworthy had misjudged his effect: "You have refined and spiritualized that poor wretch into a remote resemblance to those lunatics—there are such—who try to cut off locks of women's hair in crowds."

Conrad showed himself at this point a poorer critic of his friend's work than Galsworthy was of his, for he seems unable to credit that this effect was intended and that Galsworthy could be so merciless a judge of a character he presents with so much subjective sympathy. He shows in Hilary the wish to do good and the dread of an overwhelming commitment that possess the liberal-humanitarian reformer.

It is not as a realistic treatment of an abortive love affair that *Fraternity* wins respect, but as an intimate, imaginative attack on the ideal of the gentleman, as savage in its import as anything D. H. Lawrence would launch on postwar society. Galsworthy's treatment of the rather similarly named

Hillcrist, in *The Skin Game*, is a faint echo of what he had done in *Fraternity*, though the indebtedness of the gentlemanly ideal to a watered-down Christianity is there made a distinct point of focus. In young Jolyon of *In Chancery* and *To Let*, he was to give a kinder, more conventional portrait of the true gentleman—though even there Galsworthy represents the ultimate effort of acting in accordance with his beliefs, taking on himself the responsibility of telling his son Jon the truth about the past, as enough to kill him. Young Jolyon's successor, Michael Mont, is of a tougher, more practical breed.

Conrad had been sufficiently impressed by *Fraternity* to engage in serious criticism of it instead of sending his usual rather emptily effusive congratulations. He warned Galsworthy, with an allusion back to *The Island Pharisees*: "Beware of Sheltonism . . . don't abandon Shelton; he's your creation, your embodied conscience, your unrestful spirit going about on the earth . . . but don't let him write your novels." In reply Galsworthy defended himself by claiming that his friend had not appreciated the "negative method" he was using; in other words, what Conrad had seen as a fault was in fact a carefully designed and quite subtle way of combining satire and tragedy, the intimate and sympathetic presentation of a human type with an unempathetic, detached exposure of its destructive potentiality. "Sheltonism" is a strategy of self-effacing neutrality, and Galsworthy uses it to examine and expose a weakness with which he was intimately acquainted: the weakness of idealism found in those whose moral sense is stronger than their knowledge of the world and adjustment to it.

The most extreme example of the weak, good man in all Galsworthy's writings is the curate Strangway, in the play *A Bit o' Love* (1915), who models himself on St. Francis but is exposed as scarcely this side of idiocy, a child-man clingingly dependent on a woman's affection, helpless and hopeless without it. It is nowhere more evident that John Galsworthy *used* the contempt for humanitarians, artists, and dreamers that was part of his own Forsyte heritage to impale the suspect weakness in the liberalism he had embraced as he put it on trial. The pacifist Stephen More, in *The Mob* (1914), is more acceptable because he is a version of the martyr-hero: that play has affinities with Arthur Miller's *The Crucible* (1953), despite the difference between a historical setting and a modern one; like Miller's Procter, More embodies the paradox of weakness as strength and suffering as a mode of heroic conflict.

That J. M. Barrie recognized such characters as falling within Galsworthy's special province is revealed in his comment on the "negative" hero of the latter's most underrated novel, *Saint's Progress*: "No one would have dared, except you, to make him the central figure of a novel, but the result is triumphant." Galsworthy may indeed have pondered and profited from Conrad's general reflection prompted by Hilary Dallison: "A man of forty . . . must have a formed character, that sort of knowledge of his own weakness which . . . is a sort of strength." Edward Pierson, Church of England parson in a London parish, is constantly self-critical and self-questioning; though he has blind spots, he knows and accepts the kind of man he is without pride or shame. Galsworthy was a robust nonbeliever, with no nostalgia for, or hankering after, Christian faith, but he was certainly aware of the Christian origin of the compassion he valued so highly. (The most graphic statement of his position comes in his long poem "The Dream.") *Saint's Progress*—its title a deliberate variant on John Bunyan's *Pilgrim's Progress*—is set in wartime, and, though he makes no direct judgment on the involvement of the church in the war, it is doubtful whether he would have been moved to write this book unless he had pondered the Christian dilemma in those years.

Pierson is drawn as a good man, a sincere Christian, a widower for many years whose successful struggle to subdue his appetites has set him apart from the commonplace sense of life in ordinary men and women. Consequently he is respected, but there is more of apprehension than spontaneous liking in the general attitude to him. Skillfully the novelist uncovers the split between Pierson's mental attitudes and his instinctive reactions: he believes insistently in the fair-mindedness, generosity, tolerance, and general decency of mankind, thinking better of his neighbors than he does of himself; but his mistrust of flesh and blood, his fear of the disordered and dangerous world to which sensuality can lead, betrays his good will. A passage of dialogue in which he gives his daughter his polite opinion of the South African, Captain Fort, illustrates this:

"He seems a nice man, certainly; he has a nice smile, but strange views, I'm afraid."

"He thinks the Germans are not much worse than we are; he says that a good many of us are bullies too."

"Yes, that is the sort of thing I mean." . . .

" . . . Captain Fort says that very few men can stand having power put into their hands without being spoiled. He told me some dreadful stories. . . ."

"We're not perfect, Nollie; but on the whole I think we're a kind people."

(Saint's Progress, II. 2.1)

Pierson has two daughters whose names, Gratian and Noel (Nollie), reflect their father's slightly absurd idealism as well as making a link with the family of Bunyan's Christian. Both love him dearly but find that they cannot go his way. The elder, Gratian, is married to an atheist doctor, morally on the side of the angels though he will not compromise his intellect or his practical knowledge of the world to avoid family conflict. Gradually, as events take their course, Gratian herself finds the Christian belief in which she was brought up becoming less and less tenable for her, until she stands where her husband does. The younger girl, Nollie, is impulsive and hungry for life. She falls in love with a young soldier about to leave for the front, the feelings of each being intensified by the general emotional atmosphere of the time. They want to marry but are dissuaded by her father, with the result that Nollie gives herself to the boy, Cyril, on the eve of his departure.

The actual and literary commonplace of the illegitimate wartime baby whose father has been killed provides Galsworthy with the ordeal that he needs to put his clergyman through. There is no question of Pierson's rejecting either Nollie or the child, though he believes that what has happened is a sin. His idea of the need to set an example to others, and his belief that his parishioners will respond positively to it, determine what seems the forward-looking action of keeping his daughter and the child with him and frankly presenting the situation as it is, without concealment or apology. What reveals the spiritual pride in this with a shock of horror is Pierson's notion that living so openly is an act of atonement and purification for Nollie and himself.

Galsworthy was certainly aware of all the aspects of the situation he set up. Pierson repeats the mistake of not letting Nollie marry Cyril when he opposes her marriage to the experienced older man, Captain Fort; the South African sincerely loves her but has been involved in a reluctant liaison with her father's cousin, Leila, whose way of life has been sexually free. (Like her sister, the more mature Nollie takes her own way.) The nature of Pierson's love for Nollie, the extent to which his starved emotions have found an object in her, his awareness of her temperamental resemblance to Leila, the undetected residue of possessiveness and jealousy are all deftly and unemphatically presented as factors that influence the decisions he makes, or wants to make, on her behalf; there is even a hint of punishment, the vengeance of a just God, in the moral imperatives he sets before her.

Ferrand, the vagabond Frenchman of *The Island Pharisees,* returns in this book under the guise of the artist, Lavendie, who makes a portrait of Pierson that the latter, tellingly, dislikes. It is another example of the visual images Galsworthy frequently employs to sum up his themes and artistic attitudes to them. The dominant figure in Lavendie's unfinished picture is certainly noble and ascetic, but "the eyes rested, dreamy and unseeing, on the face of a girl painted and hung on a background of wall above the piano." The two daughters discuss it:

"But why did he choose such a horrid, common girl? Isn't she fearfully alive, though? She looks as if she were saying: 'Cheerio!'"
"She is; it's awfully pathetic, I think. Poor Daddy!"
"No. That's what hurts. He isn't quite—quite all there. . . ."

(III. 9)

The scandal caused by Pierson and Nollie among his respectable parishioners forces his ecclesiastical superiors into tentative and reluctant interference, but Pierson has already decided to relinquish his post and go into the air force as a chaplain. George, Gratian's husband, applauds the move: "He'll be where he ought to be, Nollie. . . . There's no room on earth for saints in authority. There's use for a saintly symbol, . . . but there's no mortal use for those who try to have things both ways." His comment is not quite adequate to the book Galsworthy has given us. The shell-shocked painter to whom Lavendie introduces Nollie comes nearer in the triple irony of his words—against war, against fanaticism, and against rationality:

"Great souls out there, *madame.* But I will tell you a secret," and again he gave his heavy giggle, "all a little, little mad; nothing to speak of—just a little bit mad. . . . That is the discovery of this war . . . you cannot gain a great soul till you are a little mad."

(III. 2.2)

Appropriately, there is a shift away from realism of style in the middle of the book, after the idea has emerged from the detail: Nollie's nocturnal wanderings are dreamlike, hallucinatory, giving a view of the world from which she has been shut out that has affinities with expressionist visions.

V

ALTHOUGH current critical opinion tends to prefer Galsworthy's early or more neglected novels to the Forsyte chronicles, the latter form so large and ambitious a portion of his work that particular attention has to be given to them. The first novel in the series, *The Man of Property*, can be examined among Galsworthy's early fiction, but is hard to detach entirely from its sequels. The realistic narrative in serial form has such a strong popular appeal that most readers are drawn on to follow the later fortunes of the characters. One consequence is a frequent blurring of distinctions between different items in the series, though there is general agreement that none of the later full-length novels equal the first in quality.

Galsworthy began *The Man of Property* much as he was to begin *The Country House*, with an account of just such a ceremonial gathering as cements the unity of a social group. In each of these books, it gave him the occasion to introduce a gallery of portraits. In *The Man of Property*, his elderly Forsytes provide a company of burghers as solidly characterized as a Rembrandt group. With the exception of old Jolyon, they are an awesome set of elderly children, sweet or tyrannical, petulant and fretful; and their precise rituals emphasize the narrowness of their world, an impression that Galsworthy maintains through the sequels by his concentration on members of the family, even to the extent of the intermarriages and love affairs between cousins that provide the chief incidents in the continuing story. The sociological value of the book is obvious in the exactitude of detail, even the precise idioms of speech.

Even in the final sequels, Galsworthy is never primarily a teller of tales: the narrative of events is often irregular and slow-moving; character, milieu, and image dominate. And it is remarkable how, in book after book, whatever comic interludes are included, events shape themselves into a tragic pattern: especially through the death of Bosinney and defeat of Irene; two versions of the doomed love of Fleur and Jon; Soames's death virtually at the hands of his beloved daughter; and even, with a kind of echo in a connected line, the hopeless, inevitably broken bond between Dinny and Wilfred Desert in *Flowering Wilderness*. Behind the loosely named "saga" is the outline of some ancient Greek dynastic cycle of doom, retribution, purgation. The sense of loss, the frustration of desire, are major themes never submerged for long.

When Ada Galsworthy wrote a preface to *End of the Chapter* after her husband's death, she identified the figure of Irene, which winds in and out of the books and is reincarnated in younger forms, as a token of the destructive power of beauty. Almost certainly the interpretation was based as much on critical reactions to the character as on the novels themselves. Like D. H. Lawrence, Ada writes as though the Irene of *To Let* was the same character as Galsworthy put at the center of *The Man of Property*, when he took pains to emphasize her passivity and to keep her almost silent, as close to a purely symbolic figure as he could get without disturbing the realistic fabric of the latter book.

In *To Let* Galsworthy was portraying Irene as a distinctly more realistic character and one whose possessive love of her son marks her as a Forsyte herself, deserving of the name she has taken twice over. Yet the final glimpse of her restores her symbolic value, as it links the end of the saga to its beginning: "She, too, was looking back. Suddenly she lifted her gloved hand, her lips smiled faintly, her dark eyes seemed to speak." It is the very first time she has smiled at Soames, and the resemblance to Keats's "Joy, whose hand is ever at his lips/Bidding adieu" is unmistakable. Here, in the last phase of Soames's pilgrimage ("he sometimes felt as if the family bolt was shot, their possessive instinct dying out"), is the distant counterpoint to the famous final passage of *The Man of Property*:

> Young Jolyon's glance shot past him into the hall, and Soames turned. There in the drawing-room doorway stood Irene, her eyes were wild and eager, her lips were parted, her hands outstretched. In the sight of both men that light vanished from her face; her hands dropped to her sides; she stood like stone.
> Soames spun round . . .
> And in young Jolyon's face he slammed the door.
>
> (III. 9)

A similar image occurs in "The Apple Tree," and in Bianca's picture in *Fraternity*.

The initial ceremony in *The Man of Property* is an evening party to celebrate the engagement of young Jolyon's daughter, June, to the young architect Philip Bosinney, who, as a kind of artist, represents an alien and dubious quantity within the family circle. Yet an architect is someone a Forsyte can do business with, as Soames does in commissioning him to build the "place in the country," Robin Hill. Galsworthy insinuates the information that the vowel is short in the first syllable of Bosinney's name. Indeed, he proves to be a very aggressive, self-willed young man who strikes a hard bargain. It is Soames who has to make all the compromises and is forced to pay through the nose for beauty, art, culture, even while he is learning that he cannot buy love. By virtue of her symbolic quality, Irene, for whom the house is being built, can only love and give herself to artists. Galsworthy has to kill off Bosinney, as, in this book, Irene is what no one can hold. His original manner of getting rid of him was by suicide (in reaction to the knowledge that Soames has raped Irene), a solution that brought protests from those to whom the novelist showed the manuscript. The loudest and longest protest was from Garnett, who argued that suicide, especially at such a crisis, was entirely out of character for Bosinney. Eventually Galsworthy was persuaded to rewrite, and the architect now and forever vanishes in the fog, presumably falling by accident under the horse-drawn traffic; but uncertainty remains.

It is interesting to find Galsworthy remarking to his sister Lilian Sauter, in the letter mentioned earlier, that she is too much on the side of the lovers in *The Man of Property:* it was a different balance that he had tried to strike. He revealed at the same time that he was already at work (in 1905) on other books in which the same characters would appear, and the one he named was young Jolyon. The gentlemanly ideal is far from being realized by Bosinney: he is too vibrantly alive and much too uncontrolled; his nickname is "The Buccaneer." Irene, the lady, must be reserved for young Jolyon, the chastened Forsyte, the artist-gentleman with a sufficient private income from the exertions of previous generations to keep him out of the economic battle to survive.

For Irene, besides being a symbol of unattainable desires, is Galsworthy's most deeply ambiguous portrait of a lady. She is least ambiguous in "Indian Summer of a Forsyte," most like a younger version of Margery Pendyce. In the setting of the garden at Robin Hill (Galsworthy's equivalent of Forster's Howards End: a house on the edge of the country, the typical Edwardian symbol of a tenuously surviving traditional England), she is idealized, almost an allegorical figure akin to Keats's Autumn, in old Jolyon's waking dream. There is as much of the

nature deity about her as there is about Mrs. Wilcox, the spirit of Howards End mystically perceived by Forster's main character, Margaret Schlegel. Even more than at the end of *The Country House,* Galsworthy can be seen in this story to share the fabulous rainbow vision that had passed from the Pre-Raphaelites and William Morris to be glimpsed by the Georgians and passionately revived by D. H. Lawrence, whose *The Rainbow,* as well as *Sons and Lovers,* Galsworthy had read.

In *The Man of Property,* alongside the fragrant and delicate wraith, there are traces of a different view, prompting speculation that Galsworthy intended the very effect identified by Lawrence in his account of Irene as "a prostitute of property." Certainly he went on to show the personal weakness, as well as the vulnerability, of the lady (as much a favorite Edwardian theme as the gentleman), in Clare Dedham, the heroine of his play *The Fugitive* (1913), who is "too fine" to survive on her own in the rough-and-tumble of the real world. She needs a protector; and she takes poison when faced with the truth that prostitution is the only way of survival that she has been trained for, and she is not tough enough for that.

In chapter 3 of *The Man of Property,* Galsworthy emphasizes Irene's "seductive" charm and "alluring strangeness"; he allows her to speak this once, and to demonstrate the allure quite startlingly:

> "Tell me what you think of my new star, Uncle Swithin," said Irene softly.
> Among the lace in the bosom of her dress was shining a five-pointed star, made of eleven diamonds.
>
> (I.3)

It is a piece of jewelry given her by Soames, the man of property par excellence. Irene chooses to dazzle Swithin with it and, in so doing, to identify her sexual attractiveness with the pretty gewgaw that represents so much real estate. There could be no more pointed comment on the socioeconomic role of the lady, exactly as it had been defined by Thorstein Veblen in his *Theory of the Leisure Class* (1899).

Swithin takes Irene, at her request, to Robin Hill, where she has an assignation with Bosinney, and Galsworthy takes skillful pains to eroticize her within the old bachelor's consciousness. The sequence is remarkable, proceeding from his approval of the play of her eyes through her white veil and his liking her dress ("Fitted her like a skin—tight as a drum") to the strengthening of the spell she has been exercising on him: "Irene smiled. She had lifted her veil, banding it like a nun's coif across her forehead, and the smile of her dark eyes below this seemed to Swithin more charming than ever." The juxtaposition of invitation with the images of virginity prepare him, as he dozes off, to see her in his panic dream: "in the copse where the Spring was running riot . . . her pretty figure swaying, . . . slipping now—a-ah! falling, o-oh sliding—down his breast; her soft, warm body clutched, her head bent back from his lips; his kiss, her recoil. . . ." It is appropriate that the "pa-assion" that Lawrence mocked should be mediated through a Forsyte whose senses reach out to the material world even when extreme old age has taken the active sexual powers. (Galsworthy presents a more spiritualized and imaginative version of this desire in old Jolyon, a thoroughly fleshly version in Sylvanus Heythorp of "A Stoic" and the play *Old English*.) The author's consciousness outranges Swithin's dream to offer the ultimate picture of Irene, the veil wholly gone, the religious associations paganized:

There is somewhere a picture, which Swithin has not seen, of a man sitting on a rock, and by him, immersed in the still, green water, a sea-nymph lying on her back, with her hand on her naked breast. She has a half-smile on her face—a smile of hopeless surrender and of secret joy. Seated by Swithin's side, Irene may have been smiling like that.

(I.3)

It is surely the pose and the smile of an odalisque, more than a little reminiscent of the "classical" poses in the "art" photographs of Victorian pornography. However else the novelist was deploying his character, he certainly showed the power of sexuality as the central disturbing and threatening influence within the quiet, repressed, and repressive Forsyte house. In the changed world of *A Modern Comedy* and *End of the Chapter*, where the stereotype of the lady gives way to new versions of woman, and first Fleur, then Dinny Cherrell take over from Irene, this theme largely fades out.

VI

FROM 1906 Galsworthy shifted continually between the writing of novels and the writing of plays, often on related themes. Not only does he belong to a rare band of authors in being as good and prolific a playwright as he was a teller of teles, but he seems almost immediately to have mastered a different technique for his drama, accepting that certain qualities in which he excelled as a story writer were inappropriate to the kind of drama he aimed at. Rudolf Sauter published the pencil draft of a letter his uncle wrote to an unidentified correspondent, in which he discusses his dramatic method:

It is the very first technique that refuses from end to end to take *any liberty at all with perfect naturalness and sincerity of expression*. . . . It is of course a great strain on invention and device; it rules out wit (not humour) and lyricism, except such as is implicit in the theme. . . . Its sole justification is a special kind of grip of the audience that no other technique will give.

(*Galsworthy the Man*, appendix II)

This was just such a self-denial as Ibsen had imposed upon himself in writing his social plays.

Coming today to the first of the plays, *The Silver Box*, written and produced in 1906, a reader is acutely aware of what is unsophisticated in the technique —in particular, the unnecessary stressing of the irony in the final courtroom scene by the repeated device of Jack Barthwick drawing his father's attention to the parallels between Jones's case and his own. Present-day audiences are practiced in interpreting much more elliptical texts. The heavy-handedness of the exposition and symbolism in some of Ibsen's social plays is a testimony to the different expectations of late-nineteenth-century audiences, and it is worth recalling that a high proportion of the subscribers to the Independent Theatre Society who first saw Shaw's *Mrs. Warren's Profession* in 1892 seem to have gone away puzzled and uncertain as to what that profession was. Another crudity in *The Silver Box* lies in the magistrate's indulgent response to the upper-class young man, Jack Barthwick, as a witness, in the circumstances of this particular case. It would be appropriate enough in the exaggerated comic style of post-Brechtian satire; in the strictly naturalistic mode it seems quite false.

To make his point about legal discrimination on class grounds more convincingly, Galsworthy would have had to show the dangerous subtlety with which it can operate; and to do that he would have had to make his play more complex. Of the qualities that remain impressive in *The Silver Box*, one is among the last that novelists turned dramatists usually command: dramatic economy. He has kept the lines of the play simple, and the action moves steadily forward, scene by scene. He doesn't waste time or use unnecessary strokes in characterizing the persons of his play; any experienced and skillful actor will find that he has been given suggestive material to work with. Mrs. Barthwick's bitten lips and fragmentary sentences, after she learns about Jack's night with the prostitute, are signs of genuine disturbance, and her husband's irritable retorts produce a division of sympathies: he is under stress and justified in his impatience with the ignorance and false priorities of such women as his wife, and fearful of the damage they can do; but on the other hand there seems to be no affection to control his cutting manner. He need not be a crudely selfish man, but one whose preoccupation with the concerns of a Liberal member of Parliament has left him only functional ties with other human beings. The situation is enough to explain the unease that he shows through much of the play, but Galsworthy has inserted a few directions ("He stares into space," "Staring strangely"; or his pondering over the word "kind" when his solicitor has used the conventional phrase, "If the gods are kind") that invite an imaginative actor to go further and imply some deeper and more general trouble in the man, his gloom and occasionally surfacing desperation being symptoms of an illness of the soul.

It is the Barthwicks who are most likely to be dismissed on a superficial reading as stereotypes. Galsworthy's success with the Joneses, the poor couple, is more obvious; his interest in them stronger. Indeed they are very similar characters to Mr. and Mrs. Hughs in *Fraternity* (Lawrence singled out Hughs as the one authentic and vital human being Galsworthy presented). Certainly Jones is the only one in *The Silver Box* to express, as distinct from largely choking down, fierce emotion: rebellious bitterness, scorching resentment, and disillusion that still radiate some warmth toward his wife and family.

The presentation of Mrs. Jones is central to Galsworthy's method in the play: the need to avoid sentimentality was no doubt partly responsible for his decision to make her so passive a figure and so neutral-colored, so nonconductive of emotion. Monotonously she repeats the essentials of her story, almost as though it had nothing to do with her; her meekness is that of the self-identifying victim and provokes her husband's violence. The figure of the woman acquires an impersonal value, suggesting

long-suffering submissiveness, the quality of being moved only by another's will, the absence of any resolution to act that characterize the poor in general and explain their condition. Jones has the passion for rebellion, but it is canceled out by this null and nerveless quality in his wife. Yet there is nothing abstract or allegorical about either of these characters. They are convincing as individuals, based on observation; and their habits of speech indicate how carefully Galsworthy has listened, as well as observed.

The careful symmetry of the play creates an effect very different from the—perhaps equally studied—amorphousness of the "slice-of-life" school of naturalism. Galsworthy is at no pains to conceal that this is a deliberate demonstration, offered to the audience as something to ponder; and it is not his view of the partiality of the law to the rich that impresses so much as the sharp contrast between the middle class and the poor, the suspicion of the poor that the rich felt and their denying or withholding of understanding. At the same time, the symmetry, simplicity, and clarity are the only aesthetic qualities a work of this moral seriousness can admit.

A variation on the symmetry and the basic contrast occurs again in what is often regarded as Galsworthy's best play, *Strife*, completed in 1907 and produced in 1909. But he experienced failure before *Strife* appeared, when critics and public rejected his second play, *Joy*. The passage of time has not been kind to it, either: Edwardian whimsy is built into the mechanics of a play that attempts in vain to capture a tone like that of *The Country House*. It is difficult to find a thematic relationship between the main plot and subplot apart from the verbally reiterated theme of the "special case" that the egotism of each individual pleads. The idea is treated so shallowly that it does not even convey cynicism.

Strife is Galsworthy's principal study of strength, in counterpoint to his many studies of weakness. The ostensible subject is industrial relations, viewed in the crisis of the strike, which had become an increasingly alarming, recurrent feature of the national scene in the eyes of employers and shareholders in the last two decades of the nineteenth century. (The play actually anticipated the major prewar outbreaks of industrial disturbance around 1911–1913.) However, Galsworthy's deeper concern is with something as elemental as the forces that drive the sea and hold the rocks rooted against it. He saw it evinced in the struggle for power between a rebellious proletariat and those who consciously defend rights won long ago. His own humane attitude is voiced by Edgar Anthony, son of the aged chairman of the company; John Anthony's response conveys the spirit that put the Forsytes in their dominant position:

> *Edgar*: . . . They've only this one weapon!
> *Anthony*: And you're weak-kneed enough to teach them how to use it! It seems the fashion nowadays for men to take their enemy's side. I have not learnt that art.
>
> (Act III)

There is no residue or recognition of Christian values here. The old man is not uncompassionate, for instance, to the sufferings of his daughter's ex-maid, Annie Roberts; but he has no respect for any plea for compromise that is based on compassion: "These are . . . the words of a generation that I don't understand; the words of a soft breed." Galsworthy cleverly has the old man sit silent onstage through much of the action, and in Act I his comments reach the audience through the medium of the secretary, as if John Anthony himself were too feeble to make himself heard across a table. Then, as the situation grows more tense, his strength is gathered for the final throw, more a declaration than an appeal to the board:

> I have had to do with "men" for fifty years. . . . I have fought the men of this Company four times, and four times I have beaten them. . . . It has been said that Capital and Labour have the same interests. Cant! Their interests are as wide asunder as the poles. . . . This middle-class sentiment, or socialism, or whatever it may be, is rotten. Masters are masters, men are men! Yield one demand, and they will make it six. . . . I am thinking of the future of this country, threatened with the black waters of confusion, threatened with mob government, threatened with what I cannot see.

It is not only the absence of cowardice and hypocrisy that compels admiration. There is ground-down passion in the simplicity of the language and in the emphatic rhythms. The heroic quality in Anthony and his fanatical chief opponent, Roberts, is confirmed in the defeat of both, each being rejected by the herd he has led and saluting the other's tenacity, absoluteness of purpose, and vision of the future far beyond self. (The play's satire is directed mainly at the self-indulgence and pusillanimity of the well-to-do representatives of the shareholders.)

The play is a structure of interlocked conflicts, major and minor, public and intimate. The evolutionary struggle to survive, to which Galsworthy relates even the forms and procedures of modern civilized life, finds expression in different kinds of strength: with the power to appall where it runs against our sympathies in Anthony and Roberts; hardly less disturbing in the young woman of the people, Madge Thomas, impatient of the passive, negative resistance of the miners' wives, who pits her sexual attractiveness against Roberts' hold on the men. Annie Roberts' endurance is too loyal and proud to be pathetic, and it defeats the half-hearted pity of Enid Anthony. Most familiar in Galsworthy is the unheroic gathering of principle and conviction in Edgar, to the point when he painfully joins in the vote against his father. Indeed the most interesting complexity in the play rests in the contrast between liberal morality and profound illiberal conviction.

The same contrast in attitude between father and son appears, less strongly colored, as a relatively minor element in *Justice* (written in 1909 and produced in 1910), in the persons of James and Walter How. It is hard to resist the supposition that the author's relationship to his own father, involving on his part loving admiration and great difference of values, is reflected here. There is also a variation of it in the final relations between old Jolyon Forsyte and his son.

Justice is the Galsworthy play that makes the most obvious basis for a comparison of his work with that of Arthur Miller, whose position in American drama is analogous in attitude and style to Galsworthy's in English drama. As Miller was to center a tragic drama (*Death of a Salesman*, 1949) on a hero called Loman and have him end as a suicide, so Galsworthy gives us the little man Falder, equally a victim of the society in which he gets his meager living, and traces his fate to the leap from a window that finally releases him. In the context of the campaign for reform in the treatment of prisoners, it was easy to take *Justice* as a play about the machinery of the law, particular inhumanities, and the oppressiveness of this aspect of the state as it descends inexorably to crush defenseless individuals. Falder is an ordinary man, not a degenerate "criminal type," sensitive without being neurotic. Under the stress of being in love with Ruth, who is tied to a drunken and violent husband, he takes advantage of opportunity to alter a check and so get money that will take them and Ruth's children out of the country. When the alteration is detected, he is willing to let suspicion rest on another clerk, who has just left the solicitor's office where he works and is on his way to Australia.

There is nothing heroic or clever about Falder's behavior and, in his arrest, trial, and punishment, nothing out of line with approved practice, nothing "unjust" in the usual sense of the word. (Except that he lacks the assurance of an upper-class background and a daredevil temperament fostered in the hunting field and the army, he behaves much as does Captain Dancy in the later play *Loyalties.*) Galsworthy does not indulge in special pleading for him. He makes the middle-aged chief clerk, Cokeson, the center of consciousness in the play and the most fully drawn character: a practicing Christian, obviously in some nonconformist sect, and rather comically pious in an old-fashioned way; a kind but precise man of unquestionable integrity.

None of the other characters is individualized more than is necessary: we see just as much of them as the situation naturally brings out. There is a single, simple plot, and for the most part the dialogue is as sparse, stripped of every kind of grace, as any Galsworthy ever ventured on. The opening, when Cokeson is counting in the office, sets the style:

Sweedle: There's a party wants to see Falder, Mr. Cokeson.
Cokeson: Five, nine, sixteen, twenty-one, twenty-nine—and carry two. Sent him to Morris's. What name?
Sweedle: Honeywill.
Cokeson: What's his business?
Sweedle: It's a woman.
Cokeson: A lady?
Sweedle: No, a person.
Cokeson: Ask her in. Take this pass-book to Mr. James.

Galsworthy himself commented on the kind of tension such dialogue, continued through a full-length play, sets up in the audience. In the trial scene he found the type of public occasion (like the formal board meeting in *Strife*) that allowed a complete departure from this tight-lipped style. Here the legal rhetoric makes possible the explicit statement of themes; but a more important effect is a heightening of the contrast between the dominant class—the world of authority and culture—and those with no security, no reserves, even very few words. Paradoxically, the most eloquent scene in performance is quite wordless: Falder stands locked, hopeless, in the solitude of his cell, until the frenzy seizes him and he joins in the gathering chorus spreading through the prison of man after man beating on his door with all his strength. We have now moved away from the belief that only the verbal, literary element in drama counts artistically, as more recent dramatists have imaginatively exploited the possibilities of silence and visual imagery. But at the time Galsworthy was finding the way to express in powerful stage terms such emotional meaning as comes through his grim narrative account of Hughs's dumb and unresponsive homecoming from prison in the novel *Fraternity.* H. G. Wells wrote to the playwright:

It seems to me that *Justice* . . . vindicates you. . . . I've always opposed myself to your very austere method hitherto. I've not liked a sort of cold hardness in much of your work, but since it leads you at last to the quite tremendous force of the play—well, I give in!

(H. B. Marrot, *Life and Letters of John Galsworthy,* p. 260)

The kind of tragedy *Justice* represents is not easy to define. Certainly it is close to *Fraternity* in its response to the unequal fates of men. There is even some resemblance to the plain and serious treatment of simple lives in Wordsworth's *Lyrical Ballads* (1798).

None of Galsworthy's later works has the same intensity, nor did his self-denying naturalistic technique go so far again. His later plays rank high as decent professional achievements, expertly crafted even when, as in *The Forest* and *Escape*, they abandon the act structure of the well-made play for what is essentially a more episodic development; and they never slip below a respectable level of intelligence. *The Eldest Son* (written in 1909 and produced in 1912) is an admirable play in which the subject of the lady's maid pregnant by the son of the aristocratic family is treated in a highly civilized, entirely unmelodramatic way: everyone behaves decently, and the girl shows that she is no less a lady, no less moved by the Edwardian ideal of moral excellence, than her unconventionally fair and generous mistress. The irony lies in the conclusion: instead of being rewarded by marriage out of her class, Freda shows her quality and strength in refusing her lover's offer.

The Pigeon (1912), which exposes the practical inadequacy of philanthropy and yet pleads for philanthropic feeling (fraternity), is the best of the discussion plays, a tactful blend of seriousness with lightness of touch. In this vein, Galsworthy does not have Shaw's intellectual acuteness and quickness, his ability to see all around a topic and anticipate the objections and arguments that audiences and readers

287

might raise; nor does he command Shaw's infectious, zestful energy.

The Mob might be better known if Galsworthy had not brought it out in March 1914, for there was soon to be no public hearing for the sympathetic treatment of an uncompromisingly pacifist politician and for such condemnation of jingoism. Yet Galsworthy (who was drawn to the pacifist position but whose English patriotism won the public battle hands down when war broke out), while leading his audience to accept his hero's integrity, does not—as Shaw would have done—force them to face the conflict of principles and reach their own considered decision on the moral issue. The sexual blackmail tried by Stephen More's wife, who is from a regular army family, recalls the trick played by Madge Thomas in *Strife*; the blackmail complicates the otherwise too straightforward plot, but is not an adequate substitute for genuine dialectic.

The Skin Game, produced in 1920, which moves to a grim and very bitter conclusion, is probably the best of the later plays. Here Galsworthy's celebrated objectivity and detachment are certainly to be found more in technique than in content. Self-examination has contributed to the conflict between the gentleman (chivalrous and weak, with vestiges of Christian values) and the lady (sure of her ends and self-justified in the means she employs) that runs under the more overt conflict between a still-feudal aristocracy, whose writ of noblesse oblige covers only its own, and the brash nouveau riche industrialist. When the gentleman will not fight—as hard as John Anthony in *Strife*—the lady must, and neither Hillcrist nor his young daughter has the heart, in the end, to let her carry the blame. In the relationship between Hillcrist and the wife he allows to master him, and force him into a dirty and destructive campaign to keep their place, there is some parallel to the relationship between young Jolyon and Irene at the end of *To Let*, though Mrs. Hillcrist is denied the latter's saving grace of suffering.

Loyalties, one of Galsworthy's greatest commercial successes when it was produced in 1922, identified and accused anti-Semitism in the English upper class at a time when the majority of literary men more often unthinkingly embraced it. This play's demonstration of the way that a class bands together to protect its own against outsiders is effective, but no very startling revelation. It is a polished play, in which the wildness in Ronald Dancy (though the character carries less power than his prototype, the

hard-bitten, self-destructive Captain Bellew in *The Country House*) makes an effective contrast with the smoothness and order-under-discipline typical of the other characters; that the author was still trying to write his early aborted play "The Civilised" is evident in this.

Galsworthy's general falling-away into professionalism may have come about simply because the reputation he had achieved took him beyond pupilage to Garnett or anyone else who, even when their judgment was wrong, forced him to a degree of self-critical examination of his work that itself injected emotional tension into the writing. Increasing years and authority may have protected him too much from the need to take himself and his situation apart. If the English theater had had more room for new talent in that period, if Galsworthy had not been so isolated as a playwright from the jostling of younger minds, his work might have continued to grow instead of half-dwindling, as it did, into habit. Nevertheless, he remains a crucial figure in the literature of his time and worthy of considerably more probing study than he has had in recent years.

SELECTED BIBLIOGRAPHY

I. BIBLIOGRAPHY. H. V. Marrot, *A Bibliography of the Works of John Galsworthy* (New York–London, 1928); G. H. Fabes, *John Galsworthy: His First Editions* (London, 1932); H. Gerber, "John Galsworthy: An Annotated Checklist About Him," in *English Fiction in Transition*, I (Fall 1958); E. H. Mikhail, *John Galsworthy the Dramatist: A Bibliography of Criticism* (Troy, N. Y., 1971); E. E. Stevens and H. R. Stevens, *John Galsworthy: An Annotated Bibliography of Writings About Him* (De Kalb, Ill., 1980), also contains a checklist of works by Galsworthy cited in the vol.

Note: Major Galsworthy collections are cataloged in the library of the University of Birmingham (England) and the Department of Manuscripts, the British Library, London.

II. COLLECTED WORKS. *The Works of John Galsworthy*, 18 vols. (London, 1921–1925), some copies called the Popular ed., others the Uniform ed.; *The Works of John Galsworthy*, 30 vols. (New York, 1922–1936; London, 1923–1936), deluxe ed. for which Galsworthy rev. texts and prepared intros.; *The Novels, Tales and Plays of John Galsworthy*, 13 vols. (New York, 1926–1927); *The Works of John Galsworthy*, 24 vols. (London, 1927–1934), the Grove ed.; *Works*, 6 vols. (New York, 1929], Compact ed.; *Works*, 7 vols. (New York, 1931–1934), Nobel Prize ed.

III. SELECTED WORKS. *Plays*, 7 series (New York–London, 1909–1930), 1st ser.: *The Silver Box, Joy*, and *Strife* (1909); 2nd ser.: *The Eldest Son, The Little Dream*, and *Justice* (1912); 3rd ser.: *The Fugitive* and *The Mob* (1914); 4th ser.: *A Bit o' Love, The Foundations, The Skin Game*, and *The Pigeon* (1919); 5th ser.: *A Family Man, Loyalties*, and *Windows* (1922); 6th ser.: *The Forest* and *Old English* (1925); 7th ser.: *Escape, Exiled*, and *The Roof* (1930); *Three Novels of Society* (London, 1911), includes *The Country House, Fraternity*, and *The Patrician*; *Three Novels of Love* (London, 1919), includes *The Dark Flower, Beyond*, and *Saint's Progress*; *Six Short Plays* (New York–London, 1921), includes *The First and the Last, The Little Man, Hall-Marked, Defeat, The Sun*, and *Punch and Go; Caravan: The Assembled Tales* (New York–London, 1925), fifty-six items; *The Plays of John Galsworthy* (London, 1929), 1-vol. ed.; *Candelabra* (London, 1932), selected essays and addresses; *Ex Libris John Galsworthy* (London, 1933), selected by Galsworthy and his wife; A. Galsworthy, ed., *Collected Poems* (New York–London, 1934), includes *Four Dramatic Pieces*, see *The Winter Garden* under "Separate Works"; *Forsytes, Pendyces and Others* (London, 1935), short stories and essays selected by A. Galsworthy; *Ten Famous Plays* (London, 1941), with intro. by E. Gillett (1952), reiss. as *The Ten Best Plays* (London, 1976), see also *The Forsyte Saga* under "Separate Works."

IV. SEPARATE WORKS. [John Sinjohn], *From the Four Winds* (London, 1897), tales, never repr.; [John Sinjohn], *Jocelyn* (London, 1898), novel, reiss. under Galsworthy's name (Westport, Conn.–London, 1971), new ed. with intro. by C. Dupré (London, 1976; New York, 1977); [John Sinjohn], *Villa Rubein* (London, 1900), story, this version not repr.; [John Sinjohn], *A Man of Devon* (London–Edinburgh, 1901), stories, includes "A Man of Devon," "The Salvation of Swithin Forsyte," "The Silence," "A Knight" —this version not repr.; *The Island Pharisees* (London, 1904), novel, extensively rev. with subtitle "A Journey" (New York–London, 1908); *The Man of Property* (London, 1906), novel, published under the title *The Forsyte Saga* (New York, 1906), see also *The Forsyte Saga* below; *The Country House* (London, 1907), novel, included in *Three Novels of Society* (London, 1911); *A Commentary* (London, 1908), nineteen stories; *Fraternity* (London, 1909), novel, included in *Three Novels of Society* (London, 1911); *Villa Rubein and Other Stories* (London, 1909), stories, rev. versions of *Villa Rubein* and the collection *A Man of Devon; A Motley* (London, 1910), twenty-eight stories; *The Silver Box* (London, 1910), play; *Joy* (London, 1910), play; *Strife* (London, 1910), play; *Justice* (New York–London, 1910), play.

The Patrician (London, 1911), novel, included in *Three Novels of Society* (London, 1911); *The Little Dream* (New York–London, 1911), play; *The Eldest Son* (New York–London, 1912), play; *The Inn of Tranquillity* (London, 1912), studies and essays, in two sections: "Concerning Life" and "Concerning Letters"; *Moods, Songs and Dog-*

gerels (New York–London, 1912), poetry; *The Pigeon* (New York–London, 1912), play; *The Dark Flower* (London, 1913), novel, included in *Three Novels of Love* (London, 1919); *The Fugitive* (London, 1913), play; *The Mob* (New York–London, 1914), play; *The Little Man and Other Satires* (New York–London, 1915), stories, this version not repr.; *A Bit o' Love* (New York–London, 1915), play, 1st version, entitled *The Full Moon*, was suppressed; *The Freelands* (New York–London, 1915), novel, this version not repr.; *A Sheaf* (New York–London, 1916), essays; *Beyond* (New York–London, 1917), novel, included in *Three Novels of Love* (London, 1919), rev. shorter ed. (London, 1923); *Five Tales* (New York–London, 1918), stories, includes "The First and the Last," "A Stoic," "The Apple Tree," "The Juryman," "Indian Summer of a Forsyte," see also *The Forsyte Saga* below; *Another Sheaf* (New York–London, 1919), essays; *Addresses in America* (New York–London, 1919), lectures; *Saint's Progress* (New York–London, 1919), novel, included in *Three Novels of Love* (London, 1919); [A.R.P.M. (A Representative Public Man)], *The Burning Spear, Being the Experience of Mr. John Lavender in Time of War* (London, 1919), novel, reiss. under Galsworthy's name (New York–London, 1923), included in Grove ed. (London, 1927; 1950).

Tatterdemalion (London, 1920), twenty-three stories, in two sections: "Of War-Time" and "Of Peace-Time"; *In Chancery* (London, 1920), novel; *The Foundations* (New York–London, 1920), play; *The Skin Game* (New York–London, 1920), play; *Awakening* (New York–London, 1920), novel, illus. by R. H. Sauter, see *The Forsyte Saga* below; *The Bells of Peace* (London, 1921), poems; *To Let* (New York–London, 1921), novel; *Loyalties* (London, 1922), play; *A Family Man* (New York–London, 1922), play; *Windows* (London, 1922), play; *The Forsyte Saga* (New York–London, 1922), novel, includes *The Man of Property*, "Indian Summer of a Forsyte," *In Chancery, Awakening, To Let*; reiss. with intro. by A. Galsworthy (London, 1933); *Captures* (New York–London, 1923), sixteen stories; *International Thought* (Cambridge, 1923), lecture; *On Expression* (London, 1924), English Association pamphlet no. 59, presidential address to the association; *The White Monkey* (New York–London, 1924), novel, see *A Modern Comedy* below; *The Forest* (New York–London, 1924), play; *Old English* (London, 1924), play; *The Show* (New York–London, 1925), play; *The Silver Spoon* (New York–London, 1926), novel, see *A Modern Comedy* below; *Escape* (London, 1926), play; *Verses Old and New* (New York–London, 1926), poetry; *Two Forsyte Interludes: A Silent Wooing, Passers By* (London, 1927), stories, see *A Modern Comedy* below; *Castles in Spain and Other Screeds* (New York–London, 1927), essays; *Swan Song* (New York–London–Toronto, 1928), novel, see *A Modern Comedy* below; *A Rambling Discourse* (London, 1929), essay; *A Modern Comedy* (New York–London, 1929), novels, includes *The White Monkey, A Silent Woo-*

ing, *The Silver Spoon, Passers By, Swan Song; Exiled* (London, 1929), play; *The Roof* (London, 1929), play.

On Forsyte 'Change (New York-London, 1930), nineteen stories; *Two Essays on Conrad* (Cincinnati, Ohio, 1930), privately printed; *Maid in Waiting* (New York-London-Toronto, 1931), novel, see *End of the Chapter* below; *The Creation of Character in Literature* (Oxford, 1931), Romanes Lecture, 21 May 1931; *Literature and Life* (Princeton, N. J., 1931), lecture; *Flowering Wilderness* (London, 1932; lim. ed., New York-Toronto, 1932), novel, see *End of the Chapter* below; *Carmen* (London, 1932), English version of libretto by M. Meilhac and L. Halévy with A. Galsworthy; *Lyrics for Seventeen Songs* (London, [1913]), music composed by A. Galsworthy; *Over the River* (London-Toronto, 1933), novel, American title: *One More River* (New York, 1933), see next; *End of the Chapter* (New York, [1933]; London-Toronto, 1935), includes *Maid in Waiting, Flowering Wilderness, Over the River; The Winter Garden, Four Dramatic Pieces* (London, 1935), plays, includes *The Winter Garden, Escape* (episode 7), *The Golden Eggs,* and *Similes,* with foreword by A. Galsworthy; *Glimpses and Reflections* (London-Toronto, 1937), essays.

V. INTRODUCTIONS AND PREFACES. *A Justification of the Censorship of Plays* (London, 1909); H. Hamilton, *My Husband Still* (London, 1914); G. E. M. Vaughan, *The Flight of Mariette* (London, 1916); J. Galsworthy (Ministry of Pensions), ed., *The Inter-Allied Conference on the Aftercare of Disabled Men . . .* (London, 1918), reports presented at the conference; G. Howson, *Handbook for the Limbless* (London, 1922); J. Conrad, *Laughing Anne and One Day More* (London, 1924); R. H. Mottram, *The Spanish Farm* (New York-London, 1924); W. H. Hudson, *Green Mansions* (London, 1928); E. Garnett, *The Trial of Jeanne d'Arc and Other Plays* (2nd ed., London, 1931).

VI. LETTERS. *Autobiographical Letters of John Galsworthy—A Correspondence with Frank Harris* (New York, 1933); E. Garnett, ed., *Letters from John Galsworthy, 1900-1932* (New York-London, 1934); A. B. Wilson, ed., *John Galsworthy's Letters to Leon [M.] Lion* (The Hague, 1968), *Studies in Literature,* XV, see also items by H. V. Marrot, M. Morris, and R. Sauter under "Critical Studies."

VII. CRITICAL STUDIES. S. K. Smith, *John Galsworthy* (London, 1916); A. C. Chevrillon, trans., *Three Studies in English Literature: Kipling, Galsworthy, Shakespeare* (London, 1923), from the original French ed. (1921); W. Archer, *The Old Drama and the New* (London, 1923); A. E. Morgan, *Tendencies of Modern English Drama* (New York-Glasgow, 1924); V. Woolf, *Mr. Bennett and Mrs. Brown* (London, 1924), in *The Captain's Deathbed and Other Essays* (London, 1950); R. H. Coats, *John Galsworthy as a Dramatic Artist* (New York-London, 1926); J. Conrad, "John Galsworthy, An Appreciation," in *Last Essays* (London, 1926), repr. in *Tales of Hearsay and Last*

Essays (London, 1955); D. H. Lawrence, "John Galsworthy," in E. Rickword, ed., *Scrutinies* (London, 1928), collected in *Phoenix* (London, 1936); L. Schalit, trans., *John Galsworthy* (London, 1929), from the original German ed. (1928); W. L. Cross, *Four Contemporary Novelists* (New York, 1930); N. Croman, *John Galsworthy. A Study in Continuity and Contrast* (Cambridge, Mass., 1933); S. H. Davies, "Galsworthy the Craftsman. Studies in the Original Manuscripts of the Forsyte Chronicles," in *The Bookman* (London, 1933-1935), collected and privately issued; H. Alexander, "Galsworthy as Dramatist," in *Queen's Quarterly,* XL (1933); H. W. Leggett, *The Idea in Fiction* (London, 1934); H. Ould, *John Galsworthy* (London, 1934); H. V. Marrot, *The Life and Letters of John Galsworthy* (London-Toronto, 1935).

M. E. Reynolds, *Memories of John Galsworthy, by His Sister* (London, 1936); A. Galsworthy, *Over the Hills and Far Away* (London, 1937), reminiscences of travel with Galsworthy; H. Muller, *Modern Fiction: A Study of Values* (London, 1937); D. McCarthy, *Drama* (London, 1940); V. Dupont, *John Galsworthy the Dramatic Artist* (Paris-Toulouse, 1943); V. S. Pritchett, *The Living Novel* (London, 1946); W. Y. Tindall, *Forces in Modern British Literature* (New York, 1947; rev. ed., 1956); J. H. Smit, *The Short Stories of John Galsworthy* (Rotterdam, 1947); R. H. Mottram, *John Galsworthy* (London, 1953); G. Takahashi, *Studies in the Work of John Galsworthy* (Tokyo, 1954); M. Cazamian, *Le Roman et les idées en Angleterre, 1860-1914* (Paris, 1955); R. H. Mottram, *For Some We Loved; An Intimate Portrait of John and Ada Galsworthy* (London, 1956); G. Rowell, *The Victorian Theatre* (London, 1956); W. O. Ross, "John Galsworthy: Aspects of an Attitude," in A. D. Wallace and W. O. Ross, eds., *Studies in Honor of John Wilcox* (Detroit, 1958); D. B. Pallette, "Young Galsworthy: The Forging of a Satirist," *Modern Philology,* LVI (1959).

E. Starkie, *From Gautier to Eliot: The Influence of France on English Literature, 1851-1939* (London, 1960); A. D. Chaudhuri, *Galsworthy's Plays: A Critical Survey* (New Delhi, 1961); D. Barker, *A Man of Principle* (London, 1963); D. Garnett, "E. M. Forster and John Galsworthy," in *Review of English Literature,* V (1964); G. Scrigeour, "Naturalist Drama and Galsworthy," in *Modern Drama,* VIII (1964); V. S. Pritchett, *The Working Novelist* (London, 1965); M. Morris, *My Galsworthy Story* (London, 1967), with intro. by M. Deans, contains sixty-seven letters; R. Sauter, *Galsworthy the Man; An Intimate Portrait by His Nephew* (London, 1967), contains a number of letters and useful notes on the whereabouts of Galsworthy's papers; A. West, ed., *The Galsworthy Reader* (New York, 1967); D. Holloway, *John Galsworthy* (London, 1968); S. L. Hines, *The Edwardian Turn of Mind* (Princeton, N. J., 1968); V. Marković, *The Reputation of Galsworthy in England, 1897-1950* (Belgrade, 1969); E. R. Pike, ed., *Human Documents of the Age of the Forsytes*

(London, 1969); W. Bellamy, *The Novels of Wells, Bennett and Galsworthy, 1890–1910* (New York–London, 1971); R. Gill, *Happy Rural Seat. The English Country House and the Literary Imagination* (New Haven, Conn.–London, 1972); J. Gindin, "Ethical Structures in John Galsworthy, Elizabeth Bowen, and Iris Murdoch," in A. Warren, ed., *Forms of Modern British Fiction* (Austin, Tex.–London, 1975); W. J. Scheik, "Chance and Impartiality: A Study Based on the Manuscript of Galsworthy's *Loyalties*," in *Texas Studies in Language and Literature*, XVII (1975); C. Dupré, *John Galsworthy* (New York–London, 1976); J. Fisher, *The World of the Forsytes* (London, 1976), social history; J. Gindin, *The English Climate: An Excursion into a Biography of John Galsworthy* (Ann Arbor, Mich., 1979); S. B. Shukla, *Social and Moral Issues in the Plays of Galsworthy* (Salzburg, 1979).

NORMAN DOUGLAS

(1868-1952)

Ian Greenlees

I

NORMAN DOUGLAS was a humanist. He was many other things besides: novelist, travel writer, essayist, geologist, botanist, biologist. He was animated by an insatiable curiosity, which extended to a great variety of subjects and countries. In a significant passage of *Alone* (1921), when writing of children, he throws an interesting sidelight on his own point of view:

A man who has tried to remain a mere citizen of the world and refused to squeeze himself into the narrow methods and aspirations of any epoch or country will discover that children correspond unconsciously to his multifarious interests. They are not standardized. They are more generous in their appreciations, more sensitive to pure ideas, more impersonal. Their curiosity is disinterested. The stock may be rudimentary, but the outlook is spacious; it is the passionless outlook of the sage. A child is ready to embrace the universe. And, unlike adults, he is never afraid to face his own limitations. How refreshing to converse with folks who have no bile to vent, no axe to grind, no prejudices to air; who are pagans to the core; who, uninitiated into the false value of externals, never fail to size you up from a more spiritual point of view than do their elders; who are not oozing politics and sensuality, nor afflicted with some stupid ailment or other which prevents them doing this and that.

Like the child he adumbrates here, he was "ready to embrace the universe."

Douglas began to write late in life. *Siren Land* was not published until 1911, when he was already forty-three. This was his first serious book, though he had published *Unprofessional Tales*, a volume of short stories, under the pseudonym of "Normyx" in 1901, in collaboration with his wife.

He was born in 1868 at Falkenhorst, Thuringia, in Austria (now East Germany). His father was Scot-

tish and his mother half Scottish and half German. He spent his early years in Austria but was educated in England, first at a preparatory school and then at the public Uppingham. He has written of his intense dislike of Uppingham, but after spending two years there he was able to leave and continue his education at Karlsruhe in Germany. There he was happier and was able to lay the basis of a sound scientific education. Douglas held strong views on education, and some of these are expounded by Keith in *South Wind* (1917). Keith says to the Bishop:

If I had a son, I would take him from school at the age of fourteen, not a moment later, and put him for two years in a commercial house. Wake him up. Make an English citizen of him. Teach him how to deal with men as men, to write a straightforward business letter, manage his own money and gain some respect for those industrial movements which control the world. Next, two years in some wilder parts of the world, where his own countrymen and equals by birth are settled under primitive conditions and have formed their rough codes of society. The intercourse with such people would be a capital invested for life. The next two years should be spent in the great towns of Europe, in order to remove awkwardness of manner, prejudice of race and feeling, and to get the outward forms of a European citizen. All this would sharpen his wits, give him sure interests in life, more keys to knowledge. It would widen his horizon. Then, and not a minute sooner, to the University, where he would go, not as a child, but a man capable of enjoying its real advantages, attend lectures with profit, acquire manners instead of mannerisms and a University tone instead of a University taint.

(ch. 4)

Douglas himself did not go to a university, nor did he ever regret this. *Humani nihil a me alienum puto*[1] would certainly have described his approach to life.

---

[1] "I regard nothing that is of human concern as alien to me."

He remained at the Karlsruhe Gymnasium for six years, until he reached the age of twenty.

At this period his interests lay in a scientific direction, and he wrote papers in German as well as English. He was bilingual in these two languages and remained so for the rest of his life. In addition, his mastery of Italian was complete and extended to a knowledge of several Italian dialects. Even toward the end of his life he could converse at will in Russian, and his French was always fluent.

He passed the Foreign Office examination in 1893 and from 1894 to 1896 was a third secretary at the British Embassy, St. Petersburg. He resigned from the Foreign Office in 1898, when he inherited some money. In the same year he married Elsa Fitzgibbon, and they lived for the next few years on the Bay of Posilipo, in the Villa Maya, which he had bought in 1897. Later he moved to Capri, where he wrote various monographs on the island. He had first visited the island in 1888, and his love of the Mediterranean, and of Capri in particular, germinated with this first visit. He was divorced in 1903. In the years following his retirement from the Foreign Office he lived either in Capri or on the Bay of Naples, though he also traveled extensively. He was extravagant in these years and soon ran through his money, with the result that from about 1907 onward he turned to writing to earn his living. He was fond of recounting how he had been driven to write by economic necessity, almost as if he would have preferred, given financial independence, to write scientific treatises and pursue the path of scholarship.

In the next few years he wrote *Siren Land* and *Old Calabria* (1915), which were the result of many journeys to southern Italy. In 1909 he visited Tunisia for the second time, and in 1912 he published *Fountains in the Sand*, a travel book about that country. From 1910 to 1916 he lived in London, and during part of this period he was assistant editor of the *English Review*, under Ford Madox Ford. It was for him a period of great financial difficulty. *Old Calabria* was more successful than *Siren Land*, the first edition of which was mostly sold as waste paper. In 1916 he returned to Italy, where he earned a little money contributing impressions to the *Anglo-Italian Review*. Some of these were later collected and formed part of *Alone*. In 1916 he was living again in Capri, at what has now become the Albergo Ercolano, and writing *South Wind*, the first of his books to gain a widespread success, thus establishing his reputation as a writer.

In 1922 Douglas settled in Florence, where he continued to live until 1937. During this period he published privately printed editions of his new works and sold them direct to the public, a system that he found financially more rewarding than publishing them through the normal channels. Later, he would sell the copyright outright to a London publisher. From 1937 to 1940 he lived in the south of France, but at the end of 1940 he moved to Lisbon and from there to London, where he arrived in January 1941. He remained for the rest of the war in England, but was always hoping to return to Italy, for which country he eventually obtained a visa in July 1946. When he first approached an Italian diplomat at the embassy in London for a visa to return to Italy, he was told that the Italian government was not prepared to grant visas to those who wished to live in Italy, but only to those who intended to pay a short visit to the country. To this he answered that he did not so much want to live there as to die there. This reply so moved the Italian attaché that he decided to make a special effort to get an exception made in his case and was, fortunately, successful in so doing.

Douglas stopped first in Rome, where he stayed a week, then went on to Positano, and finally back to Capri, where he remained, with the exception of an occasional visit to Rome or Calabria, until his death in 1952. Capri evoked many agreeable memories for him, and he lived in a separate apartment in the villa of his old friend Kenneth Macpherson. He was of course aware of the great changes that had overtaken Capri, as he points out in the postscript to *Footnote on Capri* (1952):

At this moment Capri is in danger of developing into a second Hollywood and that, it seems, is precisely what it aspires to become. The island is too small to endure all these outrages without loss of dignity—the pest of so-called musicians who deafen one's ears in every restaurant, roads blocked up by lorries and cars—steamers and motorboats disgorging a rabble of flashy trippers at every hour of the day.

But he himself had done much to make the island known. He had studied its history, fauna, and flora, and he had used it as the background for *South Wind*; though, as he put it, "the social atmosphere of Mr. Keith is distilled out of Capri—out of the Capri as it always should have been and as it never, alas, yet was or will be."

II

ALTHOUGH Douglas' interests were manifold and his talents varied, it was as a writer of travel books that he excelled. He was the greatest travel writer of his generation and indeed takes his place among the great English writers of that genre. As R. M. Dawkins has pointed out, he was an extrovert traveler. He was interested in the history, customs, and traditions of the country or region he visited. He was amused by any eccentricities of character, and *Old Calabria* or *Siren Land,* for example, abound in conversations with individual, odd characters. An individualist himself, Douglas admired a rich, original personality in others. He despised the gradual standardization that has overtaken, and continues to overtake, contemporary society. In *How About Europe?* (1929) he wrote:

Education has been raised to a bad eminence and one or two charges can be brought against it which contain more than the proverbial grain of truth. It is a centripetal process; it creates a type instead of a character; in other words, it instils uniformity, which is an enemy of civilization. None but a strong nature can profit by its good effects and defy the bad ones; none but a small percentage of children recover before middle age, when it is too late, from that withering strain of application. It frets away their finer edges and dries up the well-springs of individualism. It destroys their originality of outlook, their curiosity, their initiative, the directness of their mental vision. They learn to see with eyes, and to think with brains, which are not their own. Their impulses, their conversations—their dreams, I daresay—are standardized; and if not, a ten years' course of schooling has certainly done its best to attain that end. Education is a state-controlled machinery of echoes.

Douglas had no use for universal education and the standardized types it produced. He had little use for any of the clichés and shibboleths so popular in his generation. He liked to think for himself. He regarded education as a voluntary process that went on throughout life, and not something that just began and ended with school. Douglas felt at home in the Mediterranean and in fact lived there the larger part of his long life, either on the Bay of Naples or in Florence. No English writer of this century has known Italy so well or interpreted it so accurately. It was a pleasure, when traveling with him, to hear him discoursing at ease with Italians in Calabria of all ages and from all walks of life. He had a predilection for the young and the very old.

Already in 1934, when I first traveled with him to Calabria, he had become something of a legend there—the English writer who had published such a detailed and learned work on their region and visited it so frequently, whether climbing up Monte Pollino from Castrovillari, or walking through the Greek Sila, or the Sila Grande, carrying the familiar rucksack, and traversing great distances either on foot or on mule. The innkeeper, the chemist and schoolmaster would gather round him as he arrived unexpectedly in the primitive hostelry in some mountain village. Most of them had not even read *Old Calabria,* for—strangely enough—it has never been translated into Italian, but they knew of it from the few who had been able to read it in English. They were flattered that he remembered and recognized them, enjoyed his laughter and his jokes, and were immediately put at their ease by his courteous manner and his familiarity with their language.

His deep knowledge of the country—gained through long residence and extensive traveling—informs all his Italian travel books—*Siren Land, Old Calabria, Summer Islands* (1931), and *Alone.* But there is much more than mere knowledge of the country (this provides the background); a humanistic Epicurean philosophy of life, a love of the absurd, profound scholarship, and humanity are there in abundance.

Douglas displays his learning in *Old Calabria* more than in the other travel books. It should perhaps be emphasized that his scholarship was genuine, and not, as has been suggested, just a bluff that he indulged in to mystify or impress the innocent reader. Considerable research went into the writing of *Old Calabria;* Douglas spent many weeks, first, in the National Library at Naples, and, later, in the British Museum reading and checking the sources to which he refers. He was indeed fond of relating how he acquired the habit of taking snuff while reading in the British Museum. Even Italian critics have not questioned the scholarship of *Old Calabria.*

Old Calabria is the masterpiece of Douglas. It was published in 1915, though written in the years before the war. Douglas had of course read and admired the books of many English travelers to Calabria—Keppel Craven, Algernon Swinburne, Craufurd Tait Ramage, Edward Lear, and George Gissing—indeed, he writes of them himself; but his own account is more comprehensive, scholarly, and ironical. Above all, as with the other travel books, it is impregnated with his personality. In *Experiments*

(1925), in the course of an essay on the *Arabia Deserta of* Charles Montagu Doughty, he defines the qualities required by a good writer of travel books:

It is not enough to depict, in however glowing hues, the landscape and customs of distant regions, to smother us in folklore and statistics and history and besprinkle the pages with imaginary conversations or foreign idioms by way of generating "local colour." It is not enough. We want to take our share in that interior voyage and watch how these alien sights and sounds affect the writer. If he lacks that compulsion of the spirit which is called character or lets his mind linger on contingencies hostile to frank utterance, he will be unable to supply that want and leave us dissatisfied. . . .

The modern author of travel-literature one suspects to be a greyish little person, uncommonly wide awake, perky and plausible, but somewhat deficient in personality— a kind of reporter, in fact, ready to adopt anybody's philosophy, or nobody's in particular. Those earlier ones were not of this sort. They derived, to begin with, from another stock, for voyages used to be costly undertakings. They were gentlemen scholars who saw things from their own individual angle. Their leisurely aristocratic flavour, their wholesome discussions about this and that, their waywardness and all that mercurial touch of a bygone generation—where is it now? . . .

That mercurial touch disappears when the conditions which gave it birth are at an end. We have ceased to be what we were, that's all. Year by year our hard-won domestic privileges have been gnawed or lopped away; the secret history of the English citizen is one long wail of liberties forfeited; we are being continentalized, standardized—a process which cannot but reflect itself in life and literature. It blunts our peculiar edges. Singularity, the hall-mark of that older Anglo-Saxon, is hardly perceptible in our modern bearing or writing. We have ceased to be mad, none but a flatterer would still call us eccentric. All kinds of other factors have contributed to this result, such as improved world communications. Dr. Arnold, again, that merciless pruner of youthful individualism, has wrought a miracle of destruction so far as originality is concerned, for his energies hit hardest the very class from whom those sturdy and idiomatic, and sometimes outrageous opinions used to come.

Douglas certainly put into practice his theories on how a travel book should be written. Contrary to what some critics have asserted, he overflowed with humanity, kindliness, and understanding of others, and these qualities make themselves felt in the pages of *Old Calabria* and his other travel books. His account of the places he visits is informative and vivacious, rouses our curiosity, and makes us long to visit the country. Douglas traveled for the pleasure of learning, seeing little-known places, meeting new people—he always had a weakness for the simpler, more elemental type of person—and, above all, satisfying his curiosity. He succeeds in communicating this pleasure to the reader. His zest for life is sensed at once and is infectious.

Douglas wrote slowly and carefully, and *Old Calabria* is the work of several years, embodying a long and varied experience. The mood changes continually. At one moment, such as in the chapters dedicated to the Flying Monk and Southern Saintliness, Douglas reveals his interest in hagiology and shows his delicate sense of irony. At another moment he sets out to prove—perhaps with tongue in cheek—that Milton had in *Paradise Lost* plagiarized the *Adamo Caduto* of Salandra. Then there are passages where Douglas expresses a mood of complete serenity, as for example:

Meanwhile it is good to rest here, immovable but alert, in the breathless hush of noon. Showers of benevolent heat stream down upon this desolation, not the faintest wisp of vapour floats upon the horizon; not a sail, not a ripple, disquiets the waters. The silence can be felt. Slumber is brooding over the things of earth. . . .

Such torrid splendour, drenching a land of austerest simplicity, decomposes the mind into corresponding states of primal contentment and resilience. There arises before our phantasy a new perspective of human affairs; a suggestion of well-being, wherein the futile complexities and disharmonies of our age shall have no place. . . . To discard these wrappings, to claim kinship with some elemental and robust archetype, lover of earth and sun. . . .

How fair they are, these moments of golden equipoise.
(ch. 40)

Compare that with the concluding paragraph of *By the Ionian Sea* (1901), where George Gissing, after having been shown by the curator of the museum of Reggio Calabria a few words written in Greek in the hand of François Lenormant, writes:

I could have desired no happier incident for the close of my journey. By lucky chance this visit to the museum had been postponed till the last morning, and, as I idled through the afternoon about the Via Plutino, my farewell mood was in full harmony with that in which I had landed from Naples upon the Calabrian shore; so hard a thing to catch and to retain, the mood corresponding perfectly to an intellectual bias—hard, at all events, for him who cannot shape his life as he will and whom circumstance ever menaces with dreary harassment. Alone and quiet, I heard the washing of the waves; I saw the evening fall on cloud-wreathed Etna, the twinkling lights come forth upon Scylla and Charybdis; and as I looked my last toward the Ionian Sea I wished it were mine to wander endlessly amid the silence of the ancient world, today and all its sounds forgotten.

How different is the mood, and how different their approach to life! Douglas, although he admired Gissing, had the more rounded and harmonious personality; and he was also more fortunate in that he was able to spend the greater part of his life in Italy. In *Alone* he asks himself why people trouble to go to Italy and replies:

A periodical visit to this country seems an ordinary and almost automatic proceeding—a part of one's regular routine, as natural as going to the barber or to Church. Why seek for reasons? They are so hard to find. One tracks them to their lair and lo! there is another one lurking in the background, a reason for a reason.

The craving to be in contact with beauty and antiquity, the desire for self-expression, for physical well-being under that drenching sunshine, which, while it lasts, one curses lustily; above all, the pleasure of memory and reconstruction at a distance. For a haze of oblivion is formed by lapse of time and space; a kindly haze which obliterates the thousand fretting annoyances wherewith the traveller's path in every country is bestrewn. . . . He forgets them; forgets that weltering ocean of unpleasantness and remembers only the sporadic islets—those moments of calm delight or fiercer joy which he would fain hold fast for ever. He does not come here on account of a certain fountain which ought never to be cleaned. He comes for the sake of its mirage, that sunny phantom which will rise up later out of some November fog in another land. Italy is a delightful place to remember, to think and talk about. And is it not the same with England? Let us go there as a tourist—only as a tourist. How attractive one finds its conveniences and even its conventionalities, provided one knows, for an absolute certainty, that one will never be constrained to dwell among them.

What lovely things one could say about England, in Timbuktoo!

Douglas' travel books are full of such golden moments of happiness induced by the atmosphere of the place he is visiting—usually rich in historical associations—or the companion with whom he is traveling. The concluding passage of *Alone* conjures up such a mood:

I thought of certain of my fellow creatures. I often think of them. What were they now doing? Taking themselves seriously and rushing about, as usual, haggard and careworn—like those rapacious ants that scurry hither and thither and stare into each other's faces with a kind of desperate imbecility, when some sportive schoolboy has kicked their ridiculous nest into the air and upset all their solemn little calculations.

As for ourselves, we took our ease. We ate and drank, we slumbered awhile, then joked and frolicked for five hours on end, or possibly six. I kept no count of what was said nor how the time flew by. I only know that when at last we emerged from our ambrosial shelter the muscles of my stomach had grown sore from the strain of laughter and Arcturus was twinkling overhead.

Although Douglas knew Italy and the Italians well, he was most familiar with the area south of Rome—the Sabine hills, the Abruzzi, the Bay of Naples, and Calabria. He liked classical Italy, and was drawn to those regions where the civilizations of Greece and Rome met and mingled. He had little knowledge of Italian literature and in fact read little Italian poetry and few novels or short stories. Neither was he interested in Italian painting nor in any kind of painting. Although he lived many years in Florence, he was prone to dismiss the architecture and pictures there with a contemptuous tone of voice as so much "Cinquecento." He was fascinated by the fauna and the flora of Italy. In addition to his love of pagan Italy for its associations with the past, he appreciated the day-to-day human contacts. His approach was thus utterly different from that of the aesthete or intellectual who saw in Italy one vast museum and ignored the vitality and humanity of the country and its people. Douglas, with his historical and scientific cast of mind, liked classical Italy, but he needed and sought the human companionship of ordinary simple Italians as well. He had a great feeling for landscape, but, particularly, for the wild, grandiose, mountainous country of the south.

The personality of Douglas vibrates in almost every paragraph of his works, most emphatically in his travel books. Although *Old Calabria, Siren Land,* or *Fountains in the Sand* fill you with a longing to visit the places described, it is possible to derive great pleasure from reading them without having traveled in one or the other of these regions, as they are knit together by the rich personality of the author and his philosophy of life. He had all the attributes of the perfect traveler: he liked walking immense distances, and he did not mind roughing it in order to see out-of-the-way places; he could put up with coarse food and wine for the sake of getting to know remote villages in southern Italy or Tunisia; he was a fine classical scholar and could relate the present to the past; he delighted in the casual conversation; and, above all, his richly stored mind was illumined by a restless curiosity. During his travels he found great pleasure in whiling away the evening in the company of those he met in inns or restaurants. As he wrote in *Old Calabria:*

> This meal [dinner] marks the termination of my daily tasks; nothing serious is allowed to engage my attention, once that repast is ended. I call for a chair and sit down at one of the small marble-topped tables in the open street and watch the crowd as it floats around me, smoking a Neapolitan cigar and imbibing, alternately, ices and black coffee until, towards midnight, a final bottle of *vino di Cirò* is uncorked, fit seal for the labours of the day.
>
> (ch. 37)

He made it a rule never to work after dinner, and he liked to linger long over the table, talking and drinking far into the night.

Douglas was always good company, but he was at his best when traveling. I can remember many journeys with him in the thirties, through Calabria, or walks across the hills near Rome, visiting places like Olevano, Genazzano, Subiaco, or Arsoli; and, although he was already well past sixty, he would think nothing of walking twenty miles a day. The hours would pass quickly as he evoked memories of previous visits, or would point out some rather unusual wild flower, or would recall some strange story connected with the village we passed through.

At the end of a long day's walking—and he nearly always carried a rucksack on these journeys—in Calabria or over the hills round Rome he would make for some inn that he knew and where he was received as an old friend. He attached great importance to the inns or restaurants on his travels, and would remember very clearly those that were good. He would order his meal with meticulous care, even in a Calabrian village. He attached importance to what he ate and despised those who were indifferent to food. Of an Englishman in *Alone* who remarks that he does not care what he eats, he comments:

> I don't care what I eat! What a confession to make! Is it not the same as saying, I don't care whether I am dirty or clean? . . . It is nothing to boast of. A man owes something to those traditions of our race which have helped to raise us above the level of the brute. Good taste in viands has been painfully acquired; it is a sacred trust. Beware of gross feeders. They are a menace to their fellow creatures. Will they not act, on occasion, even as they feed? Assuredly they will. Everybody acts as he feeds.

III

In those travels through Calabria he would often be joined after dinner by those he had known on previous visits. I remember visiting San Demetrio Corone (which he describes in *Old Calabria*) with him in 1935. We stayed at a little inn that had a few rooms above a grocer's shop. The innkeeper, a sturdy, thickset Albanian with closely shaven head, owned the shop as well as the hotel. He had known Douglas for more than twenty years and said he was the first Englishman to have visited that village—at least in his lifetime. While we were dining, the secretary of the local Fascist party came in and in rather an insolent manner asked us if we had reported to the Fascio. We had, of course, filled in the usual forms at the hotel that foreigners were supposed to complete, but neither of us had ever heard that there was any law obliging foreigners to go to the headquarters of the local Fascist party. This man was evidently exceeding his authority. A crowd of villagers gathered round, wondering what Douglas was going to say. He replied very calmly that we had filled in the usual forms but did not feel that we were obliged to do anything more. The secretary, evidently accustomed to bullying, then adopted a yet ruder tone and peremptorily shouted at us that we should have gone round to the Fascio; at this Douglas rose to his feet and declared roundly that he had visited San Demetrio long before the secretary was even born, had never gone to the Fascio before, and did not propose to do so now. He concluded by saying that he did not want his meal to be interrupted further by such nonsense. To the delight of those assembled, the secretary remained speechless and beat a hasty retreat from the room. We resumed our dinner, and the professor, lawyer, doctor, and others who had witnessed the scene were grateful that at last someone had called the bluff of this absurdly arrogant official. They all sided with Douglas, and for the rest of the evening he was the hero of these simple villagers.

"It reveals a personality. It contains a philosophy of life," is how he summed up *The Nooks and Byways of Italy* (1868) by Craufurd Tait Ramage. And no words could more appropriately or more succinctly describe Douglas' own travel books. Whether in *Old Calabria, Siren Land, Alone,* or one of the other travel books, you continually catch a glimpse of Douglas himself. *Old Calabria,* in addition, contains a mass of information about the country and its social and economic conditions; there are also many shrewd, illuminating observations about the Italian character. One young man describes how he had heard that they still hang murderers in England, as they used to do in Italy. He thought this rather barbaric. Douglas adds that the people there tend to regard the English as savages, as hopeless savages. Or again:

I pause, to observe parenthetically that this habit of uttering platitudes in the grand manner as though disclosing an idea of vital novelty (which Charles Lamb, poor fellow, thought peculiar to natives of Scotland) is as common among Italians as among Englishmen. But vested in sonorous Latinisms, the staleness of such remarks assumes an air of profundity.

He singles out the extraordinary aptitude of Italians as engineers. He points out that no people are more fundamentally sane in matters of the heart than the southern Italians. They are seldom naively enamored. They may play to the gallery and act the part of passionate lovers for a time, but in their real courtship they will be realistic and marry a girl with a dowry and will be guided by the advice of their uncles and aunts—but not until their military service is terminated: "Everything in its proper time and place." He asserts that envy is the most conspicuous native vice, and he blames this on the lack of nutrition, and, in particular, on that morning thimbleful of black coffee. He emphasizes the poverty of Calabria. It is not very different today, though postwar Italian governments have indeed made a serious attempt to ameliorate conditions.

Sometimes, rereading *Old Calabria,* I find it difficult to remember that it was written so many years before *Christ Stopped at Eboli* (1948) by Carlo Levi, since it anticipates so much of what is to be found in the later book. Both give accurate pictures of two different regions of southern Italy. Take, for instance, the following passage from *Old Calabria:* "We are disposed to associate squalor with certain artistic effects, but it may be said of this and many other Calabrian places that they have solved the problem how to be ineffably squalid without being in the least picturesque."

He remarks that Calabria is not a land to traverse

alone: "It is too wistful and stricken, too deficient in those externals that conduce to comfort." But then Douglas seldom traveled alone. He nearly always traveled with a friend, or, as in *Alone,* found his company along the way. His acute understanding of the Italian character is displayed in the series of shrewd observations that enrich and enliven the pages of his Italian travel books. For example, in *Siren Land,* the first of his travel books, he describes the country near Sorrento. It is less erudite than *Old Calabria* but remains one of the most delightful of his works. There is the same blending of scholarship, irony, and humanity. He expresses a mood of extraordinary serenity. There is a chapter on Tiberius and one on the Blue Grotto at Capri. There is a remarkable chapter on leisure in which he writes: "Everything which distinguishes man from animals is the result of leisure. . . . Leisure first made man formidable on earth. And our virtue, so far as it differs from that of animals, is purely the result of leisure. . . . Leisure is the curse of the poor in spirit."

Douglas possessed a robust sanity of outlook that stood him in good stead and that is the most distinguishing characteristic of his writing. He believed that civilized man has the right to leisure, though he should know how to use it properly. As examples of the misuse of leisure he quotes toothache, baldness, picnics, envy, fraud, codes of honor among schoolboys, army officers, and "other imperfectly civilized associations." Douglas, like Gissing, did not believe that time was money, but rather that money was time.

Incidentally, when regretting in *Siren Land* the untimely death of Gissing, he attributes this to "inefficient equipment, not of intellectuality but of outlook and attitude . . . of that tough, cheerful egotism which, sanely regarded, is but sanity itself." Douglas prided himself on possessing a certain dose of that cheerful egotism.

In addition to the Italian travel books, Douglas wrote *Together* (1923) about Austria, *Fountains in the Sand* about Tunisia, and *One Day* (1929) about Athens. In *Together* he describes a visit to the region of Austria where he was born. He evokes a mood of nostalgia as he recalls episodes of his childhood and portrays pictures of his different relations. He points a contrast between Austria and the south, partly by quoting the reactions of R, his French traveling companion, and partly by reminding us of the difference in temperature and atmosphere between Austria and Italy. *Together,* unlike Douglas' other travel books, is lively with appreciation of the north: the shade of the woods in summer, the fir trees and pines in the Lutz forest, the mountain streams, the generous hospitality and friendliness of the Austrians—it would almost give the impression of having been written in a mood of nostalgia, after many years of residence in the south.

One Day originated out of a suggestion made by the Greek government that Douglas should write a book about Greece rather in the manner of *Old Calabria*; for this purpose he received a grant from the Greek government. But, unfortunately for posterity, when Douglas arrived in Athens he stayed at the British School. There he glanced at the vast library of books about Greece, and he perceived what a formidable task he had set himself. It would clearly take him several years to write such a book. Moreover he realized that his knowledge of the language had grown rusty with the passage of years. He therefore abandoned such an ambitious task and contented himself with writing an account of a day's visit to one or two favorite haunts, in or near Athens, evoking memories of previous visits and giving rein to a few historical disquisitions. The result is a little masterpiece and was later republished in the volume *Three of Them* (1930), with *Nerinda* (1901) and *On the Herpetology of the Grand Duchy of Baden* (1894).

In *Fountains in the Sand* he writes of his visits to Tunisia at the beginning of the century and gives some superb descriptions of the landscape and life in the towns of Gafsa and Tozeur. The conversations with some of the local inhabitants are perhaps among the most striking memories of this book.

Douglas had a zest for traveling and derived from it an intense pleasure, which he communicates in his writing. In *Late Harvest* (1946) he writes:

There is this advantage in the writing of books when they are in some measure autobiographical, describing events from childhood onwards; instead of being confused memories they are authentic documents which allow a man to live his life over again and cast his thoughts backwards with assurance. There is nothing vague about a written record.

And this is perhaps the best commentary on his travel books.

South Wind, that strange, gay, fanciful novel, also contains much of Douglas' philosophy of life. It is as if, in the interval between writing *Old Calabria*

and *South Wind*, his point of view had clarified so that he expresses it in the novel in a more sharply outlined form. Although *Old Calabria* remains—for me at any rate—his finest work, *South Wind* made a greater impact and reached a wider public. It might, I suppose, be described as a novel of conversation, or a novel of ideas, rather in the manner of the novels of Thomas Love Peacock. Yet there is, as Douglas has pointed out in *Alone*, a plot. Indeed, he asserts that

it would be nearer the truth to say that it is nothing but plot from beginning to end. How to make murder palatable to a bishop: that is the plot. How? You must unconventionalize him and instil into his mind the seeds of doubt and revolt. You must shatter his old notions of what is right. It is the only way to achieve this result, and I would defy the critic to point to a single incident or character or conversation in the book which does not further the object in view. The good Bishop soon finds himself among new influences; his sensations, his intellect, are assailed from within and without. Figures such as those in Chapters 11, 18 and 35, the endless dialogue in the boat, the even more tedious happenings in the local law-court, the very externals—the jovial immoderation of everything and everybody: they foster a sense of violence and insecurity; they all tend to make the soil receptive to new ideas.

Indeed, Mr. Heard, the Bishop—a typical representative of the narrow, conventional, upper-middle classes in England, a product of the English public schools—is profoundly influenced by his brief sojourn in the Mediterranean. It might almost be described as a study of the impact made by Italy on an Englishman: *L'inglese italianizzato è il diavolo incarnato*,[2] runs the Italian proverb. Italy certainly has a leavening, softening, and civilizing influence on the Englishman who settles in, or even visits, the country. The arteries of the Bishop, which have hardened over the years, begin to soften, his conventional point of view becomes less formal, his mind more open. His values, too, change imperceptibly. He had been taught to believe that strenuousness by itself was something to be admired. Count Caloveglia points out to him that whenever anything, however fantastic, is imposed upon men by physical forces, they straightaway make a god of it and that this is why they deify strenuousness. The complex conditions under which men live in the north make life more of a struggle. They have to obtain extra clothing, footwear, mufflers, carpets, and rugs;

---

[2] "The italianate Englishman is the devil incarnate."

abundant and costly food is required to keep the body healthy; they have to contend with the difficulties of plumbing, gas, woodwork, paintings and repaintings, tons of fuel, lighting in winter, contrivances against frost and rain, never-ending repairs to houses. Such difficulties scarcely exist in the Mediterranean.

Count Caloveglia makes it clear he is interested not in the majority—he dismisses it scornfully—but in the elect few. "Living in our lands," he says to the Bishop, "men would have leisure to cultivate nobler aspects of their nature. They would be accessible to purer aspirations, worthier delights. They would enjoy the happiness of sages. What other happiness deserves the name? In the Mediterranean, Mr. Heard, lies the hope of humanity." The Bishop listens and is thoughtful. He broods about happiness. At one time he used to think it was achieved by Christianity and civilization. In China he learned that men could be happy without Christianity, and in Africa that they could be happy without civilization. Count Caloveglia, after a pause, moves relentlessly on in pursuit of his argument. He maintains that men have realized the baseness of mercantile and military ideals and will settle round the Mediterranean, there to lead more serene lives. The Bishop, "who knew something of the evils of northern industrialism," listens approvingly.

It is interesting to trace the development of the Bishop's mental processes as the story unfolds. Keith and Count Caloveglia are the main influences on him, though from afar he too admires Eames, an expatriate Englishman of meager resources who is admired by the other characters for his austere but gentlemanly way of life. Douglas expresses his own philosophy of life partly through Keith, partly through Caloveglia, and partly through Eames. Whether in his diatribe against poverty or his enthusiasm for Pepys or his admiration for Gissing, Keith seems to be the mouthpiece of Douglas himself. Keith, too, undermines the solid convictions of the Bishop. In a conversation with him he talks of the demi-vierge concessions that the English church has made to common sense and that afford seductive resting places to the intellectually weak-kneed. Mr. Heard is slightly perturbed by these words. A good fellow like Keith! "*Demi-vierge* concessions to common sense." What did he mean by that? Did his church really make such concessions?

"I'll think about it tomorrow," he decides.

Later, Keith remarks to the Bishop that his values appear perverted, and the latter begins to wonder whether this is really so. Then Keith engages him in conversation while visiting a grotto in a rowboat and draws a distinction between horizontal and vertical gods. The horizontal or downstairs gods are those invented by intellectualists who felt themselves capable of maintaining a kind of comradeship with their deities. The vertical gods are those invented by the proletariat for the use of the aristocracy. The proletariat loves to humiliate itself, and therefore manufactures a god who approves of groveling, a god who can look down upon them. Such a distinction has never occurred to Mr. Heard before, with the result that he is puzzled and still more preoccupied about his values. He consoles himself, however, by pointing out to Keith that the laws of morality have at least been written down for our guidance in letters that never change. Keith counters this by describing how the laws of good conduct do change from generation to generation, and he adds that all morality is a generalization, and all generalizations are tedious. Mr. Heard asks Keith whether he does not disapprove of Van Koppen's (an American millionaire) ladies. Keith says he cannot disapprove of things that do not impinge on his own activities.

"Is that your quarrel with what you call the upstairs god system?" asks the Bishop.

"Precisely. It does not offend me by its unsanitary tendency to multiply sins. It affects me when it impinges on my own activities; that is to say, when it transforms those sins into legal crimes. How would you like to be haled before a Court of law for some ridiculous trifle, which became a crime only because it used to be a sin and became a sin only because some dyspeptic or impotent old antediluvian was envious of his neighbours' pleasure? Our statute-book reeks of discredited theories of conduct; the serpent's trail of the theologian, of the reactionary, is over all."

(ch. 20)

The Bishop's significant comment is: "It never struck me in that light before." Mr. Heard is influenced by what he himself terms the pagan light of the Mediterranean; for the first time in many years he has the leisure in which to meditate and is no longer drugged by habit or a life of action. He succumbs to the fascination, first, of his conversations with Caloveglia, a wise pagan Italian, and, later, of those with Keith, a self-confessed hedonist. The Bishop's outlook undergoes a steady change as a consequence.

Keith gives the Bishop no relief and hammers away mercilessly at his fixed preconceptions. Mr. Heard is worn down by the combined effect of the heat and the discussion and is in no mood to argue. He has just the energy to ask Keith his opinion.

The novel is brought to a conclusion by a conversation between Count Caloveglia and Mr. Heard; the latter asks the count if he has noticed that there is an unwonted sparkle in the air, something cleansing and clarifying.

"To be sure I do," replied the other. "And I can tell you the cause of it. Sirocco is over for the present. The wind has shifted to the north. It brightens all nature. It makes one see things in their true perspective, doesn't it?"
"That is exactly what I feel," said Mr. Heard.

(ch. 39)

And the novel ends on this note, the author having accomplished his purpose of demonstrating the influence of environment on an ordinary, conventional human being.

IV

South Wind, of course, contains a great deal besides the story of the Bishop. Count Caloveglia and Keith, the two principal characters, might, as I have already pointed out, be regarded as illustrating two facets of the author's personality. Though not in every detail—for example, Douglas had a love and understanding of music that is not shared by Keith—the author uses them to express his philosophy of life: the philosophy of a temperate Epicurean, steeped in the classical tradition, a tolerant skeptic, a rationalist humanist. Douglas wrote that *South Wind* was the result of his craving to escape from the wearisome actualities of life and that his aim had been to picture himself living in a society of such instability, such "jovial immoderation" and "frolicsome perversity" that even a respectable bishop could be persuaded to approve of murder.

Keith resembles Douglas in that

he was in love with life. It dealt fairly with him. It made him loth to bid farewell to this gracious earth and the blue sky overhead, to his cooks and his books, his gardeners and roses and flaming cannas; loth to exchange these things of love, these tangible delights, for a hideous and everlasting annihilation.

(ch. 28)

Constantly Douglas himself would talk in this vein. Just as Keith loved life and hated the idea of death, so Douglas, speaking of himself in *Late Harvest* (1946), writes:

Having reached nearly twice the age at which Platen died, I no longer complain of how I squandered my days; my one regret is that I have not many more of them to squander. If one has enjoyed life and contrived to extract matter of mirth out of its not infrequent mistakes, one cannot be said to have squandered one's days. A man's days are his own. He will do well, I should think, not to listen to others as to whether he has wasted his life or not; that is his own concern. Let him analyse the past and draw conclusions, if it amuses him, as to the part he played or was made to play.

Even in the last twilight years, at Capri, he enjoyed life; he was a rare example of the intellectual who had discovered the secret of happiness, and he had the ability to infect others with his mood. He was essentially extrovert and inclined to pity those who were given to moods of introspection. His tireless intellectual curiosity and his capacity for enthusiasm no doubt contributed in part to his happiness and his joy in life. A few days before he died, when he knew there was no longer any hope of recovery, he remarked to a friend how tragic it was that he should have to die while so many others who did not care about life should be able to go on living. Keith, in *South Wind*, we may remember, disliked funerals and displayed an unreasoning hatred of death and, what was still more remarkable, not the least shame in confessing it. Keith, too, like Douglas, was ever avid of fresh things and regretted his lost opportunities.

The advice Keith gave to Denis is much the same as the advice Douglas was wont to give to the young: he should not attach too much importance to what human beings said and did; he should forsake art and books for a time and come into contact with nature and think things out for himself instead of listening to other people.

Like Keith's, Douglas' recipe for happiness was to find everything useful and nothing indispensable, and everything wonderful and nothing miraculous; and at the same time to reverence the body and avoid fundamental causes like the plague.

Similarly, there is much of Douglas in Caloveglia. There is something Greek about both of them. Color —at least in art—said little to either of them, and both were enamored of form. Like the count, Douglas could—and sometimes did—cook with passionate enthusiasm if he had the leisure and materials. Just as when Caloveglia extols the art of cooking to the Bishop, so when he contrasts progress with civilization, or compares northern ethical values with those prevalent in the Mediterranean, or talks of the withering influence of the Bible on the English spirit, we seem to hear the voice of Douglas. And, above all, when the count defines the meaning of temperance:

"Temperance," said the Bishop. "Another of those words I am always being obliged to use. Pray tell us, Count, what you mean by temperance."

"I should call it the exercise of our faculties and organs in such a manner as to combine the maximum of pleasure with the minimum of pain."

"But who is to judge what constitutes the dividing line between use and abuse?"

"We cannot, I imagine, do better than go to our own bodies for an answer to that question. They will tell us exactly how far we may proceed with impunity."

"In that case," said the millionaire, "if you drink a little too much occasionally, only occasionally I mean, you would not call that intemperance?"

"Certainly not," said the Count.

(ch. 30)

Douglas believed in the Greek virtue of moderation. He had imbibed much of what he termed the Mediterranean spirit, and latterly he was really happy only living in the south. He was in sympathy with the temperate way of life of the Italians. He liked their tolerance, their lack of hypocrisy, their pagan outlook. He liked, too, the easygoing rhythm of life, the lack of petty restrictions, such as the licensing laws. England, on the other hand, he liked to savor in small doses, rather as a tourist. In the Mediterranean, as Caloveglia points out, ethical standards of criticism are replaced by artistic standards, and this appealed to Douglas.

Again, in the distinction that Caloveglia draws between progress and civilization it is, I think, possible to detect Douglas' own view. He regarded progress as a centripetal movement, obliterating man in the mass, whereas civilization he considered a centrifugal force, permitting and postulating the assertion of personality. In his view, progress subordinates, while civilization coordinates. The individual emerges in civilization but is submerged in progress. The two are incompatible.

Douglas was an individualist. He was not interested in politics and believed it is the duty of the individual to carve out his own existence. He abhorred any form of intolerance. He agreed with his friend

Oscar Levy that the origins of both Hitlerism and Bolshevism could be traced to the Bible. Referring to *The Idiocy of Idealism* of Levy, he wrote:

The first [Hitlerism], he argues, has its roots in the Chosen People and pure-Race nonsense with which the Old Testament is saturated (good specimens in Ezra and Nehemiah) and which was eagerly sucked in by those passionate Bible-readers, the Germans, who twisted it into their contemptible Herrenvolk doctrine. The second has its roots in that envy of the rich which crops up repeatedly in the New Testament (Woe unto you that are rich, etc.; it is easier for a camel, etc.; conveniently contrary texts, as usual, are at hand). Would it be right to say that Christianity is based to an overwhelming extent on envy of the rich and glorification of the proletariat, that Bolshevism is based on Christianity, even as Hitlerism is based on the Hebrew prophets?

Thus *South Wind*, behind its gay facade, has an underlying serious purpose—the projection of Douglas' Epicurean philosophy of life. But there are other characters to whom, perhaps, a brief reference should be made: Miss Wilberforce (note the irony in the choice of the name), the incurable but happily drunken spinster; Denis, the eternal adolescent, groping his way toward a knowledge of himself; Mr. Parker, the slightly shady, coarse-grained secretary of the local club; Signor Malipizzo, the opportunist, freethinking judge; and, of course, the Russian characters.

Writing about *South Wind* in *Late Harvest*, Douglas declared that in austere moments certain passages struck him as being ornate to the verge of flabbiness. It is true that his style underwent a considerable change in his later books. It became more astringent, and in *Alone* he evolved a highly individual style that at times is almost conversational.

The other two novels, *They Went* (1920) and *In the Beginning* (1928), were less successful. Douglas described *They Went* as a "little allegory of beauty versus betterment." Just as in *South Wind* the author is concerned with morals, in *They Went* he deals with beauty and in *In the Beginning* with religion. They are both presented as myths. As R. M. Dawkins puts it in his biography *Norman Douglas*:

We find ourselves in fact facing that well-known Triad, the True, the Beautiful and the Good. Here we are accustomed to seeing the orthodox philosopher performing a few manipulations very much as a conjuror handles his rabbits. He rolls them about a little, lowers the light a moment and then shows us with triumph that the three white rabbits are really only three aspects of one white rabbit and that none of the children need be frightened. . . . He just leaves the three poles apart to fight out their triangular duel, and so far from being all of them comfortably coequal, the True, and very certainly the Good, tend to become rather hazy in their outlines, and the Beautiful proves herself a most aggressive and incompatible bedfellow. *South Wind* came first: in it the Good distinctly goes to the wall. Then came *They Went*; here the Beautiful seems simply indifferent to what happens to the others. Lastly we have *In the Beginning,* where we see that the sanity of Truth seems to have deserted mankind for good and all. But what has driven her away? Alas! It is Goodness, that fell disease.

Douglas succeeded in remaining a humanist in an age that grew increasingly hostile to humanism. He carved out his own existence. He had a refreshing way of thinking for himself and was not deceived or misled by the platitudes or shibboleths of the world around him. He knew what he wanted in life, and he made every effort to obtain it. He was happy and able to communicate his happiness and enthusiasm to others.

As he wrote in *Together,* he would not have missed the enjoyment of this life for anything, nor would he have exchanged it even then with any other creature on earth. He was at his ease with people of all kinds. If he were set down in farthest Cathay, he wrote in *Alone,* he would undertake to find, soon afterward, some person with whom he was quite prepared to spend the remaining years of his life. In *Alone,* too, he wrote:

I never pass that way without thanking God for a misspent youth. Why not make a fool of yourself? It is good fun while it lasts; it yields mellow mirth for later years, and are not our fellow-creatures, those solemn buffoons, ten times more ridiculous? Where is the use of experience if it does not make you laugh?

This Epicurean philosophy of life, adapted to the needs of the modern age, he expressed directly or indirectly in all his books. In an easy, lucid, polished prose he expressed ideas that ran counter to many of the more fashionable, ill-digested views of his day. He always seemed, however, to be talking the language of common sense. He railed against hypocrisy, puritanism, and smugness. He was the least pompous and most human of men, and the least complacent and most erudite of writers; and much knowledge of life, as well as considerable pleasure, can still be derived from reading his various books.

Douglas is a curiously isolated phenomenon in the literary history of this century, difficult to place in relation to other writers. He does not fit into any school or category. He had few points of resemblance with his own, and fewer still with the present, generation. But he would have preferred it so. His writings have that timeless quality that prevents them from being dated. *South Wind* or *Old Calabria* are as fresh today as when first written. He did not want to conform to any pattern. He was an individualist who did not feel bound by the conventions of society or of his age. He wrote naturally and superbly, but he never aspired to move in any kind of literary circle. He kept himself aloof from cliques, and his conversation concentrated on life rather than on literature. The cast of his mind was scientific, and he was primarily interested in facts and ideas. *South Wind* is a novel of ideas; he chooses the medium of the novel simply to expound his ideas, his philosophy of life, which he had already expressed to a great extent in *Old Calabria.* In *South Wind* he puts forward his ideas in a more playful, fanciful manner. Some of his characters hardly come to life; Denis, for example, remains hazy and formless. Some critics might say that the Bishop undergoes his intellectual and moral evolution too rapidly. It might strike the reader as improbable that such a transformation could take place in only twelve days.

Perhaps, too, the Bishop does not offer enough resistance to the influences surrounding him. Yet *South Wind* is not a novel in the traditional sense of the word, and Douglas' purpose was to propound certain ideas while at the same time amusing the reader. And in this he was most successful.

The novelist's touch is lacking in *They Went* and *In the Beginning;* in each he is mainly concerned with advancing a thesis. He was at his happiest and most successful in the travel books; there he was able to expound his philosophy of life, express the many facets of his glittering personality, and indulge in his quest for knowledge; he was further able to record his impressions of the landscape and people he encountered in the course of his travels. Yet the same dominant personality pervades *South Wind,* as it does the travel books, *Looking Back* (1933), and *London Street Games* (1916); and his message in the world of today is perhaps even more relevant than it was when it was written. Just as Douglas was a sun worshiper, so the lesson he has to teach us is radiant with the sunlit atmosphere of the pagan south and is impregnated with the robust sanity of his outlook.

SELECTED BIBLIOGRAPHY

I. BIBLIOGRAPHY. E. D. McDonald, *A Bibliography of the Writings of Norman Douglas* (Philadelphia, 1927), with notes by Douglas; N. Douglas, *Late Harvest* (London, 1946), includes Douglas' notes on some of his publications; C. Woolf and A. Anderson, *Memorial Exhibition of Works by N. Douglas* (London, 1952), catalog of exhibition at Edinburgh Central Library; C. Woolf, *A Bibliography of Norman Douglas* (London, 1954), repr. with corrections as *Notes on the Bibliography of Norman Douglas* (London, 1955).

II. COLLECTED WORKS. *Three Monographs* (Naples, 1906), contains "The Lost Literature of Capri," "Tiberius," and "Saracens and Corsairs in Capri"; *The Angel of Manfredonia* (San Francisco, 1929), repr. from *Old Calabria*; *Three of Them* (London, 1930), contains *One Day, Nerinda,* and *On the Herpetology of the Grand Duchy of Baden*; *An Almanac* (London, 1945), prose anthology selected by Douglas; *Norman Douglas: A Selection* (London, 1955), valuable intro. by D. M. Low.

III. SEPARATE WORKS. *Zur Fauna Santorins* (Leipzig, 1892), essay; *Contributions to an Avifauna of Baden* (London, 1894), essay; A. J. Olsen, *The Beaver in Norway*, translated by G. N. Douglas [Norman Douglas] (London, 1894); *On the Herpetology of the Grand Duchy of Baden* (London, 1894), essay; *Report on the Pumice Stone Industry of the Lipari Islands* (London, 1895), white paper; *On the Darwinian Hypothesis of Sexual Selection* (London, 1895), essay, repr. in *English Miscellany* (Rome, 1951).

Unprofessional Tales by "Normyx" [Norman Douglas] (London, 1901), fiction, in collaboration with his wife, Elsa Fitzgibbon, includes "A Mystery," "Elfwater," "The Sentence," "Nerinda," "Impromptu," "Nocturne," "In the Red Sea," "Anacreontic," "The Ignoble," "A Tyrrhenian Fable," "The Case of Mrs. Hillier," "To E. F. G.," "The Devil's Oak," "The Psychological Moment," "The Meeting of Autos and Eschata," "Belladonna"; *Materials for a Description of Capri*, 10 parts (London and Naples, 1904–1915): (1) "The Blue Grotto and Its Literature" (London, 1904), (2) "The Forestal Conditions of Capri" (London, 1904), (3) "Fabio Giordano's Relation of Capri" (Naples, 1906), (4) "The Lost Literature of Capri" (Naples, 1906), (5) "Tiberius" (Naples, 1906), (6) "Saracens and Corsairs in Capri" (Naples, 1906), (7) "The Life of the Venerable Suor Serafina di Dio" (London, 1907), (8) "Some Antiquarian Notes" (Naples, 1907), (9) "Disiecta Membra" (London, 1915), (10) "Index" (London, 1915)—republished as *Capri: Materials for a Description of the Island* (Florence, 1930).

Siren Land (London, 1911; rev. ed., London, 1923), travel; *Fountains in the Sand: Rambles Among the Oases of Tunisia* (London, 1912), travel; *Old Calabria* (London,

1915; repr. 1956), travel, the latter contains valuable intro. by J. Davenport; *London Street Games* (London, 1916; 2nd ed., rev. and enl., 1931), essay; *South Wind* (London, 1917; new ed., 1946), fiction, the latter contains an intro.

They Went (London, 1920; 3rd ed., 1921), fiction, the latter has prefatory letter and revs.; *Alone* (London, 1921), travel; *Together* (London, 1923), travel; *D. H. Lawrence and Maurice Magnus: A Plea for Better Manners* (Florence, 1924), privately printed; *Experiments* (London, 1925), essays and reviews, contains "Arabia Deserta," "The Correct Thing," "Blind Guides," "At the Forge," "Edgar Allan Poe," "Belladonna," "Intellectual Nomadism," "The Last Word," "A Mad Englishman," "Queer," "Anacreontic"; *In the Beginning* (London, 1928), fiction, also privately printed (Florence, 1927); *Some Limericks: Collected & Ensplendour'd with Introduction, Index, and Notes by Norman Douglas* (London, 1928), privately printed; *Birds and Beasts of the Greek Anthology* (London, 1928), essays, privately printed (Florence, 1927); *Nerinda* (Florence, 1929), novel; *One Day* (Chapelle-Réanville, 1929), travel; *How About Europe? Some Footnotes on East and West,* (Florence, 1929), privately printed, commentary.

Introduction to *The Last of the Medici* by John Gaston de' Medici, grand duke of Tuscany (Florence, 1930), privately printed; *Paneros: Some Words on Aphrodisiacs and the Like* (London, 1931), essay, also privately printed (Florence, 1930); *Summer Islands: Ischia and Ponza* (London, 1931), lim. ed. (London, 1944), travel; *Looking Back. An Autobiographical Excursion,* 2 vols. (London, 1933; one-vol. ed., 1934).

Late Harvest (London, 1946), autobiography; *Footnote on Capri* (London, 1952), notes with illus.; N. Douglas, ed., *Venus in the Kitchen; or, Love's Cookery Book by Pilaff Bey* [Norman Douglas] (London, 1952), intro. by G. Greene, mostly written by G. Orioli; A. Palmer, "Some Norman Douglas Letters," in *A Review of English Literature,* 6 (July 1965).

IV. BIOGRAPHICAL AND CRITICAL STUDIES. H. M. Tomlinson, *Norman Douglas* (London, 1931; enl. ed., 1952); R. MacGillivray [R. M. Dawkins], *Norman Douglas* (Florence, 1933), reiss. under author's real name (London, 1952); C. Fitzgibbon, *Norman Douglas: A Pictorial Record* (London, 1953), includes brief study; K. Macpherson, *Omnes Eodem Cogimur: Some Notes Written Following the Death of Norman Douglas, 9 February 1952* (London, 1953), privately printed; N. Cunard, *Grand Man: Memories of N. Douglas* (London, 1954), contains extracts from his letters and appreciations; R. Aldington, *Pinorman: Personal Recollections of N. Douglas* (London, 1954); R. D. Lindeman, *Norman Douglas: A Critical Study* (Ann Arbor, Mich., 1956); R. D. Lindeman, *Norman Douglas* (New York, 1965); M. Holloway, *Norman Douglas* (London, 1980).

J. M. SYNGE
(1871-1909)

LADY AUGUSTA GREGORY
(1852-1932)

Elizabeth Coxhead

I

In the 1890's, in an Ireland still firmly under English rule, there occurred a quite remarkable upsurge of creative interest in literature and the arts. Temporarily frustrated in their struggle for political independence by the fall of the great nationalist leader Charles Stewart Parnell, Irishmen of the middle and upper classes (mainly from the Protestant "Ascendancy," which had all the educational advantages) turned for consolation to the epics of Ireland's ancient heroic past, recently translated by Celtic scholars. Folklorists like Douglas Hyde taught themselves the Irish language still spoken by the peasantry along the western seaboard and made the exciting discovery that these same stories were still a living part of the folk consciousness, along with a vernacular poetry composed and handed down by wandering bards.

They also discovered that people whose first language was Irish Gaelic spoke an uncommonly musical and vivid English, partly based on spontaneous translation from the Gaelic, but also filled with rich Elizabethan turns of phrase.

Plainly, there was a wealth of poetic material here. But it might never have gotten beyond the cottage hearth and the folklore conference had there not coincided, in space and time, a handful of men and one woman with the gifts that could transmute it into a literature of universal appeal.

The leader was William Butler Yeats, already famous as a lyric poet, and hankering, as Shelley, Tennyson, and Browning had done before him, after some means of reviving the poetic drama of the Eliza-bethans. The worst of artistic forms, he pronounced, was the play about modern educated people, with its meager language and its action crushed into the narrow limits of possibility. "Educated and well-bred people do not wear their hearts upon their sleeves, and they have no artistic and charming language except light persiflage, and no powerful language at all, and when they are deeply moved they look silently into the fireplace." He was equally repelled by Henrik Ibsen's didactic "drama of ideas," the later plays of Ibsen being then unknown to him. The London stage seemed to him dominated and vulgarized by powerful actor-managers; and Ireland had no native drama and depended entirely on visiting English companies, which, if they brought Irish characters to the stage, presented them as figures of farce.

A richer dramatic language was needed, an escape from realism to heroic and universal themes. Yeats wrote: "it is only by extravagance, by an emphasis far greater than that of life as we observe it, that we can crowd into a few minutes the knowledge of years," as Shakespeare or as Sophocles had been able to do.

But Yeats was primarily a lyric poet, not a dramatic one. His early verse dramas have great verbal beauty, but they lack the spark of dramatic life. The whole playwriting movement, and the very existence of the Abbey Theatre, are due to his inspiration and leadership; but, ironically enough, the drama he envisaged was not to be written by him. It was created on the lesser scale of talent by his friend Augusta Gregory, and on the greater scale of genius by his protégé J. M. Synge.

J. M. SYNGE AND LADY AUGUSTA GREGORY

II

THEIR origins were similar. Augusta Persse was born in 1852 of a Galway landowning family. As a child she heard folktales and "rebel" talk from her Irish nurse and longed in vain to learn the mysterious language spoken all around her. She grew up into a sort of unpaid social worker on her father's enormous estate, visiting the tenants and helping those who could scarcely read and write with their letters to children in America, and thus she gained her unrivaled insight into the Irish peasant character. At the age of twenty-eight she married a much older neighbor, Sir William Gregory of Coole, a delightful and distinguished man who had been governor of Ceylon, and with him she traveled widely and came to know the great world of London politics and art. But sketches of Irish peasant life written during her married years show that she always knew this was to be her literary material, and when after twelve years Sir William died, leaving the house and estate of Coole to her in trust for their son, she flung herself into the new literary movement, learned Irish, took up the collecting of folklore, and in the years 1895–1896 got to know Yeats.

John Millington Synge[1] was born in 1871 at Rathfarnham, a Dublin suburb, of a family that had been important but had lost most of its wealth and land. His father died the next year, and he was brought up by his mother, a woman of narrow Protestant piety, to whom he was closely bound by an exasperated and rebellious affection. His holidays were spent among the peasantry of Wicklow, though because of his mother's prejudices he could never know them as closely as Augusta Persse did her Galway tenants.

He took a desultory degree at Trinity College, Dublin, then drifted into the apparently unprofitable life of a perpetual student, first in Germany, then in Paris, studying music and the Celtic languages. In fact, these were years of slow ripening, as he became acquainted with European literature and with all sorts and conditions of men—and women. With men he was shy and could appear morose, but although an unsuccessful lover—twice his proposals of marriage were refused by girls who could not see that he had any material prospects, and Molly Allgood, the beautiful young actress to whom he was engaged when he died, was rather a receiver than a giver of

adoration—he had a natural gift for securing the friendship and the confidence of women, and this helped his imagination to create the brilliant galaxy of feminine portraits in his plays.

In 1896, Yeats took a walking tour in the west of Ireland that cemented his friendship with Lady Gregory and also carried him out on a brief trip to the Aran Islands, three bare limestone plateaus that lie in the Atlantic across the mouth of Galway Bay. Later that year, Yeats met Synge in a students' boardinghouse in Paris, recognized the latent talent in this shabby dilettante who had so far failed to publish a line, and told him roundly that he was wasting his time in an alien culture and should go back to Ireland and out to Aran: a quite uncanny instance of one genius sensing another's spiritual need.

Synge's first visit to Aran in 1898 was a true renascence, a spiritual rebirth. The knowledge he had been subconsciously acquiring during his fallow years suddenly came into focus; he looked at these primitive people, and through them, into the heart of humanity. He found an almost untouched peasant culture, with Irish as the universal language, and with an extraordinary beauty and dignity in the bare cottages, the women's red dresses and the men's gray homespuns against the creamy limestone, the treasure of poems and stories that beguiled the evenings by the light of tiny cod-oil lamps. The chief industry was fishing from curraghs, or canoes of lath and canvas, and in the wild seas fatalities were frequent, so that men lived under the shadow of death, and women of bereavement; this bred in the people the passionate intensity of feeling for which the dramatist in Synge instinctively longed.

For five summers in succession he returned to the islands, living among the people as one of themselves, amusing them with conjuring tricks, absorbing their wildness and their strength—though there was one aspect of their lives, their fervent Roman Catholicism, that as an agnostic he could never reach; and a girl with whom he had made friends told him with something like revulsion that she was sure he would "go to hell by and by."

The themes of four of his plays were taken directly from the islands, those of *The Playboy of the Western World* (1907) and *Riders to the Sea* (1905) from actual happenings, those of *The Shadow of the Glen* (1905) and *The Well of the Saints* (1905) from folktales; but before he produced any plays he had produced as his first successful piece of prose a descriptive book on *The Aran Islands* (1907), still

---

[1] Pronounced "sing," and, by a charming family legend, bestowed by Henry VIII on an uncommonly sweet-voiced ancestor.

remarkably evocative of their atmosphere today. In it, and in the posthumously published *In Wicklow, West Kerry, and Connemara* (1911), can be traced much of the material he wove into the plays, and these books enshrine his continued delight in strong character and vivid personality: "These strange men with receding foreheads, high cheekbones and ungovernable eyes seem to represent some old type found on these few acres at the extreme border of Europe, where it is only in wild jests and laughter that they can express their loneliness and desolation." There we have the essence of Synge: laughter interpenetrated with desolation, "man as an angel inhabiting the body of a beast."

But he could not turn to the writing of plays about these people until a theater had been created, and actors found, capable of interpreting them; and this meanwhile was the principal labor of his new friends, Lady Gregory and Yeats.

III

WHEN Yeats confided to Lady Gregory that he had written a poetic play on an Irish subject and failed to get it produced in London, she replied that the proper place to put on Irish plays was Dublin; and with the help of a wealthy neighbor, Edward Martyn, who was another aspiring playwright, funds were raised to bring over English companies for three years in succession. And so the first performance at the Irish Literary Theatre was a production of Yeats's *The Countess Cathleen*, on 8 May 1899. But it was not a very happy compromise, as the English actors could not even pronounce the Irish names right. Then Yeats discovered that a group of Dublin amateurs, mainly workingclass, was putting on little sketches in temperance clubs, under the direction of the brothers Frank and Willie Fay, who had had some technical training and were passionate enthusiasts; they knew, in fact, a good deal more about the new continental production methods than he did himself. Finding them changed everything, for now the Irish dramatist could create in genuinely native terms. The Fays and their devoted, hard-schooled actors (who continued as unpaid amateurs right through till 1905) made possible the writing of Synge's and Lady Gregory's plays.

The performances were given on a shoestring in makeshift concert halls, and one of these, the Molesworth, saw in 1902 the production of Lady Gregory's first play, *Twenty-Five,* a touching little piece that promised great talent to come.

That year and next came Synge's *Shadow of the Glen* and *Riders to the Sea,* and Dublin uneasily recognized that this was more than promise; it was a new and disconcerting form of achievement. Then Annie Horniman, a well-to-do Englishwoman who was a fervent admirer of Yeats's poetic plays, offered to give the movement a proper home, and a former mechanics' institute in Abbey Street was converted into a simple but adequate little playhouse; and thus, what future historians will probably recognize as the most vital theater of the early twentieth century was born. The Abbey Theatre opened its doors on 27 December 1904 with a double bill comprising Yeats's Cuchulain play *On Baile's Strand* and Lady Gregory's brilliant little village scandal comedy *Spreading the News.*

The audience at the Abbey was to show itself highly individualistic and capable on occasion of quite as much violence and passion as the Aran islanders. The opposition was mainly political and chiefly to the plays of Synge. At first, relations between the movement and the political Nationalists had been friendly, and they regarded *Cathleen ni Houlihan,* the famous propaganda playlet written jointly by Yeats and Lady Gregory, as ammunition in their cause. But then came Synge, presenting an Ireland in which wives could be unfaithful, priests unworthy, and sons capable of harboring a death wish against their fathers; and many felt that he was deliberately defacing the image so earnestly built up of a country wise, mature, and ready for self-government. Nationalist indignation culminated when *The Playboy of the Western World* was given its first week of performances in January 1907 and shouted down every night. Lady Gregory and Yeats held firm and fought for it valiantly, which they were now in a position to do, since the little amateur society had been re-formed as a professional company, with themselves and Synge as unpaid directors. The authority was now theirs—and also the strenuous labor of discovering new playwrights and reading scripts.

But not till the company made its summer tour to Oxford and London was *The Playboy* properly heard; then its immense originality was appreciated, and recognition came to Synge at last. It was just in time, for already the doctors knew that he was suffering from a malignant growth and could not live much more than a year. His last play, *Deirdre of the Sorrows* (1910), was written under the shadow of death, chiefly at his mother's suburban house, where Molly Allgood would visit him and read scenes as he wrote them, and the possibility of happiness with her gradually and bitterly receded. He was never to see her create the part.

He entered a Dublin hospital in January 1909, and on 24 March he said, "It's no use fighting death any longer" and turned his face to the wall. Remarkable as his six plays are, it is possible to hold that he had only begun to do justice to his talent, and that his death was a loss to English literature comparable to the early death of Keats.

IV

THE plays of Synge and Lady Gregory are often described as "dialect," but their language does not present much serious difficulty to anyone reasonably conversant with standard English. There are not many unfamiliar words; it is rather a question of construction and usage; and though there are constructions based on Gaelic syntax (that is, the infinitive used as subjunctive: "It is a pity the banshee not to be crying for yourself"), the context makes the sense plain. "Himself" and "herself" used as nouns are the polite peasant way of referring to the man or woman of the house. "You'd have a right to" has the force of "you ought to," and "dark" applied to a person usually means "blind." "Itself" sprinkled liberally through Synge's dialogue equals "actually" or "even." One soon becomes used to these and similar turns of phrase.

Synge's first play,[2] the one-act *Shadow of the Glen*, shows his dialogue and method already mature. If it can be considered a comedy—and the figures of husband and lover are almost farcical— at any rate it is comedy shot through with feeling and pathos. He has transposed to Wicklow the very an-

cient folktale, first heard by him in Aran, of the husband shamming death in order to trap the wife suspected of infidelity. But the change is more than geographical. To the folkteller, the wife was a villainess to be exposed, but the humane and sophisticated Synge with his background of European culture is entirely on the side of the wife, bound in the all-too-common Irish peasant institution of a loveless marriage and stifled by the mists and dreariness of the lonely glen. His Nora is a free spirit, sensitive to beauty, and his moral is the wickedness of trying to keep such a one caged.

In fact, though he objected to Ibsen's "pallid and joyless words," his Nora and the Nora of *A Doll's House* have much in common. Both slam the door on the loveless marriage and take to the hard life of the outcast. Ibsen is closer to reality, however, in making Nora take it alone. If Synge's play has a weakness, it is in the not quite realized figure of the Tramp who leads her to freedom. As with all great dramatists' creations, many of Synge's figures carry symbolic overtones. But henceforward, they are all firmly grounded in human reality first.

His second play, *Riders to the Sea*, has been called the finest one-act tragedy in the English language, and its overtones are tremendous. Synge had noted of Aran that "the maternal feeling is so powerful on these islands that it gives a life of torment to the women. Their sons grow up to be banished as soon as they are of age, or to live here in continual danger on the sea." Accordingly, old Maurya, who has already lost five sons to the sea and is about to lose the sixth, becomes a universal symbol of maternal grief. But she is nonetheless a real old woman in a whitewashed Aran cottage, with nets and a spinning wheel, and white boards against the wall that are to be used as a coffin for Michael's body when it is washed up—though we realize with a shudder that instead they will make the coffin of Bartley, the last surviving son, whom we see taking leave of his mother as he, too, rides off to the sea. Maurya foresees his death in a vision, and then her vision takes shape; her tragedy is complete.

They're all gone now, and there isn't anything more the sea can do to me. I'll have no call now to be up crying and praying when the wind breaks from the south, and you can hear the surf is in the east, and the surf is in the west, making a great stir with the two noises, and they hitting one on the other. . . . It isn't that I haven't prayed for you, Bartley, to the Almighty God. It isn't that I haven't said prayers in the dark night till you wouldn't know what I'd be saying; but it's a great rest I'll have now, and it's time, surely. It's a

---

[2] The first to be acted. An earlier one-act play, *When the Moon Has Set*, remained unpublished and unacted in his lifetime, having been rejected by Yeats and Lady Gregory. It has recently been given a private production by the Abbey Theatre and is included in *Plays*, book 1, of the Oxford *Collected Works*. It is interesting as foreshadowing the development of his dialogue, but it is still the work of an amateur who has his technique to learn.

great rest I'll have now, and great sleeping in the long nights after Samhain,[3] if it's only a bit of wet flour we do have to eat, and maybe a fish that would be stinking. . . . They're all together this time, and the end is come. May the Almighty God have mercy on Bartley's soul, and on Michael's soul, and on the souls of Sheamus and Patch and Stephen and Shawn; and may He have mercy on my soul, Nora, and on the soul of every one is left living in the world. Michael has a clean burial in the far north, by the grace of Almighty God. Bartley will have a fine coffin out of the white boards, and a deep grave surely. What more can we want than that? No man at all can be living for ever, and we must be satisfied.

But although she calls on the Christian God, Maurya is not a straight portrait of an Aran woman, who would have found more direct comfort in her religion. The forces that have brought her beyond despair are those that bludgeon the protagonists in a Greek tragedy. I am told that *Riders to the Sea* is a favorite with student drama groups in Asian universities, remote indeed from Aran, because it transcends the way of life in an obscure Atlantic island and summarizes the universal predicament.

In strong contrast is the riotous two-act comedy of *The Tinker's Wedding* (1907). The lawless bands of tinkers and gypsies that carried wildness the length and breadth of Ireland's roads always fascinated Synge, and here he takes a couple who have been living together, tinker-fashion, without benefit of wedding ring, and starts the girl hankering after respectability. A priest reluctantly agrees to marry them for a bit of gold and a tin can, but old Mary, Michael's mother, who regards the whole affair as a sad waste of time and tin, steals the can and pawns it for drink. The priest backs out and threatens to call the police, and the tinkers bundle him into a sack and make their escape. The piece is still not acted in Ireland, being considered an affront to the cloth, though it is this particular priest's unworthiness that Synge is exposing, and not altogether unkindly.

The play is merry, yet full of feeling, as comedy always is with Synge, particularly in the richly Falstaffian character of old Mary, with her relish for life, her pride in her daughter-in-law's beauty and ferocity, her moments of self-pity alternating with a fierce determination not to be left out of any fun:

What good am I this night, God help me? What good are the grand stories I have when it's few would listen to an old woman, few but a girl maybe would be in great fear the

time her hour was come, or a little child wouldn't be sleeping with the hunger on a cold night? Maybe the two of them have a good right to be walking out the little short while they'd be young; but if they have itself, they'll not keep Mary Byrne from her full pint when the night's fine, and there's a dry moon in the sky. Jemmy Neill's a decent lad, and he'll give me a good drop for the can; and maybe if I keep near the peelers tomorrow for the first bit of the fair, herself won't strike me at all; and if she does itself, what's a little stroke on your head beside sitting lonesome on a fine night, hearing the dogs barking, and the bats squeaking, and you saying over, it's a short while only till you die.

(Act I)

The Well of the Saints is a three-act black comedy, based on another widespread folktale of which Synge heard a version in Aran. Martin and Mary Doul are an elderly blind couple who have got on quite happily, begging at the crossroads and fancying themselves the handsomest pair in the countryside. A traveling saint brings water from a holy well and restores their sight, so that they learn the truth about themselves and part with bitter recrimination. Martin's life is now desolate indeed; he must labor for Timmy the smith instead of begging, and must suffer an anguish of desire for Molly, Timmy's odious young fiancée. His sight begins to fade again, and so does Mary's; they come together, and grope toward a new illusion, that when her hair has turned white and he has grown a patriarchal beard they will be handsome after all. The saint returns and offers to effect another cure, and Mary is tempted, but Martin will have none of it; he strikes the can and sends the holy water flying. The villagers, greatly shocked, drive the ungrateful pair away.

Synge is often accused of pessimism, and this play instanced as an example of it, but except in the sense that all agnostics must feel life and beauty to be ephemeral, I do not think it is an accusation he deserves. His characters are finally doomed, as we all are, but while they live, they relish life. There is nothing in them of our contemporary pessimism, which affects to regard life as boring and futile and death as a release. "There isn't anything more the sea can do to me," says Maurya, and Deirdre echoes it with "in the grave we're safe, surely," but only after they have put up a tremendous struggle to keep the life that is so rich and sweet. Here, the happiness of the blind couple is built on illusion, but the illusion itself results from the divine gift of imagination—the artist's faculty—and in possessing it Martin and Mary know a creative fulfillment forever denied to Timmy and Molly, the materially successful pair.

---

[3]Samhain: 1 November, All Soul's Day, the beginning of winter.

V

MANY critics have seen in this clash between illusion and reality the main theme of Synge's work, but perhaps that is to compress into the straitjacket of a formula an approach to life that was altogether more intuitive and complex. Undeniably, however, both he and Lady Gregory were fascinated by what she calls "our incorrigible Irish talent for myth-making," and derived from it their finest effects of pathos, irony, and fun. In *The Well of the Saints*, the myth is preferred to the harshness of fact. Synge's next play, *The Playboy of the Western World*,[4] is the triumph of a myth that, because it is believed in, becomes fact before our eyes. The Playboy has felt himself to be a weakling, but on falling in with a set of people who take him for a hero, he joyously discovers a hero's capacities.

Before Synge came to write *The Playboy*, he had abandoned Aran for West Kerry, where the people were bilingual and still possessed a richly Elizabethan English idiom; and this, as well as his increasing command of his medium, may account for the firefly-brilliant, flickering, gleaming dialogue of what is unquestionably his masterpiece. And only a masterpiece could fulfill the standard he demands in his preface:

On the stage one must have reality, and one must have joy; and that is why the intellectual modern drama has failed, and people have grown sick of the false joy of the musical comedy, that has been given them in place of the rich joy found only in what is superb and wild in reality. In a good play every speech should be as fully flavoured as a nut or apple, and such speeches cannot be written by anyone who works among people who have shut their lips on poetry. In Ireland, for a few years more, we have a popular imagination that is fiery, and magnificent, and tender; so that those of us who wish to write start with a chance that is not given to writers in places where the springtime of the local life has been forgotten, and the harvest is a memory only, and the straw has been turned into bricks.

Once again, an Aran story is given a radically different twist. The islanders had sheltered a real parricide, because they felt he was sincerely repentant and had suffered enough. But Christy Mahon, who creeps frightened and dirty into the public house on the Mayo coast, has not really killed his father, he merely imagines he has; and Pegeen, the innkeeper's daughter, far from being shocked, welcomes so colorful a character into her life, as does her neighbor, the sardonic Widow Quin. "It's great luck and company I've won me in the end of time," comments Christy as he settles into a comfortable bed; "two fine women fighting for the likes of me—till I'm thinking this night wasn't I a foolish fellow not to kill my father in the years gone by."

Under admiration, the poet in him flowers. He becomes a ready fellow with his fists, at sports, and most of all with his tongue. The story of his crime, as he tells it to the village girls, brandishing a chicken bone by way of illustration, grows in ferocity:

Christy: With that the sun came out between the cloud and the hill, and it shining green in my face. "God have mercy on your soul," says he, lifting a scythe. "Or on your own," says I, raising the loy.[5]
Susan: That's a grand story.
Honor: He tells it lovely.
Christy: He gave a drive with the scythe, and I gave a lep to the east. Then I turned around with my back to the north, and I hit a blow on the ridge of his skull, laid him stretched out, and he split to the knob of his gullet.
Girls: Well, you're a marvel! Oh, God bless you! You're the lad surely!

(Act II)

The arrival of Old Mahon with nothing worse than a sore head momentarily shakes Christy's confidence, but Widow Quin sends the old man off on a wild-goose chase, and Christy plunges into a rapturous wooing of Pegeen, carrying all before him:

Christy: It's little you'll think if my love's a poacher's or an earl's itself when you'll feel my two hands stretched around you, and I squeezing kisses on your puckered lips till I'd feel a kind of pity for the Lord God is all ages sitting lonesome in His golden chair.
Pegeen: That'll be right fun, Christy Mahon, and any girl would walk her heart out before she'd meet a young man was your like for eloquence or talk at all.

(Act III)

Old Mahon discovers the trick and returns. Pegeen's illusion is shattered; she rounds on Christy with abuse, and his attempt to make a proper job of his father's murder this time only elicits from her the

---

[4]"Western World" is Synge's translation of a Gaelic term for the western seaboard of Ireland, as opposed to the "Eastern World" of Dublin and St. George's Channel.

[5]Loy: a square-sided spade for cutting peat, the common fuel in the west of Ireland.

comment that "there's a great gap between a gallous [splendid] story and a dirty deed." But Christy is no longer a scared child. He has grown into a man, able to defy Pegeen, father, villagers, and all—and none is more delighted than Old Mahon to find that he has not fathered a weakling and will be taking the orders from now on. "You've turned me a likely gaffer in the end of all," says Christy, "the way I'll go romancing through a romping lifetime from this hour to the dawning of the judgement day," and out he swaggers with his captive parent. The comedy is his, and the tragedy Pegeen's, who has failed to appreciate her handiwork, and is left to her famous lamentation: "Oh my grief, I've lost him surely. I've lost the only Playboy of the Western World."

Rebellion is built into *The Playboy*. It is an electric play, tingling, dangerous; the riotous Dublin audiences had some excuse, and for that matter a good many people in Ireland dislike it to this day. For Synge has put his finger on something very deep in human nature, applicable everywhere, though particularly to Ireland: resentment at the dead hand of tradition and the tyranny of the older generation, the son's subconscious desire to be quit of his father and to take his place. There is a truth here that few of us can face with complete equanimity, even while we laugh.

VI

Synge's dialogue, so easy and rippling to read, cost him an infinity of pains, and each play went through many drafts. *Deirdre of the Sorrows* was pieced together by Yeats and Lady Gregory after his death, and there are a few bare patches on which he would have done more work. Nevertheless, it is in all important respects the heroic tragedy on an ancient theme of which Yeats had dreamed. The peasant idiom shows itself, as already in *Riders*, fully equal to the poetic expression of tragic feeling.

The best loved of the old stories is the one about Deirdre, the beautiful child of whom it was prophesied that she would bring doom on all who loved her, and the aging King Conchubor, who had her brought up in mountain solitude in order that she might escape the curse and safely become his wife. But you cannot play for safety in love, you cannot mate youth with age, you cannot cage beauty: those are lessons that run all through Synge's drama, and

which came home to him most poignantly now that he was dying and in love with a girl much younger than himself.

Deirdre is bound to meet up with Naisi, the king's handsome nephew, and Naisi's two brothers. Inevitably, she forces them to flee with her to Alban (Scotland). There—and this is Synge's twist to the story—the same forces bend the fate of the lovers. They cannot play for safety either, or they will age and weary of each other and their love will turn to recrimination. So when Conchubor invites them home, they return, though it is almost certain that his offer is treacherous.

And for a while it seems that Conchubor will show himself generous. But he too is caught up in the web of his own weaving; the brothers are slain, and Deirdre, forever unattainable by him, makes her funeral oration before she stabs herself on the edge of their grave:

It's you three that will not see age or death coming—you that were my company when the fires on the hilltops were put out and the stars were our friends only. . . . Because of me there will be weasels and wild cats crying on a lonely wall where there were queens and armies and red gold, the way there will be a story told of a ruined city and a raving king and a woman will be young for ever. I see the trees naked and bare, and the moon shining. Little moon, little moon of Alban, it's lonesome you'll be this night, and tomorrow night, and long nights after, and you pacing the woods beyond Glen Laoi, looking every place for Deirdre and Naisi, the two lovers who slept so sweetly with each other. I have put away sorrow like a shoe that is worn out and muddy, for it is I have had a life that will be envied by great companies. It was not by a low birth that I made kings uneasy, and they sitting in the halls of Emain. It was not a low thing to be chosen by Conchubor, who was wise, and Naisi had no match for bravery. It is not a small thing to be rid of grey hairs, and the loosening of the teeth. It was the choice of lives we had in the clear woods, and in the grave we're safe, surely.

(Act III)

VII

Synge left behind him three short critical prefaces, to *The Tinker's Wedding*, *The Playboy*, and his *Poems* (1909), which contain more illumination than many a volume; and he left the *Poems* themselves, a handful composed at the end of his life out of his love for Molly and his rage against death. They have something of the clearness of vision, combined with roughness and even amateurishness of execution, that fascinate us in the poems of Emily Brontë. His prose style may be poetic, but his poetic style is stark, and in the preface he underlines what seemed to him to be insincere in the "beautiful" poetic diction of his contemporaries:

> Many of the older poets, such as Villon and Herrick and Burns, used the whole of their personal life as their material, and the verse written in this way was read by strong men, and thieves, and deacons, not by little cliques only. Then, in the town writing of the eighteenth century, ordinary life was put back into verse that was not poetry, and when poetry came back with Coleridge and Shelley, it went into verse that was not always human.
>
> In these days, poetry is usually a flower of evil or good; but it is the timber of poetry that wears most surely, and there is no timber that has not strong roots among the clay and worms. . . . It may almost be said that before verse can be human again it must learn to be brutal.

An astonishing statement for 1908, and one that foreshadows the whole of the modern movement. And the poems themselves bear it out. He rejects the faery world of the "plumed yet skinny Shee" in which poets like Yeats and George Russell were still dwelling; instead:

> We'll search in Red Dan Sally's ditch
> And drink in Tubber fair,
> Or poach with Red Dan Philly's bitch
> The badger and the hare.
> ("The Passing of the Shee," 5–8)

He tells Molly:

> I asked if I got sick and died, would you
> With my black funeral go walking too,
> If you'd stand close to hear them talk or pray
> While I'm let down in that steep bank of clay.
>
> And, No, you said, for if you saw a crew
> Of living idiots, pressing round that new
> Oak coffin—they alive, I dead beneath
> That board—you'd rave and rend them with your teeth.
> ("A Question")

He contemplates sardonically his inevitable early death:

> I've thirty months, and that's my pride,
> Before my age's a double score,

> Though many lively men have died
> At twenty-nine or little more.
>
> I've left a long and famous set
> Behind some seven years or three,
> But there are millions I'd forget
> Will have their laugh at passing me.
> ("I've Thirty Months")

Synge's theory and practice had a profound effect on his champion Yeats, who presently learned to make his own verse "brutal" and produced work of massive humanity. And Yeats's influence on all who have come after him is unquestioned. It has been justly claimed by Alan Price, among the most perceptive of the Synge commentators, that "Synge may be no more than a minor poet, but he is one of those minors who have played a part in the major changes of poetry."

VIII

In the nature of things, Lady Gregory could not be so dedicated an artist as Synge. She did not write her first actable play till she was fifty, and she had much besides playwriting on her mind. She shouldered the chief responsibility for the Abbey, and kept its precarious finances going after Miss Horniman had withdrawn her support in 1910. She found producers, produced herself when none could be found, promoted new talent—and earned her richest reward in this direction by her discovery of Sean O'Casey in the early 1920's. She ran the house and estate of Coole, and made it Yeats's poetic sanctuary for every summer from the time of their meeting; in addition, it provided holidays to those of the literary movement who needed them, and the most distinguished were invited to carve their initials on an immense copper-beech tree that is still an object of tourist pilgrimage. (The house itself, alas, was pulled down after her death in 1932.)

The last years of Lady Gregory's life were embittered by a fruitless struggle to make the English government restore to Ireland a group of impressionist paintings that her art dealer nephew, Hugh Lane, had left to Dublin in an unluckily unwitnessed codicil to his will. (This injustice has now been righted by a compromise.) Altogether, she packed so much unselfish activity into her life—was so completely, as O'Casey said, "a charwoman, but one with a star on her breast"—that much of her literary achievement was undervalued in her lifetime and has been forgotten since.

It is an unjustified neglect. Hers is talent, not genius, but it is exquisitely satisfying of its kind, and her best things, notably her one-act plays, are minor classics. Her gentler domestic note is the natural complement to the wildness of Synge, though her temper and sympathies are heroic like his—she loves the generous gesture and the lost cause. Her dialect, "Kiltartan" as her friends called it from the name of the district in which Coole stands, lacks his savagery and color, but it has a delicious trot and lilt of its own, ideal for comedy, capable of pathos but perhaps a trifle thin for tragic emotion. And her plays are models of neat, taut construction, much influenced by Molière, in whom she had steeped herself, and whose plays she regularly translated into "Kiltartan" for performance at the Abbey.

Her most successful works, judging by the number of revivals, are the *Seven Short Plays*, published in one volume in 1909, with *The Rising of the Moon* leading the field by several lengths. It is an exciting little piece about a political prisoner trying to escape by night from the Galway quays, and a police sergeant wheedled into forgoing the £100 reward; in it one may see reflected the conflict in the mind of the child Augusta Persse during the Fenian rising, with sternly right-wing parents in the drawing room and a "rebelly" nurse upstairs. Next of these plays in popularity comes *The Workhouse Ward*, where two ancient enemies are kept alive by their joy in their perpetual quarrel; listen to them boasting of their families, of their funeral glories, and of the attentions of the banshee, the spirit whose wailings were supposed to foretell death:

Michael Miskell: I tell you but for the wheat that was to be sowed, there would be more side cars and more common cars at my father's funeral (God rest his soul!) than at any funeral ever left your own door.

Mike McInerney: And what do you say to the banshee? Isn't she apt to have knowledge of the ancient race? Was she ever heard to cry for the Miskells?

Michael Miskell: It is a pity the banshee not to be crying for yourself at this minute, and giving you a warning to quit your lies and your chat and your arguing and your contrary ways; for there is no one under the rising sun could stand you. I tell you you are not behaving as in the presence of the Lord!

Mike McInerney: Is it wishful for my death you are? Let it come and meet me now and welcome so long as it will part me from yourself! And I say, and I would kiss the book on it, I to have one request only to be granted, and I leaving it in my will, it is what I would request, nine furrows of the field, nine ridges of the hills, nine waves of the ocean to be put between your grave and my own grave the time we be laid in the ground!

Michael Miskell: Amen to that!

Other gems are *Spreading the News*, baseless scandal growing at a fair; *The Jackdaw*, a benevolent deception that takes in even its perpetrators; *Hyacinth Halvey*, or "how to give a dog a good name and refuse to hang him." In every case she draws an accurate picture of Galway peasant life, and yet reaches down into the universal that lies beneath dialect and social class.

The volume also contains one moving miniature tragedy, *The Gaol Gate*: a peasant wife and a mother learn that their man, falsely accused of murder, has been hanged because he would not inform on his friends. The young wife's lament shows Lady Gregory as a prose poet in her own right:

What way will I be the Sunday, and I going up the hill to the Mass? Every woman with her own comrade, and Mary Cushin to be walking her lone!

What way will I be the Monday and the neighbours turning their heads from the house? The turf Denis cut lying on the bog, and no well-wisher to bring it to the hearth!

What way will I be in the night-time, and none but the dog calling after you? Two women to be mixing a cake, and not a man in the house to break it!

What way will I sow the field, and no man to drive the furrow? The sheaf to be scattered before spring time that was brought together at the harvest!

Lady Gregory's work in folklore opened up for her a new sort of historical drama, the "folk history," using for dialect the peasant idiom in a way that was neither anachronistic nor fancy dress, and for theme, historical happenings as preserved in the folk memory. Thus, folk history made James II escape in a barrel after the Battle of the Boyne, and declared of Queen Elizabeth I: "Whatever man she had to do with, she would send him to the block in the morning, that he would be able to tell nothing." The Queen Elizabeth theme makes the farce of *The Canavans*, and the James II theme the heroic comedy of *The White Cockade* (both 1912). One-acters are *Dervorgilla* (1912), a noble little tragedy of the woman whose faithlessness first brought the English into Ireland, and *The Wrens* (1922), an ironic comedy of two strolling players whose quarrel is the means of losing Ireland her parliament in 1799. Synge himself acknowledged that Lady Gregory's method "had made the writing of historical plays again possible," and certainly it is the method adopted by most writers of costume drama today.

And of plays based on the old legends, *Grania* (1912), which has three acts and only three characters, makes a fascinating complement to the *Deirdre* of Synge. The themes are parallel: again a pair of lovers flee the jealousy of an aging king; but Lady Gregory finds a very different clue to the situation, in her experience of the "loveless Irishman," with his preference for the company of his own sex and his habit of pushing his womenfolk into the background. Grania is the member of the trio who has the real cause for jealousy; her lover, Diarmuid, has never ceased to hanker after the king's court and the warrior band, and his death brings the moment of truth. (At first glance Lady Gregory and James Joyce may appear poles apart, but compare the role allotted to Molly Bloom in *Ulysses* for confirmation.)

IX

SYNGE and Lady Gregory wrote for the stage, and for a specifically Irish stage, and this has militated against their wider acceptance, particularly as Ireland has an ungrateful habit of neglecting the talents it produces in such profusion. One can still find dislike and disapproval of Synge among the older generation, and Lady Gregory's plays were largely ignored by the Abbey for many years after her death, though they have always been a standby of the amateur dramatic movement, and every drama festival brings what has been unkindly dubbed "the annual ritual murder of *The Rising of the Moon.*"

But now there is a welcome change of attitude toward both dramatists. Miss Horniman's theater was gutted by fire in 1951, and on 18 July 1966 a handsome, modern theater, to the design of the distinguished Irish architect Michael Scott, was opened on the same site. Since then, the company has performed Lady Gregory's *Spreading the News*, *The Rising of the Moon*, *Hyacinth Halvey*, *The Workhouse Ward*, and her translation of Molière's *The Doctor in Spite of Himself* (in *The Kiltartan Molière*, 1910). Further productions are proposed.

Of Synge's works, *The Playboy* has been played to packed houses in Dublin and at the Edinburgh Festival. *The Shadow of the Glen* formed an interesting double bill with Sean O'Casey's *The Shadow of a Gunman*, the two major Abbey styles being thus contrasted and complemented, and this program was taken successfully to the 1968 Theater Festival in Florence.

Both dramatists can stand the test of being read as literature; and indeed Synge was so studied from the first, particularly in France and Germany, where the European quality of his thinking was quickly recognized. The smallness of his output may prevent his being considered a figure of the first rank, but many have found his six plays a source of delight as inexhaustible as the six novels of Jane Austen.

It has been made a reproach that Synge's language, and Lady Gregory's "Kiltartan," proved dead ends, founded no school, were impossible to copy and fatally easy to parody (Joyce puts a crude parody of Synge into the mouth of Buck Mulligan in *Ulysses*, having contrived to quarrel with Synge as he quarreled with practically everyone). But what is significant, surely, is that their dialogue was right for their own purposes. We do not disparage Shakespeare and Webster because attempts to imitate them have produced intolerable pastiche.

Today especially, when much serious drama either consists still of "pallid and joyless words" or is downright inarticulate, there is refreshment of the spirit to be found in these plays, allying Irish charm and a rich flow of language with a universal applicability. Some have seen Synge and Lady Gregory as the last of the romantics, the last to find an idiom both poetic and dramatic, and to use it for big themes. But I think that is to take a shortsighted view. Romance, as they understood it, with its head in the stars but its feet firmly grounded in an affectionate knowledge of human nature, can never date or die. As we draw further away from them, and it is possible to put them into the perspective of literary history, they will appear as two honored names in a splendid and continuous line.

SELECTED BIBLIOGRAPHY

GENERAL

I. HISTORICAL STUDIES. E. A. Boyd, *Ireland's Literary Renaissance* (London, 1916), an early historical survey; E. A. Boyd, *The Contemporary Drama of Ireland* (Boston, 1917; Dublin, 1918); A. E. Malone, *The Irish Drama* (London, 1929), competent historical account by one who never missed an Abbey production, some critical assessments; W. B. Yeats, *Dramatis Personae* (Dublin, 1935), intensely subjective account of the movement's beginnings, with a great deal about Synge and Lady Gregory, not always accurate or fair, primarily of importance for the light it throws on Yeats's own personality and literary aims; U. Ellis-Fermor, *The Irish Dramatic Movement* (London, 1939), still the best critical work on the whole subject, particularly illuminating on Synge and Lady Gregory; L. Robinson, *Ireland's Abbey Theatre: A History, 1899–1951* (London, 1951), the Abbey's history up to 1950 by its chief producer, who was also a leading dramatist, as sequel to Lady Gregory's book it has the same merits and drawbacks, many gaps; W. B. Yeats, *Autobiographies* (London, 1955); G. Fay, *The Abbey Theatre, Cradle of Genius* (London, 1958), a detailed history for the years of the Fays's activities, 1899–1908; H. Howarth, *The Irish Writers, 1880–1940: Literature Under Parnell's Star* (London, 1958), relates principal writers of the group to the political history; W. B. Yeats, *Essays and Introductions* (London, 1961), the definitive ed.; A Saddlemyer, ed., *Theatre Business: The Correspondence of the First Abbey Theatre Directors, W. B. Yeats, Lady Gregory and J. M. Synge* (Gerrards Cross, 1982).

J. M. SYNGE

I. BIBLIOGRAPHY. M. J. McManus, *A Bibliography* (Dublin, 1930); *Catalogue of Exhibition Held in Trinity College Library* (Dublin, 1959); *The Synge Manuscripts in the Library of Trinity College, Dublin, A Catalogue* (Dublin, 1971); P. Levitt, ed., *J. M. Synge: A Bibliography of Published Criticism* (Dublin, 1973).

II. COLLECTED WORKS. *The Works*, 4 vols. (Dublin, 1910), vols. I and II: *Plays, Poems and Translations*; vol. III: *The Aran Islands*; vol. IV: *In Wicklow, In West Kerry, etc.*; *The Dramatic Works* (Dublin, 1915); *Plays, Poems and Prose* (London, 1941; repr. 1958), Everyman's Library, the latter with a delightful short intro. by M. MacLiammóir, most economical vol. for the newcomer to Synge, contains all the plays and poems and a selection from *The Aran Islands*; *The Collected Plays*, 2 vols. (London, 1952), Penguin ed.; R. Skelton, ed., *Four Plays and "The Aran Islands"* (London, 1962), World's Classics ed., includes *Riders to the Sea, The Shadow of the Glen, The Tinker's Wedding*, and *The Playboy of the Western World*; R. Skelton, ed., *Collected Works*, 4 vols. (London, 1962–1968), the Oxford ed., vol. I: R. Skelton, ed., *Poems*; vol. II: A. Price, ed., *Prose*, includes fragment of unpublished autobiography covering Synge's childhood and student days; vol. III: A. Saddlemyer, ed., *Plays*, book I, includes *Riders to the Sea, The Shadow of the Glen, The Well of the Saints, When the Moon Has Set*, and unpublished fragments; vol. IV: A. Saddlemyer, ed., *Plays*, book II, includes *The Tinker's Wedding, The Playboy of the*

Western World, Deirdre of the Sorrows—Saddlemyer reproduces most important drafts and revs., giving valuable insight into Synge's methods of work; R. Skelton, gen. ed., *The Collected Works* (Gerrards Cross, 1982), vol. I: R. Skelton, ed., *The Poems*; vol. II: A. Price, ed., *The Prose*; vol. III: A. Saddlemyer, ed., *The Plays*, book 1; vol. IV: A. Saddlemyer, ed., *The Plays*, book 2.

III. SEPARATE WORKS. *The Well of the Saints* (Dublin, 1905), also in N. Grene, ed., the *Irish Dramatic Texts* series (Washington, D.C.–Gerrards Cross, 1982); *The Shadow of the Glen and Riders to the Sea* (London, 1905); *The Playboy of the Western World* (Dublin, 1907); *The Tinker's Wedding* (Dublin, 1907); *The Aran Islands* (Dublin, 1907); *Poems and Translations* (Dundrum, 1909; enl. ed., Dublin, 1910); *Deirdre of the Sorrows* (Dundrum, 1910); *In Wicklow, West Kerry, and Connemara* (Dublin, 1911), repr. with essays by G. Gmelch and A. Saddlemyer (Dublin, 1980); R. Skelton, ed., *Translations* (Dublin, 1961), includes some unpublished; R. Skelton, ed., *Riders to the Sea* (Dublin, 1969); L. Stephens, ed., *My Wallet of Photographs* (Dublin, 1971); R. Skelton, ed., *Some Sonnets from "Laura in Death"* (Dublin, 1971).

IV. BIOGRAPHICAL AND CRITICAL STUDIES. W. B. Yeats, *Synge and the Ireland of His Time* (Dundrum, 1911); F. L. Bickley, *J. M. Synge and the Irish Dramatic Movement* (London, 1912); P. P. Howe, *J. M. Synge: A Critical Study* (London, 1912); M. Bourgeois, *John Millington Synge and the Irish Theatre* (London, 1913); J. Masefield, *John M. Synge* (London, 1915), a few personal recollections, with biographical notes; D. Corkery, *Synge and Anglo-Irish Literature* (Cork, 1931; New York, 1965), Synge seen by an extreme nationalist, with inevitable distortions; S. Synge, *Letters to My Daughter: Memories of John Millington Synge* (Dublin, 1932); L. A. G. Strong, *John Millington Synge* (London, 1941), brief but sympathetic essay; D. H. Greene and E. M. Stephens, *J. M. Synge* (New York, 1959), indispensable, fully documented biography, attempts little in the way of literary criticism; A. Price, *Synge and Anglo-Irish Drama* (London, 1961), the most thorough and perceptive critical assessment of Synge yet published; R. Skelton, *J. M. Synge and His World* (London, 1971); R. Skelton, *The Writings of J. M. Synge* (London, 1971); J. Kilroy, *The "Playboy" Riots* (Dublin, 1971); M. Harmon ed., *J. M. Synge, Centenary Papers* (Dublin, 1972); S. B. Bushrui, ed., *Sunshine and the Moon's Delight* (Gerrards Cross, 1972); D. Kiberd, *Synge and the Irish Language* (Dublin, 1979); T. O. Johnson, *Synge: The Medieval and the Grotesque* (Gerrards Cross, 1982).

The major part of J. M. Synge's papers is now in the Library of Trinity College, Dublin.

LADY GREGORY

I. SELECTED AND COLLECTED PLAYS. E. Coxhead, ed., *Selected Plays* (London, 1962), contains *The Rising of the Moon, Spreading the News, Hyacinth Halvey, The Work-*

house Ward, The Gaol Gate, Dervorgilla, The White Cockade, Grania, Dave, with intro. by ed. and preface by Sean O'Casey; A. Saddlemyer, ed., *Collected Plays*, 4 vols. (New York, 1970); T. R. Henn and C. Smythe, gen. eds., *Coole Edition of the Writings*, 21 vols. (New York, 1970–1978; Gerrards Cross, 1970–   ), not all vols. published in the U.S.; M. FitzGerald, ed., *Selected Plays of Lady Gregory* (Gerrards Cross, 1982), contains a larger selection of plays than the Coxhead ed.

II. INDIVIDUAL PLAYS. *Seven Short Plays* (Dublin, 1909), contains *Spreading the News, Hyacinth Halvey, The Rising of the Moon, The Jackdaw, The Workhouse Ward, The Travelling Man, The Gaol Gate; The Kiltartan Molière* (London, 1910), contains *The Miser, The Doctor in Spite of Himself, The Rogueries of Scapin; Irish Folk History Plays*, 2 vols. (New York, 1912), contains *Grania, Kincora, Dervorgilla, The Canavans, The White Cockade, The Deliverer; New Comedies* (New York, 1913), contains *The Bogie Men, The Full Moon, Coats, Damer's Gold, McDonough's Wife; The Golden Apple* (London, 1916); *The Image and Other Plays* (New York–London, 1922), contains *The Image, Hanrahan's Oath, Shanwalla, The Wrens; Three Wonder Plays* (New York–London, 1922), contains *The Dragon, Aristotle's Bellows, The Jester; Mirandolina* (London, 1924); *The Story Brought by Brigit* (London, 1924); *On the Racecourse* (London, 1925); *Three Last Plays* (London, 1928), contains *Sancho's Master, Dave, The Would-Be Gentleman; My First Play* (London, 1930), contains *Colman and Guaire.*

Lady Gregory collaborated with W. B. Yeats on several plays. See W. B. Yeats, *Plays in Prose and Verse Written for an Irish Theatre and Generally with the Help of a Friend* (London, 1922), contains *The Shadowy Waters, Where There Is Nothing, The Hour Glass, The Pot of Broth, The Unicorn from the Stars* (the only one with Lady Gregory's name on the title), *Cathleen ni Houlihan, Dierdre, The King's Threshold, On Baile's Strand, Diarmuid, Grania, The Green Helmut, The Player Queen, Notes,* and *Music for Plays.*

III. OTHER PUBLICATIONS. *Arabi and His Household* (London, 1882); *Over the River* (London, *ca.* 1888), a shorter unsigned booklet of the same title was published five years later and was probably by Lady Gregory; *The Phantom's Pilgrimage, or Home Ruin* (London, 1893), published anonymously; Lady Gregory, ed., *Sir William Gregory* (London, 1894), biography; *Mr. Gregory's Letter Box* (London, 1898); Lady Gregory, ed., *Ideals in Ireland* (London, 1901; repr. New York, 1976); *Cuchulain of Muirthemne* (London, 1902; 2nd ed., New York, 1903), preface by W. B. Yeats; *Poets and Dreamers* (Dublin, 1903; repr. Port Washington, N. Y., 1967; Brooklyn, N. Y., 1974); *Gods and Fighting Men* (London, 1904; repr. New York–Gerrards Cross, 1970; New York, 1971; Atlantic Highlands, N. J.–Dublin, 1976); *A Book of Saints and Wonders* (Dundrum, 1908); *The Kiltartan History Book* (Dublin, 1909; Coole ed., 1971); *Our Irish Theatre* (New York, 1913; Coole ed., 1972), the movement from within by one of its originators, indispensable; *Coole* (Dublin, 1913), also in C. Smythe, ed. (Dublin, 1971), with a foreword by E. Malins; *The Kiltartan Poetry Book* (Dundrum, 1918; Dublin, 1971); *Visions and Beliefs in the West of Ireland*, 2 vols. (New York, 1920); *Hugh Lane's Life and Achievement* (London, 1921; Coole ed., 1973); L. Robinson, ed., *Journals 1916–1930* (Dublin, 1946), of value for her own and Abbey Theatre's development, her experience in the civil war, and her struggle to retain the Lane pictures, but the literary period covered is only from 1919 to 1930.

IV. BIOGRAPHICAL AND CRITICAL STUDIES. E. Coxhead, *Lady Gregory, A Literary Portrait* (London, 1961; 2nd enl. ed., London, 1966), combines biography with some critical assessment of the plays; A. Saddlemyer, *In Defence of Lady Gregory, Playwright* (Dublin, 1966), short critical study; A. Gregory, *Me and Nu, Childhood at Coole* (London, 1971); H. Adams, *Lady Gregory* (London, 1973); E. H. Mikhail, ed., *Lady Gregory, Interviews and Recollections* (London, 1977); C. Smythe, *A Guide to Coole Park, Home of Lady Gregory* (London, 1973; rev. and enl. 1983); A. Saddlemyer and C. Smythe, eds., *Lady Gregory, Fifty Years After* (Gerrards Cross, 1983), a collection of essays.

The major part of Lady Gregory's papers is now in the Berg Collection of the New York Public Library.

FORD MADOX FORD

(1873-1939)

Kenneth Young

INTRODUCTION

FORD MADOX FORD is one of those writers who come late into their heritage. Robert Lowell, the American poet, inquired in a poem about him:

> But Master, mammoth mumbler, tell me why
> The bales of your left-over novels buy
> Less than a bandage for your gouty foot.

The answers to that question will perhaps become apparent in the course of this essay. But, today, increasingly we find mentions of him as "that neglected writer"; some of his novels have been dramatized for television; and *The Good Soldier* (1915) and his great Tietjens tetralogy—*Some Do Not* (1924), *No More Parades* (1925), *A Man Could Stand Up* (1926), and *Last Post* (1928), conveniently known in the United States under the omnibus title *Parade's End*—have been republished in both paperback and hardcover editions. There have been several excellent full-length studies of the man and his art. A plaque in his memory was erected in 1955 on a house in Winchelsea, Sussex, where he lived before World War I.

His output was large, ranging from poetry to history, biography, criticism, and novels; and it was uneven. I can discuss in detail only *The Good Soldier*, the tetralogy, and the Tudor trilogy: *The Fifth Queen* (1905), *Privy Seal* (1907), and *The Fifth Queen Crowned* (1908); but some others of his novels—for example, *The Rash Act* (1933) and *When the Wicked Man* (1932)—are of fine quality, and his volumes of memoirs and discursive works are as highly organized art as his fiction, and as entertaining.

He has been called a writer's writer; he had a deep insight into the techniques of composition, and his views influenced men as widely separated by time and nature as Ezra Pound and Joseph Conrad, and,

at the other end of his life, Ernest Hemingway, Allen Tate, and Robie Macaulay. But the solid and subtle construction of his best books also makes them fresh and attractive to the general reader when many better-known works by Ford's contemporaries begin to seem dated and stale.

THE MAN AND THE WRITER

FORD HERMANN HUEFFER—so his birth certificate has it—was born on 17 December 1873 at Merton in Surrey. He was the eldest child of Dr. Francis Hueffer, chief music critic of the *Times* newspaper and learned author of books on Wagner and Provence. His mother was Catharine, daughter of the Pre-Raphaelite painter Ford Madox Brown. Dr. Hueffer, who had established himself in England in the 1860's, came of a family of Münster bankers with offshoots in Paris and in New York. Ford went to an "advanced" coeducational school at Folkestone and then to University College School in London.

On his father's early death, Ford's home was at 37 Fitzroy Square, London, where his grandfather painted and entertained all the "big bow-wows" of late-Victorian artistic society: the Rossettis (who were related to Brown by marriage), William Holman Hunt, Alfred Tennyson, Thomas Carlyle, William Morris, and Algernon Swinburne, who was in the habit of feeding Ford on jujubes. There Ford Madox Brown painted his young grandson in the role of William Tell's son holding the neatly divided apple, and, as Ford later recorded in *Ancient Lights* (1911): "In those days as a token of my Pre-Raphaelite origin, I wore very long golden hair, a suit of greenish-yellow corduroy velveteen with gold buttons, and two stockings of which the one was red and the other green. These garments were the curse of my existence and the joy of every street boy who saw me."

Naturally he came to detest "the hot-house atmosphere of Pre-Raphaelitism," and when he left school he wished either to enter the Indian civil service or to become an army officer. This horrified his grandfather: Ford was a genius—*all* his young relatives were geniuses. Genius ran in the family. How could young Fordie think to do such things when he had already written a fairy story? This story, *The Brown Owl* (1892), was soon pressed into a publisher's hand. Ford was given £10 for the copyright; so when he was eighteen there began that long tale of financial mishandling of his books, for *The Brown Owl*, he later said, "sold many thousands more copies than any other book I ever wrote . . . and keeps on selling to this day."

Thus unwillingly was Ford launched upon the approved way. By the time he was twenty-three he had six books, including poems and a biography of his grandfather, to his name. But if he could not be a "grand gentleman," he could behave like one. He developed a drawl, a careful carelessness about clothes, an appearance of indolence; and to such effect that a few years later even so seasoned an observer as Henry James could accept him, almost if not quite, at face value. He drew Ford as Merton Densher in *The Wings of the Dove* (1902):

He was a longish, leanish, fairish young Englishman, not unamenable, on certain sides, to classification—as for instance being a gentleman, by being rather specifically one of the educated, one of the generally sound and generally pleasant; yet, though to that degree neither extraordinary nor abnormal, he would have failed to play straight into an observer's hands. He was young for the House of Commons, he was loose for the army. He was refined, as might have been said, for the city, and, quite apart from the cut of his cloth, he was sceptical, it might have been felt, for the church. On the other hand he was credulous for diplomacy, or perhaps even for science, while he was perhaps at the same time too much in his mere senses for poetry, and yet too little in them for art. . . . The difficulty with Densher was that he looked vague without looking weak—idle without looking empty. It was the accident, possibly, of his long legs, which were apt to stretch themselves; of his straight hair and well-shaped head, never, the latter, neatly smooth, and apt into the bargain . . . to throw itself suddenly back and, supported behind by his uplifted arms and interlocked hands, place him for unconscionable periods in communion with the ceiling, the tree-tops, the sky.

(bk. II, ch. 1)

Later still Ford adopted the poses of country squire (growing prize pigs), or the man in close touch with state affairs (he was friendly with a junior minister called C. F. G. Masterman), or "the *cher maître*" of "*les jeunes*" (to some of whom he really became *maître*, but that was in New York in the 1930's). In conversation he began to refer casually to his having been at school at Malvern, or Westminster, or—he was never consistent—at Eton. At an early age he began to look back at his past and to rearrange it, and, of course, rearrange other persons who appeared in it.

Was he a snob? Was he a liar? Not in any real sense. To those who knew him best he remained an endearing and delightful friend. As Stephen Crane once wrote to a fellow American: "You must not be offended by Hueffer's manner; he patronizes Mr. James, he patronizes Mr. Conrad. Of course he patronizes me, and he will patronize Almighty God when they meet; but God will get used to it, for Hueffer is all right."

Moreover, many of the poses were really Ford trying out what it felt to be, for instance, Captain Edward Ashburnham, the soldier-landowner of *The Good Soldier*, and observing the reactions of others to that particular sort of person. Again, in the memoirs and literary studies where most of the falsehoods occur—and there are not so many as has been sometimes suggested—Ford aims at presenting the essential natures of the men and writers he discusses and at recording his own true impressions of them. As he says in the dedication of *Ancient Lights*, his first book of memoirs: "This book, in short, is full of inaccuracies as to facts, but its accuracy as to impressions is absolute."

The method often worked brilliantly. Ford saw, for instance, D. H. Lawrence arriving in London like, as he put it, a fox about to raid the hen coops of literature; and H. G. Wells shouting to the world: "Humanity will advance by the Right! Move to the Right in Fours! Form F-O-U-R-S!" He pictures Hilaire Belloc in a Soho cafe shouting: "'Sussex, my birthplace. Glorious, glorious!' and sweeping his hair in several different directions whilst he drank a bumper of *pinard* from the only remaining flower vase."

And James! If this from *Mightier than the Sword* (1938) is not true of the author of *What Maisie Knew* and *The Turn of the Screw*, then life but limps after art:

I have attended at conversations between [James] and a queer tiny being who lay as if crumpled up on the stately

320

sofa in James's magnificent panelled room in Lamb House —conversations that made the tall wax candles seem to me to waver in their sockets and the skin of my forehead and hands prickle with sweat. I am in these things rather squeamish; I sometimes wish I was not, but it is so and I can't help it. I don't wish to leave the impression that these conversations were carried on for purposes of lewd stimulation or irreverent ribaldry. They occurred as part of the necessary pursuit of that knowledge that permitted James to give his readers the "sense of evil." . . . And I dare say they freed him from the almost universal proneness of Anglo-Saxon writers to indulge in their works in the continually intrusive fumbling in placket-holes as Sterne called it, or in the lugubrious occupation of composing libidinous Limericks. James would utter his racy "Ho-ho-ho's" and roll his fine eyes whilst talking to his curious little friend, but they were not a whit more racy and his eyes did not roll any more than they did when he was asking a housemaid or a parson's wife for advice as to the advisability of employing a Lady's Help. . . . It was all in the day's work.

(pp. 27–28)

Perhaps in the end Ford's mythopoeic gift did get out of hand, and, presented in his occasionally de haut en bas style, made him appear most eccentric. Wells in his *Experiment in Autobiography* (1934) remarked: "The pre-war F. M. H. was tortuous but understandable. The post-war Ford was incurably crazy. He got crazier and crazier." Yet it was this gift, this quality of imagination that shaped everything like a child its Plasticine, that produced *Parade's End*—after the war, be it noted. On the other hand, but for a chance event, the gift might have resulted in nothing more than a fluency; he himself might have become little more than an elegant poseur, which was all that Wells saw in him:

What he is really or *if* he is really, nobody knows now and he least of all; he has become a great system of assumed personas and dramatized selfs. He has written some admirable verse, some very good historical romances, two or three books in conjunction with Conrad. . . .

It was exactly that "conjunction with Conrad" that turned Ford from the storyteller into the great artist.

Conrad and Ford first met in 1897. By then Ford had unwillingly entered the Roman Catholic Church to please his rich relations in Paris. His wife, Elsie Martindale, with whom he had been at school in Folkestone, was never a Catholic, but their children, at Ford's insistence, were brought up in that faith.

They lived in Sussex in pastoral conditions reminiscent of the life-style of William Morris and by the benefit of a £3,000 legacy from the rich Hueffers; there Conrad met them.

At once Conrad and Ford recognized in each other like minds; and they talked and talked about *how* to write. Occasionally they also wrote, but their collaborations are of little moment compared with their later separate works, although *Romance* (1903) is a splendid adventure story and *The Inheritors* (1901) an interesting political roman à clef. It was the talk that mattered; and some of it Ford recorded in *Joseph Conrad* (1924), *Thus to Revisit* (1921), *Mightier than the Sword*, and *The March of Literature* (1939). What follows is extracted from these books.

In them we see two gentlemen—Ford in his early twenties, Conrad nearly fifty—sitting in a farmhouse in Sussex. At night they beat on the beams with exhilaration; in the afternoon, one plucks his beard while the other lies supine with misery. What is it all about? Simply the question of whether or not in their joint work they have achieved the proper *charpente* (construction), *progression d'effet*, cadence, time-shift, *mot juste*. Both agreed that "the writing of novels was the one thing of importance that remained to the world, and that what the novel needed was the New Form." In their view the classical English novel had triumphed, but only by the accident of genius. Its basic form, the series of strong situations linked by flat matter of various sorts, had now led to stalemate. But in the precept and practice of Stendhal, Flaubert, Maupassant, Turgenev, and James, there were new and revivifying ideas and the hope that at last the novel could achieve form. Conrad had begun his first novel on the endpapers of a copy of *Madame Bovary*, Ford was soaked in nineteenth-century French writing. Both could recite from memory long passages from Flaubert's *Félicité* and *St. Julien l'Hospitalier* and Maupassant's *La Nuit* and *Une Vie*.

So from these French writers, Ford and Conrad, "buried deep in rural greennesses," hammered out a pattern of art. They agreed that the general effect of a novel must be the general effect that life makes on mankind. Life imposes a series of impressions on the brain, but the impressions are not an orderly progression. They are a confused mass. So the novel that truly reflects life is not a continuous and logical narration, but a stringing together of impressions.

The novelist will, however, select from his impressions—"the whole of art consists in selection"—and his criterion will be whether any incident, or even word, carries the story forward. This was the *progression d'effet*; and "as the story progressed, it must be carried forward faster and faster, and with more and more intensity."

Then, "justification":

Before everything, a story must convey a sense of inevitability: that which happens in it must seem to be the only thing that could have happened. . . . [The action of any person] must be inevitable, because of his character, because of his ancestry, because of past illness or on account of the gradual coming together of the thousand small circumstances by which Destiny, who is inscrutable and august, will push us into one certain predicament.

In telling the story the writer will render, not narrate. Ford gives a simple example in *The English Novel* (1930): "If I say Monsieur Chose was a vulgar, coarse, obese and presumptuous fellow—that is narrating. But if I say he was a gentleman with red whiskers that always preceded him through a doorway, there you have him rendered as Maupassant in fact rendered him."

Naturally the author himself must not appear:

We wanted the Reader to forget the writer—to forget that he was reading. We wished him to be hypnotized into thinking that he was living what he read—or, at least, into the conviction that he was listening to a simple and in no way brilliant narrator who was telling—not writing—a true story.

The method had two other advantages. If you break up your motives

and put them down in little shreds one contrasting with the other, you would arrive at something more coloured, lifelike, animated and interesting. . . . Into that live scene you could then drop the piece of news that you wanted to convey and so you would carry the chapter a good many stages forward.

But the "contrasting shreds" would also show that your conspectus of the world was wider than would appear had you confined yourself to a straightforward narration of your basic theme.

The other advantage was this: "The juxtaposition of the composed rendering of two or more unexaggerated actions or situations may be used to establish, like the juxtaposition of vital word to vital word, a sort of frictional current of electric life that will galvanize the work of art." From this meeting,

Ford continues in *The March of Literature*, arises a third product, an "unearned increment." He explains this by an analogy of two men standing together in a field. When

each shouts separately each can only be heard at a distance of an eighth of a mile, whilst if both shout simultaneously their range of hearing will be extended by a hundred-odd yards. The point cannot be sufficiently labored, since the whole fabric of modern art depends upon it.

(p. 804)

The language used should be composed of "fresh but usual words" with just an occasional word "not common to a very limited vernacular." The word, in fact, should be perfect but not too perfect.

The principles are open to criticism. Ford amusingly imagines the objections of his friend Wyndham Lewis: "Verisimilitude—that's what you want to get with all your wheezy efforts. . . . But that isn't what people want. They don't want vicarious experience; they don't want to be educated. They want to be amused. . . . By brilliant fellows like me. Letting off brilliant fireworks. . . . Efface yourself? . . . Bilge!" But in fairness to Ford it must be said—and he said it twice with the aid of italics in *Joseph Conrad*—that:

These two writers [Conrad and Ford] were not unaware—*were not unaware*—that there are other methods of writing novels. They were not rigid even in their own methods. They were sensible to the fact that compromise is at all times necessary to the execution of a work of art.

(p. 211)

If, however, their principles require defense, we need look no further than *The Secret Agent* or *The Good Soldier, Under Western Eyes* or *Parade's End*. In fact, much of the technique was assimilated into English fiction long before Ford died; "even the timeshift," he remarked in 1938, "has been perforce adopted by every writer who has since sat down to concoct a detective story."

In writing about the canalizing of these French ideas into English, I have spoken only of Ford and Conrad, but of course James had drunk at the same springs before them. This Ford handsomely recognized in his book about the Master; but James's influence had been confined almost entirely to such intimates as Edith Wharton; he was little read and less understood until, indeed, after he was dead. He dined more often in Mayfair than Bloomsbury.

Ford, however, talked widely, and in particular he talked in the years before World War I to a strange young man in green baize trousers and a sombrero—Ezra Pound. It was thus that Pound learned about impressionism; from this his "ideogram," despite Chinese parallels, really descended. His startlingly original method of writing poetry was identical with Ford's "juxtaposition of composed rendering," which enabled the poet to achieve virtually simultaneous insights into a theme from diverse points of view. And through Pound, this technique influenced—and still influences—the writing of all Anglo-American verse of this century, as well as such landmarks as *Ulysses*.

Pound always recognized Ford's part in this: "The revolution of the word," he wrote, "began, so far as it affected the men who were my age in London in 1908, with the LONE whimper of Ford. . . . Ford read Flaubert and Maupassant in a way that George Moore did not. Impressionism meant for him something it did not for Mr. Symons." And later he said:

I don't know whether justice has *yet* been done to Ford. I went to England in 1908 to "learn" from Yeats—and stayed to learn from Yeats *and* Ford. From 1910 onwards, Fordie and I growled at each other for nigh on twenty years. *Anyway* with all his *spumare* and his rising *soufflées*, how long it would have taken me to get to the present—wherever—if I hadn't plugged up Campden Hill almost daily when the fat man was in residence, Gawd alone knows.

Ford had an equally high regard for Pound, but he remarks of the young poets in *Thus to Revisit* (1921): "They abolished not only the illusion of the subject but the subject itself." Does he there perhaps lay his finger on that tendency to extravagance, that failure to compromise, in the use of the new technique, which has laid much modern verse open to the charge of impenetrable obscurity? Ford was never tired of emphasizing that the reader must be treated considerately, and this was where he parted company with so many of "*les jeunes*" (the young writers with whom Ford was associated). This has, indeed, been held to be a failing on his part. Hugh Kenner, in his study of Pound's poetry, believes that Ford was "deprived of a revolutionary impact on the *avant-garde*" because in his own work he

wrapped his discoveries in Pre-Raphaelite elegance . . . a genial and whimsical air. . . . But the psychological pretext had only to be chiselled away from his books to yield a sequence of intensely illuminated scenes and images after the

manner of the Cantos. This step Ford never took. Probably it would have offended his notion of good manners.

I think this simply means that Ford knew where to stop; to have gone further would, certainly, have been bad manners to his invited guest, the reader.

At this point it should be said that Ford himself throughout his life wrote poetry; he published some ten books of it and his *Collected Poems* (1936) contains 320 large pages. Two of the longer poems—"On Heaven" and "Antwerp"—have a permanent value as well as a biographical interest; many have a touching lyrical charm. He said: "I attach little importance to myself as a poet. But I do attach importance to myself as a 'specimen.' . . ." Indeed, the styles in which he wrote are a sort of history by example of the progress of English verse between 1900 and 1930. His verse can be enjoyed, but the last word on it is his own: "With me the writing of poetry is not a conscious Art. It is the expression of an emotion, and I can so often not put my emotions into any verse."

The close collaboration with Conrad ended in 1902 when Ford, suffering from "neurasthenia," began touring German and Belgian spas in search of health; this was to form much of the background for *The Good Soldier*, which did not, however, appear until 1915. By then he had published seven or eight novels, including the Tudor trilogy (which Conrad himself hailed as "a noble conception—the swan song of historical Romance"); two books descriptive of London and of the country; and various literary studies.

Late in 1908 he founded and became the editor of the *English Review*. He occupied the post only just over a year, but his list of contributors was extraordinary. Among the established writers were Hardy, James, Wells, Tolstoy, W. H. Hudson, Conrad, and Masefield; among the "unknowns" whom Ford, winnowing through piles of manuscripts, discovered were Pound, Wyndham Lewis, H. M. Tomlinson, D. H. Lawrence, and Norman Douglas, though Douglas was really Conrad's discovery. The *English Review* of 1908–1909 is rightly considered the most brilliant literary periodical of the century; but at the end of 1909 financial difficulties overwhelmed it, and it passed into other hands.

Among those who had put up money to start it was Ford's friend Arthur Marwood, younger son of a Yorkshire landowner. Marwood had been a brilliant mathematician at Cambridge; this he combined, according to Ford, with an extraordinary knowledge of the form and pedigrees of racehorses and an infallible system for defeating the tables at Monaco. He was a Tory of the pre-industrial vintage who considered that the ruling classes had a positive duty to the less fortunate. In the first issue of the *English Review* Marwood wrote what is really a very early blueprint for the welfare state—"A complete actuarial scheme for insuring John Doe against all the vicissitudes of life." Christopher Tietjens of *Parade's End* is modeled more or less closely upon him.

During Ford's editorship, his estrangement from his wife deepened, but the marriage could not be ended in divorce because he was a Roman Catholic. At this time Ford met Violet Hunt, a novelist. She wished to marry, and Ford became involved in ridiculous subterfuges that led to a "marriage" in France. The real Mrs. Ford brought a lawsuit against Violet Hunt, who had described herself in print as the wife of Ford. This caused a scandal, the reverberations of which haunted Ford almost for the rest of his days. Ford never saw the two children of his first marriage again, though they wrote often to him, and he continued to pay for their education; worse still, his feelings toward Miss Hunt began to cool. The reflection of these painful experiences colors his best work. It may also be added that from this time dates that hostility to Ford's work on the part of certain reviewers, some of whom, as Douglas Goldring points out, had not come up to Ford's standards for inclusion in the *English Review*.

When the war began, Ford, although already forty, joined the army, and it is hardly surprising that, as he wrote to a friend: "I can assure you, for what it is worth, that it is as if the peace of God had descended upon me." Ford could easily have obtained a safe job writing propaganda for the organization headed by his friend Masterman, and he did in fact write two pamphlets for him; but he preferred a commission in the Welch regiment, which involved front-line service and eventually shell shock and gassing.

After the war he returned to find himself forgotten. Nauseated by the postwar atmosphere, he retired to Sussex and thence to Provence and Paris with Stella Bowen, the Australian painter, who became Mrs. Ford. They had a child, Juliet, and Ford wrote *Parade's End.* In Paris he ran a new literary paper, *transatlantic review;* and from the end of the 1920's to his death he lived mainly in France. He paid

visits, sometimes of extended duration, to America, where he influenced a whole generation of young writers. He went into residence at Olivet College (Michigan), where he wrote his immense survey of world literature, *The March of Literature,* for which the college awarded him the degree of Doctor of Letters.

In this last period he wrote his long and delightful dissertations on life called *Great Trade Route* (1937) and *Provence* (1938). These express in personal and impressionistic form his love of France, of frugality, and of the old, quiet virtues, and his fears for the future of humanity living a rushing, substitute existence, eating processed food, and increasingly subject to demagoguery of all kinds. He was not a religious man nor a political one: "One longs," he wrote in his semiautobiographical novel *No Enemy* (1929), "to discover some formula that shall make us ourselves for ever loyal to some idea or other. . . . Or perhaps it is just rest that one wants." It was man in whom he really believed, and men of good will were in the 1930's increasingly hard to find. Why? Partly because, as Goethe said, man is what man eats, and man was now eating food grown with chemical fertilizers, dehydrated, refrigerated, unfresh; and partly because, in Ford's words,

the doctrine of pride in work as work; of engrossment and serenity; of aloofness from the world and of introspection with no other purpose—is here anathema both with the Right, which hates the doctrine of Art for Art's sake, and with the Left, which hates that of Labor for the sake of Labor.

(p. 197)

What then is left? Only this: "If you have a platoon, you can make it smart; if you have a garden you may make it fine, luxuriant, producing marrows as large as barrels. Or if you write a poem, you may make it beautiful. Everything else is vanity." If you have a chance, you can find a little cottage and a plot of land and live on it; and this was Ford's own dearest wish. Yet there he was, rushing across America, lecturing to women's clubs, or being the man-about-town in top hat and flourishing a gold-topped cane in New York. For him the pastoral life was not to be, and at the end of *Provence* he knows it. He and Janice Biala, the painter with whom he spent his last years, are standing on a bridge over the Rhone when a sudden gust of wind blows the wallet containing all their money from Janice's hand into the river:

It flows at a hundred miles an hour. . . . My ducats. . . . My daughter. . . . Waiting at home over the Mediterranean, poor child. . . . For ducats. . . .

I can no more. . . . *Je ne peux plus.* . . . What is that stone face with blind, relentless eyes? . . . That gives and takes away. . . . *C'est le Destin.* . . . We are people accursed. . . . We shall never climb again up *this* slope. . . .

I hadn't been going to do any writing for a year. For two. Perhaps not for ever if I could have laid that money out on a little bastide with an acre or so and a good, always flowing noria. . . . But perhaps the remorseless Destiny of Provence desires thus to afflict the world with my books. . . .

(pt. III, ch. 3)

He died at Deauville, in the care of Sisters of Mercy, on 26 June 1939, and is buried there in the English cemetery.

THE TUDOR TRILOGY

It was the trilogy of Tudor novels—*The Fifth Queen, Privy Seal,* and *The Fifth Queen Crowned*—that first suggested to the public between 1906 and 1908 that Ford was something more than the dilettante author of Pre-Raphaelitish fairy stories or the junior collaborator of Conrad. The novels are indeed striking from the first pages, where, through the soft-stepping, precise prose, we see the arrival at court of Katharine Howard, who is to become Henry VIII's fifth queen: dressed in tattered garments muddied from the road, she rides into the courtyard upon an ancient horse; with her is her cousin, Thomas Culpepper, an ill-kempt young man who loves her but has a distracted mind and a determination to pick quarrels.

With measured accuracy the mid-sixteenth-century court opens before us: the pikemen clatter their armor across the paved yard; ladies' maids chatter down the echoing stone corridors, falling silent and curtseying deeply when they meet a knight or a lord or sometimes Thomas Cranmer, the archbishop, in flowing black-and-white robes, his face puckered with worry and ill thoughts. There, swiftly, goes "Cur Crummock" himself—Thomas Cromwell, Lord Privy Seal, master of them all, cruel, subtle, ruthless, serving only the king. A metallic blast, a crash of pikestaves upon the stones, and there is Henry himself—his head as large as a child's body, crowned with a flat cap clasped with a flashing jewel. Everyone is on his knees. The king plants his huge frame upon a stool, crooks his little finger as sign that all may rise, and with a peasant's humor shakes with laughter at an old knight trying to mount a horse.

In a small room shabbily furnished, the lady Mary sits at her desk writing in Latin—a bitter woman who, since the king's divorce from her mother, Katharine of Aragon, has been dubbed bastard. Padding softly along the corridors, feet shod in velvet, go Throckmorton, Cromwell's spy, and Lascelles, Cranmer's spy. The lady Mary is suspected of plotting with the men of "the old religion"—the Roman Catholicism whose temporal power Henry has renounced.

Into this catacomb of medieval formality and the brazen note of the trumpet, of cunning minds watching each other's every move, of petty quarrels among ladies-in-waiting and rough-and-tumble between the pages, plunges Katharine Howard. Soon the corridors are humming with rumors of the king's liking for her. The present queen, Anne of Cleves, departs, and with her the king's Protestant alliances. And Katharine is of "the old religion." Thus to Cranmer and Cromwell and such Catholics as the duke of Norfolk the possibility of her becoming queen and so influencing Henry in favor of the pope is of high importance. For this may mean not merely changes in foreign policy but the return of the church property and riches that Henry had seized and divided among his nobles to ensure their allegiance.

Attempts are made to blacken Katharine's moral character, at first without success. The king loves her, and soon her pity for this great bear, haunted in these, his latter years, by the monstrous murders and rapine done in his name, turns to love. Moreover, she sees that by becoming queen she may further her deepest desire—the return of the true faith. In this she almost succeeds, but even the Catholics are against her, for noblemen such as Norfolk have also benefited from the sequestration of church property. The plots thicken—there is a strange meeting in a darkened tennis court; and soon Lascelles has organized a host of false witnesses. The king in council hears the evidence; he is agonized, but believes. Suddenly Katharine appears and confesses that all the evidence is true. But when the council has departed and she is alone with the king, she recants; she has made the confession because she sees clearly that Henry will never bring back the faith and because it is better for him that she depart. "You are," she says, "as God made you, setting you for His own purposes a weak man in very evil and turbulent times. . . ." She has never, she says, played false with Culpepper nor with any man, though Culpepper loved her "without regard, without thought and without falter. He sold farms to buy me bread."

She went slowly down over the great stone flags of the great hall. It was very gloomy now, and her figure in black velvet was like a small shadow, dark and liquid, amongst shadows that fell softly and like draperies from the roof. Up there it was all dark already, for the light came downwards from the windows. She went slowly, walking as she had been schooled to walk.

"God!" Henry cried out; "you have not played false with Culpepper?" His voice echoed all round the hall.

The Queen's white face and her folded hands showed as she turned—

"Aye, there the shoe pinches!" she said. "Think upon it. Most times you shall not believe it, for you know me. But I have made confession of it before your Council. So it may be true. For I hope some truth cometh to the fore even in Councils."

Near the doorway it was all shadow, and soundlessly she faded away among them. The hinge of the door creaked; through it there came the sounds of the pikestaves of her guard upon the stone of the steps. The sound whispered round amidst the statues of old knights and kings that stood upon corbels between the windows. It whispered amongst the invisible carvings of the roof. Then it died away.

The King made no sound. Suddenly he cast his hat upon the paving.

Katharine Howard was executed on Tower Hill, the 13th of February, in the 33rd year of the reign of King Henry VIII, MDXLI–II.

(*The Fifth Queen Crowned*, pt. IV, ch. 5)

This cool, deliberate, yet dramatic and vivid method is typical of these historical novels. We are convinced of the existence of Henry and Katharine and such minor figures as Magister Udal and Margaret Hall because we see their faces move, as in a film close-up, and we see them in their settings. Yet we are also aware that, human though they are, they differ from us; they have a certain dreamlike quality; and by consummate art Ford makes us believe that those differences are exactly what we might expect, were we to be suddenly transported to those times, retaining our contemporary consciousnesses. It is as though history had been wired for television.

How is this done? How are we made to sympathize with men who really believed in heavenly rewards and eternal punishments and the burning of heretics?

In part it is a result of the prose style, which, although perfectly straightforward and comprehensible, develops an antique air and cadences not of our time. Occasionally it uses words that are unfamiliar—"gar" or "anan?"—but never so unfamiliar that their meaning cannot be guessed from the context nor so repetitive that they become tainted with the film-epic English of "prithee," "forsooth," and "odds bodikins." Ford's historically quite correct use of the second-person singular is most effective: "'Child,' Henry said, 'I will cherish thee as I would a young lamb. Shalt have Cromwell's head; shalt have Winchester in what gaol thou wilt.'"

Above all, however, Ford makes us see. We are never in doubt as to where the characters are, where the light comes from, what they can see through the window, where at a critical moment their hands are, what lies beyond that door. Sometimes their very movements of joint or neck are noted. They are seen as though on a stage; it is interesting to note that at about this time James was telling himself in his notebooks that he should visualize the action of his novels as though it were taking place on a stage set. Here is an example from *The Fifth Queen Crowned*:

Cranmer suddenly stretched out, with a timid pitifulness, his white hands. But, rolling his huge shoulders, like a hastening bear, the King went over the rushes. He pulled the heavy door to with such a vast force that the latch came again out of the hasp, and the door, falling slowly back and quivering as if with passion, showed them his huge legs mounting the little staircase.

(pt. I, ch. 1)

At crucial points in the story, Ford transmutes this visual process—"phanopeia" was Pound's name for it—into the highest art. As Henry, at the end of *Privy Seal*, persuades Katharine to become his queen, Ford writes:

He lulled her in his arms, swaying on his feet. "Hast a great tongue. Speakest many words. But art a very child. God send thee all the joy I purpose thee. And, an thou hast sins, weight me further down in hell therewith."

The light of the candles threw their locked shadows along the wall and up the ceilings. Her head fell back, her eyes closed, so that she seemed to be dead and her listless hands were open in her skirts.

(pt. III, ch. 2)

The hands "open in her skirts" is a flourish, almost an affectation, of art; but it completes the picture, as a clamp closes a magnetic field. It is a beautiful parallel to what Ford praised so highly—the last words of James's *The Turn of the Screw*: "We were alone with the quiet day, and his little heart, dispossessed, had stopped." Ford says of that:

Observe how that sentence is slightly mannered. That is the device of all the great writers. In great moments the convention which is a necessity for all works of art must be enhanced by just the merest motion of the screw and the language must, by the merest shade, marmorealize itself.

One thing more: both here and in his memoirs Ford lightens the theme by displays of a most delicious gift of the comic. And if that other historical novel, the medieval *Ladies Whose Bright Eyes* (1911), had no other merits, it would still be worth reading for the picture of the two tired and rather cynical knights worn out with the perpetual jousting that is altogether too medieval for them.

THE GOOD SOLDIER

In later life Ford said that his historical novels were "nothing more than a tour de force, a fake more or less genuine in inspiration and workmanship, but none the less a fake." He was not, I think, denying the exquisite artistry, but rather asserting that the writer who seeks the highest ends must come to grips with his own world; it is that alone, after all, that he may know with the deepest intimacy.

So in 1913 Ford began to write his first work truly based on his observations of contemporary life— *The Good Soldier*. The date was 17 December, and he was exactly forty years old: "I had always entertained very fixedly the idea that—whatever may be the case with other writers—I at least should not be able to write a novel by which I should care to stand before reaching the age of forty." Into it he put, as he tells us in a dedication to a new edition in 1927, all that he knew about writing, hoping to "do for the English novel what in *Fort comme la mort* Maupassant had done for the French." His reward was perhaps John Rodker's remark that *The Good Soldier* was "the best French novel in the English language."

The novel, as its subtitle emphasizes, is "a tale of passion" told by the protagonist, Dowell, an American of considerable inherited wealth and long New England lineage. His wife, Florence, uses the pretext of a bad heart to deceive him with a number of men

and finally with Captain Edward Ashburnham, an army officer and owner of great possessions in Hampshire. The latter's wife, Leonora, plays an ambiguous part in the tale, which ends with the deaths of Ashburnham and Florence, the madness of Ashburnham's young ward, Nancy Rufford, and Leonora's remarriage to a "decent" sort of chap. Dowell, still scarcely knowing what has happened to him, takes over the Hampshire estates.

This is the briefest outline of a complex story, but the story is not half of *The Good Soldier*. Almost everything that happens is capable of several interpretations, so, in a sense, the reader himself is the other half. But is that not exactly as in life? No event is complete without an observer: in this novel we approach, as it were, at an angle, a solipsistic universe. We learn, for instance, to distrust the narrator, Dowell, not because he is a liar, but because his reactions to events involving passion are unnatural: how could they not be since he himself is gradually revealed as incapable of passion, sexual or moral? Yet from another point of view, his view of events *is* correct.

As Mark Schorer says: "No simple inversion of statement can yield up the truth, for the truth is the maze, and, as we learn from what is probably the major theme of the book, appearances have their reality." We are here—the narrator himself observes—looking at events as one looks at the image on a mirror in another mirror, at the box within the box. "Nothing is but what is not."

And the point of the novel? Beneath the omnipresent irony and even comedy of this tragic story, Schorer finds a description of a world without moral point, expressed most directly in the character of Dowell, who "suffers from the madness of moral inertia."

This is but one of the conclusions we may draw— and we continue to draw them for days after finishing the book. There is scarcely a paragraph, a sentence, that does not suggest the most diverse meanings. There is, for instance, the narrator's concern with Catholicism—that recurring theme in Ford— and the belief that all is explained by his discovery that Leonora is an Irish Catholic; there is the ironic emphasis on "hearts"—Florence and Edward both have "hearts" but in their various ways are heartless; yet is not that heartlessness due to excess of heart in another sense?

But in addition, there is in the central character, the good soldier, a subtle picture of the downfall of a class. Ashburnham, the real gentleman who puts his inferiors' needs before his own, is stripped of his estate (Leonora taking charge), of his self-respect, and of his true function in life: only suicide is left for him. Why? Because of sexual peccadilloes? Hardly, since these are often played down as "weaknesses." He is defeated because of his excess of the virtues of a gentleman: he is *too* conscientious, he has *too* much sympathy for the underdog, whether it be the weeping maidservant on the train or the drunkards he rescues. It is perhaps his knowledge of his own excess of sentiment that decides him to isolate himself from too many human contacts in Nauheim. He floats, as do all these well-off, kindly disposed, youngish people, in the rootless cosmopolitanism of spas, insulated from life, in a state of inanition such as Dante pictured in one of his circles of Hell. But such insulated inanition is not natural for people of their age and class—a class, after all, with the long tradition of service to society, a society on the verge of World War I.

The reader who comes to *The Good Soldier* for the first time will be surprised and delighted. But in the end he may be surprised once too often; he may find that the novel is *too* tightly constructed, the air we breathe in it *too* rarefied. Yet that also may have been Ford's intention.

THE TIETJENS TETRALOGY

To pass from *The Good Soldier* to *Parade's End* is to emerge from a room heavy with discharged passion into a city street full of vivid personalities. Up they pop like freshly painted jack-in-the-boxes: "Breakfast" Duchemin, so called from his habit of giving lavish morning parties, the rich, cultivated parson who breaks without warning into loathsome Latin obscenities; '09 Morgan, the Welsh private in the trenches whose wife has run off with a pugilist; the sly, snobbish Macmaster, rising suavely in the civil service and to a wartime knighthood for literary services; the old squire of Groby, master of vast acres, whose gardener lays out his filled pipes in the bushes every morning, for he is not allowed to smoke in the house; Lord Portscatho, the banker, whose world crumbles when one of his officials uses his position to injure an enemy; Miss Wanostrocht, the headmistress, "her little fingers hooked together, the hands back to back: a demoded gesture ... Girton of 1897."

These minor characters are not by accident so varied. In *Parade's End* it was Ford's aim to "register my own time in terms of my own time." His registrations of the period 1910 to 1920 are as accurate as his backgrounds—country-house weekends, a golf course invaded by suffragettes, bachelor chambers in London, a trench in France, a hotel in the GHQ area, and the Groby estate in north Yorkshire. We pass briefly also inside Whitehall offices, a small cottage where a learned woman sits pounding out journalism for a livelihood, a great girls' school.

Amid these middle-class scenes ambles the central character of the four novels—Christopher Tietjens, a lumbering "meal-sack" sort of man, his fair hair patched with gray, clad usually in too bulky tweeds, exchanged some of the time for khaki uniform. He is the younger son of the squire of Groby, a brilliant mathematician, a good Latinist, of whom it is said that he passes dull train journeys in tabulating from memory the errors in the latest edition of the *Encyclopaedia Britannica.* He has a certain intellectual arrogance, an immense kindliness, even sentimentality, and he is a Tory—but a Tory whose principles were last heard of in the eighteenth century, that is to say, at a time when the Tory party was supported by the poor, the landowners, and the "clerks," in Julien Benda's sense of schoolmasters, parsons, and journalists.

Christopher has married Sylvia, a pale society beauty and a hard, selfish, and disloyal woman. He married her because, in his rather bumbling, high-minded way, he believes he compromised her by chance kisses on a train in which they were returning from a weekend house party. Sylvia, of course, would never have looked at a younger son had she not been in a panic, believing she had become pregnant in one of her affairs. By chance Christopher learns of this. A child is born, but whether it is his own or not, he cherishes it. Sylvia leaves him for her lover; tires of the latter; confesses to her mother's friend, the Roman Catholic priest Father Consett, an important influence on Sylvia. She wishes to return to Christopher, and he, though having visions of "certain Hell," agrees. And for all these things she hates him—for, as she tells a friend, it is "his lordly full-dress consideration that drives me mad. . . . He's the soul of truth like a stiff Dutch-doll. . . . I tell you he's so formal he can't do without all the conventions there are, and so truthful he can't use half of them."

She sets out to ruin him, by spreading stories of his living on her money, keeping mistresses, and so on. This results in his being "cut" in society and in various unhappinesses he bears without saying a word in his own defense. His father, the old squire, "accidentally" shoots himself when he hears that Christopher has seduced Valentine Wannop, the daughter of his great friend, Mrs. Wannop, a blue-stocking. The seduction is one of Sylvia's rumors; but Christopher has in fact, in his slow way, fallen in love with Valentine, this clean-run girl, best Latinist in England, athlete, suffragette, and something of a pacifist. The attraction is mutual; both recognize, however, that nothing can be done: Christopher has his duty to Sylvia, who, being a Catholic, will in any case never divorce him.

This insoluble situation haunts Christopher through three of the novels; it haunts him in France where he serves during the war, and so does Sylvia, still pursuing him with her malignity. Through her the disfavor of General Lord Campion, his god-father, also descends upon him, making his army life more miserable than it is of necessity.

The middle two novels—*No More Parades* and *A Man Could Stand Up*—provide one of the most vivid yet calm pictures of World War I in France, from trenches to headquarters. There is nothing harrowing; the mud and blood, the muddle and heroism, are real enough, but they are lifted to that plane where the mind reacts with breathless absorption and with the pity that classical tragedy evokes. "The poetry," as Wilfred Owen, true poet of that war, wrote, "is in the pity." Ford, like Flaubert, looks at his characters from above; yet as Flaubert is half in love with his Emma Bovary though perceiving all her foolishness, so is Ford with his Christopher, his '09 Morgan, his little blinded lieutenant Aranjuez.

But the war changes Christopher. He returns to London to find that Sylvia has dismantled his flat and gone to Groby. In the flat he meets Valentine, but before they can speak, former fellow officers arrive determined to celebrate the armistice with Christopher. Amid the laughter and noise Christopher realizes:

That girl with the refined face, the hair cut longish, but revealing its thinner refinement. . . . That girl longed for him as he for her! The longing had refined her face. . . . This then was the day! The war had made a man of him! It had coarsened him and hardened him. There was no other way to look at it. It had made him reach a point at which he would no longer stand unbearable things . . . what he wanted he was prepared to take. . . . What he had been before, God alone knew. A Younger Son? A Perpetual Second-in-Command? Who knew? But today the world changed. Feudalism was finished; its last vestiges were gone. It held no place for him. He was going—he was damn well going!—to make a place in it for . . . A man could now stand up on a hill, so he and she could surely get into some hole together!

(*A Man Could Stand Up*, pt. III, ch. 2)

The room is furnished only with a camp bed. Valentine sees it as her nuptial couch: why then are those three officers, glasses in hand, jigging up and down on it? Then comes one of the most moving endings in all fiction:

They were all yelling.
"Good old Tietjens! Good old Fat Man! Pre-war Hooch! He'd be the one to get it." No one like Fat Man Tietjens! He lounged at the door; easy; benevolent. In uniform now. That was better. An officer, yelling like an enraged Redskin dealt him an immense blow behind the shoulder blades. He staggered, smiling into the centre of the room. An officer gently pushed her into the centre of the room. She was against him. Khaki encircled them. They began to yell and to prance, joining hands. Others waved the bottles and smashed underfoot the glasses. Gipsies break glasses at their weddings. The bed was against the wall. She did not like the bed to be against the wall. It had been brushed by. . . .
They were going round them: yelling in unison:
"Over here! Pom Pom Over here! Pom Pom!
That's the word that's the word; Over here. . . ."
At least they weren't over there! They were prancing. The whole world round them was yelling and prancing round. They were the centre of unending roaring circles. The man with the eyeglass had stuck a half-crown in his other eye. He was well-meaning. A brother. She had a brother with the VC. All in the family.
Tietjens was stretching out his two hands from the waist. It was incomprehensible. His right hand was behind her back, his left in her right hand. She was frightened. She was amazed. Did you ever! He was swaying slowly. The elephant! They were dancing! Aranjuez was hanging on to the tall woman like a kid on a telegraph pole. The officer who had said he had picked up a little bit of fluff . . . well, he had! He had run out and fetched it. It wore white cotton gloves and a flowered hat. It said: "Ow! Now! . . ." There was a fellow with a most beautiful voice. He led: better than a gramophone. Better. . . .
Les petites marionettes, font! font! font. . . .
On an elephant. A dear, meal-sack elephant. She was setting out on . . .

(pt. III, ch. 2)

One interesting aspect of *Parade's End* has been pointed out by Graham Greene: the four novels are, he writes, "almost the only adult novels dealing with the sexual life that have been written in English." There is nothing, in the relations of Sylvia and

Christopher, Valentine and Christopher, Edith Ethel and Macmaster, Mark and Marie Leonie, of the mystical heights nor the crude depths of Lawrence; yet these thoughts of Christopher as he waits for the war to end are more like the sexual life as most men know it than Lawrence would ever admit, or perhaps could ever conceive:

If they would go home he could be sitting talking to her for whole afternoons. That was what a young woman was for. You seduced a young woman in order to be able to finish your talks with her. You could not do that without living with her. You could not live with her without seducing her; but that was the by-product. The point is that you can't otherwise talk. You can't finish talks at street corners; in museums; even in drawing rooms. You mayn't be in the mood when she is in the mood—for the intimate conversation that means the final communion of your souls. You have to wait together—for a week, for a year, for a lifetime, before the final intimate conversation may be attained . . . and exhausted. So that . . .

That in effect was love.

(pt. II, ch. 6)

Mark Tietjens, Christopher's elder brother and heir to Groby, who has reached high position in the civil service, is the central character of the last of the four novels, *Last Post*; but until the final page he does not speak. For when the armistice draws near he, as head of the Ministry of War Transport, is told that the Allies do not intend to pursue the Germans into their own country. To him this is so evidently a betrayal of France—indeed of all those who have fought—that he determines never to speak again. The doctors call it a stroke. So he lies in a thatched hut without walls in Groby grounds: the master of Groby, who never wished for the country life, has returned—paralyzed and speechless. He wishes to give Christopher money, for Christopher to take over the estate. Christopher, being a stubborn Yorkshireman, refuses; he goes into business with a Mr. Schatzweiler, selling antique English furniture to the Americans. But when Sylvia, whose son will be heir to Groby, tries to let the house furnished to some nouveaux riches and has the great tree cut down, Christopher and Valentine go to live there. The son has been brought up by Sylvia and "was by now a full fledged Papist, pickled and oiled and wafered and all."

In the end, while Valentine is pregnant, Sylvia arrives—and relents. With the words of her son, "Be sporting, mother!" in her ears, she tells Valentine:

"They can all, soon, call you Mrs. Tietjens. Before God I came to drive out those people" (the nouveaux riches who came to view the property). ". . . But I wanted to see how it was you kept him. . . ." There is the old flash as she says: "Damn it, I'm playing pimp to Tietjens of Groby—leaving my husband to you!" But the influence of Father Consett is too strong; she will get her marriage dissolved by Rome.

So there is some light in the darkness, and as Mark dies he mutters to Valentine the old story about the Yorkshireman on Mount Ararat, his chin scarcely above the waters, who remarked to Noah that it was bound to clear up; and he adds: "'Never let thou thy child weep for thy sharp tongue to thy good man. . . . A good man! Groby Great Tree is down. . . .' He said: 'Hold my hand.'"

Parade's End is a moving study of human beings and a beautiful work of art; but through it, if we listen carefully, we shall catch a note of lament, of elegy. The bell tolls for the passing of old ways of living and thinking. Christopher, the most obstinately conservative and deeply virtuous of men, is forced to accept the new sexual morality and to install an unmarried woman as his and Groby's mistress. It was all very well to have mistresses hidden away and from the proper class: "In their sardonic way the tenants appreciated that: it was in the tradition and all over the country they did it themselves. But not a lady: the daughter of your father's best friend! They wanted Quality women to *be* Quality." Again, it was right for Mark to have his mistress, but not to marry her; yet marry Marie Leonie he does.

The nouveaux riches, the traditionless, are battering at the gates. Groby Great Tree is down—the tree that for centuries has been regarded by the country folk as having magical properties, and whose roots reach deep into ancestral consciences. "A Papist at Groby and Groby Great Tree down. . . . The curse was perhaps off the family!" Mark thinks. In some old families, whose property came to them as a result of Henry VIII's dispossession of the monasteries, a sense of guilt lingered through the generations. Groby had originally been monastic land; perhaps, now that a Papist would inherit, the crime would be expiated. It was an idea that had haunted Ford all his life: it was, it will be recalled, for the restoration of these properties that Katharine Howard had striven in *The Fifth Queen Crowned*.

So there is interwoven in this strange and vivid story something of what Jung might call "the collective unconscious" of the English nation. But the strangeness does not end with the last page of *Last Post*. Christopher, as we know, was based on a real person, Arthur Marwood, and long after the novels appeared Ford said that he felt him to be still alive:

> With his prototype I set out on several enterprises—one of them being a considerable periodical of a Tory kind—and for many years I was accustomed as it were to "set" my mind by his comments on public or other affairs. He was, as I have elsewhere said—the last English Tory, omniscient, slightly contemptuous—and sentimental in his human contacts. . . . And I do so still. I have only to say to my mind, as the child on the knees of an adult says to its senior: "Tell us a fairy tale!"—I have only to say: "Tell us what he would here have done!" and at once he is there.
>
> So you see, I cannot tell you the end of Tietjens, for he will end only when I am beyond pens and paper. . . .
>
> And so he will go jogging along with ups and downs and plenty of worries and some satisfaction, the Tory Englishman, running his head perhaps against fewer walls, perhaps against more, until I myself cease from these pursuits.
>
> ("Dedicatory Letter," *Last Post*, pp. vii–viii)

But Mark too was based on a real person—Arthur's elder brother, Sir William Marwood, whose estate was called Busby and, like the fictional Groby, lay on the Cleveland hills in north Yorkshire. *Last Post* was published in 1928: Sir William, the hale and hearty squire, did not read it, for Ford was held in somewhat bad repute in that house on account of the scandal over Violet Hunt and because he had had a difference of opinion with Arthur shortly before the latter's death during the war.

In 1934, Sir William Marwood was struck down with cancer of the throat. A member of his family wrote to me:

> He lay without speaking for weeks unless he was desperate. The Great Tree at Busby is really a marvellous Spanish chestnut which is still there, but a huge cedar began to split the flags round the walls and had to be cut down when Sir William was ill. He died a few days later from grief about this, and at the end he said: "Hold my hand."

LAST WORDS

THE most successful of the novels Ford wrote in the last decade of his life are *The Rash Act* (1933) and its sequel, *Henry for Hugh*, which appeared, only in the United States, in 1934. In them he deals with the people who, by means of great industrial wealth, had inherited the earth from the landed gentlemen such as the Tietjenses, and whose heirs were already suffering from guilt as a result of the corrupt methods by which their money had been made; they are doubtful how they should conduct themselves, what they should do with the tremendous power they can wield, what life really means. "*The Rash Act*," Ford himself wrote, "is meant to do for the post-war world and the crisis what the Tietjens tetralogy did for the war . . . the chief characteristic of these years is want of courage—physical and moral." The tragedy of the central character of *The Rash Act* is, Ford added, "that whatever feeble action he commits himself to he always finds himself in exactly the same situation." In *Henry for Hugh* we see the main character assuming the responsibility that he cannot escape; here Ford is suggesting that somehow or other the new governing class can become as altruistically concerned with mankind as was the Tietjens class before them.

In these two novels he carries as far as possible the technique that he had spent his life hammering out; yet in so doing he shows up with startling clarity certain weaknesses that are evident even in his finest work. One is a tendency, visible even in Christopher Tietjens and Sylvia, for his characters to be either unbelievably good or quite incredibly bad; another is a dependence on coincidence that, in *The Rash Act*, does seriously interfere with our enjoyment; and sometimes, as in *The Good Soldier*, we long for some relief from the gloom and futility that is so dexterously and quietly built up in our minds. The method *is* immensely skillful and usually immensely successful, but there are moments when we feel the force of the old tag "nothing fails like success."

Yet, once come under the spell of Ford and these objections fall away. It is sometimes said nowadays that a novel must not be considered as a presentation of character or as an exposé of situation, psychological or moral, but simply as an expression of the contents of the author's mind. Whether or not this has a general validity it is particularly pertinent in the case of Ford; for, when all is said and done, it is the mind—subtle, kindly, never moralizing, never preaching, never censorious—behind the works that attracts—or does not attract. As Ford himself said: "If I have any value to the world it is simply the value of my unaffected self—and I dare say that any man's value in this world is simply that. For no man's views are worth very much. . . ."

FORD MADOX FORD

SELECTED BIBLIOGRAPHY

The name or pen name under which a work was published is given at the end of the entry. A work that was published under the name Ford Madox Ford does not have a special designation in the entry.

I. BIBLIOGRAPHY. D. D. Harvey, ed., *Ford Madox Ford: 1873–1939. A Bibliography of Works and Criticism* (Princeton, N. J., 1962).

II. COLLECTED AND SELECTED WORKS. *Collected Poems* (London, 1914), includes *High Germany, The Face of the Night,* selection from *Songs from London, From Inland,* and *Poems for Pictures* (Hueffer); *Collected Poems* (New York, 1936), intro. by W. R. Benét, mainly *Collected Poems* (1914), *On Heaven,* and *New Poems* (Ford); G. Greene, ed., *The Bodley Head Ford Madox Ford,* 4 vols. (London, 1962–1963), with intro. by Greene—vol. I: *The Good Soldier,* selected memoirs, poems; vol. II: *The Fifth Queen, Privy Seal, The Fifth Queen Crowned;* vol. III: *Some Do Not* (*Parade's End,* pt. I); vol. IV: *No More Parades, A Man Could Stand Up* (*Parade's End,* pts. II and III).

III. SEPARATE WORKS. *The Brown Owl* (London, 1892), children's story (Hueffer); *The Feather* (London, 1892), children's story (Hueffer); *The Shifting of the Fire* (London, 1892), novel (Hueffer); *The Questions at the Well* (London, 1893), verse (Fenil Haig); *The Queen Who Flew* (London, 1894), children's story (Hueffer); *Ford Madox Brown—Life and Work* (London, 1896), biography (Hueffer).

Poems for Pictures (London, 1900) (Hueffer); *The Cinque Ports* (Edinburgh, 1900), large historical volume, illus. by William Hyde (Hueffer); *D. G. Rossetti: A Critical Essay* (London, 1902) (Hueffer); *The Face of the Night* (London, 1904), verse (Hueffer); *The Benefactor: A Tale of a Small Circle* (London, 1905), novel (Hueffer); *The Soul of London* (London, 1905), descriptive-discursive (Hueffer); *Hans Holbein the Younger* (London, 1905), criticism (Hueffer); *The Fifth Queen* (London, 1905), the 1st Tudor novel (Hueffer); *The Heart of the Country* (London, 1906), descriptive (Hueffer); *Christina's Fairy Book* (London, 1906), children's stories (Hueffer); *Privy Seal* (London, 1907), 2nd Tudor novel (Hueffer); *From Inland and Other Poems* (London, 1907) (Hueffer); *An English Girl* (London, 1907), novel (Hueffer); *The Pre-Raphaelite Brotherhood* (London, 1907), criticism (Hueffer); *The Spirit of the People* (London, 1907), discursive (Hueffer); *The Fifth Queen Crowned* (London, 1908), 3rd and final Tudor novel (Hueffer); *Mr. Apollo* (London, 1908), novel (Hueffer); *The "Half Moon"* (London, 1909), novel (Hueffer).

A Call (London, 1910), novel (Hueffer); *Songs from London* (London, 1910), verse (Hueffer); *The Portrait* (London, 1910), novel (Hueffer); *High Germany* (London, 1911), verse (Hueffer); *Ancient Lights* (London, 1911), 1st vol. of memoirs (U.S. title: *Memories and Impressions*) (Hueffer); *The Simple Life Limited* (London, 1911), novel

(Daniel Chaucer); *Ladies Whose Bright Eyes* (London, 1911), novel (Hueffer); *The Critical Attitude* (London, 1911), criticism (Hueffer); *The Panel* (London, 1912), novel (U.S. title: *A Ring for Nancy*) (Hueffer); *The New Humpty-Dumpty* (London, 1912), novel (Daniel Chaucer); *The Monstrous Regiment of Women* (London, 1913), suffragette pamphlet (Hueffer); *Mr. Fleight* (London, 1913), novel (Hueffer); *The Young Lovell* (London, 1913), novel (Hueffer); *Henry James: A Critical Study* (London, 1913) (Hueffer); *Antwerp* (London, 1915), verse (Hueffer); *The Good Soldier* (London, 1915), novel (Hueffer); *When Blood Is Their Argument: An Analysis of Prussian Culture* (London, 1915), war pamphlet (Hueffer); *Between St. Denis and St. George: A Sketch of Three Civilizations* (London, 1915), war pamphlet (Hueffer); *On Heaven and Other Poems Written on Active Service* (London, 1918) (Hueffer).

Thus to Revisit (London, 1921), 2nd vol. of memoirs (Hueffer); *The Marsden Case* (London, 1923), novel; *Women and Men* (Paris, 1923), essay; *Mister Bosphorus and the Muses* (London, 1923), long satirical verse drama, illus. by Paul Nash; *Joseph Conrad* (London, 1924), criticism; *Some Do Not* (London, 1924), 1st novel of the tetralogy *Parade's End*; *No More Parades* (London, 1925), 2nd novel of the tetralogy; *A Mirror to France* (London, 1926), study of French culture; *A Man Could Stand Up* (London, 1926), 3rd novel of the tetralogy; *New Poems* (New York, 1927); *New York Essays* (New York, 1927); *New York Is Not America* (London, 1927), essays; *Last Post* (London, 1928), 4th novel of the tetralogy; *A Little Less than Gods* (London, 1928), novel; *No Enemy* (New York, 1929), semiautobiographical.

The English Novel (London, 1930), criticism; *Return to Yesterday* (London, 1931), 3rd vol. of memoirs; *When the Wicked Man* (London, 1932), novel; *The Rash Act* (London, 1933), novel; *It Was the Nightingale* (London, 1934), 4th vol. of memoirs; *Henry for Hugh* (Philadelphia, 1934), novel, sequel to *The Rash Act; Great Trade Route* (London, 1937), discursive-philosophical; *Vive le Roy* (London, 1937), thriller; *Mightier than the Sword* (London, 1938), sketches of Hardy, James, Hudson, Stephen Crane, D. H. Lawrence, Galsworthy, Turgenev, and Dreiser (American ed.: *Portraits from Life*); *Provence* (London, 1938), discursive-philosophical; *The March of Literature from Confucius to Modern Times* (London, 1939), historical-critical work.

NOTE: Ford also contributed prefaces to many books, including one to the English trans. of René Behaine's novel *The Survivors* (London, 1937); he wrote articles for such magazines as *Blast,* the *Bookman, Harper's,* the *London Mercury,* and the *Outlook,* and to the two reviews he edited, the *English Review* and *transatlantic review.*

IV. LETTERS. R. M. Ludwig, ed., *Ford Madox Ford: Letters* (Princeton, N. J.–Oxford, 1965).

V. COLLABORATIONS. With Joseph Conrad: *The Inheritors* (London, 1901), novel; *Romance* (London, 1903),

332

novel; *The Nature of the Crime* (London, 1924), fragment; with Violet Hunt: *Zeppelin Nights* (London, 1916), commentary.

VI. BIOGRAPHICAL AND CRITICAL STUDIES. V. Hunt, *The Flurried Years* (London, 1926), useful but not entirely reliable study of Ford between about 1908 and 1915 (U.S. title: *I Have This to Say*); S. Bowen, *Drawn from the Life* (London, 1940), sympathetic study of Ford between 1920 and 1930; D. Goldring, *South Lodge* (London, 1943), sketches of Ford, Violet Hunt, Mary Butts, others; D. Goldring, *The Last Pre-Raphaelite: A Record of the Life and Writings of Ford Madox Ford* (London, 1948), by a former colleague and friend of Ford's, invaluable for the student but not fully documented in dealing with Ford's later years, particularly those in America (American ed.: *Trained for Genius*); M. Schorer, "The Good Novelist in *The Good Soldier,*" *Horizon,* 20, no. 116 (August 1949), criticism of the highest importance for *The Good Soldier.*

G. Greene, *The Lost Childhood and Other Essays* (London, 1951), contains brief but illuminating sketch of Ford the writer; H. Kenner, *The Poetry of Ezra Pound* (London, 1953), should be studied for Ford's influence, through Pound, on modern poetry; H. Kenner, "Remember that I Have Remembered," in *Hudson Review,* 3, no. 4 (1951) 609, brief, brilliant study of Ford's best novels; R. A. Cassell, *Ford Madox Ford: A Study of His Novels* (Baltimore, 1961; Oxford, 1962); P. L. Wiley, *Novelist of Three Worlds: Ford Madox Ford* (New York, 1962); J. A. Meix-

ner, *Ford Madox Ford's Novels: A Critical Study* (Minneapolis, 1962; Oxford, 1963); R. W. Lid, *Ford Madox Ford: The Essence of His Art* (Los Angeles, 1964; London, 1965); F. MacShane, *The Life and Work of Ford Madox Ford* (London, 1965), not a definitive life because author was unable to use unpublished Ford letters and mss.; C. G. Hoffman, *Ford Madox Ford* (New York, 1967); H. R. Huntley, *The Alien Protagonist of Ford Madox Ford* (Chapel Hill, N. C., 1970); A. Mizener, *The Saddest Story: A Biography of Ford Madox Ford* (New York, 1971); R. A. Cassell, ed., *Ford Madox Ford: Modern Judgments* (London, 1972); F. MacShane, comp., *Ford Madox Ford: The Critical Heritage* (Boston–London, 1972); G. C. Smith, *Ford Madox Ford* (New York, 1972); S. J. Stana, *Ford Madox Ford* (New York, 1977); T. C. Moser, *The Life in the Fiction of Ford Madox Ford* (Princeton, N. J., 1980).

NOTE: Ford is mentioned in many books relating to his period, notably H. G. Wells, *Boon* (London, 1915); J. Soskice [Ford's sister], *Chapters from Childhood* (London, 1921); E. Pound, *Personae* (New York, 1926); N. Hamnett, *Laughing Torso* (London, 1932), E. Hemingway, *The Torrents of Spring* (London, 1933); H. G. Wells, *Experiment in Autobiography* (London, 1934); E. Crankshaw, *Joseph Conrad* (London, 1936); E. Jepson, *Memoirs of an Edwardian* (London, 1937); N. Douglas, *Late Harvest* (London, 1947); W. Lewis, *Rude Assignment* (London, 1947); E. Pound, *Guide to Kulchur* (London, 1952); D. Garnett, *The Golden Echo* (London, 1953).

G. K. CHESTERTON

(1874-1936)

Christopher Hollis

GILBERT KEITH CHESTERTON was born in Campden Hill in London on 29 May 1874. He was the son of a prosperous London auctioneer whose firm is still in operation. His family was Liberal in politics and Unitarian in religion. Chesterton was sent to St. Paul's School. His career there was not outstanding in the conventional academic sense. He lacked the capacity to direct his attention to subjects that did not interest him. Physically he was a large and clumsy boy, and in athletics he won no distinction whatsoever. But he, with a group of his friends, of whom the closest to Chesterton and the most distinguished in later life was E. C. Bentley, creator of the form of light verse known as "the clerihew,"[1] founded the Junior Debating Club. Chesterton's schoolboy life found its fullest expression in the life of that debating society, over which he presided, and in the friendship of his fellow members.

After leaving school he did not go to a university but went instead to the Slade School of Art. He had considerable powers as a caricaturist and draftsman, as his later illustrations for E. C. Bentley's verses and Hilaire Belloc's satirical novels were to show, but it was soon evident that his talents were primarily literary rather than artistic. He drifted out of art into a publisher's office and soon began, at first through casual contributions, to make a name for himself in free-lance journalism.

In 1899 the Conservative government of the day, under the influence of its vigorous colonial secretary, Joseph Chamberlain, had gone to war with the two small Dutch South African republics of the Transvaal and the Orange Free State. Opinion in the Liberal party was divided on that war. Some supported it as vigorously as did the Conservatives. Others were opposed, but even among the opponents opposition was for different reasons. There were the pacifists, who opposed this war because they opposed all wars. But there were others— among whom was Chesterton—who were by no means generally pacifist, but who objected to this particular war as an unjust war. Chesterton's liberalism was always a liberalism of belief in small units. He hated imperialism and large units and the uniformity that imperialism's tyranny imposed upon people of different traditions. He was in violent reaction against the popular imperialism of the day, preached by Rudyard Kipling and Cecil Rhodes. Later, in a more lighthearted mood, he was to write an extravaganza called *The Napoleon of Notting Hill* (1904), in which he imagines the growth of a passionate patriotism among the citizens of the various boroughs of London and the outbreak of war between them.

In 1899, in a more serious mood, he championed the cause of the South African republics. He was not content like others to argue that the British Empire was wrong to fight the South African republics. He argued rather that the South African republics were right to fight the British Empire. At the same time he had no sympathy with those who decried the virtue of patriotism. For the British Empire as such he cared little, but he championed as passionately the right of an Englishman to love England as of a South African to love South Africa.

These unpopular views he poured forth throughout the war, first in the columns of a small weekly paper run by himself and his friends, called the *Speaker*, and then in those of one of the large London Liberal daily papers, the *Daily News*.

At the same time he was making his first attacks on

---

[1]A form of comic biography in a quatrain verse. The lines rhyme and have a certain rhythmical form but do not scan. An example is:

> What I like about Clive
> Is that he's no longer alive.
> There's a great deal to be said
> For being dead.

the world as a poet. In 1900 he produced his first two books of poems, *Greybeards at Play* and *The Wild Knight.* In reaction against the dominant imperialism of the age, he was also in reaction against its pessimism. He imagines an unborn child dreaming what a wonderful adventure it would be to find his way into a world covered with green hair and warmed by a gigantic ball of fire, and his splendor of delight when, stepping through the door of birth, he finds himself indeed in such a magic world.

Healthy and attractive though it was as a reaction against prevailing pessimism, there was perhaps something a trifle superficial in the too exuberant optimism of the young Chesterton of this period. There was force in the mockery of the Irish critic Thomas Kettle, who complained that it was really absurd in face of all the squalors and tragedies of life—the suicides and slums—to exclaim merely, ''How jolly it all is!'' Though he had not yet reached the full maturity of his thought, Chesterton was prepared to meet the challenge.

In 1903 John Morley, who was then editing the English Men of Letters series, commissioned Chesterton to write the volume on Robert Browning. The manuscript, when it was delivered, proved to be very different from the objective, accurate record that the editor had expected. Chesterton, with a prodigious memory but a constitutional contempt for accuracy that he often carried to unpardonable lengths, quoted Browning copiously, but always from memory and often with verbal inaccuracy. Instead of describing Browning's works, he preferred to discuss his views—and sometimes, to tell the truth, Browning was little more than a peg on which to hang the discussion of Chesterton's own views. To the challenge of superficial optimism, he replied that Browning had taught us how to find good in what was apparently unmixed evil. Browning, he said, ''walked into the foulest of thieves' kitchens and accused men publicly of virtue.''

From his earliest boyhood, from the days of the Junior Debating Club, Chesterton had always loved an argument, and his articles in the *Daily News* and elsewhere, by this time one of the major excitements of English journalism, were more often than not in the form of argument and criticism of one or other of the established leaders of popular thought of the day. Couched in the paradoxical form in which his mind naturally ran, Chesterton's statements challenged alike the inequalities of life in Edwardian England, which the Conservatives defended, and the

socialistic drift toward ever larger units and more and more regulation, which so many of the moderns accepted as progress. In 1905 he collected these controversial opinions into a book called *Heretics,* in which he took to task one after another these leaders of popular thought—Kipling, George Moore, Bernard Shaw, H. G. Wells, the rationalist Joseph McCabe—and showed how in his opinion they were all mistaken. This brilliant and amusing book provoked the obvious question—uttered, as it happened, by G. S. Street—''Heretics from what? If all these other thinkers are wrong, who is right? What is Mr. Chesterton's orthodoxy from which he blames them for diverging?'' Always ready to respond to a challenge of such a sort, Chesterton in 1908 wrote *Orthodoxy,* in which for the first time he explicitly accepted the Christian position and gave his reasons for accepting it.

Until the coming of Chesterton, the defenders of orthodoxy had tended to defend it with arguments that were not only serious but also solemn, and, in most people's eyes at any rate, the weapon of laughter was a weapon on which the skeptic had almost a monopoly. It was the first of Chesterton's achievements that he turned the laugh against the skeptic, but even more important than his annexation of laughter to orthodoxy was his annexation of reason. He entirely accepted the rationalists' contention that the Christian religion must be judged by reason, but he argued that reason was the friend and not the enemy of that religion.

The universe, he argued, manifestly did not explain itself. It could be understood only as the creation of something beyond itself. Man had this strange double nature. Even when he did that which he knew to be wrong, he was able to recognize that there was a right opposed to this wrong. He was to that extent in constant conflict with himself, and such a conflict could be explained only if we understood that he was now something different from what he was made to be—if we understood and accepted, that is to say, the Christian doctrine of the Fall. Original sin was the sole firm ground of optimism. If man, as he is, was all that man could be, there was no alternative to despair. But if man had fallen and had been redeemed, then there was a sure basis for Christian hope. Christianity, he argued, was not the alternative and the antagonist of other faiths. On the contrary, it offered to man all that the other faiths and philosophies could offer but something more as well. He wrote in *Heretics:*

That a good man may have his back to the wall is no more than we knew already; but that God could have his back to the wall is a boast for all insurgents for ever. Christianity is the only religion on earth that has felt that omnipotence made God incomplete. Christianity alone has felt that God, to be wholly God, must have been a rebel as well as a king. Alone of all creeds, Christianity has added courage to the virtues of the Creator. For the only courage worth calling courage must necessarily mean that the soul passes a breaking point—and does not break. In this indeed I approach a matter more dark and awful than it is easy to discuss; and I apologize in advance if any of my phrases fall wrong or seem irreverent touching a matter which the greatest saints and thinkers have justly feared to approach. But in that terrific tale of the Passion there is a distinct emotional suggestion that the author of all things (in some unthinkable way) went not only through agony, but through doubt. It is written, "Thou shalt not tempt the Lord thy God." No; but the Lord thy God may tempt Himself; and it seems as if this was what happened in Gethsemane. In a garden Satan tempted man: and in a garden God tempted God. He passed in some superhuman manner through our human horror of pessimism. When the world shook and the sun was wiped out of heaven, it was not at the crucifixion, but at the cry from the cross: the cry which confessed that God was forsaken of God. And now let the revolutionists choose a creed from all the creeds and a god from all the gods of the world, carefully weighing all the gods of inevitable recurrence and of unalterable power. They will not find another god who has himself been in revolt. Nay (the matter grows too difficult for human speech) but let the atheists themselves choose a god. They will find only one divinity who ever uttered their isolation; only one religion in which God seemed for an instant to be an atheist.

(ch. 8, pp. 254–255)

During all these years books and articles were pouring out from Chesterton's pen with bewildering rapidity. In literary biography he followed his study of Browning with one of Charles Dickens. He used his experience as an art student in studies of G. F. Watts and William Blake. He wrote a criticism of the man with whom throughout his lifetime he remained in unending friendly controversy, Bernard Shaw. In all, Chesterton wrote eight literary biographies—of Watts, Browning, Dickens, Shaw, Blake, William Cobbett, Robert Louis Stevenson, and Geoffrey Chaucer. We may add St. Thomas Aquinas to the list if we wish to call that a literary biography. In addition, he was continually throwing at the world his passing literary judgments in works as various as his volume on the *Victorian Age in Literature* (1913) for the Home University Library or his articles that ap-

peared on the central page of the *Illustrated London News* every week for almost the last quarter-century of his life. As was only to be expected of a writer so uncritically fertile, his literary judgments varied in merit.

He had no talent at all—as he himself was the first to confess—for what is sometimes called pure literary criticism, for arguments about form and manner. His whole interest was in ideas. As a consequence, the least successful of his biographies, as is generally agreed, are those of Watts and Stevenson, where his subject threw down no clear dogmatic challenge to the ideas of his age. The study of Blake was also a failure because Chesterton's weapon was reason, and he could not be at home with one who despised reason. On the other hand, the Browning study, written when Chesterton was still young, remains to this day a favorite, even though those who prefer Browning's verse to Chesterton's arguments have continued to complain about it for decades.

Dickens' protest against the tyrannies of Victorian industrialism was exactly the protest that Chesterton himself was anxious to make. He wrote the book in 1906. Had he come to it a little later in life he might have felt irritated by Dickens' theological weakness, but as it was, he wrote it just at the time when his admiration for Dickens was most unqualified. Chaucer was a subject naturally suited to Chesterton's sympathy, but the trouble with writing a life of Chaucer is that we know so very little about him and our bricks have therefore to be made of such very scanty straw.

Undoubtedly in many ways the most satisfactory of his biographies was that of Cobbett. For Chesterton's debt to Cobbett was immense. It was Cobbett who first loudly challenged the popular Reformation view of English history. It is true that Cobbett did it not through any positive belief in, or understanding of, the Catholic religion, to which indeed he never adhered; and what were to Chesterton the most important things in life were to Cobbett a closed book. Cobbett's interests were solely political and social— they were partly to discredit the landed aristocracy of his own day, and the established church which battened on it, through discrediting its origins. But it was from Cobbett that Belloc mainly learned his view of English history, and Chesterton learned it from Belloc. Cobbett was, it is true, a great exaggerator indifferent to detailed fact, but Chesterton also had an artist's indifference to pedantry. And, if he admired Cobbett where he was like him, he admired him equally, by a law of compensation, where he was most unlike him. Chesterton, though an enemy of industrialism and a believer in "the rude peasantry," was quite practically incompetent, whether at agriculture or any other manual task. But Cobbett was a practical farmer, and Chesterton had all the impractical man's envy and admiration for the practical man. So here was a subject into which he really could enter with spirit and enthusiasm.

Among his fantastic novels, he followed *The Napoleon of Notting Hill* with *The Man Who Was Thursday* (1908)—the story of a mysterious society of anarchists named after the days of the week. One after another, every one of these anarchists, after a series of amazing adventures, is discovered to be—unknown to all the rest—really a detective, seeking to spy on and to protect his society from his colleagues. At last only one—Sunday—is left, and he symbolizes the vast forces of Nature, which society exists to tame—"huge, boisterous, full of vitality, dancing with a hundred legs, bright with the glare of the sun, and at first sight somewhat regardless of us and our desires," as Chesterton himself put it in an explanation written in later life.

He followed these novels with another fantasia, *The Ball and the Cross* (1909). It is the story of two men, one a simple Catholic from the Highlands of Scotland, the other a sincere atheist. Completely opposed to one another in their philosophies, both see no alternative but to fight their differences out. They travel over the world trying to find a place where they will be allowed to fight one another. Yet whenever they try to stage their fight, sombody from the modern world of compromise and half-faith interferes to keep the peace between them and to compel them to move on to another battlefield.

The first of the Father Brown stories, *The Innocence of Father Brown*, appeared in 1911. It was followed by *The Wisdom of Father Brown* in 1914, *The Incredulity of Father Brown* in 1926, and *The Secret of Father Brown* in 1927. All the Father Brown stories were collected into an omnibus volume in 1929, but even an omnibus volume could not kill that exuberant little priest, and Father Brown stories continued to pour from Chesterton's pen and were published in the *Strand* and other magazines. They were collected in the final Father Brown volume—*The Scandal of Father Brown*—in 1935.

The original of Father Brown was Monsignor John O'Connor, a Yorkshire priest and a great friend of Chesterton's, who in 1922 received him into the

Catholic church. Ever since Conan Doyle had published his Sherlock Holmes stories at the beginning of the century, the detective story had been—as indeed it still is—one of the most popular sorts of book in the English bookstall. Detective stories varied, and vary, in merit from the crudest murder or from a story that merely sets out a simple problem of "Who done it?" without any attempt at literary merit, upward. But a very high proportion of England's leading men of letters in the twentieth century have tried their hand at a detective story at one time or another.

Chesterton's Father Brown certainly differed from the detectives of unliterary writers in that it was the character and features of the detective—his round, smiling, babylike face—that impressed themselves on the public and won the books their popularity. Father Brown's detection differs from that of the creations of other authors in that it is, characteristically, always some psychological and often indeed some theological slip by which the criminal betrays himself, as when the murderer, disguised as a priest, is heard to dissent from the orthodox view that even God himself is bound by reason, and Father Brown knows from his heresy that he is no true priest. Or many of the plots turn on characteristically Chestertonian criticisms of the modern world, as when a witness says that no one has been to a certain house, and it turns out afterward that the milkman and the postman have been there. The modern man, Chesterton thought, in the vast anonymity of metropolitan life would easily not notice a milkman or a postman and not think of them as persons.

The year 1911 was chiefly notable in Chesterton's life for the appearance of his long poem, "The Ballad of the White Horse"—one of the two or three outstanding ballads in modern English literature. English poetry in this century has produced a number of ballad poems—or stories written in verse, as if they were to be recited by a narrator—as, for instance, the "Reynard the Fox" of John Masefield. Such a ballad needs movement and excitement and a high theme, and all these Chesterton brought to his "Ballad of the White Horse." It is certainly one of the first and the most widely quoted of all such English ballads of this century.

On a number of hillsides in the West Country are to be seen effigies of White Horses. Of these some are indeed modern and uninteresting imitations, but two, one at Edington in Wiltshire and one at Uffington in Berkshire, are of immemorial antiquity. Chesterton in his ballad tells the story of the fight for the defense of England between the Christian King Alfred and the invading heathen Danes, of the battle of Ethandune, or Edington, of Alfred's final victory, and of the acceptance of Christian baptism by Guthrum, the Danish king.

In the early stages of the war, the prospects of victory are all on the Danish side. Our Lady appears to Alfred in a vision and says to him:

> I tell you naught for your comfort,
>   Yea, naught for your desire,
> Save that the sky grows darker yet
>   And the sea rises higher.
>
>   (I. 53)

Alfred accepts this as good news. For now at least he can know that he follows the Christian cause for its own sake and not for any worldly advantage that he may hope to get out of it. Disguised as a harpist, he goes to the Danish camp. On his way there he passes the White Horse and sees that the Danes have neglected to keep it scoured. In the camp he finds the Danes singing and telling stories to one another. Harold, one of the young chieftains, is boasting frantically of the loveliness of a life of victorious violence:

> For Rome was given to rule the world,
>   And gat of it little joy—
> But we, but we shall enjoy the world,
>   The whole huge world a toy.
>
> Great wine like blood from Burgundy,
>   Cloaks like the clouds from Tyre,
> And marble like solid moonlight,
>   And gold like frozen fire.
>
> Smells that a man might swill in a cup,
>   Stones that a man might eat,
> And the great smooth women like ivory
>   That the Turks sell in the street.
>
> He sang the song of the thief of the world,
>   And the gods that love the thief;
> And he yelled aloud at the cloister-yards,
>   Where men go gathering grief.
>
>   (III. 21–24)

But Elf, the old blind minstrel, takes the harp from him and sings his sadder song:

> A boy must needs like bellowing,
>   But the old ears of a careful king
>   Are glad of songs less rough. . . .
>
> There is always a thing forgotten
>   When all the world goes well;
> A thing forgotten, as long ago,
> When the gods forgot the mistletoe
> And soundless as an arrow of snow
>   The arrow of anguish fell.
>
> The thing on the blind side of the heart,
>   On the wrong side of the door,
> The green plant groweth, menacing
> Almighty lovers in the spring;
> There is always a forgotten thing,
>   And love is not secure.
>
>   (III. 28, 35–36)

But it is from Guthrum, the great king himself, that there comes the most awful confession of nihilistic despair:

> But the hour shall come after his youth,
> When a man shall know not tales but truth,
>   And his heart fail thereat.
>
> When he shall read what is written
>   So plain in clouds and clods,
> When he shall hunger without hope
>   Even for evil gods.
>
>   (III. 52–53)

Alfred, in his disguise, makes his answer. He asks:

> What have the strong gods given?
>   Where have the glad gods led?
> When Guthrum sits on a hero's throne
>   And asks if he is dead?
>   . . .
> You are more tired of victory,
>   Than we are tired of shame.
>
> That though you hunt the Christian man
>   Like a hare on the hill-side,
> The hare has still more heart to run
>   Than you have heart to ride.
>
>   (III. 67, 70, 71)

Christianity has taken up into itself the guardianship even of the ancient pagan things, of which the White Horse is a symbol. The new paganism cannot preserve even that from which it came:

Therefore your end is on you,
    Is on you and your kings,
Not for a fire in Ely fen,
Not that your gods are nine or ten,
But because it is only Christian men
    Guard even heathen things.
                 (III. 78)

In the end the tide of battle turns. Alfred and the Christian cause gain the victory, and Guthrum accepts baptism.

In the years before the war Chesterton wrote, among other works, two more of his extravaganzas, *Manalive* (1912) and *The Flying Inn* (1914). The second of these contains his famous drinking songs, later collected in his *Wine, Water and Song* (1915). Under the influence of Bernard Shaw, he also tried his hand at a play, *Magic* (1913), but it was not a great success. These years were mainly filled for him with journalism. He had by now made the friendship of Hilaire Belloc; and Chesterton, his brother Cecil, and Belloc ran a paper called the *New Witness*. The objects of this paper were three—first, to oppose alike the capitalist solution, which would concentrate all property in the hands of rich men, and the socialist solution, which would concentrate all property in the hands of the state, and to argue that instead property should be as widely distributed as possible; second, to denounce the system of party politics, to argue that the party game was really no more than a prearranged masquerade between the two front-benches, taking their turns at office; and third, to denounce political corruption and the system by which titles of honor were awarded in return for contributions to party funds. The paper's attacks on political corruption led it in these years into a famous lawsuit in which Cecil Chesterton was prosecuted for criminal libel for allegations that he had made against certain ministers in the Liberal government of that day in connection with transactions in the shares of the Marconi Company, which the government was then taking over. Cecil Chesterton was convicted, but only a nominal fine was imposed upon him.

Chesterton had always been the supporter of small nations against large, and the Gallic influence of Belloc had taught him to look on Prussia as the evil genius of Europe. Prime Minister Lloyd George in these years had been introducing his schemes of compulsory state insurance for workers—schemes copied from those of Bismarck's Prussia—and the

New Witness had led the opposition to those schemes with the argument that they were a step on the road to the return of slavery and of the Servile State—to use a phrase that Belloc made the title of a book he published in these years. Therefore, Chesterton had no hesitation in supporting the Allied cause when war came in 1914.

In 1915 he published his first book of collected poems—poems of a wide variety, from the light satirical to the deeply devotional. The one that most caught the popular mood of the moment was his "Lepanto," in which he told the tale of the battle of Christian Europe under Don John of Austria against the Mohammedan menace. The sultan boasts:

We have set the seal of Solomon on all things under
    sun,
Of knowledge and of sorrow and endurance of
    things done,
But a noise is in the mountains, in the mountains, and
    I know
The voice that shook our palaces—four hundred
    years ago:
It is he that saith not "Kismet"; it is he that knows
    not Fate;
It is Richard, it is Raymond, it is Godfrey in the gate!
It is he whose loss is laughter when he counts the
    wager worth,
Put down your feet upon him, that our peace be on
    the earth!
            (*Collected Poems* [1927], p. 102)

Of course, Chesterton was—as he himself was always the first to insist—above all "a roaring journalist." Careful, polished, classical work was foreign to his nature, whether in prose or verse, and therefore, if we take his collected poems, we find that many pages are filled with verbal quips that are at best amusing and at worst perhaps hardly worth preserving. But to say that his work is uneven is to say something that could as well be said of almost all poets. Of the rest, there are the satirical poems, of which the most famous is that on the late Lord Birkenhead, entitled "Anti-Christ, or the Reunion of Christendom." Lord Birkenhead (then F. E. Smith) had made a speech on the Welsh Disestablishment Bill in which he had denounced it as "a Bill which has shocked the conscience of every Christian community in Europe." Chesterton thought this denunciation on Smith's lips quite insincere, and he asked in bitter irony:

In the mountain hamlets clothing
    Peaks beyond Caucasian pales,
Where Establishment means nothing
    And they never heard of Wales,
Do they read it all in Hansard[2]
    With a crib to read it with—
"Welsh Tithes: Dr. Clifford Answered,"
    Really, Smith?
    (*Collected Poems* [1927], pp. 138–139)

It is all excellent, if most powerful, fooling. In his serious narrative poems, such as "The Ballad of the White Horse" and "Lepanto," there was no fooling. They were deeply sincere works. But they were essentially works to be recited, read aloud—not to say, shouted. It may well be pleaded that, if his verse was verse to be recited, so, too, was most of the great rhetorical verse of the Elizabethans. But it is certainly true that he did not make nor attempt to make the Wordsworthian appeal to the "inward eye which is the bliss of solitude."

During the years of World War I Chesterton had a very serious illness, and physically he was never quite the same man again. Yet that did not mean that his remaining twenty years were artistically unimportant. Very far from it. It is true that with his brother's death at the end of the war, Chesterton felt it an obligation of honor to take on the editorship of the *New Witness*, and the problems of editorship occupied a great deal of his energy throughout the rest of his life. It is true, also, that—particularly after his reception into the Catholic church in 1922—demands for lectures kept him continually on the move. Yet those last twenty years of his life produced not only a number of detective stories and volumes of verse and essays. They also produced some of his most important biographies—*St. Francis of Assisi* (1923), *William Cobbett* (1925), and, above all, the last and the greatest of such studies, *St. Thomas Aquinas* (1933).

Chesterton was, of course, no professional philosopher and no professional scholar. He always used to speak of himself with characteristic and exaggerated understatement as a casual and dilettante reader. It is true that he carried his dislike for pedantry to an extreme and was unpardonably indifferent to accuracy. But in spite of his habitual carelessness, his knowledge and memory were prodigious. Throughout his

adult life, but in particular after his reception into the Catholic church, problems of religion wholly overshadowed all others in his mind. Indeed, to him politics and literature and all the other activities of man were of importance only insofar as they could be made of service to the cause of religion. His conversion to Catholicism, although it was to him the most immensely important event of his private life, had little effect on his literary development. For the religious problems that he had cared to discuss had always been the large questions of the being of God and man and Christ, rather than the precise details of the nature or residence of authority. Therefore, there was little, if anything, in such an earlier work as *Orthodoxy*, written many years before his reception into the Catholic church, that he would not have been willing to repeat at the end of his life.

Yet to attempt a biography of St. Thomas Aquinas did seem to many a challenge to fate. "Francis of Assisi," they said. "Yes. There is a man who has won the affection of all mankind. That is a natural subject for the popularizer. But would it not be wiser to leave Aquinas to the specialist?" The event proved the exact opposite. The remarkable revival of Thomism in modern Europe has indeed been the begetter of specialized works of scholarship of the greatest value. Yet there is a great danger in leaving a revival solely to the specialists—a danger that we shall not be allowed to see the forest for the trees. It was proved that Chesterton's general commentary was exactly what the general reader needed. Thomist scholars were the first and most generous in their praise. Etienne Gilson, perhaps the most learned of living Thomists, said on reading this book, "Chesterton makes one despair. I have been studying St. Thomas all my life and I could never have written such a book."

His *St. Thomas* is the last of Chesterton's connected books, published in 1933, three years before his death. Eight years before, he had published what will perhaps remain the most central of his books, *The Everlasting Man* (1925). *The Everlasting Man* is, as it were, a matured *Orthodoxy*. It falls into two parts. The first argues that, so far from man's being merely a clever sort of animal, he is different in kind from other animals. The second part argues that, so far from Christ's being merely a very good man, he is different in kind from other men.

The argument about the difference of men from animals Chesterton bases mainly on art. Whether there was or was not a special creation as a matter of

---

[2] *Hansard* is the name given to the official report of the debates of the House of Commons; Dr. Clifford was a famous Nonconformist divine of the day, a great opponent of the Welsh Establishment.

biological history, he is not concerned to argue. But, he says, one of the few things that we know about the most primitive man was that he drew—he drew on the walls of his cave. This constitutes a difference in kind between man and the animals. For the animals do not draw at all. There was no gradual declension. It was not that Rembrandt drew well and the caveman less well and the laughing jackass and the blue-faced baboon rather less well again. It was that Rembrandt and the caveman both drew, and the jackass and the hyena did not draw at all. The difference was a difference in kind.

But man with his art was also different in kind in a deeper sense. To him alone there were things more valuable than immediate victory and success, and long before the coming of Christ he found this foreshadowing of the teaching of Christ at the dawn of things in the great poetry of Homer:

But in this one great human revelation of antiquity there is another element of great historical importance; which has hardly I think been given its proper place in history. The poet has so conceived the poem that his sympathies apparently, and those of his reader certainly, are on the side of the vanquished rather than of the victor. And this is a sentiment which increases in the poetical tradition even as the poetical origin itself recedes. Achilles had some status as a sort of demigod in pagan times; but he disappears altogether in later times. But Hector grows greater as the ages pass; and it is his name that is the name of a Knight of the Round Table and his sword that legend puts into the hand of Roland, laying about him with the weapon of the defeated Hector in the last ruin and splendour of his own defeat. The name anticipates all the defeats through which our race and religion were to pass; that survival of a hundred defeats that is its triumph.

The tale of the end of Troy shall have no ending; for it is lifted up forever into living echoes, immortal as our hopelessness and our hope. Troy standing was a small thing that may have stood nameless for ages. But Troy falling has been caught up in a flame and suspended in an immortal instant of annihilation; and because it was destroyed with fire the fire shall never be destroyed. And as with the city so with the hero; traced in archaic lines in that primeval twilight is found the first figure of the Knight. There is a prophetic coincidence in his title; we have spoken of the word chivalry and how it seems to mingle the horseman with the horse. It is almost anticipated ages before in the thunder of the Homeric hexameter, and that long leaping word with which the *Iliad* ends. It is that very unity for which we can find no name but the holy centaur of chivalry. But there are other reasons for giving in this glimpse of antiquity the flame upon the sacred town. The sanctity of such towns ran like a fire round the coasts and islands of the northern

Mediterranean; the high-fenced hamlet for which heroes died. From the smallness of the city came the greatness of the citizen. Hellas with her hundred statues produced nothing statelier than that walking statue; the ideal of the self-commanding man. Hellas of the hundred statues was one legend and literature; and all that labyrinth of little walled nations resounded with the lament of Troy.

(pt. I, ch. 3, pp. 79–80)

So, too, with Christ. Chesterton's argument follows the familiar dichotomy of *aut Deus aut malus homo* (either God or an evil man). It is idle, he argues, to say that Christ was merely a good man who said some wise things about ethics or economics. For far stronger than the evidence for his ethical or economic teaching is the evidence that He made certain astonishing claims, which cannot of their nature have been the claims merely of a great ethical teacher. Either these words are the words of a deranged man or they are the words of Almighty God. There is no third choice:

Certainly it is not for us to blame anybody who should find that first wild whisper merely impious and insane. On the contrary, stumbling on that rock of scandal is the first step. Stark staring incredulity is a far more loyal tribute to that truth than a modernist metaphysic that would make it out merely a matter of degree. It were better to rend our robes with a great cry against blasphemy, like Caiaphas in the judgement, or to lay hold of the man as a maniac possessed of devils like the kinsmen and the crowd, rather than to stand stupidly debating fine shades of pantheism in the presence of so catastrophic a claim. There is more of the wisdom that is one with surprise in any simple person, full of the sensitiveness of simplicity, who should expect the grass to wither and the birds to drop dead out of the air, when a strolling carpenter's apprentice said calmly and almost carelessly, like one looking over his shoulder: "Before Abraham was, I am."

(pt. II, ch. 2, pp. 240–241)

Psychologists sometimes tell us that art is often a compensation to the artist. So far from expressing himself in his art in the straightforward sense of writing of the things that he does in his practical life, on the contrary, in his art he gives expression to those needs of his spirit—to that side of life—of which his conduct starves him. Timid men put on paper and into fiction the brave things that they are unable to do in real life. The quarrelsome, sighing subconsciously, it may be, for a tranquillity that they never allow themselves to know, write in their verse, "I strove with none, for none was worth my strife." In this sense there was a good deal of compensation in Chesterton's art. Abnormally clumsy even as a boy, in manhood growing to a corpulence that soon became a national joke appreciated by everybody—and most uproariously by himself—he was quite incapable at all times of his life of anything in the nature of an athletic feat. He quite frankly loathed physical exercise.

He could not indeed manage what to lesser mortals are the normal achievements of daily life—such things as dressing or shaving himself—others had to do these for him. He was similarly incompetent in the simplest business affairs. He could not manage his income or his income tax. Such things he left entirely to his wife, devoted companion of all his adult life, and his secretary. He could not even be trusted to effect the simplest purchase in a shop and bring back the right change. He could not make a journey. There is a well-known anecdote about one of the few occasions on which he went on a lecture tour by himself. A few days after his departure his wife received an agonized telegram: "Am in Liverpool. Where should I be?" I remember once standing with him on the landing on the first floor of a hotel. There was the elevator or there were the stairs, by either of which we could descend to the ground floor. I said to him, "Shall we take the lift or shall we go down by the stairs?" He answered at once, "My wife will come and she will decide." It never for an instant occurred to him that he could decide even so small a practical matter as that for himself.

When the war of 1914 came, Chesterton's physical condition was, as has been said, such that there could have been no question of his joining the army, but even apart from physical disability he would certainly have made a soldier of monumental incompetence. I doubt if he ever used a spade in his life and certainly he could not have used it to effect. Yet his writings are filled with praise of the soldier and the peasant, whom he greatly preferred to most of the literary men who shared his way of life. Born a Londoner and living his life in the small town of Beaconsfield, which was rapidly becoming a suburb of London, he gave his life to denouncing urbanization and to a glorification of rural life. There was nothing insincere in this. He never pretended to be other than he was. But he was an intensely humble man who never pretended that the accidents and qualities of his life were the only accidents and qualities needed for the survival of civilization.

But there was a yet deeper compensation in Chesterton's art. The fashion of the day among advanced thinkers was to profess extreme democratic theories, but at the same time to profess equally extreme contempt for the opinions and prejudices of the ordinary man. The clearest example of this was, of course, that of Bernard Shaw, who denounced almost every one of the ordinary habits and pastimes of the Englishman of his time—who would allow him neither to work nor play, to eat nor drink, to spell nor speak as he was accustomed. Chesterton in reaction to this presented himself as the champion of the ordinary man, prepared to accept him, not asking to reform him.

> Who will write us a riding song, or a hunting song,
>   or a drinking song?

he asks. The championship was certainly perfectly genuine. But of course, though his tastes may have been those of the ordinary man, his method of expression was by no means that of the ordinary man. He expressed himself almost invariably in the famous Chestertonian paradox, the formula of which was to take a common saying and invert it, standing it on itself. Thus in his *Napoleon of Notting Hill*, which he addresses to "The Human Race to which so many of my readers belong," in an imaginary history of the future he takes tendencies that he finds around him in the early twentieth century and fantastically exaggerates them:

> But the way the prophets of the twentieth century went to work was this. They took something or other that was certainly going on in their time, and then said that it would go on more and more until something extraordinary happened. And very often they added that in some odd place that extraordinary thing had happened, and that it showed the signs of the times.

> Thus, for instance, there were Mr. H. G. Wells and others, who thought that science would take charge of the future; and just as the motor-car was quicker than the coach, so some lovely thing would be quicker than the motor-car; and so on for ever. And there arose from their ashes Dr. Quilp, who said that a man could be sent on his machine so fast round the world that he could keep up a long, chatty conversation in some old-world village by saying a word of a sentence each time he came round. And it was said that the experiment had been tried on an apoplectic old major, who was sent round the world so fast that there seemed to be (to the inhabitants of some other star) a continuous band round the earth of white whiskers, red complexion and tweeds—a thing like the ring of Saturn.

343

Then there was the opposite school. There was Mr. Edward Carpenter, who thought we should in a very short time return to Nature, and live simply and slowly as the animals do. And Edward Carpenter was followed by James Pickie, D.D. (of Pocohontas College), who said that men were immensely improved by grazing, or taking their food slowly and continuously, after the manner of cows. And he said that he had, with the most encouraging results, turned city men out on all fours in a field covered with veal cutlets. Then Tolstoy and the Humanitarians said that the world was growing more merciful, and therefore no one would ever desire to kill. And Mr. Mick not only became a vegetarian, but at length declared vegetarianism doomed ("shedding," as he called it finely, "the green blood of the silent animals"), and predicted that men in a better age would live on nothing but salt. And then came the pamphlet from Oregon (where the thing was tried), the pamphlet called "Why should Salt suffer?" and there was more trouble.

(bk. I, ch. 1)

This formula was intensely annoying to those who were annoyed by Chesterton. William Ralph Inge, with whom his differences of opinion were deep, once described him petulantly as "that obese mountebank, who crucifies Truth head downwards." To most people, the manner was less irritating than this, though many, I think, would have confessed that they sometimes found the relentless, unceasing rain of paradoxes a little wearying. Sometimes, it was often said, Chesterton's formula made the most brilliant and illuminating new sense. Sometimes it was merely a paradoxical way of saying what everybody else would say straightforwardly. Sometimes he blundered into downright nonsense. His very fecundity prevented him from being a sure critic of his own epigrams. Undoubtedly an effect of his style was to make many readers take him less seriously than he would have wished. For it is not everyone who can distinguish between the solemn and the serious.

But, of course, though form may be a matter of taste, those critics did Chesterton very much less than justice who thought that he indulged in tricks of words through perversity or a desire to show off. He wrote thus because he thought thus. He wrote thus because he could not write otherwise. He wrote in paradoxes because he thought that the ultimate nature of truth lay in paradoxes, and above all in the supreme Christian paradox by which the Creator of the Universe was a little baby, lying in a manger, the child of a human mother. *Credo quia impossibile.*

To an open house in the evening
Home shall men come,
To an older place than Eden
And a taller tower than Rome,
To the end of the way of the wandering star,
To the things that cannot be and that are,
To the place where God was homeless
And all men are at home.

("The House of Christmas," st. 5)

SELECTED BIBLIOGRAPHY

I. Bibliography. J. Sullivan, *G. K. Chesterton: A Bibliography* (London, 1958).

II. Collected and Selected Works. *The Minerva Edition,* 9 vols. (London, 1926); *Collected Poems* (London, 1927; repr. London, 1933); *The Father Brown Stories* (London, 1929); *A G. K. C. Omnibus* (London, 1936); *Father Brown: Selected Stories* (London, 1955), intro. by Ronald Knox, in the World's Classics series.

III. Separate Works. *The Wild Knight and Other Poems* (London, 1900); *Greybeards at Play* (London, 1900), poems and sketches; *The Defendant* (London, 1901), essays; *Twelve Types* (London, 1902), essays; *Robert Browning* (London, 1903), criticism; *G. F. Watts* (London, 1904), criticism; *The Napoleon of Notting Hill* (London, 1904), novel; *The Club of Queer Trades* (London, 1905), stories; *Heretics* (London, 1905), essays; *Five Types* (London, 1905), essays; *Charles Dickens* (London, 1906), criticism; *The Man Who Was Thursday: A Nightmare* (London, 1908), novel; *Orthodoxy* (London, 1908), essay; *All Things Considered* (London, 1908), essays; *George Bernard Shaw* (London, 1909), criticism; *Tremendous Trifles* (London, 1909), essays; *Defence of Nonsense* (London, 1909), essay; *The Ball and the Cross* (London, 1909), novel.

What's Wrong with the World (London, 1910), essays; *William Blake* (London, 1910), criticism; *Alarms and Discursions* (London, 1910), essays; *The Innocence of Father Brown* (London, 1911), stories; *Appreciations and Criticisms of the Works of Charles Dickens* (London, 1911), criticism; *The Ballad of the White Horse* (London, 1911), poems; *Manalive* (London, 1912), novel; *A Miscellany of Men* (London, 1912), essays; *Simplicity and Tolstoy* (London, 1912), criticism; *The Victorian Age in Literature* (London, 1913), criticism; *Magic: A Play* (London, 1913); *The Wisdom of Father Brown* (London, 1914), stories; *The Flying Inn* (London, 1914), poems; *The Barbarism of Berlin* (London, 1914), essays; *Wine, Water and Song* (London, 1915), poems; *The Crimes of England* (London, 1915), essays; *Letters to an Old Garibaldian* (London, 1915), letters; *A Shilling for My Thoughts* (London, 1916), essays; *A Short History of England* (London, 1917); *Utopia of Usurers* (New York, 1917), essays; *Irish Impressions* (London, 1919), essays.

The Uses of Diversity (London, 1920), essays; *The New Jerusalem* (London, 1920), topography; *The Superstition of Divorce* (London, 1920), essays; *Eugenics and Other Evils* (London, 1922), essays; *The Man Who Knew Too Much* (London, 1922), stories; *What I Saw in America* (London, 1922), travel; *The Ballad of St. Barbara and Other Verses* (London, 1922); *Fancies versus Fads* (London, 1923), essays; *St. Francis of Assisi* (London, 1923), biography; *The End of the Roman Road* (London, 1924), essay; *The Everlasting Man* (London, 1925), theology; *Tales of the Long Bow* (London, 1925), stories; *William Cobbett* (London, 1925), biography; *The Superstitions of the Sceptic* (London, 1925), essay, incl. correspondence between the author and G. C. Coulton; *The Incredulity of Father Brown* (London, 1926), stories; *The Outline of Sanity* (London, 1926), essay; *The Queen of Seven Swords* (London, 1926), poems not incl. in *Collected Poems*; *The Catholic Church and Conversion* (New York, 1926), essay; *Culture and the Coming Peril* (London, 1927), essay; *Social Reform and Birth Control* (London, 1927), essay; *The Return of Don Quixote* (London, 1927), novel; *Robert Louis Stevenson* (London, 1927), biography; *The Secret of Father Brown* (London, 1927), stories; *The Judgment of Dr. Johnson: A Play* (London, 1927); *Gloria in Profundis* (London, 1927), poems; *Generally Speaking* (London, 1928), essays; *The Sword of Wood* (London, 1928), story; *The Poet and the Lunatics: Episodes in the Life of Gabriel Gale* (London, 1929), stories; *Ubi Ecclesia* (London, 1929), poems.

The Turkey and the Turk: A Christmas Play (London, 1930), dramatic poem; *Four Faultless Felons* (London, 1930), stories; *The Grave of Arthur* (London, 1930), poems; *Come to Think of It* (London, 1930), essays; *The Resurrection of Rome* (London, 1930), topography; *All Is Grist* (London, 1931), essays; *Chaucer: A Study* (London, 1932), criticism; *Sidelights on New London and Newer York* (London, 1932), essays; *Christendom in Dublin: Essays on the Eucharistic Congress* (Dublin, 1932); *All I Survey* (London, 1933), essays; *St. Thomas Aquinas* (London, 1933), biography; *Avowals and Denials* (London, 1934), essays; *The Scandal of Father Brown* (London, 1935), stories; *The Well and the Shallows* (London, 1935), essays; *As I Was Saying* (London, 1936), essays; *Autobiography* (London, 1936); *The Paradoxes of Mr. Pond* (London, 1936), stories; *The Coloured Lands* (London, 1938), essays, stories, poems.

End of the Armistice (London, 1940), essays; *The Common Man* (London, 1950), essays, articles, intros. written between 1905 and 1936; *The Surprise* (London, 1952), play written in 1932, preface by Dorothy L. Sayers; D. Collins, ed., *A Handful of Authors* (London, 1953), essays, articles written between 1901 and 1935; D. Collins, ed., *The Glass Walking-Stick* (London, 1955), essays from the *Illustrated London News*, 1905–1936, preface by Arthur Bryant; D. Collins, ed., *Lunacy and Letters* (London, 1958), essays from the *Daily News*, 1901–1911.

IV. BIOGRAPHICAL AND CRITICAL STUDIES. Msgr. J. O'Connor, *Father Brown on Chesterton* (London, 1937); E. Cammaerts, *The Laughing Prophet: The Seven Virtues and G. K. Chesterton* (London, 1937); C. Clemens, *G. K. Chesterton, as Seen by His Contemporaries* (London, 1939); Hilaire Belloc, *On the Place of Gilbert Chesterton in English Letters* (London, 1940); M. Ward, *Gilbert Keith Chesterton* (London, 1944); M. Ward, *Return to Chesterton* (London, 1952).

WINSTON CHURCHILL
(1874-1965)

John Connell

INTRODUCTION

THIS essay was written and published in its original form in 1956. In the intervening years I have had occasion to study, in considerable depth, Sir Winston Churchill's work as prime minister and minister of defense from 1940 to 1945. In the body of the essay of 1956 I said that his *Second World War* (1948–1954) gave a one-sided picture of the war's conduct and administration, but as he himself would have said, *some side.* It was my awareness of that one-sidedness that provided the principal motive for the studies I have mentioned. But whatever modifications this research has brought about in my view of Churchill's understanding of strategy, tactics, logistics, and the psychology of the military commanders responsible through him to Parliament and the nation, in times of harsh crisis and agonizing decision, I have seen no reason to abate or alter such judgments as I ventured to make originally on Churchill as a writer.

CHURCHILL THE WRITER

CHURCHILL'S place in the history of his country, of the British Commonwealth and Empire, and of the world is assured and magnificent. The luster of his achievements as a national leader and statesman, especially in times of crisis and danger, equals if it does not outshine that of the greatest of the great. In one facet of his genius he was, however, almost though not quite unique: throughout his life he wrote history as well as made it. He did not merely— like many politicians and military leaders—in the leisure of retirement compose his own reminiscent record of the happenings in which he played so eminent a part. From the outset of his career he was a writer, earning money by his pen; and in every period of his life in which he was not precluded, as a

servant of the state, from taking employment of this kind, he wrote to earn money. There is no need to be apologetic or mealy-mouthed about it; Churchill himself more than once proclaimed it in public and with pride. It is right therefore to consider him a professional historian and biographer (as well as journalist, essayist, orator, and even novelist) and to assess this aspect of his life's work by the same standards as we assess the writings of Edward Gibbon, Thomas Macaulay, and G. M. Trevelyan.

So closely integrated, however, in the day-to-day and year-by-year pattern of that life were the deed and the word that it is neither fair nor possible to consider the man of action and the writer in separate compartments. Each was knit inseparably into the other; each glinted with flashes of the same spiritual splendor; each at times was marred by the same faults—showiness, superficiality, misunderstanding of a person or a belief. Every judgment of Churchill's work therefore must be an imperfect attempt to assess, by incomplete standards, one of the fullest, richest, and most copious human beings that Western society has ever bred.

A mere essay in adulation would be impertinent and distasteful; but it would be equally foolish not to found an appreciation of Churchill the writer on an explicit recognition of the greatness of Churchill the statesman. It cannot be taken for granted and then left on one side; the external events of his political and military career—the battles, the narrow shaves, the crises, the controversies, the defeats, and the glories—were constantly the pith and matter of his writing. But not only did Churchill set down a record of what he himself endured and did; he used those experiences, as any true artist must, to illuminate the ordeals and achievements of others and of humanity in general; and, as every wise, mature artist must, he used what he had discovered in study and meditation to deepen, fortify, and enrich his own writings. The patterns of this reciprocation between life, thought, and the artistic creation were in Churchill as in all

347

great artists—Plato, Vergil, Rembrandt, Mozart, Beethoven—especially numerous, subtle, natural, and inseparable.

The instrument that Churchill used for the expression and fulfillment of his genius was English prose. Of English prose he was one of the greatest known masters, ranking with Joseph Addison or Jonathan Swift for clarity and masculine vigor of exposition, with Gibbon for lapidary pungency, with Macaulay for romantic color, and with (on the loftiest, most difficult plane of all) the compilers of the Authorized Version of the Bible for a supreme combination of majesty and homely simplicity.

English prose was from the beginning the instrument that lay nearest at hand. The chances and misfortunes of his childhood—amounting, as will be seen, to what a later age would have described as deprivations—did not procure for him the conventional academic education of a boy of his class. He was, however, under the artist's imperative compulsion to communicate; and the one means of communication that he possessed was the English language. This limitation in his immediately formative years proved, as often happens, to be an advantage: all the strength and richness of his genius as an artist poured, undiverted, into the channel of the only medium of expression open to it; only much later was he to discover the creative satisfaction latent elsewhere—in painting or bricklaying or breeding horses.

Mastery of his first and chief medium was not to come to him immediately, or without effort, struggles, and setbacks. But it is as an acknowledged master of English prose, in a fairly wide field, that Churchill must be judged. Prose, written or spoken, is apparently the most workaday, the humblest and most humdrum of all media of communication: in Churchill's own rapidly widening experience, after his first written examination (in which he could barely sign his name), the subaltern officer, expounding orders to the men under his command, on maneuvers or under fire, had to make use of it; the democratic politician, seeking the suffrage of the electors, had to use it; the journalist, in the first, roaring epoch of the popular mass-circulation newspaper, telling of the wonders and ardors that he knew, had to use it. Like countless other practitioners in these fields Churchill might have got along with a clumsily humdrum use of a humdrum instrument, never shining or sharpening it, never bothering to make his use of it an individual achievement,

stamped with the artist's unique, immediately apprehensible joy. Churchill, however, was an artist; and the linked challenge and satisfaction of an artist's work are always to be found in the attempt to master the difficulties and imperfections of the medium that he has chosen or that (as with Churchill) has been imposed on him because he knows no other. Churchill was a writer both born and made—born in that, given the circumstances of his heredity, environment, and upbringing, if he were to be an artist at all, it was almost impossible for him to be anything else but a writer; made in that he transformed what might have been a cramping or stultifying inhibition into one of the essential facets of his mastery. Here lies the first key to any understanding of Churchill as a writer.

Churchill's literary reputation rests on his achievements as a writer of biography, history, and autobiographical memoirs; but also, in several momentous phases of his career, as an orator. In one sense a great deal of his writing is oratorical: it can be, and it improves by being, spoken or read aloud. This of itself is evidence of a victory over a limitation; the boy and youth who suffered from an obvious, if not extremely overwhelming, impediment of speech became the most stirring and influential English orator of his time—a time, it is worth remarking, in which the weight of fashionable critical opinion was against oratory, its virtues almost as much as its defects. Spoken prose and written prose had drifted apart, further away from each other than at almost any previous epoch in the history of English literature; and it was usually considered to be a mark of good written prose that it could not possibly be spoken or read aloud. Churchill throughout his career led far too zestful and eventful an external existence to be able to submit to this subduing and maiming fashion. His spoken word and his written word were equally significant.

Some of his spoken words, however, are likely to be remembered and repeated as long as the English language is understood. His books will be read with eagerness and pleasure and profit; but as long as men have some comprehension—whether massive and detailed, or dim and obscure—of what our civilization and our culture meant, of the faith we thought worthy of our sacrifice and our effort, of the purposes and the ideals that we held, and of the kind of people we ourselves were, so long will the best and greatest of Churchill's spoken utterances survive to stir men's hearts and set their pulses racing:

I would say to the House, as I said to those who have joined this Government: "I have nothing to offer but blood, toil, tears, and sweat."

We have before us an ordeal of the most grievous kind. We have before us many, many long months of struggle and of suffering. You ask, What is our policy? I will say: "It is to wage war, by sea, land and air, with all our might and with all the strength that God can give us: to wage war against a monstrous tyranny, never surpassed in the dark, lamentable catalogue of human crime. That is our policy." You ask, What is our aim? I can answer in one word: Victory—victory at all costs, victory in spite of all terror, victory however long and hard the road may be; for without victory there is no survival. Let that be realized; no survival for the British Empire; no survival for all that the British Empire has stood for; no survival for the urge and impulse of the ages, that mankind shall move forward towards its goal. But I take up my task with buoyancy and hope. I feel sure that our cause will not be suffered to fail among men. At this time I feel entitled to claim the aid of all, and I say, "Come, then, let us go forward together with our united strength."

("Prime Minister," 13 May 1940)[1]

In its intensity, its simplicity, and its grandeur that is one of the noblest passages in English literature. It is as profoundly characteristic of its author as it is rooted in the life and thought and texture of England; it is both original and derivative. It echoes, perhaps hardly consciously, much that had been written and said before: the Authorized Version of the Bible, Shakespeare, John Bunyan, Gibbon, and Walter Scott. There are other notable echoes, too, as of Georges Clemenceau and of Giuseppi Garibaldi. The images evoked are strong and concrete. There is the thunderous repetition of the key words "war," "victory," "survival"; and there is the irresistible magnanimity and spaciousness of the final invocation. The man and the moment—Churchill was making his first major speech in the House of Commons four days after he had become prime minister in May 1940—were fused and fired with greatness.

This speech and several others made in the late 1930's and early 1940's marked the full flowering of Churchill the writer and orator, as the events in which he was involved at the same time marked the supreme summit of his career in politics. To this tremendous phase all the rest of his life, with its glittering triumphs, its difficulties and its disappointments, its controversies and its reconciliations, was a

prelude, the symbolism of which seemed so strongly appropriate that it might be believed to be purely predestined.

The challenge that, under his leadership, was answered and defeated during World War II was in essence a complex series of impulses toward evil, savagery, chaos, darkness, and death, however adroitly cloaked by a materialist and mechanistic pseudophilosophy. And his response, expressed in unwearying and sagacious political and military leadership, was in essence that of a sane, liberal, and enlightened civilization.

That civilization waxed and grew great through communication by the written and the spoken word. It is significant that in one of its fiercest and most testing crises, the man who was unanimously acclaimed as its leader in the battle for survival was by profession a writer, a large part of whose livelihood and previous reputation had been built on and sustained by his ability to communicate, by speech and on paper, as a biographer, historian, and orator. He was a man of words and of deeds; and the word did not fail to inform, mold, and fortify the deed.

THE MAKING

WINSTON LEONARD SPENCER CHURCHILL was born at Blenheim Palace, near Oxford, on 30 November 1874. His father, Lord Randolph Churchill, was the third son of the seventh duke of Marlborough. His mother, formerly Jeanette Jerome, was the daughter of a wealthy, tough, and independent-minded New York businessman, who when he was proprietor and editor of the *New York Times* (during the American Civil War) had fortified his office with rifles and cannon against furiously rioting mobs.

Lady Randolph Churchill was a woman whose luminous beauty, charm, and wit remained, long after she was dead, in the memory of all who knew her. Lord Randolph was brilliant, forceful, and ambitious, but his talents were marred by a deep, temperamental instability that cruelly cut short an almost cometlike career in British politics. During his son's boyhood Lord Randolph was obsessed with the making of this career. There was little communication and less understanding between father and son. Winston—stocky, red-haired, slow-developing in intellect, passionate, and puzzled—was in the utmost awe of his father, who thought him stupid and a little difficult. The boy's emotions focused on

---

[1]In Winston Churchill's *Blood, Sweat and Tears*, Randolph Churchill, ed. (New York, 1941).

his mother, who was herself deeply involved in the preoccupations of a leading political hostess at the pinnacle of society in late Victorian England.

The boy grew up under the regime of robust, character-hardening, apparent neglect typical of the English upper classes. He was sent at the usual tender age to a private preparatory school, where he was very unhappy. Thence he went to Harrow, where his courage, tenacity, and unabashed combativeness secured for him the respect, if not the liking or understanding, of his immediate contemporaries. He was not regarded as at all intelligent; the austere and often valuable disciplines of the traditional classical education were denied him, and he was put—along with other sturdy and aristocratic dunces—into the army class. He left school having passed no written examination of any kind, and, after a brief period in the hands of a fashionable crammer and three attempts, scraped into the Royal Military College at Sandhurst.

Here he discovered for the first time, in military history and in the training manuals of the day, that to read and to study had purpose and meaning and indeed provided joy. His mind—in a setting that the conventional intellectual of the day (outside Germany) would have thought supremely unlikely—began to burgeon. His father's career and health were in their rapid, tragic decline. In January 1895 (two months before Winston was due to receive the queen's commission) Lord Randolph died. Winston, just twenty years old, was thrust into, and assumed ardently and successfully, a mature responsibility as head of his branch of his family. He showed himself, in a crisis of grief and financial disturbance, to be self-possessed and capable. In March, with the steeling shock of experience still upon him, he was gazetted to the 4th Queen's Own Hussars; and a literary and political weekly called the *National Observer*, reporting this fact in its gossip notes, committed itself to the magnificently infelicitous forecast that "Mr. Winston Leonard Churchill, eldest son of the late Lord Randolph Churchill, evidently does not intend to follow in the political footsteps of his father."

A cavalry subaltern in those days was not well paid, his duties were few and formal, and he had five months' leave a year. Second Lieutenant Churchill's appetite for adventure and experience could not easily be contained in so dull a vessel. In November 1895, when his first leave fell due, he persuaded a brother subaltern to accompany him to the only scene of war visible in that remarkably tranquil epoch, a rebellion against Spanish imperial rule in Cuba. To help finance his share of this jaunt, he arranged with the editor of the *Daily Graphic* (to which his father had at one time been a contributor) to write a series of dispatches at £5 apiece describing the campaign. The rules governing the conduct of serving officers and of war correspondents were a good deal more lax than they subsequently became, and an enterprising officer could, and often did, combine the two roles.

Thus, just turned twenty-one, Winston Churchill was set, in an apparently haphazard and light-hearted fashion, on the career of soldier in war, observer of war, and recorder of war, which, through all the shifts of fortune and all the revolutionary changes of the epoch, he was to pursue for so long. Other strands to his making as a writer were to come later, but these were the first.

"Twenty to twenty-five! Those are the years!" he wrote long afterward. He had his baptism of fire in the Cuban jungle on his twenty-first birthday; he saw some three days' fighting, sent several zestful dispatches to the *Daily Graphic*, learned the taste of a Havana cigar, and was awarded the Spanish Order of Military Merit, first class. When he rejoined his regiment at the end of his leave, it was to be told that they were due to depart for India.

In the cold weather of 1896–1897 the 4th Hussars reached Bangalore in southern India, at this time enveloped in a profound peace. Duties and training were the reverse of onerous; polo and visits to Poona to look at the Aga Khan's racehorses were not enough to occupy Churchill's rapidly expanding mental energies. He asked his mother to send him books and soon developed the habit of serious reading over three or four hours a day. "I resolved," he wrote afterward, "to read history, philosophy, economics, and things like that. . . . Without more ado I got out the eight volumes of Gibbon's *Decline and Fall of the Roman Empire.*"

It was a process of self-education, thorough and vigorous as every other activity that he undertook. The boxes of books were bulky; the books themselves were impressive: Plato, Aristotle, Schopenhauer, Malthus, Darwin, and (most formative of all) Gibbon and Macaulay. Because his reading was self-sought, neither imposed from outside nor controlled, its very spontaneity gave to all that he learned from it a natural depth and concentration that he was never to lose. Learning never went stale on him.

It was, however, impossible for him not to fuse action with thought. He hurried home for leave in the summer of 1897—the year of Queen Victoria's Diamond Jubilee, with its mood of climax and fulfillment—and while on leave he learned that fighting had broken out on the northwest frontier of India. A telegram to the commander of the British force engaged, General Sir Bindon Blood, with whom he had some acquaintance, produced permission to join it if he could get a job as a war correspondent. Back in India, he extracted the necessary permission from his colonel, persuaded the editor of the *Pioneer* of Allahabad to employ him, and set off to join the Malakand Field Force in a lively traditional campaign—half minatory, half punitive—against the Pathan tribesmen of the frontier. Nominally attached to the 31st Punjab Infantry, he was in the thick of the fighting soon after he arrived, was commended in dispatches for his courage and resolution, and was awarded a medal with clasp.

When he returned to Bangalore he wrote, in the midst of stubborn efforts (not popular with his brother officers) to join a similar but larger expedition against Tirah, his first book, *The Story of the Malakand Field Force* (1898). This is a readable, entertaining account of the little campaign, studded, however, with extremely outspoken criticism of planning and organization. The prime minister, Lord Salisbury, read the book; the Prince of Wales sent him a letter of congratulation on it. Emboldened by this success, Churchill sat down and wrote a novel, called *Savrola* (1900), largely autobiographical, daydreaming, romantic in the Bulwer-Lytton–Benjamin Disraeli manner, yet with more than a hint of sturdy, Macaulayan, Whiggish realism in it. It is not a good book—its author in later life always advised his friends not to read it—but it was serialized in *Macmillan's* magazine and earned some £700 in royalties.

By the coming of the hot weather of 1898 Churchill knew that he could not stomach many months (or indeed weeks) of inactivity in the sleepy cantonment in South India. Learning that a large-scale campaign was being planned in Egypt to liberate the Sudan from the somber and fanatical tyranny of the Mahdi, he maneuvered, intrigued, pulled every string he knew, involved every influential person from the prime minister downward, all in the face of the marmoreal hostility of the commander in chief, Sir Herbert (later Field Marshal Lord) Kitchener, to get himself posted to the expeditionary force. He suc-

ceeded, was attached to the 21st Lancers by direct order of the War Office, and secured a commission to write dispatches, at £15 the article, to the *Morning Post*. He took part in the last great cavalry charge of the British Army at the battle of Omdurman; was awarded another medal and clasp; made the acquaintance of a young naval officer with a great future named David Beatty, who was serving with the Royal Navy detachment on the Nile; and encountered another brilliant young journalist, G. W. Steevens, a former Balliol scholar destined to die of dysentery in the siege of Ladysmith. Steevens wrote for the *Daily Mail* a highly perceptive and prophetic sketch of Churchill at this time:

> The master strain in his character is the rhetorician. Platform speeches and leading articles flow from him almost against his will. At dinner he talks and talks, and you can hardly tell when he leaves off quoting his one idol, Macaulay, and begins his other, Winston Churchill. A passionate devotion to the matter in hand, an imperturbable self-confidence, a ready flow of sonorous half-commonplace, half-lofty English, a fine faculty of striking imagery—we shall hear more about this in the course of ten years.[2]

Those ten years were exuberantly full. After the Sudan he resigned his commission, wrote a weighty two-volume account of the campaign entitled *The River War*—its vigorous censure of his seniors, including Kitchener, was by now quite in character—fought and lost his first parliamentary by-election, as Conservative candidate for Oldham, and in 1899, with the outbreak of the South African War, was appointed the *Morning Post's* special correspondent in South Africa, at (for those days) a princely salary and with a very free hand.

His adventures during the Boer War, which included being taken prisoner, escaping, and having a price put on his head, made him at twenty-six a figure of national fame. In the "khaki election" of 1900 he fought and won Oldham as a Conservative. He quickly wrote two more books about the campaign: *London to Ladysmith via Pretoria* (1900) and *Ian Hamilton's March* (1900). Six necessary, arduous, but not immediately rewarding years followed, in which—moving steadily out of sympathy with his party and into sympathy with the powerful rising forces of twentieth-century liberalism—he made his mark in politics.

[2]Reprinted in C. Eade, ed., *Churchill by His Contemporaries* (London, 1953).

His character was taking on the mold of maturity. His zest for adventure was undimmed, but he had it in control. Physical danger and combat had tempered and fortified him; he now learned certain subtler and more difficult intellectual and spiritual disciplines. Though tirelessly energetic in practical day-to-day politics in an epoch of increasing turbulence, he procured the time to read, to study, to meditate, and thus to produce his first considerable and major work, the biography of his father, Lord Randolph Churchill.

This is not merely a pious filial tribute. It is a careful, scholarly, and meticulous study of the political and social setting of the brief and tragic life of that glittering lord of the ascendant.

Judged by the highest standards it is a very good biography, sagacious, loyal, and affectionate; but it is essentially a public biography of a public man. On the private, inner life of Lord Randolph his son had no wish to intrude. The book contains no personal revelations, no attempt to explore, within the deeply tormented heart and soul, the malady (syphilis) that was Lord Randolph's doom. Winston Churchill in this, as in much else, was of the generation into which he was born, with all its sunlit and manly sense of decency, its sane awareness of when to be reticent.

The book is suffused too with another of Churchill's chief qualities: his vast and unwavering magnanimity. Perhaps at thirty or thirty-one it would have been inconceivable to him that he could be thought magnanimous toward the brilliant father whom he had hero-worshiped. But Lord Randolph had been neither particularly understanding nor helpful toward his first-born. Their rare contacts had been formal and not without embarrassment on both sides. In a later time and society such a relationship would almost certainly have been diagnosed as producing in the son a host of morbid complexes and a high degree of maladjustment. Winston Churchill, however, triumphed over all this psychological deprivation and wrote a book that retrieved his father's political reputation from the decline that had affected it, and was as timely as it was wise and generous.

Lord Randolph Churchill was published in 1906. In that year its author, having formally crossed the floor of the House and joined the Liberals, was elected in their interest for North West Manchester in the great "landslide" election and, in the government formed by Sir Henry Campbell-Bannerman, achieved ministerial office as under-secretary for the colonies.

For the next nine years he was constantly involved, at the highest levels, in the fierce and testing political and social struggles of the epoch. Next to his older colleague and friend David Lloyd George, he was probably the most controversial figure in a stormily controversial time. He was deeply involved in all the battles around the main issues: economic, fiscal, and social reform; Ireland; women's suffrage. But when in 1911, after short spells as president of the board of trade and home secretary, he was appointed first lord of the admiralty, he was committed, intellectually and spiritually, to one overmastering theme, one supreme task: preparation for the crisis and the conflict to which the nations of Europe, and with them the young peoples of all those new, remote countries colonized and developed by the Europeans, were direfully marching after close on a century of peaceful, ordered, and liberal progress.

Churchill the statesman and man of action (who, about the private and personal part of his life, could joyfully proclaim long afterward that in 1908 he married Clementine Hozier and "lived happily ever after") was moving to his first great rendezvous with destiny. Churchill the writer was on the threshold of those tremendous experiences that would turn the facile observer and commentator, the careful biographer, into the major participant-historian.

THE TEMPERING

AT the outbreak of World War I, Winston Churchill was not quite forty years old. In the course of the war and its aftermath he endured in his public career almost every conceivable vicissitude: from the high pinnacle of power and national acclaim he was flung into obscurity; he fought back with courage, skill, and agility. He was either the sponsor or the inaugurator of several major developments in the art of war—the military use of aircraft, for example, and the armored fighting vehicle. His restless energy and burning patriotic zeal could not be confined within conventional limits. At Antwerp in the early phases of the war he, a senior minister of the crown, appeared to be assuming direct command of an operation in the field. Later, with the tragic epic of Gallipoli, he was the chief proponent and vigorous advocate of a plan that, if it had been carried out as he had intended, might have markedly shortened the war and saved many lives and reputations. Involved in the catastrophe that this undertaking became, he suffered most condign punishment as a politician. He withdrew to active service and the command of an infantry battalion on the western front. From this agreeable and distinguished—and characteristic—interlude he was summoned back to be a member of Lloyd George's war-winning coalition, as minister of munitions in succession to Lloyd George himself, and later as secretary of state for war. He remained at Lloyd George's side after the general election of 1918 and in the second coalition was probably his closest and most trusted colleague. As secretary of state for the colonies he negotiated a broad-based settlement of a turbulent and critical situation in the congeries of peoples inhabiting vast stretches of the collapsed Ottoman Empire. A few months later he was one of the prime movers in the complex pattern of events leading up to the signing of the Anglo-Irish Treaty of December 1921—so key a figure that Michael Collins, the Irish revolutionary leader, said on the eve of his own assassination: "Tell Winston we could never have done anything without him."

When the Conservatives in the autumn of 1922 brought about the end of Lloyd George's administration, Churchill sided with his friend and former chief. In the next two years he was without office, and for a short time out of the House of Commons. In 1924, however, he joined Stanley Baldwin's government, after the downfall of Ramsay MacDonald's first minority Labour administration; and he served Baldwin faithfully from 1924 to 1929 as chancellor of the exchequer—the post from which forty years before his father had so precipitately resigned. During MacDonald's second administration, from 1929 to 1931, a grave difference of opinion on the constitutional and political future of India arose between Churchill and the majority of his more powerful Conservative colleagues. When MacDonald and Baldwin, who were in agreement about India as about much else, formed their "national" government in 1931, Churchill was not invited to become a member of it; and he was out of office thereafter until, at the outbreak of World War II, he joined Neville Chamberlain's administration as first lord of the admiralty—the post he had held in 1914—and the signal went out to the Royal Navy: "Winston's back."

Throughout this tumult of events across a momentous quarter of a century, Churchill, when not prevented by the urgent responsibilities of high political office, assiduously followed his chosen calling as a writer. His contribution as a statesman to the history of his time was only part of his achievement—and that the most controversial. He made himself a principal recorder of the historic happenings in which he had been so vitally concerned. Only two others in the whole history of Western European civilization had attempted a similar dual role: Thucydides and Julius Caesar. With neither of these, however, would it be wise to press the analogy too closely. He himself defined, concisely and accurately, both the motive and the theme of *The World Crisis* (1923–1931), the great historical record of World War I in four lengthy volumes on the composition of which he was engaged during the ten years after the end of the war:

> It strives to follow throughout the methods and balance of Defoe's *Memoirs of a Cavalier*. It is a contribution to history strung upon a fairly strong thread of personal reminiscence. It does not pretend to be a comprehensive record; but it aims at helping to disentangle from an immense mass of material the crucial issues and cardinal decisions. Throughout I have set myself to explain faithfully and to the best of my ability what happened and why.
>
> (p. xv)[3]

This is as seemly and modest as it is lucid. In fact, however, it does not do complete justice to the scope and the scale of a great book which, if he had never written another word, would have ensured Churchill lasting fame as a writer. Arthur Balfour, who had known Churchill as both opponent and colleague over many years, observed slyly and uncharitably that it was autobiography thinly disguised as history. But in its own fashion *The World Crisis* is a tour de force. Certainly not the best of Churchill's writings, it will live as long as any for its extraordinary combination of gusto, knowledge, piercing intuition, and steady veracity. In form it is masterly, demonstrating complete assuredness from beginning to end in the handling of its vast and majestic theme. In style and content it is less satisfactory. It is deliberately mannered: the highly colored descriptive and rhetorical passages alternate carefully with narrative and analysis. The influence of Gibbon is marked throughout, but even more so that of Macaulay, a historian whom Churchill professed to detest. The balance of the thought is Gibbonian; the

---

[3]Appears only in the preface to the abridged ed. (London, 1931).

whirling passion is Macaulayesque. There is, however, another notable influence steeping the book and hinting at that final fusion of literary and spiritual qualities that was to be Churchill's at his greatest; it is the influence of Thackeray. Churchill has that brooding sense of time, not merely of time passing but of the ever-insistent irony implicit in the very fact of passage, and of the power that it possesses to mold and change.

In *The World Crisis,* too, Churchill discloses his stature as a reflective writer, meditating somberly, but never despairingly, on the portentous drama in which he had for so long played a leading part, and on the moral and spiritual issues that it had raised. The accusation of superficiality, either in thought or in sentiment, made against Churchill the historian was for some time as conventional and as demonstrably false as the accusations of irresponsibility and inconsistency made against Churchill the statesman.

Two valedictory passages at the end of the long book give the measure of his true quality. In the first he describes the scenes in London as the clocks struck eleven on the morning of 11 November 1918, and his own reactions to them; in the second—written ten years after that unforgettable hour—he peers forward into a darkling future:

The chains which had held the world were broken. Links of imperative need, links of discipline, links of brute-force, links of self-sacrifice, links of terror, links of honour which had held our nation, nay, the greater part of mankind, to grinding toil, to a compulsive cause—every one had snapped upon a few strokes of the clock. Safety, freedom, peace, home, the dear one back at the fireside—all after fifty-two months of gaunt distortion. After fifty-two months of making burdens grievous to be borne and binding them on men's backs, at last, all at once, suddenly and everywhere the burdens were cast down. At least so for the moment it seemed. . . . It was with feelings which do not lend themselves to words that I heard the cheers of the brave people who had borne so much and given all, who had never wavered, who had never lost faith in their country or its destiny, and who could be indulgent to the faults of their servants when the hour of deliverance had come.

. . .

New youth is here to claim its rights, and the perennial stream flows forward even in the battle zone, as if the tale were all a dream.

. . . Is this the end? Is it to be merely a chapter in a cruel and senseless story? Will a new generation in their turn be immolated to square the black accounts of Teuton and Gaul? Will our children bleed and gasp again in devastated lands? Or will there spring from the very fires of conflict that reconciliation of the three giant combatants which would unite their genius and secure to each in safety and freedom a share in rebuilding the glory of Europe?

(vol. IV, ch. 23)

Out of office in the 1930's Churchill published two major works and one minor: *Marlborough: His Life and Times* (1933–1938); the enchanting autobiographical *My Early Life* (1930); and a volume of wise, trenchant, yet charitable essays, *Great Contemporaries* (1937), biographical and analytical in purpose and manner.

My Early Life is gay, lovable, and staunch; there are some who hold it to be their favorite of all Churchill's work. There is in *My Early Life* a great deal of the quality of Thackeray, whose influence has been noted earlier—the Thackeray, above all, of *Pendennis. Pendennis,* it has been said, is every young man growing up and going out into the world; through *My Early Life* as through *Pendennis* there shines the true light of remembered youth, cool and bracing, never sentimental, yet with a deep, virile understanding in it. And though Churchill's youthful experiences were as vividly particular and idiosyncratic as everything else in his life, he endows them in recollection with a Thackerayan universality, and the reader, sharing the young Churchill's vicissitudes, looks back at his own youth with a deeper wisdom, a renewed and strengthened compassion.

Though the shade of Thackeray is certainly not absent from the great book that must be regarded as Churchill's biographical masterpiece, it was with this book that he assured himself—by his originality, his profundity, his patient scholarship, the lucidity and steady brilliance of his style—his high and permanent place among the ranks of major writers of English. All his previous books, even *The World Crisis,* were in a sense works of promise; it was possible to wonder, after each of them, where he would go from it. This was no longer possible or necessary after *Marlborough.*

Churchill was concerned—passionately concerned—to justify and defend his ancestor, to bring to naught those accusations of meanness and double-dealing that had dogged him so long and smirched his noble name. But this book is no mere piece of advocacy, however justifiable and pious. There is infused into it a deep and driving passion for historical truth, especially in its dramatic and poetic aspects.

Its narrative unfolds spaciously and grandly. It is

generous and searching. Every conclusion is sustained with carefully marshaled evidence, and with the most lucid and forceful argument. These strands of thought and feeling, knit throughout the book with a polished and apparently effortless skill, are all visible in this typical passage in an early chapter:

No dreamer, however romantic, however remote his dreams from reason, could have foreseen a surely approaching day when, by the formation of mighty coalitions and across the struggle of a generation, the noble colossus of France would lie prostrate in the dust, while the small island, beginning to gather to itself the empires of India and America, stripping France and Holland of their colonial possessions, would emerge victorious, mistress of the Mediterranean, the Narrow Seas and the Oceans. Aye, and carry forward with her, intact and enshrined, all that peculiar structure of law and liberty, all her own inheritance of learning and letters, which are to-day the treasure of the most powerful family in the human race.

(vol. I, ch. 4)

Marlborough was written when Churchill was out of office and out of power; yet it is a crucial book in the unfolding pattern of his own life. Its significance as a piece of literature is considerable; but it has an even more poignant importance as an experience that was deeply formative for its author, a quest or adventure from which his spirit returned with great benefit. Contemplation of the tasks faced and accomplished by his own great ancestor fortified his soul and enriched his understanding when, a few years later, he in his turn was summoned to lead his country through the turbulence, the dangers, and the ardors, and on to the glory of victory, in a far fiercer, wider conflict. It would be difficult not to see this as deeply appropriate; for to Churchill meditation and action were never in separate compartments. To write *Marlborough* and to lead his country in the 1939–1945 war, in emulation but not in imitation of his great forebear, were for Churchill natural manifestations of the same creative impulse.

THE MATURING

OVER a period of many years Churchill contemplated writing, as a major undertaking, a history of the English-speaking peoples. His experience, his temperament, and his inheritance—half English, half American—all drew him toward this task. But the day-to-day duties and dangers of politics were, at the same time, all absorbing.

In 1929 he went into opposition with all his former Conservative colleagues under the leadership of Stanley Baldwin. In 1930 and thereafter, however, though he always remained a member of the party, he fell out of sympathy with Baldwin and his closest associates on the subject of India. He was opposed to the relaxation of British imperial authority to which Baldwin, Lord Irwin (subsequently Lord Halifax), a former viceroy of India, and Sir Samuel Hoare (later Lord Templewood), who was secretary of state for India from 1931 to 1935, were firmly committed. He was not offered any office on the formation of the Baldwin-MacDonald "national" government in 1931, and thereafter he remained out of power, isolated except for a small group of close friends, critical and formidable.

The epithet applied to Churchill in the quarters where power lay in these years was "unreliable." Baldwin and his successor, Neville Chamberlain, preferred to have men about them who, in their own terms of reference, were reliable. Even when the controversy over India appeared to have been settled— so far as the internal politics of the Conservative party were concerned—by the Government of India Act of 1935, the breach was not healed. It in fact developed into much graver, more radical difference. The leaders of the government and the party stood for piecemeal settlement of a disturbed situation by the methods of appeasement; Churchill stood for collective security, within the framework of the League of Nations, and for powerful and efficient measures of rearmament in answer to the growing challenges of Fascist Italy and Nazi Germany.

He expounded his viewpoint in a great many articles and speeches. He who was to become one of the greatest broadcasters of the age was seldom and reluctantly conceded the freedom of the microphone. In 1936 his political fortunes appeared to be at their nadir when, in a mood that curiously mingled ardent and chivalrous generosity of spirit with political maneuvering, he went to the assistance of King Edward VIII in the crisis that led to his abdication; Churchill's plea that the king might be given time to consider any decision that he might make was shouted down in the House of Commons, and frigid fear of him turned to active hostility.

When Neville Chamberlain became prime minister in 1937, any flexibility that there had been in the government's foreign policy disappeared and was replaced by fixed and stubborn determination to preserve world peace by appeasement to the demands of the dictators. Convinced alike of the impracticability and the dishonor of this policy, and aware of deep and disquieting deficiencies in Britain's armaments, Churchill was a relentless critic both of specific actions by the government and of the philosophy underlying them.

Thus in a sense this was the final formative phase of his life. He was fighting perhaps harder than ever before. His natural pugnacity, however, was now harnessed to a majestic purpose. The themes to which he addressed himself were basic and enduring: the safety, honor, dignity, and prosperity of the people whom he served. Those whom he opposed and criticized spoke a different language. The swift, inexorable passage of events was to vindicate him totally, but in the meantime his prophecies were derided, his warnings ignored, and his motives impugned. The somber irony of this experience was not lost upon him, nor was it entirely unrecognized by the people to whom he spoke, in whose name in his greatest moments he spoke. In the curious, complex interweaving of mood and aspiration that composes a nation's inner history, Churchill at this time represented, with unique tenacity and wholeness, an element, a force of the spirit, with which the political leaders then in power had utterly lost touch. Even when Churchill was at his most solitary, when it seemed that he was a voice crying in a vast and hostile wilderness, it was still impossible to pity him or to feel that he was beaten; it was still easy to be aware of the pity and the pathos in those whom he fought.

Had he been listened to, had his advice been followed, it is probable that World War II, which he himself was to describe as "the Unnecessary War," might not have been fought. Yet he in his exile from political power, and the nation in its folly, timidity, and lethargy, were both—in a manner easy to recognize, difficult to analyze—undergoing preparation for the ordeal and the challenge that lay ahead and for the remarkable relationship between the man and the nation that was to be established during that experience.

During these years after the completion of *Marlborough,* Churchill undertook no major task as a writer. The conception of *A History of the English-Speaking Peoples* was ripening slowly, richly, agreeably. The series of essays on *Great Contemporaries* was a pleasant, characteristic diversion. The essays themselves are brief, knowledgeable, and

penetrating. They combine charity with shrewdness. They deal with a number of men whom Churchill had known in what was already a period of some thirty years at the summit of political life in Britain. Many of them were of a generation, the late Victorian and Edwardian, then just beginning to pass from the scene and, as they passed, looking almost like giants in contrast with the punier figures of the interwar years. The impressive common factor in all these essays, which they share with the life of Lord Randolph, is that they satisfy the reader intellectually and emotionally, yet they never intrude into the deeper privacies of the man under discussion. They are all about public men considered in the light of their public achievements, triumph or failure. It has been observed by Malcolm Muggeridge that "as a biographer and historian, Churchill has remained obstinately Victorian and pre–Lytton Strachey." This could be considered a virtue.

For the rest there were his speeches in and out of Parliament, later assembled in book form in *Arms and the Covenant* (1938), *Step by Step* (1939), *Into Battle* (1941), and *The Unrelenting Struggle* (1942). Not all of these speeches, inevitably, rank as major literature, but they comprise, with subsequent volumes of speeches made during and after World War II, a body of political oratory unrivaled in British history except by Edmund Burke. To Churchill a speech was always a work of art, demanding as careful a sense of composition, of form and style, as an essay or a book. Even the brilliant impromptu that was part of his daunting parliamentary armory, whether in office or in opposition, was seldom the immediate improvisation that it appeared. Action in every field of his life was the logical sequel of meditation and reflection. His mind became trained to the duty of instant decision, but no decision in detail was ever made without reflection, however rapid that reflection might be.

The effect of that process of reflection is to be seen in the general observations on human conduct, the brief aphorisms—often casual and light in their immediate delivery, profoundly searching in the quality of thought sustaining them—with which Churchill deliberately interspersed long and detailed expositions of policy or strategy, in both his books and his speeches.

Two sentences such as "Things do not get better by being left alone. Unless they are adjusted, they explode with a shattering detonation" crystallize much experience and much thought. So does a trenchant use of image of this order: "A medal glitters, but it also casts a shadow." And at their best these aphorisms fuse and give concise expression to a vast store of wisdom and compassion.

A great many of his speeches therefore stand up to study and analysis as the works of art they were intended to be. To have heard them in the hour of their delivery—particularly in the House of Commons—was a great, often unforgettable, experience. To read them in print is to lose the inflections of the voice, the pauses, the facial expression, the use of emphasis and timing that are part of the orator's art; but it is to be made aware of how consistently this orator was a writer and this writer an orator. He had the gift—the magical gift, it has been called—of putting the right words in the right order, at the right time, and in the right place.

Some years before his death he recorded a number of his most famous wartime speeches. Though age and changed circumstances had altered the timbre and occasionally the inflection, given them rhetorical gravity but taken some urgency from them, the recordings bring to generations who never heard him a comprehension of his quality as an orator. Many of the speeches, it was said by Lord Justice Birkett (himself a notable orator),

will live as examples of human speech at its highest and best, and they will be woven into the fabric of our own history and the history of the world. For many of these speeches made history before our very eyes. They changed the shape of events. They proclaimed the greatness of our past and the nature of our great traditions. . . . They appealed to the noblest and deepest feelings of mankind when discouragement and despair besieged their hearts, and brought triumph out of the jaws of defeat.

Less than any other part of his work as a writer can Churchill's speeches therefore be considered in isolation, apart from his career as a statesman, the career that took so sharp and dramatic a turn in the moment when his country's plight was dire, and all the calamities he had foreseen and striven to avert seemed about to overwhelm Britain, the Commonwealth, and the Empire.

Appointed first lord of the admiralty immediately upon the outbreak of World War II, in the administration still led by Neville Chamberlain, whom he had so sternly criticized, Churchill served in that office from September 1939 to May 1940. After the debate on the disastrous outcome of the Norway campaign, and on the day of the Nazi invasion of the Low Countries, Chamberlain—already grievously ill with cancer—resigned his office as prime minister but loyally consented to continue to serve in a coalition of all three major parties in Parliament, under Churchill's leadership. This coalition in five years led Britain from the verge of terrible and total defeat to complete and overwhelming victory.

The supreme phase of Churchill's career coincided with the most perilous and the most starkly heroic epoch in his country's history, that "finest hour" to which he himself gave a name, whose attributes of valor, endurance, and self-sacrifice he embodied and symbolized. Later he was to give, in a book some million words in length, his own account of the mighty undertaking and his part in it. While it was happening, his life was one of concentrated action, momentous decision, and moments of majestic and heart-stirring oratory, which were in themselves knit into the very fabric of the history that he, the orator, was making.

Some of the greatest of these speeches were made, as was fitting, in the House of Commons. Some, as was also fitting, were broadcast. For during this phase Churchill, who had been the focus of violent controversy all his life, spoke for, as much as to, a nation united and conscious of its unity as seldom before. He was the architect of that unity as he was of the ultimate victory; that it could not be permanently sustained was merely proof of the fact that neither individual men nor nations can be wholly heroic all the time. But his speeches in 1940–1941 helped to make the people of Britain impossible to defeat, because that is what he made them tell themselves they were.

He told the truth—often a great and stirring truth against a background black with menace—in words that, sometimes simple, sometimes magnificent, were exactly right for the thought and feeling they expressed, and for the time when they were spoken:

The Battle of France is over. I expect that the Battle of Britain is about to begin. Upon this battle depends the survival of Christian civilization. Upon it depends our own British life and the long continuity of our institutions and our Empire. The whole fury and might of the enemy must very soon be turned on us. Hitler knows that he will have to break us in this Island or lose the war. If we can stand up to him, all Europe may be free and the life of the world may move forward into broad, sunlit uplands. But if we fail, then the whole world, including the United States, including all that we have known and cared for, will sink into the abyss of a new Dark Age made more sinister, and perhaps more protracted by the lights of perverted science. Let us therefore brace ourselves to our duties, and so bear ourselves that, if the British Empire and its Commonwealth last for a thousand years, men will still say, "This was their finest hour."

("Their Finest Hour," 18 June 1940)

Words such as these gave inspiration as they possessed it. It is impossible to believe that, as long as the English language is spoken, read, and understood, though the political and military crisis that called them forth may be forgotten or thought of little account, the words themselves will not stir the hearts of succeeding generations and uplift them to courage and nobility of conduct.

THE FULFILLMENT

In the last months of World War II, a general election was held in the United Kingdom that resulted in a large Labour majority. Clement Attlee, who had been Churchill's deputy prime minister in complete loyalty and amity throughout five years of war, immediately formed a Labour administration that, in fact, concluded the final phases of the conflict and strove to deal with the massive complex of postwar problems. A Greek commentator, accustomed to a different pattern of politics, is said to have observed pityingly: "Poor Mr. Churchill, and now I suppose he'll have to take to the hills."

Churchill, however, assumed the task of leader of the opposition, which he was to fulfill with vigor and pertinacity for six years until in the autumn of 1951 he again became prime minister, this time at the head of a purely Conservative administration. In 1945 he was in his seventy-first year. Though given staunch support by the war cabinet and the chiefs of staff, he had inevitably borne the main burden of responsibility and decision, day by day and hour by hour, for five harshly testing years. It was a burden under which few men would not weary or break. Only the strongest would be unlikely not to suffer a severe form of reaction when the responsibility ended and the power was abruptly shut off.

Churchill adopted rapidly and zestfully a new rhythm of existence. He was in the thick of an arduous and often embittered political party conflict in the United Kingdom; he was the widely acclaimed statesman of world renown, going abroad to receive the thanks and the rewards he had so richly earned and making the appropriate thoughtful and penetrative speeches. He was also the historian, with matchless sources of personal experience and of documentation, determined to set down, as swiftly and as fully as he could, his own account of the momentous events in which he had played so great a part, whose course he had so largely determined.

He had been at the summit of power in his own country. Throughout the Commonwealth he had exerted a comradely leadership, only equaled in skill and sagacity by that of his veteran companion General Smuts, whose aid and counsel he frequently invoked. He had dealt on terms of subtle, easy, yet emotionally complicated friendship with President Roosevelt. He had been neither shocked nor daunted by encounters with Stalin. He had watched a host of younger men, in politics and in the higher ranks of the armed forces of the crown, wield authority and attain fame; but he was the man who, again and again, had picked them, who issued them their orders. Finally, the nature of the experience that he and his country had shared was both glorious and tragic. The battle they had waged was both right and necessary; their endurance, their ingenuity, their enterprise, and their generosity of spirit had earned them victory. But Britain at the end of World War II was drained of wealth and power, as at the end of World War I it had been drained of men.

The formidable task, therefore, that Churchill set himself as a writer, the task in which he took a strong delight, was to weld this vast mass of unique experience into the coherent form of a work of art with all its strands and patterns closely and tellingly interconnected. The experience, tremendous as it had been, mattered less than the artist's vision with which it was beheld. A child throws a twig into a mountain stream on a sunlit spring morning and stands intently watching it; there is the whole tale of humanity's passage through time and into eternity for the poet whose vision can behold it, whose words can trap and interpret it. Vast, ponderous, and important volumes of official history are painstakingly assembled; every politician, every military leader publishes his own account of the happenings in which he had his part to play. With the rarest exceptions they have neither the impetus nor the form of a work of art. The factor that profoundly and permanently differentiates Churchill's work as a historian from these others is that—whatever their virtues and his defects—his writing was from beginning to end suffused and sustained by the powerful creative impulse by which, as an artist, he was animated.

His *Second World War* is in six volumes (totaling about a million words), which were published at frequent intervals from 1948 to 1954. During the latter part of the execution of this enormous work its author was again prime minister, leading, in conditions of acute difficulty and grave challenge, an administration supported by one of the narrowest majorities in modern parliamentary history. In the year of its completion he was eighty. When it was finished and he retired from the leadership of the government and of his party, he addressed himself to his long-postponed task of a history of the English-speaking peoples. Many of his younger contemporaries—all of whom had grown up under the shadow (sometimes the stormy shadow) of his achievements—accustomed themselves to taking these facts for granted.

These facts, Churchill's dual and lifelong role as statesman and as historian of the events in which he participated, are clearly relevant when it is understood how remarkable, in his time and society, they are. They are relevant too to any consideration of the stature of *The Second World War* as an artistic undertaking. The work has never been condemned by any responsible critic, nor is it likely to be, on the grounds of prolixity. For so far-ranging and so thorough a survey of so enormous a field, it is agreeably concise, even laconic. It is refreshingly and unerringly readable, even in those chapters in which the reader may disagree with Churchill's analyses and conclusions. The main valid line of criticism of the work as a whole has been that of haste. Some sense of the compulsion of time in a man who had passed seventy when he began the first volume must be admitted; its absence would be unnatural.

Churchill in this ultimate phase of his long career as a writer was at his most natural, his least inhibited, his least mannered. In an old man's writing there might be signs of fatigue; none have been discovered, not even by the most hostile critic. The last volume has the same fresh, manly, clear-ringing strength as the first, and the same resolute sense of purpose. The avowed model remains, as it was for *The World Crisis*, Daniel Defoe's *Memoirs of a Cavalier*, knitting the chronicle and discussion of great military and political events upon the thread of the personal experiences of an individual. In his preface to the first volume Churchill argued that if *The World Crisis*, including its last two volumes,

The Eastern Front and *The Aftermath*, were considered together with the new work, the whole assemblage would comprise an account of another Thirty Years' War. An important difference, however, was that for five years of the second conflict the author was the head of the government of the United Kingdom; he wrote therefore from a special standpoint and with special authority. He added:

I doubt whether any similar record exists or has ever existed of the day-to-day conduct of war and administration. I do not describe it as history, for that belongs to another generation. But I claim with confidence that it is a contribution to history which will be of service to the future.

(vol. I, p. vii)

The reservations implicit in these remarks could not completely absolve their author from a delicate and indeed dangerous responsibility, of which he was quite aware. The memoirs were written and published so soon after the events they describe, and at a time when the author himself was still in the full tide of political life, that inevitably they themselves are a series of political documents, contributions to many fierce and deep-rooted controversies that were by no means stilled. It was impossible to disentangle the processes and purposes of faithful reporting from those of brilliant, persuasive advocacy and self-justification. A minor defect in the method of compilation was a not entirely negligible contributory cause: in an appendix to each volume there is a liberal selection of the day-to-day minutes, memoranda, and directives with which Churchill assisted his subordinates in the performance of their duties; but in the appendix there is no indication—and in the main text too little indication—of the way in which these subordinates reacted to the endless series of questions, vigorous prods, and stern summonses to "action this day." Their explanations, their protests, their occasional outraged and absolute negatives are not given. The memoirs, therefore, give a one-sided picture of the war's conduct and administration, but as he himself would have said, *some side*.

Any tendency to facile self-justification is sternly held in check throughout by certain deeper, more majestic impulses—by an irresistible candor, by a broad and sober sense of the debt that the present owes to the future, and by a persistent magnanimity that scorned to condemn any policy or act on which the author had not previously, in public and formally, recorded his opinion.

It is therefore on the highest plane that the work as a whole deserves to be considered. The dominant impression left by it is of a radiant consistency—through all the vicissitudes, the tribulations, the trials, and the triumphs of war—in belief and action. The actions are often a complicated and subtle interweaving of dozens of tactical and strategic strands, in politics and economics, in defense and offense. They would appear tortuous and meaningless were they not animated by a simple, strong, steady belief. Meditation upon, and the written recording of, any specific course of action may therefore produce understandings of how and why it failed or succeeded, regrets at blunders made, thankfulness for opportunities granted and taken. But these are within the stable framework of a robust, unshaken consciousness that the motive and the purpose were good.

The integrity of the work is not the result of technical skill, of which there is plenty. It is of the very spirit in which the whole massive design was conceived and executed. The moral, which is repeated at the beginning of every volume, is a lapidary statement of the outlook in which the task was undertaken: "In War: Resolution. In Defeat: Defiance. In Victory: Magnanimity. In Peace: Goodwill." Each volume, like the opening of a movement in a symphony, states its own theme; and the six great chords of which they are composed make as firm and as full a summary of the whole work as it would be possible to give:

Volume I: How the English-Speaking Peoples through their Unwisdom, Carelessness and Good Nature, allowed the Wicked to Rearm.
Volume II: How the British People held the Fort ALONE till those who hitherto had been Half Blind were Half Ready.
Volume III: How the British fought on with Hardship their Garment until Soviet Russia and the United States were drawn into the Great Conflict.
Volume IV: How the Power of the Grand Alliance became Preponderant.
Volume V: How Nazi Germany was Isolated and Assailed on all sides.
Volume VI: How the Great Democracies Triumphed, and so were able to resume the Follies which had so nearly cost them their Life.

The design of the six volumes of *The Second World War* can now be seen to be part of an even more spacious design that had long been brooded upon in the writer's mind, to whose fulfillment he had moved steadily through long years of toil and danger in the service of the state. The passion of patriotic service to the state had been knit with, and in a manner subordinated to, the passion of the creative artist. History was his material and history his theme, and the history, above all, of the race whence he was sprung. In that history his own name must, for his deeds, stand high forever. But the passion of the word must be fulfilled. Son of an English father and an American mother, born when the people of one branch of his ancestral stock were at their zenith and those of the other emerging from the harsh pangs of a nation's birth, he was conscious that his task would be accomplished and his work done when he had written, for succeeding generations to contemplate and act upon, the *History of the English-Speaking Peoples.*

It was, for Churchill, the fulfillment of a destined responsibility, far from novel but long postponed, since he had, after all, tarried on other duties. The first two volumes of *A History of the English-Speaking Peoples* were published in 1956, when their author was eighty-two, the third in 1957, the fourth and final volume in 1958. A new school of historians and historiographers was beginning to emerge: few of its members were willing to accept Churchill's broad and simple view of events; sociological and economic factors, in the view of most of them, mattered more than battles and dynasties and constitutional changes. The work as a whole was received respectfully but coolly.

The narrative ends with a brief, vivid account of the South African War, in which Churchill had himself served as a war correspondent. There is a sunset glow suffusing the writing: the sunset, not only of the author's own life, but of that Atlantic apparatus of power and that English-rooted civilization of which his long career, in all its facets, was at once the climax and the individual vindication.

His last printed words are, characteristically, free from nostalgia and steeped in that brooding courage, that unique mixture of awed awareness of danger and robust and manly optimism, that had always sustained him:

Here is set out a long story of the English-Speaking Peoples. They are now to become Allies in terrible but victorious wars. And that is not the end. Another phase looms before us, in which alliance will once more be tested and in which its formidable virtues may be to preserve Peace and

Freedom. The future is unknowable, but the past should give us hope. Nor should we seek to define precisely the exact terms of ultimate union.

(vol. IV, ch. 12)

In the closing years of his life Churchill no longer wrote and no longer spoke in the House of Commons, though he continued his parliamentary attendances with punctilious regularity until, at last, he resigned his seat before the general election of 1964. A generation grew up to whom he was a figure of legend. On the morning of Sunday, 24 January 1965, less than two months after his ninetieth birthday and seventy years to the day after the death of his brilliant and ill-starred father, his great heart ceased beating.

It is not to be believed that posterity will assess Churchill solely—or indeed chiefly—as a writer. Nor indeed would he have wished it so, although it was as a writer that he earned his living from his early twenties onward. Yet it is impossible to consider the rest of his achievements apart from his writings. He once observed that writing a book was an adventure. Perhaps in that almost casual and not overwhelmingly original aside lies the key to Churchill: from early boyhood to extreme old age, he sought adventure; not the least noble, and in the final analysis perhaps the most enduring, of his countless adventures was in the realm of the spoken and the written word.

SELECTED BIBLIOGRAPHY

I. BIBLIOGRAPHY. *Catalogue of an Exhibition of MSS and Printed Books* (London, 1954), in honor of Churchill's eightieth birthday, 30 November 1954, at the Times Bookshop, London; F. Woods, *A Bibliography of the Works of Sir Winston Churchill* (London, 1963).

II. SEPARATE WORKS. *The Story of the Malakand Field Force* (London, 1898); *The River War*, 2 vols. (London, 1899); *Savrola* (London, 1900), novel; *London to Ladysmith via Pretoria* (London, 1900); *Ian Hamilton's March* (London, 1900); *Lord Randolph Churchill*, 2 vols. (London, 1906), new ed. with hitherto unpublished correspondence (London, 1952); *My African Journey* (London, 1908); *The World Crisis*, 6 vols. (London, 1923–1931), vol. I: *1911–1914* (1923), vol. II: *1915* (1923), vols. III–IV: *1916–1918* (1927), vol. V: *The Aftermath* (1929), vol. VI: *The Eastern Front* (1931); *My Early Life* (London, 1930); *Parliamentary Government and the Economic Problem* (London, 1930), the Romanes lecture; *Thoughts and Adventures* (London, 1932; repr. 1948), includes "Painting as a Pastime"; *Marlborough: His Life and Times*, 4 vols. (London, 1933–1938); *Great Contemporaries* (London, 1937); *The Second World War*, 6 vols. (London, 1948–1954): *The Gathering Storm* (1948), *Their Finest Hour* (1949), *The Grand Alliance* (1950), *The Hinge of Fate* (1951), *Closing the Ring* (1952), *Triumph and Tragedy* (1954); *A History of the English-Speaking Peoples*, 4 vols. (London, 1956–1958), vol. I: *The Birth of Britain* (1956), vol. II: *The New World* (1956), vol. III: *The Age of Revolution* (1957), vol. IV: *The Great Democracies* (1958); *Frontiers and Wars* (London, 1962), a one-vol. reiss. of *The Malakand Field Force, The River War, London to Ladysmith*, and *Ian Hamilton's March*.

III. COLLECTIONS OF SPEECHES. *Mr. Brodrick's Army* (London, 1903); *For Free Trade* (London, 1906); *For Liberalism and Free Trade* (London, 1908); *Liberalism and the Social Problem* (London, 1909); *India* (London, 1931); *Arms and the Covenant* (London, 1938); *Step by Step* (London, 1939); R. Churchill, ed., *Into Battle* (London, 1941), American ed. entitled *Blood, Sweat and Tears* (New York, 1941); *The Unrelenting Struggle* (London, 1942); *The End of the Beginning* (London, 1943); *Onwards to Victory* (London, 1944); *The Dawn of Liberation* (London, 1945); *Victory* (London, 1946); *Secret Session Speeches* (London, 1946); *The Sinews of Peace* (London, 1948); *Europe Unite* (London, 1950); *In the Balance* (London, 1951); *War Speeches*, 3 vols. (London, 1951), E. Eade, comp.; *Stemming the Tide* (London, 1953).

IV. BIOGRAPHICAL AND CRITICAL STUDIES. C. L. Broad, *Winston Churchill* (London, 1941); P. Guedalla, *Mr. Churchill: A Portrait* (London, 1941); M. Thomson, *The Life and Times of Winston Churchill* (London, 1945); G. Eden, *Portrait of Churchill* (London, 1945).

E. Hughes, *Winston Churchill in War and Peace* (London, 1950); J. G. Lockhart, *Winston Churchill* (London, 1951); V. S. Cowles, *Winston Churchill: The Era and the Man* (London, 1953); C. Eade, ed., *Churchill by His Contemporaries* (London, 1953); C. R. Coote and P. D. Bunyan, eds., *Sir Winston Churchill: A Self-Portrait* (London, 1954); G. Willans and C. Roetter, *The Wit of Winston Churchill* (London, 1954); J. Marchand, ed., *Winston Spencer Churchill: Servant of the Crown and Commonwealth* (London, 1954); A. Leslie, *The Fabulous Leonard Jerome* (London, 1954), includes interesting material on Churchill's mother and her family background; F. Urquhart, *W.S.C.: A Cartoon Biography* (London, 1955); F. B. Czarnomski, ed., *The Wisdom of Winston Churchill* (London, 1956); A. L. Rowse, *The Later Churchills* (London, 1958).

S. R. Graubard, *Burke, Churchill and Disraeli* (Cambridge, Mass., 1961); G. Pawle, *The War and Colonel Warden* (London, 1963); I. Berlin, *Mr. Churchill in 1940* (London, 1964); V. Bonham-Carter, *Churchill as I Knew Him* (London, 1965); C. M. W. Moran, *Churchill: The Struggle for Survival* (London, 1966); R. S. Churchill,

Winston Spencer Churchill, vol. I: *Youth, 1874–1900* (New York–London, 1967), a 2-pt. companion (1968); vol. II: *The Young Statesman, 1901–1914* (1969), a 3-pt. companion (1969).

M. Gilbert, *Winston Spencer Churchill,* vol. III: *The Challenge of War, 1914–1916* (1971), a 2-pt. companion (1974); vol. IV: *The Stricken World, 1916–1922* (1975), a 3-pt. companion (1977); vol. V: *The Prophet of Truth, 1923–1939* (1977), a 3-pt. companion (1981)—Gilbert is completing the study begun by Churchill's son; R. Hyam, *Elgin and Churchill at the Colonial Office* (London, 1968); A. J. P. Taylor, *Churchill: Four Faces and the Man* (London, 1969); A. Leslie, *Lady Randolph Churchill* (London, 1969); R. Fedden, *Churchill at Chartwell* (London, 1969); C. Thompson, *An Assessment of Winston Churchill* (London, 1969); F. Woods, ed., *Young Winston's Wars* (London, 1972); R. R. James, *Churchill: A Study in Failure* (London, 1972); A. Stansky, *Churchill: A Profile* (London, 1973); R. Lewin, *Churchill as War-Lord* (London, 1974); E. Longford, *Winston Churchill* (London, 1974); M. Gilbert, *Churchill: A Photographic Portrait* (London, 1974); R. G. Martin, *Lady Randolph Churchill* (London, 1974), vol. I: *1854–1895,* vol. II: *1895–1921;* J. Mitchell and P. Churchill, *Lady Randolph Churchill* (London, 1974); J. Fishman, *Lady Randolph Churchill* (London, 1974); R. Pelling, *Winston Churchill* (London, 1974); W. Lash, *Roosevelt and Churchill* (London, 1977); S. Roskill, *Churchill and the Admirals* (London, 1977); E. Barker, *Churchill and Eden at War* (London, 1978); I. Curteis, *Churchill and the Generals* (London, 1979); R. J. Moore, *Churchill, Cripps and India* (Oxford, 1979); M. Soames, *Clementine Churchill* (London, 1979).

I. Finlayson, *Winston Churchill* (London, 1980); J. M. Lee, *Churchill Coalition 1940–1945* (London, 1980).

W. SOMERSET MAUGHAM

(1874-1965)

Anthony Curtis

I

"THE lucidity of Maugham, last of the great professional writers . . ." wrote Cyril Connolly in *Enemies of Promise* (1938). It is a curious distinction that, one feels, could have been made only by an English critic writing about an English author. Who, pray, are the great amateur writers? Yet one knows what Connolly meant. Maugham always looked to the market and wrote to supply the needs of the market. "No man but a blockhead ever wrote, except for money," Dr. Samuel Johnson declared forthrightly on 5 April 1776, so Boswell tells us in his *Life of Johnson*, and Maugham's life might be described as one long "Hear, hear!" in support of Johnson's declaration.

What, you may ask, is wrong with writing for the market? Did not Shakespeare write for the market? Did not Dickens write for the market? Yes, if one dare mention them in the same breath as Maugham, they did; but literate society was more homogeneous in their day than in his. By the end of the nineteenth century a hairline fissure had begun to appear between the popular and the serious reading public that in the twentieth was to widen to an apparently unbridgeable gap.[1] Maugham remains the test case of whether it could at any point be bridged.

Maugham desperately wanted to be both a popular writer and a serious writer. He wanted to become rich by his pen, and he wanted to be praised by the best judges. After about ten years of struggle he achieved the former aim; only intermittently did he achieve the latter. Against the praise of Desmond MacCarthy and Cyril Connolly, the leading London critics of their time, both of whom had some personal acquaintance with Maugham, we must put the devastating attacks on Maugham by D. H. Lawrence and Edmund Wilson. Enough time has passed since

Maugham's death, perhaps, to make a fresh view possible, one that is less clouded by the animosity that Maugham the man aroused in his contemporaries.

Maugham made no secret of the importance he attached to money in literary life. Money, he often said, is like a sixth sense without which you cannot fully use the other five. This sounds good, but it is not really confirmed by his own prose, which though admirably lucid, as Connolly says, is noticeably weak in the re-creation of sense experience, one of the most immediate pleasures we receive from literature. Although we read through the eye, imaginative writing often comes to life by arousing other senses—aural, tactile, olfactory. The first obvious difference between Maugham and those writers we think of as "modern" in the first half of the twentieth century is his indifference to all but the visual sense, his lack of sensuousness. Even a writer whom he greatly admired, Herman Melville, Maugham castigates for his overindulgence in sensuous exuberance. The American novelist strained every nerve in *Moby Dick* (1851) to communicate the sights, the sounds, and especially the smells experienced by his characters: "But few thoughts of Pan stirred Ahab's brain, as standing like an iron statue at his accustomed place beside the mizzen rigging, with one nostril he unthinkingly sniffed the suggary must from the Banshee isles (in whose sweet woods mild lovers must be walking), and with the other consciously inhaled the salt breath of the new found sea. . . ." Maugham's comment on this passage, in *Ten Novels and Their Authors* (1954), is: "To smell one odour with one nostril and at the same time, another with the other; it is more than a remarkable feat; it is an impossible one." If Maugham is at his weakest when it is a question of smells, sounds, touch, he showed from his earliest days as a writer a quick and sure eye for surroundings, ap-

[1]See Q. D. Leavis, *Fiction and the Reading Public* (London, 1935).

pearances, belongings. He is infallible when it comes to material possessions, solid structures, things. It is no surprise that the novelist whom Maugham admired most was Balzac, who showed how to reveal character through the cumulative description of possessions. Maugham wrote:

I believe he was the first novelist to dwell on the paramount importance of economics in everybody's life. He would not have thought it enough to say that money is the root of all evil; he thought the desire for money, the appetite for money, was the mainspring of human action.

(*Ten Novels and Their Authors*)

It is not my purpose in this essay to deal with Maugham's obsession with money as fully as a biographer might wish to, but I propose to consider the question briefly. Obviously Maugham's loss of both his parents before he had reached the age of ten had a great deal to do with it. Life for young Willie Maugham was a precarious business; however rich and eminent he subsequently became, it never ceased to be a precarious business. His boyhood environment, his uncle's vicarage at Whitstable, in Kent, was not poor, but it was grim, austere, parsimonious. As soon as he arrived there Maugham felt deprived, a feeling exacerbated by the instant dismissal of the woman who had looked after him in Paris. His position in the family as the youngest brother, with a big age gap between him and his next of kin, his smallness, his stammer, all contributed to his feeling of insecurity and caused him, as a precociously intelligent child, to look forward to the day when, in the words of Malvolio in *Twelfth Night*, he would be revenged on the pack of them. The choice of authorship as a profession was a break with the tradition of the Maughams: the family had risen to eminence through the law. Maugham's writing confirmed him in his isolation as well as offering him opportunities to overcome the humiliations, fancied and real, of childhood. Fearful, though, of suffering financial insecurity, he played it safe by first providing himself with an alternative profession, medicine, training at St. Thomas' Hospital, in South London. But when the moment came for him to set up as a fully qualified practitioner, he decided to write as his sole means of earning a livelihood. His office was his home, an apartment he shared in Victoria with a friend, Walter Payne, who was an accountant. When *Liza of Lambeth* was published in 1897, Maugham was twenty-three.

II

In that year Payne gave him a present, James Boswell's *Life of Johnson* in six volumes. The work must have struck a chord in Maugham. The situation of the young Johnson, coming to London from Lichfield to make his way by literature and wit, was similar to his own. Here was a supreme example of a man who had worked in isolation, cut off from the academic life, in which his abilities would have enabled him to excel; staking everything on acquiring a reputation; beginning by attracting a small circle of admirers until his fame spread. But what Maugham required was not only a patron saint but practical models of the art of writing. He had an infinite capacity to learn by example, blessed as he was with formidable energy and determination; and he had a further resource in an enviable facility for languages. Maugham's father had been the lawyer in charge of the affairs of the British embassy in Paris. By a quirk of fate Maugham had been born inside the embassy building. French came almost as naturally to him as English. His first literary enthusiasms were for French writers. Maugham described in *The Summing Up* (1938) how he haunted the galleries of the Odéon, standing there reading the novels and short stories of Guy de Maupassant, cutting the pages of books he could not afford to buy. Apart from France —a country with which Maugham always had a special relationship, going there to live after he became successful—he was exposed to other continental influences as a young man. Before taking up medical studies, Maugham had been educated in Germany, at the University of Heidelberg. He heard talk of Wagner and the new music drama, and he saw performances of plays by Henrik Ibsen and Henri Becque, both of whom were bringing a new kind of realism to the theater. While a medical student, Maugham had begun to learn Spanish and Italian, after visiting Spain and Italy for long periods.

With so much to read and so much to take in, Maugham could hardly have had a more bewildering choice of models. Without benefit of an official tutor—such as he would have had if he had gone to Cambridge like his brother Freddie[2]—to monitor his undergraduate essays, whom should he elect as his unofficial tutor? One of the masters of English prose, such as Jeremy Taylor or Jonathan Swift? Or one of

[2]Frederic Herbert Maugham (1866–1958), first Viscount Maugham, Lord Chancellor of England (1938–1939).

the French realists, who earlier in the nineteenth century had wrought major changes in the art of the novel, such as Émile Zola, Gustave Flaubert, or their most brilliant disciple, Guy de Maupassant? In fact, he elected them all, and many others. Such freedom is one of the advantages of belonging to a one-pupil university administered by oneself. Maugham read widely, insatiably, greedily. He was then, and always remained, receptive to good prose wherever he found it. Toward the end of his life he wrote essays on both the seventeenth-century English divine Archbishop Tillotson and the American mystery writer Raymond Chandler. The period of the 1890's offered almost as extreme contrasts between the lofty and the popular. Inevitably, the aesthetic cult, then at its height in England thanks to the genius of Oscar Wilde (1854–1900), made an impression on Maugham.

Wilde and other men of letters, through whom thoughts of the new, ill-educated reading public sent shudders of horror, argued that literature could survive only by becoming more demanding, more remote from ordinary life, more artificial. For the Wildean aesthetes the common enemy was vulgarity. One of the gilded young men who took this view was the essayist and caricaturist Max Beerbohm, a friend of Maugham's, some of whose work had appeared in *The Yellow Book*, a review associated in the public mind with the spirit of decadence. Several of its writers took their tone from Walter Pater, the high priest of the aesthetic movement, who had died in 1894. In his studies of the art of the Italian Renaissance and his imaginary portraits Pater wrote some of the most ornate prose ever penned by an English writer. Maugham dutifully studied Pater and attempted for a time to write like him. There are faint traces of the Pater manner in some of his early work, and some set-piece descriptions survive in *A Writer's Notebook* (1949).

But he soon abandoned this enervating prose style for a plainer approach. Afterward he would mock his youthful Pateresque pretensions. Perhaps, though, he never completely suppressed the aesthete in himself. There is a portrait of Maugham, "The Jester," by his friend the painter Gerald Kelly, made after Maugham's first successful plays were produced, that shows him immaculately attired in top-hat and frock coat as a typical English dandy of the 1890's. Maugham's urbanity; his love of that most civilized form, the essay; his insistence on the terrible sacrifices demanded by art, in many stories and novels, not least *Of Human Bondage* (1915) and *The Moon and Sixpence* (1919), demonstrate the lasting influence of the aesthetic ideal.

III

THAT ideal suffered its most grievous setback with the public humiliation and downfall of Oscar Wilde in 1895. Although Wilde's performance under prolonged cross-examination at his trial was a brilliant one, the aesthetic approach to life was thoroughly discredited; and not only aestheticism but homosexuality, with which it often coexisted. All this, one may be sure, made a deep impact on young Maugham, who was just discovering his own homosexual nature in the company of English Wildean aesthetes who lived in Italy. In consequence, part of his most intimate experience would be closed to him when he began to write fiction. One of Maugham's contemporaries, E. M. Forster (1879–1970), solved this problem by writing fiction about homosexual love but not permitting it to be published until after his death. Although the subject deeply preoccupied Maugham and conditioned the whole course of his life, it rarely crops up in all the voluminous pages of his work (save impersonally in discussions of Melville and El Greco), until his notorious newspaper confessions, *Looking Back* (1962).

Early in his career Maugham cast himself in the part of the observer, the noncommittal recorder of experience. This, after all, was what Maupassant had been. It was the perfect stance for an astute literary artist who wished never to give his deepest secret away. There were examples much nearer than Maupassant of the telling effect that could be made by a quasi-documentary approach, of seeming merely to record events and conversations with the greatest possible verisimilitude. The outlook of the French realists had been shared on the English side of the Channel by George Gissing (1857–1903) and by the Anglo-Irish novelist George Moore (1852–1933). Both had made working people, and their sufferings, the main characters in stories and novels. But Maugham's immediate model was a rather more obscure contemporary, Arthur Morrison (1863–1945), whose *A Child of the Jago* (1896) and *Tales of Mean Streets* (1894) had given vivid, firsthand accounts of the lives lived by people caught in the poverty trap of late-Victorian England. Morrison's work had appeared originally in magazine form and had appealed to the railway bookstall public, which did not want to read only stories about cozy village life and people in fashionable drawing rooms. Edward Garnett, T. Fisher Unwin's literary adviser, spotted Maugham's model immediately, but also the talent and individuality. He wrote in his report that Maugham's story *Liza of Lambeth* was not as powerful a study as *A Child of the Jago*, but that it was

a very clever realistic study of factory girl and coster life. The women; their roughness, intemperance, fits of violence, kind-heartedness, slang,—all are done truthfully, Liza and her mother Mrs Kemp are drawn with no little humour and insight. The story is a dismal one in its ending, but the temper and tone of the book is wholesome and by no means morbid. The work is *objective,* and both the atmosphere and the environment of the mean district are unexaggerated.

(George Jefferson, *Edward Garnett:
A Life in Literature,* 1982)

Morrison had himself been raised in the East End, though he afterward concealed the fact. He knew a great deal more than Maugham about the criminal underworld of London. Where Maugham scored was through his penetration of the slum interior at its most frequent moment of emergency—the delivery of a baby, unplanned and unwanted; for obstetrics was the practical work Maugham had undertaken as a medical student. Morrison had given no hint of extramarital romance in these dim regions; Maugham made such a romance the core of his tale. Its first cynical title was "A Lambeth Idyll." The stirring of love in the resplendent Liza on the one hand, the horror of her death as an unmarried mother on the other provide Maugham's story with its time scale. It has the organic movement of a single life, *une vie* (as Maupassant called one of his novels). The natural rhythm of the seasons accompanies the heroine's passage through life. We first see her on a bright day of early summer; she dies in the winter of the following year. One of the aims of the realist writers was to capture a natural process—the rise and fall, growth and decay, flowering and withering of a human organism, an individual, a group, a family, a society, even a whole nation—and to trace its course with scientific accuracy. The terms *realism* and *naturalism* are sometimes used more or less interchangeably when referring to writers of this kind. But with realism the emphasis is on the method (objective description), with naturalism on the subject (a

natural or inevitable progression seen in its entirety). Maugham practiced both. He sought to create an illusion of objective reality in his fiction, and he saw his subjects as in bondage to the processes of nature.

The publication of *Liza of Lambeth* confirmed Maugham in his decision to abandon medicine for professional authorship. The largely favorable notices that the story attracted gave him the confidence in his powers that was to see him through the next decade of hard work, until he established himself as a fashionable writer of comedies for the London theater. During that period he was to experiment with tales long and short, with novels set in the present and the past, with domestic and exotic backgrounds, with travel writing and essay writing as well as fiction. From all this industry he learned two things: that he possessed an uncommon gift for narrative, for arousing the reader's curiosity at the start of a book and sustaining it until the end; and that the style of writing best suited to exploiting that gift was a plain, serviceable, simple prose in which the sentences were never too long and the vocabulary was largely that of ordinary conversation. The dandified style of Beerbohm, now writing a weekly essay on the current theater for the *Saturday Review,* was not for Maugham. Like many writers, he kept a journal, jotting down ideas for stories, fragments of description, snatches of dialogue, insights into the personalities of his friends, notes toward a philosophy of life. Eventually it extended to fifteen volumes. Most of it he destroyed as part of a general strategy of covering his tracks and frustrating the task of a future biographer, but enough survived to make a book of 350 pages, published with a preface by Maugham in 1949 as *A Writer's Notebook.* It is illuminating to read the entries for the end of the nineteenth century and to compare the Gallic aphorisms ("Respectability is the cloak under which fools cover their stupidity") and moral aperçus with the pieces of descriptive prose, enshrining Green Park in London in winter or the fields of Kent in summertime. Maugham worked assiduously to fashion the lucid, easy manner that suited him best.

Above all he used his eyes. Little escaped his clear-sighted vision. He was always looking for those telltale details that give the game away. The profession of intelligence agent into which he was recruited during World War I, being posted on a secret mission to Russia, came naturally to him because he was a practiced observer of the stratagems of people who wish to avoid exposure. In the stories he wrote featuring the British agent Ashenden, based on his own experience, he showed what potential for entertainment there was in tales of espionage, and he may be said to have unwittingly invented the genre that became so hugely popular after World War II. As a young man, it was just such a genre that he was looking for after he had launched his career with *Liza.* Maugham studied the market and tried his hand at various forms. He wrote short tales aimed at magazines; some were accepted by *Punch* and the *Strand.* He wrote one—an exceedingly brief one—for the *Daily Mail,* the newspaper started in 1896 whose short, topical items required minimum effort on the reader's part. As an author, Maugham endorsed this approach.

Soon he had enough short stories for a book, *Orientations* (1899). He also set to work producing different kinds of currently popular novels. He wrote a historical novel set in Italy during the Renaissance; another about a soldier returning from the Boer War; another concerning a white man leading an expedition into deepest Africa; another about the marital problems of a farmer's wife in rural Kent. This apprentice work need not detain us, save perhaps for *Mrs. Craddock* (1902), which with its disillusioned heroine, a martyr to sexual passion, is the real successor to *Liza.* The novel opens in the naturalistic mode, with gray skies mirroring the heroine's moods. The countryside is that of Kent, where Maugham grew up, and there is mention of Blackstable (Whitstable) and Tercanbury (Canterbury), places to which he returned when his talent had matured.

He has no difficulty in painting this rural landscape in the somber and subdued tones favored by his naturalistic masters. Where he fails is in bringing to life the passion felt by his lady of gentle birth for the rough, virile, insensitive, socially ambitious yeoman farmer whom she marries. The subject demands the inward, incandescent, sensually aware manner of D. H. Lawrence. But when Maugham observes the social awkwardness, the flouting of the unwritten codes governing social behavior prompted by such a union, he is on his home ground. He may not be convincing in depicting the heroine's passion, but he leaves us in no doubt about her disillusionment when the true nature of the man she has married becomes apparent to her. Although the novel was written in the last years of Victoria's reign, Edwardian heartlessness is already apparent. There is among the characters an elderly spinster, the maiden aunt beloved of writers of this period, who possesses a pithy turn of phrase and a refreshingly candid manner. She could easily have stepped out of a comedy by Oscar Wilde. A perceptive reader might have thought that the young man who wrote this novel had it in him to write an effective play. Indeed, the playwright Henry Arthur Jones (1851–1929), one of whose daughters was to provide Maugham with the model for Rosie, in *Cakes and Ale* (1930), had thought so on reading *Liza;* and it was toward the theater that Maugham's ambitions were now directed.

IV

MAUGHAM's first play to be produced, *A Man of Honour* (1903) (which he did not include later in his *Collected Plays*), explores the consequences of social suicide. The hero, a young man of gentle birth, marries a common barmaid whom he has made pregnant, a marriage that ensures his exile from polite society. The play was harrowing but dramatically effective, according to contemporary critics. The pain was mitigated by some moments of comedy between the hero's genteel friends and the heroine's coarse relations. Noting how well these scenes performed, Maugham decided that it was with comedy that his immediate future lay. He then wrote several plays in the *fin-de-siècle* Wilde mold. Titled personages, mute footmen, orchidaceous epigrams are all in evidence, but there is a mellower tone than in the work of Maugham's predecessors, as if the great social taboos had by now become a bit of a joke, more honored in the breach than the observance; and there appears too a greater willingness to be frank about money and the part it may play in affairs of the heart.

A favorite device of the earlier writers had been a bundle of letters, tied up with ribbon, suddenly produced from the attic at about the end of Act II, providing incontrovertible evidence of the sexual lapses of the respected patriarch, this somehow getting into the possession of the ostracized heroine. Maugham used this motif in *Lady Frederick* (written 1903, performed 1907), his first great hit. In a brilliant *coup de théâtre* he makes the heroine nonchalantly throw the letters into the fire in the sight of her enemies, whom they could harm, out of sheer goodness of heart. This prepares the audience for the even more effective scene, a sensation in its day, in which she deliberately disillusions her young lover by admitting him to her morning toilette, so that he can see the ravages time has made on her face before cosmetics have done their work.

The success of *Lady Frederick* marked a turning point in Maugham's life. The royalties from its long run gave him the income he craved, enabling him to live like a gentleman instead of a struggling literary hack, while the many appreciative reviews led the hitherto indifferent theatrical managements to fall over one another in the rush to produce his work. Artistically, Maugham felt that his work was part of the long tradition of English comedy in which amorous misunderstanding is exposed in elegant conversation pieces, and current attitudes about sex and money are dissected. The tradition stretched back past Arthur Wing Pinero (1855–1934) and Henry Arthur Jones, his immediate predecessors, through Wilde, to Richard Brinsley Sheridan, to John Dryden, and even to Shakespeare, as in the loving quarrels of Beatrice and Benedict in *Much Ado About Nothing*. When Maugham succeeded in having four plays running simultaneously in London's West End, *Punch* published a caricature showing a pensive Shakespeare standing beside the billboards advertising Maugham's four hits. Maugham was gratified, but he kept his head amid the ballyhoo. No one knew better than he that triumph and disaster were both impostors. He had a long-term strategy for his career of which this was merely a preliminary phase. Today, reading the texts of Maugham's early comedies, *Lady Frederick, Mrs. Dot* (1904), and *Jack Straw* (1905), in the austere surroundings of a university library may induce considerable puzzlement as to why anyone ever thought they were at all funny.

This view may be modified if one has the opportunity, as occasionally occurs, to see one of them in production, where the neatness of the repartee and the author's cunning control of the audience's reactions become apparent. Maugham always insisted that his plays were written not to be read but to be performed. As he grew in stature and confidence, he imperceptibly stopped giving audiences what he thought they wanted and gave them instead what he thought they ought to have, keeping his sights focused on contemporary society but widening their range to take in sections other than the impoverished aristocracy—although, as he revealed in *Our Betters* (1915), he had not yet finished with them. Maugham's first theatrical assault on the middle

class was in *Smith* (1909), where he made an example of one bridge-playing Kensington set. Here we are in stockbroker-land, with the husband away at his office, while the wife occupies her afternoons playing rubbers of bridge with a man who in a Latin country would be called her gigolo, a penniless woman friend whose bridge earnings are her sole means of subsistence, and a woman who is married to a rich Jewish man and who neglects her newborn baby because of her love of the game and the gossip that goes with it. Maugham paints these typical English middle-class people before World War I in pretty harsh tones.

In one of his final plays, *For Services Rendered* (1932), a portrait of an English middle-class family during the Depression, Maugham offers no alleviation of the general misery; among the characters there is no one whose life is not a hideous mess. But in *Smith* there are two such: the sturdy young parlormaid who gives the comedy its name, and Tom Freeman, the hostess's brother, who has returned home from Rhodesia, where he has a farm. The misalliance across the class barrier that was shown to bring such tragic consequences in *A Man of Honour* here yields a happy ending. Tom lightly vaults over the divide, repelled by the behavior of his sister's bridge set, and takes Smith back with him to Rhodesia, where no doubt she will make him an excellent wife.

The dramatist's manipulation of the basic antithesis is, as often in Maugham, a trifle crude; babies do not often die as a result of their mothers' playing too much bridge. Nonetheless, there are moments of realistic observation that render the play an authentic comment on its period. Gone is the epigrammatic never-never-land of Edwardian England; in its place we have an insight into the Great Britain over which George V will shortly reign, with its appalling waste of human energy, its crumbling class structure, its unashamed anti-Semitism, its incredible complacency, its colonial opportunities.

Today the most often performed of Maugham's plays is the one entitled *Home and Beauty* in England and *Too Many Husbands* in America, written in 1919 while he was ill with tuberculosis in a sanatorium in Scotland, after his espionage activities in World War I. Maugham may have been confined to his room, but he seems to have been keenly aware of what was going on in the country at large. We can, if we like, see the heroine, Victoria, an unwitting bigamist, as a wicked symbol of the Britain of the Armistice—a more self-centered individual never existed—but in doing so we stifle by critical solemnity one of Maugham's most delightful works. There is a Mozartian gaiety in the to-ings and fro-ings of the main trio, a young prima donna of a wife with a pair of gallant husbands, both bent on escaping from her clutches.

A fragment of dialogue in a scene between the heroine and her mother touches on a central concern of many of Maugham's plays, the nature of marriage:

Mrs. Shuttleworth: The difference between men and women is that men are not naturally addicted to matrimony. With patience, firmness, and occasional rewards you can train them to it just as you can train a dog to walk on its hind legs. But a dog would rather walk on all fours and a man would rather be free. Marriage is a habit.
Victoria: And a very good one, Mother.
Mrs. Shuttleworth: Of course. But the unfortunate thing about this world is that good habits are so much easier to get out of than bad ones.

Many of Maugham's plays show people in one way or another getting out of the habit of marriage. Maugham observed among the French and in French novels, not to mention among his smart friends in London, how marriage as a social institution could have its limits stretched. He himself had made a marriage in America, in the early part of World War I, to Syrie, the daughter of Dr. Thomas John Barnardo. This formidable lady, who became known internationally as an interior decorator of impeccable taste, was to be a kind of facade of respectability for Maugham in society; at least that seems to have been his bizarre intention. At the same time he had a male lover, his secretary, Gerald Haxton, with whom he traveled the world. It need scarcely be added that this arrangement, if one may so dignify it, did not work at all harmoniously for either Syrie, Haxton, or Maugham. He did, though, while under considerable stress from the breakdown of his marriage, write a series of successful plays in which he showed people adopting various tactics to avoid altogether, or escape from, the imprisonment of socially respectable marriages. He introduced a new, more ferocious tone in the working out of this well-tried comic formula, one that he may have found in Henri Becque's *La Parisienne* (1885), which he had seen as a student in Heidelberg. One finds it in comedies like *Penelope* (1908), *Caroline* (1915), and *The Constant Wife* (1926), growing in ferocity with the years. His most savage play is *Our Betters* (1915), in which he pitches into the world of Syrie and her friends, including the millionaire store-owner Gordon Selfridge, who had been her protector; this kept the play off the London stage until 1923. It was a sensation in its day, but recent revivals in the provinces suggest that it may have aged as much as its American-born heroine; whereas *The Circle* (first produced in 1921), by common consent Maugham's best play, continues to flourish whenever it is performed. With its shapely symmetry of construction and its generous parts for the elderly, it contains a perfect balance of astringency and sentiment. Maugham has the best of both worlds, the Edwardian and the modern. He gazes nostalgically upon his own youth and remembers that great society beauty, his own mother, in the scene in which Lady Kitty turns the leaves of the photograph album. And Maugham looks at the world around him when the young wife deliberates over whether or not to bolt from her humorless husband, an ambitious politician. If there was a model for this character Maugham never divulged it. Let us remember the pact that Winston Churchill made with Maugham: Maugham would not put him into one of his works. They thus succeeded in staying friends for life.

The theater suited Maugham. The lack of sensuous urgency in his prose, which I have already noted, never worried the actors; his innate sense of dramatic form and timing made up for it. Before he was through, he had covered a wide variety of subjects within the conventions of the well-shaped comedy or drama, including pioneering in Manitoba (*The Land of Promise*, 1913), mercy killing (*The Sacred Flame*, 1928), and disbelief in God (*The Unknown*, 1920). His settings included China (*East of Suez*, 1922), Egypt (*Caesar's Wife*, 1918), and Malaya (*The Letter*, 1926). The last named was the only play that Maugham adapted from one of his own short stories. Usually he left that task to lesser hands, as in the case of *Rain* (1922).

V

THE kinship that exists between the arts of playwriting and short-story writing has often been noted; consider Anton Chekhov or Luigi Pirandello, or, for that matter, Noel Coward. In both forms the writer has to convey a vast amount of information in a minimum number of words; the signals are often multiple while seeming to be simple. You can be a born novelist but lack the ability required to execute either the play or the short-story form successfully. By contrast, you can be a novelist who escapes occasionally into the short story like a man snatching a weekend's break away from home; and you can be by vocation a short-story writer who occasionally attempts the novel. On this question Graham Greene, in the introduction to his *Collected Stories* (1972), writes:

I remain in this field a novelist who has happened to write short stories, just as there are certain short story writers (Maupassant and Mr V. S. Pritchett come to mind) who have happened to write novels. This is not a superficial distinction—or even a technical distinction as between an artist who paints in oil or watercolour; it is certainly not a distinction in value. It is a distinction between two different ways of life.

Maugham happened, like Maupassant, to write novels; one or two of them have become famous. But he was a born short-story writer, one of the most skillful and fertile ever to have practiced the art. He appeared to be able to conjure stories out of the air. His *Notebook* abounds in excellent ideas for stories he never bothered to write up, and so, according to those closest to him, did his table talk. He destroyed one unpublished group, relating to his espionage activities, for security reasons. Many of the earliest he never bothered to reprint after their magazine appearances. Nevertheless, there remain readily accessible in different editions about ninety stories. They range from the very short ones collected in *Cosmopolitans* (1936), written originally to be printed on opposite pages of *Cosmopolitan* magazine, such as "Mr Know-All" and "Salvatore," to those occupying some forty to fifty printed pages, including such famous tales as "Before the Party," "The Outstation," "P. & O.," "The Alien Corn," "Gigolo and Gigolette," and "The Colonel's Lady."

The magazine origin of these stories is not fortuitous. The Maugham short story is a form of journalism: the point at which journalism becomes literary art. Let us pick one to look at closely. I have selected "P. & O.," from *The Casuarina Tree* (1926), almost at random. The whole of the action occurs on board an elegant Peninsular and Orient liner that is carrying an assorted group of British passengers back home after their tour of duty as planters or members of the administration of the Federated

Malay States. Maugham fixes on one of the passengers, a Mrs. Hamlyn, as the mediating consciousness for his tale. In her early forties, she is returning to England without her husband, from whom, it soon emerges, she is estranged. He has fallen in love with the wife of a business colleague who, to Mrs. Hamlyn's mortification, is considerably older than she is. At the beginning of the story, Mrs. Hamlyn sits in her deck chair in the early morning, while the ship is tied up in Singapore. Like the good journalist he is, Maugham rapidly establishes the multiracial background, the structure of ethnic strains, that is so relevant to his story:

Singapore is the meeting place of many races. The Malays, though natives of the soil, dwell uneasily in towns, and are few; and it is the Chinese, supple, alert and industrious, who throng the streets; the dark-skinned Tamils walk on their silent, naked feet, as though they were but brief sojourners in a strange land, but the Bengalis, sleek and prosperous, are easy in their surroundings, and self-assured; the sly and obsequious Japanese seem busy with pressing and secret affairs; and the English in their topees and white ducks, speeding past in motor-cars or at leisure in their rickshaws, wear a nonchalant and careless air. The rulers of these teeming peoples take their authority with smiling unconcern. And now, tired and hot, Mrs. Hamlyn waited for the ship to set out again on her long journey across the Indian Ocean.

It is that long journey that provides Maugham with the natural linear progression for his story. By the time the ship sights land at Aden, Mrs. Hamlyn will have come to terms with her life of separation, and a fellow passenger will have died a mysterious death. He is an Irishman named Gallagher who has made his money from the rubber boom and is on his way back home for an early retirement. Mrs. Hamlyn learns from his Cockney foreman, one of the second-class passengers on the ship, that while working up-country Gallagher had lived for some ten or twelve years with a Malay girl who, on being abandoned, put a curse on him. Here, as in the play *The Circle*, we have a neat symmetry of construction: the situations of Mrs. Hamlyn and Mr. Gallagher mirror each other.

The material of firsthand observation in this story has been arranged with precision to make a number of dramatic points. As soon as the ship leaves port Mr. Gallagher begins to suffer from uncontrollable attacks of hiccups. At first this is treated as a joke by the other passengers, but his condition becomes so serious that he has to retire to the sick bay under the care of the ship's doctor (who, incidentally, is having a flirtation with the wife of one of the other passengers). The curse has started to take effect; Gallagher's life may be in danger. One senses that the germ of the story lay in some traveler's tale that Maugham (or Haxton) overheard. By showing the impact of Gallagher's mortal sickness on the whole shipboard community, passengers and crew, Maugham gives us a portrait of British society in the last days of the colonial era. The irony in his initial statement, "The rulers of these teeming peoples take their authority with smiling unconcern," reverberates as the ship plows its way home.

The class divisions ruling on board between the first-class passengers, the second-class passengers, and the lower decks, containing the humble members of the crew, lascars and others, correspond neatly to those within the British Empire. The first-class passengers are planning a fancy dress ball for Christmas. The great question is, should they drop the protocol for once and invite the second-class passengers? Some argue in favor, but the majority are against. All are concerned lest the death of Mr. Gallagher—if it occurs—cause the ball to be canceled. It is only a second-class passenger, the Irishman's Cockney assistant, who goes out of his way to do something practical that might help his employer. He takes the unprecedented step of applying to the third- and fourth-class citizens, the native members of the crew, to perform a magical ceremony to exorcise the curse Gallagher's mistress has cast over him. They agree to the assistant's request and slit the throat of a cockerel, intoning curious chants. "We're no match for them, us white men, and that's a fact," he tells Mrs. Hamlyn in explanation. But the exorcism does not work, and Gallagher continues to languish.

As his death approaches, "a definite malaise" overcomes the entire ship, and the reader senses a deeper malaise still: it is as though Maugham had foreseen the collapse of the whole paternalistic imperial system some thirty years before it happened. Mrs. Hamlyn observes two Japanese passengers playing deck quoits: "They were trim and neat in their tennis shirts, white trousers and buckram shoes. They looked very European, they even called the score to one another in English, and yet somehow to look at them filled Mrs. Hamlyn with a vague disquiet."

Maugham's stories had a huge readership. They seemed to appeal to all classes throughout the world save one, the professional literary critics. Turning through the pages of the prewar *New Statesman* we can find plenty of critical attacks on Maugham's tales by people like Rebecca West; let us turn instead to the view taken by Cyril Connolly in *The Modern Movement: 100 Key Books from England, France, and America, 1880–1950* (1965):

In these Far Eastern short stories . . . and in the secret service tales of *Ashenden* (1928), Maugham achieves an unspoken ferocity, a controlled ruthlessness before returning to sentimentality with Rosie in *Cakes and Ale*. He tells us—and it had not been said before—exactly what the British in the Far East were like, the judges and planters and civil servants and their womenfolk at home, even as *Ashenden* exposes what secret service work is really like. That would not be enough without his mastery of form, if not of language. His bloodless annexation of the Far East pays off in *The Casuarina Tree*, which includes "The Yellow Streak," "The Out Station," "Before the Party" and "The Letter"—about a coward, a snob, a murderess and a blackmailer.

Nor was it only the Far East, and Europe on the eve of the Bolshevik revolution, to which Maugham applied his "controlled ruthlessness" in short-story form. He viewed the exiled aristocracy and the nightclub entertainers of the French Riviera, where he had made his home, the smart world of Syrie's friends, the inmates of a French penal colony, and a dozen other milieus across the world in the same manner. As far back as his medical student days he had been a great traveler, and now, as a rich man, he toured the world at will. His travel books have the same easy readability, the same journalist's flair for an arresting incident, as his best stories, but they rely more on direct observation and less on manipulation of the material. No one who wishes to know Maugham should neglect books like *On a Chinese Screen* (1922), *The Gentleman in the Parlour* (1930), or *Don Fernando* (1935).

Maugham found a statement of the aims of the short-story writer in Edgar Allan Poe's review of Nathaniel Hawthorne's *Twice-Told Tales*. "In the whole composition," Poe wrote, "there should be no word written, of which the tendency, direct or indirect, is not to the pre-established design." After quoting Poe, Maugham gives his own formulation of a good short story in his 1939 selection:

It is a piece of fiction, dealing with a single incident, material or spiritual, that can be read at a sitting; it is original, it must sparkle, excite or impress; and it must have unity of effect or impression. It should move in an even line from its exposition to its close.

(Introduction to *Tellers of Tales*)

This formulation admirably suits the Maupassant-Poe-Maugham type of story, but not those by Chekhov or Joyce or Lawrence or Katherine Mansfield: these writers reacted against the short story based on a single anecdote, with its dramatic manipulation and linear development. They favored an approach that allowed the writer freedom within the confines of his tale to follow the inner consciousness of his characters, to allow those characters to behave in a spontaneous fashion instead of always behaving in a way determined by the pre-established design. They sought not to spring neat dramatic surprises on the reader but to lead him poetically toward the perception of sudden moments of universal truth about the human condition.

In considering Chekhov, Maugham had no doubt that he was dealing with a great master of the short story, although one who had a completely different conception from his own. "I find," he wrote of Chekhov's stories, "that the impression they make on me is powerful but indeterminate." Chekhov's people are "shadowy." He goes on:

I despair of making myself clear when I say that they strike me less as persons than as human beings. Each one is as it were a part of everyone else, and the hurt that one does to another is bearable because in a way it is a hurt that he does to himself. And because they are shadowy they remain secret. We understand them as little as we understand ourselves. And so Chekhov gets the effect which is perhaps the most impressive that the writer of fiction can achieve: he fills you with an overpowering sense of the mystery of life.

(Introduction to *Tellers of Tales*)

VI

THIS, if evasive, is generous: Maugham profoundly disliked and mistrusted the indeterminate in fiction. He felt that, great as Chekhov was in his native Russia, his influence abroad, especially on the short story, was unfortunate. Maugham had made what he called experiments. He had written one early novel, *The Merry-Go-Round* (1904), with a multiple plot, and in middle age he developed a literary persona in his fiction that permitted the introduction of passages of authorial comment; but he was suspicious of anything that broke the immaculate surface of the prose or muddied the logical connections of the narrative. His literary conservatism blinded him to the importance of the experiments in the art of fiction that Virginia Woolf and others were attempting. Nor did Virginia Woolf and her friends, in their turn, think much of Maugham's fiction. "Class Two. Division One," wrote Lytton Strachey crushingly, on finishing one of Maugham's novels. Influential critical opinion—the intelligentsia (to use the Marxist term of the time), the review pages in papers like the *Times Literary Supplement* and the *Statesman*—tended, whether consciously or not, to take its tone from Bloomsbury. Maugham felt aggrieved, while continuing to publish more books than ever. "I must bear my misfortune with fortitude," he told himself. He brooded on the whole process through which literary reputations were made in London.

The literary salons and the literary press were full of a method of developing character that seemed suddenly to have become available to the novelist, "the stream of consciousness"; it had been seen in Proust and Joyce, although its antecedents could be traced back to more obscure writers, and it had continued in England with Dorothy Richardson and Virginia Woolf. Looking back on all this after half a century with the wisdom of hindsight, it is clear to us, as it was not in the first intoxicated flush of this discovery, that the exploration of a character's inner being by a novelist through an association of thoughts and feelings is not incompatible with linear narrative. On this point I should like to quote part of a discussion I had with Iris Murdoch in the BBC Radio series *Novels Up to Now*. She said:

Tolstoy produces the most tremendous amount of stuff, exhibiting to us the immediate thoughts and feelings of Natasha and Pierre and Prince Andrew and so on. . . . I am interested in the relationship between immediate thoughts and feelings and the whole of the person, whatever the whole of the person may be, and I like to write and read novels in which the interior of somebody's mind is explored in enormous detail. . . . A lot of people, I think, rather object to this. I think there has been a reaction against the sort of Virginia Woolf version of this, which isn't just a case of stream of consciousness but is a case of a certain very highly wrought, semipoetic method of presenting it.

Maugham, although dedicated to realism and linear narrative, was by no means uninterested in "the relationship between immediate thoughts and feelings and the whole of the person" and wished at least once to explore the interior of somebody's mind in enormous detail. The "somebody" was himself, especially as his mind and the whole of his person had developed from the time of the death of his mother in Paris, when he was six, to the time when, as a young man on his own in London, he embarked on his literary career. Many novelists in their early days produce a novel describing, under the cover of a fictional story, their own early years; Maugham was no exception. He wrote it first after he had given up medicine. Written about 1898, it was then named "The Artistic Temperament of Stephen Carey." It opens with his nurse informing Stephen that his mother has died; tells of his unhappy years at Tercanbury School (the King's School, Canterbury, where Maugham was educated); and then is occupied with a protracted, self-destructive love affair between Stephen and a waitress in a London tea shop, here named Rosie Cameron. Maugham sent it to his publisher, T. Fisher Unwin, and presumably Edward Garnett had some doubts about it. At any rate, it was rejected and failed to find a publisher elsewhere. After World War II Maugham presented the manuscript to the Library of Congress (where it may be read by students of Maugham) with an embargo on its ever being published.

Although the manuscript languished in a drawer after its tour of rejections, as Maugham wrote comedies and less personal novels, the notion of writing a longer and fuller autobiographical novel, using the "Stephen Carey" script as a first draft, preoccupied him. There was so much in his youth of which he wished to disburden himself. He regarded the opportunities for such private catharsis as one of the main compensations for the hardships of a writer's lot. The result was his longest, most deeply felt work, *Of Human Bondage*, published in 1915.

Far from renouncing or modifying his naturalist principles in approaching this highly subjective material, he applied them as rigorously as ever. Here is Maugham in the person of Philip Carey from the age of about six to twenty-six—as seen by Maugham, aged about forty. Of course, much is omitted. There are no homosexual encounters, for example, and the hero's isolating disability is attributed to a club foot—not, as in real life, a stammer. Some Maugham-watchers have even suggested that the character of Mildred may in real life have been a man, a waiter instead of a waitress. Possibly, but we have no means of confirming this; and cer-

tainly Maugham did have some affairs with women before he married Syrie. In spite of alterations, however, the novel is remarkably faithful to the history and the spirit of his youth.

If you wish to learn the facts about Maugham's upbringing by the vicar of Whitstable and his German-born wife, about his years at the King's School, Canterbury, about his bohemian existence in Paris among expatriate artists, about his training as a doctor at St. Thomas' Hospital, this novel must be your first port of call, however many biographies you may wish to consult later on. Sometimes he includes an episode—like Philip's time as a floorwalker in a department store—based on hearsay. As far as is known, Maugham himself never actually went hop-picking, as the hero does in the rather unconvincing happy ending; but as a Whitstable boy Maugham must have had many opportunities to observe the annual hop-picking festival in Kent. He probably exaggerates the extent of his unhappiness when he was young, but we all do that, especially when we know that we have a sympathetic audience. The book stands, in the first instance, as a remarkably interesting social document. Very occasionally Maugham steps forward and summarizes Philip's developing philosophy of life, or lack of it (as after the Paris episode, when he ponders on the meaning of the figure in the carpet), but these pauses in the continuing action are rare and not without their own dramatic point.

However, *Of Human Bondage* is not merely a historical record; it is a novel, a work of art with its own inner life, and it must ultimately be judged as such. The first thing to be said about it artistically is that it seems to have gotten out of hand. Overwhelmed by the abundance of material he finds in his own past, the author has been deserted by his habitual sense of overall form. He keeps his chapters short, and they certainly grip us individually, but they do not fit together in the satisfying architectural proportions of his short stories and plays. This tends to be true in general of Maugham's longer fiction. He solves the structural problem by breaking up the novels into separate short-story sequences, connected only by the fact that each sequence involves the principal character in some way; in a true novelist, someone for whom the novel is a "way of life" in Greene's sense, the sequences are much more organically interrelated, or they are indistinguishable from the whole.

The main sequence, from which the book derives

its title, is the affair with Mildred, a harrowing account of the degrading bondage of one human being to another. This by itself might well have provided enough material for a complete novel, with its own extended linear progression. The novel, as it were, that precedes it is the account of Philip's relations with his adoptive parents, containing the unforgettable figure of the Reverend Carey—one of the most ironic portraits in English fiction—and his efforts to achieve independence from them. Then there is at least one further novel in the episodes concerned with the peculiar joys and sorrows of a life dedicated to art and centered on the Left Bank in the happy-go-lucky days of Paris before World War I.

Maugham had treated this milieu earlier in a novel called *The Magician* (1908). The preposterous figure of Aleister Crowley (1875–1947), exponent of black magic and prolific author, dominated that book, whereas in *Of Human Bondage* Maugham drew on the whole circle of his formative acquaintances at this time, including the painters Gerald Kelly, James Morrice, and Roderick O'Connor, and the connoisseur Ellingham Brooks. All of them engage in a dialectic with Philip Carey through which he arrives at the stoical, agnostic position that he reaches at the end of the book, having at last liberated himself from the rigorous, mean-spirited Anglican upbringing of the rectory. In the Parisian section, the agonies of students who yearn to become artists but lack the requisite amount of talent offer the author yet another self-contained dramatic theme. He dealt with it again in terms of music and anglicized Jews in the story "The Alien Corn," published originally in *Six Stories Written in the First Person Singular* (1931), where, because it is the whole of the predetermined pattern, it has more power.

To write *Of Human Bondage* may have been a liberating act for the author, but it is less of one for the reader. The Darwinian struggle for survival in which all the characters are engaged (Darwin's "great book" is mentioned as coming as a revelation to Philip) communicates itself all too depressingly; and, if the hero just barely holds our sympathy as he makes his way through life in search of his identity, he never becomes endearing. It is a book that one is glad to have read but to which one is reluctant to return.

In Maugham's next novel, *The Moon and Sixpence*, there emerges someone who is to be our constant companion through the rest of Maugham's work. How shall I describe him? As "Somerset Maugham"? Or as the "I" in the story? Or, pompously, as "the authorial presence"? Or simply as "the narrator"? It matters little which term I choose, because every reader of Maugham will know who I mean: that wise and waspish fellow who has knocked about the globe a good deal and who in his own leisurely but compelling fashion has a story to tell us.

Maugham has not abandoned naturalism even now, but he has stretched its limits to include his own observations, conditioning our response to the narrative. While he was baring his soul in the figure of Philip Carey he remained invisible, telling the story in the third person; but now that he is bent on baring the souls of his fellow men he feels free to come before the footlights himself in the role of a one-man chorus. There came a time in 1938 when he decided to hold the stage alone as a one-man show. This was *The Summing Up*, where he distilled into a single volume the observations of a lifetime devoted to successful authorship. In the same vein are the later volumes of essays: *The Vagrant Mood* (1952), *Ten Novels and Their Authors*, and *Points of View* (1958).

It is this author-narrator who holds together the different parts of the narrative in Maugham's last three major novels, *The Moon and Sixpence*, *Cakes and Ale*, and *The Razor's Edge* (1944). The Maugham we meet in these books is no longer the awkward misfit of *Of Human Bondage*; he is the professional author (hence Connolly's description), completely at ease among both the highest and the lowest in the land, and at many levels between those extremes. Even when he does look back on his own youth, either as a scholar or as a young writer with a name still to make, he does it with an amused tolerance. As a boy Maugham may have been bored having to listen every Sunday to his uncle's sermons, but in his own mature work he is by no means averse to adopting a homiletic tone. In one sense Maugham's novels are parables for people who no longer believe in God, nor in anything very much, apart from their own respectability and innate superiority. His favorite text is that of the world well lost, not for love, which he presents as an ephemeral thing killed by habit, but for a sense of vocation, a calling, or even just a whim, provided it turns into a commitment.

I do not know whether the Reverend Maugham ever preached on the theme "If any man come to me, and hate not his father, and mother, and wife and children, and brethren, and sisters, yea, and his own life also, he cannot be my disciple" (Luke 14:26), the saying of Jesus that is so hard to reconcile with the sanctity of the family. Perhaps not; but it became by implication, and in his way of life, his nephew's favorite text. Maugham's heroes abandon their loved ones to follow not the Christian God but the god of their own creativeness, although a Christian might not see a great distinction there. At any rate, his heroes follow their daimons—the need to paint (Strickland, in *The Moon and Sixpence*), to discover the eternal philosophy (Larry, in *The Razor's Edge*), or just to live within one's own artistic strength (Driffield, in *Cakes and Ale*)—with the single-mindedness, the inflexibility, the utter ruthlessness that Maugham applied to his own life.

Maugham was himself Strickland, telling everyone and everything who got in the way of his work to go to hell, but he was also the courteous narrator-figure, full of fun, good advice, and scandalous stories, capable of forming friendships with men and women of many different types, particularly if they had a title of some kind. The personalities of most artists are bifurcated in this way, but few have shown the two sides of themselves in their work with such compulsive clarity. Charles Strickland is in essence much closer to Maugham than to Paul Gauguin, even though the painter's life suggested the book, the last part of which was researched in Tahiti.

The Moon and Sixpence is Maugham's most uncompromising statement of this attitude in the form of a novel. More than any other work of art it has spread the myth of the artist as someone who ruthlessly severs all human claims and emotional ties to be able to follow the dictates of his genius with single-minded commitment. It seems strange that Maugham was planning and researching this particular book at precisely the time he himself was embarking on matrimony.

When it appeared, most of the reviewers rejected Charles Strickland as being too much of a monster to be credible; yet at the same time they praised Maugham's narrative technique. One critic, particularly infuriated by Strickland's antics, was the New Zealand–born short-story writer Katherine Mansfield, who had begun reviewing books for the *Athenaeum*, of which her lover, J. Middleton Murry, had recently been appointed editor. Her view was that a genuine artist does not sever human ties in the way Maugham describes, and that anyone who felt compelled to behave in that fashion should not try to become an artist. She wanted to say to

him: "If you have to be so odious before you can paint bananas, pray leave them unpainted." Several reviewers failed to make a connection between the book and Gauguin; the writer in the *Saturday Review*, for instance, described Strickland as "a crypto-Monet." As Maugham was the first to admit, there are as many differences between Strickland and Gauguin as there are similarities.

The main difference is that Strickland is an Englishman, and what he escapes from is the genteel world of the near-rich in fashionable London, a world manipulated by women and centered on the tea party, the dinner party, and the drawing room. Maugham had acquired a great distaste for this world, which he had frequented when he first went to London. His rudeness at social functions became legendary and increased with his age and celebrity, although on home ground among his friends he could be a most charming host. *The Moon and Sixpence* should be read as a social satire as well as an apologia for artistic selfishness and intolerance.

If we look at its structure, again we see the familiar Maugham scheme of separate narratives, connected only by the presence of the hero (or anti-hero) mediated through the consciousness of the author (who appears in the first person, sometimes narrating events of which he has no direct knowledge). These distinct narrative sections may be seen in terms of their settings. There is the London setting, preceded by a fine parody of the art of biography in the Max Beerbohm manner, followed by sections set in Paris, Marseilles, Tahiti, and Papeete. Each of these locations represents a different stage of Strickland's journey to artistic martyrdom. In Tahiti Maugham uses material he acquired on his tour there (possibly in part an intelligence mission) during World War I in the company of Haxton. In Marseilles he relies on literary sources and cleverly fakes the scruffy society of sailors' bars and doss-houses, with the help of Captain Nichols, a likable old ruffian Maugham was to use again, more centrally, in a later novel with an exotic backdrop, *The Narrow Corner* (1932). In Paris and London Maugham is drawing directly on his own youthful memories. In the French capital Maugham introduces a figure necessary to any account of a genius: the disciple. Dirk Stroeve, an amiable clown, is one of Maugham's most accomplished comic creations. The twist in the narrative, in which Stroeve so willingly cooperates, is that instead of the disciple betraying the master, the master betrays the disciple.

The novelist's insight into the behavior of both during this crisis seems highly accurate.

Maugham scores some telling points when he describes the effect made on strangers by the reconstructed Strickland. He is even more accurate in describing the effect of the unreconstructed, about-to-become-reconstructed Strickland upon his own kith and kin. The initial drama of Strickland's disappearance, the total misunderstanding of his motivation on the part of his wife, her sister, and the sister's husband, is a fine example of Maugham at his most ironic. Here he wickedly apologizes to the reader for a certain "shadowiness" in his description of the Stricklands at home:

My only excuse is that the impression they made on me was no other. There was just that shadowiness about them which you find in people whose lives are part of the social organism so that they exist in it and by it only. They are like cells in the body, essential, but, so long as they remain healthy, engulfed in the momentous whole. The Stricklands were an average family in the middle class. A pleasant, hospitable woman, with a harmless craze for the small lions of literary society; a rather dull man doing his duty in that state of life in which a merciful providence had placed him; two nice healthy-looking children. Nothing could be more ordinary. I do not know there was anything about them to excite the curious.

Maugham's sense of remoteness from such people in England was exacerbated by the decision of the authorities to classify Haxton, an American, as an undesirable alien and to refuse him entry. For this and other personal reasons Maugham removed himself to the French Riviera, where he had bought a villa at Cap Ferrat, the Villa Mauresque. It became his permanent residence. He was forced to leave during World War II, which he spent largely in the United States, but returned to France as soon as the war was over. After the war his appearance in London was usually confined to a visit of a few weeks in the summer, when he would stay in a private suite at the Dorchester Hotel.

As a story writer and novelist, Maugham picked up plenty of ideas along his beat in the south of France, on his regular travels with Haxton, in the Far East, and among his many friends in America. However, by 1930 he had not completely finished with the world of his childhood in Whitstable, Kent; nor had he quite finished with those hospitable English women of the middle class who had a compulsion for the small and not-so-small lions of literary society.

Maugham's continuing, horrified fascination with these women becomes apparent in *Cakes and Ale.* This novel, he tells us in the preface to the Everyman's Library edition, started out as a short story about Rosie, its voluptuous heroine; and it kept growing. The lady who is supposed to have suggested the character of Rosie has been identified as Ethelwyn Sylvia Jones, the second daughter of the playwright Henry Arthur Jones.[3] She jilted Maugham in the early days of his fame, some time before he met Syrie; and the pain of his rejection stayed with him, waiting to be put to some good literary use.

In spite of the trauma that contributed to its conception, *Cakes and Ale* is one of the most life-enhancing of Maugham's novels. The satirical description of the lionizing literary hostesses and all the wheeling and dealing in literary reputations that goes on within their drawing rooms alternates with a much more genial mood of romancing about the world of the author's boyhood. He re-creates for us the prosperous, gossipy oyster port, with the full-throated and full-bosomed Rosie presiding over the bar of the local tavern, and the raffish rascal "Lord George" paying court to her.

This is the childhood Maugham never had but would have liked to have had—carefree, athletic, exhilarating. It is all a retrospective daydream, but these happy-go-lucky scenes set in Blackstable provide a pleasant corrective to the harsher portrait of Whitstable in *Of Human Bondage.* The novelist's basic plan is linear: he tells the story of a moderately successful writer (based on Maugham himself in the days before he succeeded in getting his plays produced) who becomes involved in the biography of a grand old man of literature. Maugham makes us aware of the pressures brought to bear on the writer-character to conceal or doctor the truth; and in addition he reveals to us the charmed circle of a literary salon, with its ephemeral admirations and its ruthless mode of operation.

However, these ironic scenes of metropolitan life alternate with those set some twenty years earlier in Blackstable. The narrator boasts a previous acquaintance with the "grand old man," and he knows the full story of his youthful follies and indiscretions. Hence the subtitle: "The Skeleton in the Cupboard." Had Maugham been reading Proust and decided to

---

[3]See R. L. Calder, *W. Somerset Maugham and the Quest for Freedom* (London, 1972).

turn Blackstable into his Combray? At any rate he handles smoothly the shifts from past to present in the narrative, and through this technical device he escapes from the linear mode of story-telling.

Apart from the narrator himself, and the splendidly vulgar, erotic figure of Rosie, the other main characters in the novel are the two novelists at the center of it, Alroy Kear and Edward Driffield. The former has perfected a way of "buttering up" the book reviewers and employs other dubious means of promoting his own career with great energy. By contrast, Driffield does not appear to care about the critics or about promoting his career. He leaves all that to the second Mrs. Driffield, who is Kear's great friend. Driffield sprang from the soil, the people. He has total self-possession, a natural genius whose present eminence has been achieved, Maugham cruelly suggests, largely by reason of his longevity rather than any great intrinsic talent.

The novel created a sensation when it was first published. The London literary world thoroughly relished being told by Maugham that the emperor had no clothes. Kear and Driffield were said to have been suggested by Hugh Walpole and Thomas Hardy. Certainly the caps fitted them, as the expression goes. Walpole, who read an early copy for the Book Society, of which he was on the selection committee, felt as if he were looking into a mirror. Maugham denied that any single author was the model for either novelist, claiming that both were composite portraits with aspects borrowed from different individuals, including himself. But after Walpole's death he admitted in the preface to an American reissue of *Cakes and Ale* that he had indeed had him in mind.

The cause of Maugham's animus against Walpole —who had been a friend and had helped him in his younger days and who was also a fellow alumnus of the King's School, Canterbury—has never been fully explained. It hardly matters at this distance of time any more than the supposed identification of Hardy, with whom the resemblances are just as cogent. Hardy covered his own tracks with a posthumously published biography, which he had written himself but which was published under his wife's name. What matters is the enduring account of making a reputation in literary London. Maugham's description prompted (Mrs.) Q. D. Leavis to make a comparison between his novel and Gissing's *New Grub Street*,[4]

[4]See *Scrutiny*, vol. VII (1938).

which observes the same society slightly earlier in its evolution. Gissing's may be the greater novel of the two; Maugham's is undoubtedly the more readable.

VII

WITH *Cakes and Ale* Maugham settled his literary account with London. He went on writing plays for another few years. His farewell drama, *Sheppey* (1933), reworked the theme of a very early short story about a working man who, suddenly possessed of a fortune, decides to give it to the poor in emulation of Jesus. His family is furious and tries to have him declared insane. The play is full of beautifully controlled irony, but it was not a success and has rarely been revived. Maugham was glad to depart from the theater at the age of sixty. Writing plays, he said, was work for a younger man, and he hailed the era of Noel Coward. Maugham had not, however, finished, as a writer, with the theme of the world well lost. He returned to it in at least two more novels. In *Christmas Holiday* (1939), set in Paris on the eve of World War II, a young man from a family background not unlike the Stricklands' has an eye-opening encounter with the French criminal underworld. In his case the world is not wholly lost because he does at the end return to respectability. The book closes with the author reflecting: ". . . only one thing had happened to him, it was rather curious when you came to think of it, and he didn't just then know quite what to do about it: the bottom had fallen out of his world."

For the hero of *The Razor's Edge*, which Maugham wrote while he was in America, the bottom falls out of his world early on, and he takes possession of another one through his knowledge of Vedanta. Larry is an early example of the drop-out in twentieth-century fiction. Maugham had been in contact with Aldous Huxley and Gerald Heard in California, and he had been on an extensive tour of India in 1936 (see his essay "The Saint," in *Points of View*), but for much of the plot he re-uses the story line of an unperformed and still unpublished play entitled "The Road Uphill."

Maugham was a much more effective satirist than he was a describer of religious experience, and the real triumph of *The Razor's Edge* is the preposterous figure of Elliott Templeton, the American "socialite" of the Riviera, with his indomitable snobbery and keen nose for a smart party. He stands alongside

Alroy Kear as one of Maugham's most brilliantly malicious achievements.

At the beginning of *Cakes and Ale* Maugham attempts to place himself in the literary world of pre-war England, intellectually dominated as it was by Bloomsbury. He once compared his own position with that of the Reverend George Crabbe, who persisted in his habit of writing narrative poems in rhymed couplets well into the heady, revolutionary romantic era of the young William Wordsworth. This is rather too flattering a comparison, but it may nonetheless help us to view Maugham in relation to his contemporaries. He was a literary conservative who believed in the power of linear narrative and descriptive realism at a time when other, greater, writers were breaking with this tradition. Although claiming to be no more than a mere entertainer, Maugham showed how much was worth conserving in the tradition.

SELECTED BIBLIOGRAPHY

I. BIBLIOGRAPHY. F. T. Bason, *A Bibliography of the Writings of W. Somerset Maugham* (London, 1931), with a preface by Maugham; K. W. Jonas, *Bibliography of the Writings of W. Somerset Maugham* (New Brunswick, N. J., 1950); R. T. Stott, *Maughamiana. The Writings of W. Somerset Maugham* (London, 1950), with an intro. by Stott; R. T. Stott, *The Writings of William Somerset Maugham* (London, 1956), a supp. (1961; rev. ed., 1973).

II. COLLECTED WORKS. *The Collected Plays*, 6 vols. (London, 1931–1934), in 3 vols. (London, 1952); *The Collected Edition*, 25 vols. (London, 1934–1959); *Altogether* (London, 1934), with a preface by Maugham and an appreciation by D. MacCarthy; *The Pocket Edition*, 14 vols. (London, 1936–1938); *The Complete Short Stories*, 3 vols. (London, 1951); *Collected Short Stories*, 4 vols. (London, 1975–1976).

III. SELECTED WORKS. *Six Comedies* (New York, 1937), contains *The Unattainable, Home and Beauty, The Circle, Our Betters, The Constant Wife,* and *The Breadwinners; The Round Dozen* (London, 1940), stories selected by Maugham; *Here and There* (London, 1948), stories that appeared in *Cosmopolitans, The Mixture as Before,* and *Creatures of Circumstance; The Selected Novels*, 3 vols. (London, 1953); *The Partial View* (London, 1954), contains *The Summing Up* and *A Writer's Notebook; The Travel Books* (London, 1955); *Selected Plays* (London, 1963), contains *Sheppey, The Sacred Flame, The Circle, The Constant Wife,* and *Our Betters; Selected Prefaces and Introductions* (London, 1964).

IV. SEPARATE WORKS. *Liza of Lambeth* (London, 1897), novel; *The Making of a Saint* (London, 1898), novel; *Orientations* (London, 1899), short stories.

The Hero (London, 1901), novel; *Mrs Craddock* (London, 1902; new, rev. ed., 1928), novel; *A Man of Honour. A Play in Four Acts* (London, 1903); *The Merry-Go-Round* (London, 1904), novel; *The Land of the Blessed Virgin: Sketches and Impressions in Andalusia* (London, 1905); *The Bishop's Apron: A Study in the Origins of a Great Family* (London, 1906), novel, founded on his play *Loaves and Fishes* (London, 1924); *Flirtation* (London, 1906), short story; *The Explorer* (London, 1908), novel; *The Magician* (London, 1908), novel.

Lady Frederick. A Comedy in Three Acts (London, 1912); *Jack Straw* (London, 1912), drama; *Mrs. Dot* (London, 1912), drama; *Penelope* (London, 1912), drama; *The Explorer* (London, 1912), drama; *The Tenth Man* (London, 1913), drama; *Landed Gentry* (London, 1913), drama; *Smith* (London, 1913), drama; *The Land of Promise. A Comedy in Four Acts* (London, 1913); *Of Human Bondage* (London, 1915; new ed., 1946); *The Moon and Sixpence* (London, 1919), novel.

The Unknown (London, 1920), drama; *The Trembling of a Leaf. Little Stories of the South Sea Islands* (London, 1921), also issued under titles *Sadie Thompson and Other Stories of the South Sea* (London, 1928) and *Rain and Other Stories of the South Sea Islands* (London, 1931); *The Circle. A Comedy in Three Acts* (London, 1921); *Caesar's Wife* (London, 1922), drama; *On a Chinese Screen* (London, 1922), travel and sketches; *East of Suez* (London, 1922), drama; *Our Betters. A Comedy in Three Acts* (London, 1923); *Home and Beauty. A Farce in Three Acts* (London, 1923); *The Unattainable. A Farce in Three Acts* (London, 1923); *Loaves and Fishes. A Comedy in Four Acts* (London, 1924); *The Painted Veil* (London, 1925), novel; *The Casuarina Tree* (London, 1926), short stories; *The Letter. A Play in Three Acts* (London, 1927); *The Sacred Flame. A Play in Three Acts* (London, 1928); *Ashenden; or, The British Agent* (London, 1928), short stories.

The Gentleman in the Parlour: A Record of a Journey from Rangoon to Haiphong (London, 1930); *Cakes and Ale; or, The Skeleton in the Cupboard* (London, 1930), novel; *The Breadwinner. A Comedy in One Act* (London, 1930); *Six Stories Written in the First Person Singular* (London, 1931); *For Services Rendered. A Play in Three Acts* (London, 1932); *The Book Bag* (Florence, 1932), short story, later included in *Ah King* (London, 1933); *The Narrow Corner* (London, 1932), novel; *Sheppey. A Play in Three Acts* (London, 1933); *Ah King* (London, 1933), short stories; *The Judgment Seat* (London, 1934), short story, later included in *Cosmopolitans* (London, 1936); *Don Fernando: or, Variations on Some Spanish Themes* (London, 1935, new, rev. ed., 1950), travel; *Cosmopolitans* (London, 1936), short stories; *My South Sea Island* (Chicago,

1936), essay; *Theatre* (London, 1937), novel; *The Summing Up* (London, 1938), autobiography; *Christmas Holiday* (London, 1939), novel.

Books and You (London, 1940), essays; *France at War* (London, 1940), essay; *The Mixture as Before* (London, 1940), short stories; *Up at the Villa* (London, 1941), novel; *Strictly Personal* (New York, 1941; London, 1942), autobiography; *The Hour Before the Dawn* (London, 1942), novel; *The Unconquered* (New York, 1944), short story, later repr. in *Creatures of Circumstance* (London, 1947); *The Razor's Edge* (London, 1944), novel; *Then and Now* (London, 1946), novel; *Creatures of Circumstance* (London, 1947), short stories; *Catalina. A Romance* (London, 1948), novel; *Quartet* (London, 1948), short stories, contains "The Facts of Life," The Alien Corn," "The Kite," and "The Colonel's Lady"; *A Writer's Notebook* (London, 1949), belles lettres.

Trio (London, 1950), short stories, contains "The Verger," "Mr. Know-All," and "Sanatorium"; *The Writer's Point of View* (London, 1951), lecture; *Encore* (London, 1952), short stories, contains "The Ant and the Grasshopper," "Winter Cruise," and "Gigolo and Gigolette"; *The Vagrant Mood* (London, 1952), essays; *A Choice of Kipling's Prose* (London, 1962), selected by Maugham, his intro. contains valuable observations on the short-story genre; *The Noble Spaniard* (London, 1953), drama, first produced in London in 1909; *Ten Novels and Their Authors* (London, 1954), criticism; *Points of View* (London, 1958), essays; *Purely for My Pleasure* (London, 1962), color plates of Maugham's pictures, with an account by him of how he came to buy them.

V. BIOGRAPHICAL AND CRITICAL STUDIES. C. H. Towne et al., *W. Somerset Maugham* (New York, 1925); P. Dottin, *W. Somerset Maugham et ses romans* (Paris, 1928); S. Guéry, *La Philosophie de Somerset Maugham* (Paris, 1933); D. MacCarthy, *William Somerset Maugham—The English Maupassant. An Appreciation* (London, 1934); C. S. McIver, *William Somerset Maugham. A Study of Technique and Literary Sources* (Upper Darby, Pa., 1936); R. H. Ward, *W. Somerset Maugham* (London, 1937); R. A. Cordell, *William Somerset Maugham* (Edinburgh, 1937; rev. ed., 1961); P. Dottin, *Le Théâtre de W. Somerset Maugham* (Paris, 1937); R. Aldington, *W. Somerset Maugham. An Appreciation* (New York, 1939); K. W. Jonas, ed., *The Maugham Enigma. An Anthology* (London, 1954); R. Mander and J. Mitchenson, *Theatrical Companion to Maugham* (London, 1955), with an appreciation by J. C. Trewin, a pictorial record of first performances of Maugham's plays; K. W. Jonas, ed., *The World of Somerset Maugham. An Anthology* (London, 1959); L. Brander, *Somerset Maugham* (London, 1963); R. Maugham, *Somerset and All the Maughams* (London, 1965); G. Karin, *Remembering Mr. Maugham* (London, 1966); A. Curtis, *The Pattern of Maugham* (London, 1974); F. Raphael, *Somerset Maugham and His World* (New York–London, 1977); A. Curtis, *Somerset Maugham* (London, 1977); R. Fisher, *Syrie Maugham* (London, 1978); T. Morgan, *Somerset Maugham* (London, 1980).

LIST OF SHORT STORIES AND SKETCHES

(The titles in italics refer to the volumes in which the stories appear. If a story is included in *The Complete Short Stories,* the appropriate volume number is given in parentheses.)

"Adios," *The Land of the Blessed Virgin;* "The Alcazar," *The Land of the Blessed Virgin;* "The Alhambra," *The Land of the Blessed Virgin;* "The Alien Corn," *First Person Singular, The Round Dozen, Quartet* (II); "The Altar of Heaven," *On a Chinese Screen;* "The Ant and the Grasshopper," *Cosmopolitans, Here and There, Encore* (I); "Appearance and Reality," *Creatures of Circumstance, Here and There* (I); "Arabesque," *On a Chinese Screen.*

"The Back of Beyond," *Ah King* (III); "Bad Example," *Orientations;* "The Beast of Burden," *On a Chinese Screen;* "Before the Bull-Fight," *The Land of the Blessed Virgin;* "Before the Party," *The Casuarina Tree* (I); "Behind the Scene," *Ashenden;* "Boabdil the Unlucky," *The Land of the Blessed Virgin;* "The Book Bag," *Ah King* (III); "The Bridge of Calahorra," *The Land of the Blessed Virgin;* "The Bunn," *Cosmopolitans* (II); "By the Road," *The Land of the Blessed Virgin.*

"The Cabinet Minister," *On a Chinese Screen;* "Cadiz," *The Land of the Blessed Virgin;* "Calle de las Sierpes," *The Land of the Blessed Virgin;* "A Casual Affair," *Creatures of Circumstance* (III); "The Cathedral of Seville," *The Land of the Blessed Virgin;* "A Chance Acquaintance," *Ashenden;* "Characteristics," *The Land of the Blessed Virgin;* "Choice of Amyntas," *Orientations;* "The Churches of Ronda," *The Land of the Blessed Virgin;* "A City Built on a Rock," *On a Chinese Screen;* "The Closed Shop," *Cosmopolitans* (II); "The Colonel's Lady," *Creatures of Circumstance, Quartet* (II); "The Consul," *On a Chinese Screen* (II); "Cordova," *The Land of the Blessed Virgin;* "Corrida des Toros," *The Land of the Blessed Virgin;* "The Court of Oranges," *The Land of the Blessed Virgin;* "The Creative Impulse," *First Person Singular, The Round Dozen* (II).

"Daisy," *Orientations;* "The Dance," *The Land of the Blessed Virgin;* "The Dark Woman," *Ashenden;* "Dawn," *On a Chinese Screen;* "De Amicitia," *Orientations;* "Democracy," *On a Chinese Screen;* "The Dining-Room," *On a Chinese Screen;* "Dinner Parties," *On a Chinese Screen;* "A Domiciliary Visit," *Ashenden;* "Don Juan Tenorio," *The Land of the Blessed Virgin;* "The Door of Opportunity," *Ah King, The Round Dozen* (III); "The Dream," *Cosmopolitans* (II); "Dr. MacAlister," *On a Chinese Screen.*

"Ecija," *The Land of the Blessed Virgin;* "El Genero

Chico," *The Land of the Blessed Virgin;* "The End of the Flight," *Cosmopolitans, Here and There* (III); "Envoi," *The Trembling of a Leaf;* "Episode," *Creatures of Circumstance, Here and There* (III); "The Escape," *Cosmopolitans* (I).

"The Facts of Life," *The Mixture as Before, Here and There, Quartet* (I); "Failure," *On a Chinese Screen;* "Faith," *Orientations;* "The Fall of Edward Barnard," *The Trembling of a Leaf* (I); "The Fannings," *On a Chinese Screen;* "Fear," *On a Chinese Screen;* "A Feast Day," *The Land of the Blessed Virgin;* "The Flip of a Coin," *Ashenden;* "Flotsam and Jetsam," *Creatures of Circumstance, Here and There* (I); "Footprint in the Jungle," *Ah King* (III); "The Force of Circumstances," *The Casuarina Tree, The Round Dozen* (I); "The Four Dutchmen," *Cosmopolitans* (III); "The Fragment," *On a Chinese Screen;* "French Joe," *Cosmopolitans* (II); "A Friend in Need," *Cosmopolitans* (II).

"A Game of Billiards," *On a Chinese Screen;* "Gaol," *The Land of the Blessed Virgin;* "German Harry," *Cosmopolitans* (III); "Gigolo and Gigolette," *The Mixture as Before, Here and There, Encore* (I); "The Giralda," *The Land of the Blessed Virgin;* "The Glory Hole," *On a Chinese Screen;* "God's Truth," *On a Chinese Screen;* "Granada," *The Land of the Blessed Virgin;* "The Grand Style," *On a Chinese Screen;* "The Greek," *Ashenden;* "Giulia Lazzari," *Ashenden* (II); "Gustav," *Ashenden.*

"The Hairless Mexican," *Ashenden* (II); "The Happy Couple," *Cosmopolitans, Here and There* (I); "The Happy Man," *Cosmopolitans, Here and There* (I); "Henderson," *On a Chinese Screen;* "Her Britannic Majesty's Representative," *On a Chinese Screen;* "His Excellency," *Ashenden* (II); "Home," *Cosmopolitans, Here and There* (I); "Honolulu," *The Trembling of a Leaf* (I); "The Hospital of Charity," *The Land of the Blessed Virgin;* "The Human Element," *First Person Singular* (II).

"In a Strange Land," *Cosmopolitans, Here and There* (II); "The Inn," *On a Chinese Screen.*

"Jane," *First Person Singular, The Round Dozen* (II); "The Judgment Seat," *Cosmopolitans* (I); "The Kite," *Creatures of Circumstance, Quartet* (III).

"The Last Chance," *On a Chinese Screen;* "The Letter," *The Casuarina Tree, The Round Dozen* (III); "A Libation to the Gods," *On a Chinese Screen;* "The Lights of the Town," *On a Chinese Screen;* "The Lion's Skin," *The Mixture as Before* (I); "Lord Mountdrago," *The Mixture as Before, Here and There* (II); "Los Pobres," *The Land of the Blessed Virgin;* "The Lotus Eater," *The Mixture as Before, Here and There* (III); "Louise," *Cosmopolitans, Here and There* (I); "Love and Russian Literature," *Ashenden;* "The Luncheon," *Cosmopolitans, Here and There* (I).

"A Man from Glasgow," *Creatures of Circumstance* (I); "A Man with a Conscience," *The Mixture as Before* (III); "The Man with the Scar," *Cosmopolitans, Here and There* (II); "A Marriage of Convenience" (III; see "The Wash-Tub"); "Masterson" (III); "Mayhew," *Cosmopolitans* (III);

"Medinat Az-Zahra," *The Land of the Blessed Virgin;* "Metempsychosis," *On a Chinese Screen;* "Mirage," *On a Chinese Screen* (III); "Miss King," *Ashenden* (II); "The Missionary Lady," *On a Chinese Screen;* "Mr. Harrington's Washing," *Ashenden, The Round Dozen* (II); "Mr. Know-All," *Cosmopolitans, Trio* (I); "The Mongol Chief," *On a Chinese Screen;* "The Mosque," *The Land of the Blessed Virgin;* "The Mother," *Creatures of Circumstance* (I); "My Lady's Parlour," *On a Chinese Screen.*

"Neil MacAdam," *Ah King, The Round Dozen* (III); "Nightfall," *On a Chinese Screen;* "The Normal Man," *On a Chinese Screen;* "The Nun," *On a Chinese Screen.*

"An Official Position," *The Mixture as Before, Here and There* (III); "The Old Timer," *On a Chinese Screen;* "On Horseback," *The Land of the Blessed Virgin;* "One of the Best," *On a Chinese Screen;* "The Opium Den," *On a Chinese Screen;* "The Outstation," *The Casuarina Tree, The Round Dozen* (III).

"The Pacific," *The Trembling of a Leaf;* "P. & O.," *The Casuarina Tree* (III); "Puerta del Puente," *The Land of the Blessed Virgin;* "The Philosopher," *On a Chinese Screen;* "The Picture," *On a Chinese Screen;* "The Plain," *On a Chinese Screen;* "The Poet," *Cosmopolitans* (I); "The Point of Honour," *On a Chinese Screen, Creatures of Circumstance* (I); "The Pool," *The Trembling of a Leaf* (I); "The Portrait of a Gentleman," *Cosmopolitans* (III); "Princess September," *Gentlemen in the Parlour* (III); "The Promise," *Cosmopolitans* (I); "The Punctiliousness of Don Sebastian," *Orientations;* "The Question," *On a Chinese Screen.*

"'R,'" *Ashenden;* "Rain," *The Trembling of a Leaf, The Round Dozen* (I); "Raw Material," *Cosmopolitans* (III); "Red," *The Trembling of a Leaf* (III); "The Rising of the Curtain," *On a Chinese Screen;* "Romance," *On a Chinese Screen;* "The Rolling Stone," *On a Chinese Screen;* "Romance," *On a Chinese Screen;* "The Romantic Young Lady," *Creatures of Circumstance* (I); "Ronda," *The Land of the Blessed Virgin;* "The Round Dozen," *First Person Singular, The Round Dozen* (II).

"Salvatore," *Cosmopolitans, Here and There* (III); "Sanatorium," *Creatures of Circumstance, Here and There, Trio* (II); "The Sea-Dog," *On a Chinese Screen;* "The Servants of God," *On a Chinese Screen;* "The Seventh Day Adventist," *On a Chinese Screen;* "Seville," *The Land of the Blessed Virgin;* "The Sinologue," *On a Chinese Screen;* "The Skipper," *On a Chinese Screen;* "The Social Sense," *Cosmopolitans, Here and There* (II); "The Song," *The Land of the Blessed Virgin;* "The Song of the River," *On a Chinese Screen;* "The Spirit of Andalusia," *The Land of the Blessed Virgin;* "Straight Flush," *Cosmopolitans* (III); "The Stranger," *On a Chinese Screen;* "A String of Beads," *Cosmopolitans, Here and There* (I); "The Stripling," *On a Chinese Screen;* "A Student of Drama," *On a Chinese Screen;* "Sullivan," *On a Chinese Screen;* "The Swineherd," *The Land of the Blessed Virgin.*

"The Taipan," *On a Chinese Screen;* "The Three Fat

Women of Antibes," *The Mixture as Before, Here and There* (I); "The Traitor," *Ashenden* (II); "The Treasure," *The Mixture as Before* (II); "A Trip to Paris," *Ashenden*; "Two Villages," *The Land of the Blessed Virgin*; "The Unconquered," *Creatures of Circumstance, Here and There* (I).

"The Verger," *Cosmopolitans, Here and There, Trio* (II); "The Vessel of Wrath," *Ah King, The Round Dozen* (I); "The Vice-Consul," *On a Chinese Screen*; "Virtue," *First Person Singular* (II); "The Voice of the Turtle," *The Mixture as Before* (I).

"The Wash-Tub," *Cosmopolitans* (appears in III as "A Marriage of Convenience"); "Wind and Storm," *The Land of the Blessed Virgin*; "Winter Cruise," *Creatures of Circumstance, Here and There, Encore* (III); "A Woman of Fifty," *Creatures of Circumstance* (III); "Women of Andalusia," *The Land of the Blessed Virgin*; "The Yellow Streak," *The Casuarina Tree* (I).

G. M. TREVELYAN
(1876-1962)

J. H. Plumb

GEORGE MACAULAY TREVELYAN was the heir of a great tradition. His great-uncle was Thomas Babington Macaulay, who, with Edward Gibbon, is the chief glory of English historical writing. His father, Sir George Otto Trevelyan, was also a historian of great distinction, a most important figure in the development of Anglo-American understanding, for his great work on the American Revolution did much to dispel ancient prejudice. With this inheritance it is not surprising that G. M. Trevelyan had a high sense of the duty of a historian. For him the writing of history, like the writing of poetry, was but a part of English culture, a culture not limited to the few but available to all men, so that it might deepen their understanding. History, for him, had a literary and moral purpose. His inheritance made this attitude clear enough to himself, but it required an obstinate courage to maintain it, for the view was no longer fashionable among academic historians. They preferred to treat history as a science, to concentrate on evidence, techniques, statistics; and if the public found the results unreadable that did not matter, for history was a specialized study by professionals for professionals. In the face of such opposition, Trevelyan had to define and defend his attitude, and this he did in his volumes of essays, *Clio: A Muse* (1913) and *An Autobiography and Other Essays* (1949). For anyone wishing to study the whole of Trevelyan's works, these books should be read first and be followed by *Sir George Otto Trevelyan: A Memoir* (1932), *The Poetry and Philosophy of George Meredith* (1906), the biography *Grey of Fallodon* (1937), and the delightful little history *Trinity College* (1943), for these make clear his personal inheritance, the background of tradition that fed that rare poetic imagination, perhaps his greatest gift.

I

IN his *Autobiography*, written in the evening of his life, Trevelyan explained:

More generally, I take delight in history, even its most prosaic details, because they become poetical as they recede into the past. The poetry of history lies in the quasi-miraculous fact that once, on this earth, once, on this familiar spot of ground, walked other men and women, as actual as we are today, thinking their own thoughts, swayed by their own passions, but now all gone, one generation vanishing after another, gone as utterly as we ourselves shall shortly be gone like ghost at cock-crow.

He made the same moving affirmation when he became regius professor of modern history at Cambridge in 1927:

The appeal of history to us all is in the last analysis poetic. But the poetry of history does not consist of imagination roaming at large, but of imagination pursuing the fact and fastening upon it. That which compels the historian to "scorn delights and live laborious days" is the ardour of his own curiosity to know what really happened long ago in that land of mystery which we call the past. To peer into that magic mirror and see fresh figures there every day is a burning desire that consumes and satisfies him all his life, that carries him each morning, eager as a lover, to the library and the muniment room. It haunts him like a passion of almost terrible potency, because it is poetic. The dead were and are not. Their place knows them no more and is ours to-day. Yet they were once as real as we, and we shall tomorrow be shadows like them.
(The Present Position of History)

There is one beautiful example of "imagination pursuing the fact and fastening upon it" in his own early work *Clio: A Muse,* which illustrates how much his poetic imagination, blended with such wide-ranging human sympathy, was stirred by the visible memorials of a past time.

The garden front of St. John's, Oxford, is beautiful to everyone; but for the lover of history, its outward charm is blent with the intimate feelings of his own mind, with images of that College as it was during the great Civil War.

383

Given over to the use of a Court whose days of royalty were numbered, its walks and quadrangles were filled, as the end came near, with men and women learning to accept sorrow as their lot through life, the ambitious abandoning hope of power, the wealthy hardening themselves to embrace poverty, those who loved England preparing to sail for foreign shores, and lovers to be parted forever. There they strolled through the garden, as the hopeless evenings fell, listening, at the end of all, while the siege-guns broke the silence with ominous iteration. Behind the cannon on those low hills to northward were ranked the inexorable men who came to lay their hands on all this beauty, hoping to change it to strength and sterner virtue. . . . The sound of the Roundhead cannon has long ago died away, but still the silence of the garden is heavy with unalterable fate, brooding over besiegers and besieged. . . .

This has an incomparable beauty of tone. Having read such words as these, who could doubt that here was a great artist at work, at work in a medium, the writing of history, in which scholars have been plentiful and artists rare. But why did Trevelyan choose to use his gifts of imagination in history rather than in poetry? The answer to this question is manifold, but one overwhelming reason cries aloud in the three quotations given above, that is, his preoccupation with time. Many artists—William Wordsworth and Marcel Proust immediately spring to mind—have been deeply moved, one might almost say that their art has been controlled, by the sense of the loss involved in the nature of time. But nowhere more than in the study of history is the artist so acutely aware of the tragedy of man caught inexorably in the temporal world of flesh. Each historical fact is implicit with our doom, as the long story of man's achievement is our one straw of hope. And this contrast is made keener for a historian unable to accept the fact of personal immortality as he looks back over the countless lives, as numberless as the sands of the sea, that go to make our story.

Those wide Border lands in which Trevelyan grew to manhood—there were the lasting physical memorials of unknown men that haunted him with their sense of destiny. The walls and forts of the Romans, the villages of Saxon and of Dane, the ruined abbeys and peel towers, the battlefields with their forgotten dead—these to Trevelyan were what the lakes and the woods and the trees were to Wordsworth: the symbols of man's tragedy and hope.[1]

The circumstances of Trevelyan's life did much to strengthen this feeling for the passing of time, just as the social and cultural interests of his family had their say in directing his historical interests. Trevelyan was born in 1876. His family background was both aristocratic and upper middle class. His father's family could trace their ancestry back through the centuries, from Northumberland to Somerset, from Somerset to Cornwall, a long line of typical English gentry, never of national distinction but playing their part in the local affairs of their day. His grandfather, a successful Indian civil servant, married Macaulay's sister, who introduced the atmosphere of middle-class culture, with its piety and its liberal views on politics and society. Trevelyan's father knew the great figures of Victorian civilization intimately, at the same time that he was accepted as a member of aristocratic society.[2] His marriage with Caroline Philips, daughter of a Manchester merchant, free-trader, Unitarian, friend of the economist Richard Cobden and of the statesman Herbert Gladstone, strengthened the family ties with both liberalism and the middle class. And so Trevelyan grew up amid all that was best in the late Victorian world of art and politics, imbibing its liberalism, its free-thinking, and its culture, to which his own nature was so responsive. The background to his life were the country houses of an earlier age, particularly Wallington Hall, the great house in Northumberland that his father inherited in 1886. Here he was able to savor that stable English country life that had endured for centuries.

Time has not been kind to this early world of Trevelyan's. Of the great houses in which he lived as a boy, Welcombe, his mother's house near Stratford-upon-Avon, is a British Railways hotel, and Wallington Hall has been given to the National Trust, of which he himself was an ardent supporter and a munificent benefactor. The trust has helped to preserve many of the great houses of England and much of the loveliness of the wilder countryside of cliff and fell that meant so much to him. But far more has been lost, and now the pace has accelerated. In another generation the civilization that Trevelyan knew as a young man will have passed, and then his occasional works, his essays, memoirs, and biographies of his friends, will not only help readers to understand his own works but also have great value as historical documents in their own right. Yet one cannot doubt

[1] See "The Middle Marches," in *Clio: A Muse*.

[2] Not the same, as Trevelyan is careful to stress in his admirable memoir of his father.

that the passing of this world, of which he was intensely aware, gave a keener edge to his preoccupation with history, particularly with those aspects of nineteenth-century English history that are linked with his own and his parents' past.

Trevelyan's education was the same as that of any rich young man of his day—preparatory school in Berkshire, Harrow, and then Trinity College, Cambridge—but of course with him it was more formative. His interest in history had developed very early, particularly in military history. At Harrow he was exceptionally fortunate in his history masters, Robert Somervell and George Townsend Warner. Somervell had a rare gift of teaching boys to write well, and Townsend Warner was a scholar of distinction.[3] As a freshman at Cambridge he fell under the spell of Frederic Maitland, the great English medieval and legal historian, of William Cunningham, who was founding the study of economic history, and of John Acton, one of the greatest Catholic historians of modern times, whose learning and wisdom were unrivaled. But he fell afoul of John Seeley, Acton's predecessor in the regius chair of history. Seeley was an ardent champion of scientific history and loved to denounce Macaulay and Thomas Carlyle; to the one Trevelyan had his family loyalty and the other had illuminated his first year's work at Cambridge. Ever after he was a devoted admirer of the superb imaginative quality of Carlyle's work, especially *Oliver Cromwell's Letters and Speeches* and *The French Revolution.*

Naturally, with his background, Trevelyan was drawn to the liberal intelligentsia, and he became a friend of Bertrand Russell, Desmond MacCarthy, and G. E. Moore. Many young men at the university reject the beliefs in which they were nurtured, but the circles in which Trevelyan mixed at Trinity helped to strengthen the liberal attitude to life that he had derived from his family. This attitude was essentially Protestant, infused as it was with a strong skepticism of all doctrinaire beliefs, in either religion or politics. When Trevelyan came to start historical research it was natural that his interest should be aroused in a historical movement deeply concerned with the belief in individual freedom. His imagination was caught by the Lollards, by the Peasants' Revolt, by the first stirrings of national consciousness in En-

gland. It was this work that won for him the fellowship at Trinity: it was published in 1899 with the title *England in the Age of Wycliffe,* and in the same year he issued with Edgar Powell a collection of documents that he had used as evidence and that he thought deserved a wider currency.

England in the Age of Wycliffe achieved immediate success, and it has enjoyed a continuing popularity, having been reprinted fourteen times. It was an astonishing achievement for so young a man. Many of the views, especially on economic and legal matters, would now require modification; about the whole work there is a slight but definitely archaic air, probably derived from its militant anti-Romanism. It is very well written—even as early as this Trevelyan's style was completely under his control, and what a marvelously flexible instrument it is. The narrative moves with exceptional speed; his descriptive passages evoke the dark and the light of Chaucer's England; the analysis of social causes and human motives is crisp and clear. The book has a pace and élan that will carry it on through many editions yet to come. Although there is a marked bias toward Lollardy and its protest for freedom of thought, Trevelyan's historical judgment is never darkened by prejudice, and the facts, truly ascertained, are made to give their own evidence. Even more remarkable are the skill with which Trevelyan uses narrative writing and his capacity to reveal motive by the description of events. In this way the reader is made aware of why these conflicts and battles took place without the tedium of detailed analysis. Remarkable, too, is the certainty of both the writing and the convictions of the author. In his work there is the steady affirmation of a faith that would last a lifetime, whatever time brought forth, for it was a faith begot by inheritance and by tradition, and it is made explicit in the closing words of the book.

In England we have slowly but surely won the right of the individual to form and express a private judgment on speculative questions. During the last three centuries the battle of liberty has been fought against the State or against public opinion. But before the changes effected by Henry the Eighth, the struggle was against a power more impervious to reason and less subject to change—the power of the Medieval Church in all the prestige of a thousand years' prescriptive right over man's mind. The martyrs who bore the first brunt of that terrific combat may be lightly esteemed to-day by priestly censure. But those who still believe that liberty of thought has proved not a curse but a blessing to England and to the peoples that have sprung

---

[3] Winston Churchill said that Somervell taught him his mastery of English. To have helped produce two such masters of our language as Churchill and Trevelyan is indeed a claim to fame.

from her, will regard with thankfulness and pride the work which the speculations of Wycliffe set on foot and the valour of his devoted successors accomplished.

II

FOR his work on the age of Wycliffe, Trevelyan had been awarded a fellowship at Trinity in 1898, and a straightforward career as a professional academic historian was open to him. He began to teach for his college; he started to lecture. He had accepted the offer of a publisher, Methuen, to write a textbook on Stuart history as one of their series on the history of England. These were all easily recognized stages in the making of a don. Then suddenly he left Cambridge. The reason he gives in his *Autobiography* is that he knew that he wanted to write literary history and that "I should do so in more spiritual freedom away from the critical atmosphere of Cambridge scholarship." The artist in him had dominated and instinctively bolted from an uncongenial world, although to the outsider it must have seemed a curiously willful gesture for a young professional historian to desert the citadel of his profession.

In the event, Trevelyan's decision was fully justified. His output has been far greater than that of the majority of his generation because he was able to avoid the time-consuming hack work of academic life—the endless supervisions and lectures and examinations. But more important, he escaped from the withering atmosphere of hypercritical scholasticism that has grown stronger and more powerful in Cambridge during the twentieth century. The fine points of argumentative scholarship exercised with equal zest on the important and the trivial had no fascination for Trevelyan, and he had an even stronger distaste for the shifting quicksand of historical abstraction. Again, the fields of history upon which Cambridge historians were concentrating—economic, diplomatic, constitutional—were fields that offered little attraction to Trevelyan. They lacked story; they lacked drama; they lacked the warmth of human life. Because of these things, the artist insisted on escape.[4]

---

[4]Of course, Trevelyan was a young man of means and could afford to quit an assured position. In any case he could easily have maintained himself by his writing, but whether the choice would have been so easy had he been without private means is an interesting speculation.

Away from the inhibiting influence of Cambridge, Trevelyan produced a book of outstanding quality. His *England Under the Stuarts* (1904) was far and away the most impressive volume in the series published by Methuen. When the others have been forgotten, it will still be read, for it may be generations before the most dramatic century in English history is so finely portrayed between the covers of a single book. The advance on his first book is obvious but remarkable. The nineteenth century had been profoundly interested in the struggle between Crown and Parliament, for the feeling was that the triumph of Parliament had made democracy in England possible. Nor were the Victorians dismayed by the intensely biblical language of Puritan thought and action, for the middle classes of the nineteenth century were equally capable of testing political issues by religious principles and expressing themselves with force in Old Testament terms. Nevertheless, the old Whig attitude of seeing Charles and his cavaliers as dissolute despots and Cromwell and the Roundheads as apostles of liberty had mellowed by Trevelyan's day. It was fashionable to be more than scrupulously fair to opponents in debate, and, in consequence, although Trevelyan was, in his final reckoning, on the side of the Roundheads, his sympathies do not at any point in his book inhibit his imaginative insight. In many ways it has remained the least biased summary of the seventeenth century, for the twentieth century has witnessed the development of a concealed apologia for the Stuarts under the cloak of a more exact scholarship. The same movement has sought to denigrate Cromwell as the prototype of a fascist dictator because of his grave failure to secure constitutional government and his resort to force—for neither of which is he spared by Trevelyan. These Tory historians—as dangerous as their Whig counterparts—should read and reread Trevelyan's magnificent paragraphs on the execution of Charles I, which must be quoted in full, for they demonstrate one of his greatest virtues as a historian.

If there was any chance that the establishment of a more democratic form of government could gradually win the support of the people at large, that chance was thrown away by the execution of the King. The deed was done against the wish of many even of the Independents and Republicans; it outraged beyond hope of reconciliation the two parties in the State who were strong in numbers and in conservative tradition, the Presbyterians and the Cavaliers; and it alienated the great mass of men who had no party at all. Thus the Republicans, at the outset of their career, made it impossible for themselves ever to appeal in free election to the people whom they had called to sovereignty. Their own fall, involving the fall of democracy and of religious toleration, became therefore necessary to the re-establishment of Parliamentary rule. The worship of birth, of pageantry, of title; the aristocratic claim to administrative power; the excessive influence of the large land-owner and of inherited wealth; the mean admiration of mean things, which became so powerful in English society after the Restoration—all these gained a fresh life and popularity by the deed that was meant to strike them dead for ever.

It is much easier to show that the execution was a mistake than to show what else should have been done. Any other course, if considered in the light of the actual circumstances, seems open to the gravest objection. It is not possible to say with certainty that if Charles' life had been spared Cromwell could have succeeded in averting anarchy and the disruption of the empire until opinion was again ripe for government by consent.

> This was that memorable hour
> Which first assured the forcéd power:—

—that was the verdict on the King's execution privately passed by Cromwell's secretary, Andrew Marvell, a man of the world if a poet ever was such, who in the same poem wrote the lines we all still quote in praise of Charles' conduct on the scaffold. The situation at the end of 1648 was this—that any sort of government by consent had been rendered impossible for years to come, mainly by the untrustworthy character of the King, and by the intolerant action of Parliament after the victory won for it by the Army. Cromwell, in the Heads of the Proposals, had advocated a real settlement by consent, only to have it rejected by King, Parliament and Army alike. The situation had thereby been rendered impossible, through no fault of his. But he was not the man therefore to return to his private gardens and let the world go to ruin. He took upon his massive shoulders the load of obloquy inherent in a situation created chiefly by the faults of others. Those Herculean shoulders are broad enough to bear also the blame for a deed pre-eminently his own, inscribed like a gigantic note of interrogation across the page of English history.

(England Under the Stuarts, ch. 9)

This is a complete realization of all that is important in a historical incident of profound significance, beautifully and confidently expressed. And the book abounds in similar passages.

Along with a deepening historical judgment, there was a growth in craftsmanship. In his earlier book, Trevelyan had been most humanly tempted to spend many pages on those aspects of his subject that contained a deeply personal interest, but *England Under the Stuarts* witnesses a more rigorous personal discipline. Military and social history are kept firmly, at times almost too firmly,[5] in their place and never allowed to clog the narrative, which moves at a furious pace; surely no textbook has ever before or since been written with such gusto. Although the general reading public gave the book an ardent reception, the professional historians received it rather coldly. It was considered worthy of only a short notice in the *English Historical Review*, and the space was largely devoted to a consideration of Sir Charles Oman's preface—only ten lines being given to the book itself. The reviewer, C. Sandford Terry (whoever he may have been), thought the chapter mottoes platitudinous and the success of the book questionable,[6] so great had become the gulf between professional and literary history. But Trevelyan had no cause to complain, for this book fully justified his decision to break with academic life.

In the same year as the publication of *England Under the Stuarts*, there took place what he described as "the most important and fortunate event of my life"—his marriage to Janet Penrose, a daughter of Mrs. Humphry Ward, the novelist and social worker. Among the wedding presents was a collection of books on Italian history, including Giuseppe Garibaldi's *Memoirs* and Belluzzi's *Ritirata di Garibaldi da Roma nel 1849* (*Garibaldi's Retreat from Rome in 1849*).

Immediately the creative artist in Trevelyan saw the story of Garibaldi as a subject that exactly fitted his genius. It touched some of the deepest springs of his nature, and the work and study necessary for the undertaking could be woven into the fabric of his personal life, for his wife had a passion for things Italian perhaps even keener than her husband's. From a public point of view the choice could not have been more judicious had it been made by a sophisticated journalist in search of a best-seller. The year in which Trevelyan wrote *Garibaldi's Defence of the Roman Republic* was 1906, and it was published in 1907. These were the years of the greatest liberal victory in English politics for a generation. The intellectual world responded to the optimism of the politicians. Here was the manifest triumph of that long nineteenth-century tradition of liberal humanism; the final defeat of obscurantism was at hand. It was one of those rare moments in history in

---

[5] The battle of Dunbar is dealt with in five lines.
[6] *English Historical Review* 20: 403–404 (1904).

which the atmosphere of life is lyrical and charged with hope, when man seems his own master and his destiny secure. Trevelyan's personal life was completely in tune with the world at large. Newly married, father of a son and heir,[7] an established success in his chosen career in which risks had been taken and justified, he too was enjoying a time of hope.

The Garibaldi story fitted these moods. The struggles, defeats, and ultimate success of Italian liberalism in the nineteenth century had seemed to many Victorians a demonstration by Providence of the justice of their attitude to life and of its capacity to save other nations from spiritual and political obscurantism. Again, it was heroic, and personally heroic. It did not seem to be the long culmination of an anonymous historical process but the dramatic act of individual men, and of those Garibaldi was the greatest. Hence a consideration of the story of his achievement did not appear to disturb historical truth. For Trevelyan personally it touched perhaps deeper springs, not only of his mind but of his heart, for within the Garibaldi story there was one of the world's great love stories—the passionate and tragic love of Anita.

As with many great historians, Trevelyan had a very strongly developed topographical sense. The very act of standing on the battlefield of Blenheim or on the heights of the Janiculum, where Garibaldi conducted his defense, released the springs of his historical imagination. It would have been impossible for him to write well about any historical events of whose setting he was ignorant. It was necessary for him to walk over and to see, to experience with all of his senses, the locality of history. And this he had already done for Italy, as he tells us in his *Autobiography:*

But eight years went by before I ever thought of writing on any Italian theme, although during those years my chief walking-grounds were the Tuscan and Umbrian hills, and the Alban and Sabine heights that look down on the Campagna of Rome. I kept the high ground as much as I could, with the help of ordnance map and compass. I used to prolong my walks till late into the charmed Italian night, under those brilliant stars, known and named so long ago; at the right time of year I could walk after dark, mile after mile, to the continuous song of innumerable nightingales.

So the topographical setting for his Garibaldi was, when he came to write it, as well known to him as the wide Border lands of Northumberland. All was prepared—his love of nature, his personal romance, his beliefs and attitude to life, all were pointing to Italy and to Garibaldi; but it needed that chance wedding present to release the springs of imagination. He wrote:

I began one day to turn over their pages and was suddenly enthralled by the story of the retreat from Rome to the Adriatic, over mountains which I had traversed in my solitary walks: the scene and spirit of that desperate venture, led by that unique man, flashed upon my mind's eye. Here was a subject made to my hand, if ever I could write "literary history," this was the golden chance.

Just as he had been unconsciously prepared to write it, so the public had been unconsciously prepared to receive it.[8] It established Trevelyan, and rightly so, as the foremost historian of his generation. It is a wonderful book, and it is a miracle that all the detailed work and the writing could have been accomplished in twelve months, yet the pace with which it was done adds undoubtedly to its quality. Had the writing been prolonged it is unlikely that the note of intense lyricism could have been sustained, for in many ways it is the most poetic of Trevelyan's longer works, certainly the most completely so. Apart from the beauty of the writing, its greatest strength lies in the handling of the narrative. This dramatic and exciting story has enthralled, and will continue to enthrall, generations of readers, yet never once is historical accuracy sacrificed for the sake of literary effect. In his characters, too, Trevelyan was fortunate; both Garibaldi and Anita were simple, direct, lacking in psychological subtlety and complication: a man and a woman of epic quality. Their thought was action and their action thought. Their words expressed, and never attempted to conceal, their response to life. With them Trevelyan seems to have felt a kinship of spirit, and he was able to re-create not only the history of their deeds but also the warm human reality of their lives.

The reception of *Garibaldi's Defence of the Roman Republic* was so enthusiastic that it was impossible for Trevelyan to leave the rest of the story of the Risorgimento untold even if he had wished to do so. *Garibaldi and the Thousand* was published in 1909, and two years later he completed the trilogy with *Garibaldi and the Making of Italy.* He had not,

---

[7]Theodore Macaulay Trevelyan, who tragically died in 1911, aged five.

[8]What Italy meant to men of culture in the nineteenth century is described by Trevelyan himself in his essay "Englishmen and Italians," published in *Clio: A Muse.*

however, finished with Italy, for he spent the years of World War I as the commandant of the British Red Cross Ambulance Unit and worked with the Italian army on the Isonzo and Piave fronts from 1915 to the end of the war. He summarized his experiences of these years in *Scenes from Italy's War*, published in 1919, which proves one thing—if nothing else—that great as Trevelyan was as a historian he would have found it difficult to earn a living as a journalist. The book is fascinating to read because of its singular lack of merit: history-in-the-making failed to quicken his imagination.

He wrote his last book on Italian history in 1922, *Manin and the Venetian Revolution of 1848* (published 1923), the result of many visits to Venice and of contacts with Venetian intellectuals during his war service. It gave him great pleasure to write, but the public received it with less enthusiasm, and, I think, rightly so, for the intricacy of Venetian politics and society, twisted and encrusted with traditional and personal attitudes, and, moreover, a society as far gone in decay as it was developed in sophistication, was not a world for the great simplicities of Trevelyan's heart and mind.

But to return to the Garibaldi books: they have weathered the years remarkably well, and they have achieved a permanent position in the historical literature of the world. In my estimation, they rank with the works of William Prescott and Francis Parkman; in fact, with the world's best narrative histories. They have, of course, their weaknesses: the motivation of nationalism is largely unexplored, especially the economic and social causes; the papacy and papal policy, as well as the motives of Louis Napoleon and the French, are judged too harshly; the self-interest of British policy is too consistently ignored. Yet for many years it remained the best and the least-biased account of the Risorgimento in any language, and it was acclaimed by a generation of Italian scholars for whom the movement for Italian liberation was too recent and too political to allow such an objective attitude as Trevelyan maintained. In many ways, these three books are the highest achievement of Trevelyan: never again were his theme and his imagination so completely fused. But as long as English literature is read, these works will remain a contribution of outstanding worth to historical scholarship. As darkness rolls over the world, this evocation of liberal idealism and hope, one of the greatest contributions of nineteenth-century Europe to the world, may acquire the stature and the significance of a saga.

III

TREVELYAN was now established as the foremost literary historian of his time, and naturally as soon as the war was over he was eager to return to his study; but it was less easy to find a theme that matched his gifts as absolutely as the Italian books. Like many writers of great natural creative power he was always wary of themes that failed to touch the deepest springs of his own experience. Through his mother's family he was connected with the great movement for free trade, associated with Manchester, of the mid-nineteenth century; and before World War I he had written *The Life of John Bright* (1913). It was not favorably received, and nowadays it comes in for little notice and less reading. The weaknesses are obvious, and Trevelyan himself was conscious of them: he did less than justice to the opponents of Bright, and the complexity of the political difficulties that faced Robert Peel are simplified to Peel's disadvantage. Yet the book has a very real and positive value that far outweighs these shortcomings. His grandfather had been a friend of Cobden and Bright's, and he had acquired from him and his mother an understanding of the rugged moral power of the great nineteenth-century liberals. In the re-creation of the past it is essential for the historian to recapture the conscious aspirations of men and to do full justice to their ideals as well as to lay bare whatever unconscious grasp they may have had of the purpose and destiny of the social class to which they happened to belong. And this Trevelyan achieves. It should never be ignored by anyone wishing to understand the power and force of the Manchester School.

His next choice was less happy: *Lord Grey of the Reform Bill* (1920). "The theme of glorious summer (in this case the summer of Reform) coming after a long winter of discontent and repression, is, as I have said, congenial to my artistic sense. And then the background of Grey's life was my own—Northumberland." But here his local, political, and personal loyalties, his instinctively Whig attitude to life and history, got in his way, made him visualize too clearly and too simply issues that were dark and involved. The intricate interplay of social dynamics and political activity of which, at times, politicians are the ignorant marionettes was not a field for the exercise of his talents. He was too consciously aware of the final achievement of Victorian constitutional development to appreciate fully the desperate insecurity and the sharp revolutionary edge of these years; and this achievement prevented him from seeing the Reform Bill for what it was, a rapid and instinctively cunning readjustment to new conditions by those selfsame social classes that had dominated eighteenth-century politics and were to dominate English political life until the introduction of the ballot box. The real difficulty lay in this: that neither personalities nor the detailed narrative story were the crux of the historical situation; its reality lay outside formal politics and within the strained structure of society, and massive sociological research has been required to reveal it. And much remains to be done. Because of this, *Lord Grey of the Reform Bill* has become outmoded, a fate that has not overtaken any other of Trevelyan's books.

The early twenties must have been a difficult period for Trevelyan. His last three books, judged by the high standard of success of his Garibaldi trilogy or even of *England Under the Stuarts*, had been failures. No theme had captured his imagination in the same way. Much of his creative energy was being absorbed in public work; he was a member of the Royal Commission on Oxford and Cambridge and a strenuously active supporter of the National Trust. The writing of *The Life of John Bright* before World War I and of *Lord Grey* after it had entailed a great deal of work and thought on the whole range of nineteenth-century history that, no doubt, like all good artists, Trevelyan thought it a pity to waste. Whatever the reason may have been, *British History in the Nineteenth Century* appeared in 1922. It was avowedly a textbook—in many ways far more of a textbook than *England Under the Stuarts*—but its success was great. A well-balanced, well-constructed, comprehensive book, even in texture, beautifully written, it became the staff of life for generations of adolescent historians bent on examination success. And for the general reader as well as for the student it remains the best introduction to nineteenth-century British history, weak though it certainly is on the economic side, to which very little space is devoted. But the importance of the book lay not entirely in itself but in the idea it gave to both Trevelyan and his publishers: its success showed that it filled a real need. There was a greater: no comprehensive, single-volume *History of England* of any merit had been published for over fifty years, since J. R. Green had written his *Short History of the English People* (1874), and it remained for Trevelyan to fill the gap.

This venture entailed an immense amount of work, intensive reading in fields with which he had little acquaintance; and the book took three years to write. Trevelyan's own comment in his *Autobiography* on this really great achievement is almost absurdly modest.

> In April 1926 my *History of England* came out. It has been, as regards sales, the most successful of my books, except the *Social History*, because it treated so necessary a subject as the history of England at the length, and to some extent in the manner, which suited a large public, including schools and Universities. Some day, very soon perhaps, it will be replaced, but it will have served its generation.

Not only has it served its generation, there is no doubt that it will outlast it, and many more, taking its place by the side of J. R. Green's masterpiece. Let us admit its faults at once. Too little space is devoted to the development of industry, trade, and finance; it has—although one might almost say "Thank God!"—a bias: it is frankly liberal and Protestant. The archaeologists might grumble a little at the brevity of its prehistory; specialists can no doubt attack it on points of detail; yet what a massive achievement remains. Within seven hundred pages the story of the English people is told with an unmatched verve and gusto; rarely has the craft of narrative been so brilliantly sustained. Its judgments on men and affairs glitter with wisdom. Once more the deepest springs of Trevelyan's creative imagination had been released by the story of the people to which he belonged and of the countryside he so deeply loved, and in which—and this is important—he had faith. For this book could only have been written by a liberal and a humanist.

Conscious though he was of the disastrous weakness of men confronted by the problem of their own destiny, he was never without hope.[9] This enabled him to give full and true value to the positive contributions of Englishmen to civilization and to do full justice to the aspirational side of their endeavors. His book glows with human warmth, and some of the best chapters are those in which he re-creates the

---

[9] Compare *An Autobiography* (1949): "I used to look askance at Gibbon's dreadful saying that history is 'little more than the register of the crimes, follies, and misfortunes of mankind' [*Decline and Fall*, ch. 4]. Nor do I even now wholly subscribe to it. But the war of 1914–18 enlarged and saddened my mind, and prepared me to write English history with a more realistic and a less partisan outlook. Yet, even after that war, the Reign of Queen Anne and the History of England up to the end of Victoria's reign, still seemed to me, when I came to write them, to be stories of happy endings" (p. 34). This, too, was written in 1949.

world of ordinary men and women, the medieval peasants, the Tudor yeomen, the Hanoverian squires, the working men of Victorian England, all nameless now and forgotten.

But the *History of England* has a social as well as an intrinsic worth. Millions of Englishmen have derived from this book the little history that they will ever know.[10] Hence the importance of Trevelyan's attitude and beliefs. He wrote in his introduction to the book: "In answer to the instincts and temperament of her people, she evolved in the course of centuries a system which reconciled three things that other nations have often found incompatible—executive efficiency, popular control, and personal freedom."

It is his stress on these qualities, as well as on the material and spiritual contribution of Englishmen, that gives the book such enduring worth. He lays bare the common ground of tradition, possessed by rich and poor alike, and fortifies their belief in their way of life, which is today so desperately challenged. And it is well that this should be liberal and humanist, stressing the genius of the English for compromise, tolerance, social justice, and freedom of the spirit. Yet he did not gloss the lapses. The brutality of Irish policy is not ignored, nor is the human suffering entailed in the Industrial Revolution left undescribed. This wise, just book would by itself have secured Trevelyan's place in the great tradition of English historical writing.

IV

AFTER the publication of the *History of England*, the circumstances of Trevelyan's life changed once more. In 1928 his parents died. He inherited Wallington Hall in Northumberland from a distant relative; and Stanley Baldwin had offered him the regius professorship of modern history at Cambridge, which he accepted in 1927. Many honors quickly followed, but none gave him greater pleasure than the conferment of the Order of Merit in 1930, a distinction his father had held before him. The return of Trevelyan to academic life did not mean, however, a return to the academic chores from which he had escaped a quarter of a century before, for the duties

of administration and lecturing of a professor are not onerous and rightly allow plenty of time for creative work; and, although there was still a powerful atmosphere of destructive criticism abroad in Cambridge, his confidence in his own abilities was now unassailable.[11] And the third phase of Trevelyan's historical writing began—his great three-volume book on the reign of Queen Anne.

Before dealing with this major contribution to English historical studies, let us turn to three other books of this period that are too often neglected. He published a charming memoir of his father, Sir George Otto Trevelyan, in 1932, that in many ways is a document of great worth for the social and cultural history of late-nineteenth-century England and is invaluable for understanding the compulsions in Trevelyan's own nature that made him a historian. In the same genre is his biography *Grey of Fallodon*, a labor of love for his great and distinguished Northumbrian neighbor; this book is pervaded with nostalgia for the way of life that Grey represented and that Trevelyan knew to be passing. In both of these works one is made keenly aware of Trevelyan's preoccupation with the poetry of time and of nature. Then, in 1938, there was a masterpiece in miniature, *The English Revolution, 1688–1689*, published in the Home University Library. The social analysis of politics was never Trevelyan's strong point, but in this book his descriptions of the social forces that brought about the revolution are profoundly stimulating, and his realistic intuitions have been fully justified by subsequent research.

The motivation for writing the chief historical work of his life, *England Under Queen Anne*, is best described in his own words:

The idea of taking up the tale where my great-uncle's history [Lord Macaulay's *History of England*] had broken off, was perhaps a fancy at the back of my consciousness.

---

[10]Over 200,000 copies have been sold, but in schools copies are used time and time again, and, of course, many schoolmasters base their lessons on it.

[11]One of the duties of a professor is the supervision of the research of postgraduate students, and because I had the honor of being one of Trevelyan's perhaps I may be allowed one personal reminiscence. I would take my written work round to his study at Garden Corner in West Road. He would peer at it through his steel-rimmed spectacles; his long legs would twine and untwine impatiently; he would growl a little to himself and then I would find myself by his side at an enormous desk while he attacked my prose with his pencil. Unnecessary adjectives would fly out, commas would be removed and then appropriately replaced, phrases would be inserted, so apt that I knew at last what I meant; and I would come away happy and inspired by sentences that were, of course, his, but I liked to think mine.

But I was more seriously attracted by the dramatic unity and separateness of the period from 1702–14, lying between the Stuart and Hanoverian eras with a special ethos of its own; the interplay and mutual dependence of foreign and domestic, religious and political, English and Scottish, civil and military affairs; the economic background and the social scene and their political outcome; the series of dramatic changes of issue, like a five act drama, leading up to a climax of trumpets proclaiming King George. . . . In Anne's reign, it seemed to me, Britain attained by sea and land to her modern place in the world, having settled her free constitution and composed by compromise and toleration the feuds that had torn her in Stuart times.

It was planned, therefore, on the most considerable scale and intended to be his greatest contribution to the study of English history. But what of the achievement? Personally, I feel that in the choice of subject Trevelyan's intuition for once failed him. The reign of Anne, unlike the Italy of Garibaldi or England of the Stuarts, was not a heroic age. Even Marlborough, who most nearly approximates to the hero, has none of the hero's simplicity and emotional force, that direct response in action to emotional need that marks a Garibaldi or a Cromwell. The other chief characters in this part of English history—Harley, Bolingbroke, Godolphin—were men of exceptional psychological complexity, tortuous in thought, feeling, and deed, whose words often bore little relation to intention and whose intentions bore no relation to avowed aspiration. Backstairs politics, the worldliness and cynicism of men seeking power at all costs, twisting and debauching institutions to get it, is not a world in which Trevelyan moved with instinctive ease.

Furthermore, Trevelyan's traditional outlook on English politics distorted his vision of the Augustan age. He was a firm believer in the historical continuity of the two-party English political system.[12] In the reign of Anne, party politicians, it is true, used party clichés, exploited for their own purposes social animosities that lay concealed under party names, and were prepared to enforce legislation of a party nature; but this is only the surface story, concealing the real drive for power and for the fruits of office. The failure of the Whigs to obtain any clear-cut and detailed definition of the constitution in 1689 led to the disintegration of politics, making the growth of

oligarchy easy, desirable, and certain. The system of Robert Walpole was based on the system of Harley, sometimes using the same men and their connections; what had been fostered by the Tories was easily adaptable to Whig purposes, for the motives were the same. The straightforward conception of a two-party system does not forward the analysis of this intricate and involved period of English political history; such an analysis must come from the detailed study of factions and connections as yet largely undescribed. Nor was the unity of the period as actual as Trevelyan would have us believe. In all aspects of English history—social, economic, political, religious, constitutional, and diplomatic—the play had got well and truly into its second act by 1702. In consequence, the structure of these books is to some extent artificial and does not arise naturally from the historical situation, as it does in the Garibaldi trilogy.

But it is, of course, a work of tremendous quality. The opening chapters, which draw a picture of England at the start of the eighteenth century, are outstanding for their imaginative insight and for the warm spirit of human reality that breathes through them. Actual and vivid, they compel belief even though Trevelyan lays major stress on the ease, virtue, and sweetness of life of the possessing classes and glosses somewhat the brutality and suffering that were the lot of the common man. Perhaps this is right, for the quality of an age is not the work of common men; they but labor namelessly to support it. Apart from the social background, the best part of the work is that which deals with naval and military history. Certainly, too, by far the best character study is of Marlborough, whom Macaulay had detested and to whom Trevelyan, conscious of a major family blunder, was determined to do full justice. Full justice is, indeed, done both to his capacity as a general and to the persistence of his will in diplomacy.

As in all of Trevelyan's work the narrative is treated very cunningly. The pace of the book is intense, especially in *Blenheim* (1930), the first of the three volumes, for the battle gives a natural and dramatic climax to the book. In the second two parts, *Ramillies and the Union with Scotland* (1932) and *The Peace and the Protestant Succession* (1934), there is no such natural climax, and inevitably the story is more broken up, with a consequent loss of intensity. Stylistically, these are the most beautiful of Trevelyan's books. In his earlier works there are

---

[12]Compare his Romanes lecture, "The Two-Party System in English Political History," delivered at Oxford in 1926 and reprinted in *An Autobiography and Other Essays*, pp. 183–199.

strong traces, especially in the descriptive passages, of John Ruskin and Carlyle, which to our modern taste impart a sense of straining after effect. It is possible that the writing of the *History of England*, in which every word had to count, helped to simplify his style without weakening his gift for a memorable phrase. Whatever may have been the cause, words in these books are used with absolute mastery: passage after passage stirs the heart and mind with elegant clarity and evocative beauty. *England Under Queen Anne* is a great work and a great achievement, but one cannot help regretting that, in the fullness of his powers, Trevelyan was not drawn to a subject more apt to his genius.

The mastership of Trinity College, Cambridge, is a crown appointment, and it must have given Winston Churchill great pleasure to confer it on Trevelyan when the vacancy was created by the death of J. J. Thomson in 1940. They had been contemporaries at school and, in a sense, rival historians, for Churchill's *Life of Marlborough* was published at about the same time as *England Under Queen Anne*. This last and greatest distinction of his academic life made, as Trevelyan has written, "my life as happy as anyone's can be during the fall of European civilization." The depth of his feeling for his college, great in men and history, and for the beauty of the stone buildings in which it lives its corporate life may be seen in the pages of the little book *Trinity College*, which he published in 1943. It will continue to give pleasure to generations not only of Trinity graduates but of all whom Cambridge has enriched.

But the most outstanding success was yet to come. Before the war Trevelyan had been working on a social history of England as a companion volume to his *History of England*, which had been mainly concerned with politics and war. In 1940, he decided to drop the early part of the work and begin with Chaucer.[13] From that point onward the book was already written, but owing to war shortages it was not published in England until 1944, when it appeared under the title of *English Social History: A Survey of Six Centuries*. By 1949 it had sold 392,000 copies and has since far exceeded this large total. This book must have reached thousands who do not normally read history. I was told by a friend who did

his military service in the Suez Canal Zone that he saw it being read by soldiers who had left school at fourteen and who had probably never held a hardcover book in their hands since. And my friend said that they lay in their bunks for hours, reading with all the keen and eager enjoyment they might have derived from an adventure story. In many homes it must be the one and only history book. The work is not only a social history but a social phenomenon.

Once more, as with the Garibaldi books, Trevelyan was exceptionally fortunate in the moment of his publication—1944. The war, which we were bringing to a successful end, had jeopardized the traditional pattern of English life, in some ways destroyed it forever. This created among all classes a deep nostalgia for the way of life we were losing. Then, again, the war had made millions conscious that our national attitude to life was historically based, the result of centuries of slow growth, and that it was for the old, tried ways of life we were fighting. Winston Churchill, in his great war speeches, made us all aware of our past as never before. And in this war, too, there were far more highly educated men and women in all ranks of all of the services. The twenties and thirties of this century had witnessed a great extension of secondary school education, producing a vast public capable of reading and enjoying a book of profound historical imagination once the dilemma of their times stirred them to do so.

Trevelyan's book was a beautifully timed response to the need that so many were unconsciously feeling, and its nature widened its appeal, for it is the story of how the ordinary men and women of England had lived out their lives, enduring their times as best they might; and it was read by just such ordinary men and women, who were enduring times as hard as the English people had ever faced and perhaps with far less hope for their future. In such tribulation it was natural to read with avid longing of ages more gracious and more secure, and to draw strength from our checkered past.

Intrinsically the book deserved its fame, its continued and continuing success. Throughout his life the poet in Trevelyan had been drawn to a contemplation of the ordinary nameless man, caught up inexorably in time. In volume after volume that he published on English history there are chapters that evoke the past life and lost countryside of our island. It is usually in these chapters that his writing acquires its most lyrical note. The subject, therefore, of the *Social History* touched the deepest springs of his

---

[13]Unused fragments of the projected earlier part may probably be detected in two essays in *An Autobiography and Other Essays*. They are "Social Life in Roman Britain" and "The Coming of the Anglo-Saxons."

temperament and was one he had long contemplated. By and large, during the centuries about which Trevelyan wrote, the great contributions to our civilization were made by the aristocrats and squires and yeomen, by merchants and craftsmen, by owners of wealth, great or small; in fact, by those classes with which he was instinctively familiar and from which he derived his ancestry. Their world is dead; their opportunity past. It is as well that their elegy should be pronounced by one who loved their ways of life so well, who could respond to their aspirations and to the beauty of the material civilization they created, and who could accept, if uneasily, the poverty and suffering upon which it was, of necessity, based. This attitude gives a sunset glow to the whole work, softening the edges, obscuring some of the harshness, bitterness, and conflict that have, at times, distracted England, but in the main fulfilling the great purpose Trevelyan set himself.

Each one, gentle and simple, in his commonest goings and comings, was ruled by a complicated and ever-shifting fabric of custom and law, society and politics, events at home and abroad, some of them little known by him and less understood. Our effort is not only to get what glimpses we can of his intimate personality, but to reconstruct the whole fabric of each passing age, and see how it affected him; to get to know more in some respects than the dweller in the past himself knew about the conditions that enveloped and controlled his life.

There is nothing that more divides civilized from semi-savage man than to be conscious of our forefathers as they really were, and bit by bit to reconstruct the mosaic of the long-forgotten past. To weigh the stars, or to make ships sail in the air or below the sea, is not a more astonishing and ennobling performance on the part of the human race in these latter days, than to know the course of events that had been long forgotten, and the true nature of men and women who were here before us.

Few books have responded so nobly to the demands of their age.

V

SUCH are the many triumphs and the few failures of Trevelyan's contribution to English historical literature. He died in 1962, and it remains to assess his achievement. What perhaps is most frequently forgotten, or ignored, is the skill of his literary craftsmanship. Trevelyan was a born writer and a natural storyteller; and this, among historians, is a rare gift. Only William H. Prescott, among the great histori-

ans, had this facility in equal or greater measure. In consequence, those episodes of history that were full of dramatic action, with a firm beginning and obvious end, have brought forth some of his best writing—the Garibaldi books, *England Under the Stuarts,* much of the *History of England,* and perhaps *Blenheim.* As a stylist he cannot be compared with Gibbon, Macaulay, or even Lord Clarendon, and in his own generation he would have to concede the first place to R. H. Tawney; but he has written passages of greater lyrical beauty than any of them, when the heart of the poet has been stirred. A poet at large in history is a unique phenomenon of our literature and will create for Trevelyan a special place in the history of English letters. Certainly, I think, it will secure a permanent niche for *Garibaldi's Defence of the Roman Republic,* which, were it fiction, would live as one of the greatest love stories, told with exquisite feeling and poetic power. The same poetic temperament has been responsible for some of the best evocations of times past that have been written in English. They are scattered throughout his works but are brought together and continuously sustained in the pages of *English Social History.* If one quality is to be singled out, it should be this, for all historians he is the poet of English history.

His work has one other great and enduring merit: the tradition within which it was written. The Victorian liberals and their Edwardian successors have made one of the greatest contributions to science and to culture ever made by a ruling class. To these by birth and by instinct Trevelyan belonged. Therefore, as time passes, his work will acquire fresh significance and become the material of history itself, for these books of his will show how these liberal humanists considered their past, whence they derived their tradition, by what they would like themselves judged. And because he has written from such a standpoint, he has helped to inculcate in the hearts of men and women born in more desperate times a regard for human justice and personal freedom.

SELECTED BIBLIOGRAPHY

I. COLLECTED EDITIONS. *Garibaldi* (London, 1933), a one-vol. ed. of *Garibaldi's Defence of the Roman Republic, Garibaldi and the Thousand,* and *Garibaldi and the Making of Italy.*

II. SEPARATE WORKS. *England in the Age of Wycliffe* (London, 1899; 2nd ed., 1904; 3rd ed., 1909); G. M. Trevelyan and E. Powell, eds., *The Peasants' Rising and the Lollards: A Collection of Unpublished Documents Forming an Appendix to "England in the Age of Wycliffe"* (London, 1899); *England Under the Stuarts* (London, 1904; rev. ed., 1925); *The Poetry and Philosophy of George Meredith* (London, 1906); *Garibaldi's Defence of the Roman Republic* (London, 1907); *Garibaldi and the Thousand* (London, 1909); *Garibaldi and the Making of Italy* (London, 1911); *The Life of John Bright* (London, 1913; 2nd ed., 1925); *Clio: A Muse, and Other Essays Literary and Pedestrian* (London, 1913), retitled *The Recreations of an Historian* (London, 1919), new ed. with original title (London, 1930); 1913 ed. contains "Clio: A Muse," "George Meredith," "If Napoleon Had Won the Battle of Waterloo," "John Woolman, the Quaker," "The Middle Marches," "Poetry and Rebellion," "Poor Muggleton and the Classics," "Walking"; 1919 ed. contains "Englishmen and Italians," "George Meredith," "The Hegira cf Rousseau," "If Napoleon Had Won the Battle of Waterloo," "John Woolman, the Quaker," "The Middle Marches," "The Muse of History," "The News of Ramillies," "Poetry and Rebellion," "Poor Muggleton and the Classics," "Two Carlyles," "Walking"; 1930 ed. contains "Clio: A Muse," "Englishmen and Italians," "History and Fiction," "If Napoleon Had Won the Battle of Waterloo," "John Bunyan," "John Woolman, the Quaker," "The Middle Marches," "The News of Ramillies," "Poetry and Rebellion," "Poor Muggleton and the Classics," "Present Position of History" (the inaugural lecture at Cambridge, 1927); *De Haeretico Comburendo: or, The Ethics of Religious Conformity* (Cambridge, 1914), address delivered to "The Heretics" in October 1913; *Scenes from Italy's War* (London, 1919); *Englishmen and Italians: Some Aspects of Their Relations Past and Present* (London, 1919), annual Italian lecture to the British Academy (1919), *Proceedings of the British Academy*, 9.

Lord Grey of the Reform Bill: Being the Life of Charles, Second Earl Grey (London, 1920); *The War and the European Revolution in Relation to History* (London, 1920), the Creighton lecture for 1919; *British History in the Nineteenth Century, 1782–1901* (London, 1922), 2nd ed. retitled *British History in the Nineteenth Century and After, 1782–1919* (London, 1937); *Manin and the Venetian Revolution of 1848* (London, 1923); *The Historical Causes of the Present State of Affairs in Italy* (London, 1923), Sidney Ball Memorial lecture, 1923, Barnett House Papers; *The Two-Party System in English Constitutional History* (Oxford, 1926), the Romanes lecture; *History of England* (London, 1926; 2nd ed., enl., 1937; 3rd ed., 1945); *The Present Position of History* (London, 1927), inaugural lecture as Regius Professor of Modern History in the University of Cambridge, repr. in *Clio: A Muse*, 3rd ed.; *Must England's Beauty Perish? A Plea on Behalf of the National Trust for Places of Historic Interest or Natural Beauty* (London, 1929); *England Under Queen Anne*, 3 vols. (London, 1930–1934), vol. I: *Blenheim* (London, 1930), vol. II: *Ramillies and the Union with Scotland* (London, 1932), vol. III: *The Peace and the Protestant Succession* (London, 1934); *The*

Call and Claims of Natural Beauty (London, 1931), the Rickman Godlee lecture, University College and University College Hospital Medical School, London; *Sir George Otto Trevelyan: A Memoir* (London, 1932); *Grey of Fallodon: Being the Life of Sir Edward Grey, Afterwards Viscount Grey of Fallodon* (London, 1937); *The English Revolution, 1688–1689* (London, 1938).

A Shortened History of England (London, 1942); *Trinity College [Cambridge]: An Historical Sketch* (Cambridge, 1943); *English Social History: A Survey of Six Centuries: Chaucer to Queen Victoria* (London, 1944), repr. in 4 vols. (London, 1949–1952), illus., with notes by R. C. Wright; *History and the Reader* (London, 1945), 3rd annual lecture sponsored by the National Book League; *Biography: A Reader's Guide* (London, 1947), bibliography comp. for the National Book League; *Admiral Sir Herbert Richmond, 1871–1940* (London, 1948), from *Proceedings of the British Academy*, 32; *An Autobiography and Other Essays* (London, 1949), includes "Autobiography of an Historian," "Bias in History," "The Call and Claims of Natural Beauty," "The Coming of the Anglo-Saxons," "Cromwell's Statue," "Friends Lost: (1) Sir John Clapham, (2) Admiral Sir Herbert Richmond, (3) Denys Arthur Winstanley," "History and the Reader," "The Influence of Sir Walter Scott on History," "Jonathan Swift," "Milton's *Areopagitica*," "Religion and Poetry," "Social Life in Roman Britain," "Stray Thoughts on History," and "The Two-Party System in English Political History"; *English Literature and Its Readers* (London, 1951), presidential address to the English Association; *A Layman's Love of Letters* (London, 1954), the Clark lectures, Cambridge, 1953; *Speech . . . Made on the 12 November 1955 at the Dinner in Christ's College, Cambridge . . . to Celebrate the Publication of "Studies in Social History": A Tribute to Trevelyan,* J. H. Plumb, ed. (London, 1956), printed for private circulation.

III. WORKS EDITED OR CONTAINING CONTRIBUTIONS BY TREVELYAN. "The Past and the Future," in *The Heart of the Empire* (London, 1901); G. M. Trevelyan, ed., *The Meredith Pocket Book* (London, 1906), a selection from Meredith's prose works; W. J. Stillman, *The Union of Italy, 1815–1895* (Cambridge, 1909), with epilogue by Trevelyan; R. de Cesare, *The Last Days of Papal Rome, 1850–1870* (London, 1909), trans. by H. Zimmern, with intro. ch. by Trevelyan; *English Songs of Italian Freedom* (London, 1911), chosen and intro. by Trevelyan; *The Poetical Works of George Meredith* (London, 1912), notes by Trevelyan; H. E. H. King, *Letters and Recollections of Mazzini* (London, 1912), ed. by Trevelyan; R. J. Fruin, Sr., *The Siege and Relief of Leyden in 1574* (The Hague, 1927), trans. by E. Trevelyan, intro. by G. M. Trevelyan; T. B. Macaulay, *Lays of Ancient Rome and Other Historical Poems* (London, 1928), intro. by Trevelyan; G. M. Trevelyan, ed., *Select Documents for Queen Anne's Reign Down to the Union with Scotland, 1702–1707* (Cambridge, 1929); "Memoir of R. Geikie," in R. Geikie and I. A. Montgomery, *The Dutch Barrier, 1705–1719* (Cambridge,

1930); Henry St. John [Viscount Bolingbroke], *Bolingbroke's Defence of the Treaty of Utrecht: Being Letters VI–VIII of "The Study & Use of History"* (Cambridge, 1932), intro by Trevelyan; S. A. Buchan, *John Buchan* (London, 1947), preface by Trevelyan; G. M. Trevelyan, ed., *The Seven Years of William IV: A Reign Cartooned by J. Doyle* (London, 1952), with notes by ed.; G. M. Trevelyan, ed., *Carlyle: An Anthology* (London, 1953); G. M. Trevelyan, comp., *Selected Poetical Works of George Meredith* (London, 1955), with notes by comp.

IV. Biographical and Critical Studies. S. W. Halperin, ed., *Some 20th Century Historians* (Chicago, 1961), includes essay on Trevelyan by H. R. Winkler; G. K. Clark, "G. M. Trevelyan as an Historian," in the *Durham University Journal*, December 1962, pp. 1–4; Sir G. N. Clark, "George Macaulay Trevelyan," in *Proceedings of the British Academy*, 49 (1963), 375–386; Lord Adrian, "George Macaulay Trevelyan," in *Biographical Memoirs of Fellows of the Royal Society* (1963), 315–321; M. Moorman, *G. M. Trevelyan* (London, 1980).

E. M. FORSTER

(1879-1970)

Philip Gardner

I

In addition to being one of the finest novelists of his generation—and of this century—E. M. Forster was also the longest-lived. When he died, on 8 June 1970, he was in his ninety-second year. His longevity assisted official recognition of the enduring quality of his work: in 1953 he was made a Companion of Honour, in 1968 appointed to the Order of Merit. In Forster's case, these honors seem also to be tokens of collective esteem for the man himself, revealed by his writings to be a liberal humanist, sensitive and tolerant (though not lacking a salutary astringency), concerned with the individual conscience and the individual heart.

But, as Forster said in a broadcast in 1940, "by the time writers have become eminent they have usually done their best work." Forster's novels, on which his major reputation rests, belong to the first half of his life, and *A Passage to India*, the last and best of them, appeared in 1924. Between then and 1951, the year of *Two Cheers for Democracy*, Forster continued to respond eloquently to the world about him, to the pressures of book, person, and event, but in the form of lectures, essays, and broadcasts rather than by means of the deeper and more wide-ranging transformations of fiction. His last two books, *The Hill of Devi* (1953) and *Marianne Thornton* (1956), though often fascinating and never less than interesting, are evocations of the past consisting largely of letters written many years earlier. They are in effect a return by Forster to his origins: to those Indian experiences that he had so memorably transmuted into fiction, and to the families from which he sprang and the great-aunt whose generous legacy made his career as a writer possible.

Part of Forster's reason for abandoning fiction (as to all appearances he had) was no doubt indicated in the answers he gave, always kindly, to those whose regret prompted them to question him about it. As he put it to me: the postwar world was not one in which his imagination felt at home—too much had changed. One such change, which he lamented in 1946, was the sudden expansion of Stevenage into a large new satellite town of London; it was near that erstwhile village—in the house that was the original for *Howards End* (1910)—that he had spent his happiest childhood years. But there was something else, as became clear after his death with the publication in 1971 of *Maurice* (written in 1914) and in 1972 of *The Life to Come*, of which seven stories had been written after *A Passage to India* (the last in 1958): not many, but enough to show that Forster had not in fact dried up. But the homosexual content of these stories and of *Maurice* understandably kept Forster from publishing them when the law was hostile and the public likely to be intolerant. Forster's recognition of this central aspect of himself seems eventually (for a sense of impatience with conventional human configurations shows itself as early as a diary entry of 1911) to have prevented his imagination from setting it aside in exchange for publication. His problem may perhaps be expressed by a sentence from *Aspects of the Novel* (1927): "It is a pity that Man cannot be at the same time impressive and truthful." If Forster could not publish fiction as a homosexual, he would not publish it as if he were not one.

The posthumous appearance of *Maurice* and *The Life to Come* was thus for the majority of Forster's readers like the shaking of a kaleidoscope, substituting new patterns for old, or at least altering their proportions and perspectives. Since then, the immense extensions to our knowledge of Forster made by the scrupulous Abinger editions of Oliver Stallybrass, by the unemphatic frankness of Forster's biographer P. N. Furbank, and not least by Forster's own manuscripts and papers, left by him to King's College, Cambridge, have provided a larger context than existed in Forster's lifetime within which the various elements present in his fiction may perhaps be brought into steady focus. This necessarily brief survey cannot hope to be more than an attempt to do so.

II

EDWARD MORGAN FORSTER was born on 1 January 1879 in a house in London near Marylebone Station: 6 Melcombe Place, Dorset Square. He chose as a writer to be known by his initials, but to family and friends he was always Morgan, his second Christian name preferred to the first possibly because that was intended to have been Henry—an early instance, as John Colmer has pointed out, of the phenomenon of "muddle" that often crops up in his novels. Another phenomenon there, sudden death, may have been suggested by the death from consumption of Forster's father in October 1880, at the early age of thirty-three.

The consequence of his father's death was that Forster's childhood was dominated by women: by his mother, Alice (Lily) Clara Whichelo, to whom he was very close and with whom he lived until her death in 1945; and to a lesser extent by his maternal grandmother (on whom he modeled one of his most likable women characters, Mrs. Honeychurch, in *A Room with a View*, 1908), and by his paternal great-aunt, Marianne Thornton. The latter on her death in 1887 left him £8,000, which provided for his education, his early travels, and his start as a writer. Forster may have derived much of his high-minded humanism from the Thorntons, influential nineteenth-century bankers and philanthropists with strong Evangelical connections. From his mother's family, poorer but more artistic than the Thorntons, and from his father, an architect, came the seeds of his creativity and the value he attached to form.

Forster was eventually to live in a house built by his father, West Hackhurst, near Abinger in Surrey, but this was not until 1925. In 1883 he and his mother moved into a former farmhouse, of faded red brick, set in the rolling Hertfordshire countryside near Stevenage; it can still be glimpsed to the left as one hurtles down the Great North Road from Baldock— photographs do not do justice to its charm. This house his mother named Rooksnest, after the tiny hamlet in which it lay, and in it and its adjacent meadow, orchard, and garden (with its tall wych-elm tree) Forster enjoyed a happy only childhood.

His earliest surviving piece of writing is a detailed description, dating from 1894, that reveals Rooksnest as the blueprint for *Howards End*; to this Forster added in 1901 a note on his friendship with one of the garden boys there, "my beloved Ansell," the memory of whom he partly fictionalized in an early short story ("Ansell") and in *Maurice*, and whose name he borrowed for a character in *The Longest Journey* (1907).

By 1894 Forster's unregimented years in the country had ended. From 1890 to 1893 he had boarded at a small preparatory school in Eastbourne, where he was told that "school is the world in miniature." In 1893, the lease on Rooksnest having expired, he found himself uprooted into a suburban world of narrow-minded, snobbish gentility and insensitive heartiness to which he later gave the name "Sawston"—a choice that, though evocative of sawdust and "wise saws," seems unfair to the real village of that name near Cambridge. In plain terms, Forster and his mother went to live at Tonbridge in Kent, and later at Tunbridge Wells, so that he could attend Tonbridge School as a day boy. As his descriptions in *The Longest Journey* indicate (there is something of Forster in A. C. Varden, the boy whose ears are pulled, as well as in Rickie Elliot), he and the school—which "aimed at producing the average Englishman," characterized by Forster elsewhere as having a well-developed body, a fairly developed mind, and an undeveloped heart—did not suit each other. The first half of his time there was acutely unhappy, and he was glad enough to leave in the summer of 1897.

King's College, Cambridge, where he spent the next four years reading first classics and then history (he gained second-class honors in both), was an altogether different, open-minded world, a harmonious society of undergraduates and dons. It inspired in Forster "the only unforced loyalty I have ever experienced." With two of his teachers he formed close and lasting friendships: the energetic, unconventional Nathaniel Wedd, his tutor in classics, who first encouraged him to write; and Goldsworthy Lowes Dickinson, the political scientist, Hellenophile, and author of *The Greek View of Life*, whose biography Forster published in 1934. There, as well as in *The Longest Journey*, he recorded his love for Cambridge and his gratitude for its liberating influence. Among other things Cambridge revealed to Forster his homosexual nature: the Platonic relationship between Maurice Hall and Clive Durham is partly based on his love for his fellow Kingsman H. O. Meredith, through whom in his final year Forster was elected to the eminent Cambridge debating society known as the Apostles (at some of whose meetings homosexuality was freely discussed). It was to Meredith ("H.O.M.") that Forster dedicated *A Room with a View*, the first notes for which, made late in 1901, carried his initials in the list of projected characters.

Having graduated from Cambridge, Forster expanded his horizons further, adding gradually to the stock of raw material that, once fructified by his developing imagination, was to issue in short stories and his first three novels. Much of 1901 and 1902 he spent traveling in Italy, Sicily, and Greece, experiencing not only the curious, insular life of the English middle classes abroad (particularly at a pension in Florence), but also the unmediated freshness and challenge of Europe—Italian painting and opera, the historic hill towns of Tuscany (like San Gimignano, the original of Monteriano), and the Pan-haunted landscapes of the south that thrust straight into his mind two of his earliest short tales, "The Story of a Panic" and "The Road from Colonus." By the time, in 1904, that the itinerant Forster and his mother had found another English home (an unlovely house in Weybridge in which they lived until 1925), Forster had built up a confidence in his literary powers that helped to keep the conventionalities of Sawston at bay, a sense of larger intellectual and spiritual values to set against them, and a context of character and incident within which to embody the struggle between the two. It is to Forster the writer that I now turn.

III

SINCE Forster began his career in fiction as a writer of short stories, it is convenient to mention them first, though they overlap with four prewar novels. His earliest published story, "Albergo Empedocle," a fine mixture of poetry and ironic observation, appeared in *Temple Bar* in 1903 and was inexplicably not seen again until after his death. The others, spanning 1902 to 1912, were published (or reprinted from the Liberal *Independent Review*, jointly edited by Dickinson and Wedd) in two widely separated collections, *The Celestial Omnibus* (1911) and *The Eternal Moment* (1928). As revealed by these volumes

(Forster's homosexual stories, written from 1922 onward, are of a different type and are treated later), the short story was useful to Forster as a more poetic, more "fantastic" vehicle for his feelings and ideas than he allowed his novels to be.

In his use of fantasy, that "muddling up of the actual and the impossible" that permits a horse bus driven by Dante and Sir Thomas Browne to ply between Surbiton and Heaven, and a girl harassed by her conventional fiancé to turn into a tree ("Other Kingdom"), Forster was in part influenced by his admiration for Samuel Butler's *Erewhon* (1872). But what one feels more strongly is his own belief in the individual's need for freedom, whether attained through literature (an allegorical Heaven inaccessible to those who, like the culture-snob Mr. Bons, cannot abandon *baldanza*—self-importance) or expressed in the metaphors of mythology: the transformation of Daphne; the liberating influence of Pan ("The Story of a Panic" and "The Curate's Friend"); the song of the Siren, which may bring inspiration, total understanding, or death. For if most of Forster's early stories—short but not lightweight, their tone ranging from the whimsical to the mystical—celebrate various kinds of liberating encounter (such as that of Mr. Lucas in "Colonus"), they also intimate a sense that extinction, or separation from others (as with Harold's final insanity in "Albergo Empedocle"), may be the price that needs to be paid for illumination. The "supreme transfiguring event" that Mr. Lucas is deprived of by not staying at Colonus turns out to be death; and the "escape" of Eustace into the primitive energy of nature, at the end of "The Story of a Panic," is accompanied by the death of the Italian boy Gennaro, who in a sense dies to save him.

Less ambiguous, more straightforwardly powerful, is Forster's only exercise in science fiction, "The Machine Stops" (1909), a reaction against Wellsian views of progress. Here, against first an ironic and then a despairing vision of a civilization that has banished direct awareness of people and nature, Forster asserts his belief that "Man is the measure" and that his divine essences are his soul and body, "those five portals by which we can alone apprehend."

Stimulating as Forster's fantasies are ("Co-ordination" is the only one that falls flat), they are not entirely satisfactory. Their fables and metaphors, didactic in apparent intention, tend to outrun literal application, and it is sometimes hard to distinguish imaginative subtlety from obscurity. In my view, the best of the stories, the most austere and controlled, is "The Eternal Moment" (1905), whose investigation of the power of emotion to transfigure everyday experience takes place in a beautifully realized and entirely real world. Revisiting, with Miss Raby, the town of Vorta, in which the most important event of her life has occurred, we are in fact entering the world of Forster the novelist, who also, in his first novel, depicted the collision between England and Italy.

Where Angels Fear to Tread (1905) was referred to by Forster as "my novelette," but it is in fact an astonishingly accomplished first performance. It originated in a scrap of gossip Forster overheard on his travels in Italy, about an English tourist who contracted a misalliance with an Italian. Out of this he spun a complex plot that he handles with great skill; the crucial part of it concerns the attempts of a middle-class Sawston family, the Herritons, to gain possession of a baby, sole fruit of the hasty and short-lived union between their widowed daughter-in-law, Lilia, and the much younger Gino Carella, the son of a small-town Italian dentist.

The wish to be free of narrow Sawston respectability has made Lilia susceptible to the charm of Italy and led her to fall in love with a man who, though handsome and impetuous, takes a decidedly conventional, male-chauvinist view of his role as a husband. The breakdown of the marriage, from which Lilia pathetically and ineffectually tries to escape, is powerfully conveyed in chapter 4, at the end of which Lilia dies in giving birth to Gino's son. (It is remarkable how often the motif of remarriage, as well as that of sudden death, occurs in Forster's novels.)

The Herritons' attempt to get hold of the baby (their reasons, described in chapter 5, are a muddled mixture of rivalry, the need to appear respectably concerned, and a little genuine feeling for Irma, Lilia's daughter by Charles Herriton) ends in disaster. Though Philip Herriton and Caroline Abbott, a family friend, at last realize the extent of Gino's elemental pride in his fatherhood (splendidly rendered in chapter 7), the obsessional bigotry of Philip's sister, Harriet, causes her to steal the baby when Gino is out. The carriage in which she takes it to the station goes too fast in the darkness and overturns on the muddy road; the baby is thrown out and killed. If this seems melodramatic in a summary, it is not so in the novel. Nor is the following scene, in which Philip, taking the blame for Harriet's action on himself, has his arm (broken in the accident; For-

ster broke his own arm in Italy) painfully twisted by Gino and is methodically half-strangled. This sadistic vengefulness on Gino's part has been prepared for much earlier by his silent but terrifying reaction to Lilia's suggestion that she can keep him in order by denying him money. Now, at any rate, he has the nobler motive of grief. But there is more to the scene than Gino's paternal feelings. There is a sexual element in this physical confrontation in the dark room ("You are to do what you like with me, Gino," Philip says) that Forster recognized many years later; and the fundamentally sympathetic relationship between Philip and Gino adumbrates the closer one (emphasized by a closer family link) between Rickie and Stephen in *The Longest Journey*, a novel to which the words of Gino's friend Spiridione—"Sono poco simpatiche le donne" (Women are not very likable)—apply particularly well.

The scene ends with the reconciliation of the brothers-in-law, which is brought about by the intervention of Caroline Abbott, the first of those women in Forster's novels who are given not only intuition but an aura of the superhuman—both Philip and Gino in their different ways worship her. But she is a woman, not a goddess, revealing as she and Philip return with Harriet to England that she has all along been physically in love with Gino. Details of her earlier behavior, once puzzling, are suddenly made clear, and one again appreciates Forster's skill in preparing revelations. Philip, by now in love with her, is surprised by the news, but he has been so matured by the climactic events of the novel that he can silently rise above personal disappointment. As Caroline has helped him earlier, so he helps her now, and the novel ends on a note of "great friendliness," a phrase that, though chasteningly not "love" (Forster's supreme absolute), conveys the hard-earned value of personal relations. The novel also ends with protective tolerance toward those less able to respond to life's opportunities for self-enlargement, as Philip and Caroline return to their railway carriage "to close the windows lest the smuts get into Harriet's eyes," as they had done also when, some hundred pages earlier, she had opened the window to clear the air of "filthy foreigners" as the train passed through the San Gotthard tunnel on the outward journey.

The novel's title has some aptness: the Herritons' interference in Gino's love for his child, "something greater than right or wrong," is partly a case of fools rushing in. But Forster did not like the title, which was his publisher's choice. His own was "Monteriano," which emphasized the importance of the Italian town in which, by the end, "all the wonderful things had happened." It is in Monteriano that the narrow and joyless, if dutiful, Sawston conformities are confronted by something more vibrant, if more vulgar. This is not to say that Gino Carella is not a conformist too, in his own man-centered world, nor that Forster feels Italy to be perfect; but what Monteriano has is an instinctive sense of the importance of the emotions and of human relationships that Sawston either lacks or smothers. Mrs. Herriton's concealment from Irma of the fact that she has a "lital brother" contrasts with Gino's unthinking but more natural attempt to establish an awareness of him in the girl's mind by sending picture postcards.

The people of Monteriano are capable of wholehearted, unembarrassed enjoyment, displayed in chapter 6 at the performance of *Lucia di Lammermoor* (an opera Forster himself had heard in Italy). Music always plays a significant part in Forster's novels, and this scene is particularly rich. While for Harriet the opera is "culture," demanding a reverent silence, for the Italians it is life, to be actively entered into. And to Philip it brings "an access of joy" that "promised to be permanent," opening his heart to the later experiences that turn him from an ineffectual, priggish aesthete with a merely romantic, spectator's view of Italian history and art into a full human being.

For Forster, indeed, "the object of the book is the improvement of Philip," and Philip, though based in some details on Forster's Cambridge friend E. J. Dent (later a renowned musicologist), is more essentially a portrait of Forster himself, as the wry description at the start of chapter 5 suggests. There is a strong feeling in the book that action, even if it involves mistakes, is preferable to observation; and that mistakes can themselves lead to right action. Philip's "improvement," subtly charted and culminating in his painful confrontation with Gino, which Forster in 1905 called "sacramental," causes him to learn the truth of the text that he preaches so glibly to Lilia at the beginning: "Love and understand the Italians, for the people are more marvellous than the land." The novel begins and ends with a train journey, the first an unthinking departure, the second a sadder but wiser return.

Forster once said that he had learned from Jane Austen "the possibilities of domestic humour." Comedy is not the dominant mode of *Where Angels*

Fear to Tread, though—a mixed approach to life being characteristic of Forster—neither is tragedy. But there is certainly a sharpness in his observation of the two contrasting, close-knit societies of Sawston and Monteriano, together with an overall crispness and economy of presentation, that Austen may well have taught him. In his first novel Forster is obviously writing about matters of great moment to him, but he seems to hold them at a distance: it is a minor masterpiece of artistic detachment. *The Longest Journey* is a fuller, heavier book, and a more pressingly personal one. It is neither neat nor altogether clear; nevertheless, in later life Forster described it not only as the novel "I am most glad to have written" but as the one in which "I have got nearer . . . to saying what I wanted than I have elsewhere."

It is appropriate at this point to suggest thematic concerns in terms of which Forster's novels may all be seen. Three seem particularly important: the individual's search for and achievement of self-realization; the attempt to harmonize different life-styles and schemes of value; and the individual life as set against something larger than itself—a country, the universe, the human urge for continuance or expansion. The first two concerns carry with them a sense of the primacy of personal relations and the inner life; the last sometimes involves the suspicion (as in the mind of Mrs. Moore in *A Passage to India*) that the individual may be of small account. All of them may be unified under one single heading, Forster's epigraph to *Howards End* (1910): "Only connect." His key characters are shown trying to connect with themselves, substituting intellectual and emotional honesty for catchwords and conventional stances; with other people (they may succeed or fail); and with some spiritual reality sensed behind and beyond human life. It is perhaps because *The Longest Journey* shows these connections being painfully sought by a character admitted by Forster to be very close to himself—Rickie Elliot—that Forster valued the book so highly. It is to a large extent a working out of his own inner tensions, a projection of conflicting aspects of himself into different characters and life-styles. It is also, next to *A Passage to India*, his most mystical book, and one in which symbolism reinforces plot.

The novel's title is taken from a passage in Percy Bysshe Shelley's poem "Epipsychidion" in which the poet contrasts his own preference, the love of mankind (or of a wide range of friends), with the habit of most people of taking one mate and thus narrowing their horizons. Marriage, for Shelley, is "the dreariest and the longest journey." Forster's novel is divided into three sections—Cambridge, Sawston, Wiltshire—that partly represent chronological stages in Rickie Elliot's clouded pilgrimage, in the increasingly uncongenial company of his wife, Agnes Pembroke, a woman older and less imaginative than himself, toward death and a vicarious immortality. More important, the three divisions represent three ways of life that Rickie is offered and in none of which he is completely at home. Each of these ways (two good, one bad) is epitomized by a character who is narrower yet tougher than Rickie and who survives: Stewart Ansell, Agnes Pembroke, and Stephen Wonham. Rickie, who seems to have the potential to comprehend them all, fails through some weakness (objectified in his lameness, but its source never made quite clear) to make much of his life. Through his attitudes, the novel seems to recommend the impulse toward tolerance, but through his experience, to suggest its dangers. This is surely what is meant by Rickie's "Primal Curse," which is "not the knowledge of good and evil, but the knowledge of good-and-evil."

Forster described *The Longest Journey* as being "about reality and the need for accepting it." For Rickie, an orphan devoted to the memory of his mother and detesting (rightly) that of his father, the problem of reality—of discovering what is really there and what is illusory—becomes bound up with discovering his own deepest nature and to whom he is related: specifically, with acknowledging his illegitimate half-brother, Stephen Wonham, who has been brought up in Wiltshire and stands for the life of simple emotion and instinct. Rickie's journey begins in Cambridge, which in the person of his uncompromising friend Stewart Ansell stands for the life of the mind, the search for the central reality. (Ansell was modeled on Forster's fellow Apostle, the argumentative, pipe-smoking Alfred Ainsworth.) To the clarity of this life Rickie is attracted but not suited, by reason of his romantic imagination (he writes short stories, one of them obviously Forster's own "Other Kingdom"). This leads him, unfortunately, to invest ordinary people with qualities they do not possess and to expect more of them than they can perform.

It is in such an idealizing spirit that Rickie comes to marry Agnes Pembroke (who for the rude but perceptive Ansell is "not really there") and enter the world of Sawston, the ambitious minor public school in which her brother Herbert has full scope for his meaningless activities of organization and regulation. Forster called the Pembrokes a "compensation device" for his unhappy school days, and the world of petty pomposity and hypocrisy that he builds around them is devastating and memorable. Nevertheless, he is too fair-minded entirely to condemn them ("For Agnes also has her tragedy": chapter 24), and one may see Rickie's spiritual ruin and sense of unreality at Sawston as the result partly of values false in themselves and partly of his simply marrying a woman who is as wrong for him as she had been right for Gerald Dawes, her athletic fiancé most improbably "broken up in the football match" in chapter 5.

Rickie's emancipation from Sawston is brought about by Ansell. In chapter 1 Ansell has been described drawing squares inside circles ad infinitum: reality is "the one in the middle of everything." This image becomes a symbol in chapter 13, when the fact that Rickie has a half-brother is gradually revealed to him by his paternal aunt, the clever but cold Mrs. Failing, as they walk through the two concentric circles of "Cadbury Rings" (Figsbury Rings, an Iron Age earthwork near Salisbury). That Stephen is his half-brother dawns on Rickie just as they reach the central tree; but this basic "real thing" immediately changes for Rickie into an image of his hated father, whose illegitimate son he assumes Stephen to be. Partly because of this, partly because Agnes' concern for respectability is stronger than his desire for truth, Rickie conceals the relationship (of which Stephen at this point is unaware) for two years. But then Stephen is thrown out of Cadover, Mrs. Failing's home; and Ansell, happening to meet him and learning his story (this is less merely coincidental than it seems), determines that the truth shall be heard, not only by Rickie but by a whole dining hall full of Sawston boys. (We believe in this scene because of its theatrical appropriateness rather than its likelihood; Rickie's complacency badly needs shaking up by now.) In the process Rickie learns something he has not bargained for: Stephen is the son of his idolized mother. The reader, also kept in ignorance, is enlightened by the flashback of chapter 29, whereas Rickie's reaction—the shock to his rather priggish illusions—is conveyed by the beautiful extended metaphor of chapter 28: the soul's "coinage," its bankruptcies, its chances of recovery.

But although in the final section Rickie leaves his false life with Agnes and sees that Sawston values had "ignored personal contest, personal truces, personal love," such as he now feels in relation to Stephen, he still errs by idealizing: Stephen is to him not simply a man, whose virtues and faults (he is prone to drunkenness) are alike earthy, but the reborn image of his mother, "a symbol for the vanished past." On his ride through Wiltshire with Stephen he feels "confirmed by the earth" (sufficiently to reject Mrs. Failing's assertion of the majesty of conventions), but his lately gained sense of reality is so precarious that it cannot withstand the discovery that Stephen, a "hero," has broken his promise and got drunk. A second time (Agnes was the first) he is bankrupted of his belief in the reality of people, and though one is sorry for his weakness, one also sympathizes with the "chill of disgust" that passes over Leighton, Mrs. Failing's manservant and Stephen's less sensitive friend. Finding Stephen sprawled over the level crossing (whose dangerousness has been mentioned many times in the novel), Rickie "wearily" pulls him to safety but is unable to save himself. Nor, one feels, does he wish to.

Yet the conclusion of this confused but moving book (which may in crude terms be said to show the survival of the fittest, and perhaps is Forster's burning in effigy of flaws in himself) is not pessimistic. Overlaid on Rickie's pathetic story of failure—which rises, however "wearily," to self-sacrifice at the end—is a mystical sense of continuance. Not only does Rickie achieve some posthumous reputation with his short stories; it is as if, in the last few paragraphs, some of his sensitivity passes into the stronger and now maturer Stephen, through whom and through whose small daughter, "to whom he had given the name of their mother," he gains a portion of immortality.

The last three paragraphs of *The Longest Journey*, which crystallize Forster's feeling for the Wiltshire landscape whose endurance underlies the human life of the novel, are among the most beautiful in his work. Their poignant tranquillity is foreshadowed by the last paragraph of chapter 33, in which Rickie and Stephen launch a burning paper boat into a stream. It is a brilliant poetic symbol of their difference and their unity, and perhaps the high point of the novel:

The paper caught fire from the match, and spread into a rose of flame. "Now gently with me," said Stephen and they laid it flower-like on the stream. Gravel and tremulous weeds leapt into sight, and then the flower sailed into deep water, and up leapt the two arches of a bridge. "It'll strike!" they cried; "no, it won't; it's chosen the left," and one arch became a fairy tunnel, dropping diamonds. Then it vanished for Rickie; but Stephen, who knelt in the water, declared that it was still afloat, far through the arch, burning as if it would burn for ever.

A Room with a View (which Forster unjustly called "slight, unambitious and uninteresting") is a simpler and sunnier book, beginning in Florence with the discovery of love and, after an interval of "muddle," ending there with what promises to be a happy marriage. Forster's third published novel, it was in fact the first he started, and it took its origin from his experiences, in 1901, at a boardinghouse in Florence very like the Pension Bertolini in the novel. It progressed through two drafts, the first a rather pedestrian notation of tourist manners and Italian art called "Lucy"; the second, begun at the end of 1903, a more lively and more emotional story called "New Lucy," which ended with George Emerson being killed by a falling tree while cycling to meet Lucy at Summer Street and elope with her. (This version also contains a scene in which the liberal-minded parson, Mr. Beebe, talks to George Emerson at night in a wood and calls him "irresistible"; there is a homosexual tinge in this that may provide an alternative explanation to that of the published novel for Mr. Beebe's sudden hostility when he learns that Lucy loves George.)

Though Forster rejected his earlier unhappy ending, *A Room with a View* by no means lacks seriousness. Mostly deft and light in its handling, and blending in its social comedy the spirit of Jane Austen and that of George Meredith, it is committed no less than *The Longest Journey* and *Where Angels Fear to Tread* to the idea that life is a battleground of conflicting impulses, with naturalness, truth, and "greatness" as the prizes to be gained by right choices and lost by wrong ones. As Caroline Abbott says to Philip Herriton: "There's never any knowing . . . which of our actions, which of our idlenesses, won't have things hanging on it for ever." The conflict in *A Room with a View* is summed up in its title, which from the start of Lucy Honeychurch's acquaintance with Italy and with the unconventionally truthful Emersons takes on symbolic overtones. Rooms stand for social conventions, deadening by themselves; views for naturalness, freedom, whatever makes it possible for the spirit to breathe and expand. Like *Where Angels Fear to Tread*, *A Room with a View* is about the improvement of its protagonist, and it too uses Italy ("the eternal league of Italy with youth") as the place where that improvement can be begun. Lucy, though subject to the conventional restraints of her prim spinster chaperone,

Charlotte Bartlett, has come to Italy not from Sawston but from a house with the promising name Windy Corner and a wide view of the Weald of Sussex. She has already shown to one sympathetic observer, the clergyman Mr. Beebe, the capacity for greatness in her playing of Beethoven. It is his hopeful prophecy that the novel fulfills, though his belief in celibacy cannot tolerate the form of its fulfillment: "If Miss Honeychurch ever takes to live as she plays, it will be very exciting."

She takes a long time to do so, even though it is soon apparent to the reader that she responds instinctively to the melancholy, lower-class George Emerson, who is awkward of speech but physically direct and eloquent. The first important encounter comes about as a result of a stabbing in the Piazza Signoria, when Lucy faints and George holds her in his arms; it is a tacit assertion of youth and life in the face of death. The second takes place on a hillside covered with violets and with a panoramic view of Florence and the Arno Valley: here George, the "good man" to whom the percipient Italian cab driver has directed her, suddenly kisses her—the lyrical climax to a delightful chapter whose message is that spring in nature and spring in man are the same. But the spell is broken by Charlotte Bartlett, "brown against the view," and before Lucy has had time to respond, Charlotte's propriety and Lucy's own unwillingness to face her feelings have created "a shame-faced world of precautions and barriers" in which good form triumphs over the stirrings of love.

Part II, set in Lucy's English village, where Forster gradually contrives the reassembly of most of the pension cast, shows Lucy's slow realization—in all senses—of what Italy and George Emerson have so simply offered her. Her path to love, freedom, and truth (which for Forster are all bound up together) is the more tortuous since she must first perceive the imperfections of Cecil Vyse, the supercilious aesthete to whom in her unadmitted retreat from George she has become engaged. It is plain to the reader that George's criticisms of Cecil lead Lucy to reject him, and equally plain that Cecil, essentially ascetic, is less physically attractive to Lucy than George, whom she encounters after the naked bathing scene in chapter 12, "barefoot, barechested, radiant and personable"; but, tangled in a web of petty lies, social embarrassment, and sexual inhibition, Lucy still refuses to admit that she loves George, and for a time joins what Forster, in one of those judgment-passing asides characteristic of his work, calls "the armies of the benighted, who follow neither the heart nor the brain" and have "sinned against passion and truth." It is the intuitive penetration and passionate honesty of old Mr. Emerson —whose ideas resemble those of Samuel Butler— that finally burn through Lucy's conventional armor, equip her instead with "courage and love," and save her from the fate of such as Charlotte Bartlett. The novel ends with Lucy and George united and back in Florence, looking out of their room at the view and listening to "the river, bearing down the snows of winter into the Mediterranean." They have gained happiness, but there is no doubt that it has been touch and go.

Shortly before *A Room with a View* was published, Forster wrote to Nathaniel Wedd that he was "getting much more interested in public affairs"; at the end of 1908 he repeated the sentiment in his diary. Hitherto his novels had mostly concerned themselves with the individual's inner life and its development; the pretensions of the great world offered little of which Forster could approve. But in *Howards End*, whose appearance established Forster's reputation with a larger public, he made a concerted effort to determine whether the life of feeling and imagination could run in double harness with the life of business, action, and convention. Behind the book lies a desire to "see life steadily and see it whole," and with this in mind Forster expands his canvas to include the poor clerk Leonard Bast as well as two contrasting middle-class families, the intellectual and artistic Schlegels and the commercial Wilcoxes, and wills himself to perceive merit in an unimaginative world that had seemed, in *The Longest Journey*, almost wholly uncongenial.

By *Howards End* Forster clearly thought of himself as the creator of a fictional empire, since the reader's attention is directed to other of his novels. In chapter 13 Tibby Schlegel's lack of interest in a profession is discussed in terms of a "weedy" Mr. Vyse and an admirably industrious Mr. Pembroke; and chapter 9 mentions a piano-playing Miss Quested, who will play a more important part in *A Passage to India*.

Howards End is a consciously "big" book, with a wide range of incidents and interests (one of these, the position of women, is carried over from *A Room with a View*). The unfolding of its action is leisurely, too complex to summarize, and covers a longer period of time than that of any other Forster novel except

Maurice; indeed, the passing of time, and the concomitant gradual encroachment of London, "a tract of quivering grey," on the countryside around, is an important aspect of it. Its two major elements, however, and those on which the story turns, are indicated by the title and the epigraph. Howards End, the house in Hertfordshire that Forster based down to the smallest detail on Rooksnest, has an indefinable numinous quality that transcends not only the materialism of the Wilcoxes (father and children) but the intellectualism of the Schlegels. Like its owner, the retiring, intuitive Mrs. Wilcox, it represents permanence, suggests the "unseen," and is the spiritual touchstone of the novel. Here the story begins, with the impressionable Helen Schlegel visiting and falling briefly in love with Paul Wilcox; here it ends, with Margaret Schlegel at last in possession of the home Mrs. Wilcox had left her so many chapters before, only to be disregarded by her "sensible" family. The passage in chapter 11 where her wishes are set aside is perhaps Forster's finest authorial judgment: with scrupulous fairness he marshals the arguments in favor of the Wilcoxes' action, then adds with steely finality the one that surely outweighs them: "They did neglect a personal appeal. The woman who had died did say to them, 'Do this,' and they answered, 'We will not.'"

Howards End, like Wiltshire in *The Longest Journey,* is Forster's symbol of England, an immemorial rural England resisting the "red rust" of advancing suburbia and opposed to the impersonal flux of London, where "month by month things were stepping livelier, but to what goal? The population still rose, but what was the quality of the men born?" England is symbolized also by Oniton Grange, remote at the western edge of Shropshire; another house loved by Margaret, it means nothing to its casual Wilcox owners and they mean nothing to it: "It is not their ghosts that sigh among the alders at evening." In large part, *Howards End* is a fair-minded novelist's attempt to answer, through the detailed texture of representative human lives, the question about England that his poetic alter ego poses at the end of chapter 19, as Helen Schlegel watches the sunset from the downs between Swanage and Poole Harbour. There is perhaps rather too much of a catch in his voice, but his words are moving nonetheless:

England was alive, throbbing through all her estuaries, crying for joy through the mouths of all her gulls, and the north wind, with contrary motion, blew stronger against her rising seas. What did it mean? For what end are her fair complexities, her changes of soil, her sinuous coast? Does she belong to those who have moulded her and made her feared by other lands, or to those who have added nothing to her power, but have somehow seen her, seen the whole island at once, lying as a jewel in a silver sea, sailing as a ship of souls, with all the brave world's fleet accompanying her towards eternity?

The epigraph, "Only connect . . . ," is a quotation from the novel itself, and appears in its full form in chapter 22: "Only connect the prose and passion, and both will be exalted, and human love will be seen at its height." The idea of "connection" recurs throughout the novel; its meaning ranges from being honest with oneself (as by avoiding the hypocrisy of the sexual "double standard," which Mr. Wilcox in the climactic scene between himself and Margaret in chapter 38 shows himself unable to do), to bringing together in one partnership the Wilcox outer life of business, practicality, and imperialism and the Schlegel inner life of culture, personal relations, and individual responsibility. Forster's conscious urge toward this imagined wholeness (which stems partly from the honest liberal intellectual's refusal to spurn the practical world in which he functions, and partly from loss of nerve, the fear that, by themselves, "personal relations lead to sloppiness in the end") is embodied in Margaret Schlegel, the elder of the two sisters—she is twenty-nine when the novel begins, which was Forster's age when he started to write it. But it is hard to feel either that her relationship with Henry Wilcox succeeds in building a "rainbow bridge" or that the love that keeps it going is more than a requirement of plot and theme. Henry is a cut above his brusque and hidebound son, Charles, but Margaret is too clear-sighted not to notice his lack of imagination, his conventionality of response, his lapses from honesty. In his depiction of their relationship Forster's instincts pull strongly against his intentions, and the reader resists Margaret's overtolerant progress toward what seems a decidedly arranged marriage.

Margaret's aim is worthwhile, certainly, and Margaret herself is an admirable character, sensitive as well as reasonable. But it is her younger, prettier, and more impulsive sister, Helen, whom the reader may find more sympathetic. If Margaret makes one think of a less vulnerable Rickie, Helen is something of a less single-minded Ansell. It is she who first responds to the apparent masculine strength of the

Wilcoxes, who are "keen on all games" and "put everything to use"; but she soon discovers, behind their life of "telegrams and anger," no resources for dealing with emotion, and regains her conviction that only personal relations matter. Where they are missing, as she is reminded in chapter 5, listening in the Queen's Hall to the third movement of Beethoven's Fifth Symphony, there is only "panic and emptiness."

Leonard Bast, who enters the novel at this point as an insignificant but aspiring clerk who goes to concerts and reads "improving" authors like Ruskin (meanwhile his flat is dark, as well as stuffy), grows in importance and stature as the novel proceeds. Forster describes his life with tartness yet compassion: he had spent some time teaching in London at the Working Men's College. From being a deserving case taken up by the liberal Miss Schlegel, he becomes vital not only to the plot but to the novel's theme of connection. Leonard loses his job as an indirect result of bad advice from Henry Wilcox; and Helen's simultaneous failure to right matters and her discovery that Leonard's older wife, Jacky, was once Wilcox's mistress cause her to give herself to Leonard. (Some critics have found this unconvincing; on the basis of the descriptions in chapters 40 and 41, I disagree.) Out of that brief half-hour of love at Oniton come Helen's pregnancy (a revelation Forster dramatically withholds, while Helen is absent in Germany); Margaret's realization of the hollowness of her marriage; the moving reunion of the sisters at Howards End, despite the self-righteous and "unconnecting" prohibition of Henry Wilcox; and the death of Leonard himself, through heart disease and Charles Wilcox's notions of chivalrous behavior.

It is not for nothing, however, that Leonard's death ("They laid Leonard, who was dead, on the gravel; Helen poured water over him") has a likeness to baptismal rebirth. Though Margaret's kindness keeps her with Henry, who needs her support now that his son has been imprisoned by a law "made in his own image," all her efforts have failed to make a bridge between her world and that of her husband. Howards End is hers, belatedly, but it is to the illegitimate child of Leonard and Helen—the fruit of impulse, the "connection" of middle-class culture and working-class aspiration—that it will pass, thus in a sense restoring the urban, uprooted Leonard to the land from which his agricultural forebears sprang. There is no facile optimism in Forster's

pastoral ending; the "shiver" of Margaret and the "infectious joy" of Helen are too closely juxtaposed for that. But the inner life has won a kind of victory, and what Forster many years later called "the possession of England" has been achieved by those who have deserved it.

Howards End is a remarkable piece of work and enlarges the area of contemporary life on which Forster comments (making his heroines half-German seems partly a device allowing him to use impressions gathered while in Pomerania in 1905, as tutor to the daughters of the countess von Arnim, the Elizabeth of *Elizabeth and Her German Garden*). But it is not entirely characteristic of him, this liberal intellectual's excursion (as he later felt it to be) into the realistic, essentially metropolitan world of Galsworthy and Wells; at times the novel moves heavily, at times Forster's addresses to the reader lack his usual authority and aplomb (in the last paragraph of chapter 2, for instance), and it is perhaps symptomatic that he chooses to educate Tibby Schlegel not at his own Cambridge but at Oxford, which "wants its inmates to love it rather than to love one another." Where the novel is Forsterian is in its defense of the inner life, its preference of the country to the city, its transcendence of materialism (the Wilcox world of motorcars and money) by an awareness of greater values—all that is implied by Helen Schlegel's cryptic and visionary phrase, "Death destroys a man; the idea of Death saves him."

In 1911 Forster started a new novel that he called "Arctic Summer." (The title refers to the aim of one of its protagonists, a successful civil servant named Martin Whitby, who wants a "new era . . . in which there will be time to get something really important done.") It was again intended to contrast, and apparently to bring together, two human types, the civilized intellectual and, this time, the romantic, chivalrous "man of instinct," represented by a fair-haired young officer, Clesant March. Forster later salvaged this name for his stories "Dr. Woolacott" and "The Other Boat"; but the novel, which opened promisingly with a vivid scene at Basle station and proceeded to Italy, was abandoned in 1912 because he "had not settled what was going to happen."

In October 1912 Forster set off on the first of his two visits to India. He stayed for six months and traveled widely: to Aligarh to see his Muslim friend Syed Ross Masood, whom he had first met in Weybridge in 1906, tutored for Oxford entrance, and fallen in love with; to the native state of Dewas

Senior near Indore, where his Cambridge friend Malcolm Darling was tutor to the young maharajah; to Bankipore in Bengal (the original of Chandrapore) and the nearby Barabar Caves. On this visit he drafted the first seven chapters of *A Passage to India* and parts of the novel up to the outing to the Marabar Caves; he knew that something important was to happen there but (as with "Arctic Summer") not yet what. But this, at least, eventually became clear, some ten years later.

Meanwhile, a visit that Forster paid in September 1913 to the sixty-year-old thinker Edward Carpenter realized in him the wish and the ability to write directly about homosexuality. Carpenter (himself a homosexual who shared his "simple life" with a young working-class man) had written courageously on sexual matters, and in his essay "The Intermediate Sex" there is a description of the male homosexual that fits Forster well enough: he "tends to be of a gentle, emotional disposition," and his mind "is generally intuitive and instinctive in its perceptions, with more or less of artistic feeling." To this feminine temperament, expressed indirectly in the heterosexual framework of his conventional novels, may be credited both his heroes' response to other men (even Rickie's marriage to Agnes seems partly a vicarious possession of Gerald) and his empathy toward his heroines. It is not too fanciful to see in the sisterly tenderness of Helen and Margaret (chapters 37 and 40 of *Howards End*) another kind of love relationship, and in their embattled unity against Wilcox maleness a declaration by their creator. One may also sense in Margaret's defense of "eternal differences" (chapter 14) a meaning beyond the immediate context, an increasing pressure within Forster himself: "people are far more different than is pretended. All over the world men and women are worrying because they cannot develop as they are supposed to develop. Here and there they have the matter out, and it comforts them." It was in *Maurice*, begun immediately after his visit to Carpenter and finished in July 1914, that Forster "had the matter out," though factors external and personal delayed the publication of his fictional catharsis until after his death.

The four parts into which *Maurice* is symmetrically divided can be considered virtually as two, each dealing with one of Maurice's relationships: his intense but Platonic one with his fellow undergraduate Clive Durham, and his frankly physical one with the gamekeeper Alec Scudder. The two large sections are related by motifs; in each occurs the yearning invocation "Come!" and both relationships reach fulfillment by means of contrasted entries at windows, Maurice leaping up to Clive's, Alec climbing into Maurice's. But counterpointed against the chronological four-part or two-part structure of the novel—which charts Maurice's "improvement" through self-realization—is another, thematic, one, tripartite and akin to that of *The Longest Journey*: one may call it "Sawston, Cambridge, Wiltshire." Though, as a distancing device, Forster makes Maurice in some externals unlike himself—he is the son of a stockbroker, has sisters, is fairly good at games, and is not an intellectual—Maurice's discoveries are Forster's and give him the opportunity to present the plight of the homosexual in an unsympathetic and largely uncomprehending world: the portraits of Dr. Barry, Dr. Lasker-Jones, and the clergyman, Mr. Borenius, are notable additions to his gallery of minor characters. Nor, while rendering sympathetically Maurice's loneliness and his search for the friend of his boyhood dream, does Forster's honesty fail to record the seamier side of his experience, in the earlier chapters of part III.

Maurice's journey begins in the pleasant but clouded world of suburbia—mother-dominated home, preparatory school (at the seaside, like Forster's), public school (here called Sunnington) —where he has fitful intimations of his homosexual nature, inherited from his father. He moves on to Cambridge, where his mind is progressively liberated: by the perception that talk can matter (Risley, the garrulous Trinity B.A., is based on Lytton Strachey), by music (Tchaikovsky's "Pathetic" Symphony, which recurs as an example of homosexual composition), by the reading of Plato's *Symposium*, and finally by the realization that he returns the love of the more intellectual Clive Durham. Their relationship is a mixture of tenderness, high-minded restraint, and youthful ragging, its perfection beautifully caught in chapter 13, the motorcycle excursion that ends in the fens beyond Ely, and is both ordinary and outside time and society. But for Clive, inheritor of a country estate, homosexuality proves only a phase, and his terse announcement from Greece, "Against my will I have become normal," plunges Maurice into "the abyss where he had wandered as a boy." Only an iron effort of will that involves a total separation of his public and his private personalities keeps him going.

It is from Penge, Clive's estate "on the Wiltshire

and Somerset border," that Maurice's salvation eventually comes, in the form of Alec Scudder, an under-gamekeeper. Scudder is at first a shadowy, barely articulate figure, a servant in a middle-class world; but by a number of slight touches (some literal) Forster makes credible his intuitive response to Maurice's need, which is now physical as well as emotional. But it is not until class differences and class mistrust have been fully confronted (in the tense British Museum scene, extensively revised in 1932, and the chapter following, added then) that a real relationship between two people is established—one which, after Alec has decided not to sail for Argentina on the *Normannia*, can survive only if he and Maurice drop out of stratified society and take like outlaws to "the greenwood." The final scene, in which Maurice confronts Clive and then seems almost to vanish poetically into air, is thus a declaration both of sexual and of social nonconformity, of ideal freedom, the world well lost for love; an ending that, in the words of Edward Carpenter, "though improbable is not impossible." (The 1914 text contained an epilogue, removed by 1932, in which Maurice's sister Kitty comes across her brother and Alec working as woodcutters somewhere in Yorkshire—a life of "connection" that "combined daily work with love." It was the sort of life Carpenter had himself achieved on his farm near Sheffield.)

Though it lacks the complexity and symbolism of other Forster novels (its simple forward thrust gives it some likeness to *A Room with a View*), and though it chooses to emphasize the sexual psychology of its hero above other possible aspects of his life, *Maurice* is not thinly disguised autobiography or wish fulfillment but a created fictional world. Forster's style, whether in lively or in somber mood, is admirably terse, adapted both to express Maurice's character and to keep a difficult subject under control. If the occasional phrase embarrasses, one needs to remember that Forster was breaking new ground, an incidental indication of his difficulties being given in chapter 16: "No convention settled what was poetic, what absurd." But in general the novel's presentation of the many aspects of homosexuality is illuminating and moving.

Forster spent most of World War I (from late 1915 to early 1919) in Alexandria, collecting information from the wounded as a search officer for the Red Cross. He also contributed articles to the *Egyptian Mail* under the pen name Pharos (the famous light-house of ancient Alexandria), compiled a very comprehensive *History and Guide* that was published there in 1922, and wrote a number of essays on aspects of Alexandria, classical and modern, that appeared in England in 1923 under the title *Pharos and Pharillon*. Among them is one on the Alexandrian poet C. P. Cavafy, whose work Forster consistently championed; others reveal an interest in byways of the early Christian church and an awareness of Alexandria as a historic meeting point of West and East.

In 1921 Forster revisited India, acting for six months as private secretary to the maharajah of Dewas Senior. This fascinating experience (fully documented in 1953 in *The Hill of Devi*) gave Forster the material for the final section of *A Passage to India*, but he was able to continue work on the book only when he had returned from the country it "purported to describe," and it was completed with difficulty and self-doubt.

A Passage to India was eventually published in 1924, to a chorus of praise that may have allayed Forster's worries about its adequacy as a picture of the country. Even for an Anglo-Indian critic, who pointed out technical inaccuracy in the trial scene and in the portrayal of the collector and other officials, there was no lack of emotional verisimilitude (it should be said that, in political terms, the novel—in the words of K. Natwar-Singh—"depicts a pre-1914 India"). Though much of its material is disturbing, Forster's handling of it is not, and the novel has an impressive air both of authority and of truth.

The comments of T. E. Lawrence, comparing it with his own *Seven Pillars of Wisdom*, are particularly illuminating: "If excellence of materials meant anything, my book would have been as good as yours: but it stinks of me: whereas yours is universal: the bitter hopeless picture a cloud might have painted, of man in India." The last three words, and their juxtaposition, are significant. Forster's novels have always dealt with people, and *A Passage to India* does so too, finding in the misunderstandings and rapprochements of English and Indians both a new and special example of human relationships and a final metaphor for their general difficulty. They have also presented human development, people reexamining themselves in relation to a country or the sense of one, and here India takes the place of an invigorating Italy or a quietly enduring England. But in *A Passage to India* the variety of races and types—English, Anglo-Indian, Indian (Moslem and

Hindu)—is so much wider that "men" become "man"; and the country is so much bigger, so much more deeply challenging in its diverse religions and manifestations of the unseen, so baffling a mixture of mystery and muddle, that it comes to represent the universe itself, against which man's values seem so uncertain and man's activities so trivial.

It is this contrast that makes *A Passage to India* such a profound and poignant book: despite the pessimism voiced by (and through) Mrs. Moore, people matter in it, but nothing could be less true than D. H. Lawrence's statement that Forster here sees "people, people and nothing but people." The novel's detachment is twin to its universality and is demonstrated in two specific differences from its predecessors: it contains virtually no authorial asides, no glosses on its characters' behavior, which is left to explain itself; and it begins (as do its second and third sections) not with people talking but with a description of the context in which they exist: city and sky; dry hills and caves; God. Without denigrating the earlier novels, one may say of Forster in *A Passage to India* what he says in chapter 26 about the symbolically named Adela Quested, the transplanted denizen of the cultured London of *Howards End*: "she was no longer examining life, but being examined by it."

A Passage to India is a realistic and a symbolic novel, of such rich and even texture, so successfully doing so many things at once, that it is difficult to separate its varied strands without falsifying the total impression it gives. Out of the confrontation between the English and India, and the simple but gripping plot that dramatizes it, Forster makes his most comprehensive statement of human possibilities and limitations. The drama is played out against a larger, and in some sense divine, background that is suggested by the book's division into three sections named after vital elements of the Indian experience: "Mosque," "Caves," "Temple." The outer sections represent the Moslem world of Dr. Aziz and the Hindu world of Professor Godbole respectively, and are broadly positive in tone. But the central one, which in terms of action displays the worst attitudes of the British Raj and sets them against the open mistrust and dislike of the Indian governed, represents the enigmatic and frightening side of spiritual experience, the sense of chaos and nothingness whose effects spill over and make the conclusion of the novel equivocal. The sections are also, however, appropriate seasons of the year, states of mind, and

stages in an evolving pattern: coolness, rationality, the search for understanding; heat and dryness, climactic hysteria, loss of faith, hostility, fragmentation; rain, rebirth, a kind of reconciliation. (The movement from "Caves" to "Temple" suggests a possible link between Forster's novel and T. S. Eliot's *The Waste Land*, published two years earlier.)

"Mosque" is concerned with building up a scene, with human interaction, and with certain particular relationships, rather than with anything as definite as plot. But its splendid opening chapter (one of Forster's best pieces of writing) presents a clear indication of the novel's scope, describing first the two worlds of Chandrapore—shapeless Indian town and neat British civil station—linked only by the "overarching sky"; and ending, with apparent casualness yet a touch of foreboding, with a mention of the distant "fists and fingers" of the Marabar Hills, "containing the extraordinary caves." The adjective (which recurs like a leitmotif in chapters 12 and 32) has its original, literal force in this novel: the caves—outside nature, superhuman—are the ground where the ordinary, the familiar, the positive will be tested and strained. While they wait, Forster with a multitude of small details and lively touches shows the failure of "official" relations between British and Indians at Mr. Turton's "bridge party" (Forster does not like the group mentality of Anglo-India—especially that of the memsahibs—but he is by no means as blindly hostile to it as is sometimes supposed), and the more successful attempts at communication between individuals. The most important of these is between the mild and humane principal of the Government College, Cyril Fielding (whose response in chapter 32 to Venice's "beauty of form" makes him seem an older Martin Whitby), and the volatile, poetic Moslem doctor, Aziz, whose impetuosity is brilliantly rendered by the opening of chapter 2. Aziz also establishes an instinctive relationship, through their meeting in the mosque, with Mrs. Moore, who believes in goodwill and, in her intuitive capacity, resembles Mrs. Wilcox. It is through her that the religious uneasiness of the novel is transmitted, first by her puzzlement when the Christian "God is love" is faced by Godbole's Hindu god who "refuses" or "neglects to come," then through her terrifying experience of "panic and emptiness" in the Marabar Caves.

Here, on the expedition planned by Aziz to cement his friendship with the two visiting English ladies, things fall apart. The introductory chapter of

"Caves" contains a perfect natural symbol for attempted union (with fellow man, or perhaps with God) in its description of the striking of a match in the polished interior chamber: "Immediately another flame rises in the depths of the rock and moves towards the surface like an imprisoned spirit. . . . The two flames approach and strive to unite, but cannot, because one of them breathes air, the other stone."

But on Adela and Mrs. Moore the caves (sacred places in India) have a totally malign effect, destructive of human friendship and of sustaining faith. Their claustrophobic atmosphere causes the former to imagine she has been assaulted by Aziz (she has not, but what has happened cannot be dismissed by the easy term "hallucination") and sets off all the latent hostility of rulers and ruled, its last reverberations—after the trial—even upsetting the mutual trust and generosity of Aziz and Fielding. For Mrs. Moore it is the cave's dull, monotonous echo, "bououm" or "ou-boum," that generates horror: "It had managed to murmur, 'Pathos, piety, courage—they exist, but are identical, and so is filth. Everything exists, nothing has value.'" The echo, it is important to notice, is heard by Mrs. Moore "at a time when she chanced to be fatigued," and so its message of futility and blankness can hardly be taken as Forster's final vision of life, particularly in view of the end of chapter 23; but its pessimism lurks at the edges of human endeavor in this novel. It is present in Adela's statement to Fielding, in chapter 29, that "all these personal relations we try to live by are temporary"; and (though here the effect is ironic and humbling rather than disillusioning) in Forster's use, as a frame for the fiasco of the trial scene, of the untouchable punkah-wallah, to whom nothing has any meaning and who, when it is all over, continues "to pull the cord of his punkah, to gaze at the empty dais and the overturned special chairs, and rhythmically to agitate the clouds of descending dust."

"Temple," the mystical concluding section—in which the quality of Forster's writing, as if borne on some hidden current of understanding, touches what he called "prophecy"—offers a knitting-together, a reconciliation, as well as the "scene of separation" that Forster had recommended in 1906, in a lecture entitled "Pessimism in Literature," as the only close to a novel that offered "rest with honour." Fielding and Aziz come together again not in British India but in the native state of Mau (actually Dewas Senior), whose function in the novel resembles that of Oniton

in *Howards End:* a place enduring "somewhere else," where something mysterious and good goes on. They compose their differences, the misunderstanding about Adela (whom Aziz supposes Fielding to have married) is cleared up, the two are friends again; but "socially they had no meeting-place," and we are made to feel that for them, "here" and "now," parting is inevitable—a condition not merely of India but, it seems, of human life. Yet around them, in the rainy season, the lovingly described sacred and funny rituals of Gokul Ashtami—the festival of the birth of Krishna—are going on: a topsy-turvy world of "God is love" in which, as Godbole sings his song of appeal and holds within his mind both Mrs. Moore and a wasp (like the one she had called "pretty dear" in chapter 3), it may be said that everything exists and everything has value. The dead Mrs. Moore is also present through her daughter, Stella (whom Fielding has married), and through her son, Ralph, quick to sense the nuances of human feeling and thus "an Oriental," as Aziz calls him in the identical phrase he had used to Mrs. Moore herself. All of them seem comprised within the divine chaos of the Hindu festival, and in the collision of their two boats with each other and with the mud replica of Krishna's village of Gokul as it is carried into the waters of the tank, Forster offers a magnificent natural symbol of baptismal rebirth, as humans touch each other and what is beyond them. Thus, though the last ride of Aziz and Fielding takes sad note of "the divisions of daily life" and the particular obstacles to friendship in India, we are able to sense in the final negatives "not yet" and "not there" the presence, the possibility, of "sometime" and "somewhere."

IV

AFTER *A Passage to India* Forster published no more fiction in his lifetime. Had he actually written no more (and he wrote little enough), the technical mastery of his last novel, and the feeling of completeness it gives, would be enough in themselves to account for his silence: it is hard to see how *A Passage to India* could be bettered as a statement of the human experience sub specie aeternitatis. But we now know, from Forster's correspondence and private papers, and from the stories of *The Life to Come*, both that he retained the wish to express the homosexual outlook on life and that, from time to time, he succeeded in doing so. He felt unable, however either to publish the results or to suppress the wish (or express it in a form compatible with censorship, as to some extent his earlier novels had done, the friendship of Fielding and Aziz being perhaps the last, though very faint, example). His dilemma is suggested by a letter of 1928 that he and Virginia Woolf addressed to the *Nation and Athenaeum* in connection with Radclyffe Hall's lesbian novel *The Well of Loneliness:* "The sense that there is a taboo list [of prohibited or prohibitable subjects] will work on [the novelist], and will make him alert and cautious instead of surrendering himself to his creative impulses." For Forster, the effect was to separate his career after 1924 into two pieces, the public and the private.

In 1927 he gave the Clark lectures at Trinity College, Cambridge. These were published as *Aspects of the Novel* and express with admirable lucidity and organization a host of insights into the ways in which novels work, some of them—particularly the notions of pattern, rhythm, expansion, and the affinity between fiction and music—being invaluable as indications of Forster's own aims as a novelist. Forster's essays of many years were collected in *Abinger Harvest* (1936) and *Two Cheers for Democracy* (1951): they are obviously the work of a man who loved writing, and who valued it not only as a way of expressing delight and giving language permanence, but as a weapon in the fight against the darker tendencies of the twentieth-century world. It is in his essays that Forster most clearly appears as a liberal humanist, concerned for the life of the individual and of the spirit, against philistinism, intolerance, and any kind of political totalitarianism. His later writings have a largely retrospective flavor, that of a man less and less at home in the organized world about him, and feeling piety and gratitude toward the past: toward the tradition of the countryside in his pageant play, *England's Pleasant Land* (1940), toward individuals in his biographies, *Goldsworthy Lowes Dickinson* (1934) and *Marianne Thornton* (1956), and toward a vanished India, "the great opportunity of my life," in *The Hill of Devi.* As great an opportunity had been furnished by his undergraduate years at King's College, Cambridge, and some return to that life was offered when, in 1945, King's made him an honorary fellow and invited him, unusually, to reside. There he spent his last twenty-five years: it was an appropriate conclusion, and one as beneficial to others as to himself.

But Forster had not entirely given up fiction, as the publication in 1972 of *The Life to Come* made clear. At the International Writers' Congress in Paris in 1935 he had complained again about censorship and declared that "sex is a subject for serious treatment and also for comic treatment." In his eight homosexual short stories, written between 1922 and 1958, both methods are used. "The Obelisk" (1939) is the best of the comic ones, but it is not merely a phallic joke. The suggestive double entendre at the end ("It's fallen into the landslip upside-down, the tip of it's gone in ever so far") is extremely funny, as is Hilda's dawning realization that if she and her handsome sailor did not reach the obelisk, then neither did her husband, Ernest, and his odd one. But it is also a genuinely happy and liberating story, in which the secret dreams of husband and wife are satisfied (both, in another sense, reach the obelisk), and a tacit appeal for equal tolerance of the two routes to it, homosexual as well as heterosexual. The more fanciful, Ruritanian "What Does It Matter?" is also such an appeal (though less well executed), an attempt to deflate the pressure of sexual intolerance by laughing at it.

The serious stories admit the pressure and powerfully convey the unhappiness it brings. "Arthur Snatchfold" (1928), the story of a brief but not sordid weekend encounter between a rich businessman and a milkman, emphasizes the vindictiveness of the law and suggests the dignity of homosexual feeling by associating it with self-sacrifice—that of the working-class partner: it is as if *Maurice* had taken a grimmer turn at the end. "The Life to Come" (1922), with its bleak, tragic misunderstanding between a missionary and a native chief, and between two kinds of love, is strangely imaginative and haunting, and ends in a violence that, Vithobai hopes, will unite him with Paul Pinmay beyond the grave. But the violence that ends the finest, longest, and most physically explicit of all these stories, "The Other Boat" (begun in 1913 and finished in 1957–1958), is surely that of defiance and despair. Set in the second decade of the century, on a boat bound for India (the *Normannia,* as in *Maurice*), the story brilliantly creates the two worlds of Lionel March: that of convention and racial superiority in which as a young army officer he appears to belong, and that below decks which he shares with the half-caste, "Cocoanut," his childhood playmate on the boat going the other way, and now his lover. The complex tension between his loyalties, public and personal, and between his knowledge of his real nature and his orthodox revulsion from it, lead to his strangling Cocoanut at the point of orgasm and then to his suicide, jumping into the sea "naked and with the seeds of love on him." It is a magnificent and terrible climax, and suggests—particularly coming from a man of nearly eighty—Forster's frustration as a writer unable to express his full self publicly. Such was the price he paid for reticence. When he wrote on the final text (1960) of *Maurice* the wry comment "Publishable—but worth it?" (which—if it is not mere tautology—means "Is it worth stirring up a fuss?"), he indicated that he did not wish to pay whatever price frankness in his lifetime might involve. In view of the public and legal attitude to homosexuality as late as the early 1960's (as evidenced, for instance, by the contemporary British film *Victim*, 1961), criticism of Forster's choice seems out of place.

The conclusion of a short essay like this, on a writer as complex and subtle as Forster, can be no more than the précis of a précis. He is both an intellectual novelist and a poetic one. He moves easily from the realistic into the symbolic and the mystical. Beneath a sometimes comic manner he is profoundly serious. Aesthetically, his novels have pattern, harmony, order. To the mind they offer more wisdom than most; in both mind and emotions they generate a sense of liberation and excitement, and go on doing so. Forster has his blind spots and his prejudices, but his conscientious fairness strives to reduce them. He is occasionally clumsy and unconvincing. But here we should remember what he said, in *Aspects of the Novel*, about Sir Walter Scott: "If he had passion he would be a great writer—no amount of clumsiness or artificiality would matter then." Unlike Scott, Forster has much more than "a temperate heart and gentlemanly feelings and an intelligent affection for the countryside." Forster has passion, and is a great writer.

SELECTED BIBLIOGRAPHY

I. Bibliography. B. J. Kirkpatrick, *A Bibliography of E. M. Forster* (London, 1965; rev. ed., 1968); F. P. W. McDowell, "E. M. Forster: An Annotated Secondary Bibliography," *English Literature in Transition* 13, 2 (1970), very comprehensive.

II. Collected Works. Uniform Edition (London, 1924), *A Passage to India* first published in this edition, 1926; Pocket Edition: novels (London, 1947), *Aspects of the Novel* (London, 1949), *Goldsworthy Lowes Dickinson* (London, 1962); *Collected Short Stories* (London, 1947); repr. 1966), intro. by Forster; O. Stallybrass, ed., Abinger Edition (London, 1972–   ).

III. Separate Works. *Where Angels Fear to Tread* (London, 1905), novel, Abinger ed. (1975); *The Longest Journey* (London, 1907), novel, World's Classics ed. (London, 1960), with intro. by Forster; *A Room with a View* (London, 1908), novel, Abinger ed. (1977); *Howards End* (London, 1910), novel, Abinger ed. (1973); *The Celestial Omnibus and Other Stories* (London, 1911; repr. 1920 and 1924), contains "The Story of a Panic," "The Other Side of the Hedge," "The Celestial Omnibus," "Other Kingdom," "The Curate's Friend," "The Road from Colonus."

The Story of the Siren (London, 1920), short story; *The Government of Egypt: Recommendations by a Committee of the International Section of the Labour Research Department* (London, 1920), includes "Notes on Egypt" by Forster; *Alexandria: A History and a Guide* (Alexandria, 1922), repr. with new intro. by author (New York, 1961; Gloucester, Mass., 1968; Woodstock, N. Y., 1974); *Pharos and Pharillon* (London, 1923; repr. 1926, 1961), essays; *A Passage to India* (London, 1924), novel; *Aspects of the Novel* (London, 1927), criticism, the Clark lectures, Cambridge, Abinger ed. (London, 1974); *The Eternal Moment, and Other Stories* (London, 1928), contains "The Machine Stops," "The Point of It," "Mr. Andrews," "Co-ordination," "The Story of the Siren," "The Eternel Moment"; *Goldsworthy Lowes Dickinson* (London, 1934), biography, Abinger ed. (London, 1973), with intro. by W. H. Auden; *Abinger Harvest* (London, 1936), sixty assorted pieces contributed to various journals from 1903 to 1934.

Nordic Twilight (London, 1940), political essay, Macmillan War Pamphlet no. 3; *England's Pleasant Land; A Pageant Play* (Toronto–London, 1940); *Virginia Woolf* (Cambridge, 1942), criticism, the Rede lecture, Cambridge, 1941, repr. in *Two Cheers for Democracy; The Development of English Prose Between 1918 and 1939* (Glasgow, 1945), the W. P. Ker Memorial lecture, Glasgow, 1944, repr. and rev. in *Two Cheers for Democracy; Two Cheers for Democracy* (London, 1951), sixty-seven essays and reviews from 1925 to 1951, Abinger ed. (London, 1972); *The Hill of Devi: Being Letters from Dewas State Senior* (London, 1953); *Marianne Thornton, 1797–1887: A Domestic Biography* (London, 1956).

A. Gishford, ed., *Tribute to Benjamin Britten on His Fiftieth Birthday* (London, 1963), contains "Arctic Summer: Fragment of an Unfinished Novel" by Forster; *Maurice* (New York–London, 1971), novel, intro. by P. N. Furbank; *Albergo Empedocle and Other Writings* (London, 1971), ed. with intro. and notes by G. H. Thompson, contains Forster's earliest published story and other uncollected essays and reviews from 1900 to 1915; *The Life to Come, and Other Stories* (New York–London, 1972), Abinger ed., contains "Ansell," "Albergo Empedocle," "The

Purple Envelope," "The Helping Hand," "The Rock," "The Life to Come," "Dr. Woolacott," "Arthur Snatchfold," "The Obelisk," "What Does It Matter? A Morality," "The Classical Annex," "The Torque," "The Other Boat," "Three Courses and a Dessert"; *The Lucy Novels: Early Sketches for "A Room with a View"* (London, 1977), Abinger ed.

IV. SHORTER PIECES. "'Reflections in India—Too Late,' by our Indian correspondent [E. M. F.]," *Nation and Athenaeum* (21 January 1922), 614–615; E. Fay, *Original Letters from India 1779–1815* (London, 1925), intro. and notes by Forster; G. Beith, ed., *Edward Carpenter: In Appreciation* (London, 1931), includes "Some Memories" by Forster, pp. 74–81; A. W. Lawrence, ed., *T. E. Lawrence by His Friends* (London, 1937), includes section by Forster, pp. 282–286; A. Craig, *The Banned Books of England* (London, 1937)), intro. by Forster; "The Ivory Tower," *London Mercury* (Christmas 1938), 119–130; "The Art of Fiction I: E. M. Forster," *Paris Review* (Spring 1953), 28–41, interview by P. N. Furbank and F. J. H. Haskell; "Indian Entries," *Encounter* 18 (January 1962), 20–27, extracts from Forster's diary describing his first visit to India (8 October 1912 to 2 April 1913).

V. BIOGRAPHICAL AND CRITICAL STUDIES. V. Woolf, "The Novels of E. M. Forster," *Atlantic Monthly* 115, no. 5 (November 1927), repr. in *The Death of the Moth and Other Essays* (London, 1942); D. M. Hoare, *Some Studies in the Modern Novel* (London, 1938), contains ch. on Forster; R. Macaulay, *The Writings of E. M. Forster* (London, 1938); L. Trilling, *E. M. Forster: A Study* (Norwalk, Conn., 1943); E. K. Brown, "The Revival of E. M. Forster," *Yale Review* 33 (June 1944), 668–681; P. Ault, "Aspects of E. M. Forster," *Dublin Review* (October 1946), 109–134; D. Cecil, *Poets and Story Tellers* (London, 1949), contains essay on Forster; R. Warner, *E. M. Forster* (London, 1950), rev. by J. Morris (London, 1960); J. K. Johnstone, *The Bloomsbury Group* (London, 1954), a study of Forster, Strachey, Woolf, and their circle; J. McConkey, *The Novels of E. M. Forster* (Ithaca, N.Y., 1957).

H. J. Oliver, *The Art of E. M. Forster* (Melbourne, 1960);

J. B. Beer, *The Achievement of E. M. Forster* (London, 1962); F. C. Crews, *E. M. Forster: The Perils of Humanism* (Oxford, 1962); K. W. Gransden, *E. M. Forster* (Edinburgh, 1962); V. A. Shahane, *E. M. Forster: A Reassessment* (Allahabad, India, 1962); K. Natwar-Singh, ed., *E. M. Forster: A Tribute, with Selections from His Writings on India* (New York, 1964), with intro. by ed.; A. Wilde, *Art and Order: A Study of E. M. Forster* (New York, 1964; London, 1965); H. T. Moore, *E. M. Forster* (New York–London, 1965); D. Shusterman, *The Quest for Certitude in E. M. Forster's Fiction* (Bloomington, Ind., 1965); M. Bradbury, *Forster: A Collection of Critical Essays* (Englewood Cliffs, N. J., 1966), repr. of essays by D. S. Savage, F. R. Leavis, I. A. Richards, P. Burra, and E. K. Brown; W. Stone, *The Cave and the Mountain: A Study of E. M. Forster* (Stanford, 1966); G. H. Thompson, *The Fiction of E. M. Forster* (Detroit, 1967); N. Kelvin, *E. M. Forster* (Carbondale, Ill., 1967); L. Brander, *E. M. Forster: A Critical Study* (London, 1968); D. Godfrey, *E. M. Forster's Other Kingdom* (Edinburgh–London, 1968); F. P. W. McDowell, *E. M. Forster* (New York, 1969); O. Stallybrass, ed., *Aspects of E. M. Forster: Essays and Recollections Written for His Ninetieth Birthday* (London, 1969); H. H. Anniah Gowda, ed., *A Garland for E. M. Forster* (Mysore, 1969), includes letters from Forster to R. C. Trevelyan.

J. R. Ackerley, *E. M. Forster: A Portrait* (London, 1970); E. Barger, "Memories of Morgan," *New York Times Book Review* (16 August 1970); J. P. Levine, *Creation and Criticism: A Passage to India* (London, 1971); E. Ellem, "E. M. Forster's 'Arctic Summer,'" *Times Literary Supplement* (21 September 1973), 1087–1089; P. Gardner, ed., *E. M. Forster: The Critical Heritage* (Boston–London, 1973); J. Colmer, *E. M. Forster: The Personal Voice* (London, 1975); J. S. Martin, *E. M. Forster: The Endless Journey* (London, 1976); I. Stephens, *Unmade Journey* (London, 1977), ch. 55 treats Forster; J. L. Pinchin, *Alexandria Still: Forster, Durrell and Cavafy* (Princeton, N. J., 1977); P. N. Furbank, *E. M. Forster: A Life* (New York, 1978; pbk. ed., 1981).

POETS OF WORLD WAR I

John Press

INTRODUCTION

WHEN Europe went to war in August 1914 it had not witnessed a major conflict since the defeat of Napoleon at Waterloo in 1815, although the war for the liberation of Italy and Bismarck's wars against Denmark, Austria, and France had reminded politicians that violence might be an effective instrument of policy. Britain's only adventure on the continent, the Crimean War, had revealed the criminal incompetence of the army command, the scandalous state of the hospital services as exposed by Florence Nightingale, and the blundering stupidity of military tactics, seen at its most notorious in the charge of the Light Brigade. But all that was over fifty years before. A study of the American Civil War might have prepared the men of 1914 for what lay before them: the employment of artillery on a very large scale; the devastation of the countryside; the destruction of towns and the wandering of refugees from homes they had been forced to abandon. Yet nobody would have believed that the particular kind of savagery endured in the United States in the 1860's would have marked a conflict between the chivalrous professional armies of Europe fifty years later.

Leonard Woolf describes how he walked over the Sussex Downs in the summer of 1914 and how they looked almost as if unchanged since Domesday. World War I was to transform far more than the landscape of Sussex and of the other English counties. The face of the world was changed and, together with the millions who perished on the battlefields or in the influenza epidemic after the war, the civilization of Europe died. The pages that follow record how some English poets fought in the trenches and wrote poems by which they are remembered.

SOME ESTABLISHED POETS

MANY of the older poets, who were well over military age, felt the impulse to write patriotic verse about the war. It is better not to quote Sir William Watson's lines about Germany or his address to the Kaiser, but to remark only that he sank to depths of vulgarity and hysteria unplumbed by any other poet in both world wars. Thomas Hardy's "Men Who March Away" is on a different level of achievement, but it moves with an uncharacteristic jaunty religious fervor that has not worn well. Charles Sorley, a great admirer of Hardy, believed that one line of the poem, "Victory crowns the just," was the worst Hardy had ever written.

Rudyard Kipling (1865–1936) summoned his fellow countrymen to brace themselves for the coming struggle and to gird themselves for sacrifice. "For All We Have and Are" is an accomplished call to arms, an attempt to stiffen the sinews and to strengthen the will. Kipling warns all patriots that "The Hun is at the gate," adroitly seizing on the Kaiser's admonition to his troops at the time of the Boxer rebellion that they should behave like the ancient Huns. Kipling's poems on the war are varied in mood and theme; some are diatribes against politicians who hid the truth before the war and sent men ill-equipped into battle after war had come. He also wrote some memorable epigrams, including one on a soldier executed for cowardice, toward whom he shows an unexpected compassion. Under most of his wartime poems one can detect anger and grief at the death in action of his beloved son.

Unlike Kipling, who was well attuned to the mood of the public, A. E. Housman (1859–1936) caused some offense by his tribute to the regular army, which fought with such courage in the early days of the war and saved the Allies from defeat. People objected to the title of his poem "Epitaph on an Army of Mercenaries," on the grounds that it was an insult to a heroic body of men, even though the word "mercenaries" was an accurate description of their calling. Nor did the pious relish the poem's last two lines:

415

What God abandoned, these defended,
And saved the sum of things for pay.

Today one admires the laconic precision of the phrasing, the lapidary force of the encomium bestowed by Housman on men who practiced two of the virtues he most cherished: stoical courage and devotion to duty.

One should pay a brief tribute to Ford Madox Ford (1873–1939), who insisted on joining the army and who fought in the trenches, even though overage. It is true that he was probably more of a menace to his military superiors than to the Germans, and that he had enlisted partly to get away from his mistress, Violet Hunt, who was proving even more tiresome than his wife. Nevertheless, it was a gallant gesture, and although Ford was not a very good poet, his "Antwerp" is an interesting example of an attempt to adapt and to enlarge imagistic technique for the purpose of describing war without emotion. The Belgian, with a smoking gun, is an uncomely man in an ugly tunic, and when he is killed he "lies, an unsightly lump on the sodden grass." As late as November 1917, T. S. Eliot described "Antwerp" as "the only good poem I have met with on the subject of the war," which makes one wonder what poems about the war Eliot had read.

"For the Fallen" by Laurence Binyon (1869–1943) is probably familiar to more people than any other poem of World War I. It is so widely known because it is frequently declaimed at memorial services, including services in memory of those who died in the Falkland Islands in 1982. The poem has a solemn, liturgical quality that commends it to those mourning their dead, and since it is free of any tincture of Christian devotion, it appeals to those who want religious dignity without Christian dogma:

They shall grow not old, as we that are left grow old:
Age shall not weary them, nor the years condemn.
At the going down of the sun and in the morning
We will remember them.

(st. 4)

Although there is no warrant in the text, congregations habitually supplement the words of the officiating clergyman by intoning a repetition of the last line: "We will remember them." The poem of an individual poet is transformed into a communal liturgical rite. None of Binyon's subsequent poems attained anything like the popularity of "For the Fallen." Halfway through World War II Binyon

wrote a poem called "The Burning of the Leaves," which is concerned with the necessity of laying aside all that is ended and done. It may not be fanciful to suppose that he was looking back to the previous war and drawing courage from the experience of 1914–1918 when he achieved the mingled doubt and affirmation of the poem's final line: "Nothing is certain, only the certain spring."

Most of the younger poets who had begun to make a reputation by 1914 were associated, at least in the minds of poetry readers, with the Georgians or the imagists, although these were rough and often misleading classifications. D. H. Lawrence, for example, wandered cheerfully between the two camps, glad to win whatever sustenance he could from either group.

There were obvious links between the Georgians and the war poets, mainly because Edward Marsh printed their work in the anthologies with which he followed up his initial *Georgian Poetry 1911–1912*. His editorial labors did much to spread the fame of Rupert Brooke and to make more widely known the work of Siegfried Sassoon and of the largely forgotten but by no means untalented W. W. Gibson. Edmund Blunden and Ivor Gurney had strong affinities with Georgianism; and even Wilfred Owen was proud to be held peer by the Georgians, greatly though he surpassed them in technical mastery and imaginative force.

Imagism, on the other hand, had little influence on the war poetry written between 1914 and 1918. The younger imagist poets who served in the trenches included Richard Aldington (later famous as a novelist of the war), Herbert Read, and T. E. Hulme, who was killed in 1915, leaving no war poems. Long after the war Herbert Read sought to explain in *The Contrary Experience* (1963) why the aesthetic theories of imagism were inadequate to explain the "terrorful and inhuman events" of the conflict. Certainly Aldington's war poems, though well constructed, are too decorative and remote to move us greatly. Perhaps his best war poem is "Sunsets," the first stanza of which can be read simply as an impressionistic evocation of the sky at evening:

The white body of evening
Is torn into scarlet
Slashed and gouged and seared
Into crimson,
And hung ironically
With garlands of mist.

(1–6)

416

It is only after reading the second stanza that one understands the sinister import of the first, in which the bloody violence of war is mirrored upon the canvas of the natural world:

> And the wind
> Blowing over London from Flanders
> Has a bitter taste.
>
> (7–9)

Ezra Pound alone among the imagists found adequate expression for the inner meaning of the war, in *Hugh Selwyn Mauberley;* but that poem lies outside the scope of this essay, since it was written by a man who, though living in England, was a civilian and an American.

Just as the avant-garde poetry of the immediate prewar years exerted only a marginal influence on the war poets, so the poetry of 1914–1918 barely affected the modernist movement of the 1920's. Eliot, Pound, and William Butler Yeats seem to have learned nothing even from Owen and Isaac Rosenberg; and although W. H. Auden and the poets of the 1930's professed a deep reverence for Owen, they assimilated little of his achievement except a few technical devices and a tendency to invoke pity as an emotional gesture. It was left to the poets of World War II to discover that certain poems written between 1914 and 1918 gave imaginative shape to unchanging truths about the nature of war and of human life.

MORNING HEROES

WHATEVER might be said against the landed aristocracy and other members of the British ruling classes in 1914, nobody could gainsay their physical courage. The main fear of the young men among them was that the war might be over by Christmas, thus preventing them from killing Germans. Almost all of them had been educated at public schools, where they had absorbed the codes of honor and duty that governed all who grew up there. The poems of Henry Newbolt (1862–1938), though written mainly during the 1880's and 1890's, still expressed the ethics of the public schools. Indeed, Newbolt in 1914 had not felt it necessary to write any new poems: he merely published a collection of his earlier work, of which 70,000 copies were sold.

Poems such as "Vitai Lampada" may nowadays seem ludicrous, but young officers in 1914 accepted the injunction, "Play up! play up! and play the game!" Many of these young officers, most of whom were in no sense professional poets, wrote poems that recorded their experience of combat during the period of the war that ran from August 1914 to the end of June 1916, the eve of the Battle of the Somme. After that the world became darker: the experiences, terrifying but sometimes joyful, of Julian Grenfell and Charles Sorley were replaced by the purgatorial twilight in which Sassoon, Owen, and Rosenberg found themselves.

Raymond Asquith (1878–1916), eldest son of the prime minister, practiced at the bar after a career of exceptional brilliance at Oxford. He left no war poems and indeed was not a poet, although he wrote extremely skillful parodies and pastiches. He deserves to be remembered for his parody of Kipling's jingoistic "Soldiers of the Queen," which begins:

> The sun like a Bishop's bottom
> Rosy and round and hot. . . .

He was typical of his class and his generation in that he volunteered for military service when there was no pressure on him to do so; rejected a safe job as a staff officer for the danger and discomfort of the trenches; and died with courage and composure on the Somme in September 1916, during what the divisional commander called "the greatest of all the war achievements of the Brigade of Guards."

Herbert Asquith (1881–1947), Raymond's younger brother, managed to go through the war from beginning to end unscathed. He is remembered chiefly for a competent though old-fashioned and conventional sonnet, "The Volunteer," about a city clerk who is afraid that he will never break a lance in life's tournament. He volunteers, is killed, and lies content. This poem, with its imagery drawn from medieval knight errantry, is typical in its loftiness and total divorce from reality, the mood in which many young men went to war in 1914. This is not invalidated by the fact that Herbert Asquith wrote "The Volunteer" in 1912.

One of the closest friends of the Asquiths was Julian Grenfell (1888–1915). His father, William Grenfell, a remarkable athlete, was created Lord Desborough in 1905; his mother, "Etty," was probably the most celebrated hostess of her day. Before he was two he had displayed his vigorous enjoyment of killing: "Determined to kill a mouse. Hammer it with a hammer" (Mosley, *Julian Grenfell,* p. 13). He was a man of considerable intelligence, educated at Eton and Balliol, who in 1909 collected but did not publish a book of essays on social and political themes that his strong-minded mother and her friends heartily disliked. He received a commission in the Royal Dragoons in 1910, having passed first among all university graduate entrants to the army. After service in India and then in South Africa, Grenfell planned to give up his army career so that he might devote himself to painting. Etty, with whom his relations were always complex, mocked him and incited her circle of friends to join in the mockery. He capitulated.

On October 1914 Grenfell sailed for France. Although he had never enjoyed the mass slaughter that had characterized Edwardian and Georgian shooting parties, Grenfell had always loved solitary killing, because it represented a link with the earth and furthered his pursuit of primitive things. He perfected a technique that enabled him to stalk Germans after dark, to creep close to them and then shoot them. In mid-November he shot a German on each of two successive evenings, for which he was awarded the Distinguished Service Order. When he went home on leave he made an entry in his game book to the effect that on 16 and 17 November 1914 he had bagged a Pomeranian.

Grenfell's attitude to the war was unambiguous: it is to his credit that he did not drape his naked ferocity in sanctimonious moralizing. He was a killer from the egg, describing war as all the most wonderful *fun.* More sinister is his verdict on the life that he was leading:

I have never, never felt so well, or so happy, or enjoyed anything so much. It just suits my stolid health, and stolid nerves, and barbaric disposition. The fighting—excitement vitalises everything, every sight and word and action. One loves one's fellow-man so much more when one is bent on killing him.

(*Julian Grenfell,* p. 241)

Yet he was not devoid of human feelings. After a passage in a letter from Flanders written in October 1914: "I *adore* war. It is like a big picnic without the objectlessness of a picnic" (p. 239)—Grenfell goes on to express his sense of pity at the wretchedness of the inhabitants who had been forced to leave their homes.

At the end of January 1915 Grenfell returned to France, taking with him three greyhounds—he had always loved the breed and before the war had written a poem entitled "To a Black Greyhound." On 29 April he wrote "Into Battle," the poem that is his surest title to immortality. At 4:00 A.M. on 13 May he was grievously wounded, and although his friends believed that his toughness would pull him through, his wounds proved fatal. On his deathbed, presided over by the indomitable Etty, he quoted Phaedra's song from the *Hippolytus* of Euripides, a play that he had admired since his boyhood. When on 25 May a shaft of sunlight fell across his feet, Grenfell said, "Phoebus Apollo," and did not speak again except once to say his father's name. He died on 26 May with a radiant smile on his face.

"Into Battle" is one of those poems by gifted amateurs that have taken their place in the corpus of English poetry. It brings together many of the strands woven into Grenfell's nature: his love of killing that brought him closer to the earth; the sheer exhilaration of battle; a strain of mysticism. (At the age of thirteen, during a thunderstorm, he suddenly seemed to realize God, and he became devoted to Saint Thomas à Kempis.)

The poem opens with a celebration of the spring, which will enrich the fighting man. Then follows a section in which Grenfell affirms the kinship between the fighting man and the forces of the universe: "the bright company of Heaven"; the woodland trees; the kestrel and the little owls:

The blackbird sings to him, "Brother, brother,
  If this be the last song you shall sing,
Sing well, for you may not sing another;
  Brother sing."

(st. 6)

Grenfell ends by envisaging the joy of battle, expressing his trust in the Destined Will, and committing himself to the powers of Day and Night.

Another intimate of the Asquith circle was Patrick Shaw-Stewart (1888–1917), whose career at Oxford was only slightly less brilliant than Raymond Asquith's. After leaving Oxford, he joined Baring's Bank, where he rapidly attained a senior position. Soon after the outbreak of war he became a lieutenant-commander in the Royal Naval Division and fought at Gallipoli. He was killed in action in France late in 1917, having refused to quit the field after his ear had been torn off by shrapnel. An untitled poem was found in Shaw-Stewart's copy of Housman's *A*

Shropshire Lad, a book whose influence on him it is difficult to overemphasize. The poem begins:

> I saw a man this morning
> Who did not wish to die.

It then considers the fighting in the Dardanelles, reflecting for a moment on Helen of Troy and incorporating into the poem a pun on her name that derives from Euripides. Shaw-Stewart's attainments as a classical scholar rivaled those of Raymond Asquith, and, like Julian Grenfell, he turned quite naturally in moments of crisis and fear to the world of classical Greece. He communes with Achilles, asking him if it was very hard to die, and the poem concludes on a note of affirmation, in which the figure of Achilles is invoked:

> I will go back this morning
> From Imbros over the sea;
> Stand in the trench, Achilles,
> Flame-capped, and shout for me.
>
> (25–26)

Robert Nichols (1893–1944), although now largely forgotten, was once a name to conjure with, cherished by the reading public as all that a young heroic poet should be, and admired by Edward Marsh as one of his favorite Georgian poets. Marsh was an influential figure, a cultivated member of the English upper classes, private secretary to Winston Churchill, a patron of the arts and editor of the widely read anthology *Georgian Poetry 1911–1912,* the first of five such collections. Although Nichols' army career was in no way discreditable, he was invalided home suffering from shell shock and after five months' treatment in military hospitals received his discharge. Robert Graves, who did not like Nichols, thought him almost a phony, perhaps because after leaving the army he scored a great success with his lectures in the United States on the war, in spite of having experienced active service only for what Graves would have regarded as a ridiculously brief period.

Nichols' wartime poetry, with its mixture of homosexual eroticism and religiosity, has not worn well. Even among his contemporaries there were those who found his work distasteful. Douglas Goldring savagely but justly called "The Assault" "a masterpiece of drivel"; and Wilfred Owen regarded him as "self-concerned and *vaniteux* in his verse" (*Wilfred Owen: Collected Letters,* p. 511). Yet some-

thing survives of the romantic vitality and élan that awoke a response in Nichols' first readers. His description of "Dawn on the Somme" was written during the Battle of the Somme while he was being treated for neurasthenia in a hospital:

> Oh, is it mist, or are these companies
> Of morning heroes who arise, arise
> With thrusting arms, with limbs and hair aglow,
> Towards the risen gold, upon whose brow
> Burns the gold laurel of all victories,
> Hero and heroes' gold, th'invincible Sun?
>
> (7–12)

After the war his reputation faded, although a selection of his poems, *Such Was My Singing,* appeared in 1942, and he edited *An Anthology of War Poetry* in 1943. Some of his lyrical pieces deserve to be remembered, while "The Sprig of Lime," a poem of about ninety lines, surpasses in gravity and tenderness everything else that Nichols wrote. It remains one of the neglected masterpieces of our time.

A far more formidable figure than Nichols was Rupert Brooke (1887–1915), for whom Edward Marsh felt a deeper affection than for any other Georgian poet. His legendary fame persists to the present day for a variety of reasons. He had many friends of widely different callings, ranging from Virginia Woolf to Geoffrey Keynes, the distinguished surgeon and literary scholar, and Hugh Dalton, chancellor of the exchequer in the Labour government of 1945. In conversations, diaries, memoirs, and letters they united to celebrate Brooke's physical splendor, intellectual power, and literary gifts. The cult of Rupert Brooke still flourishes, given fresh impetus by the revelation that he and Virginia Woolf once bathed naked; and it is possible even now to wax sentimental over the Old Vicarage, at Grantchester, and to get honey for tea in a tea shop in the village.

The building of Rupert Brooke into a legend began almost as soon as he was dead, and it is clear that, in part at least, those who fabricated the edifice did so in order to encourage young men to volunteer for the armed forces. Winston Churchill eulogized him as joyous, fearless, and ruled by high, undoubting purpose. Brooke confessed soon after the outbreak of war that the perils of the time and the darkness of the world made him uneasy and vaguely frightened. Nor was he joyous: he was deeply neurotic, especially in his dealings with women. In a letter of August 1912 to Ka Cox, with whom he had a long affair, Brooke confessed his fear that he was incapable of any fruitful sexual relationship, and testified to his self-disgust. He probably never recovered from the nervous breakdown that ended the affair. After he left Tahiti, where he had found brief happiness with a girl called Taatamata, Brooke received a letter from her full of misspellings in French and English, and he "gulped a good deal."

Brooke had achieved a reputation as a poet before 1914. He was one of the six people who met for luncheon in Edward Marsh's rooms on 20 September 1912 and planned the genesis of *Georgian Poetry*. He was probably the most valued contributor to the first anthology, *Georgian Poetry 1911–1912*, which appeared before the end of 1912.

Brooke's response to the war, a group of war sonnets, appeared in *New Numbers*, December 1914, without attracting much attention. In September, Brooke had received a commission in the Royal Naval Division, which early in 1915 sailed for the Dardanelles in the hope of striking a decisive blow against the Turks. Before he was able to accomplish anything of note, Brooke contracted blood poisoning caused by a bite from a mosquito or a scorpion. He died in a French military hospital on the Greek island of Scyros on Saint George's Day, 23 April. The firing party at his grave on the island, traditionally associated with Achilles, was commanded by Patrick Shaw-Stewart.

Even before Rupert Brooke's death one of his five war sonnets had begun to reach a wide audience. On 5 April 1915, Easter Day, the dean of Saint Paul's, W. R. Inge, had taken as the text for his sermon Isaiah 26:19—"The dead shall live, my dead bodies shall arise. Awake and sing, ye that dwell in the dust." Inge went on to quote one of Brooke's sonnets, "The Soldier," remarking that "the enthusiasm of a pure and elevated patriotism had never found a nobler expression." Three days after Brooke's death Winston Churchill praised the war sonnets in the *Times*. On 16 June 1915 the sonnets were gathered into *1914 and Other Poems*, edited by Edward Marsh. A few months later they were given a separate edition under the title *1914. Five Sonnets*.

Brooke had a gift for the striking phrase and the rhetorical assertion, as the opening lines of three of his sonnets demonstrate:

> If I should die, think only this of me:
> That there's some corner of a foreign field
> That is for ever England.
>
> ("The Soldier")

> Blow out, you bugles, over the rich Dead!
> There's none of these so lonely and poor of old,
> But, dying, has made us rarer gifts than gold.
>
> ("The Dead")

> Now, God be thanked who has matched us with His hour,
> And caught our youth, and wakened us from sleeping,
> With hand made sure, clear eye, and sharpened power,
> To turn, as swimmers into cleanness leaping,
> Glad from a world grown old and cold and weary,
> Leave the sick hearts that honour could not move,
> And half-men, and their dirty songs and dreary,
> And all the little emptiness of love!
>
> ("Peace")

Yet the sonnets are inadequate, poetically and morally. Even Julian Grenfell had been content to proclaim his love of killing without prating about the cleansing power of war. Nobody since the emotionally disturbed hero of Tennyson's *Maud* (1855), who resolved to plunge into the slaughter of the Crimea, had supposed that war was likely to offer a regenerative experience. Read in the light of what we know about Brooke's psychological difficulties, these sonnets represent the struggle of a highly strung, desperate man to escape from the emotional problems in which he lay trapped. There was a conscious drive toward simplification and self-sacrifice, a barely conscious drifting toward death.

It is significant that three of his contemporaries, all poets who died in battle, were unimpressed by Brooke's sonnets. In a letter to his mother dated 28 November 1914, Charles Sorley remarks that Brooke "is far too obsessed with his own sacrifice, regarding the going to war of himself (and others) as a highly intense, remarkable and sacrificial exploit. . . . He has clothed his attitude in fine words; but he has taken the sentimental attitude" (*Letters*, p. 263). Isaac Rosenberg, who was admittedly jealous of Edward Marsh's devotion to Brooke and to his memory, refers in a letter to Mrs. Cohen, probably written at midsummer 1915, to the commonplace phrases in Brooke's "begloried sonnets" (*Collected Works*, p. 237). Rosenberg thought that his "Clouds" was a magnificent poem, and, in a letter to Sydney Schiff dating from about August 1916, he singles out for praise Brooke's "Town and Country," but remarks of his other poems that "they remind me too much of flag days" (*Isaac Rosenberg 1890–1918: Catalogue with Letters*, p. 16). Edward Thomas, in a letter to Robert Frost of 19 October 1916, while acknowledging that Brooke had "succeeded in being youthful and yet intelligible and interesting (not only pathologically) more than most poets since Shelley," passes a severe judgment on him: "He was a rhetorician, dressing things up better than needed. And I suspect he knew only too well both what he was after and what he achieved" (*Rupert Brooke: A Biography*, p. 502).

It would be ungenerous to conclude on a sour note. When Brooke encountered the reality of war in the retreat from Antwerp in late 1914 he was moved to pity by the spectacle of refugees. In the "Fragment" written on his troopship in April 1915 he describes how, after dark, he remains on deck, watching his friends, unobserved by them. The poem is infused with a profound sadness, an awareness of human fragility. It is worlds away from the mood of the sonnets. Brooke's reaction to Dean Inge's sermon evinces something of his old irony and good sense. When he lay dying, his friend Denis Browne came to his cabin to talk about the dean's sermon, of which Brooke already knew, having received a newspaper clipping from Marsh. The clipping contained Inge's reservation about "The Soldier": "And yet it fell somewhat short of Isaiah's vision and still more of the Christian hope." Brooke murmured his regret that the dean didn't think him quite so good as Isaiah. They were his last coherent words.

Charles Hamilton Sorley (1895–1915) had an intense passion for truth:

The voice of our poets and men of letters is finely trained and sweet to hear; it teems with sharp saws and rich sentiments: it is a marvel of delicate technique: it pleases, it flatters, it charms, it soothes: it is a living lie.

(*The Letters with a Chapter of Biography*, pp. 37–38)

This passage has sometimes been quoted as Sorley's response to the jingoistic poetry of 1914: in fact, it comes from a paper on John Masefield read to the Literary Society of Marlborough College on 3 November 1912.

Sorley, who went to school at Marlborough, was planning to enter Oxford in September 1914, but, after leaving school at the end of 1913, he went to live in Germany in January 1914. He loved Germany, despite his loathing for such evil manifestations as the student corps, with their drunkenness, aggressiveness, and hatred of Jews. Nor did he care for Germany's bigotry and conviction of spiritual superiority. When war broke out he was on a walking tour; he was briefly imprisoned, released, and expelled. As soon as he reached England he applied for a commission.

Sorley was unique among English poets who fought in the war in having an intimate knowledge of Germany. He was in a very small minority of people who detested the tawdry elements in official propaganda, the nauseating humbug preached by journalists and churchmen, whom he stigmatized collectively as Annas and Caiaphas. Even his beloved Hardy's "Men Who March Away" incurred his displeasure. It is, he says, in a letter of 30 November 1914, "the most arid poem in *Satires of Circumstance*, besides being untrue of the sentiments of the ranksman going to war: 'Victory crowns the just' is the worst line he ever wrote—filched from a leading article in *The Morning Post*" (*Letters*, p. 246).

As early as August 1914 Sorley had grasped the truth that Britain and Germany were engaged in a fratricidal conflict. His sonnet "To Germany" opens:

You are blind like us. Your hurt no man designed,
And no man claimed the conquest of your land.

The theme of mutual blindness sounds at the end of the octet:

And in each other's dearest ways we stand,
And hiss and hate. And the blind fight the blind.

None of Sorley's poems compares in quality with the finest poetry written during the war: his command of poetic technique was inadequate to bear the charge of his imaginative vision. It is in his superb *Letters*, still available in the original edition of 1919, that one finds the best evidence of his intellectual keenness and searing honesty. Nowhere are these qualities more vigorously exhibited than in Sorley's letter to Arthur Watts of August 1915, describing the excitement of the encounter with the enemy:

. . . the wail of the exploded bomb and the animal cries of the wounded men. Then death and the horrible thankfulness when one sees that the next man is dead: "We won't have to *carry* him in under fire, thank God; dragging will do": hauling in of the great resistless body in the dark, the smashed head rattling: the relief, the relief that the thing has ceased to groan: that the bullet or bomb that made the man an animal has now made the animal a corpse. One is hardened by now: purged of all false pity: perhaps more selfish than before. The spiritual and the animal get so much more sharply divided in hours of encounter, taking possession of the body by swift turns.

(pp. 305–306)

One of Sorley's best poems is the untitled "All the hills and vales along," which owes something in mood to Housman. Written before Sorley had seen active service, it ironically celebrates the fact that the marching men are going to their death, urges them to be joyful, and reminds them that Nature will rejoice at their death as it rejoiced at the death of Socrates and of Christ:

> Earth that never doubts nor fears
> Earth that knows of death, not tears,
> Earth that bore with joyful ease
> Hemlock for Socrates,
> Earth that blossomed and was glad
> 'Neath the cross that Christ had,
> Shall rejoice and blossom too
> When the bullet reaches you.
>
> (st. 3)

Sorley's awareness of mortality and his sense of communion with the dead, which go back to his school days, find expression in two sonnets on death dated 12 June 1915 and in the sonnet "When you see millions of the mouthless dead," found among his possessions after his death in action on 13 October 1915. In that final sonnet, as in the June sonnets, one can detect an attempt to resolve a deep ambiguity in his attitude to death. Perhaps it would be truer to say that there coexisted in Sorley a devout belief in the Christian doctrine of the resurrection and a deep subconscious acceptance of the knowledge that death is final.

The final sonnet prefigures in certain ways Owen's apprehension of war as a tragedy in which numberless men meet their deaths:

> When you see millions of the mouthless dead
> Across your dreams in pale battalions go. . . .
>
> (1–2)

The sonnet emphasizes the deadness of the dead, the futility of praise or tears, the remoteness of the dead from the living. It might almost be a rejoinder to Rupert Brooke, whose war sonnets had not commended themselves to Sorley. The final line of the sonnet is difficult to read as other than a denial of immortality: "Great death has made all his for evermore."

During the last five months of his life Sorley wrote one or two poems that are no better than the average run of verse in a hymnal or the memorial tributes in a public school magazine. It is not easy to account for this descent into banality of thought and diction; but despite his rebellion against certain aspects of the ethos inculcated at Marlborough, Sorley remained deeply attached to the school and to the downs nearby, where he loved to take his long solitary runs. Perhaps, in the physical and emotional turmoil of the trenches, he at times found solace in reverting to the idiom and the values of his adolescence.

Sorley died so young that his potential as a poet had scarcely begun to develop. He had probably the keenest intelligence and the most admirable nature of all the poets of World War I. The visitor who wishes to enter the chapel at Marlborough, a splendid example of Victorian Gothic, must first pass through the antechapel. He will see, affixed to the walls, a number of memorial tablets that honor distinguished sons of the school. Most of them commemorate Victorian admirals, generals, and governors of remote colonies. One is in memory of Charles Hamilton Sorley: it is fitting that it should be there.

Sorley's view of the war was shared by few of those fighting in the trenches. When Siegfried Sassoon and Vivian de Sola Pinto, his platoon commander, first read Sorley's poems in 1916 they could scarcely believe that anybody who had died in action in October 1915 could have taken such an attitude to the war. Young poets continued to write under the influence of Rupert Brooke as late as mid-1916. One such was W. N. Hodgson (1893–1916), an athlete and an exhibitioner[1] of Christ Church, Oxford, who enlisted at the outbreak of the war and won the Military Cross in 1915. His poems, couched as they are in the deplorable idiom of late-nineteenth-century romanticism, display barely a vestige of talent. However, one poem, "Before Action," can still move the reader with its poignant intensity, partly because one knows that it was written by a brave man on 29 June 1916, two days before he died on the first day of the Battle of the Somme. The poet moves from a Ruskinian adoration of natural beauty in the opening stanza to a recognition that he has watched

> . . . with uncomprehending eyes
> A hundred of Thy sunsets spill
> Their fresh and sanguine sacrifice.
>
> (18–20)

Finally the poet faces the knowledge that he

> Ere the sun swings his noonday sword
> Must say goodbye to all of this;—
> By all delights that I shall miss,
> Help me to die, O Lord.
>
> (21–24)

[1]A student who attends school by benefit of a scholarship.

422

The Battle of the Somme ushered in a new and even darker phase of the war. Hitherto it had been just possible to keep up the pretense that there were elements of chivalry in the conflict. At Christmas 1914 in certain parts of the line British and German troops had fraternized, exchanging gifts, singing carols, playing football. The authorities had sternly forbidden the repetition of such gestures and court-martialed Sir Iain Colquhoun and another captain of the Scots Guards for permitting their men to fraternize with the Germans on Christmas Day 1915. A new era of mass slaughter was about to begin. Before the attack on 1 July 1916, Field Marshal Douglas Haig had bombarded the German trenches for a week. Unfortunately, the German dugouts were so deep and well constructed that their machine gunners were able to scramble into position unharmed and mow down the British soldiers as they mounted their assault. The British army lost 60,000 killed and wounded on 1 July, the heaviest casualties it had ever sustained on any one day in its annals. The pattern established on the Somme repeated itself from then on: artillery bombardment, waves of infantrymen assaulting positions defended by heavy concentrations of machine guns, and an advance of a few hundred yards. At Passschendaele the following summer, a new element of horror pervaded the fighting: the sea of mud where rain fell on ground churned up by the British artillery. Not until March 1918 was the stalemate broken, when a German offensive appeared to have won the war. Yet the impetus petered out; on 8 August an Allied counteroffensive broke through the German positions and on 11 November the war was over.

One needs to bear this background in mind when considering the work of Sassoon, Owen, and Rosenberg, all of whose best poems were written after the summer of 1916. The public at home still preferred the romantic falsities of Robert Nichols to the savage truths of Siegfried Sassoon. Nichols' *Ardours and Endurances*, published in May 1917, sold more copies than Sassoon's *The Old Huntsman*, which appeared at the same time. But no serious poet could write about the war with the devotional highmindedness that one finds in W. N. Hodgson. He was the last of the morning heroes.

Even before the Somme one or two poets were beginning to make some adequate response to the ghastly realities of the war. Sassoon was writing the first of his trench poems that aimed at presenting an objective picture of life at the front. There was also Arthur Graeme West (1891–1917), who suffered a total revulsion from the war in August 1916, returned to France, and was killed by a bullet in April 1917. His *Diary of a Dead Officer* (1919) records his growing disillusionment. It is mainly prose, with a few poems added, of which the finest is "Night Patrol," dated March 1916. West anticipates Sassoon in his determination to record the true visage of war:

> . . . and everywhere the dead.
> Only the dead were always present—present
> As a vile sickly smell of rottenness.
> The rustling stubble and the early grass,
> The slimy pools—the dead men stank through all,
> Pungent and sharp. . . .
>
> (19–24)

His polemic in "God! How I Hate You, You Young Cheerful Men," against those who wrote lyrical poetry in the manner of Rupert Brooke, forms part of his desire to clarify in his own mind the nature of the struggle in which he was enmeshed. In that same poem he makes a more subdued but perhaps more heartfelt protest against the popular concept of God, foreshadowing Wilfred Owen in his speculations about the love of God and the suffering on the battlefield:

> Ah how good God is
> To suffer us be born just now, when youth
> That else would rust, can slake his blade in gore
> Where very God Himself does seem to walk
> The bloody fields of Flanders He so loves.
>
> (34–38)

Even from these brief quotations one observes how far West had traveled from the landscape of the mind portrayed by Grenfell, Brooke, and Shaw-Stewart; how near he was to the no-man's land delineated by Sassoon, Owen, and Rosenberg. Before considering that somber region, one must turn to the achievement of three men who, belonging to no school, made highly distinctive contributions to the poetry of war.

EDWARD THOMAS, IVOR GURNEY, EDMUND BLUNDEN

IN one sense Edward Thomas (1878–1917) can scarcely be called a war poet: he wrote no poems about fighting or about life in the trenches; almost all his poems that refer to the war do so glancingly; and he probably wrote no poems after he had landed in France. Yet in one way Thomas was essentially a war poet: he owed his existence as a poet to the war. He had married very young, and his struggle to support his wife and three children condemned him to a round of ceaseless publishing on a wide variety of subjects—the countryside, queens of England, English men of letters. Although some of his literary criticism, notably *Algernon Charles Swinburne* (1912) and *Walter Pater* (1913), contains perceptive insights and there are passages worth reading in most of his books, this merely proves his extraordinary stamina and his determination to do honest work for his meager pay. Being commissioned in the army meant that the worst of his financial worries were over and that he was free of the literary treadmill. Between 3 December 1914 and 24 December 1916, Edward Thomas wrote the body of verse by which he is primarily remembered.

It is not necessary to consider in any detail the debt owed by Thomas to Robert Frost. The strong-minded widows of the two poets turned into a matter of dispute something that Frost and Thomas would have discussed amicably. Frost certainly told Edward Thomas that he should write certain paragraphs of his prose in verse form and keep exactly the same cadence. This may account for the fact that although Thomas' poems are unmistakably poetry they never, even at their most formal, lose touch with the movement of prose.

Thomas' most overt declaration about the war occurs in "This Is No Case of Petty Right or Wrong," in which he disclaims all conventional patriotism. When Eleanor Farjeon asked him if he knew what he was fighting for, he picked up a pinch of the earth and said, "Literally, for this." So, in the poem, Thomas affirms his irrational love for his country:

> I am one in crying, God save England, lest
> We lose what never slaves and cattle blessed.
> The ages made her that made us from dust.
>
> (21–23)

A subtler, finer poem, "Tears," explores Thomas' feeling for his country and tells us even more about his own nature. Although not directly relevant to the war, it gives us more than a hint about his attitude toward the soldiers in the trenches and toward his native land. One April morning he stepped out of "the double-shadowed Tower" into a courtyard:

> They were changing guard,
> Soldiers in line, young English countrymen,
> Fair-haired and ruddy, in white tunics. Drums
> And fifes were playing "The British Grenadiers."
> The men, the music piercing that solitude
> And silence, told me truths I had not dreamed,
> And have forgotten since their beauty passed.
>
> (12–18)

There are poems by Thomas that seem to have no connection with the war until a phrase arrests one's attention, compelling one to read the poem in a new light. In "Rain," one of his most characteristic poems, one encounters a reference to those whose sympathy cannot relieve human suffering, but who lie awake,

> Helpless among the living and the dead,
> Like a cold water among the broken reeds,
> Myriads of broken reeds all still and stiff.
>
> (12–14)

The image of the last line is almost certainly suggested by the victims of slaughter on the battlefields of France and of Flanders.

The war is present even more explicitly in "The Owl." As in so many of his poems, Thomas writes here in the first person, describing how hungry, cold, and tired he was, until he had satisfied his needs at an inn. An owl's "most melancholy cry" leads him away from a preoccupation with his solitary pains into an imaginative sympathy with others:

> And salted was my food, and my repose,
> Salted and sobered, too, by the bird's voice
> Speaking for all who lay under the stars,
> Soldiers and poor, unable to rejoice.
>
> (st. 4)

The conjunction of soldiers and poor recalls Isaac Rosenberg's observation that privates in the army are akin to slaves. For Thomas, soldiers are not heroes or our gallant boys in the trenches, but rather men low on the social scale, on a level with the poor. They suffer passively, unable to rejoice.

The four-line poem "In Memoriam (Easter, 1915)" is both a beautiful elegy and a powerful comment on the war:

> The flowers left thick at nightfall in the wood
> This Eastertide call into mind the men,
> Now far from home, who, with their sweethearts, should
> Have gathered them and will do never again.

The emphasis falling on "should" makes us aware that it may be read in two ways: the simple observation that the soldiers would have gathered the flowers had they been home; and the implication that the war, by destroying the dead men, has broken the ritual of courtship, the gathering of flowers that the dead men ought to have performed. Once again Thomas is showing how a tiny incident in a peaceful countryside may help us to grasp the significance of war.

One observes the same kind of strategy in "As the Team's Head-Brass." A soldier who has not yet been out to the war is watching a man plowing a field. Lovers disappear into the wood, and the plowman stops from time to time to have a word with the soldier. Their conversation veers toward the war: the fallen elm on which the soldier is seated won't be taken away until the war is over; the soldier could spare an arm but would be reluctant to lose a leg; one of the plowman's mates died on his second day in France. The talk is inconsequential and casual, yet the poem gradually pieces together a picture of the way in which the war demands and deprives. The poem ends with what is almost certainly something more than a straightforward description of the landscape:

> The lovers came out of the wood again:
> The horses started and for the last time
> I watched the clods crumble and topple over
> After the ploughshare and the stumbling team.
> (34–37)

The menace hidden in the phrase "for the last time" may remind the reader that the soldier, like the men who will never again gather the flowers, will perhaps, as he fears, lose not just an arm or a leg in battle, but his head as well. There is even a hint that the lovers and the age-old relationship between man and the soil are under threat from the destructiveness of war.

Edward Thomas is the quietest, most introspective of all the war poets, but the keenness of his observation and the probing quality of his imagination enable him to penetrate beyond the outer semblance of things into the heart of sadness.

Ivor Gurney (1890–1937) was that rare creature, a poet who was also a composer, equally gifted in the two arts. The son of a Gloucester tailor, he grew up and was educated in the cathedral city that he never ceased to love. His intelligence and his musical gifts augured well for his future, and nobody found it ominous that his fellow schoolboys gave him the nickname of "Batty Gurney."

In the autumn of 1911 Gurney won a scholarship to the Royal College of Music, where he showed his precocious skill in 1912 by his setting of five Elizabethan lyrics, a composition that he called "The Elizas." In 1912–1913 he began to write poetry, an activity that was not only of value in itself, but also an influence on his music; for Gurney was to set poems by most English poets of merit who flourished during the first two decades of the twentieth century. His joining the army did not put an end to his composition of music or of poetry: in 1916–1917 he achieved what may well be the unique feat of writing five songs while undergoing a spell of duty in the trenches. He sent home to a friend the poems that he had been writing, and in 1917 they appeared under the title *Severn and Somme*, names of the river that he had loved in childhood and the river associated with the terrible fighting that Gurney had known, and in which on 7 April 1917 he was wounded. In September 1917 he was gassed and sent home, then transferred to a mental hospital at Warrington and later to a similar hospital at St. Albans. His military career was over, formally terminating with his discharge in October 1918. There seems to be something mysterious about Gurney's last thirteen months in the army, since little is known about the circumstances of his gassing or of his confinement to the two mental hospitals. By 1919 he had apparently recovered.

From 1919 to 1921 he cut something of a figure at the Royal College of Music and in the literary world of London, a second book of poems, *War's Embers*, having appeared in 1919. Even so, he depended for his survival on a weekly allowance from a fund raised by his teacher Vaughan Williams and by friends. Back in Gloucester, he talked brilliantly and tumultuously, received financial help from Edward Marsh, and grew ever wilder. He was incarcerated in September 1922 at Barnwood House, Gloucester, and in December at the City of London Mental Hospital, Dartford, Kent. There he remained until his death on 26 December 1937, St. Stephen's Day, at a time of year that meant much to him.

Although Gurney's friends never deserted him, the story of his life at Dartford is heartrending. Apart from his bitter resentment at what he believed to be his betrayal by his country, Gurney was tormented by delusions that he was suffering from tortures inflicted from a distance by electricity. He claimed to have composed the works of Shakespeare, Beethoven, and Haydn. It is likely that he enjoyed (if that be the word) periods of lucidity. When in 1937 a friend told him that Oxford University Press was about to publish a collection of his songs, he merely said, "It is too late."

The poems written before he finally went mad are mostly acceptable exercises in the pastoral mode and reflections on various aspects of beauty. Two war poems stand out from the rest of those early poems. "To His Love," written when Gurney received a false report that his friend F. W. Harvey had died in battle, deploys in the first three stanzas the conventional properties of pastoral elegy—grazing sheep, the small boat on the Severn, the violets from the riverside. The final stanza opens decorously, but suddenly administers a shock:

> Cover him, cover him soon!
>   And with thick-set
> Masses of memorial flowers
> Hide that red wet
> Thing I must somehow forget.
>
>   (st. 4)

Calling a dead man a "red wet / Thing" strikes one with a raw violence, and it is almost as brutal to suggest that one should cover the corpse with masses of flowers partly in tribute and partly to blot it from sight.

Even finer is Gurney's "Ballad of the Three Spectres," a poem that somehow captures the spirit of the Border Ballads without lapsing into archaism or pastiche. The first two stanzas may yield some idea of the poem's merit:

> As I went up by Ovillers
>   In mud and water cold to the knee,
> There went three jeering, fleering spectres,
>   That walked abreast and talked of me.
>
> The first said, "Here's a right brave soldier
>   That walks the dark unfearingly;
> Soon he'll come back on a fine stretcher,
>   And laughing for a nice Blighty.

The curt off-rhymes in both stanzas enhance the atmosphere of menace and strangeness, just as it is sinister that one of the apparitions should speak the slang of the trenches, prophesying that the soldier will get a "nice Blighty"—a wound bad enough to ensure his return to England.

Yet the best of the poems that he wrote during his madness surpass even the most accomplished examples of his early work. One has to face the question of his insanity before turning to consider the poems composed in the asylums, and the evidence is probably inadequate for anybody to reach a verdict. The latest opinion is that he, like his mother, suffered from paranoid schizophrenia. Should this be so, one cannot lay the blame on the war for driving him mad, though the war almost certainly intensified his madness and determined the pattern that it took. Although the power to compose music left him after 1926, he was able to produce a mass of poetry throughout his confinement at Barnwood and at Dartford from 1922 to 1937.

Some of his poems are painful to read. Two long letters in verse to the metropolitan police ramble on about his war service and the pain that he is wrongfully enduring. All the sentences taken separately are logical, but something has gone wrong with the links between them, and gradually one realizes that the writer has lost his reason. A poem written at Barnwood House in December 1922 is far more controlled, despite the anguish that racks the poet as he draws up his indictment. The opening lines of "To God" are both tragic and comic in a pathetic way. Gurney's first example of God's cruelty toward him is that there are prayers with meals:

> Why have You made life so intolerable
> And set me between four walls, where I am able
> Not to escape meals without prayer, for that is possible
> Only by annoying an attendant.

What is so unnerving in the poem is the mixture of factual observation about forced meals, mere delusion about torture by electricity, and the prayer for death:

> Forced meals there have been and electricity
> And weakening of sanity by influence
> That's dreadful to endure. And there are others
> And I am praying for death, death, death.
>
>   (9–12)

Gurney's bitter sense of having been betrayed by his country is certainly linked with his insanity, although nobody has explained precisely how. He seems to have felt outraged in that his sufferings during the war had not brought him merited fame. He may also have experienced anger and pity at the recollection of the suffering endured by others who fought. The prime emotion of "There Is Nothing" is certainly pain at his own betrayal. The poem, dated February 1925, bears the note "in torture":

Soldier's praise I had earned having suffered soldier's pain,
And the great honour of song in the battle's first gray show—
Honour was bound to me save—mine most dreadfully slain.

(12–14)

During the years at Dartford, Gurney continually reverts to his memories of the war. Some of the poems he wrote on that theme are so lucid that it is hard to believe he was other than sane when he was composing them. They display an unwavering control of mood and of tone as he remembers the killing of comrades or calls to mind with stoical irony those who for a while, until death took them, contrived to beat the system. These poems have no parallel in the work of any other war poet: the voice is Gurney's alone, speaking clearly and with authority from the depths of a mental hospital.

Two poems in particular yield a taste of Gurney's quality. "The Silent One" begins curtly in the middle of the story:

Who died on the wires, and hung there, one of two—
Who for his hours of life had chattered through
Infinite lovely chatter of Bucks accent:
Yet faced unbroken wires; stepped over, and went
A noble fool, faithful to his stripes—and ended.

It is all there in five lines: the tale of an honest countryman, a loyal NCO, obedient to his orders, who ended up hanging on the barbed wire. Then an officer, with "a finicking accent," unlike the Bucks accent of the dead man, politely asks the narrator of the poem if he'd mind crawling through a hole in the wire. The courteous exchange between the officer and the narrator derives its savor from the fact that it is taking place in the middle of the battlefield, where one might expect orders to be rapped out. There is a measure of anger smoldering away in the poem, whose irony points at the upper-class voice of the officer, at God, and at the narrator himself. The apparent casualness hides a cool artistry. The narrator lay down under unbroken wires,

Till the politest voice—a finicking accent, said:
"Do you think you might crawl through there:
    there's a hole"
Darkness, shot at: I smiled, as politely replied—
"I'm afraid not, Sir." There was no hole no way to
    be seen,
Nothing but chance of death, after tearing of
    clothes

Kept flat, and watched the darkness, hearing bullets
    whizzing—
And thought of music—and swore deep heart's
    deep oaths
(Polite to God). . . .

(9–16)

Equally fine is "The Bohemians," a portrait of Gurney and his friends, who found army regulations irksome, who wanted to be left alone:

Certain people would not clean their buttons,
Nor polish buckles after latest fashions,
Preferred their hair long, puttees comfortable.

(1–3)

He describes how they never adapted themselves to military ways,

Surprised as ever to find the army capable
Of sounding "Lights Out" to break a game of Bridge,
As to fear candles would set a barn alight.

(14–16)

Only in the last line of the poem does Gurney move almost imperceptibly from gentle irony into the starkness of an epitaph:

In Artois or Picardy they lie—free of useless fashions.

It is impossible to say just how good a poet Gurney was, because most of his work remains unpublished. Michael Hurd, who has labored so long and so effectively on the texts of Gurney's poems, reckons that 600 out of his 900 poems have not been published. About 300 are viable, many of them of the highest quality. It is sad to think that such richness lies neglected in the Gurney archive of the Gloucester public library. The cruel mischance that confined him to mental hospitals for the last fifteen years of his life still has the power to obscure his fame.

Edmund Blunden (1896–1974) remains an undervalued poet, partly because even his war poems are often held to be academic and pastoral, especially by those who have not read them. Joining the army early in 1915, he had already published two small collections and was to bring out a third in 1916, *Pastorals*, which was, like the two earlier volumes, devoted to the countryside in time of peace. Yet he was rapidly changing, as he tells us in *War Poets: 1914–1918*:

In May and June 1916, in my notebooks, the grimness of war began to compete as a subject with the pastorals of peace. By the end of the year, when madness seemed totally to rule the hour, I was almost a poet of the shell-holes, of ruin and of mortification.

(p. 24)

Blunden was awarded the Military Cross and saw as much hard fighting as any other war poet. In Raymond Asquith's letters home, printed in John Jolliffe's *Raymond Asquith: Life and Letters*, one learns that, despite the killing, the pain, the fear, the acute discomfort, and the boredom, there were moments of exaltation and pleasure during the war: the singing of nightingales or the enjoyment of splendid food and drink. Such moments seldom find their way into the poems of the most powerful war poets, such as Sassoon, Owen, or Rosenberg. It is a mark of Blunden's rare honesty and range of sympathies that he can reveal the less dark sides of war:

> O how comely it was and how reviving,
> When with clay and with death no longer striving
> Down firm roads we came to houses
> With women chattering and green grass thriving.
> . . .
> Gazed on the mill-sails, heard the church-bell,
> Found an honest glass all manner of riches.
> ("At Senlis Once," 1–4; 11–12)

It is typical of Blunden that the first, Miltonic line should lead us not into deep metaphysical speculation but into a remembrance of lesser mercies.

Blunden knows that, in war, innocent relaxation may for an hour or so charm away the ferocity of killing. Both are aspects of war. In "Concert Party: Busseboom," the audience, delighted by the entertainment, reluctantly leaves the world of illusion:

> We heard another matinée,
>   We heard the maniac blast
>
> Of barrage south by Saint Eloi,
>   And the red lights flaming there
> Called madness: Come, my bonny boy,
>   And dance to the latest air.
>
> To this new concert, white we stood;
>   Cold certainty held our breath;
> While men in the tunnels below Larch Wood
>   Were kicking men to death.
> (15–24)

Blunden grew up in a Kent village where, as in Leonard Woolf's Sussex, life still went on much as in the days of the Domesday Book. Even at school he was a scholar and a poet, deeply versed in the pastoral tradition of English poetry. But his own poetry is pastoral not only because of his literary learning but because he was genuinely a countryman. The weakness of his verse over the years is that he tends to retreat into archaism and whimsy, but his love for the fields and woods that he discovered in France lends an element of strength and perceptiveness to his war poetry. He loathes the war because it violates the pieties of nature no less than the sanctity of man. As early as May 1916 he linked the two in "Festubert: The Old German Line":

> Sparse mists of moonlight hurt our eyes
> With gouged and scourged uncertainties
> Of soul and soil in agonies.
> (1–3)

One of his most moving poems, "Report on Experience," published in the collection *Near and Far* (1929), takes up the earlier theme. The good man and the enchanting Seraphina, "like one from Eden," are victims of the war, which has also devastated a landscape:

> I have seen a green country, useful to the race,
> Knocked silly with guns and mines, its villages vanished,
> Even the last rat and the last kestrel banished—
> God bless us all, this was peculiar grace.
> (st. 2)

The poem ends with an affirmation, not of faith as a Christian would understand it, but of a belief that we live in an ambiguous universe presided over by a distant God:

> Say what you will, our God sees how they run.
> These disillusions are His curious proving
> That He loves humanity and will go on loving;
> Over there are faith, life, virtue in the sun.
> (st. 4)

The war continued to haunt Blunden's imagination. He collected many of his best war poems as a supplement to the prose narrative of *Undertones of War* (1928). One of the finest is a singularly beautiful elegy, "Their Very Memory," that reveals Blunden as a master of rhythmical subtlety. The imagery of the poem evokes running water, green valleys, a spring, a fountain, a greenwood, music. Although Blunden's memory of his comrades is fading, it has not wholly vanished:

428

When they smiled,
Earth's inferno changed and melted
Greenwood mild;
Every village where they halted
Shone with them through square and alley.

(st. 3)

Even when Blunden is not ostensibly writing about the war, it presides over his meditations. His justly admired poem "The Midnight Skaters," from *English Poems* (1925), evokes death at watch within the pond's black bed:

What wants he but to catch
Earth's heedless sons and daughters?
With but a crystal parapet
Between, he has his engines set.

(9–12)

The word "parapet" intrudes into a tranquil, Wordsworthian scene like an icy wind blowing from no-man's-land.

Even after World War II, the memory of World War I steals into poems far distant in time and place. When Blunden was working in Hong Kong, the Communists allowed him to visit the Great Wall of China, because he was a poet and because they rightly believed that he would make no political use of his visit. His sonnet "At the Great Wall of China" is, sadly, one of the few poems of his later years fit to rank with the best of his work. The parapet reappears in the sonnet's octet, more appropriately perhaps than in "The Midnight Skaters." We look from a tower and imagine

Where these few miles to thousands grow, and yet
Ever the one command and genius haunt
Each stairway, sally-port, loop, parapet,
In mute last answer to the invader's vaunt.

(5–8)

It is in the sextet that the memories of Blunden's war loom unmistakably clear:

But I half know at this bleak turret here,
In snow-dimmed moonlight where sure answers quail,
This new-set sentry of a long dead year.

(9–11)

For there are two ghosts at the bleak turret: that of a young Chinese soldier and that of a British sentry on the Ancre or the Somme. They merge insensibly in the mind of an English poet.

Blunden's war poetry is tougher than commonly supposed. Even though he wrote pastoral verse and, at the end of *Undertones of War* (p. 314), called himself "a harmless young shepherd in a soldier's coat," he was adopting a strategy that enabled him to confront the war and record what he observed. In old age he went to live in Suffolk at the village of Long Melford with his wife and daughters, wrote a guide to the magnificent church, and composed an obituary for his old friend Siegfried Sassoon, who was, like Blunden, a survivor of the trenches, a holder of the Military Cross, and an honored poet.

It is time now to consider the work of two men whose view of the war is darker and more tragic than that of the poets so far discussed. (There will not be an account of Wilfred Owen, since he is the subject of a separate essay in this volume.)

SIEGFRIED SASSOON

SIEGFRIED SASSOON (1886–1967), who was born into a rich Jewish family, left Cambridge without taking a degree and in the years before 1914 devoted himself to hunting, cricket, golf, ballet, opera, and evenings at his London club. He also began to develop a taste for literature, bringing out his privately printed collection *Poems* in 1906 and *The Daffodil Murderer* in 1913. This poem, which appeared under the pseudonym Saul Kain, was a parody of John Masefield but also a serious attempt to portray the feelings of the poor and the degraded.

Sassoon, who had joined the army on the first day of the war, rapidly acquired a reputation for courage that bordered on the insane. He stood several inches over six feet, and was lean, athletic, and reckless: it is not surprising that this formidable killer acquired the nickname "Mad Jack." His poem "The Kiss," whatever he may have thought of it later, is written in praise of "Brother Lead and Sister Steel." In the Somme offensive of July 1916 he fought with such gallantry that he was awarded the Military Cross. But his attitude toward the war had already begun to change.

It is not easy to chart the logical progress of that change, if only because Sassoon lived by generous passion rather than by calm reason. He may have reacted strongly against lectures on "the spirit of the bayonet," given at the Fourth Army School at Flixécourt in the spring of 1916, lectures that aroused the disgust of poets as various as Edmund Blunden, Robert Graves, and David Jones.[2] He had begun writing early in 1916 what he himself called genuine trench poems that were the first things of their kind. Further stages in his pilgrimage include meetings at Garsington Manor, Oxfordshire, the home of Philip Morrell, MP, and Lady Ottoline Morrell, with a number of prominent pacifists, including Bertrand Russell; and a spell in a hospital after being invalided home with a bullet wound in his lung, sustained at the battle of Arras in April 1917, the engagement in which Edward Thomas was killed.

By February 1917 Sassoon was already losing his belief in the war, and in July he made a protest against its needless prolongation. This "act of wilful defiance of military authority," as Sassoon described it, rendered him liable to court-martial and imprisonment. Thanks largely to the intervention of Robert Graves, an alternative procedure was followed, and Sassoon, who had meanwhile thrown his Military Cross into the Mersey, agreed to appear before a medical board. Graves testified that Sassoon suffered from hallucinations typical of shell shock, and himself burst into tears three times while making his statement. The board dispatched Sassoon to Craiglockhart War Hospital, appointing as his escort Robert Graves, who missed the train that was carrying Sassoon to his destination.

At Craiglockhart the doctors cured Sassoon of whatever illness had prompted him to issue his act of defiance, and he asked for a posting abroad. He arrived in Egypt at the end of February 1918, then moved to France in May. His fighting days came to an end on 13 July 1918, when, on a daylight patrol, he was accidentally shot through the head by a British sentry and sent home to pass the rest of the war in a hospital.

Two volumes of poetry, *The Old Huntsman* (1917) and *Counter-Attack* (1918), contain almost all the enduring poems that Sassoon wrote about the war. The judgment that he is primarily a satirist is questionable, but his satirical poems retain to this day their incisiveness and power. In "They," Sassoon launches an attack not only on a complacent, stupid bishop but on the apparent subservience of the Anglican church to the state, and on the windy rhetoric that was one of the main civilian contributions to the war:

---

[2]Robert Graves is the subject of a separate essay in this series. Therefore, there is no discussion of his poetry here. His war poems form only a minor part of his work.

The Bishop tells us: "When the boys come back
They will not be the same; for they'll have fought
In a just cause; they lead the last attack
On Anti-Christ."

(st. 1)

The next stanza contrasts the stale abstractions by which the bishop lives with the raw truths that are the products of war:

"We're none of us the same!" the boys reply.
"For George lost both his legs; and Bill's stone blind;
"Poor Jim's shot through the lungs and like to die;
"And Bert's gone syphilitic; you'll not find
"A chap who's served that hasn't found *some* change."
And the Bishop said: "The ways of God are strange."

(st. 2)

In view of his official and social position, Edward Marsh showed courage when he published the poem: the mention of syphilis was an offense against decorum and an affront to patriotic feeling.

There are moments when Sassoon's rage may seem to be in excess of its object. In January 1917, just before returning to France, Sassoon went to a revue at the Hippodrome in Liverpool and wrote a poem designed to be his farewell to England:

. . . prancing ranks
Of harlots shrill the chorus, drunk with din;
"We're sure the Kaiser loves our dear old Tanks!"

I'd like to see a Tank come down the stalls,
Lurching to rag-time tunes, or "Home, sweet Home."
And there'd be no more jokes in Music-halls
To mock the riddled corpses round Bapaume.

("Blighters," 2–8)

It is a little hard on the inoffensive chorus girls to stigmatize them as harlots, and the audience hardly deserves to be massacred. But Sassoon believed that the ignorance of civilians about what was happening on the battlefield was criminal. Songs in music halls about tanks were blasphemous insults to the troops and to their dead comrades. Viewed in this light, "Blighters" is a valid testament of justified indignation. Its final line, particularly when spoken aloud, delivers a searing curse on those who thoughtlessly mock the agony of their fellow men.

Some of Sassoon's other satirical poems have become anthology pieces, such as "Base Details," "Glory of Women," "Does It Matter?" "The General," and "Fight to a Finish," a savage attack on civilians, especially journalists and members of Parliament.

Most of his poems have scarcely any satirical element, but take as their theme trench warfare, presented with an almost brutal realism, although the underlying tenderness aroused by the spectacle of the wounded and the dead redeems what would otherwise be almost intolerable. In "Attack," Sassoon, while playing down the worst of the horror, describes what it was like to go over the top:

> Lines of grey, muttering faces, masked with fear,
> They leave their trenches, going over the top,
> While time ticks blank and busy on their wrists,
> And hope, with furtive eyes and grappling fists,
> Flounders in mud. O Jesus, make it stop!
> (9–13)

Some reviewers of *Counter-Attack* condemned Sassoon for his insistence on the ugly aspects of war. In the title poem he portrays as faithfully as a Dutch seventeenth-century painter the contents of a captured trench:

> The place was rotten with dead; green clumsy legs
> High-booted, sprawled and grovelled along the saps
> And trunks, face downward, in the sucking mud,
> Wallowed like trodden sandbags, loosely filled;
> And naked sodden buttocks, mats of hair,
> Bulged, clotted heads slept in the plastering slime.
> And then the rain began,—the jolly old rain.
> (st. 1)

This is no mere catalog of horrifying items: the dense particularity of the description achieves a sensuous richness. The green legs are ghastly because the adjective suggests both the fertility of spring and the gangrenous texture of the rotting corpses. In a similar way the word "slept" has associations of repose that are mocked by the way in which the clotted heads sink into the slime. The stanza's last line, with its casual irony, provides a moment's relief from one's scrutiny of the dismembered bodies.

Although Sassoon wrote nothing else so richly complex as "Counter-Attack," he produced a number of memorable poems about various aspects of trench warfare. One of the most effective is "The Rear-Guard," set in a tunnel under the Hindenburg Line in April 1917 and based on an experience of his own. The narrator, who has not slept for days, is furious when a sleeping figure over whom he stumbles fails to wake up and answer his questions:

> Savage, he kicked a soft, unanswering heap,
> And flashed his beam across the livid face
> Terribly glaring up, whose eyes yet wore

> Agony dying hard ten days before;
> And fists of fingers clutched a blackening wound.
> (st. 3)

Two of Sassoon's poems are unusual in that they are explicitly elegiac. "To Any Dead Officer" mingles anger, mockery, and compassion, passing from a lament for one particular officer to a fine passage in which Sassoon mourns all who were reported "wounded and missing":

> Next week the bloody Roll of Honour said
>   "Wounded and missing"—(That's the thing to do
> When lads are left in shell-holes dying slow,
>   With nothing but blank sky and wounds that ache,
> Moaning for water till they know
>   It's night, and then it's not worth while to wake!)
> (st. 4)

"To One Who Was with Me in the War," written in 1926, is not so much a formal elegy as a "game of ghosts," in which the poet imagines going back with a fellow officer after the war to "some redoubt of Time," where they may relive their experience of the trenches. It is a less urgent, mellower poem than those Sassoon wrote during the war, yet it conveys something of his complex emotions toward that war:

>   Round the next bay you'll meet
> A drenched platoon-commander; chilled, he drums
>   his feet
> On squelching duck-boards; winds his wrist-watch;
>   turns his head,
> And shows you how you looked,—your ten-years-
>   vanished face,
> Hoping the War will end next week . . .
>   What's that you said?
> (32–37)

After the war was over Sassoon returned to his old life, combining his sporting interests with literary activity. He became widely known for a series of prose autobiographies that cover his life from the closing years of the nineteenth century to the end of the war. He continued to write poetry during the rest of a long life, happy to employ the diction and the meters of his youth, unswayed by the innovatory techniques of Pound, Eliot, and the imagists. His poems include gentle satires on, for example, the first performance of Stravinsky's *Rite of Spring* and the destruction of Devonshire House; reminiscences of the war; and explorations of religious and mystical themes. But it is by virtue of thirty or forty poems that delineate the agony of the fighting in the trenches that he holds an honored place among English poets.

ISAAC ROSENBERG

ISAAC ROSENBERG (1890–1918) is one of the few Englishmen to have achieved distinction as a poet and a painter. He was born in the East End of London and was the son of Lithuanian Jews who had emigrated to Britain in the 1880's. After leaving school in 1904 he was apprenticed to a firm of art publishers, but chafed at the narrowness of his life. Thanks to the generosity of some Jewish ladies, he was able in October 1911 to enroll at the Slade School, where he met gifted fellow students such as David Bomberg, Mark Gertler, Dora Carrington, Edward Wadsworth, Paul Nash, and Stanley Spencer. He published at his own expense in 1912 a booklet of poems, *Night and Day*, in which he was already expressing his perplexities about the significance of suffering and the nature of God.

On 10 November 1913 Gertler introduced Rosenberg to Edward Marsh at the Café Royal. For the rest of Rosenberg's life Marsh gave him all manner of help, buying his paintings, paying for the publication of his second book of poems, *Youth* (1915), and doing what he could to relieve Rosenberg's difficulties after he had joined the army.

The relationship between a man and his patron is always subject to strains of various kinds, and it must be admitted that Rosenberg and Marsh were seldom in perfect accord. Marsh was a cultivated member of the English upper classes, private secretary to Winston Churchill, a man of conservative tastes, editor of the Georgian anthologies, a passionate admirer of Rupert Brooke. It is easy to draw up an indictment of Marsh, pointing at his failure to recognize the genius of Rosenberg; at his exclusion of him from his anthologies, except for a speech from *Moses*; at his inability to admire "Dead Man's Dump." It is even held against Marsh that, years after the end of the war, he could still talk of "poor little Rosenberg."

Yet Marsh proved a true friend to Rosenberg. It was Marsh who ensured that Rosenberg's mother received from the army the allowance due her, just as it was Marsh who did all in his power to have Rosenberg moved to safer and less exacting military duties. Despite his failure to respond to "Dead Man's Dump," he took the trouble, before returning the manuscript to Rosenberg, to copy out the poem for fear that it might be lost. Nor did Marsh call him "poor little Rosenberg" in a spirit of upper-class condescension. Mark Gertler, a poor, working-class, East End, Jewish painter, described Rosenberg affec-

tionately as a "funny little man." It is possible to be a poet of the first order and also a poor, funny little man.

In June 1914 Rosenberg visited Cape Town, where he stayed with his married sister, Minnie. He wrote there "On Receiving News of the War," a poem that anticipates the end of the old order, a poem of foreboding deeper than any experienced by his compatriots at home. For over a year before the outbreak of war he had been concerned with the need to reject the orthodox male God, and at about the same time he was working on a poem on the outbreak of the war, he was composing a strange poem entitled "The Female God," an exploration of the sexual and the sacred.

Rosenberg went back to England in February 1915, although he could have stayed on in Cape Town indefinitely, especially as he was much in demand as a portrait painter. Apparently he felt that he had reached an emotional and spiritual dead end. But in London things were little better, and in the autumn of 1915 he enlisted in the army, partly to obtain an allowance for his mother and partly, it has been surmised, to fulfill a long-suppressed death wish. He wrote to Marsh that he had not joined the army for patriotic reasons.

Rosenberg's life in the army was unutterably wretched. He wrote to Lascelles Abercrombie on 11 March 1916: "the army is the most detestable invention on this earth and nobody but a private in the army knows what it is to be a slave" (*Collected Works*, p. 230). On 26 January 1918, in a passage canceled by the censor, he wrote to Edward Marsh: "what is happening to me now is more tragic than the 'passion play.' Christ never endured what I endure. It is breaking me completely."[3] Everything conspired to make Rosenberg's army life a long nightmare. He detested the coarseness of his fellow soldiers' behavior and the crudity of their minds. His lot was worsened by the anti-Jewish prejudice that he encountered among officers and private soldiers alike. Because the boots issued by the army did not fit him, he suffered the agony of sore heels, not nearly as trivial a matter as civilians at home might reckon. His awkwardness, stubbornness, and forgetfulness must have made matters worse: he was punished for leaving behind his gas helmet, and the injustice of army discipline rankled with him. The continual labor that was his lot imposed severe strains on his

---

[3]From an unpublished letter quoted in J. Cohen, *Journey to the Trenches* (London, 1975), p. 3.

physique. Dragging heavy coils of barbed wire into no-man's-land and setting them up, or digging latrines in the hard earth or in the excremental mud, weighed upon his body and his spirit. He refers several times to the difficulty of writing and of perfecting his poems in such conditions. The lives of officers were at least as dangerous as those of their men, but they enjoyed some compensations. They had the services of a batman, who would keep their uniform clean; their food and sleeping quarters were better; they were exempt from physical labor and from punishments such as pack drill for trivial breaches of discipline; they could afford to relax in decent hotels and restaurants on short leaves instead of in the bistros where private soldiers congregated; they might even make the acquaintance of cultivated Belgian or French civilians; and with luck they would find one or two congenial fellow officers in their regiment or company.

It is probably true that Rosenberg never met in the army a single person who cared for any of the arts or with whom he could have the kind of talk that meant so much to him. One of his officers, Frank Waley, asked Rosenberg for copies of some of his poems. Rosenberg was always short of paper, being obliged to write some poems on the backs of envelopes; nevertheless he gave Waley a few poems that baffled him so completely that he chucked them away. The only one Waley could remember was "Break of Day in the Trenches," and since he didn't think it was poetry he threw it out with the rest.

In 1916, at his own expense, Rosenberg published in a volume entitled *Roses* an unfinished play of that name, together with some shorter poems. It is convenient to group it with another play, *The Unicorn*, a work of only a few pages, completed in the summer of 1917, although in March 1918 he was planning to write a fuller treatment of the play, which he had always regarded as a sketch for a larger version.

Although only 470 lines long, *Moses* is an extremely complex work about whose significance there is still no general agreement. Rosenberg wrote to the poet R. C. Trevelyan in a letter postmarked 15 June 1916: "Moses symbolizes the fierce desire for virility, and original action in contrast to slavery of the most abject kind" (*Collected Works*, p. 235). Knowing Rosenberg's views about the slavery of private soldiers, one is entitled to say that *Moses* presents Rosenberg's situation in 1915–1916. It also marks the culminating stage in his rejection of the divinity whom he had scrutinized in a number of poems and stigmatized in "God" as "this miasma of a rotting God." ("This miasma of a rotting god" also occurs as line 144 of *Moses*.) One may also read the play as Rosenberg's attempt to define the historical destiny of the Jews and of the proletariat. It expresses his preoccupation with violence as a force that may possibly regenerate a crumbling, sick society, a notion that he had played with even before the outbreak of war. The only overt act of violence occurs at the end of the play, when Moses strangles the brutal Egyptian overseer, Abinoah, father of his mistress, Koelue. She may also stand for the incarnate sexuality of the earth goddess whom Rosenberg had long envisaged as the supplanter of the orthodox male God.

The Unicorn is even shorter and stranger than *Moses*. It is about a decaying race who have never seen a woman, and whose chief, named Tel, is mounted on a unicorn. The two other main characters, Saul and his wife, Lilith, belong to another tribe, as does Enoch, the only other character. The climax of the play is best described in the final stage direction:

Through the casement they see riding under the rainbow a black naked host on various animals, the Unicorn leading. A woman is clasped on every one, some are frantic, others white or unconscious, some nestle laughing. ENOCH with madness in his eyes leaps through the casement and disappears with a splash in the well. SAUL leaps after him shouting "The Unicorn." TEL places the unconscious LILITH on the Unicorn and they all ride away.

(*Collected Works*, p. 173)

In a letter to Winifreda Seaton dated 8 March 1918 Rosenberg wrote of his ambitions for an expanded version of *The Unicorn*: "I mean to put all my innermost experiences into the 'Unicorn.' I want it to symbolize the war and all the devastating forces, let loose by an ambitious and unscrupulous will" (*Collected Works*, p. 270).

Some of the themes of *Moses* reappear in *The Unicorn*, notably those of sexuality and violence as the instruments of liberation and change. Before starting work on the fragments that became *The Unicorn* Rosenberg had contemplated writing a play about Judas Maccabeus, who reconquered Jerusalem from the Romans in 165 B.C. He may also have had in mind a quotation from the Book of Numbers: "God brought them out of Egypt; he hath as it were the strength of a unicorn."

It is the richness and complexity of the themes and the way in which they mirror Rosenberg's psychological turmoil that constitute the fascination of these plays, whether one ranks them among his greatest achievements or regards them as only partially successful despite their imaginative force and the magnificent passages of verse found in them.

Although Rosenberg was a mature artist by the outbreak of war and had written some hauntingly original poems by the spring of 1916, it is on a handful of poems written between midsummer 1916 and his death on 1 April 1918 that his reputation securely rests. He wrote to Edward Marsh on 4 August 1916, enclosing "A Worm Fed on the Heart of Corinth" and "Break of Day in the Trenches." The former prophesies, in ten astonishing lines, the destruction of England by a creature akin to the invisible worm of William Blake's "The Sick Rose." With this poem Rosenberg takes his place among the Hebrew prophets and the English poets. "Break of Day in the Trenches," actually written in the trenches, is a flawless, ironical meditation, that opens with an ominous strangeness:

> The darkness crumbles away.
> It is the same old druid Time as ever.

In his letter to Marsh, Rosenberg observes: "I am enclosing a poem I wrote in the trenches, which is surely as simple as ordinary talk. You might object to the second line as vague, but that was the best way I could express the sense of dawn" (*Collected Works,* p. 239). The sight of a rat that leaps over the poet's hand as he plucks a poppy to stick behind his ear moves him to meditate sardonically on the rat's cosmopolitan sympathies, which lead him to touch first an English, next a German, hand. He then imagines the rat's grin as he watches men in all their bodily pride reduced to short-lived creatures with terror in their eyes. At the very end of the poem the image of the poppy returns.

The poppy held great emotional potency for the soldiers in France and Flanders: indeed Englishmen still wear paper poppies in their buttonholes on Armistice Day. John McCrae, a Canadian, wrote the most popular poem of the war, "In Flanders Fields," which begins:

> In Flanders fields the poppies blow
> Between the crosses, row on row.

The first half of McRae's poem is reasonably competent versifying, although the second half represents a sad decline. But Rosenberg has made the symbol of the plucked poppy ironically resonant with our sense of life's brevity and of the mortality that is the lot of rat and poppy and men:

> Poppies whose roots are in man's veins
> Drop, and are ever dropping;
> But mine in my ear is safe—
> Just a little white with the dust.
> ("Break of Day in the
> Trenches," 23–26)

In May 1917, Rosenberg sent Marsh a seventy-nine-line poem, "Dead Man's Dump," based on his own experience of carrying wire up to the line on limbers and running over dead bodies. It contains Rosenberg's only realistic descriptions of the battlefield, yet his main concern is still his search for the meaning of human existence, his desire to discover the metaphysical significance of war. He is capable of writing lines that convey with horrifying exactness the sensation of driving a cart over dead bodies:

> The wheels lurched over sprawled dead
> But pained them not, though their bones crunched.
> (7–8)

The poem ends in a similar vein, but at the middle of it the sight of the dead moves Rosenberg to compose a passage unrivaled in any other poem of war except in Wilfred Owen's finest work:

> None saw their spirits' shadow shake the grass,
> Or stood aside for the half used life to pass
> Out of those doomed nostrils and the doomed mouth,
> When the swift iron burning bee
> Drained the wild honey of their youth.
>
> (27–31)

The imagery here of honey and iron occurs also in "August 1914," a beautiful short lyric written in the summer of 1916.

Two further poems of 1917 show Rosenberg's imagination at its strangest and most potent. "Daughters of War" evokes mysterious Amazons whose lovers are soldiers killed in battle and washed clean of mortal dust. He believed it to be his best poem, and during the year that he spent on it he had "striven to get that sense of inexorableness the human (or inhuman) side of this war has" (*Collected Works,* p. 260).

Again, in "Returning, We Hear the Larks," Rosenberg explores in this brief lyric themes to which he continually recurs: war, beauty, sexuality, the menacing power of women. The lark song that at first brings only joy carries a somber reminder:

Death could drop from the dark
As easily as song—
But song only dropped,
Like a blind man's dreams on the sand
By dangerous tides,
Like a girl's dark hair for she dreams no ruins lie there,
Or her kisses where a serpent hides.

(10–16)

Rosenberg continued to write poems of high quality until a few days before his death. In a letter to Marsh dated 28 March 1918 he enclosed his last poem, "Through These Pale Cold Days," the third of three meditations on Jewish history and Jewish destiny. On 30 and 31 March Rosenberg's regiment suffered heavy casualties while resisting the German advance, and in the early hours of the morning on 1 April his company was making its way back in order to gain a brief respite from the fighting. Rosenberg volunteered to return to the battle and within an hour was killed in close combat near the French village of Fampoux.

WHAT THE SOLDIERS SANG

THE British army sang on the march, in trenches, in billets, in bistros, and in concert halls. The songs that gave strength and comfort to the troops are often ignored by literary critics, who have failed to recognize in them the most considerable body of poetry in English composed and sung by the common man.

Not all the songs were anonymous products of the trenches. "Tipperary," arguably the most famous of marching songs, although the troops came to loathe it, was written in 1912 by a professional composer. "Keep the Home Fires Burning," which belongs to 1915–1916 and the march to the Somme, brought fame and money to the youthful Ivor Novello, who after 1918 wrote, acted in, and directed a long series of spectacular musical comedies at Drury Lane.

Yet the overwhelming majority of trench songs were by anonymous soldiers. Some of them may have been written by one man for performance at a concert, before being adopted, embroidered, or parodied by troops in different parts of the line. Others may have been the work of soldiers, put together during a rest period and then transmitted by word of mouth to men of other regiments. A few songs, some of which went back to the eighteenth and nineteenth centuries, were inherited from the pre-1914 regular army.

The words sung with such gusto were often parodies of well-known hymns, ballads, and musical comedy and music-hall songs: they were usually fitted to existing tunes, sacred and profane. The authors of these songs, whoever they may have been, portrayed themselves as cowardly, lecherous, skeptical of victory, disrespectful toward their military superiors, unappreciative of the charms or the morals of French women such as "Mademoiselle from Armenteers," longing only to get back to England. "I Don't Want to Die" begins:

I want to go home,
I want to go home,
I don't want to go to the trenches no more,
Where whizz-bangs and shrapnel they whistle and roar.

That inglorious declaration finds a parallel in "I Don't Want to Be a Soldier," a parody of "On Sunday I Walk Out with a Soldier," a song of the kind loathed by Sassoon, which was sung in a revue, *The Passing Show of 1914*, produced at the London Hippodrome:

I don't want to be a soldier,
I don't want to go to war.
I'd rather stay at home,
Around the streets to roam,
And live on the earnings of a well-paid whore.

Not all the songs referred to the war. "Wash Me in the Water," widely sung throughout the war, seems to bear no relevance to the fighting, probably because it is said to have been sung by the regular army before 1914. It was set to a Salvation Army hymn tune:

Wash me in the water
That you washed your dirty daughter
And I shall be whiter
Than the whitewash on the wall.

When no officers were present, "your dirty daughter" might become "the colonel's daughter."

But almost all the finest songs have deep roots in the daily lives of those who composed and sang them. "The Old Barbed Wire" provides a superb example of the way in which contemptuous humor, apparent callousness, and deadly accuracy combine to make an unforgettable song:

If you want to find the sergeant,
I know where he is, I know where he is.
If you want to find the sergeant,
I know where he is,
He's lying on the canteen floor.

The quarter-bloke (the quartermaster sergeant) is miles behind the line; the sergeant-major is boozing up with the private's rum; the CO is down in the deep dugouts. Then comes the final dramatic twist:

If you want to find the old battalion,
I know where they are, I know where they are.
If you want to find the old battalion,
I know where they are,
They're hanging on the old barbed wire.

In 1963 Joan Littlewood's musical extravaganza *Oh What a Lovely War* made brilliant use of these songs; yet it would be wrong to think of them merely as part of a theatrical entertainment. They commemorate, more fittingly than the headstones of the Imperial War Graves Commission, the lives and deaths of those gallant though unheroic common soldiers who, when the noise of the guns had died down, were found lying in the mud or hanging on the old barbed wire.

THE AFTERMATH:
HERBERT READ AND DAVID JONES

In the early 1920's and during the rest of the decade, English novelists tried to give order and coherence to their experience and memories of the war by writing prose fiction. No poet of any merit essayed this task by means of his art until the next decade. There then appeared two poems of some length, *The End of a War* (1933) by Herbert Read and *In Parenthesis* (1937) by David Jones. Neither can be described as a novel in verse or even as an orthodox narrative poem, yet both attempt to assimilate certain qualities of modern prose fiction and to build something less impressionistic and lyrical than the war poems that we have considered in this essay.

Herbert Read (1893–1968) fought with distinction in the war, earning the Distinguished Service Order and the Military Cross. His book of poems *Songs of Chaos* (1915) was followed by a second, *Naked Warriors* (1919). Although Read was to enjoy a long career as a literary critic and aesthetician, he had not in 1919 seen any of those works by Antonio Pollaiuolo or other Florentine painters conjured up by the book's title, whose progenitor is almost certainly Wordsworth's "Character of a Happy Warrior," a poem that is a happy source book of high-minded schoolmasters and of politicians eager to sanctify their wartime speeches with an edifying quotation from a great poet:

Who is the happy Warrior? Who is he
That every man in arms should wish to be?

Read gives his answer to Wordsworth's query of 1805:

Bloody saliva
Dribbles down his shapeless jacket.

I saw him stab
And stab again
A well-killed Boche.

This is the happy warrior,
This is he. . . .

(6–12)

"The Execution of Cornelius Vane" anatomizes the life and death of a soldier who shoots away his right index finger and works thereafter in a cookhouse. Required to fight in an emergency, he points to his mutilated hand that cannot fire a rifle, only to be told by a sergeant, "But you can stab." Vane deserts, is tried by court-martial, and is sentenced to death. His executioners, men of his own regiment looking very sad, blindfold him, and just before he is shot he says to the assembly:

"What wrong have I done that I should leave these:
The bright sun rising
And the birds that sing?"

(130–132)

"Kneeshaw Goes to War" analyzes a soldier whose passivity and failure to respond to the world of experience are perhaps more ignoble than Vane's cowardice. He loses a leg in battle and, after returning to England, accepts after long meditation the need to live by the truth and to discipline oneself. The poem anticipates, in its probing of a man's inner life, the intricate analysis of character found in Read's *The End of a War*.

Read's poetry is almost invariably marked by cool

intelligence and firm restraint. Very occasionally he permits his emotion to speak nakedly and movingly; such a moment occurs in "My Company":

> But, God! I know that I'll stand
> Someday in the loneliest wilderness,
>
> . . .
>
> I know that I'll wander with a cry:
> "O beautiful men, O men I loved,
> O whither are you gone, my company?"
> (26–27; 32–34)

It is this kind of passion, this kind of rhythmical vitality, that one finds wanting in Read's most ambitious poem, *The End of a War*.

The poem comprises three interwoven monologues: "Meditation of the Dying German Officer," "Dialogue Between Body and Soul," and "Meditation of the Waking English Officer." The prose Argument summarizes the main incident of the poem (it can hardly be called the main action, for it is an almost wholly static poem). Briefly, on 10 November 1918 a wounded German officer tells a British officer that a village nearby is undefended. German machine-gunners hidden in the church tower fire on the British battalion resting in the village square, killing or wounding a hundred men. The survivors bayonet the hidden machine-gunners and a corporal dispatches the German officer, who dies impassively. Later, the British find the dismembered body of a French girl who had been raped and tortured by the Germans. The English officer falls asleep, exhausted and nauseated. When he wakes in the morning the church bells are ringing in the armistice.

Despite the grandeur of his theme, Read fails to give his poem life, and the characters are only mouthpieces through whom the poet utters his leaden, monochrome soliloquies. The language remains so inert that even the armistice bells cannot stir it into activity. Extensive quotation would not substantiate that judgment, because the reader might suspect that the hostile critic had picked out the worst passages to prove his case. Here is a short extract, which shows Read in a comparatively sprightly mood, taken from the English officer's meditation:

> . . . First there are the dead to bury
> O God, the dead. How can God's bell
> ring out from that unholy ambush?
> That tower of death! In excess of horror
> war died.
> (26–30)

The reader must discover for himself whether that extract is representative of Read's poem.

The End of a War is a praiseworthy attempt to confront some philosophical questions that have preoccupied thoughtful men and women for centuries: the existence of God, the significance of war and violence in society, the limits of political obligation. Yet although the poem has won critical acclaim during the past half-century, it can rank only as an honorable failure. One suspects that *The End of a War* has been more often referred to than read, and more frequently read than enjoyed.

David Jones (1895–1974) was, like Isaac Rosenberg, both poet and painter. He was educated at Camberwell Art School from 1909 to 1914 and enlisted in the Royal Welsh Fusiliers, serving at the front as a private soldier from December 1915 to March 1918. He became a convert to Roman Catholicism in 1921 and lived by his painting until the mid-1930's, thereafter dividing his time between his work as painter, engraver, and typographer, and his work as a writer.

In Parenthesis, begun in 1928 and published in 1937, could be described as an epic in verse about World War I, although it is unlike traditional epic, contains long passages of prose, and celebrates wars much older than the conflict of 1914–1918. It is an extremely difficult, highly allusive poem, although Jones provides thirty-five pages of notes designed, unlike those of *The Waste Land*, to elucidate rather than to tantalize. Yet even the notes offer a formidable array of theological speculation, assorted myth, army jargon, and references to historical events.

Jones sets his poem between early December 1915 and early July 1916, telling us in the preface that after the Somme battle everything became more impersonal, mechanical, and relentless. He could not have written *In Parenthesis* about the mass slaughter that characterized the war after the midsummer of 1916.

The story concerns a battalion in an infantry camp in England preparing to embark for France. It lands in France and makes its way by stages to the trenches, these preliminary movements being completed on Christmas Day 1915. The opening three sections of the poem are followed by three sections that describe a typical day in the trenches and the southward marches toward the Somme. The final section concentrates on the part played in the disastrous Somme offensive in July 1916 by number 7 platoon, under the command of Lieutenant Jenkins. We follow in particular one of its members, Private Ball, who is indeed the sole survivor of the attack. The poem ends, after the nightmare of battle, with the garlanding of the dead by a figure from Jones's private mythology, the Queen of the Woods, who is in part the goddess Diana and in part the dryad of folklore.

The poem is difficult for a variety of reasons: Jones has at his fingertips and within his imagination a wealth of allusions drawn from heterogeneous and complex sources, of which the principal are Roman history, the Gospels, the so-called Matter of Britain (the Arthurian legends), the whole Romano-Celtic tradition, early English and medieval literature, and the rites of the Roman Catholic Church, especially the Mass. Jones attempts to fuse the raw material of the epic with the technique employed in a modernist poem such as *The Waste Land*, wherein the impressionistic use of imagery and evocative incantation of rhythm largely supersede the formal logic of argument and the orderly unfolding of narrative.

Yet behind these highly elaborate literary devices one senses the presence of the private soldiers with their routine blasphemies, their cockney speech, and their daily suffering. Nor must one forget Jones's constant sardonic humour. Even Private John Ball, hero of the epic tale (insofar as there is one), is so called not only because his namesake was the priest who led the Peasants' Revolt in 1381. As Jon Stallworthy observes in his *Survivors' Songs in Welsh Poetry* (1982), Ball's name has a further significance: coming after that of Private Leg in the sergeant's roster, and following the last two digits, 01, in his army number, it is both ballistic and anatomical.

When Private Ball lies wounded he finally abandons his rifle, even though he remembers the admonitions of the instructors in musketry:

> Marry it man! Marry it!
> Cherish her, she's your very own.
> Coax it man coax it—it's delicately and
>   ingeniously made
> —it's an instrument of precision—it costs us tax-payers
> money—I want you men to remember that.
>
> (pp. 183–184)

That might well come from a work of naturalistic fiction, yet it coexists with the boast of Dai-Great-Coat, uttered after the men of number 1 section have shared a meager benefit of bread and rum. In his lengthy boast Dai, a character in Thomas Malory's *Morte Darthur*, who stands here for the private soldier throughout the ages, claims to have participated in all kinds of historical and mythical events involving the use of hand weapons from the war in Heaven onward:

> I served Longinus that Dux bat-blind and bent;
> the dandy Xth are my regiment;
> who diced
> Crown and Mud-hook
> under the Tree, . . .
>
> (p. 83)

This is a fairly simple example of Jones's elaborate allusiveness. The Xth Fretensis is reputed to have furnished the escort party at Jesus' crucifixion, and the dicing under the Cross is equated with the gambling game Crown and Mud-hook, or Crown and Anchor, that was popular among the troops in World War I. Jones's repeated collocation of exalted moments from the past with the brutal or trivial events of the war is not designed to glorify the war or, indeed, to diminish the splendor of history and legend. He wants us to apprehend the timelessness of human action. In a later poem, "The Fatigue," he imagines that the execution of Christ is carried out not by the Xth Fretensis but by a party of British soldiers of World War I.

The prose of *In Parenthesis* ranges from the demotic to the hieratic, the brutally simple to the densely allusive. The verse covers an equally wide gamut of form and of emotional resonance. The closing pages of the poem attain a climax of rare poetic intensity, when the Queen of the Woods comes to deck with garlands all who have died in the battle, officers and other ranks, the loved and the detested, German and British alike. Nothing in the poetry of the war excels this luminous requiem:

> For Balder she reaches high to fetch his.
> Ulrich smiles for his myrtle wand.
> That swine Lillywhite has daisies to his chain—you'd
> hardly credit it.
> She plaits torques of equal splendour for Mr. Jenkins and
> Billy Crower.
> Hansel with Gronwy share dog-violets for a palm, where
> they lie in serious embrace beneath the twisted tripod.
>
> (p. 185)

Jones ends *In Parenthesis* with René Hague's translation of lines from the *Chanson de Roland*:

> The geste says this and the man who was on the field . . .
> and who wrote the book . . . the man who does not know
> this has not understood anything.
>
> (p. 187)

Those words may serve as an epitaph for the poets of 1914–1918, whether they appear in the pages of this essay or not, and as a commemoration of all who suffered and bore witness on the battlefields of World War I.

SELECTED BIBLIOGRAPHY

LAWRENCE BINYON

I. COLLECTED WORKS. *The Four Years: War Poems* (London, 1919); *Collected Poems*, 2 vols. (London, 1931).

II. SEPARATE WORKS. *The Anvil* (London, 1916); *The Cause: Poems of the War* (Boston, 1917); *For the Fallen* (London, 1917).

EDMUND BLUNDEN

I. BIBLIOGRAPHY. B. J. Kirkpatrick, *A Bibliography of Edmund Blunden* (Oxford, 1979).

⁍ II. COLLECTED WORKS. K. Hopkins, ed., *Edmund Blunden: A Selection of Poetry and Prose* (London, 1950; New York, 1961); *Poems of Many Years* (London, 1957); R. Marsack, ed., *Selected Poems* (Manchester, 1982).

III. SEPARATE WORKS. *Undertones of War* (London, 1928), verse and prose, with new preface by author (New York, 1956); *War Poets 1914–1918* (London, 1958), criticism.

IV. CRITICAL STUDIES. A. M. Hardie, *Edmund Blunden* (London, 1958; rev. ed., 1971); M. Thorpe, *The Poetry of Edmund Blunden* (Wateringbury, 1971).

RUPERT BROOKE

I. BIBLIOGRAPHY. G. Keynes, *A Bibliography* (London, 1954; 2nd ed., rev., 1959).

II. COLLECTED WORKS. *Collected Poems: With a Memoir by E[dward]. M[arsh].* (London, 1918); G. Keynes, ed., *The Poetical Works* (London, 1947), paperback ed. (London, 1960); C. Hassall, *The Prose* (London, 1956); G. Keynes, ed., *Letters* (London, 1968).

III. SEPARATE WORKS. *Poems* (London, 1911); *1914 and Other Poems* (London, 1915); *John Webster and the Elizabethan Drama* (London, 1916); *Letters from America* (London, 1916), preface by Henry James.

IV. CRITICAL STUDIES. W. de la Mare, *Rupert Brooke and the Intellectual Imagination* (London, 1919); M. Browne, *Recollections of Rupert Brooke* (London, 1927); A. J. A. Stringer, *Red Wine of Youth: A Life of R. Brooke* (Indianapolis, 1948); C. Hassall, *Rupert Brooke: A Biography* (New York, 1964); M. Hastings, *The Handsomest Young Man in England: Rupert Brooke* (London, 1967), lavishly illus.; G. Keynes, *Rupert Brooke: Drafts and Fair Copies in the Author's Hand* (London, 1974).

FORD MADOX FORD

I. COLLECTED WORKS. *Collected Poems* (New York, 1936), intro. by W. R. Benét.

JULIAN GRENFELL

I. SEPARATE WORKS. *Battle: Flanders* (London, 1915).

II. CRITICAL STUDIES. V. Meynell, *Julian Grenfell* (London, 1917), memoir with poems; M. Mosley, *Julian Grenfell* (London, 1976), based on Grenfell family papers.

IVOR GURNEY

I. COLLECTED WORKS. *Poems by Ivor Gurney* (London, 1954), with memoir by E. Blunden; *Poems of Ivor Gurney, 1890–1937* (London, 1973), intro. by E. Blunden and bibliographical note by L. Clark; P. J. Kavanagh, ed., *Collected Poems of Ivor Gurney* (London, 1982), first major collection of Gurney's work, includes over 300 poems, 100 not previously collected; R. K. R. Thornton, ed., *War Letters of Ivor Gurney* (Manchester, 1983).

II. SEPARATE WORKS. *Severn and Somme* (London, 1917); *War's Embers, and Other Verses* (London, 1919).

III. CRITICAL STUDIES. M. Hurd, *The Ordeal of Ivor Gurney* (London, 1978).

W. N. HODGSON

I. COLLECTED WORKS. *Verse and Prose in Peace and War* (London, 1916; 2nd ed., 1917).

A. E. HOUSMAN

I. COLLECTED WORKS. *Collected Poems* (London, 1939; New York, 1940; 1959).

DAVID JONES

I. COLLECTED WORKS. H. Grisewood, ed., *Epoch and Artist: Selected Writings* (London, 1959), prose; R. Pryor, ed., *David Jones: Letters to Vernon Watkins* (Cardiff, 1976), foreword by G. Watkins, notes by ed.; R. Hague, ed., *Dai Greatcoat: A Self-Portrait of David Jones in His Letters* (Boston, 1980); J. Matthias, ed., *Introducing David Jones: A Selection of His Writings* (Boston, 1980).

II. SEPARATE WORKS. *In Parenthesis* (London, 1937), verse and prose; *The Anathemata: Fragments of an Attempted Writing* (London, 1952; 2nd ed., 1955), verse and prose; *The Sleeping Lord and Other Fragments* (London, 1974), verse and prose; although these later writings do not have World War I as their theme, they all throw light on *In Parenthesis*.

III. CRITICAL STUDIES. D. Blamires, *David Jones: Artist and Writer* (Manchester, 1971; Toronto, 1972); R. Hague, *David Jones* (Cardiff, 1975); J. Hooker, *David Jones: An Exploratory Study of the Writings* (London, 1975); R.

Mathias, ed., *David Jones: Eight Essays on His Work as Writer and Artist* (Llandysul, 1976); S. Rees, *David Jones* (New York, 1977), includes bibliography; W. Blissett, *The Long Conversation: A Memoir of David Jones* (London, 1981).

ROBERT NICHOLS

I. COLLECTED WORKS. *Such Was My Singing: A Selection from Poems 1915–1940* (London, 1942).

II. SEPARATE WORKS. *Invocation: War Poems and Others* (London, 1915); *Ardours and Endurances* (London, 1917).

HERBERT READ

I. COLLECTED WORKS. *Collected Poems* (London, 1966).

II. SEPARATE WORKS. *Songs of Chaos* (London, 1915), verse; *Naked Warriors* (London, 1919), verse; *In Retreat* (London, 1925), prose narrative; *Ambush* (London, 1930), prose narrative; *The End of a War* (London, 1933), verse.

III. CRITICAL STUDIES. F. Berry, *Herbert Read* (London, 1961).

ISAAC ROSENBERG

I. COLLECTED WORKS. G. Bottomley, ed., *Poems* (London, 1922), with memoir by L. Binyon; G. Bottomley and D. Harding, eds., *Collected Poems* (London–New York, 1949); I. Parsons, ed., *Collected Works* (London, 1979), rev. and enl. from 1937 ed., intro. by ed., foreword by S. Sassoon.

II. SEPARATE WORKS. *Night and Day* (London, 1912); *Youth* (London, 1915), poems; *Moses* (London, 1916), drama.

III. CRITICAL STUDIES. J. Cohen, *Journey to the Trenches: The Life of Isaac Rosenberg, 1890–1918* (London, 1975); J. Liddiard, *Isaac Rosenberg: The Half-Used Life* (London, 1975); J. M. Wilson, *Isaac Rosenberg, Poet and Painter* (London, 1975). Note: Catalogs of two exhibitions contain valuable material on Rosenberg: *Isaac Rosenberg 1890–1917: Catalogue with Letters*, ed. by M. de Sausmarez and J. Silkin, Leeds University Exhibition Catalog (Leeds, 1959), and the National Book League Exhibition Catalogue, ed. by J. Liddiard and C. Simmons (London, 1975).

SIEGFRIED SASSOON

I. BIBLIOGRAPHY. G. Keynes, *A Bibliography* (London, 1962).

II. COLLECTED WORKS. *The War Poems* (London, 1919); *The Complete Memoirs of George Sherston* (London, 1937), prose; *Collected Poems* (London, 1947); *Collected Poems 1908–1956* (London, 1961); *Selected Poems* (London, 1968), paperback ed.

III. SEPARATE WORKS. *The Old Huntsman and Other Poems* (London, 1917); *Counter-Attack and Other Poems*

(London, 1918), intro. by R. Nichols; *Picture Show* (Cambridge, 1919), verse; *Satirical Poems* (London, 1926; enl. ed., 1933); *The Heart's Journey* (London, 1927), verse; *Memoirs of a Fox-Hunting Man* (London, 1928), memoirs; *Memoirs of an Infantry Officer* (New York–London, 1930), memoirs; *Sherston's Progress* (London, 1936), memoirs; *The Old Century and Seven More Years* (London, 1938), memoirs, paperback ed. with intro. by M. Thorpe (London, 1968); *The Weald of Youth* (London, 1942), memoirs; *Siegfried's Journey, 1916–1920* (London, 1945), memoirs; D. R. Hart, ed., *Diaries 1920–1922* (London, 1982), intro. by ed.

IV. CRITICAL STUDIES. M. Thorpe, *Siegfried Sassoon: A Critical Study* (London, 1966).

CHARLES HAMILTON SORLEY

I. COLLECTED WORKS. *Marlborough, and Other Poems* (London, 1916; 5th ed., rev. and enl., 1922); *Letters from Germany* (Cambridge, 1916); *The Letters with a Chapter of Biography* (Cambridge, 1919).

II. CRITICAL STUDIES. T. B. Swann, *The Ungirt Runner: Charles Hamilton Sorley, Poet of World War I* (Hamden, Conn., 1965).

EDWARD THOMAS

I. COLLECTED WORKS. *Collected Poems* (London, 1920), foreword by W. de la Mare; R. G. Thomas, ed., *Letters from Edward Thomas to Gordon Bottomley* (London, 1958); R. G. Thomas, ed., *Collected Poems* (New York–Oxford, 1978).

II. CRITICAL STUDIES. J. Moore, *The Life and Letters of Edward Thomas* (London–Toronto, 1939); H. Coombes, *Edward Thomas* (London, 1956); E. Farjeon, *Edward Thomas: The Last Four Years* (London, 1958); V. Scannell, *Edward Thomas* (London, 1965); W. Cooke, *Edward Thomas: A Critical Biography 1878–1917* (London, 1970); H. Thomas, *Edward Thomas* (Edinburgh, 1974), contains *As It Was* (New York–London, 1927) and *World Without End* (London, 1931), his widow's 2-vol. account of her life with him; A. Motion, *Edward Thomas* (London, 1980).

ARTHUR GRAEME WEST

I. SEPARATE WORKS. *Diary of a Dead Officer* (London, 1919).

ANTHOLOGIES

E. H. Marsh, ed., *Georgian Poetry* (London, 1914; 1916; 1918; 1919; 1922), eds. for 1911–1912, 1913–1915, 1916–1917, 1918–1919, 1920–1922; E. H. Marsh, ed., *1914 and Other Poems* (London, 1915); F. Brereton [Frederick T. Smith], ed., *Anthology of War Poems* (London, 1930), intro. by E. Blunden; R. M. B. Nichols, ed., *An Anthology of War Poetry* (London, 1943), with long intro. in form of dialogue between Nichols and J. Tennyson; J. Brophy and E. Partridge, eds., *The Long Trail: What the British Soldier Sang and Said in the Great War of 1914–1918* (London, 1965), rev. ed. of *Songs and Slang of the British Soldier 1914–1918* (London, 1938); B. Gardner, ed., *Up the Line to Death: The War Poets 1914–1918* (London, 1965), intro. by E. Blunden; I. M. Parsons, ed., *Men Who March Away: Poems of the First World War* (New York–London, 1965); M. Hussey, ed., *Poetry of the First World War* (London, 1967).

GENERAL CRITICISM

J. M. Johnston, *English Poetry of the First World War* (London, 1964), detailed study of the leading poets of the war; B. Bergonzi, *Heroes' Twilight: A Study of the Literature of the Great War* (London, 1965); J. Silkin, *Out of Battle: The Poetry of the Great War* (London, 1972); J. Stallworthy, *Poets of the First World War* (London, 1974); P. Fussell, *The Great War and Modern Memory* (New York, 1975).

WILFRED OWEN

(1893-1918)

Dominic Hibberd

I

WORLD WAR I may have made Wilfred Owen a better poet than he would otherwise have been, but it did not make him a poet. He himself always reckoned that his poetic career began on a holiday with his mother in the Cheshire countryside some ten years before the war, and in a sense Mrs. Owen and the English landscape are more his subjects than war and the pity of war. He said of one of his poems in 1918 that it baffled his critical spirit; modern criticism has tended to be similarly baffled by his poetry. Reluctant to label him either a minor or a major poet, we keep him in the category "war poet," where we can with increasing confidence regard him as the greatest of his kind. It is not a very helpful category, however; Edward Thomas has been rescued from it, Rupert Brooke is still too often put in it as a mark of disgrace, and several thousand people who presumably belong in it, since their only verse was written about and during the war, are out of print and out of mind, probably forever. In the simple category "poet," Owen's place is not yet clear; the critic's task has not been made easier by the lack of a complete and definitive edition of the poems, but a greater obstacle is the war itself. One's prior knowledge of the slaughter on the Somme introduces a factor into one's reaction to a poem such as "Anthem for Doomed Youth" that if not present when one reads, say, *In Memoriam* (1850)[1] and remembers the death of Arthur Henry Hallam. For Owen himself, however, the war brought the fulfillment of a poetic destiny that had been taking shape all his life.

He was born on 18 March 1893 at Oswestry, on the Welsh border. His parents were probably both Welsh in origin, and he was conscious of his Celtic ancestry; he wrote in one of his early poems that Celtic blood "makes poets sing and prophets see." He shared with the family a delight in music and a rather less enthusiastic allegiance to evangelical religion. Mr. Owen preferred "Men of Harlech," his favorite record, to sermons, but Mrs. Owen came from a sternly religious background and was a pious and frequent churchgoer. Wilfred was the eldest son and the object of his mother's intense devotion; he returned her affection and was thus caught in a trap from which he was never wholly to free himself. Any doubts about religion and any interest in another woman seemed to be treason against his mother. By training her son from the start to think of himself as a future clergyman and of all other women as dangerous and undesirable, Mrs. Owen established a hold over him that was to be of fundamental importance to his poetry.

For the first four years of Owen's life, the family lived with his mother's father in comfortable rural circumstances; but when old Mr. Salter died, their finances obliged them to move to industrial Birkenhead, where Mr. Owen was employed as a stationmaster. Owen's school days were uneventful; he was a quiet and competent pupil, interested in the earth sciences as much as in literature. He was a keen amateur botanist, astronomer, and geologist (as the imagery in his war poems reminds us: soldiers are said to "die back" and "wither," their eyes are like "cold stars," their bodies fossilize into coal). These interests may have been consciously modeled on the example of John Ruskin, whom he much admired; they were shared with his cousin, Leslie Gunston, Owen's follower and companion in many early activities. After 1907, when the Owens moved from Birkenhead to Shrewsbury, he was able to reach open country easily and to pursue his scientific interests among the Shropshire hills. Writing poetry began as one activity among many and grew slowly into a habit; the subject of his earliest verse is invariably nature.

[1] Alfred Lord Tennyson's collection of elegies that were inspired by the death of his best friend, Arthur Hallam.

His world was still essentially late Victorian; his provincial, lower-middle-class upbringing gave him little contact with contemporary culture. On visits to the Gunstons, who lived at Wimbledon, he was able to make excursions to London and to acquire a regular habit of going to the annual exhibition of the Royal Academy; but the illustrations in *Royal Academy Pictures,* through which the cousins were fond of browsing, show that a visitor to those exhibitions in Owen's lifetime would have been given scarcely an inkling of the new movements that were revolutionizing the world of art. The cousins would have often seen the eccentric figure of Algernon Swinburne taking his walk on Wimbledon Common; daringly, for the Gunstons' household was even more pious than the Owens', they used to read his poems together. In general, Owen's reading before 1913 was of a standard, old-fashioned, and popular kind: he preferred Shakespeare to Milton, and Alfred Tennyson to Matthew Arnold; took little or no interest in the Augustans and Metaphysicals; read quantities of Dickens; had a passionate enthusiasm for the great romantics; and was almost completely ignorant of the writers of the day. A public school education would have given him a familiarity with the classics and some knowledge of modern literature; Charles Sorley, for instance, was discovering Thomas Hardy, John Masefield, and Homer, while Owen was adventuring into Swinburne. The war poetry of Sorley and Robert Graves has a cool, hard tone that is partly a result of their public school backgrounds. Owen's work, on the other hand, tends to be emotional, less disciplined, and sometimes archaic. Siegfried Sassoon said of him as a person that he was "perceptibly provincial," and the same might be said of him as a poet.

His lack of public school training showed itself in other ways. Whereas a public schoolboy found becoming an officer or achieving distinction something for which his training had prepared him, Owen grew up with a strong tendency to venerate anyone who seemed his superior and to value highly any mark of recognition. In no way was his habit of veneration more apparent than in his feelings for the authors he most admired. On the evidence of his letters, the first poet to capture his devotion was Coleridge; "The Ancient Mariner" (1798) influenced him throughout his life, and it may be the Mariner's compelling eye that is one of the origins of the dead man's dreadful stare in "Strange Meeting." The letters of 1911 show a sudden intoxication with Keats, who became his "great hero" for several years and whose mark is all too obvious in the poems that have survived from this period. A fragmentary sonnet written "Before reading a Biography of Keats for the first time" must have been composed in April 1911, before he began Sidney Colvin's life of the poet. Keats, whom he elsewhere speaks of as a lover, is here seen "like a god on high uprist"; but the language is borrowed from his earlier idol, since the Ancient Mariner describes how "like God's own head/The glorious Sun uprist." One can make too much of Owen's love of Keats; the infatuation did not last into the war years, although it was succeeded by a more mature admiration, and as early as 1912 Percy Bysshe Shelley was claiming as much attention. Shelley tends to be neglected in this context. It was he, more than anyone, who formed Owen's social conscience and laid the foundations for his later attitude to war.

After he left school, Owen tried unsuccessfully to get into university, and then, as a temporary measure before trying again, he found an evangelical vicar willing to tutor him in return for unpaid work in the parish. The parish of Dunsden is across the Thames from Reading; it was no doubt while he was living in the vicarage that Owen, with his strong sense of place, read Oscar Wilde's *The Ballad of Reading Gaol* (1898), from which he quotes in one of his manuscripts. A verse letter written from Dunsden in 1911 puts the village on the literary map by listing the neighborhood's associations with Tennyson, Thomas Gray, Arnold, and Shelley. The letter describes its author as listening both to the river and to Shelley; Owen would have known that the poem that Shelley composed in a boat on this stretch of the Thames was *The Revolt of Islam* (1818). Owen read *The Revolt* with much interest; there are more traces of it in his later poetry than there are of any other single work. There is an echo of it in "1914," the sonnet he wrote on the outbreak of war, and one can pick up the trail again in several of the major war poems right up to the end of his life. He was to remember Shelley's hatred of war and his insistence that the true poet, refraining from all forms of violence, should fight the battle for truth with the weapons of passive resistance and active love.

Meanwhile, at Dunsden, Shelley's poetry helped to arouse Owen's sympathy for the many poor people whose wretched cottages he visited on behalf of the vicar; it also played a part in intensifying his disenchantment with evangelical religion and the organized church. The vicar was a bachelor very fond of worldly comforts, but also a preacher equally fond of giving "horrifyingly dismal" sermons against the gratifications of the flesh. Memories of such hypocrisy probably lie behind some of Owen's first war poems in 1917, particularly "Le Christianisme" and "At a Calvary near the Ancre"; but he was too honest to be satisfied for long with attacking others and not looking into his own heart. He was never sure that he himself could live up to Shelley's, or Christ's, ideals; as he said of some Dunsden parishioners in 1912, the "Shelleyan Principle of Love, being a Law unto itself, loses its attractiveness when the Adonis is a loutish tallow-face with a blood-poisoned arm, and the Venus a bedraggled creature." In "Strange Meeting," with deliberate allusions to *The Revolt,* he was later to demonstrate the hopeless incompatibility of the roles of Shelleyan poet and dedicated officer.

He went to Dunsden partly to please his mother, who hoped it would lead to his taking orders; he himself was more interested in the promised tuition. Parish work materialized in large quantities, but the tuition, it appears, did not; such spare energy as Owen had went into writing verse and questioning religion. The verse is almost all unpublished; there is a good deal of it, but it is not particularly distinguished or interesting. His allegiance to literature had by this time become deeply entrenched, but the vicar regarded books as an "artificialized life" and so helped to set up a tension between the charms of a literary career and the stern demands of a religious one.

Religion seemed to be opposed to everything that could be enjoyed through the senses, and the young poet considered his senses to be exceptionally strong. His upbringing had not prepared him for sexual maturity, a lack that caused further complications. It seems fairly certain that he became intimate, very innocently but to the vicar's alarm, with some of the village boys. Yet another problem was the difficulty of reconciling what he knew about evolution and other scientific matters with the literal interpretation of Scripture that fundamentalist religion demanded of him. This slightly absurd tug of war between evangelicalism on the one hand and poetry, emotion, and science on the other ended in a serious crisis early in 1913. He left the vicarage for home and collapsed with what was called "congestion of the lungs"; the illness was accompanied by what he later referred to as "phantasies" or "horrors" and was clearly nervous in origin. These nightmares or hallucinations prefigured the "war dreams" he was to suffer from after his shell shock in 1917. It may have been in 1913 that he became obsessed in dreams with the horrifying face that reappears in many forms in his poems; at some stage between 1911 and 1913 he wrote a melodramatic poem about an encounter with the Medusa-like figure of Despondency who froze his blood with her stare and steeped his nights in "bloodiness and stains of shadowy crimes."

This poem, the "Supposed Confessions of a Second-rate Sensitive Mind in Dejection" (a title copied from Tennyson), is one of several that seem to reflect his revolt in 1913 against the tyranny of evangelicalism. A piece beginning "The time was aeon" describes a vision of a beautiful youth who represents "the Flesh"; a "small Jew" then appears, crying "Crucify him!" Further details in this curious piece confirm that the small Jew is St. Paul, urging his followers to "crucify the flesh" (Galatians 5:24). It is clear from the passionate tone of the description that the poet's sympathies lie entirely with "the Flesh" and not at all with St. Paul. Another biblical text, this time from St. Jude, is defiantly used in "O World of many worlds" to show how the poet, like a wandering star lighting the darkness of the world, has a destiny far above other men's and is not to be circumscribed by fixed creeds. Here, and in a series of images that extend throughout Owen's subsequent poetry, darkness is taken to be the proper environment for a poet, who is a source of light and vision. In many of these images, there is an emphasis on the brief endurance of the light; the poet is as a passing meteor or a tree bathed in lightning. Even in his early writing, there is evidence that Owen expected his life to be short.

II

THE break from his mother's kind of religion made home a difficult place to be, though Owen was always deeply grateful to his mother for her devoted nursing in the spring of 1913. In the autumn he somehow found a job for himself as a teacher of English at the Berlitz school in Bordeaux; he was not to return to England for two years. The job proved dull, exhausting, and ill paid; but he improved his already good French and tried his hand at writing a little verse in that language. On the back of one of these poems, he wrote down a list of pararhymes and so began feeling his way toward the rhyming that was to help make him famous.

Among the various kinds of incomplete rhyme, pararhyme is the most exacting: a pair of words must have similar consonant sounds before and after unlike vowels, as in "braid/brood" or "leaves/lives." This can be distinguished from half-rhyme, in which only the final consonants correspond, as in "lives/staves" or "brood/mud." These forms of rhyme had not been used since ancient times as regular patterns, but half-rhyme is quite common in those English poets who have not been prepared to abide by strict rules; there is a group of half-rhymes marked in Owen's copy of Shelley. No English poet before Owen ever used pararhyme deliberately, however; he may have worked out the system for himself, or he may have got the idea either from ancient Welsh verse or from modern French poets, a number of whom had used pararhyme in a small way. He seems not to have written any verse in consistent pararhyme until the summer of 1917, when he tried it out in "Has Your Soul Sipped" and a few other lyrics. He first used it in a complete war poem in "Wild with All Regrets," written in the following December. He was doubtful about his "vowel-rime stunt" in this poem, but Robert Graves warmly encouraged him to continue the experiment.

As John Middleton Murry said in 1919, pararhymes in a war poem were a "discovery of genius"; but Owen originally developed the device for use in lyric poetry. "From My Diary. July 1914," almost certainly written in 1917, shows his lyric technique at an advanced stage:

> Birds
>   Cheerily chirping in the early day.
> Bards
>   Singing of summer, scything thro' the hay.[2]

In addition to the full rhyme of "day/hay" and the pararhyme of "birds/bards," Owen manages to introduce an internal pararhyme ("cheer-/chir-"). This is further elaborated in the assonance of "chir-/ear-" and the approximate rhyme of "cheerily/early." The second long line has obvious and deliberate alliteration. Here, as in many other poems, Owen has carefully structured his lines around these and other devices; in this case, he produces a complicated pattern that is pleasant but rather labored and that is

present largely for its own sake. In his best poems, the pattern is an essential part of the poem's meaning, as in this stanza from "Exposure":

> Sudden successive flights of bullets streak the silence.
> Less deathly than the air that shudders black with snow,
> With sidelong flowing flakes that flock, pause, and renew;
> We watch them wandering up and down the wind's
>   nonchalance,
>   But nothing happens.

Here again, each of the long lines has its alliterating consonant (*s*, *d*, *f*, *w*); assonance and various forms of internal rhyme are also evident. These arrangements of sound direct the flow and pause of the lines, suggesting the irregular rushing of snow and bullets; a detailed analysis would show how the linked words "streak," "black," "flakes," and "flock" punctuate the movement, while the many repeated consonants mirror the unceasing sweep and eddy of the snow. These echoing sounds in the stanza are confirmed by the rough pararhymes at the ends of the lines, rhymes that are themselves nonchalant, irregular, and incomplete.

One of the principal themes in Owen's poems is that war prevents young soldiers from fulfilling their lives. Pararhymes are themselves unfulfilled; the reader expects a full rhyme and gets instead only an incomplete one. The effect is one of frustration and sadness, as though the ideal of completeness, which can still be perceived in the rhyme, is being destroyed as we read. It is one of the strange facts about Owen's life that this system of rhyming, so perfectly suited to war poetry, was something that he first used well before the war; as he toyed with it in Bordeaux in 1913, he can have had no idea of how valuable the instrument was that he had discovered.

Apart from a little experimenting with literary techniques, he was not able to write much in France until the summer of 1914, when a new job brought leisure and far pleasanter surroundings. He spent the opening weeks of the war as a private tutor in a villa high in the Pyrenees, possibly happier than at any other time in his life. Looking back three years later, he recorded his happiness in "From My Diary. July 1914." He gave the month in the title as July in order to set the poem in the last month of peace; but the month was actually August, and the somewhat ludicrous reference in the poem to bards scything hay is a memory of his having to help with the crop because the farmhands had gone off to join the army. As a civilian in a foreign country, he was not much af-

---

[2]Quotations from the poems are taken from D. Hibberd, ed., *Wilfred Owen: War Poems and Others* (London, 1973).

fected by war fever; the patriotic appeals in the English newspapers for young men to enlist took time to reach him and more time still to move him. He came to the conclusion, and declared it in a rather defensive tone, that a poet was more useful to England alive than dead.

His confidence in himself as a poet was strengthened by the friendliness of Laurent Tailhade, an elderly and celebrated French poet to whom Owen was introduced by his new employer. It is often supposed that Tailhade's principal influence on Owen was as a pacifist. There is little or no evidence for this view. Tailhade had indeed opposed war in speeches and writing years before, and had been imprisoned for his pains, but it was his poetry, not his prose, that he gave to Owen, and his poetry is not about pacifism. Tailhade had lived through several literary generations and had been friendly with many of the greatest French writers of his time. He had known Parnassians, Symbolists, and Decadents; he had been a devout attender at Mallarmé's Tuesday meetings and a close companion of Verlaine's; he was a veteran duelist and a regular spectator at the Spanish bullrings; he had been a member of occult societies and anarchist groups; and he was a great talker. He was strongly attracted to Owen. It seems a reasonable guess that some of their conversation opened up to the younger man a world he had never thought much about before. Tailhade gave him a copy of Gustave Flaubert's *La Tentation de Saint Antoine* (1874), and all through the following winter Owen soaked himself in French literature of a similar kind. Far from turning him against war, Tailhade may have been partly responsible for his eventual decision to enlist. He himself was "shouldering a rifle" later in the year, or so Owen reported in a letter home.

The history of Owen's move toward enlisting is a curious one. His parents were urging him to settle on a career, since a series of tutorships was not very promising. He insisted repeatedly in 1915 that he was now quite certain that he had an artist's temperament and that he wanted to be a poet, an insistence that must have exasperated his hard-working and puzzled father. Owen knew well enough, however, that an artist needs money. He considered an extraordinary variety of money-making activities, including a visit to America with a balloon inventor, one to Canada with a fashion designer, and one to the East with a scent manufacturer; he actually did make a brief visit to a London trade fair on behalf of the scent manufacturer. He also attempted to inveigle a rich uncle into war profiteering; in view of his fury against profiteers in 1918, it was just as well that this attempt got nowhere. It became increasingly clear that going into the army would solve his problems.

He was finally persuaded by several factors, including recruiting propaganda in newspapers sent to him from home, a quotation he encountered in an essay by Hilaire Belloc ("If any man despairs of becoming a Poet, let him carry his pack and march in the ranks"), and an enthusiastic reading of *Salammbô* (1862). This novel, Flaubert's most careful and exotic work, is one of the most gruesome books about war ever written; it describes a mutiny in ancient Carthage and contains lurid descriptions of wounds, physical suffering, and violent death. It is a revealing indication of one side of Owen's temperament that he found *Salammbô* fascinating. The book probably inspired his short-lived desire to join the Italian cavalry for the sheer romance of it; certainly it helped to convince him that war could be material for art. Perhaps it would be better after all for England that a poet should be in the army rather than out of it. He came back to London finally in September 1915 and enlisted as a cadet in the Artists' Rifles on 21 October.

His knowledge of French literature helps to explain features of his poems that otherwise may seem strange. His use of elaborate sound effects can be paralleled in the work of many late-nineteenth-century French poets. Images of red and white flowers, fatal women, pale brows, and other subjects common in French writers of the Decadence are apparent in such poems as "Anthem for Doomed Youth" and "The Kind Ghosts." Although such imagery sometimes exposes the homosexual and sadomasochistic elements in his nature, it was remarkably well suited to war poetry. The pale and soulful women clasping white lilies, who had been portrayed by many of the French Symbolist painters as well as by Dante Gabriel Rossetti and others in England, became in wartime the grieving wives and mothers in "The Send-Off," who give their men white flowers that can mean good luck or death. The fatal women of the later nineteenth century, of whom Salammbô herself is one of the first examples, caused the deaths of their lovers. As it happened, many men in the war came to feel that they had been urged to join up by the women, like the boy in "Disabled" who enlisted "to please the giddy jilts." There were, it must be admitted, some women who did urge men to go to war with an almost greedy fervor. One such was Jessie Pope, against whose appalling recruiting verses Owen aimed his "Dulce et Decorum Est" in 1917.

In October 1914, soon after meeting Tailhade, Owen wrote a description of a fatal woman ("Long ages past") into which he put every traditional detail he could discover in his new reading. The woman has killed her lovers; she has their blood on her lips and on her "brow the pallor of their death." In "Anthem for Doomed Youth," written three years later, dead soldiers are commemorated by "the pallor of girls' brows"; the image from "Long ages past" has been successfully adapted to a wartime context. Many of the war poems have similar roots in Owen's earlier work.

It is not surprising that this naive and imaginative young man of twenty-two entered upon his duties in the British Army with a certain excitement. Wearing a uniform and practicing salutes on the plane trees in a Bloomsbury square was an entertaining occupation. London had the additional attraction of Harold Monro, the Georgian poet who kept the Poetry Bookshop. Owen went into the shop and struck up an acquaintance with the proprietor soon after his arrival in London. He gave Monro some sonnets to look over. Monro's comments on them helped to direct him away from the conventional style he had so far usually employed, toward a fresher and more modern diction. Owen's letters in 1916 mention W. B. Yeats, A. E. Housman, and other established poets of the day whom he had probably not read before. He would not have been able to remain ignorant for long of the most famous poet of the war generation, Rupert Brooke. It was probably in 1916 that he drafted "An Imperial Elegy," a fragment that begins with a quotation from Brooke's "The Soldier" and goes on to be much more grandiloquent about the glory of war than anything Brooke ever said or would have wished to say.

A manuscript written at the same time as that of "An Imperial Elegy" has a note in the margin, *"How to Instruct in Aiming and Firing,"* the title of an army manual. The poem was no doubt drafted during one of the musketry courses that Owen had to take in 1916. He spent the whole year at various training camps in England and was commissioned in the summer as a second lieutenant in the Manchester Regiment. By the end of the year he was considered fit to be entrusted with the leadership of men at the front. He was sent to France and on 6 January came within earshot of the guns.

III

JANUARY 1917 was a month of bitter cold. Trench warfare had become a highly organized business in a vast, shattered landscape. The authorities had found that an officer performed best when given only short stints in the line. Although Owen was in France for some five months, he spent only five or six weeks in trenches. The rest of the time was taken up by periods of rest, further training, and two stays in a hospital, once with concussion and once with shell shock. His trench experiences are vividly recorded in his letters and were to provide the raw material for all his subsequent war poems. His description of holding a dugout in January 1917, for instance, can be seen to be the foundation for "The Sentry," a poem begun some seven or eight months later and not completed until the autumn of 1918:

My dug-out held 25 men tightly packed. Water filled it to a depth of 1 or 2 feet, leaving say 4 feet of air.
One entrance had been blown in & blocked.
So far, the other remained.
The Germans knew we were staying there and decided we shouldn't.
Those fifty hours were the agony of my happy life.
Every ten minutes on Sunday afternoon seemed an hour.
I nearly broke down and let myself drown in the water that was now slowly rising over my knees.
Towards 6 o'clock, when, I suppose, you would be going to church, the shelling grew less intense and less accurate: so that I was mercifully helped to do my duty and crawl, wade, climb and flounder over No Man's Land to visit my other post. It took me about half an hour to move about 150 yards. . . .
In the Platoon on my left the sentries over the dug-out were blown to nothing. . . . I kept my own sentries half way down the stairs during the more terrific bombardment. In spite of this one lad was blown down and, I am afraid, blinded.

(*Collected Letters:* 16 January 1917)

Owen's letters from the trenches are deservedly well known; they contain some of the most vivid personal accounts we have of conditions at the front and they would be valuable even if he had written no poems. The bulk of the letters, however, come from other periods of his life. Nearly all of them were written to his mother, and he usually told her only the things he thought she would like to know or would benefit from knowing. Since Mrs. Owen was not a literary or intellectual person, the letters offer nothing comparable to the brilliant critical insights that make Keats's letters so rewarding. What they do contain in abundance, however, is lively and often funny reporting of people and events, and, behind the reporting, the steady maturing of a highly imaginative and sensitive young man who was able to laugh at himself more often than one might expect. There are also, as in the extract quoted above, frequent allusions to Mrs. Owen's piety. These begin as reverent, gradually become gently satirical, and develop in 1917 into powerful, generalized denunciations of orthodox religion and the hypocrisy of the churches in wartime. The widening gap between mother and son in their attitudes to formal religion made him realize how much he had grown away from her. In the process of finding out what war was like, he came to recognize that he was an adult and had been one for some time.

While he was actually at the front, Owen regarded verse as a means of forgetting war, and he amused himself in the hospital by writing an assortment of sonnets in a vaguely Symbolist style. Some of these poems were the result of an old agreement with Leslie Gunston that the cousins and a literary friend had recently revived: one of the aspiring poets would choose a title and all three would then write on it. Most if not all of the sonnets Owen wrote on these agreed subjects date from late 1916 or early 1917; they include "Music," "Purple," "A Sunrise," "The Fates," "Happiness," and "Golden Hair." He had written enough of these exercises by the spring of 1917 to be able idly to plan a volume of them, bound in his favorite color, purple, and entitled "Sonatas in Silence."

Only "Sonnet to my Friend/with an identity disc," one of the poems that might have been included in "Sonatas in Silence," uses imagery drawn from war, but even this could hardly be described as war poetry. Like "Happiness" and several other poems of this period, the sonnet is about the new perceptions that come with maturity. In August, Owen wrote to his mother that the first lines of his to "carry the stamp of maturity," as a result of war experience, were three from "Happiness":

> But the old happiness is unreturning.
> Boys have no grief so grievous as youth's yearning,
> Boys have no sadness sadder than our hope.

These lines do not precisely correspond to any version of the poem published before 1974, but with the publication of the first draft in Jon Stallworthy's biography of Owen we now know that they formed the first half of the original sestet. The second half was:

> Happy are they who see not past the scope
> Of mother-arms. I loosed them, broke the bond.
> Not one day happy have I gone beyond.

We may take this with a pinch of salt. Owen rightly marked this half in the margin as "BAD" and transformed "the scope / Of mother-arms" into the fine image in the better-known version: "the wide arms of trees have lost their scope." This is a very characteristic example of the way in which his imagination associated his mother and nature. There is a more generalized image of the same kind in a draft of "Anthem": "Women's wide-spread arms shall be their wreaths." The first draft of "Happiness" is dated February 1917, but his later attribution of the maturity in the poem to war experience was the result of hindsight. As it stands, the sonnet makes no mention of war. The sadness of growing up is caused by breaking the maternal bond and, as some versions of the poem suggest, by arriving at sexual knowledge.

Other products of Owen's sonneteering in the winter of 1916–1917 include "The End" and "Storm." These were written before his shell shock, probably before he left England, and are of a much higher quality than the pieces he drafted in the hospital. There is no evidence as to whether he meant "The End" to be a poem about the war or not. Edmund Blunden placed it last, except for "Strange Meeting," in his edition of the poems. Other people have followed this misleading clue and have supposed "The End" to have been one of Owen's last works. Its grand style is not in keeping with his most mature poetry, however, and it is clear from a remark in one of his letters that he meant the style to be an imitation of that used by the literary friend with whom he and Leslie Gunston were competing. The style is actually Shelley's:

> And when I hearken to the Earth, she saith:
> "My fiery heart shrinks, aching. It is death.
> Mine ancient scars shall not be glorified,
> Nor my titanic tears, the seas, be dried."

This may be compared with a speech by the Earth in Shelley's *Prometheus Unbound* (1820):

> I hear, I feel;
> Thy lips are on me, and their touch runs down
> Even to the adamantine central gloom
> Along these marble nerves; 'tis life, 'tis joy,
> And through my withered, old and icy frame

The warmth of an immortal youth shoots down
Circling.

(III. iii. 84–90)

It is a measure of Owen's development in this period
that his lines can be compared with those of Shelley
without being wholly overwhelmed. The Earth,
which had filled with the warmth of youth under the
kiss of Prometheus the Titan, now becomes old and
chill in the knowledge of universal death; youth is
mortal and unreturning. A sonnet in a borrowed
style and on a subject set by someone else became a
sonorous and memorable prophecy, but it is a poem
more about youth, age, and mortality than about
World War I.

In two short poems that may have been written in
France, however, Owen did make a start on writing
directly about the war.[3] "At a Calvary near the Ancre" and "Le Christianisme," taken together, make a
contrast between the wayside crucifix, where Christ
and the soldiers keep company, and the buried statues of Christ and the saints in the church, "Well out
of hearing of our trouble." With his sternly Protestant background, he always found religion easier to
criticize if he could give it Roman Catholic trap-
pings, but his experience at the vicarage had predis-
posed him to condemn hypocrisy from any organized church, and nearly all the churches were busily
urging on the war effort. His first thoughts about the
war concentrated on its significance for religion.
Christ seemed to have preached "Passivity at any
price!" In urging men to slaughter their enemies, the
churches were on the side of the devil, whereas the
endurance of the soldiers had a Christ-like quality.

The wayside Calvary, damaged by shellfire as
though Christ himself were sharing the men's suffering, was an image that had already tempted a number of writers to identify the front as Golgotha and to
suggest that soldiers were undergoing a kind of
crucifixion that would redeem humanity. There was
even a propaganda story, which gave rise to at least
one poem, that the Germans really had crucified a
Canadian soldier. Many of the men themselves believed, like the bewildered sufferers in "Exposure,"
that they had been born to die and that only by their
deaths could the world purge itself of violence and
greed.

[3] I am no longer convinced by this dating. Like all the poems in
which Owen criticizes the war, these two pieces seem likely to
have been written after he met Sassoon. "Greater Love" was probably finished as late as 1918, although the idea for it had been in
his mind since 1914.

This image of the Tommy as crucified Christ was
attractive but seriously misleading. It enabled
civilians to contemplate the casualty lists with convenient piety; but it took no account of the fact that a
soldier not only suffered passively but also had to
maim and kill his enemy. The weakness of the image
is conspicuous in "Greater Love," a deplorable poem
that has sometimes been much admired. The title
had become a cliché by 1917, for a start, and the
poem is padded out with superfluities such as
"raftered loft," put in to elaborate the rhyme and
disguise the underlying lack of meaning. The dying
men are Christs trailing crosses—early drafts give
"rifles," which was at least more accurate—and
sacrificing themselves. The failure of the soldier-
Christ comparison in the poem shows up as much
stronger the parallel, erotic comparison between the
soldiers and "any beautiful Woman" (she is so
described in a canceled subtitle). It is difficult not to
feel that Owen is luxuriating in his subject without
understanding himself well enough to see what he is
doing. He has perceived, like many artists before
him, that a dying youth can be beautiful as well as
horrifying, but he has not distanced himself from his
material. In a letter of August 1917, he finally
dismissed the idea that soldiers died for "greater
love" by saying that it was "a distorted view to hold
in a general way"; he resolved to suppress a ballad he
had drafted, in which he had described Tommies as
"Kings and Christs." With the soldier-Christ image
out of the way, he was able to look more carefully at
his own reactions to war.

His time in the trenches came to an end in April,
when, in a particularly unpleasant engagement, he
was narrowly missed by a shell and left in no fit state
to command men in action. Few people then clearly
understood the nature of shock; a man who was un-
wounded but unable to fight was likely to be suspected of cowardice. Owen felt this very keenly.
One of the reasons why he decided to go back to the
war in 1918 was that he wanted a clean record as a
soldier. Thus with mixed feelings of relief and guilt he
was sent back to Craiglockhart War Hospital, near
Edinburgh.

IV

CRAIGLOCKHART was doing pioneer work in nursing
mentally injured officers. It will be remembered for
its doctors' work in this field and also as the meeting
place of two of the best poets of the war. Owen's doc-

tor encouraged him to develop his old interests, persuading him to lecture to the hospital natural history society on "Soil" and "Do Plants Think?" as well as to write verse. After six weeks during which his writing talents were usefully exercised and his love of nature strongly revived, he was in good shape for the most important literary event of his life, his meeting with Captain Siegfried Sassoon. Sassoon was already distinguished both as a poet and as a soldier. He was sent to Craiglockhart partly because he had been on the edge of a nervous breakdown and partly because the authorities wanted to silence him. He had publicly protested that Britain had lost sight of her original aim of liberating Belgium and pacifying Europe; the war had become one of "aggression and conquest." Whether or not he was right historically (and the evidence on the whole suggests that he was not), his anger against civilian incomprehension of the war was passionate and often just.

Owen read Sassoon's recently published collection of war poems and was very deeply moved. Then, in a state of "fear and trembling" similar to that in which he had sat down to read a biography of Keats six years before, he knocked on the older man's door and introduced himself. Sassoon treated him with a mixture of condescension and warm sympathy; in return, Owen adopted his new acquaintance as an idol, equivalent, he said later, to Keats, Christ, and others. By September they were close friends, discussing each other's work and spending long hours together. Soon after their first meeting, Owen abandoned all the verse he had in hand and set himself the task of writing a war poem "in Sassoon's manner." The result was the first draft of "The Dead-Beat," a piece utterly unlike anything he had written before and the first of a number of poems composed in the second half of 1917 deliberately in Sassoon's style. It took him several months to shape "The Dead-Beat" to his liking. The final draft is a representative example, though perhaps not the best, of his work "in Sassoon's manner":

> He dropped,—more sullenly than wearily,
> Lay stupid like a cod, heavy like meat,
> And none of us could kick him to his feet;
> —Just blinked at my revolver, blearily;
> —Didn't appear to know a war was on,
> Or see the blasted trench at which he stared.
> "I'll do 'em in," he whined, "if this hand's spared,
> I'll murder them, I will."
> 　　　　　　　　A low voice said,
> "It's Blighty, p'raps, he sees; his pluck's all gone,
> Dreaming of all the valiant, that *aren't* dead:

> Bold uncles, smiling ministerially;
> Maybe his brave young wife, getting her fun
> In some new home, improved materially.
> It's not these stiffs have crazed him; nor the Hun."

> We sent him down at last, out of the way.
> Unwounded;—stout lad, too, before that strafe.
> Malingering? Stretcher-bearers winked, "Not half!"

> Next day I heard the Doc.'s well-whiskied laugh:
> "That scum you sent last night soon died. Hooray!"

Owen was a versatile imitator. Several of his poems seem to have been modeled on works by other writers: "Shadwell Stair," for example, is close to Wilde's "Impression du Matin"; "Six o'clock in Princes Street" to Yeats's "When you are old"; and "Conscious" to Sassoon's "The Death-Bed." The kind of style that he first borrowed from Sassoon was colloquial, satirical, and direct. In order to use it, he had to draw on the anger he had felt against civilians when he had written "At a Calvary" in the spring; but his feelings about war had developed since then. "Dulce et Decorum Est," which attempts to tell civilians what the front was really like, is actually more concerned with the poet's own tormented dreams, the major symptom of his shell shock, than with the death of the gassed soldier. These dreams, as this poem and "The Sentry" record, seem to have centered on a contorted face with terrifying eyes. In "The Sentry," completed in September 1918, the vision is kept under control, but in "Dulce et Decorum Est," written almost a year earlier, the dream is still too immediate, and the poem becomes inarticulate. The dream-haunting faces of the gassed man and the blinded sentry are wartime versions of the vision of Despondency-Medusa that had plagued Owen's nights with "bloodiness and stains of shadowy crimes" before the war. The realization of his 1913 "phantasies" in the 1917 trenches was a factor likely to make his war poems intensely personal once they had become personal at all. It is not surprising that even in later drafts of "The Dead-Beat" he moved away from Sassoon's style. His mind was, in any case, more eccentric and original than his hero's. Sassoon could never have produced such odd imagery as "grow me legs as quick as lilac shoots" or

> Voices of boys were by the river-side.
> Sleep mothered them; and left the twilight sad.[4]

---

[4]These two lines are from the fragment "Bugles sang," written at Craiglockhart as Owen's first, unfinished attempt at a para-rhymed war poem. Parts of the fragment were used soon afterward in "Disabled" and drafts of "Anthem for Doomed Youth."

We have seen already how his imagery often has to do with maternal affection and the lives of the plants. There are often also suggestions of a mythical background. The soldier in "Disabled," for example, is a modern Adonis, a beautiful youth who has been sacrificed to female desire and who has bled purple from a thigh wound. The ease with which the coal mine in "Miners" is magnified to become an image of the war, or with which the cavern in "Strange Meeting" is described as like and yet utterly unlike a wartime dugout, shows how Owen's imagination could, without straining, invest actuality with mythical significance.

The annus mirabilis of his short poetic career began not in the trenches but with the drafting of "The Dead-Beat" in August 1917. All his finest poems were written in the following thirteen months. It was meeting Sassoon, not seeing war at first hand, that finally set his talent free. Sassoon later found this embarrassing, feeling that he could have done more to help. He did what he could to play down his influence, encouraging the mistaken belief (which held sway for many years and which still misleads critics) that some of Owen's major poems, notably "Exposure," were written before the two men met. In truth, however, Owen needed little help. He had longed for years to know a fellow poet and to be accepted by him. Sassoon praised his work and arranged for him to meet other literary people, which enabled him at last to feel recognized and independent as a writer. His progress after that August was extraordinarily rapid.

"Anthem for Doomed Youth," written in September, was almost his last and certainly his finest sonnet; in terms of his pre-Sassoon work it is a crowning achievement, but in terms of his major poetry it is a first step on the road to his own style. The imagery of music and funeral rites is skillfully handled, moving from the sounds of the European battlefield to the bugles in the English shires and finally to the simple customs of a household in mourning. The sestet offers the consolation that the dead will be remembered by their families. In some of his 1918 poems, such as "The Send-Off" and "Exposure," Owen withdraws this consolation and prophesies instead that dead soldiers will be forgotten at home. "Anthem" itself is less hopeful than "To a Comrade in Flanders," written in 1916, in which the poet expects to return home in spirit after death. As the months passed, it became increasingly apparent that people at home, including even Mrs. Owen, could not fully sympathize with the men who had to suffer in the trenches. "Anthem" is one of Owen's most famous war poems, but it does not represent his final thoughts about war.[5] As for the sonnet form, it was too strict and conventional a frame for his swiftly developing ideas. It had long been his favorite, but after "Anthem" it was largely abandoned in favor of more varied and flexible shapes. In November or early December he moved further forward by writing "Apologia pro Poemate Meo," in which he defends the gloom of his Sassoon-influenced poetry on the ground that any suggestion that war had its pleasures might allow civilians to think that soldiers were "well content." The poem seems likely to have been an answer to a complaint from Graves that "Disabled" and "Wild with All Regrets" were too disconsolate. Graves had met Owen while visiting Sassoon in October and was very much impressed: "I have a new poet for you, just discovered . . . the real thing," he wrote to Edward Marsh[6] soon afterward.

"Apologia" is not a wholly successful poem. Its hearty tone rings a little false, and one suspects that Owen is too anxious to prove himself a worthy equal of Graves and Sassoon. He alludes deliberately to "Two Fusiliers," a poem by Graves about comradeship with Sassoon at the front. In taking his stand with his new friends, he rejects the poetry of an old one by saying that love is not "the binding of fair lips/With the soft silk of eyes," as "old song" tells. In a little poem called "L'Amour," Leslie Gunston had said that love was "the binding of lips, the binding of eyes." Poems of the "Sonatas in Silence" kind now seemed to Owen to be out of date in the context of war. "Apologia" was originally entitled "The Unsaid"; now that the unsaid had been said, there was also less point than there had been in writing poems intended to convince civilians of the horrors of the trenches. He had admitted that love and beauty could be found in the thick of battle; there was more scope for poetry here than in what he came to see as the "propaganda" of Sassoon's poems. In any case,

[5] "Anthem" is one of the poems that owe some of their fame to Benjamin Britten's use of them in his *War Requiem* (1962). That work, fine though it may be as music, does not altogether do Owen justice. The poems appear to have been selected without regard to their being late or early, complete or fragmentary, major or minor. Sometimes a piece seems to have been included for the sake of its references to music, and in some cases the setting does not, in my opinion, reflect the meaning of Owen's words.
[6] Sir Edward Marsh (1872–1953) was editor of *Georgian Poetry*, an anthology of contemporary verse initiated in 1912 by Marsh, Brooke, and Monro. Five volumes appeared between 1912 and 1922, but Owen was never among the contributors.

unlike Sassoon, he had no civilian audience to convince. Although he had published two of his poems in the Craiglockhart magazine, which he edited, he had no wish to rush into print. In the end, only five of his poems were published in his lifetime.

He gave much thought in the winter of 1917–1918 to his function and status as a poet. Since Graves and Sassoon had been published in Marsh's anthology, *Georgian Poetry*, it was natural to feel more akin to the loose grouping of poets who could be called "Georgians" than to any other contemporary movement. There is evidence that Owen read widely in the work of the Georgians during this period. By the end of 1917 he had read recent books by such contributors to the anthology as Monro, Masefield, Robert Nichols, John Drinkwater, Brooke, W. W. Gibson, and probably Walter de la Mare, as well as Graves and Sassoon. Early in the following year, he felt able to call himself a Georgian along with the rest. One can see the Georgian style emerging in a poem such as "Wild with All Regrets," where the monologue is comparable in character to Sassoon's "The Old Huntsman" and to work by Gibson and Masefield.

Another line of inquiry which he actively pursued was that of the *kind* of poetry he was to write. In a list of books read in December he included a translation of Theocritus, Bion, and Moschus. The elegies of Bion and Moschus had been the foundation for *Adonais*, as Owen would have known from several of the books he had read about Shelley. There are a number of traces of Shelley's great elegy in his letters and poems of this winter. In the following April he drafted the first part of what was to become "Elegy in April and September." The manuscript has on the back a note about Matthew Arnold, whose work Owen seems to have been studying seriously for the first time. He notes several titles, including the two elegiac poems, "Thyrsis" and "The Scholar-Gipsy," and adds the epithets "lofty restrained dignified/ wistful agnostic." With this note in mind, one can see that his own "Elegy" is written in imitation of Arnold. It is clear that he spent some time investigating the elegy and its use by different poets. In his 1918 preface (see below), he refers to his war poems as "these elegies," and indeed a poem such as "Futility," with its echo of Tennyson's famous elegy, is preeminently an elegy or song of mourning.

The annotated list of poems accompanying Owen's preface suggests the development he wished his readers to follow through his projected book. The first half consists mostly of poems that he labels "Protest," but protest on its own seemed not enough.

The second half has subjects such as "Cheerfulness," "Description," "Reflection," "Grief," and "Philosophy." As an elegist, Owen saw grief and meditation as essential final stages in the progress toward understanding. When our grief is aroused, we can, of course, begin to see the waste and suffering that war causes; we can also begin to see how even the wisest men can become involved in such a nightmare. If, on the other hand, we condemn war before we grieve, we are likely to be superficial and smug, vaguely supposing that if war ever threatened *us* we would know it for what it was. It would seem, however, that when war comes really close, human knowledge and values can very easily go awry. In the physical and spiritual chaos that followed the German invasion of Belgium, grief seemed the one reaction that was humane and true beyond doubt. At the end of "Insensibility," an ode that may be read as an introduction to Owen's elegies, the poet's curse falls on those who have freely chosen to make themselves immune to "pity and whatever moans in man." The elegist incites men to pity, and to love, which is the fruit of pity; and it is by love, not by cynicism or bitterness, that men can establish order. Owen's thinking on these matters shows clearly the influence of Shelley, whose work he must have studied often during the war years.

If we read Owen as the elegist he aspired to be, we can see the inadequacy or irrelevance of such critical approaches as those by John H. Johnston, in *English Poetry of the First World War*, who vainly expects him to be a writer of epics, or by Jon Silkin, in *Out of Battle*, who strenuously tries to make him a "political" (i.e., socialist) poet. Epic tends to glorify death in war; politics tempts both reader and poet to shift guilt away from themselves onto someone else. Owen fell into neither trap.

Shelley reminded him that the poet's task is to lead society toward peace and truth. In some pararhymed couplets possibly addressed to Sassoon in December, Owen outlined the future course that true poets should follow: to break ranks from those who trek from progress, to remain aloof from fighting until war should end (at the cost, if necessary, of "rank and seniority"), and then, once the chariots of war had come to a halt, to wash men with the sweet waters of truth.

Miss we the march of this retreating world
Into low citadels that are not walled.

But when their blood has clogged their chariot wheels
We will go up and wash them from deep wells.

For now we sink from men as pitchers falling
But men shall raise us up to be their filling,

Even from wells we sank too deep for war
Even the sweetest wells that ever were.

Meanwhile, while war lasted, the elegy would be his medium. Sonnets were too frail, satire too limited; all the poet could do was to try to keep the spirit of pity active and to record for posterity the plight of doomed youth.

V

OWEN was discharged from Craiglockhart in October 1917. He was fit only for light duties and was posted to a reserve battalion of his regiment in Scarborough. Thanks to Sassoon, he was able to meet a number of literary people, a few of them nationally famous and most of them talented. During the next year, these contacts affected Owen's poetry in various ways. Having actually met H. G. Wells and Arnold Bennett, for instance, he paid attention to their newspaper articles, with which he did not always agree, and gave more thought to politics than he had done before. One result was the prophecy of postwar society embodied in "Strange Meeting." Charles Scott Moncrieff, future translator of Proust, became a firm friend and took much interest in Owen's experiments in rhyme. Several of these new acquaintances urged him to publish a volume of his war poems. In the late spring, he drafted a preface and list of contents for such a volume, but it looked too much like a propaganda exercise. The preface, which has become almost more famous than the poems, is less meaningful than many of its readers have supposed. It was no more true of him in 1918 than it ever had been that he was "not concerned with Poetry," unless by that he meant the sort of poetry he had played with in "Sonatas in Silence." Nevertheless, the idea of a book was useful; it helped him to organize his manuscripts and consider his goals. At the end of 1917 he felt able to write home: "I go out of this year a Poet, my dear Mother, as which I did not enter it. I am held peer by the Georgians: I am a poet's poet."

His task in 1918 was to make himself more than a poet's poet. The first poem of the year proved to be a milestone. "Miners" not only dealt with two topical events, a Staffordshire colliery disaster and the war itself, but also appeared in print in a national periodical only a fortnight after the pit explosion. With its immediacy and its striking use of pararhyme, it drew some attention, and Owen could feel that he was beginning to find a public voice.

In the second week of March he was declared fit for physical training as a prelude to a return to active service. He was sent to a camp at Ripon and found a room in a cottage where he could work undisturbed during his free time. Whether he actually lived in the cottage or whether he merely went there during the day is not clear, but this secret base enabled him to carry through what was probably the most productive period in his writing career. A large proportion of the manuscripts in the British Museum were written either at Craiglockhart or at Ripon. Many of the Craiglockhart manuscripts are of poems he felt did not need, or were not worth, revision in 1918.

The Ripon work is partly new poems and partly fresh versions of poems written earlier. After making several rough drafts, his habit was to take a large sheet of paper and write out the poem in a bold, round hand. In a few cases, he then destroyed earlier drafts and left the final version unaltered. More often, he kept the other versions by him and returned repeatedly to the fair copy, writing in changes until the page became too congested to be of further use. Then he would write out another fair copy and begin again. One can often see the original wording of a poem, the fair copy showing through the later revisions like a neat skeleton. The editor has to decide which manuscript is the last and then to work out a satisfactory text from the revisions. Even after the editorial labors of Edith Sitwell, Sassoon, Blunden, and C. Day Lewis, about three-quarters of the published poems were textually inaccurate in some way or other, and there are still errors to be corrected. Yet the impression one gets from Owen's manuscripts is not in the least one of muddle or incompetence; rather it is one of intense care, a refusal to be easily satisfied, and a determination to make each poem as good as it could be made.

He had just found his cottage room when the war took a sudden turn. The long stalemate had made peace negotiations seem a possibility in 1917. Sassoon's protests against the war had not been outbursts of futile rage but part of a wider campaign to influence civilian opinion, and hence the politicians, against the continuation of the fighting. In 1918, however, Germany made a sudden, supreme effort at a military victory. Having finally subdued its eastern front, Germany launched a massive offensive westward. Within a few days, the British had been driven back almost to the Channel coast. As news of the disaster filtered into the papers, Owen read of the places he had helped to capture a year before being overrun again and lost with heavy casualties. There was no more point in thinking about peace negotiations. The sympathy with human suffering that he had begun to learn at Dunsden, and that had been deepening in him ever since, now filled him as a flood tide.

His personal chances of not returning to France were now very much diminished, although Scott Moncrieff, who had friends in the right places, was trying to get him a permanent home posting. If he had been offered a home job, he would probably not have taken it: honor obliged him to get fit and return to his duty in the line. The decision could be delayed for a while, however. His awareness of his own likely fate was absorbed into a much larger pity for the men now at the front. Their endurance and his sorrow prompted "Insensibility," a formal ode that describes the common soldier in an elevated and yet unheroic style. It is an extraordinary achievement, though weakened by a final stanza in which its author succumbs, as he had done in "Hospital Barge," to the attractions of Tennysonian rhetoric as a substitute for profound thinking. The "last sea and the hapless stars," for example, do not bear much looking into; perhaps all that lies behind them is a phrase from "Oenone," "the loud stream and the trembling stars."

The criticism is sometimes made of Owen that he was always too much under the domination of the Victorians. It is true that his facility for imitation and his habit of venerating great writers made him an easy prey to the captivating music of Tennyson and Swinburne, but at his best he was able to get the upper hand. Although the influence of other poets is frequently evident in his work, his style is unmistakable and unique. Often the trace of another poet in his lines adds to the poem's meaning and is meant to do so, as in the echoes of Keats's *Hyperion* and Shelley's *The Revolt of Islam* in "Strange Meeting." The red roses in "The Kind Ghosts" are more terrible than anything Swinburne ever managed in his numerous images of blood and flowers, and "Futility" shows what Owen could do with the Tennysonian tradition:

> Move him into the sun—
> Gently its touch awoke him once,

> At home, whispering of fields unsown.
> Always it woke him, even in France,
> Until this morning and this snow.
> If anything might rouse him now
> The kind old sun will know.

> Think how it wakes the seeds,—
> Woke, once, the clays of a cold star.
> Are limbs, so dear-achieved, are sides,
> Full-nerved,—still warm,—too hard to stir?
> Was it for this the clay grew tall?
> —O what made fatuous sunbeams toil
> To break earth's sleep at all?

This is, in the opinion of many, Owen's most nearly flawless poem. Published in *The Nation* on 15 June 1918, it was almost certainly composed at Ripon and may be allowed to stand here for the other elegies that came from the cottage in Borage Lane. It is far from a damaging criticism in this case to suggest that "Futility" is in direct descent from the great stanzas in Tennyson's *In Memoriam*:

> "So careful of the type?" but no.
> From scarped cliff and quarried stone
> She cries, "A thousand types are gone:
> I care for nothing, all shall go.

> "Thou makest thine appeal to me:
> I bring to life, I bring to death:
> The spirit does but mean the breath:
> I know no more." And he, shall he,

> Man, her last work, who seemed so fair. . . .

> Who loved, who suffer'd countless ills,
> Who battled for the True, the Just,
> Be blown about the desert dust,
> Or seal'd within the iron hills?

> No more? A monster, then, a dream,
> A discord. Dragons of the prime,
> That tare each other in their slime,
> Were mellow music match'd with him.

> O life as futile, then, as frail! . . .
> (56)

Tennyson goes on, of course, to suggest that life is not futile; and Owen's poem need not be read as a cry of unrelieved despair. Present behind "Futility" is our knowledge that war is a man-made thing and not the responsibility of whatever power gave us life. Nature in many of Owen's poems is a hostile force, as in the deathly snow of "Exposure" or the "winds' scimitars" in "Asleep," but this hostility is a response to war. In "Spring Offensive," where his understanding of this problem is most fully set out, nature tries to prevent men from going into an attack, launches a violent onslaught against them when they ignore the appeal, and becomes peaceful again as soon as the attack is over. His early poems show repeatedly that he believed nature to be a source of blessing to those in harmony with the natural order, and the reader of his letters soon becomes accustomed to his odd elaborations of this belief ("we ate the Vernal Eucharist of Hawthorn leaf-buds"). His poems are consistent with the romantic tradition in this and other ways; they are not the ironic denial of it that some critics have understood them to be.

Owen is not an easy poet, yet from the details of his technique to the largest statements of his elegies there runs a consistent pattern. A line such as "Rucked too thick for these men's extrication" ("Mental Cases") shows his characteristic rhyming ("ruck-/ thick/ -tric-") and an equally characteristic use of an unexpected but simple word ("rucked") leading to the more elaborate "extrication." This kind of combination can be seen again in, for example, "Strange Meeting," where a single line contains the colloquial "thumped" and the archaic "made moan"; or in "Futility," where the startlingly simple familiarity of "kind old sun" precedes a complex image of clay that is developed from biblical and older origins. Similarly, the tunnel in "Strange Meeting" is at once a dugout and the underworld; the men in "Mental Cases" are inhabitants of a mental hospital and of the inferno; and the infantry in "Spring Offensive" charge both an unseen human enemy and the romantic landscape itself. Parallel to these ambivalences, which are wholly deliberate, are Owen's frequent allusions to earlier poets, particularly Shelley, Keats, and Dante. These, too, are deliberate and they bind his poetry into literary tradition. The echo of Keats's odes in the description of the landscape in "Spring Offensive" suggests the strange possibility that the landscape *is* that of the odes, a suggestion that, if we follow it, adds much to the significance of the poem. Yet it is easy to dismiss the echo as being unintentional, proof only of Owen's inability to get away from nineteenth-century diction. The old view of his poems as products of the war, forced out of an immature and ill-informed mind under the pressure of intense experience, is slow in dying but does not deserve to live. The major poems are the result of long years of training and preparation, finding fruit not in some hasty scribble done on the back of an envelope in the trenches but

in the meticulous, protracted labor that went on at Ripon in the spring of 1918.

If memories of World War I ever fade, much of the verse we associate with it will also be forgotten. Owen's poetry seems more likely to endure than most. It is uneven, incomplete, and sometimes of poor quality, but at his best he belongs to English literature and not just to a historical event. It is not easy to make a similar case for any of the other poets of the war, except for those like Thomas and Blunden who wrote about many other subjects. Some isolated pieces by Isaac Rosenberg, Sorley, and others should be considered, but Owen is alone in having left a substantial and largely coherent body of work. Many of his poems are unpleasant, but they have that intensity that Keats said could make "all disagreeables evaporate"; they marry beauty and terror, as Shelley required poetry to do. We feel the pity and we see the waste, because his elegies are both beautiful and true. He saw that pity was "the one thing war distilled" and that it was the most important thing, for it showed that love was stronger than hate and that truth could not be wholly overcome.

VI

OWEN was graded fit for general service on 4 June 1918 and was sent back to Scarborough. There was still a chance of a home posting, but the return to full duties was a strain. He was not really cured. His war dreams began again, caused, he thought, by the hideous faces of the advancing revolver targets, grotesque dummies that moved relentlessly forward while they were shot at. In July he heard that Sassoon, who had gone back to the trenches despite Owen's attempts to dissuade him in December, had been sent home wounded. There was some argument in the correspondence columns of *The Nation* after the war about the circumstances of Owen's having been eventually posted abroad. According to Scott Moncrieff, the authorities were of the opinion that an officer who had apparently lost his nerve at the front should be sent back there once he was fit again rather than be allowed to remain in England. There seems to be no evidence, however, that Owen did not freely make his own choice to go out again, and his letters show that it was Sassoon's return that finally decided him. A poet was needed at the front;

someone had to speak for the men. He was declared fit for overseas duty on 11 August and crossed the Channel on the last day of the month.

During his last weeks in England, he made desperate and unsuccessful efforts to get his manuscripts into good order for publication. There was not enough time. Many of his last revisions are so scribbled as to be almost illegible. For his reading, he turned to two of his old favorites, Shelley and Swinburne. At the end of July, he wrote the little Swinburnian poem "The Kind Ghosts" and sent it to Sassoon in the hospital. Its strange and frightening image of Britannia[7] as a Sleeping Beauty, in a palace built of doomed youths and yet unaware of the horrors round her, was presumably meant as a comment on civilian attitudes for Sassoon's approval. The image also expresses something of Owen's subconscious feelings about his mother, about her passivity and possessiveness, her unawareness of what her son was really doing and thinking, and her frequent spells in bed with minor ailments. Her health seems to have taken up as much of her letters as any larger event. Owen's letters of this period are full of solicitude and vehement assertions of his love for her.

Four of his 1918 poems seem to make a rough and developing sequence. In "Exposure," soldiers dying from frost attempt in a confused way to account for their presence at the front. Their argument that spring will not come again unless they endure and die is not, it would seem, meant to be accepted by the reader. It is their repetition of the old soldier-Christ image, made muddled and ineffective by years of war. The manuscript shows Owen working on a further stanza in which the soldiers eventually recognize that their only hope is in destruction: since the doors of home are closed, the door they are waiting for is a shell crater that will engulf them. The final line, "And our door opens," would have contrasted with the previous refrain of "nothing happens"; something *will* happen and the men will enter the earth. There is a similar image in the fragment "Cramped in that funnelled hole," where a crater is described as a mouth of hell. In the margin of the

paper on which this fragment is scrawled, there are draft lines for "Exposure" and "Mental Cases."

In "Mental Cases," which he wrote at Ripon, shell-shocked soldiers are described in such a way as to seem also damned souls in hell. A visitor to hell asks who these figures are and is answered by a guide. The reference is clearly to the *Inferno*, of which Owen owned a translation. The description is a revised version of a fragment he had written in 1916. The fragment in its turn is developed from a still earlier piece and did not originally have anything to do with the war. The dream of a bodily descent into hell appears in several obscure poems probably written after Dunsden or in Bordeaux. "Mental Cases" is an old nightmare transformed into a war poem. The success with which Owen has distanced himself from what had been a private horror is suggested by the way in which most readers take the word "brother" to refer to themselves, accepting a share in guilt although the wording of the poem does not in fact require them to do so.

The soldiers in "Exposure" had waited to enter hell; the poet in "Mental Cases" has arrived there. In "Strange Meeting," written at Ripon or later in the summer, a soldier-poet makes the full journey. This is Owen's most celebrated and most haunting poem, although it is neither his best nor his last work, as some have thought. The opening section is magnificently done, the half-echoing pararhymes suggesting the depth and darkness of the tunnel and the description setting up allusions to the many sleeper-filled caverns of mythology. This is a Titanic vault, a relic of those wars of the Giants that Keats had intended to describe in *Hyperion*; it is a version of the cave of Morpheus, of the inferno, and of other underworlds. The dead soldier rises; his look, the nightmare gaze of a Gorgon, tells the poet that both men are in hell.

The speech of the dead man begins with an obscure section about beauty and truth, in which the references are to Keats. It continues with a section that is unmistakably Shelleyan since it alludes to *The Revolt of Islam* and draws heavily on the lines that Owen had written for Sassoon in the previous December. There is, however, a significant change: whereas those lines had declared a positive intention of staying aloof from war until men are ready for truth, the dead soldier laments that he cannot now carry out such an intention, and he takes leave of his poetic ambitions. Owen seems to be recognizing that his likely return to war will mean an end forever of his hopes of working to a Shelleyan program, not

---

[7]The word "Brittania" (Owen's spelling was erratic) appears unexplained in a rough list of titles he jotted down that summer; it seems likely to have been a draft title for this poem. Compare Swinburne's "Perinde ac Cadaver." While Owen was in France he acquired a copy of Swinburne's *Poems and Ballads*; it was probably the last book he read.

only because he may be killed but also because he will have to kill. In the last five lines of the poem, in a simple but resonant style quite unlike that of the complex and archaic passage that precedes them, the paradoxes of "enemy" and "friend," seeing in the dark, and bayoneting with a frown sum up the dilemma of the soldier-poet. As a poet, he must make peace; as a soldier, he must make war. He had "escaped" into the tunnel but there can be no further escape, only the "encumbered" and dream-ridden sleep to which his mirror image invites him.

For fifty years after his death, the details of Owen's life were jealously guarded, first by his mother and then by his brother Harold. With the best of intentions, they suppressed anything that might make him appear odd or inconsistent. It is presumably Harold Owen's editing that is responsible for the inaccurate wording in the *Collected Letters* (p. 580) of the citation for the Military Cross that his brother won in October 1918. The *Letters* version states that Owen "personally captured an enemy Machine Gun in an isolated position and took a number of prisoners." The original citation, given in the official history of the Artists' Rifles[8] and elsewhere, says that he "personally manipulated a captured enemy machine gun from an isolated position, and inflicted considerable losses on the enemy." The machine gun and its victims need to be remembered. It would be very wide of the mark to suppose that Owen abandoned the principles of Christ and Shelley at the last merely in order to win a medal and prove to himself that his nerve was steady after all. The circumstances of war were such that no fit officer could honorably stay at home; it would have been a betrayal of the men for whom one was responsible and whose lives one's leadership could do a little to protect. "I came out in order to help these boys—directly by leading them as well as an officer can; indirectly, by watching their sufferings that I may speak of them as well as a pleader can." That was his comment after the battle. He added, "I have done the first," a claim supported by the citation ("On the company commander becoming a casualty, he assumed command and showed fine leadership").

His last poem, "Spring Offensive," may have been finished after this fighting, although it had been begun some weeks before. It is about a representative and anonymous group of "these boys." The offensive occurs in a May landscape that seems more like Shropshire than the western front. Harold Owen has recorded that the "blessed with gold" image was a phrase used by his brother Wilfred years before the war on a country walk near Shrewsbury. The further image of the clinging brambles is reminiscent of the embrace of the trees in "Happiness"; Mrs. Owen is present here, as so often. The Keatsian language of parts of the description is intentionally obvious: this is an English, poetic landscape. It contains elements of the objects of Owen's early loves: home, his mother, nature, Keats. The breaking of the maternal bond, the clinging brambles, is followed by the making of war, the sudden horror of the sun's smiling face turning to fire and fury, and the entry "in the body" into hell.

"Spring Offensive" ends and sums up Owen's achievement. It is only roughly finished, the last stanza being a hasty pencil scrawl on the back of the manuscript, but its opening stanzas have a richness peculiarly his own. The public, impersonal statement is founded upon a series of images and allusions drawn from his private experience and reading. The language of the poem, unlike that in some of his earlier work, is sparing and precise, yet resonant and memorable: "the imminent line of grass," "a lift and flare of eyes." The final rejection of the clinging maternal arms and of passivity is heroic. There is an instant of exultation as the men challenge the sun and the landscape. There can be nothing Christian or Shelleyan about such an onslaught (if there is a sacrifice, it is, as the Old Testament phrase "high place" suggests, by fire to Moloch), but the offensive against the spring has not been wholly futile. Owen remained in the fighting line, confident and admired as an officer. He was hit and killed on 4 November, while helping to lead men across a heavily defended canal. The war ended a week later.

APPENDIX

Dates of Owen's Poems

Jon Stallworthy's *The Complete Poems and Fragments of Wilfred Owen* prints the poems in the apparent order of their final drafts, but this sequence does not necessarily reflect the order of initial composition. Owen finished some poems within a few days but went on drafting others for years. Ascribing a date to a poem is often difficult, since he rarely dated his manuscripts. The list below shows when

---

[8]Major S. S. Higham, comp., *The Regimental Roll of Honour and War Record of the Artists' Rifles* (London, 1922), 3rd ed.

the better-known poems seem to have been in progress. Dates of first and/or last drafts are given only where the evidence seems certain; parentheses indicate a degree of guesswork.

Before 1913   Numerous minor poems.

1913   "On My Songs" composed in January. "O World of Many Worlds" first drafted in 1912, continued in 1914, and completed in 1915.

1914   "1914," "Long ages past," "The Sleeping Beauty," and other poems first drafted in the second half of the year, after the outbreak of war and Owen's meeting Tailhade.

1915   Draft work for various pieces, including "Maundy Thursday" and a long poem on "Perseus," a project continued in 1916 and 1917. "A Palinode" probably written in October, when Owen was enlisting.

1916   "An Imperial Elegy" drafted and abandoned. A number of sonnets first drafted later in the year, including "To———," "Music," "A New Heaven," "Storm," "Purple," and "The End."

1917   "Happiness" and "Golden Hair" first drafted in February during a rest period behind the front line. "Sonnet to My Friend" first drafted in the hospital in March. "The Fates," "The Wrestlers" (also entitled "Antaeus"), "Song of Songs," and "From My Diary" first drafted at Craiglockhart before Owen met Sassoon. After the meeting, in August, and before leaving the hospital at the end of October, Owen made first drafts of "The Dead-Beat" and "My Shy Hand" (both August); "The Next War" and "Anthem for Doomed Youth" (both September); "Disabled," "Dulce et Decorum Est," "Soldier's Dream," and "Winter Song" (all October); "Six o'clock in Princes Street," "The Sentry," "S.I.W.," "The Chances," and "Inspection." During the winter of 1917–1918, he seems to have been at work on "Asleep," "Apologia pro Poemate Meo," "Greater Love," "Conscious," "Le Christianisme," "At a Calvary," "The Letter," "The Show," and "Shadwell Stair." "Wild with All Regrets" (revised in April as "A Terre") and "Hospital Barge" were completed by early December; and in the same month Owen drafted preliminary work for "Exposure," including "Cramped in that funnelled hole."

1918   "Miners" was written "in 30 minutes" in January. "Last Words" was drafted in February and revised as "The Last Laugh." "Insensibility" seems to date from the winter or early spring. At his cottage in Ripon, Owen revised much of his existing work and composed "Arms and the Boy" (May), "The Send-Off," "Mental Cases," "Strange Meeting," "Futility," the fragment "As Bronze," and the preface and table of contents for a book of war poems. Either at Ripon, or more probably later in the summer, he drafted "The Calls," "The Roads Also," and "The Parable of the Old Man and the Young." The manuscript of "Training" is dated June and that of "The Kind Ghosts" July. In September, again in France, Owen composed "Smile, Smile, Smile" (prompted, like "Miners" by a newspaper report) and completed "The Sentry" (begun at Craiglockhart), "Elegy in April and September" (begun in April), "Exposure" (begun at the end of 1917), and "Spring Offensive" (probably begun in the summer). The final draft of "Spring Offensive" can be regarded as his last poem.

1919   Mrs. Owen sent her son's manuscripts to the Sitwells. Edith Sitwell arranged for several to be published in periodicals and began work on an edition of the major poems.

1920   Sassoon took over as editor. Chatto and Windus published *Poems* in December.

SELECTED BIBLIOGRAPHY

I. BIBLIOGRAPHY. W. White, *Wilfred Owen (1893–1918): A Bibliography* (Kent, Ohio, 1967), lists most of the many articles about Owen up to 1965.

II. COLLECTED AND SELECTED POEMS. S. Sassoon, ed., *Poems* (London, 1920), intro. by ed., contains twenty-three poems; E. Blunden, ed., *The Poems of Wilfred Owen: A New Edition, Including Many Pieces Now First Published, and Notices of His Life and Work* (London, 1931), contains fifty-nine poems; C. Day Lewis, ed., *The Collected Poems of Wilfred Owen* (London, 1963), intro. and notes by ed. and memoir by E. Blunden, contains eighty poems, including all the war poems except a few very minor pieces; D. Hibberd, ed., *Wilfred Owen: War Poems and Others* (London, 1973), intro. and notes by ed., contains fifty-six poems; J. Stallworthy, ed., *The Complete Poems and Fragments of Wilfred Owen* (London, 1982).

III. LETTERS. H. Owen and J. Bell, eds., *Wilfred Owen: Collected Letters* (London, 1967), contains 673 letters; D. Hibberd, "Wilfred Owen's Letters: Some Additions, Amendments and Notes," in *Library*, 4, 3 (September 1982), 272–287, includes some previously unpublished material.

IV. MEMOIRS AND BIOGRAPHY. S. Sassoon, *Siegfried's Journey, 1916–1920* (London, 1945); O. Sitwell, *Noble Essences or Courteous Revelations* (London, 1950), the fifth and last book of Sitwell's autobiography, *Left Hand, Right Hand*; H. Owen, *Journey from Obscurity: Wilfred Owen, 1893–1918: Memoirs of the Owen Family*, 3 vols. (London, 1963–1965); J. Stallworthy, *Wilfred Owen* (London, 1974); D. Welland, "Sassoon on Owen," in *Times Literary Supplement* (31 May 1974).

V. CRITICAL STUDIES. J. M. Murry, "The Poet of the War," in *The Nation and Athenaeum* (19 February 1921), 705–707, repr. in D. Hibberd, ed., *Poetry of the First World War: A Casebook* (London, 1981), with other essays on Owen; C. D. Lewis, *A Hope for Poetry* (London, 1934); D. Thomas, *Quite Early One Morning* (London, 1954); D. Welland, *Wilfred Owen: A Critical Study* (London, 1960; repr. with a postscript, 1978); J. H. Johnston, *English Poetry of the First World War: A Study in the Evolution of Lyric and Narrative Form* (Princeton, N. J., 1964); T. J. Walsh, comp., *A Tribute to Wilfred Owen* (Birkenhead, 1964); B. Bergonzi, *Heroes' Twilight: A Study of the Literature of the Great War* (London, 1965); D. J. Enright, *Conspirators and Poets* (London, 1966); G. M. White, *Wilfred Owen* (New York, 1969); J. Silkin, *Out of Battle: The Poetry of the Great War* (London, 1972); A. E. Lane, *An Adequate Response:The War Poetry of Wilfred Owen and Siegfried Sassoon* (Detroit, 1972); P. Fussell, *The Great War and Modern Memory* (London, 1975); D. Perkins, *A History of Modern Poetry* (Cambridge, Mass., 1976); A. Banerjee, *Spirit Above Wars: A Study of the English Poetry of the Two World Wars* (London, 1976); D. Hibberd, "A Sociological Cure for Shellshock," in *Sociological Review*, 25 (May 1977), 377–386; P. Hobsbaum, *Tradition and Experiment in English Poetry* (London, 1979); S. Bäckman, *Tradition Transformed: Studies in the Poetry of Wilfred Owen* (Lund, 1979); D. Hibberd, "Wilfred Owen and the Georgians," in *Review of English Studies*, 30, 117 (February 1979), 28–40; J. Glover, "Owen and Barbusse and Fitzwater Wray," in *Strand*, 21, 2 (Spring 1980), 22–32.